Managing Human Resources
Through Strategic Partnerships

Eighth Edition

Susan E. Jackson

Rutgers University

Randall S. Schuler

Rutgers University

THOMSON

—✷—™

SOUTH-WESTERN

Australia · Canada · Mexico · Singapore · Spain · United Kingdom · United States

THOMSON

SOUTH-WESTERN

Managing Human Resources Through Strategic Partnerships, 8th edition
Susan E. Jackson and Randall S. Schuler

Publisher
Melissa S. Acuña

Sr. Acquisitions Editor
Charles E. McCormick, Jr.

Developmental Editor
Mardell Toomey

Marketing Manager
Larry Qualls

Sr. Production Editor
Deanna Quinn

Media Technology Editor
Diane van Bakel

Media Developmental Editor
Josh Fendley

Media Production Editor
Lora Craver

Manufacturing Coordinator
Diane Lohman

Design Project Manager
Rik Moore

Internal Designer
Rik Moore

Cover Designer
Rik Moore

Cover Photograph
©Rick Fischer, Masterfile

Compositor
Trejo Production

Printer
Transcontinental Printing
Louisville, Quebec

Library of Congress
Cataloging-in-Publication Data
Jackson, Susan E.
    Managing human resources
through strategic partnerships /
Susan E. Jackson, Randall S.
Schuler.—8th ed.
    Rev. ed. of: Managing human
resources. ©2000.
    Includes bibliographical references
and index.
ISBN: 0-324-15265-5
    1. Personnel management. 2. Per-
sonnel management—Case studies.
I. Schuler, Randall S. II. Jackson,
Susan E. Managing human resources.
III. Title.
HF5549.S24895 2002
658.3—dc21

                            2001057692

These extra resources guide instructors and students through the many issues involved in effectively managing human resources.

Instructor's Manual with Test Bank
The instructor's manual portion of the supplement includes re-capped learning objectives, chapter overviews and lecture material that is enhanced with summaries of company vignettes and other special features, including end-of-chapter case notes. Answers to all review and discussion questions are included. Most chapters include experiential and skill building exercises. The test bank portion includes approximately 40 multiple choice questions, 25 true/false questions, and 5 essay questions for each chapter.

ExamView Testing Software
ExamView is a computerized version of the printed test bank that allows instructors to easily create customized tests for their students.

Teaching Transparency Acetates
Derived from the most useful exhibits found in the main text, 100 transparencies provide visual support for lectures.

Video Package
The video package is a compilation of current, CNN video segments organized around four parts: "Today's Work Environment and Context," which includes topics such as e-privacy and illegal workers; "Diversity and Fair Treatment," which includes topics such as equal pay and disabilities in the workplace; "Unionization and Collective Bargaining," which includes topics such as welfare to work and labor and the new economy; and "Compensation and Benefits," which includes employee perks and asking for a raise. Many other topics are included. The video segments complement chapter content and are useful to start classroom discussions and reinforce important topics.

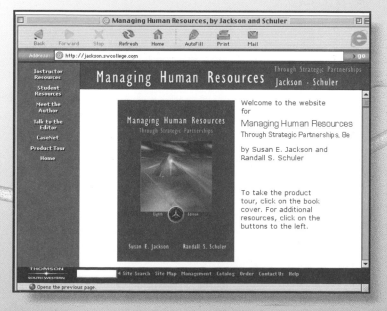

PowerPoint Presentation Software
The slide presentation includes coverage of the most salient chapter material, and compelling art, following the order in which chapter material is presented. These slides are designed to hold student interest and prompt questions that will help students learn.

Web Site
A rich Web site at **http://jackson.swcollege.com** provides many extras that will support and enrich student learning.

brief contents

c1

MANAGING HUMAN RESOURCES THROUGH STRATEGIC PARTNERSHIPS

c2

UNDERSTANDING THE GLOBAL ENVIRONMENT

c3

Ensuring Fair Treatment and Legal Compliance for a Diverse Workforce

c4

CREATING ORGANIZATIONAL ALIGNMENT

c5

HR Planning for Strategic Change

c6

USING JOB ANALYSIS AND COMPETENCY MODELING AS THE FOUNDATION FOR THE HR SYSTEM

c7

RECRUITING AND RETAINING QUALIFIED EMPLOYEES

c8

SELECTING EMPLOYEES TO FIT THE JOB AND THE ORGANIZATION

c9

TRAINING AND DEVELOPING A COMPETITIVE WORKFORCE

c10

DEVELOPING AN OVERALL APPROACH TO COMPENSATION

c11
MEASURING PERFORMANCE AND PROVIDING FEEDBACK

c12

USING PERFORMANCE-BASED PAY TO ENHANCE MOTIVATION

c13

PROVIDING BENEFITS AND SERVICES

c14

PROMOTING WORKPLACE SAFETY AND HEALTH

c15

UNDERSTANDING UNIONIZATION AND COLLECTIVE BARGAINING

c16

UNDERSTANDING THE HR PROFESSION

Managers from the very largest multinational firms to the smallest domestic firms claim that managing people effectively is vital to success in today's highly competitive marketplace. "The most important thing I do is hire bright people," says Microsoft's Bill Gates. "Hire people smarter than you and get out of their way," says Howard Schultz, chairman of Starbucks. "Without the right people in place, strategies can't get implemented," says Tom Siebel, CEO of Siebel Systems. In fact, the challenge of effectively managing human resources is recognized throughout the world. According to Floris Maljers of the British-Dutch company Unilever, "Limited human resources, not unreliable capital, are the biggest constraint when companies globalize." These industry leaders know that people are the core of any organization. To succeed, they must have the best people available working productively throughout their companies.

THE STRATEGIC PARTNERSHIP PERSPECTIVE FOR MANAGING HUMAN RESOURCES

The task of managing human resources includes all of the activities that organizations use to affect the behaviors of all the people who work for it. Because the behaviors of employees influence profitability, customer satisfaction, and a variety of other important measures of organizational effectiveness, managing human resources is a key strategic challenge. To explain how organizations meet this challenge, this book uses a "strategic partnerships" perspective. The strategic partnerships perspective is summarized in the illustration shown on the inside front cover. At the center of the illustration are human resource management (HRM) activities, including both the formal policies of the organization and the actual daily practices that people experience.

Current Practices for Managing Human Resources

Managing Human Resources Through Strategic Partnerships, Eighth Edition, offers a detailed picture of how successful companies manage human resources in order to compete effectively in a dynamic, global environment. Because organizations differ from each other in so many ways—including their locations, competitive strategies, products and services, and corporate cultures—we use many different companies to illustrate how businesses are addressing the challenge of managing human resources effectively. Examples of companies in many different industries include Southwest Airlines, Continental, Lincoln Electric, IBM, Cisco, SAS Institute, Bayer, MetLife, Royal Dutch Shell, GE, Levi Strauss, Mayo Clinic, Cirque du Soleil, Cendant Mortgage, Dell, DaimlerChrysler, Coca-Cola, Disney, Weyerhaeuser, FedEx, The Ritz-Carlton, Owens Corning, and many, many others. By combining a respect for established principles of human resource management with a willingness to experiment and try new approaches, these companies succeed year after year.

Satisfying Multiple Stakeholders

Ultimately, an organization is effective only if it satisfies its major stakeholders. Effective organizations recognize that there's more to "success" than just a good bottom line. The best companies balance their concerns over short-term, bottom-line results with the recognition that long-term success requires satisfying a variety of stakeholders. In addition to satisfying the demands of shareholders, the best organizations also address the concerns of employees and their families, customers, members of the local communities, government regulators, unions, public interest groups, and other organizations that they do business with—suppliers, distributors, alliance partners, and so on. These various stakeholders care deeply about how businesses conduct themselves, and in particular, how they treat their employees. Throughout this textbook, we explicitly consider how different approaches to managing human resources can influence the way stakeholders view an organization— for better or for worse. Although it's not always possible to satisfy all stakeholders equally well, effective organizations make a habit of analyzing the available alternatives from multiple perspectives and seeking solutions that meet as many concerns as possible. The approach of developing human resource management policies and activities that are responsive to the concerns of an organization's key stakeholders is central to the strategic partnerships perspective adopted throughout this book.

Managing Strategically

If you have worked in more than one organization, you know from experience that there are many different approaches to managing human resources. Some employers are highly selective in whom they hire, while others seem to hire anyone who walks in the door. Some provide extensive training to employees, while others let new hires sink or swim. Some pay well and offer large bonuses, others don't. Many of these differences in how organizations manage people are due to differences in the environments of organizations. Rapid changes in technologies, as well as economic, political, and social conditions, mean that few organizations can effectively compete today by just using the old tried-and-true approaches of yesterday. Nor can they simply copy other organizations. As the best organizations realize, continuous change requires continuous learning.

Increasingly, the great companies—the "Most Admired" and the "Best Companies to Work For"—manage their human resources based upon an understanding of the company and its environment. In order to recruit the right people with the right competencies and keep these people motivated to do their best work, managers and HR professionals alike need to understand the demands and nature of the business. A computer company that competes by continually offering innovative new products and services is likely to manage people differently than a retailer that competes by offering low-cost goods, or a manufacturer that competes by offering the best quality possible. Furthermore, each of these companies may adopt a different approach during good economic times than when the economy is not performing well. Finding new and better ways of doing things is the only way to get ahead and stay ahead of the competition—and that includes learning new and better ways of managing human resources. Managing human resources with this understanding of the nature of the business and the environment in which it operates is central to managing human resources through strategic partnerships.

The HR Triad: Managers, Employees, and HR Professionals

Given the importance of addressing the concerns of many stakeholders, it is not surprisingly that another quality shared by successful companies is their recognition that managing human resources is everyone's responsibility.

Naturally, HR professionals carry much of the responsibility for ensuring that the organization is applying the best knowledge available and conforming to legal requirements. But day in and day out, line managers and the employees themselves carry most of the responsibility for managing human resources. Managers translate the formal policies of the organization into daily practice. Employees, in turn, may be asked to participate in many HR practices, such as interviewing potential new hires, assisting with training, providing feedback on the performance of colleagues, suggesting improvements, and so on. This view—that managing human resources is a shared responsibility—is highlighted throughout this book in a feature called "The HR Triad." Within each chapter, it details the roles and responsibilities of HR professionals, managers, and employees.

Recurring Contemporary Themes

As organizations strive to manage employees effectively, they face many challenges. Of these, we pay special attention to four issues that companies are currently struggling to understand and resolve:

- managing teams,
- managing diversity,
- managing globalization, and
- managing change.

Managing Teams. Many managers now believe that improving the teamwork processes in their organization is essential for ensuring their organizations' success. Using team-based organizational structures, employers hope to achieve outcomes that could not be achieved by individuals working in isolation. But the payoff from teams isn't automatic. To create and orchestrate teams, people need to be selected, appraised, compensated, and trained in ways that reflect the unique relationships that develop between employees who work together. Examples of how organizations use human resource practices to maximize team effectiveness are highlighted in the "Managing Teams" feature.

Managing Diversity. Just as organizations have come to realize the benefits of teamwork, they have also discovered that the people who were being put into teams are more diverse than ever before. Today, organizations are finding that diversity management practices must be sensitive to issues of gender, ethnicity, personality, religion, sexual orientation, marital and family status, age, and various other unifying life experiences. The "Managing Diversity" feature in this book describes how effective organizations use HR practices to leverage employee diversity and create competitive advantage.

Managing Globalization. Throughout the 21st century, technological advances in transportation and communications spur the growth of international commerce. As firms evolve from domestic to global, they face several challenges related to managing human resources. One challenge is learning how to manage people in different countries effectively. Differences in employment laws, labor market conditions, and national cultures mean that companies often cannot simply assume that HR practices that work in the United States will be equally effective in other countries. Another challenge is to learn how to help employees around the world work together. Although detailed treatment of the issues raised by globalization is beyond the scope of this book, the "Managing Globalization" feature provides a glimpse of how some companies are addressing these challenges.

Managing Change. In most organizations, the current approach to managing people reflects both tradition and some new experimentation. A never-ending stream of new technologies makes possible new approaches to recruiting and training employees—not to mention the possibility of a virtual organization. Merging with another firm, spinning off a business unit, and flattening the hierarchical structure all involve changing who does what and how. A dynamic, changing environment means that even the most successful organizations can't rest on prior successes. Almost always, changes in business practices mean changes in HR practices, and examples of this are provided throughout this book in the "Managing Change" feature.

ORGANIZATION OF THIS BOOK

The many topics discussed in this book are organized according to the illustration of the strategic partnerships perspective illustrated on the inside front cover. We begin by discussing the "big picture," then we discuss each of the HR topics listed at the center of the illustration, and finally we wrap up with a discussion of the HR profession.

The Big Picture

Chapter 1 describes each component of the strategic partnerships perspective shown in the illustration. This important chapter provides an orientation for thinking about why it is so important—and difficult—for organizations to develop effective HR policies and practices. Then Chapters 2 and 3 describe in more detail the external environment, including globalization, the changing labor market, new technologies, restructuring due to mergers and acquisitions, laws and regulations, and employees' evolving view of what constitutes fair employment practices. In Chapter 4, we describe the organizational environment, focusing on competitive strategies, internal structures, and corporate cultures. As this chapter makes clear, effectively managing human resources starts at the top of the organization with leaders who understand the importance of people and are committed to addressing the needs of their employees.

Specific HR Activities

Having described the environment that shapes how companies manage their human resources, we then turn to descriptions of the specific policies and practices that organizations use to manage their workforces. An effective HRM system requires planning and coordination as well as continual evaluation and readjustment. Chapter 5 describes how strategic planning and HR planning together can be used to align HR practices with conditions in the global and organizational environments. HR planning also serves to align the various HRM activities with each other. Chapter 6 describes how job analysis and competency modeling can be used to develop an understanding of the work and the competencies employees need in order to maximize their performance in current jobs as well as their longer-term success.

To get work done, organizations need to attract people to apply for jobs and retain those who do their jobs well. Chapter 7 describes how companies recruit applicants to apply for job openings and some of the ways they can reduce unwanted turnover. After applicants have applied for a position, but before they are made a job offer, the process of selection occurs. As described in Chapter 8, employers want to select employees who will be able and willing to learn new tasks and continually adapt to changing conditions. They also want employees who fit well with the organizational culture.

With rapid changes in job requirements, existing employees must be both willing and able to develop new competencies, become proficient in new jobs, and even change their occupations. Chapter 9 describes training and development practices that enable employees to develop themselves and remain employable despite rapid changes in the world of work.

Employees work in exchange for compensation, whether monetary or otherwise. A total compensation package typically includes base wages or salary, some form of incentive pay, and various types of benefits. Chapter 10 describes how organizations design the total compensation package. To ensure that employees perform satisfactorily and receive appropriate compensation, performance must be measured and employees must receive usable feedback and the support needed to identify and correct performance deficiencies. When appropriate performance standards, measures, and feedback are provided, capable employees become a high-performance workforce. Chapter 11 describes principles for performance measurement and feedback and sets the stage for a discussion using rewards to further motivate employees. Then Chapter 12 describes the use of incentives, bonuses, and other forms of rewards that employers offer to motivate employees to perform at their peak.

The best companies often become targets for recruitment by competitors. Offering innovative benefits packages and employee services that address a wide array of employees' concerns is one tactic for warding off such poaching, as described in Chapter 13. In addition to the benefits that employers offer voluntarily, Chapter 13 describes benefits required by law. Chapter 14 focuses on what employers can do to ensure that the workplace is safe and that employees are healthy. Exposure to toxic chemicals and dangerous equipment remains a concern in some work environments, but more often air quality and ergonomic concerns top the agenda. Increasing concern about violence in the workplace is another unfortunate development described in Chapter 14. Chapter 15 addresses the current state of unionization and collective bargaining. Because unions have maintained their strength in many other countries, they play a vital role in companies that strive to be globally competitive and profitable.

The HR Profession

The design and implementation of effective HR systems requires substantial expertise. Although line managers from all areas of an organization must also be involved in the process, professional HR knowledge is essential. Chapter 16 specifically addresses readers who wish to pursue a career in human resource management, working either as a staff member within an organization or as an external consultant. What competencies will you need to succeed in this field? What professional standards will you need to meet? How are HR activities organized in different organizations? And what is the future likely to hold? The last chapter explores these questions from the perspective of HR professionals.

FEATURES OF THIS EDITION

We have already alluded to several features that appear through this book, but others have yet to be mentioned. Below are descriptions of all of the special features that we use to reinforce key ideas and bring the topic of managing human resources to life.

Contemporary Themes

Managing Through Strategic Partnerships. As an introduction to each chapter, these features describe in some detail the human resource activities of a company that is likely to be familiar to most readers. They are used to illustrate how HR professionals, line managers, and employees work together to achieve effective approaches to managing human resources based upon an understanding of the business, its environment, and its multiple stakeholders.

In each chapter, several examples illustrate how some of the best and most admired companies manage human resources to deal with the critical issues of the day. Detailed examples are organized around specific themes and appear in each chapter as

- Managing Globalization
- Managing Change
- Managing Teams
- Managing Diversity

These features reinforce two important lessons. First, successful companies follow well-established principles for managing human resources, and second, they also are willing to experiment with new ideas in order to improve upon what is known. Through these examples, we hope to convince readers that effectively managing human resources requires mastering what is known *and* then having the confidence to venture into the unknown.

The HR Triad. In each chapter, the specific roles and responsibilities of HR professionals, managers, and all other employees are discussed in the text. In addition, the HR Triad feature summarizes the key points. This feature highlights the role that each member of the triad plays in designing and implementing effective HR policies and practices.

Internet Resources. Throughout each chapter, several Internet Resources boxes direct you to the Web site for *Managing Human Resources Through Strategic Partnerships.* From there, you can easily follow the electronic links provided to learn more about various topics addressed in the chapter. Using the Internet Resources feature you will be able to investigate companies, learn about relevant professional associations that provide resources for managing people, find out about the products and services offered by HR consultants and vendors, and in many other ways enrich your understanding of human resource management.

Margin Notes. Throughout the chapters, margin notes reinforce and extend key ideas. The *fast facts* offer tidbits of information that are sometimes surprising and sometimes merely useful. The *quotes* illustrate the perspectives of real managers and HR professionals. We selected some quotes because the people who spoke them are well-known executives or public figures. Although you won't recognize the names of others, we think you'll agree that their insights are worth remembering.

Terms to Remember. A list of key concepts appears at the end of each chapter. Its purpose is to allow you to check whether you recall and understand the key vocabulary associated with the content of the chapter. If you see a term you aren't sure about, you may want to go back and review that section of the chapter again, or ask the instructor to help clarify the meaning for you. You can also improve your understanding of key terms by looking them up in the Glossary provided on the Web site for this book.

Discussion Questions. The discussion questions at the end of each chapter seek to determine your understanding of the material found in the chapter. They include material in the body of the chapter and in the "Managing . . ." features. By the time you finish reading and studying all the chapters, you should know a great deal about basic principles for managing human resources, about what particular companies are doing today, and about what companies should be preparing to do as they face the future.

Projects to Extend Your Learning. The projects at the end of the chapters reinforce the key themes of managing strategically, managing globalization, managing teams, managing change, and managing diversity. Some of these projects direct you to investigate human resource practices in companies in your neighborhood. Many others ask you to gather information by using the Internet. Finally, one project in each chapter focuses your attention on the human resource activities used by the two companies portrayed in the end-of-text integrative cases.

Endnote Citations. At the end of each chapter, you will find an extensive list of endnotes, which provide full citations to the materials used in preparing the chapter. For anyone wishing to dig deeper into the content of the chapter, the endnotes are an excellent starting point. Included are citations to the latest academic research as well as citations for coverage that has appeared in the public press and relevant Internet addresses.

End-of-Chapter Cases. A case at the end of each chapter offers challenge and variety. It is up to you to analyze what is going on and suggest improvements. In some instances, discussion questions are presented to guide your thinking; in other instances, you are on your own to determine the issues most relevant to the material in the chapter. Many of the companies in these cases are disguised, but their problems and challenges are real and they are likely to be familiar to many experienced managers.

End-of-Text Integrative Cases. At the end of the textbook we present two longer cases. They describe various human resource activities at Lincoln Electric and Southwest Airlines. By studying each case, you should gain an appreciation for how the many aspects of human resource management described throughout the text work together as a total system. By necessity, any particular chapter focuses on only one small piece of the total HR puzzle. In the real world, the pieces must fit together into a meaningful whole. The end-of-text integrative cases illustrate two very different total HR systems found in two successful organizations. These cases provide rather detailed examples of how two firms are meeting the challenge of managing human resources through strategic partnership.

SUPPORT MATERIALS

We designed a comprehensive set of support materials to guide instructors and students through the many issues involved in managing human resources effectively. Supplementary materials for *Managing Human Resources Through Strategic Partnerships*, Eighth Edition, include:

Instructor's Manual with Test Bank (ISBN 0-324-17938-3). The instructor's manual portion of the supplement was prepared by Loren Kuzuhara of the University of Wisconsin. The instructor's manual portion of the supplement includes recapped learning objectives, chapter overviews, and lecture material that is enhanced with summaries of company vignettes and other special features, including end-of-chapter case notes. Answers to all review and discussion questions are included. Most chapters include experiential and skill-building exercises. The test bank portion of the supplement was prepared by Daniel O. Lybrook of Purdue University and includes approximately 40 multiple-choice questions, 25 true-false questions, and 5 essay questions for each chapter.

ExamView Testing Software (ISBN 0-324-17935-9). ExamView is a computerized version of the printed test bank that allows instructors to easily create customized tests for their students.

Instructor's Resource CD-ROM (IRCD) (ISBN 0-324-18509-X). The instructor's resource CD-ROM includes the instructor's manual, test bank, and ExamView Electronic Test Bank (see descriptions above) along with a PowerPoint® slide presentation. The PowerPoint slides, prepared by Vicki Kaman, University of Colorado, have been improved from the last edition in terms of color, variety, and appeal. The slides include coverage of the most salient chapter material, and compelling art, following the order in which chapter material is presented. These slides are designed to hold student interest and prompt questions that will help students learn.

Teaching Transparency Acetates (ISBN 0-324-18217-1). Derived from the most useful exhibits found in the main text, 100 transparencies provide visual support for lectures.

Video Package (ISBN 0-324-07157-4). The video package is a compilation of current CNN video segments organized around four parts: "Today's Work Environment and Context," which includes topics such as e-privacy and illegal workers; "Diversity and Fair Treatment," which includes topics such as equal pay and disabilities in the workplace; "Unionization and Collective Bargaining," which includes topics such as welfare to work and labor and the new economy; and "Compensation and Benefits," which includes employee perks and asking for a raise. Many other topics are included. The video segments complement chapter content and are useful to start classroom discussions and reinforce important topics.

http://jackson.swcollege.com Web Site. A rich Web site at jackson .swcollege.com provides many extras that will support and enrich student learning. Resources include an interactive glossary, descriptions of important court decisions, additional Web site exercises, direct links to the Web sites referenced in the main text, and HRM Resources, which lists many sources for research and further learning. The Web site also includes instructor resources.

ACKNOWLEDGMENTS

As with the previous editions, many fine individuals were critical to the completion of the final product. They include Paul Buller at Gonzaga University; Paul Adler at the University of Southern California; Hugh Scullion at Strathclyde University in Glasgow, Scotland; Paul Sparrow at Manchester Business School in England; Shimon Dolan at ESADE in Barcelona, Spain; Stuart Youngblood at Texas Christian University; Gary Florkowski at the University of Pittsburgh; Bill Todor at The Ohio State University; Vandra Huber at the University of Washington; John Slocum at Southern Methodist University; Lynn Shore at Georgia State University; Mary Ahmed at Grand Forks; Ed Lawler at the Center for Effective Organizations, University of Southern California; Gerold Frick at Fachhochschule Aalen; Lynda Gratton and Nigel Nicholson at the London Business School; Chris Brewster at the South End University in London; Shaun Tyson at the Cranfield Management School; Michael Poole at the Cardiff Business School; Paul Stonham at the European School of Management, Oxford; Jan Krulis-Randa and Bruno Staffelbach at the University of Zürich; Albert Stähli and Julia Schirbach at the GSBA–Zürich; Mark Mendenhall at the University of Tennessee, Chattanooga; Helen De Cieri and Denise Welch of Monash University; Yoram Zeira of Tel Aviv University; Dan Ondrack, the University of Toronto; Moshe Banai, Baruch College; Steve Kobrin, Wharton School; Steve Barnett, York University; Carol Somers, Harvard University; Christian Scholz, University of Saarlandes; Pat Joynt, Henley Management College; Reijo Luostarinen, Helsinki School of Economics and Business Administration; Mickey Kavanagh, SUNY, Albany; Wayne Cascio, University of Colorado, Denver; Peter Dowling at the University of Tasmania in Australia; Ricky Griffin, Texas A&M University; Ed van Sluijs at GTIP in The Netherlands; Joy Turnheim, New York University; and Mark Huselid, Jim Sesil, Charles Fay, and Paula Caliguiri at Rutgers University.

In their roles of reviewers and evaluators, the following individuals provided many valuable ideas and suggestions for changes and alterations, all of which we very much appreciated:

Wendy Boswell, Texas A&M University

James Browne, University of Southern Colorado

Gary Chaison, Clark University

John Cote, Baker College

Hyacinth Ezeamii, Albany State College

Ken Kovach, University of Maryland at College Park

Mitchell Lambert, CUNY Brooklyn

Preston Lytle, Columbia Union College

Arthur Matthews, Cornell University

Gordon Morse, George Mason University

David Ozag, Gettysburg College

Several human resource managers and practicing line managers also contributed in many important ways to this edition, particularly with examples and insights from their work experiences. They include Mark Saxer, Libby Child, Mike Mitchell, Manfred Stania, Tom Kroeger, Doug Bray, Patricia Ryan, Georges Bächthold, Dick Fenton, Esther Craig, Ann Howard, Don Bohl, Bob Kenny, Jack Berry, Robert Joy, Paul Beddia, John Fulkerson, Cal Reynolds, Jon Wendenhof, Michael Losey, Debbie Cohen, Nick Blauweikel, Mike Loomans, Sandy Daemmrich, Jeffery Maynard, Lyle Steele, Rowland Stichweh, Bill Maki, Rick Sabo, Bruce Cable, Gil Fry, Bill Reffett, Jerry Laubenstein, Richard Hagan, Horace Parker, Steve Grossman, Paris Couturiaux, John Guthrie, Paul Sartori, and Johan Julin.

The following individuals graciously provided case and exercise materials: George Cooley, Richie Freedman, Ari Ginsberg, Bruce Evans, Mitchell W. Fields, Hugh L. French Jr., Peter Cappelli, Marcia Miceli, Anne Crocker-Hefter, Stuart Youngblood, Ed Lawler, John Slocum, Jeff Lenn, Hrach Bedrosian, Kay Stratton, Bruce Kiene, Martin R. Moser, James W. Thacker, Arthur Sharplin, and Jerry Laubenstein.

The support, encouragement, and assistance of many individuals were vital to the production of this work. They include Sara Cooperman and Kristin Nordfors, who worked carefully in the preparation of the many parts of the final chapter drafts; Steve Director, HRM Department Chair, and Barbara Lee, Dean of the School of Management and Labor Relations at Rutgers University, who provided an environment that supported our work; and Chuck Nanry, Elizabeth Douthitt, Ibraiz Tarique, Aparna Joshi, Jane Barnes, and Mila Lazarova—all of whom used the seventh edition and offered us their feedback. Also, several people at South-Western Publishing deserve our special thanks for their help and support: Charles McCormick, Senior Acquisitions Editor; Mardell Toomey, Developmental Editor; Deanna Quinn, Senior Production Editor; Larry Qualls, Marketing Manager; Rik Moore, Art/Design Coordinator; and Christine Wittmer, Media Developmental Editor. Without their professional dedication and competence, this book would not have been possible. We thank them all for making the completion of this eighth edition both possible and enjoyable.

We also thank our colleagues who have worked so diligently to prepare the supporting materials that accompany this book: Loren Kuzuhara, University of Wisconsin at Madison, who prepared the Instructor's Manual; Daniel Lybrook, Purdue University, who prepared the Test Bank; and Vicki Kaman of the University of Colorado, who prepared the PowerPoint slide presentation.

Finally, we thank the many students who have used prior editions of this book. Their reactions to the book and related course materials, their unique insights into how organizations treat employees, and their suggestions for improvements in prior editions of this book have helped us develop our approach to teaching and to writing *Managing Human Resources Through Strategic Partnerships*.

Susan E. Jackson and Randall S. Schuler
Department of Human Resource Management
Rutgers University

CHAPTER

1

MANAGING HUMAN RESOURCES THROUGH STRATEGIC PARTNERSHIPS

"We pay just as good wages and benefits as other airlines, but our costs are lower because our productivity is higher, which is achieved through the dedicated energy of our people. We've got exactly the same equipment. The difference is, when a plane pulls into a gate, our people run to meet it."

Herb Kelleher
Chairman
Southwest Airlines[1]

MANAGING THROUGH STRATEGIC PARTNERSHIPS

Cisco Systems

To many people, Cisco is an $18 billion high-technology stealth company: the fastest growing company of its size in history, faster even than Microsoft, with a market capitalization of over $150 billion. Cisco competes in markets where hardware is obsolete in 18 months or less and software in 6 months. It operates in the heart of Silicon Valley, where employee turnover averages almost 30 percent, and yet the turnover at Cisco is around 8 percent.

Cisco was founded in 1984 by Leonard Bosack and Sandy Lerner, a husband and wife team who invented a technology to link together separate computer systems at Stanford University. With venture funding from Don Valentine at Sequoia Capital and a new CEO in John Morridge, Cisco went public in 1990. By 2001 the company was ranked third on *Fortune*'s list of the "100 Best Companies to Work For in America." It had more than 30,000 employees operating in over 54 countries around the world. It continues to provide products that enable computers to communicate with each other, offering customers end-to-end scalable network solutions.

As part of its approach to managing human resources, Cisco espouses five core values: a dedication to customer success; innovation and learning; openness; teamwork; and doing more with less. Each of these values is continually articulated by CEO John Chambers and reinforced in the mission statement, current initiatives, human resource policies and practices, and the culture of the company. Signalling the importance of customer satisfaction as a core value, he personally reviews as many as 15 critical accounts each day, often calling on customers himself to straighten out problems.

To encourage openness, Chambers holds a monthly "birthday breakfast" meeting open to anyone with a recent birthday and answers every question put to him—no matter how tough the question. Teamwork is so important that disregarding it is one of three things that can get a person fired at Cisco. To reinforce the important link between business initiatives and the work that people do, every employee is expected to be able to recite the top initiatives. Tremendous peer pressure ensures that employees know about these initiatives. The culture and values are also reinforced through the way jobs are structured and managed. For Cisco employees in sales offices there are not even assigned spaces: It is all "hot desks" or "nonterritorial" office space.

The HR group ensures that these and other HR policies and practices are aligned with the business strategy and continually reinforced. For example, the recruitment and selection system identifies exactly the kind of people they need to hire. Cisco recruits at art fairs, microbrewery festivals, and other places frequented by potential recruits. Rather than list specific job openings, Cisco's ads feature their Web site address, which can provide up-to-the-minute information about hiring needs. As senior VP of human resources Barbara Beck explained, Cisco is a high-tech company and "If you don't leverage the technology, you won't be able to leverage HR capabilities." To select, Cisco uses a minimum of five job interviews. The reward system is also carefully aligned with the strategy and values of the company. Stock options are distributed generously, with a full 40 percent of all Cisco stock options in the hands of individual employees without managerial rank.[2]

THE STRATEGIC IMPORTANCE OF MANAGING HUMAN RESOURCES

"The industrial revolution was about economies of scale. The Internet revolution will be about economies of skill and how you empower people."

John Chambers
CEO
Cisco Systems

A firm has a competitive advantage when all or part of the market prefers the firm's products and/or services. Because competition is the name of the game, companies seek ways to compete that can last a long time and cannot easily be imitated by competitors. That is, they seek to gain a **sustainable competitive advantage**.[3] Firms attempt to establish a sustainable competitive advantage in many ways: Southwest Airlines coordinates all of its operations to ensure that customers get excellent service; Wal-Mart uses rapid market intelligence and competitive pricing so that the right products are always available in the right amounts at the lowest price. McDonald's Corporation enters into agreements with shopping mall developers to secure prime locations for their facilities. Au Bon Pain and Starbucks negotiate special supplier arrangements to ensure that they receive some of the best coffee beans. Management practices such as these can all help a firm gain a competitive advantage. But none of these strategies can create a sustainable advantage unless the organization also has the human resources it needs to successfully implement the strategy.

Leaders such as John Chambers of Cisco and Herb Kelleher of Southwest Airlines see human resources as assets that need to be managed conscientiously and in tune with the organization's needs. Tomorrow's most competitive organizations are working now to ensure they have available tomorrow and a decade from now employees who are eager and able to address their organizations' key competitive challenges. Increasingly this means attracting superior talent and then stimulating employees to perform at peak levels. When brainpower drives the business, as it does at Cisco, then attracting and keeping great intellectual talent becomes a necessity. When customer service is important to the business, as it is at Southwest Airlines, a key challenge is attracting and keeping employees who deliver ever-better service day in and day out even to the most difficult customers.

Some firms use their approaches to managing human resources to gain a sustainable competitive advantage. Exhibit 1.1 illustrates conditions an organization must meet in order to gain sustainable competitive advantage through managing human resources effectively.

Employees Who Add Value

Employees add value by using skills and knowledge to transform the organization's other resources (e.g., raw materials, component parts, equipment, real estate, information, etc.) to produce and deliver products and services that generate profits or other valued forms of return. Employees who are most closely associated with the activities that generate valued returns usually have the most opportunity to add value. Sometimes referred to as "core" employees, they are closest to the essential work of the organization. In software development firms, programmers are core employees. In pharmaceutical firms, scientists and researchers are core employees. In orchestras, musicians are core employees. In health care institutions, doctors and nurses are core employees. As these examples illustrate, core employees can add value to an organization in a variety of ways—through research and new product development, production, problem diagnosis, service delivery, and so on. In most organizations, core employees are supported by people working in a variety of staff, managerial, and support jobs. Non-core employees should also add value. For example, they can improve the organization's efficiency by keeping costs low, analyze the environment to identify new market opportunities, carry out necessary administrative tasks, facilitate coordination among core employees, and so forth.

Regardless of the specific work being done, the objective of effective human resource management is to maximize the value employees add by ensuring that the organization is staffed with the right employees doing the right things at the right time and place and under the right conditions.

Employees Who Are Rare

To be a source of sustainable competitive advantage, human resources must also be rare. If competitors can easily access the same pool of talent, then that talent provides no advantage against competitors. By being an employer of choice, an organization can gain access to the best available talent. In other words, "The Best

"People have become the key competitive differentiator in today's knowledge-based economy, but addressing these human performance or 'people issues' is still a vexing management problem for many corporate leaders, regardless of location, industry, or type of company."

David Clinton
Global Leader of the Human Performance Practice

"The relationship we have with our people and the culture of our company is our most sustainable competitive advantage."

Howard Schultz
Chairman and Chief Global Strategist
Starbucks

FAST FACT

For more than 20 years, *Fortune* magazine has been publishing an annual list of the best companies to work for.

ex 1.1 Managing Human Resources for Sustainable Competitive Advantage

Characteristics of Human Resources for Gaining a Sustainable Competitive Advantage	Implications for Managing Human Resources
Source of Value	Employees have a positive impact on the way customers perceive the organization's products and services. For example, they • Offer excellent services • Generate innovative ideas for new products • Serve as ambassadors of goodwill Employees help the firm gain access to other resources that can be used for competitive advantage. For example, they • Recruit other excellent talent • Help the organization understand and gain access to new markets Employees facilitate organizational change and adaptation. For example, they • Anticipate major environmental changes in advance of others • Are capable of making rapid changes
Rare	Employees have unusually high levels of technical knowledge and skill. Employees have unusually high levels of organization-specific knowledge. For example, they • Understand the organization's strategy and how it differs from competitors • Know the organization's history and are unlikely to repeat mistakes Employees are committed to the organization and highly motivated to contribute to its success.
Difficult to Copy	All aspects of managing human resources fit together to provide a clear, consistent guide for behavior. Authentic attitudes, values, and habits guide behavior more than do rulebooks and manuals. Approaches to managing human resources represent solutions created by the organization to address its specific needs.

Get the Best," as Cisco, The Container Store, and Southwest Airlines have learned.

Books, articles, and Web sites that purport to identify the "best" places to work are especially popular among students graduating from college, who view firms high in the rankings as desirable places to land their first postgraduation job. This is why companies want to be on the list of the "100 Best Companies to Work For in America." Dissatisfied workers who are looking for better employment situations read these lists too. Over time, a reputation for attracting, developing, and keeping good talent acts like a magnet drawing the best talent to the firm.

When Lincoln Electric Company in Cleveland, Ohio, announced it was planning to hire 200 production workers, it received over 20,000 responses.

When BMW Incorporated announced that it had selected Spartanburg, South Carolina, as the site for its first U.S. production facility, it received more than 25,000 unsolicited requests for employment. Numbers this large make it more feasible for Lincoln Electric and BMW to hire applicants who are two to three times more productive than their counterparts in other manufacturing firms.

> **FAST FACT**
>
> The Container Store, based in Dallas, is one of *Fortune's* "Best Companies to Work For." Of its new hires, 41% are friends who were recommended by the firm's enthusiastic employees.

A Culture That Can't Be Copied

Getting the best people into the firm is just a first step. Keeping the best people happy and productive is equally important. Business practices that are easy for competitors to copy don't provide sources of sustainable competitive advantage. Similarly, a corporate culture that's easily duplicated provides little advantage. Southwest Airlines and FedEx are two companies with strong corporate cultures that contribute to business success.

Southwest Airlines. The fun-loving, customer-oriented culture of Southwest Airlines—another one of the "Best Companies to Work For"—is unique in an industry known for disruptive strikes and low customer satisfaction. Besides hiring the best people, Southwest Airlines maintains a company culture that keeps employees happy and motivates them to achieve peak performance. Employees at Southwest Airlines understand the company's strategy and do everything possible to achieve outstanding company success. When a gate supervisor was asked what makes Southwest different from other airlines she said, "We're empowered to make on-the-spot decisions. For example, if a customer misses a flight, it's no sweat. We have the latitude to take care of the problem. There's no need for approvals."

A profit-sharing program is one aspect of the Southwest Airlines approach to managing human resources that keeps employees focused on the company's performance. An incident in Los Angeles illustrates the point: An agent from another airline asked to borrow a stapler. The Southwest agent went over with the stapler, waited for it to be used, and brought it back. The other agent asked, "Do you always follow staplers around?" The Southwest agent replied, "I want to make sure we get it back. It affects our profit sharing." Setting goals and targets for the performance of the company as a whole and never setting separate departmental goals is another approach to managing people that ensures employees all pull together. At Southwest, the philosophy is that everyone should share common goals and that setting up different goals for different areas would be likely to create a schism within the company.[4]

FedEx. In 1990, FedEx was the first service company to win the coveted Malcolm Baldrige National Quality Award. Since day one, its basic philosophy of doing business, as stated by Chairman, CEO and President Frederick W. Smith, has been People, Service, and Profit. Its motto is 100 percent Customer Satisfaction. In a business that relies on individuals delivering packages overnight to customers anywhere, 100 percent customer satisfaction comes only from managing human resources as if they really matter. The FedEx philosophy of managing people is represented in the following policies:

> **FAST FACT**
>
> The Baldrige Award is named for Malcolm Baldrige, who served as secretary of commerce from 1981 until his tragic death in a rodeo accident in 1987. His managerial excellence contributed to long-term improvement in efficiency and effectiveness of government.

- do not lay off employees;
- guarantee fair treatment;
- use surveys to obtain feedback and guide action;

- promote from within;
- share profits; and
- maintain an open-door policy.

Like Southwest Airlines, FedEx has developed a complex and integrated system of human resource practices designed to keep employees focused on the needs of customers and the business. Its system was not simply copied intact from another company, nor did the firm develop it by applying some formula that could guarantee a correct solution. Rather, through a period of many years, FedEx developed its own unique philosophy, policies, and practices. As a consequence, its corporate culture is difficult for outsiders to fully understand and thus impossible to copy.[5]

INTERNET RESOURCES   I.A

The Strategic Importance of Managing Human Resources

At our Web site, http://jackson.swcollege.com/, you can:

1. Learn about the strategic importance of human resources at some of the firms discussed in this section by visiting their company home pages:

   Cisco Systems

   The Container Store

   Lincoln Electric Company

   BMW

   FedEx

2. Find out about this year's "100 Best Companies to Work For in America"

A FRAMEWORK FOR MANAGING HUMAN RESOURCES THROUGH STRATEGIC PARTNERSHIPS

"At other places managers say that people are their most important resource, but nobody acts on it. At Southwest, they have never lost sight of the fact."

Alan S. Boyd
Retired Chairman
Airbus North America

Human resource management refers to all of the activities that an organization uses to affect the behaviors of all the people who work for it. Because the behaviors of employees influence profitability, customer satisfaction, and a variety of other important measures of organizational effectiveness, managing human resources is a key strategic challenge.

Exhibit 1.2 illustrates our overall framework for discussing what organizations need to consider in managing human resources effectively. At the center of the framework are human resource management (HRM) activities, which are the focus of this book. As the framework illustrates, HRM activities partly determine how well an organization satisfies the concerns of its major stakeholders. Stakeholders' various concerns are described later in this chapter. HRM activities do not occur in a vacuum, of course. They are shaped by various other forces inside the organization, which, in turn, are shaped by forces in the external global environment. We briefly describe this framework here, and then elaborate on each element in subsequent chapters.

The Importance of Changes in the Environment

If you have worked in more than one organization, you know from experience that there are many different approaches to managing human resources. Some are highly selective in who they hire, while others seem to hire anyone who walks in the door. Some provide extensive training, while others let new

ex 1.2 A Framework for Managing Human Resources Through Strategic Partnerships

Global Environment

Local Conditions   National Conditions   Multinational Conditions

Economic and Political Trends	Industry Dynamics	Evolving Technology	Labor Markets	National and Regional Cultures	Laws and Regulations	Unions and Collective Bargaining

Organizational Environment	**Human Resource Management Activities**	**Stakeholder Satisfaction**
Leadership • Vision • Mission • Values Strategy • Corporate diversification • Competitive business strategy Organizational Structure • Domestic • Global Organizational Culture	*Formal Policies and Daily Practices* • Ensuring fairness and legal compliance • Creating organizational alignment • HR planning for strategic change • Job analysis and competency modeling • Recruitment and retention • Selecting employees to fit the job and organization • Training and development • Measuring performance and providing feedback • Compensating employees • Using rewards to enhance motivation • Providing benefits and services • Promoting workplace safety and health • Understanding unionization and collective bargaining	Owners and Investors • Financial returns • Corporate reputation Customers • Quality • Speed, responsiveness • Low cost • Innovation • Convenience Society • Legal compliance • Social responsibility • Ethical practices Other Organizations • Reliability • Trustworthiness • Collaborative problem-solving Organization Member • Fairness • Quality of work life • Long-term employability

The HR Profession

hires sink or swim. Some pay well and offer large bonuses, others don't. Many of these differences in how organizations manage people are due to differences in the environments of organization.

The Global Environment. The global environment affects organizations in many ways—but its effects are not the same for all organizations. Small businesses do not have to comply with the same employment laws that apply to large organizations. Labor market conditions for businesses in high-tech industries can be very different from those in the retail industry. Global businesses face a stronger imperative to respond to differences in national cultures than do most domestic businesses.

Chapter 2 describes in detail several aspects of the global environment that can influence an organization's approach to managing human resources. In addition to the globalization of business, it reviews the important role of political organizations, industry dynamics, evolving technologies, labor market conditions, and cultural differences between countries.

Chapter 3 describes U.S. employment laws and regulations, and employees' evolving attitudes about what constitutes fair employment practice. It describes legal definitions of fairness, such as those provided by equal opportunity laws and various other regulations. This chapter also discusses how employees evaluate fairness. As Chapter 3 makes clear, complying with employment laws and regulations is only the first step in designing approaches to managing employees that they perceive as fair and equitable. Chapter 3 provides a foundation for other discussions of fairness that appear in subsequent chapters.

The Organizational Environment. Changes in the external global environment put pressure on organizations to change internally. As Chapter 4 explains, this creates the challenge of keeping the organization aligned with the global environment, and the challenge of aligning the internal organizational components. Often when major changes are needed, new leaders with different perspectives and management approaches are brought in to move the organization in new directions. In addition to developing new competitive strategies, they may restructure the business and develop a new mission and vision. Whether intentional or unintentional, major changes such as these often result in fundamental shifts in the organization's culture. Because the global environment is changing so rapidly, the internal environments of organizations seem to be in continuous flux. Human resource management activities play a central role in supporting the organization's ongoing process of adaptation and change.

Human Resource Management Activities

Every organization, from the smallest to the largest, engages in a variety of **human resource management activities.** Human resource activities include formal organizational policies, but these are just the tip of the iceberg. Also included are the many informal practices for managing people that simply evolve through daily interactions between managers and other employees in the organization. In some organizations, formal policies and informal practices are closely aligned. In most organizations, however, the formal policies represent statements of expectations and aspirations rather than actual daily practices. Over time, policies and practices evolve together. Sometimes policies are created in order to encourage new practices. Other times, new practices develop first and then formal policies are written to endorse the practices.

The many specific human resource policies and practices described in this book include the following:

- HR Planning for Strategic Change
- Job Analysis and Competency Modeling
- Recruitment and Retention
- Selecting Employees to Fit the Job and the Organization
- Training and Development
- Measuring Performance and Providing Feedback
- Compensating Employees

- Using Rewards to Enhance Motivation
- Providing Benefits and Services
- Promoting Workplace Safety and Health
- Understanding Unionization and Collective Bargaining

When an organization systematically coordinates and integrates all of these activities, it creates a **human resource management system.**

HR Planning for Strategic Change. An effective HRM system requires planning and coordination as well as continual evaluation and readjustment. Chapter 5 describes how strategic planning and HR planning together can be used to align HR practices with conditions in the global and organizational environments. HR planning also serves to align the various HRM activities with each other. Change management provides for continual evaluation of the HRM system's overall effectiveness and stimulates the organization to make adjustments that continually improve the system.

Using Job Analysis and Competency Modeling as the Foundation of the HR System. All organizations divide up the work to be done into jobs. Jobs comprise a set of task and role responsibilities. Effective HR systems are grounded in a clear understanding of the way work is allocated among jobs, the competencies needed by employees who work in those jobs, and a long-term view of how these are likely to change in the future. Chapter 6 describes how job analysis and competency modeling can be used to develop an understanding of the work and the competencies employees need in order to maximize their performance in current jobs as well as their longer-term success.

Recruiting and Retaining Employees. To get jobs done, organizations need to attract people to apply for jobs and retain those who do their jobs well. When job openings occur, recruitment may involve looking outside the organization for new employees. Alternatively, current employees may be recruited to move from their current jobs to new ones. Regardless of whether recruits come from outside or inside the organization, retaining the best employees is usually desirable. Chapter 7 describes how companies recruit applicants to apply for job openings and some of the ways they can reduce unwanted turnover. Understanding why excellent employees voluntarily leave reveals the important role of HR practices in retaining the best talent.

Selecting Employees to Fit the Job and the Organization. After applicants have applied for a position, but before they are made a job offer, the process of selection occurs. Selection involves sorting and ranking employees using a standard set of criteria. As described in Chapter 8, the criteria used to select employees flow from the results of job analysis and competency modeling. Increasingly, employers want to select employees who will be able and willing to learn new tasks and continually adapt to changing conditions. They also want employees who fit well with the organizational culture.

Training and Development. To ensure that people know what they're supposed to do, employers often provide some instruction and training. Training and retraining are critical issues in the technology-driven information era. With rapid changes in job requirements, existing employees must be both willing and able to develop new competencies, become proficient in new jobs, and even change their occupations. Chapter 9 describes the socialization, training, and development practices that enable employees to develop themselves and remain employable despite rapid changes in the world of work.

Compensating Employees. Employees work in exchange for compensation, whether monetary or otherwise. A total compensation package typically includes base wages or salary, some form of incentive pay, and various types of benefits. Chapter 10 describes how organizations design the total compensation package. It also describes in detail the process used to set the level of compensation to be offered for specific jobs.

Measuring Performance and Providing Feedback. To ensure that employees perform satisfactorily and receive appropriate recognition, performance must be measured in some way. Employees need fair and clearly stated performance standards. They deserve usable feedback and the support needed to identify and correct performance deficiencies. When appropriate performance standards, measures, and feedback are provided, capable employees become a high-performance workforce. Chapter 11 describes these activities and sets the stage for a discussion using rewards to further motivate employees.

Using Rewards to Motivate Employees. During the past decade, employers have been changing the design of total compensation. An overarching objective has been to increase the extent to which performance is a key driver of the pay that people receive. In the long run, creating a stronger linkage between performance and pay should improve motivation and productivity, which in turn should help to control labor costs. Chapter 12 describes the use of incentives, bonuses, and other forms of rewards that employees offer.

Providing Benefits and Services. As many organizations have discovered, retaining a high-performance workforce can be a major challenge. The best companies often become targets for recruitment by competitors. Offering innovative benefits packages and employee services that address a wide array of employees' concerns is one tactic for warding off such poaching, as described in Chapter 13. Such benefits include those with obvious monetary value, such as health insurance, as well as others whose monetary value is more difficult to quantify, such as flexible work arrangements and telecommuting options. In addition to the benefits that employers offer voluntarily, Chapter 13 describes mandatory benefits required by law.

Promoting Workplace Safety and Health. Chapter 14 focuses on what employers can do to ensure that the workplace is safe and that employees are healthy. As jobs in the United States have shifted out of manufacturing, and as even manufacturing jobs became less labor intensive, issues of workplace safety and health also have changed. Exposure to toxic chemicals and dangerous equipment remains a concern in some work environments, but more often air quality and ergonomic concerns top the agenda. Increasing concern about violence in the workplace is another unfortunate development described in Chapter 14.

Understanding Unionization and Collective Bargaining. Chapter 15 addresses the current state of unionization and collective bargaining activity. Although union membership has been shrinking steadily in the United

States for many years, firms such as GE, Southwest Airlines, Continental Airlines, AT&T, and the major U.S. auto companies all hold joint discussions with the unions on issues such as productivity gains, the quality of working life, and outsourcing. Because unions have maintained their strength in many other countries, they play vital role in companies that strive to be globally competitive and profitable.

Understanding the HR Profession

The design and implementation of effective HR systems requires substantial expertise. Although line managers from all areas of an organization must also be involved in the process, professional HR knowledge is essential. Chapter 16 considers the HR profession itself. The chapter specifically addresses readers who wish to pursue a career in human resource management, working either as a staff member within an organization or as an external consultant. What competencies will you need to succeed in this field? What professional standards will you need to meet? How are HR activities organized in different organizations? And what is the future likely to hold? The last chapter explores these questions from the perspective of HR professionals.

THE HR TRIAD

Used wisely, human resource management activities can transform a lackluster company into a star performer. Used unwisely, they create havoc. In some companies, existing approaches to managing human resources reflect chance and happenstance. Instead of analyzing how their HR systems affect all aspects of the business, some organizations continue to do things the same way year after year. Ask why salespeople in the shoe section are paid on commission and people in toys are not, and you are likely to be told, "That's just the way we've always done it." When companies do change the way they manage people, they may do so for the wrong reason. Why did that small retail food chain just send all its middle managers to off-site wilderness training? "Everybody in the industry's doing it—we can't be the only ones who don't." Why did your insurance company start randomly listening in on calls from customers? "The new telecommunications system we installed last year included it as a no-cost feature, so we decided we should use it."

Whether a company chooses its human resource policies and practices carefully or somewhat haphazardly, those policies and practices can have powerful effects. To be sure those effects are *positive* rather than destructive requires active involvement of three key players. We refer to them as the **HR Triad**:

- HR professionals,
- line managers, and
- the employees who are affected by the human resource policies and practices.

There's a saying at Merck that goes like this: "Human resources are too important to be left to the HR department." No department can, by itself, effectively manage a company's human resources.[6] Companies like Merck, Cisco Systems, and Southwest Airlines have developed approaches to managing people that reflect all three perspectives in the HR Triad. The special expertise of HR professionals is used by, and in cooperation with, line managers, other administrative staff, and all first-line employees in every

"Best Management Decision: Appointing the right people. Biggest Management Mistake: Appointing the wrong people."

Richard Goldstein
CEO
Unilever, United States

THE HR TRIAD Roles and Responsibilities for Managing Human Resources

LINE MANAGERS	HR PROFESSIONALS	EMPLOYEES
• Work closely with HR professionals and employees to develop and implement HR policies and practices. • Include HR professionals in the formulation and implementation of business strategy and discussions of its HR implications. • On a daily basis, consider the implications of business decisions for managing human resources. • Accept shared responsibility for managing human resources strategically and work to reduce barriers to this objective. • Learn about and apply basic accepted principles for managing human resources. • Seek input from employees and HR professionals in order to improve own competency for managing human resources.	• Work closely with line managers and employees to develop and implement HR policies and practices. • Stay informed of the latest technical principles for managing human resources. • Develop the skills and competencies needed to support change processes. • On a daily basis, consider how well the organization's approaches to managing human resources fit with the current global and organizational environment. • Be proactive in learning about how leading companies are managing human resources and what they're learning from their experiences. • Work with employees to help them voice their concerns effectively and serve as their advocate when appropriate.	• Work closely with line managers and HR professionals to develop and implement HR policies and practices. • Accept responsibility for managing their own behavior and careers in organizations. • Recognize the need for personal flexibility and adaptability. • Be committed to learning and changing continuously throughout one's career. • Learn about and apply basic accepted principles for managing human resources for HR activities in which they participate (e.g., selecting team members, appraising supervisors, and training coworkers). • Be willing to share ideas that might help the company manage its people better.

department. So, regardless of whether a line manager ever holds a formal position in human resource management, she or he is held accountable for the task of managing people.

Line Managers Have Always Been Responsible

"In many ways, I can't divorce the primary responsibilities of the CEO from the responsibilities of the senior HR person."

Irv Hockaday
CEO
Hallmark Cards

In small businesses, owners must have HR expertise as they build the company from the ground up. This reality is clearly reflected in the various popular magazines targeted to small-business owners—for example, *Inc.*, *Money*, *Success*, and *Entrepreneurship*. These publications devote a great deal of space to discussing issues related to managing the people who make up a small company. Eventually, as a company grows, the owner may contract out some of the administrative aspects related to managing people (e.g., payroll), or delegate some of the responsibilities to a specialist, or both. As the company grows larger, more specialists may be hired—either as permanent staff or on a contract basis to work on special projects, such as designing a new pay system. As with other business activities, these specialists won't bear all responsibility for the project. For example, many companies have a marketing department; nevertheless, they employ people outside that department to conduct marketing activities. Similarly, most companies have a few people with special expertise in accounting; nevertheless, employees throughout the company perform accounting activities. The same is true for managing human resources.

This book treats managing human resources as a responsibility shared by everyone in the company—line employees *and* professionals in the human resources department *and* top-level executives *and* even entry-level new hires. Consistent with the stakeholder model in Exhibit 1.3, involvement in the process of managing human resources can even extend to people outside the organization, such as managers in supplier firms, customers, union representatives, and members of community organizations.

HR Professionals Provide Special Expertise

HR professionals are people with substantial specialized and technical knowledge of HR issues, laws, policies, and practices. The leaders of HR units and the specialists and generalists staff who work within the function usually are HR professionals, although this isn't always the case. Sometimes organizations fill the top-level HR position with a person who has a history of line experience but no special expertise in HR. According to one survey of 1,200 organizations, this is a growing trend, reflecting increasing recognition of the importance of people to business success. Line managers who are doing a "tour of duty" in the HR department would be appropriately referred to as HR managers, but they would not be considered HR professionals—at least not until they gained substantial experience and perhaps took a few executive development courses devoted to HR.

External experts who serve as HR consultants or vendors for the organization *may* be HR professionals also. But don't assume that a consultant or vendor is an HR professional just because he or she offers HR products or services. In addition to a record of substantial HR experience, other things that might indicate the specialized expertise of a professional include a college-level degree in the field and accreditation from a professional association. For example, the Society for Human Resource Management provides certification for two levels of expertise for HR generalists: basic and senior. The World at Work (formerly the American Compensation Association) is an example of a professional organization that provides certification in specialized areas of HR. Whether employed on the staff or hired as consultants or vendors, HR professionals play many important roles in managing people effectively.

Employees Share Responsibility

The responsibilities of line managers and HR professionals are especially great; nevertheless, they share responsibility with the third key part of the HR Triad, namely all of the other employees who are affected by HR policies and practices. Regardless of their particular jobs, all of the employees in an organization share some of the responsibility for effective human resource management. Some employees write their own job descriptions and even design their own jobs. Many employees provide input for the appraisal of their own performance or the performance of their colleagues and supervisors, or both. Many organizations ask employees to participate in annual surveys where they can express their likes and dislikes about the organization's approach to managing people. Perhaps most significant, employees assess their own needs and values and must manage their own careers in accordance with these. Doing so effectively involves understanding many aspects of their employer's human resource management practices. As we move forward, we all need to position ourselves for the future. Learning about how effective organizations are managing human resources is an essential step for getting into position.

To help readers understand the role of the three key players in the HR Triad, each chapter includes a feature titled "The HR Triad: Roles and Responsibilities for Managing Human Resources." In this chapter, the HR Triad describes some of the general roles and responsibilities of the three key players in the Triad. Subsequently, the HR Triad focuses on roles and responsibilities that are relevant to the specific HR activities described in the chapter.

INTERNET RESOURCES   1.B

The HR Triad

At our Web site, http://jackson.swcollege.com/, you can:

1. Visit several professional associations whose members are experts in managing human resources:

   The Society for Human Resource Management

   Human Resource Planning Society

   The Human Resources Division of the Academy of Management

   WorldatWork

   Society for Industrial and Organizational Psychology

THE MEANING OF STRATEGIC PARTNERSHIPS: SATISFYING MULTIPLE STAKEHOLDERS

"If we treat employees the right way, they'll naturally treat our customers the right way."

Elizabeth Pedrick Sartain
VP of the People Department
Southwest Airlines

Ultimately, the success of an organization is determined by the evaluations of its major stakeholders. We argue throughout this book that an organization's approach to managing human resources is central to its success in satisfying key stakeholders.

Stakeholders are individuals or groups that have interests, rights, or ownership in an organization and its activities. Stakeholders who have similar interests and rights are said to belong to the same stakeholder group. Customers, suppliers, employees, society, and other organizations are examples of stakeholders, as illustrated in Exhibit 1.3.

Stakeholders benefit from the organization's successes and can be harmed by its failures and mistakes. Similarly, the organization has an interest in maintaining the general well-being and effectiveness of key stakeholders. If one or more of the stakeholder groups break off their relationships with the organization, the organization suffers.

For any particular organization, some stakeholder groups may be relatively more important than others. The most important groups—the primary stakeholders—are those whose concerns the organization must address in order to ensure its own survival.[7] When success is defined as effectively serving the interests of these groups, their needs define a firm's fundamental objectives. These objectives, in turn, drive the organization's approaches to managing employees.

Each organization weighs the concerns of stakeholders somewhat differently, but it ignores any particular stakeholder at its own peril. Executives who once enjoyed enormous autonomy and wielded considerable personal power in running their companies now focus increasingly on maximizing shareholder value. Companies that once attended little to customers now find that in almost every industry it's a buyers market, and sellers have become captives of the customer. Employers who once acted as if they were in charge of the employment relationship are now so desperate for good people that

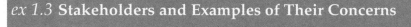

ex 1.3 **Stakeholders and Examples of Their Concerns**

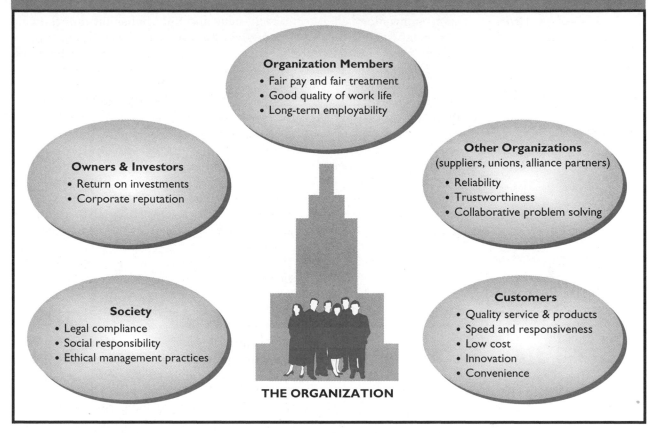

Organization Members
- Fair pay and fair treatment
- Good quality of work life
- Long-term employability

Owners & Investors
- Return on investments
- Corporate reputation

Other Organizations
(suppliers, unions, alliance partners)
- Reliability
- Trustworthiness
- Collaborative problem solving

Society
- Legal compliance
- Social responsibility
- Ethical management practices

Customers
- Quality service & products
- Speed and responsiveness
- Low cost
- Innovation
- Convenience

THE ORGANIZATION

they're beginning to let employees decide where company offices should be located, what hours they'll work, and under what conditions.[8]

The principle that effective management requires attending to all relevant stakeholders is as true for managing human resources as for other management tasks. Human resource practices cannot be designed solely to meet the concerns of employees. Nor can they be designed by considering only their consequences for the bottom line. Organizations that are the most effective in managing people develop HR systems that meet the needs of all key stakeholders. In order to develop a stakeholder-friendly approach to managing human resources, it is necessary to understand the concerns of each stakeholder group. We describe these next and briefly note how the concerns of each group can influence an organization's HR practices.

Owners and Investors

Most owners and investors invest their money in companies for financial reasons. At a minimum, owners and shareholders want to preserve their capital for later use, and ideally they want to experience a growth in their capital. To achieve these goals, their capital should be invested primarily in profitable companies. Because an organization's approach to managing human resources can enhance or diminish its profitability, many investors prefer companies with good reputations for HR management.

The job of institutional investors, which is to make money by choosing which companies to invest in, has become increasingly complex as difficult-to-measure assets have become more important. Tangible assets, such as inventory, equipment, real estate, and financial assets are relatively easy to measure. In the old economy, investors focused on measuring tangible assets in order to determine a firm's value. In the new economy, however, investors recognize that many **intangible assets** can be just as valuable as tangible assets. Intangible human assets include such things as reputation as an employer of choice, depth of employee talent and loyalty, and the firm's ability to innovate and change. In organizations such as investment banks, consulting firms, and advertising agencies, there is almost nothing there except intangible human assets. Investing in these companies often means hoping that the best employees will continue working at and for the company.[9] As one study of initial public offering (IPO) companies showed, companies that attend to human resource management issues are rewarded with more favorable initial investor reactions as well as longer-term survival.[10] Accountants may have difficulty attaching monetary values to a firm's human resources, but this doesn't stop investors from paying attention.

Because intangibles such as how employees feel and behave can be used to predict financial performance,[11] business analysts pay attention to how people are being managed. Each year, the staff at *Fortune* magazine conducts extensive interviews with employees in order to evaluate the best companies to work for.[12] To determine just how important happy workers were for achieving higher shareholder returns, *Fortune*'s research staff conducted one of the earliest efforts to look at this question. They studied the 61 publicly traded firms on their 1987 list of "100 Best Companies to Work For in America." Shareholder returns for the "100 Best" were compared with those of the "Russell 3000," an index that includes comparable companies. The bottom line? If you had invested $1,000 in the Russell 3000 in 1987, you would have had $3,976 in 1997, but if you had invested the same amount in the Best Companies to Work For, you would have had $8,188 by 1997—more than twice as much.[13] Research such as this shows that it's possible for organizations to manage employees in ways that satisfy investors as well as employees.

Several other studies have shown that the approaches companies take to managing their human resources can translate into greater profitability, higher annual sales per employee (productivity), higher market value, and higher earnings-per-share growth.[14] Exhibit 1.4 illustrates the results from a study of several hundred companies. A survey was used to measure each company's HR practices. These responses were then used to create a score between 0 and 100, which represented the extent to which the company's HR practices reflected state-of-the-art knowledge. The performance of these companies was measured using financial accounting data. As the graph shows, companies with better HR practices experienced greater increases in market value per employee. That is, firms with the best human resource management systems were rewarded the most by investors.[15]

Customers

At Siebel Systems and many other firms, improving customer satisfaction is a primary means through which human resource management practices affect success. Reducing costs, improving product quality, and improving service quality all are ways to improve customer satisfaction.[16]

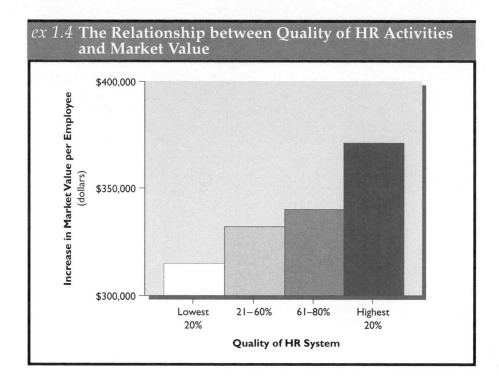

ex 1.4 The Relationship between Quality of HR Activities and Market Value

Service companies win or lose during the time of contact between employees and customers. This time of contact is now referred to by many people as the moment of truth—a phrase coined by Jan Carlzon as he was writing about his experiences as CEO and chairman of Scandinavia Airlines System.[17] The moment of truth, it turns out, is often the moment when customers get a glimpse of how a firm manages its human resources and its business. When the internal climate of the organization is positive, with employees generally getting along well and not leaving the company at too rapid a pace, customers report they're more satisfied and intend to return.[18]

The relationship between HR practices and customer satisfaction is explicit in the guidelines used to evaluate organizations vying for the Malcolm Baldrige National Quality Award. To meet customers' demands for higher quality, companies such as Weyerhaeuser, Southwest Airlines, and FedEx maintain an environment conducive to full participation and personal and organizational growth for their employees. This is the criterion for human resource utilization used by the committee that determines award recipients. Specific suggestions for how to create this environment are offered in the Baldrige guidelines. These include the following:

- Promote cooperation such as internal customer-supplier techniques or internal partnerships.
- Promote labor-management cooperation, such as partnerships with unions.
- Use compensation systems based on building shareholder value.
- Create or modify recognition systems.
- Increase or broaden employee responsibilities.
- Create opportunities for employees to learn and use skills that go beyond current job assignments.

> **FAST FACT**
>
> Averaging only 7 hours per employee per year, the retail industry spends less on training than all other business sectors.

- Form partnerships with educational institutions to develop employees or to help ensure the future supply of well-prepared employees.

Improving customer satisfaction often requires finding ways to improve the company's ability to understand the customer's perspective. For example, through its hiring practices, a company can make sure that its employees are demographically similar to customers. The assumption is that communication improves when employees and customers share similar experiences. Such reasoning led American Express to recruit gay and lesbian planners in order to improve service for gay and lesbian customers. They also sought to improve customer satisfaction among this group by educating financial advisers about the special needs of the gay and lesbian market.[19]

Society

For organizations such as public schools, nonprofit foundations, and government agencies, the concerns of owners—that is, taxpayers and contributors—often are essentially those of society at large. But for privately owned companies and those whose shares are publicly traded, the concerns of owners—that is, investors—may be quite different from those of society in general.

Under free-market capitalism, the primary managerial obligation is to maximize shareholders' profits and their long-term interests. Nobel Prize-winning economist Milton Friedman is probably the best-known advocate of this approach.[20] Friedman argues that using resources in ways that do not clearly maximize investor interests amounts to spending the owners' money without their consent—and is equivalent to stealing. According to Friedman, a manager can judge whether a decision is right or wrong by considering its consequences for the company's economic needs and financial well-being. If it improves the financial bottom line it's right, but if it detracts from the financial bottom line, it's wrong. Thus, for example, a company would be justified in hiring long-term welfare recipients if an analysis showed that this paid off given that government tax incentives and wage subsidies are available. But it could not justify such action simply by asserting that it's the right thing to do.

The average American rejects the idea that making money is the only role of business. In fact, socially responsible corporations are the more attractive alternative to prospective employees.[21] In other words, the best employers do more than simply obey the letter of the law—they seek to have a positive impact on society.

Legal Compliance. Codes of conduct for some aspects of business behavior take the form of formal laws, and many of these have implications for managing human resources. In addition, businesses are subject to regulation through several federal agencies and various state and city equal employment commissions and civil rights commissions. Finally, multinational corporations (MNCs) must be aware of the employment laws in other countries. By complying with legal regulations, firms establish their legitimacy and gain acceptance and support from the community. Ultimately, they increase their chances for long-term survival.[22] Because they affect virtually all human resource management activities, many different laws, regulations, and court decisions are described throughout this book, beginning with an overview in Chapter 3.

Community Relations. Formal laws and regulations establish relatively clear guidelines for how society expects a company to behave, but effective companies respond to more than simply these formal statements. They understand that the enactment of formal laws and regulations often lags behind public opinion by several years. Long before legislation is agreed to, communities communicate their expectations and attempt to hold organizations accountable for violations of those expectations. In turn, proactive organizations stay attuned to public opinion and use it as one source of information that may shape their own management practices. With heightened public interest in corporate social responsibility, many companies are discovering that they can't avoid having people evaluate how well they perform in this respect.[23]

A commitment to community involvement and development can have major implications for managing human resources. Voluntary labor is often a community's biggest need. Organizations that encourage employees to participate as volunteers help communities meet this need. For example, UPS recently celebrated the 30th anniversary of its Community Internship Program, a four-week program in which managers live in poor neighborhoods while working in soup kitchens and women's shelters. Another ambitious volunteer programs—one that often serves as a benchmark for other companies—is the We Are Volunteer Employees (WAVE) program, supported by the Fannie Mae and Freddie Mac Foundation. Key components of this program are described in Exhibit 1.5.[24]

Being socially responsive in these and other ways has many implications for managing human resources, including

- the type of employees the company chooses to hire,
- the criteria used to evaluate their performance,

FAST FACT

Volunteers serving in formal programs donate an average of 4.2 hours per week.

FAST FACT

When Cisco laid off 6,000 employees, it offered a unique severance package. Pink-slipped employees who agreed to work for one year at a local non-profit organization were paid one-third of their salary plus benefits and stock options, and the right to be first in line for rehiring in the future.

---

ex 1.5 The WAVE Program

Key Components of the We Are Volunteer Employees (WAVE) Program

- Volunteer matching service that helps employees connect with volunteer opportunities

- Group projects that are coordinated by "issues" committees (e.g., AIDS/HIV, homelessness)

- Corporate and regional recognition programs

- "Dollars for Doers" grants that match the hours employees work with donations for the agencies they serve

- Team building for executives based on volunteer service

- 10 hours paid leave time per month for volunteer activities

- the scheduling and coordinating of activities within work units, and
- compensation practices associated with paying employees for time spent in the community.

Other Organizations

Companies of all types are becoming increasingly interdependent with other organizations. Other organizations that can be considered major stakeholders include suppliers, unions, and alliance partners, among others.

Suppliers. Suppliers provide the resources a company needs to conduct its business. In addition to the capital of owners and investors, the resources needed by most companies include material and equipment, information, and people. Other companies usually supply material and equipment. Suppliers of people might include schools, the professional associations that serve specific occupational groups, state employment agencies, and companies that offer electronic recruiting services.

Unions. Unions may also serve as a supplier of people, but their role is much larger than this. Firms with employees who are represented by a union involve unions in joint discussions on issues such as improving productivity; outsourcing policies; improving safety, compensation, and benefits; and various other conditions of work. In recent years, union leaders and their members have moved away from their traditional adversarial relationship with management to a collaborative, problem-solving relationship. Despite this general trend, work slowdowns and strikes remain major threats to companies in which unions represent the employees. Furthermore, such work disruptions often reach far beyond the firm itself. When strikes involve transportation or communications workers, the entire country feels their effects.

Alliance Partners. Through cooperative alliances with other firms, a company seeks to achieve goals that are common to all members of the alliance. Some alliances are formed to influence government actions. In New Jersey, for example, leaders from business, government, and labor organizations formed an alliance to address the government's approach to managing the state's transportation infrastructure (including roads, rivers, and rails). Research and development needs are another common reason for alliance formation. International Sematech is an example of a multilateral alliance that supports learning through collaborative research. Through joint participation, 13 semiconductor manufacturers from seven countries share knowledge and expertise in ways that ultimately influence the entire industry.

Joint ventures represent yet another basis for forming alliances. When a bottle maker learned how to recycle plastic, it recognized the commercial opportunities of the technology. Subsequent discussions with suppliers, customers, and competitors about a collaborative venture eventually helped all the partners realize that the idea would require substantial investment in research and development. Out of this, a collaborative research network was born. Each company paid toward the research at a university and participated in quarterly board meetings. The research output became the venture's property, and all interested parties were assured licensing rights for a nominal fee. As we describe in Chapter 4, managing human resources within strategic alliances poses many special challenges.

Organizational Members

Organizational members are another key stakeholder group. Unlike the other external stakeholders we discussed above, organizational members reside within the organization. Included in this group are *all* of the people who hold positions within the organization, including the CEO and other top-level executives, other managers and supervisors, professionals and administrative specialists, line employees, part-time employees, and so on. Because they are such a diverse stakeholder group, they have a great variety of concerns. Nevertheless, most members of this stakeholder group share concerns about pay and benefits, quality of work life, and employability.

Pay and Benefits. Most organizational members want to be paid well and they want to be paid fairly. For women, the desire to receive equal pay for equal work is among the most important workplace issues, according to a national survey of 40,000 women. Nevertheless, many women as well as men feel that their employers don't live up to this principle. Of nearly equal importance to fair pay are a desire for secure and affordable health insurance, paid sick leave, and assured pension and retirement benefits. Some people may be surprised that child-care issues are considerably less important than these other concerns for the majority of women surveyed.[25] In fact, it is precisely because people's attitudes can be difficult to estimate that progressive companies use surveys to monitor the concerns of organizational members. HR policies and practices can then be developed to address the most important concerns.

Quality of Work Life. Besides earning a good living, most employees also want to enjoy a good quality of life while on the job. Starbucks' Howard Schultz grew up knowing his father felt beaten down by his work. At Starbucks, Schultz strives to make sure that workers have self-esteem no matter what the nature of their jobs. Providing a stock option program and generous health insurance benefits for everyone—even part-timers—is part of the strategy.[26] Many aspects of human resource management contribute to a good quality of working life, including

- training and development to improve employees' skills and knowledge,
- job designs that allow employees to really use their knowledge and skills,
- management practices that give employees responsibility for important decisions,
- selection and promotion systems that ensure fair and equitable treatment,
- safe and healthy physical and psychological environments, and
- work organized around teams.

    Such practices increase employee commitment, satisfaction, and feelings of empowerment, which in turn result in greater customer satisfaction.[27] In general, corporate cultures characterized by greater employee involvement and participation generate higher returns on sales and investments in subsequent years.[28]

Employability. In recent years, the changing economy and its effects on the workplace have introduced tremendous uncertainty, creating feelings of insecurity and anxiety for employees and their families. When IBM restructured its organization in the early 1990s, it terminated more than 100,000

> *"I don't want my tombstone to read, 'He shipped a billion pairs of jeans.' I can sleep better at night knowing that the package we put together for our displaced people provided them with far more benefits than what is conventional. [Nevertheless], you have to have a financially viable business or all the words about values can ring hollow."*
>
> Robert D. Haas
> Chairman
> Levi Strauss

FAST FACT

At American Century, a mutual fund and brokerage company with about 3,000 employees, more than 50% work a flexible schedule and 4% telecommute full-time.

employees. The company had long been known for its policy of job security, so employees were shocked when IBM replaced some of its managers with temporary people hired to finish ongoing projects.

In the new economy, companies like IBM now strive to develop a sense of *employment* security, not job security. Employment security increases when employees develop skills and knowledge that they need to be employable should they lose their current job. Feelings of employment security also improve when employers provide outplacement assistance as part of the severance package offered to laid-off workers.

Finding Synergy

Clearly, the primary concerns of the stakeholder groups differ somewhat, and conflict among stakeholders is common. But shared interests aren't unusual either. Effective managers determine the interests of key stakeholders and work with them to find a solution that addresses each set of concerns. More and more managers are beginning to understand that a company's human resource practices can either exacerbate apparent conflicts among key stakeholders or create synergies.

The events leading up to a settlement between the United Steelworkers and Wheeling-Pittsburgh Steel Co. illustrates the point. When steelworkers struck the company, the union put pressure on the company's major stockholders. The source of the influence was its pension funds. Over $10 billion in pension funds were managed by one of the steel company's major stockholders. After this stockholder publicly expressed support for management's position, the union sent a message: "If this is your philosophy, maybe you shouldn't be managing worker money." When the dispute was resolved, the chairman of the company that was managing the pension fund took some credit for encouraging the company to reach a satisfactory agreement with the union.[29]

As another example, consider what happens during restructuring and downsizing. Decisions to reduce layers of management or sell off a poorly performing division usually are made to improve efficiency and profitability in order to satisfy shareholders. The employees who lose their jobs in the process are victims of the conflict between their needs for employment and shareholders' desire for financial gain. However, when the compensation system is used to ensure that employees are owners themselves, managers and other employees may put more effort into finding a solution that minimizes disruption while also meeting the organization's financial goals.

FAST FACT

Union pension holdings, most of which are invested in the stock market, exceed $1.3 trillion.

INTERNET RESOURCES   **1.C**

Satisfying Multiple Stakeholders

At our Web site, http://jackson.swcollege.com/, you can:

1. Find measures for evaluating how effectively a company manages human resources at Metrus and the Saratoga Institute.

2. Learn more about research linking HR activities to financial performance.

3. Learn more about the Malcolm Baldrige Quality Award.

4. Learn more about the community involvement of Fannie Mae and Freddie Mac.

5. Learn about the members of the AFL-CIO and their current concerns.

In the chapters that follow, we argue that approaches to managing human resources can provide organizations with effective solutions to the problem of how best to align the organization with the concerns of its multiple stakeholders, even when the concerns of different stakeholders seem to conflict. In more cases than not, appropriate HR practices make it possible to create win-win situations. The approach of developing human resource management policies and activities that are responsive to the concerns of an organization's key stakeholders is what we mean by *Managing Human Resources Through Strategic Partnerships*.

LOOKING AHEAD: FOUR CURRENT CHALLENGES

As organizations strive to manage employees effectively, they face many challenges. In subsequent chapters, we pay attention to four special issues that companies are currently struggling to understand and resolve:

- managing teams,
- managing diversity,
- managing globalization, and
- managing change.

As you will see, all of the human resource activities discussed in subsequent chapters can help organizations address these special issues, as well as the ever-present issues of attracting, retaining, motivating, and improving a competitive workforce.

Managing Teams

In a recent study of U.S. and Canadian companies, half the managers responding believed that improving teamwork processes to focus on customers was the strategic initiative with the greatest potential for ensuring their organizations' success. According to a survey conducted by The Conference Board, innovation and on-time delivery were the two most common reasons for the increasing use of work teams. As described in the feature "Managing Teams: Mayo Clinic's Patient-Centered Care,"[30] improved problem solving and better patient care make the extra effort of teamwork worthwhile. Exhibit 1.6 lists several other reasons for organizing employees into work teams instead of having them work on small tasks that they can complete alone.[31]

"I love this job. Here everyone does everything. It's like a team."

Chris Robinson
Employee
The Container Store

ex 1.6 Why Organizations Use Work Teams

THE MOST COMMON REASONS FOR HAVING EMPLOYEES WORK IN TEAMS

To Satisfy Customers

- Improve on-time delivery of results
- Improve customer relations
- Facilitate innovation in products and services
- Improve quality
- Reduce costs and improve efficiency

To Satisfy Employees

- Facilitate management development and career growth
- Reinforce or expand informal networks in the organization
- Improve employees' understanding of the business
- Increase employee ownership, commitment, and motivation

MANAGING TEAMS

Mayo Clinic's Patient-Centered Care

Each year, nearly half a million patients are treated by the 2,000 physicians and 35,000 allied staff who work in the Mayo Clinic. The philosophy behind the Mayo Clinic was developed a century ago by two Minnesota physicians—Doctors Charlie and Will Mayo. Their philosophy for practicing medicine was that two heads are better than one and that five heads are even better! That philosophy is reflected in the Mayo Clinic's mission statement:

Mayo will provide the best care to every patient every day through integrated clinical practice, education and research.

Symbolizing the integration of practice, education, and research in the interest of protecting patients' health is the clinic's logo of three interlocked shields.

At Mayo, the value of teamwork is evident everywhere. Doctors are encouraged to include social workers, spiritual advisors, and psychiatrists as members of the team working with a patient. Dr. Lynn Hartmann explained the team concept: "We work in teams, and each team is driven by the medical problems involved in a case and the patient's preferences. Sometimes that means that a

team must be expanded—or taken apart and reassembled."

The importance of doctors consulting with each other when treating patients is reflected in the language used at the clinic. All doctors use the term *consultants* to refer to each other. To ensure that economic forces don't interfere with teamwork, all doctors are paid a salary. The high value placed on teamwork also shows up in the way patients are treated. They can be as actively involved in their own diagnosis and treatment as they wish. Governance of the clinic is by teamwork, too. Committees of doctors make decisions ranging from how to decorate the lobby, to how patient billings should be handled, to when and where to expand the clinic and its services.

The Mayo approach is unique, so how does the clinic find physicians who fit its culture? Most of them have been "Mayo-ized" through a process of careful selection and extensive socialization. For physicians who train at Mayo, the culture is taught from the beginning of their careers. Their days in training also give Mayo consultants time to observe whether they fit the culture. "You can tell early on. You watch people, day in and day out, and you quickly tell who has the attitude as well as the aptitude," explained neurologist Robert Brown.

The increasing popularity of team-based organizational structures reflects the belief that teamwork can achieve outcomes that could not be achieved by the same number of individuals working in isolation. But as many organizations are discovering, the payoff from teams isn't automatic. Although teams offer great potential for increased innovation, quality, and speed, that potential isn't always realized. Even when teams do fulfill their potential in these areas, team members and their organizations may experience unanticipated negative side effects, such as lingering unproductive conflicts and turnover.[32]

Human resource management practices can make the difference between success and failure for organizations using teams. To create and orchestrate teams, people need to be selected, appraised, compensated, and trained in ways that reflect the unique relationships that develop between employees who work together. Most companies know—or at least believe—that people working in teams should not be managed just the same as people who work more or less independently. Nevertheless, teamwork really is a somewhat new phenomenon in the American workplace, so considerable experimentation in how best to manage teams is still taking place around the country. Some practices now viewed as experimental will undoubtedly become commonplace within the next decade.

Because teams are rapidly becoming more prevalent in organizations, examples of how organizations are using human resource practices to maximize team effectiveness are highlighted throughout this book in the Managing Teams feature.

Managing Diversity

At about the same time that organizations began to recognize the benefits of teamwork, they discovered that the people who were being put into teams were more diverse than ever before. More and more women are working, for example, resulting in a new gender mix that's nearly balanced instead of being male dominated. Throughout this century, immigration patterns also have changed, resulting in more cultural diversity. In addition to issues of gender and ethnicity, employees differ from each other on a wide variety of values and lifestyles. Thus organizations are finding that diversity management practices must be sensitive to issues of religion, sexual orientation, marital and family status, age, and various other unifying life experiences.[33]

　　　　Throughout this book, the Managing Diversity feature describes how effective organizations use HR practices to leverage employee diversity and create competitive advantage. Before reading further, test your basic knowledge about diversity by completing the quiz in the feature "Managing Diversity: Diversity Knowledge Quiz."

Diversity Knowledge Quiz

MANAGING DIVERSITY

Indicate whether each statement is True or False.

1. T　F　Joy and fear are feelings that can be accurately recognized from facial expressions, regardless of which cultures people are from.

2. T　F　A person who is older than 65 and living in one of the world's developing regions is three times more likely to be working than a person of that age living in a developed region.

3. T　F　Worldwide, about 50 percent of women between the ages of 15 and 64 are in the labor force.

4. T　F　Most Americans with Japanese heritage come from families who have lived in the United States for two or three generations.

5. T　F　During the past decade, college graduation rates have been declining for men and increasing for women.

6. T　F　Most people could count on their fingers the number of female and minority CEOs who head one of the 500 largest firms in the United States.

7. T　F　In America's 10 largest cities, an average of one of four persons is of Latino origin.

8. T　F　Compared with other demographic groups, gay men tend to be better educated and hold higher paying jobs.

9. T　F　Compared with other employees, those with disabilities have better safety records on the job.

10. T　F　Mental speed slows down slightly but steadily beginning at about age 30, but performance of many complex mental tasks continues to improve steadily as people age.

11. T　F　As recently as 1970, interracial marriages were illegal in some parts of the United States.

12. T　F　Almost all *Fortune* 500 firms indicate that they are implementing initiatives to manage diversity.

13. T　F　The proportion of companies with at least one woman board director is greater among *Fortune* 500 companies than among companies ranked 501 through 1,000.

14. T　F　One out of every four American workers is employed by a business owned by a woman.

For the correct answers, refer to page 35.

Glass Ceilings and Glass Walls. Many of the approaches to managing people that are prevalent in today's organizations reflect old habits developed when the workplace was more homogeneous. To the extent diversity was present years ago, different demographic groups were segregated by level in the organization and job categories. Segregation within organizations is declining, albeit slowly, and with this desegregation comes the new challenge of managing workforce diversity.

In today's progressive atmosphere, it may seem hard to believe that glass walls (between occupational groups) and glass ceilings (between levels within the organization) still persist in corporate America. But it takes considerable effort and time to change some of the old patterns of managing human resources that created these phenomena.[34] A Department of Labor report, *Workforce 2000*, initially drew attention to the issue by highlighting the changing demographics of the U.S. labor force. Then, a follow-up report by the Department of Labor's Glass Ceiling Commission showed that women and non-Caucasian men were advancing up the corporate ladder more slowly than Caucasian men were. With approximately equal numbers of men and women now obtaining degrees in accounting, accounting firms are now under considerable pressure to improve these statistics. Failing to do so will greatly impair their appeal as employers for fully one-half of all entry-level accountants.

> **FAST FACT**
>
> In accounting firms, women compose about 25% of the workforce, but less than 10% of partners are women.

> **FAST FACT**
>
> The term *Hispanic* is used to refer to people with national origins from numerous different countries and cultures, including Cuba, Mexico, Puerto Rico, Spain, and the countries of Central and South America.

An organization can begin to assess whether people from different backgrounds and with different needs are being given job opportunities that match their capabilities by analyzing various employment statistics. But usually that is just the first step in building a positive organizational culture in which everyone feels equally integrated into the larger system. In such organizations, members of majority and minority subcultures feel respected, everyone has an equal chance to express views and influence decisions, and everyone has similar access to both formal and informal networks within the organization. Achieving these outcomes often requires making significant changes in recruitment, selection, training, development, performance assessment, pay, and promotion practices.

Creating Economic Value. Many organizations are striving to manage diversity effectively because they believe that they can use diversity to create greater economic value.[35] With a diverse workforce and positive organizational culture in place, many managers believe that their companies will be able to

- develop products and services for new markets,
- attract a broader range of customers,
- improve customer satisfaction and increase business from repeat customers, and
- reduce costs, including those associated with litigation.

Denny's is an organization whose negative corporate culture resulted in blatantly poor customer service for African-American customers and several consecutive years of financial losses. In 1993, on the same day that it settled one federal suit for discriminating against customers in California, six black Secret Service agents waited nearly an hour before being served in a Denny's restaurant in Maryland. Such poor customer treatment was condoned by Denny's managers all over the country. Meanwhile, competitors such as McDonald's had established strong links to minority communities and developed many loyal customers. The cost to Denny's of settling these and similar suits was enormous. As part of one settlement, Denny's paid $54 million to 295,000 aggrieved customers. In the case of Denny's, there is little doubt that corporate culture contributed to the company's financial decline during the 1980s and early 1990s. Since then, Denny's has effected a major cultural and financial turnaround. In fact, the transformation has been so complete that Denny's parent company, Advantica, was rated by *Fortune* as the best company for minority employees in 2000.[36]

Little research is publicly available to document the economic benefits of a diverse workforce and positive organizational culture. Some companies use proprietary information to establish the economic benefits of diversity. Others simply believe that there is a link and don't require research evidence to support their view. One manager was convinced of the value of the firm's diversity efforts when he and a team of his managers attended a meeting with one of their company's largest customers. Somewhat to his surprise, there wasn't a single white male on the other side of the table. When they expressed an interest in his company's diversity efforts, he was fortunate to be able to point to an excellent record, despite appearances. Christine Lagarde, chairman of Baker & McKenzie, one of the largest law firms in the world, agrees that customers expect to see diversity in the companies that they do business with. As more and more corporations hire women as high-level corporate counselors, law firms are getting the message that they need to have similarly integrated legal teams.[37]

Undoubtedly, personal experiences with customers and clients have convinced some CEOs that managing diversity poorly is risky business. But what may have grabbed the most attention of CEOs was the stock plunge that Texaco experienced after it settled a widely publicized discrimination lawsuit. At $175 million, the cost of the settlement itself was substantial. However, that paled in comparison with the nearly $1 billion decline in market value that occurred in the days immediately following the discovery of a tape recording in which a high-level executive was heard making racist remarks that were apparently accepted without comment by the other executives who were present. Texaco's share price later recovered, and management has since earned praise for its efforts to improve the company's organizational culture. But the cost of this episode to the company and its employees was enormous.[38]

For organizations that are committed to fully utilizing their human resources, having a workforce that is diverse in terms of gender, ethnicity, culture, lifestyle, religion, sexual orientation, age, and many other characteristics requires finding new ways of managing. The increasing diversity of the workforce, combined with changing attitudes about differences that may have been ignored in the past presents both challenges and opportunities for organizations and their employees.

Managing Globalization

During the past 50 years, technological advances in transportation and communications have spurred the growth of international commerce. As a result, many firms evolved from being purely domestic to becoming truly global. The first step in this evolution was simply to export goods for sale in one or two foreign markets. The next step was to manufacture those goods overseas

"Diversity was a concept as foreign to its all-white management team as foie gras was to a Denny's menu."

News Reporter

because it was more efficient than shipping products thousands of miles to markets. Setting up operations close to foreign markets also helped a company better understand its customers. A transnational firm has "headquarters" in several nations, and no single national culture is dominant in the firm.[39] Customers in various countries may not even think of such firms as being foreign owned. For example, many U.S. customers don't think of Shell Oil Company as a Dutch firm. As firms evolve from domestic to global, they face several challenges related to managing human resources. Staffing is one such challenge, as illustrated in the feature "Managing Globalization: Hiring Is No Laughing Matter for Cirque du Soleil."[40] When making hiring decisions in various parts of the world, Cirque du Soleil must understand the legal constraints as well as the cultural factors that apply in each country.[41]

Foreign Employees Working in U.S. Companies Abroad. One of the most difficult challenges for truly global organizations is developing an approach to managing human resources that works at home as well as abroad. Perhaps because Cirque du Soleil was founded as an international organization, it quickly learned how to conquer this challenge. Other firms have learned more slowly through painful trial and error. When Lincoln Electric began to globalize, it assumed that its very American approach to managing employees would work just as effectively in other countries as it worked in Cleveland, Ohio. It soon discovered that exporting its approach to managing human resources wouldn't work. In fact, some of its practices are illegal in other countries, just as some practices that are common in other countries are illegal in the United States. A firm's decisions about which HR practices will be used universally and which will be adapted to reflect local conditions may ultimately determine its success or failure.

Expatriate Assignments. Managing expatriates is another major HR challenge that firms grapple with as they expand beyond domestic borders. Suppose that you are a senior partner in Midland Ashby, a consulting firm. You are writing a proposal for an assignment halfway around the world, and as part of the proposal you need to describe the members of the team that would work with your client. The client is located in a country with very "traditional" views about men and women. The person with the most expertise on the client's problem is a woman, so you list her as one of the team members. Your potential client comments on this aspect of the proposal, stating that a woman team member is unacceptable. What should you do? Should you remove the woman from consideration and give her another assignment, or should you refuse to play by the client's rules?

When a panel of managers was asked this question, here's how they responded.

- One manager commented, "Business is business. Leave her on the team, where you need her. It would be ridiculous to assume that she could not be on the team even in a culture with very different attitudes about women."
- Two other managers chose to begin by trying to persuade the client to accept the woman. But if the client would not accept her, they would take her off the team in order to respect the culture of the client.

MANAGING GLOBALIZATION

Hiring Is No Laughing Matter for Cirque du Soleil

Remember the last time you sat under the big top, watching clowns entertain and acrobats tumble across the floor? Perhaps you've even seen a performance of Cirque du Soleil—one of the most unique acts in the world. With corporate headquarters in Montreal and offices in Las Vegas, Nevada, and Amsterdam, Holland, Cirque du Soleil is an international entertainment company that employs more than 1,200 people representing 17 nationalities and speaking at least 13 different languages. Its main products include a permanent show that runs in Las Vegas and several touring shows that run in countries around the world.

In this business, people are clearly the company's most important asset. Success is possible only with careful planning, recruitment, and selection. For its tours, Cirque relies heavily on temporary staff (temps) hired in each city—people who work

as ushers, ticket sellers and takers, and security personnel. For a year of tours, that adds up to some 1,800 temps. Although Cirque employs them for only a few days, good temps are essential to the company's reputation because they have the most direct personal contact with customers. To be hired, applicants must conduct themselves well during an interview designed to assess attitude, experience, and skills. For positions in the touring groups, the selection process is more intensive. Throughout these selection processes, the company must ensure that it adheres to all local labor laws. The following table illustrates differences in discrimination laws—just one aspect of employment conditions. Ideally, Cirque will also be sensitive enough to local conditions to be able to avoid practices that, although legal, are considered undesirable within local cultures.

WHO'S PROTECTED WHERE?

Country	Age	Sex	National Origin	Race	Religion	Marital Status
Canada	Yes	Yes	Yes	Yes	Yes	Yes
France	Some	Yes	Yes	Yes	Yes	Yes
Germany	No	Yes	Yes	Yes	Yes	No
Greece	No	Yes	No	Yes	Yes	Yes
Hong Kong	No	No	No	No	No	No
Indonesia	No	No	No	No	No	No
Japan	No	Yes	Yes	Yes	Yes	No
Singapore	No	No	No	No	No	No
United Kingdom	No	Yes	No	No	No	No
United States	Yes	Yes	Yes	Yes	Yes	No
Venezuela	No	No	No	No	No	No
Vietnam	No	Yes	No	Yes	Yes	No

- Acknowledging that this is one of the toughest business decisions, another manager said that the consulting company's principles against discrimination should not be compromised. He would leave her on the team and let her make presentations to the client to prove her expertise. He thought that this would probably result in loss of the contract, but that was better than discriminating against his employee.
- Two managers thought that the woman's suggestions and input should be sought before she was written into the proposal. If she was interested in the assignment, knowing the extra challenges she would face, these managers would keep her on the team. They would handle the client by stressing the importance of making a sound business decision—in this case, that means making use of the expert on the topic.
- One manager agreed that the consultant should be responsive to the cultural norms of clients. But she noted that the consultant might want to reconsider where and with whom the firm was willing to do business.

- One manager proposed handling the situation by explaining the situation to the woman and asking her to serve as a ghost member of the team. Her input would be sought and used by the team, but the client would never see her.
- One manager stated that legally, the consultant had no option but to use the best qualified person. Under Title VII, denying her the assignment because she was a woman would be illegal.

Foreign Employees Working in the United States. Yet another HR challenge for U.S. employers is managing foreign workers who work here. In the United States, domestic labor shortages in certain fields mean that some organizations cannot succeed unless they consider the entire world as their labor market. Thus, more and more employees are being hired from other countries. Many middle managers are working with a global workforce without even leaving home. These workers bring with them values, expectations, and patterns of behavior that reflect, in part, the HR philosophies, policies, and practices that they experienced in their home countries. HR practices can facilitate, or hinder, the speed with which foreign employees adapt to the U.S. culture and a specific organization. HR practices may also facilitate, or hinder, the effectiveness of the domestic employees who work side by side with foreign employees. Throughout this book, we return repeatedly to issues of how globalization affects organizations manage their human resources. Although detailed treatment of this topic is beyond the scope of this text, many of the issues that global organizations face are illustrated in the Managing Globalization feature. Readers who are particularly interested in cross-cultural and international human resource management should consult the relevant sources referenced throughout the chapters.

Managing Change

Current approaches to managing people within any particular company reflect both the past and the process of letting go of the past in order to prepare for the future. As environmental change quickens, more and more companies are concluding that some of the traditional approaches to managing human resources must be modified. A shortage of qualified employees may lead an organization to change its human resources management system in order to attract more job applicants. A never-ending stream of new technologies makes possible new approaches to recruiting—not to mention the possibility of a virtual organization. Changing laws and regulations may threaten old practices or create new opportunities. Merging with another firm, spinning off a business unit, and flattening the hierarchical structure all involve changing who does what and how. A dynamic, changing environment makes innovation and change as important—if not more important—for established organizations as they are for new organizations. Even the most successful organizations can't rest on prior successes. If they become complacent, competitors will woo away employees as well as customers.

Adopting a new organization structure, merging with another organization, or changing from a privately held to a publicly traded company are all examples of changes that affect human resource management. Such organizational changes can be stimulated by changes in the competitive environment, by persistent performance declines, by changes in top management

"The burden is on us, not the employee, to change. For many of us, that's a new recognition."

Charles R. Romea
Employee Benefits Director
ConAgra

leaders, or by the development of new technologies. Most recently, the development of the Internet has required managers in almost every industry to rethink and radically change the way their organizations function. At Hewlett-Packard, the Internet, declining share value, and a new CEO were the forces driving that company's radical change, including extensive restructuring of the business.

At Continental, a poor reputation in the industry and a new CEO were the forces that drove a major turnaround effort. The feature "Managing Change: Flying High Again at Continental" describes how changes in HR practices facilitated the recent transformation of Continental Airlines.[42]

Regardless of the cause, achieving radical change often requires huge investments in planning and implementing the change.[43] Almost always, changes in business practices mean changes in HR practices. Throughout this text, the Managing Change feature describes examples of how organizations use HR practices to create change.

> About the changes at
> Continental Airlines:
> *"I've been doing this for
> 20 years and I've never
> seen a turnaround of a
> workplace culture as
> dramatic as this one."*
>
> Robert Levering
> Coauthor of *100 Best Places
> to Work For in America*

P.S.: WHAT ARE HUMAN RESOURCES?

This book is about managing human resources. So far, we have spent a great deal of time talking about the subject, but we have not yet provided a definition of the term *human resources*. Is it just a fancy way to refer to *people* or *employees*? Does it mean anything different than the older term, *personnel*? How are human resources different from *human assets* or *human capital*?

Flying High Again at Continental

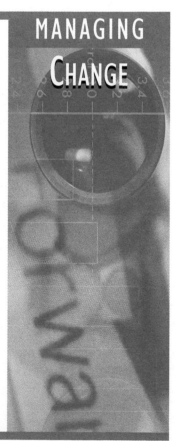

MANAGING
CHANGE

Before its turnaround, Continental Airlines was on the verge of bankruptcy for the third time. That's when the company began a complete transformation that rivaled Cinderella's at the stroke of midnight. Even the vice president of corporate communications admitted that the company had been in serious trouble: "This airline was probably, candidly, one of the least-respected airlines in corporate America. It could *not* get any worse." Two years later, Continental was celebrating its highest pretax profits ever. By 2001, it had fully regained its reputation as one of the better airlines in the United States (it had not yet matched Southwest Airlines, however).

CEO Gordon Bethune initiated the change effort by setting out the following strategic goals and specific measures of success:

1. *Fly to win.* The goal was to achieve top-quartile industry profit margins.
2. *Fund the future.* To do so required reducing interest expense by owning more hub real estate.
3. *Make reliability a reality.* Specific goals included ranking among the top airlines on the four measurements used by the U.S. Department of Transportation (DOT).
4. *Work together.* Have a company where employees enjoy working and are valued for their contributions.

When the specific goals were met, specific rewards followed. For example, one goal was to be ranked in the top five of the DOT on-time performance ratings. For each month the goal was achieved, employees would earn an extra $65. Two months later, Continental was in first place. Executives have goals and rewards, too. For example, employees regularly rate their managers on an employee survey, reporting on how well they communicate, set goals, and treat employees. Executives' bonuses reflect their performance as measured by the survey. Jobs were redesigned, which meant additional training was needed. To reduce fines the company was having to pay because of its slow turnaround times at the gate, new "supertugs" and communications equipment were purchased. Supertugs speeded up the docking and undocking of planes, but their use also changed the jobs of the mechanics and gate attendants who did this work. With the new equipment, supertug drivers operate as two-person "aircraft move teams" who are in direct communication with the control tower. According to one supertug operator, "the work is more challenging and more satisfying."

Although these sound like simple questions, we do not have simple answers. The term *human resources* gets used in a variety of ways by business journalists, managers, HR professionals, and even professors who write HR textbooks! Sorting out all the potential nuances is a task for another time and place. Here we simply wish to state what we mean when we use the term:

Human resources: *the available talents and energies of people who are potential contributors to the creation and realization of the organization's mission, vision, and goals.*

INTERNET RESOURCES   I.D

Looking Ahead: Four Current Challenges

At our Web site, http://jackson.swcollege.com/, you can:

1. Learn about how the Mayo Clinic uses teams to address patients' needs.

2. Learn about The Conference Board's most recent research results.

3. See how issues of diversity are addressed today at Denny's and Texaco.

4. Learn more about issues in international human resource management by visiting the home pages of the International Association for Human Resource Information Management and the International Personnel Management Association.

SUMMARY

Managing human resources is critical to the success of all companies, large and small, regardless of industry. The more effectively a firm manages its human resources, the more successful the firm is going to be.

Organizations define success by how well they serve their stakeholders. Stakeholders include those who have a claim on the resources, services, and products of the companies. Although stakeholders influence all parts of an organization, they affect some aspects more than others, and some aspects are affected by more stakeholders. The primary stakeholders who shape the typical organization's approach to managing human resources include (but aren't limited to) the shareholders and owners, society, customers, other organizations, and organization members. It is, in part, the existence of these powerful stakeholders that makes managing human resources such a challenging and important task.

Managing human resources involves many specific activities that, taken together, form an organization's human resource management system. Some approaches to managing human resources are more effective than other approaches. Nevertheless, there is no one best way to manage employees. Organizations need to manage human resources to fit their unique situations. This involves coordinated human resource activities. Every HR activity sends a message to employees. If all these activities send different messages, the employees are likely to respond in rather unpredictable ways. A strategic approach to managing human resources involves coordinating an organization's total set of HR activities with each other and fitting all of the HR activities to the global and organizational environment.

The complexity of managing human resources means that no one person can manage this task alone. Instead, line managers, HR professionals, and all other employees working in the organization must work together.

These three key players are referred to as the HR Triad. They share responsibility for managing human resources in a way that balances the concerns of an organization's primary stakeholders. In carrying out their roles and responsibilities, the HR Triad encounters many challenges. Four of those challenges appear as recurring themes throughout this book: managing teams, managing diversity, managing globalization, and managing change.

TERMS TO REMEMBER

Human resource management
Human resource management
   activities
Human resource management
   system
HR professionals

HR Triad
Intangible assets
Stakeholders
Sustainable competitive
   advantage

DISCUSSION QUESTIONS

1. What has Cisco Systems been doing that demonstrates the value of managing human resources? How do you think Cisco's approach is likely to change during times of economic boom and bust?
2. Refer to the list of stakeholders and their concerns in Exhibit 1.3. For each stakeholder group, add at least one additional concern that you think may shape how organizations manage human resources. Then, for each stakeholder group, give at least one specific example of how that group's concerns could affect a major HR activity (e.g., planning, staffing, appraisal, compensation, or training).
3. Explain the meaning of managing human resources through strategic partnerships.
4. Is it realistic to expect organizations to be strategic in managing human resources? What organizational and individual barriers are likely to make it difficult to adopt a strategic approach?
5. Why are the challenges of managing teams, managing diversity, managing globalization and managing change so important today? Are these challenges likely to decrease in importance during the next decade? Why or why not?

PROJECTS TO EXTEND YOUR LEARNING

Answer to Diversity Quiz on page 27: All of the statements are True.

1. *Managing Change.* HP began making significant changes under the leadership of CEO Carly Fiorina. Describe the ways in which HP is reinventing itself. How are these changes likely to affect the company's human resource policies and practices? Visit the company's home page to make your assessment.
2. *Integration and Application.* Read the two cases at the end of this textbook, entitled "The Lincoln Electric Company," and "Southwest Airlines." Then, using the stakeholder framework illustrated in Exhibit 1.3, make an illustration that identifies the stakeholders of each company and shows the relative importance of each stakeholder to each company. Here, as in the chapters to follow, you can gather your information from materials in the chapter, the cases at the end of the text, and from other

sources including newspapers, magazines, the Internet, and your experience. If you are unable to obtain information you feel is relevant, make assumptions based on your best judgment. Note any major assumptions you make. You'll want to visit the home pages of these two companies often, so bookmark them for future use.

INTERNET RESOURCES   I.E

Projects to Extend Your Learning

At our Web site, http://jackson.swcollege.com/, you can:

1. Find the company home pages for

   Hewlett-Packard

   Genentech.

2. Begin to learn more about the two companies featured in the End-of-Text Cases, Lincoln Electric and Southwest Airlines. You'll want to visit the home pages of these companies often.

LEVI STRAUSS & COMPANY

In 1872, Levi Strauss received a letter from Jacob Davis. The Nevada tailor, who had been buying bolts of fabric from Strauss's dry goods company, Davis wrote to explain how he used metal rivets to strengthen the construction of the overalls he made. Because Davis couldn't afford to file for a patent, he invited Strauss to become a partner. Strauss knew a good idea when he saw it and the two were granted the patent in 1873. Today, Levi Strauss & Company is still privately owned, and the company's approach to ethical management is as familiar to business leaders as its jeans are to teenagers. Its mission statement begins, "The mission of Levi Strauss & Co. is to sustain responsible commercial success as a global marketing company of branded apparel." Its Aspiration Statement goes on to say, "We all want a company people can be proud of," which includes "leadership that epitomizes the stated standards of ethical behavior." At Levi Strauss, ethical leadership extends well beyond company walls, to its dealings with some 500 cutting, sewing, and finishing contractors in more than 50 countries. Despite cultural differences in what is viewed as ethical or as common business practices, the company seeks business partners "who aspire as individuals and in the conduct of all their businesses" to ethical standards compatible with those of Levi Strauss. In addition to legal compliance, the company will do business only with partners who share a commitment to the environment and conduct their business consistent with

its own Environmental Philosophy and Guiding Principles. Partners must pay prevailing wage rates, require less than a 60-hour week, not use workers under age 14 or younger than the compulsory age to be in school, not use prison labor, and not use corporal punishment or other forms of coercion. Levi Strauss regularly conducts contractor evaluations to ensure compliance. It helps companies develop ethical solutions when noncompliance is discovered.

Closer to home, Levi Strauss actively promotes ethical business practices through activities such as membership in Business for Social Responsibility—an alliance of companies that share their successful strategies and practices through educational programs and materials. The company's domestic employment policies also are known for being ahead of the times. For example, during the 1950s, it was a pioneer in integrating factories in the South. In the 1990s, it was among the first companies to offer insurance benefits to its employees' unmarried domestic partners. Through this and other policies, the company has taken a strong stance in favor of the diversity that employees bring to the workplace. To assess how well the company adheres to its values, its conducts a social audit. Case Exhibit 1 shows some of the criteria used to evaluate the company.[44]

At our Web site, http://jackson.swcollege.com/, you can go to the home page of Levi Strauss & Company to learn more about its current activities.

case study

Case Exhibit 1 Social Audit Criteria Considered by Levi Strauss & Company

STAKEHOLDER GROUP	EXAMPLES OF CRITERIA CONSIDERED WHEN ASSESSING PERFORMANCE
Owners and Investors	Financial soundness
	Consistency in meeting shareholder expectations
	Sustained profitability
	Average return on assets over five-year period
	Timely and accurate disclosure of financial information
	Corporate reputation and image
Customers	Product/service quality, innovativeness, and availability
	Responsible management of defective or harmful products/services
	Safety records for products/services
	Pricing policies and practices
	Honest, accurate, and responsible advertising
Organization Members	Nondiscriminatory, merit-based hiring and promotion
	Diversity of the workforce
	Wage and salary levels and equitable distribution
	Availability of training and development
	Workplace safety and privacy
Community	**Environmental Issues**
	Environmental sensitivity in packaging and product design
	Recycling efforts and use of recycled materials
	Pollution prevention
	Global application of environmental standards
	Community Involvement
	Percentage of profits designated for cash contributions
	Innovation and creativity in philanthropic efforts
	Product donations
	Availability of facilities and other assets for community use
	Support for employee volunteer efforts

QUESTIONS

1. Knowing that its managers are willing to trade some economic efficiencies in order to operate according to their collective view of what is "ethical," would you buy shares of stock in this company? Why or why not?

2. Managers at Levi Strauss believe that they run an ethical company, but some critics view their liberal employment and benefits policies as immoral. These critics object to the policies because they're inconsistent with the critics' religious views. Analyze the pros and cons of adopting socially liberal employment policies that are viewed by some members of society (including potential employees and potential customers) as immoral.

3. Suppose you are looking for a new job. You have two offers for similar positions—one at Nike and one at Levi Strauss. Both organizations have indicated that they would like you to work for a year in one of their off-shore production plants somewhere in Southeast Asia. The two salary offers are very similar, and in both companies you would be eligible for an annual bonus. The bonus would be based largely on the productivity of the production plant where you will be located. Which offer would you accept? Explain why.

4. In recent years, Levi's has not performed well financially. Sales began declining in 1996 and since then the company has closed more than 50 plants worldwide, resulting in job losses for nearly 20,000 people. Do you think the company's approach to managing human resources is too expensive to maintain in the long term? Explain.

ENDNOTES

1 A. Diba and L. Munoz, "America's Most Admired Companies," *Fortune* (February 19, 2001): 64–80; N. Stein, "The World's Most Admired Companies," *Fortune* (October 2, 2000): 183–196.

2 R. Levering and M. Moskowitz, "The 100 Best Companies to Work For," *Fortune* (January 8, 2001): 148–168; Adapted from C. A. O'Reilly, III, and J. Pfeffer, *Hidden Value: How Great Companies Achieve Extraordinary Results with Ordinary People* (Boston: Harvard Business School Press, 2000): 49–77.

3 M. A. Hitt, L. Bierman, K. Shimizu, and R. Kochhar, "Direct and Moderating Effects of Human Capital on Strategy and Performance in Professional Service Firms," *Academy of Management Journal* 44 (2001): 13–28; S. A. Snell, M. A. Youndt, and P. M. Wright, "Establishing a Framework for Research in Strategic Human Resource Management: Merging Resource Theory and Organizational Learning," *Research in Personnel and Human Resource Management* 14 (1996): 61–90; J. B. Barney, "Firm Resources and Sustained Competitive Advantage," *Journal of Management* 17(1) (1991): 99–120; M. E. Porter, *Competitive Advantage* (New York: Free Press, 1985).

4 B. Leonard, "Ready to Soar," *HR Magazine* (January 2001): 52–56; W. Zellner, "Southwest: After Kelleher, More Blue Skies," *Business Week* (April 2, 2001): 45; F. E. Whittlesey, "CEO Herb Kelleher Discusses Southwest Airlines' People Culture: How the Company Achieves Competitive Advantage from the Ground Up," *ACA Journal* (Winter 1995): 8–25.

5 D. Roth, "My Job at the Container Store," *Fortune* (January 10, 2000): 74–78.

6 M. A. Huselid, S. E. Jackson, and R. S. Schuler, "Technical and Strategic Human Resource Management Effectiveness as Determinants of Firm Performance," *Academy of Management Journal* 40 (1997): 171–188.

7 D. Robson, "The Green Utility That's in the Black," *Business Week* (March 26, 2001): 108; C. Schmitt, "Corporate Charity: Why It's Slowing," *Business Week* (December 18, 2000): 164–166; O. C. Richard, "Racial Diversity, Business Strategy, and Firm Performance: A Resource-Based View," *Academy of Management Journal* 43 (2000): 164–177; M. B. E. Clarkson, "A Stakeholder Framework for Analyzing and Evaluating Corporate Social Performance," *Academy of Management Review* 20 (1995): 92–117; R. E. Freeman, *Strategic Management: A Stakeholder Approach* (Boston: Pittman/Ballinger, 1994); T. M. Jones, "Instrumental Stakeholder Theory: A Synthesis of Ethics and Economics," *Academy of Management Review* 20 (1995): 404–437.

8 T. Davenport, "Workers Are Not Assets," *Across the Board* (June 2000): 30–34.

9 M. F. Barney, "Human Capital," *The Industrial-Organizational Psychologist* 32(2) (October 2001): 58–62.

N. Wong, "Let Spirit Guide Leadership," *Workforce* (February 2000): 33–36; C. Handy, "A Better Capitalism," *Across the Board* (April 1998): 16–22.

10 T. M. Welbourne and A. O. Andrews, "Predicting the Performance of Initial Public Offerings: Should Human Resource Management Be in the Equation?" *Academy of Management Journal* 39 (1996): 891–919.

11 T. A. Stewart, "Real Assets, Unreal Reporting," *Fortune* (July 6, 1997): 207–208.

12 D. Whitford, "A Human Place to Work," *Fortune* (January 8, 2001): 108–120.

13 L. Grant, "Happy Workers, Happy Returns," *Fortune* (January 12, 1998): 81. Also see G. E. Fryzell and J. Wang, "The Fortune Corporation 'Reputation' Index: Reputation for What?" *Journal of Management* 20 (1994): 1–14.

14 For descriptions of other studies that show the linkage between managing human resources and organizational effectiveness, see E. Zimmerman, "What Are Employees Worth?" *Workforce* (February 2001): 32–36; J. Bae and J. J. Lawler, "Organizational and HRM Strategies in Korea: Impact on Firm Performance in an Emerging Economy," *Academy of Management*

Journal 43 (2000): 502–517; T. M. Welbourne and A. O. Andrews, "Predicting the Performance of Public Offerings: Should Human Resource Management Be in the Equation?" 891–919; B. E. Becker and M. A. Huselid, "High Performance Work Systems and Firm Performance: A Synthesis of Research and Managerial Implications," in G. Ferris (ed.), *Research in Personnel and Human Resources Management*, (Greenwich, CT: JAI Press, 1998); and the following articles, which all appeared in the *Academy of Management Journal*'s "Special Research Forum on Human Resource Management and Organizational Performance," Vol. 39(4) (August 1996): B. Becker and G. Gerhart, "The Impact of Human Resource Management on Organizational Performance: Progress and Prospects," 779–801; J. E. Delery and D. H. Doty, "Modes of Theorizing in Strategic Human Resource Management: Tests of Universalistic, Contingency, and Configural Performance Predictions," 802–825; M. A. Youndt, S. A. Snell, J. W. Dean, Jr., and D. P. Lepak, "Human Resource Management, Manufacturing Strategy, and Firm Performance," 836–867; R. D. Banker, J. M. Field, R. G. Shroeder, and K. K. Sinha, "Impact of Work Teams on Manufacturing Performance: A Longitudinal Field Study," 867–890.

15 Based on data presented in B. E. Becker, M. A. Huselid, and D. Ulrich, *The HR Scorecard: Linking People, Strategy, and Performance* (Boston: Harvard Business School Press, 2001); and M. A. Huselid and B. E. Becker, "High Performance Work Systems and Organizational Performance," Paper presented at the 1995 Academy of Management Meetings, Vancouver, BC (August 1995).

16 A. Wilkinson, G. Godfrey, and M. Marchington, "Bouquets, Brickbats and Blinkers: Total Quality Management and Employee Involvement in Practice," *Organization Studies* 18(5) (1997): 799–819.

17 J. Carlzon, as quoted in C. Grunroos, *Service Management and Marketing* (Lexington, MA: Lexington Books, 1990): xv.

18 J. W. Johnson, "Linking Employee Perceptions of Service Climate to Customer Satisfaction," *Personnel Psychology* 49 (1996): 831–846.

19 R. Abelson, "Welcome Mat Is Out for Gay Investors," *New York Times* (September 1, 1996): Section 3: 1, 7.

20 M. A. Friedman, "Friedman Doctrine: The Social Responsibility of Business Is to Increase Its Profits," *New York Times Magazine* (September 13, 1970): 32ff.

21 K. H. Hammonds, W. Zellner, and R. A. Melcher, "Writing a New Social Contract," *Business Week* (March 11, 1997): 60–61.

22 W. R. Scott, "The Adolescence of Institutional Theory," *Administrative Scientific Quarterly* (1987): 493–511; and L. G. Zucker, "Institutional Theories of Organization," *Annual Review of Sociology* (1987): 443–464; J. W. Meyer and B. Rowan, "Institutionalized Organizations: Formal Structure as Myth and Ceremony," *American Journal of Sociology* (1977): 340–363.

23 To learn how researchers attempt to measure corporate social performances, see D. Kirkpatrick, "Looking for Profits in Poverty," *Fortune* (February 5, 2001): 175–176; B. M. Ruf, K. Muralidhar, and K. Paul, "The Development of a Systematic, Aggregate Measure of Corporate Social Performance," *Journal of Management* 24 (1998): 119–133.

24 B. Leonard, "Supporting Volunteerism," *HRM Magazine* (June 1998): 84–93.

25 T. Lewin, "Equal Pay for Equal Work Is No. 1 Goal for Women," *New York Times* (September 5, 1997): A20.

26 K. F. Clark, "Leaders of the Pack," *Human Resource Executive* (May 6, 1997): 80–82.

27 E. E. Lawler III, *The Ultimate Advantage: Creating the High Involvement Organization* (San Francisco: Jossey-Bass, 1992); E. E. Lawler III, S. A. Mohrman, and G. E. Ledford, *Employee Involvement in America: An Assessment of Practices and Results* (San Francisco: Jossey-Bass, 1992).

28 E. E. Lawler III et al., *Employee Involvement and Total Quality Management* (San Francisco: Jossey-Bass, 1992); D. R. Denison, *Corporate Culture and Organizational Effectiveness* (New York: John Wiley, 1990).

29 A. Berstein, "Working Capital: Labor's New Weapon?" *Business Week* (September 29, 1997): 110–112.

30 P. Roberts, "The Best Interest of the Patient Is the Only Interest to Be Considered." *Fast Company* (April 1999): pp. 149–162.

31 H. Axel, "Teaming in the Global Arena," *Across the Board* (February 1997): 56; S. A. Mohrman and A. M. Mohrman Jr., *Designing and Leading Team-Based Organizations: A Workbook for Organizational Self-Design* (San Francisco: Jossey-Bass, 1997); R. D. Banker, J. M. Field, R. G. Schroeder, and K. K. Sinha, "Impact of Work Teams on Manufacturing Performance: A Longitudinal Field Study," *Academy of Management Journal* 36 (1996): 867–890.

32 S. E. Jackson, K. E. May, and K. Whitney, "Understanding the Dynamics of Diversity in Decision Making Teams," in R. A. Guzzo and E. Salas (eds.), *Team Effectiveness and Decision Making in Organizations* (San Francisco: Jossey-Bass, 1995); S. E. Jackson and R. N. Ruderman (eds.), *Diversity in Work Teams: Research Paradigms for a Changing Workplace* (Washington, DC: American Psychological Association, 1995).

33 For a description of the cultural experiences of Latino Americans, see R. Suro, *How Latino Immigration Is Transforming Us* (New York: Knopf, 1998).

34 P. D. Jennings, "Viewing Macro HRM from Without: Political and Institutional Perspectives," *Research in Personnel and Human Resource Management* 12 (1994): 1–40.

35 G. Robinson and K. Dechant, "Building a Business Case for Diversity," *Academy of Management Executive* 11(3) (1997): 21–31.

36 F. Rice, "Denny's Changes Its Spots," *Fortune* (May 13, 1996): 133–142; E. LaBlanc, L. Vanderkam, and K. Vella-Zarb, "America's Best 50 Companies for Minorities," *Fortune* (July 10, 2000): 190–200.

37 M. Petersen, "Her Partners Call Her Ms. Chairman," *New York Times* (October 9, 1999): C1, C4.

38 K. Labich, "No More Crud at Texaco," *Fortune* (September 6, 1999): 205–212; "Rooting Out Racism," *Business Week* (January 10, 2000): 66–67.

39 N. Adler and S. Bartholomew, "Managing Globally Competent People," *Academy of Management Executive* 6 (1992): 52–65.

40 C. Hall, "Ringmasters Turn a Circus into an Empire," *Dallas Morning News* (February 8, 1998): H1–H2; G. Flynn, "Acrobats, Aerialists, and HR: The Big Top Needs Big HR," *Workforce* (August 1997): 38–45. Table adapted from L. B. Pincus and J. A. Belohlav, "Legal Issues in Multinational Business Strategy: To Play the Game You Have to Know the Rules," *Academy of Management Executive* 10(3) (1996): 52–62; J. P. Begin, *Dynamic Human Resource Systems: Cross-National Comparisons* (New York: de Gruyter, 1997); R. Orzechowski and B. Berret, "Setting Up Shop in Vietnam," *Global Workforce* (May 1998): 24–27.

41 For a discussion of how culture impacts hiring practices, see A. M. Ryan, L. McFarland, H. Baron, and R. Page, "An International Look at Selection Practices: Nation and Culture as Explanations for Variability in Practice," *Personnel Psychology* 52 (1999): 359–391.

42 A. Farnham, "Worst Airline?" *Forbes* (June 11, 2001): 105–115; B. O'Reilly, "The Mechanic Who Fixed Continental," (December 20, 1999): 176–182; G. Bethune and S. Huler, *From Worst to First: Behind the Scenes of Continental's Remarkable Comeback* (New York: John Wiley, 1999).

43 K. E. Weick and R. E. Quinn, "Organizational Change and Development," *Annual Review of Psychology* 50 (1999): 361–386.

44 K. Schoenberger, "Tough Jeans, a Soft Heart and Frayed Earnings," *New York Times* (June 25, 2000): Section 3: 1, 12, 13; J. Makower, *Beyond the Bottom Line: Putting Social Responsibility to Work for Your Business and the World* (New York: Simon & Schuster, 1994).

CHAPTER

2

UNDERSTANDING THE GLOBAL ENVIRONMENT

"Our commitment to build a workforce as broad and diversified as the customer base we serve in more than 160 countries isn't an option. For us, this is a business imperative as fundamental as delivering superior technologies in the marketplace."

Lou Gerstner
CEO
IBM

MANAGING THROUGH STRATEGIC PARTNERSHIPS

DaimlerChrysler

From the day it was first announced, many outsiders believed that the culture differences between Daimler and Chrysler would create major problems during the post-marriage period of adjustment. The quintessential values and attitudes of each company's host country were reflected in everything—from product design to manufacturing, marketing, and approaches to managing human resources. Top executives in the new firm seemed to believe that the two company cultures could simply be put in a blender and poured out as a new synergistic company. Cultural issues were all but ignored. To many observers, it seemed as if the only time cultural issues were addressed was when executives made general statements to the media regarding the differences in the two companies. Either top management at Daimler and Chrysler did not fully realize the implication of cultural differences, or they chose to focus on operational and business synergies while simply hoping that cultural differences would resolve themselves.

Recalling his first meeting at the Mercedes-Benz U.S. headquarters, Chrysler marketing chief Jim Holden described the relationship between the two companies this way: "Many Daimler-Benz executives initially viewed Chrysler as a primped-up matron would regard an earnest young suitor. We felt like we were marrying up, and it was clear that they thought they were marrying down. As the Germans presented their view of the brand hierarchy—Mercedes on top and everything else far, far below—the tension in the room was palpable."

During the initial stages of the merger, Chrysler president Thomas Stallkamp indicated that Daimler intended to adopt Chrysler's product development methods, which emphasized teamwork rather than individual-oriented work procedures. Chrysler in turn would adopt many Daimler operating practices, including rigid adherence to timetables and their methodical approach to problem solving. The required cooperation failed to emerge, however. The battle became public knowledge when Daimler executives refused to use Chrysler parts in Mercedes vehicles.

Despite evident problems, Daimler's chief of passenger cars, Jürgen Hubbert, declared, "We have a clear understanding: one company, one vision, one chairman, two cultures." Since the departure of Robert Eaton (Chrysler's former chairman), it's true that only one chairman (Jürgen Schrempp) runs the company. Hubbert's other assertions are questionable, however. DaimlerChrysler may be "one" company in name, but two separate operational headquarters are maintained; one in Michigan and one in Germany. Business operations continue under separate paradigms, as evidenced by "Daimler's" decision to allow "Chrysler" more leeway in the design and production of its vehicles, which more closely emulated the practices of the "old Chrysler." Daimler and Chrysler each focus on different aspects of the automobile market, making one vision difficult to see. With the acknowledged existence of two cultures, can Daimler-Chrysler truly become one company with one vision?[1]

The DaimlerChrysler cross-border merger illustrates some of the management challenges created by globalization. Competitive forces in the global auto industry initially led the two companies to merge. The combination looked good on paper, but cultural differences interfered with management's ability to quickly reap the economic benefits it had anticipated. Had there been a partnership between the HR leaders and the top managers at both Daimler and Chrysler, it is possible that (1) the impact of the country cultures of the two companies would be significant in their relationship and (2) the creation of a common culture with one vision would have been possible.

THE STRATEGIC IMPORTANCE OF UNDERSTANDING THE GLOBAL ENVIRONMENT

Managing cultural differences is just one of the human resource challenges created by the forces of rapid globalization. Our guiding framework for managing human resources, which was summarized in Chapter 1 and Exhibit 1.2, emphasizes the importance of the global environment as a dynamic force that influences HR activities in U.S. organizations.

The **global environment** encompasses local, national, and multinational conditions. In this chapter, we briefly describe some of the implications of global conditions for human resource management. This discussion focuses on U.S. firms, but keep in mind that these same forces affect companies worldwide—from the smallest domestic firms to giant conglomerates with worldwide operations. The specific global conditions discussed in this chapter are the following:

- economic and political conditions,
- evolving technologies,
- industry trends (including mergers and acquisitions),
- differences in national and regional cultures, and
- labor markets.[2]

Two other important aspects of the external environment—legal issues and unions—are discussed later in Chapters 3 and 15, respectively.

Poorly managed human resources account for many business failures in the international arena. The primary cause of failure in multinational ventures is a lack of understanding of the essential differences in managing human resources in foreign environments—differences due to culture as well as those due to political and economic trends. Domestic firms with no international operations also can fail if they don't appreciate how the global environment affects their business.

Systematic Environmental Scanning

Despite the importance of the global environment for managing effectively, firms differ greatly in their use of systematic environmental scanning—especially when it comes to using the resulting information for making decisions about how to manage the firm's human resources. In the most competitive firms, formal and systematic analysis of the environment generally includes

1. scanning all segments of the environment to detect changes that are already under way and to identify early signals of potential changes,
2. regularly monitoring key aspects of the environment in order to more precisely determine the nature of changes as they unfold,
3. using forecasting techniques to make projections about what might actually happen and when, and
4. assessing the timing and significance of environmental changes for key decisions related to managing the firm (e.g., strategy selection).[3]

In many organizations, managers engage in these formal activities according to a regular schedule, for example, annually. Often, however, key events of special importance—such as an unexpected and major new action by a competitor or a military coup—can trigger a formal analysis.

The process of conducting a formal analysis is designed to ensure that the analysis is reasonably systematic. Structure is imposed on the process so that all of the available information is used and considered. As any experienced manager understands, however, there are many informal processes that influence how the information collected through formal analysis is eventually translated into decisions. Internal politics and simple habits from the past can shape the decisions made almost as much as the information itself.

Although seldom recognized, one of the most fundamental steps in conducting an environmental analysis is choosing who participates in the process of interpreting the results and using them to guide future action. If marketing is viewed as the most important activity, people who are viewed

"Merging a U.S. and a European company, as we have done, is a particularly complicated process. The management styles are totally different. People have different views on how to manage a global organization. The British and American philosophies are so apart on those subjects they're almost impossible to reconcile."

Jan Leschly
Former CEO
GlaxoSmithKline

as relevant to marketing activities may have more influence than others. If research and innovation are key concerns, then people with expertise about R&D issues will be included in the process. When a firm's human resources are recognized as essential to business success, people with knowledge of HR issues will be included. When human resource management issues are viewed as central to the success of the business, the organization is likely to be more systematic in gathering and interpreting information about labor markets and relevant cultural conditions. They may also be more systematic in analyzing the HR implications of changes in technology, economic trends, and political events.

Role of the HR Triad

To meet the challenges created by a dynamic environment, partners in the HR Triad must work together to gather relevant information about the environment, share it with all relevant stakeholders, and collaboratively develop action plans to address the challenges. When members of the HR Triad attend to their roles and responsibilities for global scanning and analysis, which are shown in the HR Triad feature, the firm's HR activities are more likely to stay in tune with the changing global environment. In the remainder of this chapter, we describe some of the changes occurring in the global environment and comment on their potential implications for managing human resources.

THE EVOLVING GLOBAL ECONOMY

Depending on your perspective, you may believe the United States is either too open to foreign competition or not open enough. Regardless of one's perspective, it's clear that the size and wealth of the U.S. market make it a desirable target for foreign competitors. In comparison with other markets of similar size, it has remained relatively open regardless of which political party is in power. Imports of shoes, textiles, and electronics continue to increase, even as the intense pressure they create for domestic producers threatens to put them out of business. Less than 10 years ago, U.S. companies dominated the office copier business here and abroad. Today their share of the domestic market is approximately 50 percent. Similar trends have occurred in several other industries during the last 25 years.

Deregulation has contributed to some of the changes, both here and abroad. In Japan, there has been deregulation of several industries that previously enjoyed protection, including financial services, distribution, and agriculture. New foreign competition requires drastic changes in these industries. Beginning in 1998, the financial services industry began consolidating through massive merger-and-acquisition activity, repeating a pattern that occurred years earlier in the United States. Massive layoffs followed—something that was almost unheard of before in Japan.[4]

Currently, in the United States the process of deregulation is affecting utilities, which were once thought of as essential natural monopolies that had to be regulated by the government. Today, utilities are beginning to compete in a more open environment. For utility companies, this means shifting their focus from worrying about the concerns of regulators to worrying about the actions of competitors and the preferences of consumers. For consumers, this should mean more choices about where to purchase power supplies. For employees of utilities companies, it is likely to mean layoffs and other cost-cutting measures that are

FAST FACT

McDonald's opens two outlets every three days in Europe.

Roles and Responsibilities for Understanding the Global Environment

Line Managers	HR Professionals	Employees
• Stay informed about economic conditions and their possible implications for the organization. • Investigate potential new markets for products and services. • • Encourage discussion of the potential implications that you learn. • Investigate new technologies relevant to the business to learn how they can be used to gain competitive advantage. • Advocate and support the use of new HRIM technology as appropriate. • Develop an understanding of the culture of selected countries of likely importance to the business. • Develop language and interpersonal skills for working in a multicultural environment. • Encourage and facilitate the development of cross-cultural skills among employees. • Develop an understanding of newly emerging structural forms and their implications for managerial jobs. • Develop skills needed for managing alliances. • Keep employees and HR professionals informed of environmental trends that are likely to have a significant impact on the business.	• Stay informed about economic conditions and their possible implications for the organization. • Investigate foreign labor market qualifications and conditions. • Encourage discussion of the potential implications that you learn. • Learn to use advanced HRIM technologies and understand how they can be used to gain competitive advantage. • Advocate and support the use of new HRIM technology as appropriate. • Educate the organization about the new issues to be addressed as the organization expands beyond domestic borders. • Provide resources for managers and other employees to learn about cultural differences and to develop skills in cross-cultural interaction. • Provide information to managers and employees about the skills needed in newly emerging organizational structures and provide the resources needed to develop those skills. • Keep line managers and employees informed about the implications of environmental trends for individual skills development, career management, and changes in approaches to managing human resources.	• Stay informed about economic conditions and their possible implications for the organization. • Develop a basic understanding of how global conditions are likely to affect your organization and career. • Take responsibility for continuously developing skills needed to use new technologies. • Be proactive and creative in thinking about how available HRIM technologies can be used advantageously in your own work area and by you personally. • Develop an understanding of at least one culture other than your own. • Develop an understanding of the unique aspects of your own culture and how people from other cultures view it. • Help employees from other cultures learn about your culture. • Develop teamwork skills needed for working across organizational boundaries. • Recognize that changes in the environment can have unpredictable consequences for your employment situation and be prepared for unexpected disruptions.

likely to affect their pay and working conditions. As the energy crisis in California during 2001 highlighted, the process of deregulation is filled with uncertainties.

Two decades of change in the telecommunications industry provide a glimpse of what may be ahead for electric utilities. Once highly regulated and stable, the telecommunications industry now changes every day. The environment is filled with new competitors, including many small and entrepreneurial firms, who battle intensely for individual and institutional customers with increasingly sophisticated needs. A century ago, farmers were content to use the barbed wire on their fences as the wires that enabled them to take advantage of the

FAST FACT

In Denver, the starting pay for telephone equipment salespeople is $40,000—twice what it was in 1992.

newest technology—telephones.[5] Today, customers want a fully integrated communication system, combining the benefits of the TV cable system, computer software capabilities, and satellite technology. To give them what they want, telecommunications companies are changing the very definition of an industry by acquiring and merging with cable TV providers, satellite operations, and software companies.[6]

Selling to the World

To compete effectively, many U.S. companies can no longer depend on the domestic market as their sole source of customers. To thrive, they must expand to serve a global market that's growing at a much faster pace. In some industries, it's now typical that foreign sales account for between one-third and two-thirds of a U.S. company's total sales. These industries include

- computers and office equipment (59 percent foreign sales),
- machinery (51 percent foreign sales),
- autos and auto parts (44 percent foreign sales),
- chemical products (39 percent foreign sales), and
- transportation equipment (34 percent foreign sales).[7]

In other industries that have lower foreign sales overall, particular firms can be found that depend heavily on foreign sales. Coca-Cola, for example, generates 80 percent of its sales in other countries; for Gillette, the figure is 65 percent.

Services also are being offered to expanding global markets, although in many cases they aren't "exported" in the way products are exported. For service firms, expanding into global markets often means setting up operations in those markets. Examples of U.S. service firms that generate substantial sales in other countries include Hilton Hotels, KPMG, EDS, and IBM.

Worldwide Operations

At the same time that companies are learning to meet the needs of a global marketplace, they're also learning new approaches to producing and delivering their goods and services. At Hewlett-Packard, providing service to a global market meant creating worldwide sales and marketing groups so that multinational clients could get all their worldwide needs met at a single source. At Philips, the Dutch electronics giant, operations were reorganized and moved to the hottest regions for new trends: Its set-top box business moved to California and the audio business moved to Hong Kong. Philips audio production was struggling in Europe due to high costs there and the fact that Europe is a long way from the center of innovation and manufacturing for the industry, which is in Asia.[8]

As firms globalize their operations, they create conditions that speed the transfer of management practices around the globe—including many human resource management practices. For example, like many U.S. companies, Hewlett-Packard was initially slow to adopt the total quality management practices that were prevalent in Japan by the 1970s. But after its Japanese subsidiary was honored in the 1980s with the prestigious Deming Prize for quality, it quickly began transferring total quality management processes to other operations throughout the world.[9] With the new approach to quality management came changes in the way work was structured, employee involvement in decision making, performance measurement

"We are all heads of international. The scope of every manager is the world."

Pasquale Pistorio
CEO
ST Microelectronics

systems, and so on. (Chapter 4 describes the HR implications of total quality management in more detail.)

The staffing of foreign operations with expatriates, and the challenges of managing expatriation, is the most obvious HR activity affected by the globalization of a firm's operations. According to a worldwide survey of global relocation trends, the countries to which the most expatriates are assigned are the United Kingdom and the United States. The next most popular destinations are quickly rising in importance, however. The survey also revealed that predictions for the near future show that China, Brazil, and Mexico are emerging as the new active locations for expatriates.[10]

INTERNET RESOURCES   2.A

The Evolving Global Economy

At our Web site, http://jackson.swcollege.com/, you can:

1. Update your knowledge about the integration of DaimlerChrysler.

2. Discover what facts the CIA provides about countries around the world.

3. Obtain statistics on international trade from several sources.

4. Examine the business information provided to companies by the Chamber of Commerce.

THE POLITICAL LANDSCAPE

The globalization of business operations is unfolding against a political landscape that also is changing. In this political landscape are sown the seeds of many business threats and opportunities. Among the many aspects of the political landscape affecting companies are political turmoil and nongovernmental political or community action groups.

It is apparent that political events within a country shape business activity. Similarly, international firms are affected by the local political events in every country where they operate. Furthermore, both domestic and international firms can be influenced by the actions of international governmental and nongovernmental organizations. Among the most significant consequences of international political cooperation in recent years is the emergence of regional free trade zones.

"China is moving from one kind of orderly system, socialism, to another, free-market capitalism. In between, you have a chaotic period."

Dong Tao
SC First Boston, China

Local Politics

When Mexicans elected Vicente Fox to the presidency in 2000, they tossed out a party that had ruled the country since 1929. Mexico's stock market rose 6 percent the day the election results were announced. Although U.S. businesses had learned to live with the prior ruling party, the Institutional Revolutionary Party (PRI), they expressed optimism about the changes that might occur under the new leadership.[11] The future seemed certain to hold new opportunities. For example, telecommunications companies were hopeful that Fox would privatize the phone company, making room for foreign competitors to gain access to that market.

The events in Mexico stood in sharp contrast to those that had unfolded a few years earlier in Indonesia. At the beginning of 1997, Indonesia was experiencing 10 percent GDP growth. But by the end of the year, the value of the rupiah and the stock market had both plunged 50 percent while GDP slowed to nearly zero. Student protests against political corruption

Comment on the election of Mexican president Vicente Fox: *"It's comparable to the fall of the Berlin Wall, the end of apartheid, and the vote to oust [Chilean military dictator Augusto] Pinochet, all rolled into one."*

Aguilar Zinser
Senator
Mexico

forced Indonesia's president of 30 years to step down in 1998, creating great political uncertainty. The rupiah plunged another 25 percent. Most foreign businesses vacated the country, including the many Chinese enterprises that served as the foundation of the economic engine, and by mid-year GDP growth hit minus 4 percent.[12] Will future business in Indonesia will be marked by the political corruption and cronyism of the past? Or will successful political reform help reopen this huge market to more open competition? The two possible futures have vastly different consequences for human resource management within Indonesia. These two possible futures also have vastly different implications for HR practices of non-Indonesian firms, who must decide whether and how to utilize the 225 million people who live there.

International Political Organizations

In response to the competitive pressures of globalization, governments may respond by imposing regulations on taxation and tariffs, pollution, labor issues, and so on. They may also coordinate their policies, agree to treaties that regulate international business activities, and even form new governmental bodies. Through such actions, political leaders and country representatives work in partnership with business leaders to create new rules for economic growth and development.

Members of nongovernmental consortia generally have no official authority to impose rules of business conduct. Instead, the force of their appeals to business is limited by the strength of the support they receive in the social realm. The members of nongovernmental consortia may include government officials, labor leaders, human rights activists, religious leaders, consumer organizations, student groups, community groups, and and/or various other stakeholders. Such consortia may be domestic or international in scope, and they operate as grassroots organizations or as formal agencies.

Some students may be familiar with the Worker Rights Consortium, a grassroots movement that has established a code of conduct requiring disclosure of labor practices by factories that produce goods bearing university names.[13] Nongovernmental agencies that are better known to employers include the International Labor Organization, Social Accountability International, and the World Trade Organization.

> **FAST FACT**
>
> Trade among members of the WTO accounts for 95% of world trade.

International Labor Organization. The International Labor Organization (ILO) is housed within the United Nations. Founded in 1919, its mandate is to promote "social justice and internationally recognized human and labor rights." Representatives within the ILO include workers, employers, and governments. Together, these stakeholders formulate international labor standards regarding the right to organize, collective bargaining, forced labor, equality of opportunity and treatment, and an array of other working conditions.[14] The ILO has no authority to enforce these standards, however, so compliance is completely voluntary.

> **FAST FACT**
>
> The ILO's organizing theme for 2002–2005 is "Putting the Decent Work Agenda into Place."

Social Accountability International. Another nongovernmental group that promotes socially responsible approaches to conducting business is Social Accountability International (SAI). SAI administers a certification process called Social Accountability 8000 (SA 8000). Companies that wish to be considered for SA 8000 certification volunteer to undergo an intensive audit and to permit additional scheduled and unscheduled inspections. To obtain certification, the company must satisfy standards in the areas of child labor, forced labor, health and safety, collective bargaining, discrimination, disciplinary action, working hours, and compensation. SA 8000 standards were developed by representatives representing diverse perspectives, including Amnesty International, Avon Products, Toys R Us, Body Shop, the National Child Labor Committee, KPMG Peat Marwick, Reebok, Amalgamated Bank, and the International Textile Garment and Leather Workers Federation.[15]

Successful completion of the certification process gives a company the right to use the SA 8000 logo, which serves as a social seal of approval. Companies that depend on suppliers who operate in countries with few protective regulations may put pressure on their suppliers to obtain SA 8000 certification, which serves as a form of insurance. By requiring suppliers to be certified, global companies such as Avon and Toys R Us can feel more confident that their goods and services will not be subject to protests over unethical management practices.

World Trade Organization. The **World Trade Organization (WTO)** was established in 1995. An outgrowth of the 1947 General Agreement on Tariffs and Trade (GATT), the WTO provides a forum for members to conduct trade negotiations and settle trade disputes. It is the only global body able to enforce its decisions through its own court. The WTO also monitors national trade policies and provides technical assistance and training for people in developing countries.

WTO agreements influence the costs of imported goods and services. For example, the WTO requires that taxes and tariffs applied to imported goods and services must be applied equally to their domestic equivalents, unless a concession is negotiated and approved. Based on the **most favored nation principle**, businesses operating in WTO countries also know that concessions offered to one WTO member country will automatically apply to all other WTO members.

As the most inclusive international trade organization, the WTO promotes harmonization through the agreements negotiated among member countries. Further promoting global harmonization of trade policies are the cooperative relationships maintained between the WTO's various other international trade organizations, including three major regional ones: NAFTA, the EU, and ASEAN. These organizations and their associated trade zones are described next.

Commenting on SA 8000:
"The process of law will correct most abuses, but this is a gentler way to resolve or head off issues."

Martin Bennett
VP of Training and Consulting
Cendant Intercultural

INTERNET RESOURCES   2.B

The Political Landscape

At our Web site, http://jackson.swcollege.com/, you can:

1. Read the code of conduct that students helped develop to ensure that goods bearing university labels were produced under fair labor conditions.

2. Find a list of members of the World Trade Organization.

3. Discover the ILO's strategic objectives and explore the many types of useful information they provide.

4. Read opinions about how globalization is and should be shaped by political (versus economic) forces.

REGIONAL TRADE ZONES

Trade relations often are strongest among countries that are geographically close to each other. Besides shared trade, countries within geographic regions often share similar languages, cultures, and environmental concerns. Thus, the development of regional cooperation seems only natural as a strategy for survival amidst global competition. By forming regional trade zones, smaller countries can reap the benefits of economies of scale in consumer markets and gain easier access to a larger labor pool.

Many attempts at regionalism have not yet succeeded—for example, in Africa and Latin America. Others, such as APEC, have been effective in promoting greater cooperation but do not yet have formal, binding treaties or agreements. NAFTA and the EU are examples of regionalism that has succeeded to the point of creating free trade zones and permanently changing the competitive landscape.

Asia-Pacific Economic Cooperation

The **Asia-Pacific Economic Cooperation (APEC)** is a regional association that promotes open economic cooperation and open trade. Its 21 members, which include China, account for nearly 25 percent of the world's total trade.

> **FAST FACT**
>
> The combined populations of APEC member countries total 2.5 billion people.

APEC holds annual Ministerial Meetings that engage representatives in discussions about key economic issues in the region. Throughout the year, committees such as the Committee on Trade and Investment (CTI) seek to further promote cooperation among members. For example, CTI addresses issues related to tariffs, customs procedures, intellectual property rights, deregulation, and dispute mediation, among others. As committees reach consensus on issues, APEC representatives communicate the organization's views back to their country leaders.[16]

North American Free Trade Agreement

In 1993, the Canadian Parliament, the U.S. Congress, and the Mexican Congress each approved a historic agreement designed to allow for eventual free trade among these three countries. Their agreement went into effect the following year, marking the first time that a developing country entered into a free trade agreement with developed countries. The **North American Free Trade Agreement (NAFTA)** creates a free trade zone among the three member countries by removing numerous trade barriers such as tariffs, quotas, and licensing requirements. Immediately all tariffs were removed for some classes of goods (e.g., computers, telecommunications, aerospace, and medical equipment) as well as for all new services. Tariffs for other goods and services were scheduled to decrease gradually over a period years, with nearly all tariffs being eliminated within 15 years. The same year that NAFTA went into effect, Mexico became the 25th member of the Organization for Economic Cooperation and Development, the first Latin American country to join.[17]

> **FAST FACT**
>
> The United States is the largest export market of Canada and Mexico.

Maquiladoras. Since passage of NAFTA, dozens of major U.S. manufacturing companies have expanded operations in Mexico. Often they set up operations along the U.S.–Mexico border, in plants referred to as **maquiladoras.** In many cases, this has meant moving low-skill, low-pay jobs from the U.S.

side of the border to the Mexican side, where wages were substantially lower. Predictably, unemployment levels in U.S. border towns went up, often to levels that were two and three times higher than the national average. What was perhaps less predictable was that average wages in the area also rose, on both sides of the border. Wages for maquiladora workers remain much lower than they would be in the United States, but their average wage is five times Mexico's minimum wage.[18]

FAST FACT

The population of Mexico-Texas border towns grew about 30% during the 1990s. Growth rates on the Mexican side are twice those on the U.S. side.

Because of wage disparities between the United States and Mexico, early opponents of NAFTA feared that low-wage assembly jobs would quickly leave the United States and Canada and move to Mexico, where labor costs are much lower. That happened, of course. But others point out that without NAFTA, these jobs would probably have moved to low-wage countries in Asia. Furthermore, if the assembly work took place in Asia, local suppliers would soon go out of business. By keeping the assembly jobs in Mexico, U.S. suppliers prosper. In fact, Mexican assembly plants get 82 percent of their parts from the United States.[19]

Canada's Brain Drain. Wage differences between Canada and the United States play out quite differently along the northern border of the United States. For Canada, the problem is that its most talented professionals can easily work in the United States and earn higher wages. To keep the talent in Canada, employers there must adapt by raising wage rates for talent that is in high demand. But doing so can create equity problems for other employees in the organization. The feature "Managing Globalization: Borderline Pay in Canada" describes one approach to handling this problem.

Long-term Outcomes. Nearly a decade after NAFTA took effect, growth is on the rise in towns on both sides of the border. Warehouses, offices, distribution centers, and truck depots have expanded to support the growing trade traffic.[20] GM, for example, uses its facilities in Juárez, just across the border from El Paso, as a basic training location for its network of global managers. While many of the plant managers that GM will eventually send to other countries are Mexican nationals, managers from all over the world also receive their training in Mexico.[21] Unfortunately, local governments have not always been able to keep up with the growth, which puts enormous pressure on the physical infrastructure and social services like health care, education, and crime prevention.[22]

Not all observers agree about whether the economic benefits of NAFTA outweigh its negative social consequences, but supporters seem to be in the majority. Now talk has turned to expanding NAFTA to cover the entire Western Hemisphere. Besides expanding the geographic scope of NAFTA, some leaders—including Vicente Fox, Mexico's president—would like to see NAFTA transformed into a broader social agreement. Fox would have the United States and Canada provide aid to Mexico to help it develop the country's infrastructure, including roads and schools. In return, Mexico would agree to enforce stricter labor and environmental standards. The incorporation of broader social issues into a trade agreement may take years to evolve in North America. In Europe, however, social and economic issues were inextricably linked together during the formation of the European Union.[23]

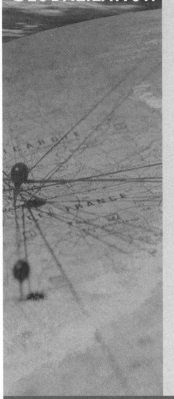

MANAGING GLOBALIZATION

Borderline Pay in Canada

The problem of perceived pay inequity is one that must be solved by the many companies that straddle the Canada–U.S. border. Typically, employees who hold jobs at lower pay levels are paid more in Canada than in the United States. In contrast, Canadian professionals and managers typically earn one-third less than their U.S. counterparts, as shown in the table below. Demand for managers and professionals is strong in the United States, so many Canadians comparing inputs and outcomes to those of similar executives in the United States may conclude that they are underpaid and seek employment across the border. As more Canadian professionals and managers seek employment in the United States, Canadian companies face the possibility of a "brain drain."

To attract new talent and avoid losing their best employees, some Canadian companies try to minimize pay inequity by using a formula that blends the pay levels in the two countries. The following is an example of the formula used to determine the salary of a top information systems executive:

Weighted blending. A weight of 0.2 is given to pay rates in Canada, and a weight of 0.8 is given to pay rates in the United States. The exchange rate used to convert U.S. to Canadian dollars is 1.37. Thus

$(0.2 \times \$98,000) + (0.8 \times \$110,000 \times 1.37) = \$140,160$ Canadian.

The formula takes into account managers' natural tendencies to compare their inputs and outputs to those of similar U.S. managers. Using the blended approach to setting the manager's pay helps reduce perceived inequities that might arise from such comparisons and knowing that subordinates are being paid as much as or more than the manager.

Job	Canada	United States	Canadian Pay as a Percentage of U.S. Pay
CFO of $300 million packaging company	$161,000	$247,500	65%
Information system executive	98,000	150,300	65
Treasurer	109,100	153,200	71
Machine operator	27,000	19,900	136
Salesclerk	24,500	16,800	146

Note: Amounts are in Canadian dollars.

European Union

"The single most important regulatory change anywhere in the world is the European Monetary Union."

Mac Heller
Cochair, Mergers and Acquisitions
Cohead, Investment Banking Division
Goldman Sachs

The **European Union** (previously known as the European Community) describes itself as "an institutional framework for the construction of a united Europe." This institution developed out of a desire to reduce conflict in the region and prevent another event like the devastating World War II. Similar to NAFTA, the European Union (EU) has a primary goal of creating a single market through the removal of trade barriers, such as tariffs. But the EU also differs from NAFTA in important ways. Besides the obvious difference in the number of member countries is both a broader agenda and a more sophisticated governance structure. As of 2002, the European Union had 15 members. Can you identify them? Find out by taking the quiz shown in Exhibit 2.1.

In addition to establishing an economic free trade zone that permits free movement for goods and services, the EU establishes free movement of people across its members' borders, provides recognition for educational degrees earned in member countries, and seeks to institute a common monetary system based on the *euro*. In January 2002, banks in 12 EU countries began withdrawing their national currencies from the market, with the goal

ex 2.1 European Union Membership Quiz
(correct answers appear below)

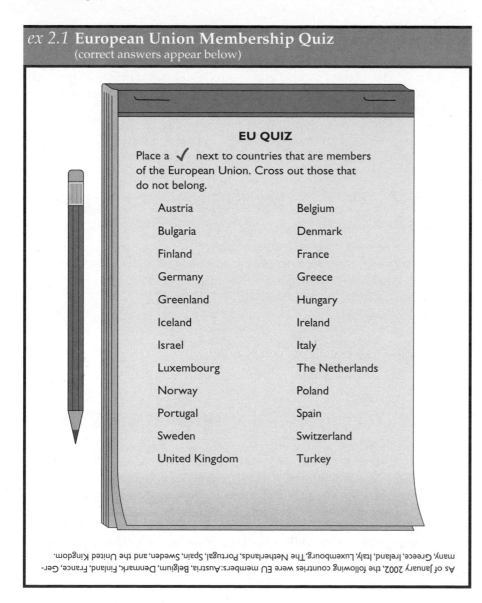

EU QUIZ

Place a ✓ next to countries that are members of the European Union. Cross out those that do not belong.

Austria	Belgium
Bulgaria	Denmark
Finland	France
Germany	Greece
Greenland	Hungary
Iceland	Ireland
Israel	Italy
Luxembourg	The Netherlands
Norway	Poland
Portugal	Spain
Sweden	Switzerland
United Kingdom	Turkey

As of January 2002, the following countries were EU members: Austria, Belgium, Denmark, Finland, France, Germany, Greece, Ireland, Italy, Luxembourg, The Netherlands, Portugal, Spain, Sweden, and the United Kingdom.

of completing full conversion to the euro by July of that year. French francs, German marks, Italian lira, and Spanish pesetas became extinct. [At this writing, Sweden, Britain and Belgium had not agreed to join the monetary union.] The euro establishes participating countries as the second largest economic zone (after the United States), with countries linked together through common economic policies. Through monetary union, and the trade agreement that the EU can make with other countries, EU members expect to reduce costs associated with currency conversions and increase economic stability within the region. Businesses, in turn, should reap the benefits of improved efficiencies and reduced economic uncertainty.

Despite their adoption of a common currency and regional governance institutions, countries belonging to the European Union differ from each other in many ways—politically, economically, and culturally. Countries will continue to elect their own leaders, and most issues will be governed by

"We think the unions could cause trouble when their members start comparing wages across borders."

J. C. Tavares
CEO
Gastronómica da Alcoava

local laws. Prices will still vary considerably between countries, as will unemployment rates. Currently, for example, unemployment rates range from 2 percent in Luxembourg to 9 percent in Germany, and 19 percent in Spain. Wages for similar jobs in Portugal and Spain differ by as much as 300 percent. Such differences will become more apparent when prices are denominated in a single currency.[24] Cultural and language differences rooted in hundreds of years of history will not disappear soon, either. As described later in this chapter, removing cultural barriers to economic cooperation is proving more difficult for some companies than removing trade barriers was for countries within free trade zones.

INTERNET RESOURCES   2.C

Regional Trade Zones

At our Web site, http://jackson.swcollege.com/, you can:

1. Read more about APEC and the issues it is currently debating.

2. Read the trade provisions created by NAFTA.

3. Explore the human resource services offered to Canadian employers.

4. Find out how the European Union's official institutions make and enforce policies.

5. Study the trade agreements between the United States and the EU.

6. Learn about the euro and its current value against the dollar.

INDUSTRY DYNAMICS

The industry in which a company competes is an important aspect of the global environment. Economic and political events may have different implications for different industries. Changes in national policies regarding tariffs or wages may be viewed as favorable for one industry and unfavorable for another. As another example, an overall trend in the direction of increasing productivity at the national level can mask the fact that some industries are enjoying substantial gains while other industries may actually be declining.

Industry boundaries are both fuzzy and unstable, so the question "What industry are we in?" isn't always easy to answer. Furthermore, some companies compete by constantly pushing at the boundaries of the industry and, eventually, redefining the industries in which they compete.[25] Nevertheless, at any point in time, the relevant industry for most organizations is composed of a group of companies that offer similar products and services. Companies within an industry experience similar patterns of growth, and eventually a common industry culture may develop. Generally, companies within the same industry are a firm's most significant competitors, as well as their most likely partners in various strategic alliances, including mergers and acquisitions and joint ventures.

Industry Life Cycles

FAST FACT

The typical life span of a company is about 12.5 years.

Like people and the organizations they work in, industries have life cycles. This is illustrated in Exhibit 2.2. Companies within the same industry may experience these life cycles in tandem, which creates certain similarities in the issues they face and the solutions they adopt. When there are many opportunities for growth (e.g.,

ex 2.2 Industry Life Cycle

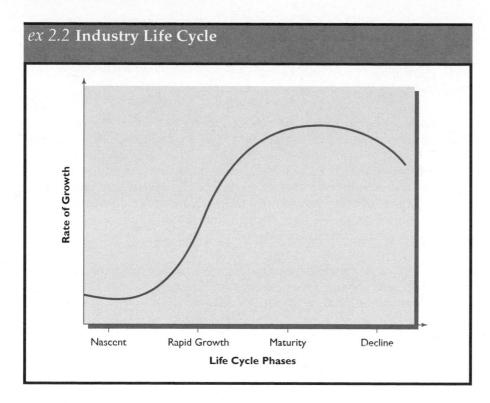

because of strong demand or government deregulation), many firms can thrive within the industry. Eventually, however, competition is likely to intensify, and eventually growth of the industry levels off or even contracts.[26]

Nascent. During the nascent stage of an industry's life cycle, firms are competing to establish a distinctive reputation and to create customer loyalty. At this stage, there are relatively few competitors, so each company has many options. Because the industry isn't yet well established, there is a great deal of risk associated with this stage of an industry's life cycle. Many start-up companies will fail, so simply surviving is the primary concern for the company. Survival is still the primary concern of thousands of service providers specializing in creating electronic marketplaces, electronic procurement, supply management, Web content distribution and management, e-marketing, e-commerce, and other start-up businesses created after the development of the Internet. These companies compose industries in the nascent stage. Before the industry shakeout that began in the year 2000, the entire country was swept up in the excitement that can accompany the latter days of this stage and the early days of the growth stage.

Growth. Companies that survive the shake-ups that often occur during the early phase of an industry's creation usually enjoy a period of rapid growth. If the new product offered by the industry is easily standardized, this growth phase may be characterized as a period of rapid franchising. For example, during the 1980s, the franchising of premium quality coffee bars resulted in extremely rapid growth of that industry. Most industries do not grow

FAST FACT

Nearly 80% of businesses in Turkey were established after 1980.

through franchising, however. Instead, the dominant firms each grow their market share by developing new products to meet consumers' evolving demands. As organizations grow, issues of acquiring and retaining talent and coordinating the activities of the expanding enterprise often become central. Many high-tech industries currently face this challenge.

Mature. In most industries, the rate of growth eventually slows and the industry moves into a mature stage. Now there are a few large firms all striving to become more efficient while also improving the quality of their products. Often it's at this stage that companies begin to expand into international markets, which are viewed as opportunities for continued growth. Industry maturity may also stimulate consolidation through mergers and acquisitions, as is currently occurring in the financial services industry.[27]

Decline and Renewal. Finally, an industry may go into decline as the products and services on which it's based become obsolete. At this stage, companies in the industry must eventually go out of business or transform themselves to offer new products and services and, effectively, enter a new industry.

Changing managerial priorities characterize organizations in various developmental stages. In addition, companies within the same industry tend to draw upon the same labor pool for people working in the technical areas that define the industry. Thus common approaches to managing human resources tend to evolve within industries. At the senior level, for example, changes in the role of the CEO and top management team correspond to changes in the stage of the industry's life cycle and often organizations seek outside executives to help the organization move into the next stage. The top management teams, in turn, are likely to initiate major changes in the firm's strategy, design, and/or culture.

Cooperative Relationships Between Firms

The media often portray business organizations as warring enemies who define their own success by the demise of their competitors. Executives sometimes use similar imagery to motivate their "troops." What such images ignore are the strong interdependencies among business organizations and the degree to which cooperation results in mutual gains. Just as nations have discovered the benefits of economic cooperation, businesses have learned that success often depends on forming strategic alliances. Through these alliances, industries are sometimes completely transformed.

Strategic Alliance. A **strategic alliance** involves two or more firms agreeing to cooperate as partners in an arrangement that's expected to benefit both firms. Sometimes strategic alliances involve one firm taking an equity position in another firm. Ford, for example, has equity in both foreign and U.S. auto parts producers. It also owns 49 percent of Hertz, the car rental company, which is one of Ford's major customers. Other alliances do not affect legal ownership. In the airline industry, a common type of alliance is between an airline and an airframe manufacturer. For example, Delta agreed to buy all its aircraft from Boeing. Boeing has a similar deal, valued at billions of dollars, with American Airlines. Through these agreements, Boeing guarantees that it will be able to sell specified models of its aircraft for several decades to come. The airlines, in turn, can develop a schedule for retiring old aircraft and can begin to adapt their operations to the models they will be flying in the future.[28]

In high-tech industries, strategic alliances allow older, established firms to gain access to the hot new discoveries being made by scientists in universities and in small, creative organizations. For example, the U.S. bio-technology industry is characterized by networks of relationships between new biotechnology firms dedicated to research and new product develop-ment and established firms in industries that can use these new products, such as pharmaceuticals. In return for sharing technical information with the larger firms, the smaller firms gain access to their partners' resources for product testing, marketing, and distribution.[29] Big pharmaceutical firms such as Merck or Eli Lilly gain from such partnerships because the smaller firms typically develop new drugs in as little as five years, versus an eight-year average development cycle in the larger firms.[30]

International Joint Ventures. An **international joint venture (IJV)** is one type of strategic alliance. Alliance partners form a joint venture when they create a separate legal organizational entity representing the partial holdings of two or more parent firms. In international joint ventures, the headquarters of at least one partner is located outside the country of the joint venture. Joint ventures are subject to the joint control of their parent firms. The parent firms, in turn, become economically and legally interdependent of each other.

Firms form international joint ventures for many reasons. In some countries, the host government provides strong incentives to foreign firms to use joint ventures as a mode of entry into their markets. Another reason to form joint ventures is to gain rapid access to new markets. Learning is an-other objective behind many international joint ventures. By partnering with local companies instead of entering a market on their own, foreign firms can more quickly develop their ability to operate effectively in the host country. Strategic alliances also provide a means for competitors within an industry to leverage new technology and reduce costs. In the auto industry, for exam-ple, Ford, General Motors, DaimlerChrysler, Nissan, and Renault formed an international joint venture, Covisint, in order to manage their supply chains using business-to-business e-commerce.[31] Ford's former CEO Jac Nasser explained the reasoning behind the formation of this IJV: "We see this tech-nology [e-business] as so powerful that, for it to be optimized, we need it to become an industry standard. So, rather than have 15 different standards out there . . . we figured out that it would be more efficient if the basic architec-ture was common." Assuming Covisint succeeds, it will fundamentally alter supply chain relationships within the automobile industry.

For various reasons, managing IJVs successfully is diffi-cult, and many ultimately fail. IJV failures often stem from poor management of human resources issues. Exhibit 2.3 illustrates four stages of the IJV process and the HR implications for each.[32] The

> **FAST FACT**
>
> Up to 50% of IJVs fall short of expectations.

exhibit highlights the important role of HR practices in joint venture success. Prior to formation of an IJV, human resource professionals can help the potential partners assess their cultural compatibility. As the new entity is formed, recruiting and selecting of key executives to staff the IJV becomes critical. With the staff in place, HR practices that align employees' skills and motivations with the business objectives of the IJV can determine whether it ultimately achieves the desired outcomes.

ex 2.3 Key HR Activities in the Four Stages of the IJV Process

MANAGEMENT TASKS	KEY HR ACTIVITIES
	Stage 1—Formation
• Identifying reasons for IJV	• Participate in initial planning
• Planning for utilization	• Assist in selecting business development manager
• Selecting dedicated manager	• Assess compatibility with potential partners
• Finding potential partners	• Facilitate communication processes
• Selecting likely partners	• Ensure extensive communications
• Negotiating the arrangement	• Select skilled negotiators
	Stage 2—Development
• Locating the IJV	• Help surface concerns of all stakeholders
• Establishing the right structure	• Evaluate proposed structure for likely impact on learning and knowledge management
• Getting the right senior managers	• Assist in recruiting and selecting senior staff
	Stage 3—Implementation
• Establishing the vision, mission, values, strategy	• Assist in selecting participants for discussions of vision, mission, values, strategy
• Developing HR policies and practices	• Facilitate discussions
• Staffing and managing the employees	• Assist with design of HR policies and practices, taking into account global considerations
	• Assist managers to ensure effective implementation of HR policies and practices
	Stage 4—Advancement and Beyond
• Learning from the partner	• Evaluate and revise HR systems to support knowledge flow to the parent and learning by the parent
• Transferring the new knowledge to the parents	
• Transferring the new knowledge to other locations	

Mergers, Acquisitions, and Takeovers

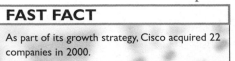

FAST FACT

The merger of Exxon and Mobil had to be approved by regulators in 60 countries.

Companies today need to be fast growing, efficient, profitable, flexible, adaptable, future-ready, and dominant in market position. Without these qualities, it is virtually impossible to be competitive in today's global economy. In addition to participating in strategic alliances to develop the capabilities they need to compete, many firms evolve and grow by mergers or acquisitions. Among the most significant transnational merger and acquisition deals in recent years are Daimler–Chrysler, Chase–J. P. Morgan, McKinsey–Envision, UBS–Paine Webber, Credit Suisse–DLJ, Celltech–Medeva, SKB–Glaxo, NationsBank–Bank of America, AOL–Time Warner, Pfizer–Warner Lambert, Nestlé–Purina, and Deutsche Telekom–Voice Stream. The future appears ripe for a continuation of annual increases in merger and acquisition (M & A) activity.

In a **merger,** two companies agree to join their operations together to form a new company in which they participate as equal partners. In an **acquisition,** one firm buys controlling or full interest in another firm with the understanding that the buyer will determine how the combined operations will be managed. The majority of acquisitions are friendly—that is, the acquired firm solicits bids and enters into an acquisition voluntarily. Sometimes, however, a firm becomes a

FAST FACT

As part of its growth strategy, Cisco acquired 22 companies in 2000.

takeover target. A **takeover** acquisition usually occurs when an unsolicited bid is made for a poorly performing firm. Shareholders may agree to the takeover because they lack faith in the current managers' ability to return the firm to sound financial health. Although mergers, acquisitions, and takeovers are technically different, it's common to refer to all three means for combining the operations of two firms as mergers and acquisitions, or just **M&As.**[33]

Reasons for M&As. Through mergers and acquisitions, firms seek to

- increase their market share,
- increase their geographic reach,
- fill out their product lines,
- respond to new deregulation,
- acquire new technologies and product innovation, and
- gain key talent.[34]

In the computer industry (hardware and software) and the biotech industry, a major objective of M&As is gaining access to the skills and talents of people employed by another company. Any technology or pharmaceutical discovery that a company owns will quickly become outdated. But if the people who created that technology or drug stay and remain energized, they're likely to create new products that will continue to succeed in the marketplace.

Some observers argue that the increased pace of transnational M&As is a major driving force behind the development of multigovernment agreements and rules for business conduct.[35] M&A deals can have enormous economic and social consequences. They can quickly put the major competitors within a country out of business, and they can determine whether, how, and where people work. Gaining government approval for transnational M&As is sometimes difficult, but the initial step of gaining approval usually proves to be far easier than successfully managing the new entity.

"Between 1909 and 1919 there were 120 car companies. How many are left in the United States today? Two."

Lee Iacocca
Former Chairman and CEO
Chrysler

Failure Rates. With the importance of and need for mergers and acquisitions growing, and the base of experience expanding, it may seem reasonable to also assume that success is more likely to occur than failure in these types of combinations. Indeed, the opposite is true. Only 15 percent of M&As in the United States achieve their financial objectives, as measured by share value, return on investment, and profitability. In Europe, a study of deals valued at $500 million or more showed that 50 percent destroyed shareholder value, 30 percent had minimal impact, and only 17 percent created shareholder returns.[36]

FAST FACT

Statistics show that two out of three M&As are financial failures.

Reasons for Failure. Mergers and acquisitions fail for a variety of reasons. Among the reasons most often cited are culture clashes, incompatibility, and loss of key talent—all human resource issues.[37] Plans that look logical on paper often fall apart when managers try to implement them. People, it seems, get in the way. When a firm with a fairly uniform culture introduces diversity in the form of another organizational culture, the clash can be so severe that the financial benefits of a merger can't be realized. This is what happened at DaimlerChrysler.[38] Through experience, some companies have discovered the importance of different organizational cultures. These companies now evaluate cultural compatibility before closing an M&A deal. GE Capital Services took this idea a step further to create their Pathfinder model, which is described in "Managing Diversity: GE Capital's Pathfinder Model for Cultural Integration."[39]

"If you are very successful, you start thinking you can walk on water."

Dieter Zetsche
Daimler executive who took
over as Chrysler's CEO

MANAGING DIVERSITY

GE Capital's Pathfinder Model for Cultural Integration

GE Capital Services has made the successful management of acquisitions a cornerstone of its strategy for growth. Every business group has a business development officer whose job is to find potential acquisition targets. The company has made more than 100 acquisitions during the past five years, growing by 30 percent in the process. GE Capital's experience has shown that acquisitions are much more likely to be successful if the employees who end up working together share the same values and mindsets. Therefore, conducting a cultural audit and identifying cultural barriers are tasks that GE Capital's managers complete before an acquisition decision is final.

Its cultural audits identify cultural differences at all levels—societal, industry-wide, and organizational. Regarding industry-level similarities and differences, the companies are compared in terms of costs, brands, technologies, and customers. If the differences seem so great that they could cause the acquisition to fail, GE drops the planned acquisition. If the differences seem manageable and an acquisition deal is concluded, a systematic process for integrating the cultures then begins.

One of the first steps is to appoint an integration manager, who is responsible for integrating the cultures and the business and operational systems. As soon as the deal is final, key people from the two businesses are brought together to socialize, exchange information, and share their feelings about the new situation. Managers of the acquired company are quickly informed of GE Capital's 25 central policies and practices. Integration goals are developed, a 100-day deadline is set, and managers from the two companies meet for a three-day session devoted to exploring the cultural differences. Managers tell each other about their companies' histories, folklore, and heroes. Other topics include approaches to market penetration, the amount of focus on cost, and reliance on authority versus shared decision making.

These discussions culminate in a written plan for the next six months or more. Such plans generally include short-term projects that require people from the two companies to work together to achieve some quick results, such as reducing costs. The plans, as well as other information related to the integration process, are posted on the company's intranet, where managers throughout the company can study them and learn from each new acquisition experience.

As is true for joint ventures, mergers and acquisitions unfold through many stages. At each stage, success requires effectively managing human resource issues. Exhibit 2.4 describes the stages of M&A implementation and the key associated HR issues to be addressed at each stage.[40] Recognizing the complexity of M&A implementation, Novell wanted to ensure that its executives thought through all of the key HR issues before merging companies. To assist Novell's executives, the HR staff developed the Merger Book. Its two thousand questions serve as a road map for Novell's M&A activities. Information gathering and analysis are the heart of the process.[41]

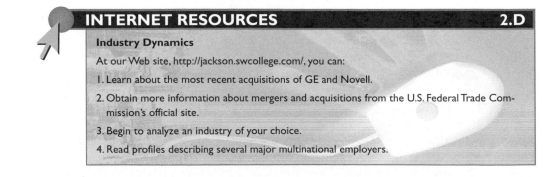

INTERNET RESOURCES   2.D

Industry Dynamics

At our Web site, http://jackson.swcollege.com/, you can:

1. Learn about the most recent acquisitions of GE and Novell.

2. Obtain more information about mergers and acquisitions from the U.S. Federal Trade Commission's official site.

3. Begin to analyze an industry of your choice.

4. Read profiles describing several major multinational employers.

ex 2.4 Key HR Activities in Three Stages of the Mergers and Acquisition Process

MANAGEMENT TASKS	KEY HR ACTIVITIES
Stage 1—Precombination	
• Identifying reasons for the M&A • Forming M&A team/leader • Searching for potential partners • Selecting a partner • Planning for managing the process • Planning to learn from the process	• Participate in preselection assessment of target firm • Assist in conducting thorough due diligence assessment • Participate in planning for combination • Assist in developing HR practices that support rapid learning and knowledge transfer
Stage 2—Combination	
• Selecting the integration manager(s) • Designing/implementing transition teams • Creating the new structure/strategies/leadership • Retaining key employees • Managing the change process • Communicating to and involving stakeholders • Developing new policies and practices	• Assist in recruiting and selecting integration manager(s) • Assist with transition team design and staffing • Develop retention strategies and communicate to top talent • Assist in deciding who goes • Facilitate establishment of a new culture • Provide assistance to ensure implementation of HR policies and practices
Stage 3—Solidification and Assessment	
• Solidifying leadership and staffing • Assessing the new strategies and structures • Assessing the new culture • Assessing the concerns of stakeholders • Revising as needed • Learning from the process	• Participate in establishing criteria and procedures for assessing staff effectiveness • Monitor the new culture and recommend approaches to strengthen it • Participate in stakeholder satisfaction • Assist in developing and implementing plans for continuous adjustment and learning

EVOLVING TECHNOLOGIES

Technology refers to the process of making and using tools and equipment plus the knowledge used in this process. Technology has been evolving for thousands of years. In early civilization, the available technology was limited to simple tools—hammers, levels, pulleys, shovels, picks, spears—and related knowledge about how to use them. The relatively simple technology of ancient civilization, combined with a system of organizing the people who used it, made possible the creation of objects that continue to inspire awe centuries later—the pyramids, fireworks, and Stonehenge are just a few familiar examples.

> **FAST FACT**
>
> Approximately 90% of medium and large companies provide employees with access to e-mail.

Throughout the history of economic development, changes in technology have been a key factor that shaped the way people worked, the evolution of new industries, and the development of global interdependencies. The rate of technological evolution greatly accelerated after reliable technology was created for generating power. The steam engine, introduced in the late 1700s, was a revolutionary technology. By powering ships and trains, it greatly expanded the speed and reach of trade and commerce. By powering machines such as the "spinning jenny," it lowered production costs, lowered prices, and in doing so expanded markets for the goods produced. The expanding demand required more workers, more machines, and a larger scale of production, and soon another fundamentally new technology evolved—the factory.

Factories and Mass Production Technologies

With the factory system came myriad new challenges related to managing human resources. First, people had to be convinced to leave their farms or small workshops and move near the factory—usually in a large city and often far away. Once recruited to the factory, people had to be convinced to work in a completely new way. On their farms and in their small shops, workers had previously enjoyed a great deal of personal autonomy and flexibility in their approach to the work. Now they had to accept the authority of factory owners and their agents and they had to accept the highly standardized procedures used to complete the work. Whereas the quality or creativity or speed of their previous work had created some feelings of personal pride, factory work was highly routine and depersonalized. What motivated people to accept this change in their work life? Usually it was the prospect of more income and/or more reliable income.

Finally, factory owners had to address the issue of skills. Most of the existing labor force had little education. They were unable to read instruction sheets or procedures manuals. They had little experience with complex machinery. They knew little about how to plan large-scale production processes or how to manage other workers. The skills they had simply didn't match those needed in the factory. All of these challenges had to be addressed in order to run a factory.[42]

Approaches to solving these human resource challenges have evolved and changed, just as the technology used has continued to evolve and change. A full appreciation of current approaches requires some understanding of their historical evolution. Exhibit 2.5 presents a thumbnail sketch of the changing concerns of human resource management within the United States.[43]

The Age of Computers and Information Technology

In the Factories. By 2000, there were fewer manufacturing jobs than government jobs in this country. Those who still work in factories, like the employees at Lincoln Electric, do so along side sophisticated robots. In many cases, the robots are being used to produce the computers that will help design the next generation of products to be manufactured—by the robots!

At the New Balance Athletic Shoe Inc. factory in Maine, factory employees using computer technology work in teams to produce shoes similar to those that most competitors are producing overseas using low-tech workers. Among the jobs performed by New Balance employees is operating computerized equipment that runs 20 sewing machine heads at once. Another job involves controlling a camera-guided automated stitcher that increases a worker's productivity sixfold. This technology allows U.S workers to produce a pair of shoes in 24 minutes, versus three hours in China. Although the total labor cost per shoe is still somewhat higher in the United States, reduced shipping costs, improved speed to market, and other gains more than compensate for the difference.[44]

ex 2.5 Changing Concerns of Human Resource Management

Time Period	Primary Concerns	Employee Perceptions	Techniques of Interest
Before 1900	• Production technologies	• Indifference to needs	• Discipline systems
1900–1910	• Employee welfare	• Employees need safe conditions and opportunity	• Safety programs, English-language classes, inspirational programs
1910–1920	• Task efficiency	• Need high earnings made possible with higher productivity	• Motion and time study
1920–1930	• Individual differences	• Employees' individual differences considered	• Psychological testing, employee counseling
1930–1940	• Unionization • Productivity	• Employees as adversaries • Group performance	• Employee communication programs, anti-unionization techniques • Improving conditions for groups
1940–1950	• Economic security	• Employees need economic protection	• Employee pension plans, health plans, fringe benefits (pensions, etc.)
1950–1960	• Human relations	• Employees need considerate supervision	• Foreman training (role-playing, sensitivity training)
1960–1970	• Participation • Employment laws	• Employees need involvement in task decision	• Participative management techniques
1970-1980	• Task challenge and quality of working life	• Employees from different groups should be treated equally	• Affirmative action, equal opportunity
1980–1990	• Employee displacement; quality, cost, and customers	• Employees need work that is challenging and congruent with abilities	• Job enrichment, integrated task teams
1990–2000	• Productivity • Competitiveness • Globalization • Change	• Employees need jobs (lost through economic downturns, international competition, and technological changes) • Employees need to balance work and nonwork and make contributions; need to be flexible	• Outplacement, retraining, total quality management, organizational learning • Linking the needs of the business, training, ethics, diversity, and workplace accommodation
2000–Present	• Globalization • Strategic alliances • Mergers & acquisitions • Domestic labor shortages	• Job insecurity will remain high for some, yet employees will remain valued • Continuous learning and development will be essential	• Using practices to be an employer of choice • Telecommuting • Virtual workplace • Phased retirement of baby boomers

"In" the Office. For the majority of U.S. workers who don't work in factories, information technology is more relevant to their daily lives than robotics. **Information technology (IT)** encompasses a broad array of communication devices that link together people with information hardware and software. Included are voice and video conferencing, the Internet, corporate intranets, groupware and shareware, cell phones, faxes, personal digital assistants, and so on. Such devices promote information sharing and collaboration throughout and between organizations.[45]

Before the advent of Internet-based services, most service organizations were fairly low tech (medical services are a notable exception, however). Information technology was used primarily as a record-keeping tool. It

> **FAST FACT**
>
> According to a recent study, the typical office worker receives 52 phone calls, 36 e-mails, and 18 pieces of postal mail per day.

was through social skills and technical knowledge that employees created value for the company and developed a sense of personal accomplishment. But now, "expert systems" (also called, appropriately, artificial intelligence) capture and store technical knowledge, which often is then accessed and used by nonexperts. In addition, technologies are used to mediate and reduce the need for personal transactions between service providers and customers. As customers, we often must negotiate an electronic menu before speaking with a person. When we do speak with a customer service employee, it is likely to be someone working in a call center. Charles Schwab used the Internet and call centers to create a powerhouse in the brokerage industry. Exhibit 2.6 illustrates the rapid increase in Internet-generated revenue since the mid-1990s.

Benefits of IT. Research shows that within organizations, using information technology for group problem solving is generally more effective than face-to-face meetings.[46] Information technology also increases efficiency and improves labor productivity by increasing the speed of communication, reducing the cost of communication, and reducing the need for managers to spend time monitoring.[47]

At Chiat/Day, the advertising firm, the IT system promotes collaboration and speeds communication by making it easier for people to access information. When advertising copy is delivered to the firm, the IT system posts it to the intranet and informs the person who needs it. The giant manila folders and mechanical files that were used in the past to store photos and other account information have been replaced with "electronic job jackets." Because clients' accounts no longer have physical files to keep track of, the need for "traffic managers" is greatly reduced.[48] The explosive growth of computer-mediated business-to-business e-commerce, such as Covisint, suggests that

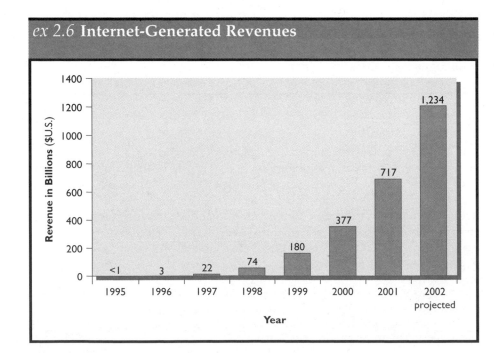

ex 2.6 **Internet-Generated Revenues**

(Revenue in Billions ($U.S.) by Year)
- 1995: <1
- 1996: 3
- 1997: 22
- 1998: 74
- 1999: 180
- 2000: 377
- 2001: 717
- 2002 projected: 1,234

managers expect to reap similar benefits by using information technology to improve interorganizational communication and problem solving.

In the medical profession, IT is revolutionizing patient care and patient management. Electronic medical records help reduce the incidence of recording errors. Electronic orders for prescriptions, X-rays, and lab tests make it possible to instantly check for possible problems such as drug interactions and allergies. Digital radiology makes it possible for physicians around the country to simultaneously view an X-ray and discuss its implications. By making such innovations possible, IT promises to improve patient care and perhaps reduce its costs at the same time. Soon, new innovations will make remote monitoring and diagnosis of patients a routine part of medical practice.[49]

Implications for Managing Human Resources

Like the steam engine, information technology has revolutionized jobs, organizations, and industries. It also is revolutionizing human resource management. Perhaps the most dramatic consequence of the IT revolution is that it makes it possible for an organization to employ a virtual workforce, with employees located all over the world. In addition, human resource information systems are changing the nature of the HR profession and the HR services available to organizations.

Virtual Workforce. Members of the **virtual workforce** perform their jobs anywhere and anytime, often on an as-needed basis. They work out of sight of their supervisors, though not out of mind. Common forms of virtual working include telecommuting, teleworking (e.g., from hotels and airports while traveling), and virtual teams. By eliminating the need for office space for employees who telecommute, IBM reduced its real estate expenses by about 50 percent per office site. Hewlett-Packard reported that it doubled revenue per salesperson after adopting virtual work arrangements.[50]

A **virtual work team** meets and carries out its tasks without everyone being physically present in the same place or even at the same time. Virtual work teams can be functional, problem solving, multidisciplinary, or self-managing. As described in the feature "Managing Teams: NCR's Virtual Success,"[51] communications technologies such as the Internet, voice mail, and video allow virtual work teams to extend the reach of organizations far beyond their traditional physical and cultural boundaries.

Of course, the benefits of a virtual workforce are not won without overcoming significant challenges. Employees working under such arrangements may feel isolated and detached from their employer. If their actions are closely monitored electronically, their morale may suffer. If they have not been properly trained in the use of IT, their insensitive electronic interactions with others may create misunderstandings or resentment among coworkers or even clients. As we discuss in subsequent chapters, a variety of human resource activities can be used to address these challenges and enable organizations and their employees alike to enjoy the benefits of a virtual workforce.

HRIM. New technologies change not only the nature of work in organizations but also change the way workers are managed. When computer technologies are used to gather, analyze, and distribute information about the people in an organization, the resulting system is referred to as a

> *"I remember when IBM meant 'I've been moved.'"*
>
> Heidi Toffler
> Author, Futurist, Consultant
> Toffler Associates

MANAGING TEAMS

NCR's Virtual Success

When NCR was founded more than a century ago, it produced and sold cash registers. Back then, employees of the National Cash Register (NCR) Company knew nothing about working in virtual teams—the term hadn't even been coined and the technology necessary for such teams to function hadn't even been thought of, much less invented. Today, such teams are vital to the firm's survival. Although you may still be able to buy an antique cash register from NCR, most of the company's customers are more interested in products such as its WorldMark enterprise computer server. A virtual team of more than 1,000 people working in 17 locations created this product. The U.S. team members were scattered across five states, and they in turn worked with others who lived in China, India, and Ireland. With such a complex project (imagine designing a computer that weighs about 10 tons!), the most amazing feat of this team may have been completing its work on time and within budget.

One factor contributing to its success was that everyone on the team understood his or her mission and its importance. In addition, all team members knew the basics of good project management—setting goals, identifying tasks and the ultimate results to be achieved, scheduling work, and so on. And, perhaps most important, this team had the benefit of using the latest and best communications technologies. As they worked together each day, they relied heavily on a continuously available high-speed, full-bandwidth communications link through which they could send audio, video, and data signals. The team nicknamed this link "Worm Hole." In science fiction stories, wormholes make it possible for people to be transported instantly from galaxy to galaxy. NCR's "Worm Hole" didn't actually transport people from one location to another—but it came close. Team members could see everyone at all the locations, visually present material to each other, exchange documents, use flip charts, and discuss or argue about any topic. In just 11 months, this team created a new generation of computer systems.

human resource information management (HRIM) system (also referred to as HRIS, for human resource information system). Sophisticated human resource information management systems keep track of who's doing what jobs and where. CitiGroup maintains a database that provides basic information about all employees in the 100+ countries where it does business. In addition, it has more detailed information for about 10,000 key managers who are considered part of the company's global talent pool. When openings occur within the company, the database can be searched for potential internal candidates to fill the position.[52]

The prevalence of HRIM systems today is particularly interesting when compared with predictions made by human resource executives a decade earlier. Then, the revolutionary impact of information technology was not anticipated. At the time, most companies didn't yet have e-mail systems, intranets, and Internet access. Today, these technologies are considered essential for activities such as recruitment and staffing, succession planning, performance management, and career development.

FAST FACT

Different countries have different laws regulating the use of HR information that can be stored and shared electronically.

Low-level HRIM applications merely allow employees to access general information (e.g., policies, procedures, company events) using a company intranet. A bit more complex are systems that allow employees to access specific information contained in their own employee records, such as retirement plan balances and vacation days accrued. Sometimes referred to as employee self-service, such systems may also handle purchase requisitions and other simple requests. Much more complex are systems that give employees and managers a way to administer their own HR data and processes, without paperwork or administrative support.

A sophisticated HRIM architecture allows employees and managers to enter performance data, display and analyze it for trends over time, and use the data as input for both the employee's personal development plan and the organization's longer-term workforce and succession planning. When appropriate, third-party vendors (e.g., pension fund managers, insurance providers, accountants) can be brought into the process, also. As they become more common, sophisticated applications will greatly facilitate cooperative planning and problem solving by the HR partnership triad.[53]

INTERNET RESOURCES 2.E

Evolving Technologies

At our Web site, http://jackson.swcollege.com/, you can:

1. Read summaries of recent court decisions regarding the conduct of e-commerce.

2. See what advice is being offered to employers who wish to set up telecommuting arrangements.

3. Learn how companies in the aerospace industry use the IT services of AeroTech Service Group to operate virtual factories.

4. Access the Journal of Organizational Virtualness and read about the most recent research on virtual organizing.

5. Discover what issues in technology are being discussed by professional engineers.

6. Learn about recent developments in HRIM technology from the International Association for Human Resource Information Management.

THE GLOBAL WORKFORCE

Just as firms must compete for customers, so must they compete for employees. Like customers, employees can be sought in the domestic market only, or employers can broaden their horizons to include the entire global labor market. Increasingly, U.S. employers looking for highly skilled workers have turned to the global labor market to cope with domestic labor shortages. In addition to benefiting from liberal immigration policies, U.S. employers can now use information technologies to essentially import labor electronically. Thus, labor market conditions are yet another force contributing to the process of globalization.

"I will put my job anywhere in the world where the right infrastructure is, with the right educated workforce, with the right supportive government."

John Chambers
CEO
Cisco

Domestic Labor Shortages

In recent years, several factors have contributed to domestic labor shortages within the United States, including population demographics, low unemployment, and the inadequate skills of those employees who are available. Although unemployment levels can be expected to ebb and flow over time, the structural problems created by population demographics, business demand, and inadequate skills are likely to persist into the foreseeable future for the **domestic labor market**.

Population Demographics. With a population of more than 280 million today, projections indicate that the U.S. population will continue to grow, reaching 383 million by 2050. Despite this change, the rate of growth in the working population is expected to slow each year between now and 2020.[54] The biggest reason for the slowing growth in the size of the workforce is the impending retirement of baby boomers (those born between 1946 and 1961).

Between 1990 and 2000, the number of U.S. workers aged 48 to 53 increased by 67 percent. In contrast, those aged 35 to 47 increased by only 38 percent. Chapter 7 describes in more detail how the overall aging of the workforce is making it more difficult to recruit needed talent, as well as how employers are responding to this challenge.

Unemployment. After rising to 7.5 percent in 1992, unemployment levels in the United States declined steadily through 2000. Beginning in 2001, they again began to rise slightly. Nevertheless, they remain comparatively low by historical standards, as shown in Exhibit 2.7. A weak economy could partially ease the labor shortages employers experienced throughout the past decade, but most observers expect that even a weak economy will not solve the problem of domestic labor shortages. This is because simply having more people available to work is not enough. Employers also need more highly skilled workers.

FAST FACT

Approximately 25% of U.S. adults are functionally illiterate, compared with 5% in Japan.

Skill Shortages. In many industries experiencing worker shortages, companies cannot find workers with the needed skills. After installing millions of dollars worth of computers in its Burlington, Vermont, factories, the IBM Corporation discovered, much to its dismay, that it had to teach high school algebra to thousands of workers before they could run the computers. Lincoln Electric understands the problem IBM faced. Most of the 1,000+ applications submitted to Lincoln each month are rejected because applicants don't have the needed skills. The company needs skilled tool-and-die makers, mold makers, and machinists. When Lincoln asked the Ohio Bureau of Employment Services to search its databases for candidates for the tool-and-die openings, the bureau couldn't

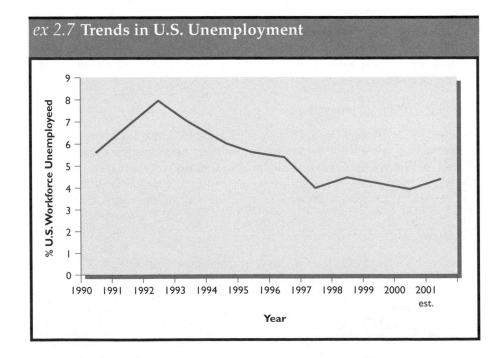

ex 2.7 **Trends in U.S. Unemployment**

come up with a single candidate in the entire state—even though Ohio has one of the highest numbers of machine-tool companies in the country.

Lincoln is willing to train new recruits, but few of the thousands of applicants who apply for jobs at Lincoln can do high school trigonometry or read technical drawings, and many don't show an aptitude for learning how to operate computer-controlled machines—skills that Lincoln says even entry-level workers need.[55] The severe labor shortage forced this 100-year-old company to adopt some unusual recruiting tactics. Along with advertising on local radio stations, managers have met with local ROTC units and the Interchurch Council of Greater Cleveland to discover candidates. Lincoln won't specify how much it spends on recruiting but says it recently spent more in two years than in the previous 100 years put together. It holds frequent open houses for high-school teachers, career counselors, and students and sends recruiting teams to neighboring counties in Ohio and Pennsylvania.

Labor shortages are even more severe for so-called new economy jobs, which is why Congress agreed to raise the cap on H-1B visas in 2000. From 1996 to 2006, projections indicate there will be more than a 100 percent increase in computer-related jobs.[56] Given that enrollments in college engineering programs have been dropping steadily during the past decade, it is clear that the people to fill these jobs will not come from the U.S. workforce alone. Nor are they likely to come from Europe, which is experiencing the same problem. According to a 2001 survey of 350 European managers, labor shortages were having severe adverse consequences for about half of their businesses.[57]

Global Labor Market

The lack of skilled labor in the domestic labor market has led many U.S. companies to look elsewhere for their employees. There is no shortage of people when one considers the **global labor market** as a potential source of employees.

> **FAST FACT**
>
> Since 1995, Asia's workforce has grown by 240 million, while Europe's has grown by only 6 million.

Where People with Skills Live. Currently there are more than 6 billion people on this planet. Projections indicate that the labor force in developing nations alone will expand by about 700 million people by the year 2010, while the U.S. labor force will grow by only 75 million. To get a sense of where in the world people live, study the figures presented in Exhibit 2.8.[58]

Consider next the data shown in Exhibit 2.9 regarding the skills of populations around the world. The math and science scores of 8th graders provide further insight into the issue of where employers are likely to find the workers they need in the future.[59]

> **FAST FACT**
>
> GE employs more people in India than in the United States.

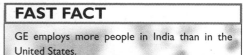

Increasingly, well-educated entry-level workers can be found in developing countries. Furthermore, educational gains are being made more rapidly in developing countries. In 1970, less than 25 percent of all college students were in developing countries; today, the figure has risen to about 50 percent.

Global Recruiting. For employers seeking flexible and adaptable workers, the young and newly educated workforces in developing countries are particularly attractive. Workers from other countries also fill professional-level jobs. U.S. companies are increasingly hiring highly skilled workers in Asia and in countries that were part of the former Soviet bloc to perform jobs once reserved for American professionals.[60] Texas Instruments Inc., IBM, and

ex 2.8 Selected Characteristics of the World Population

If the world's population were shrunk to a village of 100 people but the existing ratios remained the same, the population breakdown would be as shown below:

	1990	Est. 2025
Asians	57	61
Europeans	21	9
North and South Americans	14	13
Africans	8	17
Nonwhite	70	80
White	30	20

FAST FACT

The Senate overwhelmingly endorsed legislation in 2000 to increase the yearly limit on H-1B visas from 95,000 to 165,000.

scores of other companies have contracted with Indians, Israelis, and others to write computer programs. Film and TV producers increasingly bring in foreign film professionals.

For U.S. companies that require high skill levels in areas such as science and engineering, adopting an international approach is no longer questioned. These foreign workers do not represent a search for cheaper labor: According to a study by the U.S. Department of Labor, 99 percent of employees holding work visas are paid the prevailing wage rate.[61]

For lower-skill jobs that don't satisfy H-1B visa requirements, bringing foreign workers into the United States is not a feasible solution to domestic labor shortages. When companies can't move needed workers to the United States, they often move the jobs abroad. Of course, for low-skill jobs, this approach often reduces labor costs substantially as well. When companies like American Express and Citigroup set up back office operations in India, their labor costs may be reduced by as much as 40 to 50 percent. At the same time, they are likely to get better quality work from employees. After

ex 2.9 A Sampling of Test Scores from a 41-Nation Study of Eighth Graders

Math Scores		Science Scores	
Singapore	643	Singapore	607
Japan	605	Czech Republic	574
Czech Republic	564	Japan	571
Slovak Republic	547	Australia	545
Australia	530	Slovak Republic	544
Ireland	527	Ireland	538
Germany	509	United States	534
United States	500	Germany	531
Latvia	493	Spain	517
Spain	487	Greece	497
Greece	484	Latvia	485

E-Funds International, a division of Deluxe, the check printer, set up operations near New Delhi, it cut data processing errors by 90 percent and reduced the days taken to close a client's monthly accounts from five to three.[62]

India is a particularly desirable labor market for U.S. employers due to the prevalence of English language skills and various technical skills. The successes experienced by companies like GE and American Express have convinced other companies that it is an excellent location for IT-enabled jobs—those which can be done anywhere using information technology. Some of the work that is migrating most quickly to India involves customer service call centers, medical transcription, finance and accounting services, and pre-press and digital pre-media.[63]

CULTURAL DIVERSITY IN THE GLOBAL ENVIRONMENT

Increasingly, a firm's total diversity is created by cultural differences associated with nationality. Perhaps the greatest challenge to managing human resources in a global economy is learning to manage across different cultures. Entire volumes have been devoted to describing national differences in culture and approaches to managing human resources around the world,[64] and the space here isn't nearly sufficient to summarize this work. Nevertheless, it is important to recognize that the challenge of managing in a global environment requires developing new approaches to managing people.

> **FAST FACT**
>
> Current predictions suggest that quick and accurate electronic language translation will be routine by 2012.

Cultural differences have many far-reaching consequences for managing organizations.[65] At the most fundamental level, bringing together different cultures often means that language differences interfere with smooth communication. At a 3Com plant in the United States, 65 nations are represented in the workforce. Explained one worker, "Around here you point a lot." For U.S. firms working in other countries, cultural differences mean that the company's U.S. managers must understand a variety of societal cultures and be able to work with the local managers who run sales offices in those countries.

> **FAST FACT**
>
> "English-only" rules for U.S. employees are likely to be considered discriminatory and illegal unless there is a clear business necessity. Requiring the use of English during breaks is seldom justified.

Differences can be significant even when comparing cultures that we may think of as similar (e.g., because they share the same language). For example, compared with those in the United States, companies in Australia place much less emphasis on merit and they tend to adopt a more top-down approach, command-and-control management style.[66] Expatriates who lack cultural sensitivity experience problems in communication and feelings of isolation. Managers working in a culture that they don't understand are likely to make poor decisions about how to staff their organizations and motivate employees.[67] This is one reason why expatriates who have been sent abroad to manage a firm's foreign operations often fail, despite the exceptional financial and marketing skills that made them seem like the ideal candidates for such conditions.[68]

Dimensions of National Culture

Describing cultural differences has been the objective of hundreds of research projects. Out of all these investigations have come several different frameworks for comparing and contrasting country cultures. The best-known framework was developed by Geert Hofstede based on research conducted at IBM several decades ago. Hofstede's work continues to serve as a foundation for research on cultural differences. As research progressed, however, it became apparent that some modifications to Hofstede's original framework were needed to better capture the full range of cultural differences found around the world today. In this section, we use results from the Global Leadership and Organizational Behavior Effectiveness (GLOBE) research project to describe cultural differences. GLOBE is a team of 150 researchers who have collected data on cultural values from 18,000 managers in 62 countries. The GLOBE results indicate that cultural comparisons are best described using the dimensions shown in Exhibit 2.10. Examples of countries that are high and low on each dimension are also shown in Exhibit 2.10.[69]

Consequences of Culture

U.S. employers cannot simply impose their domestic HR practices on employees around the world and expect them to be effective. Cultural differences result in workers elsewhere reacting differently to some U.S. HR practices. For example, one study found that workers in the United States, Mexico, and Poland responded well to HR practices that empowered them to make work-related decisions, but Indian employees responded negatively to empowerment. On the other hand, employees in all of these countries responded well to HR practices that support continuous improvement.[70] Another study using data from 18 countries documented the importance of using HR practices that fit the country culture. The study showed that European and Asian work units had better financial performance when HR practices in the units were congruent with the national culture.[71]

Some HR practices that are common in the United States are actually illegal elsewhere. For example, compared to those in the United States, workers in Europe are eligible for more social benefits and live in greater economic egalitarianism. In addition, various laws have protected workers from layoffs. Centralized wage-setting institutions have kept wage disparities down relative to the United States, and educational and work apprenticeship programs generally ensure high levels of skills. Many of these differences may eventually diminish in response to competitive pressures. Competitive pressures may also eventually diminish the high standards of corporate social responsibility to which European businesses are currently held. Even as changes continue to evolve within Europe, however, significant differences are likely to remain between Europe and the United States well into the foreseeable future. Differences in approaches to managing human resources are even greater when one compares U.S. practices with those in non-European countries.[72]

To cope with the cultural diversity present in their global operations, many large corporations seek to create a strong transnational corporate culture that glues together operations flung across great distances. The Swiss-Swedish firm Asea Brown Boveri (ABB) is one global firm with a strong corporate culture. The corporate culture—focused on making money, taking action, using a hands-on approach, and traveling to wherever business opportunities arise—isn't insensitive to national cultures, however. Indeed, the firm insists that its 213,000 employees working in 1,300 national companies adapt the corporate culture to blend with the local cultural scene. Local activities, in turn, influence the ABB corporate culture because local learning is shared across borders. For example, ABB's approach to equal employment opportunity in Europe reflects its U.S. experience. This is because European countries have become actively concerned with issues of equal employment

ex 2.10 Dimensions for Comparing National Cultures

CULTURAL DIMENSION — Behaviors That Society Encourages and Rewards	SAMPLE COUNTRIES — Low-Scoring Countries or Regions	SAMPLE COUNTRIES — High-Scoring Countries or Regions
Assertiveness — Toughness, confrontation, competitiveness (v. modesty, tenderness)	Sweden Switzerland Kuwait	Spain United States Greece
Future Orientation — Planning, investing in future, delaying gratification	Russia Argentina Poland	Netherlands Switzerland Singapore
Gender Differentiation — Males and females expected to behave differently and be treated differently (vs. accepting gender neutral behavior)	Hungary Poland Slovenia	South Korea Egypt Morocco
Uncertainty Avoidance — Orderliness, consistency, following formal procedures and laws	Russia Hungary Bolivia	Germany (former West) Sweden Switzerland
Power Distance — Recognizing and showing respect for people and groups with greater authority, prestige, status, material possessions than oneself	Denmark Netherlands South African (blacks)	Thailand Argentina Morocco
Institutional Collectivism — Participating in legislative, economic, and political processes (vs. personal autonomy). Behaviors that support the collective good are encouraged through formal institutions, taxes, etc.	Greece Hungary Germany (former East)	Japan South Korea Sweden
In-Group Collectivism — Taking pride in one's membership in smaller groups such as family, circle of close friends, employer	Denmark Sweden New Zealand	China India Iran
Performance Orientation — Performance improvements and excellence, acceptance of feedback	Russia Argentina Greece	New Zealand Hong Kong Singapore
Humane Orientation — Being fair, generous, altruistic, kind toward others	Germany (former West) Spain France	Malaysia Ireland Philippines

opportunity only recently, whereas the United States has many years of experience addressing these concerns.

For companies with little experience beyond their domestic borders, cultural clashes often are more disruptive than anticipated. Even experienced executives can be surprised by the powerful impact of cultural differences, as the DaimlerChrysler example revealed. Some of the firm's managers argue that differing management philosophies and organizational cultures caused the problems—not national differences. Arguments such as these miss the point. Separating organizational culture from national culture is difficult, if not impossible. Organizational cultures almost always develop first within a national context; they reflect and incorporate local values and practices. It is true that organizations within a culture are likely to have different organizational cultures. Nevertheless, it is also true that, on average, predictable differences can be found when comparing organizations in different cultures. The key challenge of managing human resources in a global environment is finding a balance that respects local differences while enabling global success.

INTERNET RESOURCES   2.F

The Global Workforce and Its Cultures

At our Web site, http://jackson.swcollege.com/, you can:

1. Obtain statistics about the U.S. population and the U.S. labor force.

2. Obtain statistics about the global labor market.

3. Learn more about the implications of the aging of the U.S. workforce from:

   The American Society on Aging

   The Administration on Aging

   The National Council on Aging

4. Learn about resources available to expatriates and their employers.

SUMMARY

The environment in which organizations operate is complex and dynamic, creating a constant flow of new opportunities and challenges for organizations and the people who work there. We began this chapter by briefly describing the nature of global competition. To meet this challenge, partners in the HR Triad must work together to gather relevant information about the environment, share it with all relevant stakeholders, and work collaboratively to develop action plans.

The intensity of competition is one reason many U.S. companies become involved in international activities. International competition is not shaped by economic conditions alone. Political events and regional trade alliances also play important roles.

To compete in the international arena, companies engage in various forms of transnational strategic alliances, including international joint ventures as well as mergers and acquisitions. Whether these strategies succeed or fail can depend on whether the associated human resource issues are recognized and effectively managed.

Labor shortages at home and the wealth of talent and skills elsewhere in the world further contribute to globalization. Employing a global labor force is made possible, in part, by information technologies. Many types of skilled jobs can be performed anywhere in the world—no longer is it necessary for office work to be performed at a centrally located office. Besides making new forms of organizing work possible, technology is changing various human resource management activities. HRIM systems often shift HR tasks to line managers and their employees and out of the hands of specialized HR staff.

One consequence of the ways that firms have responded to the many environmental forces described in this chapter has been an increase in the amount of cultural diversity within organizations. Learning how to manage cultural diversity has become one of the major challenges for managing human resources. Because this is so difficult and so important, the firms that meet this challenge most quickly will gain a source of sustainable competitive advantage.

TERMS TO REMEMBER

Acquisition
Asia-Pacific Economic Cooperation
  (APEC)
Domestic labor market
European Union
Global environment
Global labor market
Human resource information
  management (HRIM)
Information technology (IT)
International joint venture (IJV)
M&As

Maquiladoras
Merger
Most favored nation principle
North American Free Trade
  Agreement (NAFTA)
Strategic alliance
Takeover
Technology
Virtual work team
Virtual workforce
World Trade Organization (WTO)

DISCUSSION QUESTIONS

1. Describe the forces that have increased the speed of globalization during the past two decades. Which of the changes in the global environment do you think are most important to managing human resources? Why?
2. Choose an industry of interest to you. How would you rate the relative level of domestic and international competition in this industry at the current time? Explain your evaluation. What are the specific indicators of competitiveness in the industry? Is the level of competitiveness likely to intensify in the next five years? Why or why not?
3. You are working at a local bank in a midlevel management position. You learn on the evening news that your company has agreed to a merger with a competitor. The rationale that's given for the merger is: "There are many synergies that a merger will allow us to exploit. This merger isn't about becoming more efficient—it's about growing revenues." Assume this is true. What will be the three most significant HR issues for the new organization? Why?
4. Think about the most recent technological developments. What are the likely implications of these developments for employers during the next 10 years?
5. Which characteristics of the domestic and global labor markets are most significant for a consumer products company like Coca-Cola? Which are most significant for a pharmaceutical company like Merck? Describe the nature of the effects.
6. Some people argue that organizations can develop their own corporate culture, and that doing so will make differences in country cultures irrelevant to effectively managing human resources. Do you agree? Explain your opinion.

PROJECTS TO EXTEND YOUR LEARNING

1. *Managing Change.* Your company is exploring the idea of acquiring another firm. It has never completed an acquisition before, and everyone wants to make sure they make the right decision. After learning about GE Capital Services' Pathfinder model, you are convinced this is just what your company needs to do. You need much more information in order to actually use the model, however, so you have arranged a one-hour interview with the director of human resources at GE Capital Services. What are the most important things you need to learn during your interview with this person? If you could interview one other person, who would it be, and what would you want to learn? Explain your rationale.

2. *Managing Globalization.* Working with a class partner, choose two countries of interest to you and learn as much as you can about the characteristics of the labor markets in those two countries. What are the biggest differences between the labor forces in the two countries? How would these differences be likely to affect approaches to managing human resources in these countries?

3. *Integration and Application.* Review the end-of-text cases.
   a. Describe the impact/relevance of the following environmental factors for Lincoln Electric's approach to managing human resources:
      * the global economy
      * the national culture of the United States
      * changes in technology
   b. Describe the impact/relevance of the following possible events for Southwest Airlines' approach to managing human resources:
      * The unemployment rate continues to decline, putting pressure on wages.
      * A tax law change makes it more difficult for business travelers to treat airfare as a deductible expense.
      * OPEC members agree to substantially reduce oil production in an attempt to boost prices.

INTERNET RESOURCES   2.G

Projects to Extend Your Learning

At our Web site, http://jackson.swcollege.com/, you can:

1. Before preparing your interview questions, learn more about GE Capital Services and its recent acquisitions. Be sure to read its latest annual report before deciding who else in the company you would most want to interview.

2. Go to the Web site of the International Labor Organization for information about labor force characteristics in different countries. You may also find the country descriptions provided by the CIA useful.

3. Before preparing your answer, learn more about the global economy and U.S. unemployment rates. You may also want to read more about oil production and processing from the Web sites of Shell Oil Company and BP Norge.

IMPLICATIONS OF A COMPETITIVE ENVIRONMENT FOR MANAGING HUMAN RESOURCES AT BARDEN BEARINGS

case study

The Barden Bearings Corporation manufactures high-precision ball bearings for machine tools, aircraft instruments and accessories, aircraft engines, computer peripherals, textile spindles, and medical and dental equipment. Currently, it employs about 1,000 people and includes a marketing department and a small corporate staff. It was founded during World War II to manufacture the special bearings needed for the Norden bombsight and has been nonunion since the beginning. Mr. Donald Brush, vice president and general manager of the Precision Bearings Division, gave the following description of his division:

Reporting directly to me is a small staff comprising a manufacturing manager, a quality manager, an engineering manager, a director of manufacturing planning, and a manager of human resources (see Case Exhibit 1). We meet several times a week to discuss current problems, as well as short- and long-range opportunities and needs. On alternate weeks, we augment this group by including the supervisors who report to the senior managers listed above. I might interject here that all supervisors meet with hourly

employees on either a weekly or biweekly basis to review specific departmental successes and failures, and to otherwise keep employees informed about the business and to encourage ownership of their jobs. The managers themselves meet on call as the Employee Relations Committee to discuss and recommend approval of a wide range of issues that include the evaluation and audit of hourly and salaried positions, as well as the creation and modification of all divisional personnel policies.

A few words about our Human Resource Department: There are six employees who together provide the basic services of employment, affirmative action, employee activity support, labor relations, interpretation of the federal and state laws, benefits administration, wage and salary administration, records preparation and maintenance, cafeteria supervision, and so on. There are, in addition, two people who coordinate our rather extensive training activities.

As currently organized, the Medical Department comes under the supervision of the manager of

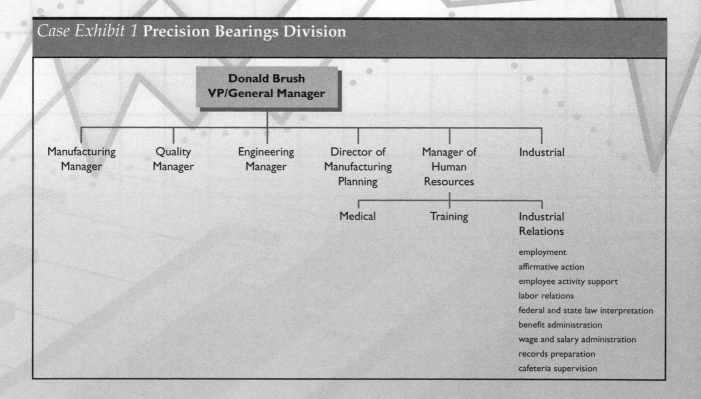

Case Exhibit 1 **Precision Bearings Division**

human resources. Its authorized staff includes a medical director, the manager of employee health and safety (who is an occupational health nurse), a staff nurse, a safety specialist, and a secretary/clerk.

The development and execution of plans and programs, including those of a strategic nature, almost invariably involve the active participation of HR. And that's how we want it to be. On the other hand, the HR Department doesn't run the business. By this I mean they don't hire or fire, promote or demote. They don't write job descriptions or determine salaries or wages. All these things are done by the line managers with the HR Department providing a framework to ensure consistency and that all actions are appropriate to company goals. You might say that HR is our "Jiminy Cricket"—they're there for advice, consent, and, importantly, as a conscience.

BUSINESS OBJECTIVES

During the past several months, we have been running into many issues that affect the very essence of our business objectives: growth, profits, survival, and competitiveness. Because the issues involve our human resources, these must be our major HR objectives. Would you please give us your experience, expertise, and suggestions as to how we can solve them? Thanks! The following briefly describes the nature of each of the four HR objectives.

Recruiting and Training New Hourly Employees. The need to recruit and train approximately 125 new hourly workers to respond to a surge in business is very challenging. By midyear, it became evident that we had an opportunity to significantly increase our business. In order to achieve otherwise attainable goals, we need to increase our hourly workforce by a net of about 125 employees (that is, in addition to normal turnover, retirements, etc.) in one year. I have asked HR to test the waters, recognizing that the unemployment in the Danbury labor market for skilled workers has reached an unprecedented low of about 2.5 percent.

Safety and Occupational Health Improvement. The need to create a heightened awareness by the workforce for safety and occupational health considerations is very important. This is an evolving mission born of a dissatisfaction on our part about "safety as usual." Over the years, Barden employees

have assumed that, because we are a metalworking shop, people were just going to get hurt. But we cannot afford to have people get hurt and miss work anymore. Yet, as our workforce ages, the employees seem to get out of shape and become more injury- and illness-prone.

Managing Health Costs of an Aging Workforce. The spiraling health costs of an aging and, sometimes, out-of-shape workforce are very costly. All employers face this. Barden's problem is a little unique in that hourly employees tend to stay with the company and retire from the company. For example, we still have several employees whose careers began with us 45 years ago, shortly after the company was founded. Our average age approaches 45 for employees and their dependent spouses. Generally, our jobs do not require much physical effort, and it's easy to become out of shape. As a consequence, employees get sick, use hospitals, and have accidents.

New Machines and the Development of Qualified Workers. The technological evolution of increasingly complex machinery and related manufacturing equipment, and the development of trained workers to operate and maintain this equipment, are important facts of life. This process is unceasing and requires a good deal of planning for both the short and the long run. For example, what should we do in the next year, or five years out, in order to remain competitive in terms of cost, quality, and service? Buying and rebuilding machines is part of the story. Running them efficiently is quite another. As you know, modern equipment of this sort requires operational people who are not only knowledgeable about the turning or grinding of metals, but also conversant with computerized numerical controls. The employee who sets up and operates a $500,000 machine must be well trained. Yet finding trained people is getting more difficult.

SUMMARY

Mr. Brush knows that these HR objectives all reflect the increasing diversity of the workforce. Because of this, he knows these issues will be around for a long time. He requests that you provide him with your general ideas and suggestions. He doesn't want details at this time.

QUESTIONS

1. Which of the HR objectives facing Mr. Brush are really the most important to the success of the business? Prioritize them and justify your list.

2. Now consider this list of objectives from the perspective of employees. Using the employees' perspective, how would you prioritize the list? What are the implications of any differences in the two lists of priorities for Mr. Brush?

3. Choose two objectives. For each, describe the key roles and responsibilities of the HR manager, the line managers, and other employees.

Source: This case was prepared by Randall S. Schuler, who expresses his appreciation for the cooperation of Donald Brush.

ENDNOTES

1 "The DaimlerChrysler Emulsion," *Economist* (July 29–August 4, 2000): 5; A. Blanco, "When a Merger Turns Messy," *Business Week* (July 17, 2000): 90–93; F. Gibney Jr., "Daimler-Benz and Chrysler Merge to Daimler-Chrysler," *Time* (May 24, 1999); C. Tierney, "Defiant Daimler," *Business Week* (August 7, 2000): 89–93; B. Vlasic and B. A. Stertz, "Taken for a Ride," *Business Week* (June 5, 2000): 84–89; "Daimler to Adopt Aspects of Chrysler Culture, Stallkamp Says," http://www.geocities.com /MotorCity/Downs/9323/dc.htm.

2 These trends and their implications for managing human resources in 10 countries are described in detail in a special issue of the *International Journal of Manpower*, titled "Trends and Emerging Issues in Human Resource Management: Global and Transcultural Perspectives" Volume 22 (3) (2001); also see P. Budhwar and Y. Deborah, *Human Resource Management in Developing Countries* (London: Routledge, 2001).

3 M. A. Hitt, R. D. Ireland, and R. E. Hoskisson, *Strategic Management: Competitiveness and Globalization* (Cincinnati, OH: Thomson, 2001).

4 J. Selmer, "Human Resource Management in Japan: Adjustment or Transformation," *International Journal of Manpower* 22 (2001): 235–243.

5 D. B. Sicilia, "How the West Was," *Inc.* Tech 2 (1997): 74–78.

6 P. Elstrom, C. Arnst, and R. O. Crockett, "At Last, Telecom Unbound," *Business Week* (July 6, 1998): 24–27.

7 D. Kirkpatrick, "From Davos, Talk of Death," *Fortune* (March 5, 2001): 180–182; J. Gurley, "Why Wi-Fi Is the Next Big Thing," *Fortune* (March 5, 2001): 184; J. Kotkin, "The Future," *Inc.* (December 2000): 108–114; S. Strom, "In Japan, Start-Up and Risk Are New Business Watchwords," *New York Times* (April 23, 2000): 1–6; "Questioning Authority," *Across the Board* (January 2001): 15–16; "Readers Report," *Business Week* (July 17, 2000): 14–18; "The Treadmill of the New Economy," *Across the Board* (January 2001): 33–38; "To Cut or Not to Cut," *Economist* (February 10, 2001): 61–62.

8 G. Edmonson, "See the World, Erase Its Borders," *Business Week* (August 28, 2000): 113–114.

9 R. E. Cole, *Managing Quality Fads: How American Business Learned How to Play the Quality Game* (New York: Oxford, 1999).

10 *Global Relocation Trends: 2000 Survey Report* (New York: GMAC GRS/Windham International, 2000).

11 G. Smith and E. Malkin, "Mexican Revolution," *Business Week* (July 17, 2000): 38–40; G. Smith, "Tax Reform: Fox Is Pushing the Case," *Business Week* (July 24, 2000); 52–54.

12 M. Landler, "Gloom Over Asia Economies Spreads as Yen Drops Again," *New York Times* (June 12, 1998): D1, D6.

13 L. Compa, "Wary Allies, Trade Unions, NGOs, and Corporate Codes of Conduct," *American Prospect* (Summer 2001): 8–9.

14 Based on information posted on the ILO home page, http:// webfusion.ilo.org/public/ (July 13, 2001).

15 R. E. Thaler-Carter, "Social Accountability 8000," *HR Magazine* (June 1999): 105–112.

16 Y. Luo, Guanxi and Business (Singapore: World Scientific, 2000); home page of the Asia-Pacific Economic Cooperation, http://www.apecsec .org.sg/ (July 13, 2001).

17 For a full discussion of cultural differences among the three NAFTA countries, see R. T. Moran and J. Abbott, NAFTA: *Managing the Cultural Differences* (Houston, TX: Gulf Publishing, 1994).

18 T. Stundza, "Trade Approaches $600 Billion," *Purchasing* (March 9, 2000): 70; see also http://www.mac.doc.gov/nafta/, July 2, 2000.

19 C. J. Watlan and P. Magnusson, "NAFTA's Scorecard: So Far, So Good," *Business Week* (July 9, 2001): 54–56.

20 S. H. Verhoveck, "Free Trade's Benefits Bypass Border Towns," *New York Times* (June 23, 1998): A1, A16.

21 G. Smith, "Mexican Revolution," *Business Week* (July 17, 2000): 38–40; G. Smith, "Tax Reform: Fox Is Pushing the Case," *Business Week* (July 24, 2000): 52–54; M. A. Gowan, S. Ibarreche, and C. Lackey, "Doing Things Right in Mexico" *Academy of Management Executive* 10 (1996): 74–81; J. Millman, "Mexico Is Becoming Auto-Making Hot Spot," *Wall Street Journal* (June 23, 1998): A17.

22 C. Juarez, "Between Here and There," *Economist* (July 7, 2001): 28–30.

23 J. Faux, "The Global Alternative," *American Prospect* (Summer 2001): 15–18.

24 D. Fairlamb, "Ready, Set, Euros," *Business Week* (July 2, 2001): 48–50; E. L. Andrews, "The Euro Unites Twelve Countries," *New York Times* (December 30, 2001): Section 5, p. 2.

25 G. Hamel, "Avoiding the Guillotine," *Fortune* (April 2, 2001): 139–144; G. Hamel and C. K. Prahalad, *Competing for the Future: Breakthrough Strategies for Seizing Control of Your Industry and Creating the Markets of Tomorrow* (Boston: Harvard Business School Press, 1994).

26 K. Lucenko, "Strategies for Growth," *Across the Board* (September 2000): 63; T. J. Galpin and M. Herndon, *The Complete Guide to Mergers and Acquisitions* (San Francisco: Jossey-Bass, 1999: 107–08); I. M. Jawahar and G. L. McLaughlin, "Toward a Descriptive Stakeholder Theory: An Organizational Life Cycle Approach," *Academy of Management Review* 26 (2001): 397–414.

27 E. Zuckerman, "Focusing the Corporate Product: Securities Analysts and De-diversification," *Administrative Science Quarterly* 45 (2000): 591–619; see M. A. Hitt, R. D. Ireland, and R. E. Hoskisson, *Strategic Management: Competitiveness and Globalization* (Cincinnati: South-Western,

2001); C. M. Grimm and K. G. Smith, *Strategy as Action* (Cincinnati, OH: South-Western, 1997).

28 M. Brannigan and J. Cole, "Delta to Buy All Its Planes from Boeing Co." *Wall Street Journal* (March 20, 1997): B2.

29 J. P. Liebeskind, A. L. Oliver, L. G. Zucker, and M. Brewer, "Social Networks, Learning, and Flexibility: Sourcing Scientific Knowledge in New Biotechnology Firms," *Organization Science* 7 (1996): 428–443.

30 C. Robertson and T. Jett, "Pro-Environmental Support: The Environmental and Industrial Benefits of Project XL at Merck & Co., Inc.," *Organizational Dynamics* (Autumn 1999): 81–88; E. Schonfeld, "Merck vs. the Biotech Industry: Which One Is More Potent?" *Fortune* (March 31, 1997): 161–162; and I. Sager, "The New Biology of Big Business," *Business Week* (April 15, 1996): 19.

31 L. Greenhalgh, "Ford Motor Company's CEO Jac Nasser on Transformational Change, E-business, and Environmental Responsibility," *Academy of Management Executive* 14 (3) (2000): 46–51.

32 Adapted from R. S. Schuler, "HR Issues and Activities in International Joint Ventures," *International Journal of Human Resources Management* (February 2001): 1–52.

33 N. Deogun and K. Scannell, "Market Swoon Stifles M&A's Red-Hot Start, But Old Economy Supplies a Surprise Bounty," *Wall Street Journal* (January 2, 2001): R4; A. Charman, "Global Mergers and Acquisitions: The Human Resource Challenge," *International Focus* (Alexandria, VA: Society for Human Resource Management, 1999); http://members.tripodasia.com.sg/batsmile/article05.htmlmembers.tripodasia.com.sg/batsmile/article05.html.

34 G. Colvin, "M&A and You: Career Power," *Fortune* (June 22, 1998): 173–175.

35 L. D. Tyson, "The New Laws of Nations," *New York Times* (July 14, 2001): A15.

36 C. D. Charman, "A CEO Roundtable on Making Mergers Succeed," *Harvard Business Review* (May–June 2000): 145–154.

37 For a full discussion of reasons for failure, see M. A. Hitt, R. D. Ireland and R. E. Hoskisson, *Strategic Management: Competitiveness and Globalization* (Cincinnati, OH: South-Western, 2001); see also D. A. Nadler, *Champions of Change* (San Francisco: Jossey-Bass, 1998).

38 A. Taylor, "Bumpy Roads for Global Auto Makers," *Fortune* (December 18, 2000): 18.

39 R. N. Ashkenas, L. J. DeMonaco, and S. C. Francis, "Making the Deal Real: How GE Capital Integrates Acquisitions," *Harvard Business Review* (January–February 1998): 165–178.

40 Source: R. S. Schuler and S. E. Jackson "HR Issues in Mergers and Acquisitions," *European Management Journal* (June 2001): 59–73.

41 J. Bower, "Not All M & A's Are Alike—and That Matters," *Harvard Business Review* (March 2001): 93–101; A. Charman, "Global Mergers and Acquisitions: The Human Resource Challenge," *International Focus* (Alexandria, VA: Society for Human Resource Management, 1999); A. Barrett, "Addicted to Mergers?" *Business Week* (December 6, 1999): 84–91; D. Anfuso, "Novell Idea: A Map for Mergers," *Personnel Journal* (March 1994): 48–55; "Doing Mergers by the Book Aids Growth," *Personnel Journal* (January 1994): 59; A. F. Buono and J. L. Bowditch, *The Human Side of Mergers and Acquisitions: Managing Collisions between People, Cultures, and Organizations* (San Francisco: Jossey-Bass, 1989).

42 D. A. Wren, *The Evolution of Management Thought* (New York: John Wiley, 1994).

43 Portions of this exhibit were adapted from S. J. Carroll and R. S. Schuler, "Professional HRM: Changing Functions and Problems in the 1980s," in S. J. Carroll and R. S. Schuler (eds.), *Human Resource Management in the 1980s* (Washington, DC: Bureau of National Affairs, 1983): 8–10. Also see A. Howard, "A Framework for Work Change," in A. Howard (ed.), *The Changing Nature of Work* (San Francisco: Jossey-Bass, 1995).

44 A. Berstein, "Low-skilled Jobs: Do They Have to Move?" *Business Week* (February 26, 2001): 94.

45 For an excellent review of research, see T. Dewett and G. R. Jones, "The Role of Information Technology in the Organization: A Review, Model and Assessment," *Journal of Management* 27 (2001): 313–346.

46 M. L. Maznevski and K. M. Chudoba, "Bridging Space Over Time: Global Virtual Team Dynamics and Effectiveness," *Organization Science* 11 (2000): 473–492; G. DeSanctis and P. Monge, "Introduction to the Special Issue: Communication Processes for Virtual Organizations," *Organizational Science* 10 (1999): 693–703.

47 J. Rosenfeld, "Information," *Fast Company* (March 2000): 204–219; M. Sawhney and D. Parikh, "Where Value Lives in a Networked World," *Harvard Business Review* (January 2000): 79–86.

48 R. Kuperman, "An Advertising Agency without Walls," in E. Halal (ed.), *The Infinite Resource: Creating and Leading the Knowledge Enterprise* (San Francisco: Jossey-Bass, 1998): 213–222.

49 E. Licking, "This Is the Future of Medicine," *Business Week e.Biz* (December 11, 2000): 77–78; W. C. Symonds, "How E-Hospitals Can Save Your Life," *Business Week e.Biz* (December 11, 2000): 70–74.

50 W. F. Cascio, "Managing a Virtual Workplace," *Academy of Management Executive* 14 (3) (2000): 81–90; see also A. J. Walker, "Visions of the Future: The Workforce of the Future," *IHRIM Journal* (October–December 2000): 8–12.

51 J. Lipnack and J. Stamps. "Virtual Teams: The New Way to Work," *Strategy & Leadership* (January–February 1999), 14–19. Also see E. Carmel, *Global Software Teams: Collaborating Across Borders and Time Zones* (Upper Saddle River, NJ: Prentice-Hall), 1999.

52 L. K. Stroh, S. Grasshoff, A. Rude, and N. Carter, "Integrated HR Systems Help Develop Global Leaders," *HRM Magazine* (April 1998): 15–17.

53 W. F. Cascio, "Managing a Virtual Workplace," J. F. LeTart, "A Look at Virtual HR: How Far Behind Am I?" *HRM Magazine* (June 1998): 33–42.

54 Bureau of Labor Statistics, as reported in S. J. Wells, "Looking for Trouble," *HR Magazine* (January 2001): 38–48.

55 A. Borrus, "Workers of the World: Welcome," *Business Week* (November 20, 2000): 129–133; H. Gleckman, "High-Tech Talent: Don't Bolt the Golden Door," *Business Week* (March 16, 1998): 30.

56 "Shifting From . . . Shifting To," *Fast Company* (March 2000): 215–218.

57 "Bridging Europe's Skills Gap," *Economist* (March 2001): 55–56.

58 D. G. Albrecht, "Getting Ready for Older Workers," *Workforce* (February 2001): 56–62; D. Fandray, "Gray Matters," *Workforce* (July 2000): 27–32; Society for Human Resource Management, "Human Resources Yearly Outlook: What to Expect in the Coming Year," *Workplace Visions* 6 (2000): 2–7; Society for Human Resource Management, "The Aging Workforce as Baby Boomers Retire, Employers Will Face New Challenges," *Workspan* (January 2001): 30–32; "Earth Population Breakdown," *ACA News* (July/August 1996): 17.

59 A. M. Konrad and J. R. Deckop, "Human Resource Management Trends in the United States: Challenges in the Midst of Prosperity," *International Journal of Manpower* (August 2001); B. Murray, "America Still Lags Behind in Mathematics Test Scores," *APA Monitor* (January 1997): 44.

60 A. Rahunathan, "Thanks for Coming: Now Go," *New York Times* (July 15, 2001): Section 14, 1, 7.

61 C. Joinson, "Strength in Numbers?" *HR Magazine* (November 2000): 43–49; S. Ante, "The New Software Whizzes," *E.Biz* (December 11, 2000): 30–42; M. Simons, "Retired, Rehired: Dutch Fill Crucial Work Force Gap," *New York Times International* (April 23, 2000): 8.

62 "Outsourcing to India: Back Office to the World," *Economist* (May 5, 2001): 99–101.

63 "Outsourcing to India: Back Office to the World."

64 R. B. Freeman (ed.), *Working Under Different Rules* (New York: Russell Sage, 1997); P. J. Dowling, R. S. Schuler, and D. E. Welch, *International Dimensions of Human Resource Management,* 3rd ed. (Cincinnati, OH: South-Western/ITP, 1999).

65 S. C. Schneider and J.-L. Barsoux, *Managing Across Cultures* (New York: Prentice-Hall, 1997); P. C. Earley and M. Erez (eds.), *New Perspectives in International Industrial/Organizational Psychology* (San Francisco: New Lexington Press, 1997).

66 B. Kabanoff and J. P. Daly, "Values Espoused by Australian and U.S. Organizations," *Applied Psychology: An International Review* 49(2) (2000): 284–314.

67 B. Schlender, "Microsoft: First America, Now the World," *Fortune* (August 18, 1997): 214–217; R. Tung and V. Worm, "East Meets West: Northern European Expatriates in China," *Business and the Contemporary World* 9 (1997) 137–148; and N. Rogovsky and R. S. Schuler, "Managing Human Resources Across Cultures," *Business and the Contemporary World* 9 (1997): 63–75.

68 "Expatriate Activity Still Expanding, But at Slower Rate, Survey Says," *HR News* (February 2001): 10; M. A. Shaffer and D. A. Harrison, "Expatriates' Psychological Withdrawal from International Assignments: Work, Nonwork, and Family Influence," *Personnel Psychology* 51 (1998): 87–118; W. A. Arthur Jr., and W. B. Bennett Jr., "The International Assignee: The Relative Importance of Factors Perceived to Contribute to Success," *Personnel Psychology* 48 (1995): 99–114; D. C. Thomas and E. C. Ravlin, "Responses of Employees to Cultural Adaptation by a Foreign Manager," *Journal of Applied Psychology* 80 (1995): 133–146.

69 To learn more about GLOBE, see M. Javidan and R. J. House, "Cultural Acumen for the Global Manager," *Organizational Dynamics* 29 (4): 289–305; GLOBE Research Team, *Culture, Leadership, and Organizational Practices: The GLOBE Findings* (Sage, 2002 in press).

70 C. Robert, T. M. Probst, J. J. Martoccio, F. Glasgow, and J. J. Lawler, "Empowerment and Continuous Improvement in the United States, Mexico, Poland, and India: Predicting Fit on the Basis of Dimensions of Power Distance and Individualism, *Journal of Applied Psychology* 85 (2000): 643–658.

71 K. L. Newman and S. D. Nollen, "Culture and Congruence: The Fit Between Management Practices and National Culture," *Journal of International Business Studies* (1996): 753–776.

72 Z. Aycan, R. Kanungo, M. Mendonca, K. Yu, J. Deller, G. Stahl, A. Kurshid, "Impact of Culture on Human Resource Management Practices: A 10-Country Comparison," *Applied Psychology: An International Review* 49 (2000): 192–221.

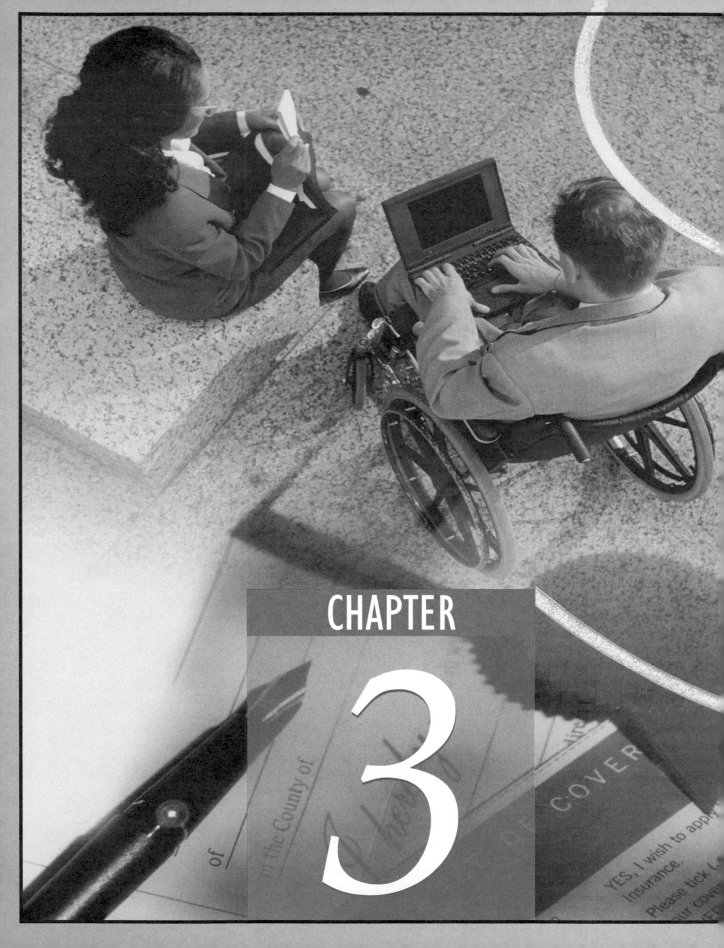

CHAPTER

3

ENSURING FAIR TREATMENT AND LEGAL COMPLIANCE FOR A DIVERSE WORKFORCE

"Eighty percent of the ethics issues that came across my desk were human-resources related [involving] people who thought they should have been allowed to try for a particular job opening, or someone who thought they were unfairly disciplined, where the boss yelled at them unfairly in front of others, showing a lack of mutual respect."

Bill Prachar
Former Ethics Officer
Teledyne Inc.[1]

MANAGING THROUGH STRATEGIC PARTNERSHIPS

Coors

The Coors Brewing Company, headquartered in Golden, Colorado, is famous for its beer and for its procedures for managing employees fairly. But that hasn't always been true. For many years, employees relied on their union to deal with management around issues of fairness. But after a failed strike against the company, employees voted to decertify the union. This left employees without protection from what they saw as the "potential abuses of management."

Employees were afraid that management would take control from them and give them no recourse in such matters as employee discipline. To their way of thinking, "if management wants to get us out of here, they'll do it and do it without a fair hearing." Representatives for the workers told Bill Coors, who was head of the company: "Our employees are frightened because they've had this union here that was taking care of our needs and making sure that discipline was meted out fairly. Now we don't have that and we've got to either find a way to provide it or ultimately the employees will bring in another union."

The company acted swiftly. Borrowing from a Coors subsidiary, Coors Container Company, the HR department set up a peer review system designed to give employees a chance to air their complaints and have their peers take part in evaluating whether their complaints were legitimate. HR believed that such a system would benefit employees and management alike. Others in senior management, including the Coors family members, were not so positive. They feared that every disciplinary action would be considered unfair. So disciplinary actions would always be reviewed by the peer review system. This, in turn, would mean that the disciplinary action would always be reversed. Despite their concerns, they agreed to put the system in place.

To appease senior management's fears, HR said it would use the system only for debates over termination actions. But the company found out early on that some employees get very upset even about a first written warning—long before termination action is taken. So they expanded the system to include hearings for all forms of discipline including first warnings, final warnings, suspensions without pay, and terminations. Coors' Peer Review system works like this:

Step 1. An employee who's unsatisfied with the application of a company policy—but not the policy itself—may file an appeal with his or her employee relations representative within seven working days. The employee relations representative then sets up an appeal board by randomly selecting two members of management and three employees from the same job category as the appellant.

Step 2. A hearing is held, orchestrated by the employee relations representative. At the hearing, the supervisor describes the circumstances and the employee explains why the supervisor's action was unfair. Board members may ask questions of both parties during the proceedings and also may request testimony from witnesses.

Step 3. When board members have all the information they need, they privately discuss the case. They decide by majority vote whether to uphold the action, reduce the severity, or overturn the action completely. The board's decision is final. The employee relations representative notifies the supervisor and the appellant of the decision through a brief, written summary, signed by all the board members. In the past decade, the board has overturned a supervisor's actions in about 10 percent of the appeals.

Management now recognizes an added value of the review board: Coors has never lost a wrongful termination case in court. The company credits the appeals process for its success in court. If it can't substantiate or uphold a termination internally with its appeal board, it can almost guarantee that the action wouldn't be upheld by a jury. And if it's upheld internally, a jury will generally agree that the action was justified. The experience of Coors, as well as a great deal of research on the topic, shows that the process and procedures used to make decisions are as important to employees as the decisions themselves.[2]

THE STRATEGIC IMPORTANCE OF FAIRNESS AND LEGAL COMPLIANCE

In an idealized capitalistic economic system, managers on behalf of shareholders seek to maximize profits free of noneconomic external constraints—that is, without constraints other than those imposed by consumers and competitors. In the real world, however, effective businesses address the concerns of many stakeholders, including society and employees. They take a proactive stance in their relationship with society and employees, going beyond codified laws and regulations in order to live up to society's ethical principles. At the other extreme, some companies allow managers and other employees to flagrantly violate existing laws and regulations.

Dayton-Hudson, a division of Target Corporation, considers issues of managing diversity effectively in its department stores to be essential to its business success, while Dillard's department store has been criticized severely for racially biased practices in its Kansas City stores. As part of a lawsuit, police officers who worked while off duty as security guards for Dillard's testified that the company instructed them to follow black customers and that some guards used special codes over the walkie-talkie system to alert the store to the presence of black shoppers. After losing the case, which was brought by a black human resources manager who was searched by a security guard at an upscale suburban store, Dillard's issued no apologies and appealed the verdict. Meanwhile, the mayor asked the city's pension managers to ensure that the city didn't own any Dillard's stock.[3] As Dillard's learned, fairness is a topic that concerns society in general as well as members of the workforce.

"If the only thing we do is reside in the rules-based, compliance-based legal focus, I don't think we challenge our organizations to revise and grow."

Keith Darcy
Senior Vice President
IBJ Schroder Bank and Trust

Society and the Law

The concept of fairness has many connotations, so ensuring fair treatment can be a major challenge.[4] Society's view of what constitutes fair treatment of employees is in constant flux. Practices that were considered fair at the beginning of the 20th century had become illegal by the middle of the 20th century. Similarly, practices considered fair today may no longer be legal in 5 or 10 years. Companies must continually adjust to society's changing attitudes about fairness. To make matters more complicated, operating internationally requires companies to be responsive to the different views of fairness held within multiple societies.

> **FAST FACT**
>
> At Harley-Davidson, 86% of employees say they are paid fairly. Turnover is 3%.

Legal institutions provide one channel for the labor force to use in communicating their fairness concerns to employers. In the United States, the legal system helps define and interpret the meaning of fair treatment within employment settings. Through elected government representatives, members of the labor force initiate and ultimately create federal and state laws. Through their tax payments, employees pay for the operations of a vast array of government agencies and courts, which are responsible for interpreting and enforcing the laws. Thus, employment laws should be thought of not only as legal constraints; they're also sources of information about the issues that potential employees are likely thinking about as they decide whether to join or leave an organization. Simply complying with laws and regulations is seldom enough to ensure employees feel they are fairly treated, however.

Concerns of the Labor Force

People believe that fairness is a desirable social condition—we want to be treated fairly, and we want others to view us as being fair.[5] Companies that rank high as the best places to work generally emphasize fairness as part of their corporate culture. Fairness creates the feeling of trust that's needed to "hold a good workplace together."[6]

Members of the labor force communicate their fairness concerns to employers in many ways. As free agents, they communicate their concerns to employers directly. When deciding where to work, a potential employee evaluates whether a company pays a fair wage, whether it offers desirable benefits, whether the corporate culture is appealing, and so on. In making these evaluations, perceptions of what is "fair," "desirable," and "appealing" reflect the applicant's fairness concerns. The free agency of job applicants, combined with the diversity of the U.S. labor force, means that companies must consider a broad array of labor force concerns in order to attract and hire the best talent.

Once hired, employees continue to express their concerns about fairness and evaluate whether their employer is addressing those concerns. Employees may voice their concerns informally and indirectly through daily conversations at work. If they feel unfairly treated, they may "vote with their feet" and seek employment elsewhere.[7] Or, like Kim Miller, who says she complained more than a dozen times about her treatment at Wal-Mart, they may eventually file a lawsuit.[8] To avoid such departures and surface problems before they become severe, many companies offer formal channels of expression, such as employee surveys and employee grievance systems. Finally, union members voice their concerns directly when they collectively bargain with employers over working conditions and compensation.

In this chapter, we first explain how employees evaluate whether they have been treated fairly and how this affects their behavior at work. Then we describe workplace policies and practices that support fair treatment of employees. As you will see, some approaches to managing workplace fairness—like the one used at Coors—mirror the procedures used in U.S. courts. Finally, this chapter concludes with an overview of the legal rights and responsibilities of employers and employees.

The HR Triad

Fairness and legal compliance are complex issues that implicate all three members of the HR Triad, as shown in "The HR Triad: Roles and Responsibilities for Ensuring Fair Treatment and Legal Compliance." HR professionals, with the assistance of legal experts, share responsibility for enforcing the legal responsibilities of employers and protecting the legal rights of employees. They may participate in policy development, monitor HR actions and their consequences, provide training, and serve as mediators when conflicts arise. Managers carry out their responsibility for ensuring fairness and legal compliance through daily interactions with employees. Besides treating job applicants and employees fairly and legally, they help set a tone that communicates what behaviors the company endorses and tolerates. Managers play a key role in determining whether the workplace is a hostile or welcoming place for members of a diverse workforce. Finally, all employees share responsibility for reporting illegal workplace behaviors, respecting the property rights of employers, and safeguarding the company's intellectual capital. These responsibilities are described in more detail later in the chapter.

WHAT FAIRNESS MEANS TO EMPLOYEES

Imagine that you are the employees involved in the following two situations. How do you feel? And what will you do?

A Missed Promotion—Michelle Chang graduated with her MBA five years ago. Since then, she has worked for a large financial services company as an industry

"I worked there longer than most people are married these days and I never got a promotion."

Kim Miller
Greeter
Wal-Mart

Roles and Responsibilities to Ensure Fair Treatment and Legal Compliance

THE HR TRIAD

LINE MANAGERS	HR PROFESSIONALS	EMPLOYEES
• Be informed about laws and regulations protecting employees' rights and behave in accordance with them. • Set policy for fair treatment of employees in workplace issues in collaboration with HR professionals. • Learn the steps involved in the organization's procedures for due process and follow them. • Be proactive in attempting to understand and respond to employees' views about fairness. • Be proactive and intervene if you observe discriminatory or other illegal behavior among subordinates, colleagues, or superiors. • Keep accurate and current records regarding employee problems and performance.	• Stay up to date about new legal developments in employment law; consult with legal experts as needed. • Set policy for fair treatment of employees in workplace issues in collaboration with line managers. • Encourage managers to use societal views of fairness as guides to policies and behaviors rather than adopting a narrow legalistic model. • Assist in developing and implementing policies and practices that support and are consistent with fair and ethical behavior by everyone in the organization. • Help keep employer and employee rights and responsibilities in balance. • Administer grievance procedures and participate in alternative dispute resolution activities.	• Be informed about laws and regulations protecting employees' rights and behave in accordance with them. • Work with HR professionals in establishing procedures for dealing fairly with workplace issues. • Report discriminatory or other illegal behavior among subordinates, colleagues, or superiors to an HR professional. • Accept and fulfill responsibilities to behave fairly toward employer and the organization's assets. • Help educate employees from other cultures about U.S. employment laws. • Use employer's procedures for reporting harassment.

analyst. Her performance reviews have always been positive. She and her peers assumed she was on the company's informal fast track. But recently, she has begun to wonder. After the manager of her unit left last month for a better opportunity at another firm, Michelle applied for the job. She didn't get the promotion. To her surprise, the person chosen to be the new boss for her unit was Jim Johnson, a 20-year veteran of the firm who was transferred from another unit. After three weeks at his new job, it was obvious that Jim's previous experiences had not provided him with the knowledge he needs. Michelle feels that the company's decision to give Jim the job is a signal that her future may not be as bright as everyone thought. Perhaps it's time to look into possibilities at other companies.

An Unexpected Layoff—Bill Markham works for the same firm as Michelle and Jim. He has been with the organization about 7 years, coming there after working for 12 years at a large computer company and for 8 years as an independent consultant. As manager of the Information Services Department, he has been responsible for managing all the company's computer specialists. Last week, the firm unexpectedly disclosed plans for a major reorganization of Information Services. To "improve efficiency," the company has decided to decentralize several staff activities. In the new structure, the activities of Information Services will be carried out by generalists who will work within each of the firm's several divisions. Of course, everyone knew that the words improve efficiency were code, meaning the size of the Information Services staff would be reduced. But Bill was not worried when he heard the *announcement; he expected to be assigned to the largest division and had already begun discussing the idea of a major move with his family. He was shocked when he learned that he was going to be let go. He appreciates the firm's offer to pay for out-placement counseling, but he wonders whether he should accept its decision as final. As a 50-something white male, he imagines that finding a new job will be pretty tough. Maybe he should put up a fight.*

How much trust in their employer do Michelle and Bill feel? Has each person been treated fairly? What other information might you want before deciding whether this company is treating employees fairly?

Since the mid-1970s, social and organizational scientists have conducted numerous studies designed to improve our understanding of concepts such as fairness and justice. This research has shown that people's perceptions of fairness reflect at least three features of the situations they find themselves in: the actual *outcomes*, the *procedures* used in arriving at these outcomes, and the *interactions* the employees have with their managers. These features are referred to as distributive justice, procedural justice, and interactional justice, respectively.[9]

Distributive Justice

Employees feel a sense of **distributive justice** when they believe that outcomes they experience are fair in comparison with the outcomes of others. Is pay distributed fairly among people from the top to the bottom of the organization? Are performance evaluations distributed fairly among good and poor performers? Not surprisingly, people prefer favorable outcomes for themselves. In the cases of Michelle and Bill, a promotion is better than no promotion and a transfer is better than being let go. In another case, nonsmokers will view a new policy banning smoking at work as more fair than will smokers.[10]

Nevertheless, we do not necessarily feel that we have been treated unfairly when we do not get the best possible outcome.

Perceptions of fairness hinge on how our own outcomes compare with the outcomes of other people, taking into account our own situation and the situations of others. In evaluating the fairness of her situation, for example, Michelle compares her outcome with Jim's. If Michelle felt that the outcomes she and Jim experienced reflected their relative qualifications, then Michelle probably would accept the situation as fair even though she didn't get promoted. Furthermore, Michelle and Jim's coworkers use similar heuristics in evaluating their employer. When Michelle's coworkers see that she has been unfairly treated, they not only feel bad about what happened to Michelle, they may also conclude that their employer generally treats employees unfairly.[11]

Distributive justice also influences how people react to pay practices. Generally, people see pay as fair when they believe that the distribution of pay across a group corresponds to the relative value of the work being done by each person. Similarly, when the relative sizes of raises correspond to the relative performance levels of people in the unit, people tend to accept the systems as fair.

As these examples illustrate, U.S. employees typically experience distributive justice under conditions of equity, or merit-based decision making.[12] Employees from other countries and cultures may see things quite differently, however. American culture is individualistic, whereas many other cultures are more collectivistic. In collectivistic cultures—like many of those found throughout Asia—concern for social cohesion is greater than in the United States. Going along with a perspective that focuses more on groups, people from collectivistic cultures value *equality* of treatment and treatment based on *need*, and they allocate rewards accordingly.[13] From a collectivistic perspective, Michelle might be viewed as having been treated fairly because she was treated the same as her coworkers (equally), and perhaps Jim needed the job more than did Michelle.

Procedural Justice

Perceptions of justice depend on more than the relative distribution of outcomes. Also important to perceived fairness are beliefs about the entire process used to determine outcomes. The term **procedural justice** refers to perceptions about fairness in the process. For example, Michelle and Bill might wonder *how* their company made its decisions in their situations. Research suggests that in U.S. culture, employees consider a formal procedure to be fair if it meets the conditions shown in Exhibit 3.1.[14]

Interactional Justice

The formal system is only one aspect of the procedures that employees react to. Employees also take into account how they personally are treated in their

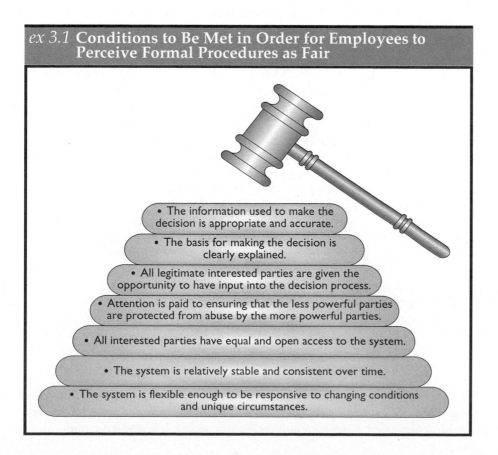

ex 3.1 Conditions to Be Met in Order for Employees to Perceive Formal Procedures as Fair

- The information used to make the decision is appropriate and accurate.
- The basis for making the decision is clearly explained.
- All legitimate interested parties are given the opportunity to have input into the decision process.
- Attention is paid to ensuring that the less powerful parties are protected from abuse by the more powerful parties.
- All interested parties have equal and open access to the system.
- The system is relatively stable and consistent over time.
- The system is flexible enough to be responsive to changing conditions and unique circumstances.

interactions with the managers who carry out the formal procedures. Perceptions of **interactional justice** reflect whether employees feel managers are sensitive to their situation and treat them politely and respectfully as well as whether employees feel they are given sufficient and timely information about the procedures.[15] Employees respond more favorably when they feel they are given a full and reasonable account of what happened.[16]

Reactions to Unjust Treatment

Consider again the situation of Michelle and the actions she might take. If you were Michelle, you would probably consider actions that fall into one of the following categories:

A. Exit the organization and put the incident behind you;
B. Stay and simply accept the situation as something you must tolerate;
C. Stay but engage in negative behaviors that help you restore your sense of fairness (e.g., shorten your hours a bit; stop attending unnecessary meetings and functions);
D. Voice your concern to people inside the organization (e.g., discuss the situation with your colleagues; talk about it with a mentor; talk to someone in the employee relations office); or
E. Voice your concern to external authorities (e.g., explore possible legal action; talk to the press).[17]

Quit? For high performers like Michelle, choice A, quitting, may be the best alternative. From the organization's perspective, however, having Michelle leave and perhaps join the competition may be the least desirable alternative. From society's perspective, turnover caused by feelings of injustice is undesirable because it tends to reduce productivity.[18]

Stay and Accept the Situation? Alternative B would be better for Michelle's employer, but it's probably not very common because few people easily shrug off injustices suffered at the hands of their employers. Instead, their outlook sours. Employees who stay in situations that they believe are unfair lose confidence in the competence of management and feel they cannot trust it.[19] Employees who feel unfairly treated also report feeling more distressed, dissatisfied, and uncommitted to both their employers and the goals their employers set for them.[20]

FAST FACT

Employers lose $40 billion per year due to theft, most of which is committed by employees.

Seek Revenge? Feelings of injustice affect behavior, not just attitudes, even for employees who decide not to quit because of unfair treatment. Therefore, reactions that fall into categories C and E are possible. Employees attempt to maintain a sense of balance in their relationship with employers. If a legal issue is involved, employees may seek legal solutions. Often, however, feelings of unfairness arise in response to perfectly legal management behavior. This was illustrated quite dramatically in a company that temporarily cut employees' pay. The company was a large manufacturer of aerospace and automotive parts.

Owing to the loss of two contracts, temporary pay cuts were required at two of the company's three plants. Everyone at the two plants took a 15 percent pay cut for 10 weeks, including management. The situation created a natural opportunity for the company and a researcher to learn more about how best to implement pay cuts, so a small experiment was conducted. In one plant, the company tried to convey how much it regretted the pay cuts, explained that the pay cuts would eliminate the need for layoffs, and assured employees that no favoritism would occur. At a full meeting with the employees, top management spent an hour answering employees' questions. At the second plant involved, the pay cut was announced at a brief 15-minute meeting with no apology and very little explanation. The third plant was used as a control group. Employees' reactions were assessed in terms of theft rates, turnover, and responses to a survey.

At both plants taking pay cuts, theft rates went up during the weeks the cuts were in effect and then went back down again when full pay was restored, particularly at the plant where the inadequate explanation was given. Turnover in this plant also soared, from 5 percent to 23 percent. Survey results confirmed that employees at this plant didn't understand how their pay cut was determined and felt they were treated unfairly.[21] As this company found out, people are sensitive to changes that disturb their sense of equity and will seek ways to rebalance the scales if they're tipped.[22]

Talk to Others in the Organization? The way companies manage situations can greatly influence how employees react.[23] One aspect of managing situations effectively involves using formal organizational systems to deal with conflicts and disputes. By fully explaining how decisions are made and by offering employees opportunities to *voice* their concerns and have their questions answered (choice D), employers can minimize negative employee reactions. In well-managed companies, employees' feelings of dissatisfaction are intentionally surfaced and used to stimulate positive changes that actually benefit both employees and employers.[24]

Complain to External Authorities? As described later in this chapter, employees who feel they have been treated unfairly can seek redress through the legal system. Substantial research exists to show that perceptions of distributive and procedural injustice are likely to result in a lawsuit.[25] Depending on their circumstances, employees may sue their employer claiming unfair discrimination, wrongful termination, failure to comply with laws regulating pay, and so on. If they win, employees who bring such lawsuits may be reinstated in their old jobs, given promotions, given payments to cover lost compensation, and so on. Regardless of whether the employee wins or loses, the cost of litigating and settling such lawsuits can end up costing employers millions of dollars as well as immeasurable reputational loss in the eyes of the public.

> **FAST FACT**
>
> In 2000, Coca-Cola settled a class action racial discrimination suit for a record-breaking $192.5 million.

Managing to Ensure Fair Treatment

Because employees' perceptions of fairness can have such far-reaching consequences, employers ensure fairness by using a variety of policies and practices. Various laws and regulations mandate some, while others are voluntary. Issues of fairness and legal compliance pervade almost every area of human resource management. In Chapters 7 and 8, for example, you will learn about laws governing staffing procedures and the means that employers can use to ensure that job applicants are treated fairly. In Chapters 10, 12, and 13 you will learn about laws governing compensation and practices that improve employees' perceptions of pay fairness. In those and other chapters, the laws, policies, and practices that are especially important to the activities will be described in more detail.

In this chapter, we set the stage for discussions in subsequent chapters by describing some of the most sweeping legislation and the agencies that enforce it. In addition to describing the legal landscape, we describe proactive management practices that can reduce the likelihood of lawsuits. As you read about these, keep in mind that good policies are not enough. Inevitably, employees sometimes feel that a decision or procedure is unfair. Sensitive supervisors and managers who acknowledge these situations and express their concern can minimize the disruptive effects of the situations. As simple as it seems, apologies reduce anger.[26]

LEGAL MEANS TO ENSURE FAIR TREATMENT

"It's really a matter of where you spend your money—at the front to avoid the lawsuit, or at the end during litigation."

Doug Towns
Employment Attorney
Jones, Day, Reavis, & Pogue

U.S. companies must act in accordance with several different types of laws, including constitutional laws, statutory laws, administrative regulations, executive orders, and common laws. Laws are simply society's values and standards that are enforceable in the courts. The legal environment communicates society's concerns through state and federal laws, regulations, and court decisions. In general, the legal system is designed to encourage socially responsible behavior.[27] That is, it considers the outcomes of all parties concerned and attempts to impose decisions and remedies that balance the perspectives of employees and employers as well as other stakeholders.[28] Failure to comply with employment laws may result in monetary fines, imprisonment, and court orders that constrain future activities, as well as employee turnover and customer boycotts.

The legality of an employer's actions and decisions doesn't necessarily make them ethical, however. At one time, U.S. employers could legally discriminate against women and minorities in hiring and promotions. As a consensus developed that such discriminatory practices were unethical, laws such as the *Civil Rights Act* were passed to stop the practices and ensure equal employment opportunities for all citizens. In addition, the federal government issued regulations requiring government agencies and federal contractors to work at correcting the effects of past discrimination.

FAST FACT

Federal employment discrimination lawsuits have increased about 300% during the past decade, a rate that is nine times higher than all other types of federal civil litigation.

To understand how the legal environment affects the way companies manage human resources, it's necessary to understand several major employment laws and regulations that are promulgated and enforced by our legal system.[29]

U.S. Constitution

In countries that have one, the constitution is the fundamental law of the land. The U.S. Constitution is the oldest written constitution still in force in the world. It defines the structure and limits of the federal government and allocates power among the federal government and the states. All 50 states also have written constitutions. State and federal laws must be consistent with the U.S. Constitution.

FAST FACT

Surveys show that 90% of Americans believe that hiring persons with disabilities is good.

In the area of employment, one particularly important section of the U.S. Constitution is the Fourteenth Amendment, which guarantees due process and equal protection when the state takes certain actions involving the life, liberty, and property of citizens. This amendment also prohibits state actions that are inconsistent with federal law. Because of its equal protection clause, the Fourteenth Amendment often plays a role in cases involving reverse discrimination. The best known of these was *Regents of the University of California v. Bakke*, which effectively rendered illegal the University of California's affirmative action program for minority students. Because the Fourteenth Amendment applies only to state actions, the affirmative action programs of private employers are not directly affected by this decision. Nevertheless, this ruling made it clear that efforts to ensure nondiscrimination against one group (e.g., ethnic minorities) must not result in reverse discrimination against another group (e.g., those of European descent).

Within the legal framework established by the Constitution have flourished numerous other state and federal laws, regulations, and court decisions that further define the legal contours of the relationship between an employer and its employees.

Title VII of the *Civil Rights Act*

The U.S. Constitution gives Congress all power to make laws on behalf of the federal government. State constitutions give lawmaking power to state-level governmental bodies. The resulting federal and state laws are called statutes.

One especially important federal employment law has been Title VII of the *Civil Rights Act*. It was originally enacted in 1964, and later revised in 1978 and 1991. The 1991 law reinforced the intent of the *Civil Rights Act* of 1964 but states more specifically how cases brought under the act should proceed.[30] Today, **Title VII of the *Civil Rights Act*** prohibits discrimination by employers, employment agencies, and unions on the basis of race, color, religion, sex, national origin, and pregnancy.

> **FAST FACT**
>
> U.S. citizens employed elsewhere by a firm controlled or owned by an American parent are protected by Title VII, the ADEA, and the ADA.

Title VII is one of several key statutory laws that affect the employment relationship. Other important laws are summarized in Exhibit 3.2. We cannot fully discuss all of these laws here, but you should familiarize yourself with them in preparation for future chapters, where they will be referred to again.

State Laws

As already noted, state laws must be consistent with federal law, but this does not mean that state and federal laws must be the same. Three important differences between state and federal laws are common. First, state laws often cover companies that are not covered by federal laws. For example, federal employment laws such as Title VII often apply only to businesses with 15 or more employees, but similar state laws often apply to even smaller businesses. Second, state laws often offer greater protection to employees than do federal laws. For example, 11 states and the District of Columbia prohibit discrimination on the basis of sexual orientation, but at this time, no federal law prevents such discrimination.[31]

> **FAST FACT**
>
> Only Michigan and the District of Columbia have laws intended to protect people who are overweight against employment discrimination.

The third difference between state and federal laws is that state laws often precede federal laws and in this sense tell us what to expect in the future at the federal level. For example, Massachusetts passed the first minimum wage legislation in 1912, which was a predecessor of the federal *Fair*

ex 3.2 Major Federal Employment Laws and Regulations

Act	Jurisdiction	Basic Provisions
National Labor Relations Act (Wagner Act, 1935)	Most nonmanagerial employees in private industry	Provides right to organize; provides for collective bargaining; requires employers to bargain; unions must represent all members equally
Fair Labor Standards Act (FLSA; 1938)	Most nonmanagerial employees in private industry	Establishes a minimum wage; controls hours through premium pay for overtime; controls working hours for children
Equal Pay Act (1963)	Most employers	Prohibits unequal pay for males and females with equal skill, effort, and responsibility working under similar working conditions
Title VII of the Civil Rights Act (1964; 1991)	Employers with 15 or more employees; employment agencies; unions	Prevents discrimination on the basis of race, color, religion, sex, or national origin; establishes EEOC; provides reinstatement, back pay, compensatory and punitive damages; permits jury trials
Executive Order 11246 (1965)	Federal contractors with large contracts and 50 or more employees	Prevents discrimination on the basis of race, color, religion, sex, or national origin; establishes Office of Federal Contract Compliance (OFCC)
Age Discrimination in Employment Act (ADEA; 1967)	Employers with more than 20 employees	Prevents discrimination against persons age 40 and over, and states compulsory retirement for some employees
Occupational Safety and Health Act (OSHA; 1970)	Most employers involved in interstate commerce	Assures as far as possible, safe and healthy working conditions and the preservation of our human resources
Rehabilitation Act (1973)	Government contractors and federal agencies	Prevents discrimination against persons with physical and mental disabilities
Employee Retirement Income Security Act (ERISA; 1974)	Most employers with pension plans	Protects employees covered by a pension plan from losses and benefits due to mismanagement, job changes, plant closings, and bankruptcies
Pregnancy Discrimination Act (1978)	Employers with 15 or more employees	Identifies pregnancy as a disability and entitles the woman to the same benefits as any other disability
Worker Adjustment and Retraining Notification Act (WARN; 1988)	Employers with more than 100 employees	Requires 60 days' notice of plant or office closing or substantial layoffs
Americans with Disabilities Act (ADA; 1990)	Employers with 15 or more employees	Prohibits discrimination against individuals with disabilities
Family and Medical Leave Act (1993)	Employers with 50 or more employees	Allows workers to take up to 12 weeks' unpaid leave for childbirth, adoption, or illness of employee or a close family member

Labor Standards Act of 1938 (FLSA). New York had adopted a fair employment law in 1945, and about half of the states had similar laws by the time the Civil Rights Act of 1964 was passed at the federal level. Florida, Maine, and the District of Columbia had each adopted family leave legislation before the federal *Family and Medical Leave Act of 1993* was enacted.

California's Proposition 209 may be another example of a state law that predates a similar federal law. By passing Proposition 209, California voters agreed with the opponents of affirmative action who argue that such programs cause reverse discrimination. Proposition 209 outlawed *state*-sponsored affirmative action programs. After passage of this law, the University of California discontinued its affirmative action programs for student admissions. Proposition 209 doesn't affect businesses directly, but the logic of this law can easily be applied to employment situations. Because California is known as a bell-wether state on social issues, it can't be ignored.

> **FAST FACT**
>
> Research shows that investors reward companies with high-quality affirmative action programs by bidding up the price of their stock and punish companies that have been found guilty of discrimination.

Administrative Regulations

At both the federal and state levels, the legislative and executive branches of government can delegate authority for rule making and enforcement to an administrative agency. In carrying out their duties, administrative agencies make rules (often called standards

> **FAST FACT**
>
> In most states, employees have up to 300 days after an alleged discriminatory event to file a charge with the EEOC.

or guidelines), conduct investigations, make judgments about guilt, and impose sanctions. In practice, this means these federal agencies have the responsibility and authority to prosecute companies they believe are violating the law. Administrative regulations refer to the rules, guidelines, and standards that such agencies produce in order to enforce the law. In other words, administrative regulations explain how the agency will put legislation into practice.

Three administrative agencies of particular importance for managing human resources are

- the Equal Employment Opportunity Commission (EEOC),
- the Occupational Safety and Health Administration (OSHA), and
- the National Labor Relations Board (NLRB).

EEOC. **The Equal Employment Opportunity Commission** is one of the most influential agencies responsible for enforcing employment laws. The EEOC administers Title VII of the *Civil Rights Act* as well as the *Equal Pay Act of 1963* and the *Age Discrimination in Employment Act of 1967.* For each of these acts, the EEOC has produced regulations that inform employers of how the agency will assess whether or not a legal violation has occurred. As you read subsequent chapters, you will see that EEOC regulations have implications for nearly all human resource activities—recruitment, selection, training, pay, performance measurement, termination, and so forth.

Each year, the EEOC receives approximately 80,000 complaints from employees. As Exhibit 3.3 shows, the monetary benefits that the EEOC won for employees grew substantially during the 1990s. Large monetary settlements often occur when the EEOC files a class action suit against an employer. In a **class action lawsuit**, a group of similar employees (i.e., a "class") asserts that all members of an employee class suffered due to an employer's unfair policies

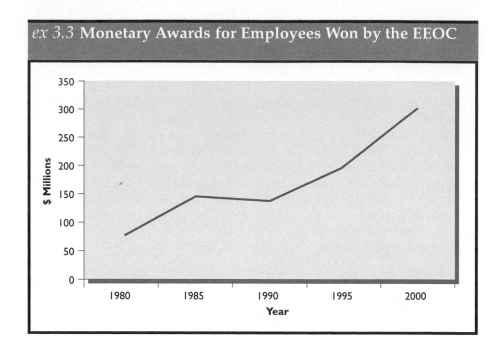

ex 3.3 Monetary Awards for Employees Won by the EEOC

and practices. For example, the $34 million paid by Mitsubishi Motor Manufacturing to settle several sexual harassment cases was distributed to nearly 500 former and current female employees (in addition to the lawyers).

The EEOC and other agencies do not limit their activities to promulgating and enforcing rules; they also have the authority to adopt practices that reduce the need for litigation. In recent years, for example, the EEOC developed a voluntary mediation program. More than 25,000 employees have used this program instead of the courts to resolve complaints against their employers. The program is one reason why the EEOC was able to reduce its backlog of unresolved claims from 111,000 in 1995 to 41,000 in 2001.[32]

> **FAST FACT**
>
> OSHA estimates that 1.8 million workers experience injuries related to repetitive motion and overexertion. About a third of those injuries require taking time off from work.

OSHA. The **Occupational Safety and Health Administration** administers the *Occupational Safety and Health Act*. As described in Chapter 14, OSHA conducts safety and health inspections, investigates accidents and alleged hazardous conditions, issues citations for violations, levies fines, collects mandatory reports prepared by employers, and compiles statistics on work injuries and illnesses.

NLRB. The **National Labor Relations Board** administers the *National Labor Relations Act*. The NLRB's responsibilities include protecting the rights of employees to engage in group actions for the purpose of influencing their work conditions. As described in Chapter 15, the NLRB focuses much of its attention on group activities related to union organizing and collective bargaining. This is not the NLRB's only area of jurisdiction, however. In recent years, for example, the NLRB has become involved in several cases concerning nonunion employees who protested their company's actions using their company's e-mail system. As discussed in Chapter 10, the *National Labor Relations Act* also provides for a fair minimum wage, establishes employees' right to overtime pay, and constraining working hours for children.

Executive Orders

U.S. presidents shape the legal environment by approving and vetoing bills passed by Congress and by influencing how vigorously administrative agencies carry out their duties and responsibilities. In addition, the president can create law by issuing executive orders. An **executive order** specifies rules and conditions for government business and for doing business with the government.

In employment, the actions of government contractors (organizations that do work for the federal government) are most affected by Executive Order 11246, issued in 1965 by President Lyndon B. Johnson. Like Title VII, Executive Order 11246 prohibits discrimination on the basis of race, color, religion, or national origin. It applies to federal agencies and to federal contractors and subcontractors. In 1966, Executive Order 11375 was issued to prohibit discrimination based on sex by these employers.

Whereas Executive Orders 11246 and 11375 parallel federal law that applies to all employers, Executive Order 11478, issued in 1969, has no parallel in federal statutory law. Executive Order 11478 requires that employment policies of the federal government be based on merit. Although most employees agree that merit-based employment policies are a good idea, there is no federal law that *requires* businesses to make merit-based employment decisions.

Common Law

Common law is a set of rules made by judges as they resolve disputes between parties. The U.S. system of common law is rooted in English common law, which was established after the Normans conquered England in 1066. To help unify the country, William the Conqueror established the King's Court. Its purpose was to develop a common set of rules and apply them uniformly throughout the kingdom. Decisions were based on the opinions of judges. Important decisions were recorded and subsequently referred to as **legal precedents** (examples) for making future decisions. When new types of disputes arose, judges created new law to resolve them. This system is still in effect today in England.

The U.S. Court of Appeals for the Ninth Circuit applied the logic of common law when it ruled that workers who were on Microsoft's payroll for more than a few months were common-law employees regardless of whether they were employed as independent contractors or so-called perma-temps. Like a common-law spouse, such employees are not officially married to the company but by virtue of living with it for a long period of time, they are entitled to the same benefits as "permanent" staff. In this case, the ruling meant that more than 6,000 temporary employees would have to be allowed to participate in its stock purchase plan.[33]

Unlike English judges, U.S. judges do not make laws, they only interpret and apply them. But their interpretations continue in the tradition of setting precedent to decide new cases. The use of precedent to decide cases helps employers anticipate how the courts might rule should they find themselves involved in a similar case. When interpreting the implications of court decisions, keep in mind that rulings made by the Supreme Court carry the most weight because the decisions of all other federal and state courts are subject to review by the Supreme Court.

INTERNET RESOURCES   **3.A**

Strategic Importance and Meaning of Fair Treatment and Legal Compliance

At our Web site, http://jackson.swcollege.com/, you can:

1. Learn more about the organization, administration, and operation of U.S. federal courts.

2. Read the official wording of U.S. labor codes and federal regulations, including those that pertain specifically to small businesses.

3. Read summaries of the latest Supreme Court decisions.

4. Find out about the activities of the courts within a particular state.

SETTLING DISPUTES

Even the best companies occasionally experience disputes over the treatment of employees. In the most extreme cases, such disputes may end up in court, where they are eventually resolved by a legal decision or through a legal settlement. More often, however, disputes are resolved through alternative dispute resolution procedures before they reach a court.

Using the Courts to Settle Disputes

For employment law cases that are resolved by a court decision, two common remedies for violations are monetary damages and settlement agreements.

Monetary Damages. If an employee's legal right has been violated and injury has resulted, the employer may be required to pay monetary damages to the plaintiff. Compensatory monetary damages are intended to help victims retrieve what they have lost—for example, back pay and attorneys' fees. Punitive monetary damages are intended specifically to punish wrongdoers and deter future wrongdoing. Most civil lawsuits never actually reach the stage of a formal trial. Court proceedings can be lengthy and costly—sometimes outrageously so. The U.S. Department of Justice and administrative agencies can speed the process of ensuring that employers engage in responsible behavior by negotiating a settlement.

Settlement Agreements. When lawsuits are resolved by a **settlement agreement**, the defendant (employer) usually does not admit to wrongdoing. Nevertheless, it may agree to pay money to the plaintiff or plaintiffs. For example, when Coca-Cola settled the racial discrimination lawsuit brought against it on behalf of African-American employees, it denied any wrongdoing. At the same time, it agreed to pay an average of $40,000 to each of the company's 2,000 black employees, set aside $59 million for a fund to cover claims of emotional distress, and set aside nearly $67 million to be used to correct past pay disparities and eliminate pay disparities in the future.[34] As is common in settlement agreements, Coca-Cola did more than agree to pay money to the plaintiffs. It also agreed to make significant changes in its human resource management policies and practices, as directed by the court.

As described in the feature "Managing Change: Texaco's Plan for a Cultural Shift," litigation may lead to many changes in HR practices.[35] Texaco agreed to change its management practices as part of a settlement

MANAGING CHANGE

Texaco's Plan for a Cultural Shift

The seriousness of Texaco's problems became public in 1996, when secretly recorded conversations revealed that senior executives used racial epithets and plotted to destroy documents demanded by the courts in a discrimination case. Other evidence presented during the case revealed that it was common for supervisors to refer to members of racial subgroups in derogatory terms. Many employees did nothing to protest such treatment, for fear of losing their jobs. Others quit. And eventually, some took their evidence to court.

As part of the lawsuit settlement, Texaco agreed to pay $140 million—at the time, it was the largest settlement ever for a case of racial discrimination. The massive cultural change effort that the company agreed to initiate is outlined below.

Components of Texaco's Cultural Change Initiatives

Recruitment and Hiring
- Ask search firms to identify wider arrays of candidates
- Enhance the interviewing, selection, and hiring skills of managers
- Expand college recruitment at historically minority colleges

Identifying and Developing Talent
- Form a partnership with INROADS, a nation-wide internship program that targets minority students for management careers

- Establish a mentoring process
- Refine the company's global succession planning system to improve identification of talent
- Improve the selection and development of managers and leaders to help ensure that they're capable of maximizing team performance

Ensuring Fair Treatment
- Conduct extensive diversity training
- Implement an alternative dispute resolution process
- Include women and minorities on all human resources committees throughout the company

Holding Managers Accountable
- Link managers' compensation to their success in creating "openness and inclusion in the workplace"
- Implement 360-degree feedback for all managers and supervisors
- Redesign the company's employee attitude survey and begin using it annually to monitor employee attitudes

Improve Relationships with External Stakeholders
- Broaden the company's base of vendors and suppliers to incorporate more minority- and women-owned businesses
- Increase banking, investment, and insurance business with minority- and women-owned firms
- Add more independent, minority retailers and increase the number of minority managers in company-owned gas stations and Xpress Lube outlets

agreement. In 1990, in the process of its normal monitoring activities, the Department of Labor found that Texaco was deficient in its minority representation, and in 1995, the EEOC issued a similar finding. Although the company's employment numbers indicated it had been making some progress in terms of hiring a more diverse workforce, promotion and pay rates lagged other companies in the industry. Too many managers within the company ignored the company's nondiscrimination policies and allowed their personal prejudice to affect their actions at work.

Eventually, the EEOC took Texaco to court. As part of the lawsuit settlement, Texaco agreed to implement broad-reaching diversity management initiatives.

Company Grievance Procedures

Grievance procedures (also referred to as complaint resolution procedures) encourage employees to voice their concerns to the company instead of the courts. They provide a formal means for employees to seek constructive resolutions without litigation. In unionized settings, the presence of such procedures had already become nearly universal by 1950.[36] Almost all public and private unionized employees are covered by contracts that specify formal written grievance procedures, and most of these culminate in final and binding arbitration by a third-party arbitrator.[37] Historically, the picture has been quite different for nonunion employees. In 1950, formal procedures were almost never available to these employees. Now more than half of America's largest corporations have some type of formal complaint resolution system.[38]

The growing popularity of formal complaint resolution is consistent with managers' beliefs that employees have a right to fair treatment.[39] It helps establish a positive corporate culture in which conflicts are resolved through compromises that acknowledge the legitimate interests of both disputing parties.

Fairness systems like the one at Coors are particularly helpful in environments where employees lack the representation and negotiating power of a union.[40] Coors's appeal process gives employees a voice in how they're treated. This voice combined with peer review ensures a better balance of power, which may in turn result in employees being more willing to continue working for an organization even if they have some complaints.[41]

As is true of most administrative systems, the specific details of the policy are not as important as the way the policy is carried out on a daily basis. When they work well, grievance procedures not only help lower the legal costs associated with resolving disputes in the courts; they also increase employee loyalty.[42]

Mediation and Arbitration

Company grievance procedures typically involve a panel of employees—usually peers of the parties involved in the dispute—to reach a resolution. When disputes cannot be resolved through this internal process, a final step may be taken before resorting to the courts. Because the courts are a slow, expensive, and difficult way to resolve serious disputes, a growing number of businesses are using alternative dispute resolution when employees make charges of unfair treatment.

Alternative dispute resolution (ADR) involves making an agreement to forgo litigation and instead resolve disputes by either internal or external mediation or arbitration. Working out a dispute before it reaches litigation can promote goodwill between management and employees and reduce the adverse publicity often associated with legal disputes.[43] It can also reduce legal costs to both employers and society. Mediation and arbitration are the two most common forms of alternative dispute resolution. In the future, on-line approaches for resolving disputes may become common.

Mediation. Mediation is the most popular form of ADR, partly because its format is less formal, more flexible, and less public than that of other proceedings. Parties to a civil dispute may be ordered into mediation by the court, or they may volunteer to submit to the process in an effort to settle the dispute without litigation.

In **mediation**, all concerned parties present their case to a neutral third party—the mediator. Mediators may be appointed by a judge, selected by the parties or their attorneys, or recommended by agencies such as the EEOC. Often, the disputing parties are required to prepare a confidential written statement of their case and a statement of the resolutions they would find acceptable. Each side then presents its views in a private meeting with the mediator. Like a diplomat shuttling between warring parties, the mediator's role is to help the parties understand each other's views and to also understand the strengths and weaknesses in their own cases. During these meetings, the ultimate goal is to steer the parties toward compromise and construct a fair settlement.[44]

Arbitration. Compared with mediation, **arbitration** is a more formal process for alternative dispute resolution, yet not so formal that the rules of a court must be followed. Employees must be permitted to have a representative for their case (usually an attorney) and attorneys must present their cases in a formal manner. Typically, decisions are rendered by a panel of arbitrators. Unlike court judges, arbitrators do not need to provide a written decision or use previous cases in rendering their decisions.

Often, arbitrators are selected by employers, making their neutrality questionable. For example, until recently, Wall Street firms usually used industry executives as arbitrators. The practice appeared to be so biased in favor of the employer that a federal judge ruled that Merrill Lynch couldn't force a former financial consultant to arbitrate her claim instead of using the courts. In stating her decision, the judge noted that she was "deeply troubled" by the "structural bias" in the industry's arbitration system.[45] Learning from the experience of Merrill Lynch, other Wall Street firms have since begun to use professional arbitrators rather than industry executives.[46] To be most fair, a panel of arbitrators should be open—that is, both parties should be allowed to select some members of the panel.

The use of arbitration procedures has skyrocketed since the early 1990s. Many employers ask employees to sign contracts upon being hired stating that they'll accept arbitration as a means to settle any potential future discrimination complaint. Usually employees are asked to agree to binding arbitration in which the arbitrator's decision is final, subject to a very limited right of appeal. In most cases, employees who sign arbitration agreements give up their right to a court hearing. Because of the requirement that employees sign away their right to pursue other legal action, the legal status of such employment agreements has long been considered controversial. In 2001, however, much of the controversy was resolved by a Supreme Court decision. In the case of *Saint Clair Adams v. Circuit City*, the court ruled that Adams could not pursue a complaint of sexual harassment through the California state courts because he had signed an arbitration agreement upon accepting employment at Circuit City.[47]

The Supreme Court's decision in *Saint Clair Adams v. Circuit City* was split 5 to 4. Like the justices, other experts disagree about whether the benefits of arbitration outweigh its potential problems. Exhibit 3.4 summarizes the arguments for and against mandatory arbitration practices.[48] Before signing an arbitration agreement, job applicants should investigate the details of an employer's arbitration process and be sure that they fully understand and are willing to accept the consequences of signing these agreements.

Resolving Disputes On-Line

The newest approaches to alternative dispute resolution take advantage of Web-based technology to prevent, manage, and resolve employment grievances. According to Janet Rifkin, codirector of the Center for Information Technology and Dispute Resolution, "We're at the beginning of a whole new age." On-line dispute resolution initially evolved to address e-commerce

ex 3.4 Weighing the Pros and Cons of Using Mandatory Arbitration to Settle Disputes

Pros	Cons
Quick dispute resolution	Relinquishment of employees' statutory rights to a trial as a condition of employment
Lower personal, professional, and financial costs for both parties	Availability of "user-friendly" arbitration may stimulate a flood of claims
Reduction in employers' advantage in litigation by outspending and outlasting an employee	May prevent better guidance for future action since courts are better able to provide consistent and clear interpretations of law
More business-related experience and expertise of professional arbitrators	Arbitrators may not be competent or impartial
Reduction in exposure to unpredictable jury awards for emotional distress and punitive damages	Small monetary penalties may reduce their effectiveness as remedies in the case of a wronged employee
Permits disputes to remain private	Confidentiality of the process may reduce its deterrence effect; conversely, confidentiality isn't guaranteed
May improve communication and employee relations	May deter some talented employees from accepting employment

disputes, but the technology has since migrated to employment disputes. Among the pioneers in this area were mediators working for the Federal Mediation and Conciliation Service (FMCS). They began experimenting in 2001 with software that allows parties in a dispute to view a mediator's proposals for resolution, see notes submitted by each party, keep track of open issues, and participate in a chat line.[49] Because this approach to employment dispute resolution in so new, little is known about its effectiveness in comparison with traditional face-to-face approaches.

DIVERSITY INITIATIVES FOR ENSURING FAIR TREATMENT

When employees turn to grievance procedures, alternative dispute resolution, or litigation, it indicates that an organization is not succeeding in its goal of treating all employees in ways that they consider fair. Effective means for resolving disputes quickly will always be needed, but many employers realize that these reactive measures alone are not sufficient. Proactive measures that reduce the occurrence of disputes also are needed. One goal of a proactive approach to fairness is to reduce the need for employees to go to court in order to assert their fairness rights. But this is not the only objective. Other benefits associated with workplace fairness include a reputation that attracts the best talent, lower turnover of valued employees, improved productivity, and better customer service.

Beginning in about 1990, many companies began to proactively address employees' fairness concerns by initiating a variety of diversity management policies and practices. In most organizations that have them, **diversity management initiatives** refer to policies and practices that the organization adopts voluntarily (not because of legal requirements) for the purpose of ensuring that all members of a diverse workforce feel they are treated fairly. Some diversity management initiatives look very similar to the Texaco plan that was imposed in the court settlement. The difference is that the courts forced Texaco to adopt the plan for diversity management after concluding that many Texaco employees had suffered the consequences of discrimination.

Who Is Covered by Diversity Initiatives?

When they first appeared, diversity management initiatives targeted the issues of fairness among women and minority employees. Today, it's increasingly evident that members of many demographic groups sometimes are victims of unfair discrimination. Diversity initiatives generally address the concerns of groups that are protected legally, but they may also address the concerns of some groups that enjoy no legal protections. Federated Department Stores, parent of Macy's and Bloomingdale's, provides a typical example. In 1996, its diversity initiatives covered only two employee groups—women and minorities. Today, Federated's diversity initiatives cover more than two dozen employee groups, including seniors, the disabled, homosexuals, atheists, the devout, and many others.[50]

Critics of a broad approach to diversity management argue that all-inclusive diversity initiatives dilute the impact of the organization's efforts. According to this view, a broad approach robs women and ethnic minorities of the resources and attention required to address persistent problems rooted in long histories of systemic sex and race discrimination. Supporters of a broad approach argue that focusing on the concerns of only a few groups ignores the legitimate concerns of many other groups and may also stimulate backlash and feelings of ill will among some employees. Exhibit 3.5 shows the diversity areas typically covered by corporate initiatives.[51]

The accounting firm of Deloitte and Touche became serious about diversity initiatives about a decade ago when the firm's employment numbers revealed that only 5 percent of the company's partners were women and that the turnover for women was 30 percent. The turnover rates and promotion patterns for men and women led some women to feel they were not treated fairly. As described in "Managing Diversity: More Women Become Partners at Deloitte and Touche" on page 105, the numbers have been transformed since the company introduced changes aimed at making it more "women friendly."[52]

What has become increasingly apparent is that simply trying to "obey the law" is not a very effective way for employers to ensure they treat employees fairly. A better approach to meeting employees' and society's concerns about fairness is to create a corporate culture in which all employees respect each other and in which decisions are made on the basis of merit rather than personal demographic attributes. As the Deloitte and Touche example

"There is no limit to what we can accomplish if we crack the code of valuing diversity on a global basis as we move forward in the 21st century."

Michael Critelli
Chairman
Pitney Bowes

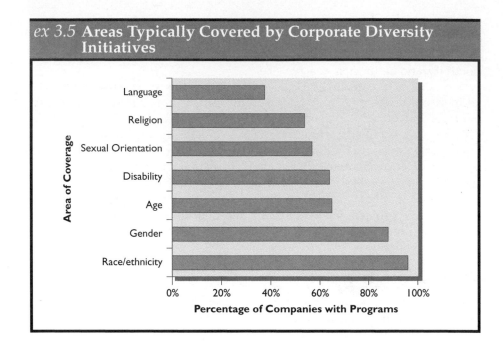

ex 3.5 **Areas Typically Covered by Corporate Diversity Initiatives**

demonstrates, through their diversity initiatives employers can create a positive organizational culture in which everyone feels equally integrated into the larger system. Members of majority and minority subcultures feel respected; everyone has an equal chance to express views and influence decisions; and everyone has similar access to both formal and informal networks within the organization. When all members of the workforce feel they have equal opportunities and access within the company, they are less likely to feel the need to exercise their right to resort to legal means for ensuring fair treatment.

Fairness Must Be Reciprocated

FAST FACT

According to the Association of Certified Fraud Examiners, the average company loses $9 per day per employee to fraud and abuse.

It's easy to emphasize the responsibility of employers to treat employees fairly. Fairness is a two-sided coin, however, and the other side is the responsibility of employees to treat their employers fairly. Unfortunately, employee misconduct is as much a problem as employer misconduct. A National Business Ethics Survey conducted in 2000 identified the following types of prevalent misconduct: lying, withholding needed information, misreporting actual time or hours worked, and abusive or intimidating behavior. A similar survey conducted by the Society for Human Resource Management found that employees are quite aware that such behaviors occur. Although they may not report it, the following figures indicate they see it happen:

- 27% of employees had observed stealing or theft;
- 36% of employees observed lying on reports or falsifying records;
- 45% of employees observed lying to supervisors.[53]

The prevalence of such behaviors reflects, and at the same time contributes to, the fraying of trust between employers and employees. Of increasing concern to employers is another violation of trust—leaking or failing to keep secure valuable information about the firm's products,

MANAGING DIVERSITY

More Women Become Partners at Deloitte and Touche

When Diana O'Brien left Deloitte and Touche in 1990 to work elsewhere, she was just one of many women who had concluded that she needed a change. When Lynne Noonan left in 1995, it was because she found it difficult to balance 70-hour work weeks and the responsibility of being a new mother. Incidents like these along with a systematic study of turnover rates among men and women at the firm finally helped the partners at Deloitte and Touche realize that the company's culture needed to change. Today, the new culture is so good that both Diana O'Brien and Lynne Noonan have returned. "Before I left, I couldn't have a life and still do consulting. Now, enough has changed that I have been able to do that," O'Brien explains. One of the most significant changes has been the company's new flexible work arrangements. Noonan returned with an agreement to work 80 percent of normal hours. She works full-time January through March, which are the busiest times for the firm, but takes extra time off during the rest of the year.

To help the company create a new culture, Deloitte and Touche formed an outside group comprising a former U.S. secretary of labor, the first female member of the New York Stock Exchange, and other notables. The group met quarterly and set achievement goals for the company. Within three years, the company had developed a new set of work life policies designed to make work life more family-friendly for men and women alike. These policies now include compressed work weeks, flexible work arrangements, telecommuting, job sharing, and two weeks of paid child-care leave. Compensation is prorated for employees who work a reduced work week, but in every other way, the company signals that there is no penalty for taking advantage of the new policies. For Jeff McLane, the new policies have made it possible to have a more balanced personal life, which includes training to compete as an Olympic cyclist. For Diana O'Brien, who was promoted to partner while working an alternative schedule, the policies make it possible to raise a family that includes triplets diagnosed with autism.

Some of the alternative arrangements are offered only to high-performing employees, so managers have a great deal of say about how particular employees are treated. To ensure that managers are fair, the company keeps track of who is permitted to work flexibly. To ensure that the arrangements don't hurt employee performance, managers are trained to manage flexibly. And for good measure, the company also tracks employees' attitudes about the policies. In a recent survey of those using the new policies, 95 percent said they would have left had it not been for the company's flexible approach.

services, competitive strategies and intellectual property. In many firms, the responsibilities of employees are spelled out in a code of ethics. A **code of ethics** informs employees that they are expected to conduct business in a way that upholds high standards of integrity. Typically, a code of ethics communicates that *employees* are expected to do the following:

- Act with personal and professional integrity.
- Understand and comply fully with the letter and spirit of laws and regulations, as well as the firm's rules and policies.
- Safeguard the firm's reputation.
- Preserve the confidentiality of information about clients, colleagues, and the firm.

In exchange, the *company* often agrees to these behaviors:

- Engage in business activities that are consistent with its reputation for integrity.
- Articulate its standards and rules clearly.
- Provide support in making legal and ethical decisions.
- Refuse to tolerate illegal, unethical, or unprofessional conduct.

Perhaps the best indicator of how fairly employees feel they're being treated is the degree to which they're willing to accept responsibility for behaving fairly in all dealings with their employers.

CHALLENGES FOR THE 21ST CENTURY

Managers will always need to be alert to employees' concerns about fairness. Yet, at particular times in history and in particular organizations or industries, specific fairness issues are salient and in need of attention. Today, in addition to the issue of diversity, four other significant fairness concerns are harassment, employment-at-will, privacy, and managing fairness in other cultures. We conclude this chapter by discussing these current fairness issues in a bit more detail.

Harassment in the Workplace

"Smart employers will stop sexual harassment in their shop because they realize the worst thing they can do to hurt their self-interest is to do nothing."

Ellen Bravo
Executive Director of 9-to-5
National Organization of Working Women

Like diversity management initiatives, policies and practices aimed at reducing the problem of workplace harassment focus on improving relationships among employees from differing demographic groups. Despite this similarity, companies often manage these two issues as if they were separate from each other. One reason behind this separation of the issues is history. Most modern-day diversity initiative grew out of concerns about inequality in access to jobs and upward career progress. In contrast, the issue of harassment deals simply with the daily interactions among coworkers and the consequences of those interactions for how coworkers *feel*. Under EEOC regulations, employers have a duty to maintain a working environment free of harassment based on sex, race, color, religion, national origin, age, or disability.[54]

FAST FACT

Men's claims account for 13.5% of all sexual harassment charges brought to the EEOC.

What Is Harassment? **Harassment** refers to conduct that creates a hostile, intimidating, or offensive work environment; unreasonably interferes with the individual's work; or adversely affects the individual's employment opportunities. Harassing conduct includes such things as racist epithets, raunchy jokes, and ethnic slurs. Usually, though not always, the conduct has to be repetitive or systematic.

In several cases, the offending behavior has taken the form of inappropriate e-mail or Internet messages.[55] For example, in one well-publicized case, Salomon Smith Barney discharged two managing directors for sharing X-rated material on their office computers. A month earlier, Morgan Stanley settled a lawsuit brought against it by two black employees who charged that they lost out on promotions because they had complained about the distribution of e-mail messages containing racist jokes.[56]

The perpetrators of sexual harassment often feel that women who complain about it are overreacting to men who are just having a little fun and trying to relieve some of the stress that builds up in high-pressure environments. But such explanations carry little weight. The standard for evaluating harassment is whether a "reasonable person" in the same or similar circumstances would find the conduct intimidating, hostile, or abusive. The perspective of the victim—reflecting her or his race, gender, age, place of origin, and so forth—has an important place in the evaluation. This is an expansion of the "reasonable woman" standard articulated in *Ellison v. Brady* (1991). There the court said that "unsolicited love letters and unwanted attention . . . might appear inoffensive to the average man, but might be so offensive to the average woman as to create a hostile working environment." The "average woman" in this case became the "reasonable woman."[57] In 1998, in the case of *Oncale v. Sundown Offshore Service Inc.*, the Court further clarified the rules by stating that employers could be held liable for same-sex harassment.[58]

The Consequences of Harassment. Harassment creates an offensive, hostile, and stressful work environment that prohibits effective performance; often it leads to expensive financial settlements and negative publicity. Ultimately, it interferes with the ability of the organization to attract and retain the best talent. Indeed, whole industries can be hurt when the public learns about unfavorable workplace climates.[59] After extensive media coverage of Lew Lieberbaum & Co.'s exploitive culture (which included lewd language, racists jokes, hiring strippers for office parties, and promising promotions in exchange for sexual favors), the company saw its business drop off dramatically, which is perhaps what led Lieberbaum to change the firm's name to First Asset Management.[60]

According to one attorney who specializes in defending companies against sexual harassment lawsuits, employers spend an average of $200,000 on each complaint that's investigated in-house and found not to be valid. For claims that are valid and end up in court, you can add the cost of the average court verdict for sexual harassment, which is $225,000. Given that 90 percent of the *Fortune* 500 companies have dealt with sexual harassment complaints, and 25 percent have been sued repeatedly, it's easy to see why one labor lawyer compares the total cost of harassment to the cost of asbestos cleanups—in the $1 billion range.[61] And, like asbestos, harassment's true cost can never be adequately expressed in dollar terms.

Preventing Harassment. The EEOC guidelines clearly state that employers are liable for the acts of those who work for them if they knew or should have known about the conduct and took no immediate, appropriate corrective action. Employers who fail to develop explicit, detailed antiharassment policies and grievance procedures may put themselves at particular risk.

Reporting Harassment. Companies can be held liable for incidents that aren't reported if there are no readily available means for such reporting to occur. In other words, if no procedures for dispute resolution are in place, employers can't plead innocent by reason of being uninformed. Conversely, employees may forfeit their right to pursue a legal case against the company if they fail to use the procedures that are in place to detect and eliminate offensive behavior. In

> Comment about Mitsubishi's efforts to eliminate widespread sexual harassment:
> *"The way I look at it, you know what a factory is about. They're trying to turn it into a Sunday school."*
>
> Male employee
> Mitsubishi Motor Manufacturing

FAST FACT

According to a *Wall Street Journal/NBC* poll, 31% of American women experience workplace harassment.

FAST FACT

If an outside contractor's employees sexually harass the on-site workers, those workers can sue their employer who hired the outside contractor.

other words, if a company develops a good internal reporting process, employees who experience harassment are obligated to use it (*Faraghar v. City of Boca Raton*, 1998).[62]

Employers can protect themselves against complaints by having and enforcing a "zero tolerance" policy. For a **zero tolerance policy** to have meaning, companies need clear procedures for dealing with complaints about harassment, effective training to teach employees about what is and isn't acceptable, and strong enforcement. Awareness-training programs help employees understand the pain and indignity of harassment. If they're comprehensive and used aggressively, such programs can be highly effective. According to one study, the estimated cost for training ranges from $5,000 for a small company to $200,000 for a large one. Being willing to dismiss problem employees is also part of a zero tolerance approach. When Salomon Smith Barney discharged two top executives, it signaled that the firm was serious about adopting a zero tolerance approach to dealing with harassment.

Exhibit 3.6 describes the components that should be part of a sexual harassment policy.[63] Such policies may not eliminate harassment, but they do help communicate the company's expectations and provide a fair means for enforcing appropriate behavior.

Employment-at-Will

As the industrial era was beginning, employers managed their businesses under the assumption that they had the right to terminate employees for any reason. This right is known as the **employment-at-will rule**, a common-law rule with historical roots in medieval England. In the United States, one Tennessee court explained it as follows:

ex 3.6 Preventing Harassment in the Workplace

Guidelines for Effective Harassment Policies

- Raise affirmatively the issue of harassment. Acknowledge that it may be present in the organization, and make all employees aware of the company's position on harassment.
- Provide a clear and broad statement defining what constitutes harassment.
- State that employees who experience or witness harassment are required to report it.
- Set up reporting procedures for harassed employees to use; include a list of names and positions to whom complaints can be made. The list should make it clear that employees who are harassed by supervisors have alternative reporting options.
- Specify that offenders will be subject to appropriate discipline, up to and including discharge.
- Establish procedures for investigating and corroborating a harassment charge.
- Give the person accused of harassment opportunity to respond immediately after charges are made. Due process must be provided the alleged perpetrator as well as the alleged victim.
- Build in checkpoints designed to detect harassment. For example, review all discharges to ensure that the employee was clearly performing poorly and had been given adequate opportunity to improve.
- Specify a set of steps in a framework of progressive discipline for perpetrators of harassment. These could be the same steps used by the organization in treating any violation of organizational policies.
- Assure employees that they won't be subjected to retaliation for reporting incidents of harassment.

All may dismiss their employee(s) at will, be they many or few, for good cause, for no cause, or even for cause morally wrong without being thereby guilty of legal wrong."
(Payne v. Western and A.R.R. Company, 1884)

Limits to Employment-at-Will. The courts still recognize the force of at-will employment. Nevertheless, over the years there has been a shift in the balance of power between employers and employees. The courts give employers wide latitude, but they also acknowledge that employers should not have absolute autonomy to end a person's employment. Giving employers too much self-government would be harmful to employees and essentially nullify all employee rights.

Since 1884 many laws have been enacted to limit the rights of employers. The *Civil Rights Act*, the *Age Discrimination in Employment Act*, and the *Americans with Disabilities Act* curtail employers' use of the employment-at-will doctrine by stating that certain personal characteristics cannot be used as justification for employment decisions of any kind, including termination. In addition, the *National Labor Relations Act* prohibits discharge for union-organizing activities or for asserting rights under a union contract, even if the employee in question had a record of poor performance. Other acceptable and unacceptable reasons for terminating employees are listed in Exhibit 3.7.[64]

ex 3.7 Acceptable and Unacceptable Reasons to Terminate Employees

Acceptable Reasons for Dismissal
- Incompetence in performance that does not respond to training or to accommodation
- Gross or repeated insubordination
- Civil rights violations such as engaging in harassment
- Too many unexcused absences
- Illegal behavior such as theft
- Repeated lateness
- Drug activity on the job
- Verbal abuse
- Physical violence
- Falsification of records
- Drunkenness on the job

Unacceptable Reasons for Dismissal
- Blowing the whistle about illegal conduct by employers (for example, opposing and publicizing employer policies or practices that violate laws such as the antitrust, consumer protection, or environmental protection laws)
- Cooperating in the investigation of a charge against the company
- Reporting Occupational Safety and Health Administration violations
- Filing discrimination charges with the Equal Employment Opportunity Commission or a state or municipal fair employment agency
- Filing unfair labor practice charges with the National Labor Relations Board (NLRB) or a state agency
- Filing a workers' compensation claim
- Engaging in concerted activity to protest wages, working conditions, or safety hazards
- Engaging in union activities, provided there is no violence or unlawful behavior
- Complaining or testifying about violations of equal pay or wage and hour laws
- Complaining or testifying about safety hazards or refusing an assignment because of the belief that it's dangerous

Note: These decisions apply to nonunion situations. When employees are represented by a union, the union contract replaces the termination-at-will doctrine and specifies the conditions under which an employee may be fired.

Procedural Justice. Most court decisions regarding an employer's right to terminate employees emphasize the value of procedural justice. That is, termination of employment should be the last step in a series of documented steps designed to ensure that an employee understood that performance problems existed and had opportunity to improve. Even though an employer may have the right to discharge an employee, the employer may be required to show evidence that none of the protections against wrongful termination were violated. All evidence and material relevant to each step should be documented and filed. Employers may also terminate an entire workforce in a plant or location, if proper procedures are followed. According to the *Worker Adjustment and Retraining Act of 1988 (WARN)*, employers are required to provide workers with 60 days' notice of a plant or office closing. Employers are also required to offer training programs in order to assist workers in adjusting to new employment conditions elsewhere.

Implied Contracts. In the 1970s, the courts began applying the doctrine of implied contracts to limit the conditions under which employers could terminate employees. An **implied contract** refers to employees' beliefs about an employer's agreement with employees regarding their conditions of employment. These beliefs may be grounded in verbal assurances made by managers, explanations given during performance appraisal meetings, and many other daily experiences of employees. When Wayne Pugh was fired by See's Candies in 1973, Pugh filed a lawsuit charging wrongful termination. Pugh argued that an implied contract existed between See's and its employees. Based on his 32 years of experience in the company, Pugh argued that employees expected that they would not be terminated without good cause. The court agreed that See's management practices created such an implied contract in the minds of employees, and that such contracts were just as binding on the employers as a formal policy. Therefore, when See's terminated Pugh at-will, they broke a legally valid contract.[65] Since the Pugh case, many states have passed laws that state the limits of employers' ability to discharge employees.

FAST FACT

When Amazon.com downsized in 2001, laid-off employees received 12 weeks of severance pay if they waived their right to sue; otherwise they received only 2 weeks of severance pay.

Explicit Contracts. In an effort to avoid wrongful termination lawsuits based on the doctrine of implied contracts, many employers have become more explicit in stating their policies about termination. Their policy manuals are **explicit contracts** that contain clear language stating that accepting employment with the company carries no guarantee of security and employees may be terminated at the employer's option. To further protect themselves, many employers require employees to sign agreements in which they waive their rights to sue as a condition for accepting severance packages during layoffs. At Lucent, laid-off employees get no severance pay at all unless they sign such a waiver. For 33-year veteran Kathy Fionte, the decision to sign was one she put off until the last minute. But in the end, she was willing to waive her rights in order to collect 30 weeks of severance pay.[66]

Critics of such practices argue that employees have little choice when they sign such agreements and they may be giving up too many rights. They argue that employees do not enter into such agreements voluntarily. Instead, they sign under duress when threatened with the loss of an employment opportunity or a large severance package. Because employers wield such power, employees feel they have little choice but to sign away rights that they would otherwise have under current law.

Employee Privacy

Simply stated, the right to privacy is the right to keep information about ourselves to ourselves. Earlier in our history, Henry Ford faced no resistance from the government when he sent social workers to the homes of employees to investigate their personal habits and family finances. Such invasions of privacy went hand in hand with the doctrine of employment-at-will. This changed in 1965, when the U.S. Supreme Court concluded that various guarantees stated in the Constitution (e.g., the Fourth Amendment's protection against illegal search and seizure) have the effect of creating zones of privacy. Since then, new state and federal legislation has begun to address employee privacy rights more explicitly.[67]

Most statutes simply give individuals the right to access and verify the information others already have. The *Privacy Act of 1974* was the first major statute to address issues of privacy directly. This act, which applies only to federal agencies (not private employers), gives individuals the right to verify information collected about them and used in selection and employment decisions. It allows individuals to

- determine which records pertaining to them are collected, used, and maintained;
- review and amend such records;
- prevent unspecified use of such records; and
- pursue civil suit for damages against those intentionally violating the rights specified in the act.

The *Privacy Act* is consistent with the *Freedom of Information Act of 1974*, which allows individuals to see all the material a federal agency uses in its decision-making processes.

In contrast to federal employees, private-sector employees are relatively unprotected against employers, who can access and use information, often without the knowledge or consent of employees or job applicants. Two laws establish exceptions to this generalization. The *Fair Credit Reporting Act of 1970* permits job applicants to know the nature and content of their credit files. The *Employee Exposure and Medical Records Regulation of 1980* gives employees the right to access their on-the-job medical records and records that document their exposure to toxic substances. New regulations released by the Clinton administration that were to take effect in 2003 would provide additional privacy protection to employees. Among other things, they would require that employers who have access to their employees' medical records

- have written privacy policies,
- designate privacy officers,
- provide training on privacy procedures, and
- limit the information that could be exchanged between employers and health plan providers.

Observers expect the Bush administration to lobby for changes to the proposed regulations before they take effect, however, so the degree of

FAST FACT

Henry Ford and other early industrialists were free to monitor whether employees went to church and to check up on the dating habits of their young female employees.

FAST FACT

Employees have more privacy rights in the public sector than the private sector.

"Privacy is a hot potato— it's beyond the scope of an HR person to completely solve this problem. It involves policy development, technology implementation, and contractual issues."

Bart Lazar
Attorney
Seyfarth Shaw

privacy protection employees will enjoy remains open at the time of this writing.[68]

Concerns about privacy also are addressed by state-level legislation. Several state laws—for example, in California, Connecticut, Maine, Michigan, Oregon, and Pennsylvania—give employees access to their human resource files and define what information employees are and are not entitled to see, as well as where, when, and under what circumstances employees may view their files.

Issues of privacy continue to be debated. Two topics of continuing discussion are employers' access to medical information and the monitoring of employees' behaviors.[69]

> **FAST FACT**
>
> People in the workforce with a disability: 32 million. Of these, 79 % are not working, but want to.

Access to Medical and Lifestyle Information. Health insurance costs have grown so dramatically since the mid-1980s that many employers now feel pressure to do whatever is necessary to reduce them. One way to lower costs is to employ people who make little use of health care services, because insurance for such employees is less expensive. Information about lifestyles and genetic makeup could help an employer determine who is likely to need extensive and expensive health care. Some employee conditions are clearly protected by the *Americans with Disabilities Act* (ADA), however. The ADA also states that a medical exam may be given only after a conditional job offer has been made. Then, the offer may be rescinded only if the exam reveals a condition that would prevent the applicant from performing the job, and cannot be accommodated. Under the ADA, medical records are supposed to be kept separate from other human resource records and treated as confidential.

Like insurance companies, employers can predict how much health care a person is likely to need if they have information about factors that put people into high-health-risk categories: Does she smoke? Is he overweight? Does she abuse alcohol? Other drugs? Does he exercise regularly? Like to bungee jump or drive too fast? Employers can penalize, refuse to hire, or even terminate employees because of some conditions associated with high health care costs.

Data about the link between behaviors such as these and a person's use of health care support the policy of General Mills to lower workers' insurance premiums if they lead healthy lives. They also support Turner Broadcasting System's policy of not hiring people who smoke. Insurance costs also help explain why drug testing has quickly gone from a rare to a routine practice: whereas in 1987, only about 20 percent of employers conducted drug testing, now more than 90 percent do so.[70]

> **FAST FACT**
>
> To settle a lawsuit brought by the EEOC, Burlington Northern Santa Fe Railway agreed to discontinue its practice of testing employees without their knowledge to see if they were predisposed to repetitive motion injuries in an effort to prove those injuries weren't caused by their jobs.

Access to Genetic Information. The ADA protects primarily people with disabilities. It does not directly address the question of how employers might use information about genetic makeup. Advances in our understanding of the link between genetics and disease susceptibility raise new concerns about medical privacy. Should a 25-year-old applying for a sales job be required to undergo genetic screening for diseases that may be experienced in middle age? Is it fair to penalize workers with high cholesterol, given that genes as well as diet affect cholesterol levels? Federal legislation that would prohibit employers from using genetic testing for staffing decisions has been proposed but has not yet been passed by Congress.[71]

Employers who seek medical and genetic information usually do so for good reasons. They may be concerned about how to keep health insurance costs as low as possible, which benefits the company's bottom line and may ultimately mean that healthy employees see a bigger paycheck. Or they may be concerned about protecting employees from diseases. Genetic information may be directly relevant to such concerns. But as the list of possible legitimate employer concerns grows, so do the misgivings of those who value their privacy.

Monitoring Communications. Research has shown linkages between watching violent TV and movies and engaging in violent behavior.[72] With violence in the workplace becoming a major issue in our society, should employers be allowed, perhaps even expected, to attempt to screen out employees whose viewing behaviors suggest they're likely to be violent?[73] Or suppose an employer wants to ensure that employees do not engage in illegal behaviors of various sorts, such as industrial espionage, drug dealing, or insider trading. Does this give the employer the right to listen in on employees' telephone calls? Do employers have the right to access and use all computer files on employees' office PCs? May employers monitor all employee e-mail communications?[74]

How would you feel if you discovered that your employer, as part of an effort to detect the illegal behavior of another employee, made a videotape of you while you were in the bathroom or locker room, installed a monitoring device to learn what magazines you were reading during your lunch break, and hired undercover agents to pose as employees as a way to keep tabs on workers? This is what the Campbell Soup Company did—before terminating 62 employees.[75]

Even when employees acknowledge that employers have a right to prevent certain types of employee behavior, most resent the idea of being too closely monitored. Employers are not likely to discontinue the practice voluntarily, however. Too often their monitoring efforts uncover behavior that is so inappropriate it results in terminating an employee—from spending several hours shopping on-line or trading stocks to gambling, viewing and distributing pornography, distributing company secrets, and even running a private business.[76] Thus, the challenge is finding approaches to monitoring that employees agree are legitimate and acceptable.[77]

> **FAST FACT**
>
> A 2001 survey by the American Management Association found that 80% of major U.S. companies monitor their employees through e-mail, phone connections, and/or video.

As technology continues to make monitoring both easy and unobtrusive, employers are likely to continue increasing their use of it, absent new legal restrictions. Current regulations make it clear that employers must inform employees before listening in on their personal telephone conversations, but the rapid speed of technological change means that the language of existing laws quickly becomes obsolete. As an example, consider a 1987 Supreme Court ruling that concluded employers generally have no right to go thorough a purse, brief case, or piece of luggage brought into the workplace: would the Court draw the same conclusion now that laptop computers fit inside all of these? The intermingling of work and nonwork both at home and on the employer's property introduce additional complexity and ambiguity. Precedent establishes that employers generally are permitted to gain access to voice mail messages if they have a business purpose for doing so: does that right hold for employees who work from home but do not have a separate company-paid phone line?[78]

> **FAST FACT**
>
> A 2001 survey of HR professionals found that most agree that privacy issues are involved when employers use genetic and medical information, but most do not agree that monitoring of phone and computer communications are privacy issues.

One common approach employers use to cope with the possible negative reactions that employees might have to electronic monitoring is to explicitly ban all nonbusiness and/or personal use of e-mail and the Internet and inform employees that their use of these will be monitored. But the NLRB has argued that this amounts to banning people from talking about anything other than their work while in their "work area." E-mail has become so ubiquitous that for many employees it's the primary mode of communication with their coworkers. The NLRB's logic in recent years has been that the more computer intensive the workplace, the less appropriate it is for employers to enforce highly restrictive e-mail policies.[79]

Fairness in the Global Context

FAST FACT

The U.S.–Japanese Treaty of Friendship states that foreign corporations are allowed to discriminate in favor of citizens from their own country in filling specified high-level positions within the United States.

Clearly, keeping up with both legal requirements and employees' attitudes about various employment practices requires substantial time as well as expertise. Some developing countries have few laws to protect employees' rights. And even if laws exist, citizens may seldom pursue litigation against their employers in court. On the other hand, the laws of many countries provide greater protection to employees than do U.S. laws. Laws relevant to almost every imaginable aspect of the employment relationship exist, and they take dozens of different forms in countries around the world.[80] In Chapter 1, using the example of Cirque du Soleil, we provided a glimpse of the range of legal regulations that may govern an international company's staffing activities. Similar variations occur around the world for laws and regulations governing work conditions, compensation, terminations, and so forth.

Work Conditions and Pay. The feature "Managing Globalization: Are U.S. Employers Heels in China?" describes how some manufacturers have struggled to manage their businesses across countries with huge differences in laws and local practices related to work conditions and compensation.[81] Clothing manufacturers with offshore plants in developing countries have learned that it's not just the locals who watch what employers do. People back home are watching too.

A Chinese woman explaining her decision to sue for wrongful termination:
"We've seen a lot of Hollywood movies—they feature weddings, funerals, and going to court. So now we think it's only natural to go to court a few times in your life."

Chen Wei
Former Employee
HealthTrends, a Beijing magazine

Terminations and Layoffs. Globalization creates many challenges for U.S. employers accustomed to using layoffs to adapt to changing business conditions in two ways. One set of challenges arise when conducting layoffs in other countries, another when laying off or and terminating H-1B visa holders working in the United States.

Most countries have some traditional or legally required practices that come into play in the event of a plant closing or a substantial reduction of the workforce.[82] In general, laws and regulations regarding layoffs and terminations in other countries create more extensive and costlier employer obligations than do layoffs in the United States and Canada. In many countries, termination of employment is viewed as a harsh action that's potentially harmful to employees. In fairness to employees, it should occur only for good cause, and employers are held responsible for minimizing its negative consequences.

One obligation employers may have when terminating employees in other countries is payment of cash indemnities that are in addition to individual termination payments required by law, collective bargaining agreements,

Are U.S. Employers Heels in China?

MANAGING
GLOBALIZATION

Most U.S. apparel manufacturers rely heavily on the low production costs in developing countries. Taking full advantage of low-cost offshore suppliers has its drawbacks, however. Conditions in a shoe manufacturing plant in Donguann, China, illustrate the problem. Some 50,000 employees, many of them younger than the Chinese minimum age of 16 for working in factories, were making products for Adidas, LA Gear, New Balance, Nike, Puma, and Reebok. Many weren't even being paid the Chinese minimum wage of $1.90 per day, with no benefits. They worked under conditions that were typical in the region but harsh by global standards. Mandatory overtime hours typically amounted to 80 hours per month, or double the amount allowed by Chinese law. Meal breaks lasted only 10 to 15 minutes. At other factories in the area, conditions were even worse. To manage the high turnover rates, some local employers required employees to pay a "deposit" equivalent to two weeks' pay. Employees forfeited the deposit if they left before their contracts expired. Other employers confiscated migrant workers' identification papers so that they couldn't job hop or even leave the city.

Public interest groups concerned about human rights and students on many U.S. campuses protested these conditions. At first, the companies shrugged off the protests. But eventually Nike and the others agreed to provide workers worldwide with the protection of various American health and safety standards (e.g., air quality) and to include representatives from labor and human rights groups in a team of independent auditors for monitoring compliance with the standards globally. Extending the protection of U.S. laws to non–U.S. citizens is not legally required, but Nike concluded that going beyond what is legally required is good business practice.

or individual contracts. In Germany and Italy, for example, termination for sexual harassment may not be considered good cause. Consequently, employers who terminate harassers may be required to pay termination indemnities. Furthermore, in many countries, a company that wishes to close down or curtail operations must develop a "social plan" or its equivalent, typically in concert with unions and other interested stakeholders. The plan may cover continuation of pay, benefit plan coverage, retraining allowances, relocation expenses, and supplementation of statutory unemployment compensation. Frequently, a company planning a partial or total plant closing must present its case to a government agency. In the Netherlands, for example, authorities may deny permission for a substantial workforce reduction unless management is able to demonstrate that the cutback is absolutely necessary for economic reasons and that the company has an approved social plan.

Managing H1-B Visa Holders. Each year, nearly 195,000 foreign workers are granted H-1B visas permitting them to work in the United States. This figure grew substantially in 2001, after Congress raised the annual limit of those allowed into the country on H-1B Visas by 80,000. H1-B visa are granted only for jobs that require a minimum of a bachelor's degree, and only to people whose education or experience are equivalent to that degree.[83] The growth and survival of many firms that employ highly skilled technical workers depend on the productivity of such employees. Nevertheless, when economic conditions tighten, these workers may be among the first to go. Under current regulations, employers may not stop paying H-1B visa holders who they wish to terminate until after notifying the Immigration and Naturalization Service (INS). As soon as the INS is so notified, technically the person has no legal basis for remaining in the country—they become illegal aliens and must leave the country more or less immediately. But further technicalities mean that in

FAST FACT
Immigrant visas, often called "green cards," allow someone to stay in the United States permanently. H-1B visas allow someone (e.g., tourists, students, employees) to stay on a temporary basis for a specific reason.

actual practice, the terminated person may be able to obtain permission to stay and accept another job. Under the law, employers are further obligated to provide travel funds for the employee's return home, although this rarely happens.[84] When the need for labor is strong, it seems, employers do not need to worry over some of the more confusing legal technicalities. But if unemployment rates rise, or the political climate shifts, enforcement of legal technicalities related to H-1B visas could quickly become stricter.

When operating abroad, as when operating at home, complying with legal regulations is one step toward managing fairly. To be truly effective, however, managers need to realize that perceptions of fairness reflect cultural assumptions and values—not just legal realities. Managers who are insensitive to the broader social fabric will find it difficult to anticipate employees' reactions to how they're treated. Unenlightened managers run the risk of triggering negative employee reactions.[85]

INTERNET RESOURCES   3.C

Challenges for the 21st Century

At our Web site, http://jackson.swcollege.com/, you can:

1. Visit the Privacy Rights Clearinghouse for facts and additional resources related to privacy in the workplace.

2. Read the recommendations for safe and effective genetic testing that were developed by the National Human Genome Research Institute.

3. Learn more about employment laws around the world.

SUMMARY

Treating employees fairly and legally is a strategic challenge faced by all employers. Failure to meet this challenge can result in litigation, legal penalties and fines, consumer boycotts, employee turnover, reduced numbers of new job applications, lower productivity, and service quality, among other negative consequences. When managers and HR professionals ask the question "What is fair?" they may find it difficult to answer. The law helps to provide clarity in some situations. Historically, the power to determine workplace conditions rested largely in employers' hands. Gradually, society recognized that this was unfair and a shift in the power balance was needed. Numerous laws now punish some employer actions because they're clearly unfair to employees. Some practices that employers once considered fair are now illegal. A first step toward ensuring workplace fairness, therefore, is legal compliance. By following the laws, employers should at least be able to protect themselves from losing lawsuits alleging unfair employment practices.

Workplace fairness is more than an issue of legal compliance, however. Individual feelings and perceptions as well as societal norms also come into play. Even legal employer actions may be considered unfair by employees. Employee monitoring practices have become routine. Does this mean employees agree that such monitoring is fair? Not necessarily. Managing human resources fairly requires an understanding of how employees evaluate fairness.

Managing in ways that meet the principles of distributive and procedural justice is one approach to creating fair employment conditions.

Managers also need to understand that the same policy and the same outcome can be perceived as relatively fair or unfair depending on the attitudes they display and the amount of respect they show personally for the concerns of employees. Managing diversity initiatives is one way that organizations can improve perceptions of fairness among members of a diverse workforce. In addition to meeting the legal and fairness challenges that arise in a diverse domestic organization, four issues of particular concern at the beginning of the 21st century are harassment, termination-at-will, privacy, and addressing fairness and legal concerns in the context of global business operations.

TERMS TO REMEMBER

Alternative dispute resolution (ADR)
Arbitration
Class action lawsuit
Code of ethics
Common law
Distributive justice
Diversity management initiatives
Employment-at-will rule
Equal Employment Opportunity Commission (EEOC)
Executive order
Explicit contract
Fairness

Grievance procedures
Harassment
Implied contract
Interactional justice
Legal precedents
Mediation
National Labor Relations Board (NLRB)
Occupational Safety and Health Administration (OSHA)
Procedural justice
Settlement agreement
Title VII of the *Civil Rights Act*
Zero tolerance policy

DISCUSSION QUESTIONS

1. Why does the peer review system at Coors Brewing Company work so well? To what extent does Coors ensure procedural, distributive, and interactional justice?
2. Why should companies be concerned about ensuring fair treatment and legal compliance for a diverse workforce? What strategic objectives can be achieved by meeting this challenge successfully?
3. Describe some of the key federal regulatory agencies and the employment laws and regulations that they administer and enforce.
4. Suppose you had a complaint against your employer regarding your lack of salary and career advancement in the company. Would you prefer to resolve it using mediation, arbitration, or the court system? Explain why.
5. What kinds of behaviors might constitute sexual harassment? How can grievance procedures protect the victim of the alleged harassment? Can these same procedures protect those who are unjustly accused of harassment? Explain.
6. Develop counterarguments for the following arguments in support of the employment-at-will doctrine:
   a. If the employee can quit for any reason, the employer can fire for any reason.
   b. Because of business cycles, employers must have the flexibility to expand and contract their workforce.
   c. Discharged employees are always free to find other employment.

d. Employers have economic incentives not to discharge employees unjustly; therefore, their power to terminate should not be restricted by laws.

7. Do you think employees have adequate legal protection from invasion of their privacy, or do you think employers have too much freedom to access medical records and monitor employees' behavior?

PROJECTS TO EXTEND YOUR LEARNING

1. *Managing Diversity.* The following 10 questions might be asked during an employment interview. Some of them are illegal and should never be asked. Employers who ask illegal questions may be subject to legal prosecution for employment discrimination. Place a check mark in the appropriate column to indicate whether the question is legal or illegal. Before taking this quiz, visit the home page of the Equal Employment Opportunity Commission (EEOC).

	Legal	Illegal
1. How old are you?	___	___
2. Have you ever been arrested?	___	___
3. Do any of your relatives work for this organization?	___	___
4. Do you have children, and if you do, what kind of child-care arrangements do you have?	___	___
5. Do you have any handicaps?	___	___
6. Are you married?	___	___
7. Where were you born?	___	___
8. What organizations do you belong to?	___	___
9. Do you get along well with other men [or women]?	___	___
10. What languages can you speak and/or write fluently?	___	___

Note: Answers appear on the following page.

2. *Managing Globalization.* Many U.S. companies have located some or all of their manufacturing facilities in other countries. As described in this chapter, employment conditions at those facilities may not meet the standards we have come to expect in the United States. Nike, the athletic apparel manufacturer, is an example of a company that has received a great deal of criticism for the actions of its foreign suppliers. How has Nike responded to this criticism? Compared with some of its competitors, does Nike seem to be more or less concerned about issues of fairness? Compare Nike with New Balance and Reebok.

3. *Integration and Application.* Review the end-of-text cases before answering the following questions for both Lincoln Electric and Southwest Airlines:

• What is the evidence that each company manages employees fairly and legally? Are there company practices that you would consider unfair? Why?

• Describe what management appears to expect from employees in each company. What does Lincoln agree to give employees in return? How do the expectations and responsibilities of management relate to notions of distributive, procedural, and interactional justice?

INTERNET RESOURCES   **3.D**

Projects to Extend Your Learning

At our Web site, http://jackson.swcollege.com/, you can

1. Learn more about what's legal and illegal in an interview at the home page of the EEOC.

2. Learn more about New Balance, Nike, and Reebok.

Answers to Questions under Projects to Extend Your Learning.

The following evaluations provide clarification rather than strict legal interpretation because employment laws and regulations are constantly changing.

1.   How old are you?
This question is legal but inadvisable. An applicant's date of birth or age can be asked, but telling the applicant that federal and state laws prohibit age discrimination is essential. Avoid focusing on age, unless an occupation requires extraordinary physical ability or training and a valid age-related rule is in effect.

2.   Have you ever been arrested?
This question is illegal unless an inquiry about arrests is justified by the specific nature of the organization—for instance, law enforcement or handling controlled substances. Questions about arrests generally are considered to be suspect because they may tend to disqualify some groups. Convictions should be the basis for rejection of an applicant only if their number, nature, or recent occurrence renders the applicant unsuitable. In that case the question(s) should be specific. For example: Have you ever been convicted for theft? Have you been convicted within the past year on drug-related charges?

3.   Do any of your relatives work for this organization?
This question is legal if the intent is to discover nepotism.

4.   Do you have children, and if you do, what kind of child-care arrangements do you have?
Both parts of this question are currently illegal; they should not be asked in any form because the answers would not be job related. In addition, they might imply gender discrimination.

5.   Do you have any handicaps?
This question is illegal as phrased here. An applicant doesn't have to divulge handicaps or health conditions that don't relate reasonably to fitness to perform the job.

6.   Are you married?
This question is legal, but may be discriminatory. Marriage has nothing directly to do with job performance.

7.   *Where were you born?*
This question is legal, but it might indicate discrimination on the basis of national origin.

8.   *What organizations do you belong to?*
As stated, this question is legal; it's permissible to ask about organizational membership in a general sense. It's illegal to ask about membership in a specific organization when the name of that organization would indicate the race, color, creed, gender, marital status, religion, or national origin or ancestry of its members.

9.   *Do you get along well with other men [or women]?*
This question is illegal; it seems to perpetuate sexism.

10.   *What languages can you speak and/or write fluently?*
Although this question is legal, it might be perceived as a roundabout way of determining an individual's national origin. Asking how a particular language was learned isn't permissible.

WHAT'S WRONG WITH WHAT'S RIGHT?

Stuart Campbell, now 35, moved slowly down the front steps of the courthouse and squinted as the last rays of sunlight pierced through downtown Cleveland. It had been a long day in the life of Stuart Campbell, who had spent the entire day in court recalling the details of his past employment with Nako Electronics, a major marketer of audio tapes in the United States. Nako Electronics had—and still has—a considerable stake in Stuart Campbell. The arbitrator's decision and the award of $500,000 plus interest of $82,083.50 was a bitter pill for Nako to swallow for having terminated their Midwest sales representative.

Stuart had agreed to meet his attorney, Jim Baldwin, for a couple of drinks and to unwind from the courtroom tension. His spirits began to pick up as he maneuvered through the city traffic, but he couldn't help thinking how, within a year's time, his good job had soured.

Five years ago, Stuart Campbell was riding high as the Midwest representative for Nako covering Ohio, West Virginia, and Pennsylvania. Stuart, a hard worker, contracted with Nako Electronics and then boosted the sluggish sales of Nako audio tapes from less than $300,000 to a $2 million business in about 14 months. In fact, business was going so well for Stuart that he began driving a Mercedes-Benz 450 SEL. But that's when Mike Hammond, vice president of marketing at Nako Electronics, took notice of Campbell. On one of his visits to Campbell's terri-

tory, Hammond commented to Stuart that he really liked his car. Mike remarked that he was making a trip to California soon. "I distinctly remember Mike saying he would like to have a Buick," Stuart testified. "He didn't want anything as fancy as I had, because a new Buick would be adequate and, after all, he wanted me to bear the expense!"

Mike Hammond unfortunately couldn't be in court that day to defend himself; Hammond had died unexpectedly the prior year of a heart attack. During the trial, though, Nako Electronics had to defend a number of allegations made against Mike Hammond. It seems that some of Stuart Campbell's coworkers suffered a similar fate. Not only had Stuart refused to go along with Hammond's car scheme, but he also refused to invest in a cartridge business begun by Hammond, which Stuart believed was a phony. Hammond, in fact, had approached all the sales representatives of Nako Electronics to invest in the cartridge company at $1,250 a share, a company for which Hammond and two other associates paid $1 a share for 80 percent of the stock. Stuart's attorney, Jim Baldwin, made sure that two of Stuart's former fellow sales representatives testified at the court proceedings that they were mysteriously fired after refusing Mike Hammond's demands to invest in his side company.

In the year following Stuart's successful boost in the sales of Nako audio tapes and Hammond's thwarted attempts at commercial shakedown, Nako increased Campbell's sales quota by more than 75 percent. As Campbell further testified, Nako sabotaged a substantial proportion of his sales by refusing to give his large customers promotional assistance. In the fall of that year, Nako fired Stuart without explanation. Nako argued in court that it didn't need a reason to fire Campbell and, besides, Campbell wasn't meeting his new, increased sales quota. Moreover, the company argued, Mr. Hammond could not defend himself against the charges of Campbell and others.

Stuart rehashed these details many times with his attorney, both during the private arbitration hearing and during numerous rehearsals for the trial. As he arrived at the restaurant, he hoped he could put these memories behind him. As they talked, Jim summarized the day's proceedings and expressed cautious optimism for the final outcome. "But you know, Stuart," mused Jim, "If you would have kicked in the $10 or $15K that Hammond demanded, you would have outlived him, you'd have a business worth over $4 million in sales today, and we wouldn't be having this drink!"

QUESTIONS

1. Why did the arbitrator award Stuart so much money?
2. Was the arbitrator's decision a just and fair one?
3. Did Nako have to give Stuart a reason for firing him?
4. If his firing was due to his failure to invest in Hammond's side company, could this be defended in court?
5. Do you think there was anything Stuart could have done, legally, to avoid being fired?
6. How do you think Stuart's old coworkers at Nako would react to what happened to Stuart?

Source: Stuart A. Youngblood, Texas Christian University.

ENDNOTES

1 T. Kelley, "Charting a Course to Ethical Profits," New York Times, Section 3 (February 8, 1998): 1, 12.

2 D. Anfuso, "Coors Taps Employee Judgment," Personnel Journal (February 1994): 56.

3 L. Louise, "Dillard's Is Meeting with Minorities to Talk of Diversity: Years of Silence End as a Store Chain Acts to Resolve Race-Bias Allegations," Wall Street Journal (April 8, 1998): B4.

4 "EEOC Issues Guidelines on ADA for Contingent Workers," HR News (February 2001): 5; P. Petesch, "Popping the Disability-Related Question," HR Magazine (November 2000): 161–172; D. A. Kravitz and S. Klineberg, "Reactions to Two Versions of Affirmative Action among Whites, Blacks, and Hispanics," Journal of Applied Psychology 85 (2000): 597–611; G. Dutton, "The ADA at 10," Workforce (December 2000): 41–46; E. Paltell, "FMLA: After Six Years, a Bit More Clarity," HR Magazine (September 1999): 144–150.

5 S. Naumann and N. Bennett, "A Case for Procedural Justice Climate: Development and Test of a Multilevel Model," Academy of Management Journal 43 (2000): 881–889; J. Greenberg, "Looking Fair vs. Being Fair: Managing Impressions of Organizational Justice," in B. M. Staw and L. L. Cummings (eds.), Research in Organizational Behavior, vol. 12 (Greenwich, CT: JAI Press, 1990): 111–157.

6 M. Konovsky, "Understanding Procedural Justice and Its Impact on Business Organizations," Journal of Management 26 (2000): 489–511; W. C. Kim and R. Maugorgne, "Fair Process: Managing in the Knowledge Economy," Harvard Business Review (July–August 1997): 65–75; R. Levering, A Great Place to Work (New York: Random House, 1988); see also F. Fukuyama, Trust: The Social Virtues and the Creation of Prosperity (New York: Free Press, 1995).

7 J. C. Morrow, P. C. Morrow, and E. J. Mullen, "Intraorganizational Mobility and Work-Related Attitudes," Journal of Organizational Behavior 17 (1996): 363–374.

8 M. Conlin and W. Zellner, "Is Wal-Mart Hostile to Women?" Business Week (July 16, 2001): 58–59; see also R. Garonzik, J. Brockner, and P. Siegel, "Identifying International Assignees at Risk for Premature Departure: The Interactive Effect of Outcome Favorability and Procedural Fairness," Journal of Applied Psychology 85 (2000): 13–20.

9 J. A. Colquitt, D. E. Conlon, M. J. Wesson, C. Porter, and K. Y. Ng, "Justice at the Millennium: A Meta-Analytic Review of 25 Years of Organizational Justice Research," Journal of Applied Psychology 86 (2001): 425–445; H. Schroth and P. Shah, "Procedures: Do We Really Want to Know Them? An Examination of the Effects of Procedural Justice on Self-Esteem," Journal of Applied Psychology 85 (2000): 462–471; C. Wanberg, L. Bunce, and M. Gavin, "Perceived Fairness of Layoffs among Individuals Who Have Been Laid Off: A Longitudinal Study," Personnel Psychology 52 (1999): 59–84. For good reviews of research on these topics, see R. Folger and R. Cropanzano, Organizational Justice and Human Resource Management (Thousand Oaks, CA: Sage, 1998); J. Greenberg, The Quest for Justice on the Job: Essays and Experiments (Thousand Oaks, CA: Sage, 1997) ; R. Cropanzano (ed.), Justice in the Workplace: From Theory to Practice (Mahwah, NJ: LEA, 2000); R. Cropanzano (ed.), Justice in the Workplace: Approaching Fairness in Human Resource Management (Hillsdale, NJ: Lawrence Erlbaum, 1993).

10 K. James, "The Social Context of Organizational Justice: Cultural, Intergroup, and Structural Effects on Justice Behaviors and Perceptions," in Cropanzano, Justice in the Workplace (1993).

11 D. M. Mansour-Cole and S. G. Scott, "Hearing it Through the Grapevine: The Influence of Source, Leader-Relations, and Legitimacy on Survivors' Fairness Perceptions," Personnel Psychology 51 (1998): 25–53.

12 C. Lee, K. Law, and P. Bobko, "The Importance of Justice Perceptions on Pay Effectiveness: A Two-Year Study of a Skill-Based Pay Plan," Journal of Management 25 (1999): 851–873; M. P. Miceli, "Justice and Pay System Satisfaction," R. Cropanzano, Justice in the Workplace; R. L. Heneman, D. B. Greenberger, and S. Strasser, "The Relationship between Pay-for-Performance Perceptions and Pay Satisfaction," Personnel Psychology 41 (1988): 745–761; M. P. Miceli et al., "Predictors and Outcomes of Reactions to Pay-for-Performance Plans," Journal of Applied Psychology 76 (1991): 508–521.

13 James, "Social Context of Organizational Justice"; H. C. Triandis, "Cross-Cultural Industrial and Organizational Psychology," in H. C.

Triandis, M. D. Dunnette, and L. M. Hough (eds.), *Handbook of Industrial and Organizational Psychology*, vol. 4 (Palo Alto, CA: Consulting Psychologists Press, 1994): 103–172.

14 Cropanzano, *Justice in the Workplace* (1993); B. L. Sheppard, R. J. Lewicki, and J. W. Minton, *Organizational Justice: The Search for Fairness in the Workplace* (New York: Lexington Books, 1992).

15 J. A. Colquitt, "On the Dimensionality of Organizational Justice: A Construct Validation of a Measure," *Journal of Applied Psychology* 86 (2001): 386–400.

16 R. J. Bies and J. S. Moag, "Interactional Justice: Communication Criteria for Fairness," in B. L. Sheppard (ed.), *Research on Negotiation in Organizations*, vol. 1 (Greenwich, CT: JAI, 1986): 43–55.

17 B. B. Dunford and D. J. Devine, "Employment At-Will and Employee Discharge: A Justice Perspective on Legal Action Following Termination," *Personnel Psychology* 51 (1998): 903–934; C. E. Rusbult et al., "Impact of Exchange Variables on Exit, Voice, Loyalty and Neglect: An Integrative Model of Responses to Declining Job Satisfaction," *Academy of Management Journal* 31 (1998): 599–627; J. Brockner and B. Wiesenfeld, "An Integrative Framework for Explaining Reactions to Decisions: Interactive Effects of Outcomes and Procedures," *Psychological Bulletin* 120 (1996): 189–208.

18 R. B. Freeman and J. L. Medoff, *What Do Unions Do?* (New York: Basic Books, 1984).

19 T. R. Tyler and S. L. Blader, *Cooperation in Groups: Procedural Justice, Social Identity and Behavioral Engagement* (New York: Taylor and Francis, 2000).

20 M. Elovainio, M. Kivimaki, and K. Helkama, "Organizational Justice Evaluations, Job Control and Occupational Strain," *Journal of Applied Psychology* 86 (2001): 418–424; D. B. McFarlin and P. D. Sweeney, "Distributive and Procedural Justice as Predictors of Satisfaction with Personal and Organizational Outcomes," *Academy of Management Journal* 35 (1992): 626–637; R. Kanfer, and P. C. Earley, "Voice, Control, and Procedural Justice: Instrumental and Noninstrumental Concerns in Fairness Judgments," *Journal of Personality and Social Psychology* 59 (1990): 952–959.

21 D. P. Skarlicki, R. Folger, and P. E. Tesluk, "Personality as a Moderator of the Relationship between Fairness and Retaliation," *Academy of Management Journal* 42 (1999): 100–108; D. P. Skarlicki and R. Folger, "Retaliation in the Workplace: The Roles of Distributive, Procedural and Interactive Justice," *Journal of Applied Psychology* 82 (1997): 434–443; J. Greenberg, "Employee Theft as a Reaction to Underpayment Inequity: The Hidden Cost of Pay Cuts," *Journal of Applied Psychology* 75 (1990): 561–568.

22 See Freeman and Medoff, *What Do Unions Do?*; D. G. Spencer, "Employee Voice and Employee Retention," *Academy of Management Journal* 29 (1986): 488–502; G. E. Fryxell and M. E. Gordon, "Workplace Justice and Job Satisfaction as Predictors of Satisfaction with Union and Management," *Academy of Management Journal* 32 (1989): 851–866.

23 R. H. Moorman, "Relationship between Organizational Justice and Organizational Citizenship Behaviors: Do Fairness Perceptions Influence Employee Citizenship?" *Journal of Applied Psychology* 76(6) (1991): 845–855.

24 M. P. Miceli and J. P. Near, *Blowing the Whistle: The Organizational and Legal Implications for Companies and Employees* (New York: Lexington, 1992).

25 B. M. Goldman, "Toward an Understanding of Employment Discrimination Claiming: An Integration of Organizational Justice and Social Information Processing," *Personnel Psychology* 54 (2001): 361–386; E. A. Lind, J. Greenberg, K. S. Scott, T. D. Welchans, "The Winding Road from Employee to Complainant: Situational and Psychological Determinants of Wrongful Termination Claims," *Administrative Science Quarterly* 45 (2000): 557–590.

26 J. Greenberg, "The Social Side of Fairness: Interpersonal and Informational Classes of Organizational Justice," in Cropanzano (ed.), *Justice in the Workplace* (1993).

27 This discussion is based mostly on R. E. Ringleb, and A. H. Meiners, *Legal Environment of Business* (Cincinnati, OH: South-Western, 2001; Use-

ful overviews also appear in R. D. Arvey and R. H. Faley, *Fairness in Selecting Employees*, 2d ed. (Reading, MA: Addison-Wesley, 1988); and A. Gutman, *Law and Personnel Practices* (Newbury Park, CA: Sage, 1993).

28 J. Ledvinka, "Government Regulation and Human Resources," in A. Howard (ed.), *The Changing Nature of Work* (San Francisco: Jossey-Bass, 1995).

29 For a more detailed discussion of relevant federal and state laws and regulations, see B. A. Lee and D. R. Sockell, "Regulation of the HRM Function," in J. B. Mitchell, M. A. Zaidi and D. Lewin (eds.), *The Human Resource Management Handbook* (Greenwich, CT: JAI Press, 1997): 199–232.

30 H. R. Fox and L. P. Karunaratne, "EEOC Updates on Sexual Discrimination," *The Industrial-Organizational Psychologist* (January 2001): 150–151; McAfee & Taft, *Age Discrimination in the Workplace* (Alexandria, VA: SHRM, 1999); P. E. Varca and P. Pattison, "Evidentiary Standards in Employment Discrimination: A View toward the Future," *Personnel Psychology* 46 (1993): 239.

31 D. Ambrosio, "Sexual Orientation Discrimination," http://www.workforce.com/feature/00/06/60/.

32 R. Abelson, "Anti-bias Agency Is Short of Will and Cash," *New York Times* (July 1, 2001): Section 3: 1, 12.

33 A. Bernstein, "Now, Temp Workers Are a Full-Time Headache," *Business Week* (May 31, 1999): 46.

34 L. Lawrence, "Coca-Cola Agrees to Record Discrimination Settlement," *HR News* (January 2001): 1, 4, 8.

35 "Rooting Out Racism," *Business Week Online*, http://www.businessweek.com/reprints/00-02/b3663022.htm; *Texaco Task Force Report on Equality and Fairness Issues: Third Annual Report* (2000) http://www.texaco.com; A. Bryant, "How Much Has Texaco Changed? A Mixed Report Card on Anti-Bias Efforts," *New York Times* (November 2, 1997): Section 3: 1, 16, 17; V. C. Smith, "Texaco Outlines Comprehensive Initiatives," *Human Resource Executive* (February 1997): 13; and "Texaco's Workforce Diversity Plan," as reprinted in *Workforce* (March 1997): Supplement.

36 "Arbitration Provisions in Union Agreements in 1949," *Monthly Labor Review* 70 (1950): 160–165.

37 See M. E. Gordon and G. E. Fryxell, "The Role of Interpersonal Justice in Organizational Grievance Systems," in Cropanzano, *Justice in the Workplace* (1993).

38 R. Ganzel, "Second-Class Justice?" *Training* (October 1997): 84–96; A. J. Conti, "Alternative Dispute Resolution: A Court-Backed, Mandatory Alternative to Employee Lawsuits," *Fair Employment Practices Guidelines* (October 10, 1997): 1–15; P. Feuille and J. T. Delaney, "The Individual Pursuit of Organizational Justice: Grievance Procedures in Nonunion Workplaces," *Research in Personnel and Human Resources Management* 10 (1992): 187–232.

39 D. W. Ewing, "Who Wants Employee Rights?" *Harvard Business Review* 49 (November–December 1971): 22–35.

40 K. S. Robinson, "Employees Engaging in Deceptive Behaviors at Alarming Rates," *HR News* (September 2000): 22; R. B. Peterson, "The Union and Nonunion Grievance System," in D. Lewin, O. S. Mitchell, and P. D. Sherer (eds.), *Research Frontiers in Industrial Relations and Human Resources*, (Madison, WI: Industrial Relations Research Association, 1992): 131–164.

41 J. B. Olson-Buchanan, "Voicing Discontent: What Happens to the Grievance Filer After the Grievance?" *Journal of Applied Psychology* 18 (1996): 52–63; C. Handy, "A Better Capitalism," *Across the Board* (April 1998): 16–22.

42 C. Gopinath and T. Becker, "Communication, Procedural Justice, and Employee Attitudes: Relationships Under Conditions of Divestiture," *Journal of Management* 26 (2000): 63–83; M. T. Miklave, "Why 'Jury' Is a Four Letter Word," *Workforce* (March 1998): 56–64; K. Aquino, R. F. Griffeth, D. G. Allen, and P. W. Hom, "Integrating Justice Constructs into the Turnover Process: A Test of a Referent Cognitions Model," *Academy of*

Management Journal 40 (1997): 1208–1227; M. Schminke, M. L. Ambrose, and T. W. Noel, "The Effect of Ethical Frameworks on Perceptions of Organizational Justice," *Academy of Management Journal* 40 (1997): 1190–1207; S. P. Schappe, "Bridging the Gap Between Procedural Knowledge and Positive Employee Attitudes: Procedural Justice as Keystones," *Group & Organization Management* 21(3) (September 1996): 337–364.

43 V. C. Smith, "Sign of the Times," *Human Resource Executive* (April 1997): 57–63; S. Caudron, "Blow the Whistle on Employment Disputes," *Workforce* (May 1997): 51–7; R. Furchgott, "Opposition Builds to Mandatory Arbitration at Work," *New York Times* (July 20, 1997): F11; "Employee Relations," *HR Reporter* 14 (12) (December 1997): 1–12; "NASD Votes to Nix Mandatory Arbitration," *Fair Employment Practices* (August 21, 1997): 99.

44 P. Salvatore, "Mediation and Arbitration of Employment Law Claims," *Legal Report* (March-April 2001): 7–8; R. J. Weinstein, *Mediation in the Workplace: A Guide for Training, Practice, and Administration* (Westport, CT: Quorum Books, 2000); P. Petesch and J. Javits, "Mediation's On—Grab a Spoon," *HR Magazine* (April 2000): 163–170.

45 M. A. Jacobs, "Judge Finds Merrill Lynch Can't Force Ex-Consultant to Arbitrate Case," *Wall Street Journal* (January 27, 1998): B8.

46 P. Truell, "Smith Barney Plaintiffs Agree to Incentives for Settlement," *Wall Street Journal* (November 7, 1997): D1, D7.

47 G. Flynn, "High Court Weighs in on Arbitration," *Workforce* (June 2001): 100—M. Meece, "The Very Model of Conciliation," *New York Times* (September 6, 2000): C1; D. Casey and B. Lee, "Mandatory Arbitration Clauses in Individual Employment Contracts: Enhancing Fairness and Enforceability," *Employee Relations Law Journal* 25 (Winter 1999): 57–75; G. Glynn, "Mandatory Binding Arbitration—Ensure Your Plan Is Usable," *Workforce* (June 1997): 121–127.

48 M. L. Bickner and C. Feigenbaum, "Developments in Employment Arbitration," *Dispute Resolution Journal* (January 1997): 234–251; S. Caudron, "Blow the Whistle on Employment Disputes," *Workforce* (May 1997): 51–57.

49 B. P. Sunoo, "Hot Disputes Cool Down in Online Mediation," *Workforce* (January 2001): 48–52.

50 J. Kahn, "Diversity Trumps the Downturn," *Fortune* (July 9, 2001): 114–116.

51 *SHRM Survey Report on the Impact of Diversity Initiatives on the Bottom Line*, http://www.shrm.org/surveys (May 2001).

52 S. J. Wells, "Smoothing the Way," *HR Magazine* (June 2001): 52–56; K. Townsend, "Female Partners Double Thanks to Gender Initiative," *Financial Times* (May 8, 2000): 35.

53 K. S. Robinson, "Employees Engaging in Deceptive Behaviors at Alarming Rates," *HR News* (September 2000): 22.

54 G. Maatman Jr. (ed.), *Worldwide Guide to Termination, Employment Discrimination, and Workplace Harassment Laws* (Chicago: Baker & McKenzie/CCH, 2001); R. Abelson, "If Women Complain, Does Ford Listen?" *New York Times* (January 28, 2001): Section 3, 1, 13; K. Schneider, R. Hitlan, and P. Radhakrishnan, "An Examination of the Nature and Correlates of Ethnic Harassment Experiences in Multiple Contexts," *Journal of Applied Psychology* 85 (2000): 3–12; V. Magley, C. Hulin, L. Fitzgerald, and M. DeNardo, "Outcomes of Self-Labeling Sexual Harassment," *Journal of Applied Psychology* 84 (1999): 390–402; "Liability for Sexual Harassment Still in the Air," *Fair Employment Practices Guidelines*, Number 441 (October 10, 1997); "EEOC Proposes Harassment Guidelines," *Fair Employment Practices Guidelines* (July 29, 1993): 87.

55 A. M. Townsend, M. E. Whitman, and R. J. Aalberts, "What's Left of the Communications Decency Act?" *HRM Magazine* (June 1998): 124–127.

56 P. McGeehan, "Two Analysts Leave Salomon in Smut Case," *Wall Street Journal* (March 31, 1998): C1, C25.

57 J. Steinhauer, "If the Boss Is Out of Line, What's the Legal Boundary," *New York Times* (March 27, 1997): D1, D4; "Reasonable Woman Standard Gains Ground," *Fair Employment Practices Guidelines* (June 25, 1993): 4.

58 K. M. Jarin and E. K. Pomfert, "New Rules for Same Sex Harassment," *HRM Magazine* (June 1998): 115–123; A. Gutman, "So What's New at www.eeoc.gov?" *The Industrial-Organizational Psychologist* 39(2) (October 2001): 78–84.

59 "A Question of Ethics," *Bulletin to Management* (July 9, 1992): 211.

60 B. Weiser, "Brokerage Settles Lawsuit on Racial and Sexual Bias: Firm to Pay $1.75 in Federal Case," *New York Times* (April 9, 1998): B5.

61 "$10 Million Sexual Harassment Settlement," *Fair Employment Practices* (February 19, 1998): 24; A. B. Fisher, "Sexual Harassment: What to Do," *Fortune* (August 23, 1993): 84–88.

62 P. Dorfman, A. Cobb, and R. Cox, "Investigations of Sexual Harassment Allegations: Legal Means Fair—Or Does It?" *Human Resource Management* 39 (Spring 2000): 33–49; S. R. Garland, "Finally, A Corporate Tip Sheet on Sexual Harassment," *Business Week* (July 13, 1998): 39; S. G. Gibson and H. Roberts-Fox, "Supreme Court Rulings on Sexual Harassment Disputes," *Industrial-Organizational Psychologist* 36 (2) (October 1998): 33–36.

63 A. B. Malamut and L. R. Offerman, "Coping with Sexual Harassment: Personal, Environmental and Cognitive Determinants," *Journal of Applied Psychology* 86 (2001): 1152–1166; "Preventing Sexual Harassment: Helpful Advice and Another Reason," *Fair Employment Practices* (February 19, 1998): 21; M. Raphan and M. Heerman, "Eight Steps to Harassment-Proof Your Office," *HR Focus* (August 1997): 11–12; D. E. Terpstra and D. D. Baker, "Outcomes of Federal Court Decisions on Sexual Harassment," *Academy of Management Journal* 35 (1992): 181–190; B. A. Gutek, A. G. Cohen, and A. M. Konrad, "Predicting Social-Sexual Behavior at Work: A Contact Hypothesis," *Academy of Management Journal* 33 (1990): 560–577.

64 M. Conlin, "Revenge of the 'Managers,'" *Business Week* (March 12, 2001): 60–62; L. Guernsey, "The Web: New Ticket to a Pink Slip," *New York Times* (December 16, 1999): G1, G8; M. W. Walsh, "More Than Just a Wrongful Termination," *New York Times* (January 31, 2001): G1; "Policy Guide: What Constitutes 'Good Cause' for Firing?" *Bulletin to Management* 49(3) (January 22, 1998): 24; "How Employers Can Use Employment-at-Will Disclaimers Effectively," *Fair Employment Practices Guidelines* (November 10, 1997): 6–8; "A Pledge of Job Security Can Alter At-Will Status," *Bulletin to Management* (August 14, 1997).

65 M. Heller, "A Return to At-Will Employment," *Workforce* (May 2001): 42–46.

66 J. D. Glater, "For Last Paycheck More Workers Cede Their Right to Sue," *New York Times* (February 24, 2001): 1, 4.

67 For detailed information about state and federal privacy laws, see D. Safon and Worklaw Network, *Workplace Privacy: Real Answers and Practical Solutions* (Toronto: Thomson, 2000).

68 M. Minehan, "HHS Releases Latest Medical Privacy Regulations," *HR News* (February 2001): 1, 13.

69 E. Eddy, D. Stone, and E. Stone-Romero, "The Effects of Information Management Policies on Reactions to Human Resource Information Systems: An Integration of Privacy and Procedural Justice Perspectives," *Personnel Psychology* 52 (1999): 335–358; J. Lipson, "HR Struggles with Fine Lines of Workplace Privacy," *HR News* (March 2001): 15, 19; D. Saton and Worklaw Network, *Workplace Privacy: Real Answers and Practical Solutions* (Toronto: Thompson, 2000).

70 W. L. Holstein, "From Rare to Routine," *New York Times* (November 28, 1993): 3–11.

71 T. Raphael, "Testing Issue Still Unsettled," *Workforce* (June 2001): 19.

72 W. Wood, F. Y. Wong, and J. G. Chachere, "Effects of Media Violence on Viewers' Aggression in Unconstrained Social Interaction," *Psychological Bulletin* 109 (1991): 371–83.

73 H. F. Bensimon, "Violence in the Workplace," *Training and Development Journal* (January 1994): 27–32; M. Braverman and O. M. Kurland, "Workplace Violence," *Risk Management* 40 (1993): 76–77; D. J. Peterson and D. Massengill, "The Negligent Hiring Doctrine—A Growing Dilemma for

Employers," *Employee Relations Law Journal* 15 (1989–1990): 419–432; *A Post Office Tragedy: The Shooting at Royal Oak*. Report of the Committee on Post Office and Civil Service, United States House of Representatives, 1992.

74 R. Behar, "Who's Reading Your E-Mail?" *Fortune* (February 3, 1997): 57–70; "Telephone and Electronic Monitoring: A Special Report on the Issues and the Law," *Bulletin to Management* 48(14) (April 3, 1997): 1–8; P. D. Samuels, "Who's Reading Your E-Mail? Maybe the Boss," *New York Times* (May 12, 1996): F11; "Policy Guide: Curbing the Risks of E-Mail Use," *Bulletin to Management* (April 10, 1997): 120; M. J. Cronin, "Tough Rules for Web Access," *Fortune* (August 4, 1997): 218–219; D. F. Linowes, "Maintaining Privacy in the Electronic Technology Age," *HR Reporter* 13(8) (August 1996): 6–8.

75 "Video Surveillance Withstands Privacy Challenge," *Bulletin to Management* 48(16) (April 17, 1997): 121; "Secret Video OK'd as Inspection Tool," *Bulletin to Management* (February 12, 1998): 44.

76 "Big Bro Is Eyeing Your E-Mail," *Business Week* (June 4, 2001): 30.

77 J. Lipson, "HR Struggles with Fine Lines of Workplace Privacy," *Inside SHRM* (March 2001): 1, 19; W. S. Hubbartt, *The New Battle Over Workplace Privacy* (New York: AMACOM, 1998).

78 L. Guernsey, "The Web: New Ticket to a Pink Slip," *New York Times* (December 16, 1999): G1, G8, G9.

79 J. E. Lyncheski and L. D. Heller, "Cyber Speech Cops," *HR Magazine* (January 2001): 145–150.

80 For an excellent review of how U.S. discrimination laws apply abroad, see W. A. Carmell, *International Focus: Application of U.S. Antidiscrimination Laws to Multinational Employers* (Alexandria, VA: SHRM, 1999).

81 M. Roffer and N. Sanservino Jr., "Holding Employees' Native Tongues," *HR Magazine* (September 2000): 177–184; R. Thompson, "Federal Anti-bias Protections Extended to Undocumented Workers," *HR News* (December 1999): 7, 13; D. M. Truxillo and T. Bauer, "Applicant Reactions to Test Score Banding Entry-Level and Promotional Contexts," *Journal of Applied Psychology* 84 (1999): 322–339; V. Dobnik, "Study: Chinese Workers Abused While Making Nike, Reebok Shoes," *Corpus Christi Caller-Times* (September 21, 1997): A8; A. Chan, "Boot Camp at the sShoe Factory," *Washington Post* (November 3, 1996): C1, C4; W. A. Carmell, "Will U.S. Employee Protection Laws Extend Overseas to Non-Citizens?" *International Update* (April 1999): 6.

82 P. J. Dowling, D. E. Welch, and R. S. Schuler, *International Dimensions of Human Resource Management*, 3rd ed. (Cincinnati, OH: South-Western/ITP, 1999).

83 For more details about H-1B visas, see C. Shusterman, "Focus on Global HR Management," *HR Magazine* (March 2001): 79–84.

84 K. S. Robinson, "The Care and Feeding of H-1B Visa Holders," *HR News* (July 2001): 11.

85 S. Wasti, M. Bergman, T. Glomb, and F. Drasgow, "Test of the Cross-Cultural Generalizability of a Model of Sexual Harassment," *Journal of Applied Psychology* 85 (2000): 766–778; W. A. Carmell, "U.S. Law Heads Abroad," *International HR Update* (July 1998): 5.

CHAPTER

4

CREATING ORGANIZATIONAL ALIGNMENT

"For companies to be globally competitive they need to be managed as effectively as possible. For me, this means I have to make sure that the way we manage our people is closely aligned to the rest of the business."

Steve Grossman
Senior VP, Human Resources
Hoffman-La Roche Pharmaceuticals

MANAGING THROUGH STRATEGIC PARTNERSHIPS

General Electric

General Electric (GE) Company's dramatic changes during the past three decades illustrate one company's continuous adjustment to an increasingly competitive environment. Changes in top management brought with it changes in corporate strategy, which in turn required changes in many other organization systems—including the human resource management system. Through his creative leadership, Jack Welch changed GE's business and its culture. In the process, he supported the development of new approaches to managing the GE workforce and grew the firm's reputation as a corporate training ground for top business talent.

Before Welch became CEO, Reginald H. Jones had built the firm into a strong financial performer. His approach was to create a broadly diversified firm. Through diversification, Jones put the company into about one hundred different businesses, ranging from manufacturers of appliances and light bulbs, to coal mines and producers of TV sets and computer chips.

In the process of building a profitable and diverse conglomerate, Jones created a massive organization mired in bureaucracy. Reporting requirements were legendary. One manager finally had to stop computers from generating seven daily reports on sales of hundreds of thousands of products; the paper from just one of those reports stood 12 feet high!

Jack Welch assumed the post of GE's chief executive officer in 1981. In picking Welch as his successor, Jones supported Welch's objective of making the $27-billion GE a "world class competitor," able to thrive in an increasingly global marketplace. Welch took the helm of a strong yet somewhat complacent firm. A key task would be to "instill in managers a sense of urgency when there is no emergency," and prepare the company to meet the challenges of the future.

To compete effectively, Welch believed, GE had to operate only in markets in which it could be the first or second player worldwide. GE exited all but about 14 businesses and quickly reduced its 420,000-person labor force by 25 percent.

To increase productivity in the remaining businesses, Welch restructured the firm. He shifted responsibility for decision making down the line and consolidated the layers of line management. Managerial spans of control went from an average of 6 or 7 subordinates to an average of about 15. Welch's reasoning? "Overstretched" managers perform better on important tasks because they have no time for trivia and no time to interfere with subordinates' tasks. Larger spans of control mean people down the line take on more responsibility and show their ability to perform. Welch also reduced corporate staff and forced remaining staff to ask how they could help people on the line "be more effective and competitive." By the mid-1990s, GE had reduced its workforce to 200,000 employees through layoffs, attrition, and divestiture of businesses.

In recent years, improving quality became a primary focus for the firm. Welch understood that one way to beat competitors and maximize a company's profitability was by improving quality control. To focus his managers' attention on quality control, Welch tied 40 percent of executive bonuses to implementing a quality improvement initiative called Six Sigma. By the year 2000, the company trained a cadre of 10,000 "Black Belts" in quality control techniques. After completing the training, each Black Belt went back to a plant or office to set up and organize quality improvement projects. GE invested hundreds of millions of dollars to carry out the training, run projects, and put in place the computer systems needed to measure quality and analyze problems. Jeff Immelt, Welch's hand-picked successor, was one of the first senior managers to embrace GE's Six Sigma initiative.

To improve communication and further reduce bureaucracy, GE initiated a program called Work-Out. The heads of the business units meet regularly with subordinates to identify and eliminate unnecessary activities—meetings, reports, and unproductive work. The process identifies better ways to evaluate and reward managers. Training is another top priority. Welch took his message directly to employees during training sessions at GE's in-house university in Crotonville, New York, which trains five thousand employees annually. When staffing business units, Welch sought leaders who were open and willing to change. This meant they must be able to "create a vision, articulate the vision, passionately own the vision, and . . . relentlessly drive it to completion." Identifying and preparing future leaders is so important that Welch and now Immelt regularly review files of selected employees from the time they join the firm and evaluate each person's potential for future positions. According to Immelt, the new CEO, managing human resources effectively is part of the solution for managing GE into the future.[1]

STRATEGIC IMPORTANCE OF THE ORGANIZATIONAL ENVIRONMENT

In Chapter 2, we described a variety of forces in the global environment that affect the way organizations conduct business. Besides creating the conditions within which organizations compete for customers and resources, the external environment was portrayed as having an important influence on how organizations manage human resources. For example, domestic labor shortages have led many employers to hire employees from other countries. Increased reliance on international sources of labor in turn introduces greater diversity into the workforce. As described in Chapter 3, managing a diverse workforce effectively involves designing management systems that everyone perceives as fair while also being mindful of the legal rights and responsibilities of employers and employees alike.

While the global environment clearly influences how organizations manage their workforce, it does not fully determine their approach. A more accurate portrayal is to think of the global environment as a set of constraints and opportunities. Each organization's response to these is unique, depending on the organization's internal strengths and weaknesses.

Effective organizations seek to create an internal organizational environment that fits well with the current external environment yet is also flexible enough to change as new conditions arise. Because the external environment changes constantly, changes in the internal organizational environment often are needed. The **organizational environment** includes the company leadership, corporate and business strategies, organizational structure, and organizational culture. These aspects of the organizational environment provide an immediate context for managing human resources.

As is true of the external environment, components of the organizational environment are highly interdependent. At GE, competitive forces in the external environment stimulated then-CEO Jack Welch to change the firm's corporate strategy, from competing in 100 businesses to focusing on being the best in only a few businesses. The new corporate strategy, in turn, stimulated GE to restructure the organization. Restructuring at GE involved exiting several businesses and flattening the bureaucracy. But a new structure alone would not automatically improve the firm's competitiveness—new processes were also needed. So, GE learned about and adopted total quality management (TQM) processes in all of its businesses. Implementing TQM, in turn, required new technical skills and a new philosophy about how to manage people. Thus, more change was in GE's future as its culture and approaches to managing human resources were aligned to fit the new strategic imperatives.

> **FAST FACT**
>
> It is estimated that GE's Six Sigma program added over $6 billion in earnings over the past five years.

In this chapter, we describe the major components of the organizational environment and consider how it influences a firm's approach to managing human resources. Whereas Chapters 2 and 3 emphasized the importance of aligning HR practices to fit the external context, here in Chapter 4 we emphasize the importance of aligning HR practices with other aspects of the internal organizational environment.

COMPANY LEADERSHIP: VISION, MISSION, AND VALUES

A company's leaders should provide a vision of what the company stands for, the mission it seeks to fulfill, and the values that will guide the means it uses to achieve its mission. Leadership sets the stage for managing human resources by providing a broad set of guidelines that help people make choices and direct their energies. Effective leadership ensures that people are generally working to achieve the same results, and that by achieving those results the organization will satisfy the organization's key stakeholders.

The organization's vision, mission, and values convey to employees answers to questions such as Where are we going? Why are we going there? And how will we get there? Because the answers to these questions are of major importance when managing human resources, the HR leader and staff often are involved in the creation, maintenance, and revision of the organization's vision, mission, and values statements. Of course, HR professionals also participate in developing HR practices intended to ensure that managers behave in ways that are consistent with the corporate vision, mission, and values.

Vision

"One of the things I'm very fond of saying is, our firm is a firm not of leaders and followers, it's a firm of leaders."

Rajat Gupta
Managing Director
McKinsey & Company

A **vision** is top management's view of the kind of company it is trying to create. It can be thought of as a best case scenario of where the company will be in the future.[2] Jack Welch envisioned a corporation in which every business was number one or number two in its industry. At American Express, the vision is "to become the world's most respected service brand." Southwest Airline's vision is "to be the airline of choice." The vision of The Ritz-Carlton states, "we want to be the world's No. 1 hospitality provider." The success of each company in pursuit of its vision rests in part upon employees: for Southwest to be the airline of choice, employees (i.e., associates) have to be treated well enough to satisfy their customers.

"A CEO lacking a clear vision is an individual probably short on real leadership qualities."

John F. Budd Jr.
Advisory Board Member
National Association of Corporate Directors

Mission

A **mission** statement defines a company's business and provides a clear view of what the company is trying to accomplish for its customers. A mission statement is more specific than the vision. It provides more guidance for developing plans that can be implemented to fulfill the vision. At State Farm Insurance, the mission is to

- Provide quality insurance products
- Offer friendly policyholder service
- Settle claims fairly and quickly
- Charge reasonable rates for our insurance products
- Maintain financial stability to fulfill our commitment to our policyholders
- Uphold the State Farm marketing partnership

"We're not just a hamburger company serving people; we're a people company serving hamburgers."

Jack Greenberg
CEO
McDonald's

For Merck Pharmaceuticals, the mission is to

- Provide society with superior products and services—innovations that improve the quality of life and satisfy customer needs
- Provide employees with meaningful work and advancement opportunities
- Provide investors with a superior rate of return

As these examples show, a mission statement usually is more specific than a vision statement. Often the mission statement addresses issues that more directly reflect the interests of the organization's different stakeholders, including employees.

Values

Values are the strong enduring beliefs and tenets that the company holds dear—they help to define the company and differentiate it from other companies. Harley-Davidson's values are simple:

- Tell the truth
- Keep promises
- Be fair
- Respect individuals

The values of State Farm Insurance include:

- Providing customers with the best possible service and value
- Building lasting relationships among customers, agents, employees, and communities through respect, understanding, and mutual trust
- Being financially strong
- Keeping promises by always dealing fairly and with integrity

Value statements have a direct impact on managing human resources because they state how employees are expected to behave—toward each other, toward customers, toward suppliers, and toward the community.

Together, an organization's vision, mission, and values create a framework that points people in one direction. They state the firm's aspirations for what it would like to be, though few organizations fully live up to these expectations. In comparison with the enduring aspirations reflected in a statement of vision, mission, and values, a firm's strategy describes a specific approach to conducting its business.

INTERNET RESOURCES   4.A

Leadership: Mission, Vision, and Values

At our Web site, http://jackson.swcollege.com/, you can:

1. Decide whether GE's statement of values is personally compelling to you.

2. Visit the Ethics Resource Center and the Business Ethics Institute to learn about the many creative practices organizations are using to encourage ethical employee conduct.

3. Learn about the HR practices that the European Business Network for Social Cohesion recommends for organizations seeking information about what valuing diversity involves.

4. Learn about how the Body Shop evaluates its performance against its stated values.

STRATEGY

A **strategy** is a set of integrated and coordinated commitments and actions intended to achieve a stated goal. A strategy reflects a firm's vision and mission. Like values, a strategy serves as a guide for action.[3] However, as will soon become apparent, strategies are much more closely linked to the nature of one's business than are values.

To fully describe an organization's "strategy" can be complicated—especially if the organization is large and complex. Such organizations often have many types of strategies, including a corporate strategy, competitive strategies for each business, a strategy for how to internationalize, and perhaps a strategy for developing and managing a network of cooperative relationships with other organizations. Functional units within each business unit may also develop strategies to guide their actions. One way to understand an organization's many strategies is to identify strategies for different levels in the organization.

Levels of Strategy

Three common levels for strategy formulation are the corporate, business, and functional levels. In many firms, strategies are formulated for more than one of these levels.

Corporate Diversification Strategy. A **corporate diversification strategy** describes how the corporation will select and manage a portfolio of businesses to ensure that the whole is greater than the sum of its parts.[4] The central issue addressed is usually how much diversification (low, high) and what type of diversification (related, unrelated) to pursue. In the automobile industry, most of the major corporations have low levels of diversification, and the business units are highly related to each other. In contrast, GE's corporate strategy involves a higher level of diversification. Many of its businesses are only weakly related to each other—for example, lighting, NBC, and Medical Systems. On the other hand, several other businesses share a common financial basis—for example, Employers Reinsurance, Capital Services, Structured Finance, and Global Consumer Finance. Corporate-level strategies often have implications for how the human resources function is structured. This topic is addressed in Chapter 16.

Business-Level Competitive Strategy. A **business-level competitive strategy** describes how a business unit competes against other direct rivals offering the same products and services. More specifically, a competitive strategy states how the business will attract and retain customers—what value will the business offer that its competitors will find difficult to match? Domestic firms that compete in only one business or industry may articulate only one competitive strategy. Southwest Airlines follows a competitive strategy that emphasizes creating value for customers by providing them with low-cost, reliable airline transportation. For many decades, Nordstrom, the Seattle-based department store, followed a competitive strategy of offering outstanding customer service.

A competitive strategy applies to a specific type of business or a single business unit. So, if a company has multiple business units, it should have a competitive strategy for each business. The competitive strategies may be similar across the business, or each business may have a distinctive strategy. After Nordstrom's expanded from a single store in Seattle to a national retail chain—complete with Internet shopping—it restructured into several business units (divisions). Although the divisions are somewhat autonomous, their business strategies are quite similar—all seek to offer excellent customer service to the customers they serve. In contrast, each of GE's several businesses follows a strategy specific to that organization. Several business-level competitive strategies are described in detail later in this chapter.

Functional Strategy. In organizations with strong, centralized functional departments, each department may develop a **functional strategy** to support the business strategy. For example, the heads of marketing, R&D, finance, and human resources may each develop strategies intended to support the business strategy. Suppose the intended corporate strategy is to grow by acquiring businesses that currently provide supplies to the company. In that case, the functional strategy for the human resource department would probably focus on evaluating the workforces and corporate cultures of potential acquisition candidates and developing HR practices that facilitate integration of newly acquired firms. Alternatively, if the corporate strategy calls for internally driven growth, the functional strategy for the human resources department would probably focus on recruiting, hiring, and perhaps training a sufficient number of new employees to meet the expected demand for labor.

Developing a Competitive Strategy

The processes through which firms develop their strategies vary greatly. Although most large companies eventually adopt a fairly systematic approach to strategy formulation, the strategy of smaller firms may reflect the founder's intuitions and passions as much as his or her formal analysis. Here we consider currently popular prescriptions about what firms should consider when developing their business-level competitive strategies, while recognizing that firms may be somewhat unsystematic or may use a systematic approach that considers different issues than the ones described. We focus on competitive strategies because they often have the most direct consequences for managing human resources.

Within an industry, firms compete for customers by trying to differentiate themselves from other firms. Thus, strategy development benefits from competitive analysis, which helps to identify threats and opportunities within the industry. A competitive strategy should also take into account the firm's own strengths and weaknesses. Effective strategies are built upon the firm's strengths. The analysis of this combination of factors—strengths, weaknesses, opportunities, and threats—is often referred to as a **SWOT analysis.**

Identifying Opportunities and Threats. **Competitive analysis** is a systematic approach for identifying opportunities and threats within an industry. The best-known framework for competitive analysis is the **five-forces model**, developed by Michael Porter.[5] This model identifies the following major sources of competitive pressure:

- threat of new firms entering into competition (e.g., the Internet made it possible for firms to begin selling worldwide without a large sales force or many physical assets)
- intensity of the rivalry among existing firms that compete directly for customers, (e.g., the Internet increased rivalry in many industries because information about prices and product features became easier for customers to obtain and compare)
- suppliers' ability to exercise bargaining power and leverage (e.g., in business-to-business markets, the Internet gave suppliers easier access to more customers, making them less dependent on any one customer)
- buyers' ability to exercise bargaining power and leverage (e.g., in business-to-business markets, buyers also have access to more possible suppliers who can meet their needs)
- other firms that may take away customers by offering substitute products or services (e.g., Internet services are making it possible to rent computer services instead of buying them)[6]

"In theory, anyone can hang out a shingle and open a child care center. But our relationships with employers create formidable entry barriers for our competitors."

Roger Brown
Co-Founder
Bright Horizons

Consideration of current competitors and their likely moves illustrates the types of questions an organization must answer to conduct a complete analysis. Specific questions to be answered about competitors include these:

- What drives the competitor? That is, what are its objectives? Answering this question involves understanding who the competitor defines as its key customers and the basis on which the competitor tries to attract and retain customers.
- What is the competitor's current strategy and what strategy *could* it adopt?
- What assumptions does the competitor make about the industry? Answering this question involves discerning whether the competitor seems to be operating in a status quo mode or is preparing for major changes, and if so, the nature of change it anticipates.
- What are the competitor's capabilities? Included here is information about marketing strategies, distribution methods, size of the sales force, terms and conditions of sales, size and location of operations, research and development activity, and just about every other aspect of doing business.

"We strive to create an environment where employees can achieve company goals and personal goals simultaneously."

Paul Beddia
Former Vice President, Human Resources
Lincoln Electric

Competing for Labor. Just as firms compete for customers in the product market, they engage in similar competition in the labor market. To attract and retain the best talent, firms may try to differentiate themselves from others on the basis of compensation or benefits, flexibility of work schedules, opportunities for skill development and use, and so on. If one firm begins to offer signing bonuses of several thousand dollars to new MBAs, the competitors will be under considerable pressure to match that competitive move. If one firm gives middle managers more degrees of autonomy or more influence in key strategic decisions, other firms may find their best talent is soon hired away unless they match these working conditions.

Although similar dynamics among competitors hold in the labor market, however, the systematic use of competitive analysis for understanding competition for labor isn't widely used. A related activity that *is* quite common is benchmarking. **Benchmarking** refers to a process that involves three key steps. The first step is identifying the "industry leaders"—for example, firms that have reputations for excellence in the area of managing human resources. The second step is investigating and analyzing the "best practices" that set these leading firms apart from the competition. The third, and most important, step is transferring what is learned about the best practices used by the leaders to one's own organization. Can some of the best practices observed during benchmarking be copied? Or, better yet, what additional improvements can be made before the best practices found in other firms are developed for application at home?

Benchmarking differs from competitor analysis in some important ways. Competitor analysis focuses specifically on understanding one's direct competitors. As a consequence, the process tends to be covert and involves little cooperation between the competing firms. In contrast, benchmarking usually is a collaborative effort among several firms that, ostensibly, aren't in direct competition. In addition, benchmarking studies usually focus on one or two specific aspects of human resource management, such as recruiting practices *or* use of flexible schedules *or* use of team-based job designs. Thus, benchmarking does not yield a complete, integrated picture of a particular competitor.

Assessing Organizational Strengths and Weaknesses. Firms generate profits by capitalizing on their own strengths and, whenever possible, exploiting the weaknesses of competitors. One approach to evaluating a firm's strengths and weaknesses is to consider the firm's available resources, capabilities, and core competencies.

Resources include tangible assets (e.g., equipment, real estate holdings, access to financial capital) as well as intangible assets (e.g., reputation for excellence, recognized brand name, patents, trademarks). Resources that are unique to the firm can serve as a basis for creating a sustained competitive advantage. For UPS, an important resource is its fleet of 150,000 brown trucks, which reach virtually every address in the United States. Using this resource, UPS is able to match FedEx's delivery speed for intermediate distances (under 500 miles) at a much lower cost. UPS built its fleet over decades, and the cost of matching it would be prohibitive for FedEx. Thus, for UPS, this is a key resource to utilize as part of its strategy.[7]

In knowledge-intensive industries, people with unique knowledge or those with the ability to create new knowledge can be a source of advantage. Scientists and engineers, for example, are key resources in many high-tech industries. In sports, the unique talents of star players are quite different from those of engineers and scientists, but those talents are no less valuable as sources of competitive advantage. At BMW, designers are key to creating a product with unique qualities that will command high prices. If an organization wants to assess whether a particular group of its employees are a key resource, two key questions it should ask are: Is the talent associated with another strategic resource (e.g., customers, brands, patents)? Is the talent highly sought after by key competitors? When the answer to these questions is yes, the people in question represent resources that should be managed with care.[8]

When resources are managed well and integrated, they create a **capability** that enables the organization to accomplish a task or achieve an outcome. Capabilities are often associated with specific functional areas. For example, General Electric's effective and extensive management development programs represent its exceptional capability in human resources. Sony's miniaturization of electronic components represents its capability in R&D and manufacturing.[9] Examples of several capabilities for textile firms and hospitals are shown in Exhibit 4.1.[10]

As noted in Chapter 2, organizations such as NCR have learned to combine their human and technical resources to create a capability for performing work in a virtual organization. For firms like NCR and Verifone, virtual teamwork capabilities are essential to the ability to operate as a global organization.[11] The feature "Managing Teams: Integrating People and Technology to Create a Capable Workforce" explains how Verifone's capability for virtual working helps it satisfy customers. Here's an example of how a Verifone global team works: When an employee was trying to sell the company's services in Greece, the prospective customer expressed some doubt about the ability of the company to deliver the service as described. He needed some convincing. Immediately after leaving his meeting with the prospective customer, the employee found the nearest telephone, hooked up his laptop, and sent an e-mail SOS to other employees around the world. The purpose of his message was to recruit a team to help him make the sale. He wanted testimonials from other customers who could vouch for Verifone's

> *"I've tried to figure out why Mickey appealed to the whole world. Everybody's tried to figure it out. So far as I know, nobody has."*
>
> Walt Disney
> Creator of Mickey Mouse
> Founder of Walt Disney Co.

FAST FACT

McDonald's founder Ray Kroc specified that its hamburgers weigh exactly 1.6 ounces, measure exactly 3.875 inches, and be served with exactly .25 ounces of onions, and his restaurants were capable of producing them.

ex 4.1 Examples of Organizational Capabilities for Hospitals and Textile Firms

CAPABILITIES THAT MAY SERVE AS SOURCES OF COMPETITIVE ADVANTAGE IN TWO INDUSTRIES

Textiles

- Expertise in international transport logistics
- Technological capacity that facilitates easy production changes, e.g., to accommodate new fabrics and designs
- Ability to link operational goals to compensation plans
- Process-reengineering know-how to improve efficiency and reduce costs
- Marketing knowledge and skills for global competition
- Cost control

Hospitals

- Capacity for change—to start new programs, close programs, seize opportunities
- Expertise across the full continuum of care, including pre-hospital, in-hospital, and post-hospital
- Information management capacity, such as on-line medical records and imaging services
- Attracting and retaining skilled top-level executives
- Ability to quickly and effectively train physicians and other staff on new medical knowledge and technology
- Risk management

Note: These capabilities become core competencies when an organization uses them as a basis for achieving a sustainable competitive advantage.

---

performance, and he was open to any other advice about how to make the sale. It was near the end of the day in Greece, so he was looking for people who could work on this while he slept. A San Francisco employee took up the challenge and organized a conference call with marketing employees in Atlanta and Hong Kong. These three people agreed on a plan for what type of data they should collect from customers. By the end of their day, the two Americans had drafted a sales presentation. They forwarded it to Hong Kong so the Asian data could be added. When the rep in Greece was ready to get started the next day, he retrieved the presentation from his e-mail account and used his laptop to present it to the prospective client, who was so impressed by what had been accomplished while he was asleep that he placed an order with Verifone.

Core competencies are the resources and capabilities that produce a firm's competitive advantage and result in its success.[12] Like a capability, a core competency reflects a firm's knowledge about how to accomplish something. However, whereas most organizations have many capabilities, only a few of these represent core competencies. In developing their strategies, firms need to identify their core competencies. Over time, they must continue to invest in developing their competencies in order to stay ahead of rivals.[13]

Successful firms understand what their own core competencies are, which competencies are essential for success in their industry given a particular strategy, and also how to leverage their existing competencies to move into new areas of business. They also understand that some of their core competencies will become obsolete with time, and new ones will be needed to replace them.[14] According to PepsiCo's president, Stephen Reinemund, one of his firm's core competencies is marketing. But its marketing competency is stronger for suburban markets than for urban markets. Reinemund recognizes that opportunities for future growth lie in urban markets, so expanding its marketing competency to address these new markets is imperative for future success.[15]

Capacity management is a core competency for FedEx. FedEx competes by offering fast, reliable delivery service. To make good on their

"In my quest to convince nondesigners that a BMW, like a fine wine, cannot be hurried, I often appeal to a deeply held, almost nonverbal sense about BMW-ness—a certain pride of product shared by everyone that expresses itself in the classic quality of our cars, from the purring engines to the buttery seats."

Chris Bangle
Director of Design
BMW

Integrating People and Technology to Create a Capable Workforce

MANAGING
TEAMS

At Verifone, employees create virtual teams on an as-needed basis. Some virtual teams last for only a day or two—just long enough to solve a pressing problem. Other teams are more permanent. Any employee can establish a virtual team as long as he or she follows a few simple rules. These rules help ensure that people use the available technology in the most appropriate ways and thus leverage the resources as much as possible.

At NCR, the first rule for creating a virtual work team is that there must be a clear and specific purpose for the team. The team's purpose guides the design of the team and its work: Who should be on it? What information will they need? How will they evaluate their effectiveness? Second, the teams must be kept small—usually only three to five people. The small size keeps communication and coordination problems in check. Third, the team should be designed to leverage differences in time zones. The counterintuitive lesson is that the ideal design is one where each team member is in a different time zone. These teams aren't spending a lot of time chatting together. Each member has certain tasks to do, and often there is some sequencing of tasks that makes the most sense. With people in different time zones, someone on the team is always making progress, regardless of what time it is. Another rule is that the duration of the team must be stated. This makes individual planning much easier and helps ensure that people don't join a team that they can't stay with until the task is accomplished. The final rule is that employees must match the technology they use to the type of task they're working on. They understand that e-mail is a good way to send information to each other, but if much discussion is needed, then telecommunication technology should be used, or, if it's not available, a "live" team might be the best solution.

promise of reliable delivery service, employees absolutely must be where they are needed when they are needed. Excellent human resource management makes this possible and is central to the company's success in pursuing this strategy. By using more part-time employees and paying bonuses for making extra deliveries, FedEx maintains a flexible and productive workforce. The capacity of the workforce easily expands when demand is high and contracts when demand is low. Fixed costs are kept low because the size of the permanent workforce is kept somewhat low, which also eliminates cycles of rapid hiring followed by unwelcome layoffs. Part-time staff are kept motivated by aggressive incentives.

During the past decade, many companies identified organizational learning as an important core competency. **Learning organizations** continually find new ways to satisfy customers and other stakeholders. A learning organization skillfully integrates the resources of information, technology, and people to produce and then effectively use new knowledge. As Exhibit 4.2 reveals,[16] developing learning as a core competency has many implications for HR practices. Together with other elements of the organization environment (leadership, culture, structure), HR policies and practices support the behaviors needed to facilitate learning. These behaviors include experimentation, learning from others, documenting what is learned, and several others listed in Exhibit 4.2.

Types of Competitive Strategies

Firms describe their competitive strategies using a variety of terms, but basically competitive strategies reflect two decisions: Who are the customers? Which customer needs will the firm seek to satisfy? Michael Porter developed a well-known taxonomy for describing competitive strategies by considering these two questions:

ex 4.2 Aligning Human Resource Management with the Organizational Environment to Support Organizational Learning

Organizational Environment for Learning Organizations → **Managing Human Resources to Support Continuous Learning** → **Needed Behaviors**

LEADERSHIP
Lead by personal example based on an understanding of how knowledge and learning link to strategic objectives and stakeholders' concerns

STRATEGY
Identifies organizational learning as a core competency that contributes to a sustainable competitive advantage

CULTURE
Values include continuous innovation and change; sharing best practices; and focus on learning as a common objective

DESIGN AND STRUCTURE
Fluid, flexible, flat, team-based, networked with alliance partners

STAFFING
Recruit, hire, and promote based on actual knowledge and the capacity for future learning

TRAINING AND DEVELOPMENT
Knowledge on any topic is accessible to everyone, anywhere, all the time

PERFORMANCE APPRAISALS
Assess the individual's growth and development and contributions to others' growth and development

REWARDS
Monetary rewards and recognition encourage long-term growth and development of self and others

LEARNING ORIENTATION AND CAPACITY

- Think critically
- Create new knowledge
- Work across boundaries
- Learn through experience
- Learn from others
- Revise and update old knowledge
- Create and adjust to change
- Share knowledge
- Apply knowledge
- Document what is known

- *Who is the customer?* Firms can target a broad population of customers, or narrow its scope to only certain groups of customers.
- *Which customer needs does the firm seek to satisfy?* Fundamentally, a firm can choose to satisfy the desire to buy at the lowest possible price, or it can charge a premium by offering something that is unique, or at least very different.

Exhibit 4.3 illustrates how different strategies can be categorized into Porter's four types based on a firm's answers to these two questions.[17]

A firm can't compete by focusing completely on one type of customer need and ignoring the others. Investors would not use Vanguard's low-cost services if they didn't receive an acceptable quality of service, and fashion bugs won't pay unreasonable prices for Lauren's newest styles. There are few products or services that customers will buy based solely on price, and there are few products or services for which quality or image is so important that customers will pay any price to have it.[18]

ex 4.3 Four Types of Competitive Strategy

WHICH CUSTOMER NEEDS DOES THE FIRM SEEK TO SATISFY?

	Desire for Low Cost	Desire for Something Unique
WHO IS THE CUSTOMER? — **Broad Target Market**	**Cost Leadership:** Seeks to serve a broad market by satisfying the desire for low cost products and services. *Example:* Wal-Mart offers low-cost goods to all types of people in several countries.	**Differentiation Strategy:** Seeks to serve a broad market by satisfying the desire for products and services that are unique in some way (e.g., quality, function, style, image). *Example:* Ralph Lauren offers stylish, high-quality clothing for customers of all ages around the world.
Narrow Target Market	**Focused Cost Leadership:** Seeks to serve a narrow market by satisfying the desire for low-cost products and services. *Example:* Dollar General seeks to serve lower-income shoppers who are shopping simply to obtain basic products and who prefer to do so in a smaller store that's located in their neighborhood.	**Focused Differentiation:** Seeks to serve a narrow market by satisfying the desire for products and services that are unique in some way (e.g., quality, function, style, image). *Example:* McKinsey & Co. offers its unique approach to consulting primarily to large business firms.

Similarly, effective organizations are likely to change their competitive strategies over time, in response to a changing external environment. When the Hunter Fan Company started up in 1886, it had an innovative new product—large ceiling fans that could be used to cool factories. Continuous improvement in the design of the product allowed the company to maintain a large market share. But changes in technology—the invention of air conditioning—cut sharply into its business and the firm went into decline. When energy prices rose rapidly in the 1970s, however, Hunter Fan was able to use its capabilities to exploit a new market for high-quality ceiling fans for home use. Thus, while strategic change may be stimulated by the environment, the direction of change should be strongly influenced by a firm's existing capabilities and competencies.[19]

Behavioral Imperatives for Alternative Strategies

Associated with different business strategies are several unique challenges for managing human resources. For competitive strategies to be successfully implemented, employees have to behave in certain ways and they must be willing to do so within some labor cost constraints. We use the term *behavior imperatives* to refer to the behaviors needed from employees in order to implement a strategy. In this section, we describe the behavioral imperatives associated with cost leadership strategies and those associated with two different ways to pursue differentiation: innovating and offering excellent quality.

Differentiation through Innovation. When a desirable new product or service is created, its uniqueness and limited availability mean that a company can charge a premium price and a sufficiently

FAST FACT

Intel, Texas Instruments, and 3M want a substantial portion of revenue to be generated by products developed within the past five years.

large number of customers will be willing to pay it. However, this opportunity arises only if the firm also has the capabilities needed to develop the new invention into a marketable product and then bring that product into the marketplace. Celtrix, a California biotech firm, holds patents on a cell-regulating protein that may prove useful in helping cells heal. However, Genetech was able to more quickly develop the process for producing this protein. This situation effectively forced Celtrix to enter into a joint venture with Genetech in order to realize at least a portion of the future profits from its invention. As this example illustrates, the behavioral imperatives for innovation include behaviors that lead to the birth of new ideas as well as behaviors that lead to developing new ideas into usable products or services that can be delivered to the market in a timely manner. Experimentation, risk taking, accepting failure as normal, project management, and teamwork are some of the behavioral imperatives associated with a differentiation strategy based in offering new and unique products and services.

Continuing to innovate over long periods of time turns out to be rather difficult. The success of early innovations usually results in the organization growing in size. Eventually, procedures and rules are imposed to minimize the chaos that accompanies rapid growth. Ways of doing things that succeeded in the past become institutionalized as "the best way" of doing things, creating rigidities that block creativity.[20] Solutions to such problems can be found in human resource management practices that support creativity and change.

Because the management practices (including HR) that support creativity often conflict with those of older established firms, a firm may not want to adopt them on a company-wide basis. So, some innovative organizations intentionally create separate "skunkwork" units. A skunkwork unit is a new venture team that has considerable leeway in its activities. Often it even moves to another location that's out of sight and out of mind, where it can more easily operate outside the normal model. Within these islands of entrepreneurial activity, formal rules and procedures are ignored in favor of experimentation and innovation. Top management may tolerate violations of reporting policies and review procedures, as long as the team stays focused on helping the company bring new products and services to market ahead of competitors.[21]

Creative employees working in skunkwork units usually are selected because of their specialized expertise, and they tend to be highly motivated by their projects. Nevertheless, skunkworks create special HR challenges. One challenge is ensuring that key talent stay with the employer rather than venturing off to start up their own firm. Legal contracts give the employer some protection. Incentive plans that allow the creators of new products to reap financial rewards after a successful product launch may be more effective in the long run, however.

Differentiation through Quality. Another basic way to differentiate one's products and services from those of others is to offer outstanding quality. Organizations are continually confronted with the need to deliver quality goods and services. In the international arena, the standards of quality keep going up: what was acceptable quality yesterday is unacceptable today. Thus, organizations such as General Electric, Archway Cookies, Motorola, and Honeywell pursue quality improvement with a vengeance.

Delivering total quality depends on all parts of the organization working together. Increasingly, these efforts are guided by feedback from customers, because quality is in the eyes (and ears and hands and taste buds!) of customers.[22]

The specific aspects of products and service that go into customers' judgments of quality are listed in Exhibit 4.4.[23] From this exhibit you can see the behavioral imperatives associated with competing on the basis of quality excellence. The beneficial outcomes of pursuing total quality strategies include increased productivity, profits, jobs, customer satisfaction, and employee skill levels. The desirability of these and related outcomes provide strong incentives for undergoing the necessary organizational design and cultural changes and dealing with the implications for managing human resources.[24]

Cost Leadership. The most common approach to pursuing a cost leadership strategy is to generate a high volume of sales to make up for the low margin associated with each sale. Because volume is so important, companies pursuing this strategy usually seek the broadest possible customer base. Appealing to the typical or average customer is the objective.

The central business objective for firms pursuing a cost leadership strategy is reducing their costs. Investments in more efficient production systems, tight cost monitoring and controls, low investment in R&D, and a minimal sales force are characteristic of this strategy. Highly efficient systems that link the firm to its suppliers and distributors and "trouble-free" products and services that keep recalls and customer returns low also are important for success. In the retail business, links to suppliers who will sell at rock-bottom prices also are especially important.[25]

Human resource management practices also must support the goal of maximizing efficiency. This usually implies keeping labor costs low. One

> *"Sure it's cheaper here.*
> *They don't call it a dollar*
> *store for nothing."*
>
> John Brown
> Customer
> Dollar General Store No. 2392

FAST FACT

Wal-Mart's founder, Sam Walton, flew first class only once in his life—on a trip to Africa.

---

ex 4.4 What Does Quality Mean to Customers?

Products

- *Performance:* A product's primary tangible operating characteristic. Examples are a car's ability to accelerate and a television set's picture clarity.
- *Features:* Supplements to a product's basic functioning characteristics, such as one-touch power windows on a car.
- *Reliability:* A probability of not malfunctioning in a specified time period.
- *Conformance:* The degree to which a product's design and operating characteristics meet established standards.
- *Durability:* A measure of product life.
- *Serviceability:* The speed and ease of repairing a product.
- *Aesthetics:* How a product looks, feels, tastes, and smells.
- *Perceived Quality:* Quality as defined and judged by the individual customer.

Services

- *The Tangibles:* The appearance of the physical setting for the service, including the location, people, communication materials, and equipment.
- *Reliability:* The ability to perform the promised service dependably and accurately.
- *Responsiveness:* The extent to which an employee helps customers and provides prompt service.
- *Assurance:* An employee's knowledge, courtesy, and ability to convey trust and confidence.
- *Empathy:* Caring, individualized attention.
- *Insight:* The ability to anticipate the customer's needs.
- *Problem Solving:* The ability to diagnose problems with the customer and develop solutions the customer finds appropriate.

common cost-cutting tactic that shapes the behaviors needed from employees is reengineering, which is described in detail later in this chapter. Other behavioral imperatives often associated with cost leadership strategies include accepting part-time work and shift work, performing repetitive behaviors efficiently and accepting the boredom that this often engenders, working under Spartan conditions, and accepting minimal fringe benefits.

INTERNET RESOURCES   4.B

Strategy

At our Web site, http://jackson.swcollege.com/, you can:

1. Find out what types of benchmarking resources are available by visiting the International Benchmarking Clearinghouse service provided by the American Productivity and Quality Center.

2. Use VeriFone's product descriptions. Do they compete on the basis of cost or differentiation? Do they appeal to a broad market or have they targeted one or more narrow markets?

3. Learn what current research is discovering about strategic management by perusing research issues of the *Strategic Management Journal*.

4. Learn about Business Insight, which provides software designed to help managers conduct a competitive analysis, and MRC, a consulting company that claims competitive analysis as one of its core competencies. Evaluate the offerings of Business Insight and MRC. Do you think they would be helpful for a nonprofit organization, such as the Modern Museum of Art in New York City?

ORGANIZATIONAL STRUCTURE

To support and implement a strategy effectively, other elements of the organization environment must be aligned with the strategy.[26] In this section, we describe the choices about organization structure that can be made when deciding how to organize people and their work in order to achieve a strategy. **Organizational structure** describes the allocation of tasks and responsibilities among individuals and departments. A structure designates the nature and means of formal reporting relationships as well as the groupings of individuals within the organization.[27]

The structural forms generally recognized for domestic firms include departmentalization (such as the human resource department, or the marketing department), divisionalization based on products or geographic location, and matrix organization. As an organization grows and ages, it may progress through all of these forms.[28] The vast majority of medium and large companies in the United States are structured around departments, divisions, or a matrix of these. In addition, many organizations are linking up with other firms to create various network forms and structures that cross organizational borders.

Each structural form poses different challenges for managing human resources.[29] Exhibit 4.5 summarizes some of the benefits and potential pitfalls of the structural forms described below.

Departmental Structure

In organizations having a **departmental structure**, work is divided into tasks that are assigned to specialized groups within the organization (e.g., sales, manufacturing, accounting). Decision making is centralized at the top of the

ex 4.5 Types of Organizational Structures and Their Potential Benefits and Pitfalls

POTENTIAL BENEFITS	POTENTIAL PITFALLS
Departmental Structure **(based on functions)**	
• Efficient for small, single-product firms • Encourages development of specialized expertise • Easy for internal and external constituents to access specialized knowledge • Provides clear paths for employee development and advancement	• Coordination becomes difficult as firm grows • Turf battles may erupt as departments compete for resources • Focuses employees on concerns of their department instead of organization-wide goals; managers develop narrow focus • Employees may not understand how their work fits within larger context
Divisional Structure **(based on product lines, customer markets, or geographical locations)**	
• Facilitates fast changes within each division • Employees develop ability to think and work across functional areas • Provides better external visibility to key constituents (e.g., for a product line, of a customer group) • Support functions (e.g., HR, marketing) may develop specialized expertise and thus provide better service to line managers	• May be more difficult to make organization-wide changes • Experts within functional areas may not coordinate and learn from each other due to turf battles between divisions • Desire to satisfy external constituents may lead employees to put key constituents' concerns above organization-wide concerns • Duplication of support functions across divisions is costly
Matrix Structure **(dual reporting to functional and divisional heads)**	
• Reduces duplication of costs for support functions • Facilitates sharing of employees across organizational units • Facilitates knowledge sharing and transfer so organizational learning can occur	• Requires managers with excellent communication and collaboration skills • Employees may have less job security (but, potentially, more organizational security) • Lines of authority may be ambiguous for employees, creating ambiguity about priorities
Horizontal Structure **(based on processes)**	
• Cost-efficient due to flat hierarchical structure • Employees gain detailed understanding of how activities are interrelated • Use of teams facilitates individual learning and rapid knowledge transfer, supporting quick and continuous improvement in products/services	• Fewer opportunities for upward career progress • Requires broad skill development, which may be associated with higher compensation costs • Managers may underestimate the need to change management systems in order to structure work around teams
Network Structure **(many outsourced activities)**	
• Leverages information technologies to coordinate work carried out in several locations • Provides flexibility by reducing fixed costs and increasing the number of potential sources of supplies, services, etc. • Managing the network form is a rare capability, so it can be a source of competitive advantage	• Requires high levels of employee expertise in technology use and investments in continuously updating this expertise • Increases employment volatility; employees may feel reduced commitment and loyalty • The firm may lose its ability to manage and control outsourced activities, and it's more difficult to tailor outsourced activities to specific needs of the firm

ex 4.5 Types of Organizational Structures and Their Potential Benefits and Pitfalls (continued)

POTENTIAL BENEFITS	POTENTIAL PITFALLS
CROSS-BORDER STRUCTURES (for firms with operations in more than one country)	
International	
Company is able to grow outside its own domestic borders without having to change its current structure and ways of operating	Company may not reap advantages of economies of scale or of learning about how the rest of the company could operate internationally
Global Regions	
Company is able to grow outside its domestic borders with a limited number of products or services that can be adapted to the local culture and tastes	Company may not reap the advantage of economies of scale nor manage a broad array of products or services
Global Product	
Company can expand outside its domestic borders with a wide variety of products or services and also reap economies of scale	Company is not able to easily incorporate or adapt to the local cultures and tastes
Transnational	
Company can expand outside its domestic borders with a variety of products or services and still incorporate and adapt to local cultures and tastes	A major challenge to develop managers who can operate in this environment and coordinate all the parts of the company simultaneously

organization, and a clear vertical chain of authority is used to communicate decisions downward.[30] Sales and operations departments often wield the most power. Careers in these types of companies generally focus narrowly on developing single-department, "silo-like" expertise. Businesses with a single product or service often have a departmental structure.

Ben & Jerry's Homemade, the ice cream company, was in business for 10 years before it divided the work and assigned different tasks to two different departments. By that time, the company had grown so large that professional managers had to be brought in to oversee some of the specialized tasks. A director of retail operations oversaw the franchisees; a controller supervised the accounting and finance departments, and a director of manufacturing oversaw plant operation. In recalling the change from one big family to a departmentalized organization, the former CEO remarked, "The up side was that more work was getting done. The down side was that as people became more task-oriented, they began to lose their connection to the whole of the organization."[31]

Departmentalization can easily engender feelings of commitment and loyalty to department groups (accounting, marketing, R&D), and it supports specialized skill development. On the negative side, it can turn organizational decision making into a competitive sport in which departments battle over turf and resources.

Divisional Structure

Multiproduct and multiservice firms often adopt a **divisional structure**, with each division serving a different customer need (product-based divisions) or a different customer base (geographic divisions). Divisionalized firms tend to be more externally focused than are firms structured around departments, and they emphasize bottom-line results over smooth internal functioning. They tend to serve broad markets and in general must respond to an environment characterized by considerable complexity.[32] In the 1970s, GE reorganized into 43 divisions, with each division being essentially a complete business that could clearly identify its potential customers and competitors, could design strategies to address them, and could be held accountable for achieving business objectives. These divisions were called Strategic Business Units (SBUs). Since the 1980s, this structure has been adopted by several other large corporations and the term SBU is now widely used to refer to highly autonomous divisions.[33] Different SBUs may adopt different business strategies and coordination between divisions may be modest, at best.

For many years, Colgate-Palmolive was organized around regional divisions: North America, Latin America, Eastern Europe, and so on. In 1997, however, the firm reorganized as part of its new strategic plan. In the new structure, the type of business strategies being pursued are the basis for organizing. These strategies differ according to whether the market for a product is relatively mature or newly emerging.[34] At Colgate-Palmolive, for example, issues of establishing brand-name recognition would be more important in emerging markets, while reducing costs may be more important in mature markets. In addition, goals related to market share and sales growth would be quite different for the different divisions despite the fact that they're selling the same product.

As is true in departmentalized organizations, too little coordination among the major groups—in this case, divisions—can create problems for the total corporation. Nordstrom, the department store chain, experienced this problem after its rapid expansion during the 1990s. As it expanded from the west coast to the east coast and other regions, the number of groups of buyers, who choose merchandise for the stores, expanded to more than a dozen. Each division placed separate orders with suppliers, who were sometimes driven to distraction. As Paul Charron, president of Liz Claiborne put it, "The fragmentation of the buying organization works at cross-purposes sometimes."[35] To offset such coordination problems, many large companies began to adopt matrix structures during the 1970s and 1980s.

Matrix Structure

The matrix form of organization began to emerge as corporations faced markets that demanded both efficiency (a strength of the departmental form) and responsiveness (the strength of the divisional form).[36] In a **matrix structure**, employees report to more than one boss, with each boss responsible for a different aspect of the organization.[37] For example, a fashion design artist might report to the vice president of marketing and the vice president of outerwear. These vice presidents, in turn, might report to a general manager for manufacturing and a general manager for the North American region. In this type of structure, managers enjoy a great deal of autonomy but they also must coordinate with each other in assigning work to their subordinates, evaluating employee performance, and so on.

For matrix designs to work effectively, the managers with matrixed responsibilities must communicate well with each other and work well together as a team. When disagreements arise, they must be resolved through effective problem solving and collaboration. Problems can't be allowed to fester, nor can they be solved by simply passing them up to the next level in the hierarchy. Teams of employees representing the areas in an organization often are used to address the coordination challenges posed by the matrix structure.

Process-Based Horizontal Structure

Organizations have learned that achieving outcomes such as great quality or low cost requires managing the relevant value creation processes. Thus, in some organizations, processes define the organizational structure. **Process-based horizontal structures** are relatively flat, and many different tasks are clustered together within an organizational unit.[38] When organizing around processes—such as those needed to ensure total quality or those needed to maximize the cycle times and efficiency with which a set of tasks is performed—the structure reflects the flow of work. A basic process would include everything that occurs between the point at which the organization receives inputs from suppliers until it satisfies a customer.

In the horizontal structure, work is performed by teams. Thus, HR practices that fit team-based work designs are appropriate. Typically, process teams are self-managing. They are empowered to make decisions and take quick action, as needed. Training programs help teams improve their problem-solving and decision-making skills. Performance is likely to be measured using indicators that reflect the team's performance as a whole. For example, the performance of a team that handles order generation and fulfillment might be evaluated using cycle time as the primary criterion. At Xerox, the performance of customer service is measured using indicators such as how quickly the team responds to requests for service and the performance of the machines they service. Incentive pay is awarded solely on the basis of team performance measures such as these.

Process-based horizontal structures are most common in U.S. organizations pursuing competitive strategies that focus on offering excellent quality. Two popular approaches for improving quality are total quality management and reengineering.

Total Quality Management. **Total Quality Management (TQM)** is a process used to create products and services that meet the highest possible quality standards.[39] Since its inception in 1987, the guidelines created for selecting winners of the Malcolm Baldrige National Quality Award have been used by hundreds of U.S. companies to redesign their business processes. The Baldrige Award is given to companies that excel in the activities in Exhibit 4.6.

Somewhat similar to the Baldrige Award criteria for quality are the standards of the International Organization for Standardization (ISO) in Geneva, Switzerland. Any company that meets the set of specified standards receives ISO certification—it isn't a contest. Nevertheless, the standards are very difficult to meet. The ISO standards, which are identified by numbers (e.g., ISO 9000), have been adopted by many companies within the European Union. Most of the areas addressed in the ISO criteria are covered in category 6.0 of the Baldrige criteria, Process Management.[40]

"We realized that a capability comes only by combining a competence with a reliable process."

Jan Leschy
Former CEO
GlaxoSmithKline

FAST FACT

A study by Accenture found that investments in customer relationships accounted for half of the difference between top and average financial performance. The most important form of investment was in approaches to motivating and rewarding employees.

FAST FACT

At Sun Microsystems, 40 top engineers from Sun Labs were reassigned from developing new products to finding new ways to measure product quality. They're called the Rascals (which stands for reliability, availability, serviceability, and computer analysis lab).

ex 4.6 Scoring the Baldrige Award

2002 EXAMINATION CRITERIA AND POINT ALLOCATIONS

General Category and Specific Items	Item Point Values	Total Category Points
1 Leadership		120
1.1 Organizational Leadership	80	
1.2 Public Responsibility and Citizenship	40	
2 Strategic Planning		85
2.1 Strategy Development	40	
2.2 Strategy Deployment	45	
3 Customer and Market Focus		85
3.1 Customer and Market Knowledge	40	
3.2 Customer Relationships and Satisfaction	45	
4 Information and Analysis		90
4.1 Measurement and Analysis of Organizational Performance	50	
4.2 Information Management	40	
5 Human Resource Focus		85
5.1 Work Systems	35	
5.2 Employee Education Training and Development	25	
5.3 Employee Well-being and Satisfaction	25	
6 Process Management		85
6.1 Product and Service Processes	45	
6.2 Business Processes	25	
6.3 Support Processes	15	
7 Business Results		450
7.1 Customer-focused Results	125	
7.2 Financial and Market Results	125	
7.3 Human Resource Results	80	
7.4 Organizational Effectiveness Results	120	
Total		**1,000**

Although not directly specified as a criterion for the Baldrige Award, many firms pursuing total quality rely heavily on **employee empowerment**.[41] Empowered employees have the autonomy and responsibility to make key decisions about how work gets done, without seeking approval from their supervisors. For example, at GE's aircraft engines plant in Durham, North Carolina, employees work in nine teams, and each team "owns" the engines it builds. When a team is assigned to build an engine, the only instruction it receives is the date on which the engine is to be shipped from the plant. Their job is to make a perfect engine quickly, safely, and cheaply. Exhibit 4.7 shows the responsibilities that teams take on as they move from low to high levels of empowerment.

Empowering workers appears to be critical to getting employees more committed and involved, making it one of the important capabilities needed to turn TQM into a core competency for gaining a competitive advantage. Compared with many other aspects of TQM procedures, empowerment is much more difficult to imitate; thus, organizations that learn to use empowerment effectively cannot be easily copied by competitors.[42] The feature "Managing Change: Weaving a Better Basket" describes how empowered basket weavers helped Longaberger save $3 million a year.[43]

Process Reengineering. **Process reengineering** also focuses on creating new ways to get work done. It most often involves the redesign of processes related to logistics, manufacturing, and distribution. The goal is to design the most effective process for delivering a service or product.[44] Effective processes are those that cost the least while at the same time produce goods and provide services of excellent quality rapidly.

Successful reengineering requires managers and employees to examine the breadth of activities to be redesigned and the depth of the changes needed. In terms of *breadth*, although reengineering a single activity or function may be important to an organization, including more activities is likely to extend its benefits throughout the organization.[45] Often, reengineering a process requires employees to think across departments. Reengineering

"What drove our reengineering effort was the recognition that we couldn't rest on our past success at delighting customers. Most of our reengineering dealt with how we could do things faster."

Louis Zambella
Senior VP, Operations
L.L. Bean

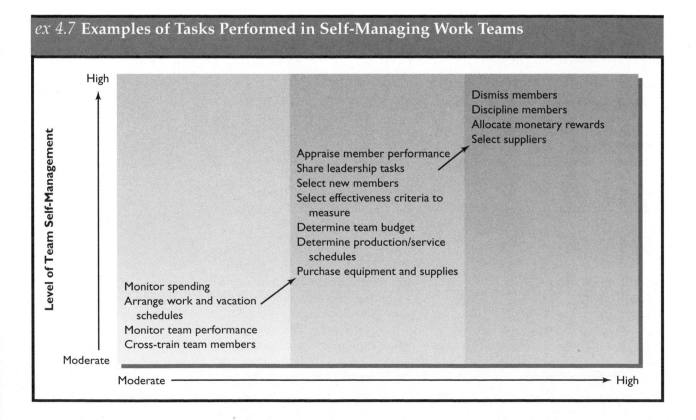

ex 4.7 Examples of Tasks Performed in Self-Managing Work Teams

Level of Team Self-Management (vertical axis: Moderate to High)
(horizontal axis: Moderate to High)

Monitor spending
Arrange work and vacation schedules
Monitor team performance
Cross-train team members

Appraise member performance
Share leadership tasks
Select new members
Select effectiveness criteria to measure
Determine team budget
Determine production/service schedules
Purchase equipment and supplies

Dismiss members
Discipline members
Allocate monetary rewards
Select suppliers

Weaving a Better Basket

Located in Frazeyburg, Ohio, Longaberger is a world-renowned purveyor of handmade baskets. Even if you don't own one of their baskets, you may be familiar with their headquarters office building, which looks like a giant version of the baskets they produce.

Longaberger weavers are paid on a piece-rate basis, not by the hour. So, they want to be able to work as efficiently as possible. A source of inefficiency that frustrated some workers was that they did not always have the materials they needed at hand when they needed them. If the materials weren't there, they engaged in trading with nearby workers, which stole time from everyone involved. Variability in their access to supplies resulted in some weavers being able to produce only 25 percent of what others could produce. With the approval of the CEO and head of manufacturing, three weavers set out to design a new process that would ensure everyone would have the correct mix of maple veneer in the correct amount at the correct time. Their specific goals were to reduce weaver downtime by 50 percent and reduce leftover material by 75 percent.

To design the new system, the team of three weavers took a paid sabbatical from weaving. They were trained to use flow-charting, cause-and-effect analysis, and other problem-solving techniques. They also were trained in all of the job functions that would eventually be affected by changes in the system—sorting, sawing, stamping, and so on. After studying 40 basket makers for nearly three weeks, they concluded that the biggest problem was in the quality of material delivered to each weaver. Weavers were given adequate quantities, but often the raw materials were moldy or too dry to use. A new sorting and delivery system was designed to fix the problem. Before the new system was in place, weavers at the 1,200 work stations ran out of materials an average of 52.5 times per day. After putting the new system in place, the figure dropped to 9.1. By boosting the productivity of weavers, the company lowered its costs, and at the same time employees' pay checks got bigger.

---

can reduce the amount of "hand-offs" between departments by increasing the amount of resources that are brought together simultaneously to meet customers' needs. Benefits may include faster delivery time, more accurate billing, and fewer defective products that must be returned.

The *depth* of a reengineering effort is measured by the number of roles, responsibilities, rewards, incentives, and information technologies to be changed. Successful reengineering requires deep change. If reengineering efforts are sufficiently deep, the old support systems (e.g., accounting, performance measurement, training, and compensation) will become obsolete. Starting from scratch, in effect, the organization can redesign itself and new support systems will emerge. In the short run, the change process may create excess capacity and financial stress. Unless the organization is growing, such pressures can lead to layoffs.[46] Firms capable of growth can undergo changes to improve efficiency without having to suffer this short-term side effect.

Network Structure

The structures described so far—those organized by departments, divisions, or a matrix that includes both—evolved to address the problem of how to divide up the responsibilities of people working in a fairly stable organization that serves a fairly stable customer base. As changes in the global environment put more and more pressure on organizations to adapt rapidly, new forms of organization are evolving. The network structure is one of these new forms. Industries where the network structure is most common include fashion, toys, publishing, motion pictures, and software.

Firms with a **network structure** subcontract substantial portions of the work to other firms. The subcontracted work may be assembly work, customer service, sales, marketing, distribution, and even some human resource management practices. Information technologies often facilitate coordination among the various players. Nike provides an example of the network structure. The core of the organization is headquartered in Beaverton, Oregon, which is where most of the design and product development work occurs. Production and assembly of the shoes is done by firms located throughout the Pan-Pacific region. When new products, such as golf balls, are introduced, new suppliers are added to the network. For marketing expertise, Nike turns to professional advertising agencies.

Network organizations provide many advantages for firms that need to constantly change and adapt. They also pose special management challenges. Employees working in network organizations may have low commitment to the total enterprise. In fact, they may not even understand it. At best, they may feel committed to their employer within the network. Unless Nike's interests and those of its network partners are perfectly aligned, people working within the network are not likely to always be aligned with Nike's strategic needs.

Structures That Cross Country Borders

"We had to resolve conflicts with individuals who felt their position was to defend their home country or their particular function. On a global team, you are a voice, an expert on that topic."

Barry Simmonds
Senior VP, Personnel
Corange London Limited

As companies move into the international arena, they face the same problems of how to organize tasks and how to integrate and coordinate the parts of the organization, but structural options for achieving these objectives differ. Four basic structures for global firms are international, global regions, global product, and transnational.[47]

Basic Structures. For many companies, the first step in globalization is to adopt an **international structure**, which simply involves having a separate group in the company responsible for all the international activity. Major human resource activities here are expatriate staffing and helping the human resource departments in the local subsidiaries in the countries of operation. In many respects, the operations in different countries act as separate companies that are very much tied to the local conditions.

Over time, the firm moves from the international structure into a phase of growth through production or service diversification (offering more products or services) or through expanding the geographical areas of operations. If companies expand through diversification they typically use a **global product structure**. Here the firm gains economies of scale through a more rationalized, centralized approach to decision making. This enables a company to produce products or deliver services more efficiently throughout the world. The human resource function thus becomes more concerned with planning and coordination around the world and the development of managers who can perform well in different environments but typically within the same product or service. Alternatively, if the company expands geographically without expanding into many new products and services, they are likely to adapt a **global regions structure**. This structure enables the company to be more sensitive to local conditions. Here the control and coordination are focused around regional groupings that seem similar in economic development, culture, and tastes. The human resource function focuses on the development of all the human resource activities for that particular region.

Whether the company has a global product or global regions structure, however, the concerns of the human resource professionals at the corporate headquarters is the same as that of the CEO: how to gain both global economies of scale and local responsiveness at the same time. Often, the challenge of balancing global and local concerns leads the company to evolve further and move toward the adoption of the **transnational structure**. The transnational structure is essentially a matrix structure in a global environment. It tries to maximize the economies of the global product structure and the sensitivity of the global regions structure at the same time. Here the company tries to act as a truly global firm that considers the needs and issues of everyone. A major challenge for human resource professionals becomes the development of managers who can manage in the matrix and coordinate teams of employees across borders.

These are just a few of the basic forms of organizational structures found in firms as they become more global in operation.[48] Each structure has unique implications for how people are managed, but the fundamental challenge that's common across these alternatives is how to coordinate the dispersed units while also adapting to the societal requirements of host societies.

Coordinating with Global Teams. For many companies, making the transition from an international structure through to a transnational structure proves to be a significant challenge for human resource management. Regardless of how the company is structured—for example, by region or by products—the autonomous units become focused on succeeding in the domain over which they have authority. Coordinating with other units for the good of the company as a whole seems to fall to the bottom of the priority list. To deal with this problem, many companies use teams as cross-cutting structures for linking together autonomous units. For example, General Motors used global teams in its R&D activities to examine the feasibility of producing "global" cars. PricewaterhouseCoopers has been using global teams to serve clients for many years, but they have seen rapid growth in the need for such teams in the last decade as the clients served by the firm have globalized.

When The Conference Board conducted research on global teams, it found that the most common objectives of such teams were those listed below. The percentage of companies using global teams for each objective is also shown:[49]

Objectives to Be Achieved with Global Teams

On-time delivery of results	69%
Innovations in product/service offerings	63%
Better understanding of the business	59%
Expand informal networks in the firm	50%
Improve customer relations	47%
Provide a means to develop employees	40%

Its research also investigated the nature of the global teams. Team composition varied greatly. Sometimes teams included members from across several departments, while other times teams were composed of specialists from the same department. Some teams were intentionally short lived, while others endured for years. Some were formal, while others were better described as informal networks. Some included people from only one level in the company, others mixed people from many levels, and some even included people from other companies, such as customers or suppliers.

Despite the many differences in the types of teams a company set up, however, there was agreement on one point. All of the respondents in the study expected the use of global teams to continue to grow in the next few years.

HRIM Systems Facilitate Coordination. In addition to global teams, human resource information management systems are proving to be useful for improving coordination and consistency in global firms. Such systems make it easier to communicate the same message to everyone regarding the company's values and strategy. They also make it easier for firms to design and implement HR systems that are common across different cultures, assuming that is something the firm wishes to do. When Dow Chemical changed its structure from international to transnational, it also restructured its HR function. For HR, supporting the firm's new business-driven model meant helping the company break out of its old habits of making decisions and allocating resources on a country-specific basis. As part of the change process, HR professionals sought to involve employees more directly in managing their careers. The feature "Managing Globalization: Dow Chemical's Self-Sufficient Employees" explains how the company's HRIM system supports its multinational structure.

INTERNET RESOURCES   4.C

Organizational Structure

At our Web site, http://jackson.swcollege.com/, you can:

1. Investigate the growing coffee chain of Starbucks, which adopted a structure of divisions organized according to geographic location. Does it still have that structure now? Find out by examining the titles of the company's top executives.

2. Learn how GlaxoSmithKline manages its quality processes.

3. Learn more about two head-to-head competitors—Levi Strauss and The Gap. Have they adopted the same corporate structure? What do you think explains the similarity/difference in the structures of these two companies?

4. Read the newsletter of the Association for the Management of Organization Design. Are any new forms of organization structure emerging that were not described in this chapter?

ORGANIZATIONAL CULTURE

An **organizational culture** is the unique pattern of shared assumptions, values, and norms that shape the socialization activities, language, symbols, rites, and ceremonies of people in the organization. As illustrated in Exhibit 4.8, assumptions, values, and norms form the base of a culture, but they can't be observed directly. They can only be inferred from a culture's more visible elements—its socialization activities, symbols, language, narratives, and practices. Like personality, organizational culture affects in predictable ways how people behave when no one is telling them what to do.[50]

People often find it difficult to describe an organization's culture. Sometimes the easiest way to understand the culture of one organization is by contrasting it with a different organization. Such contrasts occur naturally when two firms merge. Mergers that bring together contrasting cultures create a unique type of diversity that organizations may find they are not prepared to manage. When the Cuningham Group, an architectural

---

FAST FACT

The mascot of Rosenbluth International is a salmon, which the company explains this way: "Swimming against the current, like the salmon, we incorporate swiftness, persistence, and dedication into everything we do."

MANAGING GLOBALIZATION

Dow Chemical's Self-Sufficient Employees

Based in Midland, Michigan, Dow Chemical is an $18 billion business that generates 40 percent of its revenues from outside the United States. Until the mid-1990s, each country manager was free to develop a country-specific business strategy. Then Dow decided country managers needed to coordinate their activities to serve the firm's 14 different businesses, and the firm began to reorganize around a transnational structure. As part of the change, the HR function was reorganized into three groups: Business Partners serve the business operations, making sure that each business has the HR services it needs. Business Partners also provide input to the Strategy Centers. Strategy Centers design new policies and programs, for adoption worldwide. Resource Centers then administer and implement those programs.

Facilitating worldwide coordination is a global HRIM system that makes it possible for managers working from any workstation in the company to get information about employees working anywhere in the company. Conversely, employees around the world can access

- information about the performance expectations and competencies required for all types of jobs in the company;
- their personal development plans and tools for managing their own development;
- descriptions of job openings and employment opportunities everywhere in the company; and
- compensation information—including benefits—for all job families on a country-by-country basis.

With this system, employees are expected to take a proactive approach to managing their careers. If they are interested in possibly changing jobs, they can keep informed of the 3,000 or so jobs that become available in a typical year. If they are considering an international move, they can study the compensation and benefits likely to be available to them before deciding which country to target and prepare themselves accordingly. Managers, in turn, serve as coaches and mentors to employees, while also being more proactive in identifying potential internal hires for open positions.

firm in Minneapolis, Minnesota, decided to merge with Solberg + Lowe Architects, with offices in Los Angeles and Phoenix, the top management teams in both organizations thought that their cultures would meld easily. For the Cuningham Group, the goal of the merger was to expand geographically and to broaden its range of projects. Partners Rick Solberg and Doug

ex 4.8 The Culture Iceberg

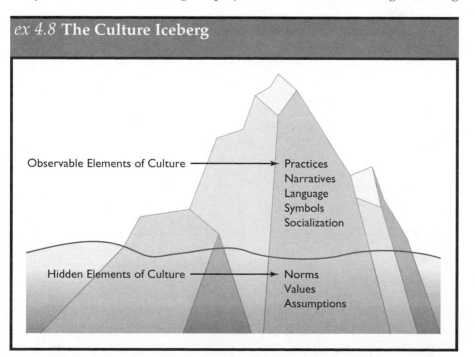

Observable Elements of Culture → Practices
Narratives
Language
Symbols
Socialization

Hidden Elements of Culture → Norms
Values
Assumptions

"Nice perks may help somewhat in recruiting, but to keep people here we've got to demonstrate that we offer a culture where they are respected and treated as adults, one that shows people that we really do care about them."

Patricia Brown
First Tennessee Bank

MANAGING DIVERSITY

Building on Contrasting Corporate Cultures

When Cuningham and his team visited the offices of Solberg + Lowe, they liked the look and feel of the work environment. The physical spaces reminded them of their own offices, and they could see that the principal partners still liked to be actively involved in project design. "I felt it would be easy for me to work there," recalled Cuningham. Solberg recalls feeling the same way when he visited Minneapolis. "I wanted to see live, vibrant contributors on the ownership side. I didn't want a bunch of dead initials on the door." What he and his partner saw led them to conclude, "This is where we'd want to be." Subsequent visits to each others' homes reinforced their beliefs that the two teams would work well together.

The honeymoon lasted less than a year. By then, the fundamental value differences between the two firms became more apparent. Although neither had a formal dress code, the Minnesotans often wore ties to work, whereas the staff in Los Angeles and Phoenix preferred knit shirts. The Minnesota group worked a full five-day week, but on Friday afternoons, they couldn't reach anyone in Phoenix or Los Angeles because those offices routinely closed at midday on Friday. "At first we wondered if they were just lazier than we were. But we just had to adjust," admits Cuningham.

Communication patterns within the firms also differed. The Cuningham Group didn't hold nearly as many meetings as Solberg + Lowe. And when they did meet, there was always a clear agenda. Solberg and Lowe admit that some of their partners' meetings were more like family fights than discussions between professionals. Solberg and Lowe's frankness with each other was beneficial, but the screaming shocked Cuningham's team, which Solberg described as using a "Minnesota nice" style. There were even differences in how the two firms handled bill collections. The easy-going approach of Solberg + Lowe meant that they didn't press people whom they considered trustworthy for over-due payments. Cuningham disapproved: "If you don't pay your gas bill, they cut off your gas. It isn't mean or kind; it's just policy. And it has to be the same for everyone," he explained.

Five years after the merger, the two groups are working together well enough to consider expanding again through another merger. This time, Solberg says that he would make even more effort to ensure that there is totally open communication with the other management team, as well as with the staff. "You can't hold anything back. Chances are, what you're concealing will be the problem. Better to find out today than after you've committed to the transaction."

Lowe of Solberg + Lowe were well known for their work in hotels and the entertainment industry, but economic conditions in the Los Angeles area meant that they needed to look for opportunities elsewhere. As is often the case, the managers at both firms discovered that, although analyzing whether a merger makes financial and strategic sense is easy, successfully merging two corporate cultures is much more difficult. At Solberg + Lowe, the shared assumptions, values, and norms created a familylike atmosphere that contrasted with the more professional atmosphere created by the shared assumptions, values, and norms of the Cuningham Group as illustrated in the feature "Managing Diversity: Building on Contrasting Corporate Cultures."[51]

Types of Organizational Cultures

There are many ways to describe organizational cultures. Different organizational cultures may be appropriate under different conditions, with no one ideal type of culture for every situation. Regardless of how appropriate they may be, however, different cultures tend to coincide with different types of strategies and organizational structures. Furthermore, some employees may prefer one culture over another. Employees who work in organizations with cultures that fit their view of an ideal culture tend to be committed to the organization and optimistic about its future.[52]

Of the many frameworks that have been proposed, a useful one is presented in Exhibit 4.9.[53] The vertical axis reflects the formal control orientation, ranging from stable to flexible. The horizontal axis reflects the focus of attention, ranging from internal functioning to external functioning. The extreme corners of the four quadrants represent four pure types of organizational cultures: bureaucratic, clan, entrepreneurial, and market.[54] In a culturally homogeneous organization, one of these basic types of culture will be predominant. In a culturally fragmented organization, multiple cultures are likely not only to exist but also to compete for superiority.

Bureaucratic Culture. An organization that values formalization, rules, standard operating procedures, and hierarchical coordination has a **bureaucratic culture**. The long-term concerns of a bureaucracy are predictability, efficiency, and stability. Its members highly value standardized goods and customer service. Behavioral norms support formality over informality.[55] Managers view their roles as being good coordinators, organizers, and enforcers of written rules and standards. Tasks, responsibilities, and authority for all employees are clearly defined. The many rules and processes are spelled out in great detail, and employees believe that their duty is to "go by the book" and follow legalistic procedures. Most local, state, and federal governments have bureaucratic cultures, as do many companies organized by specialized departments.[56]

Clan Culture. Tradition, loyalty, personal commitment, extensive socialization, teamwork, self-management, and social influence are attributes of a **clan culture**. Its members recognize an obligation beyond the simple exchange of labor for a salary. They understand that contributions to the organization (e.g., hours worked per week) may exceed any contractual agreements. The individual's commitment to the

FAST FACT

CEO Meg Whitman describes eBay's culture as "of the people, by the people, for the people."

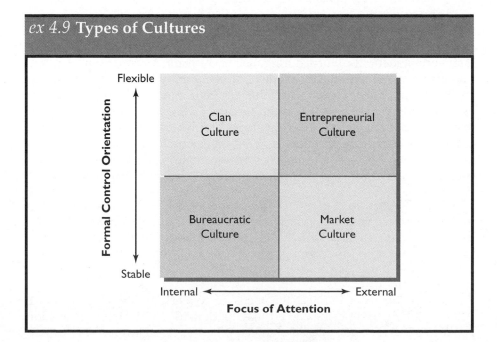

ex 4.9 **Types of Cultures**

Formal Control Orientation (vertical axis, ranging from Stable at bottom to Flexible at top)

Focus of Attention (horizontal axis, ranging from Internal at left to External at right)

- Clan Culture (flexible, internal)
- Entrepreneurial Culture (flexible, external)
- Bureaucratic Culture (stable, internal)
- Market Culture (stable, external)

organization is exchanged for the organization's commitment to the individual. The clan culture achieves unity with a thorough socialization process. Long-time clan members serve as mentors and role models for newer members. These relationships perpetuate the organization's values and norms over successive generations of employees. The clan is aware of its unique history and often documents its origins and celebrates its traditions in various rites. Members have a shared image of the organization's style and manner of conduct. Public statements reinforce its values.

Fel-Pro, an auto parts maker in Skokie, Illinois, had a clan culture. Maintaining that culture was made a condition of selling the company to Federal-Mogul. The Fel-Pro culture valued having a family atmosphere. It operated a summer camp for children of its employees, always sent parents a treasury bond upon the arrival of a new child, and funded scholarships for employees and their children. Teamwork among employees was promoted, and turnover was unusually low. The family programs cost the company 57 cents per worker hour, and company data indicated that employees who took advantage of the programs were more likely to participate in team problem solving and offer suggestions for operational improvements. When Chairman Richard Snell of Federal-Mogul approached Fel-Pro about buying the company, he was told that a deal could be worked out only if Fel-Pro's culture was protected. Although he worried about how Federal-Mogul's employees might react, Snell agreed to continue operating Fel-Pro's summer camp for at least two years and to continue the scholarship fund for at least five years.[57]

Entrepreneurial Culture. High levels of risk taking, dynamism, and creativity characterize an **entrepreneurial culture**. There is a commitment to experimentation, innovation, and being on the leading edge. This culture doesn't just quickly react to changes in the environment, it creates change. Effectiveness means providing new and unique products and rapid growth. Individual initiative, flexibility, and freedom foster growth and are encouraged and well rewarded.

An entrepreneurial culture suits a new company's start-up phase. Internet-based start-ups such as Yahoo! and Amazon.com were well known for their entrepreneurial cultures during their early years. An entrepreneurial culture also fits well with the demands faced by employees who are seeking to create and develop new products within the environment of a larger company. However, for managing products and services that have already been brought to market and may be entering later stages of the product life cycle, a market culture may be more appropriate. By 2000, for example, many who had happily invested in dot-com start-ups when they were unprofitable began to pressure those same companies to produce financial results for shareholders.

Market Culture. In a **market culture**, the values and norms reflect the importance of achieving measurable and demanding goals, especially those that are financial and market based (e.g., sales growth, profitability, and market share). Hard-driving competitiveness and a profit orientation prevail. Companies with strong market cultures include PepsiCo, Aramark, and CitiGroup, among others.

As the term implies, the focus of a market culture is outward. Although the market being served may be quite dynamic, the organization usually strives for some internal stability. When a person is hired at Frito-Lay,

"A duck who is tamed will never go anywhere anymore. We are convinced that any business needs its wild ducks. And in IBM we try not to tame them."

Thomas J. Watson Jr.
Former CEO and Chairman
IBM

"At E*Trade, we're an attacker. We're predatory. We believe we have a God-given right to market share."

Christos Cotsakos
CEO
E*Trade

the obligations of each party are agreed upon in advance and the relationship between individual and organization is contractual. The employee is responsible for delivering results, and Frito-Lay promises a specified level of rewards in return. The contract, renewed annually if each party adequately performs its obligations, is utilitarian because each party uses the other to further its own goals. Thus, rather than promoting a feeling of membership in a social system, a market culture values independence and individuality. For example, the salesperson who increases sales will make more money, and the firm will earn more profits through the salesperson's greater sales volume.

A market culture doesn't exert much informal social pressure on an organization's members. Superiors' interactions with subordinates largely consist of negotiating performance—reward agreements and/or evaluating requests for resource allocations. Social relations among coworkers aren't emphasized, and few economic incentives are tied directly to cooperating with peers. Managers in one department are expected to cooperate with managers in other departments only to the extent necessary to achieve their performance goals.

Organizational Subcultures

For an organizational culture to be of any consequence, it must have a base of shared assumptions, values, and norms. At the same time, however, various individuals and groups in the organization may hold different assumptions, values, and norms. An **organizational subculture** exists when assumptions, values, and norms are shared by some—but not all—organizational members.

It's not unusual to find several subcultures within a single organization. Before they merged, the cultures of the Cuningham Group and Solberg + Lowe were similar in many ways. No doubt, both were shaped by the assumptions, values, and norms that pervade their profession. Yet, even after five years of existence as a unified organization, distinct subcultures rooted in past histories persisted at the firm's three offices.

Organizational subcultures occur for a variety of reasons. As with the Cuningham Group and Solberg + Lowe merger, subcultures are likely to exist after established organizations come together to form a new organization. Organizational subcultures also are common in international firms, where societal cultures combine with organizational cultures to create distinct subcultures. In domestic companies, subcultures may emerge among employees from different demographic groups or among employees working in different divisions or occupations. All of these situations are reasons that managing cultural diversity has emerged as a key business issue in recent years.

Subcultures Reflecting National and Regional Differences. In organizations that operate in several countries, subcultures that reflect national differences are likely to exist even when there is a common organizational culture. At each location where a company has operations, organizational and societal cultures in combination create a unique organizational subculture.

Experienced travelers know that societal cultures are not uniform within a country, however. National culture may change dramatically from one side of a mountain range to the other, from north to south, and from seashore to landlocked interior. The U.S. subcultures found in Midwestern Minnesota and Western Los Angeles were readily apparent to employees of the Cuningham Group and Solberg + Lowe.

A study of more than 700 managers in large cities in each of China's six major regions suggests that there are at least three distinct subcultures in China: one in the southeast, another in the northeast, and a third covering much of the central and western parts of the country. The subculture of the southeast region is the most individualistic, whereas the subculture of the central and western areas is the most collectivistic. The culture of the northeast region falls between these two extremes. Thus a manager whose company operates at several locations in China needs to understand the organizational subcultures that are based on these regional differences.[58]

Subcultures based on national and regional differences have many potential implications for HR practices. Consider training programs, for example. In the United States, employees generally appreciate trainers who sprinkle some humor in with the more serious information and involve participants in active discussions. This same approach may not work as well in Japan, however, if the trainer fails to first fully establish his or her credibility.

Subcultures Reflecting Industry Differences. Dutch researcher Geert Hofstede, who is best known for his studies of societal cultures, has also studied industry cultures. His research indicates that industry cultures can be compared by using the following dimensions:[59]

Employee Oriented (focus on people) vs. Results Oriented (focus on goals)

Parochial (employees identify vs. Professional (employees identify with employer)   with professions)

Open (many types of people fit in) vs. Closed (it takes time to feel at home)

Loose Control (codes of conduct allow vs. Tight Control (rules control behavior) for much variation)

"One thing that eroded our culture very fast was bringing in a huge amount of new people from blue chip corporations."

Anita Roddick
Founder
The Body Shop

As an industry, higher education has long been more people oriented than results oriented. It is also a relatively closed system that requires several years of training to enter and whose members exert strong control over who is allowed to remain (e.g., through granting or denying tenure). The entertainment industry is also relatively people oriented, with the concerns of artists being at least as important as the concerns of entertainment consumers. Relative to higher education, it is more open, however. A wide variety of people, some with relatively little specific experience, can easily move into the industry and expect to achieve success.

When SBUs in a company compete in different industries, industry-based subcultures often clash. Andersen Worldwide experienced debilitating internal conflicts for several years, owing in part to the two different subcultures that evolved in its accounting and consulting units. Founded in 1913, the accounting firm of Arthur Andersen was so internally cohesive that employees were sometimes referred to as "Androids." In 1954, the firm began its consulting activities, which focused on information technology. For years, people who specialized in accounting and consulting coexisted in a firm dominated by the culture of the original accounting firm. By the 1980s, however, industry-based differences had emerged within the firm. Some partners in the consulting business came to the firm later in their careers and weren't CPAs. The consultants began to question the assumption that the two businesses were better off combined than they would be as separate firms. The consultants eventually persuaded the accountants to establish Andersen Consulting as a separate business unit. Face-to-face meetings between the two groups were rare, and the adversarial relationship between the presidents of the two divisions was public knowledge. The two business units continued to grow apart, each with its own culture and vision of the future. Battles between the units peaked in 2000, when they entered arbitration in order to settle disagreements about the nature of their respective legal obligations. The arbitrator's ruling cleared the way for the two businesses to sever their relationship completely. When it became independent, Andersen Consulting renamed itself Accenture.[60]

Strategic Importance of Organizational Culture

An organization is said to have a **strong culture** when the more observable cultural elements project a single, consistent message. In such organizations, managers and employees share a common behavioral style. They use the same basic approach to solve problems, meet goals, and deal with important customers, suppliers, and other stakeholders. They share common norms that guide how they relate to one another. Results are measured the same way throughout the organization. And a common set of rules governs the use of rewards and punishments.[61] In other words, a strong organizational culture results in predictable, well-specified behavior patterns.

Organizational culture has the potential to enhance organizational performance, individual satisfaction, the sense of certainty about how problems are to be handled, and other aspects of work life. However, if an organizational culture gets out of step with the changing expectations of external stakeholders, it can hinder effectiveness.[62]

The need to determine which attributes of an organization's culture should be preserved and which should be modified is constant. In the United States during the 1980s, many companies began changing their cultures to be more responsive to customers' expectations for high-quality products and excellent customer service.[63] During the 1990s, when unemployment levels reached historic lows and labor shortages made it difficult for organizations to take advantage of market opportunities, many top managers began to reassess how well their organizational cultures fit the expectations of their workforces. Rapid rates of globalization and the need for business models that are effective in a variety of countries continue to press organizations to scrutinize their cultures.[64] Finally, the continuation of merger and acquisition activities has focused attention on the importance of understanding, assessing, and melding differing organizational cultures. As Exhibit 4.10 shows, many executives recognize that they have often failed to merge cultures successfully.[65]

Regardless of the specific type of culture an organization has, a strong culture that's well matched to an organization's objectives and criteria for measuring success can enhance organizational performance as well as individual performance and satisfaction. Strong cultures provide clear guidelines for how people in the organization should behave. In a strong market culture, for example, people understand that ultimately their performance will be

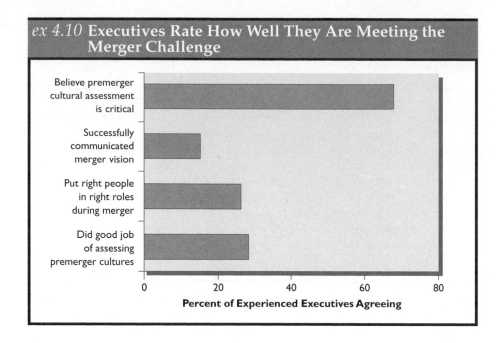

ex 4.10 Executives Rate How Well They Are Meeting the Merger Challenge

judged in terms of quantifiable, bottom-line results. An overarching feature that enhances the impact of these strong cultures is that they respect the employees. In a strong clan culture, people understand that focusing on the bottom line and ignoring interpersonal relationships is a recipe for disaster. In and of itself, however, a strong culture is of no particular usefulness for achieving business objectives. This is because culture addresses the question of "*How* do we do things around here." A culture becomes useful when paired with a clear answer to the question "*Where* are we going?" This is answered though the vision, mission, values, strategy, and leadership of the company.

INTERNET RESOURCES   4.D

Organizational Culture

At our Web site, http://jackson.swcollege.com/, you can:

1. Learn more about the cultures of Arthur Andersen and Accenture. What type of culture does each organization have today? Which culture do you think suits you best?

2. Find out whether the old Fel-Pro culture survived after this firm was acquired by Federal-Mogul. Visit Federal-Mogul to find out. What type of culture does Federal-Mogul have today?

PARTNERSHIP ROLES FOR CREATING ORGANIZATIONAL ALIGNMENT

As the foregoing synopsis of the components of the organizational environment implies, managing the organizational environment is a complex and critical task. To achieve excellence requires creating an organization that's both aligned internally and well suited to the conditions in the external environment. A clear direction supported by an integrated HR system and the partnership perspective all facilitate alignment.[66]

HR Linkage and HR Integration

To keep people focused on what everyone is striving for, many companies create visions, missions, and values as described earlier in the chapter. In a study of over 300 chief executives, when asked to write down their vision statement, all but one were able to do so.[67] At the 35,000-employee Weyerhaeuser lumber and paper company, the vision is to be *The Best Forest Products Company in the World.* McDonald's vision statement includes this: *Our People Vision defines what we aspire to be as an employer. Simply put, McDonald's aspires to be the best employer in each community around the world.*

While a company's vision statement may seem very general to outsiders, if formulated with the deliberation and input of many employees, it can take on great meaning especially for the company's approach to managing human resources. In addition, company values often suggest how employees are to be treated and what is expected from them in return. Business strategies provide further guidance. Systems for selecting and socializing new employees, managing performance, and providing rewards and recognition should all be designed to support the behaviors needed to innovate, deliver high quality goods and services, and/or continuously increase efficiency and reduce costs, as called for by the competitive strategy.

At Levi Strauss, a company known for its strong, values-based culture, the company's philosophy about how to treat employees is spelled out in an Aspirations Statement. The specific aspirations of the company include:

- For management to exemplify "directness, openness to influence, commitment to the success of others, and willingness to acknowledge our own contributions to problems."
- To value "a diverse workforce (age, gender, ethnic group, etc.) at all levels of the organization; diversity will be valued and honestly rewarded, not suppressed."
- The company will "provide greater recognition—both financial and psychic—for individuals and teams that contribute to our success [including] those who create and innovate and those who continually support day-to-day business requirements."
- Management should epitomize "the stated standards of ethical behavior. We must provide clarity about our expectations and must enforce these standards throughout the corporation."
- Management must be "clear about company, unit, and individual goals and performance. People must know what is expected of them and receive timely, honest feedback."
- Management must "increase the authority and responsibility of those closest to our products and customers. By actively pushing responsibility, trust, and recognition into the organization, we can harness and release the capabilities of our people."[68]

Formal statements such as these may help large companies keep their HR systems aligned with the broader vision, but they aren't essential. More important than the formal statements are the way people are treated and the messages they're sent about the importance of innovation, quality, costs, and so on.

At Mobil and many other companies, managers participate in developing strategy maps using the balanced scorecard. The **balanced scorecard** was developed as a tool for managers to use to gain an understand-

"Fit not only increases competitive advantage, but also makes strategy harder to imitate. Rivals can copy one activity or product feature fairly easily, but will have much more difficulty duplicating a whole system of competing. Without fit, discrete improvements . . . are quickly matched."

Michael Porter
Professor and Management Guru
Harvard University

ing of how three key drivers—employees, operations, and customers—contribute to a firm's bottom-line financial performance. For example, at Mobil, return on capital is an important financial indicator of success. Using the balanced scorecard approach to mapping the drivers of this performance indicator, Mobil's managers determined that three important human resource objectives were to help employees develop expertise in several key functional areas of importance to the firm, develop everyone's leadership skills, and develop an integrated view of the company among all employees. Achieving these HR objectives would contribute to operational excellence, which is needed in order to satisfy Mobil's customers (dealers) and establish a win-win relationship with them. Through win-win relationships with dealers, Mobil improves both the performance of the dealers and their own performance, which ultimately makes more capital available as well as ensuring that investments in innovation and cost reduction yield long-term returns.[69]

Partnership Perspective

Forces in the external environment constantly stimulate companies to reassess elements of the organizational environment, making the goal of achieving alignment a continuous business activity. The process of striving to achieve alignment sometimes requires major organizational transformations. More often, however, it involves making continuous small changes. Because the external environment is changing so rapidly, companies need to be constantly involved in changing. Consequently, companies need to understand the process of change, which is the topic of Chapter 5.

Regardless of how much change is needed to achieve strategic alignment, success depends on the understanding and cooperation of managers, HR professionals, and all other employees. The implications of the partnership perspective are summarized in "The HR Triad: Roles and Responsibilities for Creating Alignment."

SUMMARY

The organizational environment includes the company leadership, corporate and business strategies, organizational structure, and organizational culture. These aspects of the organizational environment provide an immediate context for managing human resources. Effective firms align the internal organizational environment with the current external global environment, while at the same time remaining flexible enough to change as new conditions arise. Continuous change in the external environment means that adjustments and change often are needed in the organizational environment.

Leadership sets the stage for managing human resources by providing a broad set of guidelines that help people make choices and direct their energies. Effective leadership ensures that people are generally working to achieve the same results, and that by achieving those results the organization will satisfy its key stakeholders. The organization's vision, mission, and values convey to employees answers to questions such as Where are we going? Why are we going there? And how will we get there?

A strategy is a set of integrated and coordinated commitments and

Roles and Responsibilities for Creating Alignment

THE HR TRIAD

LINE MANAGERS	HR PROFESSIONALS	EMPLOYEES
• Understand, communicate and behave in line with the vision, mission, and values. • Recognize the importance of organizational culture for firm performance and direct efforts to building an appropriate culture. • Assist HR professionals in determining the behaviors needed to implement the firm's strategy and encourage these behaviors among employees. • Understand and communicate implications of firm's structure for employees' development and career advancement. • Understand and hone the new managerial behaviors needed for an empowered workplace. • Continuously monitor the internal environment to ensure the many components are aligned.	• Align HR policies and practices with the vision, mission, and values. • Help line managers and other employees understand the importance of organizational culture; develop HR practices that send a clear and consistent message about the desired culture. • With line managers, determine the behaviors needed to implement the firm's strategy and develop policies and practices to support the needed behaviors. • Develop HR policies and practices that enhance development of expertise that fits firm's structure and supports collaboration across units. • Help line managers and employees adjust to empowerment and teamwork. • Assist in monitoring the alignment of the human aspects of the internal environment; recommend and help implement changes when needed.	• Focus efforts on contributing to the mission; behave consistent with the values. • Seek to understand the organization's culture and its implications for own behavior; adapt to changing conditions, if appropriate. • Learn which behaviors are needed to implement the firm's strategy; develop the skills needed for strategy implementation; assist other employees with needed behaviors and skills. • Recognize possible conflicts that arise due to the development of loyalty to organizational units; channel efforts into activities that are consistent with the organizational goals. • Accept the need for job design improvements; assist in job redesign efforts by providing input for improvements and feedback about the effects of changes to job design. • Monitor own needs and requirements and seek changes as needed.

actions intended to achieve a stated goal. Three common levels for strategy formulation are the corporate, business, and functional levels. At the level of a business, competitive strategies describe how the firm seeks to create value for customers and gain an advantage over competitors. When developing a competitive strategy, a firm considers several forces within the industry that are likely to shape the competitive landscape, as well as the firm's own resources, capabilities, and competencies. Effective strategies exploit the weaknesses of competitors and leverage the strengths of the firm. Because competitive strategies have many implications for the behaviors needed from employees, organizations need to tailor their approaches to managing people to fit their strategies.

Organizational structure describes the allocation of tasks and responsibilities among individuals and departments. A structure designates the nature and means of formal reporting relationships as well as the groupings of individuals within the organization. When deciding how to organize people and their work in order to achieve a strategy, firms choose among several possible forms, including departmental, divisional, matrix, horizontal, network, and cross-border structures. Associated with each form are a variety of potential benefits and pitfalls, many of which have implications for managing human resources.

The leadership, strategy, and structure of an organization evolve throughout the life of the organization and give rise to its distinctive organizational culture. A strong culture provides clear guidelines for how people in the organization should behave. When matched with the organization's objectives and the concerns of multiple stakeholders, a strong culture can enhance organizational performance as well as individual performance and satisfaction. HR practices usually reflect the current culture, and they also can be used to create a new culture.

TERMS TO REMEMBER

Balanced scorecard	Market culture
Benchmarking	Matrix structure
Bureaucratic culture	Mission
Business-level competitive strategy	Network structure
Capability	Organizational culture
Clan culture	Organizational environment
Competitive analysis	Organizational structure
Core competencies	Organizational subculture
Corporate diversification strategy	Process reengineering
Departmental structure	Process-based horizontal structure
Divisional structure	Resources
Employee empowerment	Strategy
Entrepreneurial culture	Strong culture
Five-forces model	SWOT analysis
Functional strategy	Total quality management (TQM)
Global product structure	Transnational structure
Global regions structure	Values
International structure	Vision
Learning organization	

DISCUSSION QUESTIONS

1. Describe how a powerful and clear statement of an organization's vision, mission, and values can be helpful to employees of the organization. Are these useful for other stakeholders? Explain your rationale.
2. Higher education is an industry in which changes in the global environment are creating many pressures for changes in how colleges and universities operate. Using the five-forces model, describe the most important trends in the global environment and how they may affect this industry. What are some possible consequences for managing human resources?
3. Select a business for which effective knowledge management could be a source of competitive advantage. Explain how effective knowledge management could contribute to competitive success. Is knowledge manage-

ment more likely to be an important core competency for firms with certain competitive strategies, or is this a competency that is relevant to all competitive strategies?

4. Select a company familiar to you and describe how it is organized (by departments, divisions, matrix, etc.). From the perspective of customers, what are the strengths and weaknesses of the structure?

5. What type of organizational culture do you think you would prefer? How can you assess whether you are likely to fit into an organization's culture before taking a job?

6. How are employees likely to behave when they work in an organizational culture that does not fit their personal preferences? What are the implications for organizations—should they try to have only employees who fit into the corporate culture, or are there advantages to having some employees who do not fit in well with the culture?

PROJECTS TO EXTEND YOUR LEARNING

1. *Managing Globalization.* Compare the organizational structures of two great competitors: Pepsi and Coca-Cola. What do the formal structures of these companies suggest about the type of culture you could expect to find in each company?

2. *Managing Change.* For IBM, the past decade has been a time of significant change. After downsizing during the early 1990s, the company had rebounded by 1996. Much of its new growth came from acquisitions. Read the chairman's letter to shareholders in IBM's most recent annual report. Identify one or two current strategic issues facing IBM and speculate about the challenges for managing human resources that these issues are likely to create.

3. *Integration and Application.* Review the Lincoln Electric Company and Southwest Airlines cases and then answer the following questions.
   a. What is the company's competitive strategy?
   b. Describe the basic structure of the company.
   c. Which of the four types of organizational culture best describes the company?
   d. Which elements of the internal environment do you think are most likely to change within the next five years? Why?

INTERNET RESOURCES   4.E

Projects to Extend Your Learning

At our Web site, http://jackson.swcollege.com/, you can:

1. Visit the home pages of Pepsi and Coca-Cola to see how these companies are organized.

2. Read IBM's latest annual report.

MIRROR, MIRROR ON THE WALL: SHOULD I REFLECT THE BUSINESS STRUCTURE?

"Getting our people invited to the key strategy meetings in the business units is my number one goal this year," says Margaret Woodward, senior vice president of human resources for the Transatlantic Insurance Company (TIC). She knows that there are many things to do to achieve this goal but thinks that changing the way HR is organized is the place to begin. She believes that she must consider mirroring TIC's structure in the HR department. Of course, Woodward is facing the same situation as many other HR executives in an era when firms seem to be constantly changing the way they do business. As the environment has become more competitive, firms have had to reconsider whether or not their businesses are organized in the most effective way.

Presently TIC is organized around several distinct businesses: individual life insurance, pensions, reinsurance, and a number of smaller businesses. Each line of business serves distinct customers, is bound by distinct regulations, and uses different work processes. The HR function is currently centralized, as were the businesses of TIC until two years ago. Woodward and her staff have not been thinking in terms of different businesses. In the past, it didn't seem necessary. In the past, everyone seemed to accept the idea that all employees should be managed alike—the idea of having different pay systems or different performance appraisal processes for different sets of employees was never seriously considered.

But now managers in the different businesses have begun to ask Woodward to reconsider some of the firm's approaches to managing human resources. Woodward wants to be responsive to their needs, but she also is concerned about the potential drawbacks of developing different HR practices within each line of business.

QUESTIONS

1. Tailoring HR practices to each line of business may keep line managers satisfied, but won't it be less efficient and more costly for the firm as a whole? Help Woodward weigh the potential costs and benefits of restructuring the HR unit by listing the pros and cons of the current structure and an alternative structure in which HR staff are assigned to serve particular business units. Be sure to consider the perspectives of customers, line managers, and other technical and support employees in the firm.

2. Woodward is considering centralizing some HR activities and not others. Which HR activities do you think are the best candidates for centralizing? Why?

3. If the HR group does decide to restructure around the businesses, what are some of the likely implications for current members of the HR staff, including Woodward? What new skills will they need? How will their careers be affected?

© Randall S. Schuler, Rutgers University

case study

ENDNOTES

1 A. Serwer, "A Rare Skeptic Takes on the Cult of GE," *Fortune* (February 19, 2001): 237–238; J. Useem, "Meet 'Da Man,'" *Fortune* (January 8, 2001): 102–106; G. Colvin, "The Ultimate Manager," *Fortune* (November 27, 1999): 185–187; W. M. Carley, "Charging Ahead: To Keep GE's Profits Rising, Welch Pushes Quality Control Plan," *Wall Street Journal* (January 13, 1997): A1, A8; P. M. Gunther, "How GE Made NBC No. 1," *Fortune* (February 3, 1997): 92–100; S. G. Richter, "General Electric's Victory in Europe," *New York Times* (November 30, 1997): B11; J. Curran, "GE Capital: Jack Welch's Secret Weapon," *Fortune* (November 10, 1997): 116–134; A. Bernstein, S. Jackson and J. A. Byrne, "Jack Cracks the Whip Again," *Business Week* (December 15, 1997): 34–35; Koenig, "If Europe's Dead, Why Is GE Investing Billions There?" *Fortune* (September 9, 1996): 114–118.

2 J. F. Budd Jr., "A Vision of a Mission," *Across the Board* (July/August 2001): 8.

3 This definition is adapted from the one provided by M. A. Hitt, R. D. Ireland, and R. E. Hoskisson, *Strategic Management: Competitiveness and Globalization* (Cincinnati, OH: South-Western Publishing, 2001): 144.

4 M. E. Porter, "From Competitive Advantage to Corporate Strategy," *Harvard Business Review* 65(3) (1987): 43–59.

5 M. E. Porter, *Competitive Strategy: Creating and Sustaining Superior Performance* (New York: Free Press, 1985).

6 M. E. Porter, "Strategy and the Internet," *Harvard Business Review* (March 2001): 63–78.

7 C. Haddad and J. Ewing, "Ground Wars," *Business Week* (May 21, 2001): 64–68.

8 "Measuring an Employee's 'Worth,'" *Workforce* (May 2001): 68.

9 R. M. Grant, *Contemporary Strategy Analysis* (Cambridge, England: Blackwell Business, 1991).

10 A. W. King, S. W. Fowley, and C. P. Zeithaml, "Managing Organizational Competencies for Competitive Advantage: The Middle Management Edge," *Academy of Management Executive* 15(2) (2001): 95–106.

11 W. Pape, "Group Insurance," *Inc. Tech* 2 (1997): 29–31.

12 C. K. Prahalad and G. Hamel, "The Core Competence of the Corporation," *Harvard Business Review* 68 (May–June 1990): 79–91.

13 For a review see R. Sanchez and A. Heene, "Reinventing Strategic Management: New Theory and Practice for Competence-Based Competition," *European Management Journal* 15(3) (1997): 303–317.

14 G. Hamel and C. K. Prahalad, *Competing for the Future: Breakthrough Strategies for Seizing Control of Your Industry and Creating the Markets of Tomorrow* (Boston: Harvard Business School Press, 1994).

15 N. Byrnes, "The Power of Two at Pepsi," *Business Week* (January 29, 2001): 103–104.

16 Adapted from S. E. Jackson and R. S. Schuler, "Turning Knowledge into Business Advantage," *Financial Times* (January 15, 2001): Mastering Management Supplement. Copyright held by S. E. Jackson and R. S. Schuler. Used with permission.

17 M. E. Porter, *Competitive Strategy: Creating and Sustaining Superior Performance* (New York: Free Press, 1985); D. Miller, "Generic Strategies: Classification, Combination, and Context," *Advances in Strategic Management* 8 (1992): 391–408.

18 G. Hamel, "Avoiding the Guillotine," *Fortune* (April 2, 2001): 139–144; S. Shepard, "A Talk with Meg Whitman," *Business Week* (March 19, 2001): 98–99; T. A. Stewart, "Want Innovation? Oil the Machine and Water the Garden," *Fortune* (May 7, 2001): 224; "Taking Stock: More Lawyers and Engineers, Fewer Inventors," *New York Times* (December 2, 2000): B13.

19 A. Bianco, "The New Leadership," *Business Week* (August 28, 2000): 101–108; J. B. Barney, "Looking Inside for Competitive Advantage," *Academy of Management Executive* 9(4) (1995): 49–61.

20 R. S. Kaplan and D. P. Norton, "Having Trouble with Your Strategy? Then Map It," *Harvard Business Review* (September–October 2000): 167–176; D. Leonard-Brown, "Core Capabilities and Core Rigidities: A Paradox in Managing New Product Development," *Strategic Management Journal* 13 (Summer 1992): 111–126; D. Dougherty, "Interpretive Barriers to Successful Product Innovation in Large Firms," *Organization Science* 3 (1992): 179–202.

21 M. E. McGill and J. W. Slocum Jr., *The Smarter Organization: How to Adapt to Meet Marketplace Needs* (New York: John Wiley, 1994); G. T. Lumpkin and G. G. Dess, "Clarifying the Entrepreneurial Orientation Construct and Linking It to Performance," *Academy of Management Review* 21 (1996): 135–172. Note, however, that this approach to innovation structures is more pronounced in some cultures than others—see S. Shane, S. Venkataraman, and I. C. MacMillan, "Cultural Differences in Innovation Championing Strategies," *Journal of Management* 21 (1995): 931–952.

22 L. Clifford, "Why You Can Safely Ignore Six Sigma," *Fortune* (January 22, 2001): 140; N. Shirouzu, "Why Toyota Wins Such High Marks on Quality Surveys," *Wall Street Journal* (March 15, 2001): A1; G. Tucker and B. Shearer, "Winning Over Main Street and Wall Street," *Across the Board* (October 1996): 33–35; W. M. Carley, "To Keep GE's Profits Rising, Welch Pushes Quality-Control Plan," *Wall Street Journal* (January 13, 1997): A1, A8.

23 H. Hertz, *Criteria for Performance Excellence* (Gaithersburg, MD: Baldrige National Quality Program, 2001); R. B. Lieber, L. Grant, and J. Martin, "Now Are You Satisfied? The 1998 American Customer Satisfaction Index," *Fortune* (February 16, 1998): 161–168; T. A. Stewart, "A Satisfied Customer Isn't Enough," *Fortune* (July 21, 1997): 112–113; D. A. Garvin, "How the Baldrige Award Really Works," *Harvard Business Review* (November–December 1991): 80–95; V. A. Zeithaml, A. Parasuraman, and L. L. Berry, *Delivering Quality Service* (New York: Free Press, 1990).

24 R. S. Schuler and D. L. Harris, *Managing Quality* (Reading, MA: Addison-Wesley, 1992): 32.

25 M. E. Porter, *Competitive Strategy*.

26 D. Barber, M. A. Huselid, and B. E. Becker, "Strategic Human Resource Management at Quantum," *Human Resource Management* 38 (Winter 1999): 321–328; D. A. Nadler and M. B. Nadler, *Champions of Change: How CEOs and Their Companies Are Mastering the Skills of Radical Change* (San Francisco: Jossey-Bass, 1998).

27 W. A. Randolph and G. G. Dess, "The Congruence Perspective of Organization Design: A Conceptual Model and Multivariate Research Approach," *Academy of Management Review* 9 (1984): 114–127.

28 L. E. Greiner, "Evolution and Revolution as Organizations Grow," *Harvard Business Review* (May–June 1998): 55–67. [An earlier version of this classic article appeared in 1972.]

29 L. Baird and I. Meshoulam, "Managing Two Fits of Strategic Human Resource Management," *Academy of Management Review* (1988): 116–128.

30 P. V. Marsden, C. R. Cook, and A. L. Kallenberg, "Bureaucratic Structures for Coordination and Control," in A. L. Kallenberg, D. Knoke, P. V. Marsden, and J. L. Spaeth (eds.), *Organizations in America: Analyzing Their Structures and Human Resource Practices* (Thousand Oaks, CA: Sage, 1996).

31 F. C. Lager, *Ben & Jerry's: The Inside Scoop* (New York: Crown Trade, 1994): 143.

32 P. V. Marsden, C. R. Cook, and A. L. Kallenberg, "Bureaucratic Structures for Coordination and Control."

33 D. Channon, "SBU Structure," in C. L. Cooper and C. Argyris (eds.), *The Concise Blackwell Encyclopedia of Management* (Malden, MA: Blackwell, 1998).

34 N. Schwartz, "Colgate Cleans Up," *Fortune* (April 16, 2001): 179; T. Parker-Pope, "Colgate Gives Management New Structure," *Wall Street Journal* (January 15, 1997): B6.

35 S. Brouder, "Great Service Wasn't Enough," *Business Week* (April 19, 1999): 128–129; L. Lee, "Nordstrom Cleans Out Its Closets," *Business Week* (May 22, 2001): 105–106.

36 G. B. Voss, D. M. Cable, and Z. G. Voss, "Linking Organizational Values to Relationships with External Constituents: A Study of Nonprofit Professional Theatres," *Organizational Science* 11 (May–June 2000): 330–347; R. E. Miles and W. E. D. Creed, "Organizational Forms and Managerial Philosophies: A Descriptive and Analytic Review," *Research in Organizational Behavior* 17 (1995): 333–372.

37 S. M. Davis and P. R. Lawrence, *Matrix* (Reading, MA: Addison-Wesley, 1977).

38 D. H. Pink, "Who Has the Next Big Idea?" *Fast Company* (September 2001): 108–116; F. Ostroff and D. Smith, "The Horizontal Organization," *McKinsey Quarterly* 1 (1992): 148–168.

39 D. A. Garvin, "Leveraging Processes for Strategic Advantage: A Roundtable with Xerox's Allaire, USAA's Herres, SmithKline Beecham's Leschley, and Pepsi's Weatherup," *Harvard Business Review* (September–October 1995): 77–90.

40 J. Conkling, "A Firm Reaches for and Achieves Excellence," *Workforce* (May 1997): 87–90; National Institute of Standards and Technology, *Baldrige National Quality Program, 2002: Criteria for Performance Excellence.* Gaithersburg, MD: Baldrige National Quality Program, 2002).

41 R. Forrester, "Empowerment: Rejuvenating a Potent Idea," *Academy of Management Executive* 14(3) (2000): 67–73.

42 T. C. Powell, "Total Quality Management as Competitive Advantage: A Review and Empirical Study," *Strategic Management Journal* 16 (1995): 15–37; also see M. R. Kelley, "Participative Bureaucracy and Productivity in the Machined Products Sector," *Industrial Relations* 5 (3) (1996): 374–399; F. K. Pils and J. P. MacDuffie, "The Adoption of High-Involvement Work Practices," *Industrial Relations* 35(3) (1996): 423–455.

43 D. Kiley, "Crafty Basket Makers Cut Downtime, Waste," *USA Today* (May 10, 2001): 3B.

44 E. Brynjolfsson, A. A. Renshaw, and M. V. Alstyne, "The Matrix of Change," *Sloan Management Review* (Winter 1997): 37–54; M. Hammer

and J. Champy, *Reengineering the Corporation* (New York: HarperCollins, 1993); M. Hammer, *Beyond Reengineering: How the Process-Centered Organization Is Changing Our Lives* (New York: HarperBusiness, 1996); and J. Champy, *Reengineering Management: The Mandate for New Leadership* (New York: HarperBusiness, 1996).

45 A. Majchrzak and Q. Wang, "Breaking the Functional Mind-set in Process Organizations," *Harvard Business Review* (September–October, 1996): 93–99.

46 J. D. Sterman, N. P. Repenning, and F. Kofman, "Unanticipated Side Effects of Successful Quality Programs: Exploring a Paradox of Organizational Improvement," *Management Science* 43 (1997): 503–521; R. L. Harmon, *Reinventing the Business: Preparing Today's Enterprises for Tomorrow's Technology* (New York: Free Press, 1996).

47 R. Wellins and S. Rioux, "Solving the Global HR Puzzle," *Workspan* (February 2001): 26–29; S. Ghoshal and C. A. Bartlett, "The Multinational Corporation as an Interorganizational Network," *Academy of Management Review* 15 (1990): 603–625; A. V. Phatak, *International Dimensions of Management* (Boston: PWS-Kent, 1992); also see L. Eden, *Multinationals in North America* (Calgary, Alberta: University of Calgary Press, 1994).

48 M. Hansen and B. von Oetinger, "Introducing T-Shaped Managers: Knowledge Management's Next Generation," *Harvard Business Review* (March 2001): 107–116; P. D. Dowling, D. Welch, and R. S. Schuler, *International Dimensions in Human Resource Management* (Cincinnati, OH: South-Western, 1999); Y. L. Doz and C. K. Prahalad, "Managing DMNCs: A Search for a New Paradigm," in R. P. Rumelt and D. J. Teece, eds., *Fundamental Issues in Strategy: A Research Agenda* (Boston: Harvard Business School Press, 1994): 495–526.

49 H. Axel, *HR Executive Review: Company Experiences with Global Teams* (New York: Conference Board, 1996).

50 Z. Aycan, R. Kanungo, M. Mendonca, K. Yu, J. Deller, G. Stahl and A. Kurshid, "Impact of Culture on Human Resource Management Practices: A 10-Country Comparison," *Applied Psychology: An International Review* 49 (2000): 192–221; D. R. Denison, "What Is the Difference between Organizational Culture and Organizational Climate? A Native's Point of View on a Decade of Paradigm Wars," *Academy of Management Review* 21 (1996): 619–654; C. A. O'Reilly, III, and J. A. Chatman, "Culture as Social Control: Corporations, Cults, and Commitments," in B. M. Staw and L. L. Cummings (eds.), *Research in Organizational Behavior* 18 (1996): 157–200.

51 C. Caggiano, "Merge Now, Pay Later," *Inc.* (April 2000), pp. 86–96.

52 S. G. Harris and K. W. Mossholder, "The Affective Implications of Perceived Congruence with Culture Dimensions During Organizational Transformation," *Journal of Management* 22 (1996): 527–547.

53 Adapted from R. Hooijberg and F. Petrock, "On Cultural Change: Using the Competing Values Framework to Help Leaders Execute a Transformational Strategy," *Human Resource Management* 32 (1993): 29–50; R. E. Quinn, *Beyond Rational Management: Mastering the Paradoxes and Competing Demands of High Performance* (San Francisco: Jossey-Bass, 1988).

54 R. Hooijberg and F. Petrock, "On Cultural Change."

55 D. A. Morand, "The Role of Behavioral Formality and Informality in the Enactment of Bureaucratic Versus Organic Organizations," *Academy of Management Review* 20 (1995): 831–872.

56 R. Kanter, "A More Perfect Union," *Inc.* (February 2001): 93–98; B. Elgin, "Running the Tightest Ships on the Net," *Business Week* (January 29, 2001): 125–126; J. A. Byrne, "Management by Web," *Business Week* (August 28, 2000): 84–96; P. V. Marsden, C. R. Cook, and A. L. Kallenberg, "Bureaucratic Structures for Coordination and Control."

57 R. A. Melcher, "Warm and Fuzzy, Meet Rough and Tumble," *Business Week* (January, 26, 1998): 38.

58 D. A. Ralston, Y. Kai-Cheng, X. Wang, R. H. Terpstra, and H. Wei. "The Cosmopolitan Chinese Manager: Findings of a Study on Managerial Values across the Six Regions of China," *Journal of International Management* 2 (1996): 79–109.

59 Adapted from G. Hofstede, *Cultures and Organizations: Software of the Mind* (New York: McGraw Hill, 1995); G. Hofstede, B. Neuijen, D. D. Ohayv, and G. Sanders, "Measuring Organizational Cultures: A Qualitative and Quantitative Study of Twenty Cases," *Administrative Science Quarterly* 35 (1990): 286–316.

60 *Wall Street Journal* (February 26, 1998): A9; A. Bryant, "The Andersen Family Feud: Two Units Split on New Leadership," *New York Times* (June 28, 1997: B35, B37; D. Whitford, "Arthur, Arthur. . . ." *Fortune* (November 10, 1997): 169–178; D. Leonhardt, "Andersen Consulting's Chief Make E-commerce a New Goal," *New York Times* (November 2, 1999): C3; R. O. Crockett, "Next Stop, Splitsville," *Business Week* (January 18, 1999): 100–102; "Andersen Consulting Wins Arbitration Case: Will Formally Separate from Arthur Andersen," Arbitrator's News Release at http://newsroom.ac.com/news/arbitration/release.shtml/ (September 6, 2000).

61 E. H. Schein, "What Is Culture?" in P. J. Frost, L. F. Moore, M. R. Louis, C. C. Lundberg, and J. Martin (eds.), *Reframing Organizational Culture* (Newbury Park, CA: Sage, 1991): 243–253.

62 D. R. Denison and A. K. Mishra, "Toward a Theory of Organizational Culture and Effectiveness," *Organization Science* 6 (1995): 204–222.

63 For a historical perspective on quality fads, see R. R. Cole, *Managing Quality Fads: How American Business Learned How to Play the Quality Game* (New York: Oxford University Press, 1999).

64 M. J. Mandel, "The New Economy: It Works in America. Will It Go Global?" *Business Week* (January 31, 2000): 73–77.

65 P. L. Giles, "The Importance of HR in Making Your Merger Work," *Workspan* (August 2000): 16–20. Also see A. T. J. Tetenbaum, "Beating the Odds of Merger & Acquisition Failure: Seven Key Practices that Improve the Chance for Expected Integration and Synergies," *Organizational Dynamics* (Autumn 1999): 22–36; S. DeVoge and S. Spreier, "The Soft Realities of Mergers," *Across the Board* (December, 1999): 27–32.

66 O. C. Richard and N. B. Brown, "Strategic Human Resource Management Effectiveness and Firm Performance," *International Journal of Human Resource Management* 12 (2001): 299–310; G. B. Voss, D. M. Gable, and Z. G. Voss, "Linking Organizational Values to Relationships with External Constituents: A Study of Nonprofit Professional Theatres," *Organizational Science* 11 (2000): 330–347; M. A. Huselid, S. E. Jackson, and R. S. Schuler, "Technical and Strategic Human Resource Effectiveness as Determinants of Firm Performance," *Academy of Management Journal* 40 (1997): 171–188.

67 L. Larwood, C. M. Falbe, M. P. Kriger, and P. Miesing, "Structure and Meaning of Organizational Vision," *Academy of Management Journal* 39 (1995): 740–769.

68 R. Mitchell and M. Oneal, "Managing by Values: Is Levi Strauss' Approach Visionary—or Flaky?" *Business Week* (August 1, 1994): 46–52.

69 R. S. Kaplan and D. P. Norton, "Having Trouble with Your Strategy? Then Map It," *Harvard Business Review* (September–October 2000): 167–176; B. E. Becker, M. A. Huselid, and D. Ulrich, *The HR Scorecard: Linking People, Strategy and Performance* (Boston: Harvard Business School Press, 2001).

CHAPTER

5

HR Planning for Strategic Change

"In three years, Ameritech has gone from a sleepy bureaucratic company to a nimble, market-driven global communication company. We tapped new leadership and recruited new people. We compressed management layers. We pushed for those closest to customers to drive major company decisions. We outsourced and trimmed our workforce. We reorganized and consolidated. And the change continues."

William M. Oliver
Former Senior VP, Human Resources
Ameritech, now part of SBC

MANAGING THROUGH STRATEGIC PARTNERSHIPS

Weyerhaeuser Company

With yearly sales of about $12 billion, Weyerhaeuser Company is one of the largest paper and forest products companies in the world. Headquartered in Federal Way, Washington, it spreads most of its forty thousand employees throughout North America. Major competitors include Georgia-Pacific Corporation, International Paper Company, and Westvaco Corporation.

Today, the company's vision is in clear focus, but before competition intensified to its present level, its importance was not so apparent. Through the 1970s, the firm enjoyed fairly consistent growth and financial success. In the 1980s, the business environment began to change: global and domestic competition roared in at the same time that the national economy went into recession and the housing industry entered a major slump. These conditions created overcapacity in the paper industry. Suddenly the company's successful strategy of being a large-commodity lumber and paper business was no match against the tactics of new, smaller, and speedier competitors who focused more on the customer.

Faced with a do-or-die crisis situation, top management decided to decentralize operations and concentrate attention on the customer. They restructured the company into three major divisions: forest products, paper products, and real estate. The decentralized structure was motivating for many people, but it created new problems, too: people began to lose a feeling of identity with the larger company; inefficiencies due to duplication crept in, and some resources were underutilized.

The challenge of reducing the disadvantages of decentralization without losing its advantages was tackled by Jack Creighton, then CEO. He and a new senior management team established the company's new vision: "To be the best forest products company in the world." They also defined a set of common values, which are also shared by everyone in the company:

Customers: *We listen to our customers and improve our products and services to meet their present and future needs.*

People: *Our success depends upon people who perform at a high level working together in a safe and healthy environment where diversity, development, and teamwork are valued and recognized.*

Accountability: *We expect superior performance and are accountable for our actions and results. Our leaders set clear goals and expectations, are supportive, and provide and seek frequent feedback.*

Citizenship: *We support the communities where we do business, hold ourselves to the highest standards of ethical conduct and environmental responsibility, and communicate openly with Weyerhaeuser people and the public.*

Financial Responsibility: *We are prudent and effective in the use of the resources entrusted to us.*

To achieve these behavioral changes, the company needed to revise many of its human resource policies and practices. Compensation, training and development, and performance management systems were all revised to deliver a clear and consistent message that encourages and supports new behaviors that are consistent with the new organization and the new expectations. For example, performance appraisals and compensation were revised to evaluate and reward decision making, customer focus, and innovation.

The past 20 years of strategic change have not been easy for Weyerhaeuser. But through extensive planning, restructuring, and new ways of managing human resources, considerable success has been achieved. Today, Steven Rogel leads the company toward its vision. His challenge is to continue to uphold the company's values while implementing the company's current strategic plan, which includes the following objectives:

- making total quality the Weyerhaeuser way of doing business,
- relentlessly pursuing full customer satisfaction,
- empowering Weyerhaeuser people,
- leading the industry in forest management and manufacturing excellence, and
- producing superior returns for shareholders.

As business conditions continue to change, Weyerhaeuser's structure is likely to continue to evolve, and new approaches may be needed for managing the company's human resources. Continuous HR planning will surely accompany this firm's continuous process of strategic adjustment and realignment.

THE STRATEGIC IMPORTANCE OF HR PLANNING

As the Weyerhaeuser example illustrates, changes in the global environment are a major impetus for strategic change efforts. In order to succeed under new competitive conditions, companies may change their vision, values, structure, strategy, and even their corporate culture. As described in Chapter 4, these elements of the organization are closely intertwined—changes in any one of them is likely to require changes in the others. At Weyerhaeuser, a new vision, a clarification of the company's values, was accompanied by a major change in strategic objectives and organization structure. All of these changes had significant implications for the behaviors needed from people in the organization. To encourage and support the behaviors required in the new organization, many of the company's HR practices required changing. Ultimately, over a period of several years, Weyerhaeuser succeeded in repositioning itself to become a highly successful global competitor.

For Indianapolis mayor Stephen Goldsmith, the vision was to dramatically improve how the city delivered services. From this vision flowed a new model for managing city employees. Hundreds of job descriptions and regulations were eliminated, and people were encouraged to focus on teamwork. Employees from various departments were put together to work on projects and told to let their actions be guided by "thoughtful risk taking." When employees made mistakes, Goldsmith told them to "make a new mistake next time."[1]

Weyerhaeuser recognized the need for strategic change 20 years ago. Other firms in the industry were not as quick to act. For example, Champion International, a paper producer headquartered in Stamford, Connecticut, began its similar transformation nearly a decade later. Although its timing was different, Champion underwent many changes similar to those at Weyerhaeuser. Mark Childers was senior vice president of organizational development and human resources when he spearheaded the strategic change effort at Champion. He explains: "Champion was an old-line paper manufacturing company with classic characteristics solidly in place. We had a traditional management structure that dealt with employees in a parental manner, an adversarial relationship with unions, and information systems that reflected that type of thinking. In little more than a decade, we've changed our hierarchy, opened up our information systems, developed cooperative partnering relationships with employees and unions, and established accountability within supervisory groups."[2] Exhibit 5.1 summarizes some of the specific strategic changes at Champion International and shows their impact on the firm's performance.

Changes such at those at Weyerhaeuser and Champion are being repeated in hundreds of firms in every industry. As described in Chapters 2 and 4, major change initiatives may be stimulated by the need to drastically reduce costs, changing global labor market conditions, the availability of new technologies, growth strategies that depend on multiple mergers and acquisitions, fundamental changes in the structure and dynamics in some industries, and so on. Regardless of the reasons for strategic change, it has become omnipresent. And regardless of the type of change an organization undertakes, successful strategic change almost always requires changes in policies and practices for managing human resources.[3]

Strategic change refers to major transformations in the structure, size, or functioning of an organization for the purpose of achieving strategic

> *"Operating in this more complex and volatile business environment requires the capacity to cope with change—at a very rapid pace. We have to create a new organization that can evolve, that can modify itself as technology, skills, competitors and the entire business change."*
>
> Paul Allaire
> Chairman
> Xerox Corporation

> *"HR has input and control over the processes that can make a company stay like it is or change—the compensation and reward systems, the career planning systems, the training and development systems. If these don't change, the company won't budge."*
>
> Mark Childers
> Senior Vice President of Forestry Products
> Champion International

ex 5.1 Strategic Change at Champion International and Its Consequences

Key Changes Made at Champion International . . .

- New technology and restructuring of 10 of its 11 paper mills.
- Jobs redesigned for 7,500 of 24,000 employees.
- Hierarchical management structure changed to team-based structure, reducing management layers from 5 to 2.
- Functional support groups (accounting, purchasing, marketing, etc.) restructured horizontally to support business process.
- Shift to high-involvement management approach means employees now work with managers and customers to improve product and service quality.
- Employees participate in hiring process, evaluating peers on performance, and promotion decisions.
- Major investments made in training to improve business knowledge, technical skills, problem-solving, and team operating skills.
- Performance-based pay and gain sharing introduced.
- New, more cooperative approach to negotiations with unions results in more "partnership agreements" and fewer traditional labor contracts.

. . . and Their Consequences

- Company moved up in *Fortune*'s list of Most Admired Companies six years in a row
- Reduced administrative costs
- Mill production increased 32%
- Productivity increased 47%

"We view layoffs as darn-near the last resort."

Christopher Dobbs
Chief Financial Officer
Charles Schwab

objectives. It can be stimulated by conditions in the external environment or by people within the organization who have a vision about how to do things differently. At Hewlett-Packard, the Internet, declining share value, and a new CEO were the forces driving that company's radical change, including extensive restructuring of the business. In addition to many reasons for change, there are many different types of change. It can be radical or incremental, and it can occur in anticipation of future events or as reactions to current conditions.[4] Exhibit 5.2 illustrates how the degree and timing of change create four basic types of change.

Degree of Change

Radical change occurs when organizations make major adjustments in the ways they do business. Adopting a new organization structure, merging with another organization, or changing from a privately held to a publicly traded company are all examples of radical change.

Radical change is relatively infrequent and generally takes a long time to complete. Managers undertake radical change intentionally, often making huge investments in planning and implementing the change.[5] Radical

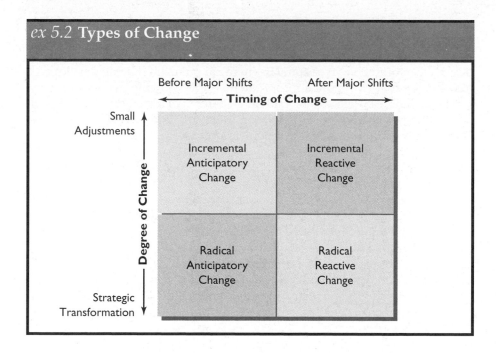

ex 5.2 Types of Change

	Before Major Shifts	After Major Shifts
	← Timing of Change →	
Small Adjustments ↑	Incremental Anticipatory Change	Incremental Reactive Change
Degree of Change		
Strategic Transformation ↓	Radical Anticipatory Change	Radical Reactive Change

change touches everyone and everything in the organization. It changes the daily lives of every employee, as well as other key stakeholders, such as customers, suppliers, and alliance partners. Radical change suggests that one "big bang" can transform an organization into something new.

In contrast, **incremental change** is an ongoing process of evolution over time, during which many small changes occur routinely. After enough time has passed, the cumulative effect of these changes may be to transform the organization totally. Yet while they are occurring, the changes seem to be just a normal aspect of revising and improving the way that work gets done. Total quality management (TQM) is an approach that relies heavily on incremental change. Employees routinely look for ways to improve products and services, and they make suggestions for changes day in and day out. Incremental change is also important in learning organizations. The desire to improve performance continuously in order to stay ahead of competitors is a common reason for smaller organizational changes.[6] Successful organizations are equally adept at making both radical and incremental changes.

Timing of Change

In addition to the differences in the magnitude of change are differences in the timing of change. **Reactive change** occurs when an organization is forced to change in response to some event in the external or internal environment. New strategic moves made by competitors, new scientific or technological discoveries, and performance problems are common reasons for reactive change. Reactive change can be incremental or radical. Weyerhaeuser's change was reactive and radical. If an organization adapts to a change in the environment without undergoing a substantial reorientation in its strategy or values, the change is reactive and incremental.

When the economy turned down in 2001, CEO Thomas Seibel led his computer software company, Seibel Systems, through an incremental strategic change intended simply to keep the company on track under changing business conditions. Armed with statistics that showed a slowing market, he realized that steering a high-growth company through an economic downturn required swift action. His financial planners quickly developed a new budget that was more appropriate given the slowing demand for projects. To meet the budget, Seibel laid off 10 percent of his workforce and postponed bonuses. Spending on travel was cut in half, and recruiting costs were cut from $8 million to $1 million. Some people were reassigned to serve as reinforcements on sales teams, who were directed to focus their energies on closing big contracts. These quick change efforts helped Seibel Systems outpace its competitors during a difficult business downturn.[7]

FAST FACT

"The species that survive are not the biggest but the most adaptable."
Charles Darwin

Charles Schwab also introduced incremental reactive change when the stock market stalled in 2000 and 2001 and affected the firm's financial performance. A drop in trading activity resulted in a 27 percent earnings decline and reduced profitability. Like Seibel Systems, Charles Schwab took quick action to cut costs, but its approach was quite different. At first, Schwab tried to get by without implementing layoffs and instead made changes that would spread the cost-cutting effects across the firm while leaving its workforce intact for the hopefully brighter future. Executives saw their salaries cut by as much as 50 percent. A hiring freeze was put in place, and spending limits were instituted for travel and entertainment. Employees were encouraged to take unpaid leaves and use up their vacation days. For several weeks, about half the 26,000 employees were told to take Fridays off, saving an estimated $10 to 15 million in compensation costs. By spreading the cost-cutting measures across the firm, Schwab hoped to avoid layoffs. But when the economy remained soft, it eventually announced that 2,000 (out of 25,000) jobs would be cut. To build goodwill with downsized employees, the severance package included a $7,500 hire-back bonus that people can receive if they are rehired within 18 months.[8] The research evidence suggests this is a good HR strategy. In a study of the 250 largest U.S. companies, those that had announced workforce reductions of at least 3 percent showed short-term financial improvements, but these were not sustainable in the longer run.[9]

As both the Seibel Systems and Charles Schwab examples illustrate, a systematic approach to HR planning helps organizations align their human resource policies and practices with the company's longer-term strategy while remaining responsive to short-term critical events.

Anticipatory change occurs when managers make organizational changes in anticipation of upcoming events or early in the cycle of a new trend. The best-run organizations always look for better ways to do things in order to stay ahead of the competition. They constantly fine-tune their policies and practices, introduce technological improvements, and set new standards for customer satisfaction. Often, anticipatory change is incremental and results from constant tinkering and improvements. Occasionally, anticipatory change is discontinuous, however. Visionary leaders within the organization become convinced that major changes are needed even though there is no apparent crisis. Because there is no crisis, the change can be planned carefully and implemented gradually.

Most organizations go through years of continuous, reactive change as a normal part of steady growth. In addition, many organizations attempt to anticipate the future and initiate change before there is an obvious need for it. Successful companies are adept at managing both reactive and anticipatory

"How many of you feel comfortable being here? About half. Okay. Well, I hope to change that this week. I want you all to be comfortable. Because if you're comfortable, you can really be a revolutionary, can't you?"

Janine Bay
Director of Vehicle Customization for Ford Motor Co.'s Automotive Consumer Service Group, speaking to participants in Ford's New Business Leader program

change. Increasingly they are also adept at learning from their experiences so that they can be more effective in making future changes. As described in Chapter 4, learning from experience—including experiences related to strategic change—has become a core competency for some of the most successful companies.[10]

A FRAMEWORK FOR UNDERSTANDING HR PLANNING

Radical strategic changes seldom occur without a bit of chaos. Indeed, a few organizations seem to thrive on chaos. But most organizations strive to impose some order and keep chaos under control during strategic change by engaging in systematic planning. The process of HR planning during strategic change comprises the steps shown in Exhibit 5.3. The planning process doesn't always proceed exactly as shown. Nevertheless, regardless of the

ex 5.3 Phases in HR Planning for Strategic Change

"In IBM, HR is right there at the table whatever the issues are—shutting a plant down, hiring workers, downsizing. We work with management on the decision, help craft the action plan, and then implement it with line management."

Laura Russell
Resource Program Director
IBM

FAST FACT

Since the introduction of its Trac II razor 30 years ago, Gillette has always included a consideration of HR implications when planning to launch new products.

---

sequence, the steps shown constitute the basic components of a systematic approach to planning for, and implementing, strategic change efforts.[11]

Exhibit 5.3 is not intended to be a precise map that shows all the alleys and valleys of HR planning. It's more like a snapshot of a famous skyline. You can see most of the landmarks, but you recognize that it would take several days to explore them all.

Synchronizing Business Planning and HR Planning

The framework shown in Exhibit 5.3 highlights the importance of systematically and continuously evaluating all the global and organizational elements described in Chapters 2 through 4 and considering their implications for managing the firm's human resources. Research on integration following mergers and acquisitions, for example, shows that the HR implications of strategic change should not be treated as an afterthought or left out of the business planning process. By planning for the human side of the integration, merging companies can build trust and prepare people for the changes they are about to undergo.[12]

Human resource issues are a major part of any strategic change effort—whether the change leaders recognize that or not. Similarly, HR planning should not occur in isolation from business issues. Possible changes in HR policies and practices should be considered in the context of issues related to other tangible and intangible resources, including finances, technology, physical resources, and the firm's current and desired reputation. The need for close coordination and collaboration between line managers and HR professionals during strategic planning is shown by the double-headed arrows in Exhibit 5.3.

Elements of Human Resource Planning

The term **human resource planning** refers to the activities highlighted in the box shown on the right side of Exhibit 5.3. It begins with early involvement of HR professionals during discussions of possible changes in the company's leadership or its corporate and/or competitive strategies, as discussed in Chapter 4. It continues with more focused efforts aimed at specifying the HR objectives for change. **HR objectives** for change state what is to be achieved with regard to the firm's human resources. Objectives may be stated in both quantitative and qualitative terms. Ideally, if the stated objectives for HR change efforts are met, the firm will meet its overall strategic objectives for change. Once the objectives for change are clearly specified, **HR plans** for achieving the objectives can be developed. The HR plans can be thought of as blueprints for action. They specify who needs to do what, when, where, and how. As plans are developed, close coordination is required between the HR professionals and other managers involved in creating corporate-level and business-level plans. At this stage, HR plans need to address two key issues: What procedures should be used to design new HR policies and practices? How will the new HR policies and practices be introduced to the workforce? Once the plans are developed, implementation of the plans can begin. As change unfolds, its effects on all stakeholders should be reviewed. In any change effort, the process of reviewing and evaluating success inevitably leads to revisions and refocusing.[13]

Historically, the goal of human resource planning was simply to ensure that the right number and type of people were available at the right time and place to serve relatively predictable business needs. For example, if the business was growing at 10 percent, top management would continue to add to the workforce by 10 percent: it worked before, it would work again.

Today, because the environment is changing so dramatically, human resource planning has become more dynamic and more focused on strategic issues.[14] Because the environmental changes often are unpredictable, managers often use scenario planning. With scenario planning, several alternative business scenarios are developed and the strategic issues that would be associated with each scenario are identified. Human resource planning for the possible future scenarios still involves numbers, but it often also involves

- crafting and communicating mission and value statements:
- ensuring that managers as well as all other employees understand and buy into the process of continuous change and adaptability;
- crafting HR strategies to help ensure that the company has the competencies and behaviors it needs;
- systematically designing and aligning HR activities to address the concerns of multiple stakeholders;
- developing methods to monitor the effects of change;
- being alert to signals indicating that plans should be reconsidered or modified; and
- integrating all of these activities with other change efforts in areas such as finance, marketing, and operations.

Planning Time Horizons

Human resource planning considers change from both long- and short-term perspectives, paralleling the business planning process.[15] In many organizations, the process of planning begins with a vision of where the organization needs to be in 5 (or even 10) years, and then works backward to understand the near-term implications of the long-term vision. In some organizations, the longer-term perspective might play little role in the planning process. Two common reasons for not paying much attention to the long-term are (a) a belief that the future is so unpredictable that trying to predict it is a waste of time, or (b) an implicit assumption that the future will be pretty much the same as the present.

For either long- or short-term planning, the phases shown in Exhibit 5.3 seldom unfold linearly. Nevertheless, planning activities generally precede implementation. Although even this distinction is not clear-cut, we use it here to organize our discussion of the planning process. We begin by considering HR issues that might arise during the earliest phases of strategic planning and then move to describing the process of developing HR objectives and specific plans.

"I wouldn't put together a five-year plan for a turnaround. I would put together a five-year direction. But I would put together a two-year plan and then manage the company with these two-year marks in mind."

Charlie Feld
Founder and CEO
The Feld Group

ASSESSING THE GLOBAL AND ORGANIZATIONAL ENVIRONMENT

The first phase of planning for change involves gathering data to learn about and understand all aspects of the environment. As described in Chapter 2, the global environment includes local, national, and multinational conditions, since all of these may be of importance even for a domestic company. More specifically, recall that the global environment includes the following:

- Economic and political trends
- Industry trends
- Technology
- Labor markets
- National and regional cultures
- Laws and regulations
- Unions and labor relations

Of course, the likely and possible changes in customers' needs and preferences also must be considered.[16]

Chapter 4 described the elements of the internal organizational environment. Recall that these include

- Company leadership (vision, mission, values)
- Strategy
- Structure
- Culture

Global Environment

During this early phase of planning for change, HR expertise is especially relevant for assessing labor market conditions, making predictions about how new employment laws and regulations might affect the organization, and alerting managers to relevant trends in union activity and labor relations. Examples of how changing laws and regulations affect organizations were provided in Chapter 2. Trends in union activity and labor relations are described in Chapter 15. Therefore, in this chapter we focus on labor market trends to illustrate how the changing global environment can create the need for organizational change.

Domestic labor shortages can be anticipated for many occupational groups. Understanding labor market conditions is essential for organizations that hope to experience significant growth, as is developing a long-term plan for how to meet the company's anticipated needs. The Boeing Company was hiring 150 to 200 employees each week in an effort to keep up with the growth in demand for aircraft. To meet its needs, it even began hiring people away from some of its suppliers—a move it eventually regretted.[17]

Exhibit 5.4 shows the trend of slowing workforce growth during the next 20 years. In the year 2000, just before the economy began to slow down a bit, polls revealed that 85 percent of corporate officers reported that their firms experienced chronic talent shortages.[18] Of course, similar shortages may not exist in the global labor market, which is predicted to continue expanding well into the future. Furthermore, the overall trend masks several important subtleties. For example, as Exhibit 5.5 shows, the average age of available workers also is expected to change, as the baby boomers continue to push through their careers. In fact, after taking into account factors such as likely retirement patterns and the trend of younger people delaying their entry into the workforce in order to continue their education, current projections show a 9 percent *reduction* in workers age 25 to 34, and a 54 percent *increase* in workers age 55 to 64.[19]

Organizational Environment

Changes in the global environment seldom have direct and obvious implications for organizations—their meaning and implications depend on each

---

"Cutbacks in education and a lack of emphasis on the skill sets needed for the information age are taking a toll. Finding people with both the aesthetic and technical capabilities is becoming more difficult all the time."

John Hughes
President
Rhythm and Hues

FAST FACT

Free detailed information about U.S. population and workforce demographics is available on-line from the Bureau of Labor Statistics.

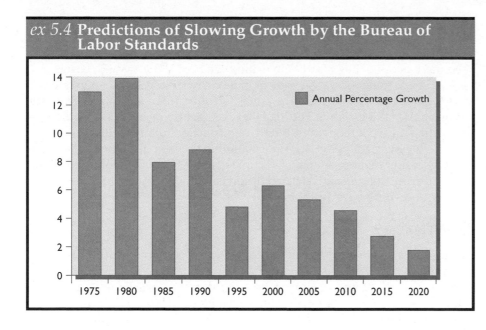

ex 5.4 **Predictions of Slowing Growth by the Bureau of Labor Standards**

firm's situation. Consider the age trends described earlier and depicted in Exhibit 5.5. For some firms, the aging workforce may mean that older workers will experience increasing frustration as they realize that a glut of senior talent means fewer of them will be able to continue their climb up the corporate ladder. For many firms, like Chevron, having a glut of workers nearing retirement makes downsizing easier—generous buyout packages can be used to encourage voluntary early retirement, eliminating the need for layoffs. For Deloitte and Touche, these trends mean that the number of partners over age 50 will double in five years, to make up 25 percent of the total. Partners are highly paid, and they become vested in the firm's pension plan at age 50. Retirement at age 50 is likely to be financially feasible for most

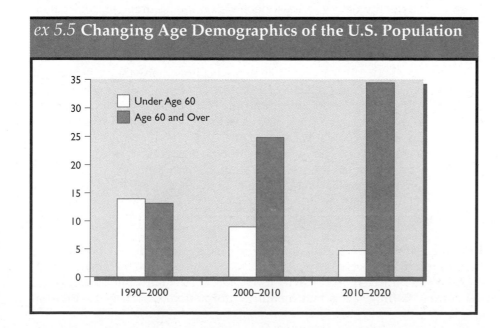

ex 5.5 **Changing Age Demographics of the U.S. Population**

partners. Whereas some companies might welcome mass retirements, they could be disastrous for Deloitte and Touche, because partners are a very valuable source of experience and talent. Unless the firm does something to keep these people, they may begin exiting the firm at a very high cost.

An organization's assessment of its current situation is often referred to as **organizational analysis**. The aim is to fully understand the current situation before taking action. The idea that organizational analysis should precede action may seem obvious, but its importance is often underestimated.[20]

Reviewing a variety of information is the best approach when conducting an organizational analysis. Three general types of information used during organizational analysis are HR forecasts, behavioral cause-and-effect models, and employees' opinions.

HR Forecasts

HR forecasts estimate the firm's future human resource needs. Earlier, in times of greater environmental stability, forecasting human resource needs and planning the steps necessary to meet those needs was largely a numbers game. Forecasting efforts focused on (a) developing estimates of how many people with which skills would be needed, (b) forecasting the likely supply of people and skills, and (c) implementing plans to ensure that the right number and type of people were available at the right time and place. If the supply of people was expected to exceed the projected needs, downsizing plans might be developed. If the projected needs were greater than the anticipated supply, aggressive recruiting plans might be developed.

In many organizations, quantitative forecasts of future human resources continue to be one important ingredient in an organizational analysis. At Chevron, for example, all operating units must conduct a demographic analysis each year to identify where talent shortages or surpluses are likely to occur. In addition to information about the supply and productivity of employees, data about skills, competencies, education levels, turnover and absenteeism rates, and attitudes may all be used to forecast future human resource needs.

The quality of any forecast depends on the accuracy of information used and the predictability of events. The shorter the time horizon, the more predictable the events and the more accurate the information. For example, organizations are generally able to predict how many graduates they need for the coming year, but they are less able to predict how many they will need for the next five years. And predicting the behavior of new college graduates is easier than predicting the behavior of people at the other end of their employment cycle. You can count on new graduates to be looking for jobs, but at what age should you expect older workers to be thinking about retirement?

Forecasting involves approximations, not absolutes or certainties. A variety of forecasting methods—some simple, some complex—can be used to predict an organization's demand for human resources and the likely supply that will be available to meet the demand. Two commonly used methods are statistical projections and judgmental forecasts.

Judgmental Forecasts. **Judgmental forecasting methods** rely on the opinions of informed experts (usually managers), who provide their estimates of current and projected productivity levels, market demand, and sales, as well as current staffing levels and mobility information. One way to arrive at agreement about what estimates to use is the Delphi technique. At a Delphi meeting, experts take turns at presenting their forecasts and assumptions to the others, who then make revisions in their own forecasts. This combination process continues until a viable composite forecast emerges. The composite may represent specific projections or a range of projections, depending on the experts' positions. Although judgmental forecasts rely on less data than those based on statistical methods, they tend to dominate in practice.

Statistical Forecasts. In contrast to judgmental methods, **statistical forecasting methods** rely heavily on objective data and formal models. For example, statistical methods might be used to predict labor needs under various conditions of business growth or decline. Statistical projections are possible when large amounts of historical data are available for analysis and to serve as the basis for projecting the future. Statistical projections often are used to

> **FAST FACT**
>
> Long known for its stable workforce and low attrition rates, PeopleSoft was taken by surprise when turnover rates for program developers jumped to 30% due to low morale and generous job offers from rival firms.

estimate the likely supply of labor in the external labor market, for example. In that case, data about birth rates, typical retirement ages, and educational trends can be used to forecast future labor supplies.

Within the organization, statistical projections also can be used to focus supply and demand—but only if the organization keeps track of the information needed to make projections. In order to make statistical forecasts, an organization needs a well-specified model of how changes in demand for products and services translate into changes in the company's operations, and thus the number, types, and locations of employees needed. Although HRIM systems are making it much more feasible for companies to collect and analyze such data, the reality is that relatively few companies currently use this forecasting method.

Regardless of the method used, forecasts of future labor needs and supplies should be considered rough estimates, at best. Accurate forecasts depend on the ability to predict both changing conditions in the external labor market and current employees' future employment attitudes and behaviors.

Behavioral Cause-and-Effect Models

Behavioral cause-and-effect models are another important ingredient in organizational analysis. **Behavioral cause-and-effect models** provide insight into why employees behave as they do and they identify the business consequences of employees' behaviors. When Sears set out to design a turnaround strategy to pull the firm back from the brink of extinction, it conducted a highly sophisticated organizational analysis using this approach. Its objective was nothing less than learning how the business worked at the most fundamental level. Sears knew it needed to improve customer satisfaction, but what caused customers to be satisfied or dissatisfied? Instead of relying on the hunches, intuitions, and experiences of Sears managers, the company conducted research on itself.

Like many U.S. retailers, Sears had lost track of how important customer satisfaction is to success in this industry. When employees were asked, "What do you think is the primary thing you get paid to do here?" more than half said it was to protect the assets of the company. So it should come as no surprise that Sears was getting some of the lowest customer satisfaction ratings in the industry. In the mid-1990s, the company committed to regaining its reputation as a world-class retailer. A group of 120 top executives were organized into task forces. Their objective was to define what world-class meant—to shareholders, employees, and customers. They developed six key measures that the company could use to assess its performance and then developed a theory about what caused performance on these measures to rise and fall. Their theory viewed employee and customer attitudes as the primary causes of financial performance.

Their theory seemed reasonable, but they decided they should test it before engaging in a massive change effort based on that theory. The data they used came from the records they kept at all 820 of their full-line stores. Included were 13 financial performance measures, hundreds of thousands of employee-satisfaction data points, and millions of data points on customer satisfaction. Statistical analyses confirmed the general sequence of effects and added some more specific information. The two particular types of employee satisfaction that were predictors of how employees behaved with customers were attitudes about the job itself and attitudes about the company. These predicted customer retention and customers recommending Sears to other shoppers. Furthermore, they learned that increasing employee satisfaction by five points on their survey would translate into a two-point increase in customer satisfaction the following quarter, which in turn would improve financial performance by .5 percent. That small percentage improvement is worth millions.

Based on this analysis, Sears changed its compensation and developed a new way to get customer satisfaction data to individual employees. It also instituted town meetings for educating employees about such things as the competitive environment, how Sears compares to its competitors in ratings of customer satisfaction, and how the revenue generated by the sales employees is related to profit figures.[21]

Recently, cause-and-effect models such as the one developed by Sears have been referred to as **strategy maps**. The goal of a strategy map is to help managers understand what causes what in an organization. Most strategy maps focus on depicting the factors that determine the organization's ability to execute its strategy. For example, if a pharmaceutical company's strategic objective is growing revenues, its strategy map would probably show that revenues are determined, in part, by the ability of the firm to develop innovative drugs and marshall them through the regulatory approval process. Developing innovative drugs, in turn, requires managing an effective R&D unit, which in turn requires both skilled managers and excellent technical talent. In other words, strategy maps are one way to help managers see the connection between human resource management activities and the firm's success in meeting its strategic objectives.[22]

Employees' Opinions

Employees' opinions are another one of the many sources of information that can be useful when conducting an organizational analysis. Opinions about both problems and potential solutions can be helpful when planning for change. **Employee surveys** are one method for finding out employees' opinions. The content of the survey depends on the areas of most concern to the organization. For example, if the organization's strategy requires innovation and creativity, managers could use a survey to monitor whether employees feel that innovation and creativity are truly valued.

Opinions also can be solicited in ways that more actively engage employees in the planning process. As described in the feature "Managing Globalization: Building Global Leaders at Best Foods," employees' opinions can be more than a source of diagnostic information—they may also form the basis of a plan to address key strategic issues.[23]

INTERNET RESOURCES 5.A

Assessing the Global and Organizational Environment

At our Web site, http://jackson.swcollege.com/, you can:

1. Learn about assessment tools that can be used during organizational analysis, including

   a survey to assess the organization's climate for creativity

   a general organizational diagnosis survey

   an expert system intended to identify strategic misalignments

2. Visit the home pages of several professional organizations whose members have special expertise in the area of strategic change, including

   The Human Resource Planning Society

   The Academy of Management's Division of Organizational Change and Development

   The Tavistock Institute

   The Human Resource Institute

3. Locate articles in the *Journal of Organizational Change Management* describing recent research on the topic of strategic change.

4. Read the latest reports about labor market and economic conditions, available from The Economic Policy Institute and The Conference Board.

SPECIFYING THE OBJECTIVES FOR A CHANGE EFFORT

Successful strategic change is guided by clear objectives. The strategic objectives of a major change effort typically flow directly from discussion about corporate and business-level strategies, as described in Chapter 4. At Best Foods, the company's international growth strategy stimulated a discussion about how to ensure the company would have the global leaders it would need to succeed in the future. When Anne Mulcahy took over as CEO of Xerox, the strategic objective was to engineer a major turnaround. That was also the objective of her predecessor, but he had clearly failed after more than a year at the helm. Prior to becoming CEO, Mulcahy served as president of the company. That was when she began to communicate the strategic objectives for the turnaround. An immediate objective was cutting $1 billion in annual costs and returning the company to financial health. This meant laying off thousands of employees and closing some plants. The longer-term objective is to turn Xerox into a business services firm.

An example of how the organization's strategic objectives can set the stage for change was provided by the example of Continental Airlines, described Chapter 1. Recall that, when CEO Gordon Bethune took over beleaguered Continental Airlines, he was charged with turning around a losing operation. His battle cry was "From worst to first." Bethune realized early on that achieving the company's strategic objectives required several changes in the company's HR system. Employees were give specific, companywide goals, and incentives were offered to reward them for achieving the goals. To improve the performance of managers, employees regularly rate their managers on an employee survey. Besides improving the bottom line, the changes

"The sequence should be to figure out where you're going before you figure out how to get there."

William Byham
CEO
Development Dimensions International

MANAGING GLOBALIZATION

Building Global Leaders at Best Foods

Headquartered in Englewood Cliffs, New Jersey, Best Foods is one of the largest branded food companies in the United States. Its operations are spread across more than 60 countries and its products—which include Hellmann's mayonnaise, Mazola corn oil, Skippy peanut butter, and Thomas' English muffins—are sold in more than 110 countries. More than 60 percent of revenues currently come from markets outside the United States, and the company's projections are that future growth will come primarily from Africa, Asia, Eastern Europe, the Middle East, and the countries of the former Soviet Union.

When Best Foods learned that more than 80 percent of purchasing decisions for its products were made by women, they decided it was time to develop and promote more women into senior leadership positions within the company. To begin to address this strategic issue, the CEO worked with the Corporate Strategy Council to convene a week-long Women's Global Leadership Forum. Attended by 55 women from 25 countries, the event was an intensive work session that sought to document women's beliefs about the current situation, identify barriers to advancement, and provide suggestions for an action plan that the company could implement. To inform discussions at the forum, the company conducted a survey of its 20

corporate officers and the next 125 most senior executives. The survey results, which were presented by the CEO at his kick-off address to the forum, documented top management's perceptions of the benefits associated with having more women in leadership positions and also solicited suggestions for what the company could do to increase the number of high-ranking women leaders.

Throughout the week, global teams met to develop recommendations for how the company could begin to create change, which fell into three categories: enhancing career opportunities, increasing women's representation in senior positions, and addressing issues of work/life balance in order to enable women to perform at their highest capabilities. For each category, suggestions were made for implementation at both global and local levels within the company. Within two months, the company's Strategic Council had reviewed and approved the suggestions and launched a company-wide change effort based on the recommendations received.

In the example of Best Foods, employees' opinions were the primary method of organizational analysis as well as the basis for a large-scale plan to ensure that the company's top leadership understood and became connected to its key customer base—women around the world.

resulted in higher pay for employees, while use of sick leave, turnover rates, workers' compensation costs, and on-the-job injuries all went down.

Involving Employees

"In my experience, this is the stage at which most CEOs make their first major mistake—failing to involve enough people and build enough initial support."

David Nadler
CEO
Delta Mercer, a unit of Mercer

An important role for HR professionals during the early stages of planning for strategic change is finding ways to involve people throughout the organization. For a change effort to be effective, those who are affected must buy into it. The best way to ensure that is through early involvement.[24] It seems obvious that employees should be involved when planning change, but often even experienced managers forget this principle. Task forces, focus groups, surveys, hot lines, and informal conversations are just a few of the ways managers can involve employees and other stakeholders in planning change efforts.

To involve managers in developing plans for how to meet strategic objectives, Motorola designed coursework experiences at Motorola University, its training and development facility. Over a period of six months, 30 teams of managers spent a week each in places like Mexico City, Santiago, and São Paulo. Their assignments included interviewing customers, suppliers, and employees; holding discussions with bankers and government officials; and immersing themselves in the local culture. These experiences helped develop the managers' understanding of how the markets in these locations work, and that enabled them to think more meaningfully about possible new approaches to competing effectively in those markets.[25]

Siemens University also uses action learning to involve employees in creating change. Its in-house corporate training gives responsibility for solving real business problems to analysts and engineers from around the world, who work together in "student" teams. Students share their analyses with business units and debate the benefits and costs of their plans.

As described in the feature "Managing Change: Involving Employees at Royal Dutch/Shell," strategic change doesn't occur simply because top-level managers recognize the need for change. Grassroots involvement is required, too.[26]

Accountability

When specifying objectives, it is important to state not only what is to be achieved, but also who is responsible for making the needed changes. If the change is a success, will only managers reap the rewards? If things don't go well, will the lower-level employees be the ones who suffer most? Involvement is likely to be most effective when people also have a stake in the outcomes that result.

Holding people accountable for achieving the objectives of a change can have a variety of implications for human resource management practices. Typically, accountability translates into new approaches to awarding incentive pay and bonuses. Depending on the nature of the strategic objectives, and whether they are qualitatively different from those of the past, new performance measurement systems may be required. Procedures for deciding on future promotions may also be affected. At Best Foods, for example, the compensation system was changed as part of the HR plan to improve the representation of women in leadership positions. Senior managers were given goals for developing and retaining high-performing women, and incentive pay was linked to success in achieving the goals.

Link to Business Objectives

Strategic business objectives help focus attention on several important aspects of managing employees, including (a) the number of employees that will be needed as a consequence of anticipated growth or decline, (b) new competencies and behaviors that will be required as a consequence of aspiring to provide higher-quality customer service, and (c) higher levels of productivity needed as a consequence of identifying the reduction of operating costs as an objective. Once the strategic objectives for a change effort have been specified, the implications for HR become more clear. For example, if strategic objectives call for involvement in mergers and acquisitions, an HR objective may be to develop the competencies needed for their involvement in "soft" due diligence activities in order to assess the compatibility of potential new partners in terms of corporate culture and specific HR policies and practices. If the strategic objectives call for improving the organization's learning capacity, an HR objective may be to help the various businesses learn from each other and derive more synergies from their common membership in the larger corporate entity. If strategic objectives call for involvement in joint ventures, HR objectives may be developed for all of the activities required to staff the new organization and ensure its success.

To illustrate how strategic objectives can be translated into HR objectives for change, consider the example of United Stationers. As of 2001, this wholesaler of office products was an amalgamation of several smaller

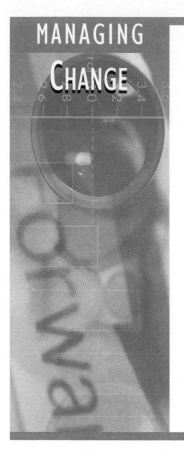

MANAGING CHANGE

Involving Employees at Royal Dutch/Shell

With 101,000 employees and $128 billion in annual revenues, Royal Dutch/Shell (known to many people simply as "Shell") is one of the largest firms in the world. Worldwide, it has more than 47,000 filling stations, which serve more that 1 million customers daily. But Shell's size couldn't protect it from the intense competition being created by European hypermarkets, new competitors throughout the world, and business customers that needed a truly global supplier.

Recognizing the need for strategic changes, Shell began a change initiative intended to transform the company. Beginning at the top, and working down, managers at each level attended workshops that explained the changes needed. Over a period of two years, the company reorganized and downsized, but more fundamental change was still needed. Although the company's leaders agreed that Shell had to move into the Internet age, they couldn't agree on how to implement that idea and so the change effort stalled.

Steve Miller, Shell's managing director, concluded that empowered employees would help the company find its way into the future. According to him, "once the folks at the grassroots find that they own the problem, they find that they also own the answer—and they improve things very quickly." One of the challenges facing Shell was figuring out how better to use its 47,000 retail outlets to boost sales of all the company's products. To begin tackling that problem, Miller set up a five-day "retailing boot camp." Cross-functional teams (e.g., a trucker, a dealer, and a marketing employee) went to the "camp" and then went home to develop a new business plan. Later they returned to camp and received feedback on their plans from their peers. After another cycle of revising their plans and getting more feedback, they went home to put their plans into action. After two more months, they returned to camp for a follow-up session that focused on what had worked, what had failed, and what they had learned. "The grassroots employees got to touch the new Shell, and participate in a give-and-take culture," Miller explained. "The energy of our employees spread to the managers above them. These frontline employees taught us to believe in ourselves again."

Miller is convinced that creating change is a bottom–up task. "As people move up, they get further away from the work that goes on in the field—and as a result they tend to devalue it. People get caught up in broad strategic issues, legal issues, stakeholder issues. But what really drives the business is the work that gets done down at the coalface [the frontline]."

companies that were put together in the prior decade. Its customers include Staples, Office Depot, and thousands of distributors throughout the United States. In 1998, it set a strategic objective of growing revenues from $2.3 billion to $6 billion. To achieve that objective, top management concluded it needed to make substantial changes in the organization's structure, from one based on departments to one based on products. As it turned out, for this company, changing the structure really meant clarifying who was accountable for what and helping people see how they fit into the big picture. Thus, clarifying managerial accountability and addressing employees' desire for a clear picture of their role in the company became key HR objectives.[27]

INTERNET RESOURCES   5.B

Specifying the Objectives for a Change Effort

At our Web site, http://jackson.swcollege.com/, you can:

1. Learn more about benchmarking and how it can be used to guide strategic change efforts.

2. Read more about the balanced scorecard and its usefulness as a strategic planning tool.

DEVELOPING THE HR PLAN, MEASUREMENTS, AND TIMETABLES

A plan is the blueprint for action. For major change efforts, the strategic plan for the organization as a whole can be quite complex because it includes plans for all levels and all units involved in the change effort. If an organization is structured along functional departments, then each department develops a strategic plan; if it is organized by region, then plans for each region are developed, and so on. Thus, depending on the specific circumstances, the human resources component of the strategic plan may be prepared as a plan for the functional area of human resources management, or HR issues may be addressed within the strategic plan for the entire division. Regardless of how the HR plan is structured, its development begins with a full consideration of alternatives. After evaluating the pros and cons associated with different alternatives, choices are made about which HR activities and policies will change. This part of the planning process also includes identifying the HR measurements that will be used to track the effects of the company's change efforts.

Considering Alternatives

For almost any set of objectives, the list of alternative ways to achieve it is likely to be long and varied. For example, some of the alternatives available to employers who face a shortage of skilled workers are listed in Exhibit 5.6.

> **FAST FACT**
>
> Interest in benchmarking against Walt Disney World in Orlando, Florida, is so strong that Disney created the Disney Institute, which offers seminars such as "The Walt Disney Approach to HR Management" to interested professionals.

As Exhibit 5.6 reveals, most alternatives have both potential advantages and potential disadvantages. Solutions that might work in the short term may create new problems in the long term. Solutions that might work in the long term may do little to address short-term needs. Similarly, different alternatives have different advantages. Some alternatives contribute by lowering costs, while others contribute more by increasing skill levels. For

ex 5.6 Alternatives to Coping with Labor Shortages

Possible Solution to a Labor Shortage	Possible Negative Consequences
• Raise base wages to attract more applicants	• May attract more applicants, but new applicants may not be any more qualified. Recruiting costs per hire go up as number of applicants to be screened goes up.
• Offer more financial incentives in an effort to motivate employees to boost their productivity	• If productivity increases don't keep up with increased labor costs, margins will shrink unless consumers are willing to pay higher prices.
• Reduce turnover rates to lessen the need for new hires	• May drive up labor costs if wages tend to increase with time at the company. Too little turnover may stifle creativity. Skills obsolescence may become a problem.
• Hire people without the skills needed and train them	• Productivity of new hires is low. Increased supervision of new workers is required, which raises costs. Can be costly, takes time, and workers once trained, may leave to work for competitors.
• Buy up other companies to acquire their workforce	• The challenge of integrating the acquired company may cause productivity declines in the short term. Success rates for mergers and acquisitions are only about 50 percent.
• Buy new technologies that reduce the number of people needed	• Major changes in technology require major organizational changes, which take time. New technologies may require even higher levels of skill to operate.
• Utilize foreign labor markets	• The organization learning curve is steep for domestic firms with no prior international experience. Competition for labor in the global market may be just as stiff as in the domestic market.
• Make business decisions that will reduce the need for more skilled workers	• May be possible, but would probably involve major changes in strategy and even changing the businesses in which the company competes.

example, retaining current workers is an excellent way to reduce costs. According to a study of over 200 companies, conducted by consulting firm William M. Mercer, turnover costs reach $40,000 per person for 10 percent of all vacancies when you take into account lost productivity due to the vacancy, search fees, management time used to interview, and training costs. For 30 percent of all vacancies, the costs range between $10,000 and $40,000.[28] For highly technical work in fields that change rapidly, however, the skills of new college graduates may be much more current than those of current employees.

When developing the HR plan, consider all possible alternatives, along with the pros and cons. Major issues usually require multipronged solutions. All chosen solutions cannot usually be implemented en masse, however, so priorities must be decided upon, taking into account both short- and long-term needs. Nevertheless, a comprehensive HR plan for change is likely to have many components, just as a companywide plan for change has many components. To illustrate what some of the components of an HR plan might be, we briefly describe examples for the HR activities of staffing, training, leadership development, and managing benefits.

FAST FACT

Service Marine Industries, a shipbuilding company, offers $50 just for qualified applicants to show up and take a craft test.

Staffing Plans

FAST FACT

According to Alan Blinder, former vice chairman of the Federal Reserve Board, economists generally agree that most recessions last 9 to 11 months.

The plans for staffing arise out of forecasts about future labor demand and supply. Earlier in this chapter, we described how domestic labor shortages and the age demographics within an organization may make staffing the organization a strategic issue. For growing businesses, HR objectives often focus on ensuring that new people are available to support the projected growth. For businesses undergoing global expansion, the HR plan may include developing new approaches to evaluating the ability of new hires and current employees to work in multicultural settings and their effectiveness in working on projects completed in virtual teams.

For businesses undergoing a turnaround, such as Xerox, strategic objectives for HR often include identifying where to cut staff levels, reducing staff levels without demotivating those who remain, and restaffing the organization with people who have the new skills that are needed for the future. Alternatively, instead of cutting staff, the organization may choose to reduce pay, offer sabbatical leaves, or in other ways reduce labor costs without eliminating jobs. Because managing layoffs and the process of downsizing is so important, Chapter 7 provides more details about how to plan for these strategic events.[29]

FAST FACT

Prior to being named CEO of Xerox, Anne Mulcahy served as VP of human resources, chief of staff, and president.

Forecasting human resource demand and supply is essential for succession planning and the development of replacement charts. The objective of **succession planning** is to ensure that the organization is prepared to fill key positions when the current incumbents leave, for whatever reason. For employees, succession planning provides useful information about the direction their career is likely to take if they continue to work in the organization. Succession planning for CEOs often receives attention in the business press, because staffing for this position is so important to shareholders. Sometimes a company's succession plan for the CEO slot is quite public. Up to a year prior to the CEO's planned retirement, a successor may be named so that there is no uncertainty about the company's plans. Or, several possible successors may be identified, with the understanding that their performance will be closely monitored during the next year and used as a basis for making a final decision when the CEO steps down. Although less public, many organizations conduct similar succession planning for all executive positions and some also engage in succession planning for all managerial positions.

Succession plans may be formalized by tracking talent pools and preparing replacement charts. A **talent pool** refers to a list of employees who have been identified as having high potential for advancement—usually because they are top performers in their current positions. The employees in a talent pool are the people that the organization is especially interested in retaining and developing. Ensuring that employees in the talent pool are considered when job openings occur is one tactic for successful long-term staffing of the organization. A replacement chart is one tool that organizations use to keep track of opportunities for people in the talent pool. In a **replacement chart**, the titles of key jobs in the organization are displayed along with the names of current incumbents. Also included are the names of current employees who might be used to fill potential vacancies—that is, the most appropriate employees from the talent pool. Besides serving the career objectives of employees in the talent pool. Replacement charts also alert the organization to possible areas of vulnerability in the event of an unexpected departure.

Training Plans

At United Stationers, the HR objectives of clarifying managerial accountability and helping employees see how they fit into the big picture led to HR plans that emphasized training activities. To help managers perform in their new roles, the HR group developed a leadership framework and offered to train interested managers (note that it was up to managers to decide whether or not to receive training in the leadership framework). To help employees see how they fit into the picture, HR professionals worked with line managers to develop business awareness training modules for employees. HR experts made sure the training modules met professional quality standards, but line managers were responsible for the actual business content and for delivering the training to employees.

Leadership Development Plans

At Weyerhaeuser, the HR plan for creating strategic change emphasized leadership development activities. Leadership development activities also are likely to be important for firms whose strategic objectives include adopting a truly transnational organizational structure.[30] As organizations globalize, meeting the leadership challenge is often a top priority. In addition to answering the question of who will be available for the senior leadership roles, HR plans should provide a means to ensure that the available people have the competencies required to do the work. Exhibit 5.7 illustrates some of the different skills needed by international and transnational managers. As Exhibit 5.7 suggests, managers who competently perform traditional international roles can do so without having developed the skills needed in a transnational organization.

Because transnational organizations are a relatively recent development, there are few managers in the world with fully developed transnational skills. Even if an organization is prepared to pay any price to hire

ex 5.7 Examples of Differing Skill Levels Needed by International and Transnational Managers

Skill	International Managers	Transnational Managers
Global Perspective	• Understand a single foreign country and manage relationships between headquarters and that country.	• Understand worldwide business and manage relationships among parts located in dozens of countries.
Synergistic Learning	• Work with and coach people in each foreign culture separately or sequentially.	• Work with and facilitate learning among people from many cultures simultaneously.
Collaboration	• Interact within clearly defined hierarchies of structural and cultural dominance.	• Interact with all foreigners as equals and facilitate the same behavior in others.
Career Perspective	• Expatriation and repatriation occurs primarily to get a specific job done.	• Transpatriation experiences are accepted in anticipation of long-term career and organizational development.
Cross-cultural Interaction	• Use cross-cultural skills primarily on foreign assignments.	• Use cross-cultural skills on a daily basis throughout one's career.

such managers, it will not be able to find them. They have to be grown by the organization and then retained long enough to reap the rewards of a long-term investment. According to one study of 1,500 executives in 50 different transnational companies, the degree to which the human resource system is transnational lags far behind that of the other systems. For example, on average, these firms generated 40 percent of their business from other countries, yet only 8 percent of their top 100 executives were from other countries. Furthermore, only one-third of the executives in the study reported having any expatriate experience and less than 20 percent spoke a second language. Clearly, to begin developing their talent pool of the future, these firms must develop new practices to encourage and support the development of transnational leaders.[31]

Plans for Changes in Benefits

For organizations that are growing as well as those that need to reduce costs or downsize, HR plans for creating strategic change often include changes in employee benefits. As will be described in Chapter 7, offering an attractive benefits packages is one way to attract top talent, so growing firms may want to upgrade the benefits they offer. When AT&T set as its objective eliminating 10,000 jobs, the HR staff designed a retirement incentive program to encourage people to leave voluntarily. Qualified employees were offered more liberal retiree health care benefits, pension incentives, and even financial assistance in making career changes. People who left to start up their own business were eligible for $10,000 in start-up funds.[32]

Measuring Progress

FAST FACT

Hard, specific goals provide both clarity and motivation.

Effective change efforts have a clear link to the business strategy. Recall the example of GE Medical Systems, described in Chapter 4. The firm had developed a new approach to recruiting in response to its need for more technical workers. It needed workers with skills that precisely matched the type of work that would be done for the specific new products being developed. Because the company is always innovating, it was important to have very specific recruiting goals. And because cost considerations were also important, new approaches to measuring the effectiveness of the new approach were important. In order to achieve its staffing goals, the firm would need to work with only the most talented suppliers.

Recruitment Yield Rates. To judge the efficiency of professional recruiters, GE calculated "first-pass" and "second-pass" yield figures. First-pass yield refers to the percentage of resumes submitted that lead to interviews. Second-pass yield is the percentage of interviews that result in offers. To improve recruiters' performance, GE provided feedback on why it didn't choose to hire someone it interviewed. It also offered bonuses to the most productive recruiters.

Offer Acceptance Rates. GE assessed the effectiveness of its intern program by examining the hiring rates for interns compared with other job applicants. It found that summer interns were twice as likely to accept a job offer as other applicants, so hiring interns was an efficient recruiting method. To get more interns, procedures were developed for interns to assess their bosses. The company weeded out bosses who used interns for menial tasks like photocopying and put managers in a position of having to earn good evaluations from past interns in order to be able to get more interns in the future.

When goals related to recruiting and hiring are established, measures that might be used to assess progress toward goals can include the number of minimally qualified applicants who apply for jobs, the skill levels of applicants, the length of time needed to fill vacancies, yield rates such as those used by GE Medical, turnover rates for employees who have been with the company less than a year, and so on. Such measures can generally be created and tracked with ease.

> **FAST FACT**
>
> Of the *Fortune* Most Admired companies, 40% monitor retention, career development and other employee-oriented measures—more than triple the percentage of companies that didn't make the list.

Customer Satisfaction. In many companies, change efforts are stimulated by the company's design to better satisfy customers. A study by The Conference Board found that the customer-driven changes were common in the manufacturing and service sectors. Exhibit 5.8 summarizes some of the findings from that study.[33] For the goals listed, how would *you* measure the organization's progress?

Intangibles. If an HR objective is to create a learning organization, developing measures to gauge progress can be particularly challenging. Intangible assets, such as knowledge and learning, account for a large part of a company's value. Yet traditional performance indicators provide little to guide investment in knowledge and learning. Recognizing the importance of measuring organizational learning, Leif Edvinsson developed a management model at Swedish financial services group Skandia built around the concept of intellectual capital. Consultants now offer help to companies that wish to monitor their progress toward achieving the goal of building knowledge resources and learning capabilities.

To judge improvement, an organization needs to know where it was before and where it is now. Measurement tools make assessing improvement possible. Once developed, measures of progress toward goals can become an important element of new approaches to managing human resources. In learning organizations, employees have access to data about customer

> *"In the end, a customer centric culture sustains itself during times of great change. What we must have . . . is a core competence in reinventing ourselves as the needs of our customers change in the marketplace."*
>
> Dawn Gould Lepore
> Vice Chairman & Chief Information Officer
> Charles Schwab

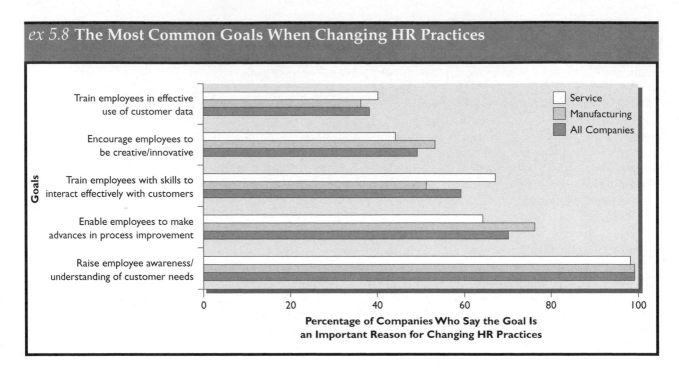

ex 5.8 **The Most Common Goals When Changing HR Practices**

satisfaction, profits and losses, market share, employee commitment, and competitors' strategies, among other things. Data are gathered, monitored, disseminated, and used throughout the organization.

Timetables

In the early 1990s, L.L. Bean began a major change effort to improve customer service. After he had five years of experience under his belt, the senior vice president of operations was asked, "If you had to start your reengineering all over again, what would you do differently?" His reply: "We would specify a time limit on when we needed an end result. We should have set specific dates for individuals and departments to make the changes."[34]

Change is tough work that often involves making difficult and sometimes painful decisions. If people can put it off, they will. Building in deadlines and scheduled check points into the change process is one way to keep the process moving ahead. The challenge is to set deadlines that are challenging but achievable. Realistic expectations about how quickly change will occur are important to the long-term success of change efforts. Changes designed to help employees balance their work and nonwork commitments might be effective within only a year or two. More fundamental changes can require much longer. Usually even changes that seem relatively simple occur more slowly than expected. Xerox began changing its culture to be more receptive of diversity more than 30 years ago and continues to do so. It is doubtful that managers anticipated how long their companies' change efforts would continue to evolve.

When a computer manufacturing company that produced leading-edge specialty products for business decided to change its strategy to include the consumer market, it knew it would also need managers with a different set of skills. The company estimated it would need five years to build the talent pool. The first year was spent analyzing the environment, developing a model of the skills that would be needed, and developing a strategy for building the talent pool. The initiatives taken during the next four years included

- assessing their current managers to determine who had the skills needed for the new business strategy,
- training managers on the meaning of the new strategy,
- externally recruiting new managers with the needed skills, and
- meeting quarterly with senior executives to keep them informed of progress.

In addition, as these planned initiatives were rolled out, it became clear that changes were needed in most other aspects of the HR system, including a variety of additional training programs, the organizational structure, and the compensation system.[35]

INTERNET RESOURCES   5.C

Developing the HR Plan, Measurements, and Timetable

At our Web site, http://jackson.swcollege.com/, you can:

1. Discover resources available from The Conference Board related to HR planning activities during mergers and acquisitions.

2. See examples of HR metrics that can be used to assess the effectiveness of strategic change efforts.

3. Read the international code of ethics for professionals who assist organizations in planning and implementing change.

IMPLEMENTING THE PLANS FOR STRATEGIC CHANGE

The focus so far has been on developing a plan. Eventually, the time comes to move from planning to action. We turn next to issues that arise when plans are taken out of the drafting room and into the offices and plants where people do their work.

> **FAST FACT**
>
> A study of how Russians and Westerners view planning in organizations revealed that Russians tend to view plans as something that must be executed as initially designed while Westerners view plans as needing continuous adjustments.

The Change Has Already Started

If the people who are responsible for drawing up the blueprint for strategic change efforts have followed the principle of involvement, the implementation stage is actually already well under way by the time the plans have been fully developed. People already have a good grasp of the vision—they had to understand it in order to be involved in the planning process. Although a leadership team may have been responsible for getting the plan put together, many details (goals, timetables) were developed using substantial input from the people who will be expected to implement the plan. If honest two-way communication has occurred throughout the planning process, major obstacles to implementing change have already been identified and removed. If empowered employees have been energized by the challenges identified, some are already experimenting with new approaches to their work. To the extent this is true, problems of resistance—the major barrier to implementing change—will be lessened. Even in the best of circumstances, however, pockets of resistance will be found.

Resistance to Change

Few planned organizational change efforts proceed smoothly. Most run into some amount of resistance. The various forms that resistance can take include immediate criticism, malicious compliance, sabotage, insincere agreement, silence, deflection, and in-your-face defiance.[36] The reasons for such resistance include fear, misunderstandings, and cynicism.[37]

Fear. Some people resist change because they fear that they'll be unable to develop the competencies required to be effective in the new situation. When Mercedes-Benz Credit Corporation set out to restructure its operations in the United States, employees seemed to have good reason to be fearful of the future. Weren't layoffs sure to follow? The company's president, Georg Bauer, knew that fear could be a problem and would make getting needed help from employees difficult. "It was absolutely essential to establish a no-fear element in this whole change process," he said. Rather than resist change, he wanted employees to help create a new, more efficient organization by expressing their ideas about where to cut and how to do work differently. Besides empowering employees to make decisions about how to change their work, he offered an incentive to convince employees that even cutting their own jobs wouldn't harm them financially.[39]

Misunderstandings. People resist change when they don't understand its implications. Unless quickly addressed, misunderstandings and lack of trust build resistance. Top managers must be visible during the change process to spell out clearly the new direction for the organization and what it will mean for everyone involved. Getting employees to discuss their problems openly is crucial to overcoming resistance to change.[40]

When wide-ranging changes are planned, managers should anticipate that misunderstandings will develop and take steps to minimize them. At Prudential Insurance, a specially designed game was used to help employees understand the implications of the company's impending change from a mutual association to a public company. Small groups of employees at all levels and in all types of jobs throughout the company were brought together to play the game, which was both informative and fun. Top management was convinced that this approach to informing the workforce about the implications of the change they were about to experience would enable the change process to go smoothly—and it did.

Cynicism. In some organizations, initiating change efforts is seen simply as something that new managers do to make their mark.[41] Over time, employees see change efforts come and go much like the seasons of the year, as managers implement one fad after the other. Eventually, cynicism sets in and employees refuse to support yet another change "program." Without employee support the change efforts fail, which further contributes to cynicism.[42] Cynicism is difficult to combat, once it sets in. Perhaps the best approach is to prevent it from developing by avoiding the temptation to always adopt the latest management fad. Organizations that take a strategic and systematic approach to developing and implementing change efforts are less likely to initiate a change effort simply because it is the latest new craze.

Creating Readiness for Change

Perhaps the best approach to reducing resistance to change is to create readiness for change—even before the decision to undertake a specific change has been made. Of course, that takes great forethought and planning! For organizations that anticipate the need for eventual change, taking steps to enhance organizational readiness for change is a wise investment. Exhibit 5.9 describes several actions that managers should take in order to create an organization that is in a continual state of readiness.[43]

INTERNET RESOURCES 5.D

Implementing Change Plans and Managing Resistance

At our Web site, http://jackson.swcollege.com/, you can:

1. Study the competencies needed by professionals who specialize in organizational change.

2. Assess whether you might benefit by attending a program designed to help managers and executives assess their strategic leadership strengths and weaknesses.

---

ex 5.9 Guidelines for Creating Organizational Readiness for Change

Develop a Pro-Learning Orientation Among Employees

- Provide frequent opportunities for employees to take responsibility for problem identification and problem solving.
- Develop open communication channels and ensure that they are used frequently to inform employees of organizational successes and failures.
- Do everything possible to keep employees informed of customers' preferences and the evaluations of the services and products offered by the organization.
- Encourage small-scale experimentation to produce solutions to emerging problems before large-scale solutions are needed.

Develop a Resilient Workforce

- Use resilience-to-change as a basis for hiring and promotion decisions.
- Educate the workforce about the fundamentals of organizational change processes.
- Train employees to understand the symptoms and causes of resistance and cynicism, and train managers in effective means for reducing resistance and cynicism.
- Celebrate successful change efforts—large and small—to build confidence in the organization's capacity for change.

Build the Architecture to Support Change Initiatives

- Develop a means for recording lessons learned from change efforts and ensuring these lessons are used to guide future change efforts.
- Train managers in structured approaches to change rather than allowing them to rely on their intuition and instincts.
- Create opportunities for employees to work in cross-functional teams as a means of developing the teamwork and communication competencies often needed for large-scale change efforts.
- Identify key measures that can be used to regularly measure organizational performance. Regularly assess the organization against these measures to establish a baseline against which future change can be assessed.

REVIEW, REVISE, AND REFOCUS

When a company offers a product to the external marketplace, it almost certainly reviews and evaluates the success of that product using objective indicators. Likewise, the success of products and services offered in the company's internal marketplace should be monitored. At this point, the measures developed to track the progress of change efforts come into play. The measures define the criteria for evaluating whether a program or initiative is successful or needs revision. For example, if personal self-development is the only goal one hopes to achieve from holding diversity awareness workshops, then asking employees whether the workshop experience was valuable may be the only data that should be collected. However, when large investments are made for the purposes of reducing turnover, attracting new or different employees to the firm, or improving team functioning, or all three, then data relevant to these objectives should be examined.

A human resource information management (HRIM) system facilitates evaluation by allowing for more thorough, rapid, and frequent collection and dissemination of data. Based on what is learned, people can make informed decisions about whether to stay the course as planned, or revisit and perhaps revise the original plan. Overall objectives for the change effort are not likely to be changed at this point, but new goals might be added and timetables might be adjusted.

Change expert John Kotter believes that change can be facilitated by virtually guaranteeing that the review and evaluation process produces some positive results, which can then be used as a cause for celebration. He calls these "short-term wins." The slowness of change can be demotivating. After several months of all-out effort, employees will almost certainly be asked to rededicate themselves for another several months of effort. Without some evidence that the new ways of doing things are paying off, too many people may give up and join the ranks of the resisters. Rather than leave to chance the question of whether there will be anything to celebrate after a year or two of effort, Kotter suggests specifically assigning a few excellent people to the task of creating a short-term win. And when they meet the challenge, be sure to involve everyone in the celebration.[44]

Whether or not the evaluation of progress against goals is accompanied by celebration, pausing to reflect on the process is an essential part of any effective change. This ensures the change process will be self-correcting and should prevent most misjudgments made during planning from turning into major fiascoes.

Working together, managers and HR professionals can prepare their organizations for successful organizational change by following these guidelines prior to initiating a change effort. The objective should be to ensure that the organization maintains a state of readiness for change so that it can move quickly and effectively when major changes are needed and then learn from its experiences. Like all other activities involved in successful organizational change, developing a state of organizational readiness requires collaboration. The many opportunities for collaboration among line managers, HR professionals, and employees during planning and change processes are described in "The HR Triad: Roles and Responsibilities for HR Planning and Strategic Change."

"Most companies go to great lengths to avoid any kind of change. For them, change is like a snakebite—one hit and they're paralyzed. For MCI, change has always meant new opportunities."

Gerald H. Taylor
CEO
MCI Communications Corp.[38]

Roles and Responsibilities for HR Planning and Strategic Change

THE HR TRIAD

LINE MANAGERS	HR PROFESSIONALS	EMPLOYEES
• Learn about effective change processes and act as a role model for effective learning and change. • In the early phases of planned change, participate by providing information about the current environment and forecasting labor needs. • Participate in the process of generating and evaluating alternative approaches to change. • Share information with and involve HR professionals during development of change objectives and business plans, measures, and timetables for change. • Collaborate in the collection and interpretation of data to assess progress toward HR objectives. • Communicate constantly with employees concerning planned changes using formal and informal means.	• Serve as the facilitator of change; help line managers and other employees develop an enhanced capacity for leading and accepting change. • Manage the organization's HR planning activities, including forecasting labor needs and supplies, and identifying the HR implications of planned strategic changes. • Facilitate discussions about and evaluations of alternative approaches to change. • Develop detailed HR change objectives, plans, measures, and timetables for strategic change. • Develop, collect, and analyze measures to assess progress toward HR objectives. • Work with line managers to develop and disseminate formal communications about planned changes in HR activities; respond promptly and candidly to questions about planned changes in HR activities.	• Recognize that change is constant and develop a personal capacity for frequent change. • Provide input during the early phases of planning for change as needed. • Participate in the process of generating and evaluating alternative approaches to change. • Provide input during the development of HR plans, measures, and timetables. • Collaborate in the collection and interpretation of data to assess progress toward HR objectives. • Take personal responsibility for ensuring own understanding of planned changes and their implications.

SUMMARY

The dynamic global environment often creates the need for strategic change in organizations. In order to achieve their strategic objectives, organizations may need to focus on a new vision, restructure their operations, expand, downsize, or otherwise transform who they are and what they do. As managers realize that a capability for successful change and continuous learning is a sustainable competitive advantage, employees are being asked to expect and accept continual change as part of their normal work situation.

Because strategic changes always affect the people in an organization, the process of planning for strategic changes should always incorporate human resource planning. Human resource planning refers to the efforts of firms to identify and respond to the short- and long-term human resource implications of a company's strategic business objectives created by the changing environment. The several phases of HR planning are depicted linearly in Exhibit 5.3, although change is seldom a linear experience. The HR planning phases include assessing the global and organizational environment, specifying HR objectives for change, and developing specific HR plans, with measurements and timetables. A comprehensive HR plan for strategic change is likely to address a variety of HR activities, including staffing, training, leadership development, benefits, and so on.

Significant change almost always involves unforeseeable sources of resistance and unintended consequences. Although these cannot be avoided, their detrimental effect can be minimized by involving the entire organization in planning for and evaluating the change process. Managers and other employees who will be affected by strategic changes should be involved in developing the plan for change and in monitoring the outcomes of changes made. Monitoring key indicators of success throughout the change process makes it possible for an organization to quickly detect when corrective action is needed, as well as detect when key milestones have been reached and can be celebrated.

Effective HR planning and change improve the ability of organizations to satisfy customers while also addressing the concerns of other stakeholders. HR planning and change, in turn, requires an understanding of specific HR practices and their impact on employees. By studying the remaining chapters, you will begin to gain the insight and understanding required to design and implement an HR system that is appropriate for an organization's specific strategic objectives and change initiatives.

TERMS TO REMEMBER

Anticipatory change	Organizational analysis
Behavioral cause-and-effect models	Radical change
Employee surveys	Reactive change
HR forecasts	Replacement chart
HR objectives	Statistical forecasting methods
HR plans	Strategic change
Human resource planning	Strategy maps
Incremental change	Succession planning
Judgmental forecasting methods	Talent pool

DISCUSSION QUESTIONS

1. Review Chapters 2 through 4, which describe several aspects of the global and organizational environment. Which aspects of the environment are more likely to lead to incremental vs. radical change? Is strategic change more likely to be incremental or radical? Explain.

2. A thorough approach to planning for change can take a great deal of time. When time is short, which steps in the planning process can be eliminated most readily? What are the potential risks of skipping these steps? Explain your logic.

3. Describe one of your own experiences with strategic change in an organization. Which HR policies and practices in the organization were affected by the change effort? Were these effects on HR policies and practices part of the initial plan? Why or why not?

4. Imagine you are the HR director of a large energy company like Royal Dutch/Shell. Projections of future demand for the company's products indicate the company should continue to expand for at least the next decade, but there is also evidence to suggest that young people around the world have a negative image of large oil companies and view them

as undesirable employers. Describe how you would go about developing a long-term plan to address this strategic issue. Who would you involve in developing the plan, and why?

5. Throughout your career you will often be expected to lead and facilitate radical change initiatives. What can you personally do now to become better prepared to be an effective change leader and facilitator?

PROJECTS TO EXTEND YOUR LEARNING

1. *Managing Globalization.* As domestic companies begin to expand overseas, they face many new challenges. Among these is deciding how to compensate the people who fill top-level management positions in the global operations. Two basic alternatives are (a) pay managers by matching the compensation of local executives in the non-U.S. locations, or (b) pay managers by matching the compensation of their U.S. counterparts. What are the pros and cons of each alternative? What HR objectives might best be achieved by each approach? Choose one approach to this strategic issue. Assume your company adopted this approach a year ago when it opened a new facility in France. Now it is time to evaluate whether the approach that was selected was the right choice. Describe how you would evaluate the effectiveness of the company's approach to managerial compensation. What would you measure to assess whether there were any unexpected negative consequences associated with the company's compensation approach?

2. *Managing Diversity.* Imagine you were recently appointed to a task force charged with conducting a benchmarking study to identify state-of-the art approaches to leveraging diversity to enhance your organization's performance. The CEO has asked the task force to prepare a report describing how HR practices are being used to leverage diversity in at least five outstanding companies. Identify the companies that you would recommend for participation in the benchmarking study. Then, focusing on the issue of how to plan *and* implement change, prepare a list of questions that you would seek to answer as part of the benchmarking study.

3. *Integration and Application.* Lincoln Electric has had experience with operating overseas, but it has not always been positive. Nevertheless, it realizes that survival depends on learning to operate effectively in a global environment. Imagine you are a member of the planning committee that has been charged with setting up operations in Shanghai. The company has decided to build a new plant and staff it entirely with local nationals. Develop a strategic plan complete with goals and timetables for the staffing process.

MANAGING STRATEGIC CHANGE AT CISCO SYSTEMS

After 40 quarters of sales, earnings growth, and stock market acceptance (market capitalization), the roof came down on Cisco! Of course it came down on virtually all technology companies, beginning in the third quarter of 2000 and continuing throughout 2001. During this time, neither the Federal Reserve nor the politicians in Washington were able to do anything to significantly change the direction of the stock markets and the success of companies that were once the "high fliers" of the economy.

With no apparent end in sight, CEO John Chambers announced that the earnings projections for 2001 were far too optimistic. Orders from the telecommunications companies were dropping fast, with no visible signs of a turnaround. Market analysts used the term "poor visibility" to describe the future of the economy and the future of high-tech companies in particular. "This may be the fastest any industry our size has ever decelerated," Chambers observed. Chambers compared the slowdown to a 100-year flood. "We never built models to anticipate something of this magnitude," he said.

Before the downturn, Cisco had grown to more than 30,000 employees, after doubling in only three years' time. Suddenly, the strategic business objective changed from "maintain high levels of growth in highly competitive environments," to "reduce costs and hope to survive." Although a cause of the economic slowdown appeared to have been excess inventory buildup and excess production capacity, it wasn't clear to Chambers and others just how long a correction and recovery would take. Therefore, it wasn't clear if costs would need to be reduced for one year, two years, etc.

QUESTIONS

1. What type of change was Cisco facing—radical or incremental? Reactive or anticipatory?
2. Refer to Exhibit 5.3. Assume you are Barbara Beck, Cisco's senior VP of human resources. Chambers has invited you and the other top executives to a three-day strategic planning retreat. What information about the global and organization environment should you collect in anticipation of the meeting? Why?
3. Suppose the business forecast predicted that the economy was likely to languish for at least a year, and perhaps longer. State two or three strategic objectives that Cisco's executives would probably focus on during this strategic planning retreat. What HR objectives might be associated with each strategic objective?
4. How might the business objectives and HR objectives be different if the forecast was for an economic turnaround to occur within four to six months?

case study

ENDNOTES

1 M. Mercer, *Absolutely Fabulous Organizational Change: Strategies for Success from America's Best-Run Companies* (New York: Castlegate Publishers, 2000).

2 A. Rosenthal, "Champion of Change," *Human Resource Executive* (June 18, 1999): 75–77.

3 M. Beer and N. Nohria, "Cracking the Code of Change," *Harvard Business Review* (May–June 2000): 133–141; for reviews of the academic literature on managing change, see A. Armenakis and A. Bedeian, "Organizational Change: A Review of Theory and Research in the 1990s," *Journal of Management* 25 (1999): 293–315; K. E. Weick and R. E. Quinn, "Organizational Change and Development," *Annual Review of Psychology* 50 (1999): 361–386.

4 C. Fishman, "Creative Tension," *Fast Company* (November 2000): 358–388; D. Rousseau and S. Tijoriwala, "What's a Good Reason to Change? Motivated Reasoning and Social Accounts in Promoting Organizational Change," *Journal of Applied Psychology* 84(4) (1999): 514–528.

5 Radical change is also referred to as discontinuous or fundamental change, retrofit, transformation, change and reinvention. Incremental change is also referred to as evolutionary change. See D. A. Nadler and

M. B. Nadler, *Champions of Change: How CEOs and Their Companies Are Mastering the Skills of Radical Change* (San Francisco: Jossey-Bass, 1998); K. E. Weick and R. E. Quinn, "Organizational Change and Development."

6 M. Beer and N. Nohria, *Breaking the Code of Change* (Boston: Harvard Business School Press, 2000); R. A. Johnson, "Antecedents and Outcomes of Corporate Refocusing," *Journal of Management* 22 (1996): 439–483.

7 J. Kerstetter, "Silicon Seer," *Business Week* (August 27, 2001): 112.

8 P. McGeehan, "Schwab Tells Some Workers to Stay Home," *New York Times* (January 31, 2001): C1–C2; A. Bernstein, "The Human Factor," *Business Week* (August 27, 2001): 118–122.

9 V. Wayhan and S. Werner, "The Impact of Workforce Reductions on Financial Performance: A Longitudinal Perspective," *Journal of Management* 26(2) (2000): 341–363.

10 A. Van De Ven, H. Angle, and M. S. Poole, *Research on the Management Innovation* (New York: Oxford University Press, 2000); Y-T. Cheng and A. H. Van de Ven, "Learning the Innovation Journey: Order Out of Chaos," *Organization Science* 7 (1996): 593–614.

11 M. S. Poole, A. Van De Ven, K. Dooley, and M. Holmes, *Organizational Change Processes* (New York: Oxford University Press, 2000); M. L. Tushman and C. A. O'Reilly III, *A Practical Guide to Leading Organizational Change and Renewal* (Boston: Harvard Business School Press, 1997); A. H. Van de Ven and M. S. Poole, "Explaining Development and Change in Organizations" *Academy of Management Review* 20 (1996): 510–540; P. J. Robertson, D. R. Roberts, and J. I. Porras, "Dynamics of Planned Change: Assessing Empirical Support for a Theoretical Model," *Academy of Management Journal* 36 (1993): 619–634.

12 J. A. Schmidt, "The Correct Spelling of M&A Begins with HR," *HR Magazine* (June 2001): 102–108; J. Birkinshaw, H. Bresman, and L. Hakanson, "Managing the Post-Acquisition Integration Process: How the Human Integration and Task Integration Processes Interact to Foster Value Creation," *Journal of Management Studies* 37 (2000): 395–425; M. L. Marks and P. H. Mirvis, "Making Mergers and Acquisitions Work: Strategic and Psychological Preparation," *Academy of Management Executive* 15(2) (2000): 80–92.

13 R. S. Schuler, S. E. Jackson, and J. Storey, "HRM and Its Link with Strategic Management," in J. Storey (ed.), *Human Resource Management: A Critical Text* (London: Blackwell, 2001): 137–159; A. Armenakis and A. Bedeian, "Organizational Change: A Review of Theory and Research in the 1990s," *Journal of Management* 25(3) (1999): 293–315; J. W. Walker, "The Ultimate Human Resource Planning: Integrating the Human Resource Function with the Business," in G. R. Ferris (ed.), *Handbook of Human Resource Management* (Oxford, England: Blackwell, 1995); B. J. Smith, J. W. Boroski, and G. E. Davis, "Human Resource Planning," *Human Resource Management* (Spring–Summer 1992): 81–94; M. London, E. S. Bassman, and J. P. Fernandez (ed.), *Human Resource Forecasting and Strategy Development: Guidelines for Analyzing and Fulfilling Organizational Needs* (Westport, CT: Quorum Books, 1990); E. H. Burack, "Linking Corporate Business and Human Resource Planning: Strategic Issues and Concerns," *Human Resource Planning* 8 (1985): 133–146; D. Ulrich, "Strategic Human Resource Planning," in R. S. Schuler, S. A. Youngblood, and V. L. Huber (ed.), *Readings in Personnel and Human Resource Management*, 3rd ed. (St. Paul: West, 1988): 57–71.

14 M. Mercer, *Absolutely Fabulous Organizational Change*; M. S. Poole, A. H. Van De Ven, K. Dooley and M. Holmes, *Organizational Change Process*; R. S. Schuler and J. W. Walker, "Human Resources Strategy: Focusing on Issues and Actions," *Organizational Dynamics* (Summer 1990): 5–19; G. T. Milkovich, L. Dyer, and T. M. Mahoney, "The State of Practice and Research in Human Resource Planning," in S. J. Carroll and R. S. Schuler (eds.), *Human Resource Management in the 1980s* (Washington, DC: Bureau of National Affairs, 1983).

15 Adapted from S. E. Jackson and R. S. Schuler, "Human Resource Planning: Challenges for I/O Psychologists," *American Psychologist* (February 1990): 223–239.

16 M. Beer and N. Nohria, "Cracking the Code of Change"; S. B. Bacharach, P. Bamberger, and W. J. Sonnenstuhl, "The Organizational Transformation Process: The Micropolitics of Dissonance Reduction and the Alignment of Logics of Action," *Administrative Science Quarterly* (1996): 477–506; P. H. Mirvis, "Human Resource Management: Leaders, Laggards, and Followers," *Academy of Management Executive* 11(2) (1997): 43–56; and M. Hammer and S. A. Stanton, "The Power of Reflection," *Fortune* (November 24, 1997): 291–296.

17 S. Kuczynski, "Hiring In," *HR Magazine* (March 2000): 60–64; J. J. Laabs, "Paving the Way to Profitability," Workforce (March 2000): 66–70; J. Markoff, "William Hewlett Dies at 87; A Pioneer of Silicon Valley," *New York Times* (January 13, 2001): B9; S. Greengard, "HR Can Unlock a Prosperous Future," *Workforce* (March 1998): 45–54.

18 B. Panus, "Talent Mining," *Workspan* (August 2000): 47–49.

19 J. Reingold, "Brain Drain," *Business Week* (September 20, 1999): 112–126.

20 A. Howard and Associates, *Diagnosis for Organizational Change: Methods and Models* (San Francisco: Jossey-Bass, 1994); see also J. Waclawski and A. H. Church, *Organizational Development: Data Driven Methods for Change* (San Francisco: Jossey-Bass, 2002).

21 "Bringing Sears into the New World: An Interview with Anthony Rucci," *Fortune* (October 13, 1997): 183–184.

22 R. S. Kaplan and D. P. Norton, *The Strategy-Focused Organization: How Balanced Scorecard Companies Thrive in the New Business Environment* (Boston: Harvard Business School Press, 2000); B. E. Becker, M. A. Huselid, and D. Ulrich, *The HR Scorecard: Linking People, Strategy, and Performance* (Boston: Harvard Business School Press, 2001); C. Creelman, "Mark Huselid and the HR Balanced Scorecard," (February 20, 2001) http://www.hr.com/Hrcom/index.cfm/WeeklyMag/.

23 N. Adler, L. Brody, and J. Osland, "The Women's Global Leadership Forum: Enhancing One Company's Global Leadership Capability," *Human Resource Management* 39(2 & 3) (Summer–Fall 2000): 209–225.

24 C. Wanberg and J. Banas, "Predictors and Outcomes of Openness to Changes in a Reorganizing Workplace," *Journal of Applied Psychology* 85(1) (2000): 132–142.

25 M. Hopkins, "Zen and the Art of the Self-Managing Company," *Inc.* (November 2000): 54–63; T. T. Baldwin, C. Danielson, and W. Wiggenhorn, "The Evolution of Learning Strategies in Organizations: From Employee Development to Business Definition," *Academy of Management Executive* 11 (1997): 47–58.

26 R. Pascale, "Change How You Define Leadership and You Change How You Run a Company," *Fast Company* (April–May 1998): 110–120; G. Hamel, "Reinvent Your Company," *Fortune* (June 12, 2000): 99–118.

27 T. Helton, "Implementing the Requisite Organization," *HR.Com* (March 6, 2001), http://www.hr.com/HRCom/index.cfm/Weekly Mag/.

28 "Job Turnover Tab," *Business Week* (March 20, 1998): 8.

29 F. Jossi, "Take the Road Less Travelled," *HR Magazine* (July 2001): 46–51; J. C. McElroy, P. C. Morrow, and S. N. Rude, "Turnover and Organizational Performance: A Comparative Analysis of the Effect of Voluntary, Involuntary, and Reduction-in-Force Turnover," *Journal of Applied Psychology* 86 (2001): 1294–1299.

30 M. L. Maznevski and J. DiStefano, "Global Leaders Are Team Players: Developing Global Leaders Through Membership on Global Teams," *Human Resource Management* 39 (Summer/Fall 2000): 195–208; M. Harvey, M. Novicevic, and C. Speier, "An Innovative Global Management Staffing System: A Competency-Based Perspective," *Human Resource Management* 39(4) (Winter 2000): 381–394; Y. Baruch and M. Peiperl, "Career Management Practices: An Empirical Survey and Implications," *Human Resource Management* 39(4) (Winter 2000): 347–366; S. Greengard, "Why Succession Planning Can't Wait," *Workforce* (December 2001): 34–38.

31 Adapted from S. L. Davis, "Assessment as Organizational Strategy," in R. Jeanneret and R. Silzer (eds.), *Individual Psychological Assessment: Predicting Behavior in Organizational Settings v(San Francisco: Jossey-Bass, 1998).

32 R. K. Miller, "Going the Distance," *HR Executive* (February 22, 2001), http://www.hrexecutive.com/weir.htm.

33 K. Troy, *Change Management: Striving for Customer Value: A Research Report* (New York: Conference Board, 1996).

34 "Growing Pains," *Across the Board* (February 1997): 43–48.

35 S. Michailova, "Contrasts in Culture: Russian and Western Perspectives on Organizational Change," *Academy of Management Executive* 14(4) (2000): 99–112; D. Pottruck and T. Pearce, "Creating Culture," *Business 2.0* (May 2000): 362–378; R. Silzer, "Shaping Organizational Leadership: The Ripple Effect of Assessment," in R. Jeanneret and R. Silzer (eds.), *Individual Psychological Assessment: Predicting Behavior in Organizational Settings.*

36 W. Echikson, "Nestle: An Elephant Dances," *Business Week e.Biz* (December 11, 2000): 44–48; R. Maurer, *Beyond the Wall of Resistance* (Austin, TX: Bard Books, 1996).

37 R. Kanter, "The Ten Deadly Mistakes of Wanna-Dots," *Harvard Business Review* (January 2001): 91–100; J. Kerstetter, "PeopleSoft's Hard Guy," *Business Week* (January 15, 2001): 76–77; K. Skoldberg, "Tales of Change," *Organization Science* 5 (1994): 219–238.

38 G. H. Taylor, "Knowledge Companies," in W. E. Halal (ed.), *The Infinite Resource: Creating and Leading the Knowledge Enterprise* (San Francisco: Jossey-Bass, 1998): 97–109.

39 T. Petzinger Jr., "Georg Bauer Put Burden of Downsizing into Employees' Hands," *Wall Street Journal* (May 10, 1996): B1.

40 C. Heckscher, *White-Collar Blues* (New York: Basic Books, 1995).

41 Research shows change initiatives are more often undertaken earlier in the careers of executives, and less likely to occur later; e.g., see D. Miller and J. Shamsie, "Learning Across the Life Cycle: Experimentation and Performance Among the Hollywood Studio Heads," *Strategic Management Journal* 22 (2001): 724–745.

42 J. W. Dean, Jr., P. Brandes, and R. Dharwadkar, "Organizational Cynicism," *Academy of Management Review* 23 (1998): 341–352; A. E. Reichers, J. P. Wanous, and J. T. Austin, "Understanding and Managing Cynicism about Organizational Change," *Academy of Management Executive* 11 (1997): 48.

43 J. L. McCarthy, *A Blueprint for Change: A Conference Report* (No. 1149-96-CH) (New York: Conference Board, 1996); T. J. Galpin, *The Human Side of Change* (San Francisco: Jossey-Bass, 1996); Price Waterhouse, *Better Change: Best Practices for Transforming Your Organization* (Burr Ridge, IL: Irwin, 1995); and B. Schneider, A. P. Brief, and R. A. Guzzo, "Creating a Climate and Culture for Sustainable Organizational Change," *Organizational Dynamics* 24(4) (1996): 6–19.

44 J. P. Kotter, "Leading Change: Why Transformation Efforts Fail," *Harvard Business Review* (March–April 1995): 59–67.

CHAPTER

6

USING JOB ANALYSIS AND COMPETENCY MODELING AS THE FOUNDATION FOR THE HR SYSTEM

"The CEO's primary job is to cultivate a corporate culture that benefits all employees and customers." [1]

Tom Siebel
Chairman and CEO
Siebel Systems

MANAGING THROUGH STRATEGIC PARTNERSHIPS

Aetna

Aetna Life and Casualty Company is a leading provider of insurance and financial services. Its lines of business include health care, casualty coverage for commercial and personal property, life insurance, and asset management. After years of great success, Aetna's profits started to decline in 1987. This happened partly because the company had a product line that was too large and too diversified and because some of its businesses were unprofitable. Also, overhead expenses exceeded the industry average in many cases.

In the early 1990s, then CEO Ronald E. Compton set about the task of making the company more profitable. Like other large insurers in the industry, such as ITT Corporation, Hartford Fire Insurance Company, and Cigna Corporation, Aetna started eliminating unprofitable lines of businesses. These included its individual health and reinsurance operations. Soon Compton announced plans to stop selling guaranteed investment contracts (GICs) and single-premium annuities to pension plans. At the same time, he announced that 10 percent of the workforce would be laid off.

In addition to eliminating people and lines of business, Aetna reengineered many areas of the business and introduced new technologies. Throughout the process, corporate HR staff partnered with managers to implement the new strategy. Specifically, it sought to ensure that the new work environment was consistent with Aetna's vision:

Aetna's employees have worked together to create one of the world's leading providers of insurance, financial and health care services. We strive to offer unmatched customer service and to achieve superior financial performance. To attain greatness, we have become a multi-niche company that is quick, flexible and right in a challenging environment. Our employees demonstrate the highest levels of integrity and competency. In all we do, our policy is to go beyond the expected.

Aetna's three core values are to invest in people, build trust, and inspire excellence. The first core value—invest in people—shapes how work is structured throughout the company. Aetna's commitment is to be sure that all employees have the opportunity to reach their potential. This implies career progress along logical paths within the company. With all the changes that were occurring, employees found it hard to see how what they were being asked to do in this time of turmoil might relate to their own longer-term career objectives. To address this issue, new career paths were developed using job analysis and broadbanding.

The human resource professionals, along with input from other employees and managers, helped the company reduce more than seven thousand individual job titles to two hundred job families. In effect, they redesigned jobs to give more latitude to the employees and to managers. The old job classification system specifically delineated the tasks that employees were supposed to do. This discouraged employees from taking on additional responsibilities. With the new job families, employees can perform many tasks and be rewarded for doing so, without having to go through a promotion procedure and without having to revise the job description. Aetna used job analysis to define the boundaries and content of its job families.[2]

Job analysis and **competency modeling** refer to two related procedures for systematically understanding the work that gets done in an organization. The basic goals of both procedures are to understand what people do, how they do it, and what skills they need to do the work well.

Among HR practitioners, there is some disagreement about whether job analysis and competency modeling are two different procedures, or just two variations on the same theme. Our view is that competency modeling represents one particular approach to job analysis. In other words, job analysis is a broader and more general term, with competency modeling being one approach to job analysis.[3] This chapter describes the competency modeling approach—which currently enjoys great popularity—as well as other more traditional approaches to job analysis.

Regardless of which specific procedures one uses to conduct a job analysis, the results of the job analysis are used to write job descriptions. A **job description** spells out essential job functions, describes the conditions in which the job is performed, and states special training or certification requirements for the job. For employees, a job description produced through job analysis serves as a guide to work behavior. For supervisors and managers, a job description serves as a guide to performance evaluation and feedback. Job descriptions also serve as the basic building blocks for designing pay policies and training programs. In other words, job analysis provides the foundation upon which to build virtually all components of the HR system. It can be used to ensure that an organization's entire system for managing people is internally consistent and appropriate for the organization's context, as shown in Exhibit 6.1.

THE STRATEGIC IMPORTANCE OF JOB ANALYSIS AND COMPETENCY MODELING

The strategic importance of job analysis and competency modeling is grounded first and foremost in their usefulness as systematic procedures that provide a rational foundation on which to build a coherent approach to managing human resources. This role for job analysis and competency modeling becomes especially obvious during periods of strategic change, when jobs in an organization are like to be suddenly transformed. Legal considerations

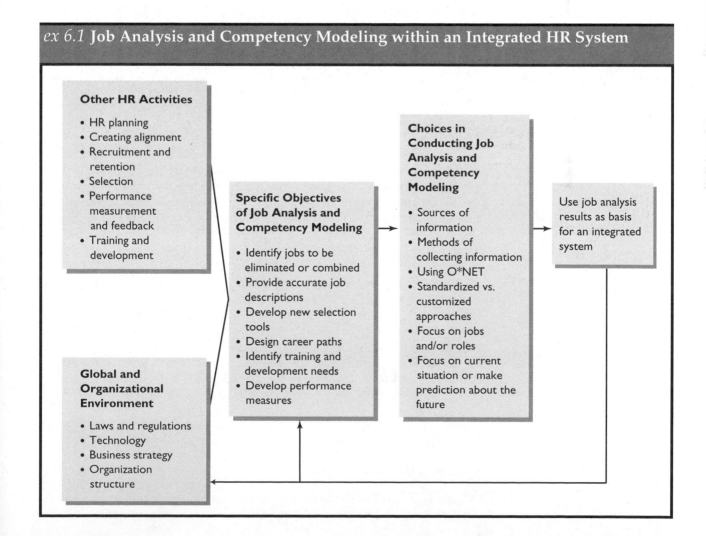

ex 6.1 **Job Analysis and Competency Modeling within an Integrated HR System**

Other HR Activities

- HR planning
- Creating alignment
- Recruitment and retention
- Selection
- Performance measurement and feedback
- Training and development

Specific Objectives of Job Analysis and Competency Modeling

- Identify jobs to be eliminated or combined
- Provide accurate job descriptions
- Develop new selection tools
- Design career paths
- Identify training and development needs
- Develop performance measures

Choices in Conducting Job Analysis and Competency Modeling

- Sources of information
- Methods of collecting information
- Using O*NET
- Standardized vs. customized approaches
- Focus on jobs and/or roles
- Focus on current situation or make prediction about the future

Use job analysis results as basis for an integrated system

Global and Organizational Environment

- Laws and regulations
- Technology
- Business strategy
- Organization structure

also contribute to the strategic importance of job analysis. As described in Chapters 1 and 3, compliance with various employment laws and regulations is one of the many objectives of effective organizations.

Strategic Change

As the example of Aetna illustrates, the nature of jobs can change radically when an organization undergoes a strategic change, such as restructuring the organization around key processes. When the nature of jobs in an organization changes, many aspects of the human resource management system are likely to be affected as well. At Aetna, broader jobs and reduced layers of management meant there were fewer opportunities for advancement through promotion. Job analysis helped the HR professionals address this problem by providing a new map of how people could achieve career advancement in the new organizational structure.

For many organizations, the process of restructuring occurs in the context of a merger or acquisition. M&As are another form of strategic change that illuminates the strategic importance of job analysis. During a merger or acquisition, job analysis provides a systematic basis for comparing the content of jobs that existed in the separate companies. When the companies are brought together, a key challenge is treating people fairly. For example, if two people are doing essentially the same work, they should be paid essentially the same following the merger. Job analysis provides a means for determining which jobs are essentially the same in the merged company. During a merger, job analysis also can be used to identify redundant jobs that might be candidates for elimination. Other uses of job analysis following a merger or acquisition include specifying the competencies needed to perform a job, redesigning jobs to accommodate employees with disabilities, developing measures of job performance, and designing training programs.

At Hewlett-Packard, job analysis was used to help managers understand the implications of the company's new strategy for the specific roles, behaviors, and skills that employees would need in the new environment. For HP, the new business strategy called for a shift from a traditional manufacturing operation to a service delivery business. During the strategic planning phase of the change process, managers created a "vision matrix" that specified key changes that would be needed in business operations. Then job analysis procedures were used to help managers define the roles, behaviors, and competencies needed to perform in the new business environment. The results of the analysis served as the basis for developing new job descriptions and rewards aimed at supporting the new business strategy.[4]

Regardless of why an organization undergoes restructuring, job analysis provides the information needed to develop new HR policies and practices that are appropriate for the organization's new jobs. According to recent research by William M. Mercer, Inc., driving strategic change is one of the key reasons that organizations are turning to competency-based job analyses. For example, when a company moves into a new market or a new business area, job analysis can be used to identify the new skills and competencies that will be needed to succeed in the new venture.[5]

Legal Considerations

Because it serves as the basis for selection decisions, performance appraisals, compensation, and training, job analysis has received considerable attention from legal and regulatory bodies. By regularly conducting job analysis studies and documenting the results in written job descriptions, employers can better protect themselves against claims of unfair treatment. Principles for conducting appropriate job analyses have been articulated in federal regulatory guidelines and several court decisions.[6]

> **FAST FACT**
>
> Section 14.C.2 of the *Uniform Guidelines* states that "there shall be a job analysis which includes an analysis of the important work behaviors required for successful performance."

Nondiscrimination. During the past three decades, the courts have clearly indicated that employers should conduct thorough job analyses for all positions in the organization and use the results of those job analyses as the basis for a variety of personnel decisions. By conducting job analyses and documenting job requirements, employers can reduce the role of stereotypes and uninformed opinions about the skills needed to perform a job. For example, in *Rowe v. General Motors* (1972), the court ruled that to prevent discriminatory practices in promotion decisions, a company should have written objective standards for promotion. In *United States v. City of Chicago* (1978), the court stated that, in addition to having objective standards for promotion, the standards should describe the job to which the person is being considered for promotion. These objective standards can be determined through job analysis.[7]

The *Americans with Disabilities Act of 1990* (ADA) also draws attention to the importance of job analysis. The ADA makes it unlawful to discriminate against a qualified individual who has a disability. It applies to anyone who has a physical or mental impairment that substantially limits one or more major life activities. A person is considered qualified for a job if he or she can perform the job's "essential functions," although some accommodation may be necessary on the part of the employer. For example, a hearing impaired employee may be able to perform the essential functions of a proofreading job, provided the employer makes some reasonable accommodations in the procedures used to assign work to the individual. In this example, it would not be legal for the employer to use the employee's hearing disability as a basis for refusing to allow her to work as a proofreader.

> **FAST FACT**
>
> About 1.6 million blind people live in the United States, of which about 70% are unemployed.

Although the extent of employers' responsibilities for making accommodations is still being clarified, the EEOC has been very clear in stating that compliance with the law requires employers to conduct job analyses to identify the essential functions of jobs and formulate job descriptions. When the EEOC investigates an employer's compliance with ADA, a written job description—the product of job analysis—is one of the first documents they ask to see.[8]

> **FAST FACT**
>
> Microsoft agreed to pay $97 million to settle a lawsuit brought by former workers whom the company had classified as independent contractors. The court ruled they should be classified as regular employees, and so were entitled to back pay and the value of stocks they didn't receive.

Independent Contractors. For purposes of compensation and taxation, the law treats independent contractors and regular employees quite differently. For example, for regular workers employers must withhold and pay Social Security and Medicare taxes and they must pay for unemployment insurance. None of these are required for contract workers. Another major difference is that regular workers enjoy the right to certain benefits and overtime pay that contract workers are not entitled to. During the 1990s, as Microsoft thrived, it hired thousands of workers through local personnel agencies and treated them as "temps"—paying them no company benefits and clearly stating that full-time employment in the future was not guaranteed. These temps stayed around so long that they took on the nickname "permatemps." As Microsoft learned, simply labeling someone an independent contractor does not relieve the employer of responsibility for fairly treating people who qualify as regular workers. Nor did the courts agree that workers forfeited their rights when they signed a waiver stating that they understood their "temporary" status.[9] Thoroughly documenting a worker's job duties is a better approach to determining whether he or she qualifies as an independent contractor or a regular employee.[10]

Job analysis results are one source of information that employers can use to assess whether a worker who has been classified as an independent contractor should be reclassified and treated as a regular employee. Some of the key questions that job analysis can clarify are these:

- Does the job description tell the worker *how* to do the job, or indicate that a supervisor will tell the person *how* to do the job? An employer should not tell independent contractors how to do their jobs.
- Does the job description state that the work performed on the job is an essential part of the business? Independent contractors should not be hired to perform essential tasks or services.
- Does the job description state that the worker must personally do the work? An independent contractor should be allowed to hire some else to do the work.
- Does the job description specify the hours to be worked? An independent contractor should be allowed to determine the hours of work needed to complete the job.
- Does the job description indicate that the worker is expected to work full-time? An independent contractor should not be prevented from doing work for other employers.
- Does the job description specify that the work is to be performed at the company's facilities? An independent contractor chooses where to do the work.[11]

Partnership Roles in Job Analysis and Competency Modeling

As this chapter will describe, the process of conducting a thorough job analysis or competency study can involve many different groups of people. HR professionals almost always have primary responsibility for overseeing the process, but they cannot conduct an adequate analysis on their own. The people who work in a job and the people who observe a job being done day in and day out are the experts when it comes to describing a job, so their involvement in the process of conducting a job analysis is essential. During the restructuring at Aetna, job analysis required the cooperation of nearly everyone in the organization. The feature "The HR Triad: Roles and Job Responsibilities in Job Analysis and Competency Modeling" summarizes the major ways that HR professionals, managers, and other employees get involved in job analysis. In the remainder of this chapter, we describe these roles in more detail.

BASIC TERMINOLOGY

In everyday conversations, people often use the word *job* whenever they refer to an employment situation. But when an entire system for managing

---

FAST FACT

Estimates place the percentage of contract workers at about 20% of the workforce.

Roles and Responsibilities in Job Analysis and Competency Modeling THE HR TRIAD

LINE MANAGERS	HR PROFESSIONALS	EMPLOYEES
• Participate in strategic planning and organizational change. (See Chapters 4 and 5.) • Work with HR managers to determine whether jobs need to be analyzed or reanalyzed. • Help decide who should conduct the job analysis and for what purposes. • Help identify incumbents to participate in job analysis. • Provide technical documents to the job analyst. • Participate in job analysis through interviews and questionnaires. • Facilitate job incumbents' participation in job analysis.	• Participate in strategic planning and organizational change. (See Chapters 4 and 5.) • Communicate with line managers and employees about the importance of job analysis. • Work with line managers to determine whether jobs need to be analyzed or reanalyzed and for what purposes. • Serve as a job analysis expert, or help select an external vendor to conduct job analysis. • Ensure that line managers and employees are aware of legal considerations. • Prepare and update job descriptions with line managers and employees. • Keep up to date on new techniques and changing trends in job analysis and competency modeling.	• Participate in strategic planning and organizational change. (See Chapters 4 and 5.) • Understand the purposes and importance of job analysis. • Help line managers recognize when major changes in a job indicate the need for job analysis or reanalysis. • Provide accurate information for the job analysis process. • Adapt to the changing nature of the job and be willing to show flexibility in performing new job tasks. • Use job analysis results for career planning and job choice decisions. • Understand the relationships among job analysis, competency modeling, and other HR practices.

human resources depends on understanding the jobs in an organization, more specific terminology is needed. More precise use of several related terms facilitates clear communication.

Positions, Jobs, and Job Families

Human resource professionals use the term **position** to refer to the activities carried out by any single person. They use the term **job** to refer to positions that are functionally interchangeable in the organization. In small organizations, each job may have only one position associated with it; no two employees are expected to do the same thing. An example of this situation would occur if Raol's position is Account Manager and only Raol holds the job of Account Manager. As organizations grow, the number of positions associated with some jobs increase. A family bakery may eventually hire more people to work as bakers as well as more people to work at the sales counter. The bakery's growth requires adding positions without increasing the number of jobs. If the bakery continues to expand, new jobs may eventually be added. If the bakery adds seating and coffee service for customers, the job of waiter might be added. Additional jobs could also be created through increased specialization. In a small bakery, the job of baker includes baking breads as well as pies and cakes, but as the organization grows, the baker's job is split into two jobs: bread baker and pastry maker.

A **job family** refers to a group of jobs that can be treated as similar for administrative purposes. Jobs in the same family generally require similar competencies, although each job involves different tasks. Job families are closely related to what many people think of as occupational categories. In the bakery example, the jobs of bread baker and pastry maker would fall into the same job family.

Job Analysis

Job analysis is a systematic process of describing and recording information about job behaviors, activities, and worker specifications.[12] Typically, the information described and recorded includes the following:

- purposes of a job;
- major duties or activities required of job holders;
- conditions under which the job is performed; and
- competencies (i.e., skills, knowledge, abilities, and other attributes)[13] that enable and enhance performance in the job.

HR experts have devoted a great deal of attention to developing systematic job analysis techniques, and there are many different techniques available. In fact, according to one recent review of the available techniques, there are at least 15 major job analysis approaches.[14]

The focus of a job analysis is a major feature that accounts for why there are so many techniques. Most techniques are either task oriented or worker oriented. Traditional approaches tend to focus on tasks. In a **task-oriented job analysis**, the focus is on *what* the job involves in terms of activities and outcomes. Time and motion studies are a task-focused method of job analysis, as are most other traditional approaches to job analysis.

A **worker-oriented job analysis** focuses on the characteristics of job incumbents that are required to perform the job well. The objective is to provide a description of the skills, abilities, attitudes, personality characteristics, and so forth, that lead to successful job performance. Here the question is *who* can do the job. Competency modeling is a worker-focused approach to job analysis.

Each of the available job analysis techniques has certain strengths and weaknesses. Indeed, the reality is that no one technique is perfect. The usefulness of a particular technique often depends on the purpose for conducting the job analysis. For example, if the results of a job analysis will be used to design a new selection procedure, a worker-focused approach may be best. On the other hand, the results of a task-focused approach may be more useful for designing a job training program. For these reasons, HR professionals often rely on information from a combination of job analysis techniques when developing an organization's HR policies and practices.

Competency Modeling

As already noted, we consider competency modeling to be a specific approach to conducting a job analysis. Although some consultants prefer to use the new language of competency modeling to describe the services they offer, the basic procedures and objectives of competency modeling are firmly grounded in traditional job analysis procedures. What distinguishes the competency modeling approach is that it places much more emphasis on specifying the individual characteristics that are associated with effective performance in a job. That is, the primary objective of competency modeling is to describe the skills, knowledge, abilities, values, interests, and personality of successful employees.

The competency modeling approach to job analysis is somewhat new in the United States. Indeed, it has really taken hold only in the past decade or so. But the philosophy of focusing on the worker rather than the job has a long tradition in Japan. Traditionally, Japanese organizations have hired individuals under the assumption that they would perform many different jobs during a long career with the company. Thus, selection decisions focused on assessing the person's capacity to learn rather than the ability to do a specific job. In essence, individuals were organizational applicants rather than job applicants.

The competency-based approach is also used in the United Kingdom,[15] where the goal is to use competency information to design more effective education and training programs. Traditionally in the UK, the status of one's family within the class structure largely determined educational opportunities and educational achievement, and in turn was often *presumed* to result in competence at work. Demonstration of one's job skills often wasn't required to land good managerial jobs.

In 1981, the Manpower Services Commission published a report that suggested a strategy for improving vocational education standards to align them more closely with competencies needed to perform modern jobs. The objective was nothing short of developing a more flexible and highly skilled national workforce. Subsequent documents emphasized the need for major reform and began to sketch out the details of a new national policy. One stated that "vocational qualifications need to relate more directly and clearly to the competence required (and acquired) at work." In 1986, the National Council for Vocational Qualifications was formed to develop national occupational competency standards.

Responsibility for developing managerial competencies and standards was given to the National Forum for Management Education and Development. To accomplish this task, it analyzed the roles of thousands of managers from hundreds of organizations using interview and questionnaire techniques. Its work was guided by a well-specified set of procedures developed and disseminated by the Manpower Services Commission. The set of procedures closely approximates the procedures for the customized approach described in this chapter.

Job Descriptions

Often, the most immediate use of job analysis results is writing job descriptions that detail what the jobholder is expected to do and the competencies needed for the job. Job descriptions are part of the written contract that governs the employment relationship. Exhibit 6.2 shows an example of a job description. During recruitment, clear job descriptions provide job applicants with realistic information.

Once on the job, employees use their job descriptions to guide their behavior. Good job descriptions help employees direct their energies to the most important aspects of the job. Supervisors use job descriptions in evaluating performance and providing feedback. Well-written job descriptions can also guide supervisors in writing references and incumbents in preparing resumes. Typically, a well-written job description includes the elements listed in Exhibit 6.3.[16]

"Friendly and caring personality. Competent in handling difficult situations. Able to communicate effectively with people from all parts of the world. Supportive of colleagues. Able to remain calm and efficient under pressure. Self reliant and independent. Willing to treat everyone as an individual."

British Airways vacancy announcement

FAST FACT

Companies that use the Internet for recruiting generally post electronic job descriptions on their recruiting pages.

"Flight Attendants ensure that Customers' safety and comfort come first, and create a memorable experience by providing friendly, enthusiastic, courteous and fun service."

Southwest Airlines recruiting announcement for the job of flight attendant

ex 6.2 Job Description

Title: Corporate Loan Assistant   Department: Corporate Banking
Date: June 2002   Location: Head Office

Note: *Statements included in this description are intended to reflect in general the duties and responsibilities of this classification and are not to be interpreted as being all inclusive.*

Relationships

Reports to: Corporate Account Officer or Sr. Corporate Account Officer
Subordinate staff: None
Internal customers: Middle and Senior Managers within the Corporate Banking Department
External contacts: Major bank customers

Summary Description

Assist in the administration of commercial accounts to ensure maintenance of profitable Bank relationships.

Domains

A.   Credit Analysis (Weekly)
Under the direction of a supervising loan officer, analyze a customer company's history, industry position, present condition, accounting procedures, and debt requirements. Review credit reports, summarizing analysis and recommending courses of action for potential borrowers; review and summarize performance of existing borrowers. Prepare and follow up on credit reports and Loan Agreement Compliance sheets.

B.   Operations (Weekly)
Help customers with banking problems and needs. Give out customer credit information to valid inquirers. Analyze account profitability and compliance with balance arrangements; distribute to customer. Direct Loan Note Department in receiving and disbursing funds and in booking loans. Correct internal errors.

C.   Loan Documentation (Weekly)
Develop required loan documentation. Help customer complete loan documents. Review loan documents immediately after a loan closing for completeness and accuracy.

D.   Report/Information System (Weekly)
Prepare credit reports, describing and analyzing customer relationship and loan commitments; prepare for input into Information System. Monitor credit reports for accuracy.

E.   Customer/Internal Relations (Weekly)
Build rapport with customers by becoming familiar with their products, facilities, and industry. Communicate with customers and other banks to obtain loan-related information and answer questions. Prepare reports on customer and prospect contacts, and follow up. Write memos on events affecting customers and prospects.

F.   Assistance to Officers (Monthly)
Assist assigned officers by preparing credit support information, summarizing customer relationships, and accompanying on calls or making independent calls. Monitor accounts and review and maintain credit files. Coordinate paper flow to banks participating in loans. Respond to customer questions or requests in absence of assigned officer.

G.   Assistance to Division (Monthly)
Represent bank at industry activities. Follow industry/area developments. Help Division Manager plan division approach and prospect for new business. Interview loan assistant applicants. Provide divisional backup in absence of assigned officer.

H.   Competencies (Any item with an asterisk will be taught on the job)
Oral communication, including listening and questioning. Intermediate accounting proficiency. Writing. Researching/reading to understand legal financial documents. Organizational/analytical skills. Social skills to represent the Bank and strengthen its image. Sales. Knowledge of Bank credit policy and services. Skill to use Bank computer system. Knowledge of bank-related legal terminology. Independent work skills. Ability to work efficiently under pressure. Knowledge of basic corporate finance.

I.   Physical Characteristics
See to read fine print and numbers. Hear speaker 20 feet away. Speak to address a group of five. Mobility to tour customer facilities (may include climbing stairs).

J.   Other Characteristics
Driver's license. Willing to: work overtime and weekends occasionally; travel out of state every three months/locally weekly; attend activities after work hours; wear clean, neat businesslike attire.

ex 6.3 Elements of a Job Description and What They Should Specify

Element	What Should Be Specified
Job title	• Defines a group of positions that are interchangeable (identical) with regard to their significant duties.
Department or division	• Indicates where in the organization the job is located.
Date the job was analyzed	• Indicates when the description was prepared and perhaps whether it should be updated. A job description based on a job analysis conducted prior to any major changes in the job is of little use.
Job summary	• An abstract of the job, often used during recruitment to create job postings or employment announcements and to set the pay levels.
Supervision	• Identifies reporting relationships. If supervision is given, the duties associated with that supervision should be detailed under work performed.
Work performed	• Identifies the duties and underlying tasks that make up a job. A *task* is something that workers perform or an action they take to produce a product or service. A *duty* is a collection of related, recurring tasks. Duties should be ranked in terms of the time spent on them as well as their importance. Specified duties are used to determine whether job accommodations for individuals protected under the *Americans with Disabilities Act* are reasonable, whether the job is exempt from overtime provisions of the *Fair Labor Standards Act*, and whether two jobs with different titles should be treated as equal for purposes of compliance with the *Equal Pay Act*.
Job context	• Describes the physical environment that surrounds the job (e.g., outdoors, in close quarters, in remote areas, in extremely high or low temperatures, exposed to dangerous conditions such as fumes and diseases) as well as the social environment in which work is performed (e.g., teamwork, flexibility, and continuous learning). Increasingly, the degree of change and uncertainty associated with the job, the corporate culture, and elements of the organizational mission or vision statement are specified.

INTERNET RESOURCES   6.A

Strategic Importance and Basic Terms

At our Web site, http://jackson.swcollege.com/, you can:

1. Visit the home page of Aetna Life and Casualty Company.

2. Review extensive information about job analysis and its uses provided by the Management Assistance Program for Nonprofits. Learn more by visiting their Web site.

3. Study the Uniform Guidelines, which are available on-line from the U.S. Department of Labor, to learn more about the legal reasons for conducting a job analysis.

4. Read a job description for the chair of the board of directors and peruse a database of dozens of other job descriptions.

SOURCES OF INFORMATION

Information about a job can be obtained from anyone who has specific information about what the work involves. The people used as sources of information about specific jobs are often referred to as **subject matter experts (SMEs)**. They can include current job incumbents, supervisors, trained job analysts, and customers. Each of these sources sees the job from a different perspective. Associated with each source of information about a job are different advantages and disadvantages.

By using several sources, there is less chance of error in the final result. Some common job analysis errors and the conditions that can cause them are described in Exhibit 6.4.[17] To conduct the most comprehensive job analysis, the best strategy is to include as many different sources as possible.[18]

Job Incumbents

"The auto worker is almost a scientist in a technical way. He's required to know so many trades, he's required to know so much."

Joe Lo Galbo
Machinery repairman turned trainer
Ford Motor Company

Job incumbents—the people who are currently doing the job—have the most direct knowledge about tasks and competencies associated with a job. Incumbents usually provide data through participation in an interview or by responding to a questionnaire.

One concern in job analysis is selecting the particular job incumbents to include. If your publishing firm employs 30 copy editors, do you need to obtain information from them all in order to understand the job of a copy editor? Many companies feel that it is inefficient to survey everyone, so they select only a sample. When a sample is used, it must be a **representative sample**. That is, it should include men and women, members of different ethnic groups and nationalities, younger people as well as older ones, people who work in different divisions or regions, and so on.[19] A representative sample captures the full variety of perspectives among people in the job.

Line managers and incumbents usually agree about whether an incumbent performs specific tasks and duties. However, incumbents tend to see their jobs as requiring greater skill and knowledge than do line managers or outside job analysts. One reason for this difference is that job-specific

ex 6.4 Job Analysis Inaccuracy

Source of Error	Possible Consequences	Conditions Likely to Cause Error
Low accuracy motivation	Incomplete information about job	Tasks aren't meaningful, the group is large, individuals do not feel accountable.
Impression management	Inflated descriptions of job or competency requirements	Job incumbents feel the job analysis results will be used to evaluate them as individuals.
Demand effects	Inflated agreement and inflated descriptions of job or competency requirements	Supervisors convey their preference for employees to portray their jobs as challenging and/or as more complex than in the past.
Reliance on heuristics and job stereotypes	Incomplete and unreliable task ratings	Too many items on a questionnaire, creating fatigue and loss of ability to differentiate among similar tasks.
Use of extraneous and irrelevant information	Inaccurate ratings, either inflated or deflated	Extraneous information about things such as employees' salaries and tenure levels are known.
Halo	All job tasks are given similar ratings	The rater has insufficient job information available, little personal knowledge of the job, or low motivation.
Leniency and severity	All job tasks are given high (lenient) *or* low (severe) ratings	Leniency is more likely when it can result in benefits for the raters (e.g., a possible pay raise). Severity may occur if the job analyst thinks it may benefit the organization (e.g., help justify elimination of a job or low wages).

information is more salient to incumbents who perform the work than it is to outsiders. The difference may also be due to self-enhancement. Because job analysis is related to many human resource outcomes—for example, performance appraisal and compensation—incumbents, and, to a lesser extent, their supervisors may exaggerate job duties in order to maximize organizational rewards and self-esteem.[20]

Although incumbents may inflate the difficulty of their jobs, there are still good reasons to include them in the job analysis process. First, they're the source of the most current and accurate information about the job. Second, their inclusion allows line managers and incumbents to gain a shared perspective about job expectations. Third, including incumbents can increase perceptions of procedural fairness and reduce resistance to changes that might be introduced on the basis of job analysis results.

Supervisors

> **FAST FACT**
>
> In most convenience stores, 25 inches separate a cashier and customer, 80 inches separate two cashiers, and managers are far from the work floor.

Like incumbents, supervisors have direct information about the duties associated with a job. Therefore, they're also considered SMEs. Yet, because they're not currently performing the job, supervisors may find it more difficult to explain all the tasks involved in it. This is especially true of tasks the supervisors cannot observe directly, such as mental tasks or tasks performed out in the field. On the other hand, supervisors who have seen more than one job incumbent perform a job bring a broader perspective to the job analysis process. Supervisors also may be in a better position to describe what tasks should be included in the job, and what tasks could be included if the job is to be redesigned.[21]

Trained Job Analysts

Some methods of job analysis require input from trained job analysts. Supervisors or incumbents can be taught to serve as job analysts, but usually outside consultants or members of the company's HR staff perform this role.

An advantage of enlisting the help of trained job analysts is that they can observe many different incumbents working under different supervisors and in different locations. Trained job analysts also can read through organizational records and technical documentation and provide information culled from these indirect sources. Furthermore, trained experts are more likely to appreciate fully the legal issues associated with conducting job analysis. Nevertheless, like every other source of information, trained job analysts are imperfect. One drawback to using their skills is that, like supervisors, they cannot observe all aspects of a job. They can see the physical aspects, but not the mental and emotional demands. Also, they may rely too much on their own stereotypes about what a job involves, based on the job title, rather than attend to all the available information. Finally, especially in the case of outside consultants, their services may be expensive.

Customers

> **FAST FACT**
>
> Replacement window salespeople at Everest used to need a week to produce an estimate for customers. Today they use hand-held computers to produce instant cost estimates as well as instant postreplacement images of the house.

If satisfying customers is a strategic imperative, it seems obvious that customers should also be used as subject matter experts. In actuality, this is seldom done. Collecting information from customers has been considered a marketing activity rather than an HR activity. Yet, in some jobs, customers are clearly an excellent source of information about a job. For example, cashiers spend 78 percent of their time interacting with customers and only 13 percent of their time interacting with managers.[22] For jobs like these, it seems obvious that using customers as SMEs is likely to become more common as organizations increasingly incorporate the perspectives of customers when designing jobs and assessing employee performance.

METHODS OF COLLECTING INFORMATION

Just as many sources provide information about jobs and the organization as a whole, many methods are used to obtain that information. The three most common ways to collect job and organizational analysis information are observations, interviews, and questionnaires.

Observations

FAST FACT

Almost all freight trucks are fitted with electronic engines programmed to control speed and gear-shifting and satellite dishes used to monitor the trucks' exact location at all times.

Observing workers as they perform their work provides rich information about the tasks involved. Observation may include simply watching people do their job, videotaping, audiotaping, and computer monitoring. Physical measurements of activities performed, such as measuring objects that must be moved, and descriptions of how equipment is operated often require some observation of the job as it is performed. Through observation of a "filler" in the original Ben & Jerry's Homemade ice cream factory, an observer could learn that this job involved two basic tasks. At a time when hand-filled pints of ice cream were unusual in the industry, the filler job at Ben & Jerry's required holding a pint container under a pipe that exuded ice cream and then pulling the pint away at just the moment it was filled. At the same time the filler moved another container under the pipe. As the second container filled, the other hand was used to print a production code on the bottom of the filled container and slide it along a table to the next work station. Fillers did this over and over again, all day long.[23]

Observation can be very time consuming, especially if the work tasks and conditions change depending on the time of day or on a seasonal basis. To be practical, the use of observation generally requires sampling. **Work sampling** refers to the process of taking instantaneous samples of the work activities of individuals or groups of individuals. A haphazard work sampling approach—which yields equally haphazard results—is to simply observe the work being performed when it's convenient for the job analyst. Systematic work sampling yields better information. To be systematic, a job analyst can observe the incumbent at predetermined times.

One disadvantage of observation as a method for analyzing jobs is that employees may feel as if they're under surveillance. Their privacy is invaded by close observation, and they may feel their judgments will be called into question. As competition in the freight delivery business intensifies, managers have begun using high-tech observation methods to analyze every aspect of a truck driver's job. Often the results of the job analysis are used to make efficiency-enhancing changes in how truckers perform their jobs. To resist such intrusions, some drivers put buckets or aluminum foil over their satellite dishes. Others seek shelter by parking beneath a wide overpass when they feel they need to a short nap. "It's getting worse and worse all the time," according to one experienced driver. "Pretty soon they want to put a chip in the drivers' ears and make them robots."[24]

"They do everything through computers. The supervisor says you have to do 20.2 stops an hour and you can only do 15. Next day the supervisor tells you it took you two hours longer than the computer says it should take; it's terrible."

Edward Martin
Package Truck Driver
UPS

Interviews

Some jobs include tasks that are difficult to observe. The components of the larger organizational system—the structure, culture, and strategy—also may be difficult to discern through simple observation. A better way to understand some jobs and the organizational context may be to conduct interviews with the various people touched by them. For example, to really understand the job of a software designer who develops customized graphics programs for commercial printers, you might interview job incumbents, their supervisors, members of their product design teams, staff members who write the computer codes to implement their design, and the customers who ultimately define their objectives.

Questionnaires

Questionnaires are useful for collecting information from many different people because they're more economical than interviews or observations. This is especially true when the questionnaires are administered electronically (e.g., using the organization's intranet). Questionnaires may be developed for specific circumstances, or standardized questionnaires may be purchased from external vendors. Standardized questionnaires are more economical. Often an added benefit is that the vendor can also provide useful information from a larger database. On the other hand, customized questionnaires usually yield information that is more specific to the particular jobs involved. This feature is especially useful for writing meaningful job descriptions and for developing performance measures.

> **FAST FACT**
>
> Information technology has made collecting and analyzing job analysis ratings much quicker and easier, thus removing a major obstacle to its regular use.

METHODS ANALYSIS

Methods analysis focuses on analyzing job elements, the smallest identifiable components of a job. Methods analysis can be used to assess minute physical movements. These movements can then be assessed to determine whether they're efficient and whether they cause undue strain. Methods analysis has been used for decades at UPS. Some companies also find it's helpful as a tool that can guide the redesign of jobs during process reengineering.

> **FAST FACT**
>
> Research in Germany shows that workers become markedly dissatisfied when the cycle time for repeating a task is less than 1.5 minutes.

Time and Motion Studies

At UPS, methods analysis has helped the company thrive, despite stiff competition. In the business where "a package is a package," UPS has always understood that the way people do their work has direct consequences for the company's profitability. In the 1920s, UPS engineers cut away the sides of UPS trucks to study the drivers. Changes in equipment and procedures were then made to enhance workers' efficiency. Today, the study of workers' behavior on the job continues. In one project, a time-and-motion study was used to discover how drivers naturally carried packages and how they handled money received from customers. Job design experts then determined the best way to carry packages (under the left arm) and how to handle money (place it face-up before folding). Training programs now incorporate this information.

> **FAST FACT**
>
> Zap Courier uses expert bike riders to deliver messages in the San Francisco Bay area. Riders listen on a two-way radio as a dispatcher constantly calls out jobs. Each rider decides which calls to take and the best route to follow when making the delivery.

As job have become more knowledge intensive and less labor intensive, many organizations have shifted away from methods analysis. Nevertheless, it's still used by companies that rely heavily on human labor to carry out repetitive and routine tasks accurately and efficiently.

Process Reengineering

Methods analysis also may be used in conjunction with process reengineering. Flow process charts are familiar to anyone who has participated in a reengineering effort. Such charts detail the overall sequence of an operation by focusing on either the movement of an operator or the flow of materials. Flow process charts have been used in hospitals to track patient movements, in grocery stores to analyze the checkout process, in small-batch manufacturing facilities to track the progress of material from machine to machine, in banks to examine the sequence associated with document processing, and in performance appraisal interviews to track supervisor-incumbent interactions. When jobs are reengineered, methods analysis can be used to help the organization develop a detailed understanding of the processes through which work gets done. Developing this detailed understanding is the initial step that must occur before jobs can be redesigned.

GENERIC JOB ANALYSIS

"The first 25 years of our history we provided data to people. For the next 25 years, we'll handle interactions between people."

Hasso Plattner
Cochairman and CEO
SAP

For some situations, generic job analysis results may be sufficient to meet an organization's needs. Generic job analysis results are published by the federal government in the *Dictionary of Occupational Titles (DOT)* and electronically on *O*NET*.

The Dictionary of Occupational Titles

The U.S. Training and Employment Service developed a method called **functional job analysis (FJA)** during the 1950s and 1960s to improve job placement and counseling for workers registering at local state employment offices. Sidney A. Fine, the acknowledged father of this technique, first used

FAST FACT

The *DOT* described 12,000 "different" occupations.

functional job analysis to analyze the jobs of social workers for the Rehabilitation Service of the U.S. Department of Health. Since then, hundreds of thousands of jobs have been analyzed using FJA.

As in methods analysis, trained observers conducted FJA. With FJA, the observers used a complex rating system to describe the activities of jobs. The rating system focused on the data, people, and things associated with a job. For each of these aspects, the analysts provided a rating of the level of functioning required by the job.[25]

The U.S. Department of Labor has used FJA as a basis for describing thousands of jobs. These job analysis results have been made available to the public in the *Dictionary of Occupational Titles (DOT)*. Although the *DOT* is now in the process of being replaced by the O*NET, described below, it is likely to be many years before all organizations fully replace the HR systems that have been built around job descriptions found in the *DOT*. An example of a *DOT* job description follows:

JOB ANALYST (profess. & kin.) alternate title: personnel analyst.
Collects, analyzes, and prepares occupational information to facilitate personnel, administration, and management functions of organization. Consults with management to determine type, scope, and purpose of study. Studies current organizational occupational data and compiles distribution reports, organization and flow charts,

and other background information required for study. Observes jobs and interviews workers and supervisory personnel to determine job and worker requirements. Analyzes occupational data, such as physical, mental, and training requirements of jobs and workers and develops written summaries, such as job descriptions, job specifications, and lines of career movement. Utilizes developed occupational data to evaluate or improve methods and techniques for recruiting, selecting, promoting, evaluating, and training workers, and administration of related personnel programs. May specialize in classifying positions according to regulated guidelines to meet job classification requirements of civil service system and be known as Position Classifier.

Occupational Information Network

The U.S. Department of Labor's new job analysis service, which was first released to the public in 1998, is titled the *Occupational Information Network (O*NET)*. Available on the Internet, the function of O*NET is "to provide a comprehensive database system for collecting, organizing, describing and disseminating data on job characteristics and worker attributes."[26] O*NET describes jobs as having six content areas, as shown in Exhibit 6.5. The goal is to provide this information for all major occupations represented in the U.S. economy by the end of 2003.

Perhaps the most innovative aspect of O*NET, compared with other approaches to job analysis, is that O*NET attempts to place information about jobs and the people who fill those jobs into an organizational and economic context. For example, the O*NET will provide descriptions of the labor market conditions, wages, and future occupational outlook for the jobs it describes, and it will describe the typical organizational context in which a job is likely to be found. Such information should be especially useful to HR professionals interested in projecting future labor supplies and recruitment strategies.

O*NET is intended to serve as a resource for anyone who seeks to make informed employment decisions. Employers and employees can get facts about occupations and jobs by visiting O*NET's home page and searching the database. For example, a search for information about the occupation of "actuaries" yielded five pages of descriptive information about this occupation. Included were details about

FAST FACT

Approximately half of all actuaries who are wage and salary workers are employed in the insurance industry.

- specific tasks actuaries perform,
- work conditions of typical jobs,
- education that's needed to become an actuary (including recommendations that can be used when selecting college courses),
- examinations and occupational certifications that are required for advancement in the profession,
- predictions about the job outlook through the year 2006,
- average salaries for actuaries at different stages of their careers, and
- suggestions about where to get additional information about this occupation.

O*NET is an important resource for private and public employers. The O*NET method for conducting a job analysis represents state-of-the-art practice. In addition, O*NET results from thousands of jobs are available. Suppose you're a line manager in a small business. You want to provide job descriptions for all of your employees. How can you do this given your

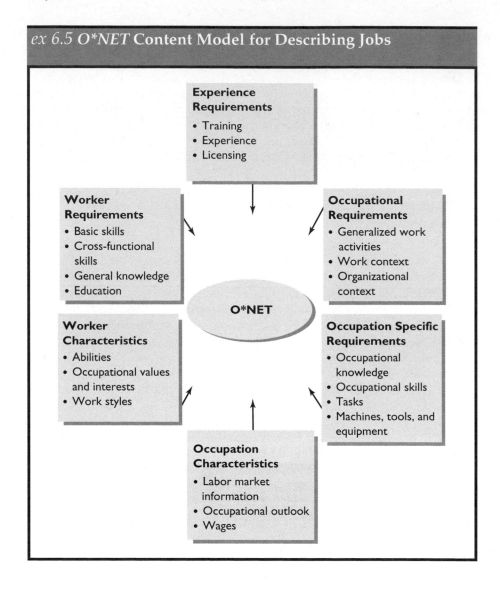

ex 6.5 O*NET Content Model for Describing Jobs

limited resources? O*NET offers one solution. You could find a detailed job description and then adapt it to fit the specific conditions in your company. O*NET is quick, and it's essentially free. Furthermore, the job descriptions available through O*NET are based on hundreds of observations.[27]

With a bit of research, you'll soon discover that O*NET is not the only resource of this kind. You also could purchase a commercial software product that includes hundreds of job descriptions, ready for you to edit and tailor to your needs. The quick and inexpensive software package may be a good alternative to O*NET, but before deciding whether to purchase it, you need to know whether the information used to generate the job descriptions is equally reliable. What sources of information were used to generate the job descriptions? Were acceptable job analysis procedures followed to create the job descriptions, or are the job descriptions just convenient examples? Unless you can be certain that systematic job analysis procedures were applied to very large samples of incumbents in each job of interest to you, O*NET is probably the best solution for this hypothetical small business.

STANDARDIZED JOB ANALYSIS QUESTIONNAIRES

Standardized job analysis questionnaires rely on ratings of job behaviors made by incumbents, supervisors, or perhaps a human resource manager. The advantage of this approach is that it does not require trained job analysts to observe and rate jobs.

The items on standardized questionnaires are intentionally written to be generally applicable to a wide variety of jobs. Consider the job of salesperson in an ice cream parlor. Relevant items from a standardized questionnaire might read "Works in an enclosed area that is cold" and "Chooses among items that differ in terms of color." The value of using such general statements is that they allow you to analyze all types of jobs using the same items. You could use the same questionnaire to analyze the jobs performed by the production workers who make ice cream, the packers who prepare it for shipping, the drivers who deliver it to locations around town, and the salespeople who eventually serve it to customers. Two of the most widely used standardized job analysis questionnaires are the Position Analysis Questionnaire and the Management Position Description Questionnaire.

Position Analysis Questionnaire

The **Position Analysis Questionnaire (PAQ)** can be applied to the activities and behaviors of all workers, regardless of the specific jobs they perform. The creator of the PAQ, Ernest J. McCormick, started with two assumptions: (a) a relatively small set of work behaviors is common to all jobs, and (b) all jobs can be described in terms of how much they involve each of these behaviors. Based on these assumptions, he developed a structured questionnaire containing 194 statements that describe worker behaviors. Each statement is rated on scales such as extent of use, importance to the job, and amount of time spent performing the job. The statements are organized into the six divisions shown in Exhibit 6.6.[28]

The PAQ has been used to analyze hundreds of jobs held by thousands of people. The results from many of these job analyses have been centrally stored in a database to allow comparisons between similar jobs in different organizations. The PAQ database also contains information about the relationships between PAQ responses, job aptitudes, and pay rates for the labor market. Thus, the PAQ can be used to decide what selection criteria to

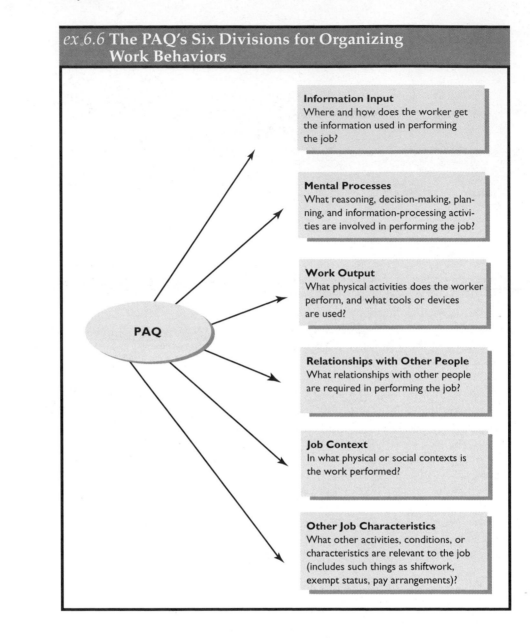

ex 6.6 The PAQ's Six Divisions for Organizing Work Behaviors

Information Input
Where and how does the worker get the information used in performing the job?

Mental Processes
What reasoning, decision-making, planning, and information-processing activities are involved in performing the job?

Work Output
What physical activities does the worker perform, and what tools or devices are used?

Relationships with Other People
What relationships with other people are required in performing the job?

Job Context
In what physical or social contexts is the work performed?

Other Job Characteristics
What other activities, conditions, or characteristics are relevant to the job (includes such things as shiftwork, exempt status, pay arrangements)?

PAQ

use when making hiring decisions, and it can be used to design pay packages. However, the PAQ must be bought from a consulting firm; consequently, direct costs appear high. Another potential drawback to using the PAQ is that it requires a postcollege reading comprehension level. Thus, the PAQ shouldn't be given to raters who have lower levels of reading skill or language fluency.[29]

Management Position Description Questionnaire

The **Management Position Description Questionnaire (MPDQ)** is a standardized questionnaire containing 197 items related to managers' concerns, responsibilities, demands, restrictions, and miscellaneous characteristics.[30] These items have been condensed into 13 essential components of managerial jobs, as illustrated in Exhibit 6.7.

The MPDQ is designed for analyzing all managerial positions, so responses are expected to vary by managerial level in any organization and also across different organizations. The MPDQ is appropriate for creating job families and placing new managerial jobs into the right job family; developing selection procedures and performance appraisal forms; determining the training needs of employees moving into managerial jobs; and designing managerial pay systems.

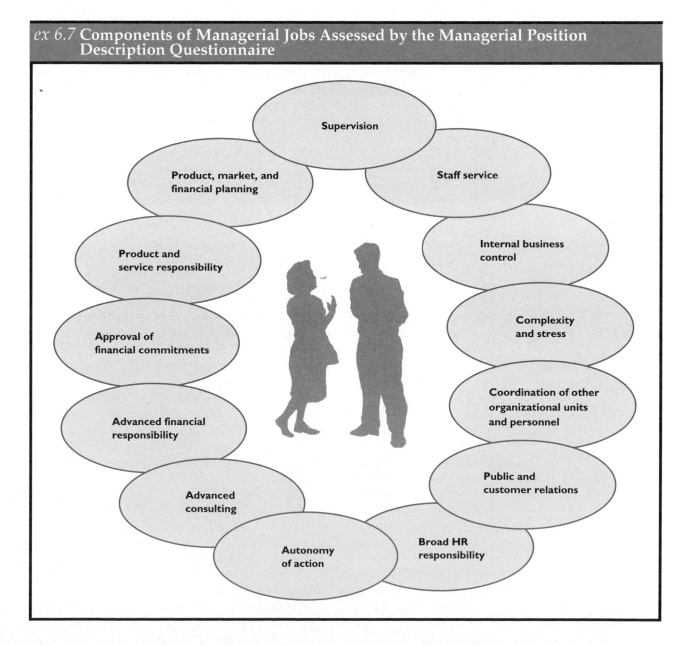

ex 6.7 **Components of Managerial Jobs Assessed by the Managerial Position Description Questionnaire**

CUSTOMIZED TASK INVENTORIES

A **customized task inventory** is a listing of tasks or work behaviors, called items, for the jobs or group of jobs being analyzed. The items in the inventory are not standard items—they are developed as part of the job analysis process and are unique to the jobs being studied. The inventory is customized in that it is developed from the ground up for each new customer, such as a company or a unit within a company or a manager.[31] If the job of HR analyst were analyzed using a customized task inventory, a part of the inventory might look like Exhibit 6.8.

The development of customized task inventories depends heavily on the cooperation of employees. Usually, they must be willing to have their behavior observed, participate in interviews, and respond to lengthy questionnaires. Furthermore, analyzing the results from this method requires complex statistical analysis. Consequently, the use of these instruments is usually limited to organizations that employ many people in the same occupation (police, firefighters, data entry clerks). Reliance on customized job analysis inventories is fairly widespread in city and state governments, the military, and large corporations.

The process of conducting a job analysis using a customized inventory involves using multiple sources of information and multiple methods for collecting information. Usually, observations and interviews are used to learn about the basic activities involved in the jobs being analyzed. Then questionnaires are developed and used to systematically collect more detailed information. In the end, the payoff for this effort is a very detailed understanding of the jobs being analyzed. Exhibit 6.9 illustrates how the job of an administrative assistant was described following a job analysis that used a customized inventory.

Developing the Customized Inventory

The items that appear in a customized job analysis inventory can be generated in a variety of ways. Usually, a job analyst begins by observing the job being performed by incumbents and reviewing samples of the materials, forms, and equipment used in the job. Brief, informal interviews may be conducted during this phase, if needed, to clarify observations and identify the purpose of employee activities. This step familiarizes job analysts with various aspects of the job.

During this phase, some job analysts also ask job incumbents and supervisors to describe critical incidents that represent effective or ineffective performance.[32] Those describing the incidents are asked to describe what led up to the incidents, what the consequences of the behavior were, and whether the behavior was under the incumbent's control. Here is a critical incident report written by a librarian, as an example of effective job performance:

A person who was apparently somewhat disturbed came into the library and started yelling obscenities. When I heard the commotion, I came out of my office and tried to calm him down. I was really afraid he might hurt someone or cause some damage to our collection. I spoke with him for about ten minutes and finally convinced him to step outside. As soon as he did so, I had a staff member call the police and I went outside to try to keep him from leaving the area until the police arrived. Luckily, nothing more happened once we went outside. Later that day, however, a reporter from the local TV news came by and wanted the full story. I told her the basic flow of

ex 6.8 Job Analysis Questionnaire for Human Resource Analyst I

Work Behaviors	A. Is the work behavior performed in the position? 1 = Yes 0 = No	B. Indicate the percentage of time spent performing it. The percentages must total exactly 100.	C. How important is it that this work behavior be performed acceptably? 4 = Critical 3 = Very important 2 = Moderately important 1 = Slightly important 0 = Of no importance	D. Is it necessary that employees new to the position be able to perform this work behavior? 1 = Yes 0 = No
	(circle one)	(fill in)	(circle one)	(circle one)
1. *Counsels employees* on various matters (career opportunities, insurance and retirement options, personal problems relating to employment, etc.) by listening, asking relevant questions, and noting alternative courses of action.	1 0	_____%	4 3 2 1 0	1 0
2. *Disseminates information* (job vacancies and requirements, insurance and retirement programs, merit system rules, etc.) to applicants, employees, and the public verbally through written materials and/or using electronic means.	1 0	_____%	4 3 2 1 0	1 0
3. *Prepares reports* (e.g., management reports, HUD reports) by collecting, organizing, and summarizing statistical data, historical documents, or verbal records, or all three.	1 0	_____%	4 3 2 1 0	1 0
4. *Interviews applicants or employees* in a structured or unstructured manner to investigate applicant or employee complaints, grievances, or adverse action appeal cases and to identify qualified applicants for specific job vacancies.	1 0	_____%	4 3 2 1 0	1 0
5. *Conducts job analyses* by reviewing written records (e.g., job descriptions, class specifications), observing and interviewing job experts, and administering questionnaires.	1 0	_____% Total = 100%	4 3 2 1 0	1 0

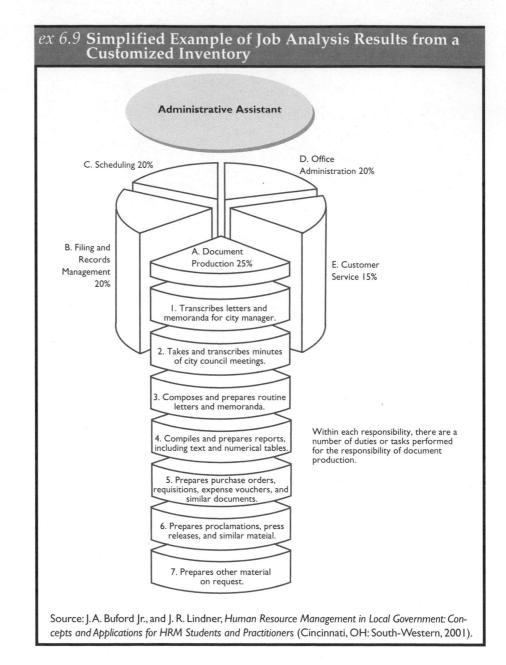

ex 6.9 Simplified Example of Job Analysis Results from a Customized Inventory

Administrative Assistant

C. Scheduling 20%

D. Office Administration 20%

B. Filing and Records Management 20%

A. Document Production 25%

E. Customer Service 15%

1. Transcribes letters and memoranda for city manager.

2. Takes and transcribes minutes of city council meetings.

3. Composes and prepares routine letters and memoranda.

4. Compiles and prepares reports, including text and numerical tables.

5. Prepares purchase orders, requisitions, expense vouchers, and similar documents.

6. Prepares proclamations, press releases, and similar mateial.

7. Prepares other material on request.

Within each responsibility, there are a number of duties or tasks performed for the responsibility of document production.

Source: J.A. Buford Jr., and J. R. Lindner, *Human Resource Management in Local Government: Concepts and Applications for HRM Students and Practitioners* (Cincinnati, OH: South-Western, 2001).

events but tried not to say anything that would reflect poorly on the library or compromise the rights of our intruder. We were all happy to see that the story wasn't carried on the ten o'clock news that evening.

Based on observations, interviews, and reports about critical incidents, the job analyst writes task statements. For example, the librarian's critical incident report was used to create task statements like these:

- Handles serious disturbances created by users of the library.
- Represents the library to members of the news media (e.g., reporters).

Typically, a long list of statements is generated by the job analyst at this stage. These items are used to create a job analysis questionnaire like the one shown in Exhibit 6.8.

Analyzing the Data

Ratings from the custom-designed questionnaire are arithmetically combined to arrive at a description of the job. Finally, work behaviors included in the job description are screened on the basis of combined ratings. Each work behavior must meet several minimum criteria in order to be a "qualifying" work behavior that goes into the job description. For instance, a "qualifying" work behavior would be one performed by the majority of job incumbents.

Exhibit 6.10 shows partial results of work behavior ratings for the job of HR analyst. Statement 5 would now be eliminated because it doesn't qualify as being part of the job for most incumbents.

Advantages and Disadvantages

A major advantage of customized task inventories is that they generate vivid descriptions of the job. Reading a job description developed with this method, it's easy to picture what the job involves. Rather than generate abstract descriptions that could apply to any job, this method creates specific descriptions that clearly outline the tasks required. This advantage also makes it easier to develop training programs for people who will do the job.[33]

The major disadvantages of customized inventories are the time required to develop the task statements and the complex data analysis required after the ratings have been obtained. For example, one job analysis conducted for an organization with 120 positions (i.e., 120 employees) involved 106,000 task ratings; another job analysis for an organization with 3,600 positions involved 1.8 million ratings. Desktop software, computers, intranets, and even artificial intelligence systems can ease the task of collecting and analyzing data sets like these, so this disadvantage is not as significant as

ex 6.10 Job Analysis Results for Human Resource Analyst I

		WORK BEHAVIOR RATINGS		
Item	Work Behavior	Percentage Who Perform	Mean Percentage of Time Spent	Median Importance Rating*
1	Counsels employees	100	15	2
2	Disseminates information	100	33	3
3	Prepares reports	100	33	3
4	Interviews applicants	100	24	2
5	Conducts job analyses	0	0	0

Note: Importance ratings are based on the responses of only SMEs who perform the task.

*Scale for importance rating: 4 = Critical
3 = Very important
2 = Moderately important
1 = Slightly important
0 = Of no importance

it was just a few years ago.[34] Nevertheless, even large firms often rely on consultants who specialize in this work rather than perform complex analyses themselves.

ANALYZING NEEDED COMPETENCIES

Competencies are the skills, knowledge, abilities, and other characteristics that someone needs to perform a job effectively. Information about required competencies is essential if job analysis results are going to be used to develop procedures for selecting people to perform jobs and designing training programs. Competency information can be obtained using either a standardized or a customized approach.

Standardized Approach

A well-known standardized approach to assess ability requirements is the Ability Requirements Approach.[35] Using 50 different ability dimensions, it can be used to assess the level of ability needed in a job. Usually, job incumbents are trained to understand what each ability involves, and then they use a rating scale to report the level of ability required in their work.

Many consulting firms that perform job analysis collect competency information using fairly standardized procedures that they have developed for their own use. For example, Personnel Decisions Inc. developed a taxonomy of managerial competencies that includes the following basic domains:

- Thinking, which includes analytical agility, creativity, planning, strategy development, and business-specific knowledge;
- Communications, which includes verbal, written, listening, and public speaking;
- Inter/Intrapersonal, which includes teamwork, influencing, adapatability, and dependability;
- Leadership, which includes supervision, motivation, decisiveness, and work commitment;
- General Operations Management, which includes materials management, facilities and security, information management, and international operations; and
- Functional Business Knowledge, which includes economics, accounting and finance, marketing and sales, and managing human resources.[36]

When a company hires this firm to conduct a job analysis for managerial jobs, the consultants use a fairly standardized process to assess the required levels of competencies for the focal jobs.

Customized Approach

The examples of job analysis and competency rating questionnaires for a human resource analyst shown in Exhibits 6.8 and 6.10 illustrated the customized approach for assessing competencies. The procedure involves asking subject matter experts (usually incumbents and supervisors) to identify all the skills, knowledge, attitudes, values, and so on that they think may be necessary to perform the work. A group interview meeting may be held to create the list of possible competencies to examine. Based on the results of the group interview meeting, a competency rating questionnaire is created and distributed to subject matter experts. Respondents rate the competencies along a number of dimensions: whether the competency is used at all in the position, importance, whether a new incumbent needs the competency upon entry to the job, and the extent to which the competency distinguishes a superior incumbent from an adequate one. Exhibit 6.11 shows a portion of a competency rating questionnaire.

Exhibit 6.12 shows results for the competency items. Based on these results, the organization may conclude that it should ensure that new hires have a good knowledge of HR procedures and good computer skills, as well as some familiarity with relevant laws and ethical standards. To maximize performance, the organization may want to offer additional training in both HR procedures and legal and ethical standards. Investing in computer training for new hires may not pay off as much, however. While computer skills are necessary, they do not contribute much to outstanding performance.

Global Leadership Competencies at 3M

At 3M, two forces put pressure on the organization to invest in conducting a customized competency-based job analysis. As was true at many other companies, the decade of the 1990s saw increased global competition for 3M. The fierce competition, in turn, highlighted the need for highly effective leaders who could steer the company through a period of shrinking margins, pressures on pricing, and the ever-present demand for more innovations. This environment also highlighted the importance of succession planning as an activity that could promote the company's long-term viability. Due to the breadth of businesses and technologies within 3M, it takes years of experience before executives learn to function effectively in the company. Thoughtful succession planning efforts would ensure that the occasional managerial and executive job openings were leveraged as opportunities for leadership development.

Customized Approach. The decision to use a customized approach to developing a leadership competency model for the company fit well with this company's culture. Innovation is a core competence for 3M, and employees are constantly tinkering with products and systems in order to improve them.

Partnership Perspective. The customized approach also served the objective of involving all key players in the process: HR professionals worked closely with a team of key executives. Rather than simply hand the executives an off-the-shelf competency model, the HR professionals held meetings and discussions with the executives to solicit their ideas, craft the language used in describing the competencies, and so on. After all, the leadership competency model would have important implications for the careers of key talent within the company. Involving executives early in the process would contribute to the validity of the model and also enhance their acceptance of it.

Global Involvement. 3M is a global company, and its leadership competency model is applied all over the world. Thus, the process of developing the leadership competency model required getting input from not only the CEO and those reporting directly to him but also representatives of Europe, Asia, Latin America, Canada, and the United States.

ex 6.11 Competency Rating Questionnaire

Competencies	E. Is the competency used in the position? 1 = Yes 0 = No	F. How important is this competency to acceptable job performance? 4 = Critical 3 = Very important 2 = Moderately important 1 = Slightly important 0 = Of no importance	G. Is it necessary that employees new to the position possess this competency? 1 = Yes 0 = No	H. To what extent does this distinguish between superior and adequate new employees? 3 = To a great extent 2 = Considerably 1 = Moderately 0 = Not at all
A. *Knowledge of HR procedures:* Knowledge of the working rules and regulations. Included are policies on overtime, absences, vacations, holidays, sick leave, court leave, selection, promotion, reassignment, disciplinary actions, terminations, grievance procedures, performance appraisals, and so forth, as outlined in relevant manuals.	(circle one) 1 0	(circle one) 4 3 2 1 0	(circle one) 1 0	(circle one) 3 2 1 0
B. *Knowledge of organizational structure:* Knowledge of whom to contact when various situations arise. Included is the knowledge of interrelationships between organizational units, lines of authority, and responsibility within organizational units.	1 0	4 3 2 1 0	1 0	3 2 1 0
C. *Knowledge of laws and ethics:* Knowledge of legal and ethical standards to be maintained in HR work. Included are ethical considerations governing general professional practice (e.g., confidentiality of records) as well as state and federal regulations governing fair employment practices (e.g., EEO legislation and the *Uniform Guidelines on Employee Selection Procedures*).	1 0	4 3 2 1 0	1 0	3 2 1 0
D. *Computer skill:* Skill in the use of a computer. Included is a basic knowledge of the keyboard and of computer terminology.	1 0	4 3 2 1 0	1 0	3 2 1 0

ex 6.12 Competency Rating Results for Human Resource Analyst I

		COMPETENCY RATINGS			
Item	Competency	Percentage Who Use It	Median Importance Rating*	Percentage Rating It Necessary at Entry	Median Rating for Distinguishing Superior Employees**
A	Knowledge of HR procedures	100	2.5	70	3.0
B	Knowledge of organizational structure	100	2.0	0	2.0
C	Knowledge of laws and ethics	100	2.0	60	2.5
D	Computer skill	100	2.5	80	0.5

Note: Ratings provided by job incumbents. Results are shown only for SMEs who reported they use the competency.

*Scale for importance ratings:
    4 = Critical
    3 = Very important
    2 = Moderately important
    1 = Slightly important
    0 = Of no importance

**Scale for extent to which competency distinguishes superior from average employees in the job:
    3 = To a great extent
    2 = Considerably
    1 = Moderately
    0 = Slightly or not at all

Strategic Importance. The dimensions of 3M's global leadership competency model are described in the feature "Managing Globalization: 3M's Global Leadership Competencies."[37] The competencies listed reflect the corporate values and business strategy. 3M's stated values are these:

- We satisfy customers with superior quality, value, and service.
- We provide our investors with a fair rate of return through sustained quality growth.
- We respect our social and physical environment.
- We work to make 3M a company employees are proud to be a part of.

    These values are apparent in the "fundamental" and "essential" categories. The company's corporate strategy is reflected in the "visionary" competencies.

Behavioral Anchors. Associated with each of 3M's Global Leadership Competencies are specific behaviors that illustrate exemplary levels of competency. Information about the specific behaviors displayed by top-level executives is used by the CEO during their annual review. Elsewhere in the company, executives and managers refer to the specific behaviors when setting performance expectations, judging performance, and discussing the development needs of their employees. As an example, specific behaviors associated with the competency of "global perspective" include the following:

- Respects, values, and leverages other customs, cultures, and values.
- Uses global management team to understand and grow the total business.
- Able to leverage the benefits from working in multicultural environments.

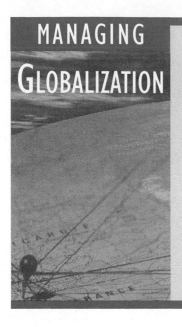

MANAGING GLOBALIZATION

3M's Global Leadership Competencies

The foundation of many HR practices at 3M is their Global Competency Leadership model, which specifies the following major competencies required for success as a leader in this global corporation.

Fundamental Leadership Competencies
New employees should possess these when hired and refine them through experience in successive managerial assignments.
- Ethics and integrity
- Intellectual capacity
- Maturity and judgment

Essential Leadership Competencies
These competencies are developed through experience leading a function or department, and set the stage for more complex executive positions.

- Customer orientation
- Developing people
- Inspiring others
- Business health and results

Visionary Leadership Competencies
These competencies develop as executives take on responsibilities that require them to operate beyond the boundaries of a particular organizational unit and are used extensively in higher-level positions.
- Global perspective
- Vision and strategy
- Nurturing innovation
- Building alliances
- Organizational agility

- Optimizes and integrates resources on a global basis, including manufacturing, research, and businesses across countries, and functions to increase 3M's growth and profitability.
- Satisfies global customers and markets from anywhere in the world.
- Actively stays current on world economies, trade issues, international market trends, and opportunities.

INTERNET RESOURCES   6.C

Specific Tools for Job Analysis and Competency Modeling

At our Web site, http://jackson.swcollege.com/, you can:

1. See sample questions and learn more about the PAQ and the PMPQ.

2. Visit the home page of Job-Analysis, which provides on-line assistance for creating a job description and try creating a job description for a job you have held.

3. Investigate the competency modeling services offered by consultants to learn more about this approach to job analysis and its uses for building an integrated HR system.

4. Learn more about the history of 3M and the nature of this global business today. You can also learn about the McKnight Management Principles, which underlie the company's corporate culture.

JOB FAMILIES AND CAREER PATHS

The initial results of job analyses are typically many separate and unique job descriptions and employee specifications—as many as there are unique jobs. Often, however, these unique jobs aren't greatly different from each other. That is, employees who perform one job may be able to perform several others. And increasingly, as at Aetna, this flexibility is what employers need. This is why organizations group jobs into families. Jobs are placed in the same family to the extent that they require similar competencies or have similar tasks or are of similar value to the organization.[38]

Managing Careers

Grouping distinct jobs into families can also benefit organizations by helping employees see the logical progression that their careers might take if they stay with the company for a period of years. The challenge of providing employees with a satisfying and longer-term career is one that Hovnanian, a large national construction company, faced during the 1990s when a boom in the housing market created a very tight labor market for this industry. The company used job analysis to design a "homebuilding career path." Typically, employees begin their careers working as construction technicians, doing basic carpentry and trade work. As they develop the necessary skills, they can move up to positions that involve greater scope and responsibility. For example, community administrators become involved in sales and service activities, as well as basic construction work. At higher career levels, the work involves supervising various aspects of the company's building projects, while at the highest levels the work includes activities related to building and sustaining a competitive corporation. Using job analyses, Hovnanian identified a logical progression of jobs that employees could move through if they wanted to advance up the corporate ladder. For jobs at all levels, the analyses also pinpointed the skills and knowledge needed to perform the work. Based on this information, the firm could then develop training modules and procedures for assessing the competencies of their employees. Finally, the results were used to develop job performance measures that reflected the key responsibilities associated with each job.

> *"Creating a well-understood path for personal development within our organization enables our Associates to be the best in the business, achieve individual aspirations, and contribute to our strategic business vision."*
>
> Ara Hovnanian
> President and CEO
> K. Hovnanian Companies

Broadbanding

When jobs are grouped into only a very small set of categories, as at Aetna and Hovnanian, the term **broadbanding** is used. Broadbanding involves clustering jobs (or even job families) into wide tiers. One use of broadbanding is managing employee career growth—which is what Hovnanian did. Another common reason to engage in broadbanding is to simplify the company's pay system. When used for pay administration, broadbanding collapses multiple salary grades with narrowly defined pay ranges into fewer salary grades with more pay potential. Flatter and broader pay scales are appropriate for flatter organizational structures, where job descriptions encompass a broad class of jobs rather than specific jobs.[39] Chapter 10 presents a more detailed discussion of how broadbanding is used for pay administration.[40]

MetLife Auto and Home used a modified broadbanding approach to support a new corporation culture that placed less emphasis on rules and more emphasis on flexibility. Its broadbanding approach is described in the feature "Managing Change: Revising Job Analysis to Achieve Business Objectives at MetLife."[41]

TRENDS IN JOB ANALYSIS

At some organizations, such as AT&T and Microsoft, technological changes occur so rapidly that traditional job analysis is all but impossible. And increasingly, job requirements are hard to specify because companies expect employees to do "whatever the customer wants." In these situations, job analysis must be dynamic and fluid. Here, the HR professionals, line managers, and employees all need to value flexibility and adaptability. The fast-paced world of the 21st century poses particularly great challenges for job analysis.

MANAGING CHANGE

Revising Job Analysis to Achieve Business Objectives at MetLife

MetLife Auto and Home was a traditional company with a traditional culture. "We loved job titles and job descriptions," explained Carolyn MacDonald, the director of human resources. "There was a sense of security with our job titles." With 732 job descriptions, there seemed to be more than enough security to go around. But competition was heating up in the insurance industry and MacDonald sensed the need for change.

After studying what was needed to succeed in the future, MacDonald and her staff concluded that employees should be valued and rewarded based on their individual contributions rather than job titles. Broadbanding seemed to offer one solution. With a broadbanding approach, MacDonald could reduce hundreds of narrowly defined jobs to a few dozen more broadly defined jobs. After several months of research aimed at better understanding both the needs of the organization and employees' concerns, MacDonald and her staff decided to completely eliminate job descriptions and salary ranges. The new approach would give managers the flexibility needed to move employees around the organization and it would give employees opportunities to accept new challenges without worrying about whether taking a new position would result in lower pay or status.

A new organizational architecture was designed. Its four key elements are career bands, corporate profiles, functional profiles, and employee development continuums.

Career bands describe the five types of careers followed by most employees: leadership, professional, technical, management, and administrative.

Corporate profiles describe seven areas of competencies that *all* employees should display: knowledge, customer relations, impact/execution, decision making, innovation, communication, and ethics/quality. For each career band, a corporate profile details the responsibilities of people who are moving along that career ladder. For example, for the domain of "Innovation," professionals "encourage and foster a learning environment that encompasses a theoretical or scientific area of expertise and its applicability to MetLife Auto and Home." Within this system, no profile is superior to the other, and there are no salary ranges associated with the profiles.

Functional profiles describe departmental roles and are used in place of traditional job descriptions. The functional profiles describe what is to be achieved and the competencies needed to achieve it. For example, the function of a trainer is to "develop and/or administer programs that will educate claims personnel and enhance the skills necessary to facilitate individual personal and professional development." Performing this function requires knowledge of the company's claims procedures and state regulations, basic understanding of learning and instructional techniques; effective communication skills, the ability to work independently, and several other specified competencies.

Finally, an *employee development continuum* describes how an employee can continuously develop competencies. In this new culture, titles do little more than indicate one's general function. An employee's level of development is what determines value to the organization, regardless of career track or department.

The Decline of Job Analysis?

Decreased job specialization, increased job sharing, and the increased prevalence of work teams are just a few of the reasons why people have begun to question the usefulness of traditional job analysis techniques. Traditional techniques force boundaries to be drawn between jobs and are inconsistent with the trend toward increased sharing of responsibilities across jobs and across levels in the organization.[42]

The apparent inconsistency between the assumptions of traditional job analysis and new approaches to managing employees is so great that it has led some human resource professionals to raise the question: "Do we need job analysis anymore?" We think the answer to this question is clearly yes. What seems to be changing, however, is the preference for competency-based approaches to job analysis over other traditional approaches. As we stated at the beginning of this chapter, job analysis and competency modeling can be valuable tools during strategic change. Also, job analysis is essential to any organization concerned about legal compliance and its ability to defend its employment practices (the legal status of competency modeling is not as well established, however). Clearly, organizations will continue to use job analysis in some form as a foundation upon which to build integrated HR systems.

While job analysis will not disappear, the procedures used are likely to evolve and change to meet the new needs of organizations. The increasing popularity of competency modeling (instead of task-focused job analysis) is one example of how job analysis is evolving. Part of the appeal of competency modeling seems to be that it is more useful for identifying the "core" competencies and behaviors that are *similar* across all jobs in a department, business unit, or organization. When these are included in employees' job descriptions, competency modeling serves as a tool for defining and communicating a consistent corporate culture.

From "My Job" to "My Role"

Traditional job analysis techniques were developed in a time when organizations and jobs were more stable and predictable. People could be hired to do a particular job, and they could expect to do basically the same job in the same way for many months or even years. This arrangement was convenient for management and workers, except when management wanted the workers to change or do something "not in their job descriptions."

Flexibility. Today's environment requires adaptable organizations and flexible individuals. Organizations focus on how they can get flexibility without worker resistance, while also satisfying workers' needs for comfort. Organizations such as Nissan and Honda hire applicants to work for the company rather than to do a specific job. At Southwest Airlines, Libby Sartain, vice president of people, likes to say that they hire people to do work, not jobs. Thus we are seeing a shift in the employee's attention—from thinking only about doing "my job" to thinking about doing whatever is necessary to accomplish the organization's work.[43] Corresponding to this, some human resource professionals have argued that the term *role analysis* should be used in place of the term job analysis.[44] Focusing on roles when conducting job analysis and writing job descriptions is consistent with the philosophy of emphasizing results over procedures, and it works well in organizations that allow employees to use flexible work arrangements, such as telecommuting and flextime, to adapt work requirements to their personal needs.[45]

Teamwork. This shift from a focus on "the job" to work roles is almost inevitable in organizations where work is organized around teams instead of individuals. In a team environment, the tasks performed by a particular individual may depend on the talents and interests of the other people in the team. The team as a whole is assigned duties and may be held accountable for specific tasks. If the team is self-managed, members can organize the team's work any way they wish. In such situations, asking individuals about their roles as a team members may be much more useful than asking them to describe their "individual job."[46]

Future-Oriented Job Analysis and Competency Modeling

To address the reality of constant change, traditional job analysis and competency modeling procedures can both be easily modified to provide information

"The shelf-life of job analysis results is only as long as the duration of the current job configurations."

Karen E. May
Partner
Human Resource Solutions

"At one point we were hiring hands and arms and legs, and now we are hiring total people—with minds more important than the other."

Robert J. Eaton
Former Chairman and CEO
Chrysler

FAST FACT

Telecommuting is growing at an annual rate of 20.6 % according to research by the International Telework Association & Council.

"The job is just a social artifact. Most societies since the beginning of time have done fine without jobs. In the preindustrial past, people worked very hard, but they did not have jobs."

William Bridges
Author
Job Shift

about the likely nature of future job tasks and the competencies that employees are likely to need to perform those new tasks. In a **future-oriented job analysis**, the emphasis shifts from *descriptions* of the present to *prescriptions* about what the future should be like.

For example, suppose an organization has decided to downsize. Traditional job analysis could be used to identify all the tasks currently performed by employees. Then, a future-oriented job analysis could be conducted to focus attention on which tasks the organization *should* continue doing, and which it should eliminate or outsource. Thus, in this example, a future-oriented job analysis would be included as part of the organization's strategic planning processes. Following the process of HR planning described in Chapter 5, the results of the future-oriented job analysis would serve as a foundation for developing new HR policies and practices related to hiring, training, performance measurement, pay, and so on.

A large Southern energy company used future-oriented job analysis and competency modeling as part of its integration process following the acquisition of another similar company. In addition to the merger, the industry was moving from a period of regulation to deregulation. During this time of strategic change, managers recognized the value of thinking systematically about what would be the appropriate new culture for the company. To define the new culture, the company conducted a future-oriented job analysis to identify the key competencies that would be needed and specify the appropriate cultural behaviors. Executives in both companies participated in the job analysis interviews, and managers in both companies participated by describing critical incidents that revealed exemplary cultural behaviors. When managers were selected for key positions in the merged company, they were assessed against the competency model that had been created.[47]

Job Analysis for Customers

A desire to maximize customer satisfaction drives many organizations to look for new approaches to managing. Having nearly run out of new ideas, some progressive companies began to realize that there are many parallels between managing customers and managing employees. Peter Mills, a business professor and service management expert, even suggested that customers should be thought of as "partial employees" of the organization.

If one thinks of customers as partial employees, the next logical step is to consider how human resource management practices might be used with customers. Professors Benjamin Schneider and David Bowen have done just that. They advise organizations to use job analysis techniques to assess their current customer role and to develop a description of the ideal role that customers could play.

For many organizations, customers are given tasks to do before they arrive on site (e.g., mortgage companies send forms for customers to complete and checklists of items to attach to the forms; surgical outpatient clinics give patients dietary instructions to follow the day before they're to have surgery, etc.). Once on site, the organization is likely to want customers to engage in some behaviors and avoid others. Job analysis procedures can help the organization identify customer behaviors and competencies that increase or decrease the probability of a successful service encounter. Detailed "job" analysis results describe the behaviors and competencies needed from customers. The organization can then decide whether customer behaviors are best modified by

- selecting different customers (e.g., sell to a different market),
- training customers (e.g., give them better instructions), and/or
- increasing their motivation to engage in the desired behaviors (e.g., change the service fee structure).

Human Factors Approach to Job Analysis and Job Redesign

The objective of the **human factors approach** to analyzing jobs, also referred to as *ergonomic analysis,* is to minimize the amount of stress and fatigue experienced as a result of doing work. An ergonomic analysis of a job focuses on how job tasks affect physical movements and physiological responses.[48] For example, with an understanding of the biomechanics of the wrist, arm, and shoulder, ergonomic analysis of office jobs can be used to identify sources of unnecessary strain. Office equipment that causes unnecessary strain might then be replaced, workers may be trained to operate the equipment in ways that minimize strain, or other accommodations may be made to safeguard employees' health.

> **FAST FACT**
>
> Eighty percent of us will sustain a back injury during our lifetime.

The human factors approach to job analysis and redesign has proved useful in automobile factories, where the physical capabilities of the workforce have changed as this workforce has aged. On average, U.S. autoworkers are now more than a decade older than their counterparts in Japan. This makes it increasingly difficult to achieve productivity gains using the old approach of just speeding up the assembly line. Ergonomic analysis of these jobs helped U.S. auto companies identify the sources of strain that affect their older workers and guided the auto industry's efforts to redesign plants and install equipment to ease the strain. For example, overhead conveyor belts tilt auto bodies at angles that make assembly work less physically demanding, and the air guns used to drive screws are designed to reduce the stresses that cause carpal tunnel syndrome. Gyms have been installed, and workers have taken "back classes" to learn how to lift without injuring themselves.

Just before leaving office, former president Bill Clinton sought to enact new regulations that would have held employers accountable for meeting higher ergonomic standards in the workplace. Ultimately, this regulatory effort was unsuccessful. Nevertheless, this event stimulated public discussion of the potential negative health consequences of poorly designed offices, equipment, and tools. When new ergonomic regulations are eventually adopted, the human factors approach to job analysis will quickly become more widespread.

INTERNET RESOURCES 6.D

Trends

At our Web site, http://jackson.swcollege.com/, you can:

1. Learn more about the trend toward telecommuting from the International Telework Association & Council.

2. Visit the home page of the Society for Industrial and Organizational Psychology, which has many members who are experts in job analysis and competency modeling. Search for experts and learn about the services they offer.

3. Track other trends in job analysis and competency modeling by visiting the Job-Analysis.Net Work.

SUMMARY

The creation and maintenance of effective organizations require a comprehensive understanding of the work that needs to be done and the way work is structured into jobs. Job analysis and competency modeling provide systematic information about the duties associated with jobs, the behaviors required to fulfill those duties, and the competencies needed by jobholders. In turn, this information is helpful for determining hiring criteria, designing training programs, developing measures of performance, creating career paths, and setting pay policies. Thus, job analysis and competency modeling results serve as a basis for linking together all human resource activities and also linking these activities to the needs of the business.

Job analysis can be conducted in a variety of ways. When choosing a method for conducting job analysis, the best choice depends on the intended purpose. Standardized methods make it easy to compare the results for a particular job with results found for many other similar or dissimilar jobs—including jobs in other organizations. Thus, it can be useful for setting pay schedules and creating career ladders. Compared with standardized approaches, customized job analysis methods provide more job-specific details. Such details are particularly useful for designing training programs and creating performance measurement and feedback systems.

Regardless of the approach, job analysis serves as the foundation for nearly all the human resource practices described in the chapters ahead. In addition to helping to create consistency across the entire HR system of practices (e.g., by providing content that can be used in job descriptions, training programs, career planning, performance appraisals, and so on), job analysis can be adapted for use as a strategic planning tool. Future-oriented job analysis is one way to help managers envision how anticipated changes in the business are likely to affect the nature of people's future jobs and the competencies that people will need to perform them.

TERMS TO REMEMBER

broadbanding
competency modeling
customized task inventory
Dictionary of Occupational Titles (DOT)
functional job analysis (FJA)
future-oriented job analysis
human factors approach
job
job analysis
job description
job family
job incumbents
Management Position Description Questionnaire (MPDQ)

methods analysis
*Occupational Information Network (O*NET)*
position
Position Analysis Questionnaire (PAQ)
representative sample
standardized job analysis questionnaire
subject matter experts (SMEs)
task-oriented job analysis
work sampling
worker-oriented job analysis

DISCUSSION QUESTIONS

1. Describe how job analysis and competency modeling can be useful during times of strategic organizational change, such as a merger, downsizing, or rapid growth.

2. Domestic labor shortages are predicted to persist for at least the next decade. How can job analysis and competency modeling improve the ability of employers to attract and retain the talent they need during labor shortages?

3. What special challenges are likely to arise when global organizations conduct job analyses around the world?

4. Describe the possible uses of job analysis results. What does it mean to say that job analysis serves as a foundation for an organization's integrated HR system?

5. What are the advantages and disadvantages of standardized and customized approaches to job analysis and competency modeling?

6. The courts have recognized task-based job analysis as useful for preventing unfair discrimination, but some HR professionals worry that competency-based approaches are more susceptible to stereotyping and bias. From an employee's perspective, would you prefer to have a job description and performance appraisal based on a task-oriented job analysis or a competency modeling study? Explain why.

PROJECTS TO EXTEND YOUR LEARNING

1. *Managing Teams.* In a local organization (e.g., business, hospital, or service organization), identify one or more jobs that seem to require a great deal of teamwork. Obtain the job descriptions for these jobs. First analyze each job description in terms of its completeness, as described in this chapter. To what extent do they provide information regarding performance standards, worker activities, equipment used, job context, job characteristics and worker specifications, or personality requirements? Interview the job incumbents to get their views about whether the job description is complete. Find out what job analysis methods were used by the organization to collect the information in the descriptions, who provided the information, and how long ago the information was collected. Suggest specific improvements in the job analysis methods used to create the job description.

2. *Managing Globalization.* Conduct a future-oriented job analysis focusing on how globalization is likely to affect the way an existing job might be performed in the future. Follow these steps:

    a. Select a job you might like to perform during some stage of your career. Pick a professional job (e.g., manager, financial analyst, chemical engineer, museum curator, dietician), not a skilled or semiskilled job.

    b. Select a method to conduct your job analysis. To do this exercise, you will have to modify whatever technique you choose in order to make it a future-oriented job analysis.

    c. Select a person or persons to interview, observe, and so forth. Identify that person and give her or his telephone number.

    d. Conduct a future-oriented job analysis. Focus on learning how the job is likely to change during the next five years. What changes might result in the job becoming more globally oriented? What implications would greater globalization have for the competencies needed to do the job?

   e. Prepare a complete job description for the position as it is likely to exist in five years. Rank the job duties in order of their importance. Indicate the amount of time spent on each task. Also indicate the criticality of error if this task is performed incorrectly.

   f. Respond to this question: "From the perspective of (1) an employee and (2) the employee's manager, why is it important to conduct future-oriented job analysis?"

3. *Integration and Application.* After reviewing the end-of-text cases of Lincoln Electric and Southwest Airlines, answer the following questions:

   a. Compare the objectives of job analysis in these two cases.

   b. Explain how job analysis helps each organization meet its strategic objectives.

   c. For each company, describe the advantages and disadvantages of using standardized versus customized job analysis techniques.

JOB DESCRIPTIONS AT HITEK

Jennifer Hill was excited about joining HITEK Information Services after receiving her BA. Her job involved examining compensation practice, and her first assignment was to review HITEK's job descriptions. She was to document her work and make recommended changes, which would include reducing more than six hundred job descriptions to a manageable number.

BACKGROUND

To its stockholders and the rest of the outside world, HITEK is a highly profitable, highly aggressive company in the computer business. In addition to its numerous government contracts, it provides software and hardware to businesses and individuals. From its inception in the late 1970s, it has maintained its position on the leading edge by remaining flexible and adaptable to the turbulent environment in which it operates. It's a people-intensive organization that relies enormously on its human resources; therefore, it's in HITEK's best interests to establish policies and procedures that nurture productivity and enhance the satisfaction of its employees.

Because the computer industry is growing at an incredible pace, opportunities for placement are abundant, and the competition for high-quality human resources is tremendous. HITEK has grown about 30 percent in the last three years, and its management knows that, as easily as it attracts new employees, it can lose them. However, its turnover rate (14 percent) is about average for its industry.

HITEK remains relatively small at one thousand employees, and it prides itself on its "small team company culture." This culture is maintained partly by extensive use of the company's intranet and by the utilization of open office spaces. The relatively flat, lean organizational structure (shown in Case Exhibit 1) and the easy accessibility of all corporate levels also supports an open-door policy. All in all, employees enjoy working for HITEK, and management is in touch with the organization's "pulse."

With the notable exception of the HR department, there are few rules at HITEK. In other departments, employees at all levels share the work, and positions are redefined to match the specific competencies and interests of the incumbent. "Overqualified" and "overachieving" individuals are often hired but are then promoted rapidly. Nothing is written down; and if newcomers want to know why something is done a certain way, they must ask the person(s) who created the procedure. There is extensive horizontal linkage between departments, perpetuating the blurring of distinctions between departments.

THE HR DEPARTMENT

The HR department stands in stark contrast to the rest of HITEK. About 30 people are employed in the department, including the support staff members, or

Case Exhibit 1 HITEK's Organizational Chart

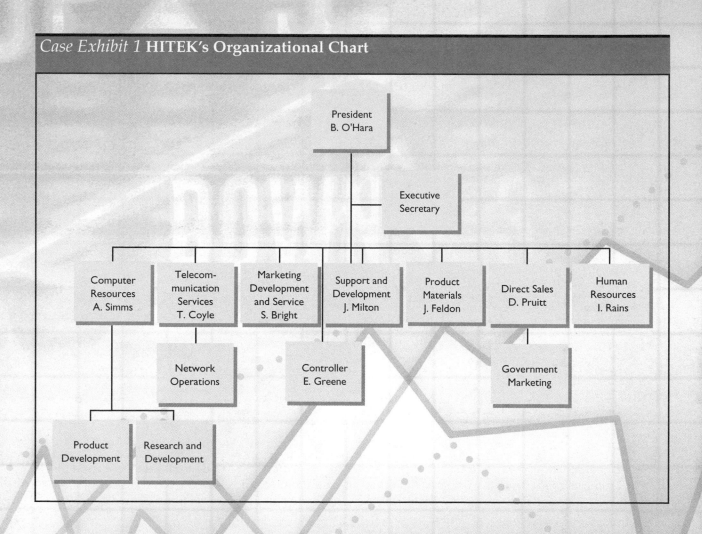

about one HR employee per 33 HITEK employees. The vice president for human resources, Isabel Rains, rules the department with an "iron fist." Employees are careful to mold their ideas to match Rains's perspective. When newcomers suggest changes, they're told that "this is the way things have always been done" because "it's our culture." Written rules and standard operating procedures guide all behavior. Department employees know their own job descriptions well and there is little overlap in employees' duties.

With the exception of one recruiter, all 12 of the incumbents whose positions are represented in Case Exhibit 2 are women. Only half of them have degrees in industrial relations or HRM, and only one-fourth have related experience with another company. Most of them have been promoted from clerical positions. In fact, some employees view the vice presidency as a "gift" given to Isabel, a former executive secretary, the day after she received her

bachelor's degree at a local college. In other departments, it's widely believed that professional degrees and related experience lead to expertise.

One incident that conveyed the department's image to Jennifer Hill occurred during her second week on the job. While preparing a job description with Dave Pruitt, Jennifer explained that she would submit the job description to Janet Voris for final approval. Dave became confused and asked, "But Janet is only a clerical person; why would she be involved?"

JENNIFER HILL'S DUTIES

At HITEK, the pool of job descriptions had grown almost daily as newcomers were hired, but many of the old job descriptions were not discarded, even when obsolete. Other job descriptions needed updating. Jennifer spent some time thinking about how to proceed. She considered the uses of the job descriptions and what steps she would need to take to

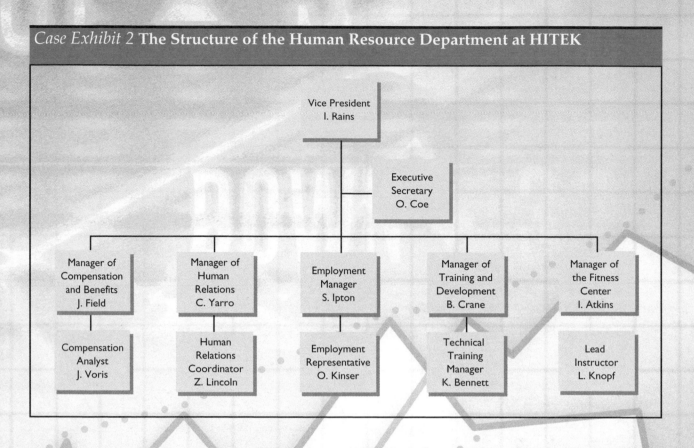

accomplish all that was expected of her. Support from within the department was scarce because other employees were busy gathering materials for the annual review of HITEK's hiring, promotion, and development practices conducted by the Equal Employment Opportunity Commission.

After six harried months on the job and much frustration, Jennifer had revised all the descriptions that were still needed (examples of "old" and "new" job descriptions appear in Case Exhibits 3 and 4). She was also beginning to develop some strong opinions about how the HR department functioned at HITEK

Case Exhibit 3 **An "Old" Job Description**

ASSOCIATE PROGRAMMER

Basic Objective	Perform coding, testing, and documentation of programs, under the supervision of a project leader.
Specific Tasks	• Perform coding, debugging, and testing of a program when given general program specifications. • Develop documentation of the program. • Assist in the implementation and training of the users in the usage of the system. • Report to the manager, management information services as requested.
Job Qualifications	Minimum: • BA/BS degree in relevant field or equivalent experience/knowledge • Programming knowledge in Java or C# • Good working knowledge of business and financial applications Desirable: • Computer programming experience in a time-sharing environment • Some training or education in XML, UML, and HTML

ASSOCIATE PROGRAMMER

General Statement of Duties Performs coding, debugging, testing, and documentation of software under the supervision of a technical superior or manager. Involves some use of independent judgment.

Supervision Received Works under close supervision of a technical superior or manager.

Supervision Exercised No supervisory duties required.

Examples of Duties (Any one position may not include all the duties listed, nor do listed examples include all duties that may be found in positions of this class.)
- Confers with analysts, supervisors, and/or representatives of the departments to clarify software intent an programming requirements.
- Performs coding, debugging, and testing of software when given program specifications for a particular task or problem.
- Writes documentation for the program.
- Seeks advice and assistance from supervisor when problems outside of realm of understanding arise.
- Communicates any program specification deficiencies back to supervisor.
- Reports ideas concerning design and development back to supervisor.
- Assists in the implementation of the system and training of end users.
- Provides some support and assistance to users.
- Develops product knowledge and personal expertise and proficiency in system usage.
- Assumes progressively complex and independent duties as experience permits.
- Performs all duties in accordance with corporate and departmental standards.

Minimum Qualifications
- Education: BA/BS degree in relevant field or equivalent experience/knowledge in computer science, math, or other closely related field.
- Experience: No prior computer programming work experience necessary.
- Knowledge, skills, ability to exercise initiative and sound judgment.
- Knowledge of a structured language.
- Working knowledge in operating systems.
- Ability to maintain open working relationship with supervisor.
- Logic and problem-solving skills.
- System flowchart development skills.

Desirable Qualifications
- Exposure to Java, C# and data transfer languages.
- Some training in general accounting practices and controls.
- Effective written and communication skills.

and what needed to be done to improve its effectiveness and its image. She decided to arrange a confidential lunch with Billy O'Hara, HITEK's president.

QUESTIONS

1. What are the strategic objectives of HITEK? Of the HR department? Why does the conflict create problems for HITEK?
2. Jobs change frequently at HITEK. What approach to job analysis makes the most sense in such a fast-changing environment: Customized? Standardized? Task-focused? Competency modeling? Broadbanding? Evaluate the strengths and weaknesses of the alternative approaches and make recommendations to Jennifer about how to proceed.
3. Is the "new" job description (Case Exhibit 4) better than the "old" one (Case Exhibit 3)? Why or why not? Consider the employee's perspective as well as the perspective of the person supervising this job. Does your answer change depending on the way the job description is being used?

Source: Written by M. P. Miceli, Georgetown University, and Karen Wijta, Macy's.

ENDNOTES

1 B. Fryer, "Siebel Systems," *Harvard Business Review* (March 2001): 122.

2 J. B. Treaster, "Aetna Is Said to Seek Deal in Health Care," *New York Times* (February 28, 1998): D1; J. B. Treaster, "Aetna Deal for New York Life's Health Unit is Expected Today," *New York Times* (March 16, 1998): D1; S. Jackson, "Aetna's Brave New World," *Business Week* (March 30, 1998): 180; S. Caudron, "Master the Compensation Maze," *Personnel Journal* (June 1993): 64D; C. Roush, "Aetna's Heavy Ax," *Business Week* (February 14, 1994): 32. Aetna Life and Casualty Company, *Our Vision and Our Values* (internal company document, Hartford, CT, 1994).

3 See J. Shippmann, R. Ash, M. Batitista, L. Carr, L. Eyde, B. Hesketh, J. F. Kehoe, K. Pearlman, E. Prien, and J. I. Sanchez, "The Practice of Competency Modeling," *Personnel Psychology* 53 (2000): 703–740; S. B. Parry, "The Quest for Competencies," *Training* (July 1996): 48–56.

4 T. R. Athey and M. S. Orth, "Emerging Competency Methods for the Future," *Human Resource Management* 38 (Fall 1999): 215–226.

5 D. Rahbah-Daniels, M. L. Erickson, and A. Dalik, "Here to Stay: Taking Competencies to the Next Level," *WorldatWork Journal* (First Quarter 2001): 70–77.

6 The essence of the Civil Rights Act of 1964 and 1991, the Equal Opportunity in Employment Act of 1972, and various court decisions is that employment decisions be made on the basis of whether the individual will be able to perform the job. Chapter 8 expands on the job relatedness of selection procedures.

7 "Objective Employee Appraisals and Discrimination Cases," *Fair Employment Practices* (December 6, 1990): 145–146.

8 M. M. Harris. "Practice Network: ADA and I-O Psychology," *Industrial-Organizational Psychologist* 36(1) (1998): 33–37. "Job Analyses and Job Descriptions Under ADA," *Fair Employment Practices* (April 22, 1993): 45; see also K. Tyler, "Looking for a Few Good Workers?" *HR Magazine* (December 2000): 129; B. P. Sunoo, "Accommodating Workers with Disabilities," *Workforce* (February 2001): 86–93; E. Tahmincioglu, "Job Aides Open Doors for Those Who Can't," *New York Times* (January 24, 2001): G1.

9 R. Lieber, "The Permatemps Contretemps," *Fast Company* (August 2000): 198–214.

10 N. E. McDermott, "Independent Contractors and Employees: Do You Know One When You See One?" *Legal Report* (November–December, 1999): 1–4.

11 S. Bates, "A Tough Target: Employee or Independent Contractor?" *HR Magazine* (June 2001): 69–74.

12 R. J. Harvey, "Job Analysis," in M. D. Dunnette and L. M. Hough (eds.), *Handbook of Industrial Organizational Psychology*, 2d ed. (Palo Alto, CA: Consulting Psychologists Press, 1991).

13 Throughout this book, we use the term *competency* to refer to a cluster of related knowledge, skills, abilities, and other personal characteristics and qualities that affect performance on the job.

14 J. S. Schippmann, *Strategic Job Modeling: Working at the Core of Integrated Human Resources* (Mahwah, NJ: Lawrence Erlbaum, 1999).

15 G. Lane and A. Robinson, "The Development of Competency Standards for Senior Management," *Executive Development* 8(6) (1995): 13–18.

16 *How to Analyze Jobs* (Stanford, CT: Bureau of Law & Business, 1982); Equal Employment Opportunity Commission, *Uniform Guidelines on Employee Selection Procedures*, 43 Federal Register, 38290–38315 (1978); J. Ledvinka and V. G. Scarpello, *Federal Regulation of Personnel and Human Resource Management*, 2d ed. (Boston: Kent Publishing, 1990).

17 F. P. Morgenson and M. A. Campion, "Social and Cognitive Sources of Potential Inaccuracy in Job Analysis," *Journal of Applied Psychology* 82 (1998): 627–655.

18 For a detailed discussion of how to maximize accuracy in job analysis results, see J. I. Sanchez and E. L. Levine, "Accuracy or Consequential Validity: Which is the Better Standard for Job Analysis Data? *Journal of Organizational Behavior* 21 (2000): 809–818; F. P. Morgenson and M. A. Campion, "Accuracy in Job Analysis: Toward an Inference Based Model," *Journal of Organizational Behavior* 21 (2000): 819–827; R. J. Harvey and M. A. Wilson, "Yes, Virginia, There Is an Objective Reality in Job Analysis," *Journal of Organizational Behavior* 21 (2000): 829–854.

19 M. K. Lindell, C. S. Clause, C. J. Brandt, and R. S. Landis, "Relationship Between Organizational Context and Job Analysis Task Ratings," *Journal of Applied Psychology* 83 (1998): 769–776; F. J. Landy and J. Vasey, "Job Analysis: The Composition of SME Samples," *Personnel Psychology* 44 (1991): 27–50.

20 R. D. Arvey, "Sex Bias in Job Evaluation Procedures," *Personnel Psychology* 39 (1986): 315–335; A. P. O'Reilly, "Skill Requirements: Supervisor-Subordinate Conflict," *Personnel Psychology* 26 (Spring 1973): 75–80.

21 J. I. Sanchez and E. I. Levine, "Accuracy or Consequential Validity: Which Is the Better Standard for Job Analysis Data?" J. Shippmann, *Strategic Job Modeling: Working at the Core of Integrated Human Resources.*

22 D. E. Bowen and D. A. Waldman, "Customer-driven Employee Performance," in D. R. Ilgen and E. D. Pulakos (eds.), *The Changing Nature of Work Performance: Implications for Staffing, Personnel Actions and Development* (San Francisco: Jossey-Bass, 1999).

23 F. C. Lager, *Ben & Jerry's: The Inside Scoop* (New York: Crown, 1994).

24 A. W. Mathews, "New Gadgets Trace Truckers' Every Move," *Wall Street Journal* (July 14, 1997): B1, B2.

25 For a full description of FJA as it is practiced today, see S. A. Fine and S. E. Cronshaw, *Functional Job Analysis: A Foundation for Human Resources Management* (Mahwah, NJ: Lawrence Erlbaum, 1999).

26 Information about O*NET is provided by the Department of Labor at http://www.doleta.gov/programs/onet/. See also N. G. Peterson et al., "Understanding Work Using the Occupational Information Network (O*NET): Implications for Practice and Research," *Personnel Psychology* 54 (2001): 451–492.

27 Fundamental changes to the DOT—a monumental undertaking—has been under way for several years.

28 Our description of the PAQ and its development is based on E. J. McCormick, P. R. Jeanneret, and R. C. Mecham, "A Study of Job Characteristics and Job Dimensions as Based on the Position Analysis Questionnaire," *Journal of Applied Psychology* 56 (1972): 347–367; E. J. McCormick and J. Tiffin, *Industrial Psychology*, 6th ed. (Englewood Cliffs, NJ: Prentice-Hall, 1994).

29 For additional discussion of the PAQ, see E. T. Cornelius III, A. S. DeNisi, and A. G. Blencoe, "Expert and Naive Raters Using the PAQ: Does It Matter?" *Personnel Psychology* (Autumn 1984): 453–464; E. J. McCormick, A. S. DeNisi, and B. Shaw, "Use of the Position Analysis Questionnaire for Establishing Job Component Validity of Tests," *Journal of Applied Psychology* 64 (1979): 51–56.

30 W. W. Tornow and P. R. Pinto, "The Development of a Managerial Job Taxonomy: A System for Describing, Classifying, and Evaluating Executive Positions," *Journal of Applied Psychology* 61 (1976): 410–418.

31 J. I. Sanchez and S. L. Fraser, "On the Choice of Scales for Task Analysis," *Journal of Applied Psychology* 77 (1992): 545–553; M. A. Wilson and R. J. Harvey, "The Value of Relative Time-Spent Ratings in Task-Oriented Job Analysis," *Journal of Business and Psychology* 4 (1990): 453–461.

32 J. C. Flanagan, "The Critical Incident Technique," *Psychological Bulletin* 51 (1954): 327–358.

33 I. L. Goldstein, *Training in Organizations: Needs Assessment, Development, and Evaluation* (Pacific Grove, CA: Brooks/Cole, 1993).

34 R. J. Harvey, "Job Analysis."

35 E. A. Fleishman and M. D. Mumford, "Ability Requirement Scales," S. Gael (ed.), *The Job Analysis Handbook for Business, Industry, and Government*, vol. 2 (New York: John Wiley, 1988).

36 J. S. Schippman, *Strategic Job Modeling: Working at the Core of Integrated Human Resources*.

37 For a detailed discussion of the 3M leadership competency model, see M. Alldredge and K. Nilan, "3M's Leadership Competency Model: An Internally Developed Solution," *Human Resource Management* 39 (2&3) (Summer/Fall 2000): 133–145; for other examples, see T. R. Athey and M. S. Orth, "Emerging Competency Methods for the Future."

38 Detailed discussions of issues related to creating job families are provided in J. Colhan and G. K. Burger, "Constructing Job Families: An Analysis of Quantitative Techniques Used for Grouping Jobs," *Personnel Psychology* 48 (1995): 563–586; M. K. Garwood, L. E. Anderson, and B. J. Greengart, "Determining Job Groups: Application of Hierarchical Agglomerative Cluster Analysis in Different Job Analysis Situations," *Personnel Psychology* (1991): 743–762; J. C. Hogan, "Structure of Physical Performance in Occupational Tasks," *Journal of Applied Psychology* 76 (1991): 495–507.

39 ACA/Hewitt Associates, *Life with Broadbands* (Phoenix, AZ: American Compensation Association, 1998); K. S. Abosch, "Confronting Six Myths of Broadbanding," *ACA Journal* (Autumn 1998): 28–35.

40 For other examples of using broadbanding, see M. Enos and G. Limoges, "Broadbanding: Is That Your Company's Final Answer?" *World at Work Journal* (Fourth Quarter 2000): 61–68.

41 L. Sierra, "The Next Generation of Broadbanding: Insurance Company Overhauls Hierarchy with CareerBanding," *ACA News* (February 1998): 21–24; see also D. Gilbert and K. S. Abosch, *Improving Organizational Effectiveness through Broadbanding* (Scottsdale, AZ: American Compensation Association, 1996).

42 R. B. Morgan and J. E. Smith, *Staffing the New Workplace: Selecting and Promoting Quality Improvement* (Milwaukee: ASQC Quality Press, 1996); K. P. Carson and G. L. Stewart, "Job Analysis and the Sociotechnical Approach to Quality: A Critical Examination," *Journal of Quality Management* 1 (1996): 49–64.

43 R. Lieber, "The Permatemps Contretemps," *Fast Company* (August 2000): 198–214; W. Bridges, *Job Shift: How to Prosper in a Workplace without Jobs* (Addison-Wesley, 1995).

44 C. Joinson, "Refocusing Job Descriptions," *HR Magazine* (January 2001): 67–72; J. I. Sanchez, "From Documentation to Innovation: Reshaping Job Analysis to Meet Emerging Business Needs," *Human Resource Management Review* 4(1) (1994): 51–74.

45 N. B. Kurland and T. D. Egan, "Telecommuting: Justice and Control in the Virtual Organization," *Organizational Science* 10 (1999): 500–513.

46 For a discussion of how to analyze the work of teams, see S. A. Mohrman, S. G. Cohen, and A. M. Mohrman Jr., *Designing Team-Based Organizations: New Forms for Knowledge Work* (San Francisco: Jossey-Bass, 1995).

47 D. Rahbar-Daniels, M. L. Erickson, and A. Dalik, "Here to Stay: Taking Competencies to the Next Level," *World at Work Journal* (First Quarter 2001): 70–77.

48 W. C. Howell, "Human Factors in the Workplace," in M. D. Dunnette and L. M. Hough (eds.), *Handbook of Industrial-Organizational Psychology*, vol. 2 (Palo Alto, CA: Consulting Psychologists Press, 1991): 209–270.

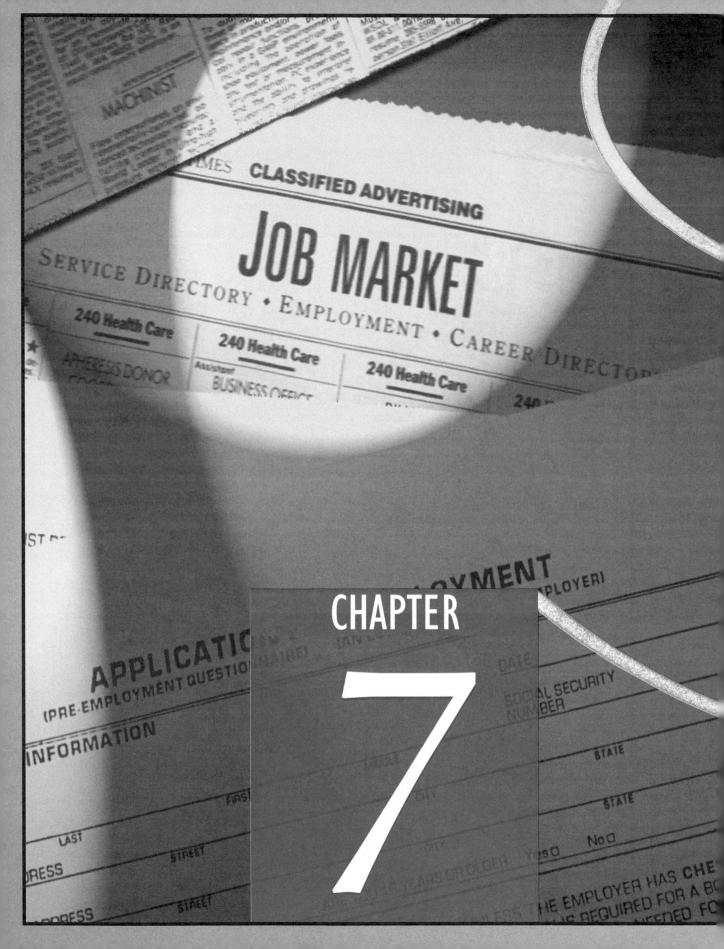

CHAPTER

7

RECRUITING AND RETAINING QUALIFIED EMPLOYEES

" We've always used the Web to recruit, but now we want to use it more effectively. "[1]

Jeff Chambers
Director, Human Resources
SAS Institute

MANAGING THROUGH STRATEGIC PARTNERSHIPS

SAS Institute

SAS Institute is the largest private software developer in the world. It has about 4,000 employees and revenues exceeding $1 billion. Headquartered in Cary, North Carolina, it is No. 2 on the list of the "100 Best Companies to Work For." Surprisingly, SAS Institute was a late adopter of automated on-line recruiting. Jeff Chambers, director of human resources, acknowledged that this was an activity "that we don't do as progressively as other companies."

The main reason the company was slow to adopt new recruiting technologies was that it was unnecessary until recently. SAS employees provide a continuing source of leads for potential hires—about 20 percent of the total last year. A very informal recruiting method worked well, according to Chambers: "A lot of our people will recommend friends, neighbors, and family members because they think we are such a good place to work. We have been known as an employer of choice for a long time." Even without on-line recruiting, the company received 20,000 applications for 200 job openings.

Another rationale Chambers gives for the company's slow shift to Internet recruiting is the belief that most of the best people aren't looking to change their job, implying that those looking for new work aren't the best talent. Chambers observes: "When you look at the IT talent market, there is such a hot demand that if anybody is looking for a job, all they need to do is submit a resume to one of hundreds of companies, and they will have tons of interviews. So you get the impression that the people out there who are looking for you as an employer—rather than you looking for them—are in some way inferior talent."

As a software company, SAS looks to its internal staff to enhance its present system. "Our philosophy has been that we build our own rather than go out and find somebody else, and in that respect, I think we have been underutilizing the potential of the Web," Chambers acknowledges. "We have never had the ability to interface with potential applicants online. We just let them apply without having to send in a resume."

Under the new system, SAS describes its current needs and accepts electronic resumes from people who may have some interest in working at the company. It no longer requires candidates to apply solely for open positions. Instead, people can simply let the company know that they may be interested at some point if there is a potential opportunity to advance. Information about both current employees and potential future employees will be kept in a database that records their competencies. The database will make it possible to scan for critical job skills and keep track of people—something SAS has never done before. Under the new system, "when we have a future need, we can go into the system and pull out the people that meet the search criteria," explains Chambers.

Chambers calls the new approach "an evolution, rather than a revolution. We used to receive a whole slew of resumes, which someone had to go through by hand. Now we are going to be able to do much of that through Web-based technology, to prequalify candidates, to give managers a better range of choices sooner. It's simply using technology to make us more efficient."

RECRUITING AND RETENTION WITHIN THE HR SYSTEM

Recruitment involves searching for and obtaining qualified applicants for the organization to consider when filling job openings. It is the first step in the hiring process. Recruitment stops short of making decisions about which particular applicants should be hired.

The initial recruiting experience—when an employee is first considered for a position in the organization—is an employee's first exposure to the organization's recruiting activities, but it is not the last one. Employees may again become involved in recruiting activities as they help (or hinder) their employer's efforts to attract others to the company. When employees eventually consider applying for other jobs in the organization, they again become actively involved in recruitment activities. At this point, employees learn how the organization handles recruitment within its own workforce. These later experiences with the organization's recruiting activities may be especially important in determining whether talented employees are retained.

Recruitment versus Selection

To complete the process of hiring someone into a job, some selection occurs. Interviews, reference checks, and tests of various sorts are all part of the selection process. Described in Chapter 8, selection involves sorting and ranking potential employees and making decisions about which individuals will receive offers of employment. Recruitment and selection are closely related activities that together form the backbone of the hiring process. In this chapter, we discuss the recruiting activities involved in hiring people into jobs. Recent surveys indicate that recruitment and selection activities are often the *top* HR priorities in companies today.[2]

Retention

We also discuss the issue of retention in this chapter. **Retention** activities refer to everything an employer does to encourage qualified and productive employees to continue working for the organization. The objective of retention activities is to reduce unwanted voluntary turnover by people the organization would like to keep in its workforce. Together effective recruitment and retention attracts individuals to the organization *and* increases the chance of retaining the individuals once they are hired. Thus, these activities seek to satisfy the needs of job applicants as well as the needs of managers.[3]

Links to Other HR Activities

This chapter focuses on recruiting as if it is a somewhat discrete aspect of managing human resources, but it important to recognize that this is not the case. In a fully integrated, strategically aligned system for managing human resources, recruiting activities are developed with a full appreciation for how they may affect other parts of the system, and how other parts of the system may affect recruiting activities. For example, in this chapter, we discuss how an applicant's decision about whether to accept a job offer can be affected by the company's compensation plan, benefits, work arrangement, and approach to career development. All come into play as applicants consider whether to accept a job offer. For applicants, it is clear that the effectiveness of world-class recruiting practices will be limited if other HR practices are not world-class also.

For managers, the connections between recruiting activities and other aspects of the HR system also become apparent—with experience. Inexperienced managers often focus on speed when evaluating the effectiveness of the organization's recruiting activities. They want jobs filled quickly and with as little effort as possible. Experienced managers recognize that, while speed is important, the quality of people hired is ultimately more important. If the hiring process does not succeed in getting qualified employees, managers will then need to provide more training to new employees or they will soon be looking for more replacements. Similarly, if qualified people are found and convinced to accept job offers, they will be productive and stay only as long as the organization addresses their desire for rewards, work flexibility, career advancement, and so on. In other words, recruiting activities work in concert with the entire HR system to determine the flow of people through jobs.

Exhibit 7.1 illustrates the relationship between recruiting activities and other aspects of the HR system, and summarizes the many sources of potential job applicants and the methods organizations can use to reach them.

"Our philosophy is simple—if you have the best people in the industry to fit into your culture and you motivate them properly, then you're going to be an industry leader."

John Chambers
CEO
Cisco Systems

ex 7.1 Recruitment and Retention within an Integrated HR System

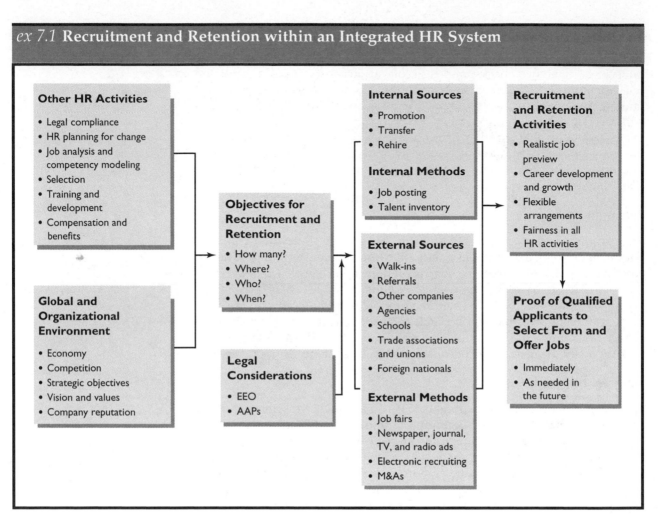

Other HR Activities

- Legal compliance
- HR planning for change
- Job analysis and competency modeling
- Selection
- Training and development
- Compensation and benefits

Global and Organizational Environment

- Economy
- Competition
- Strategic objectives
- Vision and values
- Company reputation

Objectives for Recruitment and Retention

- How many?
- Where?
- Who?
- When?

Legal Considerations

- EEO
- AAPs

Internal Sources

- Promotion
- Transfer
- Rehire

Internal Methods

- Job posting
- Talent inventory

External Sources

- Walk-ins
- Referrals
- Other companies
- Agencies
- Schools
- Trade associations and unions
- Foreign nationals

External Methods

- Job fairs
- Newspaper, journal, TV, and radio ads
- Electronic recruiting
- M&As

Recruitment and Retention Activities

- Realistic job preview
- Career development and growth
- Flexible arrangements
- Fairness in all HR activities

Proof of Qualified Applicants to Select From and Offer Jobs

- Immediately
- As needed in the future

External Forces Affecting Recruitment and Retention

Also shown in Exhibit 7.1 are several aspects of the global and organizational environment that influence recruitment and retention. Clearly, labor market conditions and competitive pressures can be powerful determinants of the resources companies invest to attract and retain top talent. As illustrated by the opening example of SAS Institute, new technologies also influence the design and implementation of a company's recruitment and retention activities. As described later in this chapter, a dynamic and changing legal environment is another important factor that organizations must take into account. But perhaps the most important influence on recruitment and retention activities is that managers in an organization do (or do not) understand how effective recruitment and retention contribute to achieving strategic objectives.

THE STRATEGIC IMPORTANCE OF RECRUITING AND RETAINING TALENTED EMPLOYEES

At SAS and many other companies, getting good people into the organization is so important that the chairman gets personally involved in the firm's recruiting and selection. At SAS, managers devote time and attention to recruiting because they believe it is vital to the success and long-term survival of the business. Effective approaches to recruitment and retention begin during the strategic planning process when managers determine the organization's immediate and long-term labor needs. The major objectives to be served by recruitment and retention efforts influence both the level of investment a company makes and the company's specific actions. Exhibit 7.2 illustrates how different strategic objectives may result in different approaches to recruitment and retention.

> **FAST FACT**
>
> Ernst & Young's research shows that the stock purchasing decisions of institutional investors take into account a company's ability to attract talented people.

Strategic Choices

Effective recruiting efforts are consistent with the strategy, the vision, and the values of the company as described in Chapter 4. Consequently, recruiting activities vary across companies, even in the same industry such as insurance. Questions to be addressed during strategic planning might include these:

- How many new hires do we need in the near term and three to five years from now?
- Do we want to recruit people who are motivated to stay with the company for a long time, or are we looking for a short-term commitment?
- Are we prepared to pay top dollar, or should we look for people who will be attracted to our company despite the modest compensation we offer?
- Are we interested in finding people who are different from our current employees to bring in new perspectives, or is it important to maintain our status quo?

ex 7.2 Examples of How Strategic Choices May Influence Recruitment and Retention Objectives

Strategic Objective ⟶	Examples of Implications for Recruitment and Retention Objectives
Increase Market Share by Offering Lowest-Cost Service	• Important to retain current talent as company grows. • Need to predict rate of growth and translate changes in market share to increases needed in size of workforce. • Continuously improve efficiency of recruitment practices needed to keep costs down. • Low-cost strategy puts pressure on compensation and benefits costs, so need to be creative in finding low-cost ways to attract and retain talent.
Increase Return on Investment by Offering Innovative Products and Maintaining High Margins	• Recruiting practices need to focus on attracting highly qualified applicants at the cutting edge of their fields. • Best talent not likely to be looking for jobs, so need to go to them (not wait for them to come to us). • Excellent retention strategy for top talent needed, as workforce will be an attractive pool that other companies will try to raid. Knowledge retention is key strategic concern, also.
Respond to Declining Industry Trends by Diversifying into New Businesses	• May need to develop and implement layoff plans, creating the challenge of how to attract new talent and retain best talent at the same time. • Recruiting efforts for new business areas should include plan for lateral transfers from declining business areas, to minimize need for layoffs. • For new businesses, HR will need to develop strategies for recruiting key talent in those industries.

- What behaviors and competencies do we need from our employees, and how rapidly will these change?

"Executives worldwide who say that by 2010 attracting and retaining people will be the No. 1 force in strategy: 80%."

Economist Intelligence Unit

To illustrate how different answers to questions such as these can lead to different approaches to recruitment and retention, consider two successful insurance companies, Chubb and AIG. To implement its business strategy, Chubb aims its recruitment efforts at inexperienced undergraduates and graduates who mirror Chubb's customers. Chubb looks for applicants who have good interpersonal competencies, because these are important and very difficult to develop. The technical competencies needed by Chubb employees are unique to the firm, so Chubb can't expect to find applicants who already have the expertise they need. Instead, Chubb seeks out applicants who are capable of learning and then invests in training programs to develop the firm-specific skills it needs. To reap satisfactory returns on its investments, Chubb must be able to retain new recruits. Chubb's recruitment approach wouldn't work at AIG. Because it enters and exits markets so quickly, AIG doesn't have time to train inexperienced employees. Its recruitment efforts seek to create a pool of applicants who already know the industry and can quickly jump into a new job and perform it well.[4]

Strategic discussions focus on the general needs of the organization. Once those needs are understood, the focus turns to defining the needs of specific units or departments and the requirements for specific positions. At this stage, job analysis results become relevant. An appropriate job analysis yields answers to questions such as the following:

- What are the characteristics of the ideal recruit?
- Which competencies must people have when they first enter the organization, and how important is it that new hires be eager to learn new competencies?
- What career opportunities can we discuss with applicants?

At GE Medical Systems, the strategic planning process links recruitment planning directly with product development planning. When developing new products, managers draw up a "multigenerational product plan" *and* a "multigenerational staffing plan." These clarify the skills that will be needed as a product moves through three iterations of development. For example, suppose a development plan for a CT scanner that will complete 1-second scans in its first generation, ¾-second scans in the second generation, and ½-second scans in the third generation. Then the recruitment plan specifies the number of "absolute algorithm" experts who will be needed to write code for each product generation.

Improving Productivity and Reducing Expenses

Today, concerns about recruitment and retention are salient for many employers. Even as many companies continue to downsize, finding the talent needed remains a concern. The current environment is especially challenging for organizations. For many companies, the combination of strong competitive business pressures and tight labor market conditions mean that an effective approach involves finding a balance that keeps costs under control and at the same time ensures that the organization has the workforce it needs to grow, diversify into new areas of business, expand internationally, and so on.

A survey conducted by The Conference Board found that nearly all companies believe that being an "employer of choice" is an important objective today if they're to remain viable in the years ahead. At the same time, 43 percent of them reported having problems in achieving this objective. Recruiting problems were slightly worse among service companies than manufacturers, perhaps due to their faster growth rates and relatively lower rates of compensation. Across the country, the occupational groups that accounted for most of the concerns were technical workers and senior managers as highlighted in the opening SAS feature. Both of these groups were difficult to recruit and difficult to retain.[5]

At Nationwide, an ineffective recruiting process was irritating managers and employees alike. Employees were becoming upset because the firm would advertise open positions in the external market before first giving internal candidates a chance to apply for the jobs. They complained that the company said human capital was its most important resource, yet it seemed to ignore that resource when good jobs became available in the company. Line managers complained that they were being given resumes that were already 90 days old, so many candidates were no longer available. Inability to fill openings quickly was cutting into the productivity of their business units. The HR department responded to these problems by fundamentally changing the recruiting process, as described in "Managing Change: Nationwide Speeds Up Hiring."[6]

The Value of Retention

Recruiting people to meet the organization's human resource needs is only half the battle in the war for talent. The other half is keeping these people. An organization that keeps its employee turnover rates lower than the competitors gains in two ways—by reducing costs and improving productivity.

The true costs of turnover include both easy-to-quantify, out-of-pocket expenses and intangible opportunity costs associated with lost productivity. A study of the costs associated with turnover in supermarkets included the expense of filling the empty positions as well as the costs created by inexperienced employees, such as errors in making change, paperwork mistakes, and damaged products. For professional work, turnover can lower productivity because projects are lost when a client's favored employees leave and because the firm decides not to bid for projects due to staff shortages. Other "costs" associated with turnover include lower morale among overworked employees who must pick up the extra work created when a colleague leaves, lost knowledge that only the departing employee has, and the business contacts that employees may have been able to use to build the business.

For some organizations, inability to cope with turnover threatens the firm's strategic competitiveness. At Schering-Plough, high turnover appears to have significantly contributed to the firm's repeated failure to meet government manufacturing standards for its prescription drugs. The quality of the company's manufacturing process was so unreliable that the Food and Drug Administration withheld approval for one new allergy drug until the manufacturing problem was fixed. The company also ordered several large recalls of products after discovering they had been contaminated during the manufacturing process. What was causing these problems? According to an auditor's report, "excessive turnover, shortage and pharmaceutical inexperience of supervisors [had] resulted in inadequate training and oversight of subordinates and manufacturing operations."[7] In this example, the costs of turnover included significant damage to the firm's reputation and brand image.

"The productivity of a sales rep selling very sophisticated products like software continues to rise for as long as three years."

Warren C. Culpepper
CEO
Culpepper & Associates

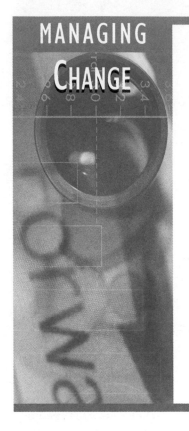

MANAGING CHANGE

Nationwide Speeds Up Hiring

Nationwide Insurance is a multibillion-dollar company headquartered Columbus, Ohio, with essentially three businesses—personal property/casualty insurance, financial services, and commercial services (which helps other firms manage risk, workers' compensation, and related activities). Before the company changed its recruiting practices, it took an average of 45 days to get someone hired. To the frustration of everyone, it actually took longer to hire internal candidates than to hire external candidates! According to Patti Cotter, who headed up the change effort, "We didn't have a step-by-step process. Typically, if someone would respond to an ad, his resume might sit somewhere. By the time we got to them, they had moved on to the next ad." That was a pretty unsatisfactory state of affairs for a company that hires 300 to 400 people every month.

Cotter began her change efforts by sending a survey to everyone in the company who had hired anyone in the past year, asking about the recruiting staff's responsiveness, speed in filling open positions, and ideas for how to make improvements. Out of 100 points, the average satisfaction scores were 63, 63, and 79 for the three divisions. Handling internal candidates was one of the problems identified. From the managers' perspective, the recruiting staff didn't do enough screening. A manager would get 10 or 15 internal candidates for a position, and then would have to call as many as 15 people to tell them they weren't qualified. This wasted managers' time and also made them uncomfortable!

One change the company made is that managers who post jobs now are contacted by a recruiting staffer within 48 hours to facilitate the process. The staffer might help by organizing a targeted job fair with interviewers and screeners in attendance. For key occupations, such as IT, the recruiting staff will put candidates through the entire recruiting and hiring process in five days. Another change was putting a "careers" link in a prime location of the Web site. Software for handling electronic resumes helped address the problem of having frustrated job seekers call to find out whether their applications were received. Now, all of the nearly 20,000 applicants who apply each month get an instant message acknowledging their inquiry, and another message follows 24 hours later.

Within a year, the time needed to fill positions had dropped 30 percent, and satisfaction scores on the survey of managers were up to 79, 84, and 85.

Addressing Societal Concerns Through Legal Compliance

Obtaining a pool of qualified applicants is the primary objective of recruiting, but legal compliance is also very important. As described later in this chapter, legal compliance requires careful record keeping. Although managers sometimes deride such record keeping as a bureaucratic nuisance, the records used to document legal compliance can also be very useful for evaluating the effectiveness of recruitment efforts and for linking recruitment activities to other aspects of the human resource management. A study of 3,200 employers in Atlanta, Boston, and Los Angeles supports this view. The results indicated that employers who actively engaged in affirmative action efforts, which require extensive recording keeping, were also more likely to carefully evaluate performance and provide training to new hires. Furthermore, the study indicated that effective *recruitment*—not preferential selection—was the key to the success.[8]

Involving Everyone

HR professionals usually take the lead in designing a systematic and integrated approach to recruitment and retention, but these cannot be implemented without the involvement and cooperation of line managers and other employees who will work with new recruits. At Cisco Systems, the active involvement of employees is essential to the company's recruiting efforts. Employees participate in focus groups designed to brainstorm ideas about where to find qualified applicants. The folks Cisco wants to hire aren't spending their time looking through want ads. They are more likely to be found attending local art festivals and garden shows. So Cisco recruiters go to those events and work the crowds. When an interested prospect is identified, Cisco pairs the person with a current employee who has similar interests and skills—a "friend." Friends help screen out unsuitable applicants and serve as advocates to convince the best applicants to accept Cisco's job offers.[9] Other ways that employees and managers can be involved in recruitment and retention are summarized in "The HR Triad: Roles and Responsibilities for Recruiting and Retaining Employees."

INTERNET RESOURCES   7.A

The Strategic Importance of Effective Recruitment and Retention

At our Web site, http://jackson.swcollege.com/, you can:

1. Visit recruiting Web sites that are considered among the best and therefore useful as benchmark examples:

GE Power Systems

Advance Micro Devices

Booz Allen Hamilton

Nations Bank

Kodak

2. Evaluate the possible advantages of aggressively recruiting from the growing ranks of "seniors" by learning more about this population and their work habits. Information is available from

AARP

Senior Community Service Employment Program

Senior Job Bank

3. Evaluate the possible advantages of aggressively recruiting people with disabilities. Learn more about the Able to Work consortium and read about best practices related to the employment of people with disabilities.

RECRUITING METHODS AND SOURCES

Once the recruiting objectives are specified and job analysis results have been considered, specific recruitment activities can be planned and implemented. In designing recruitment activities, two central issues to address are the methods to use and the sources to target.

Employers inform potential applicants about employment opportunities using a variety of methods. They place ads, post notices on the company bulletin board, accept applications from people who simply walk into their recruiting offices, and so on.

Different methods may reach different sources of applicants. Posting announcements on company bulletin boards is a good way to recruit employees. Employees are called the **internal labor market**. Potential applicants who don't work for the organization are called the **external labor market**. Placing ads in local newspapers or trade publications are common methods used to reach those in the external labor market.

Many studies have considered whether recruiting from different sources results in different employee outcomes, such as performance, turnover, loyalty, and job satisfaction. If different sources of applicants were

> **FAST FACT**
>
> The U.S. Postal Service, which is the largest U.S. employer, starts recruiting in August for the 40,000+ temporary workers it needs to handle the holiday mail.

THE HR TRIAD Roles and Responsibilities for Recruiting and Retaining Employees

Line Managers	HR Professionals	Employees
• Work with HR staff to develop recruitment objectives and plans that meet the organization's strategic objectives and address employees' concerns. • Develop an understanding of the linkages that exist between recruitment and retention activities and other aspects of the HR system. • Help disseminate information about open positions to all potentially qualified internal candidates. • Stay informed of labor market trends in order to anticipate their implications for recruitment. • Understand and abide by relevant legal regulations. • Facilitate retention efforts through effective management and employee development.	• Work with line managers to develop recruitment objectives and plans that meet the organization's strategic objectives and address employees' concerns. • Design recruitment and retention activities that contribute to the development of an integrated, internally consistent HR system. • Develop recruitment plans that meet legal guidelines and generate a diverse pool of qualified internal and/or external candidates. • Evaluate recruitment outcomes and be innovative in developing practices to ensure a sufficient number of qualified applicants. • Provide training as needed to line managers and employees involved in recruitment activities. • Monitor retention patterns to diagnose potential problems. • Use exit interviews, employee survey, etc., to identify needed improvements.	• Openly discuss your short-term and long-term objectives in order to facilitate the development of recruitment plans that address your concerns. • When applying for jobs, consider all aspects of the HR system when making a decision about whether to change jobs and employers. • Participate in recruitment efforts such as referring others to the company. • Use knowledge of competitors' recruitment approaches to help the organization develop innovative and more effective practices. • Work with HR professionals and line managers in the organization's efforts to effectively manage workforce diversity. • Seek out information about openings within the company and actively pursue those that fit your personal career objectives.

found to have different outcomes, companies could target their recruitment efforts to the most appropriate sources, given their strategic needs. Overall, however, research shows no clear differences in the employment experiences of new employees recruited from different sources.[10]

Instead of targeting one source of applicants, most employers recruit from multiple sources using multiple methods. This approach helps the organization generate a large applicant pool. In addition, recruiting from multiple sources is a good way to increase the diversity of the applicant pool. Below we describe the most common methods used for recruiting applicants from internal and external labor markets.

Recruiting from the Organization's Internal Labor Market

In an era when labor shortages and low unemployment are constantly in the news, a natural tendency may be to assume that recruiting efforts should focus on finding *new* employees to hire. But wise employers understand the value of beginning their recruiting efforts by looking first for candidates inside the organization.[11]

For jobs other than those at entry level, current employees should be considered a primary source of applicants for any job opening. Current employees usually become applicants by informing their employer of their interest in an announced opening. That is, employees learn about appropriate job openings and express their interest in a position in order to be considered. Having expressed their interest in a position, internal applicants typically go through the recruitment process in much the same way as external applicants, becoming candidates for promotions, transfers, and job rotations. However, as illustrated in the Nationwide example described earlier, employers may want to be particularly careful to manage how internal candidates experience recruiting activities. If they have negative experiences when they apply for jobs within the organization, it may trigger them to consider looking outside the organization for other opportunities.

Internal applicants for job vacancies can be located using several methods. Some (e.g., the grapevine and job postings) assume that potential applicants should take most of the responsibility for learning about opening positions and applying for those they find interesting. Others (e.g., using talent inventories) place more responsibility on the HR staff and line managers.

Job Postings. **Job postings** prominently display current job openings to all employees in an organization. They are usually found on bulletin boards (cork as well as electronic). Other than word of mouth, job postings are the most commonly used method for generating a pool of internal applicants. Job postings usually provide complete job descriptions. A well-constructed job description communicates competencies needed, organizational goals, and objectives. By also including information about compensation and performance standards, job postings send signals to employees about what is valued. Astute employees realize that observing postings over time yields information about turnover rates in various departments, as well as information about the competencies that are most in demand.

Job postings can reduce turnover by communicating to employees that they don't have to go elsewhere in order to find opportunities for advancement and development. Posting jobs also creates an open recruitment process, which helps to provide equal opportunity for advancement to all employees. Job posting has many advantages, but it's not foolproof. If hiring decisions are already made when postings appear, the system will soon lose credibility. Managers who merely go through the motions of posting jobs generate ill will and cynicism.

Talent Inventories. Almost every organization has a reservoir of qualified employees that it can tap when recruiting to fill open positions. Like savings accounts, these reservoirs of internal talent contain easily accessed resources that can be "withdrawn" as needed. In addition, the future value of the organization's reservoir pool can be enhanced through investments in selection procedures, training programs, and retention efforts.

As described in Chapter 5, some organizations identify high-potential employees to create talent pools and replacement charts to use for leadership succession planning. Similarly, some organizations have a systematic method for keeping track of the entire reservoir of talent at all levels and in all positions, and ensuring that it's used wisely. Rather than rely on employees to identify appropriate openings in the organization, proactive employers maintain a talent inventory to systematically monitor their internal talent and facilitate the process of matching internal applicants to suitable opportunities. By maintaining talent inventories,

> *"Online job hunting is going to be the standard approach of the emerging workforce."*
>
> Bruce Skillings
> Executive Vice President
> Hodes Advertising

FAST FACT

Adecco sets up Job Shop Kiosks in shopping malls so that companies can post job openings.

FAST FACT

At Hallmark, 90% of management positions are filled internally.

proactive employers can ensure that they consider *all* internal candidates with the necessary qualifications, regardless of whether taking the open position would involve a promotion, transfer, or temporary job rotation.

A **talent inventory** is a database that contains information about the pool of current employees. Talent inventories usually include employees' names, prior jobs and experiences, performance and compensation histories, and demonstrated competencies. The employees' work-related interests, geographic preferences, and career goals also should be included. With an up-to-date talent inventory to consult, there is no need to rely on employees to nominate themselves for job openings. Instead, qualified potential applicants can be identified and encouraged to apply when jobs become available. Citibank uses its talent inventory to identify suitable positions for staff members who wish to transfer or who are seeking another job because of technological displacement or reorganization. The system ensures that suitable internal candidates won't be overlooked before recruiting begins outside the organization.

Promotions. Regardless of how an employee becomes an applicant, recruitment activities can result in three types of career moves within the organization. A promotion generally involves moving into a position that's recognized as having higher status—and often, higher pay. Understandably, current employees often feel they should be given priority as applicants for jobs that represent opportunities for promotion. When this doesn't happen, as was true at Nationwide, they are dissatisfied.

Transfers. A transfer involves moving into a position of similar status, often with no increase in pay. Chapter 6 explained that many organizations have replaced the traditional system of jobs that are organized into clear status hierarchies with job families and broadbanding. Under these new arrangements, taking a new position within the company often involves a lateral job transfer rather than a promotion. After several transfers, employees develop a broader perspective and can better understand how the entire organization functions as a system. Because lateral transfers play such an important role in the long-term development of employees, they represent a valuable opportunity for employees. Thus, it is important that the company's recruitment procedures alert employees to such opportunities when they arise.

Pros and Cons of Internal Recruitment. There are several potential benefits associated with recruiting applicants who are eligible for promotions and transfers. Compared with external recruitment, internal recruitment can reduce labor costs because outside recruits tend to receive higher salaries. The organization may also pay a one-time signing bonus to external recruits.

In addition to reducing these monetary costs, internal recruitment is valued by employees. Recruiting externally can reduce employee morale and diminish employees' willingness to maximize their productivity in order to be eligible for future career opportunities. Gaining a reputation for excellent employee development is one of the best ways to become an "employer of choice," according to a recent study conducted by The Conference Board.[12] Firms in the "Most Admired Companies to Work For" all have great opportunities for employee development.

Counterbalancing these advantages of internal recruitment are several disadvantages. If internal recruitment is used in place of external recruitment, the most qualified candidates may never be considered. Other disadvantages include infighting between candidates vying for a position, and inbreeding. Inbreeding exists when someone who is familiar with the organization has come to accept its ways of doing things. Such people are less likely to come up with creative and innovative ideas for improvement.

Recruiting from the External Labor Market

Rapidly growing organizations and those that require large numbers of highly skilled professionals and managers seldom can meet their labor needs without recruiting from the external labor market.[13] Internal recruitment simply can't produce the numbers of people needed to sustain continued growth. During one of its growth spurts, for example, Cisco Systems was taking on about 1,000 new hires each quarter, which amounted to nearly 10 percent of total job growth in Silicon Valley.[14]

> **FAST FACT**
>
> Being seen as an "Employer of Choice" draws a larger applicant pool.

Labor shortages sometimes even force a company to pull up roots and move to the location of the talent. Gateway's founder Ted Waite grew up in South Dakota and for the first 13 years of its life, that is where Gateway's company headquarters were. During its early years, Gateway's business strategy required people to assemble and ship products, and little else. Within a dozen years of its founding, the company employed 5,500 assembly workers, which helped to substantially reduce the region's unemployment rate. But this simple strategy could not sustain continued growth forever. Eventually, Waite decided to expand in new directions. As part of the new strategy, he planned to develop new software and cutting-edge product designs. To implement the new strategy, Gateway needed highly talented engineers as well as managers with competencies in marketing and finance. Attracting the best people in these fields to South Dakota proved difficult. After a year of trying to fill 250 such job openings, Waite concluded that the company would have to move in order to attract the caliber of talent needed. To choose the company's new location, Gateway hired a labor market study of several cities. San Diego—the current home for the company headquarters—came out on top as a location with a large pool of available high-tech workers.[15]

Even when companies are not growing, or are shrinking, they may not be able to generate large numbers of internal applicants with the competencies needed under changing business conditions. If internal candidates would require training in order to be qualified, it may be cheaper, easier, and quicker to go outside the firm and hire people who already have the competencies needed. In addition, recruiting from the outside brings in people with new ideas, which is especially important for organizations that require innovation and creativity.[16]

Walk-in Applicants. Some individuals become applicants by simply walking into an organization's employment office and declaring they are interested in working for the organization. They may be motivated by an advertisement indicating that the company is recruiting, or they may simply have a good impression of the organization and want to explore the possibility of working there. Before the Internet explosion, walk-ins were especially prevalent for clerical and service jobs; managerial, professional, and sales applicants were seldom walk-ins.[17] New technology is quickly changing that. Now, applicants for almost any type of job can "walk in" to an organization through its electronic, cyberspace doors.

> **FAST FACT**
>
> Warmer metropolitan areas attract job seekers far more than seasonal environments, according to the Department of Labor.

Holding an open house is an excellent way to attract walk-in applicants. An open house can serve to introduce the organization to the community and attract individuals who might not otherwise become applicants. Such events give the firm a chance to look at potential applicants in a fairly informal setting.

Electronic and Other Media. Virtually every company now has a Web site that applicants (internal and external to the company), as well as customers, can go to and learn about the company. Many of these sites have specific information about job postings, required competencies, career progression programs, mentoring, diversity initiatives, and benefits. Increasingly, company Web sites accept—even encourage—electronic applications.[18] Companies like Southwest Airlines, Cisco Systems, and SAS Institute have moved as much as possible of their application process to the Internet. This saves a great deal of time and cost. It also enables the companies to be accessible to a wide range of applicants.

The use of the Web enables applicants to select themselves out of the application process if the descriptions provided are not appropriate for them. Thus those remaining are more likely to have evaluated themselves as fitting into the company even before the application process really starts. This can lead to a more effective hiring process and a potentially longer-term relationship between the individual and the company.

The Internet is a very popular way to contact potential applicants, but it is still quite new. Therefore, most organizations that recruit using the Internet also continue to use more traditional approaches, such as placing ads in newspapers and journals, hiring billboard space, making announcements on local radio and television, and simply putting "help wanted" signs in the window.

Employee Referrals. **Employee referrals** occur when current employees inform someone they know about an opening and encourage them to apply. Informal referral programs consist of informing current employees about job openings and encouraging them to have qualified friends and associates apply for positions. Companies such as New York Life Insurance facilitate employee referrals by supporting on-line alumni networks. Other companies make it easy for their employees to send electronic job announcements to their friends. This is a very low-cost approach. Formal referral programs reward employees for referring qualified applicants. The financial incentives may be linked to a recruit's completion of an application, acceptance of employment, or completion of work for a specified time period.

Compared with other external recruiting methods, for most occupations, employee referrals result in the highest one-year survival rates. One explanation for this success is that employees provide a balanced view of organizational life. The more information that is available, the better the referral decision is likely to be. Another explanation is that employees tend to recruit applicants who are similar to them in interests and motivations. Since employees are already adjusted to the organizational culture, this matching process increases the likelihood that applicants also will fit into the environment.[19]

The referral approach seems to be good for applicants as well as employees. At Citibank, referral applications present more appropriate resumes, are more likely to apply under favorable market conditions, perform better in the interview, and are more likely to get hired.[20] A potential disadvantage of referrals is that employees tend to refer others who are similar in age, gender, ethnicity, and religion. If relied on too heavily, this recruiting approach may be detrimental to equal employment opportunity goals.

Employment Agencies. Public and private **employment agencies** are good sources of temporary employees and permanent employees. American public employment agencies operate under the umbrella of the U.S. Training and Employment Service; it sets national policies and oversees the operations of state employment agencies, which have branch offices in many cities. State employment agencies offer counseling, testing, and placement services to everyone and provide special services to military veterans, members of some minority groups, colleges, and technical and professional people. Their services are supported by employer contributions to state unemployment funds. The Social Security Act provides that, in general, workers who have been laid off from a job must register with the state employment agency in order to be eligible for unemployment benefits. Thus, most state agencies have long rosters of potential applicants.

> **FAST FACT**
>
> The *Personal Responsibility and Work Opportunity Act of 1996* requires that adult welfare recipients return to work within two years after they start receiving welfare.

Private employment agencies—sometimes called headhunter, placement, or search firms—serve professional, managerial, and unskilled job applicants. Agencies dealing with unskilled applicants often provide job candidates that employers would have a difficult time finding otherwise. Many employers looking for unskilled workers do not have the resources to do their own recruiting or have only temporary or seasonal demands for these workers.

Private agencies such as Korn/Ferry, Spencer Stuart, and Heidrick & Struggles play a major role in recruiting professional and managerial candidates. The executive recruiting industry grew at a phenomenal pace during the past decade. Predictably, now it is going through a period of consolidation, with the larger players buying out their smaller competitors.

Executive search firms can be an expensive recruitment method for the employer, who may have to pay fees as high as one-third of the first year's total salary and bonus package for a job that's filled. More troublesome are the hidden costs of using search firms. A search firm generally cannot approach executives it has recently placed, and it may have agreements with its clients that limit its ability to approach the clients' employees. This restricts the pool of applicants considered by a search firm and runs counter to the objective of creating the large pool of qualified applicants. In addition, search firms typically present employers with very few possible candidates to consider. They prescreen heavily before letting the employer and applicant meet. This protects applicants' privacy and saves the employer time. But it also places a great deal of weight on the judgment of the search firm. Because search firms have much less information about the needs of the organization, compared with managers, search firms are more likely to err by rejecting a candidate who would do well. To minimize such costs, close monitoring of the search firm's activities is necessary. In spite of these drawbacks, headhunter firms are doing well, especially when it comes to helping talented people who work in troubled companies find new positions. Exhibit 7.3 offers suggestions for how to select a search firm when one is needed.[21]

> *"I get calls from headhunters and such, offering bigger salaries, signing bonuses and such. But the excitement of what I'm doing here is equal to a 30% pay raise."*
>
> Jorgen Wedel
> Executive Vice President
> Gillette

> **FAST FACT**
>
> The association for search firms is Bluesteps.

ex 7.3 Tips for Selecting an Executive Search Firm

- Learn about the search industry; be sure to understand its weaknesses.
- Investigate the firm's "completion" rate. Some firms fill the positions they are hired for more than 90% of the time. Others fill the positions less than 70% of the time.
- Be sure you know how many restrictions the firm is under. If a firm you want to use is obligated to not recruit from a long list of clients, you may need to hire more than one firm.
- Determine the ratio of "lions" (the partners who often are essential to arranging a meeting and closing a deal) to "squirrels" (researchers and recruiters who help put together a list of possibilities). Be sure you meet the squirrels before hiring the lions.
- Understand and carefully consider the fee structure. Most fee structures are designed to benefit the search firm making few performance commitments to clients. Negotiate a flat fee rather than a fee based on the new hire's compensation and insist on a refundable retainer.
- Understand the search process used by the firm and evaluate how likely it is that the process will yield candidates who meet your recruitment objectives.

School Placement Services and Trade Associations. Schools are important sources of recruits for most organizations, although their importance varies depending on the type of applicant sought. If an organization is recruiting managerial, technical, or professional applicants, then colleges and universities are the most important source. These institutions become less important when an organization is seeking production, service, office, and clerical employees.

For some jobs, the recruitment process begins in the high schools even though the hiring process doesn't kick in until college graduation. Gannett, owner of the *Detroit News*, the *Asheville Citizen-Times*, and 80 other newspapers, targets high school students who show even a glimmer of interest in journalism. Editors speak with the students, talking up the glamorous aspects of a career in journalism. In addition to sponsoring workshops for the staff working on high school newspapers, Gannett's editors offer to critique the papers and invite students into their newsrooms to give them exposure to the excitement. For college students, working as an intern provides additional experience. These and other efforts help Gannett compete effectively for college graduates despite the fact that the publishing industry pays much less than many others.[22]

Many trade and professional associations also provide recruiting opportunities. Often jobs can be announced through their newsletters or through links to the association's Web site. Annual trade conferences provide a more personal forum where employers and potential job applicants can meet. Communities and schools have adopted this idea and now bring together large numbers of employers and job seekers at **job fairs**. At a job fair, usually several employers are present to provide information about employment opportunities at their company. The setting is often somewhat informal. The public is invited to attend to gather information and ask questions.

Increasingly, job fairs incorporate electronic screening in order for employers to use their time at the fairs more efficiently. Employers set up an

FAST FACT

To guard against trivial assignments being given to student interns, who may then get turned off, J. P. Morgan Chase requires supervisors to describe intern projects to the HR staffers who oversee recruiting.

FAST FACT

Merck committed to giving $10 million to the United Negro College Fund for scholarships and internships in an effort to expand the pool of outstanding minority researchers.

electronic site that contains information about openings and a link to the company Web site, where applicants can learn more. The site is active for a two- to four-week period just prior to a scheduled job fair. Interested candidates use the site to submit their applications. Employers can then screen applicants in advance and contact those they are most interested in to schedule a meeting at the job fair.

Foreign Nationals. In some professions—such as chemical engineering, software engineering, and others that involve high-tech skills—labor shortages cause employers to recruit foreign nationals. Foreign nationals may be employed in operations in the United States or abroad. When they work abroad, they serve as **host-country nationals** (persons working in their own country, not the country of the parent company) or **third-country nationals** (persons working in a country that's neither their own nor that of the parent company). Under the *Immigration Reform and Control Act of 1986*, the *Immigration Act of 1990*, and the *American Competitiveness in the Twenty First Century Act of 2000*, it's unlawful for employers to hire foreign nationals to work in the United States unless they are authorized to do so. Those hired must be paid the prevailing wage. For professional-level workers, employers typically spend an additional $100,000 to $200,000 in relocation costs.[23]

> **FAST FACT**
>
> Costa Rica requires high school students to take English, its workforce includes 12,000 engineering students, and its per capita computer usage rate is higher than in the United States and Canada.

As described in Chapter 2, one way for a foreign worker to enter the U.S. labor market is by obtaining an H-1B visa. A quicker alternative for foreign employees working abroad in U.S. companies is to obtain an **L-1 Intracompany Transferee visa**. Such visas are not subject to annual quotas. Another advantage of an L-1 intracompany transferee visa is that it is easier for transferees to bring along family members.

TN NAFTA visas are another alternative, but only Canadian and Mexican citizens can obtain these visas. With appropriate documents in hand, newly hired Canadian and Mexican workers can obtain a TN NAFTA visa at the border as they enter the United States to begin work.[24]

Recruiting foreign employees to work in the United States is a useful approach to dealing with labor shortages, but it involves some extra administrative work and planning. Several of the activities associated with recruiting foreign workers are summarized in the feature "Managing Globalization: Employing Foreign Workers."

Recruiting foreign nationals successfully requires making an extra effort to understand other cultures from which applicants are sought. For example, whereas U.S. applicants can be expected to recognize the names of many large companies, the names of those companies may be very unfamiliar to applicants outside the United States. Or, even if the name is recognizable, applicants may have little information about what it would be like to work in a particular U.S. city. Many French students recognize Coca-Cola's brand name, but few are likely to have a clear image of what it would be like to work in the Atlanta headquarters.

> **FAST FACT**
>
> Most employees in Iceland receive the same government-sponsored benefits plan, and when searching for a new job they are not used to comparing different benefit plans, flexible benefits, cafeteria plans, and so on.

The job searching approaches used in other countries are another factor to consider when recruiting outside the United States. In Japan, for example, a tradition of long-term employment security means that many excellent potential applicants have had little need to hone their job-seeking skills. Also, they are less likely than U.S. applicants to use the Internet for job hunting, and more likely to rely on magazines and newspapers for information.[25]

MANAGING GLOBALIZATION

Employing Foreign Workers

Complying with federal regulations and facilitating the successful relocation of foreign workers are two responsibilities that must be accepted by employers of foreign workers. Specific activities include those listed below.

- Publicize job openings in foreign labor markets using methods that are culturally appropriate to the location (as well as legally acceptable in the United States).
- Document domestic recruiting efforts and their lack of success, in order to meet Department of Labor regulations governing employment of foreign workers.
- Monitor salary and benefits of foreign and domestic workers to ensure that foreign workers are treated equally with domestic workers, as required by H-1B visa regulations.

- Monitor the percentage of employees holding various types of visas to ensure that legal limits are not exceeded within the company.
- Provide relocation support to foreign employees, including assistance with immigration, travel, permanent residence applications, visa renewals, bank accounts, credit cards, driver's licenses, and so on.
- Develop and provide training and acculturation programs for both domestic and foreign employees.
- Develop a long-term strategy on how to handle visa expirations.
- Assist foreign employees with the process of repatriation to their home country at the end of their employment assignment.

Acquisitions and Mergers. In contrast with other external methods, hiring new employees by acquiring the firm they work for is a recruiting approach that can facilitate the immediate implementation of an organization's strategic plan. Cisco, Lucent, Nortel, and Tyco used this strategy to grow.[26] When an organization acquires a company with skilled employees, this ready talent may enable the organization to pursue a business plan—such as entering a new product line—that would otherwise be unfeasible. However, the need to displace employees and to integrate a large number of them rather quickly into a new organization means that the human resource planning and selection process becomes more critical than ever.

> **FAST FACT**
>
> About 550,000 Americans work for Japanese companies located in the United States.

Even when a company doesn't acquire a company, M&A activity can provides a good source of applicants. Several months after Thomas Weisel's former firm, Montgomery Securities, was acquired by NationsBank, Weisel realized he needed a change. So, he left NationsBank to start up a new investment bank. Many of the first staff members were former Montgomery employees. Because of possible competitive concerns, Weisel had to cut a deal with NationsBank in order to take his colleagues along on his new venture. To fill out the staff, which grew to 800 people in just two years, Weisel recruited many other people in the wake of major acquisitions and mergers in the industry. When word was out that a firm was about to be acquired, Weisel or others in the firm quickly approached the best talent and invited them to consider joining the firm. With a compelling business plan and Weisel's track record of success in the industry, they were able to persuade much of the industry's top talent to join them.[27]

Contingent Employees, Rehires, and Recalls

Contingent workers are hired by companies to cope with unexpected or temporary challenges—part-timers, freelancers, subcontractors, and independent professionals. Recently, contingent workers have also been called **free agents**. Usually, employers hire contingent workers from the external labor market. The Internet has proved to be a useful tool for recruiting and job search within this corner of the labor market. Vendors serve both free agents and employers by helping establish rates of pay, contract terms, standardized billing, and other arrangements.[28]

> **FAST FACT**
>
> Estimates place the number of contingent workers at about 8% of the U.S. workforce.

Members of the contingent workforce understand that they'll be frequently entering into and exiting from employment relationships. The temporary assignments generally last 3 to 12 months. Therefore, even when they are working on temporary assignments, they nurture their connections to a wide range of possible future employers. In effect, contingent workers must continually maintain their status as members of the applicant pool in order to ensure their continued employment.[29]

Some contingent workers are recruited directly, but many are recruited indirectly by using the services of temporary help agencies such as Manpower. As more and more companies find it preferable to hire temporary workers, temporary help agencies have experienced a boom. Organizations are using temporary help

> **FAST FACT**
>
> In the United States, 3% of the workforce are temps versus 1.3% in 1990. About 55% of these people have no health insurance coverage.

agencies more than ever because some hard-to-get skills are available nowhere else. This is especially true for small companies that aren't highly visible or can't spend time recruiting. Getting short-term employees without an extensive search is an obvious advantage of temporary help agencies.

Fluctuating Demand. Many employers recruit from the contingent workforce as part of a planned strategy. Rehiring and recalling are particularly beneficial to organizations that have seasonal fluctuations in the demand for workers, such as department stores, canneries, construction companies, and ski resorts. Each summer and fall during the apple harvest, canneries in eastern Washington State recall large numbers of employees—some who have been on

> **FAST FACT**
>
> Manpower, which is based in Milwaukee and has 3,700 franchises and independent offices in 59 countries, is the world's largest temporary services firm. About 50% of revenues come from overseas. France is the largest market, followed by the United States and the UK.

the payroll for more than 20 years. Mail-order companies like L.L. Bean continually bring back a large share of their laid-off workforces between September and December, the busiest months of the year.

Recalls and rehires aren't always planned, however. American Express had not planned to recall its retired head of the Travel-Related Services unit, but this is just what it did when it found it had been weakened by a steady drain of its marketing talent. Recalls and rehires also occur in organizations coping with unexpected staffing problems created by downsizing. A survey of large U.S. companies conducted by the American Management Association found that more than half of the respondents who had downsized said they had lost so many talented people that their ability to compete had been severely damaged. When this happens, many downsized companies end up rehiring as temporary employees the people they have just laid off. Indeed, an estimated 17 percent of contingent employees have been regularly employed by the same company that now employs them on an as-needed basis. At some companies, as many as 80 percent of contingent workers were previously working as regular employees.[30]

Advantages and Disadvantages. Rehiring former or laid-off employees is a relatively inexpensive and effective method of recruiting. The organization already has information about the performance, attendance, and safety

> When the economy sours, *"the typical response is to put pressure on head count and push for layoffs, but you'll find that destroys the fabric of the workforce. Lincoln shows how a different process can work, but it requires more creativity and imagination."*
>
> Ray Vogt
> Vice President of HR
> Lincoln Electric

records of these employees. Rehires are already familiar with job responsibilities, so they need less time to settle in—*unless* the job has changed substantially while they were away.

The growing reliance on contingent employment is often considered a negative trend for employees, however. As the name suggests, such workers lead uncertain lives, and they almost never receive benefits. Nevertheless, some employees prefer contingent arrangements because it allows them to work on a schedule of their own choosing. Highly skilled temporary workers often are paid more on an hourly basis than are permanent employees doing similar work. Temporary employment also provides a way to preview different jobs and work in a variety of organizations. For employees, temporary work is a good way to learn about possible new careers. Good temporary employees often receive permanent job offers. Contingent employment also serves the needs of core employees because it facilitates implementation of temporary leave policies.

Recalls, rehires, and contingent employees have some unique disadvantages, however. The commitment of rehired employees who would have preferred to keep a steady, full-time job may be low. Alternatively, permanent employees who know they are paid less per hour than comparable temporary hires may feel resentful. For these and other reasons, conflict between permanent and temporary employees is common. L.L. Bean is very aware of these possible disadvantages and realizes that relying on rehires would backfire if all employees weren't fully committed to providing high-quality service. To prevent this, it works very hard to recruit employees who prefer seasonal employment and then to establish positive employment relationships.

INTERNET RESOURCES   7.B

Recruiting Methods and Sources

At our Web site, http://jackson.swcollege.com/, you can:

1. Learn about executive search firms and employment agencies by visiting the company home pages of

    Bluesteps

    Adecco

    Manpower

    Korn Ferry Future Step

    Spencer Stuart

2. Visit an on-line marketplace for free agents and employers at

    http://www.Guru.com

    http://www.artemisintl.com/opus360

    http://www.eworkexchange.com

3. See examples of the reports that can be generated by applicant tracking software available from

    BrassRing Systems

    Icarian

    Recruitsoft

    PeopleSoft

ex 7.4 Tips for Saying Good-Bye to Employees

Do	Don't
Ask employees how they prefer to spend their time on their last day.	Assume employees will want a party to celebrate their departure (ask).
Treat all departing employees the same.	Wait until the employee's last day to plan the employee's exit (think this through in advance).
Let departing employees know their work has been appreciated.	Cut off access to supplies and resources prior to the employee's last day, unless it's necessary for security reasons.
Give employees plenty of opportunity to say good-bye to friends, coworkers, and mentors.	Be stingy when deciding what the employee is entitled to (e.g., number of vacation days) upon departure (it's better to err in favor of the employee).
Conduct a thorough exit interview.	Expect employees to continue to be available to offer assistance after they leave, unless you pay for that assistance.
Be flexible in addressing the needs of individual employees.	Make departing employees feel they are just a statistic being processed by an uncaring bureaucracy.
Make every effort to ensure employees leave with a positive image of the company, regardless of the circumstances surrounding their departure.	Assume the employee will never return in the future.

In order for a strategy of using recalls and rehires to be effective, employees who have left the company must be eager to return if an opportunity arises. Treating departing employees well is one way to set the stage for their subsequent re-recruitment. Exhibit 7.4 offers advice for employers who want to say "good-bye" to applicants with style. Of course, employees will appreciate a dignified send-off even if they are never recalled.[31]

FAST FACT

During the economic slowdown in 2001, financial institutions were reluctant to lay off employees because they knew they would soon need to hire them back!

RECRUITING FROM THE APPLICANT'S PERSPECTIVE ENHANCES RETENTION

Regardless of who the applicants are or how they became applicants for positions, events that occur during recruitment can determine whether they accept the organization's employment offer or choose to reject it. Recruiting activities should create positive experiences for all applicants—even those who aren't offered positions. If the firm's recruitment methods promote a favorable image of the company, rejected applicants may try again in the future and encourage their friends to view the company as an employer of choice. In other words, recruitment addresses current labor needs while also anticipating future labor needs.

For organizations to effectively attract *and* retain potentially qualified candidates, they need to understand the behaviors and preferences of the diverse workforce. What do candidates consider when searching for, and choosing, a new job? How do candidates differ in their job search activities? Where do they get their information regarding job availability and what do they react to the most?[32]

Building a Corporate Reputation

"Publicity is one of the key brand builders we have. Positive press shows people that this is a great place to work."

Andy Lorenzen
Manager
Chik-fil-A

For many applicants, the reputation of the firm they work for is an important consideration. Generally, people prefer to work for an organization that they can be proud of. By the time a job opening needs to be filled, it may already be too late to begin convincing potential applicants that a particular company is a good place to work.

Planning. Building a reputation takes time and requires a long-term planning horizon. Chik-fil-A is proud of the achievements of its employees and it makes sure local newspapers communicate that message. Since 1975, this restaurant chain has awarded employees with scholarships worth more than $13 million—and local newspapers cover the stories. Chik-fil-A also informs newspapers when employees earn big incentive rewards—like the "Symbol of Success," which includes the keys to a new automobile. CIGNA Insurance uses a similar strategy to build the company's reputation as a good employer. CIGNA rewards top achievers by making them members of the President's Club. Of those who make the club, 99 percent get their picture published in their local newspaper.[33]

"There are considerable risks in presenting myself as an employer of choice."

Martin McGinn
Chairman and CEO
Mellon Financial Corp.

Risks. With all the talk about becoming an employer of choice, it's worth pointing out that organizations should think carefully about whether to mount a public campaign to raise public awareness. Unless a company really is a great place to work, employers should not claim that it is. And, if managers aren't ready to make significant investments in order to become a great place to work, the company is better off not jumping on this bandwagon. After Merrill Lynch made *Working Woman*'s list of best companies in 2000, a group of female stockbrokers started a writing campaign to have the company removed from the list. They also hired an airplane to fly banners at sporting events, informing spectators that the group had sued the company for sex discrimination. When Martin McGinn announced that Mellon Financial was undertaking an employer-of-choice campaign, his customers warned him that he might be in worse shape if he tried and failed, suggesting that it might be better to not even try. Consider the exposure such a campaign creates. In order to be considered for the "best company" lists, employees must be polled and the company must participate in benchmarking studies to determine whether the pay-and-benefits structure falls below the competition. The exercise revealed that Mellon was underpaying employees relative to the competition. Thousands of employees had to be given raises, which cost the company several million dollars.

McGinn has no regrets that he embarked on an employer-of-choice campaign, but many managers remain skeptical. According to one study of 7,000 corporate officers, only 7 percent thought their company had enough talent to pursue the most promising business opportunities, and only 11 percent thought the company had enough talented managers to substantially increase its performance relative to competitors. Yet, only 7 percent said they were updating their recruiting and retention strategies.[34]

Making It Easy to Apply

From the applicant's perspective, making it easy to apply for a job is a good way to increase the number of applications received. User-friendly on-line application software that accepts applicants' resumes is one way to make it easy. Allstate Insurance makes it easy for independent contractors to apply by using software that instantly conducts the initial screening process and gives immediate feedback to the applicant. Successful applicants are told on the spot that

> **FAST FACT**
>
> For drivers, FedEx relies heavily on owner operators employed as independent contractors. They can learn all about the contract terms, submit resumes on-line, and get on-line assistance for running their business more efficiently.

an interview will be scheduled as the next step. There is literally no waiting required for the applicant to learn whether the company is a good prospect. J. P. Morgan Chase went one step further. It made it *fun* to apply on-line by creating a job-hunting game that helps applicants match their interests to alternative jobs in the company.[35]

Making a Good Personal Impression

To develop an understanding of how job applicants view recruiting practices, one team of researchers decided to conduct intensive, open-ended interviews with a few job hunters. The researchers asked placement directors from four colleges of a large university to identify job seekers who were as different from each other as possible in terms of gender, race, grade point average, and so on. Forty-one job seekers were identified and then interviewed early in the campus recruiting season and again near the end, 8 to 10 weeks later. The interviews were recorded, transcribed, and then content analyzed.

The results showed that job seekers' early perceptions of how well they fit a job were affected most by job and company characteristics, then by contacts with recruiters, and then by contacts with other people in the company besides recruiters. In many instances, recruiters made jobs that initially appeared unattractive seem attractive. Positive impressions were created by the status of recruiters and whether recruiters made applicants feel "specially" treated. On the other hand, almost all job seekers reported that some recruiters or recruiting practices or both created poor impressions and made some jobs seem less attractive. Timing was especially important here: slow or late decisions were a major reason for negative impressions. Another interesting finding was that the best applicants were more likely than weaker applicants to interpret recruiting practices as indications of what the employing organization was like rather than assuming the practices were just a poor reflection on the particular recruiter involved.[36] Effective recruiters show sincere interest in applicants, and, in return, applicants show more interest in the job.[37]

At Dell Computers, applicants feel special because so many people are involved, as described in the feature "Managing Teams: The Dell Recruiting Team."[38]

> *"I was impressed that these women executives would take the time out to interview me, a mid-level person. I was delighted to find people that embrace the same values I embrace."*
>
> Teri Robinson
> Vice President
> Darden Restaurants

MANAGING TEAMS

The Dell Recruiting Team

The job of the head of staffing for Dell Computers is to hire world-class people. Regardless of how many new recruits are needed, the company never lowers its standards for quality. Dell wants to hire only the best, and to do so it uses the best recruiters—its own employees, including the CEO, when necessary. Besides getting referrals from employees, Dell's recruiting managers use a "leads team." Like a SWAT team, its job is to act quickly and aggressively to tackle hiring problems—such as an unexpected vacancy in a key position. Acting almost like spies, the "leads team" studies newspapers, the Web, trade journals, and anything else they can think of to come up with the names of people who might consider a job change. Dips in stock prices, mergers, or plans for downsizing all provide clues.

When good people are found, they often visit the company headquarters in Austin, Texas, before making a final decision. At this point, Dell may involve other people from the community to help. When a recruit wanted to know about the ice hockey opportunities for his son, a Junior Olympian, Dell had the local youth league president meet with the candidate to provide the information. That was somewhat unusual. More typical would be involving realtors, medical experts, school administrators, or religious leaders, depending on candidates' particular concerns. For a company that depends on the talent of its employees for success, all this effort is worth it.

Making an Offer Applicants Will Accept

Recruiters and the recruitment process help create a good (or bad) impression, but other things matter too. Especially for younger applicants, deciding whether to accept an employment offer may be entangled with choosing an occupation. These choices are influenced by economic issues, including the realities of the labor market; psychological issues, such as individual needs, interests, and abilities; and sociological issues, including exposure to the occupation through parents and relatives.[39]

> **FAST FACT**
>
> A survey of 2,000 college students found that they have the following job priorities: flexibility, stock options, vacation time, and ability to telecommute.

Work Context. It is often assumed that the attractiveness of an offer depends in part on what other offers the applicant is considering. This line of thinking follows from the image of a job seeker who invests a great deal of time and effort to generate as many options as possible and then simultaneously evaluates them. In reality, except for new college graduates, job seekers have only a hazy notion of their options.[40] The objective of most job seekers is to find an acceptable, rather than ideal, job. They usually evaluate opportunities sequentially. If an offer meets minimum criteria, it's accepted; if it doesn't, the sequential search process continues. In other words, alternative offers are less important than past experiences and beliefs about what is realistic to expect.

"There's never a question that you would get a job. There's just the question of will you get bored."

A Computer Science Graduate Student
Stanford University

Location, job attributes, company attributes, and perceptions that the organization's values match the applicant's own all influence an applicant's decision.[41] Important company characteristics include its size, general reputation and management ethics as presented in the media, attitudes toward the product, and HR practices—such as whether the company is hiring new managers and at the same time laying some people off. Important job characteristics include the status of the functional area the job is in and opportunities for personal development through the job, as well as the nature of the work itself.[42] Savvy recruiters understand the importance of these and make an effort to inform applicants about the company as well as the job.

Pay. Another important consideration is the applicant's **noncompensatory reservation wage**, which is the minimum pay necessary to make a job offer acceptable. Prior compensation levels, length of unemployment, and the availability of accurate salary information all affect an individual's reservation wage. In general, males have higher reservation wages than females. One explanation for this is that females tend to undervalue their work abilities.[43] Another may be that males are exposed to more job opportunities. Increasingly, when applicants evaluate compensation offers, they consider the value of signing bonuses in addition to salary, benefits, and incentive offers.[44]

> **FAST FACT**
>
> The Society for Human Resource Management estimates that signing bonuses are offered by 40% of employers.

Benefits and Work Arrangements. Once a reservation wage is met, job seekers adopt a **compensatory approach**. That is, they make trade-offs between different job attributes.[45] As described in Chapter 13, benefits and flexible work arrangements often are among the most important considerations. Both sexes prefer companies that offer more flexibility and opportunities to learn quickly.[46] With the exception of workers under age 30, almost everyone agrees that benefits such as health insurance are among the most important factors to consider. For those at the bottom of the earnings scale, job security is one of the most important concerns.[47]

> **FAST FACT**
>
> When JigZaw Inc. places job ads, it includes the phrase "people interested in flextime are encouraged to apply."

Giving Applicants the Information They Need

In their efforts to attract a large pool of applicants, many employers oversell their virtues and cover over their flaws. Just as applicants work to create the best possible impression,[48] so do employers. Some recruiters tell job applicants about only the positive aspects of a job and the company. This tactic follows from a desire to increase offer acceptances. In the short run, this tactic may work.[49] Longer-term, it's counterproductive. Allstate Insurance communicates what employees can expect from the company, as well as what the company expects from employees, in a booklet titled "The Allstate Partnership: Meeting Mutual Expectations." Exhibit 7.5 summarizes the key points discussed in the booklet.[50]

Honesty Pays (Saves). Describing both the positive and negative aspects of a job and organization—that is, providing a **realistic job preview**—is a better approach. Research shows that using realistic job previews actually increases the number of eventual recruits. In addition, recruits who receive both types of information are more committed and less likely to quit once they accept the job.[51]

> **FAST FACT**
>
> According to the Bureau of Labor Statistics, the average worker holds nine different jobs between the ages of 18 and 32.

Being overly optimistic also is questionable from an ethical perspective. Accepting a job offer can have far-reaching implications for a person's life—it can affect where the person lives, how much stress the person experiences commuting to work, where the person's children attend school, where a partner works, income levels, and so on. Viewed in this light, persuading a person to take a job becomes a big responsibility. Clearly, the only ethical approach is to engage in an honest exchange of information with job applicants. In fact, recent research shows that applicants appreciate the concern shown by employers who provide negative as well as positive information.[52]

If a firm's representatives make false promises to job candidates, the firm can face costly lawsuits. Truth-in-hiring lawsuits have yielded damage awards as high as $10 million.[53] Withholding information is just as dangerous as making false statements. In one case (*Berger v. Security Pacific Information*

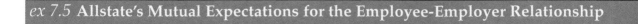

ex 7.5 Allstate's Mutual Expectations for the Employee-Employer Relationship

What the Company Expects from Employees

1. Perform at levels that significantly increase our ability to outperform the competition.

2. Take on assignments critical to meeting business objectives.

3. Continually develop needed skills.

4. Willingly listen to and act upon feedback.

5. Demonstrate a high level of commitment to achieving company goals.

6. Exhibit no bias in interactions with colleagues and customers.

7. Behave consistently with Allstate's ethical standards.

8. Take personal responsibility for each transaction with our customers and for fostering their trust.

9. Continually improve processes to address customers' needs.

What Employees Can Expect from the Company

1. Offer work that is meaningful and challenging.

2. Promote an environment that encourages open and constructive dialogue.

3. Recognize you for your accomplishments.

4. Provide competitive pay and rewards based on your performance.

5. Advise you on your performance through regular feedback.

6. Create learning opportunities through education and job assignments.

7. Support you in defining your career goals.

8. Provide you with information and resources to perform successfully.

9. Promote an environment that is inclusive and free from bias.

10. Foster dignity and respect in interactions.

11. Establish an environment that promotes a balance of work and personal life.

Systems), Colorado's highest court upheld a jury's award of $451,600 because a company withheld information about its financial difficulties from a prospective employee.

More accurate information allows employees to make better decisions about whether a situation is right for them. By helping applicants who won't be satisfied self-select out of the hiring process, organizations prevent unnecessary turnover. Applicants and employers both benefit. New or potential employees usually have inflated ideas or expectations about what a job involves. A realistic preview usually reduces these overly optimistic expectations. Of course, employees share responsibility for getting a realistic job preview. In order to make sure they know what they are getting into, applicants should ask questions until they get detailed answers about things such as the ex-

FAST FACT

A survey of 400 international assignments in 80 companies around the world revealed that 40% wouldn't take another international assignment after learning what it was like.

pected results, the timetable available to achieve the results, and the resources available to them.[54]

Sources of Information. Realistic job previews take many forms, including advertisements, formal job descriptions, film or video presentations, and samples of the actual work. A study involving several large companies found that potential applicants are attracted to companies that provide more information in their ads. When ads tell about the company, the job, and the job benefits, job seekers are more likely to follow up and apply for the job.[55] Another study found that applicants who obtained information through both formal and informal means had more knowledge about the job than those who relied on only one type of information.[56] In general, more information is better, and informal means of communicating about the job often produce more accurate perceptions.[57]

Rejecting with Tact

When Mirage Resorts received 57,000 applications for 6,500 job openings, it had to tell thousands of applicants they wouldn't be hired. Southwest Airlines sends the same message to thousands of applicants year after year. If rejected candidates feel angry, they may never again purchase services from the organization. If recruiting procedures are viewed as unfair, too lengthy, or too impersonal, rejected candidates may share their dissatisfaction with friends and associates. For "high-demand" organizations, rejecting with tact is an extremely important step in the total recruitment process.

Most applicants receive the news of their rejection in written form. Whether it's a traditional letter or an e-mail message, the same basic principles apply. To leave a positive impression, a rejection letter should include statements that are friendly, a personalized and correct address and salutation, and a summary of the applicant's job qualifications. Including statements about the size and excellence of the application pool reduces disappointment and increases perceptions of fairness.[58] Applicants also appreciate timely rejection notices. A recruitment and selection timetable should be specified for applicants and the organization should meet its self-imposed deadlines.

INTERNET RESOURCES   **7.C**

The Applicant's Perspective

At our Web site, http://jackson.swcollege.com/, you can:

1. See examples of how companies make it easy for applicants to check whether they are a good "fit" for the organization by visiting

   Texas Instruments

   Ernst & Young

2. Find out about companies that are "Employers of Choice," as identified by *Fortune's* list of "The 100 Best Companies to Work For in America."

3. Find out about the services that placement firms offer to employees who are searching for new jobs and careers, including

   Lee Hecht Harrison

   Manchester

EQUAL OPPORTUNITY AND NONDISCRIMINATION

Legal considerations play a critical role in the recruitment and hiring processes of most companies in the United States. As described in Chapter 3, U.S. employment laws prohibit discrimination in recruiting as well as other human resource management activities.

EEO-1 Reports

One method the federal government uses to track compliance with nondiscrimination laws is requiring most employers with more than 100 employees to file annually an **Employer Information Report (EEO-1)**. Exhibit 7.6 illustrates the information an employer must supply. Briefly, the report gives an accounting of the composition of the workforce using four factors: job family (9 categories), sex (2 categories), race/ethnicity (8 categories), and employment status (5 categories).

Electronic **applicant tracking systems** often collect and store the needed information automatically, making record keeping quick and easy. The typical applicant tracking software provides a standard format for input of a job requisition, which lists the job content and skill requirements (based on a job description.) These systems also capture data from applicants (e.g., from resumes) and provide for reports to be entered based on interviews and other selection procedures. In addition to tracking the number and qualifications of applicants, applicant tracking systems make it easy for employers to track the demographic characteristics of applicants who learned about job openings from different sources (e.g., a job fair, job boards, recruitment agencies). Note, however, that it is important for tracking systems to store demographic information about applicants separately from information about qualifications, as it is illegal to use most demographic information as a basis for hiring decisions. Finally, applicant tracking systems usually make it easy to generate reports of many types; they can be used to assess the speed of recruiting procedures, the number and quality of applicants from different sources, and so on.[59] While convenient, the electronic applicant tracking systems do not relieve employers of the strategic decisions that must be made when developing a recruiting strategy and designing specific recruiting practices.

Employers should take care to consider whether their practices are likely to reach and be equally effective for all types of applicants. On-line recruiting methods in particular should be scrutinized. Because these are relatively new, the potential sources of unintended discrimination are not well understood. Similarly, many vendors who offer electronic recruiting services have relatively little experience. They may have gotten into the business of recruiting primarily as a result of their technical computer knowledge—not their professional HR expertise. If their recruiting methods turn out to discriminate unfairly, the employer who hired the vendor is the one who will be held legally accountable.

Affirmative Action Programs

The U.S. employment laws most directly relevant to recruitment are those describing **affirmative action programs (AAPs)**. Affirmative action programs are intended to ensure proportional representation or parity, or to correct underutilization, of qualified members of protected groups in an organization's relevant labor market. Title VII of the *Civil Rights Act of 1964*

FAST FACT

In 1997, non-Hispanic white males were the largest group hired by state agencies under federally mandated affirmative action programs.

ex 7.6 Employer Information Report EEO-1 (Excerpt, Part B)

	American Indian or Alaska Native	Asian	Black or African American	Native Hawaiian or Other Pacific Islander	White	Hispanic or Latino (all races)	Hispanic or Latino (White race only)	Hispanic or Latino (all other races)
Officials, Managers Male								
Female								
Professionals Male								
Female								
Technicians Male								
Female								
Operatives Male								
Female								
Sales Workers Male								
Female								
Office, Clerical Male								
Female								
Craft Workers Male								
Female								
Laborers Male								
Female								
Service Workers Male								
Female								

Column groups: APPLICANTS, HIRES, PROMOTIONS, TERMINATIONS, ALL FULL TIME AT END OF YEAR identifies the following as protected groups: women, African Americans, Hispanics, Native Americans, Asian Americans, and Pacific Islander Americans. As Exhibit 7.7 shows, most firms have AAPs.[60]

Some AAPs are required because the company is a federal contractor. Others were adopted as part of a consent degree. Finally, many are voluntary efforts.

FAST FACT

There are about 65,000 companies that are federal contractors.

Federal Contractors. If a company has a federal contract greater than $50,000 and has 50 or more employees, it's referred to as a federal contractor. Executive Order 11246, which became effective in 1965, requires federal contractors to

1. have and abide by an equal employment policy;
2. analyze its workforce to assess possible underutilization of women and ethnic minorities; and
3. when underutilization is revealed, develop a plan of action to eliminate it and make a good faith effort to implement the plan.

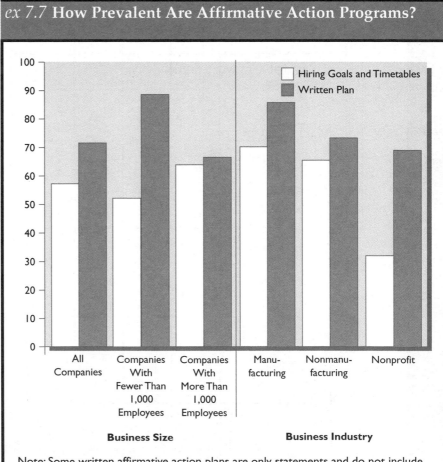

ex 7.7 How Prevalent Are Affirmative Action Programs?

Note: Some written affirmative action plans are only statements and do not include goals and timetables.
Bureau of National Affairs. Used by permission.

Regulatory guidelines and subsequent Supreme Court decisions make it clear that such plans must not include strong preferential treatment or strict quotas. Instead, plans should emphasize recruitment activities that increase the representation of protected groups and employment practices that eliminate bias.

In addition to protecting members of the groups identified in Title VII, federal contractors are required to take affirmative action to employ and advance qualified disabled individuals (section 503 of the *Rehabilitation Act of 1973*). The rules further provide that employers with 50 or more employees who hold federal contracts totaling more than $50,000 must prepare written affirmative action programs for disabled workers in each of their establishments—for example, in each plant or field office.

Federal contractors are required to file written affirmative action plans with the **Office of Federal Contract Compliance Programs (OFCCP)**, which is charged with overseeing the employment practices of federal contracts and enforcing relevant federal regulations. The Department of Labor specifies the required components of the written plans:

> **FAST FACT**
>
> More than 20% of the U.S. workforce is covered by OFCCP affirmative action regulations.

1. A **utilization analysis.** The analysis determines the number of minorities and women employed in different jobs within an organization. Under the new regulations, this requirement can be met with a one-page organizational profile.
2. An **availability analysis.** This measures how many members of minorities and women are available to work in the relevant labor market of an organization. The **relevant labor market** is generally defined as the geographic area from which come a substantial majority of job applicants and employees. If an organization is employing proportionately fewer members of protected groups than are available, a state of **underutilization** exists. Under the new regulations, this analysis was simplified to require the use of only two factors—down from the old requirement of using eight factors.
3. **Goals and timetables.** Goals and timetables specify how the organization plans to correct any underutilization of protected groups. Because goals and timetables become the organization's commitment to equal employment, they must be realistic and attainable. When a protected group is found to be underutilized, the timetable for addressing the problem is likely to stretch over several years.

> **FAST FACT**
>
> At the end of the year 2000, the OFCCP instituted new regulations for Federal Contractors' Affirmative Action Plans.

These plans are intended to reduce discriminatory practices among employers who receive federal funds. Several studies indicate that for federal contractors, representation of black males and black females has grown rapidly.[61] A review of the status of women and minorities in these firms suggests that AAPs may not eliminate discrimination, however. In summarizing their findings, an OFCCP official concluded, "In nearly every review we do, we're finding inequities in the compensation for women and minorities compared to white men."[62]

Consent Decrees. Employers that are not federal contractors may nevertheless be subject to a government-regulated affirmative action plan. A federal court may require an AAP if it finds evidence of past discrimination in a suit brought against the organization through the Equal Employment Opportunity Commission. The evidence that leads to such conclusions often comes from a utilization analysis conducted by the EEOC. **Consent decrees** specify the affirmative action steps the organization will take.

Since the 1960s, hundreds of consent degrees have put AAPs into place. Their effectiveness to date is difficult to judge, however. Women and minorities have made some progress in their employment status. Whether progress would have been faster or slower in the absence of consent decrees is impossible to know. When *Fortune* put together its list of the 50 Best Companies for Asians, Blacks, and Hispanics, the vast majority of the 50 companies selected had aggressive EEOC recruiting plans in place.[63] Some programs were put in place years ago in response to consent decrees. It's likely that many others were developed to avoid lawsuits or minimize the damages that would be caused by a lawsuit. One thing *is* clear, however: perceptions of unfair discrimination persist even among African Americans who are generally optimistic about their futures.[64]

Voluntary Affirmative Action. If a company develops a reputation for being a difficult place for minorities to work, it's likely to make recruiting in a tight labor market all the more challenging. Elgin Clemons described an incident he experienced while working as an attorney at the prestigious law firm of Shearman & Sterling. A graduate of Princeton University and New York University Law School, Clemons worked as an associate for the law firm for two years. One day he decided not to call for a messenger and instead personally delivered to the firm's mail room a stack of work to be sent to a client. A mail clerk told him he would have to get an attorney's signature. "What makes you think I'm not an attorney?" Clemons, who is black, asked. He knew that the mail clerk was reacting to his race. The stereotyping was even more painful because the mail clerk also was black.

A mail clerk's stereotyping habits may have little consequence for an attorney, but when the firm's partners engage in stereotyping, the consequences are significant. At Shearman & Sterling, the partners, all of whom were white, acknowledged that they assumed that blacks as a group have more problems with legal writing than whites. When stories such as this spread—through the informal grapevine as well as national newspapers—they naturally reduce the size and diversity of the firm's applicant pool.[65]

Designing AAPs. The content of a voluntary AAP depends on the organization and the extent to which various groups are underrepresented. It may also depend on the company's strategic business objectives. American Express, for example, proactively recruits women and minority managers in particular, recognizing that its diversity is a particularly valuable asset in today's competitive environment.

The EEOC publishes guidelines for organizations that wish to establish voluntary affirmative action programs, and it offers the annual Exemplary Voluntary Efforts Award to recognize companies with the best voluntary programs. Winning the award appears to have value beyond simply good public relations. A study of firms that have won this award showed that investors bid up the stock prices of the winning companies after the award was announced. By comparison, stock prices fell following announcements of discrimination settlements.[66]

Risks of AAPs. Exhibit 7.8 summarizes some of the arguments made for and against affirmative action activities. Despite research that documents the

ex 7.8 Two Sides of the Affirmative Action Debate

Arguments Supporting Affirmative Action

- Historical inequities in the treatment of members of protected groups cannot be corrected unless affirmative efforts are made to bring these groups up to parity.
- Affirmative action efforts that are appropriately designed and implemented do not result in reverse discrimination.
- They increase the diversity of the applicant pool; they do not involve lowering standards for making hiring decisions.
- Affirmative action efforts benefit society as a whole by ensuring that the country's human resources are not squandered. Without such efforts, significant portions of the population will be caught in a vicious cycle of low economic achievement.
- Some groups may have to suffer temporary reverse discrimination due to affirmative action efforts, but the greater good that such efforts serve justify this.

Arguments Against Affirmative Action

- Affirmative action efforts inadvertently harm those who are intended to be the beneficiaries by lowering their self-esteem and causing others to view them as less qualified.
- Affirmative action efforts result in reverse discrimination.
- Any efforts to help one group necessarily mean discrimination occurs against the groups that do not receive such help.
- By classifying employees into protected and unprotected groups, affirmative action efforts create polarizing and separation between men and women and between majority and minority ethnic groups. Pitting groups against each other leads to greater racism and prejudice.
- Affirmative action efforts create innocent victims. The males and nonminorities who experience reverse discrimination today are not the same individuals who are responsible for the historical events that resulted in present-day inequities.

benefits of AAPs, mandatory and voluntary AAPs have come under increasing political attack. It's unclear how long they'll remain legal. Employers who thought they were being socially responsible by taking affirmative actions have lost lawsuits for taking measures that the courts viewed as reverse discrimination. The case of *Piscataway Board of Education v. Taxman* (1997) illustrates this legal trend. The case involved a layoff affecting two equally qualified teachers who had been hired on the very same day and so had identical job tenure. A white teacher (Sharon Taxman) was laid off while an African-American teacher (Debra Williams) was retained in order to maintain the school's racial diversity. The courts ruled that the Board of Education engaged in illegal employment practice because under Title VII employers may not use race as a basis for employment decisions except for compelling reasons. Because the school district had no record of past discrimination or underutilization, maintaining a diverse workforce was not viewed as a sufficiently compelling reason to consider race in the layoff decision.[67]

In another recent case, a federal appeals court struck down affirmative action practices intended to increase job opportunities for minorities and women in the broadcasting industry. This case is described in more detail in the feature "Managing Diversity: Court Strikes Down Affirmative Action in Broadcasting."[68] When deciding whether to implement a voluntary affirmative action plan, employers must consider the threats posed by the shifting legal and political landscape.[69]

Some opponents of affirmative action argue that preferential treatment often backfires, causing harm to the intended beneficiaries of AAPs. Consistent with this argument, studies have shown that affirmative action hires are *perceived* as being less competent than *equally qualified* employees not hired under an AAP.[70] During the 1990s, organizations began developing new approaches to managing diversity. These include offering cultural awareness training programs and the development of decision-making procedures that reduce the impact of any individual's personal prejudices and

"It hurt her self-esteem. With all she had put into education, and then to be told that the only reason she has her job is because she's black."

Alvin Williams
Husband of Debra Williams

biases. According to numerous opinion polls, Americans strongly support efforts designed to ensure equal opportunity and eliminate bias, and they oppose practices that they believe involve giving any group preferential treatment.[71]

Breaking the Glass Ceiling

Regardless of why organizations develop AAPs, their presence often stimulates people to think more systematically about their recruitment efforts. Until recently, the disciplined approach associated with AAPs—that is, defining the relevant labor market and tracking how recruitment efforts affect both who is offered a position and who accepts job offers—was used only for lower-level positions and external recruitment efforts.

"The critical factor for the advancement of women is commitment from the top."

Sheila Wellington
President
Catalyst

Many companies have found that a decade or two of affirmative action recruiting at lower levels ensured that by the late 1980s there were plenty of women in the pipeline for higher-level positions. Yet, women still seem to be trapped below a glass ceiling. Based on its intensive study of nine large corporations, the Department of Labor concluded that the recruiting methods typically used to hire managerial talent contributed to the problem of glass ceilings.[72] Exhibit 7.9 summarizes how several common recruiting practices can contribute to the problem. The challenge for these companies is how to balance their desire to recruit the best available talent with their desire to break the glass ceiling.

Colgate's approach is one way to overcome these problems. For Colgate-Palmolive, focusing the firm's recruitment efforts on women seemed like a reasonable solution. When one of the four regional vice presidents stepped down, Colgate's CEO decided he wanted to fill the position with a woman. According to CEO Reuben Mark, the company "wanted the best person we could possibly get, but that person had to be a woman." Colgate hired Lois Juliber in 1988 and put her in charge of its Far East and Canada Opera-

---

ex 7.9 Recruiting Practices That May Create a Glass Ceiling

Reliance on Networking——Word-of-Mouth: Middle- and upper-level positions often are filled through word-of-mouth referrals. Corporate executives may learn of individuals, interview them casually at luncheons or dinners, and make them an offer, without a formal recruitment process. Diminished opportunity occurs for people not in the executive network result.

Reliance on Networking—Employee Referrals: In some companies, elaborate employee referral systems are in place. If employees in the company do not represent the full diversity of the labor force, the pool of applicants created by their referrals also will not reflect this diversity.

Executive Search Firms: Employers are responsible for obtaining a diverse pool of applicants. Companies may not make executive recruitment firms aware of their equal employment and affirmative action obligations and objectives, or they may not use success in this area in deciding which search firm to hire.

Job Postings: Some companies post job notices for lower-level jobs, but not for mid- to upper-level jobs. At the higher levels, employees learn about openings only through their informal networks. Informal communications tend to flow more intensely among people who are demographically similar, which means that members of many protected groups are less likely to hear about openings for higher-level positions.

Recruiting Venues: Recruiting often occurs at conferences for trade and professional associations and interviews often are scheduled to take place in a hotel room. A Wellesley College Center for Research on Women study found that holding job interviews in hotel rooms can be intimidating for many women and reduces the possibility of finding qualified women applicants.

Court Strikes Down Affirmative Action in Broadcasting

MANAGING
DIVERSITY

In 1998, some of the nation's largest broadcasters decided to continue their affirmative action efforts even after a court ruled that they were no longer required to follow guidelines published by the Federal Communications Commission (FCC). The guidelines essentially stated that, as a condition for keeping their license, broadcast companies must make good-faith efforts to recruit and hire minorities. When the court ruled that such guidelines were not enforceable, the FCC rules were revised to clearly state that a company's record would not be a factor in deciding whether to renew a broadcaster's license. The revised FCC rules for broadcasters set out initiatives to recruit more minorities and women through activities such as career fairs and internships. Broadcasters were required to undertake four such initiatives. Alternatively, they could develop their own outreach efforts. But if those efforts yielded "few or no applications from women or minorities," the FCC promised to investigate. In explaining the FCC's position, William Kennard stated, "We're at a time when there is a troubling disconnect between images people see on TV and the reality of our multicultural society."

The revised rules were challenged too, and the case eventually was heard again in a federal appeals court, which handed down its decision in 2001. That decision supported the lower court. It stated, "The rule does put official pressure upon broadcasters to recruit minority candidates, thus creating a race-based classification that is not narrowly tailored to support a compelling governmental interest and is therefore unconstitutional." The decision was handed down on the same day that the government released a report showing that the number of television stations owned by minorities had dipped to the lowest level in at least a decade. Kennard, the first black chairman of the FCC, described the court's decision as "outrageous." The new FCC chairman, Michael Powell, took over the job shortly after the appeals court made its ruling. Powell stated that he believed there was insufficient evidence to show a connection between diversity in employment and diversity in the content offered by broadcasters.

tions. A decade later, she was promoted to Executive Vice President and put in charge of North America and Europe, which constitute half of the company's worldwide operations. The appointment was widely viewed as a signal that she was being considered as a top contender for the CEO position.[73]

Other companies use other approaches. Many have developed management intern programs aimed at recruiting recent minority and female college graduates, as well as sponsoring scholarships for minorities and women in disciplines related to the company's business. Some companies have tried to remedy problems related to the glass ceiling with better use of search firms and other forms of recruitment, record keeping, and internal monitoring. Other approaches include awareness training for top executives and cultural audits, which can be used to identify obstacles or barriers that hinder individuals from meeting their career goals.[74]

"If you stick to hiring the best and brightest diversity will take care of itself. That's not to say that people don't have to be trained to develop a comfort level. That's what we're working on."

Archyne Woodward
Diversity Coordinator
The Chubb Corporation

REDUCING RECRUITING NEEDS THROUGH RETENTION

For some organizations, rapid growth is the primary reason that new employees must be recruited. Growth may be steady over a long period of time, or it may occur in short bursts when new facilities are opened. But the need to replace workers who leave is a far more common force driving most recruitment activities. Turnover, not growth, creates most recruitment pressures.

Understanding the Reasons for Turnover

Some turnover is unavoidable, of course. People retire or move for non–job related reasons. As described in Chapter 5, turnover due

FAST FACT

When Ernst & Young learned that women were much more likely than men to leave this firm to work elsewhere, they created an Office of Retention.

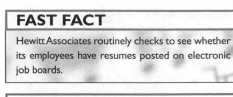

FAST FACT

Hewitt Associates routinely checks to see whether its employees have resumes posted on electronic job boards.

FAST FACT

In the fast-food industry, turnover of hourly workers averages 140% annually.

to the upcoming retirement of baby boomers is expected to have major implications for future recruiting activities. Furthermore, not all turnover is bad. Sometimes organizations encourage employees to leave. The objective may be to shrink the size of the workforce overall, or simply to help unproductive workers realize that they may be better off finding alternative employment. But the lion's share of turnover—that caused by dissatisfied employees—is not desirable and may be avoidable. Exhibit 7.10 illustrates some of the known causes of voluntary turnover.[75]

Exit Surveys

It is not necessary for *all* of the possible problems suggested by Exhibit 7.10 to exist in order for an organization to have turnover problems, especially under tight labor market conditions. In order to understand the reasons behind employees' decisions to seek other employment, some organizations conduct **exit surveys**. At about the time the employee leaves the organization, he or

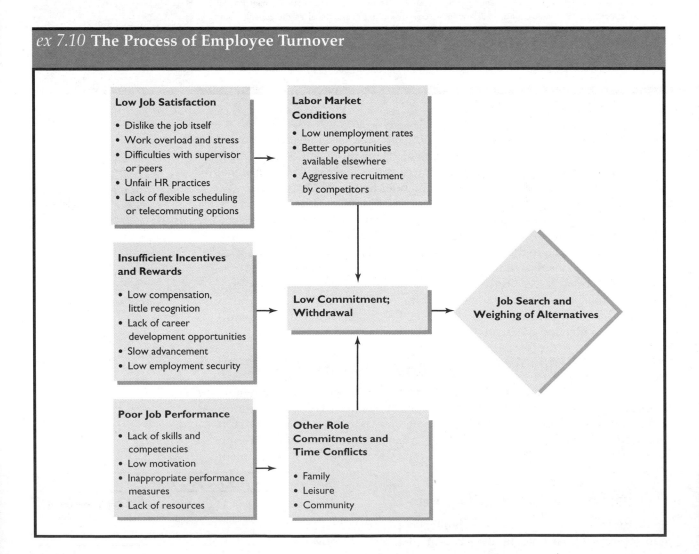

ex 7.10 **The Process of Employee Turnover**

Low Job Satisfaction
- Dislike the job itself
- Work overload and stress
- Difficulties with supervisor or peers
- Unfair HR practices
- Lack of flexible scheduling or telecommuting options

Labor Market Conditions
- Low unemployment rates
- Better opportunities available elsewhere
- Aggressive recruitment by competitors

Insufficient Incentives and Rewards
- Low compensation, little recognition
- Lack of career development opportunities
- Slow advancement
- Low employment security

Low Commitment; Withdrawal

Job Search and Weighing of Alternatives

Poor Job Performance
- Lack of skills and competencies
- Low motivation
- Inappropriate performance measures
- Lack of resources

Other Role Commitments and Time Conflicts
- Family
- Leisure
- Community

she is asked several questions—usually they focus on assessing satisfaction with things such as benefits, work conditions, career advancement and development, supervision, and pay. Such information may be gathered using an interview, a paper-and-pencil survey, or an on-line survey. Regardless of the method used, the information gathered will not be useful to the employer unless the employee is quite candid. There are many reasons why departing employees may not fully disclose their reasons for leaving, however, so getting candid responses can be difficult. Among the reasons for not being completely open when responding to an exit survey are these:

- wanting to put any negative experiences behind and move on,
- fear that any negative comments made may reach their new employer,
- cynicism regarding the employers' true level of interest in fixing any problems that exist,
- concern that colleagues who remain may in some way suffer as a result of what is said, and
- a desire to "not burn any bridges" because the employee may anticipate wanting to return to the organization sometime in the future.

From Exhibit 7.10, it's easy to see that many causes are under the control of employers. Unfair HR practices clearly are under employers' control. Examples of unfair HR practices that employers can change include electronic monitoring and travel schedules that require extended time away from home. Employers also may be able to offer better pay and benefits in order to decrease the rate at which employees voluntarily leave.[76] And, with sufficient effort, they can remove the glass ceilings that prevent otherwise qualified applicants from being promoted and encourage them to look elsewhere for advancement opportunities. Even causes of turnover that may not seem to be under an employer's control can probably be at least partially addressed by employers who want to make the effort.

Turnover and Recruiting Difficulties

Many of the conditions that cause people to leave also make it difficult to attract new applicants to replace them. For example, if employees are leaving a company due partly to their inability to manage both work and nonwork demands, that company will also have a more difficult time recruiting new employees with the same concern. If employees are leaving the company because they have ineffective relationships with their managers, they are likely to discourage their friends from working at that company.

> **FAST FACT**
>
> Two-thirds of women professionals say they desire top-level positions, and more than half say they'll move to another company if they are passed over for them.

According to a recent study of people of color aged 21 to 30 who had recently quit their jobs, poor work relationships with supervisors and peers was a common reason for their leaving. People of color aren't the only ones who leave for this reason, of course. In fact, a study of 25 years of Gallup interviews with more than a million employees found that employees' relationships with their supervisors were a major determinant of whether or not they stayed in a job. Among the things that more effective managers do are taking the time to understand their employees interests and concerns, providing regular and honest feedback, discussing employees career plans, and providing suggestions for career development.[77]

In general, retaining good employees involves nothing less than doing an excellent job in all aspects of managing human resources. This may be more difficult than it sounds, however. Learning about what other companies do can be helpful. But the reality is that every company is likely to face at least a few unique challenges.

Companies in the inner cities face some of the biggest challenges. The first challenge is that many of the available jobs are boring and routine. A. J. Wasserstein tries to enliven work at his records storage company by holding a monthly "breakfast club" meeting with his employees and offering monthly prizes to workers in unannounced categories—pulling the most orders, making the most deliveries, and so on. Another tactic he uses to control turnover is a "Pay to Stay" bonus—$100 for every six months of continuous service. Another common challenge, especially for low-skill jobs, is that many potential employees don't have well-developed work skills and habits. Reducing turnover among these employees may require making an investment in basic training—teaching them how to get to work on time, how to fill out a time sheet, and the rudiments of customer service.[78]

Managing Workforce Reductions and Layoffs

"It is not our culture to be laying off people in one division and hiring in another."

Cheryl Smith
Staffing Representative
3M

Facing the threat of job loss and seeing others lose their jobs can be a traumatic and bitter experience.[79] This is one reason why many excellent companies do everything possible to avoid layoffs. Instead, they work to maintain an internal labor market from which to recruit applicants for job openings.[80] Despite their best efforts, however, even the most employee-friendly companies may deal with difficult economic conditions by reducing their workforces. How such reductions in the workforce are managed can have long-ranging implications for employee loyalty and turnover.

Avoiding Layoffs. After the attack on the World Trade Center and the Pentagon sent the airlines industry into a tailspin in the autumn of 2001, most major airlines soon began announcing plans to cut their workforces by as much as 20 percent. But Herb Kelleher was determined to do everything possible to avoid layoffs. Instead of cutting costs through layoffs, the company scrapped its growth plans, delayed deliveries of new aircraft, and prepared for possible damage to its stock price. This approach to dealing with the economic downturn was possible in part because the company was debt-free and had $1 billion in cash. Southwest is one of only a few companies that have long records of avoiding layoffs. Another is Pella, the window manufacturer. Even during the Depression, Pella chose to keep employees on the job washing windows over and over again instead of resorting to layoffs.

The 3M company, based in St. Paul, Minnesota, works hard to keep employees even when its own business units eliminate jobs. Instead of being fired, displaced employees are given first consideration for other job openings within the unit. If no suitable placement can be found, they are put on the Unassigned List, which makes them eligible for jobs in other units. They can stay on the list for six months. During that time, finding employment is the employees' responsibility. The company supports their efforts, however. Before recruiting externally to fill open positions, managers first check the qualifications of people on the Unassigned List. The company also sponsors an optional three-day workshop that covers topics such as outplacement, coping with job loss, resume writing, and interviewing skills. For the first four months that they are on the Unassigned List, employees have the option of taking a severance package and leaving the company. Approximately 50 percent of the people on the list find other jobs at 3M within the four-month window. When that happens, both employees and the company are winners.[81]

Internal transfers are just one of many alternatives to massive layoffs. Others include:

- Restricting overtime
- Reducing the hours in a standard workweek
- Not renewing contracts for temporary and part-time workers
- Temporary leaves
- Job sharing
- Retraining
- Providing seed funds and entrepreneurship training and encouraging employees to start their own businesses
- Transferring staff to other companies (e.g., suppliers, customers)
- Early retirement with preferential conditions
- Reducing executive salaries and incentive pay
- Partnering with government agencies and professional societies to find jobs for displaced employees
- Employee buyouts of the company[82]

The Consequences of Layoffs. In choosing to adopt a no-layoffs policy, companies such as 3M have decided that the costs associated with maintaining their workforce are justified to avoid the hidden costs associated with layoffs. These costs include:

- Severance payments made to departing employees
- Fees paid to consultants who assist with the downsizing process
- Litigation from aggrieved workers
- Loss of trust in management
- Lack of staff needed to grow when the economy rebounds
- Loss of reputation in the labor market, making future hiring more difficult
- Cynical and paranoid behaviors among layoff survivors
- Declining customer satisfaction resulting from low employee morale[83]

Exhibit 7.11 shows the frequency of some consequences that follow layoffs. The data were collected through a survey of human resource professionals conducted by the Society for Human Resource Management.[84]

Downsizing with Respect. When employees must be let go, the process by which jobs are eliminated can make a difference. Loss of attachment, lack of information, and a perception of apparent managerial capriciousness as the basis for decisions about who will be terminated cause anxiety and an obsession with personal survival.[85] The negative cycle of reactions may not be inevitable. If survivors feel that the process used to decide whom to let go was fair, their productivity and the quality of their job performance may not suffer as much. It's not the terminations *per se* that create bitterness—it's the manner in which the terminations are handled. Survivors often express feelings of disgust and anger when their friends and colleagues are fired. If they believe their own performance in no better than those who are let go, survivors may feel guilty

> **FAST FACT**
>
> A survey by the Society for Human Resource Management found that 30 % of employers took *no* actions to deal with the stress experienced by layoff survivors.

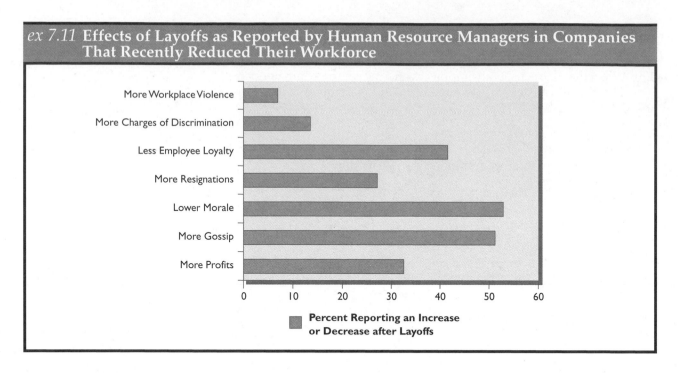

ex 7.11 **Effects of Layoffs as Reported by Human Resource Managers in Companies That Recently Reduced Their Workforce**

Percent Reporting an Increase or Decrease after Layoffs

---

that they have kept their jobs.[86] Statistics showing that older displaced workers who find new work earn about one-third less than they did in their old job contribute to the survivors' angst.[87] Thus, in developing human resource policies, procedures, and practices for effective downsizing and layoffs, even the needs of survivors require attention.

As with any major organizational change, the steps of diagnosing the current situation and developing a careful plan to implement change are essential. But the process of downsizing isn't just about strategies and plans; it's also about relationships between the people in a company and it's about personal character. The greatest challenges for companies and their managers are maintaining employee morale and regaining their trust while the actions of the company seem to say, "You are not valuable."[88]

INTERNET RESOURCES   **7.D**

Equal Employment and Nondiscrimination

At our Web site, http://jackson.swcollege.com/, you can:

1. Learn more about affirmative action plans from the Office of Federal Contract Compliance Programs.

2. Read the Department of Labor's Glass Ceiling report.

3. Learn more about how some organizations have addressed the problem of a glass ceiling by visiting

   Catalyst

   American Express

   J. P. Morgan Chase

4. Get more information about conducting exit interviews and how on-line software can help.

SUMMARY

Organizations are dynamic, and the need to attract and retain the right people is perpetual. Two important HR activities that guide effective recruitment and retention are the strategic planning process and job analysis. Planning establishes close linkages between longer-term strategic objectives and activities that address issues related to recruitment and retention. Job analysis enables the organization to convey information accurately (via job descriptions and job specifications) to applicants so that both individuals and organizations are well-matched. Selection is another activity that should be closely aligned with recruitment, as described in the next chapter. Selection decisions are constrained by the size and quality of the applicant pool, which is created through recruitment and retention activities.

Recruitment involves internal and external searches. Although organizations vary considerably in terms of the types of jobs available, both external and internal labor markets exist for the recruitment of suitable applicants. Over time, organizations weigh costs and benefits of internal and external methods in order to choose the most effective ones. The choice of recruitment methods and the implementation of a recruiting plan should take into account the perspective of applicants, as well as the needs of the organization.

For applicants, the recruitment is fundamentally a search for information. Applicants deserve to be given accurate and complete information in order to make the best possible employment decisions. Employers also benefit from this approach, as it reduces post-hire dissatisfaction and premature turnover. Retaining employees is one way to reduce the need for extensive recruiting and its associated costs. The development of an effective human resource management system requires understanding the causes of voluntary turnover.

Recruitment and retention activities take place within a dynamic legal environment. While the objectives of nondiscrimination legislation are clear, the means that society finds acceptable for creating equal employment opportunities are under debate. Sharply different opinions prevail concerning the best ways to use and design Affirmative Action Programs. It is increasing difficult for employers to simply "follow the law" when recruiting—they must consider the strategic and social objectives to be achieved and design recruitment strategies to meet those objectives.

TERMS TO REMEMBER

affirmative action programs (AAPs)
applicant tracking system
availability analysis
compensatory approach
consent decree
contingent workers
employee referrals
Employer Information Report (EEO-1)
employment agencies
exit survey
external labor market

free agents
goals and timetables
host-country nationals
internal labor market
job fairs
job postings
L-1 Intracompany Transferee visa
noncompensatory reservation wage
Office of Federal Contract Compliance Programs (OFCCP)
realistic job preview
recruitment

relevant labor market
retention
talent inventory
third-country nationals

TN NAFTA visa
underutilization
utilization analysis

DISCUSSION QUESTIONS

1. How is the Web likely to help SAS recruit? What are the possible disadvantages of Web-based recruitment at SAS?
2. After reviewing Chapter 4, describe the recruitment and retention implications that might follow from a strategic objective of offering low-cost products to a broad consumer market. Compare these implications with those that might follow from the strategic objective of offering innovative business services to owners of small businesses.
3. According to some estimates, one-third of all executive-level hires prove to be unsatisfactory. What role might executive recruitment practices play in creating this situation?
4. Why do some organizations use mostly external searches, whereas others use mostly internal searches?
5. What information should be contained in a realistic job preview by a firm seeking to attract the best MBA students? Does your answer depend on the type of industry? The geographic location of the job? Whether it involves an overseas assignment?
6. Do you think firms such as Colgate-Palmolive, American Express, and General Mills should address the glass ceiling problem by explicitly stating that they want to fill a specific managerial position with a woman? Explain your opinion.

PROJECTS TO EXTEND YOUR LEARNING

1. *Managing Through Strategic Partnerships.* Employers can easily advertise their employment opportunities over the Web. They can list openings on the company Web site or list them on public sites. Visit several available public recruiting sites. Compare and contrast the features of these sites from the perspective of employers and applicants. What are the major strengths and weaknesses of the sites you visited? If you were an employer and could list an opening on only one public site, which one would you choose? Explain your choice.
2. *Managing Diversity.* Shearman & Sterling is an international law firm headquartered in New York City, with offices in Abu Dhabi, Beijing, Dusseldorf, Tokyo, Paris, and elsewhere. As in other law firms, much of the necessary work is carried out by entry-level professionals, including student interns and associates who have just completed law school. The firm is dependent on these sources of labor and is eager to attract the best and the brightest. Visit the Web site for Shearman & Sterling to investigate the professional opportunities described (e.g., summer programs, continuing education, and career development). Analyze the firm's formal communication. What messages are conveyed through the Web site? Describe the specific cues that you react to as part of the message. Prepare a one-page memo to Shearman & Sterling describing the strengths and weaknesses of its approach to communicating via the Internet. How could improving its Web site contribute to its recruitment effectiveness?

3. *Integration and Application.* After reviewing the two end-of-text cases, answer the following questions by comparing and contrasting the recruitment efforts of the two firms.
   a. Which company do you think needs to be most concerned about recruitment? Why?
   b. What should be the objectives of each company's recruitment efforts? Relate the recruitment objectives to each company's strategic objectives.
   c. Which company is likely to have the most difficult time creating a large pool of qualified applicants? Explain your reasoning.
   d. For each company, describe the practices that are most likely to influence employee turnover. Does low turnover contribute to the success of these companies? Explain.

INTERNET RESOURCES 7.D

Resources for Projects

At our Web site, http://jackson.swcollege.com/, you can:

1. Investigate several on-line sites where applicants and employers can hook up.

2. Learn more about Shearman & Sterling's diversity recruiting activities.

DOWNSIZING: ANATHEMA TO CORPORATE LOYALTY?

case study

Jim Daniels was unprepared for the dilemma facing Defense Systems, Inc. (DSI). Jim, vice president of human resources for DSI, joined the company one year ago when he was pirated away from one of the company's major competitors. DSI manufactures electronic components used in weapons supplied to the Air Force and many other firms. In addition, DSI makes semiconductors used in many of the weapons systems as well as in personal computers and automotive computers.

When Jim joined DSI, a major drive to build up the staff in engineering was undertaken in anticipation of a major upturn in the semiconductor market. Unfortunately, industry analysts' projections were optimistic, and the semiconductor market failed to pick up. DSI recently completed an aggressive hiring policy at the major universities around the United States, wherein the company had selected 1,000 engineers who were among the cream of the crop with an average GPA of 3.4. Without a pickup in business, however, DSI is confronted with some fairly unpleasant alternatives.

From one point of view, potential cutbacks at DSI fit the overall pattern of cutbacks, restructuring, and downsizing facing many major U S. companies.

The motives among firms who have trimmed their workforces vary—some to please Wall Street and the stockholders, others to keep pace with foreign competitors or to shrink an unwieldy organizational structure. To Jim, the DSI layoffs or terminations are poor alternatives to dealing with a turbulent environment.

The major problem, as Jim sees it, is to preserve as many of these jobs as possible until business picks up. To terminate these new hires would irreparably harm DSI's future recruitment efforts. On the other hand, underemploying these talented recruits for very long is bound to lead to major dissatisfaction. Although terminations would improve the balance sheet in the short run, Jim worries about the impact of such a move on corporate loyalty, a fragile and rare commodity at other major firms that have had to cut their white-collar workforce.

Jim is scheduled to meet with the executive committee of DSI in three days to discuss the overstaffing problems and to generate alternatives. In preparation for this meeting, Jim is trying to draw on his experience with his past employer to generate some ideas. A number of differences between DSI and Jim's old employer, though, make comparisons difficult. For one, DSI does not employ nearly the number of temporaries or student interns as did his old employer. Nor does DSI rely on subcontractors to produce parts needed in its assembly operation. Because of extra capacity, DSI can currently produce 50 percent of the parts it purchases, whereas Jim's ex-employer could produce only 5 percent.

Another major difference is the degree of training provided by DSI. At Jim's old employer, each employee could expect a minimum of 40 hours of additional training a year; at DSI, however, training consists of about 10 hours per year, much of it orientation training.

Jim wonders whether there might be some additional ways to remove slack from the system and at the same time preserve as many jobs as possible. For example, overtime hours are still paid to quite a few technicians. Would the engineers be willing to assume some of these duties in the interim until business picked up? Some older employees have accumulated several weeks of unused vacation.

Could employees be encouraged to take unpaid leaves of absence? Perhaps early retirement incentives could be offered to make room for some of the bright young engineers. DSI also has 14 other geographic locations, some in need of additional workers. Could a recruiting plan for internal transfers address this problem?

As Jim thinks these options, one thing is clear: he needs to organize and prioritize these ideas concisely if he is to be prepared for his upcoming meeting.

QUESTIONS

1. Why is Jim sensitive to DSI's recruitment efforts?
2. What are some potential problems for the current class of engineers recruited at DSI?
3. How could the use of temporaries, student interns, or subcontractors potentially help DSI?
4. Evaluate Jim's alternatives for reducing DSI's labor surplus. What do you recommend?

ENDNOTES

1 W. C. Rappleye Jr., "How High is Humanizing Human Resources," Workforce (March 2001); and Web site of SAS Institute (http://www.sas.com), March 2001.

2 A. Bernasek, "Help Wanted. Really," Fortune (March 5, 2001): 118–120; C. Whalen, "Economic Trends," Business Week (March 5, 2001): 30; Special Survey Report: Human Resources Outlook 49(4) (Washington, DC: Bureau of National Affairs, 1998).

3 J. Breaugh and M. Starke, "Research on Employee Recruitment: So Many Studies, So Many Remaining Questions," Journal of Management 26(3) (2000): 405–434; J. A. Breaugh, Recruitment: Science and Practice (Boston: PWS-Kent, 1992).

4 Based on P. Cappelli and A. Crocker-Hefter, Distinctive Human Resources Are the Core Competencies of Firms, Report No. RQ00011-91 (Washington, DC: U.S. Department of Education, 1994).

5 S. Gale, "Formalized Flextime: The Perk That Brings Productivity," Workforce (February 2001): 39–42; B. Parus, "Talent Mining: Digging for Gold in Your Own Back Yard," Workspan (August 2000): 46–49; A. Poe, "Refugees to the Rescue," HR Magazine (November 2000): 86–92; G. Anders, "Talent Back," Fast Company (February 2000): 93–99; D. Brady, "Brain Drain," Business Week (September 20, 1999): 111–126; M. W. Walsh, "Luring the Best in an Unsettled Time," New York Times (January 30, 2001): G1, 10; L. S. Csoka, HR Executive Review: Competing as an Employer of Choice (New York: The Conference Board, 1996).

6 T. Raphael, "Nationwide Speeds Up Hiring, Increases Satisfaction," http://www.workforce.com/feature/00/07/00.

7 M. Petersen, "Faults Found at a Schering Plant," New York Times (March 2, 2001): C3.

8 "Does Hiring Minorities Hurt?" Business Week (September 14, 1998): 26.

9 A. B. Fisher, "Surviving the Market Turmoil," Fortune (April 2, 2001): 98–106; P. Nakache, "Cisco's Recruiting Edge," Fortune (September 29, 1997): 275–276.

10 A. E. Barber, Recruiting Employees: Individual and Organizational Perspectives (Thousand Oaks, CA: Sage, 1998); R. P. Vecchio, "The Impact of Referral Sources on Employee Attitudes: Evidence from a National Sample," Journal of Management 21(5) (1995): 953–965.

11 J. Pfeffer, "Fighting the War for Talent Is Hazardous to Your Organization's Health," Organizational Dynamics (in press, 2001).

12 J. Reingold, "For the Class of 2000, the Sellers' Market Intensifies," Business Week (May 8, 2000): 54; T. A. Stewart, "Have You Got What It Takes?" Fortune (October 11, 1999): 318–322; H. Axel, HR Executive Review: Competing as an Employer of Choice (New York: The Conference Board, 1996).

13 A. Bernstein, "Low-Skilled Jobs: Do They Have to Move?" Business Week (February 26, 2001): 94–95; A. Sewer, "Missing Persons," Fortune (February 19, 2001): 34–36; A. Poe, "Time, For a Change," HR Magazine (August 1999): 77-81; K. Tyler, "Looking for a Few Good Workers?" HR Magazine (December 2000): 129–134.

14 P. Nakache, "Cisco's Recruiting Edge."

15 R. O. Crockett, "Gateway Loses the Folksy Shtick," Business Week (July 6, 1998): 80–84.

16 K. A. Bantel and S. E. Jackson, "Top Management and Innovations in Banking: Does the Composition of the Top Management Team Make a Difference?" Strategic Management Journal 10 (Summer Supplement 1989): 107–124.

17 C. Joinson, "Capturing Turnover Costs," HR Magazine (July 2000): 107–119; B. Davidson, "The Importance of Cost Per Hire," Workforce (January 2001): 32–34. For information about sources in recruiting salespeople, see S. L. Martin and N. S. Raju, "Determining Cutoff Scores That Optimize Utility: A Recognition of Recruiting Costs," Journal of Applied Psychology 77 (1992): 15–23.

18 S. Hays, "Hiring on the Web," Workforce (August 1999): 76-84; B. Leonard, "Online and Overwhelmed," HR Magazine (August 2000): 37–42; B. Parus, "The Sky's the Limit in Online Recruiting," Workspan

(January 2001): 54–56; P. Cappelli, "Making the Most of On-Line Recruiting," *Harvard Business Review* (March 2001): 139–146; M. Schneider, "GE Capital's E-Biz Farm Team," *Business Week* (November 27, 2000): 110–111; "Headhunting 2000," *Business Week* (May 17, 1999): 74–84; "Job Candidates Judge Employers by Their Web Sites," *HR Magazine* (July 2000): 30–35; C. Patton, "Searching in Space," *Human Resource Executive* (October 6, 1997): 36–38.

19 A. Van Vianen, "Person-Organization Fit: The Match Between Newcomers' and Recruiters' Preferences for Organizational Cultures," *Personnel Psychology* 53 (2000): 113–149; T. A. Judge and D. M. Cable, "Applicant Personality, Organizational Culture, and Organizational Attraction," *Personnel Psychology* 50 (1997): 359–394; A. M. Saks and B. E. Ashforth, "A Longitudinal Investigation of the Relationships Between Job Information Sources, Applicant perceptions of Fit, and Work Outcomes," *Personnel Psychology* 50 (1997): 395–426; R. W. Griffeth, P. W. Hom, L. S. Fink, and D. J. Cohen, "Comparative Tests of Multiple Models of Recruiting Sources Effects," *Journal of Management* 23 (1997): 19–36.

20 R. M. Fernandez and N. Weinberg, "Sifting and Sorting: Personal Contacts and Hiring in a Retail Bank," *American Sociological Review* 17 (December 1997): 883–902.

21 M. N. Martinez, "Get Job Seekers to Come to You," *HR Magazine* (August 2000): 45–51; C. McCreary, "Get the Most Out of Search Firms," *Workforce* (Supplement) (August 1997): 28–30.

22 R. S. Johnson, "The 50 Best Companies for Asians, Blacks & Hispanics," *Fortune* (August 3, 1998): 94–122.

23 V. Infante, "The Pros of Hiring Ex-Cons," *Workforce* (December 2000): 30; S. Overman, "Winning Ways," *HR Magazine* (July 2000): 87–96; M. Thompson, "Border Crossing," *ACA News* (May 2000): 33–38.

24 L. West and W. Bogumil, "Foreign Knowledge Workers as a Strategic Staffing Option," *Academy of Management Executive* 14(4) (2000): 71–84.

25 S. Overman, "Recruiting in China," *HR Magazine* (March 2001): 87–93; J. L. Laabs, "Recruiting in the Global Village," *Workforce* (April 1998): 30–33.

26 "Cisco Systems' HR Is Wired for Success," *Personnel Journal* (January 1996): 59.

27 G. Anders, "Talent Bank," *Fast Company* (May–June 2000): 93–97.

28 P. Cappelli, "Making the Most of On-Line Recruiting," *Harvard Business Review* (March 2001): 139–146.

29 L. Lawrence, "Microsoft 'Permatemp' Settlement Seen as Warning to Employers," *HR News* (February 2001): 8; see C. von Hippel, S. L. Mangum, D. B. Greenberger, R. L. Heneman, and J. D. Skoglind, "Temporary Employment: Can Organizations and Employees Both Win?" *Academy of Management Executive* 11(1) (1997): 93–104.

30 N. E. McDermott, "Independent Contractors and Employees: Do You Know One When You See One?" *Legal Report* (November–December 1999): 1–4; D. G. Albrecht, "Reaching New Heights: Today's Contract Workers Are Highly Promotable," *Workforce* (April 1998): 42–48.

31 M. Boyle, "The Not-So-Fine Art of the Layoff," *Fortune* (March 19, 2001): 209–210; Adapted from R. Kessler, "Say Good-bye with Style," *HR Magazine* (June 1998): 171–174.

32 S. L. Rynes and A. E. Barber, "Applicant Attraction Strategies: An Organizational Perspective," *Academy of Management Review* (1990): 286–310; R. E. Herman, *Keeping Good People: Strategies for Solving the Dilemma of the Decade* (New York: McGraw-Hill, 1991); K. G. Connolly and P. M. Connolly, *Competing for Employees: Proven Marketing Strategies for Hiring and Keeping Exceptional People* (Lexington, MA: Lexington Books, 1991).

33 J. Juergens, "Read All About It," *HR Magazine* (November 2000): 142–150.

34 M. W. Walsh, "Luring the Best in an Unsettled Time," *New York Times* (January 30, 2001): G1, G10; B. Breen, "Where Are You on the Talent Map," *Fast Company* (September 2000): 102–125; McKinsey & Company, *War for Talent 2000* (Boston, MA: McKinsey & Company, 2000).

35 B. Parus, "The Sky's the Limit in Online Recruiting," *Workspan* (January 2001): 54–56; P. Cappelli, "Making the Most of On-Line Recruiting."

36 S. D. Maurer, V. Howe, and T. W. Lee, "Organizational Recruiting as Marketing Management: An Interdisciplinary Study of Engineering Graduates," *Personnel Psychology* 45 (1992): 807–833.

37 D. B. Turban and T. W. Dougherty, "Influences of Campus Recruiting on Applicant Attraction to Firms," *Academy of Management Journal* 35 (1992): 739–765.

38 C. Salter, Andy Esparza Knows What Success Sounds Like," *Fast Company* (December 1999): 218–222.

39 R. Kanter, C. R. Wanberg, and T. M. Kantrowitz, "Job Search and Employment: A Personality—Motivational Analysis and Met-Analytic Review," *Journal of Applied Psychology* 86 (2001): 837–855; J. O. Crites, *Vocational Psychology* (New York: McGraw-Hill, 1969); J. P. Wanous, *Organizational Entry: Recruitment, Selection, and Socialization of Newcomers* (Reading, MA: Addison-Wesley, 1980); K. G. Wheeler and T. M. Mahoney, "The Expectancy Model in the Analysis of Occupational Preference and Occupational Choice," *Journal of Vocational Behavior* 19 (1981): 113–122.

40 D. P. Schwab, S. L. Rynes, and R. A. Aldag, "Theories and Research on Job Search and Choice," in K. Rowland and G. Ferris (eds.), *Research in Personnel and Human Resource Management* 5 (1987): 129–166.

41 V. Corwin, T. B. Lawrence, and P. J. Frost, "Five Strategies of Successful Part-time Work," *Harvard Business Review* (July–August 2001): 121–127; A. E. Barber and M. V. Roehling, "Job Postings and the Decision to Interview: A Verbal Protocol Analysis," *Journal of Applied Psychology* 78 (1993): 845–856; T. A. Judge and R. D. Bretz Jr., "Effects of Work Values on Job Choice Decisions," *Journal of Applied Psychology* 77 (1992): 261–271.

42 A. E. Barber, M. J. Wesson, Q. Roberson and M. S. Taylor, "A Tale of Two Job Markets: Organizational Size and Its Effects on Hiring Practices and Job Search Behavior," *Personnel Psychology* 52 (1999): 841–867; E. Chambers, M. Foulon, H. Handfield-Jones, S. Hankin, and E. Michaels, "The War for Talent," *McKinsey Quarterly* 3 (1998): 44–57; S. D. Maurer, V. Howe, and T. W. Lee, "Organizational Recruiting as Marketing Management."

43 C. E. Jergenson, "Job Preference: What Makes a Job Good or Bad?" *Journal of Applied Psychology* 63 (1978): 267–276; B. Major and E. Konar, "An Investigation of Sex Differences in Pay in Higher Education and Their Possible Cause," *Academy of Management Journal* 4 (1986): 777–792; D. P. Schwab, S. L. Rynes, and R. A. Aldag, "Theories and Research," 129–166.

44 A. Poe, "Signing Bonuses: A Sign of the Times," *HR Magazine* (September 1999): 104–112; L. Uchitelle, "Signing Bonus Now a Fixture Farther Down the Job Ladder," *New York Times* (June 10, 1998): A1, D2; J. S. Lublin, "Now Butchers, Engineers Get Signing Bonuses," *Wall Street Journal* (June 2, 1997): B1.

45 R. D. Bretz, Jr., J. W. Boudreau, and T. A. Judge, "Job Search Behavior of Employed Managers," *Personnel Psychology* 47 (1994): 275–301.

46 R. C. Barnett and D. T. Hall, "How to Use Reduced Hours to Win the War for Talent," *Organizational Dynamics* 29(3) (2001): 192–210; S. F. Gate, "Formalized Flextime: The Perk That Brings Productivity," *Workforce* (February 2001): 39–42; S. Branch, "MBAs: What They Really Want," *Fortune* (March 16, 1998): 167; N. Munk, "Organization Man," *Fortune* (March 16, 1998): 63–74; T. A. Stewart, "Gray Flannel Suit?" *Fortune* (March 16, 1998): 76–82.

47 M. W. Walsh, "Money Isn't Everything," *New York Times* (January 30, 2001): G10.

48 C. K. Stevens and A. L. Kristof, "Making the Right Impression: A Field Study of Applicant Impression Management During Job Interview," *Journal of Applied Psychology* 80 (1995): 587–606.

49 R. D. Bretz, Jr. and T. A. Judge, "Realistic Job Previews: A Test of the Adverse Self-Selection Hypothesis," *Journal of Applied Psychology* 83 (1998): 230–337.

50 M. Roehling, M. Cavanaugh, L. Moynihan, and W. Boswell, "The Nature of the New Employment Relationship: A Content Analysis of the Practitioner and Academic Literatures," *Human Resource Management* 39(4) (Winter 2000): 305–320; L. Prusak and D. Cohen, "How to Invest in Social Capital," *Harvard Business Review* (June 2001): 86–93.

51 J. P. Wanous et al., "The Effects of Met Expectations on Newcomer Attitudes and Behaviors: A Review and Meta-Analysis," *Journal of Applied Psychology* 77 (1992): 288–297; J. M. Phillips, "Effects of Realistic Job Previews on Multiple Organizational Outcomes: A Meta-Analysis," *Academy of Management Journal* (1999): 156–172.

52 P. W. Hom, R. W. Griffeth, L. Palich, and J. S. Bracker, "Revisiting Met Expectations as a Reason Why Realistic Job Previews Work," *Personnel Psychology* 52 (1999): 97–112; P. W. Hom, R. W. Griffeth, L. E. Palich, and J. S. Bracker, "An Exploratory Investigation into Theoretical Mechanisms Underlying Realistic Job Previews," *Personnel Psychology* 51 (1998): 421–451.

53 M. R. Buckley, D. B. Fedor, and D. S. Marvin, "Ethical Considerations in the Recruiting Process: A Preliminary Investigation and Identification of Research Opportunities," *Human Resource Management Review* (1997): 101–134; "Truth in Hiring Gains Importance," *Bulletin to Management* (July 28, 1994): 5.

54 J. Useem, "Welcome to the New Company," *Fortune* (January 10, 2000): 62–70; A. Fischer, "Don't Blow Your New Job," *Fortune* (June 22, 1998): 159–162.

55 R. D. Gatewood, M. A. Gowan, and G. J. Lautenschlager, "Corporate Image, Recruitment Image, and Initial Choice Decisions," *Academy of Management Journal* 36 (1993): 414–427.

56 C. R. Williams, C. E. Labig Jr., and T. H. Stone, "Recruitment Sources and Posthire Outcomes for Job Applicants and New Hires: A Test of Two Hypotheses," *Journal of Applied Psychology* 78 (1993): 163–172.

57 A. M. Saks, "A Psychological Process Investigation for the Effects of Recruitment Source and Organization Information on Job Survival," *Journal of Organizational Behavior* 15 (1994): 225–244.

58 M. J. Aamodt and D. L. Peggans, "Rejecting Applicants with Tact," *Personnel Administrator* (April 1988): 58–60; S. W. Gilliland, M. Groth et al., "Improving Applicants' Reactions to Rejection Letters: An Application of Fairness Theory," *Personnel Psychology* 54 (2001): 669–703.

59 W. Dickmeyer, "The Basics of Applicant Tracking Systems," *Workforce* (January 2001): 33; W. Dickmeyer, "Applicant Tracking Reports Make Data Meaningful," *Workforce* (February 2001): 65–67. For a discussion of likely changes that may be needed in HRIS software due to changes in EEO-1 forms, see F. Jossi, "Reporting Race," *HR Magazine* (September 2000): 87–94.

60 Data provided by the Bureau of National Affairs. For a discussion of how to calculate EEO statistics in the temporary help industry, see A. M. Ryan and M. J. Schmidt, "Calculating EEO Statistics in the Temporary Help Industry," *Personnel Psychology* 49 (1996): 167–180; P. Wingate and G. C. Thornton, III, "Statistics and Employment Discrimination Law: An Interdisciplinary Review," *Personnel and Human Resource Management* 19 (2000): 295–337.

61 J. S. Leonard, "The Impact of Affirmative Action Regulation on Employment," *Journal of Economic Perspectives* 3 (1990): 47–63.

62 L. Micco, "Wilcher Describes Changes Under Way at OFCCP," *HR News* (April 1998): 6.

63 R. S. Johnson, "The 50 Best Companies for Asians, Blacks & Hispanics."

64 N. Munk, "Hello Corporate America," *Fortune* (June 6, 1998): 136–146.

65 P. M. Barrett, "Legal Separation: Prestigious Law Firm Courts Black Lawyers, But Diversity Is Illusive," *Wall Street Journal* (July 8, 1997): A1, A9; see also E. White, "'We're Wild and Wacky' Law Firms Tell Recruits," *Wall Street Journal* (June 24, 1998): B1.

66 P. M. Wright, S. R. Ferris, J. S. Hiller, and M. Kroll, "Competitiveness Through Management of Diversity: Effects of Stock Price Valuation," *Academy of Management Journal* 38 (1995): 272–286.

67 "Piscataway Settlement Hangs Heavy Over Affirmative Action," *Fair Employment Practices* (February 25, 1998): 1–2; B. Pulley, "A Reverse Discrimination Suit Upends Two Teachers' Lives," *New York Times* (August 31, 1997): A1, A18.

68 S. A. Holmes, "Broadcasters Vow to Keep Affirmative Action," *New York Times* (July 30, 1998): A12; S. Labaton, "Court Rules Agency Erred on Mandate for Minorities," *New York Times* (January 1, 2001): A16.

69 For a discussion of psychological factors that may influence a manager's voluntary affirmative action behavior, see M. Bell, D. A. Harrison and M. McLaughlin, "Forming, Changing, and Acting on Attitude Towards Affirmative Action Programs in Employment: A Theory-Driven Approach," *Journal of Applied Psychology* 85(5) (2000): 784–798.

70 M. E. Heilman and V. B. Alcott, "What I Think You Think of Me: Women's Reactions to Being Viewed as Beneficiaries of Preferential Selection," *Journal of Applied Psychology* 86 (2001): 574–582; M. E. Heilman, C. J. Block, and P. Stathatos, "The Affirmative Action Stigma of Incompetence: Effects of Performance Information Ambiguity," *Academy of Management Journal* 40 (1997): 603–625.

71 For a full review of this and other research on affirmative action, see D. A. Kravitz et al., *Affirmative Action: A Review of Psychological and Behavioral Research* (Bowling Green, OH: Society for Industrial and Organizational Psychology, 1997); E. H. James, J. Dietz, A. P. Brief, and R. R. Cohen, "Prejudice Matters: Understanding the Reactions of Whites to Affirmative Action Programs Targeted to Benefit Blacks," *Journal of Applied Psychology* 86 (2001): 1120–1128.

72 See http://www.catalystwomen.org for more recent developments. J. P. Fields, *Women and the Corporate Ladders: Corporate Linkage Project* (Wellesley, MA: Wellesley College Center for Research on Women, July 31, 1994); U.S. Department of Labor, *A Report on the Glass Ceiling Initiative* (Washington, DC, 1991).

73 T. Parker-Pope, "Colgate Puts Lois Juliber in Line for Top," *Wall Street Journal* (January 20, 1997): B5.

74 Chicago Area Partnerships, *Pathways & Progress: Corporate Best Practices to Shatter the Glass Ceiling* (Chicago: Chicago Area Partnerships, 1996).

75 Hundreds of studies have examined the reasons for voluntary employee turnover. A detailed discussion is beyond the scope of this chapter. Interested readers can begin to learn more by consulting R. W. Griffeth, P. W. Hom, and S. Gaertner, "A Meta-Analysis of Antecedents and Correlates of Employee Turnover: Update, Moderator Tests, and Research Implications for the Next Millennium," *Journal of Management* 26(3) (2000): 463–488; R. W. Griffeth and P. W. Hom, "The Employee Turnover Process," *Research in Personnel and Human Resources Management* 13 (1995): 245–293; C. O. Trevor, "Interactions Among Actual Ease-of-Movement Determinants and Job Satisfaction in the Prediction of Voluntary Turnover," *Academy of Management Journal* 44 (2001): 621–638; R. D. Iverson and S. J. Deery, "Understanding the 'Personological' Basis of Employee Withdrawal: the Influence of Affective Disposition on Employee Tardiness, Early Departure and Absenteeism," *Journal of Applied Psychology* 86 (2001): 856–866.

76 J. D. Dawson, J. E. Delery, G. D. Jenkins Jr., and N. Gupta, "An Organizational-Level Analysis of Voluntary and Involuntary Turnover," *Academy of Management Journal* 41 (1998): 511–525.

77 K. Dixon-Kheir, "Supervisors Are Key to Keeping Young Talent," *HR Magazine* (January 2001): 139–142; M. Buckingham and C. Coffman, *First, Break All the Rules: What the World's Greatest Managers Do Differently* (New York: Simon & Schuster, 1999); "War for Talent II: Seven Ways to Win," *Fast Company* (May–June, 2000): 98–99; K. S. Lyness and M. K. Judiesch, "Are Female Managers Quitters? The Relationships of Gender, Promotions, and Family Leaves of Absence to Voluntary Turnover," *Journal of Applied Psychology* 86 (2001): 1167–1178.

78 E. Barker, "The Company They Keep," *Inc.* (May 2000): 85–91.

79 R. L. Knowdell, E. Branstead, and M. Moravec, *From Downsizing to Recovery——Strategic Transition Options for Organizations and Individuals* (Palo Alto, CA: CPP Books, 1994); G. E. Prussia, A. J. Kinicki, and J. S. Bracker, "Psychological and Behavioral Consequences of Job Loss: A Covariance Structure Analysis Using Weiner's (1985) Attribution

Model," *Journal of Applied Psychology* 78 (1993): 382–394; C. R. Leana and D. C. Feldman, *Coping with Job Loss: How Individuals, Organizations, and Communities Respond to Layoffs* (New York: Lexington Books, 1992).

80 E. Zimmerman, "Why Deep Layoffs Hurt Long-Term Recovery," *Workforce* (November 2001): 48–53. A detailed discussion of internal labor markets can be found in L. T. Pinfield and M. F. Berner, "Employment Systems: Toward a Coherent Conceptualization of Internal Labor Markets," *Research in Personnel and Human Resource Management* 12 (1994): 41–78.

81 P. J. Kiger, "At First USA Bank, Promotions and Job Satisfaction Are Up," *Workforce* (March 2001): 54-56; P. Cappelli, "A Market-Driven Approach to Retaining Talent," *Harvard Business Review* (January-February 2001): 103–111; M. Nealy Martinez, "Retention: To Have and To Hold," *HR Magazine,* (September 1998): 131-138.

82 "Companies Continue to Increase Staff Size," *HR Magazine* (January 2001): 35-36; "To Cut or Not to Cut," *Economist* (February 10, 2001): 61-62; S. Kuczynski, "Help! I Shrunk the Company," *HR Magazine* (June 1999): 40-45; T. Mroczkowski and M. Hanaoka, "Effective Rightsizing Strategies in Japan and America: Is There a Convergence of Employment Practices?" *Academy of Management Executive* 11(2) (1997): 57-67; M. London, "Redeployment and Continuous Learning in the 21st Century: Hard Lessons and Positive Examples from the Downsizing Era," *Academy of Management Executive* 10(4) (1992): 67–79; W. N. Davis III, D. L. Worrell, and J. B. Fox, "Early Retirement Programs and Firm Performance," *Academy of Management Journal* 39(4) (1996): 970–984; R. Maurer, "Alternative to Downsizing," *Solutions* (October 1996): 40–48.

83 M. Conlin, "Where Layoffs Are a Last Resort," *Business Week* (October 8, 2001): 42.

84 B. McConnell, "HR Should Be a Player in Layoff Decisions, SHRM Survey Finds," *HR News* (December 2001): 12.

85 E. W. Morrison, "When Employees Feel Betrayed: A Model of How Psychological Contract Violation Develops," *Academy of Management Review* 22 (1997): 226–256; E. M. Mervosh, "Downsizing Dilemma," *Human Resource Executive* (February 1997): 50–53.

86 D. M. Schweiger, J. M. Ivancevich, and F. R. Power, "Executive Actions for Managing Human Resources Before and After Acquisition," *Academy of Management Executive* 1 (2) (1986): 127–138.

87 G. Koretz, "Downsizing's Painful Effects," *Business Week* (April 13, 1998): 23.

88 H. Axel, *HR Review: Implementing the New Employment Compact* (New York: The Conference Board, 1997).

CHAPTER

8

Selecting Employees to Fit the Job and the Organization

" No strategy, however well designed, will work unless you have the right people, with the right skills and behaviors, in the right roles, motivated in the right way and supported by the right leaders. Adopting new technologies without having the right people to use them, wastes billions of dollars of investment by companies throughout the world. "

Chris Matthews
CEO
Hay Group

MANAGING THROUGH STRATEGIC PARTNERSHIPS

Honeywell

When Larry Bossidy became CEO of Allied Signal (which later merged into Honeywell), he and everyone else knew the company was in bad shape. Morale, the stock price, operating margins, and return on equity were all low. As he considered how to turn the company around, Bossidy realized that a major weakness in the firm was a lack of management talent. "It wasn't up to par with our competitors, and we were unlikely to produce future leaders because we didn't have the bench strength." A decade later, when Allied Signal and Honeywell merged, the turnaround had been completed. Morale, stock price, operating margins and return on equity had all gone up sharply. So too had the quality of the firm's managers. One indication of that quality was the fact that Allied Signal had become a hunting ground for head hunters, who helped other firms lure several of the firm's executives away for CEO jobs at other companies. "We weren't happy to see any of them leave, but at the same time, it was a testament to our efforts at Allied." Bossidy credited the change in management quality to the investments he and his staff made in selecting and developing talent.

During his first two years at Allied, Bossidy estimates that he spent 30 to 40 percent of his time and emotional energy to hiring and developing leaders. "We had to go outside for nearly all of our early hires," he recalled. Bossidy interviewed hundreds of applicants, including people who would be reporting directly to him, the direct reports of his direct reports, as well as over 300 newly minted MBAs. His philosophy? "You hire a good person, they will hire a good person."

When selecting people Bossidy did more than just interview them. In fact, he doesn't think much of job interviews. "I feel strongly that the job interview is the most flawed process in American business." Why? Because some people interview well and others don't, and sometimes the one that doesn't interview well is the best person for the job. Besides interviews, Bossidy relies heavily on information about past job performance. When evaluating internal candidates, Bossidy looked carefully at the performance reviews they had received from peers, supervisors, and even subordinates. To evaluate outside candidates, "it's essential to talk directly to references. I personally checked references for dozens of candidates. I remember fellow CEOs asking, 'Why are *you* calling? I would answer that it's a personal concern of mine . . . If I'm going to hire someone, I want to check them out myself."

What was Bossidy looking for in all of this information? He was trying to assess four characteristics that he believes good leaders need:

- *Ability to Execute:* A demonstrated history, with concrete examples of real accomplishment and execution, is important.
- *A Career Runway:* He likes to hire people who have plenty of runway left in their careers; he hires people in anticipation of the *next* job they'll be in.
- *Team Orientation:* A person who tries to do a job alone, and take all the credit, has limited leadership ability, in Bossidy's view.
- *Multiple Experiences:* A person who has worked in a variety of environments—preferably in different industries—is more likely to be effective in a highly competitive industry.

Despite all his efforts, Bossidy admits to having made some mistakes. "Our success rate was roughly 70 percent—and we set a high bar for success—so that's a good percentage. Of course you'll make some mistakes. But if you're willing to learn from them, you'll make better decisions the next time."[1]

THE STRATEGIC IMPORTANCE OF SELECTION

Selection is the process of obtaining and using information about job applicants in order to determine who should be hired for long- or short-term positions. It begins with an assessment of the requirements to be met by the new hire, including the technical aspects of a job and the more-difficult-to-quantify organizational needs. Applicants are then assessed to determine their competencies, preferences, interests, and personality. Done well, selection practices ensure that employees are capable of high productivity and motivated to stay with the organization for as long as the organization wants to employ them. In order for this to occur, selection practices need to do more than assess the technical capabilities of applicants; they must also assess whether the organization is likely to satisfy the applicants' preferences and keep them motivated over the long term.[2]

Uses of Selection Decisions

Typically, the objective of these assessments is to predict the likely future performance of applicants—in the job that is open, as well as other jobs that they might hold over a period of several months or years. Being good at predicting who is likely to do well in the future has many useful purposes. Clearly, it is important when hiring new people into the organization. When it hired Larry Bossidy, the board of directors made one of the most important selection decisions for that organization—choosing its new CEO.[3]

The decision about when to promote or transfer a current employee—and in which job—is another example of selection. And, as Larry Bossidy experienced when he became CEO, selection also comes into play when making termination decisions. Bossidy selected who would be asked to leave the organization (or perhaps be eased into retirement) based on his assessment of who was *not* likely to perform well in the future.

Finally, a variety of less salient decisions also involve selection. When a special task force is created and a manager decides who to recommend or appoint, she or he makes a selection decision. In organizations with mentoring programs, participating mentors make selection decisions when they decide who to mentor, if anyone. When managers develop replacement charts and succession plans (as described in Chapter 5), they are making selection decisions. Although no one may be promoted when the chart is prepared, several people have been selected for further consideration.

Selection and Strategy Implementation

Although there is little rigorous research to show it, many executives think it is obvious that different business strategies demand different types of people to implement them effectively. It follows that selection practices contribute to (or detract from) an organization's strategic capabilities. The selection of top executives, key expatriate managers, and lower-level employees all drive firm performance.

> **FAST FACT**
>
> For productivity and retention, companies such as Southwest, Lincoln Electric, Honda, GE, and Toyota hire on the basis of whether an individual matches the job requirements and the corporate culture.

Executives. The entrepreneur who starts up a company in the garage and grows it into a successful firm is not always able to manage the larger organization very well. Managers who excel when the strategy calls for innovation may fail when cost-cutting pressures intensify. The competencies needed by managers in a firm that is growing through the acquisition of many smaller firms are likely to be different from those needed by managers in a firm that slowly grows organically from within. Thus, in selection decisions to staff positions at the top of an organization, or at the top of a business unit, making the right selection is critical to the success or failure of the business. Larry Bossidy understood this close connection between implementing a strategy and selecting the executives who were responsible for implementing it. His assessment was that the talent at Allied Signal would not succeed in implementing his new strategic agenda.

Expatriates. When an organization's strategic plans call for expanding into global markets, the selection of expatriates becomes a key determinant of success. The globalization strategy will require operating facilities overseas. The plan may call for building new facilities or acquiring existing operations. Either way, decisions about how to staff the facilities will be among the first strategic choices made. Three choices are to send a parent-country national (PCN or expatriate), hire a host-country national (HCN), or hire a third-country national (TCN). U.S. companies have generally favored sending expatriates—but it is common knowledge that U.S. expatriates often do not perform well in such assignments. The pros and cons of selecting these three types of individuals are listed in Exhibit 8.1.[4]

The choice about whether to staff with an expatriate, HCN, or TCN is likely to reflect a judgment about how difficult it will be to find an expatriate who is qualified, versus finding other talent. This judgment takes into consideration both the nature of the job and the qualifications of people in the two talent pools (at home and abroad). Expatriate managers must carry out daily activities with the concerns of the parent company clearly in focus, while also responding to the host country's societal concerns and a local culture that's often quite different from their home culture. In addition, expatriate managers typically operate in a culture with a different language—a major obstacle for many of them.[5]

For expatriate managers to succeed, they need the competencies required to perform their specific job as well as those needed to effectively manage many types of relationships, including those with

ex 8.1 Selecting Managers: Pros and Cons of PCNs, HCNs, and TCNs

PARENT-COUNTRY NATIONALS (PCNs)

Advantages

- Organizational control and coordination is maintained and facilitated.
- Promising managers are given international experience.
- PCNs are the best people for the job.
- The subsidiary will likely comply with the company objectives, policies, and so forth.

Disadvantages

- The promotional opportunities of HCNs are limited.
- Adaptation to the host country may take a long time.
- PCNs may impose an inappropriate headquarters style.
- Compensation for PCNs and HCNs may differ.

HOST-COUNTRY NATIONALS (HCNs)

Advantages

- Language and other barriers are eliminated.
- Hiring costs are reduced, and no work permit is required.
- Continuity of management improves, since HCNs stay longer in positions.
- Government policy may dictate the hiring of HCNs.
- Morale among HCNs may improve as they see the career potentials.

Disadvantages

- Control and coordination of headquarters may be impeded.
- HCNs have limited career opportunities outside the subsidiary.
- Hiring HCNs limits opportunities for PCNs to gain overseas experience.
- Hiring HCNs could encourage a federation of national rather than global units.

THIRD-COUNTRY NATIONALS (TCNs)

Advantages

- Salary and benefit requirements may be lower than for PCNs.
- TCNs may be better informed than PCNs about the host-country environment.

Disadvantages

- Transfers must consider possible national animosities.
- The host government may resent the hiring of TCNs.
- TCNs may not want to return to their own countries after assignment.

- their coworkers,
- their families,
- the host government,
- their home government,
- the local clients, customers, and business partners, and
- the company's headquarters.

Assessing how well applicants are likely to manage these relationships is necessary regardless of where the applicants are found.[6] However, the selection procedures used may differ depending on whether they are used to assess U.S. applicants or applicants from the local labor market. Expatriates and TCNs are usually selected using U.S practices, while host-country nationals (HCNs) are usually selected using host-country practices.[7]

A strategic decision to expand globally sets in place a chain of decision making concerning how to staff the new facilities. Eventually, a selection process will unfold and people will be hired into these key positions. If the selection process results in qualified people being hired, the company improves its chances of successfully implementing its new strategy. Poor selection decisions may end up costing millions. The feature "Managing Globalization: World Staffing for Regus" describes selection practices for one rapidly growing global company.[8]

Other Employees. The strategic importance of people who fill key roles is apparent, but other selection decisions are not less important. Hiring a scientist who invents or discovers a new product may also be worth millions or even billions of dollars to a company. Conversely, hiring a person who engages in fraud or illegal activity may end up costing the company millions. To implement Lincoln Electric's strategy, it is essential to select employees who will thrive working in an environment that demands a high level of productivity as well as flexibility. At Lincoln, the selection of production workers is so important that new hires are put on probation for six months, after which time coworkers decide whether they can stay. At Southwest Airlines, it's important to hire employees with a fun-loving attitude who work well in a team-oriented culture. Increasingly, employers seek to select new hires who can perform their jobs well and *also* be good corporate citizens.

The Economic Utility of Effective Selection Practices

The **economic utility** of an organization's selection practices refers to the net monetary value associated with using a set of selection practices to decide who to place in which jobs. In general, economic utility is a function of the costs incurred to design and use the selection practices and the value of outcomes gained by doing so.[9]

Value. When the job being filled is that of CEO, the value of making a good selection decision can be millions, or even billions, of dollars. Some of the economic gains are returned to the CEO as compensation, but usually most of the gains are returned to shareholders, employees, and the government.

When considered individually, the economic value of any single selection decision is usually not so large. Clearly, the potential value of a good CEO selection decision is the exception. Nevertheless, it is important to realize that the potential to reap large economic gains from effective selection is not limited to selecting people into a few key positions. In fact, the real value

"We prefer to recruit country nationals for each new location simply because they have the local language and culture in their blood. They know the local market, customs and how to motivate other local talent. [But] we are increasingly importing and exporting nationals of different countries . . . so we get international experience into each center."

Mark Dixon
CEO
Regus

FAST FACT

At Lucent, formal selection programs rarely cost more than $1,000 per applicant.

MANAGING GLOBALIZATION

World Staffing for Regus

Mark Dixon is the founder and chairman of a company with 250 offices in more than 45 countries. His vision? To be in 140 countries by 2004. The business, called Regus, operates "instant offices"—full-service facilities that are available to rent by the hour, the day, the week, the month, or the year. Regus serves businesses that want to move into new markets but aren't yet ready to make capital expenditures. You make a reservation in advance of arriving at the location, and when you get there you walk in, fill out a rental agreement, and then get right to work. Facilities can be altered as needed within a day.

The rapid growth of this firm means Regus needs to hire thousands of new employees per year. Because the business center industry is relatively new, Dixon can't poach employees from competitors—he has to develop the skills in-house. Finding people with technical and commercial real estate experience has proved to be a challenge. "Senior managers and country managers also are a rare breed," he says. To find people, Dixon really has to search for them. Getting applicants isn't the problem, but "sorting the wheat from the chaff is more difficult." The selection task is carried out by RIOT (for Regus International Opening Team). RIOT is a team of "glopats"—managers who are frequently on the move taking short-term assignments. Selected by Dixon, the glopats generate applicants through employee referrals, print advertising, the Internet, and search agencies. The center manager is usually hired first, and then other applicants are interviewed by the RIOT team and the center manager. When they want a second opinion from company headquarters, which is in the UK, they set up a video conference.

Dixon says hiring around the world is a challenge due in part to country differences in hiring practices. "In America, for example, you can't ask a lot of questions. You have to stay on your toes, be careful of what you say and how you say it." This is one reason Dixon hired an American HR director for the region. It's also why members of the RIOT team must be trained in local employment laws—"so we don't get sued," Dixon says. Asia presents a different challenge for Regus: "Interviewing can be very frustrating in Asia. Because everything is so formal, it can be hard to engage them in a conversation, so it's extremely difficult to get to know the person." In Germany, Dixon learned, the general practice is to return applicants' CVs, which often are very beautifully prepared. To help the RIOT team get things right, Regus has an intranet site where members are expected to post what they learn as soon as they learn it.

of effective selection practices often accumulates by making good decisions when hiring people at lower levels in the organization. In large organizations, the accumulated benefits of making thousands of good selection decisions add up quickly. Effective selection also minimizes the risk of harm and the costs of lawsuits brought by victims of criminal, violent, or negligent acts perpetrated by employees who shouldn't have been hired or kept in their jobs.

Cost. The cost of selection decisions includes the value of all of the time and resources used to collect the information about job applicants that is used to make final decisions. Information gleaned from resumes and brief screening interviews costs relatively little to acquire compared with information from multiple interviews, background investigations, and medical exams. Furthermore, the time used by highly paid employees in the organization (e.g., the CEO) costs more than the time used by those who are paid less (e.g., a product manager). Expensive means of acquiring information may be worthwhile if they enable the organization to make better decisions *and* if substantial consequences are attached to making better decisions. Generally, more expensive procedures may be justified when

- tenure in the job is expected to be relatively long,
- incremental increases in performance reap large rewards for the organization or
- many applicants are available.

Expensive procedures might not be justified if

- progressively higher tax bites are associated with increased profits,
- labor costs are variable and rise with productivity gains, or
- labor markets are tight, which makes it less likely that the best candidates, once identified, can be enticed to take the position.[10]

Calculating Utility. A variety of sophisticated approaches have been developed to assess the economic utility of selection practices, and in the past two decades numerous studies have demonstrated that well-designed selection practices can pay off handsomely. Although a full discussion is beyond the scope of this chapter, the following practical example illustrates how utility analysis can be used to assess the value of selection practices. When Kroger Co., the grocery store chain, wanted to assess the economic utility of a new interview procedure for selecting entry-level workers, it conducted a small experiment using 90 stores. During a nine-month period, some stores began to use the interview to make selection decisions and others did not. Several months later, Kroger compared the financial performance of stores using the new interviews with stores that did not use the interview. The value of any improvement in financial performance minus the cost of administering the test represents the economic utility of the interview procedure.[11] (For details about how to conduct an economic utility analysis, consult Appendix A.)

The value of using several selection techniques in combination was demonstrated in a study of 201 companies from several industries. Companies reported their use of practices such as validation studies, structured interviews, and cognitive tests. The researchers showed that companies that used these practices had higher levels of annual profit, profit growth, and overall performance. The relationship between use of these practices and bottom-line performance was especially strong in the service and financial sectors.[12]

Other Costs and Benefits. Calculating the economic value of any HR practice is extremely difficult. On the one hand, it is fairly easy to add up all the costs of interviewing, administering and scoring tests, conducting background checks, and so on. On the other hand, it is very difficult to put dollar values on all of the potentially important positive consequences of making a good selection decision and the negatives of making a poor one. Exhibit 8.2 summarizes several of the other consequences that result from making correct versus incorrect selection decisions. These also should be taken into account when determining how much is too much to spend on improving an organization's selection practices.

OVERVIEW OF THE SELECTION PROCESS

Exhibit 8.3 illustrates several components of selection and shows how they are interrelated with other aspects of an integrated HR system. Clearly, one of the most important activities that must take place prior to making a selection decision is recruitment. Unless the organization attracts a pool of qualified applicants, there is little need to invest time and energy in making a selection decision. The number of applicants who are eventually hired as a proportion

ex 8.2 The Consequences of Correct and Incorrect Selection Decisions

	Do Not Offer Applicant the Open Position	Offer Applicant the Open Position
High Performance	• Applicant and employee continue to pay costs of continued searching, unnecessarily. • Applicant may decide to accept alternative job that's less well suited to his or her competencies and interests. • Applicants may remain unemployed unnecessarily and forgo rewards they could have earned. • Applicant may file discrimination lawsuit. • Employees may be required to carry an overload until job is filled. • Customers' expectations may not be met while employer is understaffed. **Reject a Qualified Candidate (Incorrect decision)**	• Employee performs well. • Employee receives rewards associated with good performance. • Employee enjoys work. • Peers benefit from employee's good performance and high morale. • Managers achieve their objectives. • Customers receive products and services that meet their expectations. **Accept a Qualified Candidate (Correct decision)**
HOW EMPLOYEE DOES/WOULD PERFORM **Low Performance**	• Applicant continues to look for more suitable work. • Employer continues to search for more suitable employee. • Applicant may decide to get more training. • Employer may decide to offer more training so that more applicants can be accepted. • Customers do not suffer from the mistakes of a poor performer. • Employees may continue to carry an overload while search continues, but they do not suffer from the errors produced by an ineffective peer. **Reject an Unqualified Candidate (Correct decision)**	**Accept an Unqualified Candidate (Incorrect decision)** • Employee performs poorly. • Employee loses self-esteem due to poor performance, and forgoes the rewards associated with good performance. • Peers suffer consequences of poorly performing employee. • Customers' expectations aren't met due to employee's poor performance. • Managers fail to meet their objectives. • Injuries, accidents, and other serious problems may occur due to employee's poor job performance. • Employee eventually must find new job, creating additional costs associated with turnover.

EMPLOYER'S SELECTION DECISION

of the initial pool is called the **selection ratio**. The lower the selection ratio, the more opportunity there is for an employer to find a few applicants who are outstanding compared with the others. On the other hand, if an employer must essentially hire every person who walks in the door, it does not make sense to invest time and money in assessing how well each person will perform. Effective recruitment practices contribute to low selection ratios, as does high unemployment.

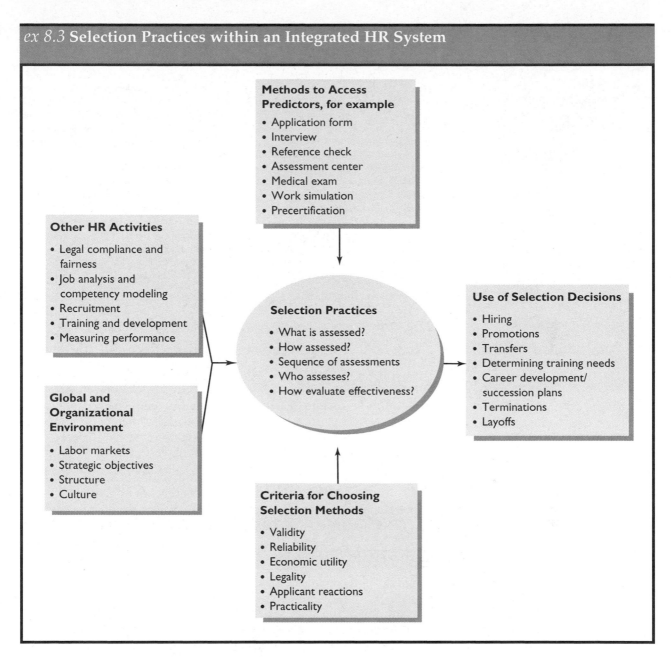

ex 8.3 Selection Practices within an Integrated HR System

Methods to Access Predictors, for example
- Application form
- Interview
- Reference check
- Assessment center
- Medical exam
- Work simulation
- Precertification

Other HR Activities
- Legal compliance and fairness
- Job analysis and competency modeling
- Recruitment
- Training and development
- Measuring performance

Global and Organizational Environment
- Labor markets
- Strategic objectives
- Structure
- Culture

Selection Practices
- What is assessed?
- How assessed?
- Sequence of assessments
- Who assesses?
- How evaluate effectiveness?

Use of Selection Decisions
- Hiring
- Promotions
- Transfers
- Determining training needs
- Career development/ succession plans
- Terminations
- Layoffs

Criteria for Choosing Selection Methods
- Validity
- Reliability
- Economic utility
- Legality
- Applicant reactions
- Practicality

As Exhibit 8.3 shows, job analysis is another HR practice that is closely aligned with selection practices. The important role of job analysis is described in detail later in this chapter. Finally, it is worth noting that selection practices should be aligned with an organization's training and development practices. If extensive training will be provided, the selection process may focus on identifying applicants who are likely to learn quickly and succeed after exposure to training. The feature "Managing Change: An HR System for a New Plant" illustrates some of these interrelationships between selection practices and other aspects of the HR system.[13]

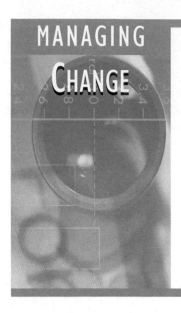

MANAGING CHANGE

An HR System for a New Plant

Cirent, a computer chip manufacturer, was originally created as a joint venture between Lucent Technologies and Cirrus Logic. In 1995, Cirent built a new $600-million clean room in Orlando, Florida. In order to operate the facility, it needed to fill many new jobs, and often those jobs required the skills of trained technicians. Cirent's job analysis for the new jobs indicated that the technicians would need expertise in robotics, pneumatics, vacuum technology, and silicon processing, as well as interpersonal communications, writing, and teaching. Of course, they would also need to continuously learn and adapt to change. To assess these aptitudes, Cirent developed a selection procedure that included written tests to assess knowledge and cognitive ability, along with interviews to assess interpersonal and communication skills. But a problem that Cirent ran into was finding the skills it needed in the local labor market. There simply weren't enough people who had the skills it needed. To address this problem, Cirent developed a training curriculum. For the short term, the company offered a series of courses to newly hired employees, giving them time off from their jobs to attend classes. But the longer-term objective was to develop a larger pool of local labor that it could select from to hire trained technicians. Toward that end, it collaborated with a local community college. Cirent helped the college design the curriculum for an associate degree program that would train technicians with the skills Cirent needed.

The selection process generally involves the following basic steps:

1. Assess the job tasks and organizational context to establish the criteria of interest.
2. Choose valid predictors to assess when making the selection decision.
3. Design a selection process that allows both the organization and the applicant to gather the information they need to make a decision.
4. Synthesize the information collected and make the selection.

Selection does not end when the organization makes its decision. The candidate must ultimately make a final decision about whether to accept the new position and under what conditions. As the person enters the new position, accommodation, socialization, and training activities may all be involved. As time passes, both the organization and the new job incumbent will reevaluate their decisions.

Assess the Job Tasks and Organizational Context

"When people are not successful, more times than not it's because of the inability to work effectively within the culture as much as it is a lack of technical skills."

Jackie Brinton
(no job title—no one at
the company has one)
W. L. Gore & Associates

An understanding of the specific tasks involved in a job and the competencies needed to perform those tasks is the objective of job analysis and competency modeling (described in Chapter 6). An understanding of the organizational context surrounding the job develops from conducting an organization analysis of the company's culture, values, business strategy, and structure, as described in Chapter 4. Ideally, organizational and job analysis information provides a solid foundation for all selection decisions made within the company—including those that determine who the new hires will be and those used in promotion decisions, firings, and layoffs. In reality, job analysis is more likely to be conducted for lower-level and midlevel jobs and for jobs that encompass many positions. For positions near the top of the organization, "job analysis" may or may not be systematic and very likely will be subjective rather than quantitative. At the level of CEO, for example, it may consist of a discussion among members of the board of directors.[14]

Whether it's formal or informal, based on quantitative data or "soft" judgments, the objective of job and organizational analyses is to determine the outcomes that will be affected by selection decisions. These outcomes are referred to as **criteria.** Often, the primary criteria of interest are how the person will perform in the job and whether he or she is likely to be a good corporate citizen. For a corporate loan assistant job, speed and accuracy in documenting decisions would probably be important criteria, as would willingness to help out colleagues during times of work overload. Increasingly, employers also consider criteria other than job performance. As described in Chapter 7, organizations seek to lower their voluntary turnover rates, and they may use the selection process as one tool for achieving that objective. In such a situation, turnover is a criterion that the organization wants to influence through the selection process. Employers also are looking for employees who will adapt quickly in an organization that is continually changing.[15] And, companies like W. L. Gore, the makers of GORE-TEX, seek to hire for people who will fit into the corporate culture and embrace the philosophy of the organization.[16]

Choose Valid Predictors

When making selection decisions, employers are making predictions about how people will perform in the future, how long they are likely to stay, whether they will be good organizational citizens, and so on. This is why the various pieces of information used to make selections are referred to as **predictors.** Predictors serve as the basis for estimating how likely applicants are to perform well in a particular job, whether they'll fit the organization's unique culture, whether they are likely to stay for a while, and so on. Generally, organizations assess skill, ability, knowledge, personality, and behavioral styles and use these as predictors—that is, they use competencies as predictors.[17]

When a job involves a great deal of teamwork, personality and interpersonal skills are likely to be useful predictors.[18] To select people to work in their theme parks, Walt Disney's employees judge the personalities of applicants and assess their ability to fit into the Disney culture. The Disney approach is described in the feature "Managing Teams: Selecting the Walt Disney Cast."[19]

The Concept of Validity. A great deal of information often can be gathered and used to evaluate candidates; whether that information *should* be gathered and used depends on the likelihood that it will lead to better selection decisions. Put simply, information that predicts the criteria of concern should be used, and information that doesn't predict these outcomes should be avoided. The term **validity** refers to the usefulness of information for predicting the future job behavior of applicants.

High validity is present when low predictor scores translate into low scores on the specified criteria and high predictor scores translate into high scores on the criteria. For most predictors, validity depends on what you want to predict. A personality test that assesses gregariousness might be valid for predicting performance as a fund-raiser for the city ballet company, but it's probably useless for predicting performance as a highway landscape designer.

> **FAST FACT**
>
> When Disney opened its theme park outside Paris, French job applicants protested Disney's strict, and very American, standards for dress and grooming.

> *"I finally got accepted somewhere because they didn't just see the wheelchair."*
>
> Wilfredo "Freddy" Laboy
> Salesclerk
> The Gap

MANAGING TEAMS

Selecting the Walt Disney Cast

The next time you visit Walt Disney World in Florida or Disneyland in California, consider the complexity of finding more than 25,000 people needed to fill more than 1,000 types of jobs that make the entertainment complexes so effective. With over 50 million visitors to Disney World and Disneyland yearly, the company is a reigning star in the entertainment business. Since the mid-1980s, when it went through a major change in senior management and strategic direction, the Walt Disney Company has developed a reputation for creativity, strong financial management, and very effective approaches to managing people.

The managers and employees of the Walt Disney Company view themselves as members of a team whose job is to produce a very large show. This is reflected in the way they speak of themselves, their activities, and the process of selecting new members. Eager applicants to the firm are cast for a role rather than hired for a job. Rather than being employees, applicants who join the firm become cast members in a major entertainment production. A casting director interviews applicants.

For hourly jobs, a casting director spends about 10 minutes interviewing every applicant. The interviewer's (casting director's) major objective is to evaluate the applicant's ability to adapt to the firm's very strong culture. Does the applicant understand and accept the fact that Disney has strict grooming requirements (no facial hair for men, little makeup for women)? Is the applicant willing to work on holidays—even ones that almost everyone else will have off? After the first screening, the remaining applicants are assessed as they interact with each other and judged as to how well they might fit with the show. Current employees who are experts in their roles participate in this entire process—they assess the applicants' behaviors and attitudes while also providing first-hand information about their role in the production.

Once people join the firm, they become cast members whose inputs and talents are highly valued by the Walt Disney Company. The company fills 60 to 80 percent of its managerial positions by promoting existing cast members. In addition, the firm draws on suggested referrals from current cast members for help in hiring the 1,500 to 2,000 temporary employees required during particularly busy periods—Easter, Christmas, and summers.

How can you be sure that a given measure is valid for the situation of interest? Three basic strategies are used to ascertain whether inferences based on predictor scores will be valid:

- content validation,
- criterion-related validation, and
- validity generalization.

All these strategies begin with job and organizational analysis. Then, the three strategies diverge. (For more detailed information on these strategies, consult Appendix A.)

Content Validation. **Content validation** is the most commonly used strategy. It involves using job analysis results to build a rational argument for why a predictor should be useful. In the simplest case, the job analysis uses a competency modeling approach, and then an expert job analyst determines which predictors appear to map onto the competencies identified. Suppose competency modeling reveals that senior managers should have competencies related to managing relationships with the firm's strategic partners—suppliers, customers, members of an alliance network, and so on. From this, the job analyst might conclude that it is logical to assess the extent of applicants' past experience in managing such relationships.

This basic content validation strategy can be substantially improved by involving a wider range of people in judging whether a predictor is likely to be useful. Although such judgments are necessarily subjective, one's confidence is increased when several experts agree that a particular skill is needed.[20]

When an organization is creating new jobs and experiencing major organizational change, a content validation strategy may be the only feasible validation approach. It's the approach Levi Strauss & Co. used when it began the biggest change effort in the company's history. As described in the feature "Managing Change: Levi's Changes Jobs and Staffing Requirements," when hundreds of new jobs were created at the company, employees were asked to facilitate the change process by actively seeking new job placements.[21]

Criterion-Related Validation. **Criterion-related validation** uses more definitive data to establish a relationship between predictor scores and criteria. It involves assessing people on the predictor and also assessing their actual performance in the job. If a ballet company wanted to decide whether gregarious people are better fund-raisers, it could ask all its current fund-raisers to take a personality test. Then it could correlate the fund-raisers' scores on gregariousness with their performance as fund-raisers. If gregariousness and fund-raising performance were correlated, criterion-related validity would be established.

Criterion-related validity replaces judgments about which predictors are most useful with statistical analyses that demonstrate the predictive usefulness of criteria. CapOne, a credit card and financial services firm, used criterion-related validity to establish the usefulness of the on-line tests it uses to select call center reps. After choosing the test to be given and developing the on-line technology that would be used, the company had its current call center reps take the tests. Then it developed statistical models to show that the test results were correlated with the performance of sales reps currently in the job. In this example, the criteria used included sales rates and dollars collected per hour. The predictors included scores on math tests and scores on a simulated over-the-phone interaction, among other things.[22]

Validity Generalization. **Validity generalization** is a relatively new approach that has been gaining acceptance during the past decade and may continue to gain popularity in the 21st century. The validity generalization strategy assumes that the results of criterion-related validity studies conducted in other companies can be generalized to the situation in your company. For example, suppose 10 other organizations have already shown that gregarious people tend to be more successful fund-raisers. Even if the correlation between this personality characteristic and fund-raising performance was not strong in all those organizations, and even if the type of fund-raising was quite different, you might nevertheless conclude that gregariousness is likely to be a valid predictor of fund-raising success for your ballet company. If you accepted this conclusion, then your company should evaluate gregariousness and use it when selecting people whose roles include fund-raising.[23]

Validity generalization analyses have been conducted for a large number of applicant characteristics that an employer might assess during the selection process. The results indicate that each of the techniques described in this chapter *can* be effective predictors of performance across a variety of jobs.[24] Whether or not a technique such as a mental ability test or an interview *is* actually a good predictor of performance for a particular job in a particular organizational setting depends on many things, however. Most importantly, the predictors must be selected because they're relevant to the job.[25]

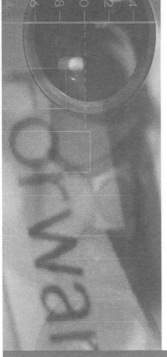

MANAGING CHANGE

Levi's Changes Jobs and Selection Practices

Recognized as one of the world's most successful companies, Levi's top management recognized that success wouldn't last unless the company underwent significant change. Levi's had great products and great marketing skills. So why the need for change? Because its customers—store managers and purchasing agents—were saying they had poor service.

Leading the change effort was a team of 200 people, organized into 20 teams. Their task was to reinvent the supply chain. They invented thousands of new jobs, specifying everything from the title and formal job description to the required competencies. Examples of some new titles include process leader, performance consultant, source relations manager, and system relationship coordinator. The teams concluded that these new jobs would require many new behaviors. How could the company predict who was likely to succeed in these new jobs? Because the jobs were new, a content validity approach was used to choose what to assess when selecting people to fill the new jobs. The teams of experts concluded that people would need to understand the big picture, work in a team, and think in terms of the entire organizational system.

To fill the new jobs, Levi's designed a new recruitment and selection process. Consistent with its philosophy of participation and accountability, this process depended on current employees to apply for the new jobs. Job descriptions were posted via e-mail. Employees submitted applications and were screened to determine whether they qualified for a panel interview. The details of this procedure were described in a document that came to be known as "The Lunch Box." It explained the principles behind the design of the new organization, included posters that traced the steps in the process for making selection decisions, and developed a career-planning workbook. Levi's distributed 4,500 lunch boxes in English and Spanish and followed them up with workshop sessions.

Even with this help, many employees applied for new jobs and didn't get them. Sometimes the process was painful. But the process was also enlightening. Employees were forced to assess their strengths and weaknesses and consider how they could add value. As managers participated in selecting people to staff their new organizations, they discovered that many employees had talents and skills that were underutilized and even unknown to the company. By placing such employees into new jobs, Levi's supported its change initiative while also managing human resources more effectively.

Advantages and Disadvantages. Each of these strategies has associated advantages and disadvantages. The criterion-related validation strategy has the advantage of documenting empirically that a predictor is correlated with the criteria of interest in a particular job in a particular organization. CapOne can be very sure that its new automated selection tests will help the company select better call center reps. However, the criterion-related strategy can be costly and is not applicable to jobs that have only a few incumbents (e.g., CEO). Content validation strategies are more feasible, but they also depend more on subjective judgment. In the Levi example, the company believes that it developed an effective selection practice for filling its new jobs, but it can't really prove that this is true. Finally, validity generalization may be cost-effective, but you won't know whether results from other organizations will hold in your organization until after you make a selection decision. Furthermore, whereas the legal credibility of the other strategies is well established, validity generalization has not been sufficiently tested in the courts.

Design the Selection Process

For each predictor of interest—each competency, personality characteristic, and so forth—there are many means that can be used to assess applicants. Information can be obtained using application forms, resumes, reference checks, written tests, interviews, physical examinations, and other measurement approaches. Exhibit 8.4

FAST FACT

Circle K convenience stores have computers in them to allow customers to apply for a job.

illustrates how a company might use several different methods to capture all the information it wishes to use in selecting a corporate loan assistant (refer to Chapter 6, Exhibit 6.2 for information about what is involved in this job). Thus, an important step in designing a selection practice is choosing how to measure the predictors of interest.

Choose Reliable Measures. Each bit of information contributes to the final selection decision, so the quality of information used determines the quality of the final outcome. One aspect of information quality that's especially important is **reliability**. The reliability of a measure (e.g., an interview, a mathematical reasoning test, or a work simulation) is the degree to which the measure yields dependable, consistent results. Unreliable measures produce different results depending on the circumstances. Different circumstances

ex 8.4 **Selection Matrix: Possible Selection Methods for Several Competencies**

CORPORATE LOAN ASSISTANT

			Methods Used to Assess							
Code	Competencies	Used to Rank?	SAF	WKT	WS	PCD	SPI	DMI	BI/REF	PAF
MA	1. Communication	Yes	X				X	X	X	X
MQ	2. Math		X		X					
MQ	3. Writing		X							X
MQ	4. Reading		X		X					X
MQ	5. Researching		X							
MQ	6. Organizing	Yes	X							X
MQ	7. Listening	Yes	X				X			X
MQ	8. Social skills		X				X			X
MQ	9. Sales	Yes								X
MQ	10. Interpreting	Yes						X		
WT	11. Bank policy									
WT	12. Bank services	Yes	X	X					X	X
MT	13. Computer				X					

MQ	=	Is a minimum qualification
MT	=	May be acquired through training or on the job (desirable); preference may be given to those who possess this competency
MA	=	Can be accommodated within reason
WT	=	Will be acquired through training or on the job; not evaluated in the selection process
SAF	=	Supplemental Application Form
WKT	=	Written Knowledge Test
WS	=	Work Sample
PCD	=	Physical Capability Demonstration
SPI	=	Structured Panel Interview
DMI	=	Departmental Manager Interview
BI/REF	=	Background Investigation/Reference Check
PAF	=	Performance Appraisal Form (internal hires only)

could include having different people administer and score the measure (e.g., having several different interviewers screen applicants), or administering the measure while different events are occurring (e.g., giving a mathematical reasoning test in August versus during the week immediately after everyone files tax returns). When purchasing a test of any sort, information about reliability should be requested. Reputable test developers will be able to demonstrate that they have performed and documented all of the steps needed to create a reliable and valid test.

"You can't spend too much time or effort on hiring smart. The alternative is to manage tough, which is far more time consuming."

Pierre Mornell
Independent Consultant

Decide When to Measure Each Predictor. Often, selection decisions progress through several steps, with each progression to a new step based on some information about how the candidate scores in terms of multiple predictors. Exhibit 8.5 illustrates a typical progression. Typically, information collected early in the process is used to disqualify people from further consideration. Because more people go through the earlier steps, employers generally try to use less expensive procedures early in the process; this reduces the costs of selection. Clearly, each piece of information used throughout this process has the potential to determine the final outcome. Perhaps less clearly, information used early in the process is, in effect, weighted the most heavily—applicants who fail to do well early in the process fail by default on all the later steps.

Synthesize Information and Choose Appropriate Candidates

Upon reaching this final step, a large amount of information of many types—some of it easily quantified and some of it very "soft"—may be available for a large number of applicants. To complicate things further, some applicants might be considered simultaneously for more than one job opening. Combining and synthesizing all available information to yield a yes-or-no decision for each possible applicant-job match can be a fairly complex task. Alternative approaches to combining and synthesizing information might lead to very different final decisions, so this step takes on great significance for both applicants and the organization. When multiple predictors are used, the information can be combined in three ways.

Multiple-Hurdles Approach. In the **multiple-hurdles approach**, an applicant must exceed fixed levels of proficiency on all the predictors in order to be accepted. A higher-than-necessary score on one predictor can't compensate for a score lower than the cutoff on another predictor. Underlying this approach is the assumption that some skills or competencies are so critical that inadequacy guarantees the person will be unsuccessful on the job.

Compensatory Approach. Because most jobs do not have absolute requirements, a **compensatory approach** is commonly used. It assumes that good performance on one predictor can compensate for poor performance on another—for instance, a high score on an interview can compensate for a low score on a written examination. With a compensatory approach, no selection decisions are made until the completion of the entire process. Then, a composite index that considers performance on all predictors is developed.

Combined Approach. Many organizations use a **combined approach**. First, one or more specific requirements—for instance, pass the state bar or the

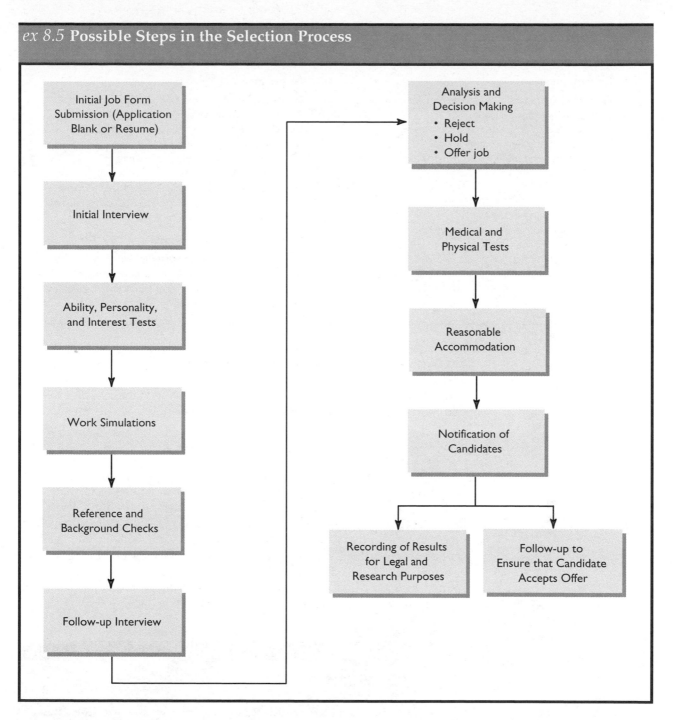

ex 8.5 **Possible Steps in the Selection Process**

CPA examination—must be met. Once these hurdles are met, scores on the remaining predictors are combined into an overall measure of suitability. Kinko's, the copy shop, uses a combined approach. The first hurdle involves a short screening test, which is completed by calling a toll-free number and answering some simple questions using automated procedures. The first hurdle assesses basic experience and availability. Applicants who pass this

ex 8.6 Competencies Required for Teamwork

I. Communication

    A. Understand verbal and nonverbal communications
    B. Listen without evaluation
    C. Give feedback to others that can be used
    D. Encourage others to contribute
    E. Facilitate communication across teams

II. Problem Solving

    A. Identify problems with others
    B. Gather data to diagnose
    C. Propose and analyze alternative solution
    D. Implement solutions
    E. Evaluate results

III. Group Member

    A. Understand group stages of development
    B. Manage group dynamics
    C. Understand social, task, and individual roles
    D. Understand team project planning, goal setting, execution, evaluation, and learning
    E. Manage group conflict
    F. Understand interaction styles of group members
    G. Recognize the variety of types of teams used in organizations

IV. Performance Management

    A. Understand need for team mission and objectives
    B. Monitor and measure group performance
    C. Understand self and team management concepts
    D. Have ability to learn from the past

---

hurdle enter a second phase when they are asked questions designed to assess their fit with Kinko's culture and business strategy. This is also done using automated telephone technology. Applicants who make it past the second hurdle (about 50 percent) are invited for interviews. The results of interviews and other selection information are then combined into a composite score that determines the final selection decision.[26]

Companies that are trying to enhance their competitiveness by improving quality seem to agree that the employees at the front line are key to improving and delivering quality. Thus, they devote considerable time and effort to selecting front-line production workers. In high-quality manufacturing environments, work is organized around teams, so selecting people who can be effective as team players is essential. The same is true in many service organizations, where employees work in teams that serve specific customers. Exhibit 8.6 lists several types of competencies that are likely to be needed in team-based organizations.[27] To assess these competencies, some organizations use very sophisticated approaches, including those listed in

INTERNET RESOURCES   8.A

The Strategic Importance of Selection

At our Web site, http://jackson.swcollege.com/, you can:

1. Learn about the great selection practices at some of the firms discussed in this chapter by visiting their recruiting pages:

    Disney

    Southwest

    Deloitte and Touche

    Lincoln Electric

2. Learn more about Regus and its global business.

3. Investigate the services of consulting firms that assist with expatriate selection.

ex 8.7 An Approach to Selecting Team Workers in a Total Quality Production Plant

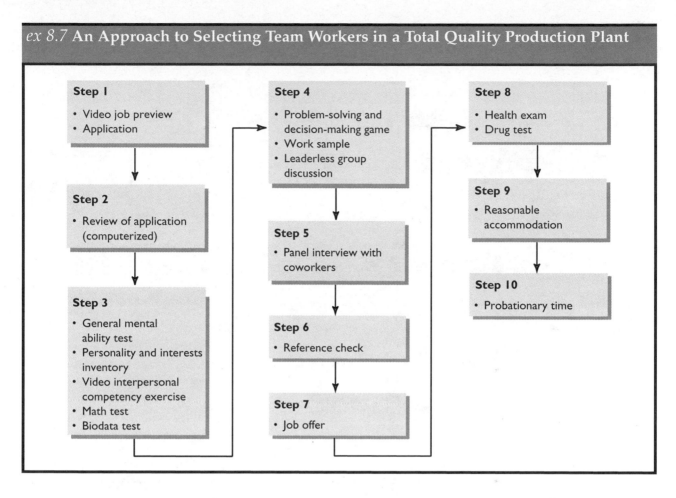

Step 1
- Video job preview
- Application

Step 2
- Review of application (computerized)

Step 3
- General mental ability test
- Personality and interests inventory
- Video interpersonal competency exercise
- Math test
- Biodata test

Step 4
- Problem-solving and decision-making game
- Work sample
- Leaderless group discussion

Step 5
- Panel interview with coworkers

Step 6
- Reference check

Step 7
- Job offer

Step 8
- Health exam
- Drug test

Step 9
- Reasonable accommodation

Step 10
- Probationary time

Exhibit 8.7. In this exhibit, each box represents one step in a series of multiple hurdles. A compensatory approach is used to combine the information within each step and decide whether to involve the applicant in the next step.

TECHNIQUES FOR ASSESSING JOB APPLICANTS

A variety of selection techniques are available for assessing an applicant's competencies, personality, values, and other relevant characteristics.

A recent study of the selection practices used around the world revealed that some of the selection techniques commonly used in the United States are also popular in many other countries—for example, educational qualifications and employer references. On the other hand, the popularity of other techniques depends on what country you look at. Exhibit 8.8 illustrates some of the country differences identified by this study.[28]

FAST FACT

Automated, on-line testing of applicants has quickly become popular due to its convenience and low cost. But verifying who actually takes an on-line test remains difficult.

Personal History Assessments

Premised on the assumption that past behavior is a good predictor of future performance, personal history assessments seek information about the applicant's background. Application blanks and biodata tests are two commonly used methods of assessing personal histories.

ex 8.8 Comparison of Practices Used in Selected Countries (Part A)

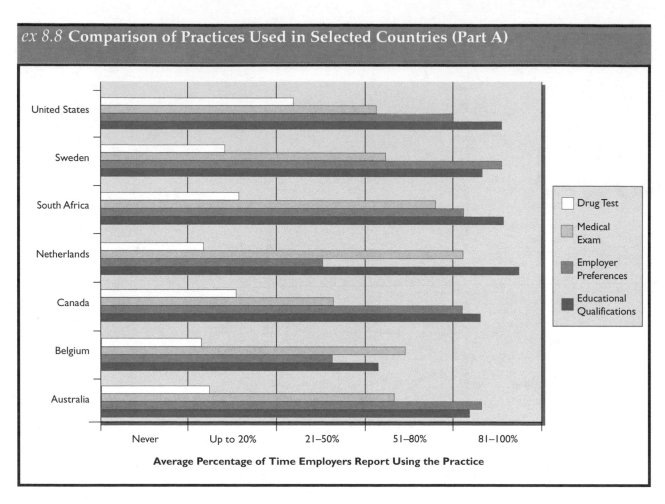

Average Percentage of Time Employers Report Using the Practice

Legend: Drug Test, Medical Exam, Employer Preferences, Educational Qualifications

Countries (top to bottom): United States, Sweden, South Africa, Netherlands, Canada, Belgium, Australia

X-axis: Never, Up to 20%, 21–50%, 51–80%, 81–100%

Application Blank. An **application blank** seeks information that the employer uses to screen candidates and assess whether they meet the *minimum* job requirements. It often is the first hurdle applicants must clear and is easily completed on-line. Application blanks usually are quite short, asking for the most basic information: educational achievements. work experience, and other background information. Validity evidence indicates that educational requirements are predictive of job tenure. Both educational and experience requirements may be useful in selecting individuals for high-level, complex jobs, not jobs that require a short learning period.[29] Application blanks may also request the applicant's willingness to work split shifts, work on weekends, or work alone. If the job does require split-shift work, items that inquire about shift preferences tend to be good predictors of turnover.[30]

Employers should be especially cautious to avoid asking for information that's not directly relevant to the job. Exhibit 8.9 lists several items that might be included on an application blank. Which items do you think might be avoided because they might lead to unfair discrimination?

Biodata Test. A **biodata test** is a variation on this theme of obtaining information about past and current activities. It asks autobiographical questions on such subjects as extracurricular activities (e.g., "Over the past five years,

ex 8.9 Designing Application Blanks with Fairness in Mind

Instructions: Indicate whether each item below is something to do or not to do in interviews and on job applications.

Do	Don't	Item
		Ask about marital status
		Ask about the number of children
		Ask about skills to do the job
		Ask for a woman's maiden name
		Ask the age of the applicant
		Ask for driver's license
		Ask about religious affiliation
		Ask about birthplace of applicant
		Ask about club memberships
		Ask if planning to have children
		Ask about preferred hours of work
		Ask about disabilities
		Ask about other names applicant has used
		Ask about arrest record
		Ask about height and weight
		Ask about nature of military discharge
		Ask about friends or relatives with the firm
		Ask for clergy as references
		Ask about credit questions
		Ask if the applicant is willing to travel

Answers appear later in this chapter.

how much have you enjoyed outdoor recreation?"), family experiences as a child, and recent and current work activities (e.g., "How long were you employed in your most recent job?"). Responses to these questions are empirically keyed, based on research that usually involves hundreds of respondents.[31] Biodata information alone can be quite effective as a predictor of overall performance, and it can also be effective when used in combination with an interview, a general mental ability test, or a personality test.[32] Besides overall performance, other criteria that biodata can predict include turnover, customer service, coping with stress, learning rate, teamwork, and promotability.[33] The validity of these tests is a major reason why they tend to be used in the insurance industry.[34]

FAST FACT

Biodata tests are used in only about 5% of selection decisions.

Despite their validity, biodata tests do have a downside: Applicants often react to them as being unfair and invasive.[35] The major reason for this reaction is that some biodata items do not appear to be job related. Another downside is that these tests often are quite long—they may include 200 to 300 items.

Reference Checks and Background Verification

The information obtained from application blanks, interviews, and biodata tests has proved to be useful in a variety of settings. But increasingly, employers question the accuracy of background information supplied by applicants. Verified Credentials reports that almost 30 percent of the resumes it checks contain false information. Distortions vary from a wrong starting date for a prior job to inflated college grades to actual lies involving degrees, types of jobs, and former employers. The most common distortions relate to length of employment and previous salary.

Because some job applicants falsify their qualifications and misrepresent their past, employers have stepped up efforts to check references thoroughly. Instead of relying on unstructured reference letters, which are seldom negative, some organizations hire outside investigators to conduct **reference verification**. Other employers personally contact prior employers to get reference information firsthand.[36] Unfortunately, the potential for defamation-of-character suits has made getting information from past employers more and more difficult. Reference checks of an applicant's prior employment record aren't an infringement on privacy if the information provided relates specifically to work behavior and to the reasons for leaving a previous job. Nevertheless, to avoid possible lawsuits many employers strictly limit the type of information they give out about former employees.[37]

Written Tests

Due to the widespread use of computer testing technology, the term "written test" is becoming outdated. Nevertheless, it continues to be used to describe tests that originally involved traditional paper-and-pencil testing measures. The most common types of written tests measure ability, knowledge, and personality.

Ability Tests. An **ability test** measures the potential of an individual to perform, given the opportunity. Widely used in the United States and Europe since the beginning of the 20th century, numerous studies document the usefulness of such tests for a wide variety of jobs.[38] The number of distinct abilities of potential relevance to job performance is debatable, but generally they fall into three broad groupings: cognitive (e.g., verbal, quantitative), psychomotor (e.g., perceptual speed and accuracy), and physical (e.g., manual dexterity, physical strength and ability).[39] Bank tellers need motor skills to operate a computer and finger dexterity to manipulate currency. Sensory tests that measure the acuity of a person's senses, such as vision and hearing, may be appropriate for such jobs as wine taster, coffee bean selector, quality control inspector, and piano tuner.

Cognitive abilities include verbal comprehension, mathematical fluency, logical reasoning, memory and many others. Such tests are useful for predicting performance in many jobs, and approximately 30 percent of employers use them when making selection decisions for some jobs. However, many employers shy away from using cognitive ability tests because they often result in adverse impact (which is explained later in this chapter). When deciding whether to use cognitive ability tests, employers must weigh their value in predicting job performance against the fact that they are very likely to screen out more members of some ethnic minority groups.[40]

Knowledge Tests. **Knowledge tests** are similar to ability tests. The difference is that a knowledge test assesses what a person knows at the time of taking the test. There is no attempt to assess the applicant's potential—that is, a knowledge test can inform employers about what applicants know now, but not whether they are likely to learn more or learn quickly in the future. Knowledge tests can be useful for jobs that require specialized or technical knowledge that takes a long time to acquire. For example, selection practices for hiring and promoting law enforcement officers usually include a test for knowledge about laws and the appropriate means for enforcing laws.

Personality Tests. A **personality test** assesses the unique blend of characteristics that define an individual and determine her or his pattern of interactions with the environment. A variety of psychological assessment tools can be used to measure personality, but paper-and-pencil tests (or their electronic equivalents) are probably the most common.[41]

> **FAST FACT**
>
> In France, graphology (handwriting analysis) often is used for making selection decisions.

Most people believe that personality plays an important role in job success or failure, but for many years U.S. employers shied away from measuring it largely because research indicated that personality seldom predicted performance. But this early conclusion may have been inaccurate.[42] Recent advances in the academic community's understanding of the nature of personality suggest that employers may have abandoned personality measures too early. The most significant advance has been the realization that most aspects of personality can be captured using only a few basic dimensions. Often referred to as the Big Five, these are

- Extraversion (sociable, talkative, assertive)
- Agreeableness (good-natured, cooperative, trusting)
- Conscientiousness (responsible, dependable, persistent, achievement oriented)
- Emotional stability (not being overly tense, insecure, or nervous)
- Openness to experience (imaginative, artistically sensitive, intellectual)[43]

One important dimension for predicting job performance across a variety of jobs and a variety of occupational groups is conscientiousness. In general, conscientious people perform better, and this seems to be even truer for managerial jobs characterized by high levels of autonomy. Not surprisingly, extraversion is somewhat predictive of performance in jobs that involve social interaction, such as sales and management, but these linkages are actually not very strong.[44]

Personal integrity and honesty is another personality characteristic that's attracting a lot of attention among employers. Employee theft is often cited as a primary reason for small-business failures, with some estimates suggesting it's the cause of up to 30 percent of all failures and bankruptcies. In retailing, inventory shrinkage (unexplained losses in cash, tools, merchandise, and supplies) is a

> **FAST FACT**
>
> During its CEO hunt, Hewlett-Packard put Carly Fiorina and other finalists through a two-hour, 900-question personality test.

major problem, requiring companies to invest large amounts in security systems. In a survey of nine thousand employees by the Justice Department, one-third admitted stealing from their employers. White-collar crime involving millions of dollars regularly makes the news.

Problems of this scope and magnitude help explain why employers administer millions of **integrity tests** annually. Undoubtedly, not all these tests are equally valid, but the better ones can predict dishonest and disruptive work behaviors—for instance, theft and disciplinary problems.[45] Applicants favor paper-and-pencil integrity tests over more invasive procedures, such as background checks and lie detectors (which were found to be highly unreliable and banned as selection tools under the *Employee Polygraph Protection Act of 1988*).[46]

Work Simulations

A **work simulation**, also referred to as a **work sample**, requires applicants to perform activities similar to those required on the job under structured "testing" conditions. Rather than measure what an individual knows, they assess the individual's ability to *do*. For example, applicants for the job of retail associate at a department store might be asked to watch a videotape that shows a typical customer and then role-play how they would handle the situation. Interactive video assessments of conflict resolution skills can be used to predict the performance of managers.[47] Work sample tests are very difficult to fake. They tend to be more valid than almost all other types of selection devices and they are the least likely to create problems due to unfair discrimination. Nevertheless, as Exhibit 8.10 shows, one-on-one interviews, panel interviews, and criminal record checks all are used more often than work samples. Unfortunately, work simulations are usually expensive to develop so they're cost-effective only when large numbers of applicants are to be examined. The total

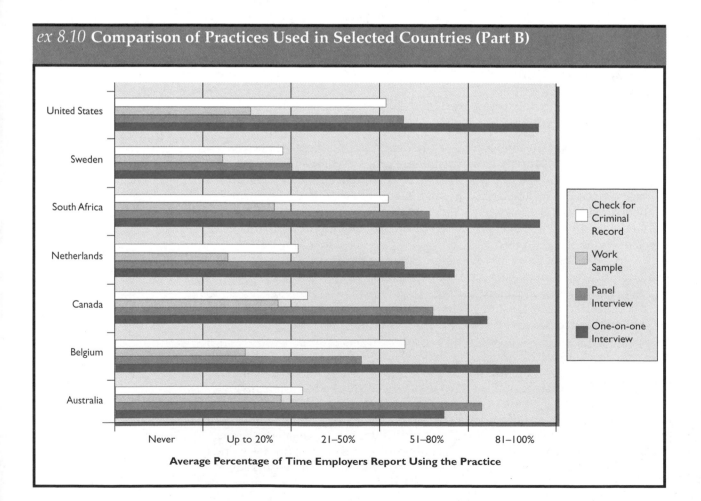

ex 8.10 Comparison of Practices Used in Selected Countries (Part B)

Legend:
- Check for Criminal Record
- Work Sample
- Panel Interview
- One-on-one Interview

x-axis: Never | Up to 20% | 21–50% | 51–80% | 81–100%

Average Percentage of Time Employers Report Using the Practice

price is lower if they're placed at the end of a selection process, when the number of applicants tested is smaller.[48] Despite the fact that work samples are excellent predictors of job performance, they are seldom used.

Assessment Centers

Assessment centers evaluate how well applicants or current employees might perform in a managerial or higher-level position. Some organizations use assessment centers only for developmental purposes. That is, they use assessment center exercises to assess employees' strengths and weaknesses and then provide feedback to employees for use in creating their personal career development plans. When used only for developmental purposes, no selection decision is involved. When an assessment center is used for selection purposes, on the other hand, the same objective is to rank-order applicants and choose the best for placement in a new job.

Assessment centers usually involve 6 to 12 attendees, although they may involve more. Customarily, they're conducted off the premises for one to three days. Usually managers from throughout the organization are trained to assess the employees or job applicants. Increasingly, team members who will work with new hires also assess the participants.[49] Assessment centers can be particularly effective for selecting team-oriented candidates, and their use grows each year.[50]

At a typical assessment center, candidates are evaluated using a wide range of techniques. One activity, the **in-basket exercise**, creates a realistic situation designed to elicit typical on-the-job behaviors. Situations and problems encountered on the job are presented to the applicant, who prioritizes them and decides what actions should be taken. To simulate a typical day, the in-basket exercise may be performed under time pressure.

Other exercises used in assessment centers include simulations and leaderless group discussions. Some simulations are designed to assess very specific skills, such as giving performance feedback to a direct report or handling an ethical dilemma. The applicant is given time to read about a situation, allowed some time to prepare to enact the situation, and then engaged in a role-play. **Business games** are another way to simulate organizational situations. Business games are living cases that require individuals to play assigned roles, make decisions, and deal with the consequences of those decisions. Usually, business games involve several people and several rounds of "play," which unfold over several hours or days. In a **leaderless group discussion**, a group of individuals are asked to discuss a topic for a given period of time. For example, participants might each be asked to make a five-minute oral presentation about the qualifications of a candidate for promotion, and defend their nomination in a group discussion with several other participants. Participants may be rated on their selling ability, oral communication skill, self-confidence, energy level, interpersonal competency, aggressiveness, and tolerance for stress.

Assessment centers appear to work because they reflect the actual job environment and measure performance on multiple job dimensions. Although they are expensive to operate, the cost seems to be justified. The annual productivity gains that are realized by selecting managers through assessment centers average well above administrative costs.[51] In addition, assessment centers appear to be nondiscriminatory as well as valid across cultures.[52] Thus, their higher cost may be further justified by lower costs related to lawsuits.[53]

> **FAST FACT**
>
> Assessments centers were developed in the 1950s at AT&T under the direction of Doug Bray. By the time he retired, about 200,000 employees had been assessed.

> *"Teams spend a lot of energy on the hiring process, and they want the new person to succeed."*
>
> Deborah Harrington-Mackin
> President
> New Directions Corporate Consulting Group

> **FAST FACT**
>
> The United Nations uses assessment centers to select managers for its operations all around the world.

Interviews

The job interview is the most widely used procedure for determining who gets a job offer. As shown in Exhibit 8.5, interviews occur both at the beginning and during the selection process. Interviews that follow sound procedures can be quite useful. Poorly conducted interviews may yield very little useful information and may even damage the organization's image.

At Southwest Airlines, candidates for flight attendant jobs are first interviewed by a panel of representatives from the People Department and the Inflight Department. Before the selection process is finished, they'll also have one-on-one interviews with a recruiter, a supervisor from the hiring department, and a peer. Southwest Airlines' interview process was developed in collaboration with Development Dimensions International, a consulting firm that specializes in designing sound selection practices. Thus, the procedures at Southwest Airlines adhere to the basic principles of good interview design: structured questions, systematic scoring, multiple interviewers, and interviewer training.[54]

Structure. An **unstructured job interview** involves little preparation. The interviewer merely prepares a list of possible topics to cover and, depending on how the conversation proceeds, asks or does not ask them. Although this provides for flexibility, the resulting digressions, discontinuity, and lack of focus may be frustrating to the interviewer and interviewee. More important, unstructured interviews result in inconsistencies in the information collected about the candidates.

In a **structured job interview**, all the applicants are asked the same questions in the same order. Usually, the interviewer has a prepared guide that suggests which types of answers are considered good or poor. Although structuring the interview restricts the topics that can be covered, it ensures that the same information is collected on all candidates. Computerized interviewing is one way to ensure the interview process is structured.[55]

Another approach that minimizes snap judgments is the **semistructured job interview**. Questions are prepared in advance, the same questions are asked of all candidates, and responses are recorded. Follow-up questions are allowed to probe specific areas in depth. This approach provides enough flexibility to develop insights, along with the structure needed to acquire comparative information. In general, structured and semistructured interviews are more valid than unstructured interviews.[56] Structured interviews also appear to be less likely to unfairly discriminate against members of ethnic minority groups.[57]

Behavior. Structured and semi-structured job interviews usually focus on behavior, and for this reason they are sometimes referred to as **behavioral job interviews**. There are two basic approaches to asking behavioral questions.[58] One popular approach is to ask the interviewee to describe specific instances of past behavior that reflect a competency that the employer is looking for in applicants. The assumption behind this approach is that past behavior is the best predictor of future behavior—an assumption that is well supported by research. Many consulting firms that specialize in the design and implementation of human resource systems use behavioral questions when they design a selection process for clients. One consultant, for example,

---

FAST FACT

An interview that would take two hours to complete with a human interviewer can be completed in about 20 minutes using a computerized interview.

conducted job analyses in many different countries for a global client. Based on the job analyses it conducted, the consultant identified relationship building as one of several important competencies required of managers. Exhibit 8.11 lists some of the types of questions the consultant developed to assess an applicant's competency in the area of relationship building.[59] Depending on the client's preference, these questions could be used as a basis for a structured or semi-structured interview.

An alternative approach to conducting behavioral interviews is to pose hypothetical situations that might arise on the job. The interviewee is then asked to describe or role-play what he or she would do. The assumption behind this approach is that behavior on the job can be predicted by an applicant's intentions. The assumption that behavioral intentions predict actual behavior is also well supported by research. One reason to use this approach is that it provides a way to assess how applicants might behave in new situations that they have never before encountered. For example, suppose an internal applicant applies for a position that involves a promotion. Clearly, the new job would involve new responsibilities. For example, newly promoted managers usually face a variety of new situations associated with coaching, providing performance feedback, discipline, dismissals, and so on.

Systematic Scoring. Job interviews vary in the degree to which results are scored. At one extreme, an interviewer merely listens to responses, forms an impression, and makes an accept, reject, or hold decision. Alternatively, raters are given specific criteria and a scoring key to evaluate responses to

> *"A candidate may be able to fool one interviewer, but he or she isn't likely to fool three people at once."*
>
> Antonio Fulk
> HR Specialist
> Rohr Inc.

---

ex 8.11 Examples of Questions to Use in a Structured Interview

COMPETENCY BEING ASSESSED: RELATIONSHIP BUILDING

Interview Questions Designed to Focus on Behavioral Descriptions

1. Sketch out two or three key strengths you have in dealing with people. Can you illustrate the first strength with a recent example? [Repeat same probes for other strengths.]
   Probes:
   - When did this example take place?
   - What possible negative outcomes were avoided by the way you handled this incident?
   - How often has this situation arisen?
   - What happened the next time this came up?

2. Tell me about a time when you effectively used your people skills to solve a customer problem.
   Probes:
   - When did this take place?
   - What did the customer say?
   - What did you say in response?
   - How did the customer react?
   - Was the customer satisfied?

3. Maintaining a network of personal contacts helps a manager keep on top of developments. Describe some of your most useful personal contacts.
   Probes:
   - Tell me about a time when a personal contact helped you solve a problem or avoid a major blunder.
   - How did you develop the contact in the first place?
   - What did you do to obtain the useful information from your contact?
   - When was the next time this contact was useful?
   - What was the situation at that time?
   - How often in the past six months have personal contacts been useful to you?

each question. This approach helps ensure that applicants are evaluated against the same criteria.

Number of Interviewers. Typically, interviewers meet with applicants one person at a time. As Exhibit 8.10 shows, this is true around the world.[60] But one-on-one meetings are time consuming, and the interviewer's impressions vary, depending on what was discussed. These problems can be overcome by using a **panel interview**, in which several individuals (typically two, three, or four) simultaneously interview one applicant. Because all interviewers hear the same responses, panel interviews produce more consistent results. They may also be less susceptible to the biases and prejudices of the interviewers, especially if panel members come from diverse backgrounds.[61] If applicants are to be interviewed by more than one person anyway, panel interviewing can be efficient, reliable, and cost-effective.[62]

Training Interviewers. Left on their own, interviewers tend to form their own impressions based on whatever criteria are most important or salient to them. One interviewer might reject an applicant for being "too aggressive," while another rates the applicant for being "assertive." In fact, interviewers' recommendations about whether to hire an applicant are strongly influenced by how much the interviewer likes the applicant and by physical attractiveness.[63] Consequently, interviewers must be trained to use job-relevant information and to apply it consistently across applicants.[64] **Frame-of-reference training** involves teaching interviewers a common nomenclature for defining the importance of each component of behavior that's to be observed in the interview.[65] This can be accomplished by having potential interviewers develop questions and a scoring key. Alternatively, an interviewer's ratings for "practice" interview questions can be compared with normative ratings given by other interviewers. Such training brings individual perceptions into closer congruence with those of the rest of the organization.

Medical Tests

Although not all organizations require medical tests, these are being given in increasing numbers. However, concerns about privacy and fear of discrimination based on medical conditions mount, creating some opposition to such testing. Three types of medical tests that employers sometimes use when making selection decisions are general health examinations, genetic screening, and drug tests.

General Health Examinations. Since the enactment in 1990 of the *Americans with Disabilities Act (ADA)*, general health examinations may be given only after a job offer has been made.[66] Before the offer is made, employers may only describe the job's functions and ask if the applicant is capable of performing the job. Prior to making an initial job offer, which may be contingent on the results of a medical exam, it is illegal to inquire about any disabilities. If a medical exam subsequently determines that the person is not able to perform the job for medical reasons, the employer may then revoke the job offer. In other words, disabilities may be used in making selection decisions only when they are job related. After Ozark Airlines refused to hire Gary Frey due to a nonfunctioning left ear, the OFCCP sued the airline on Frey's behalf. Ozark acknowledged that Frey was capable of performing the required job duties, but justified the decision not to hire him because he did not prove that he could do the job without endangering himself and others. The court ruled in favor of Frey, stating that it was Ozark's duty to show that Frey's condition would be a source of danger—Frey did not have to prove that the disability was not a source of endangerment. In this landmark decision, the court also stated that a disabled person is "qualified for employment if he [or she] is capable of performing a particular job with reasonable accommodation to his [or her] handicap" (*OFCCP v. Ozark Airlines*).

Many jobs—including police officer, firefighter, electrical powerplant worker, telephone line worker, steel mill laborer, paramedic, maintenance worker, and numerous mechanical jobs— require particular physical, sensory, perceptual, and psychomotor abilities. When job analysis documents that these are needed to perform a job (something Ozark Airlines did not have), employers may be justified in not hiring applicants without the required abilities. The exception is when the employer could make "reasonable accommodations" that would enable the applicant to perform the job despite the disability.[67] Even when accommodation is possible, however, the courts have made it clear that employers are not obligated to hire a person with a disability over a more qualified nondisabled applicant, stating that employers are not required to "give bonus points to people with disabilities" (*EEOC v. Humiston-Keeling Inc.*).[68]

> **FAST FACT**
>
> Not all disabilities are covered by the ADA, which provides protection only for physical or mental impairments that substantially limit one or more major life activities.

Genetic Screening. Each year, hundreds of thousands of job-related illnesses and deaths occur. The recent completion of a map of the human genome provides hope for reducing this number substantially. It creates almost endless possibilities for the development of medical tests to assess a person's genetically determined risks of experiencing various medical problems. For example, genetic screening can identify individuals who are hypersensitive to harmful pollutants in the workplace. Once identified, these individuals can be screened out of chemically dangerous jobs and placed in positions in which environmental toxins do not present specific hazards.

Genetic screening is not prohibited by the *ADA* or other federal legislation. On the other hand, at the state level there are numerous restrictive laws. Eventually, federal legislation is likely to be written in order to provide a common standard for determining when genetic screening is legitimate as a basis for making employment decisions. Meanwhile, many firms will continue to use it and the debate over the ethics of this practice is likely to grow.[69]

Drug and Alcohol Testing. Testing for use of illegal drugs is permissible under the *ADA*. The *ADA* protects applicants and employees who are in recovery programs, but not current drug and alcohol users. When employers first introduced drug testing programs, they were very controversial—similar to today's situation regarding genetic screening. Since then, this practice has become rather common in the United States, as shown in Exhibit 8.8. Drug and alcohol abuse costs U.S. industry more than $100 billion annually, which helps explain why more than 15 million applicants and employees are tested for drugs every year. Of those tested, between 6 and 8 percent test

> *"When you do it [drug testing] right, courts apply a balancing test between individual privacy and the safety of other workers."*
>
> Mark de Bernardo
> Executive Director
> Institute for a Drug-Free Workplace

positive. Consequently, firms are likely to continue drug testing, which requires collecting samples of urine, blood, or hair from applicants.[70]

Precertification

A comprehensive approach to selecting employees is expensive and fraught with legal risks. When employers make poor selection decisions—hiring someone who doesn't work out or not hiring someone who would have performed well—both the employer and the applicant lose. As changes in labor market conditions have made finding competent employees increasingly difficult, employers have turned to precertification selection as one solution.

In contrast to most other selection practices, precertification requires employers to form significant partnerships with local schools and colleges. These partnerships allow employers to influence the curricula of those institutions. Such influence carries with it significant responsibility. Employers must take care to base their recommendations to schools on accurate job analysis information that describes the jobs they want to fill and the competencies needed to perform those jobs. Employers using precertification also must be able to project their future needs accurately and be able to time their hiring activities to fit with the timing of precertification training schedules. In return, employers using precertification may gain a significant competitive advantage by hiring a workforce that has been trained specifically to their needs using state and federal funds.

INTERNET RESOURCES   8.B

Techniques for Assessing Applicants

At our Web site, http://jackson.swcollege.com/, you can:

1. See examples of questions in a widely used ability test.
2. Learn about computer adaptive tests.
3. Assess the potential usefulness of having a third-party vendor conduct reference checks.
4. Read about an organization for professionals who conduct assessment centers.
5. Investigate the advantages and disadvantages of many selection techniques and see examples of test items.

THE PERSPECTIVE OF APPLICANTS

Applicants almost always care deeply about the outcomes of selection decisions and can have strong reactions to their experiences as they go through the selection process. Applicants' reactions influence their decisions about whether to pursue job opportunities in a company. For applicants already employed in the organization, such as those seeking a promotion, reactions to selection practices can influence their decision to remain with the company, and perhaps even their levels of work motivation.[71] Equally important, these early experiences serve as an organization's first steps in a socialization process that will continue for several months after an applicant is eventually hired.[72] At the heart of applicants' concerns is the desire to be treated fairly. Applicants judge fairness by the content of the measures used to select people, the administration of the process, and the outcomes of the process.[73]

Content of Selection Measures

Applicants prefer a process that involves them in activities that have obvious relevance to the job opening. Work samples and simulations usually seem more relevant to applicants than cognitive paper-and-pencil tests and handwriting analysis, for example, and, perhaps for this reason, applicants consider them to be fairer.[74] Applicants react negatively to poorly conducted interviews. Offensive or discriminatory questions obviously send negative messages, but so do questions that appear to be superficial or not clearly related to the job.[75]

Administration of the Selection Process

Applicants also attend to the process: Did the company tell them what it was evaluating and why? Did it provide feedback about how they scored? Did it appear to respect their desire for confidentiality? Did the company representatives behave professionally and appear to take the task seriously? Was the company respectful of their time and need for information about their chances for a positive outcome? Did it seem to treat all candidates equally, or did it treat some more equally than others? Did the process appear to recognize the potential for applicants to misrepresent themselves, and take steps to ensure that honesty was not penalized? Effective selection includes managing these and many other aspects of the process.[76]

"You cannot expect to delight your customers unless you as an employer delight your employees."

Carla Paonessa
Partner
Accenture Consulting

Outcomes of the Selection Process

The content and administrative features of a selection process are visible primarily to applicants, but the outcomes are visible to a broader array of people. Selection decisions are usually known by the acquaintances and coworkers of applicants who tell stories about the process, the new coworkers of successful applicants, the managers inside an organization who participated in the process, and people who served as references for applicants. Based on who is selected and who is rejected, all these constituencies form opinions about whether a company uses fair procedures and makes wise choices about who to hire or promote. Even the news media offer comments about executive selection decisions. They publish reports concerning the demographic characteristics of successful applicants at specific companies. In reporting on companies that made its list of the 50 best places for minorities to work, *Fortune* applauded the fact that 60 percent of Marriott's new hires were minorities. But it also observed that senior management had a different complexion, stating: "Heady minority representation in the workplace has not yet shown gains in the executive ranks." The news story stimulated the company to set a three-year objective of doubling representation of women and minorities in the senior management ranks.[77]

INTERNET RESOURCES 8.C

The Perspective of Applicants

At our Web site, http://jackson.swcollege.com/, you can:

1. Take a popular test for assessing personality style.

2. Find out everything you ever wanted to know about the Federal Civil Service Exam, which is taken by most applicants for federal jobs.

3. Get advice about how to handle yourself well during job interviews.

LEGAL CONSIDERATIONS IN SELECTING APPLICANTS TO FIT THE JOB AND THE ORGANIZATION

Like all HR practices, selection practices must be designed with legal regulations and social norms clearly in mind.[78] These can vary greatly from one country to the next, from state to state within the United States, and from year to year. For example, in 1998, California passed a law that prohibits discrimination against people who have a genetic tendency toward disease.[79] Thirteen states have laws prohibiting employers from using information about home ownership, and a dozen states prohibit the use of questions that probe into whether an applicant "resides with parents or relatives."[80]

Numerous acts, executive orders, guidelines, professional standards, and agencies affect selection practices in most organizations. Legal constraints operate by defining what constitutes illegal discrimination and specifying how employers can successfully defend themselves if they're charged with illegal discrimination.

Laws and Regulations That Prohibit Discrimination

As described in Chapter 3, numerous acts and executive orders prohibit employers from discriminating against employees and job applicants on the basis of various personal characteristics (see Exhibit 3.2 to review these laws). Recall that *Title VII of the Civil Rights Act* and Executive Order 11246 prohibit discrimination on the basis of race, color, religion, sex, or national origin. The *Age Discrimination in Employment Act* prohibits age discrimination, and the *Rehabilitation Act* and the *Americans with Disabilities Act* prohibit discrimination against persons with disabilities.

Federal Guidelines and Professional Standards

Several federal guidelines and documents prepared by professionals with great expertise describe the procedures that organizations should use to comply with these acts and orders. They explain how to develop and use selection tools, such as tests, and how organizations can assess whether their procedures may be considered discriminatory.

Federal Guidelines. The *Uniform Guidelines on Employee Selection Procedures in 1978* is generally considered the most complete and useful legal document relevant to selection practices. It provides many specific do's and don'ts and questions and answers for hiring and promotion. The EEOC also has published many other guidelines relevant to selection. In 1980, it issued guidelines on discrimination because of national origin. These guidelines extended earlier versions of this protection by defining national origin as a *place* rather than a *country*. It also revised the "speak-English-only rules." This means employers can require that English be spoken if they can show a compelling business-related necessity. In 1981, the EEOC issued guidelines on age discrimination. *The Guidelines on Discrimination Because of Religion* explain that employers are obliged to accommodate the religious preferences of current and prospective employees unless the employer demonstrates undue hardship. To determine how to comply with the *Americans with Disabilities Act*, employers can refer to the EEOC's *Technical Assistance Manual on Employment Provisions*. It explains how to identify essential job functions, acceptable interviewing strategies, and the appropriate timing and use of medical examinations.

Professional Standards. Selection processes are monitored by the American Psychological Association (APA), which includes among its members many experts in testing and individual assessment. The APA publishes *Standards for Education and Psychological Tests*, which are updated regularly to reflect changes in scientific knowledge as well as changing legal conditions. Another useful set of professional standards is the *Principles for the Validation and Use of Personnel Selection Procedures*, published by the Society for Industrial-Organizational Psychology (SIOP).

Assessing Disparate Treatment and Adverse Impact

In a typical discrimination lawsuit, a person alleges discrimination due to unlawful employment practices. The person may first go to the Equal Employment Opportunity Commission (EEOC) office. The EEOC may seek out the facts of the case from both sides, attempting a resolution. Failing a resolution, the person may continue the case and file a suit. In the first phase of the suit, the person filing it (the plaintiff) must establish a prima facie case of discrimination. This is done by showing disparate treatment or adverse impact.

> **FAST FACT**
>
> At Southwest Airlines, 33% of corporate officers are women—at least twice the level of its airline competitors and more than most companies in other industries.

Disparate Treatment. Illegal discrimination against an individual is referred to as **disparate treatment**. A prima facie case of disparate treatment exists when an individual can demonstrate that

- the individual belongs to a protected group;
- the individual applied for a job for which the employer was seeking applicants; and
- despite being qualified, the individual was rejected; and
- after the individual's rejection, the employer kept looking for people with the applicant's qualifications.

> **FAST FACT**
>
> Research by Catalyst found that supervisors believe women are not as internationally mobile as men. Although managers assumed that men would be interested in expatriate assignments, women had to ask to be considered for an international assignment.

Demonstrating a case of disparate treatment can be difficult. One reason is that discrimination can be subtle. Unless someone makes a very blatant statement during the selection process—such as "I don't think women can do this job"—the applicant may never realize that a decision was made on the basis of personal characteristics.[81] Also, most of the decision processes aren't visible to applicants. Rejected applicants, especially external ones, seldom know how other applicants performed or even who was eventually hired. For these reasons, the law provides another means for establishing a case of illegal discrimination—demonstrating adverse impact.

Adverse Impact. Discrimination against an entire protected group is called **adverse impact** (the term *disparate impact* is also used). Statistics that reflect the consequences of a large number of hiring decisions made by an employer are used to show adverse impact. Based on the statistics, a judgment is made concerning whether employers *appear* to have discriminated against members of a protected subgroup. If the statistics show that selection practices resulted in adverse impact against a protected group, then the burden is

"I will fire you if you discriminate. Anyone who doesn't like the direction this train is moving had better jump off now."

Jim Adamson
CEO
Flagstar, parent corporation of Denny's

on the employer to prove that its selection techniques assessed job-related predictors. This so-called bottom-line approach to assessing discrimination focuses on the consequences of selection practices rather the employer's intent. From a legal perspective, this is why establishing the validity of selection practices is so important. Selection practices that result in adverse impact are not illegal if the employer can prove that they are job related.

Showing adverse impact generally requires the involvement of the EEOC, which has authority to audit the EEO-1 reports that employers file. As described in Chapter 7, employers file EEO-1 with the EEOC to report the demographic characteristics of job applicants. Without access to such information, it would be nearly impossible for an individual to show that an employer's selection practices have adverse impact.[82] The two most common approaches to assessing adverse impact are making comparisons to labor market data and the 80 percent rule.[83]

Labor Market Comparisons. Disparate impact can be shown by comparing the representation of a group in the organization's workforce to the representation of that group in the **relevant labor market**. An employer's selection practices can be said to have adverse impact if the employer's workforce does not reflect parity with the composition of the relevant labor market. For example, if the relevant labor market for a job is 50 percent male and 50 percent female, the people an employer hires for that job also should be approximately evenly split on gender. The key to this approach is determining the relevant labor market. The approach preferred by the EEOC is to identify where potentially qualified applicants reside and consider this as the relevant labor market. Employers may be able to successfully defend themselves against discrimination claims if they can show that the proportions of protected group members in their workforce mirror the proportions in the relevant labor market.

The 80 Percent Rule. The **80 percent rule** (also called the four-fifths rule) evaluates adverse impact by comparing the representation of a group in the applicant pool to the representation of that group among those who have been hired, fired, promoted, transferred, or demoted. The *Uniform Guidelines* state that adverse impact is demonstrated when the selection rate "for any racial, ethnic, or sex subgroup is less than four-fifths or 80 percent of the highest selection rate for any group." The rule applies to *each part* of the selection process as well as to the process as a *whole* (*Connecticut v. Teal*, 1982).

As an example, consider the use of a physical ability test for selecting firefighters. The test assesses whether an applicant can drag a 220-pound weight a distance of 100 feet in 3 minutes or less. Does this test have adverse impact against women? Using the 80 percent rule, you would compare the percentage of female applicants who pass the test to the percentage of male applicants who pass the test. Suppose 2 out 20 female applicants passed the test and 30 out of 100 male applicants passed the test. The 80 percent rule compares these pass rates as follows:

.10 (pass rate for females)/.30 (pass rate for males) = .67 (relative success of females compared to males)

In this example, the pass rate for females is less that 80 percent of the pass rate for males. So, according to the 80 percent rule, this test has adverse impact against women. One way the firefighters could deal with this apparent problem would be to change the way they score the test. For example, they could make it easier to pass the test by allowing more time, by using a lighter weight, or by shortening the distance involved. Suppose they made some changes. The next time the test is given, 7 out of 10 females pass and 80 out of 100 males pass. Using the 80 percent rule, the pass rate for females compared to males is now

.70 (pass rate for females)/.80 (pass rate for males) = .88 (relative success of females compared to males)

Using the new test, the employer could successfully argue that the test does not unfairly discriminate against women because, according to the 80 percent rule, the pass rates for females is sufficiently similar to the pass rate for males.

Defending Discriminatory Practices

Once a prima facie case of disparate treatment or disparate impact has been established, the employer is given the opportunity to defend itself.[84] An organization accused of illegal discrimination may be able to successfully defend its employment practices by showing that the demonstrated discrimination is legally justified. Discriminatory employment practices can be acceptable if they're used on the basis of

- job relatedness,
- business necessity,
- bona fide occupational qualifications,
- bona fide seniority systems, or
- voluntary affirmative action programs.

Job Relatedness. To demonstrate **job relatedness**, the company must show that the information used in selection decisions is related to success on the job (*Watson v. Fort Worth Bank and Trust*, 1988). Employers can use either a logical argument or statistical evidence to demonstrate job relatedness. Job relatedness can be demonstrated using any of the methods for establishing validity that were described earlier in this chapter.

Business Necessity. Showing the job relatedness of a selection practice isn't always possible. The law recognizes this, and allows companies to defend their selection practices by showing **business necessity**—that is, they must show that the selection decision was based on a factor that is *essential* to the safe operation of the business. The courts and the language of the *Civil Rights Act of 1991* define job necessity in very narrow terms. For example, employers cannot argue that business necessity exists because customers prefer employees from certain demographic groups, or because not hiring members of certain groups reduces the cost of doing business.

Bona Fide Occupational Qualifications. To use the defense of **bona fide occupational qualifications (BFOQ)** the employer must show that the

> **FAST FACT**
>
> A "no-beard" employment policy may discriminate against African-American men who have a predisposition to pseudofolliculitis barbae. It may also discriminate against some religious groups unless the policy is job related and consistent with business necessity.

discriminatory practice is "reasonably necessary to the normal operation of that particular business or enterprise." The BFOQ is sometimes used to justify hiring based on sex or religion. For example, sex is considered a BFOQ for jobs such as rest room attendant and prison guard, and religion is considered a BFOQ for some jobs in religious institutions.

Bona Fide Seniority Systems. A **bona fide seniority system** is one that a company establishes and maintains without the intent to discriminate illegally. Under these circumstances, decisions regarding promotions, job assignments, and layoffs can be made on the basis of seniority. For many occupations, women and members of ethnic minority groups are more likely to be recent hires, so using seniority often results in adverse impact. Nevertheless, using seniority as a basis for selection decisions may be legal.

Voluntary Affirmative Action Programs. As described in Chapter 7, the legal and social status of voluntary affirmative action programs is currently under debate. Nevertheless, past court decisions have held that voluntary affirmative action programs can be a defense against illegal (reverse) discrimination. Voluntary affirmative action programs are legally defensible if they are

- remedial in purpose,
- limited in duration,
- restricted in effect,
- flexible in implementation, and
- minimal in harm to innocent parties.

Legal Considerations for Global Selection

By enacting the *Civil Rights Act of 1991*, Congress affirmed its policy that American civil rights laws cover U.S. citizens employed outside the country by American multinationals. Sometimes this puts American employers in the position of having to violate local practices in order to comply. An example of one such situation is described in the feature "Managing Diversity: American Ethnocentrism or American Ethics?"[85]

The United States also holds foreign companies operating within the United States accountable for adhering to U.S. employment laws. There are some exceptions to this general rule, however. For example, a treaty between the United States and Japan permits companies of either country to prefer their own citizens for executive positions in subsidiaries based in the other country. Japanese firms usually select parent-country (i.e., Japanese) executives to run their American subsidiaries, and they provide few opportunities for promotion to the top management slots for their American managers.[86] U.S. employees often consider this practice to be discrimination based on national origin. But according to the ruling in *Fortino v. Quasar Co.*, Title VII of the *Civil Rights Act* was preempted by a subsequent trade treaty. Thus, as these examples illustrate, managing human resources effectively in a global organization is not as simple as following the advice offered by one sage: "When in Rome, do what the Romans do."

MANAGING DIVERSITY

American Ethnocentrism or American Ethics?

For many people around the world, Radio Free Europe and Radio Liberty are well-known American broadcasts. Supported by a nonprofit organization, these broadcasts often reflect America's views about a range of political, economic, and social issues. Given the prominence of U.S. employment laws prohibiting discrimination, it may seem unusual that this employer would be accused of age bias. Nevertheless, when two employees were forced to retire because of their age, the employees filed a lawsuit under the *Age Discrimination in Employment Act (ADEA)*. The employees were among a group of about 300 U.S. citizens working in a facility in Munich. Consistent with most collective bargaining agreements in Germany, the company followed a policy of requiring employees to retire at age 65. Under the *ADEA*, the policy was illegal. The employer argued that *ADEA*'s "foreign laws" exemption—allowing actions taken in order to avoid violating the laws of a foreign country—applied in this case.

The U.S. District Court in Washington, D.C., disagreed with the employer's defense and ruled that U.S. law took precedent in this situation. It stated that a German labor policy of mandatory retirement at age 65 does not mean that U.S. employers can violate the *ADEA* for American workers in Germany. Although the requirements imposed by foreign laws can sometimes be legitimate reasons for employers to violate U.S. laws, the court did not consider the German labor policy to carry the weight of a foreign law. In explaining its logic, the court stated that "where a foreign labor union policy collides" with a law of the United States, the U.S. law "cannot be expected to bow down" (*Mahoney v. RFE/RL*, 1991). Some say that this is a rather ethnocentric policy stance. Others feel it is a simple matter of doing what is ethical. What's your opinion?

INTERNET RESOURCES   8.D

Legal Considerations

At our Web site, http://jackson.swcollege.com/, you can:

1. Read more about what steps are involved in filing a discrimination charge and proving a case of discrimination.

2. Find out the recent winners of the Catalyst award for companies with practices that support the advancement of women and learn more about what these companies do.

3. Visit the Web sites of some testing companies that do a good job of describing the validity evidence that backs up their work.

4. Visit the Gallaudet Research Institute to learn about test accommodations that can be made for applicants with hearing loss.

PARTNERSHIP IN SELECTION

As we have discussed, applicants are one of the key partners in the selection process. Effective selection practices recognize and respect the applicant's concerns and sensitivities. In addition, they actively involve line managers, HR professionals, and other employees, as summarized in the feature "The HR Triad: Roles and Responsibilities for Selecting Employees."

Line Managers

To achieve the firm's strategic objectives, selection must be congruent with the external environment, as well as the organizational environment. The involvement of line managers helps ensure congruence. During strategic

THE HR TRIAD Roles and Responsibilities for Selecting Employees

Line Managers	HR Professionals	Employees
• Identify staffing needs through articulating business strategies, and strategic business issues and objectives. • Help HR professionals identify appropriate criteria for evaluating the performance of new hires and new placements. • Help HR professionals develop selection tools. • Coordinate selection process with applicants and HR professionals. • Administer and score some selection tests. • Understand and comply with relevant legal regulations. • Provide accurate information to other organizations when they conduct reference checks. • Facilitate the organization's accommodation to the *Americans with Disabilities Act (ADA)*.	• Develop/choose selection tests that are reliable and valid, given the business strategies, issues, objectives, and job openings. • Coordinate the administrative aspects of the selection process. • Participate in the selection, monitoring, and evaluation of external vendors that provide selection services. • Arrange interviews between applicant and managers and other employees. • Provide education and training to all employees involved in the selection process. • Keep complete and accurate records for possible use in defending against lawsuits. • Monitor selection outcomes to ensure equal opportunity for all. • Articulate and oversee organizational compliance with the ADA.	• May participate as applicants for internal transfers, promotions, etc. • May participate by identifying appropriate criteria for evaluating performance. • May interview candidates to work in their group. • May be involved in selecting new group members. • Attend training programs for employees involved in selection processes. • When considering whether to accept a new position, accept responsibility for self-selecting into jobs that fit you and out of jobs that you aren't likely to perform well. • Inform managers of any disabilities requiring accommodation.

planning, line managers identify the jobs to be filled and perhaps the jobs to be eliminated. They participate in the job analysis activities that are used to identify the qualifications for needed competencies and the behaviors employees must have in order to perform current and future jobs. They evaluate job applicants and may coordinate the involvement of other employees during the interview process. Eventually they evaluate employee performance, which may serve as a basis for promotions, transfers, and decisions about who should be asked to leave the organization. All these activities engage line managers in the selection process, regardless of whether hiring is from external or internal applicant pools. When internal promotions and transfers are contemplated, however, line managers' involvement often escalates. In many companies, immediate supervisors have almost total control over selection decisions, especially promotion and transfer decisions. They search for qualified candidates and help choose the best one.

Because line managers often have so much influence, it's important that they understand how to ensure that their selection decisions truly result in the most qualified person filling an open position. It's easy for a manager's personal preferences to get in the way of placing the best person in a job. When a new job is being created, managers may be able to determine exactly who will be promoted by writing the job description to fit only one person. This isn't necessarily a fair practice, but it's common. Managers can also control the final decision

FAST FACT

Ninety-one percent of FedEx managers started in nonmanagement jobs at the company.

by stacking the deck to confirm their favorite candidate. To make the selection process appear legitimate, a manager may select several candidates, in addition to the favorite, for others to evaluate. The catch is that the other candidates are far less qualified than the favorite. The whole selection process becomes superficial, allowing only one "real" choice.

It's not only the managers who will supervise a new employee who get involved in a selection decision, however. Line managers from other units also play a role. Whether acting as formal mentors or informal sponsors, managers in other units can help to ensure that others notice their protégé's strengths. They can also withhold information about poor performance of an employee in their unit, in order to increase the likelihood of that person being moved to another unit. Managers who control selection decisions should accept responsibility for making these decisions wisely.

HR Professionals

In very small organizations, there may be no HR professionals involved in selection decisions. But as small organizations experience rapid growth, they often turn to HR professionals to assist with selection processes. In large organizations, human resource professionals usually gather detailed information about applicants and arrange interviews between job applicants and line managers. They may also administer standardized tests to assess the applicants' competencies and select the most qualified applicants for managers to interview. As detailed in Exhibit 8.12, centralization of some aspects of selection benefits both the organization and the applicants.

Multi-business companies often have several human resource departments, with each serving the unique needs of its own business. The decentralization is intended to produce a closer congruence between HR activities such as selection and the strategy and culture of each business unit. Decentralization does have potential disadvantages, however. If each division or unit operates independently, each is likely to select only from among its own employees and not from the whole workforce. Decentralization may also mean that each unit relies on its own performance appraisal systems, so even if candidates from other divisions become internal applicants, they may be difficult to evaluate. This reality is magnified in global firms: regions of the world may become virtually unrelated to each other, and the human

ex 8.12 How Centralizing Selection Activities Can Benefit Job Applicants and Employers

Benefits for Applicants
- Applicants go to only one place to apply for all jobs in the company, which is convenient.
- Specialists trained in staffing techniques do hiring, so the selection decisions are often better, resulting in better employee performance.
- People who know about the many legal regulations relevant to selection handle a major part of the hiring process, which improves both legal compliance and fairness to job applicants.

Benefits for Employers
- The company can consider each applicant for a variety of jobs, which is efficient.
- Specialists trained in staffing techniques do hiring, so the selection decisions are often better, resulting in better employee performance.
- Operating managers can concentrate on their operating responsibilities, which is especially helpful during peak hiring periods.

resources of one region may be completely off limits to the others. Fundamentally, the role of a company's HR professionals is helping to ensure that the best candidates available are identified and placed into open positions. Besides ensuring that selection decisions are based only on relevant information, HR professionals should continually evaluate the effectiveness of the practices in use and look for ways to improve.

Other Employees

As organizations rely more and more on teamwork, they also are likely to involve more and more employees in selecting new coworkers. Coworkers often help determine how well an applicant is likely to fit into the company's culture. At Rosenbluth International, a travel management company, applicants for managerial jobs might be asked to play a game of softball with the company team or help repair a broken fence. The objective isn't to test the applicant's skill at softball or fence mending—it's to learn whether the applicant is able and willing to be nice.

At Worthington Industries, an Ohio-based steel processor, employees play an even bigger role. There the final selection decision is made after the applicant has completed a 90-day "probation period." At the end of the probation, an employee council of about 10 peers formally votes on whether the new hire should be allowed to stay on. Presumably, at Worthington, peers make their judgments primarily on the basis of the new hire's performance level. At Worthington, profit sharing accounts for about 40 percent of each employee's total pay. Knowing that a good hiring decision translates into more profits, current employees are motivated to help ensure that only productive people are allowed to join the company.[87]

Involving employees in the selection process is generally a good idea and is a practice that seems to be growing. When employees are involved in the selection of new team members, they seem to become more committed to making sure the new hires succeed. As employees become more involved in this important decision process, it's essential that they understand the process and receive training about how to make appropriate decisions. Just as managers can be influenced by many factors other than an applicant's ability to perform well, so too are employees susceptible to making decisions for the wrong reasons.[88]

"Peers need an opportunity to weigh in on a candidate. They need a chance to ask whether they want to split the pie with a particular individual."

Eric Smolenski
Personnel Manager
Worthington Industries

FAST FACT

Southwest Airlines flies some of its best customers to Dallas and involves them in the flight attendant hiring process, believing that they probably know best what makes a good employee.

SUMMARY

Through selection and placement procedures, organizations strive to fill job openings with the most appropriate people. By the same token, job applicants strive to obtain jobs that are appropriate to their personal objectives. Effective selection practices result in the assignment of individuals to jobs (and even career paths) that match the individuals' technical competencies, personalities, behavioral styles, and preferences. In order to achieve an effective match between individuals and job situations, organizations and job applicants need to exchange information. Organizations need to obtain information about the applicant and clearly communicate information about the job and the work setting. Applicants, on the other hand, need to seek information about the job and the work setting and also share information about their qualifications and preferences. This exchange of information begins during recruitment and continues throughout all phases of the selection process.

Applicants may use a fairly informal and unstructured approach to gathering information about organizations and jobs, but effective organizations are quite systematic in their efforts to assess applicants. Building on the results of job analyses, employers can develop valid selection practices that enable them to make job offers to those applicants who are most likely to perform well in the job, be good corporate citizens, and not leave the organization prematurely. Application forms, interviews, written and physical tests, work samples, and assessment centers are among the selection techniques that organizations use for selection purposes. Managers, HR professionals, and the future colleagues of a new hire may all be involved in using these techniques to assess job applicants.

Few organizations, if any, rely on a single predictor when making selection decisions. Typically, employers gather several types of information using a variety of methods. The information obtained may be considered sequentially, using the multiple hurdles approach, or a compensatory approach to decision making may be followed. Regardless of the approach, managing human resources effectively requires the use of predictors that are valid and nondiscriminatory. An extensive framework of legal regulations, court decisions, and guidelines provides employers with advice for how to conduct the selection process in a manner that enhances the performance of the workforce while avoiding unfair discrimination.

TERMS TO REMEMBER

80% percent rule
ability test
adverse impact
application blank
assessment centers
behavioral job interview
biodata test
bona fide occupational qualifications (BFOQ)
bona fide seniority system
business games
business necessity
combined approach
compensatory approach
content validation
criteria
criterion-related validation
disparate treatment
economic utility
frame-of-reference training
in-basket exercise

integrity tests
job relatedness
knowledge test
leaderless group discussion (LGD)
multiple-hurdles approach
panel interview
personality test
predictors
reference verification
relevant labor market
reliability
selection
selection ratio
semistructured job interview
structured job interview
unstructured job interview
validity
validity generalization
work sample
work simulation

DISCUSSION QUESTIONS

1. A frequent diagnosis of an observed performance problem in an organization is, "This person was a selection mistake." What are the short- and long-term consequences of so-called selection mistakes? If possible, relate this question to your own experiences with organizations.

2. Successful selection decisions depend on other human resource activi-
    ties. Identify these activities and explain their relationships to selection
    practices.
3. Given all the weaknesses identified with unstructured interviews, why
    do they remain so popular? How could you improve the typical job
    interview to overcome some of its potential weaknesses?
4. Describe the meaning of the partnership perspective for selection.
5. What are some of the benefits to employers who are responsive to the
    applicant's perspective throughout the selection process? Consider the
    process of selecting employees as well as the process of rejected them.
6. Do you think employers should be allowed to use the results of genetic
    tests in their selection decisions? Explain the rationale for your opinion.
7. Some people feel the government should not get involved in regulating
    business practices. To what extent do you think legal regulations affect-
    ing selection practices hinder or facilitate running an effective company?

PROJECTS TO EXTEND YOUR LEARNING

1. *Managing Through Strategic Partnerships.* FedEx and UPS are two
    companies that compete in the same industry using very different
    approaches to managing. What are the implications of these differences
    for the selection criteria that should be used when hiring first-level super-
    visors? To learn more about these companies, visit their home pages.
    a. Identify up to five competencies that you think would be important
        for supervisors.
    b. List the selection practices you would use to assess these competen-
        cies. If you will use a cognitive ability test, identify which one. If you
        will use a situational interview, describe the questions that will be
        asked. If you will use a personality test, identify the specific test. Pro-
        vide a rationale for the choice of each selection device.
    c. Outline the order in which the selection devices will be administered
        and explain the rationale for the ordering.
    d. Specify how information will be combined, using a compensatory,
        multiple hurdles, or combination approach. Detail how the selection
        devices will be scored.
    e. In what ways are the differences between these two companies
        reflected in the selection practices you described?
2. *Managing Teams.* America's Job Bank is a recruiting service that was
    established by Employment Services and is owned by the Department of
    Labor. Employers post job openings with detailed job descriptions and
    prospective employees can use AJB to search and apply for jobs. Visit
    America's Job Bank. Find at least five position announcements for jobs
    that involve teamwork. Based on these position announcements, what
    characteristics do employers seem to look for when hiring employees
    into team-oriented jobs? How does your list compare with the one
    shown in Exhibit 8.6?
3. *Integration and Application.* Review the end-of-text cases of Lincoln
    Electric and Southwest Airlines. Describe, evaluate, and compare the
    selection procedures used at Lincoln Electric and Southwest Airlines. In
    preparing your answer, consider the following issues:
    a. the objectives of selection and placement;
    b. the criteria used;

c. the methods used to assess the competencies and other characteristics of individual candidates;

d. the apparent effectiveness of the selection process;

e. the roles and responsibilities of managers, HR professionals, and other employees; and

f. the relationship between the selection process and other aspects of the HRM system (e.g., training received by employees, the pay system).

INTERNET RESOURCES 8.E

Resources for Projects and Cases

At our Web site, http://jackson.swcollege.com/, you can:

1. Visit these sites for useful information in completing the projects:

UPS	Southwest Airlines
FedEx	PepsiCo
America's Job Bank	Coca-Cola
Lincoln Electric	

Answers to Exhibit 8.9 Designing Application Blanks with Fairness in Mind

In most situations, it's probably fine to ask questions 3, 6 (when driving is required on the job), 11, and 20 (if the job requires travel). Question 12 could be asked in this way: "Is there any condition you have that might make it impossible to perform 'essential job functions' even after some accommodation?" Even here, however, the applicant should be volunteering this information. It's probably best to ask this after a decision to hire has been made. Forget about the rest.

SELECTING SOLDIERS FOR THE COLA WAR

Case study

Few products appear to be more similar than soft drinks, yet the "cola wars" between Coca-Cola and Pepsi show how even organizations with highly similar products can be differentiated by their business strategies.

COKE'S DOMINANCE

Coke is the most recognized trademark in the world. First marketed some 70 years before Pepsi, Coke is, literally, part of American history and culture. In World War I, for example, Coca-Cola bottling plants went to Europe along with the U.S. armed forces. With such enormous recognition in the market, Coke's business strategy centers on maintaining its position and building on its carefully groomed image. Compared with other companies its size, Coca-Cola owns and operates few ventures—

especially now that its brief fling with Columbia Pictures is over—and has relatively few bottling franchises with which to deal. Indeed, the largest franchisee, which controls 45 percent of the U.S. market, is owned by Coca-Cola itself.

Given its dominance, the Coke trademark is something akin to a proprietary technology, and Coca-Cola's business strategy turns on subtle marketing decisions that build on the trademark's reputation. This isn't to suggest that running Coke's business strategy is easy. Rather, the decisions are highly constrained within a framework of past practices and reputation. (One reason New Coke was a debacle, it can be argued, was that it broke away from the framework represented by Coke's tradition.)

Managing Coca-Cola therefore requires a deep firm-specific understanding and feel for the trademark that can't be acquired outside the company or even quickly inside it. What Coke does, then, is both teach that culture and hang onto it. Coke typically hires college graduates—often liberal arts majors and rarely MBAs—with little or no corporate experience and provides them with intensive training. Jobs at Coke are very secure, virtually lifetime positions for adequate performers, and a system of promotion from within and seniority-based salary increases provides the carrot that keeps employees coming back day after day. The organizational culture is often described as familylike, with a high degree of employee loyalty. Decision making is very centralized; the people management system ensures that only career Coke managers who have been thoroughly socialized into worrying about the company as a whole get to make decisions affecting the company. The company allows little autonomy and has a low tolerance for individual self-aggrandizement: no one wants an unsupervised, low-level decision backfiring on the trademark. To reinforce the centralized model, performance is evaluated at the company or division level.

PEPSI'S CHALLENGE

Pepsi is not Coke. Pepsi has prospered by seeking out the market niches where Coke isn't dominant and then differentiating itself from Coke. From its early position as a price leader ("Twice as Much for a Nickel") to contemporary efforts at finding a "New Generation" of consumers, Pepsi cleans up behind the Coke trademark. Pepsi markets more aggressively to institutional buyers like hotels and restaurants than does Coke, which is focused on individual consumers. Pepsi also has many more bottling franchises that operate with some autonomy.

Given its marketing strategy, Pepsi faces a much more diversified and complicated set of management challenges. It needs more innovative ideas to identify market niches, and it needs the ability to move fast. Its people management system makes this possible. Pepsi hires employees with experience and advanced degrees, high-performing people who bring ideas with them. In particular, Pepsi brings in advanced technical skills. Within the company, Pepsi fosters individual competition and a fast-track approach for those who are successful in that competition. The company operates in a much more decentralized fashion, with each division given considerable autonomy, and performance is evaluated at the operating and individual levels. Restructuring in the early 1990s moved the firm toward further decen-

tralization and introduced a stock option program, designed to push entrepreneurial action down to individual employees.

Pepsi employees have relatively little job security, and the company does not have a strong promotion-from-within policy. One Pepsi insider commented, "Whenever anybody is either over 40 or has been in the same Pepsi job for more than four or five years, they tend to be thought of as a little stodgy." In part because of higher turnover, Pepsi employees have significantly less loyalty to the company than do their counterparts at Coke. Indeed, the main issue that unites them, some say, is their desire to "beat Coke."

What Pepsi gets from this system is a continuous flow of new ideas (e.g., from experienced new hires), the ability to change quickly (e.g., by hiring and firing), and the means for attacking many different markets in different ways (e.g., decentralized decision making with individual autonomy).[89]

QUESTIONS

1. How do the different strategies of Coke and Pepsi affect the types of competencies these two companies need in their managerial staff?
2. If you worked for Coke, would you consider experience as a Pepsi manager to be a positive feature for a job applicant applying for a managerial job? Explain.
3. If you worked for Pepsi, would you consider experience as a Coke manager to be a positive feature for a job applicant applying for a managerial job? Explain.
4. Although Pepsi generally gives employees little security, CEO Craig Weatherup moved into that position from the inside, after serving in a variety of managerial roles over several years. When Weatherup first arrived at Pepsi, he was assigned to a position in Japan, despite the fact that he had no experience with the type of job he was assigned to, he had never before visited Japan, and he spoke no Japanese. Placing people in very challenging "stretch" assignments is typical for Pepsi. What competencies should Pepsi consider when assigning managers to jobs for which they have little direct relevant experience? What are the implications of this approach to selection and placement for employees, for the company's long-term performance, and for other aspects of the company's HRM system?

ENDNOTES

1 L. Bossidy, "The Job No CEO Should Delegate," *Harvard Business Review* (March 2001): 47–49.

2 O. Port, "Artificial Eyes, Turbine Hearts," *Business Week* (March 20, 2000): 72–73; J. Williams, "The New Workforce," *Business Week* (March 20, 2000): 64–70; V. Sessa, R. Kaiser, J. Taylor, and R. Campbell, Executive Selection (Greensboro, NC: Center for Creative Leadership, 1998); For detailed reviews, see N. Schmitt and D. Chan, *Personnel Selection: A Theoretical Approach* (Thousand Oaks, CA: Sage, 1998); N. Anderson and P. Herriot (eds.), *International Handbook of Selection and Assessment* (Chichester, UK: John Wiley, 1997); R. M. Guion, *Assessment, Measurement, and Prediction for Selection Decisions* (Mahwah, NJ: Lawrence Erlbaum, 1997); W. C. Borman, M. Hanson, and J. Hedge, "Personnel Selection," *Annual Review of Psychology* 48 (1997): 299–337; H. G. Heneman III, R. L. Heneman, and T. A. Judge, *Staffing Organizations*, 2d ed. (Homewood, IL: Irwin Publishing, 1996).

3 "Churning the Top," *Economist* (March 17, 2001): 67–69; V. C. Smith, "Staffing Strategies," *Human Resource Executive* (January 1998): 44–45; C. Patton, "Natural Bedfellows," *Human Resource Executive* (January 1998): 62–63; S. M. Colarelli and T. A. Beehr, "Selection Out: Firings, Layoffs, and Retirement," in N. Schmitt and W. C. Borman (eds.), *Personnel Selection in Organizations* (San Francisco: Jossey-Bass, 1993): 341–384.

4 P. J. Dowling, D. E. Welch, and R. S. Schuler, *International Human Resource Management*.

5 P. J. Dowling, D. E. Welch , and R. S. Schuler, *International Human Resource Management: Managing People in a Multinational Context*, 3rd ed. (Cincinnati, OH: South-Western College Publishing, 1999); Society for Human Resource Management, "Short-Term International Assignments on Upswing, Survey of Multinationals Finds," *HR News* (May 2001): 21.

6 C. Daily, S. Certo, and D. R. Dalton, "International Experience in the Executive Suite: The Path to Prosperity?" *Strategic Management Journal* 21 (2000): 515–523; G. Porter and J. Transky, "Expatriate Success May Depend on a 'Learning Orientation': Consideration for Selection and Training," *Human Resource Management* 38(1) (Spring 1999): 47–60; P. Sappal, "Hungry for Global Talent," *HR World* (May/June 1999): 20–23; C. Reynolds, "Strategic Employment of Third Country Nationals," *Human Resource Planning* 20(1) (1997): 33–39; C. A. Bartlett and S. Ghoshal, "What Is a Global Manager?" *Harvard Business Review* (September–October 1992): 132; P. M. Caligiuri, M. M. Hyland, A. Joshi, and A. S. Bross, "Testing a Theoretical Model for Examining the Relationship Between Family Adjustment and Expatriates' Work Adjustment," *Journal of Applied Psychology* 83 (1998): 598–614.

7 M. E. Mendenhall, E. Dunbar, and G. R. Oddou, "Expatriate Selection, Training and Career-Pathing: A Review and Critique," *Human Resource Management* (Fall 1987): 331; J. S. Black, M. Mendenhall, and G. Oddou, "Toward a Comprehensive Model of International Adjustment: An Integration of Multiple Theoretical Perspectives," *Academy of Management Review* 16(2) (1991): 291–317.

8 P. Sappal, "Hungry for Global Talent," *HR World* (May/June 1999): 20–23; M. Dixon, "Office of the Future" *Fast Company* (April 2000): 272–305.

9 For a readable overview, see W. F. Cascio, "Assessing the Utility of Selection Decisions: Theoretical and Practical Considerations," in N. Schmitt and W. C. Borman (eds.), *Personnel Selection in Organizations* (San Francisco: Jossey-Bass, 1993): 310–340. See also J. Zeidner and C. D. Johnson, *The Economic Benefits of Predicting Job Performance: Volume 1, Selection Utility* (New York: Praeger, 1991).

10 J. W. Boudreau, "Utility Analysis for Decisions in Human Resource Management," in Dunnette and Hough (eds.) *Handbook of Industrial and Organizational Psychology*, Vol. 2 (Palo Alto, CA: Consulting Psychologists Press, 1991).

11 T. Murphy and S. Zandvakili, "Data—and Metrics—Driven Approach to Human Resource Practices: Using Customers, Employees, and Financial Metrics," *Human Resource Management* 39(1) (Spring 2000): 93–105.

12 D. E. Terpstra and E. J. Rozell, "The Relationship of Staffing Practices to Organizational Level Measures of Performance," *Personnel Psychology* 46 (1993): 27–48.

13 K. Pearlman and M. F. Barney, "Selection for a Changing Workforce," in J. F. Kehoe (ed.), *Managing Selection in Changing Organizations: Human Resource Strategies* (San Francisco: Jossey-Bass, 2000): 3–72.

14 M. Conlin, "The CEO Still Wears Wingtips," *Business Week* (November 22, 1999): 84–90; for a detailed review of what is known about this very special selection process, see G. P. Hollenbeck, *CEO Selection: A Street-Smart Review* (Greensboro, NC: Center for Creative Leadership, 1994).

15 J. LePine, J. Hanson, W. C. Borman, and S. J. Motowidlo, "Contextual Performance Teamwork: Implications for Staffing," *Research in Personnel and Human Resource Management* 19 (2000): 53–90; M. M. Lombardo and R. W. Eichinger, "High Potential as High Learners," *Human Resource Management* (Winter 2000): 321–329; G. Porter and J. W. Tansky, "Expatriate Success May Depend on a 'Learning Orientation': Considerations for Selection and Training," *Human Resource Management* (Spring 1999): 47–60; E. E. Lawler III, "From Job-Based to Competency-Based Organizations," Journal of *Organizational Behavior* 15 (1994): 3–15.

16 L. Grensing Pophal, "Hiring to Fit Your Corporate Culture," *HR Magazine* (August 1999): 50–54; J. Werbel and S. W. Gilliland, "Person—Environment Fit in the Selection Process," *Research in Personnel and Human Resource Management* 17 (1999): 209–243.

17 A. J. Vinchur, J. S. Schippmann, F. S. Switzer III, and P. L. Roth, "A Meta-Analytic Review of Predictors of Job Performance for Salespeople," *Journal of Applied Psychology* 83 (1998): 586–597; D. E. Bowen and D. A. Waldman, "Customer-Driven Employee Performance," in D. R. Ilgen and E. D. Pulakos (eds.), *The Changing Nature of Performance* (San Francisco: Jossey-Bass, 1999); R. T. Hogan and R. J. Blake, "Vocational Interests: Matching Self-Concept with the Work Environment," in K. R. Murphy (ed.), *Individual Differences and Behavior in Organizations* (San Francisco: Jossey-Bass, 1996): 89–144; J. A. Chatman, "Matching People and Organizations: Selection and Socialization in Public Accounting Firms," *Administrative Science Quarterly* 36 (1991): 459–484; R. Dunifon and G. J. Duncan, "Long-Run effects of Motivation on Labor-Market Success," *Social Psychology Quarterly* 61 (1998): 33–48.

18 R. G. Jones, M. J. Stevens, and D. L. Fischer, "Selection in Team Contexts," in J. F. Kehoe (ed.), *Managing Selection in Changing Organizations: Human Resource Strategies* (San Francisco: Jossey-Bass, 2000): 210–241; G. Neuman and J. Wright, "Team Effectiveness: Beyond Skills and Cognitive Ability," *Journal of Applied Psychology* 84(3) (1999): 376–389; M. Stevens and M. A. Campion, "Staffing Work Teams: Development and Validation of a Selection Test for Teamwork Settings," *Journal of Management* 25(2) (1999): 207–228.

19 R. Grover and E. Schine, "At Disney, Grumpy Isn't Just a Dwarf," *Business Week* (February 24, 1997): 38; R. Grover, "Michael Eisner Defends the Kingdom," *Business Week* (August 4, 1997): 73–75; V. C. Smith, "Spreading the Magic," *Human Resource Executive* (December 1996): 28–31; J. Pfeffer, *Competitive Advantage Through People* (Boston: Harvard Business School Press, 1994).

20 I. L. Goldstein, S. Zedeck, and B. Schneider, "An Exploration of the Job Analysis–Content Validity Process," in N. Schmitt and W. C. Borman (eds.), *Personnel Selection in Organizations* (San Francisco: Jossey-Bass, 1993): 3–34.

21 D. Sheff, "Levi's Changes Everything," *Fast Company* (1997): 24–31.

22 G. Nicholson, "Automated Assessments for Better Hires," *Workforce* (December 2000): 102–109.

23 For a discussion of validity generalization and other related approaches, see C. C. Hoffman and S. M. McPhail, "Exploring Options for Supporting Test Use in Situations Precluding Local Validation," *Personnel Psychology* 51 (1998): 987–1003.

24 See F. L. Schmidt and J. E. Hunter, "The Validity and Utility of Selection Methods in Personnel Psychology: Practical and Theoretical Implications of 85 Years of Research Findings, *Psychological Bulletin* 124 (1998): 262–274.

25 A. Howard, "Identifying, Assessing, and Selecting Senior Leaders," *The Nature of Organizational Leadership* (San Francisco: Jossey-Bass, 2001).

26 S. Hays, "Kinko's Dials Into Automated Applicant Screening," *Workforce* (November 1999): 71–73.

27 Based on M. J. Stevens and M. A. Campion, "The Knowledge, Skill and Ability Requirements for Teamwork: Implications for Human Resource Management," *Journal of Management* 20 (1994): 505–530; B. Dumaine, "The Trouble with Teams," *Fortune* (September 5, 1994): 86–92; and N. R. F. Maier, "Assets and Liabilities in Group Problem Solving: The Need for an Integrative Function," *Psychological Review* (April 1967): 239–249; D. Hellriegel, S. E. Jackson, and J. W. Slocum Jr., *Management*, 8th ed. (Cincinnati, OH: South-Western College Publishing, 1999).

28 G. Nyfield and H. Baron, "Cultural Context in Adapting Selection Practices Across Borders," in J. F. Kehoe (ed.), *Managing Selection in Changing Organizations: Human Resource Strategies* (San Francisco: Jossey-Bass, 2000): 242–268; A. M. Ryan, L. McFarland, H. Baron and R. Page, "An International Look at Selection Practices: Nation and Culture as Explanations for Variability in Practice," *Personnel Psychology* 52 (1999): 359–391.

29 D. G. Lawrence et al., "Design and Use of Weighted Application Blanks," *Personnel Administrator* (March 1982): 53–57, 101.

30 C. J. Russell et al., "Predictive Validity of Biodata Items Generated from Retrospective Life Experience Essays," *Journal of Applied Psychology* 75(5) (1990): 569–580; H. R. Rothstein et al., "Biographical Data in Employment Selection: Can Validities Be Made Generalizable?" *Journal of Applied Psychology* 75(2) (1990): 175–184.

31 M. Dean, C. J. Russell, and P. Muchinsky, "Life Experiences and Performance Prediction: Toward a Theory of Biodata," *Research in Personnel and Human Resource Management* 17 (1999): 245–281; G. Stokes, M. D. Mumford, and W. Owens (eds.), *Biodata Handbook: Theory, Research, and Use of Biographical Information for Selection and Performance Prediction* (Palo Alto, CA: Consulting Psychologists Press, 1994).

32 M. D. Mumford, D. P. Costanza, M. S. Connelly, and J. E. Johnson, "Item Generation Procedures and Background Data Scales: Implications for Construct and Criterion-Related Validity," *Personnel Psychology* 49 (1996): 361–398; A. T. Dalessio and T. A. Silverhart, "Combining Biodata Test and Interview Information: Predicting Decisions and Performance Criteria," *Personnel Psychology* 47 (1994): 303–319.

33 F. A. Mael and B. E. Ashforth, "Loyal from Day One: Biodata, Organizational Identification, and Turnover Among Newcomers," *Personnel Psychology* 48 (1995): 309–333; R. D. Gatewood and H. S. Field, *Human Resource Selection* (Orlando, FL: Harcourt Brace, 1994).

34 M. McManus and M. Kelly, "Personality Measures and Biodata: Evidence Regarding Their Incremental Predictive Value in the Life Insurance Industry," *Personnel Psychology* 52 (1999): 137–148; K. Carlson, S. Scullen, F. L. Schmidt, H. R. Rothstein and F. Erwin, "Generalized Biographical Data Validity Can Be Achieved Without Multi-Organizational Development and Keying," *Personnel Psychology* 52 (1999): 731–755.

35 R. Folger and R. Cropanzano, *Organizational Justice and Human Resource Management* (Thousand Oaks, CA: Sage, 1998); F. A. Mael, M. Connerley, and R. A. Morath, "None of Your Business: Parameters of Biodata Invasiveness," *Personnel Psychology* 49 (1996): 613–650.

36 W. Bliss, *Legal, Effective References: How to Give and Get Them* (Society for Human Resource Management, 2001); for a good discussion of the benefits and risks associated with using outside vendors to conduct background checks, see C. Garvey, "Outsourcing Background Checks," *HR Magazine* (March 2001): 95–104.

37 S. Romero and M. Richtel, "Second Chance," *New York Times* (March 5, 2001): C1; L. Walley and M. Smith, *Deception in Selection* (New York: John Wiley, 1998); E. A. Robinson, "Beware—Job Seekers Have No Secrets," *Fortune* (December 29, 1997): 285; "Positive Reference Leads to Claim of Negligence," *Fair Employment Practices Guidelines* 430 (April 25, 1997): 1; "Supreme Court Decision Possible Setback to Employee Reference," *Human Resource Executive* (April 1997): 8.

38 F. L. Schmidt and J. E. Hunter, "The Validity and Utility of Selection Methods in Personnel Psychology; J. C. Hogan, "Physical Abilities," in Dunnette and Hough (eds.), *Handbook of Industrial and Organizational Psychology* (1991): 753–831; R. M. Guion, "Personnel Assessment, Selection, and Placement," in Dunnette and Hough (eds.), *Handbook of Industrial and Organizational Psychology*, (1991): 327–398.

39 E. A. Fleishman and M. K. Quaintance, *Taxonomies of Human Performance* (New York: Academic Press, 1984).

40 P. L. Roth, C. Bevier, P. Bobko, F. S. Switzer, III, and P. Taylor, "Ethnic Group Differences in Cognitive Ability in Employment and Educational Settings: A Meta-Analysis," *Personnel Psychology* 54 (2001): 297–330; N. Schmitt, C. S. Clause, and E. D. Pulakos, "Subgroup Differences Associated with Different Measures of Some Common Job-Relevant Constructs," in C. R. Cooper and I. T. Roberson (eds.), *International Review of Industrial/Organizational Psychology* 11 (1996): 115–140. For a discussion of some alternatives to cognitive ability testing, see S. Zedeck and I. L. Goldstein, "The Relationship Between I/O Psychology and Public Policy: A Commentary," in J. F. Kehoe (ed.), *Managing Selection in Changing Organizations: Human Resource Strategies* (San Francisco: Jossey-Bass, 2000): 371–396. For more details about cognitive ability tests, see R. D. Gatewood and H. S. Field, *Human Resource Selection* (Fort Worth, TX: Harcourt Brace, 2001).

41 R. T. Hogan, J. C. Hogan, and B. W. Roberts, "Personality Measurement and Employment Decisions," *American Psychologist* 51 (1996): 469–477; R. T. Hogan, "Personality and Personality Measurement," in Dunnette and Hough (eds.), *Handbook of Industrial and Organizational Psychology* (1991): 873–890.

42 D. V. Day and S. B. Silverman, "Personality and Job Performance: Evidence of Incremental Validity," *Personnel Psychology* 42 (1989): 25–36; R. P. Tett, D. N. Jackson, and M. Rothstein, "Personality Measures as Predictors of Job Performance: A Meta-Analytic Review," *Personnel Psychology* 44 (1991): 703–742.

43 L. M. Hough and R. J. Schneider, "Personality Traits, Taxonomies, and Applications in Organizations," in K. R. Murphy (ed.), *Individual Differences and Behavior in Organizations*, (San Francisco: Jossey-Bass, 1996): 31–88; J. M. Collins and D. H. Gleaves, "Race, Job Applicants, and the Five-Factor Model of Personality: Implications for Black Psychology, Industrial/Organizational Psychology, and the Five-Factor Theory," *Journal of Applied Psychology* 83 (1998): 531–544; R. R. McCrae and P. T. Costa Jr., "Personality Trait Structure as a Human Universal," *American Psychologist* 52 (1997): 509–535.

44 P. Caligiuri, "The Big Five Personality Characteristics as Predictors of Expatriate's Desire to Terminate the Assignment and Supervisor-Rated Performance," *Personnel Psychology* 53 (2000): 67–88; G. Hurtz and J. Donovan, "Personality and Job Performance: The Big Five Revisited," *Journal of Applied Psychology* 85(6) (2000): 869–879; T. A. Judge, C. A. Higgins, C. Thiresen and M. Barrick, "The Big Five Personality Traits, General Mental Ability, and Career Success Across the Life Span," *Personnel Psychology* 52 (1999): 621–652; M. K. Mount and M. R. Barrick, "The Big Five Personality Dimensions: Implications for Research and Practice in Human Resources Management," *Research in Personnel and Human Resources Management* 13 (1995): 153–200; M. R. Barrick and M. K. Mount, "The Big Five Personality Dimensions and Job Performance: A Meta-Analysis," *Personnel Psychology* 44 (1991): 1–26. For an alternative view, see R. P. Tett, "Is Conscientiousness Always Positively Related to Job Performance?" *The Industrial-Organizational Psychologist* (July 1998): 24–29; D. F. Caldwell and J. M. Burger, "Personality Characteristics of Job Applicants and Success in Screening Interviews," *Personnel Psychology* 51 (1998): 119–136.

45 K. R. Murphy, *Honesty in the Workplace* (Pacific Grove, CA: Brooks/Cole, 1993); D. S. Ones, C. Viswesvaran, and F. L. Schmidt, "Comprehensive Meta-Analysis of Integrity Test Validities: Findings and Implications for Personnel Selection and Theories of Job Performance," *Journal of Applied Psychology* 78 (1993): 679–703; W. J. Camara and D. L. Schneider, "Integrity Tests: Facts and Unresolved Issues," *American Psychologist* 49 (1994): 112–119; J. M. Collins and F. L. Schmidt, "Personality, Integrity, and White Collar Crime: A Construct Validity Study," *Personnel Psychology* 46 (1993): 295–311.

46 J. Mintz, "What Are They Hiding," *Across the Board* (July/August 2001): 34–38; W. G. Iacono and D. T. Lykken, "The Validity of the Lie Detector: Two Surveys of Scientific Opinion," *Journal of Applied Psychology* 82 (1997): 426–433; A. Mello, "Personality Tests and Privacy Rights," *HR Focus* (March 1996): 22–23.

47 J. A. Weekley and C. Jones, "Video-Based Situational Testing," *Personnel Psychology* 50 (1997): 25–49; J. B. Olson-Buchanan, F. Drasgow, P. J. Moberg,

A. D. Mead, P.A. Keenan, and M.A. Donovan, "Interactive Video Assessment of Conflict Resolution Skills," *Personnel Psychology* 51 (1998): 1–24.

48 N. Schmitt and A. Mills, "Traditional Tests and Job Simulations: Minority and Majority Performance and Test Validities," *Journal of Applied Psychology* 86(3) (2001): 451–458. For an extensive review of and guide to these tests, see L. P. Plumke, *A Short Guide to the Development of Work Sample and Performance Tests*, 2d ed. (Washington, DC: U.S. Office of Personnel Management, February 1980). Note the interchangeability of the terms *work sample* and *performance test*.

49 For a discussion of assessment center history and future trends, see B. T. Mayes, "Insights into the History and Future of Assessment Centers: An Interview with Dr. Douglas Bray and D. William Byham," *Journal of Social Behavior and Personality [Special Issue]* 12(5) (1997): 3–12.

50 B. T. Mayes, "Insights into the History and Future of Assessment Centers; D. Briscoe, "Assessment Centers: Cross-Cultural and Cross-National Issues," *Journal of Social Behavior and Personality* 12(5) (1997): 261–270; A. C. Spychalski, M. A. Quinnones, B. A. Gaugler, and K. Pohley, "A Survey of Assessment Center Practices in Organizations in the United States," *Personnel Psychology* 50 (1997): 71–90; J. N. Zall, "Assessment Centre Methods," in P. J. D. Drenth, H. Thierry, and C. J. DeWolff (eds.), *Handbook of Work and Organizational Psychology, Vol. 3: Personnel Psychology* (Basingstoke, UK: Taylor & Francis Press, 1998).

51 L. M. Donahue, D. M. Truxillo, J. M. Cornwell, and M. J. Gerrity, "Assessment Center Construct Validity and Behavioral Checklists," *Journal of Social Behavior and Personality* 12 (5) (1997): 85–108; B. B. Gaugler et al., "Meta-Analysis of Assessment Center Validity," *Journal of Applied Psychology* 72 (1987): 493–511.

52 D. R. Briscoe, "Assessment Centers: Cross-Cultural and Cross-National Issues."

53 C. C. Hoffman and G. C. Thornton III, "Examining Selection Utility Where Competing Predictors Differ in Adverse Impact," *Personnel Psychology* 50 (1997): 455–470.

54 B. P. Sunoo, "How Fun Flies at Southwest Airlines," *Personnel Journal* (June 1995): 62–71. For a detailed discussion of employment interviews, see R. W. Eder and M. M. Harris (eds.), *The Employment Interview Handbook* (Thousand Oaks, CA: Sage, 1999).

55 J. Burnett and S. J. Motowidlo, "Relations Between Different Sources of Information in the Structured Selection Interview," *Personnel Psychology* 51 (1998): 963–983; S. Strauss, J. Miles, and L. Levesque, "The Effects of Videoconference, Telephone, and Face-to-Face Media on Interviewer and Applicant Judgments in Employment Interviews" *Journal of Management* 27 (2001): 363–381.

56 R. W. Eder and M. M. Harris, *The Employment Interview Handbook* (London: Sage, 2000); E. D. Pulakos and N. Schmitt, "Experience-Based and Situational Interview Questions: Studies of Validity," *Personnel Psychology* 48 (1995): 289–308; M. A. Campion, D. K. Palmer, and J. E. Campion, "A Review of Structure in the Selection Interview," *Personnel Psychology* 50 (1997): 655–702; M. A. McDaniel et al., "The Validity of Employment Interviews: A Comprehensive Review and Meta-Analysis," *Journal of Applied Psychology* 79 (1994): 599–616; S. J. Motowidlo et al., "Studies of the Structured Behavioral Interview," *Journal of Applied Psychology* 77 (1992): 571–587.

57 A. I. Huffcutt and P. L. Roth, "Racial Group Difference in Employment Interview Evaluations," *Journal of Applied Psychology* 83 (1998): 179–189.

58 For more discussion of these, see S. D. Maurer, C. Sue-Chan, and G. P. Latham, "The Situational Interview," in R. W. Eder and M. M. Harris (eds.), *The Employment Interview Handbook* (Thousand Oaks, CA: Sage, 1999): 159–178; S. J. Motowidlo, "Asking About Past Behavior Versus Hypothetical Behavior," in R. W. Eder and M. M. Harris (eds.), *The Employment Interview Handbook* (Thousand Oaks, CA: Sage, 1999): 179–190.

59 L. Fogli and K. Whitney, "Assessing and Changing Managers for New Organizational Roles," in R. Jeanneret and R. Silzer (eds.), *Individual Psychological Assessment: Predicting Behavior in Organizational Settings* (San Francisco: Jossey-Bass, 1998).

60 G. Nyfield and H. Baron, "Cultural Context in Adapting Selection Practices Across Borders," in J. F. Kehoe (ed.), *Managing Selection in Changing Organizations: Human Resource Strategies* (San Francisco: Jossey-Bass, 2000): 242–268; A. M. Ryan, L. McFarland, H. Baron and R. Page, "An International Look at Selection Practices: Nation and Culture as Explanations for Variability in Practice," *Personnel Psychology* 52 (1999): 359–391.

61 T. Lin, G. H. Dobbins, and J. L. Farh, "A Field Study of Race and Age Similarity Effects on Interview Ratings in Conventional and Situational Interviews," *Journal of Applied Psychology* 77 (1992): 363–371; see also A. J. Prewett-Livingston, H. S. Field, J. G. Veres III, and P. M. Lewis, "Effects of Interview Ratings in a Situational Panel Interview," *Journal of Applied Psychology* 81 (1996): 178–186.

62 E. D. Pulakos, N. Schmitt, D. Whitney, and M. Smith, "Individual Differences in Interviewer Ratings: The Impact of Standardization, Consensus Discussion, and Sampling Error on the Validity of a Structured Interview," *Personnel Psychology* 49 (1996): 85–102.

63 D. M. Cable and T. A. Judge, "Interviewers' Perceptions of Person-Organization Fit and Organizational Selection Decisions," *Journal of Applied Psychology* 82 (1997): 546–561; C. M. Marlowe, S. Schneider, and C. E. Nelson, "Gender and Attractiveness Biases in Hiring Decisions: Are More Experienced Managers Less Biased?" *Journal of Applied Psychology* 81 (1996): 11–21.

64 C. K. Stevens, "Antecedents of Interview Interactions, Interviewers' Ratings, and Applicants' Reactions," *Personnel Psychology* 51 (1998): 55–85.

65 H. J. Bernardin and R. W. Beatty, *Performance Appraisal: Assessing Human Behavior at Work* (Boston: Kent, 1984), 258–260; W. C. Borman, "Format and Training Effects on Rating Accuracy Using Behavior Scales," *Journal of Applied Psychology* 3 (1979): 103–115.

66 "EEOC Issues Final Guidance for Medical Examinations Under ADA," *Fair Employment Practices Guidelines* (January 25, 1996): 5; "Past Accommodations Do Not Always Determine the Future," *Fair Employment Practices Guidelines* 436 (July 25, 1997): 1; A. Bryant, "Seeing What Really Matters," *New York Times* (December 24, 1997): D1, D4; R. R. Faden and N. E. Kass, "Genetic Screening Technology: Ethical Issues in Access to Tests by Employers and Health Insurance Companies," *Journal of Social Issues* 49 (1993): 75–88; Society for Human Resource Management, "EEOC Issues Guidelines on ADA for Contingent Workers," *HR News* (February 2001): 5.

67 For a detailed discussion of providing accommodation for people with disabilities, see W. J. Campbell and M. E. Reilly, "Accommodations for Persons with Disabilities," in J. F. Kehoe (ed.), *Managing Selection in Changing Organizations: Human Resource Strategies* (San Francisco: Jossey-Bass, 2000): 319–367.

68 D. D. Hatch and J. E. Hall, "Disabled Must Compete on Equal Basis," *Workforce* (2000): 109.

69 S. Bates, "Science Friction," *HR Magazine* (July 2001): 34–44; "Growing Sophistication in Genetic Testing Raises Insurance and ADA Concerns," *Fair Employment Practices Guidelines* (February 10, 1998): 5; S. Greengard, "Genetic Testing: Should You Be Afraid? It's No Joke," *Workforce* (July 1997): 38–44; N. Wade, "Testing Genes to Save a Life Without Costing You a Job," *New York Times* (September 14, 1997): 5.

70 S. Overman, "Splitting Hairs," *HR Magazine* (August 1999): 43–48.

71 T. Bauer, C. Maertz, M. Dolen, and M. A. Campion, "Longitudinal Assessment of Applicant Reaction to Employment Testing and Test Outcome Feedback," *Journal of Applied Psychology* 83(6) (1999): 892–903; A. M. Ryan and R. Ployhart, "Applicants' Perceptions of Selection Procedures and Decisions: A Critical Review and Agenda for the Future," *Journal of Management* 26(3) (2000): 565–606.

72 R. Ployhart, A. M. Ryan, and M. A. Bennett, "Explanations for Selection Decisions: Applicants' Reactions to Informational and Sensitivity Features of Explanations," *Journal of Applied Psychology* 84(1) (1999): 87–106; for an excellent review of this literature, see Rynes, "Who's Selecting Whom?"; S. L. Rynes, "Recruitment, Job Choice, and Post-Hire Consequences: A Call for New Research Directions," in M. D. Dunnette and L. M. Hough (eds.), *Handbook of Industrial and Organizational Psychology*, vol. 2 (Palo Alto, CA: Consulting Psychologists Press, 1991): 399–444.

73 T. Bauer, D. M. Truxillo, R. Sanchez, J. Craig, P. Ferrara, and M. A. Campion, "Applicant Reactions to Selection: Development of the Selection Procedural Justice Scale," *Personnel Psychology* 54 (2001): 387–420; R. D. Arvey and P. R. Sackett, "Fairness in Selection: Current Developments and Perspectives," in N. Schmitt and W. C. Borman (eds.), *Personnel Selection in Organizations* (San Francisco: Jossey-Bass, 1993): 171–202; see D. Chan, N. Schmitt, J. M. Sacco, and R. P. DeShon, "Understanding Pretest and Posttest Reaction to Cognitive Ability and Personality Tests," *Journal of Applied Psychology* 83 (1998): 471–485.

74 See R. D. Arvey and P. R. Sackett, "Fairness in Selection: Current Developments and Perspectives," in N. Schmitt and W. C. Borman (eds.), *Personnel Selection in Organizations* (San Franciso: Jossey-Bass, 1993): 171–202; S. W. Gilliland, "Effects of Procedural and Distributive Justice on Reactions to a Selection System," *Journal of Applied Psychology* 79 (1994): 691–701.

75 D. Chan, "Racial Subgroup Difference in Predictive Validity Perceptions on Personality and Cognitive Ability Tests," *Journal of Applied Psychology* 82 (1997): 311–320; D. Chan, N. Schmitt, R. P. DeShon, C. S. Clause, and K. Delbridge, "Reactions to Cognitive Ability Tests: The Relationships between Race, Test Performance, Face Validity Perceptions, and Test-Taking Motivation," *Journal of Applied Psychology* 82 (1997): 300–310.

76 See Rynes, "Who's Selecting Whom?"

77 R. Thompson, "Marriott HR Exec Speaks About Successes, Challenges of His Job," *HR News* (December 1999): 1–2, 37.

78 W. F. Cascio, "Reconciling Economic and Social Objectives in Personnel Selection: Impact of Alternative Decision Rules," *New Approaches to Employee Management: Fairness in Employee Selection* 1 (1992): 61–86; M. E. Baehr et al., "Proactively Balancing the Validity and Legal Compliance of Personal Background Measures in Personnel Management," *Journal of Business and Psychology* 8 (Spring 1994): 345–354; S. E. Maxwell and R. D. Arvey, "The Search for Predictors with High Validity and Low Adverse Impact: Compatible or Incompatible Goals?" *Journal of Applied Psychology* 78 (1993): 433–437.

79 L. Micco, "California Bans Employment Bias Based on Genetic Testing," *HR News* (August 1998): 13.

80 For an excellent discussion of legal issues, see J. C. Sharf and D. P. Jones, "Employment Risk Management," in J. F. Kehoe (ed.), *Managing Selection in Changing Organizations: Human Resource Strategies* (San Francisco: Jossey-Bass, 2000): 271–318.

81 To learn more about how subtle discrimination can limit opportunities for women to develop their international competencies, see K. Tyler, "Don't Fence Her In," *HR Magazine* (March 2001): 70–77; [Research Report] *Passport to Opportunity: U.S. Women in Global Business* (New York: Catalyst, 2000).

82 For discussions about how the design of selection procedures can affect adverse impact, see R. P. DeShon, M. R. Smith, D. Chan, and N. Schmitt, "Can Racial Difference in Cognitive Test Performance Be Reduced by Presenting Problems in a Social Context?" *Journal of Applied Psychology* 83 (1998): 438–451; K. Hattrup, J. Rock, and C. Scalia, "The Effects of Varying Conceptualizations of Job Performance on Adverse Impact, Minority Hiring, and Predicted Performance," *Journal of Applied Psychology* 82 (1997): 656–664; P. R. Sackett and J. E. Ellington, "The Effects of Forming Multi-Predictor Composites on Group Differences and Adverse Impact," *Personnel Psychology* 50 (1997): 707–722.

83 For other methods, see S. B. Morris and R. E. Lobsenz, "Significance Tests and Confidence Intervals for Adverse Impact Ratios," *Personnel Psychology* 53 (2000): 89–111.

84 W. Honan, "Felicia Shpritzer Dies at 87; Broke Police Gender Barrier," *New York Times* (December 31, 2000): 30; K. Tyler, "Don't Fence Her In," *HR Magazine* (March 2001): 70–77; J. Ledvinka and V. G. Scarpello, *Federal Regulations in Personnel and Human Resource Management* (Boston: PWS-Kent, 1990).

85 "Age Bias in Germany," *Fair Employment Practices Guidelines* (December 17, 1992): 145.

86 R. Kopp, *The Rice Paper Ceiling: Breaking Through Japanese Corporate Culture* (New York: Stone Bridge Press, 1994).

87 K. Ferguson, "Cisco High," *Business Week* (June 5, 2000): 102–104; C. Joinson, "HR's Seat: On the Selection Committee," *HR Magazine* (April 2000): 83–90; J. Martin, "So, You Want to Work for the Best …" *Fortune* (January 12, 1998): 77-78.

88 For example, see L. M. Graves and G. N. Powell, "The Effect of Sex Similarity on Recruiters' Evaluations of Actual Applicants: A Test of the Similarity-Attraction Paradigm," *Personnel Psychology* 48 (1995): 85–97.

89 J. R. Fulkerson, "Assessment Across Cultures," in R. R. Jeanneret and R. Silzer (eds.), *Individual Psychological Assessment* (San Francisco: Jossey-Bass, 1998): 330–362; D. Greising, *I'd Like the World to Buy a Coke: The Life and Leadership of Roberto Goizueta* (New York: Wiley, 1998); P. Sellers, "Where Coke Goes From Here," *Fortune* (October 13, 1997): 88–91; J. Huey, "In Search of Roberto's Secret Formula," *Fortune* (December 29, 1997): 230–234; G. Collins, "Left Alone at the Food Fight," *New York Times* (July 16, 1997): D1, D4; L. Bongiorno and S. Anderson, "Fiddling with the Formula at Pepsi," *Business Week* (October 14, 1996): 42; P. Sellers, "Pepsico's New Generation," *Fortune* (April 1, 1996): 110–118; P. Sellers, "Pepsi Opens a Second Front," *Fortune* (August 8, 1994): 70–75. P. Cappelli and A. Crocker-Hefter, *Distinctive Human Resources Are the Core Competencies of Firms*, Report No. R117 Q00011-91 (Washington, DC: U.S. Department of Education, 1994).

CHAPTER

9

TRAINING AND DEVELOPING A COMPETITIVE WORKFORCE

" At Toyota, we have a really tough time finding good people. Training is important. " [1]

Jim Wiseman
President of External Affairs
Toyota Motor Manufacturing North America

MANAGING THROUGH STRATEGIC PARTNERSHIPS

Trident

Based in Webster, New York, Trident Precision Manufacturing fabricates sheet metal for customers such as Xerox, Kodak, and IBM. The company seemed to be humming along back in the late 1980s. Customers were happy and profits were good. But employees were leaving the company at a brisk pace. "The irony of it all was that people were leaving for as little as a nickel [more] down the street," recalled April Lusk, the company's total quality manager. CEO Nick Juskiw knew there must be a better way. After attending a Xerox presentation titled "Leadership Through Quality," Juskiw ended up spearheading the company's total quality approach. Within 10 years, Trident was awarded the Malcolm Baldrige National Quality Award. The company attributes much of its success to a clear vision that focused on improving their approach to managing their human resources.

When the top executives began analyzing the company's weaknesses, they realized that they needed to start valuing employees more. A decade ago, Trident's managers didn't care who they hired so long as they were breathing and could do the job. The approach clearly wasn't working. Far too many products came off the line with major defects that required them to be redone completely. A change in the corporate culture was needed. Their informal motto seemed to sum up the problem: "We make it nice because we make it twice."

Top management officially recognized the importance of having truly committed employees when they identified their five key business drivers:

- Supplier partnerships
- Operational performance
- Customer satisfaction
- Shareholder value
- Employee satisfaction

Changes in the way new employees were selected could contribute to improved performance, but only somewhat. The company wasn't prepared to fire everyone and start over from scratch—so, besides being more selective in its hiring, it needed to improve the performance of current employees.

To achieve its goal of completely reshaping the corporate culture would require a major investment in education and training. It set as a goal delivering a 25-hour quality training course to every employee. In addition to basic problem solving and communication skills, employees learned to read blueprints and solve problems using trigonometry. During the past decade, Trident has spent 4.7 percent of its payroll costs on training—more than three times as much as the industry average.

Trident's investment in training has brought handsome returns. In one year, employees typically make over 2,000 process improvement suggestions, of which about 98 percent are implemented. Defects dropped from 3 percent to .007 percent. Turnover dropped from 41 percent to 3.5 percent, creating enormous savings due to reduced recruitment and selection costs. And, according to recent surveys, over 90 percent of employees report being satisfied with their work.[2]

TRAINING AND DEVELOPMENT PRACTICES WITHIN THE INTEGRATED HR SYSTEM

In the preceding chapters, we have emphasized the importance of considering HR practices as a complex system of interrelated activities. At Trident, training not only dramatically improved performance, it also reduced turnover, which in turn reduced future recruitment needs.

Basic Terminology

As is true for other HR practices, the phrase "training and development" refers to a large set of closely related activities. In general, an organization's training and development practices are its *intentional* efforts to improve current and future performance by helping employees acquire the skills, knowledge, and attitudes required of a competitive workforce.[3]

Training. More specifically, **training** refers to improving competencies needed today or very soon. Usually, the main objective of training is to improve performance in a specific job by increasing employees' skills and knowledge. Depending on an organization's recruitment and selection practices, new hires may have insufficient skills and require training before being placed in a job. For other employees, technological changes and job redesign may create the need for new job skills. Another reason that employees may need new skills or knowledge is that they have been transferred or promoted. Most training for job knowledge and skills is completed in a matter of hours or days. Trident's 25-hour course in quality management is a typical example.

Development. In comparison, **development** refers to activities intended to improve competencies over a longer period of time. The major objective of development is to prepare the workforce for roles they may have in the future. While development activities may improve performance in one's current job, that is not typically the objective. In fact, a common approach to development is giving people "stretch" assignments. When employees are given stretch assignments, often the expectation is that performance may not be optimal but a great deal of valuable learning will occur that should prove useful in the future. For this reason, development activities often are referred to as "career development" or "leadership development."

> **FAST FACT**
>
> According to a five-year study of 20,000 managers in 40 organizations, continuous personal and professional development is a key characteristic of executives who make a positive difference in their organizations.

Socialization. Closely related to training and development are an organization's **socialization** practices. Upon entry into a new job or a new organization, all employees initially need to "learn the ropes." The major objective of socialization practices is teaching employees about the organization's history, culture, and management practices. Through socialization, new employees learn how things are done in the new environment, including things they can't find written in any policy-and-procedures manual.[4] Intentional efforts to socialize employees usually occur near the time of initial hiring, but merger and acquisition activity in the firm as well as other major changes may stimulate socialization efforts at other times as well.

The activities of socializing, training, and developing are so closely related that it is difficult, and perhaps impossible, to make a clear distinction among them. Instead, the entire system of activities usually is referred to simply as "training and development" (T&D). U.S. corporations spend an estimated $60 billion annually on formal employee training and development programs that use an estimated 1.5 billion hours of time for the more than 56 million employees who participate.[5]

Learning Organizations and Knowledge Management

As described in Chapter 5, in recent years, some companies have elevated the importance of learning and related activities, recognizing them as potential sources of sustained competitive advantage. Organizations that strive to make learning an activity that occurs in many ways every day throughout all parts of the organization have been referred to as learning organizations.

To support their learning agenda, companies such as Booz-Allen and Hamilton Consulting, Siemens, Andersen, KMPG, and many others have adopted various types of knowledge management technology. Knowledge management is about making sure that knowledge from employees, teams, and units within an organization is captured, remembered, stored, and shared with others—which is the essence of a learning organization.

Knowledge management technologies provide software that makes it possible for people to share knowledge electronically. The systems, which usually operate on the organization's intranet, can capture and distribute "soft" knowledge as well as quantitative data. For example, employees might enter narrative information about their successes and failures during a project. Or they might provide information about contacts, potential customers, and environmental trends. Typically, knowledge management software also organizes the stored knowledge and provides a means to search and retrieve it using key words that reflect the everyday language and jargon used in a specific organization. To help ensure that a company's knowledge management technology is fully integrated with other learning activities—including traditional training and development programs—many learning organizations have created a position titled Chief Learning Officer or Chief Knowledge Officer responsible for knowledge management.

For knowledge management technology to facilitate learning, employees must be willing to share their knowledge and experiences; and they must be willing to use the ideas and knowledge of others. Neither of these is automatic. As is true for all of the training and development opportunities employers provide, a variety of other practices should be used to encourage, support, and reward the learning process. Managers need to reward employees for sharing their knowledge so that others can benefit. They also need to reward employees for using information and knowledge that are in a common stored database, the knowledge management library.[6]

Links to Other HR Activities

The objectives of specific training and development activities vary greatly, as will become apparent in this chapter. The differing objectives, in turn, often determine which other aspects of the HR system should be more tightly integrated with a particular training and development activity. Clearly, if the objective is socializing new hires, the training activity should be coordinated with recruitment activities. Because training for new hires often includes a discussion of important company policies, the content of the training is likely to reflect the company's entire set of HR practices. Disney begins the socialization process during recruitment as a way to discourage applicants who may not fit the corporate culture. To be sure everyone knows what to expect, one of the first steps in the hiring process involves showing applicants a video that details dress codes and rules of grooming and discipline. After they are hired, an eight-hour orientation program teaches them about the company's history, philosophy, and standards for customer service.

When the objective of training is improving job performance, the training should be designed using job analysis information about what is required to do the work. If the objective is developing employees for future promotion and advancement, the activities should be aligned with the selection criteria used when hiring people into those higher-level positions. If the objective of training is to create a culture change, it may be appropriate to link performance evaluations and rewards to completion of the training.

Exhibit 9.1 provides a general overview of training and development activities, and their relationships to other HR activities. Because there are so many possible objectives of training and development, all of the other areas

ex 9.1 Components of Training and Development within an Integrated HR System

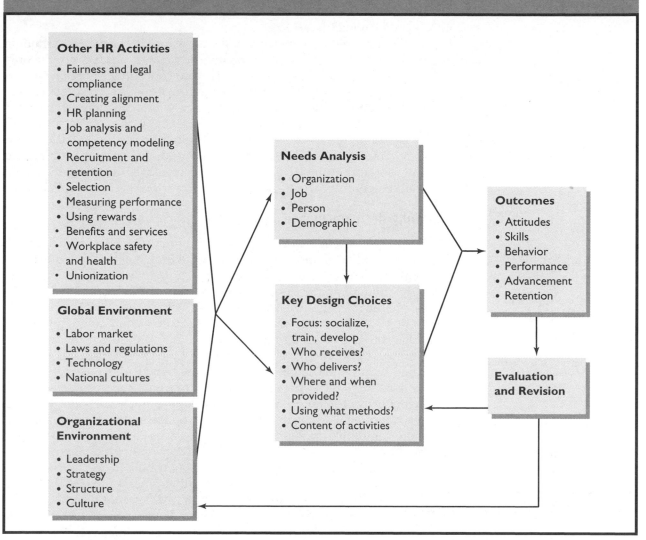

of HR activities are shown in the exhibit. Note, however, that any particular training or development program is likely to require very close alignment with only a few other HR activities.

THE STRATEGIC IMPORTANCE OF TRAINING AND DEVELOPMENT

The best competitors are using training and development practices to improve the ability of the workforce to implement their overall strategy. In the case of Trident, the strategy called for excellent quality at a low cost. Adopting a total quality management philosophy, in turn, required investing in training in order to ensure operational success. Often, changes in company strategy mean that senior managers need to adopt new leadership behavior and acquire new business

FAST FACT

Gillette invests $125 million annually in employee training.

knowledge. This was illustrated with the example of Weyerhaeuser, described in Chapter 5. In some of these cases, the need for socialization, training, and development can be immediate; in others, future needs can be anticipated and planned.[7]

Improving the competence of the workforce is one way that training and development can create a competitive advantage, but it is not the only way. Training and development activities also contribute to organizational success in less direct ways. For example, they can provide shared experiences that promote understanding among employees with many different histories and so help speed the development of organizational cohesiveness and employee commitment. Training and development activities also are a means for employers to address employees' needs. By offering training and development opportunities, employers help employees develop their own personal competitive advantage and ensure their long-term employability.

Improving Recruitment and Retention

Chapter 7 described in detail the strategic importance of being able to attract and retain qualified employees. You may recall from that discussion that one common source of employee dissatisfaction is the lack of career advancement opportunities that some employers provide. For most employees, making a significant career move involves taking a job that requires competencies not needed in their current job. How can employees acquire these competencies? One way is by seeking out educational opportunities on their own—for example, by attending classes at night or on weekends. But a more appealing way for most people is through participation in training and development activities offered by their employer. Many people seek out employers who provide training and development activities that facilitate career advancement. When they receive such opportunities, they are likely to feel more committed to their organization and are less likely to leave (see Exhibit 7.10).

Effective socialization activities also contribute to employee loyalty. Companies that have perfected the socialization process include IBM, Wal-Mart, Procter & Gamble (P&G), and Andersen. Often, the socialization process begins before the employee is hired.[8] At Procter & Gamble, for example, an elite cadre of line managers trained in interviewing skills probes applicants for entry-level positions in brand management, for qualities such as the "ability to turn out high volumes of excellent work." Through the interviewers' questions, applicants begin to learn about the organization's culture. Only after successfully completing at least two interviews and a test of general knowledge are applicants flown to P&G headquarters in Cincinnati, Ohio, where they endure a day-long series of interviews. These interviews are two-way communications that continue the socialization process at the same time that selection decisions are being made. If applicants pass the extensive screening process, they then confront a series of rigorous job experiences calculated to induce humility and openness to new ways of doing things. Typically, this phase of socialization involves long hours of work in a pressure cooker environment. Throughout this phase, new employees learn transcendent company values and organizational folklore, including the importance of product quality and stories about the dedication and commitment of employees long since retired. Intense socialization such as this increases employees' commitment

> **FAST FACT**
>
> Andersen provides employees with an average of 135 hours of training per year.

to the success of the company. Commitment, in turn, translates into a greater willingness to work long hours, less absenteeism, and lower turnover rates.

Improving Performance

A major purpose of training is to enhance the ability of employees to perform their jobs at peak levels. Such training is a routine activity in many companies. In highly competitive industries, training for immediate performance improvement is particularly important to organizations with stagnant or declining rates of productivity or customer satisfaction. Training for performance improvement is also important to organizations that are rapidly incorporating new technologies and, consequently, increasing the likelihood of employee obsolescence. A merger or acquisition is another event that may make training needs more salient, as is expansion into global markets.

Improving Service. Sometimes it takes a lot of feedback from customers before a company realizes the need for training. This was the situation at Quebecor World. Over a period of several years, it had been following a strategy of offering excellent quality at a low price, while growing through a series of acquisitions. But competition in the printing industry was tough, and eventually Quebecor realized that high-quality work at a low price wasn't enough. Customers wanted more. The feature "Managing Globalization: Training Improves Competitiveness for Quebecor World," describes how this company used training both to address customers' demands for better service and later to bring coherence to a fragmented corporate culture.[9]

Training for Customers. Increasingly, training activities are crossing organizational boundaries. Besides training their own workforce, many organizations help their customers train and develop *their* workforces. Siemens USA—one of the world's leading manufacturers of high-technology equipment—conducts a variety of training programs to meet the special needs of customers and their markets. On-the-job training for customers ensures that all the capabilities of the company's technologically advanced systems are fully utilized, and all their benefits are fully realized. When Chesterton, a company that makes sealing devices, developed a training program for its sales force, it never intended to offer it to customers. But the course proved to be very effective within the company, even among managers who initially thought it was unnecessary. Before long, Chesterton realized the training could also benefit customers by educating them in the uses and operation of their new equipment. Chesterton doesn't give the training away, however; it prefers using it to generate additional revenue.[10]

Productivity. With their longer-term focus, development activities may have a less immediate impact on the bottom line, but this does not mean they are any less valuable. When a Finnish mining and metals conglomerate bought the American Brass Factory in Buffalo, New York, company officials believed that development activities for plant employees would eventually improve the plant's productivity. The plant is one of the largest copper and brass rolling mills in the United States, making everything from buttons to ammunition shell casings to cell phone components. Until a few years ago, the blue-collar workforce understood little about their industry or how world economic conditions affected their daily lives. Many were openly

"We were hearing from our customers that our people in our plants were so different that each plant was like a different company. We needed continuity."

Marc Shapiro
Senior Vice President
Quebecor World

356   Chapter 9

MANAGING GLOBALIZATION

Training Improves Competitiveness for Quebecor World

Based in Montreal, Quebecor World is the world's largest printing company, with 160 plants in 40 countries. Back in 1998, it was losing hundreds of thousands of dollars annually due to poor customer service. Following a year-long assessment of company needs, improved customer service was identified as a top strategic priority. To remedy this and other problems, Quebecor World University was formed. Initially, the firm's customer service and account reps were trained in how to better understand customers' needs, use account management skills, and create a team-based, customer-oriented culture. The complete program included three 3-day sessions, spaced out over several weeks. To drive home the strategic importance of the training program, a senior manager or president from one of the nine business divisions was present to kick off each session, explaining the company's goals and expectations. At the end of

the training, senior managers return to listen to the participants present what they've learned and how they intend to apply it back on the job.

A year after Quebecor University began, Quebecor World merged with World Color Press. Following the merger, additional training was offered to blend these two cultures, as well as to address cultural issues that the company had not attended to in previous years as it acquired several other companies. Like the training to improve customer service, the new program adhered to three key principles for training at the company:

- Make it unique and challenging, so people want to participate.
- Involve senior management to reinforce the training goals.
- Contribute to Quebecor World's competitive advantage.

hostile toward the new foreign owners. In a long-term effort to change attitudes and improve productivity, the company began an unusual educational effort. Instructors from a local university taught about the impact of technology on the workplace, the dynamics of international competition, manufacturing costs in developing economies, how to read income statements, and the factors that influence the pricing of commodities. During the first year of the development effort, courses were offered around-the-clock so employees on all three shifts could attend. Subsequently, the plant has offered the courses every three years. In addition, management holds quarterly meetings for all 850 employees. Topics for discussion include plant operations, market conditions, and investments in equipment. According to Outokumpu president Warren Bartel, the effects of the education show. "The questions—about pricing, competition, and customers—get better every year," he says.[11]

FAST FACT

In a given year, nearly 50 percent of Hilton's hotel reservation staff will turn over. The figure is close to 150 percent at its largest call centers. Each newly hired person needs to be trained.

New Technology. New technologies account for much of the enhanced levels of productivity achieved in recent years. But new technology seldom can be introduced without also providing training in how to use it. At Gillette, significant training was needed when the company introduced the new technology it used to produce the MACH3 razor, and similar scenarios are repeated in manufacturing firms every month. The need for training in new technologies is not limited to manufacturers, however. When Hilton Hotels adopted a new reservation system called HILSTAR, it had to train 5,000 reservation agents around the world how to use it. Seeing an opportunity, Hilton folded several other training components into the program it developed to train employees using the new technology. These included professional service skills, safety training required by OSHA, and the company's harassment-free workplace guidelines.[12]

Legal Compliance and Protection

For some jobs in some industries, federal regulations require employers to provide training. OSHA, the Food and Drug Administration, and the Federal Aviation Administration are examples of agencies that monitor and enforce training requirements. In many other industries, such as financial services and real estate, employees must have a license or be certified to hold particular jobs. When licenses and certification are required, employers may wish to provide the needed training as part of their staffing strategy.

Recent Supreme Court may spur employers to provide training even when it is not required. Exhibit 9.2 summarizes several principles that employers should follow to meet the Court's standards for appropriate anti-discrimination training.[13] In *Kolstad v. American Dental Association*, the Court stated that an employer could escape liability for punitive damages if it established that an employee's conduct violated the company's equal employment policies. In two other cases, the Court established that an employer may not be held liable for discriminatory behavior by its employees if it can show that (a) it acted rea-

ex 9.2 Antidiscrimination Training Principles

The following principles are suggested by statements included in several recent court rulings. These principles represent the suggestions of an informed legal expert. They are not formal regulatory guidelines.

Training Objectives

- Inform employees of their rights, duties, and responsibilities regarding nondiscriminatory behavior.
- Create a sense of accountability and shared responsibility for creating a harassment-free workplace.

Who to Train?

- All employees should be trained, with additional training for supervisors to ensure they understand their duties and responsibilities.

When to Train?

- Upon hiring and periodically (e.g., annually) thereafter. Additional training may be appropriate if a complaint is filed.

Course Content

- Communicate the company policy, which should include a statement prohibiting all forms of harassment, and describe disciplinary action, procedures for reporting incidents of harassment, safeguards to prevent retaliation against those who report such incidents, and assurance of confidentiality.
- The legal meaning of harassment should be explained, and employees should be taught which behaviors constitute harassment. Practical examples should be discussed.
- The negative consequences of workplace discrimination and harassment should be explained. In addition to legal issues, explain the negative effects on morale and productivity.
- Supervisors should receive additional training. It should inform them of their duties and explain that the standards for their behavior are more stringent. Disrespectful behavior by rank-and-file employees may not be unlawful, while the same behavior by a supervisor is clearly illegal.

Documentation

- In order to provide protection against a lawsuit, keep records of all of the above information. It may also be useful for employees to sign a document acknowledging that they completed the training.
- Treat nondiscrimination training as you would other training for required skills. Require it as a condition of employment.

sonably to prevent the behavior, and (b) the victim acted unreasonably by not using the company's available procedures for preventing harm. Companies that can prove they offered training to inform employees of their policies and procedures should be able to defend themselves.

Mergers and Acquisitions

Following mergers and acquisitions, training that focuses on socializing employees into a new culture is probably the most common. But promoting cultural harmony need not be the only objective of postmerger training. Retaining key talent is another objective that post-merger training may serve.

When Gates Energy Products purchased a battery division from GE, the company's managers worried about how difficult it might be to integrate the plant into their existing company culture. According to Robin Kane, an HR manager at Gates, "the GE management philosophy was very strong, and deeply embedded in each manager, through extensive training and leadership classes at GE's corporate university." At Gates, on the other hand, managers had received only informal training. This caused Gates managers to worry that the experienced GE managers would abandon the division, choosing instead to seek other employment within GE. Retaining the managerial talent was a key strategic issue that Gates needed to address in order for its acquisition to pay off. Kane attacked the problem by developing a training program that emphasized the need for trust and teamwork among managers in the merged facilities. Gates wanted GE managers to see that their expertise was needed and appreciated. The company also wanted to convince these managers that they could continue to grow and develop if they remained with Gates. The training seemed to work. Turnover was low among the managers who participated, and their feedback indicated that they learned just as much from the Gates training as they had at GE.[14]

THE HR TRIAD

Training and development activities can be very expensive, requiring both time and money. Much of the expense is due to employees taking time off from work to participate. Perhaps the most important role of top-level executives is recognizing the value of training investments and supporting these activities. Most U.S. companies invest much less in training than do their competitors in other regions of the world. A study of 70 auto assembly plants from 24 companies in 17 countries showed that newly hired production workers in U.S.-owned plants received an average of only about 40 hours of training during their first six months on the job. That compares with an average of about 300 hours for similar workers in plants owned by citizens of Japan and about 260 hours for similar workers in plants headquartered in the newly industrialized countries of Korea, Mexico, Taiwan, and Brazil.[15] As organizations begin to embrace a philosophy of continuous learning and improvement, more active participation in the design and delivery of the organization's training system by all stakeholders is seen as both desirable and necessary. The feature "The HR Triad: Roles and Responsibilities in Training and Development" shows some activities for the line manager, the HR professional, and the employee.

FAST FACT

In a recent survey, senior executives said that the top HR issues facing their companies are these:
- Leadership development
- Motivational pay
- Training and development of their workforce

Roles and Responsibilities in Training and Development
THE HR TRIAD

Line Managers	HR Professionals	Employees
• Cooperate with HR professionals in identifying the implications of business plans for training and development. • Participate in the delivery of training and development programs. • Work with employees to determine their individual training and development needs. • Support employees' participation in training and development opportunities and reinforce the transfer of newly learned behaviors to the job. • Do much of on-the-job socialization and training. • Participate in efforts to assess the effectiveness of training and development activities.	• Identify training and development needs in cooperation with line managers. • Assist employees in identifying their individual training and development needs. • Communicate with employees regarding training and development opportunities and the consequences of participating in them. • Develop and administer training and development activities. • Train the line managers and employees in how to train and develop employees. • Evaluate the effectiveness of training and development activities.	• Identify their own training and development needs with HR professionals and line managers. • Accept responsibility for learning about training and development opportunities. • Consider employment opportunities from the perspective of the potential for personal learning and development. • Actively participate in training and development opportunities. • Assist with the training and development of coworkers. • Participate in efforts to assess the effectiveness of training and development activities.

Managers

Besides providing the financial resources and time needed for training and development, managers can improve the effectiveness of their organization's efforts by participating as trainers, coaches, and mentors. Without top management involvement and commitment, the major focus of an organization is likely to be on other activities. This is particularly true in organizations that focus on short-term goals and getting immediate results; this situation allows too little time to wait for the benefits of training and development. Top managers at Motorola, Dell, Microsoft, GE, GM, Coca-Cola, Gillette, The Ritz-Carlton, the Four Seasons, and PepsiCo began to emphasize training and development at the same time they recognized that they had to develop their people and businesses in order to be effective.[16]

Employees

The effectiveness of an organization's training system requires the support and cooperation of all employees in the system—top management's support alone isn't sufficient. For example, self-managed teams often take responsibility for training their own members.[17] Although most employees aren't actively involved in designing and delivering training systems, most organizations depend heavily on employees' seeking opportunities to use the available system to their advantage. For example, many companies sponsor informal events designed to provide employees opportunities to meet other people in the company, develop informal networks and support groups, and even establish mentoring relationships. Formal activities may also be offered

"My main job was developing talent. I was a gardener providing water and other nourishment to our top 750 people."

Jack Welch
Former Chairman and CEO
General Electric

to employees on a voluntary basis. Career-planning workshops, tuition reimbursement for job-related course work, and support for attending professional conferences are often available. By participating in such activities, employees facilitate their own socialization into the organization and potentially reap longer-term benefits such as greater income, job satisfaction, and a better sense of personal identity.[18] Research indicates that these opportunities are more likely to be used by employees who acknowledge their own needs for improvement and have developed a specific career plan.[19]

HR Professionals

HR professionals usually are heavily involved in the design of the training and development system and the delivery of formal training programs. As this chapter will explain, there is a vast array of training techniques available to employers and new technologies continually increase the possibilities. HR professionals take responsibility for identifying the objectives to be achieved through training and development and then choose or design training and development activities that are appropriate, given the objectives. In the best organizations, HR professionals also ensure that investments in training and development result in the desired outcomes.

DETERMINING TRAINING AND DEVELOPMENT NEEDS

Most often training is offered on the basis of need—to rectify skill deficiencies, to provide employees with job-specific competencies, to prepare employees for future roles they may be given, and so on.[20] Sometimes, however, employees receive training and development for reasons other than need. In some organizations, attendance at an executive training program serves as a reward for past performance. In other organizations, participation in training programs is a ritual that signals to newly promoted employees as well as to members of their former work groups that a change in status has occurred (e.g., a rank-and-file employee is now a manager).

Although training and development can serve these other purposes, a formal needs assessment is a vital part of a training system.[21] The four components of the needs assessment process are detailed in Exhibit 9.3.[22]

Organizational Needs Analysis

"We already had a sense that career-development . . . was an issue. The survey really threw it in our faces, and made us realize we had to do something about it."

Jeff Brown
Assistant Vice President
USA Bank

Organizational needs analysis begins with an assessment of the short- and long-term strategy and strategic business objectives of the company. This step is essentially the same as organizational assessment, described in Chapter 5, except that the focus is specifically on identifying the implications of the assessment for future training and development activities. The organizational needs analysis should result in the development of a clear statement of the goals to be achieved by the organization's training and development activities. At USA Bank, for example, it was the results of an employee survey that led the company to conclude that it needed to improve its career development activities. The survey, which was conducted following a merger, revealed that employees felt pessimistic about their future prospects at the company. The company's Opportunity Knocks program was subsequently developed to respond to the concerns employees had expressed.[23]

An organizational needs analysis may also include an assessment of the organization's current climate for training. A **supportive training climate**

ex 9.3 Four Components of Needs Assessment

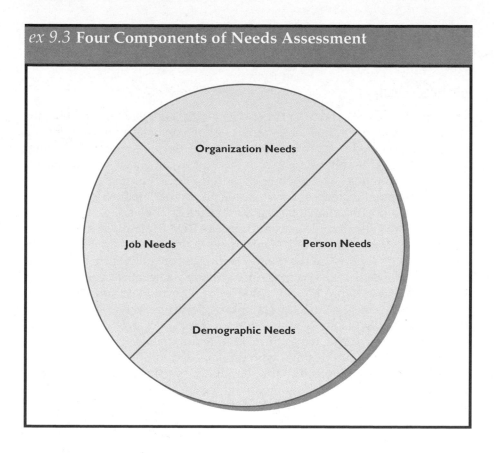

improves the chances that employees will successfully transfer what they learn from training programs to the job. Some indicators of a supportive training climate are the following:

- Incentives are offered to encourage employees to participate in T&D activities.
- Managers make it easy for their direct reports to attend T&D programs.
- Employees encourage each other to practice newly learned skills, and do not ridicule each other.
- Employees who successfully use their new competencies are recognized and rewarded with special assignments and promotions.
- There are no hidden punishments for participating in T&D (e.g., T&D activities are not scheduled to conflict with other important events; participation doesn't limit access to overtime pay).
- Managers and others who are effective providers of T&D are recognized and rewarded.

These conditions are most likely to be found in learning organizations.[24]

Finally, the organizational needs analysis should identify the available resources and any constraints that need to be considered when designing T&D programs and activities. Can employees be taken off their jobs to participate in training? If so, for how long? Will training needs differ across locations—for example, in different states or different countries? If computer-based technology is to be used to deliver T&D, do employees have access to the specific technology they will need? By addressing such questions, an organizational needs analysis can help ensure that T&D activities are practical in a specific context.

Job Needs Analysis

A **job needs analysis** identifies the specific skills, knowledge, and behavior needed in present or future jobs. A thorough job analysis with competency modeling, discussed in Chapter 6, provides the information required for job needs analysis. If training is to be provided for existing jobs, traditional job analysis and competency modeling is appropriate. If training and development are intended to address future needs, future-oriented job analysis and competency modeling should be used for the needs analysis.

Before Gillette could introduce its MACH3 triple-blade razor to the public, it needed to introduce its employees to the new machines that they would be using to produce the razor. The process of conducting the organization and job needs analysis began approximately a year before the razor hit the shelves. The HR director assembled a cross-functional team with representatives from HR, manufacturing, and engineering. Their charge was to identify the skilled-labor requirements for mechanics and operators and assess the current workforce against these requirements. The exercise provided a picture of the skills that would be needed to operate sophisticated control systems, automated parts handling systems, pneumatics, and hydraulics. It also alerted the company to the increased level of team skills that would be required by the new manufacturing system. Based on the experiences of many companies, Exhibit 9.4 profiles the competencies needed for employees in a team-oriented, total quality, modern manufacturing plant.[25] Within the year, Gillette employees had completed some 20,000 hours of required training—enough to guarantee a successful launch of the company's new product.[26]

Person Needs Analysis

After information about the job has been collected, the analysis shifts to the person. A **person needs analysis** identifies gaps between a person's current capabilities and those identified as necessary or desirable. Person needs analysis can be either broad or narrow in scope. The broader approach compares actual performance with the minimum acceptable standards of performance and can be used to determine training needs for the current job. The narrower approach compares an evaluation of employee proficiency on each required skill dimension with the proficiency level required for each skill. This approach is useful for identifying development needs for future jobs that will require a specific skill. Whether the focus is on performance of the job as a whole or on particular skill dimensions, several different approaches can be used to identify the training needs of individuals.[27]

Output Measures. Performance data (e.g., productivity, accidents, and customer complaints), as well as performance appraisal ratings, can provide evidence of performance deficiencies. Person needs analysis can also consist of work sample and job knowledge tests that measure performance capability and knowledge. Major advantages of such measures are that

- they can be selected according to their strategic importance,
- they often are easily quantified, and

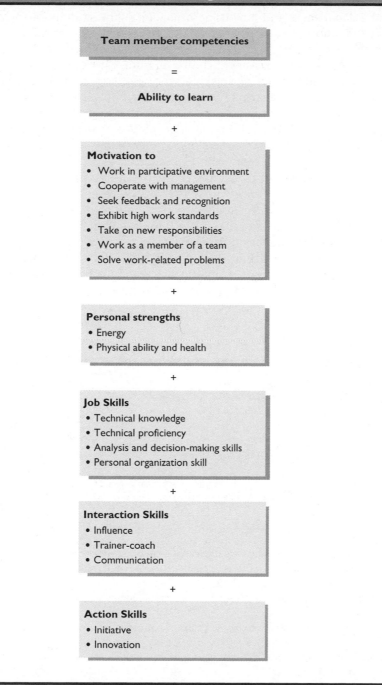

ex 9.4 **Team Member Competencies for Employees in a Total Quality Manufacturing Plant**

Team member competencies

=

Ability to learn

+

Motivation to
- Work in participative environment
- Cooperate with management
- Seek feedback and recognition
- Exhibit high work standards
- Take on new responsibilities
- Work as a member of a team
- Solve work-related problems

+

Personal strengths
- Energy
- Physical ability and health

+

Job Skills
- Technical knowledge
- Technical proficiency
- Analysis and decision-making skills
- Personal organization skill

+

Interaction Skills
- Influence
- Trainer-coach
- Communication

+

Action Skills
- Initiative
- Innovation

- when they show improvements, the value of training investments is readily apparent.

A major disadvantage is that such indicators reflect the past and may not be useful for anticipating future needs.

Self-Assessed Training Needs. The self-assessment of training needs is growing in popularity. At Motorola, for example, top managers require the employee and his or her supervisor to identify what the business needs are for the department and the business, as well as the skill needs and deficiencies of the individual. Many major U.S. firms allow managers to nominate themselves to attend short-term or company-sponsored training or education programs. Self-assessment can be as informal as posting a list of company-sponsored courses and asking who wants to attend, or as formal as conducting surveys regarding training needs.

"People instinctively want to learn."

Kent C. Nelson
Former Chairman and CEO
UPS

Surveys and worksheets are convenient tools for self-assessment.[28] At Colgate-Palmolive, high-potential employees are expected to conduct a self-assessment and use it to develop a career plan.[29] The components of this development activity are shown in Exhibit 9.5.

Self-assessment is premised on the assumption that employees, more than anyone else, are aware of their weaknesses and performance deficiencies. One drawback of self-assessment is that individuals may not be aware of their weaknesses, especially if the organization does a poor job of providing honest feedback during performance appraisals. Also, employees may be fearful of revealing their weaknesses and so may not accurately report their training needs. In both cases, reliance on self-assessment may result in individuals not receiving education that's necessary for them to

---

ex 9.5 Components of a Tool Kit for Individual Development

I. Overview of the Individual Development Process

- Assess individual competencies and values
- Define personal strengths, development needs, and options for career growth
- Identify developmental actions
- Craft individual development plan
- Meet with manager to decide a course of action (based on preceding analysis)
- Accept the challenge of implementing the plan

II. Worksheets for Individual Assessment

- Competency assessment worksheet: assesses strengths and weaknesses for a specified set of competencies
- Personal values survey: assesses preferences for types of work environments, work relationships, work tasks, lifestyle needs, and personal needs
- Development activities chart: describes on-the-job and off-the-job learning opportunities that can be used to develop key competencies
- Global training grid: lists all formal training programs offered by the company and explains how each relates to key competencies
- Individual development plan: developed by the employee, this describes specific development goals and a course of action to be taken to achieve the goals

III. Defining and Understanding Global Competencies

- This section of the tool kit is like a dictionary. It lists all the competencies considered to be important for various types of jobs throughout the company and describes the meaning of each competency. This section serves as a reference guide and encourages people across the company to use a common set of terms when discussing competencies and career development issues.

remain current in their fields. On the other hand, employees who are forced to attend programs that they believe they don't need or that don't meet their personal training needs are likely to become dissatisfied with training and lack the motivation to learn and transfer competencies.

Career Planning Discussions. To assist employees in identifying their strengths and weaknesses, some companies make sure that managers hold career planning discussions with employees. At Eli Lilly, "high potentials" discuss their strengths and weaknesses with their managers. Prior to the conversation, the manager holds conversations with other executives to get their input. The manager then communicates the key points in those discussions. Afterward, the employee prepares a career plan and reviews it with his or her manager.[30]

Attitude Surveys. Attitude surveys completed by a supervisor's subordinates or by customers or by both also can provide information on training needs for the supervisor. For example, when one supervisor receives low scores regarding her or his fairness in treating subordinates, compared with other supervisors in the organization, the supervisor may need training in that area.[31] Similarly, if the customers of a certain unit seem to be particularly dissatisfied compared with other customers, training may be needed in that unit. Thus, customer surveys can serve a dual role: providing information to management about service and pinpointing employee deficiencies.

Demographic Needs Analysis

The objective of a **demographic needs analysis** is to determine the training needs of specific populations of workers. Demographic needs analysis can also be used to assess whether all employees are given equal access to growth experiences and developmental challenges, which are known to be useful on-the-job methods for promoting skill development. For example, one large study of managers compared the developmental career experiences of men and women. In general, men were more likely to have been assigned to jobs that presented difficult task-related challenges (e.g., operation start-ups and "fix-it" assignments). Women were more likely to have been assigned to jobs that presented challenges caused by obstacles to performance (e.g., a difficult boss or a lack of support from top management).[32] If a company finds demographic differences such as these, it might conclude that an intervention is needed to assure men and women equal access to valuable developmental challenges—and equal exposure to debilitating obstacles. These demographic differences may also suggest the need for diversity training.

At Delta Airlines, an analysis of the demographic characteristics of its pilots led to a decision to focus training efforts on women and members of ethnic minority groups. Currently, only about 1 percent of Delta's pilots and flight engineers are minorities and only 5 percent are women. At the same time, Delta and other airlines have found it is increasingly difficult to recruit pilots, due in part to the smaller pool of military pilots available. To bolster the ranks of minority applicants, Delta recently awarded a grant worth $1.65 million to Western Michigan University to pay for flight training for women and minorities.[33]

SETTING UP A TRAINING AND DEVELOPMENT SYSTEM

FAST FACT

On average, wages and salaries paid to full- and part-time training staff account for 45% of all training expenditures.

Successful implementation of training and development depends on offering the right programs under the right conditions. Before moving to a discussion of issues to consider when designing programs, we consider first the importance of creating the right conditions.

Creating the Right Conditions

"You have to hit the executives over the head at the very beginning of an education program and somehow cause failure. Get them to realize they don't know how to do it and confront them with feedback that says, 'you're not as good as you think you are.'"

Jim Moore
Director of Workforce Planning and Development
Sun Microsystems

To guide the design of training and development systems, Personnel Decisions International (PDI), a large and reputable HR consulting firm, developed a simple framework with five components. By attending to these components, organizations can ensure that the right conditions are in place. Both the design of the T&D activities and a consideration of how T&D activities are integrated into the HR system contribute to ensuring that these components are in place.[34]

The five components identified by PDI are as follows:

- **Insight:** People need to know what it is they need to learn. Employees gain insight into what they need by participating in person needs analysis and receiving feedback about their current skills and competencies.
- **Motivation:** People need to be motivated by internal or external means to put in the required effort. Some employees may be eager to learn simply for the sake of learning, but most are likely to be more motivated when they believe that participation in training and development activities will lead to positive benefits. Thus, motivation to participate can be increased by integrating training and development activities with other facets of the HR system (e.g., performance measurement, promotions, incentives, and rewards), as described above.[35]

Even when explicit rewards are not directly tied to participation in training and development activities, motivation can be enhanced by clearly communicating that participation is valued by the organization. One way to send the message is by involving everyone—including top-level managers. When everyone has been targeted as needing training, as is often the case with major corporate change efforts, top managers often participate first, and other employee groups are scheduled in hierarchical sequence.

- **New Skills and Knowledge:** People must be shown how to acquire the needed competencies. The design and content of the training and development activities themselves address this issue. Alternatives to consider when developing this content are described in detail later in this chapter.
- **Real-World Practice:** Programs that engage participants in realistic activities improve the likelihood that they will apply their learning. Similarly, when at their jobs, employees should have the opportunity to practice what is learned. The program design can ensure that training and development activities are realistic, but as already noted, managers and peers share responsibility for encouraging people to practice applying their new competencies while on the job. The discussion in this chapter about choosing a learning format illustrates the advantages of some formats for providing real-world experience.
- **Accountability:** Of course, the responsibility for applying new learnings is not carried by managers and peers alone. All employees need to feel personally accountable for using what they learned. Here again, other facets of the HR system become relevant. The most direct approach to holding employees accountable is to include assessments of improvement as part of the performance appraisal process.

Who Provides?

Another key question to be addressed when setting up training and development activities is, Who provides the required guidance? Training and development activities may be provided by any of several people, including

> **FAST FACT**
>
> Many line managers spend up to 50% of their time giving and clarifying instructions to new employees.

- supervisors and other managers,
- a coworker,
- an internal or external subject matter expert, and
- the employee.

Who is selected to teach often depends on where the program is held and what skills or competencies are taught. A basic organizational orientation is usually handled by a member of the HR staff. Literacy and technical competencies are usually taught by the immediate job supervisor or a coworker, although technical competencies may also be taught by internal or external subject matter experts. Interpersonal, conceptual, and integrative competencies for management are often taught by training specialists, university professors, or consultants.

Supervisors and Other Managers. In many organizations, on-the-job training is the only form of training offered. In these circumstances, supervisors almost always are the providers of whatever training employees receive. For development activities that involve mentoring, supervisors and managers are appropriate also, as they are in the best position to assess their employees' career needs. Furthermore, because of their position in the organization, supervisors and managers are accessible to employees and have control over the employees' work assignments, which facilitates their effectiveness.[36]

Supervisors and managers may also be effective as trainers in off-the-job programs. Indeed, some CEOs consider training to be one of their

"Nobody wants to work for someone they can't learn from."

Steve Jobs
CEO
Pixar

more important duties. Craig Tysdal, CEO of NetSolve Inc., is one example. Tysdal realizes that the people joining his company come from a variety of backgrounds and are accustomed to interacting with customers in different ways. "You have to get the whole team on the same page quickly," he says. To be sure everyone gets the same message, Tysdal participates as a trainer in the monthly training sessions for new hires. His approach is to tell stories and give examples that illustrate what excellent customer service means in his company—and the negative effects of failing to provide it. The fact that the CEO considers their training to be so important sends a strong message to new employees.[37]

Coworkers. When Disney trains new hires, the company's message is delivered by some of the best "cast" members in the company. Dressed in full costume, they show through example how to create happiness—the most important aspect of their role. After the initial training session, new cast members are paired with experienced employees for 16 to 38 hours of "paired-training," which is essentially one-on-one coaching. As the Disney example illustrates, coworkers can be very effective trainers. Often, coworkers are more knowledgeable about the work than anyone else.

Coworkers also play an important role in many management development programs, which commonly bring together employees from different parts of the organization for several days of training. Participants in such programs often report that the most valuable learning occurs through conversations with their colleagues. Furthermore, exposure to the perspectives of colleagues working around the world helps employees develop more sophisticated "mental maps" of how business is conducted in different locations. Exxon's Global Leadership Workshop takes advantage of this phenomenon. Twice a year, about 30 participants from around the world participate in the workshop. IBM uses a similar model for its eight-day global leadership training program.[38]

Clearly, coworkers can be valuable providers of training. Nevertheless, their effectiveness as trainers or mentors should not be assumed. A concern with relying on coworkers as trainers is that they may not be able to instruct others. They may also teach others their own shortcuts rather than correct procedures. If coworkers are to be trainers, they should receive instruction on how to train and should be given sufficient time on the job to work with trainees.

FAST FACT

On average, payments to outside vendors account for 25% of all training expenditures.

Experts. Subject matter experts may not be familiar with procedures in a specific organizational culture. As a result, they may be respected for their expertise but mistrusted because they aren't members of the work group. Still, if no one in the immediate work environment possesses the knowledge needed, or if large numbers of individuals need to be trained, the only option may be to hire experts. Experts who are expressive when delivering training and well organized are especially effective.[39]

Employee. Self-paced instruction is also an option. With the growing popularity of computer-based training, self-paced instruction is also becoming more common. Trainees benefit from this method by learning at a speed that maximizes retention. However, if they aren't given incentives to complete the instruction in a specified period of time, they may place it on the back burner.

DEVELOPING PROGRAM CONTENT

A training program must have content congruent with its learning objectives. Three types of learning objectives that the organization may be concerned about are cognitive knowledge, skill-based outcomes, and affective outcomes.[40]

> **FAST FACT**
>
> Beck Group provides employees with a laptop and/or an Internet connection to support individual learning.

Cognitive Knowledge

Cognitive knowledge includes the information people have available to themselves (what they know), the way they organize this information, and their strategies for using this information. Of these, what people know is by far the type of cognitive knowledge that most organizations try to address through training systems.

Company Policies and Practices. **Orientation programs** are frequently used for building cognitive knowledge. These programs brief new employees on benefit programs and options, advise them of rules and regulations, and explain the policies and practices of the organization.

Typically, orientation programs inform new employees about equal employment opportunity practices, safety regulations, work times, coffee breaks, the structure and history of the organization, and perhaps the products or services of the organization. Usually, they don't tell employees about the politics of the organization—for example, that it may be merging with another company, that an extensive layoff may occur, or even that the organization may soon be going out of business.

Basic Knowledge and the Three Rs. Increasingly, organizations are concerned about cognitive knowledge of a more basic nature: the three Rs (reading, writing, and arithmetic). Training programs designed to correct basic skill deficiencies in grammar, mathematics, safety, reading, listening, and writing are still necessary in today's organization. In particular, total quality management requires basic math and statistical knowledge that many high school graduates haven't mastered. Statistical tools are fundamental to W. Edwards Deming's approach to quality, which is improvement by the numbers. The feature "Managing Change: Improving Quality at The Ritz-Carlton" shows how this applies to service-oriented firms.[41]

> **FAST FACT**
>
> The Ritz-Carlton Hotel Company's pervasive training approach is based on its rallying phrase, "We Are Ladies and Gentlemen Serving Ladies and Gentlemen."

The need for training in basic language skills is also growing as U.S. employers hire increasing numbers of recent immigrants. For employers who hire large numbers of immigrants, providing language training is an effective way to reduce errors and improve job performance, while at the same time enhancing employee loyalty. Louis Avignone is president of Uncle Wally's, a muffin manufacturer in New York. His company offers English as a Second Language (ESL) training as a solution to the tight labor market. "It is very difficult to find qualified manufacturing people on Long Island," he explained. Because he offers ESL classes, however, "I don't have to hire [only] somebody who speaks English. I can take somebody who is conscientious and hard-working and can't speak the language."[42]

The Big Picture. Employees striving for or currently in managerial positions may need knowledge about the organizational structure, the organization's products and services, the organization's business strategies, and

> *"What sets us apart is that we train people to be merchants. We let them see all the numbers so they know exactly how they're doing within the store and within the company; they know their cost, their markup, their overhead, and their profit."*
>
> Sam Walton
> Past Chairman and Founder
> Wal-Mart Stores

MANAGING CHANGE

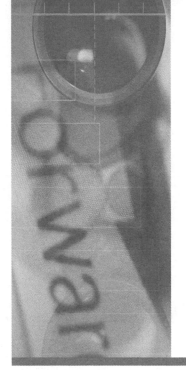

Improving Quality at The Ritz-Carlton

It seems clear that the training function in The Ritz-Carlton Hotels has earned a healthy respect as the major force in quality improvement. While this may be partly—or even mostly—a result of being in the hospitality industry, the company still serves as an interesting model for close quality/training interface.

At a time when the company had no training positions in the hotels, one of the regional vice presidents implemented a training position and presented the plan for it to the president of the company. Since then, training has been a critical part of the organization, with a training manager in each hotel. Like many other organizations, The Ritz-Carlton's training program has undergone changes as a result of the company's journey into quality management. Its decision to go for the Baldrige Award for Quality had a particularly big influence. "The Baldrige application forced us to take a look at business process design in a way that we had never really done before," explained one manager. "Right now we are looking at cycle time, such as how long it takes from the moment guests walk in, until they're in their rooms. We've done customer surveys and are studying eighteen cycle times throughout our systems to see where we are as an organization. Then we will be able to judge how to decrease cycle times by taking out the nonvalued elements from jobs. Using the

check-in example, if we want to reduce cycle time to two minutes, we may discover we can have the desk receptionists skip an explanation of the in-room bar service and have the bell staff do that job. Of course, then we must retrain." Another way that the quality initiatives feed into training is through the hotels' feedback forms. Internal Defect Reports are to be completed by any employee when systems go wrong.

"When the information is compiled and supplied to the hotel's general manager (GM) on a daily basis, it gives the manager a valuable look at what actually went on in the hotel that day. Otherwise a GM might look at the dollar and guest numbers and think, 'Well, we had a bang up day.' This way, the GM can get all the information about the hotel. And the beauty of the system is that it's tracked over time. So, something like the problem of the availability of nonsmoking rooms could be pinpointed to a certain pattern. Maybe there's a shortage only on Sundays because that's when the rooms are taken out for deep cleaning. The objective in all our work with the defect reports is to better serve guests and internal customers. The more problems we can detect, the fewer there are to be seen by guests." And, of course, the more new processes put in place to detect problems, the more training employees need in order to use those new processes effectively.

changing conditions in the environment. Much of this type of knowledge is learned through standard job assignments as well as through temporary developmental learning experiences, such as serving on a task force or taking an overseas assignment. Adapting to complex and changing environments is often a responsibility for top and middle managers, and conceptual training helps such employees make new associations. Cognitive knowledge is at the heart of today's emphasis on creativity and entrepreneurship, and on making major changes in an organization's strategy, objectives, vision, and values at firms such as Microsoft, GE, The Ritz-Carlton, Dell, GM, Weyerhaeuser, and Southwest Airlines.

Skills

"Certification for a maid? Absolutely. 'Room attendants,' as we call them, have a most important job in our organization."

Debra Phillips
Training Manager and Quality Adviser
The Ritz-Carlton New York

Whereas cognitive knowledge is essentially inside the head, skills are evident in behaviors. Whereas cognitive learning often involves studying and attending to information, skill-based learning generally involves practicing desired behaviors, such as those that demonstrate technical and motor skills.

Owing to rapid changes in technology and the implementation of automated offices, and industrial and managerial systems, technological updating and skill building have become a major thrust in training.[43] Skills in communication, conducting performance appraisals, team building, leadership, and negotiation are also increasingly in demand. The development of interpersonal competencies is essential for lower- and middle-level managers as well as for employees who have direct contact with the public, such as sales associates. Can you describe your experiences with sales people? What are good ones and bad ones like?

Affective Outcomes

When the desired result of socialization, training, or developmental experiences is a change in motivation, attitudes, or values, or all three, the learning objectives of interest are affective outcomes. The Disney Company's orientation and training programs, described earlier, are clearly intended to influence the affect of cast members. They learn about the key Disney "product"—happiness—and their roles in helping to provide it.[44]

The objectives of building team spirit and socializing employees into the corporate culture aren't the only affective outcomes of a training system. In fact, training activities often are designed in part to develop employees' feelings of mastery and self-confidence. For example, mentoring programs not only provide information, they also provide the feedback and supportive encouragement that give employees confidence in their ability to take on new tasks and make decisions that might otherwise seem too risky. Self-confidence enhances task performance. This is a point not lost on athletes, their coaches, or sportscasters—nor, apparently, is it lost on the many companies now providing wilderness training. Although the evidence is sparse, testimonials and some research indicate that participating in outdoor group adventures boosts self-confidence.[45]

Training programs designed to enhance employees' emotional intelligence are another example of efforts that target affective outcomes. Emotional intelligence involves recognizing and regulating emotions in ourselves and in others. It includes self-awareness, self-management, social awareness, and relationship management. One objective of emotional intelligence training is to teach people techniques to deal with emotions in the workplace. For example, people who work in customer service jobs may benefit from training that teaches them to keep their emotions in check when dealing with customers who are upset and angry. For people in many other jobs that create stress, emotional intelligence training can help lower the experience of stress and may contribute to overall improved health.[46]

INTERNET RESOURCES   9.B

Setting Up a Training and Development System and Developing Program Content

At our Web site, http://jackson.swcollege.com/, you can:

1. Visit the Web site of the American Society for Training and Development, an association of T&D professionals, to learn about the resources available through this organization.

2. Learn more about corporate universities by visiting the Corporate University Xchange.

3. Learn more about the Center for Creative Leadership and the research it has done on leadership development. The Center for Creative Leadership works with companies to design custom training and development programs and offers many standardized leadership development programs for individuals.

4. Investigate the role of training and development activities in companies that are being proactive in their attempts to improve how they manage diversity.

CHOOSING THE PROGRAM FORMAT

Many different formats can be used for training and development activities. Three general categories of formats are on-the-job, on-site, but not on the job, and off-site. Choices about format may be constrained by the type of learning that's to occur—cognitive, skill based, or affective—as well as by cost and time considerations. Exhibit 9.6 summarizes the advantages and disadvantages of several learning formats.

e-Learning

Note that the three major categories of training and development formats do not depend on using a specific type of technology. Before the computer, film, and communications industries began to merge, the technology used was often what most clearly distinguished one training format from another. Today, however, technology makes it possible to combine many formats and deliver them as an integrated learning system that combines, for example, computer-based quizzes, video, interactive simulations, and so on. When such technologies are used for training and development, they often are referred to as **e-learning.** The major advantage of e-learning systems is their potential for speeding up communications within large corporations. A popular example of this is the use of video teleconferencing. Here employees in separate locations can see and talk to each other. A cost study conducted by Kodak estimates that a new product training program beamed by satellite to three cities costs $20,000. Kodak also estimated that it would cost five to six times that amount to send engineers and managers on the road to do the same training. More important, six weeks of training time is saved, which is invaluable in a competitive industry.[47] These are among the reasons GM gave for creating an alliance with Unext.com, an e-learning company, and encouraging its 88,000 salaried employees to take courses in marketing, finance, and e-business.[48] Exhibit 9.7 shows how widespread e-learning has become.[49]

> **FAST FACT**
>
> By 2004, companies are expected to spend more than $23 billion yearly on on-line corporate (e-learning) education, up from $6.3 billion in 2001.

On the Job

On-the-job training (OJT) occurs when employees learn their jobs under direct supervision. Trainees learn by observing experienced employees and by working with the actual materials, personnel, or machinery, or all three, that pertain to the job. An experienced employee trainer is expected to provide a favorable role model and to take time from regular job responsibilities to provide job-related instruction and guidance. Assuming the trainer works in the same area, the trainee receives immediate feedback about performance.

One advantage of OJT is that transfer of training is high. That is, because trainees learn job skills in the environment in which they will actually work, they readily apply these skills on the job. However, on-site training is appropriate only when a small number of individuals need to be trained and when the consequence of error is low. Also, the quality of the training hinges on the skill of the manager or lead employee conducting it.[50]

Apprenticeship Training, Internships, and Assistantships. A method for minimizing the disadvantages of on-the-job training is combining it with

ex 9.6 Advantages and Disadvantages of Several Learning Formats

TYPE OF PROGRAM	ADVANTAGES	DISADVANTAGES
On the Job		
e-learning and video tele-conferencing	• Brings employees together from many locations • Speeds up communications • May reduce costs	• Start-up and equipment costs are high • Requires adaptation to a new learning format • May be done on or off the job
Apprenticeship training	• Does not interfere with real job performance • Provides extensive training	• Takes a long time • Is expensive • May not be related to job
Internships and assistantships	• Facilitate transfer of learning • Give exposure to real job	• Are not really full jobs • Provide vicarious learning
Job rotation	• Gives exposure to many jobs • Allows real learning	• Involves no sense of full responsibility • Provides too short a stay in a job
Supervisory assistance and mentoring	• Is often informal • Is integrated into job • Is expensive	• Means effectiveness rests with the supervisor • May not be done by all supervisors
On-Site, but Not On the Job		
Corporate universities	• Tailored to company needs • Supports company vision and culture	• Can be costly • Requires skilled management
Programmed instruction on an intranet or the Internet	• Reduces travel costs • Can be just-in-time • Provides for individualized learning and feedback • Provides for fast learning	• Not appropriate for some skills • Is time-consuming to develop • Is cost-effective only for large groups • Often no support to assist when trainee faces learning problems
Interactive videos	• Convey consistent information to employees in diverse locations	• Costly to develop • Do not provide for individual feedback
Off the Job		
Formal courses	• Are inexpensive for many • Do not interfere with job	• Require verbal skills • Inhibit transfer of learning
Simulation	• Helps transfer of learning • Creates lifelike situations	• Cannot always duplicate real situations exactly • Costly to develop
Assessment centers and board games	• Provide a realistic job preview • Create lifelike situations	• Costly to develop • Take time to administer
Role-playing	• Is good for interpersonal skills • Gives insights into others	• Cannot create real situations exactly; is still playing
Sensitivity training	• Is good for self-awareness • Gives insights into others	• May not transfer to job • May not relate to job
Wilderness trips	• Can build teams • Can build self-esteem	• Costly to administer • Physically challenging

off-the-job training. Apprenticeship training, internships, and assistantships are based on this combination.

Apprenticeship training is mandatory for admission to many skilled trades, such as plumbing, electronics, and carpentry. These programs are formally defined by the U.S. Department of Labor's Bureau of Appren-

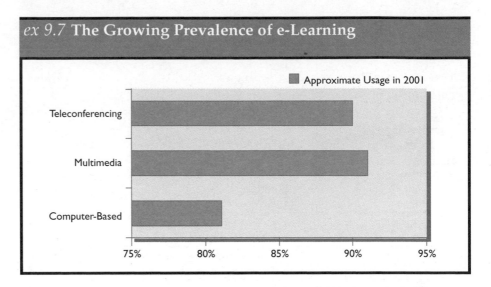

ex 9.7 The Growing Prevalence of e-Learning

ticeship and Training and involve a written agreement "providing for not less than 4,000 hours of reasonably continuous employment . . . and supplemented by a recommended minimum of 144 hours per year of related classroom instruction." The Equal Employment Opportunity Commission allows the 48,000 skilled trade (apprenticeship) training programs in the United States to exclude individuals aged 40 to 70, because these programs are part of the educational system aimed at youth.[51]

Somewhat less formalized and extensive are internship and assistantship programs. **Internships** are often part of an agreement between schools and colleges, and local organizations. As with apprenticeship training, individuals in these programs earn while they learn, but at a lower rate than that paid to full-time employees or master crafts workers. Internships are a source not only of training but also of realistic exposure to job and organizational conditions. Hewlett-Packard's internship program enables the company to evaluate college students and prepare them for future jobs.[52]

Assistantships involve full-time employment and expose an individual to a wide range of jobs. However, because the individual only assists other workers, the learning experience is often vicarious. This disadvantage is eliminated by programs that combine job or position rotation with active mentoring and career management.

Job Experiences. When development is the objective, employers may put people into jobs in order to facilitate their learning and development. **Job rotation programs** are used to expose employees to and train them in a variety of jobs and decision-making situations. Usually, job rotation programs rotate employees through jobs at a similar level of difficulty. The extent of training and long-run benefits may be limited, however, because employees aren't in a single job long enough to learn very much and may not be motivated to work hard because they know they will move on in the near future.

The philosophy of having employees learn while doing also underlies the use of **developmental job assignments.** However, with developmental job assignments, employees are placed in a new job that presents significantly more difficult new challenges. The assumption is that the process of learning to deal with the challenges will result in the employee developing new competencies. Components of a developmental job include

- Unfamiliar responsibilities
- Responsibility for creating change (e.g., to start something new, fix a problem, deal with problem employees)
- High levels of responsibility (e.g., high-stakes and high-visibility assignments; job involving many stakeholders, products, or units)
- Boundary-spanning requirements (e.g., working with important stakeholders outside the organization)
- Dealing with diversity (working with people from multiple cultures or demographic backgrounds)[53]

Supervisory Assistance and Mentoring. Often the most informal program of training and development is supervisory assistance or mentoring. **Supervisory assistance** is a regular part of the supervisor's job. It includes day-to-day coaching, counseling, and monitoring of workers on how to do the job and how to get along in the organization. The effectiveness of these techniques depends in part on whether the supervisor creates feelings of mutual confidence, provides opportunities for growth, and effectively delegates tasks.

Mentoring, in which an established employee guides the development of a less-experienced worker, or protégé, can increase employees' competencies, achievement, and understanding of the organization.[54] At AT&T, for example, protégés are usually chosen from among high-potential employees in middle or entry-level management. Each executive is encouraged to select two people to mentor and must decide how to develop the relationships. Usually, executives counsel their protégé on how to advance and network in the company, and they sometimes offer personal advice.

Coaching. For high-level executives and other employees who hold visible and somewhat unique jobs, traditional forms of on-the-job training are impractical. Yet, these employees often need to develop new competencies in order to be fully effective. In recent years, more and more executives have turned to personal **coaching** to address their training needs. A coach might sit in on a meeting to observe the employee in action and later provide feedback and guidance for how to improve interaction skills in the future. Most coaches also encourage their "trainees" to discuss difficult situations as they arise and work through alternative scenarios for dealing with those situations. Although coaching is rapidly growing in popularity, it's a relatively new technique and few guidelines are available to evaluate whether a potential coaching relationship is likely to succeed.[55] Nevertheless, the evidence of its effectiveness is beginning to accumulate.

An effective coaching program helps managers change themselves and, in the process, change their organizations. An excellent example of this is the feature "Managing Change: Improving Leadership at General Motors."[56]

> **FAST FACT**
>
> At American Express, a leadership competency model is used to set expectations and coach managers on key elements of leadership, including diversity.

On-Site, but Not On the Job

Training at the work site but not on the job is appropriate for required after-hours programs and for programs in which contact needs to be maintained with work units but OJT would be too distracting or harmful. It's also appropriate for

MANAGING CHANGE

Improving Leadership at General Motors

Bill Lovejoy, the general manager of the Service Parts Operations (SPO) division of General Motors, didn't believe that his division's employees were performing at their highest levels of productivity potential. Performing to their highest levels meant serving the needs of their customers, the GM dealers, AC Delco distributors, and other retailers, all folks who depend upon "having the right part at the right time at the right price."

To prove his point, Mr. Lovejoy brought in some of the division's customers to hear their views on the quality of the service SPO was delivering. In addition to hearing that the customers weren't satisfied, Lovejoy and his top management team read the results of a survey that SPO had participated in for warehousing and parts supplier companies: the results indicated that SPO came in 10th place out of 10 companies in their service provided. Lovejoy and his management team concluded that achieving higher levels of customer satisfaction and employee productivity would require better supervisory and leadership competencies. They hired the consulting firm of Development Dimensions International (DDI) to (1) assess the desired leadership competencies, including personal leadership characteristics, and communication and implementation competencies; (2) assess the level of competencies currently possessed by the SPO managers; (3) provide training; and (4) offer personal coaching. Although the SPO wanted to make changes affecting all 12,350 of its employees, it started by conducting a pilot program in a facility in Fort Worth, Texas.

To assess the effectiveness of the training and coaching intervention, SPO looked first at employee satisfaction measures. From these, they concluded that the culture had changed in the right direction. Lovejoy also wanted to know the impact of the training and coaching activities on the rest of the business, so the pilot location was compared with the rest of the locations on several measures:

1. scheduling attainment;
2. quality (errors per order line;
3. productivity (lines shipped per hour);
4. health and safety (recordable injuries per 200,000 hours worked; and
5. absenteeism.

The overall conclusion was that the Fort Worth facility improved its organization culture and its business performance during the time the leadership intervention was being implemented. Additional analysis indicated that that of the facility's 21 percent improvement in productivity during a three-year period, at least 30 percent could be attributed to the intervention. This represented approximately $1.2 million savings in its operating budget. To cost justify the intervention, management had estimated that the productivity improvement from the intervention would have to be 7 percent. Thus the leadership development intervention was regarded as a success and has since been expanded to the other facilities within SPO.

---

voluntary after-hours programs and for programs that update employees' competencies while allowing them to attend to their regular duties.

For example, when a major Northeast grocery store chain switched to computerized scanners, it faced the problem of training thousands of checkers spread out across three states. The cost of training them off-site was prohibitive. Yet management also was fearful about training employees on the job, lest their ineptitude offend customers. To solve the problem, the grocery chain developed a mobile training van that included a vestibule model of the latest scanning equipment. Checkers were trained on-site but off the job in the mobile unit. Once the basic skill of scanning was mastered, employees returned to the store, and the trainer remained on-site as a resource person. According to one store manager, the program was effective because employees could be trained rapidly and efficiently, yet no customers were lost owing to checker errors or slowness.

Corporate Universities and Executive Education Programs. A growing trend in the United States is the development of corporate universities that offer programs tailored to the needs of the company. **Corporate universities** focus on the education of employees and sometimes customers. McDonald's Hamburger University, begun in 1961, is among the oldest corporate universities. Started in a basement, the center now trains more than 2,500 students annually in the fine details of restaurant and franchise operations. General Electric, an advocate of training and development for years, has an up-to-date facility in Croton-on-Hudson, New York, that it uses for divisional and group training. Corporate universities have been developed by such diverse firms as AT&T, Ford, Arthur Andersen, General Motors, Motorola, United Airlines, Boeing, Kodak, Dell, and Harley-Davidson.[57] In fact, research suggests that 65 percent of all major firms offer some form of executive education. Today, many corporate colleges offer degrees, and hundreds of corporations offer courses leading to degrees. While not always the case, the executive programs at companies may be under the direction of the chief learning officer.[58]

Programmed Instruction. **Programmed instruction** is an old on-site training method that has recently become the foundation for many computer-based training programs. Here, the instructional material is broken down into "frames." Each frame represents a small component of the entire subject to be learned, and each frame must be learned successfully before the next one can be tackled.

An advantage of programmed instruction is that large numbers of employees can be trained simultaneously, with each learner free to explore the material at her or his own pace. In addition, it includes immediate and individualized feedback. Although the development of several authoring systems has eased the burden of developing programmed modules, instruction still must be carefully planned. It's estimated that 1 hour of programmed instruction requires 50 hours of development work. Consequently, this approach is effective only if canned programs (e.g., word processing and database tutorials) are used or if large numbers of employees are to be trained so that development costs for an original program can be justified. The use of intranets for delivering training makes widespread use of programmed instruction much more practical today than it was when it was first introduced several years ago.[59]

Interactive Video Training. **Interactive video training** combines the best features of programmed instruction with the best attributes of video. Interactive video programs provide a short video and narrative presentation and then require the trainee to respond to it. This sequence—packaged program, learner response, and more programmed instruction—provides for individualized learning. FedEx has a pay-for-knowledge program, which is based on interactive video training and job knowledge testing for its 35,000 customer-contact employees. Before couriers ever deliver a package, they receive at least three weeks of training. Because FedEx is constantly making changes or additions to its products and services, it also must continually update its training programs. Employees at hundreds of FedEx locations around the United States can readily access a 25-disk training curriculum, which covers topics such as customer etiquette and defensive driving. Customer-contact employees take a job knowledge test every six months; the company pays each employee for four hours of study and preparation and for two hours of test taking. The knowledge required to do well on the test is so job related that performance on the test essentially reflects performance on the job. As an incentive for employees to get serious about doing well on the test, the company links their compensation to performance on the test. Employees who excel in applying their knowledge to job performance become eligible for additional proficiency pay.

Off the Job

When the consequences of error are high, it's usually more appropriate to conduct training off the job. Most airline passengers would readily agree that it's preferable to train pilots in flight simulators rather than have them apprentice in the cockpit of a plane. Similarly, it's usually useful to have a bus driver practice on an obstacle course before taking to the roads with a load of schoolchildren.

Off-the-job training is also appropriate when complex competencies need to be mastered or when employees need to focus on specific interpersonal competencies that might not be apparent in the normal work environment. It's difficult to build a cohesive management work team when members of the team are constantly interrupted by telephone calls and subordinate inquiries. Team building is more likely to occur during a retreat, when team members have time to focus on establishing relationships.

> **FAST FACT**
>
> Ameritech Corporation puts executives to work for an afternoon in soup kitchens, housing projects, and AIDS clinics as team-building exercises.

However, the costs of off-the-job training are high. One cause for concern is that knowledge learned off the job may not transfer to the workplace. The issue of **transfer**—whether employees can readily apply the knowledge and skills learned during training to their work—is one of the most important to consider when choosing a format. Research has shown that the more dissimilar the training environment is to the actual work environment, the less likely trainees will be to apply what they learn to their jobs. For example, the transfer-of-knowledge problem is minimal when trainees work with machines that are comparable to the ones in their actual work environment. However, it may be difficult to apply teamwork competencies learned during a wilderness survival program to a management job in a large service organization.[60]

> **FAST FACT**
>
> Construction and real estate firm Beck Group reimburses workers $4,500 a year for outside courses.

Formal Courses. Formal courses can be directed either by the trainee—using programmed instruction, computer-assisted instruction, reading, and correspondence courses—or by others, as in formal classroom courses and lectures. Although many training programs use the lecture method because it efficiently and simultaneously conveys large amounts of information to large groups of people, it does have several drawbacks. Perhaps most importantly, except for cognitive knowledge and conceptual principles, the transfer of learning to the actual job is probably limited. Also, the lecture method does not permit individualized training based on individual differences in ability, interests, and personality.

> **FAST FACT**
>
> Boeing provides training for airline pilots in its flight simulators in St. Louis.

Simulation. **Simulation**, which presents situations that are similar to actual job conditions, is used for both managers and nonmanagers.[61] A common simulation technique for nonmanagers is the **vestibule method**, which simulates the environment of the individual's actual job. Because the environment isn't real, it's generally less hectic and more safe than the actual environment; as a consequence, trainees may have trouble adjusting from the training environment to the actual environment. The arguments for using a simulated environment are compelling: it reduces the possibility of customer dissatisfaction that can result from on-the-job training, it can reduce the frustration of the trainee, and it may save the organization a great deal of money because fewer training accidents occur (e.g., pilot training by all airlines is done in flight simulators). Not all organizations, even in the same industry, accept these arguments. Some banks, for example, train their tellers on the job, whereas others train them in a simulated bank environment.

Assessment Centers. Just as they are popular in managerial selection, assessment centers (described in Chapter 8) are an increasingly popular simulation technique for developing managers. Certain aspects of the assessment center, such as management games and in-basket exercises, are excellent for training.[62] When these are used for training purposes, however, it is essential that instructors help participants analyze what happened and what should have happened. The opportunity for improvement may be drastically reduced if the trainees are left to decide what to transfer from the games or exercises to the job.

Business Board Games. Companies are finding that it pays if all employees know how the company makes money, the difference between revenue and profit, and how much profit the company makes on each sale. In order to facilitate this learning, companies such as Prudential and Sears have created board games, similar in form and shape to *Monopoly*, that reveal the workings of the company. Employees actually play the game, and as they do, they learn about the company and how the company runs the business and makes a profit or loss.

Role-Playing and Sensitivity Training. Whereas simulation exercises may be useful for developing conceptual and problem-solving skills, two other types of training are used for developing human relations or process skills. Role-playing and sensitivity training develop managers' interpersonal insights—awareness of self and of others—for changing attitudes and for practicing human relations skills, such as leading or interviewing.

Role-playing generally focuses on understanding and managing relationships rather than facts. The essence of role-playing is to create a realistic situation, as in the case discussion method, and then have the trainees assume the parts of specific personalities in the situation. When the trainee does get into the role, the result is a greater sensitivity to the feelings and insights that are presented by the role.

In **sensitivity training**, individuals in an unstructured group exchange thoughts and feelings on the "here and now" rather than the "there and then." Although being in a sensitivity group often gives individuals insight into how and why they and others feel and act the way they do, critics claim that these results may not be beneficial because they are not directly transferable to the job.

Wilderness Trips and Outdoor Training. To increase employees' feelings about the here and now and raise their self-esteem, organizations sometimes use programs that involve physical feats of strength, endurance, and cooperation. These can be implemented on **wilderness trips** to the woods or mountains or water. Siemens, for example, dropped 60 managers from around the world onto the shores of Lake Starnberger, south of Munich, and

FAST FACT

Siemens uses outdoor programs to increase knowledge sharing.

gave them the task of building rafts using only logs, steel drums, pontoons, and rope. Among the rules for the exercise: No talking. The objective? To teach managers the importance of knowledge sharing. Back on the job, managers can earn bonuses for contributing their knowledge to ShareNet—the company's knowledge management software.[63]

Whereas many firms such as Siemens, General Electric, General Foods, Knight-Ridder, and Burger King use some variation of outdoor experiences in their management training with success, many others question the degree of transfer to the job that these experiences offer. Firms using outdoor experiences recognize this concern and thus articulate the link between the competencies developed in the experiences and the competencies needed by the managers on the job. They also are sensitive to employee differences in order to ensure that these experiences can be accommodated to an increasingly diverse workforce.[64]

INTERNET RESOURCES   9.C

Determining Program Format

At our Web site, http://jackson.swcollege.com/, you can:

1. Visit Sage Interactive to learn more about the computer-based training products (CBT).

2. Find out more about the wilderness training offered by Outward Bound.

3. Discover what you can learn at a distance using on-line education.

4. Experience an on-line demonstration to see what electronic learning courses are like.

MAXIMIZING LEARNING

"If, when holding a gun to an employee's head, he or she will perform, the problem isn't a training problem."

Alice Pescuric
Vice President
DDI

Even when a training technique is appropriate, learning may not take place if the experience isn't structured appropriately. Exhibit 9.8 details learning principles that increase the effectiveness of training.[65]

Setting the Stage for Learning

Before launching a training program, a trainer or manager needs to consider how information will be presented. In addition, he or she must consider the beliefs of trainees regarding task-specific competencies.[66]

Clear Instructions. If task instructions are unclear or imprecise, learning is hampered. Employees must know what is expected in order to perform as desired. Clear instructions establish appropriate behavioral expectations. Training expectations should be stated in specific terms. The conditions under which performance is or isn't expected should be identified, along with the behavior to be demonstrated.

To set the stage for desired performance, it's also useful to specify up front what the reward will be for performing as desired. Trainees are more likely to be motivated if they know that successful performance can lead to positive reinforcement (e.g., promotion, pay raise, or recognition) or can block the administration of negative reinforcement (e.g., supervisory criticism or firing).[67]

Behavioral Modeling. Even when instructions are clear, the desired behavior still may not occur if the trainee does not know how to perform it. This

ex 9.8 Learning Principles to Increase Training Effectiveness

Setting the Stage for Learning

1. Provide clear task instructions.
2. Model appropriate behavior.

Increasing Learning During Training

1. Provide for active participation.
2. Increase self-efficacy.
3. Match training techniques to trainees' self-efficacy.
4. Provide opportunities for enactive mastery.
5. Ensure specific, timely, diagnostic, and practical feedback.
6. Provide opportunities for trainees to practice new behaviors.

Maintaining Performance After Training

1. Develop learning points to assist knowledge retention.
2. Set specific goals.
3. Identify appropriate reinforcers.
4. Train significant others in how to reinforce behavior.
5. Teach trainees self-management skills.

Following Up on Training

1. Evaluate effectiveness.
2. Make revisions as needed.

problem can be overcome through **behavioral modeling**, which is a visual demonstration of desired behavior. The model can be a supervisor, coworker, or subject matter expert, and the demonstration can be live or videotaped. The important thing is to show employees what needs to be done before asking them to do it. Thus, models should show not only how to achieve desired outcomes but also how to overcome performance obstacles.

Increasing Learning During Training

Although employees should be responsible for their own learning, organizations can do much to facilitate this.

Active Participation. Individuals perform better if they're actively involved in the learning process. Organizational help in this area can range from encouraging active participation in classroom discussions to establishing a set of programs to assist managers in a major strategic change. The important point is to hook the individual on learning. Through active participation, individuals stay more alert and are more likely to feel confident.[68]

Self-Efficacy. Even with modeling, learning may not occur if people have feelings of low self-efficacy. **Self-efficacy** is a trainee's beliefs about a task-specific ability. If individuals dwell on their personal deficiencies relative to the task, potential difficulties may seem more formidable than they really are. On the other hand, people who have a strong sense of self-efficacy are likely to be motivated to overcome obstacles.[69]

Enactive Mastery. Self-efficacy increases when experiences fail to validate fears and when competencies acquired allow for mastery of once-threatening situations. This process is called **enactive mastery**.[70] To facilitate task mastery, trainers should arrange the subject matter so that trainees experience success. Whereas this may be easy when tasks are simple, it can be quite difficult when tasks are complex. Solutions include segmenting the task, shaping behavior, and setting proximal goals.

"Leaders by their actions, not by their words, establish a sense of justice in the organization."

Max De Pree
Former CEO
Herman Miller

Task segmentation involves breaking a complex task into smaller or simpler components. For some jobs (e.g., laboratory technician), the components (e.g., drawing blood, culturing a specimen, and running a blood chemistry machine) can be taught individually and in any order. For other jobs (e.g., engineer, chauffeur, and interviewer), segments must be taught sequentially because task B builds on task A and task C builds on task B.[71]

Shaping includes rewarding closer and closer approximations to desired behavior. For example, when managers are learning how to conduct a selection interview, they can be reinforced for making eye contact and for developing situational questions.

The setting of **proximal goals**, or intermediary goals, also increases mastery perceptions. Consider a software developer with an overall objective of developing a new word processing package. Proximal goals might include meeting a project specifications deadline, developing algorithms for fonts by a set deadline, developing an algorithm for formatting paragraphs, and so on. These proximal goals all lead to the attainment of the distal, or overall, objective.[72]

Feedback. For individuals to master new concepts and acquire new competencies, they must receive accurate diagnostic feedback about their performance. Feedback can be provided by a supervisor, coworkers, customers, computers, or the individual performing the task. It must be specific, timely, based on behavior and not personality, and practical. If a performance discrepancy exists, the feedback should be diagnostic and include instructions or modeling of how to perform better.[73] The topic of providing performance feedback is discussed in more detail in Chapter 11, where the focus is on performance evaluation. When studying that chapter, keep in mind that feedback is an important element of training and development.[74]

Practice. The goal of skill training is to ensure that desired behavior occurs not just one time but consistently. This is most likely to occur when trainees are able to practice and internalize standards of performance. Even mental practice appears to help improve performance.[75] Practicing the wrong behaviors is detrimental; therefore, practice must follow specific feedback.

For some jobs, tasks must be overlearned. Overlearning includes internalizing responses so that the trainee does not have to think consciously about behavior before responding. For example, if a plane is losing altitude rapidly, a pilot must know immediately how to respond. The pilot has no time to think about what should be done. The emergency routine must be second nature and internalized.

Maintaining Performance After Training

Following employees' exposure to socialization training, and development experiences, the environment needs to support the transfer of new behaviors to the job and their maintenance over time. The use of goals and reinforcers can improve performance following training.

Specific Goals. Without goals that are specific and measurable, people have little basis for judging how they're doing.[76] Specific goals for subsequent performance should be challenging but not so difficult as to be perceived as impossible. They also shouldn't be set too early in the learning process. The development of a specific action plan or contract is one approach to setting goals that relate to using what has been learned in the near future.

Reinforcers. Learning new behaviors is difficult and threatening. To ensure that trainees continue to demonstrate the skill they have learned, behavior must be reinforced. **Reinforcement** refers to a consequence that follows behavior. It can be positive (e.g., praise and financial rewards) or negative (e.g., "If you perform as desired, I will quit screaming at you"), but the consequence must be contingent on performance. Often supervisors and coworkers can be taught to reinforce desired changes. If a supervisor or coworker responds positively to a positive change in behavior, the frequency with which the new behavior will be displayed is likely to increase.

> **FAST FACT**
>
> The average Trident employee receives special recognition 10.6 times per year for behaviors that fit the culture.

Self-Reinforcement. Because it isn't always possible for significant others to reinforce an individual worker, a long-term objective should be to teach employees how to set their own goals and administer their own reinforcement. When people create self-incentives for their efforts, they're capable of making self-satisfaction contingent on their own performance. The challenge here is to ensure that personal goals are congruent with organizational goals, which leads to self-management.

TEAM TRAINING AND DEVELOPMENT

Management often rushes to form work teams without considering how the behaviors needed for effective teamwork differ from those needed for effective individual contributions. Team members may receive little or no training to ensure that they can perform the required tasks and achieve the goals set. NASA takes the opposite approach. Perhaps more than any other organization, NASA understands that training comes before effective teamwork. Before astronauts are sent into space to live in a community that relies heavily on teamwork for survival, NASA has them working together every day for a year or two in order to become a team. They share office space, spend countless hours together in flight simulators, and rehearse everything from stowing their flight suits to troubleshooting malfunctions. Formal training in procedures is part of the experience, but it isn't everything. NASA realizes that teamwork training also involves helping teammates get to know each other and develop confidence in each other.

Three main goals of most team training programs are to develop team cohesiveness, effective teamwork procedures, and work team leaders. For some teams, such as airline flight crews, team members may also need specialized training to ensure that they respond appropriately to rare and unexpected events, such as equipment failure, when lives are at risk.[77] Organizations that invest resources to train teams can increase both team and organizational effectiveness.[78]

Training to Develop Team Cohesiveness

Most organizations can't afford to give work team members a year of two of training before the teams begin working on their tasks. They look for quicker ways to achieve the same objectives that NASA has for its training program. To develop team cohesiveness, many organizations use

"Tomorrow's leader will be a team player who will seek to decentralize leadership and work towards creating an entire organization of leaders. This is a pattern the survey found to be true across all industries and geographic borders."

Windle Priem
CEO and President
Korn/Ferry International

experientially based adventure training. Evart Glass Plant, a division of the DaimlerChrysler Corporation, involved its entire 250-person staff in such training as a way to prepare its employees for working in self-managed work teams. Union members and managers trained side by side during employees' normal work hours. A hi-lo driver (similar to a forklift operator), a maintenance person, a shift supervisor, and a receptionist found themselves working together as a team throughout their training. After each activity, trainers led a discussion about the experience to identify the lesson to be learned from it. Exhibit 9.9 describes a few of the activities and associated lessons from the company's specially designed one-day program.

Was the team training at the Evart plant effective? Surveys and personal interviews were conducted to assess employees' reactions, and the results were positive. Employees commented that people now were going out of their way to help others and felt that people were doing a better job of seeking out opinions from employees at all levels. Employees also got to know each other. Explained one engineer, "Personally, I hadn't been on third shift very long and found there were three people on that shift that I had the wrong opinion of. I saw they were real go-getters and they stayed positive throughout the experience; I was surprised." Overall, the training helped break down personal walls that people had built around themselves and helped them see the benefits of being a contributing member of a team.[79]

Training in Team Procedures

Experiential training is an effective way to develop cohesiveness, but used alone it isn't likely to result in optimal work team effectiveness. Work teams can also benefit from more formal training.

Work teams of all types are being empowered to perform tasks that previously weren't employees' responsibility. The greater the degree of self-management, the more the team has authority, responsibility, and general decision-making discretion for tasks. The more self-managing a team is, the more important it is for team members to receive training.

At BP Norge, team members were taught about the characteristics of self-managed teams and provided with information about how such teams

---

ex 9.9 Examples of Team Training Activities Used at the Evart Glass Plant

The Challenging Activity	The Teamwork Lesson
• Juggle several objects simultaneously (e.g., tennis balls, hackey sacs, and Koosh balls) as a team.	• Although everyone has a different role, each person touches and affects the outcome.
• Find the path hidden in a carpet maze and move each member through it in a limited amount of time.	• Teams must find and use each individual's hidden strengths (e.g., a good memory and the ability to move quickly). Doing so allows the team as a whole to succeed.
• Balance 14 nails on the head of a nail that has been pounded into a supporting block of wood, creating a freestanding structure without supports.	• Things that may seem impossible can be achieved when people work together.
• Draw a vehicle that represents the training teams and signify which part of the vehicle each member represents.	• Each member has different strengths, and bringing these strengths together leads to task success.

have been used in other organizations. This formal training was in addition to more experiential activities, such as role-playing and sensitivity discussions, as described in the feature "Managing Teamwork: Cultural Change at BP Norge."[80] For self-managed work teams, formal training may also include company-specific procedures for obtaining resources, cost accounting, progress reports, and team evaluations.

Training for Team Leaders

New team leaders often misunderstand their role. Good team leaders are receptive to member contributions and don't reject or promote ideas because of their own personal views. Good team leaders summarize information, stimulate discussion, create awareness of problems, and detect when the team is ready to resolve differences and agree to a unified solution. Training in how to support disagreement and manage meetings is especially useful for new work team leaders.

- *Supporting Disagreement.* A skillful work team leader can create an atmosphere for disagreement that stimulates innovative solutions while minimizing the risk of bad feelings. Disagreement can be managed if the leader is receptive to differences within the team, delays the making of decisions, and separates idea generation from idea evaluation. This last technique reduces the likelihood that an alternative solution will be identified with one individual rather than the team. The absence of disagreement on a work team may be as destructive to its proper functioning as too much disagreement. The use of decision-making aids, such as brainstorming, the nominal group technique, devil's advocacy, and dialectical inquiry, creates productive controversy and can result in better-quality decisions that are fully accepted by members of the team. Training team leaders to use these simple techniques is a good first step toward stimulating constructive controversy within teams.[81]
- *Managing Meetings.* People who resist teamwork often point to time wasted in meetings as a big source of dissatisfaction. True, teams do need to meet, one way or another, but team meetings should never be a waste of time. Training team leaders in the tactics of running meetings can make meetings more efficient. In addition, training can help team leaders learn how to strike a proper balance between permissiveness and control. Rushing through a team session can prevent full discussion of the problem and lead to negative feelings and poor solutions. However, unless the leader keeps the discussion moving, members will become bored and inattentive. Unfortunately, some leaders feel that pushing for an early solution is necessary because of time constraints. Such a move ends discussion before the team has had a chance to work through a problem effectively.

CROSS-CULTURAL TRAINING

The objectives of **cross-cultural training** may be to prepare people from several cultures to work together or to prepare a person for living in another culture.[82] Within the United States, the first objective—training people from different cultures to work together—is often the aim of diversity training initiatives. The second objective—preparing a person for living in another culture—is likely to be the aim of training programs for expatriates and their families. Finally, many global firms require managers who are effective when

MANAGING TEAMS

Cultural Change at BP Norge

When the Norwegian arm of British Petroleum (BP Norge) decided that it needed to dismantle its hierarchy and move toward becoming a network of collaborators, it decided to restructure the organization around self-managing teams. If employees were willing to assume leadership and work across functions, the company believed that it could speed up decision making, reduce costs and cycle times, and increase innovation. Despite the strong business argument supporting a change to teamwork, the organization found that pushing the change was difficult.

Nine months of frustration led management to conclude that a systematic training initiative was needed to educate the organization and support the development of new teamwork competencies. The first phase of training focused on changing old thought patterns and helping people understand the link between BP Norge's business strategy and need for self-managed teams. Because employees had been through many change efforts in the past, they had become skeptical and resistant. To convince them that more change was needed, a team of American and Norwegian facilitators conducted

two-day workshops, which were attended by a mix of people from all levels and functional specialties. Oil rig workers and senior managers sat side by side, as did Norwegians and Americans—even if they couldn't speak each other's language. Prior to the workshop, everyone completed a prework assignment. First, they watched a video that explained self-managed teams and showed how other organizations had used them successfully. They also interviewed a few colleagues to find out what they thought about self-managed teams. At the workshop, discussion focused on understanding the process through which teamwork develops. Participants were taught that denial about the need for change and resistance to it are natural reactions, but they were also encouraged to share their concerns with each other and seek answers to their questions. Throughout the two-day workshops, participants also used role-plays to begin practicing the behaviors that they would need in their new team environment. These behaviors included taking risks, communicating about their feelings, and teaching others as well as learning from others.

working in a multinational context, regardless of whether they are located in their home country or abroad. We consider each of these special topics next.

Diversity Training for Employees in the United States

As the importance of learning to manage workforce diversity became more salient to U.S. employers, many companies looked to cross-cultural training programs as a solution. Their thinking was that diversity can be disruptive to the organization and create dissatisfaction among employees if people from different cultural backgrounds do not understand each other's cultures. The hope was that diversity training programs would improve cross-cultural understanding. During the 1990s, suddenly there were thousands of consulting firms offering diversity training.[83]

Cultural Awareness Training. Many diversity training programs seek to raise cultural awareness among participants. Typically, these programs are designed to teach the participants about how their own culture differs from the cultures of other employees with whom they work. In this context, "culture" is used to refer very broadly to the social group to which a person belongs. Ethnic background is one aspect of culture, but so are one's age, socioeconomic status, religion, and so on. Cultural awareness training also teaches people to understand how the stereotypes they hold about various groups can influence the way they treat people—often in subtle ways that they may not be conscious of. The main objective of this type of diversity training is increasing people's knowledge about their own and other cultures.

A typical cultural awareness program is conducted over the course of one or two days. Among the activities are information sharing intended to educate employees about the array of differences present in the workplace. Some organizations supplement formal training sessions with informal learning opportunities such as a Black History Month or a Gay and Lesbian Pride Week and use the time to focus on a group's history and cultural traditions. The hope is that raising awareness about differences will lead to attitudinal and behavior changes. Although there is scant research on the effectiveness of such awareness programs, the general consensus is that awareness programs *alone* do little to create positive change.

Building Competencies. Another approach to diversity training focuses more specifically on developing the behavioral competencies needed to work effectively in organizations characterized by diversity. Training designed to develop the interpersonal competencies that are needed in diverse workplaces often includes role-playing and practice sessions. The interpersonal behaviors taught include showing respect and treating people as equals. Videos of leaderless group discussions may also be used to help point out inappropriate behaviors that people may engage in but not be aware of. Changing behaviors and developing interpersonal skills can improve the climate within diverse workplaces.

Supplementing Diversity Training. By the year 2000, nearly all *Fortune* 500 companies had introduced some type of diversity training—and many employers required that every employee participate. As these companies quickly learned, diversity training alone cannot create fundamental changes in how effectively organizations manage diversity. As already discussed in earlier chapters, the issue of diversity should be considered during succession planning and when developing recruitment and selection practices. In addition, efforts may be needed to ensure that members of minority groups are included on advisory boards and as members of committees involved in compensation decisions. Tying compensation and other rewards to success in meeting goals for recruiting, hiring, developing, and promoting people from diverse backgrounds has been shown to improve the success of diversity training and development interventions.[84] Thus, throughout this book we will continue to return to the topic of diversity and its implications for HR practices.

Cross-Cultural Training in the International Context

A few things seem certain, and one is that "globalization" will continue to be an inescapable buzzword. Businesses will operate in an ever more interconnected world. As shown in Exhibit 9.10, the opportunities for training and development activities in global companies are many—they can focus on at least five different groups of people, and they can be offered at different times. The different groups who can benefit from training are headquarters staff, global managers, expatriates, members of expatriates' families, and members of work teams that include people from different nationalities. Training and development activities can be offered prior to the departure of expatriates, during international assignments, and upon the expatriates' return.

Clearly, a full discussion of how organizations address all of these training and development needs is not feasible here. Instead, we discuss only two widely used training and development activities: cross-cultural training for expatriates and global leadership development.

ex 9.10 **Training and Development Needs for Global Firms**

Possible Timing of T&D Activities	Upon Return from International Assignment
	During International Assignment
	Prior to Departure for International Assignment

Possible Targets of T&D Activities	Expatriates
	Inpatriates
	Families of Expatriates and Inpatriates
	Global Managers
	Headquarters Staff
	Other Staff Working with Expatriates, Inpatriates, and Global Managers

Cross-Cultural Training for Expatriates and Inpatriates

Cross-cultural training is perhaps the main growth area in the training field, and more and more companies include it as a part of predeparture programs for expatriates.[85]

Expatriates. Cross-cultural training for expatriates, and perhaps members of their families, usually takes the form of a three- to five-day immersion course in the assigned country's values, customs, and traditions. There is some debate about whether cross-cultural training is more effective if it is offered before departure or after arrival in the host country, but for now most companies have adopted the predeparture model.[86]

A typical three-day cross-cultural program might cover details about what everyday life in the country is like, typical practices that are important to doing business in the country, the role of women in the foreign culture, and a discussion of the culture shock and the stress that executives and their families are likely to experience. Such training can improve the work performance of expatriates and reduce culture shock for their families.

One available tool for cross-cultural training is called a **culture-general assimilator.** This tool was designed to develop self-awareness about one's own culture and prepare people for interaction with other cultures, and subsequent research has shown it to be effective.[87] Using scenarios that illustrate how culture influences perceptions and behaviors, it teaches people to be more understanding of cultural differences of many types, including approaches to work, time, and space; views about the importance of groups vs. individuals; class and status hierarchies; language, rituals, and superstitions. Because the culture-general assimilator does not teach about a specific culture, it may not be sufficient to completely prepare expatriates for assignments abroad. Nevertheless, this form of general training can prepare people to be alert to the effects of culture so that they can learn about other cultures more quickly. For employees who travel to many different countries within a relatively short time, learning general skills for coping in other cultural environments may be more practical that attempting to learn the specific behaviors, languages and values of each culture.

Inpatriates. Increasingly, U.S. companies also are recognizing the need for cross-cultural training for their inpatriates, or "in-pats." **Inpatriates** are employees from other countries who are sent to work in the United States. They often find relocating to the United States particularly difficult. This is due in part to the fact that so few Americans speak another language. The challenge of being a U.S. inpatriate is also partly due to the fact that U.S. employers are less likely to offer them cross-cultural training. Like expatriates, inpatriates and their families need accurate information about the local culture (as well as general assistance with the process of relocation).[88]

Training and Development for Global Managers

For expatriates, the challenge is to learn to be effective in a new and different culture. Global managers face a different challenge: they need to manage operations in several different countries simultaneously. Global leadership competency is especially important in global organizations that are structured around products rather than geographic regions. Many companies use expatriate assignments as developmental experiences intended to help managers develop the skills and mindset needed by a global leader, but success as an expatriate does not guarantee success as a global leader. Additional development is likely to be helpful.

At TRW, preparing global managers requires integrating several HR activities, including job assignments, succession planning, career planning, performance measurement, and formal training. In all of their job assignments, including expatriate positions, managers learn on the job about many aspects of the business as well as other cultures. By coordinating job assignments for individuals with the organization's succession planning and the career plans of individual managers, TRW seeks to develop a cadre of executives who have the background needed to perform as a global leader. In addition, TRW provides formal training in its executive development programs. Besides an intensive executive development program for executives with primarily domestic responsibilities, the company recently developed a program specifically for global leaders. The Global Leadership Program was developed after a needs assessment identified a gap between the company's current collective skill set and the leadership competencies it believed were needed to succeed in a global marketplace.

Similar to the programs offered at many other global companies, TRW's Global Leadership Program includes a classroom component, an action learning project, and a presentation of lessons learned. The specific content of these components has evolved as executives and the company gain experience, but the core of the program is the action learning component. For this, multicultural teams of executives are sent to different countries and given an assignment—such as developing a supply base or a marketing plan to establish a presence in the market. Through such assignments, the executives learn about their assigned country, but they also learn a great deal about the home countries of their teammates, how to manage team diversity, and how to tolerate ambiguity. At the same time, the experience serves to strengthen the network of personal relationships among executives who will be working together in the future.[89]

"So many people inbound to the U.S. think they know it through movies and TV, but they're not a good representation of what life is like here."

Tara Brabazon
Director of Intercultural Services
GMAC Global Relocation Services

FAST FACT

A recent study of global firms found that 67% lacked capable global leaders.

EVALUATING TRAINING AND DEVELOPMENT

Training and development programs have many different objectives. Not surprisingly, many measures can be used to evaluate their effectiveness, including changes in productivity, surveys to measure attitudes (e.g., satisfaction with supervisor, satisfaction with diversity programs, satisfaction with job, stress, role conflict, and knowledge of work procedures), cost savings, and attitudes toward future training.[90] The major components that can be included in the evaluation of training and development activities are shown in Exhibit 9.11.

FAST FACT

According to The Conference Board, more than half of all companies do not try to measure the value of training.

Evaluation Components

Exhibit 9.11 divides the many possible measures of T&D effectiveness into two broad categories: short-term effects and long-term consequences. Usually, employers offer training and development in hopes of reaping the long-term consequences. When it comes to evaluating the effectiveness of their efforts, however, they usually assess only short-term effects. Furthermore, evaluations usually focus on achievement of the organization's objectives to the exclusion of those of individual employees.

ex 9.11 Measurement Components for Evaluating Training and Development Activities

SHORT-TERM EFFECTS	LONG-TERM CONSEQUENCES
• Reactions to T&D activity	**Organizational**
• Learning	• Improved productivity
• Changes in behavior and attitudes	• Lower cost
• Performance on a task	• Improved customer service
	• Pool of competent global managers
	• Improved retention rates
	• Increased applicant pool
	Individual
	• Reduced stress
	• Increased job satisfaction
	• Career advancement
	• Family satisfaction
	• Employability

Assessing employees' immediate reactions to training is the most frequently used approach to evaluation. Although positive reactions to training are desirable, they may have little relationship to other important outcomes. If the objective is to assess what was learned, then paper-and-pencil tests can be used. Although testing for knowledge acquisition may indicate that learning has occurred, it won't reveal whether learning has been transferred to the job. To assess whether behavior or performance has changed, output measures, performance evaluation reports, and employee attitude surveys provide better information.

Evaluation Designs

Just as different measures of effectiveness are more or less useful, different evaluation designs can provide relatively weak or strong evidence about the effects of T&D activities. The three major categories of evaluation designs are nonexperimental, quasi-experimental, and experimental. Exhibit 9.12 summarizes these designs.[91] Each offers advantages and disadvantages.

FAST FACT

Organizations with 100 or more employees spend an estimated $60 billion annually on training.

Experiments. The most rigorous evaluation designs are **experimental designs.** In a true experiment, employees split into two groups: the "treatment" group participates in the training or development activity being evaluated, and the "control" group does not participate. Employees in both groups are assessed at Time 1—for example, they are given a knowledge test or their levels of job performance are measured. Then employees in the treatment group experience the T&D activity (X). At Time 2, employees in both groups are assessed again. By comparing the responses of employees in the treatment and control groups at Time 1 and Time 2, the following questions can be answered with a high degree of certainty:

- Did a change take place from Time 1 to Time 2—for example, did employee productivity increase?
- Was the change caused by the T&D activity (X)? If the change occurred in both groups, then it cannot be explained by the T&D activity.

ex 9.12 **Designs for Evaluating Training and Development Activities**

Nonexperimental	Quasi-Experimental	Experimental
1. One-shot case study design	1. Time-series design	1. Pretest-posttest control group design
$\quad$ X $\quad$ T_2	$\quad$ $T_1 T_2 T_3$ $\quad$ X $\quad$ $T_4 T_5 T_6$	
2. One-group pretest-posttest design	2. Nonequivalent control group design	$\quad$ T_1 $\quad$ X $\quad$ T_2
		$\quad$ T_1 $\quad$ T_2
$\quad$ T_1 $\quad$ X $\quad$ T_2	$\quad$ T_1 $\quad$ X $\quad$ T_2	
	$\quad$ T_1 $\quad$ T_2	

Note: "T" refers to the time at which the outcomes of interest (e.g., knowledge, attitudes, behavior) are assessed. "X" refers to the training or development experience received by the group.

Quasi Experiments. Organizations generally want all employees in a section trained, not just a few who are randomly selected. Consequently, they're more likely to use **quasi-experimental designs**, which do not involve randomly assigning employees to the treatment and control groups. Two quasi-experimental designs are shown in Exhibit 9.12. In the time-series design, several measures are taken before the treatment and several after. This design is easy to use and may require very little extra effort. For example, in many organizations job performance is regularly assessed. So, it is easy to compare the performance of employees before and after the T&D activity. The problem is that you cannot be certain that the T&D activity accounts for the change. A new reward system, seasonal changes, new equipment, and a variety of other changes may have occurred at about the same time as the T&D, and they may have caused the change in performance.

The nonequivalent control group design is similar to the experimental design, with one big difference. In this design employees are not randomly assigned to the treatment and control groups. Instead, employees in one location may be given training and then compared with employees at a different location. Or, if the training is voluntary, employees who chose to receive the training may be compared to those who did not. This is a practical design that allows for a comparison between those who did and did not receive training. But if a difference is found, you cannot be completely confident that the training caused it. For example, there may be many other differences between those who volunteered for the training and those who did not, and these differences may account for the change. Despite this drawback, the practicality of the nonequivalent control group design makes it a good choice.[92]

Nonexperiments. Unfortunately, in most companies, experiments and quasi experiments are never conducted to evaluate training and development activities. Despite the huge investments made in these activities, most companies do not know whether their investments really pay off. When evaluations are conducted, often they rely on the weakest design—namely, nonexperiments. The two **nonexperimental designs** shown in Exhibit 9.12 are much simpler, far less costly, and far less time consuming than the other designs. But with ease and low cost come less accuracy and confidence in measuring change that may have been the result of a training program—or any other program to produce change.

SUMMARY

Rapidly changing technology, foreign competition, and changes in organizational strategy and strategic business objectives are putting pressure on organizations to train and develop employees for competitive advantage. This requires careful attention to needs assessment, program development and implementation, and evaluation. Four types of needs analysis—organizational, job, person, and demographic—are designed to diagnose systematically the short- and long-term human resource needs of an organization. When actual performance and desired performance differ, training is needed.

Following effective needs analysis, training and development activities must be designed and implemented. Setting up these activities involves deciding who will be trained, who will train, where the training will occur, and what methods will be used. Cost considerations, as well as the types of competencies to be acquired and the format of the training affect the selection of appropriate methods. Training and development for teams and for global leaders are two especially important types of training that many organizations have been implementing recently.

Regardless of the method chosen, the content of training and development activities should be designed to maximize learning. Principles to consider include clear instructions, proper role models, active participation, feedback, and practice. These should be viewed in relationship to the trainees' self-efficacy or competency beliefs. It is also important to examine the work environment to ensure that new behaviors will be reinforced rather than punished.

The last major phase of training and development is evaluation. Typically, only short-term reactions to training are assessed, using nonexperimental design. Better approaches to evaluation employ quasi-experimental or true experimental designs, and they measure the degree of learning, changes in job behavior, and the achievement of longer-term outcomes that reflect the needs of organizations and individual employees.

TERMS TO REMEMBER

apprenticeship training
assistantships
behavioral modeling
coaching
corporate universities
cross-cultural training
culture-general assimilator
demographic needs analysis
development
developmental job assignments
e-learning
enactive mastery
experimental designs
inpatriates
interactive video training (IVT)
internships
job needs analysis
job rotation programs
knowledge management
   technologies
mentoring
nonexperimental designs

on-the-job training (OJT)
organizational needs analysis
orientation programs
person needs analysis
programmed instruction (PI)
proximal goals
quasi-experimental designs
reinforcement
role-playing
self-efficacy
sensitivity training
shaping
simulation
socialization
supervisory assistance
supportive training climate
task segmentation
training
transfer
vestibule method
wilderness trips

DISCUSSION QUESTIONS

1. Describe how Trident's training is likely to be related to other HR activities in the company.
2. What is the role of training and development in learning organizations? Do you think a pharmaceutical company could effectively manage knowledge without having well-developed training and development activities?

3. An auto dealer has hired you to help improve the performance of its sales and service staff. Your first task is to conduct a needs analysis for the organization. Describe what you will do. Then, provide examples of possible training and development activities that could be used to influence the knowledge, behavior, and attitudes of the staff.

4. A beverage producer has decided to enroll 40 members of its professional staff in a wilderness training program. The objective is to improve communications among staff members and facilitate coordination amongst them. The CEO realizes that the positive effects of the training may not transfer to the work setting. She has asked you for ideas about how to maximize the value of the wilderness training after people return to their jobs. What are your recommendations?

5. Consider the various training and development formats described in this chapter. Which three do you think would be most effective for maintaining the skills of IT engineers? Which three do you think would be least effective? Explain your rationale.

6. Imagine that your organization—a publishing company—has decided to hire an external vendor to provide diversity training. You want to begin by having the vendor conduct the training for just a small portion of the employees in order to conduct a study to assess the training's effectiveness. Describe a plan for evaluating the effectiveness of the diversity training offered by the vendor. What measures will you use and how will you design the evaluation study?

7. As a manager, what indicators would you need in order to decide whether a low-performing subordinate was a selection mistake or merely in need of training? If possible, illustrate this dilemma with an example from your own work experience.

8. Discuss the strategic role training and development activities for companies with international operations and markets.

PROJECTS TO EXTEND YOUR LEARNING

1. *Managing Change.* The feature on GM describes how the SPO division within General Motors uses training and development to more efficiently help the company achieve its strategic business objectives of better and faster customer service. More and more companies are doing the same thing, that is, learning about what is needed by the business and then tailoring their socialization, training, and development activities to serve those needs. Visit the home pages of two companies and identify some of their strategic business needs. With this knowledge, suggest some training and development needs they might have.

2. *Managing Globalization.* U.S. firms realize that the world is their marketplace. Most firms that do business abroad use some expatriates for such things as managing the operations and providing special expertise (e.g., financial management or product marketing). But the success rate of expatriates is lower than it should be, and they often return home sooner than the company had planned. The causes cited for lack of success in expatriate assignments include poor preparation for living in a foreign culture and lack of family preparation. Visit the home pages of organizations with expertise in expatriate training and develop-

ment. Then, list five recommendations that you could offer an employer as guidelines for using training to prepare expatriates and their families for an extended foreign assignment.

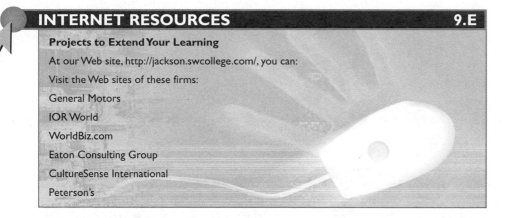

SEEING THE FOREST AND THE TREES

case study

The domestic and global competition that the leaders of the Forest Products Company (FPC) and its parent, the Weyerhaeuser Corporation, saw as they surveyed an industry on its knees in the early 1980s was far different than Weyerhaeuser and its subsidiaries had successfully competed against for so long. They knew how to compete—and win—against a large-firm, commodity lumber business. But that business was in its death throes, and what was emerging from the ashes presented an entirely new set of challenges that would require a radical change in Weyerhaeuser's strategy. The new competitors weren't the old monolithic organizations but were instead small mills, lean and mean, configured so they could tailor their products to customer demand and change their product lines rapidly if the need arose. They were nonunion, owner operated, and entrepreneurial and, in this configuration, were running the lowest-cost, most market-oriented operations around.

Going out of business was not an alternative anyone cared to think about, but if things didn't change it was a definite possibility. So Charley Bingham, the CEO of the Forest Products Company, knew that something had to be done—and sooner, not later. He gathered his top dozen managers, and together they decided that a massive reorganization was called for, accompanied by a radical change in strategy. According to Bingham, the change in strategy went something like this:

Approximately 80 percent of our sales dollars in 1982 represented products sold as commodities. By 1995, we resolved that we must reverse the proportions.

The massive reorganization at FPC mirrored that occurring at its parent company. The Weyerhaeuser Corporation decided to drastically decentralize. The three operating units, of which FPC was one, were given free rein on how to do their business. Given this scenario, Bingham and his team decided they needed to create an organization capable of acting and responding just like their competitors. Thus, they created 200 profit centers with each center largely responsible for its own bottom line.

This restructuring soon proved to be only a first step in the right direction. FPC's ability to implement its new strategy was being undermined by low morale, which was pervasive. In addition, many middle managers, those needed to actually carry out the change, were pessimistic about the possibility of sustained future success. Silently, they even questioned their own ability to operate the profit centers.

With insights from Horace Parker, director of executive development at FPC, the rest of the top team came to realize that there would have to be a total transformation of the organization: the corporate culture, knowledge base, skill levels, style of leadership, and team orientation would all have to change, for all employees. With 18,000 employees across the United States, Parker wasn't sure where to start. The others said they would help, but Horace had to tell them what to do. Horace, of course, is waiting to hear what you have to tell him.

QUESTIONS

1. Where does Horace start? What programs does he put in place to deal with the needs of corporate culture, knowledge, skills, leadership, and team orientation?

2. How does he go about developing the programs that he needs to put in place? Does he do it by himself? Can he buy off-the-shelf programs?

3. What time frame does Horace need to implement the programs to make the change successful? If he deals only with the executive development programs, does he need to be concerned with programs for middle managers and below? How does he do this?

Source: Randall S. Schuler, Rutgers University.

ENDNOTES

1 "Four Employers Score with Programs to Develop, Retain Skilled Workforces," *BNA Bulletin to Management* (October 14, 1999): 321.

2 J. L. Laabs, "Financial Impact: Quality Drives Trident's Success," *Workforce* (February 1998): 44–49.

3 For a detailed treatment of the topic of training, see I. L. Goldstein and J. K. Ford *Training in Organizations* (Belmont, CA: Wadsworth, 2002); for detailed discussions of leadership development, see B. J. Avolio, *Full Leadership Development* (Thousand Oaks, CA: Sage, 1999) and C. D. McCauley, R. S. Moxley, and E. Van Velsor (eds.), *Handbook of Leadership Development* (San Francisco: Jossey-Bass, 1998). See also L. Miller, "Initiative for Self-Development Identifies Future Leaders," *HR Magazine* (January 2001): 20.

4 C. Garvey, "The Whirlwind of a New Job," *HR Magazine* (June 2001): 111–118; R. R. Ritti, *The Ropes to Skip and the Ropes to Know: Studies in Organizational Behavior*, 5th ed. (Columbus, OH: Grid Publishing, 1997).

5 "SHRM–BNA Survey No. 63: Human Resource Activities, Budgets & Staffs, 1997–1998," *Bulletin to Management* (June 18, 1998): 2; "High-Technology Firms Lead the Way in Training," *Bulletin to Management* (February 5, 1998): 376; "1997 Industry Report," *Training* (October 1998): 33–65.

6 S. E. Jackson and R. S. Schuler, "Turning Knowledge Into Business," *Financial Times* (January 2001): Mastering Management Supplement; S. Greengard, "Will Your Culture Support KM?" *Workforce* (October 1998): 93–94; S. Greengard, "How to Make KM a Reality," *Workforce* (October 1998): 90–91; "In the Know," *Human Resource Executive* (February 1997): 31; E. Raimy, "Knowledge Movers," *Human Resource Executive* (February 1997): 32–37; S. Greengard, "Storing, Shaping and Sharing Collective Wisdom," *Workforce* (October 1998): 82–88.

7 C. Wanberg and J. Kammeyer-Mueller, "Predictors and Outcomes of Proactivity in the Socialization Process," *Journal of Applied Psychology* 85(3) (2000): 373–385; D. C. Feldman, "Socialization, Resocialization, and Training: Reframing the Research Agenda," in Goldstein and Ford (eds.), *Training and Development in Organizations*, 376–416.

8 K. Winkler and I. Janger, "You're Hired! Now How Do We Keep You?" *Across the Board* (July/August 1998): 14–23; J.C. Dannemiller, "How We Keep Good People," *Across the Board* (July/August 1998): 21; A. Baron, "Top Managers Still Don't Get It," *Across the Board* (July/August 1998): 22; M. Budman, "Show Them the Money?" *Across the Board* (July/August 1998): 23; M. R. Buckley, D. B. Fedor, J. G. Veres, III, D. S. Wiese and S. M. Carraher, "Investigating Newcomer Expectations and Job-Related Outcomes," *Journal of Applied Psychology* 83(3) (1998): 452–461; A. Newman Korn, "Gotcha!" *Across the Board* (September 1998): 30–35; G. T. Chao, "Organizational Socialization in Multinational Corporations: The Role of Implicit Learning," *Creating Tomorrow's Organizations* (New York: John Wiley, 1997): Chapter 3.

9 J. K. Laabs, "Serving Up a New Level of Customer Service at Quebecor," *Workforce* (March 2001): 40–42; S. Caudron, "Training and the ROI of Fun," *Workforce* (December 2000): 34–39.

10 E. Zimmerman, "Better Training is Just a Click Away," *Workforce* (January 2001): 36–42.

11 W. Royal, "A Factory's Crash Course in Economics Pays Off," *New York Times* (April 15, 2001): C9.

12 M. Kirk, "No Reservation," *Human Resource Executive* (June 18, 1999): 69–73.

13 M. Johnson, "Use Anti-Harassment Training to Shelter Yourself from Suits," *HR Magazine* (October 1999): 77–81.

14 L. Rubis, "Manager Training Helped Company Digest Big Bite," *HR Magazine* (December 2000): 61–62.

15 J. P. MacDuffie and T.A. Kochan, "Do U.S. Firms Underinvest in Human Resources? Determinants of Training in the World Auto Industry," *Industrial Relations* (September 1993): 145–160.

16 S. Hays, "HR Strategies Help Push New Razor to Number One," *Workforce* (February 1999): 92–93; Industry Report 1998, "Who Gets Trained? Where The Money Goes," *Training* (October 1998): 55–67.

17 C. J. Bachler, "The Trainer's Role: Is Turning Upside Down," *Workforce* (June 1997): 93–105.

18 G. T. Chao et al., "Organizational Socialization: Its Content and Consequences," *Journal of Applied Psychology* 79 (1994): 730–743; E. W. Morrison, "Newcomer Information Seeking: Exploring Types, Modes, Sources, and Outcomes," *Academy of Management Journal* 36 (1993): 557–589; C. Ostroff and S. W. J. Kozlowski, "Organizational Socialization as a Learning Process: The Role of Information Acquisition," *Personnel Psychology* 45 (1992): 849–874.

19 T. J. Maurer and B. A. Tarulli, "Investigation of Perceived Environment, Perceived Outcome, and Person Variables in Relationship to Voluntary Development Activity by Employees," *Journal of Applied Psychology* 79 (1994): 3–14. See also L. A. Hill, *Becoming a Manager: Mastery of a New Identity* (Cambridge, MA: Harvard Business School Press, 1992); T. A. Scandura, "Dysfunctional Mentoring Relationships and Outcomes," *Journal of Management* 24 (1998): 449–467.

20 T. A. Stewart, "Brain Power: Who Owns It . . . How They Profit From It," *Fortune* (March 17, 1997): 105–110.

21 R. Zemke, "How to Do a Needs Assessment When You Think You Don't Have Time," *Training* (March 1998): 38–44; "Lifelong Learning and the Skills Shortage: Policy Guide," *Bulletin to Management* (November 27,

1997): 384; "Technology and Training: A Dynamic Duo," *Bulletin to Management* 48(10) (March 6, 1997): 80; L. Saari et al., "A Survey of Management Training and Education Practices in U.S. Companies," *Personnel Psychology* 41 (1988): 731–745.

22 Adapted from I. L. Goldstein, *Training: Program Development and Evaluation*, 2d ed. (Monterey, CA: Brooks/Cole, 1986): 8.

23 P. J. Kiger, "At USA Bank, Promotions and Job Satisfaction Are Up," *Workforce* (March 2001): 54–55.

24 For more information about diagnosing the learning climate, see S. I. Tannenbaum, "Enhancing Continuous Learning: Diagnostic Findings from Multiple Companies," *Human Resource Management* 36 (1997): 437–452.

25 D. W. Bray, Chairman Emeritus, Development Dimensions International, Pittsburgh, Pennsylvania, personal communication.

26 S. Hays, "HR Strategies Help Push New Razor to Number One," *Workforce* (February 1999): 92–93; B. Calandra, "Razor Sharp," *Human Resource Executive* (June 4, 1999): 22–25.

27 For more discussion of the advantages and disadvantages of basic assessment techniques, see I. L. Goldstein, "Training in Work Organizations," *Handbook of Industrial and Organizational Psychology* 2 (1991): 507–620.

28 Modified from J. K. Ford and R. A. Noe, "Self-Assessed Training Needs: The Effects of Attitudes toward Training, Managerial Level and Function," *Personnel Psychology* 40 (1987): 39–53.

29 J. Conner and C. A. Smith, "Developing the Next Generation of Leaders: A New Strategy for Leadership Development at Colgate-Palmolive," in E. M. Mone and M. London (eds.), *HR to the Rescue: Case Studies of HR Solutions to Business Challenges* (Houston: Gulf, 1998).

30 W. Byham, "Bench Strength," *Across the Board* (February 2000): 35–41.

31 M. W. McCall, M. M. Lombardo, and A. M. Morrison, *The Lessons of Experience* (Lexington, MA: Lexington Books, 1988); C. D. McCauley et al., "Assessing the Developmental Components of Managerial Jobs," *Journal of Applied Psychology* 79 (1994): 544–560. Also see the special issue of *Harvard Business Review* (December 2001), which was devoted to the development of leaders.

32 R. Neil Olson and E. A. Sexton, "Gender Differences in the Returns to and the Acquisition of On-the-Job Training," *Industrial Relations* 35 (January 1996): 59; S. G. Baugh, M. J. Lankau, and A. Terri, "An Investigation of the Effects of Protégé Gender on Responses to Mentoring," *Journal of Vocational Behavior* 49 (1996): 309–323; P. J. Ohlott, M. N. Ruderman, and C. D. McCauley, "Gender Differences in Managers' Developmental Job Experiences," *Academy of Management Journal* 37 (1994): 46–67.

33 "Delta Air Will Give School Grant to Train Minorities as Pilots," *Wall Street Journal* (January 10, 2001): A6.

34 K. Kraiger (ed.), *Creating, Implementing and Managing Effective Training* (San Francisco: Jossey-Bass, 2001); D. B. Sloan, "Identifying and Developing High Potential Talent: A Succession Management Methodology," *Industrial-Organizational Psychologist* (2000): 80–90.

35 T. J. Maurer, "Career-Relevant Learning and Development, Worker Age, and Beliefs about Self-Efficacy for Development," *Journal of Management* 27 (2001): 123–140; J. A. Colquitt, J. LePine, and R. A. Noe, "Toward an Integrative Theory of Training Motivation: A Meta-Analytic Path Analysis of 20 Years of Research," *Journal of Applied Psychology* 85(5) (2000): 678–707.

36 See, for example, B. Ragins and J. Cotton, "Mentor Functions and Outcomes: A Comparison of Men and Women in Formal and Informal Mentoring Relationships," *Journal of Applied Psychology* 84(4) (1999): 529–550.

37 J. Reingold, "Corporate America Goes to School," *Business Week* (October 20, 1997): 66–72.

38 J. S. Black and H. Gregersen, "High Impact Training: Forging Leaders for the Global Frontier," *Human Resource Management* 39(2&3) (Summer/Fall 2000): 173–184.

39 A. J. Towler and R. L. Dipboye, "Effects of Trainer Expressiveness, Organization, and Trainee Goal Orientation on Training Outcomes," *Journal of Applied Psychology* 86 (2001): 664–673.

40 R. J. Sternberg and E. L. Grigorenko, "Are Cognitive Styles Still in Style?" *American Psychologist* 52 (July 1997): 700–712; K. Kraiger, J. K. Ford, and E. Salas, "Application of Cognitive, Skill-Based, and Affective Theories of Learning Outcomes to New Methods of Training Evaluation," *Journal of Applied Psychology* 78 (1993): 311–328.

41 "Ritz-Carlton Certifies Ladies and Gentlemen," *HR Reporter* (August 1993): 1–4.

42 K. Tyler, "Offering English Lessons at Work," *HR Magazine* (December 1999): 112–120.

43 J. Strandberg, "Training for a Technology Upgrade," *Training* (November 1997): 36–38.

44 L. Rubis, "Show and Tell," *HR Magazine* (April 1998): 110–117.

45 H. W. Marsh, G. E. Richards, and J. Barnes, "Multidimensional Self-Concepts: The Effects of Participation in an Outward Bound Program," *Journal of Personality and Social Psychology* 50 (1986): 195–204; H. W. Marsh, G. E. Richards, and J. Barnes, "A Long-Term Follow-up of the Effects of Participation in an Outward Bound Program," *Personality and Social Psychology Bulletin* 12 (1987): 465–492.

46 J. J. Laabs, "Emotional Intelligence at Work," *Workforce* (July 1999): 68–71; D. Goleman, *Working with Emotional Intelligence* (New York: Bantam Books, 1998); C. Cherniss, and D. Goleman (eds.), *The Emotionally Intelligent Workplace* (San Francisco: Jossey-Bass, 2001).

47 A. Vicere, "Ten Observations on e-Learning and Leadership Development," *Human Resource Planning* 23(4) (2000): 34–46; L. Lorek, "Computers, Cameras, Action," *Human Resource Executive* (January 1998): 36–38; L. Stevens, "Streamlined Training," *Human Resource Executive* (January 1998): 44–46; A. R. McIlvaine, "Cyber Scholars," *Human Resource Executive* (October 6, 1997): 1, 29–32; D. J. Shadovitz, "Techno Grip," *Human Resource Executive* (October 6, 1997): 4; "1997 Industry Report: Training Technology," *Training* (October 1997): 67–75; E. Santasiero, "Big Game Cyberhunt," *Training: Online Learning* (August 1998): 18–22.

48 M. Schneider, GM Gives On-line Learning a Boost," *Businessweek Online*, http://www.businessweek.com/bwdaily/dnflash/apr2001/.

49 Based on research by the American Society for Training & Development, as presented in M. Jones, "Use Your Head When Identifying Skills Gaps," *Workforce* (March 2000): 118–122. See also A. Vicere, "Ten Observations on e-Learning and Leadership Development," *Human Resource Planning* 23(4) (2000): 34–46; K. Tyler, "E-Learning Not Just for E-Normous Companies Anymore," *HR Magazine* (May 2001): 82–88; K. Brown, "Using Computers to Deliver Training: Which Employees Learn and Why?" *Personnel Psychology* 54 (2001): 271–296.

50 J. D. Facteau, G. H. Dobbins, J. E. A. Russell, R. T. Ladd, and J. D. Kudisch, "The Influence of General Perceptions of the Training Environment on Pretraining Motivation and Perceived Training Transfer," *Journal of Management* 21 (1995): 1–25; Goldstein, Training; B. M. Bass and J. A. Vaughan, *Training in Industry: The Management of Learning* (Belmont, CA: Wadsworth, 1966): 88.

51 "Delta Air Will Give School Grant to Train Minorities as Pilots," *Wall Street Journal* (January 10, 2001): A6; D. Stamps, "Will School-to-Work, Work?" *Training* (June 1996): 72–81.

52 "Internships Provide Workplace Snapshot: Policy Guide," *Bulletin to Management* 48(21) (May 22, 1997): 168; "Personnel Shop Talk," *Bulletin to Management* 48(21) (May 22, 1997): 162.

53 C. D. McCauley, *The Job Challenge Profile: Participant Workbook* (San Francisco: Jossey-Bass, 1999).

54 S. L. Willis and S. S. Dubin (eds.), *Maintaining Professional Competence: Approaches to Career Enhancement, Vitality and Success throughout a Work Life* (San Francisco: Jossey-Bass, 1990); J. A. Schneer and F. Reitman, "Effects of Employment Gaps on the Careers of M.B.A.'s: More Damaging for Men than for Women?" *Academy of Management Journal* 33 (1990): 391–406; J. H. Greenhaus, S. Parasuraman, and W. M. Wormley,

"Effects of Race on Organizational Experiences, Job Performance Evaluations and Career Outcomes," *Academy of Management Journal* 33 (1990): 64–86; A. Murrell, F. Crosby, and R. Ely, *Mentoring Dilemmas: Developmental Relationships Within Multicultural Organizations* (Mahway, NJ: LEA, 1999); M. Higgins and K. E. Kram, "Reconceptualizing Mentoring at Work: A Developmental Network Perspective," *Academy of Management Executive* 25(2) (2001): 264–288.

55 B. Filipczak, "The Executive Coach: Helper or Healer?" *Training* (March 1998): 30–36; J. Waldroop and T. Butler, "The Executive as Coach," *Harvard Business Review* (November–December, 1996): 111-117.

56 S. R. Davis, J. H. Lucas, and D. R. Marcotte, "GM Links Better Leaders to Better Business," *Workforce* (April 1998): 62–68.

57 T. A. Stewart, "See Jack. See Jack Run," Fortune (December 27, 1999): 284–290; J. Spiegel Arthur, "Virtual U.," *Human Resource Executive* (March 19, 1998): 44–46.

58 N. Byrnes, "What Really Happened to the Class of GE," *Business Week* (November 13, 2000): 98–100; L. B. Ward, "In the Executive Alphabet, You Call Them C.L.O.'s," *New York Times* (February 4, 1996): 12; "In the Know," *Human Resource Executive* (February 1997): 31; E. Raimy, "Knowledge Movers," *Human Resource Executive* (February 1997): 32–36; K. F. Clark, "The Right Track," *Human Resource Executive* (May 6, 1997): 52–55; T. Bartlett, "The Hottest Campus on the Internet," *Business Week* (October 20, 1997): 77, 80.

59 A. Bernstein, "Low-Skilled Jobs: Do They Have to Move?" *Business Week* (February 26, 2001): 94–95; Industry Report 1998, "Training by Computer: How U.S. Organizations Use Computers in Training," *Training* (October 1998): 71–76; R. Quick, "Software Seeks to Breathe Life Into Corporate Training Classes," *Wall Street Journal* (August 6, 1998): B8.

60 For a detailed list of conditions that support transfer, see L. Burke and T. T. Baldwin, "Workforce Training Transfer: A Study of the Effect of Relapse Prevention Training and Transfer Climate," *Human Resource Management* 38(3) (Fall 1999): 227–242.

61 R. Becker, "Taking the Misery Out of Experiential Training," "Training (February 1998): 78–88; M. Hequet, "Games that Teach," *Training* (July 1995): 53–58; T. A. Stewart, "The Dance Steps Get Trickier All the Time," *Fortune* (May 26, 1997): 157–160; G. C. Thornton III and J. N. Cleveland, "Developing Managerial Talent through Simulation," *American Psychologist* (February 1990): 190–199; W. M. Bulkeley, "The World of Work Is a Keystroke Away for Students in Computer-Simulated Jobs," *Wall Street Journal* (May 7, 1996): B1, B2.

62 For an excellent description of the many uses and issues of assessment centers, see the entire special issue, R. E. Riggio and B. T. Mayes (eds.), "Assessment Centers: Research and Applications," *Journal of Social Behavior and Personality* 12 (1997): 1–331; and the references in Chapter 8.

63 P. Schinzler, "Sharing the Wealth," *Business Week e-Biz* (March 2001): 36–40.

64 E. Brown, "War Games to Make You Better at Business," *Fortune* (September 28, 1998): 291–296; J. Pereira, "Leader of the Pack in Wilderness Training Is Pushed to the Wall," *Wall Street Journal* (July 24, 1997): A1, A6; C. Lawson, "Corporate Bonding Over a Hot Stove," *New York Times* (July 23, 1997): C1, C6; G. M. McEvoy and P. F. Buller, "The Power of Outdoor Management Development," *Journal of Management Development* 16(3) (1997): 208–217; C. Patton, "In Proper Conduct," *Human Resource Executive* (February 1998): 30–32.

65 C. Lee, "The Adult Learner: Neglected No More," *Training* (March 1998): 47–52; L. W. Hellervich, J. F. Hazucha, and R. J. Schneider, "Behavior Change: Models, Methods, and a Review of Evidence," *Handbook of Industrial and Organizational Psychology*.

66 For a review of related research, see J. A. Cannon-Bowers, L. Rhodenizer, E. Salas and C. Bowers, "A Framework for Understanding Pre-Practice Conditions and Their Impact on Learning," *Personnel Psychology* 51 (1998): 291–310.

67 M. A. Quinones, "Pretraining Context Effects: Training Assignment as Feedback," *Journal of Applied Psychology* 80 (1995): 226–238; V. L. Huber, " A Comparison of Goal Setting and Pay as Learning Incentives," *Psycho-*

logical Reports 56 (1985): 223–235; V. L. Huber, "Interplay Between Goal Setting and Promises of Pay-for-Performance on Individual and Group Performance: An Operant Interpretation," *Journal of Organizational Behavior Management* 7 (1986): 45–64.

68 J. K. Harrison, "Individual and Combined Effects of Behavior Modeling and the Cultural Assimilator in Cross-Cultural Management Training," *Journal of Applied Psychology* 77 (1992): 952–962.

69 S. J. Ashford and A. S. Tsui, "Self-Regulation for Managerial Effectiveness: The Role of Active Feedback Seeking," *Academy of Management Journal* 34 (1991): 251–280; S. I. Tannenbaum et al., "Meeting Trainees' Expectations: The Influence of Training Fulfillment on the Development of Commitment, Self-Efficacy and Motivation," *Journal of Applied Psychology* 76 (1991): 759–769.

70 G. May and W. Kahnweiler, "The Effect of a Mastery Practice Design on Learning and Transfer in Behavior Modeling Training," *Personnel Psychology* 53 (2000): 353–373.

71 Huber, "Interplay Between Goal Setting and Promises of Pay-for-Performance"; J. D. Eyring, D. Steele Johnson, and D. J. Francis, "A Cross-Level Units-of-Analysis Approach to Individual Differences in Skill Acquisition," *Journal of Applied Psychology* 78 (1993): 805–814; P. C. Earley, "Self or Group? Cultural Effects of Training on Self-Efficacy and Performance," *Administrative Science Quarterly* 39 (1994): 89–117.

72 B. Ragins and J. Cotton, "Mentor Functions and Outcomes: A Comparison of Men and Women in Formal and Informal Mentoring Relationships," *Journal of Applied Psychology* 84(4) (1999): 529–550; V. L. Huber, G. P. Latham, and E. A. Locke, "The Management of Impressions through Goal Setting," in R. A. Giacalone and P. Rosenfield (eds.), *Impression Management in the Organization* (Hillsdale, NJ: Lawrence Erlbaum, 1989).

73 P. Hogan, M. Hakel, and P. Decker, "Effects of Trainee-Generated vs. Trainer-Provided Rule Codes on Generalization in Behavioral Modeling Training," *Journal of Applied Psychology* 71 (1986): 469–473.

74 W. W. Tornow and M. London, "Maximizing the Value of 360-Degree Feedback: A Process for Successful Individual and Organizational Development," *Center for Creative Leadership*, (March 1998); D. E. Coates, "Don't Tie 360 Feedback to Pay," *Training* (September 1998): 68–78.

75 J. E. Driskell, C. Copper, and A. Moran, "Does Mental Practice Enhance Performance?" *Journal of Applied Psychology* 79 (1994): 481–492.

76 J. F. Brett and D. VandeWalle, "Goal Orientation and Goal Content as Predictors of Performance in a Training Program," *Journal of Applied Psychology* 84(6) (1999): 863–873; C. Frayne and G. P. Latham, "The Application of Social Learning Theory to Employee Self-Management of Attendance," *Journal of Applied Psychology* 72 (1987): 387–392.

77 See M. J. Waller, "The Timing of Adaptive Group Responses to Nonroutine Events," *Academy of Management Journal* 42 (1999): 127–137.

78 E. Salas, J. A. Cannon-Bowers, and E. Eden, *Improving Teamwork in Organizations: Applications of Resource Management and Training* (Englewood Cliffs, NJ: Lawrence Erlbaum, 2001); R. A. Guzzo and M. W. Dickson, "Teams in Organizations: Recent Research on Performance and Effectiveness," *Annual Review of Psychology* 47 (1996): 307–308; J. Cannon-Bowers, S. A. Tannenbaum, E. Salas, and C. Volpe, "Defining Competencies and Establishing Team Training Requirements," *Team Effectiveness and Decision Making* (2000): 333–380; M. London and J. Smither, "Empowered Self-Development and Continuous Learning," *Human Resource Management* 38(1) (Spring 1999): 3–15; E. Salas and J. Cannon-Bowers, "The Anatomy of Team Training," *Handbook of Training Research* (1999): 101–135.

79 H. Campbell, "Adventures in Teamland: Experiential Training Makes the Lesson Fun, *Personnel Journal* (May 1996): 56–62.

80 M. Moravec, O. J. Johannessen, and T. A. Hjelmas, "Thumbs Up for Self-Managed Teams," *Management Review* (July/August 1997); S. E. Prokesch, "Unleashing the Power of Learning: An Interview with British Petroleum's John Browne," *Harvard Business Review* (September–October, 1997); and M. Moravec, O. J. Johannessen, and T. A. Hjelmas, "We Have Seen the Future and It Is Self-Managed," *PM Network* (September 1997): 20–22.

81 J. W. Dean, Jr., and M. P. Sharfman, "Does Decision Process Matter? A Study of Strategic Decision Making Effectiveness," *Academy of Management Journal* 39 (1996): 368–396; P.W. Mulvey, J. F. Viega, and P. M. Elsass, "When Teammates Raise a White Flag," *Academy of Management Executive* 10 (1996): 40–49; and R. L. Priem, D. A. Harrison, and N. K. Muir, "Structured Conflict and Consensus Outcomes in Group Decision Making," *Journal of Management* 21 (1995): 691–710.

82 For a review of research on cross-cultural training, see D. P. S. Bhawuk and R. W. Brislin, "Cross-Cultural Training: A Review," *Applied Psychology: An International Review* 49 (2000): 162–191.

83 For a review, see S. E. Jackson and A. Joshi, "Research on Domestic and International Diversity in Organizations: A Merger that Works?", in *Handbook of Industrial, Work and Organizational Psychology* vol. 2 (Thousand Oaks, CA: Sage, 2001); see also T. F. Pettigrew, "Intergroup Contact Theory," *Annual Review of Psychology* 49 (1998): 65–85.

84 S. L. Rynes and B. A. Rosen, "A Field Survey of Factors Affecting the Adoption and Perceived Success of Diversity Training," *Personnel Psychology* 48 (1995): 247–270.

85 R. Bennett, A. Aston, and T. Colquoun, "Cross-Cultural Training: A Critical Step in Ensuring the Success of International Assignments," *Human Resource Management* 39(2&3) (Summer/Fall 2000): 239–250; D. P. S. Bhawuk and R. W. Brislin, "Cross-cultural Training: A Review," *Applied Psychology: An International Review* 49 (2000): 162–191; J. S. Black and H. Gregersen, "High Impact Training: Forging Leaders for the Global Frontier," *Human Resource Management* 39(2&3) (Summer/Fall 2000): 173–184.

86 J. S. Black (ed.), *Globalizing People through International Assignments* (Reading, MA: Addison-Wesley, 1999).

87 K. Cushner and R. W. Brislin (eds), *Improving Intercultural Interactions: Models for Cross-cultural Training Programs* (Thousand Oaks, CA: Sage, 1997).

88 C. Lachmitt, "Low-Cost Tips for Successful Inpatriation," *Workforce* (August 2000): 42–47.

89 D. B. Neary and D. A. O'Grady, "The Role of Training in Developing Global Leaders: A Case Study at TRW, Inc.," *Human Resource Management* (Summer/Fall 2000): 185–193.

90 G. Gerson and C. McCleskey, "Numbers Help Make a Training Decision That Counts," *HR Magazine* (July 1998): 51–58; G. M. Alliger, S. I. Tannenbaum, W. B. Bennett, Jr., H. Traver and A. Shotland, "A Meta-Analysis of the Relations Among Training Criteria," *Personnel Psychology* 50 (1997): 341; K. A. Willyerd, "Balancing Your Evaluation Act," *Training* (March 1997): 52–58.

91 Based on I. Goldstein, *Training: Program Development and Evaluation*, 2d ed. (Monterey, CA: Brooks/Cole, 1986): 157–167.

92 For a good example of this design, see H. Klein and N. Weaver, "The Effectiveness of an Organizational-Level Orientation Training Program in the Socialization of New Hires," *Personnel Psychology* 53 (2000): 47–66.

CHAPTER

10

DEVELOPING AN OVERALL APPROACH TO COMPENSATION

"There are no quick answers to total rewards. Total rewards are really a collection of difficult, interrelated questions about a basic, fundamental way of managing a business and the people who create value. It's also about managing costs and investments."[1]

Andrew Richter
Director of Compensation
IBM

MANAGING THROUGH STRATEGIC PARTNERSHIPS

Bayer

Bayer Corporation is a Pittsburgh-based subsidiary of the German firm named Bayer Group AG. Today Bayer Corp. is one corporation with three major divisions, but back in 1991, it was three separate operating companies: a chemical producer called Mobay Chemical Corp., a health care organization called Miles, Inc., and an imaging company called Agfa. In the aftermath of the merger that created Bayer Corp., the top executive team set out to develop a vision that would bring together the diverse workforces of the original three firms. Their vision states that Bayer Corp. will be a leader in the markets it serves and it'll be a major contributor to its parent firm. To reach this vision, Bayer would operate according to a new set of values, which emphasized the importance of

- maintaining a diversified and highly motivated workforce that was fairly compensated for its performance;
- satisfying internal and external customers through innovative problem solving, while also adhering to ethical standards;
- managing the organization in a way that minimizes bureaucracy, delegates authority, and fosters teamwork and cooperation; and
- being a good citizen of the communities in which employees work and live.

To succeed, the new organization needed employees who embraced the new values. Bayer's managers realized that employees would be more likely to embrace these new values if they received a clear and consistent message about their importance. Redesigning the job evaluation systems used within the company was high on the agenda. CEO Helge Wehmeier put this challenge to the Job Advisory Committee—a task force of 14 senior vice presidents: "Whatever you do, I want the work-valuing process you come up with to be responsive to what we're doing as a business, and I don't want to increase costs."

Prior to the merger of the three companies, jobs at Mobay had been relatively unstructured. Miles and Agfa had each used the Hay Guide Chart-Profile method, but in recent years they had grown dissatisfied because they felt it did not reflect the business values in their companies. The old system was oriented toward functional and hierarchical values. People often felt that jobs were valued according to the degrees and credentials required for the job rather than their contribution and the way those degrees and credentials were used. Another problem with the old system was that responsibility was assessed according to the size of one's budget and one's staff.

The Job Advisory Committee had to make a choice: Choose a completely new method for evaluating jobs *or* revise the content in the old Hay Guide Charts. They chose the latter alternative. The new job evaluation system used the following dimensions:

Improvement opportunity:	How much opportunity is there for people in this job to improve performance?
Contribution:	How strong are the requirements for people in this job to achieve results?
Capability:	What are the total proficiencies and competencies required in the job? Three categories were considered:
	• Expertise and complexity
	• Leadership and integration
	• Relationship building skills

This new job evaluation system is now used throughout Bayer Corporation. There is one pay system that values all work using the same dimensions, regardless of whether that work involves health care, chemicals, or imaging technology. This helps managers and employees alike because it facilitates easy cross-business transfers and promotions.[2]

TOTAL COMPENSATION

As the feature on Bayer illustrates, companies are eager to link their compensation practices with their business needs and values. The description of Bayer describes only one element of that company's total compensation—namely, base pay. At Bayer and other companies, **total compensation** typically includes a mix of several elements. The many elements of total compensation are shown in Exhibit 10.1.

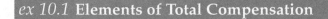

ex 10.1 Elements of Total Compensation

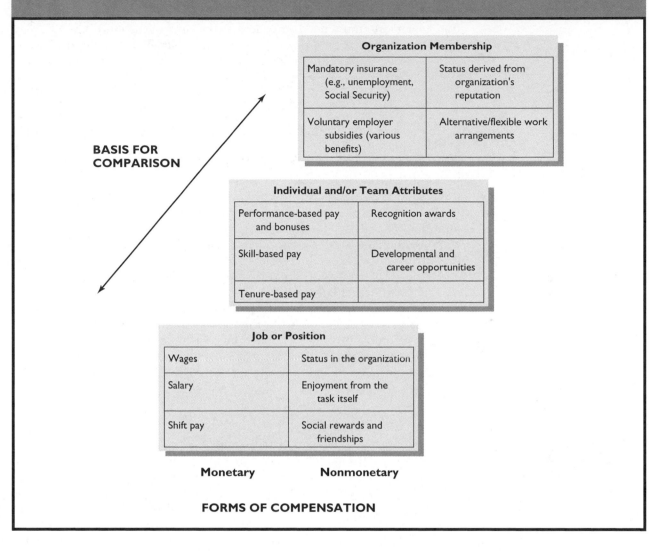

Monetary and Nonmonetary Compensation

The elements of total compensation include both monetary and nonmonetary forms of rewards. These two categories of compensation are shown on the horizontal dimension in Exhibit 10.1. **Monetary compensation** includes direct payments such as salary, wages, and bonuses, and indirect payments such as payments to cover the costs of private and public insurance plans. **Nonmonetary compensation** includes many forms of social and psychological rewards—recognition and respect from others, enjoyment from doing the job itself, opportunities for self-development, and so on.

Clearly, both monetary and nonmonetary forms of compensation are important to most employees. Nevertheless, people differ in the value they attach to these different types of compensation. For example, in one study, minority employees cited inadequate nonmonetary compensation as the

"There are two things people want more than sex and money—recognition and praise."

The Late Mary Kay Ash
Founder Chairman Emeritus
Mary Kay Cosmetics

major reason for their leaving an organization.[3] Another study found that age predicts the value employees attach to different forms of compensation. When asked what affected their decisions to stay or leave their jobs, Generation Y workers (those aged 25 or less at the time of the study) rated direct financial compensation and the nature of the job itself as less important reasons for leaving, compared to other employees.[4]

Bases of Compensation

The vertical dimension shown in Exhibit 10.1 reflects the basis for receiving the compensation. Some compensation is based solely on organizational membership. That is, the compensation is received by all, or almost all, employees in the organization, regardless of what job they perform or how well they perform it. Most forms of insurance and other benefits fall into this category. Compensation can also be based on the employee's particular job in the organization. Base wages and salaries fit here, as do social and psychological rewards derived from performing the job itself. Finally, some forms of compensation are based on attributes of the individual employee or perhaps the attributes of an employee's work team. Performance-based incentives and bonuses fit here, as do skill- or knowledge-based compensation.

This chapter begins with a discussion of the strategic importance of an organization's approach to total compensation. It then describes how organizations establish policies for job-based and skill-based monetary compensation. Approaches to managing performance-based compensation are described in Chapter 12. Chapter 13 discusses organization-based monetary compensation, which is usually referred to as employee benefits and services.

Compensation in the Context of the HR System

The many elements of total compensation mean that significant effort is needed to ensure all of the elements are aligned with each other. It can be a challenge to achieve an appropriate balance between rewards based on individual, team, and organizational performance, for example. It is also challenging to mesh compensation with the organizational culture while at the same time being sensitive to external market forces. Exhibit 10.2 shows the key choices to be made when designing total compensation and shows how these fit within an integrated HR system.

Links to the Global Environment. Perhaps more than any other aspect of the HR system, compensation practices must be responsive to the external environment. Of particular importance are conditions in the external labor market. Especially when talent is scarce relative to demand, employers must devise a compensation system that enables them to attract and retain the people they need at a cost they can afford. Here, the concerns of employees and shareholders become especially important. For employees represented by a union, most aspects of compensation must be formally negotiated. Of course, legal considerations must also be taken into account, especially when setting base pay rates and when designing the benefits package.

Links to the Organizational Environment. The organizational environment also plays a role in shaping the design of a total compensation system. Recall the description of four types of organizational culture presented in

ex 10.2 Components of Total Compensation within an Integrated HR System

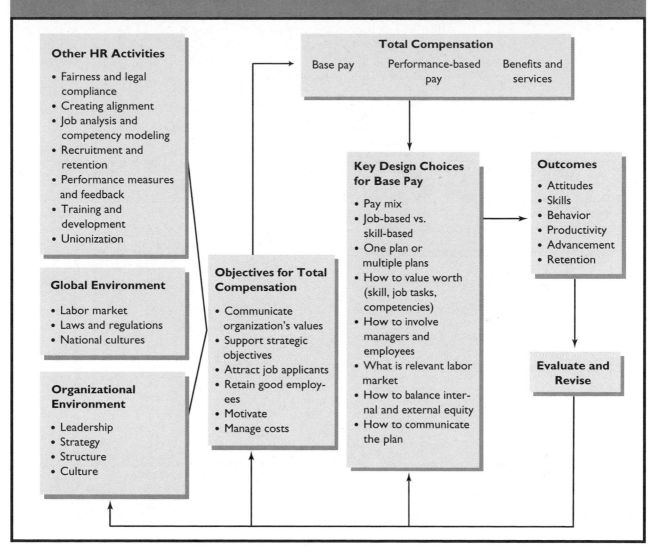

Chapter 4. In a market culture, the organization values achieving measurable and demanding goals that are financial and market based. A compensation system that includes a large component of performance-based pay is perhaps the most powerful tool the organization can use to communicate these values. In a more family-like clan culture, however, the organization is likely to rely more heavily on nonmonetary forms of compensation to convey the importance of values such as loyalty and commitment. An organization's strategy and structure also shape the compensation system, as will be described in more detail later in this chapter.

Among the many influences on an organization's culture is its life cycle. Early in the life of new firms, the entrepreneurial culture tends to predominate. As firms mature, they often transition into a culture that is more market oriented. Due partly to these cultural factors, but also due to eco-

"The components of dot-compensation are really not something new. What's different is the mix of those components."

Brian Dillon
Vice President of Total Rewards
Priceline.com

nomic factors, compensation systems tend to differ for firms at different points in the life cycle. This is illustrated in Exhibit 10.3.[5] During the start-up phase, attracting key contributors and facilitating innovation are the key HR issues. Risk is high, sales growth is slow, and earnings are low, so the company offers base salary and benefits that are below the market. Counterbalancing these are broad-based short- and long-term incentives, designed to stimulate innovation and its associated rewards.[6]

During the growth stage, sales grow rapidly, with moderate increases in earnings. Key HR issues are recruitment and training to develop

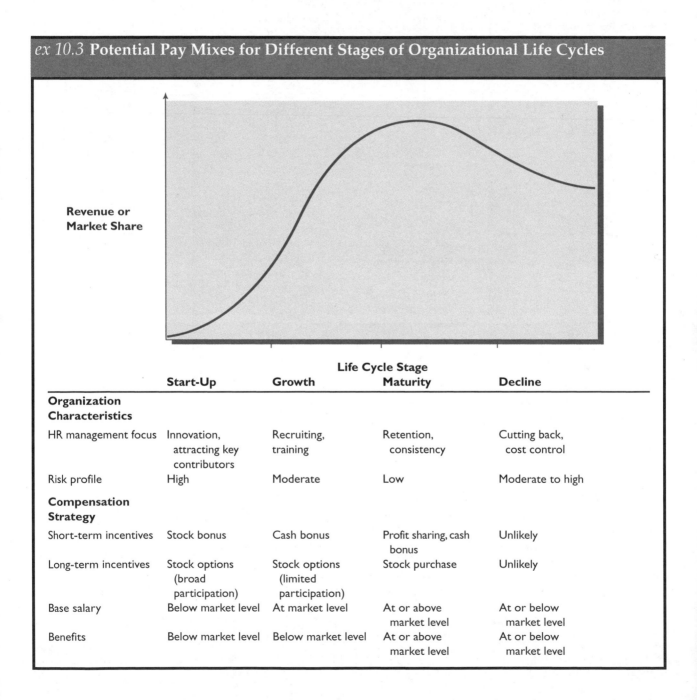

ex 10.3 Potential Pay Mixes for Different Stages of Organizational Life Cycles

Revenue or Market Share

	Life Cycle Stage			
	Start-Up	**Growth**	**Maturity**	**Decline**
Organization Characteristics				
HR management focus	Innovation, attracting key contributors	Recruiting, training	Retention, consistency	Cutting back, cost control
Risk profile	High	Moderate	Low	Moderate to high
Compensation Strategy				
Short-term incentives	Stock bonus	Cash bonus	Profit sharing, cash bonus	Unlikely
Long-term incentives	Stock options (broad participation)	Stock options (limited participation)	Stock purchase	Unlikely
Base salary	Below market level	At market level	At or above market level	At or below market level
Benefits	Below market level	Below market level	At or above market level	At or below market level

the human capital. Bonuses may be offered for innovation and sales growth, and stock options may be offered to encourage employees to think about the long-term growth of the company. For the entire high-tech industry, these dynamics were readily observable during the latter half of the 1990s.

During maturity, growth is slower and more orderly because the market is saturated with the product. High entry costs and exit barriers keep the number of competitors low, so organizations can focus on profitability. During this stage, key HR issues include performance, consistency, and retention of peak performers. Profit sharing, cash bonuses, and stock awards tied to short- or long-term growth may be offered to retain key contributors, along with competitive base pay and benefits.

During the decline stage, the human resource focus shifts to cutting back as market shares decline. Base salary and benefits are competitive at best, and may drop below market levels as management attempts to reduce expenditures.[7]

Organizational life cycles have received wide attention as a heuristic device for designing compensation systems, but the concept has critics. More than one set of compensation policies may be appropriate for any given stage in the cycle. Furthermore, organizations often have more than one product, each at a different stage of development. This complexity may make it impossible to cleanly classify a firm and its compensation mix according to a particular stage of development.[8]

Links to Other HR Practices. Added to the challenge of designing a total compensation system that is internally consistent is the challenge of making it well integrated with other aspects of the total HR system. As noted in Chapter 7, for example, the monetary and nonmonetary compensation that an organization offers is an important determinant of the number and quality of job applicants. And, once the best applicants have been selected, their decisions about whether to join the organization are likely to be influenced by the specific salary and bonus offers they receive. It should also be apparent that many of the training and development opportunities offered by employers represent valuable forms of nonmonetary compensation. Finally, as will become apparent in Chapter 12, the effective use of performance-based pay requires that it be tied to excellent performance measures.

THE STRATEGIC IMPORTANCE OF TOTAL COMPENSATION

Like many other aspects of an organization's approach to managing human resources, total compensation can facilitate (or interfere with) achieving many different strategic objectives. Three objectives of particular importance are (1) attracting and retaining the talent required for a sustainable competitive advantage, (2) focusing the energy of employees on implementing the organization's particular competitive strategy, and (3) controlling costs.

Attracting and Retaining Talent

In conjunction with an organization's recruitment and selection efforts, the total compensation program can help ensure that the rewards offered are sufficient to attract the right people at the right time for the right jobs.[9] Unless the total compensation program is perceived as internally fair and externally

"To the extent that auto insurance is a commodity, our biggest differentiator is our people. We want the best people at every level of the company, and we pay at the top of the market."

Peter B. Lewis
Chairman
Progressive Corporation

competitive, good employees are likely to leave.[10] Armed with an understanding of the determinants of pay satisfaction, organizations can develop
practices that appeal to applicants and help retain valuable talent.[11]

Pay fairness refers to what people believe they deserve to be paid in
relation to what others deserve to be paid. People tend to determine what
they and others deserve to be paid by comparing what they give to the
organization with what they get out of the organization. If they regard the
exchange as fair or equitable, they're likely to be satisfied. If they see it as
unfair, they're likely to be dissatisfied.[12]

Employees' perceptions of **equity** reflect comparisons they make
between the ratio of their inputs and outcomes to the ratios of others doing
similar work. *Inputs* are what an employee gives to the job (e.g., time, effort,
education). *Outcomes* are what people get out of doing the job (e.g., feelings
of meaningfulness, promotions, pay).[13] An example of equity comparison is
presented in Exhibit 10.4. It's a simple dollars-per-hour example to illustrate
how the ratios work. In reality the ratios can be quite complex, involving all
of the elements of total compensation.

As a result of equity perceptions, an employee or even a team will
feel equitably rewarded, underrewarded, or overrewarded. Feelings of being
overrewarded are probably rare, but when they occur they have beneficial
consequences for employers. Overrewarded employees tend to perform better in their jobs and are better members of the organization than employees
who haven't been so well rewarded.[14]

More typical are situations that result in employees feeling underrewarded. Trish Millines Dziko, executive director of Technology Access
Foundation, recalls feeling underrewarded in her first job after college—long

ex 10.4 An Example of Comparisons That Influence Equity Perceptions

	Ratio Comparison	Perception
Equity	$\frac{\$50}{5\text{ hrs. work}} = \frac{\$100}{10\text{ hrs. work}} = \$10/\text{hr.}$ $\frac{\text{Outcomes (self)}}{\text{Inputs (self)}} = \frac{\text{Outcomes (other)}}{\text{Inputs (other)}}$	"I'm being treated equally."
Inequity	$\left[\frac{\$50}{5\text{ hrs. work}} = \$10/\text{hr.}\right] < \left[\frac{\$100}{5\text{ hrs. work}} = \$20/\text{hr.}\right]$ $\frac{\text{Outcomes (self)}}{\text{Inputs (self)}} < \frac{\text{Outcomes (other)}}{\text{Inputs (other)}}$	"I'm getting less than I deserve for my efforts."
Inequity	$\left[\frac{\$50}{5\text{ hrs. work}} = \$10/\text{hr.}\right] > \left[\frac{\$25}{5\text{ hrs. work}} = \$5/\text{hr.}\right]$ $\frac{\text{Outcomes (self)}}{\text{Inputs (self)}} > \frac{\text{Outcomes (other)}}{\text{Inputs (other)}}$	"I'm getting more than I deserve."

before she retired from Microsoft as a millionaire. After Dziko, an African American, had been in her new job a few months, a white woman (who eventually became her friend) was hired at a salary $10,000 higher than Dziko's. With a degree in computer science, Dziko was a quick study for the job. The new woman, who was the same age, had majored in psychology and had to attend a training course to learn about computers. Although Dziko may have been satisfied with her salary before this incident, from then on she felt underrewarded.[15]

Generally, six alternatives are available to employees who want to reduce their feelings of inequity:

- increase their inputs (e.g., time and effort) to justify higher rewards when they feel that they are overrewarded compared with others;
- decrease their inputs to compensate for lower rewards when they feel underrewarded;
- change the compensation they receive through legal or other actions (e.g., forming a union, filing a grievance, or leaving work early);
- modify their comparisons by choosing another person to compare themselves against;
- distort reality by rationalizing that the inequities are justified; or
- leave the situation (quit the job) if the inequities can't be resolved.

Some of these reactions can harm the organization. For example, high performers who feel that their pay is too low may leave the organization. As a result, the company loses their productive talents. If dissatisfied employees stay, they may react by withholding effort in order to restrict output or lower quality. Because feelings of inequity often cause frustration, they also lead people to behave in hostile and aggressive ways. A store clerk may be hostile to customers. A factory worker may deliberately sabotage equipment. Unfortunately, such hostility can even lead to such drastic reactions as killing former colleagues and managers.[16]

Most employers understand the importance of pay fairness, and the procedures they use are intended to create a fair system. But even when employers think they have succeeded in designing "fair" systems, employees may perceive inequities. Three culprits that detract from perceptions of fairness are low pay, pay secrecy, and executive compensation practices.

Low Pay. When choosing which company to work for, employees consider many aspects of the total pay package: some focus on the predictable, guaranteed level of pay; others focus on the maximum potential pay; still others focus on the less tangible aspects of total compensation. Regardless of how employees make their assessments, however, they will be dissatisfied if they perceive the company's total pay policy as less generous than that offered by competitors. Employees who are compensated above or on par with the market average are more likely to feel fairly paid than those who are paid below the going rate.

> **FAST FACT**
>
> Henry Ford had to hire close to 1,000 workers just to keep 100 who would work on his demanding and numbing assembly line. This persuaded him to raise wages from the prevailing $2.30 per day to $5 per day.

In the past, the issue of **external equity**—fairness relative to the external market—was typically framed as a simple question: "Should we lead, lag, or match the pay rates of labor market competitors?" When almost everyone's pay was predominately a basic salary with few benefits, this simple view made sense. In today's highly competitive environment, however, external equity has become more complex because companies creatively mix several forms of pay. For example, to support a high-volume strategy, sales representatives at one company may receive a low base salary ($30,000) with a high bonus potential ($60,000). They enjoy no job security and receive minimal benefits and services. Employees who focus on the base salary and benefits will perceive this as unfairly low pay. Another company couples a higher base salary ($65,000) with merit pay increases averaging around 5 percent. Job security is good and the benefits offered are world class. Employees who focus on the maximum direct monetary compensation and place little value on the generous benefits package will view this pay as being unfairly low.

Turnover is one reaction to feeling unfairly paid, but it is not the only one. Dissatisfied employees may stay in their job and not perform as well as they could if they felt more motivated. In the worst circumstances, they may attempt to even things out by stealing from the employer. A Kinko's employee described a typical scenario: "We rip them off anyway all the time. But we don't rip them off for money that I know of. Except for that one guy who got arrested—who was actually taking money. The way people steal is just constantly making posters for their kids and doing all that kind of stuff. It feels like a fringe benefit. Because it is a low-paying kind of endless job. So people do it all the time. Like last night, I made—oh, my gosh, maybe 40 color copies of my mother-in-law's new grandchild. Which are $1.29 a piece, you know?"[17]

Pay Secrecy. Perceived inequities sometimes occur because employees have inaccurate or incomplete information. Although it is illegal for employers to forbid employee discussions of pay,[18] keeping pay secret is the norm in many U.S. organizations. According to organizational etiquette, asking others their salaries is generally considered gauche. In a study at DuPont, all employees were asked if the company should disclose more payroll information so that everyone would know everyone else's pay. Only 18 percent voted for an open pay system. At Whole Foods, a grocery retailer, employees are welcome to peruse a notebook that lists every employee's total annual compensation, but the company acknowledges that not all employees like the system. According to the company's vice president of human resources, the policy of openness made some employees so uncomfortable that they left, while others decided against taking a job offer.[19]

Managers also favor pay secrecy. It makes their lives easier. Without knowledge of pay differentials, employees are less likely to confront supervisors about inequitable pay, so managers don't have to justify their actions.[20]

Short of full disclosure about pay, employers can minimize misperceptions by involving employees in pay system design. Traditionally, HR professionals and managers had the most involvement in the design of compensation systems. During the past decade, however, employee involvement has increased. Nearly two-thirds of all labor agreements require incumbent involvement, and approximately half of all companies involve their employees in designing and implementing their compensation plans.[21] As discussed in Chapter 3, involving employees in decisions promotes acceptance of the decisions and establishes a sense of procedural justice.

Perceived inequities may also arise due to poor implementation of a well-designed system. Provisions to ensure due process address this potential problem. Union contracts often prescribe a formal appeal system for

> "*Compensation remains a sacred cow. Business owners still worry about how their workers will react when they find out someone else in the same job makes more than they do.*"
>
> Kevin Ruble
> Managing Director
> TranSolution

compensation decisions. Dissatisfied employees first file their complaints with their immediate supervisors. If no satisfactory resolution is forthcoming, the appeal moves forward to a higher level of management. Many nonunion employees have similar opportunities to appeal pay decisions.

A more radical approach to keeping employees satisfied is letting them set their own pay. This may sound far-fetched, but it is not as unusual as it may seem. Romac Industries, a pipe fitting plant, began using this approach more than 20 years ago. Employees request pay raises by completing a form that includes information about their current pay level, previous raise, requested raise, and reasons for thinking a raise is deserved. The requests are posted, along with photographs of the employees, for several working days. Then employees vote, and the majority rules.[22]

The more typical process by which employees set their own pay is when they negotiate their salary. During the latter half of the 1990s, a strong economy and tight labor market for some professionals put pressure on employers to offer higher and higher compensation. Often, the salary demands of talented employees were met—even if it meant breaking all the rules! A few thousand dollars here or there seemed like a small price to get and keep the talent that was essential to continued growth. Once the economy slowed down again, however, many companies were facing the challenge of reestablishing a feeling of fairness among those employees who were less aggressive in negotiating higher pay packages.[23]

Pay Gaps. During the past decade, employees at the middle and lower levels of organizations have watched the pay of those at the top rise rapidly at a time when increases in their own pay have been relatively modest. Moreover, as Exhibit 10.5 shows, the gap between those at the top and everyone else has been steadily increasing.[24] During the past 20 years, CEOs have seen

"We trust our employees to make decisions about everything else. Why not about their own compensation?"

Roger Sant
Chairman
AES Corporation

CEO pay:
"There's nothing like this issue. This one just galvanizes people instantly."

Betsy Leondar-Wright
Spokeswoman
United for a Fair Economy

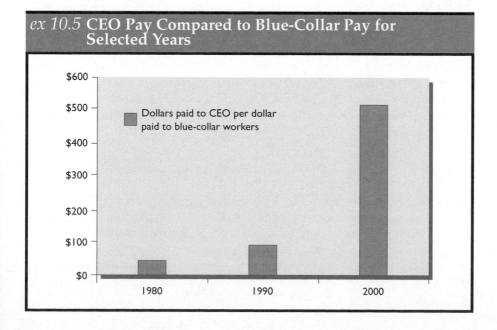

ex 10.5 **CEO Pay Compared to Blue-Collar Pay for Selected Years**

Dollars paid to CEO per dollar paid to blue-collar workers

their pay increase 514 percent, or 12 times the rate of inflation. During the same period, the federal minimum wage has increased only 36 percent and median household income has increased 43 percent. Even the stock market did not keep pace with the rapid rise in CEO pay.[25]

The pattern is stark when looking at CEO pay, but such disparities are not limited to comparisons between those at the very top and very bottom of the organization. Similar patterns are found by simply comparing the wages of employees who earn above the median with those who earn less than the median. In the United States even lower-level executives make far more than their counterparts in other advanced economies, while average workers make comparatively less.[26] Furthermore, disparities found in the United States dwarf those found in many other countries. In the United States, the typical ratio is about $185 paid to the CEO for every $1 paid to the lowest worker.[27] By comparison, the ratio for British, German, and French firms is less than $50/$1, and the ratio in Japan is just $17/$1.[28]

FAST FACT

In 2000 the top 20 highest-paid male CEOs received an average total compensation of $138.5 million. For a comparable group of females, it was $11.2 million.

How do workers feel about such disparities? Based on activity at the AFL-CIO's Web site devoted to this topic, many are angry and resentful. Here are examples of how some employees react to data about CEO pay:

No raise for us little guys for three years while the management all got bonuses and 15% raises. Do you think they will still get the same quality work from the lower ranks?

I was laid off from a small but successful software company in the early '90s at the height of the recession. And over 200 [out of 1000] other employees were also laid off [because] the company didn't want to post a losing quarter that would affect the stock price. The top five executives of the company each received a bonus that was more than my annual salary. Am I resentful? You bet.

My personal rule is that if the exec is known to receive over one million a year—I will boycott their products, period.

Do workers also boycott these companies as potential places to work? Are they more likely to leave such organizations when other employment opportunities present themselves? The extent to which such feelings translate into decisions about where to work is unknown, but it seems likely that at least some members of the workforce would prefer to decline a job offer from a firm known to have large pay disparities. As the demand for labor strengthens, others may choose to leave their current employers and move to more egalitarian companies.[29]

Implementing the Business Strategy

Do you regard a smile and a "Thank you for shopping" from the cashier of the local store as examples of quality customer-oriented service? Many people do and are willing to pay more for the goods in stores that have salespeople who engage in these behaviors. As we have seen, selection practices, socialization, and training help ensure that employees are *able* to engage in courteous, friendly behaviors. Compensation systems provide the supporting structure that *motivates* employees to display these behaviors even under the most trying circumstances.

According to one study of more than one hundred business units across 41 corporations, egalitarian pay systems facilitate a quality-driven, customer-focused strategy. Egalitarian systems are characterized by relatively less pay differential between lower-level and upper-echelon employees. As pay differentials increase, employees are less likely to feel fairly treated. At the same time, their attention to quality apparently declines. Thus, in this study, customers' ratings of quality were lower for business units with less egalitarian pay structures.[30]

An effective compensation system enhances employees' feelings of satisfaction while at the same time encouraging the behaviors needed to implement the business strategy.[31] The role of compensation in implementing competitive strategies becomes especially clear when a company changes its strategy and when it acquires or merges with another company.

Changes in Strategy. Employers like General Electric, Motorola, Sears, and IBM have discovered that a compensation system can encourage employees to embrace organizational change. Instead of handing out automatic annual pay increases based on job title and seniority—a common practice in the old economy—these companies reward teamwork, measurable quality improvements, and the acquisition of new skills. IBM's use of pay to drive its strategy is described in the feature "Managing Change: The IBM Connection."[32]

A survey of over 700 U.S. organizations found that nearly 50 percent were developing new compensation plans to fit newly emerging business strategies. In these new systems, performance-based incentive pay—for individuals and teams—plays a much bigger role, with incentives being earned through results that are clearly tied to the strategy. In fact, 70 percent of the companies had plans to introduce these elements.[33] Such changes are occurring around the world—they are not limited to the United States. In a similar study of European-based organizations, 81 percent of the companies indicated that they were changing their compensation systems in order to "improve employees' focus on achieving business goals." Although the use of incentive pay is not as prevalent across Europe as it is in the United States, the trend is clearly toward increasing use of incentives.[34]

> **FAST FACT**
>
> A study of postmerger integration found that the integration process took 9.5 months on average.

Mergers and Acquisitions. When companies combine, their cultures often clash. Because compensation systems are so closely linked to company cultures, mergers and acquisitions almost always provoke changes in the compensation system of one or both of the companies involved. Differences in pension plans, health insurance coverage, paid vacations, and collective bargaining agreements all need to be managed. As Exhibit 10.6 on page 415 illustrates, there are basically only three approaches to take when deciding how to merge the compensation plans of two firms: retain the separate plans, incorporate some aspects of one plan into the other plan, or create a totally new plan.[35] The choice a company makes should reflect other strategic decisions about how to operate in the postmerger environment. For example, if the intent is to operate the businesses as separate holdings within a corporate portfolio, then keeping the separate plans may be appropriate. Leaving the separate plans intact also

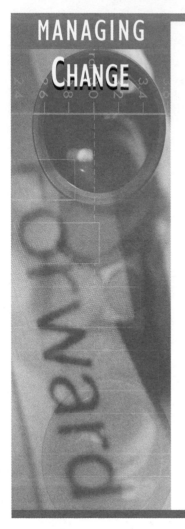

The IBM Connection

When the *Fortune* magazine published its 1993 annual list of the "most admired" companies, it revealed just how far IBM had fallen. In less than a decade, it went from being No. 1 three years in a row to being No. 324. That was the year Lou Gerstner took over as IBM's CEO and began directing its transformation back into a high-performance company. Did compensation play a role in the transformation? According to Pam Odam, Director of Total Compensation Programs for IBM Canada, it did: "Given that we spend several billion dollars on compensation and benefits worldwide, and given that our business was going through a significant transformation, we needed to take a closer look at all of our programs to determine if they were supporting our key business strategies and reflecting the changing dynamics of today's workforce."

Gerstner and his top management team developed a new strategy for IBM that focused on three key commitments:

- To Win.
- To Execute.
- To Team.

Now the challenge was to find a way for employees to connect to this strategy. Day in and day out, what exactly were the implications of the new strategy for employees? Realizing that employees needed an answer to this question, IBM made significant changes in the design, administration, and communication of several aspects of its HR system. These changes were designed:

- Attract and retain the best talent.
- Change the culture and motivate the desired behaviors needed to implement the new strategy.
- Manage costs.

One major change was to use skills or competencies as a partial basis for determining employees' base pay and their annual pay increases. IBM's new strategy required new skills. The new compensation system encourages employees to develop those new skills and rewards them for doing so. Business success also partially determines pay. This was a big change for employees who had grown accustomed to automatic salary increases. To support the shift in the culture of IBM, flexible benefits and employee-friendly practices like a new casual dress code were added. Casual dress has become fairly common in U.S. business, but for IBM'ers who had grown accustomed to the traditional blue-suit-and-white-shirt company uniform, this change was anything but easy.

To make these changes, IBM invested heavily. Their compensation and benefits costs grew from $21 billion in 1993 to a projected $50 billion in 2003. Compensation as a percentage of revenue also has grown. "It's a huge business decision and you have to work very tightly with the other areas to keep a handle on it," explained Andrew Richter, a director of compensation at IBM. The cost increases are considered appropriate by the company as it shifts to a services business that is more labor and knowledge intensive.

makes sense as a short-term strategy if the long-term strategy involves selling off significant portions of the business. However, if the business units are expected to merge and operate as an integrated whole, the other approaches may be more appropriate. If the merging companies have similar cultures, the incorporation approach may be most effective. But if the merging firms have very distinct cultures, then picking and choosing elements of their compensation plans is not likely to yield a new plan that is internally consistent. In that case, creating a new plan may be necessary.

Increasing Productivity

Whereas nonmonetary compensation influences employee satisfaction, and thus employee attraction and retention, the monetary elements of total compensation influence performance and productivity.[37] For example, gainsharing programs link financial rewards to improvements in the performance of a somewhat autonomous plant or facility. Such programs can

ex 10.6 Integrating Compensation Systems Following Mergers and Acquisitions

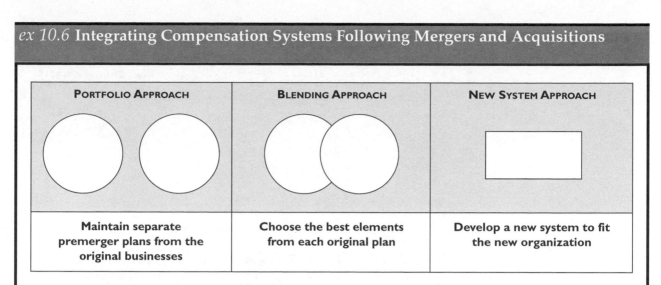

PORTFOLIO APPROACH	BLENDING APPROACH	NEW SYSTEM APPROACH
Maintain separate premerger plans from the original businesses	Choose the best elements from each original plan	Develop a new system to fit the new organization

Contrasting Corporate Cultures and Compensation Systems

Preference for risk taking vs. risk aversion:

Use of variable pay, uncapped commissions, and executive pay that's tied to shareholder value are all indicators of a risk-taking culture.

Flexibility and informality vs. rigidity and formality:

The presence of many ad hoc programs, many employees who are paid by exception rather than by the rules, few job descriptions, and the absence of detailed manuals are all indicators of a flexible and informal culture.

Decentralized vs. centralized:

Decision-making authority that's been pushed down to the divisions, a small corporate compensation staff, and bonus payouts that reflect division-level results are all indicators of a decentralized culture.

Concern for results vs. concern for people:

Few entitlements, wide variations in the bonus and merit pay given to individuals, and retirement contributions based on company performance are all indicators of a culture that emphasizes concern for results over concern for people.

Team focus vs. focus on individual stars:

Smaller pay disparities between employees at the the top and bottom rungs of the organization, cash incentives based on team performance, broad participation in employee stock ownership plans, skill- or knowledge-based pay, and team recognition programs are all indicators of a culture that promotes teamwork.

---

improve performance by focusing employees' attention on appropriate performance indicators and rewarding employees for improving over time.[38]

Incentive pay programs, the subject of Chapter 12, apply the same principles, but rewards are linked to the performance of individuals or small teams. At First Union, everyone—from branch managers to tellers—works on an incentive system that rewards selling various products and services. The incentives make up about 40 percent of an employee's total annual compensation. Some salespeople work on pure commission, with no cap.[39] Most U.S. firms use some form of incentive pay, believing that it contributes to productivity. People may or may not work harder when they are paid using incentives. However, if the incentive plan is designed well, employees are

"When I came here, they gave you a country ham and a fruitcake at Christmas if you had a good year. Now we're paying [incentives] out in cash on the barrelhead."

Edward E. Crutchfield
CEO
First Union Corporation

more likely to spend their energy working at the tasks that are most important to the firm's success.

INTERNET RESOURCES   **10.A**

The Strategic Importance of Total Compensation

At our Web site, http://jackson.swcollege.com/, you can:

1. Learn about the importance of compensating employees at some of the firms discussed in this section by visiting their company home pages:

    Progressive Insurance

    AES Corporation

    Bayer

    IBM Corporation

    Lincoln Electric

2. Learn more about the resources available through The World at Work, an association of compensation professionals, and current issues of interest to their members.

ROLE OF THE EXTERNAL ENVIRONMENT

Three forces in the external environment that directly influence the design of the total compensation system are labor market conditions, legal constraints, and unions.

Labor Market Conditions

Labor market conditions affect the overall level of pay offered and the mix of pay offered.

FAST FACT

The average hourly wage in the movie business is $32.70; in the missile production business it's $20.60.

Pay Level. The term **pay level** is used to describe how a firm's overall pay compares with that of other firms. Is the total pay package above what most others are offering, at about the same as the market, or below the market? Typically, the organizations of most interest for market comparison purposes are those competing for the same talent. If a company's pay level is too low, qualified labor won't work for the company. Thus, shortages in the labor market provide qualified workers the opportunity to negotiate better terms of employment. If employees' wage demands are too high, however, employers may react by hiring fewer people.[40]

FAST FACT

The median annual earnings for male high school graduates is about $30,000, but they can earn $100,000 a year at Lincoln Electric.

For current employees—the internal labor market—low pay is likely to create turnover, at least under conditions of low unemployment. By jumping ship, valuable employees can increase their total compensation and often their career progress. A study of recent MBAs showed this quite clearly. Comparing MBAs with equivalent backgrounds, those who left their first employer earned $24,410 per year more than those who stayed. (Unfortunately, however, the strategy was slightly less effective for women and members of ethnic minority groups compared with white males.)[41]

Under conditions of low unemployment, demand for labor drives labor prices up. Then even burger flippers and java servers may be paid as much as 30 to 40 percent above the minimum wage.[42] High prices, in turn, attract more entrants to the market—if there are any left to enter! At the same time, they push employers to seek alternatives. Introducing new technology that reduces the need for labor is one alternative. Raising prices for products and services is another, as is simply accepting smaller profit margins.[43]

Moving work abroad is another alternative. When a company moves abroad, however, wage levels, taxes and productivity all need to be considered. In Germany, for example, the cost of labor and related taxes are relatively high. In response, some German companies moved production out of the country—including to the United States. Arend Oetker, an owner of a food company named Schwartau, explained his company's recent investment in Switzerland this way: "I am a German, and I want to keep employment here as much as possible. But the more the labor costs rise and the more that taxes rise, the more difficult it is to remain in Germany. No one can be astonished that unemployment is going up."[44] Exhibit 10.7 illustrates the differing costs of labor in several countries.[45]

The procedures employers use to estimate the labor prices of competitors are described later in this chapter, as are other issues related to decisions about how to set base pay levels.

> **FAST FACT**
>
> In 2001, the average hourly wage for pilots at Delta was $201.65 and at Southwest it was $137.67.

Pay Mix. The **pay mix** in an organization's compensation system refers to the relative proportion of compensation that falls within the many categories shown in Exhibit 10.1. Over the past several years, compensation systems have included relatively greater variety. In the past, base salary and wages predominated, but this is changing as companies turn to incentive pay and as they develop new approaches to offering attractive benefits and services. Competitive pressures to keep costs down and improve productivity are causing many employers to keep fixed pay (wages and salaries) low and link

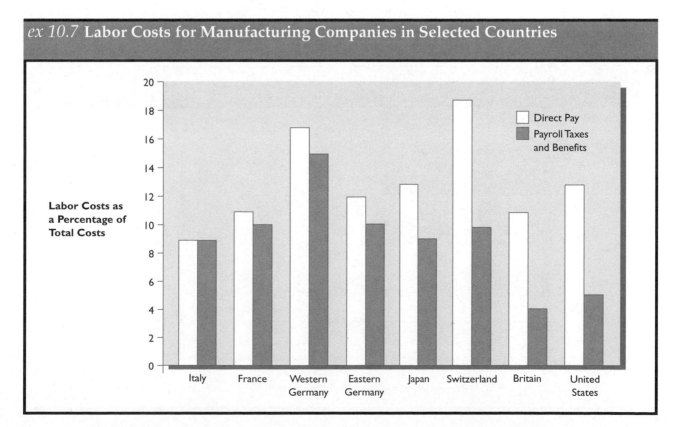

ex 10.7 **Labor Costs for Manufacturing Companies in Selected Countries**

pay increases to gains in productivity and/or profitability, which
are variable. With a well-designed variable pay component, a company's labor costs do not increase unless the company can afford it.
As part of its turnaround strategy, IBM introduced variable pay to
rank-and-file employees, which was a big change for the company.

Currently in the United States, about 90 percent of all executives
have some variable incentive pay, compared with about 25 percent of rank-
and-file wage earners.[46]

Companies differ greatly in terms of the mix of pay components they
offer employees. Furthermore, many companies offer a different mix to different groups of employees. This is illustrated in Exhibit 10.8.[47]

Legal Constraints and Social Considerations

Like other aspects of managing human resources, compensation activities are
shaped by a plethora of laws and regulations, covering topics such as
taxation, nondiscrimination, fair wages, a minimum wage, the protection of children, hardship pay for employees who work unusually long hours,
and income security through pension and welfare benefits. A sociological
analysis of all congressional bills introduced from 1951 to 1990 revealed that
different visions of work and family have been dominant at different periods,
reflecting the changing concerns of the labor market.[48] During the middle of
the 20th century, barriers between work and family were considered normal
and even desirable. Today, legislation such as the *Family and Medical Leave Act*
encourage employers to remove such barriers and actively support employees' simultaneous involvement in the spheres of work and family.[49]

Significant changes in our view of what is the normal workweek
have occurred, as well. A standard workweek now consists of five 8-hour
days. In 1840, six 13-hour days was considered normal. In 1913, when Henry

*"It never dawned on me
that there was a law
against reaching a private
agreement with someone
over work."*

Restaurant Owner
Wage Law Violator

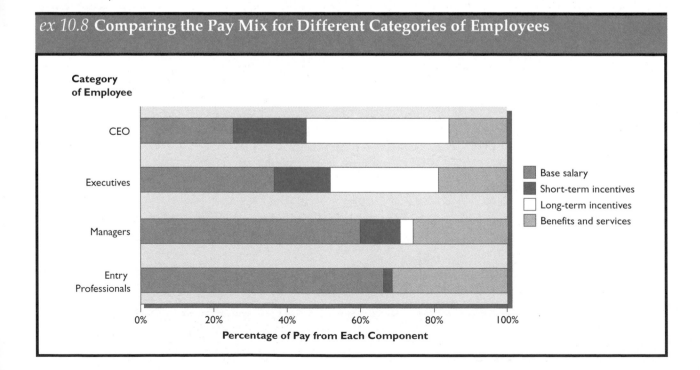

ex 10.8 **Comparing the Pay Mix for Different Categories of Employees**

Ford introduced the 8-hour day at a $5-a-day minimum wage, most of his competitors still expected 60 hours of work a week from employees. Eventually, national legislation governing hours and wages was passed.

Davis-Bacon and Walsh-Healey Acts. The first federal law to protect the amount of pay employees receive for their work was the *Davis-Bacon Act* of 1931. This act required organizations holding federal construction contracts to pay laborers and mechanics the prevailing wages of the majority of the employees in the locality where the work was performed. The *Walsh-Healey Public Contracts Act* of 1936 extended the *Davis-Bacon Act* to include all organizations holding federal construction contracts exceeding $10,000 and specified that pay levels conform to the industry minimum rather than the area minimum. The *Walsh-Healey Act* also established overtime pay at one and one-half times the hourly rate. These wage provisions did not include administrative, professional, office, custodial, or maintenance employees, or beginners, or disabled persons.

Fair Labor Standards Act. Partly because the coverage of Davis-Bacon and Walsh-Healey was limited to employees on construction projects, the *Fair Labor Standards Act* of 1938, or *Wage and Hour Law*, was enacted. This set minimum wages, maximum hours, child labor standards, and overtime pay provisions for all workers except domestic and government employees. The Supreme Court extended the coverage to include state and local government employees in 1985.

Under the *Fair Labor Standards Act*, the minimum wage began at $0.25 an hour and had reached $5.35 as of 2000. Still, subminimum wages are permitted for

- learners in semiskilled occupations,
- apprentices in skilled occupations,
- messengers in firms engaged primarily in delivering letters and messages,
- handicapped persons working in sheltered workshops,
- students in certain establishments, and
- employees who receive more than $30.00 a month in tips (up to 40 percent of the minimum requirement may be covered by tips).[50]

To prevent abuses regarding children, the act prohibits minors under the age of 18 from working in hazardous occupations. For nonhazardous positions, the minimum age ranges from 14 to 16, depending on the type of work to be performed and whether the employer is the child's parent.[51]

The act also establishes who is to be paid overtime for work and who is not. Wage earners who are covered by the act are called **nonexempt employees.** These employees must be paid time and a half for all work exceeding 40 hours a week. For nonexempt employees essentially all work-related activities required by the employer must be compensated at the hourly rate or as overtime.

Furthermore, compensation must be in the form of direct pay. Employers may not use a barter system. Thus, if a restaurant owner asks employees to come in on their days off and help spruce up their workplace, it's not legal to compensate them by giving a free pizza-and-beer party instead of overtime pay. Employers can't get around this requirement simply by claiming the work wasn't required. If an employer *permits* employees to work, it's obligated to pay them for that work.[52]

"Unless a new law has just been passed, wage/hour has always been our No. 1 category for questions."

Deborah Keary
Information Center Director
Society for Human Resource Management

FAST FACT

The worst industries for wage violations are eating and drinking establishments, apparel manufacturers, and heavy construction.

FAST FACT

For employees who are "on call" for duty, the general rule is that they do not have to be paid for the time they spend waiting if they can use that time they way they want to.

Several types of workers are considered exempt employees. **Exempt employees** are not covered by the overtime and minimum wage provisions of the FLSA. Executives, managers, professionals, administrators, and many other employees who are paid on a salary basis are exempt employees. To meet the salary criteria, exempt workers must be paid a fixed, predetermined salary, regardless of the precise number of hours they work in a given week. In addition, they must meet certain criteria regarding the content of their work. Managerial job content, for example, includes

- undertaking management duties;
- directing the work of two or more employees;
- controlling or greatly influencing hiring, firing, and promotion decisions; and
- exercising discretion.

Professional work requires a college-level or postgraduate degree in a field of *specialized* study and includes the following tasks:

- doing work requiring knowledge acquired through specialized, prolonged training,
- exercising discretion or judgment, and
- doing work that is primarily intellectual and nonroutine.[53]

Job title alone is not a sufficient basis for treating these jobs as exempt. A comprehensive job analysis is necessary to document the activities involved in executive, administrative, or professional jobs.[54]

> **FAST FACT**
>
> About one-third of all minimum wage earners are the sole earner in their household. One in six is a sole earner with one or more children.

Living Wage Laws. In addition to minimum wage laws, some employers are subject to so-called **living wage laws.** The city of Baltimore passed the first comprehensive living wage law in 1994. Although these laws affect only about 1 percent of all employees, they reflect a widespread social concern about the important need to ensure that low-wage employees earn enough to live at a reasonable level of comfort. More than 80 jurisdictions have living wage laws that require some employers—for example, those who have contracts with the local government—to pay minimum wages above federal and state levels. Some jurisdictions also specify higher minimum rates for workers who do not receive benefits. The objective of these laws is to bring the minimum wage paid to employees to a level that better reflects the actual cost of living in an area.[55]

Equal Pay Act. In 1963, the *Fair Labor Standards Act* was amended to include the *Equal Pay Act*. The *Equal Pay Act* prohibits an employer from discriminating "between employees on the basis of sex by paying wages to employees . . . at a rate less than the rate at which he pays wages to employees of the opposite sex . . . for equal work on jobs the performance of which requires equal skill, effort and responsibility, and which are performed under similar working conditions."

For monitoring purposes, employers submit compensation data when they file EEO-1 reports (described in Chapter 7). Exhibit 10.9 shows how the data are reported. To establish a prima facie case of wage discrimination, the plaintiff needs to show that a disparity in pay exists for males and females performing substantially equal, not necessarily identical, jobs. If male-dominated (e.g., janitorial) and female-dominated (e.g., clerical) jobs ex 10.9 Employer Information Report EEO-1 (Excerpt, Part C)

	MINORITY MALES / MINORITY FEMALES				NON-MINORITY MALES / NON-MINORITY FEMALES			
	Total Annual Monetary Compensation for All Minority Female Employees	Lowest Annual Monetary Compensation for Any Single Minority Female Employee	Highest Annual Monetary Compensation for Any Single Minority Female Employee	Tenure of Average Minority Female Employees With Firm	Total Annual Monetary Compensation for All Non-Minority Female Employees	Lowest Annual Monetary Compensation for Any Single Non-Minority Female Employee	Highest Annual Monetary Compensation for Any Single Non-Minority Female Employee	Tenure of Average Non-Minority Female Employees With Firm
Officials, Managers								
Professionals								
Technicians								
Operatives								
Sales Workers								
Office, Clerical Workers								
Craft Workers								
Laborers								
Service Workers								

are found to be substantially equal based on job evaluation results, wages for the lower-paid job must be raised to match those for the higher-paid position. Freezing or lowering the pay of the higher-paid job is unacceptable.

Four exceptions can be used to legally defend unequal pay for equal work: the existence and use of a seniority system, a merit system, a system that measures earnings or quality of production, or a system based on any additional characteristic other than gender. If the employer can show the existence of one or more of these exceptions, a pay differential for males and females in a similar job may be justified.

On pay for female movie stars: *"Maybe the glass ceiling has been raised a bit. But when a woman hits her head on it, she can look up and see men's loafers."*

Elaine Goldsmith-Thomas
Talent Agent
International Creative Management

Comparable Worth. The heart of the **comparable worth** theory is the contention that, although the "true worth" of nonidentical jobs may be similar, some jobs (often held by women) are paid a lower rate than others (often held by men). For example, a recent analysis of entry-level pay found that women earned 84 cents for every dollar earned by men. About 14 percent of this difference is due to differences in the skills of men and women, and another 15 percent is due to differences in career aspirations.[56] Comparable worth theory holds that the remaining differential in entry-level wages reflects wage discrimination. For example, men are placed into better-paying job categories and are more likely to have mentors, although they're equivalent on all qualifications.[57] Or, in the case of Hollywood stars, movie studios simply offer male stars higher salaries than they offer female stars, despite similar box office appeal. According to comparable worth advocates, legal protection should be provided to ensure pay equity.[58] Market rates are assumed to be biased and should not be used to justify continued pay discrimination.

Several state and local governments and unions have passed comparable worth or pay equity legislation, and many businesses have also taken action on pay equity issues. The feature "Managing Diversity: Pay Equity Pays Off," describes these issues and how they can be addressed.[59]

Labor Unions

The presence of a union in a private-sector firm is estimated to increase wages by 10 to 15 percent and benefits by about 20 to 30 percent. The wage differential between unionized and nonunionized firms appears to be greatest during recessionary periods and smallest during inflationary periods. Whether the increased compensation costs in unionized firms translate into higher output is widely debated. Some researchers contend that, by improving employee satisfaction, lowering turnover, and decreasing absenteeism, unions have a positive effect on net productivity. Others contend that the gains in productivity aren't equivalent to the increased compensation costs.[60] In addition to determining how much employees are paid, unions have shaped the way total pay is allocated among wages, performance-based pay, and benefits.[61] Chapter 15 discusses the influence of unions in more detail.

INVOLVING THE HR TRIAD IN MANAGING TOTAL COMPENSATION

Total compensation is linked to the needs and characteristics of a business when top management believes that compensation affects the company's overall performance. It is linked to the interests and preferences of employees when they have the means to voice their concerns and the power to negotiate on behalf of their interests. A compensation system that balances the

Pay Equity Pays Off

Pay equity is a policy that provides businesses the competitive edge to meet the challenges of the 21st century, according to the National Committee on Pay Equity. A consistent, fair pay policy whereby all workers are paid equally for work of equal value produces a more productive and better-motivated workforce, which, in turn, promotes recruitment and retention of good workers. "Smart employers recognize that future profits depend on current investment in their most vital resource: their people," says the coalition of labor, women's, and civil rights groups in its report *Pay Equity Makes Good Business Sense.*

Women and men of color are concentrated in lower-paying jobs. When women and men of color occupy traditionally white-male-dominated positions—even after accounting for legitimate reasons for pay differences such as differing skills, work experience, and seniority—women and men of color are still paid less. Discriminatory wage practices account for between one-quarter and one-half of this disparity in wages.

What Is Pay Equity?

Pay equity is a means of eliminating race, ethnicity, and gender as wage determinants within job categories and between job categories. Many businesses pay women and men of color less than white males due to wage structures that retain historical biases and inconsistencies that are, in fact, discriminatory.

A pay equity policy examines existing pay policies that underpay women and men of color and activates steps to correct the discrimination.

How to Achieve Pay Equity

A comprehensive audit is the first step in implementing a pay equity policy. The audit should examine the following areas for inequities and needed changes:

- job evaluation,
- external market pay levels,
- pay administration procedures, and
- recruitment practices.

In the area of pay administration, the audit should scrutinize each element of a compensation system, including salary range design, salary grades, pay differentials, promotion rates, merit increases, incentive programs, and seniority policies.

Pay Equity Is Not Costly

Following the lead of public employers, many private-sector businesses incorporate pay equity analyses in their annual budget proposals. The cost of pay equity adjustments usually has been between 2 and 5 percent of payroll. In no cases have the wages of any workers been lowered in order to achieve pay equity. The objective of pay equity is to remedy wage inequities for underpaid workers, not to penalize another group of employees.

interests of all concerned stakeholders is most likely when compensation is managed through a true partnership. If designed and implemented well, compensation policies and practices encourage and reward desired employee behaviors while at the same time treating employees fairly.

Many companies actively involve employees in the design of new compensation systems. Although involving only managers is still the norm, about one-third of companies also involve nonmanagement employees in the design process. Employee participation is especially important as a means for assuring that the diverse needs of all employees are met. Involving employees at all organizational levels and job types takes longer, but the investment seems to pay off. Several studies show that plans designed by a task force produce both higher satisfaction and better performance.[62] The roles and responsibilities of managers, employees, and HR professionals are summarized in "The HR Triad: Roles and Responsibilities for Total Compensation."

Of course, the ideal presented in the HR Triad feature is not always achieved. In fact, according to one recent study, the gap between what managers should know about compensation and what they actually know is significant. Some of the findings from the study are summarized in Exhibit 10.10. The managers may not be to blame for this knowledge gap. The study

ex 10.10 How Much Managers Know vs. What They Should Know

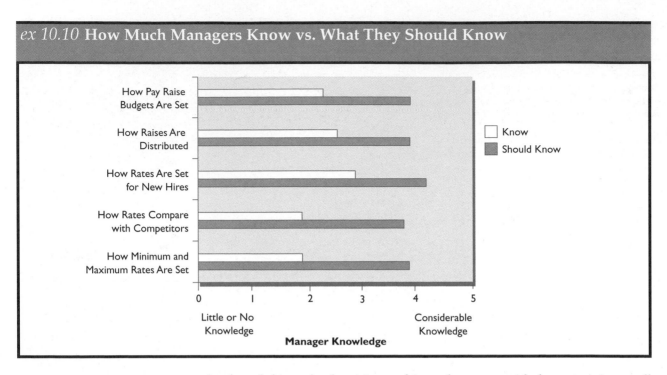

also found that only about 1 out of 6 employers provided any training at all to teach managers about the company's compensation plan. When training was provided, the most common topics were minimum wage laws and details about pay rates for new hires.

To understand the basic elements of a compensation system, managers and other employees need to know more than just how much they are paid and how much the people they supervise are paid. At a minimum, they should also understand how base pay rates are established, the rationale for any incentives that are part of the total pay package, and details of the benefits and services offered to employees. The remainder of this chapter describes how employers establish base pay rates for their employees. The topic of incentives is discussed in Chapter 12 and benefits are discussed in Chapter 13.

INTERNET RESOURCES   10.B

The Roles of the External Environment and the HR Triad in Total Compensation

At our Web site, http://jackson.swcollege.com/, you can:

1. Learn more about pay equity and comparable worth from

   the Ontario Pay Equity Commission

   the State of Minnesota's Department of Employee Relations

   the Capital Research Center

   the National Partnership

2. Find out about the AFL-CIO's position on executive pay practices.

3. Read the text of important federal laws governing compensation. Search for:

   Davis-Bacon Act (1931)

   Walsh-Healey Public Contracts Act (1936)

   Fair Labor Standards Act (1938)

   Equal Pay Act (1963)

Roles and Responsibilities for Total Compensation

THE HR TRIAD

Line Managers	HR Professionals	Employees
• Work with HR professionals to assure alignment of pay system with strategic objectives. • Work with employees to ensure pay system satisfies and motivates them. • Participate with HR professionals to determine how to value jobs and people. • Communicate pay system principles and abide by them. • Make and communicate decisions about direct pay given to individuals and small teams. • Communicate indirect components of the pay system. • Fairly administer all components of compensation. • Participate in due process appeals regarding pay.	• With line managers, assure alignment of pay system with strategic objectives. • Assess employees' preferences and reactions to pay systematically and regularly. • Monitor and analyze trends in the external market. • Develop processes to measure performances and/or skills. • Design processes for job evaluation to involve line managers and job incumbents. • Work with line managers to communicate pay system. • Work closely with line managers to finalize pay. • Ensure employees have access to due process and are free to appeal pay decisions.	• Take responsibility for understanding the total compensation system. • Indicate preferences for forms of pay. • May participate in job evaluation. • May assess the levels of performance and/or skill of self and others. • Accept responsibility for actively managing indirect compensation plans and accounts. • May provide input into pay decisions for others. • May register complaints about fairness of pay. • Participate in due process appeals regarding pay.

ESTABLISHING THE VALUE OF JOBS

An employee's **base pay** refers to the wage or salary he or she receives, exclusive of any incentive pay or benefits. In establishing base pay, employers usually use two types of information: (a) information about the job itself and its relative value within the organization, and (b) market information about what other employers pay for the job. In this section, we focus on how employers establish the relative value of jobs.

Job evaluation is a procedure for establishing the relative internal worth of jobs. Internal worth reflects a job's importance or its contribution to the overall attainment of organizational objectives. A primary objective of job evaluation is to create a system of pay rates that results in employees feeling a sense of **internal equity.** That is, job evaluation should result in employees feeling that they are paid fairly when compared with others in the same organization. By design, job evaluation focuses internally and does not take into account market forces, individual skills, or individual performance. The result is an analysis that can be used to determine a job-based pay system. In a **job-based pay** system, the pay people receive is determined *primarily* by what job they hold. The value of the job may be based on many factors, including the level of knowledge required, the responsibilities associated with the job, or the competencies required for the job.

Job evaluation is closely related to job analysis, but they are not identical. As described in Chapter 6, the objective of job analysis is to determine the content of jobs: what tasks are performed, what responsibilities employees have, and what competencies are required. Obtaining this information is an essential prior step to job evaluation. Job evaluation then asks, "What is the relative *value* of jobs with various contents and responsibilities involving the use of various competencies?"

As with any administrative procedure, job evaluation invites give and take. Consensus building is often required among stakeholders (jobholders, managers, HR professionals, union officials) to resolve conflicts that inevitably arise about the relative worth of jobs. The use of group judgments throughout the job evaluation process helps ensure that these conflicts are addressed, producing a compensation system that is congruent with organizational values and strategic objectives and not based solely on external market valuations of worth.[63]

The four major approaches to establishing the value of jobs are ranking, job classification, the traditional point rating method, and the emerging competency-based method. Traditional job evaluation methods focus on the job as the unit of interest. Some methods evaluate the whole job, whereas others evaluate components of jobs using compensable factors. Some methods evaluate jobs directly in dollar worth, whereas others assign points to jobs, and points are then converted to dollar values. In recent years, there has been a trend toward using a competency-based approach to valuing jobs. When competencies are used to value jobs, the focus shifts from the tasks involved in the work to the competencies required to perform those tasks.

Ranking Method

The simplest approach to job evaluation is the **ranking method.** One approach is to simply rank jobs according to the perceived overall market value of each job. Alternatively, jobs can be ranked on the basis of such variables as difficulty, criticality to organizational success, and the competencies required. The ranking method is convenient when only a few jobs need to be evaluated and when one person is familiar with them all. As the number of jobs increases, it becomes less likely that one person will know them all well enough to create a meaningful rank order. Thus, as the number of jobs to be ranked increases, detailed job analysis information becomes more important and input is more likely to be sought from several members of a committee.

Job Classification Method

The **job classification method** is similar to the ranking method, except that it first establishes job classes—usually referred to as pay grades—and then groups job descriptions within these broader categories. Classification standards specify the kinds and levels of responsibilities assigned to jobs in each grade, the difficulty of the work performed, and the required employee qualifications. The pay grade descriptions serve as the standard against which the job descriptions are compared. The description of a grade captures some of the details of the work that falls within the grade, yet it's general enough that several jobs can be slotted into the grade. For example, a small company might have two grades—one for managerial employees and another for everyone else. A larger company might have grades for managers, professionals doing technical work, service providers, and all other support staff.

A particular advantage of the job classification method is that it can be applied to a large number and a wide variety of jobs. As the number and variety of jobs increase, however, the classification process becomes more subjective. This is particularly true when employees work at several locations and in jobs that have the same title but not the same job content. In such cases, it's difficult to attend to the true content of each job, so job evaluators tend to rely on the job title for making a job classification.[64] Employees in these jobs may be more attuned than their managers to differences in the contents of jobs with similar titles, which is a good reason to involve them in the job classification process.

Point Rating Method

The most widely used method of job evaluation is the **point rating** (or point factor) **method.** The procedure involves using a system of points to assign value to jobs. When you read about this method, it may appear to be a very objective approach to valuing jobs, but like other job evaluation plans, the point factor method involves subjective judgments. Bias or subjectivity can enter at each of the three major steps in the process, which are:

1. selecting compensable factors to use in rating jobs,
2. assigning weights to the compensable factors, and
3. establishing the degree of each factor present in a job.

Select Compensable Factors. **Compensable factors** are the dimensions of work that an organization chooses to use when establishing the relative value of jobs. Employers compensate people more to the degree that their jobs involve tasks and responsibilities that the organization considers valuable. When selecting compensable factors, employers can choose either to use a standardized off-the-shelf system or develop their own customized set of factors.

The most widely used *standardized* point system is the **Hay Guide Chart-Profile,** which was developed by a consulting company now called the Hay Group. Recall that Bayer's old compensation system had been built using the old Hay Guide Charts. The Hay approach has been particularly popular for evaluating executive, managerial, and professional positions, but it's also widely used for technical, clerical, and manufacturing positions.

The original Hay Guide Chart-Profile method relies on three primary compensable factors: problem solving, know-how, and accountability. Point values are determined for each job, using the three factors. According to the Hay Group, a major advantage of this system has been its wide acceptance and usage. Because organizations worldwide use the system, Hay can provide clients with comparative pay data by industry or locale. Another advantage of the system is that it has been legally challenged and found acceptable by the courts.

The Hay Guide Chart-Profile Method, like any standardized system, may not reflect a particular organization's true values, however. Thus, each organization needs to consider whether the factors of problem solving, know-how, and accountability are truly congruent with the organization's values. In recognition of the idea that different companies are likely to value different aspects of a job, Hay also works with companies to create tailored point systems that fit specific organizations.

When standardized systems don't meet a company's needs, it may choose to use *custom-designed factors* to evaluate jobs. In the example of Bayer, selecting new compensable factors to use when setting base pay rates was a key strategic decision. Bayer developed new compensable factors to use in valuing jobs in an effort to improve the alignment of its pay system with its strategic objectives. To replace the standard factors from the original Hay methods, it chose the following compensable factors:

428

Chapter 10

Improvement opportunity	How much opportunity is there for people in this job to improve performance?
Contribution	How strong are the requirements for people in this job to achieve results?
Capability	What are the total proficiencies and competencies required in the job? Three categories were considered: • Expertise and complexity • Leadership and integration • Relationship building skills

Assign Factor Weights. Regardless of whether standard or customized factors are used, the next step in valuing jobs involves assigning relative weights to the factors. The weights enable the system to allocate more points to factors that are most important to the company's success. For example, Bayer may wish to give more weight to jobs in which people can make a greater contribution to the firm's performance, while giving less weight to the competencies needed to perform a job. Thus it might assign the weights of 50, 25, and 25 to the three factors listed above. These weights are reflected in the point system. A consequence of this decision might be that key sales jobs with few educational requirements would be assigned more points than some corporate staff positions that require formal degrees and certification.

To further illustrate the use of points and weights, consider the point system presented in Exhibit 10.11. It has six compensable factors. The total maximum number of points that can be assigned to a job using this system is 1,000, and the minimum is 225. Factor weights are built into the points, which makes the system easier for managers to use. The maximum points assigned to the factors can easily be translated into weights, however. To obtain the factor weights, simply divide the maximum points for each factor by the total points possible (1,000). This yields the following weights for factors 1 to 6, respectively: 20 percent, 26 percent, 24 percent, 5 percent, 10 percent, and 15 percent.

Establish Degrees of Factors Present in Job. Once factors are chosen and weighted, the next step is to construct scales reflecting the different degrees within each factor. Exhibit 10.11 also shows descriptions for five degrees of problem solving. Notice that each degree is anchored by a description of the typical tasks and behaviors associated with that degree.

After factors and degrees are delineated, a job's worth can be assessed. This involves establishing the degree of each compensable factor associated with the job. Typically, a compensation committee is chosen to assess job worth. The committee includes a cross-section of stakeholders (e.g., managers, union officials, hourly workers, and workers from various job families) who are trained in the use of the job evaluation process. They begin by evaluating each job independently—that is, each committee member determines the degree level for each factor for each job, based on job descriptions and other job analysis information. Committee members usually discuss their evaluations, and debate continues until consensus is reached on the value of each job. At the end of the process, each job has a total point value that reflects its relative worth.

ex 10.11 Example of the Point Rating Method

PART A: SAMPLE POINT EVALUATION SYSTEM

Compensable Factor	First Degree	Second Degree	Third Degree	Fourth Degree	Fifth Degree
1. Job knowledge	50	100	150	200	NA
2. Problem solving	50	100	150	205	260
3. Impact	60	120	180	240	NA
4. Working conditions	10	30	50	NA	NA
5. Supervision needed	25	50	75	100	NA
6. Supervision given	30	60	90	120	150

Note: NA = Not Applicable, which means that this degree level is not used for the relevant compensable factor.

PART B: EXAMPLE OF A COMPENSABLE FACTOR AND RELATED DEGREE STATEMENTS

Problem Solving

This factor examines the types of problems dealt with in your job. Indicate the one level that is most representative of most of your job responsibilities.

Degree 1: Actions are performed in a set order according to written or verbal instructions. Problems are referred to a supervisor.

Degree 2: Routine problems are solved and various choices are made regarding the order in which the work is performed, within standard practices. Information may be obtained from various sources.

Degree 3: Various problems are solved that require general knowledge of company policies and procedures applicable within own area of responsibility. Decisions are made based on a choice from established alternatives. Actions are expected to be within standards and established procedures.

Degree 4: Analytical judgment, initiative, or innovation is required in dealing with complex problems or situations. Evaluation is not easy because there is little precedent or information may be incomplete.

Degree 5: Complex tasks involving new or constantly changing problems or situations are planned, delegated, coordinated, or implemented, or any combination of these. Tasks involve the development of new technologies, programs, or projects. Actions are limited only by company policies and budgets.

Competency-Based Job Evaluation

As Chapter 6 explained, when organizations analyze jobs, they can focus on the tasks and responsibilities required to do the job, and/or they can emphasize the competencies required for people to perform the job. For a variety of reasons, many organizations have been moving to competency-based HR systems. The compensation plan is one aspect of the HR system that may reflect this shift. Competency-based job evaluation keeps the focus on the job, but the emphasis is on the competencies needed to perform the job rather than the job duties. The alterations Bayer made to the Hay point system involve a partial shift toward the **competency-based job evaluation** method for assigning points to jobs. In Bayer's new system, points assigned for Improvement opportunity and Contribution reflect job activities. The points assigned for Capability reflect competencies. Often the shift to a competency-based job evaluation system coincides with the adoption of the broadbanding approach described in Chapter 6. In the context of compensation, broadbanding simply means that few pay grades are used. Pay grades will be explained shortly.

Used together, competency-based job evaluation and broadbanding provide a method for defining career paths that focus on individual development instead of climbing the corporate ladder, as described in the feature "Managing Teams: New Pay at GlaxoSmithKline."[65]

Companies often adopt the competency-based approach for valuing work because it promotes individual development and growth through lateral moves in the organization. Growth through lateral moves is consistent with flatter, team-based structures. This approach does have some drawbacks, however. According to a study by Hewitt and Associates, an HR consulting firm, broadbanding may meet stiff cultural resistance in many countries. In Brazil, for example, status symbols and titles that differentiate people according to their status are highly valued forms of recognition. Similarly, in India, work often is organized hierarchically. Promotions up through the hierarchy are a major form of reward and recognition for employee loyalty. People typically expect promotions every three or four years. In Singapore, people depend heavily on clear structures and rules as guides to behavior. In contrast, competency-based broadbanding was developed to promote flexibility. It eschews rigid rules and thus may be more difficult for Singaporeans to understand and accept.[66]

Within the United States, the corporate cultures of many organizations reflect some of these same cultural values—they're still hierarchical, bureaucratic, and rule driven. When companies with such corporate cultures attempt to introduce competency-based broadbanding, the effort may ultimately fail. The most common reasons for failed implementation appear to be that

- the new system results in low morale;
- managers and their subordinates are frustrated by the system;
- managers and other employees don't understand the system;
- employees do not trust management to make fair evaluations of the competencies needed in various jobs; and
- managers continue to base their pay decisions on the old, hidden pay grade system.[67]

Single Plan versus Multiple Plans

Traditionally, organizations have used different job evaluation plans for different job families (e.g., clerical, skilled craft, and professional). This approach assumes that the work content of jobs in different families is too diverse to be captured by one plan. For example, manufacturing jobs may vary in terms of working conditions and physical effort, so these factors should be used in setting pay for those jobs. Professional jobs usually vary in terms of technical skills and knowledge, but not in working conditions and physical effort. Thus, pay for professional jobs should be based on the degree of skill and knowledge required. Proponents of multiple plans contend that these differences require the use of different job evaluation systems for different classes of job.

From a strategic perspective, using multiple systems is incongruent with the objective of communicating a coherent message about what the organization values. For example, if the strategy is to focus on customers, it may be logical to use potential for affecting customers as a variable to determine the relative worth of *all* jobs within the company. If the strategy is to

MANAGING TEAMS

New Pay at GlaxoSmithKline

GlaxoSmithKline began shifting to a competency-based organization in the mid-1990s. The first unit to make the change was Pharm Tech—a small unit that employs about 400 scientists and support staff in the United States and the United Kingdom. Like many organizations, Pharm Tech had just redesigned its organization. It replaced its old functional structure with process-driven teams. In the old culture, career advancement meant moving up the hierarchy within one's functional area. In the new organization, career advancement was conceptualized as moving through four stages. To move through the four stages, employees needed to progress through jobs that required increasing levels of seven key competencies. These seven competencies, identified as central to Pharm Tech's business strategy and culture, are

- innovation,
- teamwork,
- communication,
- use of resources,
- decision making/perspective,
- customer satisfaction, and
- technical ability.

At career stage 1, the work being performed requires relatively low levels of these competencies. At career stage 2, higher levels of competencies are required by the work, and so on. By categorizing jobs according to their fit with these four career stages, Pharm Tech structured its jobs into four broad competency bands. Salaries are tied to these four bands.

---

provide excellent quality products, it may be logical to assess the degree to which all jobs contribute to the quality of products produced.

Also, the use of a single system for valuing all jobs has been proposed as a partial solution to the problem of sex-based inequities. Proponents of pay equity assert that only if jobs are evaluated using the same criteria can the relative value of all jobs be fairly determined. When separate plans are used, it is much easier to discriminate against specific classes of jobs (e.g., clerical versus skilled) because direct comparisons of segregated jobs can be avoided.

Developing a firm-specific job evaluation system with universal variables selected in accordance with the company's strategy and culture is clearly more difficult than adopting off-the-shelf job evaluation systems developed for specific occupational groups. Nevertheless, companies such as Cisco and Hewlett-Packard have concluded that the extra effort of developing a tailored system pays off. These companies use a core set of factors to evaluate all jobs, and they supplement this with another set of factors that are unique to particular occupational groups.

Skill-Based Pay

As just described, competency-based job evaluation systems begin to shift the focus of pay systems toward the competencies of employees. **Skill-based pay** is an even more radical approach to paying people based on competencies. Companies using skill-based pay, which is also called pay-for-knowledge or multiskilled pay, determine people's pay by measuring their competencies directly. With skill-based pay, the question asked is not, "What level of competency is required to perform your job?" The relevant question becomes, "At what competency level can an employee perform?" In this system, employees are

> **FAST FACT**
>
> In 2000, about 15% of medium and large U.S. companies used skill-based pay and 20% were considering it.

paid based on their personal skill or competency level regardless of what level of competency is required in their current position.

Skill-based pay rewards employees for the range, depth, and types of skills they're capable of using. This is a very different philosophy from the conventional job-based approaches. It moves the compensation of workers toward the approaches used to evaluate many types of professionals.[68]

Research-and-development firms have valued the contributions of engineers and scientists using a related approach, called **maturity curves,** since the 1950s. With this method, a series of curves is developed to provide differing levels of worth to individuals. The underlying principle is that professionals with more experience and knowledge are more valuable to the organization. Similar approaches are used to pay elementary and secondary school teachers and apprentices in skilled crafts, who receive pay increments based on educational levels and seniority.

Skill-based pay is premised on the same assumption, namely, that a person who can do more different tasks or who knows more is of greater value and should be paid according to capabilities, not according to job assignment. The important distinction between skill-based pay and the maturity curve approach is that with maturity curves, pay increases occur automatically at particular time intervals. With skill-based pay, pay goes up only after the worker demonstrates an ability to perform specific competencies. For a machine operator, the relevant skills might include an assembly task, a material handling and inventory task, and maintenance tasks. Alternatively, pay may be pegged to the employee's *level* of skill or knowledge within a job domain. For example, supervisors might demonstrate increasing skills and knowledge in job domains such as budget planning and analysis, employee performance management, and developing client relationships.[69]

Skill-based pay creates an environment that facilitates worker rotation. This may reduce absenteeism and may ease job assignment pressures for management. Because workers are motivated to learn higher-level skills, they will likely be paid more than the job evaluation rate of the specific jobs to which they're assigned. However, overall labor costs may be lower owing to enhanced workforce flexibility and productivity.[70]

USING MARKET DATA TO SET PAY RATES

As already noted, an effective compensation system must take into account the realities of the external labor market. Allowing people to negotiate their pay is one way to do this. But even when managers negotiate pay with people they are trying to hire retain, they usually do so within a system that imposes some constraints. The constraints around the pay the people can earn for specific jobs are defined by the pay structure. The pay structure combines the results of job evaluation with market data information about pay rates. The overall objective is to ensure to ensure **external equity**. When external equity exists, employees feel there are being paid fairly relative to what people in similar jobs are paid by other employers. Achieving external equity involves (1) determining the pay rates in the external market, (2) identifying the market pay policy, and (3) establishing the organization pay policy.

Conducting a Survey to Assess External Market Rates

Data about market pay rates are generated by a **compensation survey.** Compensation surveys are usually conducted by consulting firms that sell the results to employers. To make use of data from a compensation survey, an organization needs to identify the relevant market and select appropriate benchmarks. Then, data from the market are gathered and used to establish the market policy.

Relevant Labor Market. Using survey data requires defining the relevant labor market.[71] (Recall that in Chapter 7, we discussed the concept of a relevant labor market and its role in recruitment.) In establishing pay policies, three variables are commonly used to define the relevant labor market: the occupation or skill required, the geographic location (the distance from which applicants would be willing to relocate or commute), and the other employers competing for labor. The relevant geographic labor market for a vice president of sales for Microsoft Corporation may be the entire United States. The relevant geographic labor market for an accounts receivable clerk may be Greater Seattle. In global companies, the relevant labor market for some jobs is the entire world.

> **FAST FACT**
>
> Canadian techies who move across the border to work for Microsoft can often increase their base pay 200%.

Industry differences also may become evident in definitions of the relevant labor market. If industry-specific knowledge and experience is important, an employer may consider the relevant labor market to be defined by other employers in the same industry. Exhibit 10.12 illustrates industry effects on the total cash compensation for selected jobs.[72]

Benchmark Jobs. In order to interpret survey data, benchmark jobs must be identified. Traditionally, **benchmarks jobs** are those commonly found across a range of organizations. Regardless of title, jobs make good benchmarks when the nature of the job is essentially the same regardless of where it is performed. In other words, regardless of the employer, the job description sounds pretty much the same. For example, the jobs listed in Exhibit 10.12 could be used as benchmark jobs.

When data are collected as part of a market survey, the jobs in the survey have brief job descriptions. To determine whether a job is useful as a benchmark, the job description used for the survey is compared with the job description in the employer's organization. If the two descriptions are very similar, the employer can feel confident that the market wage data provided by the survey can be applied to the job in the employer's organization. Market information about the compensation levels of benchmark jobs is used to establish the market pay policy, as explained below. (Note that for competency-based pay systems, the appropriate benchmarks would be competency profiles. For skill-based pay, the appropriate benchmarks would be identifiable skill levels. In practice, however, most companies must still rely on benchmarking against common jobs because that is the method usually used to collect market wage data.)[73]

Market Survey Data Collection. Some companies conduct their own compensation surveys, but most purchase a survey from a consulting firm or

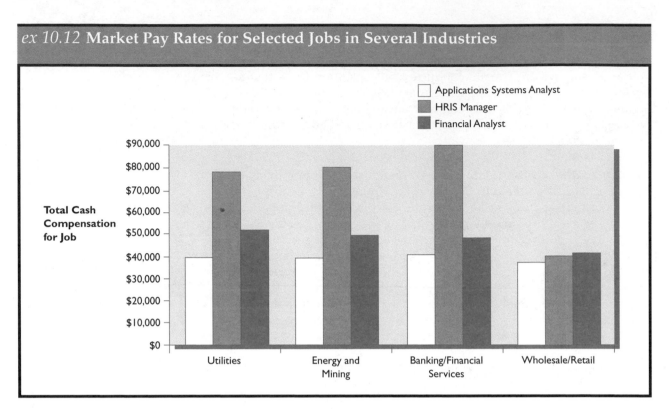

ex 10.12 **Market Pay Rates for Selected Jobs in Several Industries**

use labor market data from government sources. Regardless of who conducts the survey, the process is the same: Employers participating in the survey provide compensation information for selected jobs. Surveys often focus on specific occupational groups. For example, suppose a survey focused on sales and marketing personnel. In that case, the survey might contain brief descriptions of 100 different jobs (e.g., top marketing manager, sales trainee, account specialist). Employers are asked to identify jobs that exist in their organization and provide detailed information about the way those jobs are compensated. For sales and marketing jobs, a survey might request information about the average annual salary paid to people in the job, the lowest and highest amounts paid, the average bonus paid, the value of other cash compensation paid, the nature of long-term incentives available to people in the jobs, commission pay, and so on. Exhibit 10.13 illustrates a portion of a typical market survey questionnaire.

For global companies, it is important to understand how pay rates vary across different countries. Thus, some compensation surveys focus on country comparisons. For example, an employer with operations throughout Asia can purchase compensation survey data describing pay rates for dozens of jobs in each of several Asian countries. Exhibit 10.14 on page 436 illustrates country pay differences for the job of comptroller.[74]

Establishing the Market Pay Policy

With the appropriate market information in hand, market pay rates are plotted against the evaluation points that the company has assigned to the

FAST FACT

The cost of living in San Francisco is 31% higher than the national average.

ex 10.13 Example of Information Requested in a Market Survey

Level and Designation	Number of Employees in Position	SALARY — Average Annual Salary	SALARY — Annual Salary Range Minimum	SALARY — Annual Salary Range Maximum	BONUS — Number of Employees Receiving Bonus	BONUS — Average Bonus Paid in $ (Complete Either Column)	BONUS — Average Bonus Paid as % of Sal. (Complete Either Column)	OTHER CASH COMPENSATION — Number of Employees Receiving Other Cash	OTHER CASH COMPENSATION — Average Other Cash Paid in $ (Complete Either Column)	OTHER CASH COMPENSATION — Average Other Cash Paid as % of Sal. (Complete Either Column)	LONG-TERM INCENTIVES — Stock Options/SARs	LONG-TERM INCENTIVES — Stock Grants/Restricted Stock Grants	LONG-TERM INCENTIVES — Other Stock-Based LTIs (e.g., Phantom Stock)
Customer Service/Call Center—Inbound													
Top Customer Service Executive											☐	☐	☐
Customer Service Manager											☐	☐	☐
Customer Service Supervisor 1 Working Supervisor											☐	☐	☐
2 Supervisor											☐	☐	☐
3 Senior Supervisor											☐	☐	☐
Customer Service Representative 1 Junior											☐	☐	☐
2 Intermediate											☐	☐	☐
3 Senior											☐	☐	☐
Public Relations													
Top Public Relations Executive											☐	☐	☐
Public Relations Manager											☐	☐	☐
Public Relations Representative 1 Entry											☐	☐	☐
2 Intermediate											☐	☐	☐
3 Senior											☐	☐	☐
4 Lead											☐	☐	☐

Check type of long-term incentive(s) for which position is eligible (check any that apply)

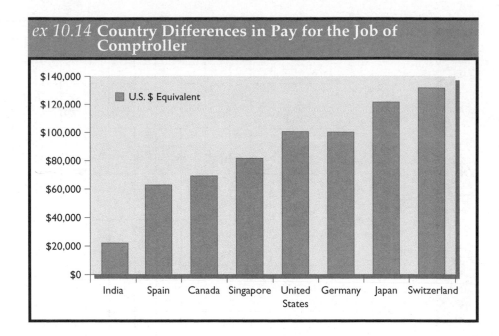

ex 10.14 Country Differences in Pay for the Job of Comptroller

FAST FACT

The average yearly salary of professional baseball players reached $2 million for the first time in 2001.

benchmark jobs. This establishes a **market pay policy line,** as shown in Exhibit 10.15. The benchmark jobs in the exhibit are labeled Job A, Job B, Job C, and so forth. The points assigned to the jobs are shown on the horizontal axis. Job E was assigned approximately 260 job evaluation points; Job B was assigned 750 job evaluation points, and so on. The average market wages for the benchmark jobs are shown on the vertical axis. For Job E, the average market pay is $35,000. For Job B, it's $73,000. The pay policy for the external market is defined by the best-fitting line relating job evaluation points to average market pay. Typically, regression analysis is used to establish the best-fitting line.

Why does an organization need to calculate the external market's policy line? Because market data won't be available for all jobs. In Exhibit 10.15, for example, Job X represents a job that exists in the organization, But for Job X, there are no market pay data available—the job was not included in the market survey. The market policy line makes it possible to estimate what the market would pay for Job X.

Setting the Organization Pay Policy

After the market policy line has been calculated, the **organization pay policy** can be established. The organization pay policy determines pay rates that will be used by a particular employer. If the company wants simply to match the market, it may set its organization pay policy line equal to the line for the external market. Alternatively, the company may choose to pay somewhat above the market or somewhat below the market. The choice of an organization pay policy is influenced by the pay rates of major competitors, the firm's profits or losses, surpluses or shortages of qualified workers, the stage of the firm's development, the role of performance-based pay, the strength of union demands, the organizational culture, and so forth.[75]

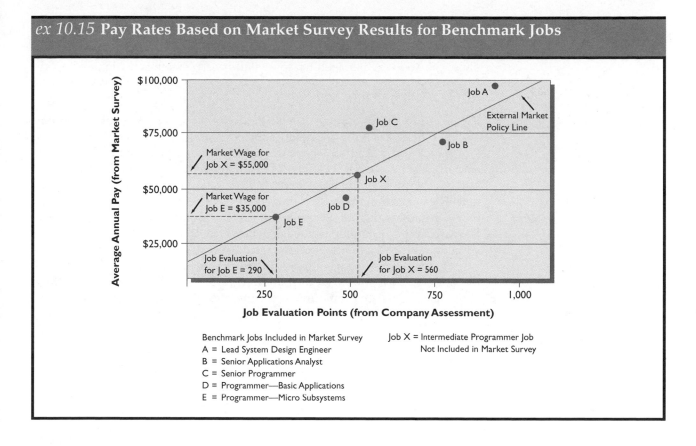

ex 10.15 Pay Rates Based on Market Survey Results for Benchmark Jobs

Benchmark Jobs Included in Market Survey
A = Lead System Design Engineer
B = Senior Applications Analyst
C = Senior Programmer
D = Programmer—Basic Applications
E = Programmer—Micro Subsystems

Job X = Intermediate Programmer Job
Not Included in Market Survey

A **lead policy,** paying somewhat above the market rate, maximizes the company's ability to attract and retain quality employees and to minimize employee dissatisfaction with pay. A lead policy signals that the firm values employees as a source of competitive advantage. A concern is whether the additional pay attracts and retains the best or merely the most applicants. It is also uncertain how much a firm needs to lead others to gain a distinct competitive advantage. Finally, the pay rates of other firms tend to escalate and eventually match the leader's rates.

By far the most common policy is to match the competition. Although the **match policy** does not give an employer a competitive advantage, it does ensure that the firm isn't at a disadvantage. When Sears restructured its pay system, it discovered from market survey data that past decisions about pay had resulted in an unintended organization policy of paying above the market. For the company, a lead policy was too costly, so the new system was designed to gradually lower the company's internal pay line in order to more closely match the market.

It is also possible to adopt a **lag policy,** where the organization intentionally pays below the market. However, a lag policy may hinder a firm's ability to attract potential employees unless other variables—such as job security, benefits, locale, and job content—compensate for the low base pay.[76]

FAST FACT

The Container Store hires fewer people and pays them two to three times the industry average, which creates fierce employee loyalty and results in high retention rates.

DESIGNING THE INTERNAL PAY STRUCTURE

With the pay policy set, a pay structure can be developed. This process differs depending on whether a job-based or skill-based system is being developed.

Job-Based Pay Grades and Ranges

Exhibit 10.16 shows a **pay grade structure** for a conventional job-based pay system. The boxes are associated with a spread of job evaluation points (the job grade) and a range of pay (the minimum and maximum that can be earned). Usually, several different jobs are covered by one box. These jobs will have similar evaluation points, but they may have very dissimilar content. The boxes that make up the structure may be the same size or may vary in width and height, but generally they ascend from left to right. This reflects the association of higher pay levels (shown on the vertical axis) with more valued jobs (shown on the horizontal axis).

In establishing pay ranges, the corporate pay line generally serves as the midpoint. Maximums and minimums are generally set at a percentage above and below that amount. The difference between the two is the pay range. Some common ranges above and below the pay grade midpoint include

Nonexempt

Laborers and tradespeople	Up to 25%
Clerical, technical, and paraprofessional workers	15–50%

Exempt

First-level managers and professionals	30–50%
Middle and senior managers	40–100%

ex 10.16 Pay Grade Structure for a Job-Based Pay System

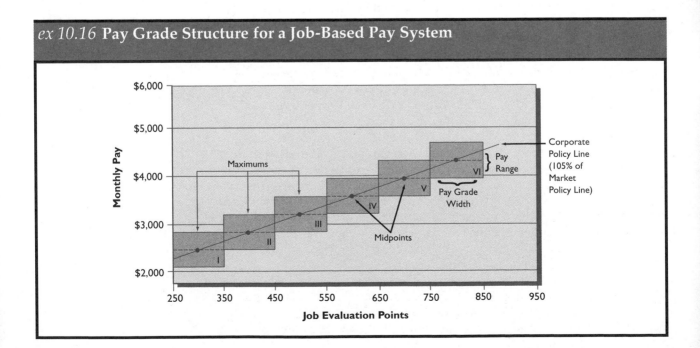

For the firm depicted in Exhibit 10.16, six equal-interval pay grades were established, each with a width of one hundred points. Each grade has a pay range of $1,000. For pay grade II, the range goes from $2,250 (minimum) to $3,250 (maximum) a month; the midpoint is $2,750 a month. Notice that the maximum annual pay for these jobs is less than $60,000, which suggests that the plan does not cover higher-level professionals or executives.

In traditional, hierarchical organizations, there are many different pay grades and each grade has a narrow range (or band). When broadbanding is used, there are fewer pay grades, and each grade has a broader range (or band). Thus, with broadbanding, there is a bigger range between the minimum and maximum pay. Also, there is a bigger difference between the midpoint of a grade and the next higher grade. As a consequence, when an employee moves from one grade to the next, the promotion has a bigger impact on pay. However, such promotions occur less often.

Competency-Based Pay Structure

Competency-based pay structures look very similar to job-based pay structures. That is, there are pay grades and ranges established, and these ascend upward along a continuum. The major difference in these systems is that the points on the horizontal axis are assigned to levels of competencies—not jobs. At the lower end of the scale would be jobs that require competencies that are of relatively less value to the organization. At the higher end of the scale would be jobs that require competencies that are more valuable to the organization. In other words, the key difference between competency-based and job-based models is not how points are used—the difference is in how points are assigned to jobs.

Skill-Based Pay Structure

With skill-based pay, increases in pay are associated with increases in skills. Employees are paid for their skills, regardless of the jobs they hold. Thus, the structure of a skill-based system really is fundamentally different from a job-based or competency-based system. The starting assumption is that base pay is more or less equal for everyone covered by the pay system regardless of the job assignment. However, additional pay can be earned by increasing one's skills. Thus, two people working side by side in the same job may be paid at different hourly rates simply because one person has more skills. The additional skills may not be needed to perform that job, but they are nevertheless valuable to the organization, so the employee is paid for them.

Approximately 85 percent of skill-based pay systems are designed to encourage employees to develop the breadth (rather than the depth) of their skills, in the interest of increasing their flexibility to perform different jobs as needed.[77] Research shows that these systems can be effective in lowering labor costs while improving quality and productivity.[78] To encourage employees to learn new skills, the pay structure is designed to increase an employee's wage rate as he or she demonstrates each new skill. For example, in an automobile plant, there may be 20 different skills that factory employees need in order to be able to move around the entire plant as needed. For each skill, a pay raise is earned when an employee demonstrates proficiency. The pay structure defines the size of the pay increase for each added skill.

BALANCING INTERNAL AND EXTERNAL EQUITY

External and internal data as well as a firm's compensation strategy differentially affect job worth decisions. Every organization must find the appropriate balance. Sometimes differences between market rates and job evaluation results can be resolved by reviewing the basic decisions associated with evaluating and pricing particular jobs. Sometimes survey data can be ignored or benchmark jobs can be changed or jobs can simply be reevaluated. In cases where the disparities persist, judgment is required to resolve them.

Pay Differentials

One way the discrepancy between internal and external pay equity can be resolved is to establish temporary market differentials. Consider the dilemma confronting a television broadcast company. The broadcast firm conducted a job evaluation study and collected market data for key positions. The job evaluation positioned the job of a broadcast engineer technician in pay grade VI. In designing the pay structure, the pay range for this grade had been set well below the average rate of pay in the external market. The discrepancy persisted even following a check of the job evaluation and wage survey data. Because engineers with broadcast experience are difficult to find, company executives considered reassigning the job to a higher pay grade (they had done this in the past). Although this would provide a "quick fix," the long-term consequences—particularly if other employees found out about the reclassification—could be disastrous, threatening the validity of the entire compensation system. To preserve the integrity of the system while meeting market demands, engineering jobs were left in the appropriate grades and a **market differential** was paid to employees in these jobs. As long as the external market rate of pay was higher than the station's policy line, engineers would receive the 10 percent market differential; when the labor market imbalance corrected itself, the differential would be eliminated.

Shift work is another common example of using pay differentials. Although people working different shifts may perform the same job, it is generally more difficult to hire people for shifts that fall outside of a standard workday. Consequently, employers pay a **shift differential** to people who work during less desirable times.

Balancing internal and external equity is especially challenging for firms operating in multiple countries. Differences in local market rates, cost of living, tax rates, and myriad other factors all must be addressed when establishing a pay policy. How these issues are addressed depends heavily on the international structure and strategy of the firm. Some firms adopt a local approach, with pay set to match local markets. Other firms attempt to establish a global pay policy, at least for higher-level executive positions. A third option is to use a blended approach, which recognizes that pay must be higher in some locations but also recognizes that many executives operate in a global context regardless of where they live.[79]

Pay Compression

Pay compression results when wages for jobs filled from outside the organization are increasing faster than wages for jobs filled from within the organization. As a result, pay differences among jobs become very small, and the traditional pay structure becomes compressed. Compression is an issue for professional organizations—such as engineering and law firms and colleges and universities—where new graduates command salaries equal to or above those of professionals with more experience.

The problem of compression has no one correct solution. Ultimately, a company considers the costs and consequences of eliminating compression problems (e.g., by raising the pay of more senior job incumbents to keep pace with the changing market) versus letting compression drive employee behavior (e.g., through psychological withdrawal or active job hunting among employees with compressed pay), and chooses the course of action that has the least negative consequences.

Communicating the Plan

Employers invest enormous resources in designing pay plans that they believe will help attract, retain, and motivate their employees. When a decision is made to revise the organization's compensation system (e.g., to change from a traditional system to broadbanding or competency-based pay), it is not uncommon for the change process to require up to a year of planning. In order for a compensation system to achieve its objectives, employees must understand the system. If employees don't fully understand how their pay is determined, they will not be motivated by the way their pay is structured.[80] Failure to adequately communicate the compensation plan is a major source of problems when employers introduce new pay systems. Even when no changes are made, communication problems may arise. With new employees continually being hired, communication lapses undermine the value of even the best-designed pay structures. An effective approach to communication helps employees understand how market rates are determined and used to establish their pay and helps them see how the structure of the plan addresses the issue of internal equity. Effective communications also educate employees about what the firm values in terms of tasks, competencies, and skills, and shows them how these values are reflected in the design of the pay system (e.g., in the way points are assigned to jobs).

When Allstate's board decided to restructure executive pay packages, it paid a great deal of attention to explaining the bases for the new packages. Allstate Insurance Company was established in 1931 by Sears, Roebuck and Company. Sixty years later, Sears spun it off to pursue a more focused strategy. When Allstate went public, an outside board of directors was established, and evaluating executive pay packages was among its first tasks. The board commissioned a study of key executives to learn how they perceived their pay and their views about how pay should be determined. The study revealed a weak link in the system. Because the pay of Allstate executives was tied to the stock movement of Sears, they felt that they had little control over it. "In many cases, our executives were not really motivated by Sears' executive pay," concluded the assistant vice president of compensation.

Allstate needed a new, simpler plan that linked pay directly to Allstate's business results. When the new pay plan was ready, experts were brought in to develop a communication strategy. They collaborated with a team of Allstate managers who had not been involved in developing the pay plan and who represented a variety of specialty areas. Before devising its formal communication strategy, team members began by making sure they understood the new pay plan themselves. "We ripped (the plan) apart, we took the staples out if it—we literally ripped it apart, not figuratively—and

> *"The pay that the vice presidents get isn't motivating the vice presidents. It's motivating the assistant vice presidents, who want to become vice presidents. Similarly, the CEO's pay isn't motivating the CEO so much—he's already there. Rather, it's serving to motivate the vice presidents who are competing against one another to become CEO."*
>
> Edward P. Lazear
> Professor
> Stanford Business School

stuck the pages up on the walls. . . . We tried to understand the plan and draw it on the board," explained one of the communication experts.

Once the team members were sure that they understood the new pay plan, the principle that proved most important as they developed the formal communication strategy was "Keep it simple." Rather than overwhelm people with all the details, the communicators emphasized the link between achieving business objectives and the pay that the executives would receive. To ensure that the executives could see "the big picture," the written material included a foldout page showing how all the pieces of the package fit together. To give personal meaning to the package, each executive received an individualized statement that showed the maximum amounts that he or she could earn if individual and group targets were achieved.

A second survey conducted after the new package was explained revealed that 85 percent of the executives felt that they now had a better understanding than before of their annual incentive pay, their stock options, and the total pay package.[81]

INTERNET RESOURCES   10.C

Developing a Pay Structure

At our Web site, http://jackson.swcollege.com/, you can:

1. Learn about pay levels in the United States and discover what other compensation information is available from the Bureau of Labor Statistics.

2. Read more about the Hay Guide Chart-Profile methods by visiting the Hay Group.

3. See what salary survey information is available on the Web.

   Advertising Age

   Job Star

   Skills Net

4. Visit HR Guide to explore extensive resources on a topic of interest to you.

COMPENSATION IN THE CONTEXT OF GLOBALIZATION

FAST FACT

The average hours worked per year in Germany is 1,573; in Canada, it's 1,790; in the United States, it's 1,943; and in Japan it's 2,031.

As the environment for many business firms in the United States becomes more global, international compensation becomes a more significant element of total compensation.[82] In developing international compensation policies, the basic objectives are the same as in a domestic context. The policy should be consistent and fair in its treatment of all employees. It should help attract and retain personnel in the areas where the company has the greatest needs and opportunities. It should motivate employees. And it should facilitate the transfer of employees across locations in the most cost-effective manner.

Basic Compensation Philosophy

FAST FACT

The Australian government mandates that all organizations must provide employees with benefits equivalent to 9% of their salary, effective in 2002.

In general, the first issue facing multinational corporations (MNCs) when designing international compensation policies is whether to establish an overall policy for all employees or to distinguish between parent-country nationals and third-country nationals. This differentiation may diminish in the future, but in the 1990s, it was very common for MNCs to distinguish between these two groups. Furthermore, separate policies may be established based on the length of assignment (temporary transfer, permanent transfer, or continual relocation). Cash remuneration, special allowances, benefits, and pensions are determined in part by such classification. Short-term expatriates—for example, those whose two- or three-year tours of duty abroad are interspersed with long periods at home—may be treated differently than career expatriates, who spend most of their time working in various locations abroad. Both of these groups are different from third-country nationals (TCNs), who often move from country to country in the employ of an MNC headquartered in a country other than their own. For example, a Swiss banker may be in charge of a German branch of a British bank. In effect, TCNs are the real global employees, the ones who can weave together the far-flung parts of an MNC. As the global MNC increases in importance, TCNs will likely become more valuable and command higher levels of compensation.

For parent-country expatriates, the most widely used policy emphasizes "keeping the expatriate whole"—that is, maintaining a pay level comparable to that of the PCN's colleagues plus compensating for the costs of international service. Foreign assignees shouldn't suffer a material loss owing to their transfer. Many companies use the **balance sheet approach** to equalize the purchasing power of employees at comparable position levels living overseas and in the home country, and to provide incentives to offset qualitative differences between assignment locations.[83] The objective of this approach is to provide a level of net spendable income in the new destination that is similar to that received in the previous (usually home) location.

> **FAST FACT**
>
> The balance sheet approach seems to be the most popular way to pay expatriates.

Base Pay

Employers usually pay expatriates in the employee's home currency at the home rate, but some companies pay in the local currency at the local rate paid for the same job. Similarly, salary adjustments and promotional practices may be fashioned according to either home-country or local standards. U.S. and Canadian companies usually pay according to the home rate, while European companies use both approaches about equally. Increasingly, however, MNCs are developing global salary and performance structures that can be applied without concern for where work is performed.[84]

The development of the European Union has brought greater use of the euro within business. This common currency will make it easier to develop a global policy that applies regardless of the organization's national origin, recognizing the need to treat European operations as truly one market and employees as truly all Europeans.

"The euro will be one of three major currencies in the world, after the dollar and the yen."

Alain Johnson
Employee Benefits Director
PricewaterhouseCoopers, Paris

Relocation Premiums

Five major categories of expenses incurred by expatriates and their families are the following:

Goods and Services: Items such as food, personal care, clothing, household furnishings, recreation, transportation, and medical care.

Housing: The major costs associated with the employees' principal residences.

Income Taxes:	Payments to federal and local governments for personal income taxes. For U.S. employees, tax liabilities usually increase when they go abroad, so most U.S. employers adopt a tax equalization policy for assignment-related income.
Reserve:	Contributions to savings, payments for benefits, pension contributions, investments, education expenses, Social Security taxes, and so forth.
Shipment and Storage:	The major costs associated with shipping and storing personal and household effects.

Not all these aspects of international compensation come into play for every expatriate; nevertheless, most U.S. companies pay expatriates a premium to cover such costs, and many also provide free housing. Consequently, the cost of posting an expatriate can be anywhere from three to seven times the expatriate's home base salary.

INTERNET RESOURCES　　　10.D

Compensation in the Context of Globalization

At our Web site, http://jackson.swcollege.com/, you can:

1. Access currency conversions and exchange rates at several sites, including

   Stat USA Internet, a service provided by the U.S. Department of Commerce

   X-rates.com

   Fxtop.com

2. Learn more about expatriate compensation from consulting firms and other organizations that provide services on this topic.

   HR Toolbox

   Bureau of National Affairs

   Organization Resources Counselors

3. Learn about the international salary surveys that are available from the Economic Research Institute.

SUMMARY

Organizations develop strategic compensation in a cost-conscious, competitive business environment that demands high quality and a continuous flow of new products. An approach to total compensation that is consistent with the organization's culture, structure, and business strategy improves the organization's ability to compete successfully. In addition, compensation practices must adhere to the *Fair Labor Standards Act*, the *Equal Pay Act*, and all other relevant regulations.

Total compensation has many components, including both monetary and nonmonetary forms of pay. Some compensation elements (e.g., mandatory insurance coverage) are offered to everyone in the organization simply on the basis of organizational membership. Other elements (e.g., base wage and salary pay) are offered on the basis of the job in which one works. Finally, pay may be offered contingent on individual or team attributes (e.g., skill-based pay and bonuses).

When designing the base pay component of a compensation system, employers can choose from many alternatives. Three basic choices are job-based, competency-based, and skill-based pay. The job-based and competency-based approaches are grounded in job evaluation, which involves a systematic assessment of the value of jobs in the organization. It is intended to establish internal equity in jobs. Ranking and job classification methods evaluate the whole job and rely heavily on intuitive judgments about job worth. Point rating systems impose a more rigorous analysis and are the most widely used. To ensure systemwide equity, a single job evaluation plan is usually preferred over multiple plans. To increase employees' acceptance and understanding of pay systems, it is helpful to involve them in the job evaluation process.

The objective when establishing the relative worth of jobs, competencies, and skills is creating internal pay equity. To establish actual wage rates, organizations use market surveys. The market pay policy is determined and then used as a guide to create the organization's internal pay policy. An organization may choose to set a pay policy that leads, matches, or lags the pay offered by competitors.

Organizations operating beyond domestic borders face additional challenges when designing their compensation system. The basic objectives to be achieved by compensation remain essentially the same, but achieving them usually requires a more complex pay system. The system must be responsive to country differences in pay practices and take into account cultural differences in the values and expectations of employees around the world.

TERMS TO REMEMBER

balance sheet approach
base pay
benchmark jobs
comparable worth
compensable factors
compensation survey
competency-based job evaluation
Davis-Bacon Act
Equal Pay Act
equity
exempt employees
external equity
Fair Labor Standards Act
Hay Guide Chart-Profile
internal equity
job-based pay
job classification method
job evaluation
lag policy
lead policy
living wage laws

market differential
market pay policy line
match policy
maturity curves
monetary compensation
nonexempt employees
nonmonetary compensation
organization pay policy line
pay compression
pay equity
pay fairness
pay grade structure
pay level
pay mix
point rating method
ranking method
shift differential
skill-based pay
total compensation
Walsh-Healey Public Contracts Act

DISCUSSION QUESTIONS

1. What are the objectives of compensation? How and why do the objectives vary across different organizations? Explain.
2. What forms of pay make up total compensation?
3. Describe the role of job evaluation. Then describe the conditions that may lead an organization to develop a customized point system to use for job evaluation.
4. Describe the similarities and differences of skill-based pay and job-based pay systems.
5. Are the CEOs of U.S. firms overpaid? Are most employees underpaid? What issues should be considered in setting pay rates for CEOs?
6. Describe the components of the typical expatriate's compensation package.
7. List the possible negative consequences that organizations are likely to experience if employees do not understand the compensation system.

PROJECTS TO EXTEND YOUR LEARNING

1. *Managing Change.* You have just been hired as the head of administrative services for a nonprofit charity fund located in Portland, Oregon. With unemployment in the area so low, it is having more difficulty than usual finding people to fill its open positions. At the moment, groundskeepers and accounting clerks are the jobs that need to be filled. You wonder whether the pay level is too low, so you decide to investigate. Use the Internet to locate information about wage levels in the local market. Then make a proposal for a total compensation system approach that will succeed in attracting qualified applicants. Include in your proposal some brief suggestions about where and how to recruit for these jobs.
2. *Managing Teams.* Imaginative Design Center (IDC) is a small business that does commercial interior design work. They specialize in renovations for the hospitality industry, providing designs for everything from bed and breakfast inns to major hotels and restaurant chains. Employees almost always work in teams, with each team having a variety of specialists. When business is booming, staffing these teams becomes difficult. The owner, Bea N. Bee, thinks this problem could be eliminated if staff members would develop a broader range of skills. She is considering changing to a skill-based pay system. Currently, employees are paid a base salary supplemented by a bit of merit pay. The merit pay is too small to make much difference, however, and usually everyone gets the same raise. IDC has hired you to provide advice. Is skill-based pay a good idea? What are the advantages and disadvantages of this approach? Regardless of whether or not you think skill-based pay is a good idea, Bea wants you to provide her with some information about the experiences of two or three other companies that have used skill-based pay.
3. *Integration and Application.* After reviewing the end-of-text cases, compare and contrast Lincoln Electric and Southwest Airlines on the following:
    a. The objectives of their total compensation systems
    b. The role of compensation in achieving competitive advantage

c. The approach used to establish base pay rates

d. The pay mix and employee's reactions to the pay mix

Which compensation system would you prefer? Explain why.

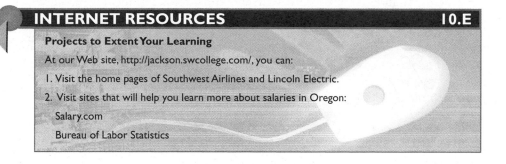

INTERNET RESOURCES   10.E

Projects to Extent Your Learning

At our Web site, http://jackson.swcollege.com/, you can:

1. Visit the home pages of Southwest Airlines and Lincoln Electric.

2. Visit sites that will help you learn more about salaries in Oregon:

Salary.com

Bureau of Labor Statistics

COMPARABLE WORTH FINDS ROCKDALE

case study

Bill Starbuck was proud to be assigned to the city beat of the *Rockdale Times*. Bill, a newspaper reporter for two years now, was paying his dues at a small-town newspaper, hoping to work his way up to a larger-circulation daily. The city beat would mean that Bill could draw on his background in journalism and political science at Wabash College to write news stories with substance. His prior assignment to the features section of the *Rockdale Times* was interesting but not intellectually stimulating.

Bill's first major assignment was coming up in two days with an invitation to cover a breakfast meeting with the city council. Clyde Langston, Rockdale's city manager, was scheduled to present the revised city budget. Bill prepared for the meeting by calling one of his contacts in the city office for some "inside" information. Bill had been dating Jill Bateman, a secretary to the personnel executive director, and he was confident he could learn something about the breakfast meeting agenda.

As Bill hung up from his call to Jill, he wondered what the rumor of a pay raise for some city employees could mean. If anything, the city was expected to trim its budget because of a slowdown in the local economy and loss of revenues due to the shutdown of two plants in the community within the past year. According to Jill, the rumor was that some of the clerical and administrative staff employees were scheduled for midyear pay adjustments. The figure working the hallways was a 3 percent pay raise, which would come as a pleasant surprise to

the 95 employees in the administrative office clerical positions.

As Bill arrived at the Wednesday morning breakfast meeting, he quickly scanned the room to identify the four city councilmen and one councilwoman. Bill wanted to interview at least three of the members for his story, which was due by 1:00 P.M. After Mayor Jim Earnie arrived, the city council, city manager, and local news reporters finished a quick and cordial breakfast.

Clyde Langston called the group to attention with a rap on his water goblet, and the cordial bantering quickly subsided. Clyde distributed a five-page report of the preliminary budget. Bill quickly scanned the report and noted that the $13.7 million total was considerably trimmed down from last year's budget of $16.4 million. Then, as Bill anticipated, Clyde pointed out a $51,000 line item increase in salaries within the pared-down budget.

Clyde proceeded to explain that the city had done an analysis of its 95 administrative office clerical positions and its 350 technical-craft positions and decided to make some pay adjustments. All but one of the administrative office clerks are women, while only 27 of the technical-craft workers are women. The pay range for office workers ranges from a low of $7.19 per hour to a high of $13.17 per hour, with an average of $8.30 per hour. The technical-craft jobs begin at $6.83 per hour and max out at $15.85 per hour, with an average of $11.69 per hour. The net effect of the $51,000 increase was to provide about a

3 percent increase to the administrative office clerical workers.

Clyde pointed out that a recently conducted job evaluation study had resulted in the merger of the previously separated job families, such that all jobs were to be evaluated on a common set of attributes. Clyde elaborated further that the impetus for this change was to avoid any litigation over the comparable worth issue. After completing the budget review briefing, Clyde offered to answer questions. When the council members sat quietly, Jim Earnie thanked the council for their time and adjourned the meeting.

Bill scurried to the door to intercept the council members as they prepared to leave, hoping to get a few reactions to this surprise comparable worth initiative by the city government. Bill caught all five of the city council members and the mayor and proceeded to ask them what they thought of Clyde's proposal for the pay adjustments. Mayor Jim Earnie, along with three of the council members, indicated that they did not understand the rationale for the raises. After Bill questioned them, they even agreed that they thought the issue deserved some further discussion.

"I did not know we were using that standard," councilman Jim Maloney said. "If we're apply-ing comparable worth throughout the system, it would be good to know that, and on what basis it's being done."

Councilwoman Marcie Rivera said she was in accord with the approach. "I'm inclined to agree with the way Clyde put it out," she said, "to avoid any problems in discrimination. If that's the concern here, I feel like it's a step in the right direction."

Amazing, thought Bill as he headed to his car with notes in hand. I just attended a city council breakfast meeting to review the upcoming city budget, and comparable worth is proposed by the city manager. And the mayor and city council hardly noticed until after the meeting was adjourned!

QUESTIONS

1. Has Rockdale really implemented a comparable worth standard?
2. How do you think the technical-craft workers will react to the announced pay raise?
3. What other approaches are available for achieving pay equity between men and women?
4. Why have state and local governments shown more interest in comparable worth than have private employers?

ENDNOTES

1 R. K. Platt, "The Big Picture at Big Blue: Total Rewards at IBM," *Workspan* (August 2000): 27.

2 Bayer is an international, research-based group active in life sciences (agriculture), polymers, health care, and chemicals. It is composed of 15 business groups, represented in virtually every country of the world. Visit its Web site for a full description of its business groups, values, relation to the environment, and job and career opportunities. Materials for this feature are based upon company documents and Annual Reports from 1995 to 2001.

3 V. J. Weaver, "If Your Organization Values Diversity, Why Are They Leaving?" *Mosaics* (July/August 2001): 1, 4; L. Gardenswartz and A. Rowe, "Diversity Q&A: Hanging on to Top Talent," *Mosaics* (July/August 2001): 3–5.

4 P. W. Mulvey, J. E. Ledford Jr., and P. V. LaBlanc, "Rewards of Work: How They Drive Retention and Satisfaction," *WorldatWork Journal* (October 2000): 6–18.

5 See D. B. Balkin and L. R. Gomez-Mejia, "Compensation Systems in High Technology Companies," in Balkin and Gomez-Mejia (eds.), *New Perspectives in Compensation* (Englewood Cliffs, NJ: Prentice-Hall, 1987): 269–277.

6 M. Wanderer, "Dot-comp: A 'Traditional' Pay Plan with a Cutting Edge," *WorldatWork Journal* (Fourth Quarter 2000): 15–24.

7 D. B. Balkin and L. R. Gomez-Mejia, "Entrepreneurial Compensation," in Schuler, Youngblood, and Huber (eds.), *Readings in Personnel and Human Resource Management* (St. Paul, MN: West): 291–296.

8 G. T. Milkovich, "A Strategic Perspective on Compensation Management," in Rowland and Ferris (eds.), *Research in Personnel and Human Resources Management*, **(AU: city, publisher, date?)**: 263–288.

9 Y. Zhang, N. Rajagopalan, and D. Datta, "Executive Characteristics, Compensation Systems, and Firm Performance," *The Nature of Organizational Leadership* (2001): 270–301; D. M. Cable and T. A. Judge, "Pay Preferences and Job Search Decisions: A Person-Organization Fit Perspective," *Personnel Psychology* 47 (1994): 339–348; A. B. Krueger, "The Determinants of Queues for Federal Jobs," *Industrial and Labor Relations Review* 41 (1988): 567–581.

10 C. O. Trevor, B. Gerhart, and J. W. Boudreau, "Voluntary Turnover and Job Performance: Curvilinearity and the Moderating Influences of Salary Growth on Promotions," *Journal of Applied Psychology* 82 (1997): 44–61; S. J. Motowidlo, "Predicting Sales Turnover from Pay Satisfaction and Expectation," *Journal of Applied Psychology* 68 (1983): 484–489.

11 M. P. Miceli and M. C. Lane, "Antecedents of Pay Satisfaction: A Review and Extension," *Research in Personnel and Human Resource Management* 9 (1991): 235–309; P. Cappelli and P. D. Sherer, "Satisfaction, Market Wages, and Labor Relations: An Airline Study," *Industrial Relations* 27 (1988): 56–73; R. W. Rice, S. M. Phillips, and D. B. McFarlin, "Multiple Discrepancies and Pay Satisfaction," *Journal of Applied Psychology* 75 (1990): 386–393.

12 S. Werner and D. S. Ones, "The Determinants of Perceived Pay Inequities: The Effects of Comparison, Other Characteristics and Pay-System Communication," *Journal of Applied Social Psychology* 20 (2000): 1300–1329; K. Klaus, "Share and Share," *ACA News* (April 2000): 22–28;

L. A. Witt and L. G. Nye, "Gender and the Relationship between Perceived Fairness of Pay or Promotion and Job Satisfaction," *Journal of Applied Psychology* 77 (1992): 910–917.

13 J. S. Adams, "Toward an Understanding of Equity," *Journal of Abnormal and Social Psychology* 67 (1963): 422–436.

14 A. S. Tsui, J. L. Pearce, L. W. Porter, and A. M. Tripoli, "Alternative Approaches to the Employee–Organization Relationship: Does Investment in Employees Pay Off?" *Academy of Management Journal* 40 (1997): 1089–1121.

15 "UI: Trish Millines Dziko," *Fast Company* (August 2000): 85.

16 K. Aquino, R. W. Griffeth, D. G. Allen, and P. W. Hom, "Integrating Justice Constructs into the Turnover Process: A Test of a Referent Cognitions Model," *Academy of Management Journal* 40 (1997): 1208–1227; R. E. Kidwell, Jr., and N. Bennett, "Employee Propensity to Withhold Effort: A Conceptual Model to Intersect Three Avenues of Research," *Academy of Management Review* 18 (1993): 429–456; J. Schaubroek, D. R. May, and F. W. Brown, "Procedural Justice Explanations and Employee Reactions to Economic Hardship: A Field Experiment," *Journal of Applied Psychology* 79 (1994): 455–461; J. Greenberg, "Employee Theft as a Reaction to Underpayment Inequity: The Hidden Costs of Pay Cuts," *Journal of Applied Psychology* 75 (1990): 561–568.

17 "Doing Whatever It Takes," *Across the Board* (March/April 2001): 56–61.

18 B. S. Murphy, W. E. Barlow, and D. D. Hatch, "Manager's Newsfront," *Personnel Journal* (December 1992): 22.

19 A. Markels, "Blank Check," *Wall Street Journal* (April 9, 1998): R11.

20 E. E. Lawler III, *Pay and Organizational Development* (Reading, MA: Addison-Wesley, 1981).

21 "Employee Involvement in Compensation Plans," *Bulletin to Management Datagraph* (May 19, 1994): 156–157.

22 M. Zippo, "Roundup," *Personnel* (September–October 1980): 43–45.

23 See J. Koechel, "Free Agent Syndrome Fueling Turnover Frenzy," *Workspan* (January 2001): 6-8; P. K. Zingheim and J. R. Schuster, "Rewards for Scarce Information Technology Talent," *ACA Journal* (Fourth Quarter 1999): 48-57.

24 A. Bernstein, "Back on the Edge," *Business Week* (April 23, 2001): 42–43; "Runaway CEO Pay" What's Happening and What You Can Do About It," *AFL-CIO Paywatch* [http://www.aflcio.org/paywatch/ceopay .htm] (July 10, 2001).

25 C. Loomis, "This Stuff Is Wrong," *Fortune* (June 25, 2001): 73–84; L. Lavelle, "For Female CEOs It's Stingy at the Top," *Business Week* (April 23, 2001): 70–71; M. Arndt, "From Milestone to Millstone?" *Business Week* (March 20, 2000): 120–122; B. R. Ellig, "CEO Pay," *WorldatWork Journal* (Third Quarter 2000): 71–78; A. Tang, "Women's Earnings: What a Difference a Degree Makes," *New York Times* (February 23, 2000): G1; H. L. Tosi, S. Werner, J. P. Katz and L. R. Gomez-Mejia, "How Much Does Performance Matter? A Meta-Analysis of CEO Pay," *Journal of Management* 26(2) (2000): 301–339; R. Veilyath, "Top Management Compensation and Shareholder Returns: Unraveling Different Models of the Relationship," *Journal of Management Studies* 36 (2000): 123–143; J. K. Galbraith, *Created Unequal: The Crisis in American Pay* (New York: Free Press, 1998); J. M. Schlesinger, "Wages for Low-Paid Workers Rose in 1997," *Wall Street Journal* (March 28, 1998): A2; L. R. Gomez-Mejia, "Executive Compensation: A Reassessment and a Future Research Agenda," *Research in Personnel and Human Resource Management* 12 (1994): 161–222.

26 L. Rivenback, "Workers Like Pay, But Not How It Is Set, Survey Finds," *HR News* 19(7) (July 2000): 1, 16; J. S. Lublin, "Pay for No Performance," *Wall Street Journal* (April 9, 1998): R1, R19; R. B. Freeman, "How Labor Fares in Advanced Economies," in R. B. Freeman (ed.), *Working Under Different Rules* (New York: Russell Sage, 1993); K. Bradsher, "Widest Gap in Incomes? Research Points to U.S.," *New York Times* (October 27, 1995): D2.

27 "Readers on CEO Pay: Many Are Angry, A Few Really Think the Big Guy Is Worth It," *Fortune* (June 8, 1998): 296.

28 M. Minehan, "The New Face of Global Compensation," *SHRM Global* (December 2000): 4–7; R. Money and J. Graham, "Salesperson Performance, Pay, and Job Satisfaction: Tests of a Model Using Data Collected in the United States and Japan," *Journal of International Business Studies* 30 (1999): 149–172; for additional data, see American Compensation Association, *CEO Pay: A Comprehensive Look* (Scottsdale, AZ: American Compensation Association, 1997).

29 For detailed discussions of the relationship between executive pay and firm performance, see H. Barkema and L. R. Gomez-Mejia, "Managerial Compensation and Firm Performance: A General Research Framework," *Academy of Management Journal* 41(2) (1998): 135–145; Y. Zhang, N. Rajagopalan, and D. Datta, "Executive Characteristics, Compensation Systems, and Firm Performance," *The Nature of Organizational Leadership* (2001): 270–301.

30 "Aligning Compensation with Quality," *Bulletin to Management* (April 1, 1993): 97.

31 For a discussion of designing pay to fit a multinational strategy, see J. Burg, I. Sisovick, and D. Brock, "Aligning Performance and Rewards Practices in Multinational Subsidiaries," *WorldatWork Journal* (Third Quarter 2000): 64–70.

32 R. K. Platt, "The Big Picture at Big Blue: Total Rewards at IBM," *Workspan* (August 2000): 27; W. Fox, "Staying a Step Ahead of the Competition with Outstanding Total Compensation," *ACA News* (October 1998): 20–22.

33 S. O'Neal, "Study Shows Compensation Programs Becoming More Strategic," *ACA News* (November–December 1996): 19–21; J. D. Shaw, N. Gupta, and J. E. Delery, "Research Notes and Commentaries: Congruence Between Technology and Compensation Systems: Implications for Strategy Implementation," *Strategic Management Journal* 22 (2001): 379–386.

34 D. Brown, "The Third Way," *WorldatWork Journal* (Second Quarter 2000): 15–25.

35 J. Bloomer and P. Shafer, "Post-Merger Reward Practices That Maximize Shareholder Value," *WorldatWork Journal* (Third Quarter 2000): 35–44; T. Zhenger and C. Marshall, "Determinants of Incentive Intensity in Group-Based Rewards," *Academy of Management Journal* 43 (2000): 149–163; P. Pascarella, "Compensating Teams," *Across the Board* (February 1997): 16–22; E. E. Lawler III, "Teams, Pay and Business Strategy: Finding the Best Mix to Achieve Competitive Advantage," *ACA Journal* (Spring 1996): 12–25; D. G. Shaw and C. E. Schneier, "Team Measurement and Rewards: How Some Companies Are Getting It Right," *Human Resource Planning* 18(3) (1996): 34–49; C. J. Cantoni, "Mergers and Acquisitions: The Critical Role of Compensation and Culture," *ACA Journal* (Summer 1996): 38–45.

36 C. J. Cantoni, "Mergers and Acquisitions: The Critical Role of Compensation and Culture," *ACA Journal* (Summer 1996): 38–45.

37 P. E. Platten and D. A. Hofrichter, "The Compensation Lag," *Across The Board* (May 1996): 27–31; L. M. Kahn and P. D. Sherer, "Contingent Pay and Managerial Performance," *Industrial and Labor Relations Review* 43 (1990): 107S–120S; M. L. Weitzman and D. L. Kruse, "Profit Sharing and Productivity," in A. S. Blinder (ed.), *Paying for Productivity* (Washington, DC: Brookings Institute, 1990); R. A. Guzzo, R. D. Jette, and R. A. Katzell, "The Effects of Psychologically Based Intervention Programs on Worker Productivity: A Meta-Analysis," *Personnel Psychology* 38 (1985): 275–291.

38 J. R. Deckop, R. Mangel, and C. Cirka, "Getting More Than You Pay For: Organizational Citizenship Behavior and Pay-For-Performance Plans," *Academy of Management Journal* 42(4) (1999): 420–428; T. M. Welbourne, "Gainsharing: A Critical Review and a Future Research Agenda," *Journal of Management* (1995): 559–609.

39 D. Greising, "Fast Eddie's Future Bank," *Business Week* (March 23, 1998): 74–77.

40 V. Infante, "The Future of the Minimum Wage?" *Workforce* (March 2001): 29; "Myth and the Minimum Wage," *Business Week* (October 12, 1998): 6.

41 G. F. Dreher and T. H. Cox, Jr. "Labor Market Mobility and Cash Compensation: The Moderating Effects of Race and Gender," *Academy of Management Journal* 48(5) (2000): 890–900.

42 J. Handel, "Job Value: Employees Are in the Driver's Seat," *Workspan* (June 2000): 29–32; L. Mannsnerus, "As Law Scrambles for New Talent, The New Talent Reaps the Rewards," *New York Times* (January 30, 2001): 4; J. J. Laabs, "What Goes Down When Minimum Wages Go Up," *Workforce* (August 1998): 54–58.

43 J. M. Brett and L. K. Stroh, "Jumping Ship: Who Benefits From an External Labor Market Career Strategy?" *Journal of Applied Psychology* 82 (1997): 331–341; B. S. Klaas and J. M. McClendon, "To Lead, Lag, or Match: Estimating the Financial Impact of Pay Level Policies," *Personnel Psychology* 49 (1996).

44 E. L. Andrews, "Germans Cut Labor Costs with a Harsh Export: Jobs," *New York Times International* (March 21, 1998): A3.

45 Andrews, "Germans Cut Labor Costs with a Harsh Export: Jobs."

46 S. Overman, "Sync," *HR Magazine* (March 2000): 87–92; B. Parus, "We've Finally Got a Piece of the Pie," *ACA News* (January 2000): 32–36; R. Platt, "The Big Picture at Big Blue," *Workspan* (August 2000): 26–28; D. J. McNerney, "Compensation: Spreading the Wealth," *HR Focus* (March 1997): 4–5.

47 M. A. Thompson, "Border Crossing: Canadian Talent Heading South," *ACA News* (May 2001): 33–37.

48 P. Burstein, R. M. Bricher, and R. L. Einwohner, "Policy Alternatives and Political Change: Work, Family, and Gender on the Congressional Agenda," *American Sociological Review* 60 (1995): 67–83.

49 V. Peckham, "The Value of Being A Child-Friendly Company," *Solutions* (October 1996): 28–29; S. J. Boyd, "Will Compensatory Time Become Law?" *ACA News* (May 1997): 18–19.

50 G. Flynn, "Overtime Lawsuits: Are You at Risk?" *Workforce* (October 2001): 36–42; R. Kuttner, "So Much for the Minimum-Wage Scare," *Business Week* (July 21, 1997): 19; "Crackdown on Child Labor Violations," *Fair Employment Practices Guidelines* 299 (June 6, 1990).

51 "Youth Employment: Child Labor Limitations Reviewed," *Bulletin to Management* (May 19, 1994): 153.

52 G. Flynn, "Pizza as Pay? Compensation Gets Too Creative," *Workforce* (August, 1998): 91–96.

53 G. Flynn, "Overtime Lawsuits: Are You at Risk?"; M. Conlin, "Revenge of the 'Managers,'" *Business Week* (March 12, 2001): 60–61; C. Hirschman, "Paying for Waiting," *HR Magazine* (August 1999): 98–105; "White-Collar Exemptions under FLSA," *Bulletin to Management: Datagraph* (February 13, 1992): 44–45.

54 See "Record Settlement under Fair Labor Standards Act," *Bulletin to Management* (August 12, 1993): 249.

55 T. Raphael, "The Push for Living Wage Laws," *Workforce* (October 2001): 24; C. Hirschman, "Paying Up," *HR Magazine* (July 2000): 35–41; S. Brull, "What's So Bad About a Living Wage," *Business Week* (September 4, 2000): 68–70; R. Sharpe, "What Exactly Is a 'Living Wage'?" *Business Week* (May 28, 2001): 78–80.

56 M. M. Marini and P-L Fan, "The Gender Gap in Earning at Entry Level," *American Sociological Review* 62 (1997): 588–604.

57 G. F. Dreher and T. H. Cox Jr., "Race, Gender, and Opportunity: A Study of Compensation Attainment and the Establishment of Mentoring Relationships," *Journal of Applied Psychology* 81 (1996): 297–308; M. M. Marini and P-L Fan, "The Gender Gap in Earning at Entry Level."

58 For an explanation of the analytic methods used to evaluate the role of gender in determining pay levels, see M. O'Malley, "Testing for Gender Difference on Pay," *ACA Journal* (Summer 1998): 16–28; P. England, *Comparable Worth: Theories and Evidence* (Hawthorne, NY: Aldine de Gruyter, 1992).

59 A. Bernstein, "Pay Equity Makes Good Business Sense," *Fair Employment Practices* (August 30, 1990): 103.

60 C. Caggiano, "The Appeasement Trap," *Inc.* (September 2000): 39–49; A. Bernstein, "Why Workers Still Hold a Weak Hand," *Business Week*

(March 2, 1998): 98; Bureau of National Affairs, "Employment Cost Index—Second Quarter 1997," *Bulletin to Management: Datagraph* (August 7, 1997): 252–254; D. C. Johnston, "On Payday, Union Jobs Stack Up Very Well," *New York Times* (August 31, 1997): Section 3.

61 R. B. Freeman and J. L. Medoff, *What Do Unions Do?* (New York: Basic Books, 1984); T. A. Kochan, H. C. Katz, and R. B. McKersie, *The Transformation of American Industrial Relations* (New York: Basic Books, 1986).

62 P. L. Gilles, "Enhancing the Participatory Process of Compensation Design," *ACA News* (May 1998): 27–29.

63 J. Koechel, "Free Agent Syndrome Fueling Turnover Frenzy," *Workspan* (January 2001): 6–8; C. O. Trevor and M. Graham, "Deriving the Market Wage," *WorldatWork Journal* (Fourth Quarter 2000): 69–76; P. Cappelli and W. F. Cascio, "Why Some Jobs Command Wage Premiums: A Test of Career Tournament and Internal Labor Market Hypotheses," *Academy of Management Journal* 34 (1991): 848–868.

64 R. Sneigar, "The Comparability of Job Evaluation Methods in Supplying Approximately Similar Classifications in Rating One Job Series," *Personnel Psychology* (Summer 1983): 371–380.

65 J. A. Green and R. W. Keuch, "Contribution-Driven Competency-Based Pay," *ACA Journal* (Autumn 1997): 62–71.

66 K. S. Abosch and B. L. Hmurovic, "A Traveler's Guide to Global Broadbanding," *ACA Journal* (Summer 1998): 38–46.

67 B. Parus, "Broadbanding Highly Effective, Survey Shows," *ACA News* (July/August 1998): 40–41; see also M. Enos and G. Limoges, "Broadbanding: Is That Your Company's Final Answer?" *WorldatWork Journal* (Fourth Quarter 2000): 61–68.

68 N. Gupta et al., "Survey-Based Prescriptions for Skill-Based Pay," *ACA Journal* (Fall 1992): 48–58; M. Rowland, "It's What You Can Do That Counts," *New York Times* (June 6, 1993): F17; M. Rowland, "For Each New Skill, More Money," *New York Times* (June 13, 1993): F16.

69 G. J. Ledford, "Three Case Studies on Skill-Based Pay," *Compensation and Benefits Review* (April 1990): 11–23.

70 D. Brown, "The Third Way," *WorldatWork Journal* (Second Quarter 2000): 15–25; S. Fournier, "Keeping Line Managers in the Know," *ACA News* (March 2000): 46–48; B. Murray and B. Gerhart, "An Empirical Analysis of a Skill-Based Pay Program and Plan Performance Outcomes," *Academy of Management Journal* 41 (1998): 68–78; Ledford, "Three Case Studies on Skill-Based Pay."

71 J. Domat-Connell, "Labor Market Definition and Salary Survey Selection: A New Look at the Foundation of Compensation Program Design," *Compensation and Benefits Review* (March–April 1994): 38–46.

72 E. R. Schultz, D. Van de Voort, and T. G. Nocerino, "Industry and Occupational Influences on Compensation," in C. H. Fay, M. A. Thompson, and D. Knight, *The Executive Handbook on Compensation* (New York: Free Press, 2001): 607–623.

73 K. Lemaire, " Competency-Based Pay: A Practitioner's Guide," in C. H. Fay, M. A. Thompson, and D. Knight, *The Executive Handbook on Compensation* (New York: Free Press, 2001): 486–495.

74 N. K. Coleman, "Local-National Employee Compensation Practices," in C. Reynolds (ed.), *Guide to Global Compensation and Benefits*, 2d ed. (New York: Harcourt, 2001): 287–306.

75 Ledford, "Three Case Studies on Skill-Based Pay."

76 D. Kiker and S. J. Motowidlo, "Main and Interaction Effects of Task and Contextual Performance on Supervisory Reward Decisions," *Journal of Applied Psychology* 84 (1999): 602–609; P. K. Zingheim and J. R. Schuster, "Rewards for Scarce Information Technology Talent," *ACA Journal* (Fourth Quarter 1999): 48–57; J. C. Kail, "Compensating Scientists and Engineers," in Balkin and Gomez-Mejia (eds.), *New Perspectives on Compensation*, 278–281; G. T. Milkovich, "Compensation Systems in High-Technology Companies," in Balkin and Gomez-Mejia (eds.), *New Perspectives on Compensation*, 269–277; C. F. Schultz, "Compensating the Sales Professional," in Balkin and Gomez-Mejia (eds.), *New Perspectives on Compensation*, 250–257.

77 N. Gupta and J. D. Shaw, "Successful Skill-Based Pay Plans," in C. H. Fay, M. A. Thompson, and D. Knight, *The Executive Handbook on Compensation,* 513–526.

78 B. Murray and B. Gerhart, "An Empirical Analysis of a Skill-Based Pay Program and Plant Performance Outcomes," *Academy of Management Journal* 41 (1998): 68–78.

79 The topic of international compensation is much too complex to address here. For detailed discussions of the issues involved, see C. Reynolds, *Guide to Global Compensation and Benefits,* 2d ed. (New York: Harcourt, 2001).

80 S. Werner and D. S. Ones, "The Determinants of Perceived Pay Inequities: The Effects of Comparison, Other Characteristics and Pay-System Communication," *Journal of Applied Social Psychology* 20 (2000): 1300–1329.

81 A. M. Healey, "Grabbing Attention for Total Compensation Plans," *ACA News* (October 1996): 11–13.

82 R. S. Schuler and N. Rogovsky, "Understanding Compensation Practice Variations Across Firms: The Impact of National Culture," *Journal of International Business Studies* 29(1) (First Quarter 1998): 159–177; P. D. Dowling, R. S. Schuler, and D. E. Welch, *International Dimensions of Human Resource Management,* 3rd ed. (Belmont, CA: Wadsworth, 1999).

83 J. Burg, I. Sisovick, and D. Brock, "Aligning Performance and Rewards Practices in Multinational Subsidiaries," *WorldatWork Journal* (Third Quarter 2000): 64–70; V. Infante, "Three Ways to Design International Pay: Headquarters, Home Country, Host Country," *Workforce* (January 2001): 22–24; V. Frazee, "Is the Balance Sheet Right for Your Expats?" *Global Workforce* (September 1998): 19–26; C. Reynolds, *Compensating Globally Mobile Employees: Approaches to Developing Expatriate Pay Strategies for the Evolving International Corporation* (Scottsdale, AZ: American Compensation Association, 1995).

84 C. M. Gould, "The Impact of Headquarters Location on Expatriate Policy," *HRM Magazine* (April 1998): 9–12; S. Spencer, "The Euro Is Coming!" *ACA Journal* (Autumn 1998): 37–44.

CHAPTER

11

MEASURING PERFORMANCE AND PROVIDING FEEDBACK

"Part of being an 'Employer of Choice' is treating our associates like valued members of the company. Giving them honest and specific feedback about their performance is a major way to do this."

Paris Couturiaux
Senior VP, Human Resources
Cendant Mortgage

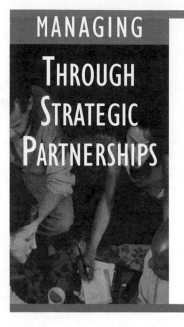

Con-Way Transportation Services

Con-Way Transportation Services is a subsidiary of CNF, the giant shipping company. It's a company in which teams are prevalent, yet it had no centralized approach to evaluating team effectiveness. So the Information System Department decided to become trailblazers. To evaluate itself, it developed the Team Improvement Review (TIR). Daily life in the department is guided by its Team Agreement, a document that sets out how to do things. According to the department's manager, "It's pretty much the common law around here." The TIR separates feedback sessions, which focus on how to improve in the future, from salary reviews, which focus on the past. The team's reasoning was that people might not be candid in evaluating each other if they knew that doing so would affect salaries. Many experts agree with that reasoning.

Before a team improvement meeting, which occurs every three months, members rate each other on 31 dimensions. To ensure that the feedback environment is "safe," these meetings usually take place with no managers present. In their place is a facilitator who helps the team manage the delicate process of providing feedback that improves rather than destroys team functioning. One trick that the team learned is to let an individual's self-assessment serve as the focus of the discussion. Each team member begins by listing a few of his or her strengths and weaknesses on a sheet of paper. The sheets are then passed around the group. By the time each sheet gets back to its owner, the sheet has comments from the other team members, indicating whether they agree or disagree with the items in the list and making suggestions for how and where to focus improvement efforts. The process encourages people to be honest with themselves and, at the same time, creates a network of support for self-initiated change efforts.[1]

Through recruitment, selection, placement, and training, organizations strive to put in place a workforce that's capable of performing the required work. The total compensation system ensures that the members of the workforce are motivated to join the company, do their job at the level needed to maintain employment, and stay with the company. In this chapter and the next, we describe the objectives and design of performance management systems. Performance management systems help to *direct* and *motivate* employees to maximize the effort they exert on behalf of the organization. For companies like Con-Way, Lincoln Electric, Cendant Mortgage, FedEx, Continental, and Southwest Airlines, this is the difference between being just okay and being the leader in the industry.

A **performance management system** is a formal, structured process used to measure, evaluate, and influence an employee's job-related attributes, behaviors, and performance results.[2] Its focus is on discovering how productive the employee is and whether he or she can perform as or more effectively in the future, so that the employee, the organization, and society all benefit.

Two components of performance management systems are (a) performance measurement and feedback for individuals and teams, which are the focus of this chapter, and (b) the rewards component of total compensation, which will be explained in Chapter 12. A well-designed performance measurement and feedback process *directs* employees' attention toward the most important tasks and behaviors. It informs employees about what's valued and provides information about whether the employees' behaviors and results meet the expectations of managers, colleagues, and customers. An effective performance measurement and feedback process is essential to the effectiveness of performance incentives and rewards, which are used to *motivate* employees. The elements of performance management and its relationship to other aspects of the HR system are shown in Exhibit 11.1.[3]

ex 11.1 Performance Management within an Integrated HR System

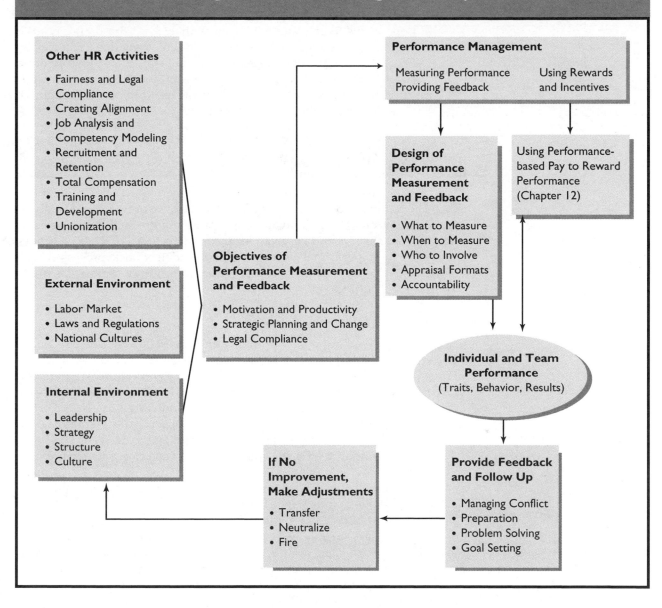

Other HR Activities

- Fairness and Legal Compliance
- Creating Alignment
- Job Analysis and Competency Modeling
- Recruitment and Retention
- Total Compensation
- Training and Development
- Unionization

External Environment

- Labor Market
- Laws and Regulations
- National Cultures

Internal Environment

- Leadership
- Strategy
- Structure
- Culture

Objectives of Performance Measurement and Feedback

- Motivation and Productivity
- Strategic Planning and Change
- Legal Compliance

Performance Management

Measuring Performance
Providing Feedback

Using Rewards
and Incentives

Design of Performance Measurement and Feedback

- What to Measure
- When to Measure
- Who to Involve
- Appraisal Formats
- Accountability

Using Performance-based Pay to Reward Performance (Chapter 12)

Individual and Team Performance
(Traits, Behavior, Results)

If No Improvement, Make Adjustments

- Transfer
- Neutralize
- Fire

Provide Feedback and Follow Up

- Managing Conflict
- Preparation
- Problem Solving
- Goal Setting

Performance appraisal is the central component of most performance management systems. **Performance appraisal** involves evaluating performance based on the judgments and opinions of subordinates, peers, supervisors, other managers, and even employees themselves. It is perhaps the most common approach to performance measurement, but it is not the only approach. Performance management systems may also use objective performance measures, such as sales figures, error rates, speed of response, and so on. For jobs that involve direct contact with customers, performance measures also include customer satisfaction data.

Regardless of how performance is measured, its usefulness requires that employees accept it as fair and use performance feedback to guide them in the future. When everything is going well, providing feedback is easy. Everyone wants to give and get feedback that says "You do not need to change." But today's competitive environment does not usually accept the status quo. Instead, it mandates improvement. In other words, the feedback often says, "We want you to do better." Effective performance management systems result in positive employee reactions to feedback even when the feedback is not positive.[4]

THE STRATEGIC IMPORTANCE OF MEASURING PERFORMANCE AND PROVIDING FEEDBACK

Performance measurement and feedback serve many purposes in organizations. The common objectives served by effective measurement and feedback are enhancing employee motivation and productivity, facilitating strategic planning and change, and ensuring legal compliance. All of these objectives are served by a performance measurement and feedback process that is aligned with the organization's competitive strategy and appropriate to the organizational culture.[5]

Enhancing Motivation and Productivity

Chapter 9 described how formal training and several developmental activities can be used to improve the knowledge and skills that employees need to perform well in their jobs. There the emphasis was on improving performance by increasing the capabilities of employees. But even the most capable employees won't perform well unless they are motivated to do so. Performance management systems address the issue of motivating employees in order to ensure that their capabilities are fully utilized.

A vast amount of research and theory has been conducted to improve our understanding of employee motivation and performance. Clearly, motivation is a complex phenomenon, with many factors coming into play. Exhibit 11.2 illustrates some of these factors.

The foundation of a model for understanding employee motivation and performance, shown in Exhibit 11.2, is expectancy theory. In this model, **motivation** has two elements: decisions about which behaviors to engage in and decisions about how much effort to expend. Usually, effective job performance requires that employees both engage in the appropriate behaviors and exert relatively high levels of effort.

Expectancy theory states that people choose their behaviors and effort levels after considering whether their behaviors and effort will lead to desired consequences (e.g., recognition and rewards). Examples of choices that are related to work performance include whether to go to work or call in sick, whether to leave work at the official quitting time or stay late, and whether to exert a great deal of effort or to work at a more relaxed pace. According to expectancy theory, people tend to choose behaviors that they believe will help them achieve their personal goals (e.g., a promotion or job security) and avoid behaviors that they believe will lead to undesirable personal consequences (e.g., a demotion or criticism).

An employee's motivation to perform well is determined by how he or she responds to three key questions: the expectancy question, the

"The average person puts only 25 percent of his energy and ability into his work. The world takes off its hat to those who put in more than 50 percent of their capacity, and stands on its head for those few and far between souls who devote 100 percent."

Andrew Carnegie
Founder
United States Steel

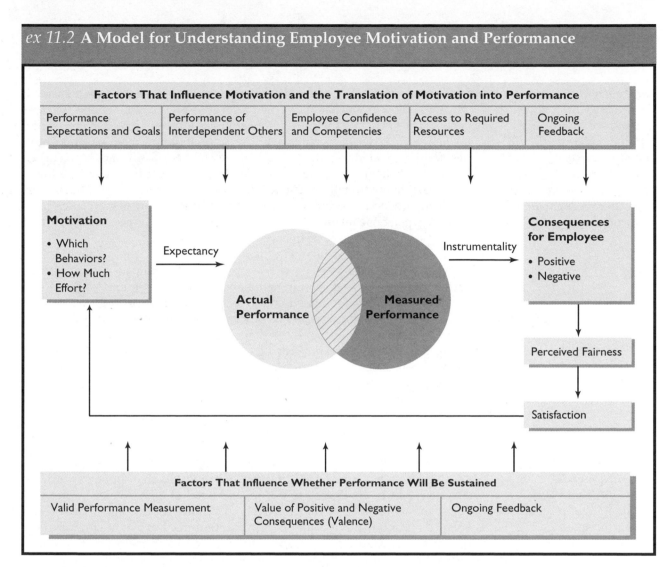

ex 11.2 A Model for Understanding Employee Motivation and Performance

instrumentality question, and the valence question. As you will see, many aspects of an organization's human resource management system can influence how employees answer these questions.

Expectancy. The **expectancy** question is: If I make an effort, will I be able to perform as intended? In order for employees to be motivated to expend effort, they must expect that their efforts will translate into performance. Employees are more likely to expect that their efforts will lead to performance if they are confident in their own skills and abilities.[6] Effective selection and training practices help ensure that employees are confident in their ability to perform. Over time, feedback about performance also can improve employees' confidence in their ability to perform. In addition, the quality of an organization's performance measures is relevant to the expectancy question. Even when employees know that they can improve their performance, their motivation may remain low if the organization uses inadequate measures. In Exhibit 11.2, the degree of overlap between "actual" and "measured" performance reflects the adequacy or validity of the organization's performance measure.

Instrumentality. The **instrumentality** question is: What consequences, if any, will follow from changes in my performance? The issue here is whether performance is of any instrumental usefulness. An HR system that uses performance as a basis for incentive pay, decisions about promotions, opportunities for personal development, discipline, and so forth should result in employees believing that the consequences that result from good performance are different from those that result from poor performance. When important consequences are influenced by factors other than performance (e.g., seniority, personal relationships, and favoritism), employees may feel that performance is of little consequence.

Medi-Health Outsourcing is a fast-growing, young company that helps hospitals and other health care organizations manage patient records and documents for inclusion in national databases. For founders Paula and Ron Lawlor, highly motivated employees are essential to a growing company, which may add as many as 60 or 70 new hospitals to its roster each year. The Lawlors' philosophy is that employees are held accountable for performance results and rewarded for achieving them. For example, if your job is to code documents for entry into a database, you might be given the goal of abstracting 100 records per week with 95 percent accuracy. If you meet the goal on Thursday, you can take the rest of the week off. Or, you can come to work and offer to take on other tasks—and some people do![7]

Valence. The **valence** question is: How much do I value the consequences associated with the intended behavior? Even when employees believe that good performers experience different consequences than poor performers, they may not be motivated to put in the required effort. Valences are personal; the same outcome may have a high valence for one person and a low valence for another. For example, a promotion from museum curator to the higher-paying position of museum director would appeal more to an individual who values financial gain and increased responsibility than to an individual who values creativity and independence. At Medi-Health, the Lawlors strive hard to make sure employees value the rewards they receive from working at the company. The company's employee-friendly approach allows employees to work from home or from the beach, arrange their weekly schedules around their personal needs, and even take three months off without worrying about losing their jobs. When it comes to keeping good performers satisfied, the Lawlors' philosophy is pretty much that "anything goes."

Satisfaction. The model shown in Exhibit 11.2 suggests that an employee's satisfaction is determined by perceptions of whether the consequences of performance are fair. Fairness can be evaluated by comparing one's own rewards with those received by others, or by comparing current rewards with those received in the past. If an employee believes that the comparison shows unfair treatment, dissatisfaction results. The topic of rewards is discussed in more detail in Chapter 12. Satisfied employees are more likely to make an effort to do their jobs well and continue to be

"In the beginning, you're the lowest paid and you're trying hard to get raises. But no matter what I did, nobody reviewed my work and I never got noticed. After awhile, I stopped being so concerned about performance."

John Ranson
Employee
Aerospace industry

"Sometimes I think we baby the heck out of them. But when you ask them to do something, you just don't hear a lot of complaining."

Chuck Hammond
Manager
Medi-Health Outsourcing

motivated. Conversely, dissatisfied employees exert less effort, which results in declining performance and a general downward spiral to ineffectiveness.[8]

It follows from this model of motivation that a company's prospects for attaining peak performance at the individual, team, and organization levels depends on a performance management system that includes monitoring performance *and* giving employees useful feedback as quickly as possible on how well they're doing.

Strategic Planning and Change

Besides motivating employees to perform at peak levels, performance measurement of individuals and teams also provides valuable information for use in strategic planning and decision making. At high levels in the organization, the performance of executives and their management teams is almost synonymous with the performance of a business unit. If the performance measures that are used to evaluate executives are designed appropriately, they should be very useful for detecting where there may be organizational problems that require attention and for evaluating change.

Detecting Problems. The role of performance management in detecting performance problems in the organization is perhaps most easily illustrated by considering performance management for CEOs. Responsibility for evaluating CEOs rests with the board of directors. The board is expected to engage the CEO in strategic planning to set goals and identify the means for achieving goals. The board also monitors the CEO's progress toward achieving organizational goals and is responsible for staying alert to significant performance problems.

Performance assessments of employees at lower levels in the organization can also be useful for detecting organizational problems. At Pepsi-Cola International, for example, performance information pointed to a deficiency in corporate training. To address the deficiency, the firm established an umbrella organization to deliver training programs around the world. The detection of performance deficiencies also led to a program that brings non–U.S. citizens to the United States for 18 months of training in the domestic Pepsi system.[9]

Evaluating Change. As described in Chapter 5, the process of strategic planning and change involves first, identifying objectives, and subsequently, assessing results against those objectives. Not *all* organizational change efforts target performance improvement as an objective—some change efforts are intended to attract more talent to the organization, others are intended to increase employee satisfaction, and so on. Nevertheless, improving organizational performance, and therefore the performance of at least some of the organization's employees, is the most common objective behind large-scale change efforts. Consequently, employee performance measures should be a key component of a plan for evaluating the success of a change initiative. If human resource issues aren't fully addressed during strategic planning, the performance management system evolves in isolation from strategic initiatives—rather than in anticipation of them.

Ensuring Legal Compliance

In almost all organizations, performance information partly determines pay, promotions, terminations, transfers, and other types of key decisions that affect both the well-being of employees and the productivity of a company. Society has a vested interest in ensuring that employers use high-quality information for these important decisions, and their interests are reflected in various laws and regulations.

A condensed set of recommended actions for developing and implementing legally defensible performance measurement is detailed in Exhibit 11.3.[10] All of these recommendations are consistent with the objective of developing a performance management system that supports the business strategy and objectives.

Three basic principles for ensuring the legality of a performance management system are similar to those for selection systems. In both cases, the measures used to assess employees should be nondiscriminatory, job related, and fair.

Nondiscriminatory. Guidance to employers regarding how to collect and use performance information is provided by numerous pieces of legislation and court decisions. Particularly relevant are the *Civil Rights Acts of 1964 and 1991*, the *Americans with Disabilities Act of 1990*, and the *Age Discrimination in Employment Act of 1967*. Each of these emphasize the importance of protecting employees against negative consequences in the workplace that may be caused by unfair discrimination and the use of inappropriate information when making employment decisions.

ex 11.3 Prescriptions for Legally Defensible Appraisal and Feedback

1. Job analysis to identify important duties and tasks should precede development of a performance appraisal system.
2. The performance appraisal system should be standardized and formal.
3. Specific performance standards should be communicated to employees in advance of the appraisal period.
4. Objective and uncontaminated data should be used whenever possible.
5. Ratings on traits such as dependability, drive, or attitude should be avoided or operationalized in behavioral terms.
6. Employees should be evaluated on specific work dimensions rather than on a single global or overall measure.
7. If work behaviors rather than outcomes are to be evaluated, evaluators should have ample opportunity to observe ratee performance.
8. To increase the reliability of ratings, more than one independent evaluator should perform appraisals whenever possible.
9. Behavioral documentation should be prepared for extreme ratings.
10. Employees should be given an opportuniy to review their appraisals.
11. A formal system of appeal should be available for appraisal disagreements.
12. Raters should be trained to prevent discrimination and to evaluate performance consistently.
13. Appraisals should be frequent, offered at least annually.

Job Related. In general, the legal system makes it clear that employers will be better able to successfully defend any legally contested employment decisions if they can show that their actions were based on valid measures of employee performance. For example, the U.S. circuit court in *Brito v. Zia Company* (1973) found that Zia Company was in violation of Title VII when a disproportionate number of employees of a protected group were laid off because of low scores on the company's measure of performance—a subjective performance appraisal. The critical point was that the company's measures of performance were based on the supervisor's overall judgments and opinions, not on assessments of how well the employee performed on specific components of the job. The best way to assure that performance appraisals are job related is to use job analysis when developing the performance appraisal measures.

Fair. Following the guidelines in Exhibit 11.3 requires careful record keeping and may limit a manager's freedom to make unilateral evaluations. Nevertheless, research indicates that managers respond favorably to the introduction of procedurally just performance management systems. A major advantage for managers is that procedurally fair performance management systems improve relationships between managers and their direct reports.[11]

> **FAST FACT**
>
> The courts have held that fair performance evaluations are tangible job benefits, and employees are protected from interference with those benefits in the form of "indefensibly harsh" evaluations.

INTERNET RESOURCES 11.A

Strategic Importance of Measuring Performance and Providing Feedback

At our Web site, http://jackson.swcollege.com/, you can:

1. Learn about managing performance and its importance at some of the firms discussed in this section by visiting their company home pages:

   CNF

   FedEx

   Nordstrom

   Cendant Mortgage

2. Visit Web sites that provide resources for learning more about issues in performance measurement and feedback at

   Zigon Performance Group

   HR Guide

DECIDING WHAT TO MEASURE

Performance criteria are the dimensions against which the performance of an incumbent, a team, or a work unit is evaluated. They are the performance expectations that individuals and teams strive for in order to achieve the organization's strategy. If jobs have been designed well, with attention paid to how job demands relate to strategic business needs, then conducting a job analysis should ensure that performance measures reflect strategic concerns. The job analysis should capture performance on specific tasks and the employee's performance as an organizational citizen.[12] Examples of **organizational citizenship** (sometimes referred to as contextual performance) include

> **FAST FACT**
>
> Employees who perform well on specific job tasks also tend to be good organizational citizens.

- volunteering to carry out task activities that are not formally a part of the job;
- persisting with extra enthusiasm or effort when necessary to complete task activities successfully;

- helping others;
- following organizational rules and procedures even when doing so is inconvenient; and
- endorsing, supporting, and defending organizational objectives.[13]

To measure task performance or organizational citizenship, three types of performance criteria can be used: personal traits, behaviors, and objective results. Regardless of which type of criteria is measured, the performance management system becomes strategic to the extent that these criteria are clearly linked to organizational goals.

Personal Traits

Trait-based criteria focus on personal characteristics. Loyalty, dependability, communication ability, and leadership exemplify traits that are often assessed. Criteria such as these address what a person is, not what a person does or does not accomplish on the job. For jobs that involve work that's difficult to observe, trait-based performance measures may be the easiest to use. Unfortunately, they may not be reliable indicators of job performance. To one manager, being dependable may mean an employee shows up to work on time every day; to another manager, it may mean an employee stays late when the boss requests it; to a third manager, it may mean that an employee doesn't use sick days even when really sick.

Performance evaluations should not depend on who is making the judgment. They should reflect what the employee does, regardless of who is evaluating. Because trait-based measures of performance are often unreliable, the courts have penalized employers who rely on them when making employment decisions.[14]

Does the position of the courts and the importance of meritocracy in U.S. culture mean that difficult-to-measure personal qualities should not be evaluated as part of the performance appraisal process? Can employers still build corporate cultures around having the right kinds of people as defined by personal qualities that extend beyond job skills? The answer is that personal qualities can be appropriately assessed by shifting the focus from traits to behaviors.

Behaviors

Behavioral criteria focus on how work is performed. Such criteria are particularly important for jobs that involve interpersonal contact. Customer service jobs and managerial jobs are examples that show how behavioral criteria can be used to measure performance.

Customer Service. Having friendly cashiers is critical to Au Bon Pain's customers and to the store's image. But Au Bon Pain doesn't use store managers' judgments of employees' friendliness to measure this critical aspect of performance. Instead, it measures friendly behaviors. To assess employees' behaviors, the company generated a list of specific actions that employees should engage in. These are behaviors that convey a "friendly" image to most customers. To assess friendliness, the store hires mystery shoppers to buy meals and fill out behavior-based appraisals.

Managing Diversity. As organizations struggle to create cultures in which diversity is valued and respected, behavioral criteria are proving useful for monitoring whether managers are investing sufficient energy in the development of employees from diverse backgrounds. Imagine how difficult it would be to evaluate whether a manager achieved a traitlike criterion such as "Values the diversity of subordinates." A trait-based criterion like this provides little guidance to the manager about what actually to *do*. It would be equally difficult for the manager's superior to interpret. (Subordinates, on the other hand, may be quite willing to express their opinions!) For the purpose of performance management, more effective criteria would be *specific* behaviors. For example, one company uses the following items to assess behaviors that managers should be exhibiting in order to manage diversity effectively in their business units:

- Does your business plan include a diversity strategy?
- Are you a member of a diversity focus group or steering committee?
- Have you attended a diversity workshop or seminar during the past 12 months?
- What percentage of employees in your organization have individual development plans?
- Has your company formed a diversity focus group?
- Has anyone in your organization filed complaints of discrimination or harassment during the past 12 months? If yes, what is their current status?

When combined with performance feedback, behavioral measures are particularly useful for employee development. With behaviors clearly identified, an employee is more likely to exhibit the acts that lead to peak performance. Behavioral criteria are less appropriate for jobs in which effective performance can be achieved using many different behaviors. Still, even in these jobs, the identification of the most appropriate behaviors serves as a useful guideline for most employees' actions.

Objective Results

FAST FACT

The best-performing employees can produce up to three times as much as the worst-performing employees.

Results criteria focus on what was accomplished or produced rather than on how it was accomplished or produced. Results criteria may be appropriate if the company does not care how results are achieved, but they are not appropriate for every job. They are often criticized for missing critical aspects of the job that are difficult to quantify. For example, the number of cases handled annually by a lawyer can easily be counted, but the results do not indicate the quality of legal counsel given or the resolution of the cases. Results criteria also can create unexpected problems if they create a results-at-all-costs mentality among employees. A collection agency used the total dollars collected by agents as its sole measure of performance. Large sums of money were collected, but the agency ended up being sued because agents used threats and punitive measures to amass collections.

Multiple Criteria

Most jobs are composed of many different duties and related tasks and require many different competencies, and job descriptions usually reflect this reality. Just as a job description describes all aspects of the job, performance measures should capture all aspects of the job. For some duties and competencies, trait-based measures may be appropriate. For other duties, behavioral performance measures or outcome measures may be best. At AT&T, for example, the performance measures for managers include both behaviors and results. Some of the results that might be measured are actual vs. budgeted expenses, revenue growth, and productivity measures of quality. Some of the behaviors that the company measures are empowerment, communication, self-awareness, and openness to learning.

Validity. A valid performance measurement system accurately reflects all aspects of the job, and nothing else. If the performance measurement process does not assess all of the behaviors and results that are important and relevant to the job, the performance measures are **deficient**. If the process assesses anything that is unimportant or irrelevant to the job, the measures are **contaminated**. Deficient and contaminated measures are quite common in organizations and are among the biggest reasons for employees' complaints about performance measurement.

Taxonomies of Performance Domains. Some researchers have argued that a limited set of performance domains can be used to capture all aspects of nearly any job. Two proposed taxonomies are useful to consider when trying to determine whether all appropriate domains of performance are being measured. These two taxonomies are summarized in Exhibit 11.4. The taxonomy in the top of Exhibit 11.4 describes the content of jobs.[15] The taxonomy in the bottom of Exhibit 11.4 was developed to address the fact that many jobs and organizations are in a state of constant flux. In organizations experiencing rapid change, the key performance domains reflect how well employees respond to stress and adapt to new work conditions—referred to as **adaptive performance**.[16]

Weighting the Criteria

For jobs involving multiple performance criteria, another question must be asked: "How should these separate aspects of performance be combined into a composite score that facilitates comparisons of incumbents?" One way is to weight all the criteria equally. If some criteria are much more important than others, then weights should be assigned to reflect these differences. The simplest approach to assigning weights is to use job analysis information—such as ratings of task frequency and importance. Statistical procedures also can be used to determine appropriate weights for each job dimension. With these procedures, greater weights are assigned to dimensions that are most strongly associated with overall performance evaluations.

"We told employees, 'You have a right to feedback and you can ask for it [any time].'"

Jeff Chambers
HR Director
SAS

TIMING

The timing of performance measurement *should* reflect strategic considerations. But often the timing of performance measurement and feedback is driven by convenience and tradition. The three most common approaches to timing performance measurement and feedback are focal-point, anniversary, and natural time span.

ex 11.4 A Two-Part Taxonomy of Performance Domains

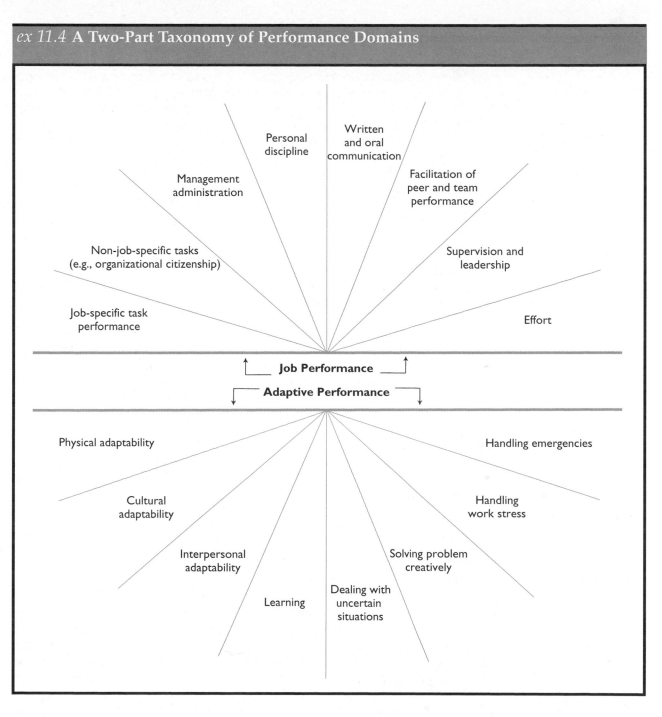

Personal discipline

Written and oral communication

Management administration

Facilitation of peer and team performance

Non-job-specific tasks (e.g., organizational citizenship)

Supervision and leadership

Job-specific task performance

Effort

Job Performance

Adaptive Performance

Physical adaptability

Handling emergencies

Cultural adaptability

Handling work stress

Interpersonal adaptability

Solving problem creatively

Learning

Dealing with uncertain situations

Focal-Point Approach

With the **focal-point approach**, performance measurement for all employees occurs at approximately the same time. Many organizations conduct formal review sessions at regular intervals, such as every quarter, every six months, or annually.

Standardization. The major advantage of this system is that supervisors find it easier to make direct comparisons among employees. They consider everyone at once and get a sense of how their performances compare during the same time period. Similarly, top management can compare the performances of different strategic business units to assess how well they're meeting corporate objectives. Such comparative information is particularly important if performance information is used for compensation decisions. Because the link to compensation is central to Lincoln Electric, its line managers spend up to two weeks doing appraisal. The HR department spends several weeks before this making sure the line managers have all the necessary data, for instance, on absenteeism and productivity.

Workload. The focal-point approach creates a tremendous workload for a concentrated period of time, which can be burdensome. The burden on managers can be reduced in two ways: first, by having clear criteria against which to evaluate performance, and second, by ensuring that subordinates share with their supervisors the responsibility for documenting accomplishments relative to performance standards.

Performance Cycles. Another concern about the focal-point approach is that it may create artificial productivity cycles that reflect merely the timing of performance measurement and feedback. For example, if a law firm measures performance each year at the end of November, an employee's billable hours may begin to peak in the weeks immediately preceding the appraisal as everyone tries to increase total billable hours. Then, after the review cycle is over, billable hours may drop below normal as everyone takes time to recover from the frenzy. This problem also occurs when performance is measured subjectively. Knowing that their manager will soon be evaluating their performances, the employees in a unit may all put in extra effort to perform at their best. Following the review, employees may reason that their performance at this time will not be remembered by the time the next review cycle begins, causing them to put in less effort for a while.

Anniversary Approach

The **anniversary approach** distributes the task of reviewing employees' performance and providing feedback across the year. Often, an employee's performance review is timed to when he or she joined the organization. As in the focal-point system, employees may receive reviews every 6 or 12 months. Assuming the organization hires throughout the year, this approach spreads out the workload, making it less overwhelming for supervisors. However, the anniversary model typically does not tie individual or team performance to the overall performance of the organization, and thus compromises the strategic benefits of the appraisal process. Furthermore, research suggests that ratings given to employees early in the calendar year are higher than ratings given later. This is particularly likely if raters or appraisers must use a "curve" so that they can allocate only specific numbers of high and low ratings.

Natural Time Span of the Job

Some experts argue that a better timing rule is to schedule reviews to correspond to the natural time span of the job. If performance is assessed too soon in the natural time span, it cannot be reasonably measured due to lack of

"Doing annual reviews is like dieting only on your birthday and wondering why you're not losing weight."

Anne Saunier
Principal
Sibson & Co.

information. If performance is measured too late, motivation and performance may suffer because the feedback comes too late to be of any use. Feedback that comes too late is particularly detrimental to a poor performer, who will likely not know how to improve performance until it's too late. In the case of some simple jobs, the time span may be only a few minutes; in the case of a senior-level management job, the appropriate time period may be as long as several years. In an advertising agency, account executives receive evaluation feedback after each presentation.

For teams working on projects, a good time for performance measurement and feedback may be about midway through the project.[17] At this point, team members are open to suggestions for improvement because they have a good understanding of the team's strengths and weaknesses, yet there remains enough time to make changes that may improve the team's performance.

PARTICIPANTS IN PERFORMANCE MEASUREMENT AND FEEDBACK

It should be apparent by now that there are many sources of performance data, including organizational records, supervisors, employees themselves, peers or team members, subordinates, and customers. Organizational records generally provide objective indicators of performance. All of the other sources—people—provide subjective judgments.

Electronic Monitoring

To gather performance data that may be perceived as more objective and less biased, some employers have turned to electronic monitoring. Using electronic monitoring, employers can gather performance information on employees who may be hard to observe, such as truck drivers, delivery drivers, and salespeople. In these cases computers can record dates, times, speeds, and places.

> **FAST FACT**
>
> Dow Chemical, Xerox, and the *New York Times* have fired employees for inappropriate use of the Internet.

Using computers to collect performance information can enhance perceptions of accuracy, but there are still important considerations of fairness and privacy as described in Chapter 3.[18] Partly because of these concerns, and partly out of necessity, most organizations rely heavily on people as the major source of performance information.

When determining which people to involve in the performance measurement process, employers need to consider the amount and type of work contact each source has with the person being evaluated.[19] Team members, customers, and subordinates see different facets of an individual's task behavior than do supervisors.[20] A customer is more likely to observe the behavior of a sales representative—for instance, greeting the customer or closing the sale—than is a first-level supervisor. No one—not even the employee—has complete information. Thus, involving multiple raters in the evaluation process generally is the best approach.

Supervisors

Many companies assume that supervisors know more than anyone else about subordinates' job performances, so they give supervisors all the responsibility for appraisal and feedback. Supervisors do appear to produce more reliable performance judgments than other sources, perhaps because they have knowledge about several aspects of employees' performance.[21] Nevertheless, because of potential legal liabilities and the desire to be as accurate as possible, organizations often invite other people to share in the appraisal process. Involving supervisors *as well as* other people increases the reliability and perceived fairness of the process. Also, it creates greater openness and enhances the quality of the superior-subordinate relationship.

Self-Appraisal

When employees assess their own performance, they conduct a **self-appraisal**. The use of self-appraisal gained popularity as a component of management by objectives, often referred to as MBO. Management by objectives, described more in the next section, combines the assessment of past performance with goal setting for the future. Subordinates who participate in the evaluation process become more involved and committed to the goals. Subordinate participation also clarifies employees' roles and may reduce role ambiguity and conflict.[22]

Inflation. Self-appraisals increase employees' satisfaction with the appraisal process[23] and are effective tools for self-development, personal growth, and goal commitment. However, self-appraisals are subject to systematic biases and distortions. Self-ratings often are more lenient than those obtained from supervisors. Also, self-appraisals often reveal blind spots—areas of poor performance that the employee is unaware of. High-performing employees appear to have fewer such blind spots than do low-performing employees.[24] Providing extensive performance feedback, building a culture of trust, and including some objective performance data are ways to reduce these problems.[25]

Cultural Differences. For global firms, and even domestic firms with culturally diverse workforces, the use of self-appraisal raises another concern—do employees from different cultures approach self-appraisal differently? If some cultures are more likely to be modest in their self-assessments, the use of this approach may be detrimental to their personal development and advancement. The feature "Managing Diversity: Cultural Differences in Self-Assessment?" describes what research says about this concern.

Peers

In team-based organizations, peer involvement in performance management is growing. Research showing that appraisals by peers are useful predictors of future performance is consistent with this trend.[26] Also consistent with this trend is research showing that, for managerial employees, the appraisals of peers and subordinates tend to be consistent with each other.[27]

Peer involvement in performance management takes many forms. Peer involvement may be limited to providing appraisals that are used only for developmental feedback, or peer appraisals can serve as the foundation for a team's self-management processes. Jamestown Advanced Products Incorporated, a small metal fabrication firm, relies on peers to help manage a variety of performance problems. One problem that came up was tardiness. One person's late arrival disrupted everyone else's schedule, reduced team performance, and consequently lowered financial bonuses. Traditionally, a tardy employee lost some wages but could still receive a quarterly performance bonus. Team members thought this was unfair. The work team was

Cultural Differences in Self-Assessment?

Do workers in collective cultures, which discourage boasting about individual accomplishments, evaluate their own performance the same as American workers do? In Western cultures, subordinates tend to evaluate themselves more favorably than do their supervisors. This effect occurs across different types of employees (clerical, managerial, blue-collar), for different types of rating scales, and for appraisals done for different purposes. The tendency to project a positive self-image to others is common in Western culture, which stresses individual achievement, self-sufficiency, and self-respect. In contrast, collectivistic cultures encourage interpersonal harmony, interdependence, solidarity, and group cohesiveness. In the interest of interpersonal harmony, people do not draw attention to their individual achievements.

Are workers in collectivistic cultures more modest than their American counterparts when it comes to rating their own job performance? To find out, an international team of researchers examined the performance ratings of over 900 pairs of supervisors and their subordinates. The ratings of people working in Taiwan were compared with those of American supervisors. When Chinese workers evaluated their own job performance and their own desire to work, they gave themselves lower ratings than did their supervisors. Their ratings were also lower than the ones American workers gave to themselves. Consistent with the value that collectivist cultures place on the wisdom that comes with aging, younger Taiwanese workers rated themselves lower than did older Taiwanese workers.

The researchers concluded that the use of self-ratings by multinational firms may create bias against Chinese employees and against other employees from collectivist cultures. Such employees may rate themselves lower than equally performing Anglo-Americans. Also, Chinese employees may be reluctant to engage in self-promotion in order to be sure that their supervisor knows about their accomplishments. As a result, their supervisors may give them lower ratings than they deserve. The result may be unintended discrimination and unfair treatment, as well as lower morale and ineffective use of the best talent.[28]

MANAGING DIVERSITY

encouraged to set performance standards for its members and to identify consequences for low performance. After the team batted around the issue of how much lateness or absenteeism it could tolerate and how punitive it should be, it reached agreement: employees could be tardy—defined as one minute late—or absent without notice no more than five times a quarter. Beyond that, they would lose their entire bonus. In addition to defining performance expectations, Jamestown team members commonly serve as evaluators; the coworker who is at an individual's side all day has an excellent opportunity to observe that individual's behavior.

Subordinates

Few subordinates have information about all dimensions of their supervisor's performance, but most have access to information about supervisor-subordinate interactions. Organizations such as Johnson & Johnson and Sears have been surveying employees for their opinions of management for years. When such surveys are used to evaluate the performance of specific managers, the process is called **upward appraisal**. Amoco adopted an upward appraisal system in response to suggestions from employees. A voluntary, computer-scored employee questionnaire solicits feedback on a supervisor's leadership style, creativity, and performance management practices. The results are incorporated into Amoco's training sessions for middle-level managers.[29]

> **FAST FACT**
>
> In a survey of executives of the nation's 1,000 largest companies, 60% said employees should be allowed to participate in a formal review of the boss.

Anonymity. One drawback to upward feedback is that subordinates don't always evaluate performance objectively or honestly, especially if their ratings are not anonymous.[30] To protect anonymity, evaluations need to be made by several subordinates, and someone other than the supervisor should average the subordinates' ratings.

Usefulness. For managers who do not already perform well, upward appraisal can be quite useful. One study followed managers over a period of five years in order to track changes in performance following upward appraisal and feedback. The results showed that managers who initially performed poorly improved significantly after receiving the results of upward appraisals. The greatest improvements occurred for managers who met with their direct reports to discuss their own performance results.[31]

Customers

At a medical clinic in Billings, Montana, patients routinely rate desk attendants and nursing personnel on behaviors such as courtesy, promptness, and quality of care. Domino's Pizza hires mystery customers who order pizzas and then evaluate the performance of the telephone operator and delivery person. The owner of a carpeting firm uses a customer checklist to monitor the on-site performance of carpet installers. When customers are used as appraisers, it is difficult for employees to discount the results because usually employers obtain the impressions of *many* customers. Nevertheless, a potential difficulty in using real customers is getting a fair sampling of customer experiences. Customers who have had particularly bad experiences may be more likely to complete a questionnaire, for example.

360-Degree Appraisals

"With 360-degree feedback, we capture input from people with whom the employee works on a regular basis. We call it their 'knowledge network.' The person who receives the evaluation views it as very accurate."

Ann J. Ewen
President
TEAMS, Inc.

When evaluations from supervisors, subordinates, peers, and employees themselves are *all* used, they are referred to as **360-degree appraisals**. In contrast to the traditional approach, where a single person—usually a supervisor—rates employee performance, 360-degree systems collect performance information from a set of colleagues and internal customers who form a circle around the employee. Many employers have adopted 360-degree appraisal and feedback systems.[32]

Multiple-source evaluations are perceived as more fair than single-source approaches. The evaluation process produces more valid results because it involves a group of people who interact with the employee in many different ways. For the same reason, the process should be less susceptible to gender and ethnicity biases than are single-source evaluations.[33]

Because the practice is relatively new, little research exists to guide organizations in developing the most appropriate 360-degree practices. However, the limited evidence that's available does suggest that the raters' identity should remain anonymous, when possible. Also, it appears that this technique works best when the full circle is represented—not just one portion of it (e.g., including only subordinates or only peers). Finally, the results should be summarized so it is easy for employees to use. Otis Elevator's Worldwide Engineering Group conducts 360-degree appraisals on its intranet. Although the employees are engineers, they were overwhelmed at first by too much information that they didn't know how to interpret.

PERFORMANCE APPRAISAL FORMATS

When performance is measured using performance appraisals (in contrast to objective measures), a method is needed to record the appraisers' judgments. Appraisals may be recorded on paper or electronically. Either way, the development of a rating form should begin with job analysis information about what the job involves. The appraisal format provides the structure for raters to record their judgments.

Norm-Referenced Formats

For many human resource decisions, employees must be compared with each other directly. Special recognition cannot be given without knowing: Who is the best performer in the group? Layoffs should not be conducted without knowing: Who are the weakest performers we can let go, given that we have to cut our workforce? Which person is most likely to be the best person to assign to a special task force? For these types of decisions, norm-referenced formats are appropriate. With a **norm-referenced format**, the rater is forced to evaluate the individual, team, or strategic unit in relation to similar others. The two most commonly used are straight ranking and forced distribution.

Straight Ranking. In **straight ranking**, the appraiser lists the focal employees (or teams of employees) in order, from best to worst, usually on the basis of overall performance. As the number of employees to be ranked increases, straight ranking becomes increasingly difficult. A problem with straight ranking is that ties usually are not allowed. Although no two subordinates perform exactly alike, many supervisors believe that some incumbents perform so similarly that making performance distinctions between them is not appropriate.

Forced Distribution. The **forced distribution method** deals with the problem of having several employees who all perform about the same. With this method, the appraiser distributes employees across several categories of performance. A typical format would use five categories, with a fixed percentage of all subordinates in the group falling within each category, as illustrated below. The forced distribution method creates problems for evaluators who believe that the pattern of performances of people being evaluated does not conform to the fixed percentages.

Lowest Performers	Next Lowest	Middle	Next Highest	Highest Performers
10%	20%	40%	20%	10%
(5 employees)	(10 employees)	(20 employees)	(10 employees)	(5 employees)

Absolute Standards Formats

Formats that use absolute standards allow evaluators to assess performance in relation to specified criteria. Graphic rating scales, behaviorally anchored rating scales, and behavior observation scales are three widely used formats that involve absolute standards.

Graphic Rating Scales. Introduced in the 1920s, **graphic rating scales** were touted as useful because direct output measures were not needed and the

"When there were just seven of us, we could just sit around the table and talk. As we've grown [to 260 employees], we've worked to find a way to keep up the continuous feedback, with more focus."

Ed Steinberg
Vice President
Synygy

"A company that bets its future on its people must remove the lower 10 percent and keep removing it every year—always raising the bar of performance and increasing the quality of its leadership."

John F. Welch, Jr.
Former CEO
General Electric

rater was free to make as fine a judgment as desired. The primary advantage of the graphic rating scale format is its simplicity. Exhibit 11.5 shows several graphic rating scales that might be used to assess the quantity of work a person completed. In this exhibit, scales A to C require the rater to define the dimension. This obviously leads to different interpretations by different raters. Scales D and E do a better job of defining work quantity, but they still provide latitude for disagreement. Scale F provides the most extensive definition of work quantity, but the rater must consider more than one aspect of quantity. In addition, scale F provides anchors for only three general groups of scale values, although 25 discrete scale values can be used. As these examples illustrate, the major disadvantage of graphic rating scales is their lack of clarity and definition. Even when raters are trained, they still might not define the performance dimensions in the same way.

ex 11.5 Sample Graphic Rating Scales for Work Quantity

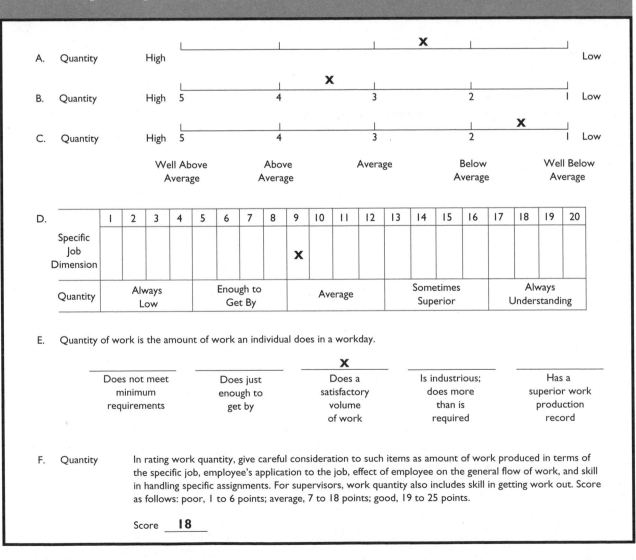

Behaviorally Anchored Rating Scales. Dissatisfaction with graphic rating scales led to the development of formats that include more specific behavioral criteria. **Behaviorally anchored rating scales (BARS)** provide information that employees can more easily use to improve their performance.

The development of a BARS performance measure involves collecting descriptions of incidents that illustrate very competent, average, and incompetent work behaviors. These performance descriptions must be obtained in advance for each dimension of performance to be rated. Typically, the behavioral incidents are collected in the process of conducting a job analysis, as described in Chapter 6. Exhibit 11.6 shows a behavioral rating scale for the performance dimension of "transacting loans." A higher scale value means higher performance.

Like any format, the BARS format has limitations. Scales can be difficult and time consuming to develop. This means they are more difficult to modify as jobs change and performance expectations shift. From a cost-benefit perspective, the development of behavioral formats should be restricted to jobs that have many incumbents or for which the job *processes* (versus results) are critical to job success. In the service sector, success often depends on *how* work is performed, so it is worthwhile to invest in the effort required to develop clear behavioral standards.

FAST FACT

A hospitality checklist reminds Red Lion Hotel employees of their company's customer service goals:
1. Greet the guest.
3. Show the guest that you care.
4. Show the guest that you can help (by going out of your way to accommodate the guest's needs).
5. Appreciate the guest's business.

---

ex 11.6 **Behaviorally Anchored Rating Scale for One Dimension of the Work Performance of a Corporate Loan Assistant**

Transacting Loans

	10	Always completes credit reports without error
Prepares follow-up documentation in a timely manner	9	
	8	Provides services desired but not asked for by customers
Helps customers in a manner that draws praise from them	7	
	6	Assists customers with loan applications
Develops loan documentation accurately	5	
	4	Prepares credit reports without having to be told
Provides information to customers, even if not asked	3	
	2	Fails to help other banks participating in loans
Conducts loan interviews in a manner that draws complaints from loan applicants	1	

For raters, problems occur when the incidents shown on the form don't correspond to any behavior the rater has observed, or when the rater has observed the employee displaying behaviors associated with both high and low performance. For example, a corporate loan assistant could prepare follow-up documentation in a timely manner and also receive complaints from loan applicants about rudeness and inappropriate questioning. In such situations, it is difficult to decide whether to give a high or low rating.[34]

> **FAST FACT**
>
> Upon opening the assembly line 80 years ago, Henry Ford issued a booklet, "Helpful Hints and Advice to Employees," warning against drinking, gambling, and borrowing money.

Behavioral Observation Scales. A more recent development in behavioral scales is called the **behavioral observation scale (BOS)**. Like BARS, these scales are derived from critical incidents of job behavior. The format is somewhat different, however. Raters are not asked to indicate the *level* of performance; they are asked to report how frequently employees engage in specific behaviors. Exhibit 11.7 illustrates the BOS format.[35] Because of the way points are assigned to behaviors, adding up all of the ratings yields an overall measure of performance together (items that describe ineffective performance are reverse scored).

BOS is just as expensive and time consuming as BARS to develop, but raters find it easier to use. Unfortunately, however, raters often don't have sufficient time or ability to accurately assess the frequency with which behaviors are observed.

Results-Based Formats

For some jobs, or some aspects of a job, the results achieved are more important than the behaviors that led those results. In such cases, it may be most appropriate to measure actual results. **Results-based formats** focus on job products as the primary criteria. As is true for the norm-referenced and absolute standards approaches, job analysis should guide the choice of results selected for measurement. Two widely used results-based formats are the direct index approach and management by objectives.

> **FAST FACT**
>
> L.L. Bean sold his first pair of hunting boots in 1912. Ninety of his first 1,000 pairs fell apart and were returned!

Direct Index Approach. The **direct index approach** measures performance using objective, impersonal criteria, such as productivity, absenteeism, and turnover. A manager's performance may be evaluated by the number of her employees who quit or by her employees' absenteeism rate. For nonmanagers, productivity measures may be more appropriate. Quality measures include scrap rates, number of customer complaints, and number of defective units or parts produced. Quantity measures include units of output per hour, number of new customer orders, and sales volume.

One advantage of the direct index approach is that it provides clear, unambiguous direction to employees regarding desired job results. Another advantage is that extraneous factors, such as the ratee's prior performance, salary, and personal characteristics like gender are less likely to introduce bias. On the other hand, important job behaviors may be ignored. This problem can be overcome by supplementing the direct indexes with other formats.

Management by Objectives. **Management by Objectives (MBO)** begins with the establishment of goals or objectives for the upcoming performance

ex 11.7 Behavioral Observation Scale Items for a Maintenance Mechanic

In completing this form, circle
0– if you have no knowledge of the employee's behavior
1– if the employee has engaged in the behavior 0 to 64 percent of the time
2– if the employee has engaged in the behavior 65 yo 74 percent of the time
3– if the employee has engaged in the beahvior 75 to 84 percent of the time
4– if the employee has engaged in the behavior 85 to 94 percent of the time
5– if the employee has engaged in the behavior 95 to 100 percent of the time

Behavior Frequency

Customer Relations

1. Swears in front of customers (e.g, operators and vendors) (R)	0	1	2	3	4	5
2. Blames customer for malfunction (R)	0	1	2	3	4	5
3. Refers to customers by name or asks for his or her name when first introduced	0	1	2	3	4	5
4. Asks operator to demonstrate what she or he was doing at the time of the malfunction	0	1	2	3	4	5

Teamwork

1. Exhibits rude behavior that coworkers complain about (R)	0	1	2	3	4	5
2. Verbally shares technical knowledge with other technicians	0	1	2	3	4	5
3. As needed, consults fellow workers for their ideas on ways to solve specific problems	0	1	2	3	4	5
4. Given an incomplete assignment, leaves a clear, written tie-in for the next day shift to use	0	1	2	3	4	5
5. Works his or her share of overtime						

Planning

1. Estimates repair time accurately	0	1	2	3	4	5
2. Completes assigned jobs on time	0	1	2	3	4	5
3. Is able to set job priorities on a daily or weekly basis	0	1	2	3	4	5
4. Even when the job is not yet complete, cleans up area at the end of the shift	0	1	2	3	4	5
5. Identifies problems or potential problems that may affect repair success or completion time						

Planned Maintenance Repairs

1. Executes planned maintenance repair, requiring no follow-up	0	1	2	3	4	5
2. Adjusts equipment according to predetermined tolerance levels; commits no errors	0	1	2	3	4	5
3. Replaces components when necessary rather than when convenient or easy	0	1	2	3	4	5
4. Takes more time than allotted to complete a planned maintenance repair (R)	0	1	2	3	4	5

Note: "R" denotes item is reverse scored (5 = 1, 4 = 2, 3 = 3, 2 = 4, 1 = 5, 0 = 0)

period. Performance is then measured against the goals that were set. Goals that are relatively objective work best. Exhibit 11.8 illustrates goals set by a graphic artist.[36] In some organizations, superiors and subordinates work together to establish goals; in others, superiors establish goals for work groups or individuals; in organizations with self-managed work teams, teams may set their own goals.

> **FAST FACT**
>
> A recent survey of executive performance management practices found that most executives have performance goals for their units, but only half translate those into personal goals.

To be effective, goals should be challenging, but not so difficult that employees don't believe they can be achieved. Easy goals don't give employees any reason to exert extra effort. If goals are too difficult, however, employees will reject them as impossible and won't even bother trying to achieve them. Goals that are challenging but doable are often called **stretch goals**.

Regardless of how goals are established, the next step is to develop a strategy for goal attainment. For managers, this strategy often includes setting goals for subordinates to achieve. The strategy that a CEO develops for

ex 11.8 Performance Goals and Subgoals for a Graphic Artist

Project: Logo Development for Casper County Park System

1. Meet all agreed-on deadlines.
2. Keep costs within the agreed-on budget.
3. Bill final hours within plus or minus 10 percent of the agreed-on budget.
4. Achieve supervisor's criteria for logo development. Subgoals include:
   a. Reproduces well in various sizes and in three dimensions
   b. Can be used in one color, line art, and halftone versions
   c. Has a strong identity
   d. Uses type in a unique manner
   e. Has high-quality art
5. Meet client's criteria for logo. Subgoals include:
   a. Conveys desired public image
   b. Message is clear
   c. Logo is easily recognizable
   d. Typeface matches the personality of the park system
6. Strive to exceed client expectations. Indicators that this goal is met include:
   a. Logo design wins an award
   b. Customers express excitement about using the logo
   c. Public learns to recognize the logo without text within one year.

achieving his or her goals is essentially the business strategy for the organization. For managers in charge of business units, some of the goals and strategies developed become the business plans for their units. Clearly delineating how a goal is to be attained reduces ambiguity and makes goal attainment more likely. Strategy development includes outlining the steps necessary to attain each objective as well as any constraints that may block attainment of the objective.

At the conclusion of the performance period, actual performance is evaluated relative to the preestablished objectives. Performance against each objective should be scored separately. Scoring algorithms can be either simple (indicating whether the objective was or was not met) or complex (signaling how far above or below the objective actual performance was). At Synygy, a professional services firm, employees who meet their goals ahead of schedule get higher scores than those who meet them on schedule.

After evaluation, the reasons for not attaining or for exceeding goals should be explored. This step helps determine training needs and development potential. The final step is to set new goals and possibly new strategies.

For an MBO system to be effective, managers must be committed to the process. Goals should cascade from the top down, helping employees see how their efforts link back to broader strategic objectives. Under these conditions, supervisory complaints are reduced, while employee satisfaction and productivity improve. Without management commitment and a shared vision, productivity gains will be meager. Even under the best conditions, MBO systems don't lead to immediate increases in productivity. On average, it takes about two years after implementation for MBO systems to work effectively.[37] At Etec Systems, goal setting and management by objectives are credited with helping the company engineer a major turnaround, as described in "Managing Change: The Goal Was a Turnaround at Etec Systems."[38]

MANAGING CHANGE

The Goal Was a Turnaround at Etec Systems

Stephen Cooper, CEO and chairman of Etec Systems, a high-tech manufacturer of expensive electronic equipment, used a combination of goal setting and MBO to turn around that company. In 1993, when Cooper took over, the company was losing $1 million a month. Believing in the power of goals both to motivate employees and to direct their attention, he set the goal of generating annual revenues of $500 million by 2000. To get there, he made sure that 800 employees had written personal plans to guide their daily work. These one-page plans included five to seven goals, to which employees assigned priority rankings. For each goal, the employee had to state how progress would be measured. Cooper views this system as essential to the company's success. He explains, "We operate on the leading edge of technology with very demanding customers. If you're going to be a technology leader, you have to execute on schedule."

For Phil Arnold, a precision optics manager, executing on schedule means achieving goals such as increasing production volume by 30 percent and reducing cycle times by 10 percent. The six junior managers who report to him, in turn, each have goals that they must achieve. And the people supervised by the junior managers all have daily checklists that reflect the junior managers' goals. Every Monday, the junior managers give a four-minute status report to Arnold. Problems are identified and solutions for dealing with them are developed immediately.

Arnold learned the hard way to monitor progress and identify problems before they turn into crises. Before he began holding his Monday meetings, Arnold didn't find out about a problem with a vendor until it was far too late to take corrective actions. He then had to spend months dealing with the damage caused by the vendor. With the current system, every week employees know what they should be doing, how much weight to give each assignment, and how their goals relate to the goals of other people in the company. The company operates efficiently, yet can respond quickly to changes in the environment.

THE RATING PROCESS

Clearly, employers can take many different approaches to measuring performance—some are more objective, but most involve some subjectivity. Some use identical standards for all employees, while others allow managers to more easily take into account individual circumstances when assessing performance. None is perfect and all cause some employees to feel uneasy. This uneasiness centers on the vulnerability of these to bias and inaccuracy.

The quality of performance judgments depends, in part, on the information-processing capabilities or strategies of the person making the evaluation.[39] As shown in Exhibit 11.9, the evaluator first attends to and recognizes relevant information. The information is stored—first in short-term memory and then in long-term memory—until a performance judgment needs to be made. That judgment reflects aggregated data retrieved from memory and any additional information used by the rater, either intentionally or unintentionally. Finally, before the evaluation is recorded officially, it may be revised depending on reactions of the incumbent or higher-level managers, the goals the rater hopes to achieve through the appraisal process, and even organizational norms.[40] Unfortunately, the fallibility of managers combines with this process to create numerous types of errors.[41]

Rating Errors

When criteria aren't clearly specified and there are no incentives associated with rating accuracy, a variety of errors occur during the rating process.

"We had 'rater error.' We had the 'contrast effect.' We had the 'halo effect.' But the biggest problem was that the feedback wasn't leading to changes in behavior."

Chris Oster
Director of Organizational Development
General Motors

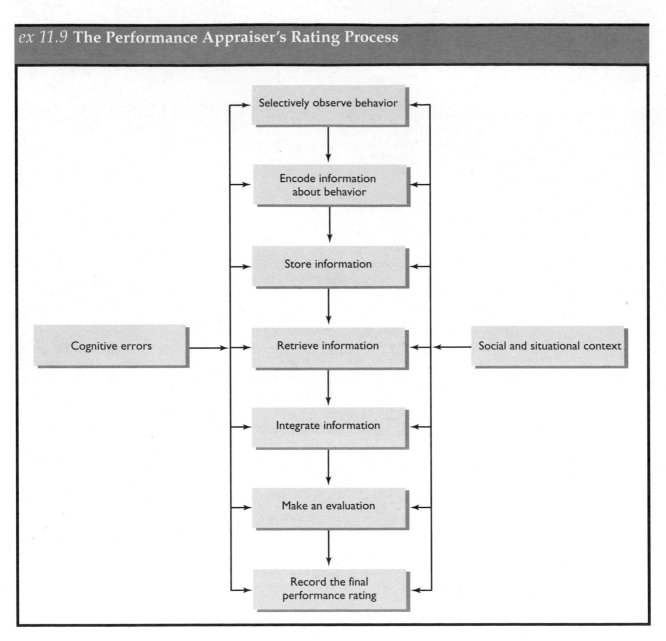

ex 11.9 The Performance Appraiser's Rating Process

Rater errors can affect all stages of the process, but their effects are most clearly seen at the final stage, after ratings have actually been recorded.[42] Exhibit 11.10 describes several types of rater errors.

Improving Rater Accuracy

Even the best performance management system may not be effective when so many extraneous errors impinge on the performance appraisal process. Fortunately, several strategies can be used to minimize appraisal errors and improve rater accuracy, as illustrated in Exhibit 11.11.

ex 11.10 Common Performance Rating Errors

Halo and Horn	A tendency to think of an employee as more or less good or bad is carried over into specific performance ratings. Or stereotypes based on the employee's sex, race, or age affect performance ratings. In either case, the rater doesn't make meaningful distinctions when evaluating specific dimensions of performance. All dimensions of performance are rated either low (horn) or high (halo).
Leniency	All employees are rated higher than they should be rated. This happens when managers aren't penalized for giving high ratings to everyone, when rewards aren't part of a fixed and limited pot, and when dimensional ratings aren't required.
Strictness	All employees are rated lower than they should be. Inexperienced raters who are unfamiliar with environmental constraints on performance, raters with low self-esteem, and raters who have themselves received a low rating are most likely to rate strictly. Rater training that includes a reversal of supervisor-incumbent roles and confidence building can reduce this error.
Central Tendency	All employees are rated as average, when performance actually varies. Raters with large spans of control and little opportunity to observe behavior are likely to use this "play-it-safe" strategy. A forced distribution format requiring that most employees be rated average also may create this error.
Primacy	As a cognitive shortcut, raters may use initial information to categorize a person as either a good or a bad performer. Information that supports the initial judgment is amassed, and unconfirming information is ignored.
Recency	A rater may ignore employee performance until the appraisal date draws near. When the rater searches for cues about performance, recent behaviors or results are most salient, so recent events receive more weight than they should.
Contrast Effects	When compared with weak employees, an average employee will appear outstanding; when evaluated against outstanding employees, an average employee will be perceived as a low performer.

ex 11.11 Improving Performance Appraisal Accuracy

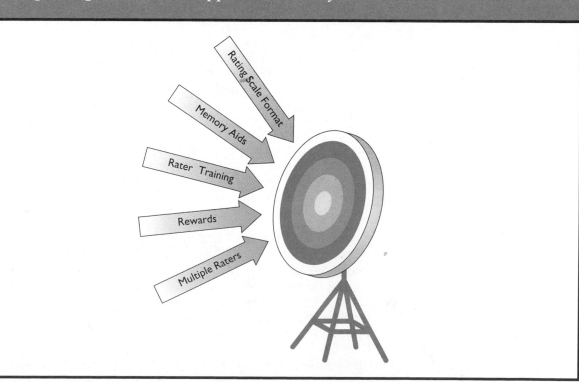

Rating Scale Format. Performance ratings tend to be more accurate when the performance criteria and the rating scales are precise. When the correct elements are in place, evaluators are more accurate in their ratings and more confident about their ratings. Features of a rating scale should include the following:

- Each performance dimension addresses a single job activity, rather than a group of activities.
- Each performance dimension is rated separately, and the scores are then summed to determine the overall rating.
- Ambiguous terms like *average* are not used because different raters have various reactions to them.[43]

Memory Aids. Everyone involved in making appraisals should regularly record behaviors or results—good or bad—that relate to an employee's or work group's performance. Reviewing these records at the time of the performance appraisal helps ensure that the rater uses all available and relevant information. Consulting a behavioral diary or a critical incident file before rating reduces recency and primacy errors, yielding more accurate measures of performance. Electronic diary-keeping software makes this task easier than ever.[44]

Rater Training. Rating accuracy can also be improved through training that focuses on improving the observation skills of raters. Frame-of-reference training is one of the most useful approaches.[45] A comprehensive frame-of-reference training program might include the following steps:

1. The raters are given a job description and instructed to identify appropriate criteria for evaluating the job.
2. When agreement is reached, the raters view a video of an employee performing the job.
3. Independently, the raters evaluate the video performance, using the organization's appraisal system.
4. The raters' evaluations are compared with each other and with those of job experts.
5. With a trainer as a facilitator, the raters present the rationales for their ratings and challenge the rationales of other raters.
6. The trainer helps the raters reach a consensus regarding the value of specific job behaviors and overall performance.
7. A new video is shown, followed by independent ratings.
8. The process continues until consensus is achieved.[46]

Rewards for Accurate and Timely Appraisals. One cause of rating inaccuracy is a lack of rater motivation. Without rewards, raters may find it easier to give high ratings than to give accurate ratings.[47] A straightforward strategy for increasing rater motivation is to base salary increases, promotions, and assignments to key positions partly on performance as a rater. Ratings done in a timely and fair manner (as measured by employee attitude surveys) should be rewarded.

Multiple Raters. Often, the ratee believes that the rater is solely responsible for a poor evaluation and any subsequent loss of rewards; the rater may also believe this. Research suggests that this negative effect can be minimized by relying on the judgments of multiple raters.[48] The diffusion of responsibility frees each rater to evaluate more accurately. Furthermore, an employee is less likely to shrug off negative information when multiple raters are involved.[48] Multiple raters acting as a group may be especially effective in producing accurate ratings, because discussion among members of the group helps overcome the various errors and biases of individuals.[49]

PROVIDING FEEDBACK

Performance management is an ongoing process, punctuated by formal performance measurement and formal feedback sessions intended to improve future performance.[51] In feedback sessions, supervisors and subordinates meet to exchange information, including evaluations of performance and ideas for how to improve.[52] Many managers feel uncomfortable providing feedback to employees, in part because the process often stimulates conflict. Understanding the sources of conflict associated with performance feedback is the first step in managing it successfully.

> **FAST FACT**
>
> Park View Medical Center in Pueblo, Colorado, doesn't believe in forms. It has an appraisal called the Annual Piece of Paper (APOP), but its only purpose is to document that a conversation focused on performance took place.

Sources of Conflict

Knowing the potential sources for conflict in the evaluation process can help improve the effectiveness of the performance appraisal system.

Evaluative and Developmental Goals. The organizational goal of evaluating employees and making employment decisions means that managers usually must give negative feedback to at least some of their subordinates. Employees, in turn, want valid feedback that gives them information about how to improve and where they stand in the organization. But employees also want to verify their self-image and obtain valued rewards. Communicating negative judgments to employees seeking rewards and recognition can be one significant source of conflict. Yet, unless areas for improvement are discussed, little problem solving occurs. To address these conflicts, supervisors must strive to be both candid about needed improvements and protective of employees' self-esteem.[53]

Attributions. Low-performance situations accentuate a natural tendency that we all share, which is to account for performance in a self-serving manner. To protect their egos, employees attribute their own poor performance to external circumstances—a difficult task, unclear instructions, lack of necessary equipment, and other situations that often implicate the supervisor. Supervisors also wish to protect their egos, so they may deny responsibility for the subordinate's poor performance and instead attribute problems to the employee's own deficiencies. These self-serving attributions can make it difficult for supervisors and their employees to come to agreement about how to improve poor performance.

Self-serving attributions may also dampen the expected effects of positive appraisals. When we perform well, the natural tendency is to take full credit for our performance. We use positive evidence to reinforce our high opinion of ourselves, discounting the role external forces may have played. The self-interested perspective of managers, however, leads them to view our success as due to such things as chance or luck and the support we received from the manager and other employees.[54] Add to this our general feeling that we are better-than-average performers, and the scene is set for a potentially dysfunctional cycle: Employees believe they perform well and deserve credit for having done so; their supervisors often evaluate their performance less favorably, and these evaluations are perceived as unfair. When supervisors do recognize good performance, employees may perceive the recognition as merely what they deserve, leaving supervisors to wonder why their subordinates aren't more grateful.

The attributions for performance made by supervisors and subordinates influence the strategies they develop for performance improvement.[55] If the employee is viewed as responsible for performance problems, strategies aimed at changing the subordinate—for example, retraining—will seem more appropriate. If performance is attributed to external circumstances, strategies that modify the environment—such as changing the job design or providing more rewards—are more likely.

Of course, not all subordinates or all employees are equally susceptible to these attribution biases, but few are completely immune, either. So all can improve by understanding these dynamics.

Timing

The delivery of performance feedback needs to be well timed. In general, immediate feedback is most useful. Feedback also should involve only as much information as the receiver can use. Providing continuous feedback is the best way to avoid information overload and maximize the value of the feedback given.[56] At Synygy, performance reviews occur once every quarter for all employees. For some managers, each review cycle consumes as much as a week of time. Yet the company feels strongly that the gains from frequent feedback make this a worthwhile investment of its resources. A recent college graduate who joined the company agreed that quarterly reviews were very helpful to him. "You don't lose a year of your time focusing on the wrong things before you get some guidance," he explained. The company also benefits by spotting the occasional problem employee very early. The extensive documentation that accumulates as a natural part of the review process puts the company on firm legal ground should it decide to fire someone.[57]

Preparation

"Schedule an appointment and have a meeting. Don't give important feedback in the hallway."

Rick Maurer
Consultant

To signal that performance matters, feedback sessions need to be scheduled in advance. In setting up the session, the manager and employee should reach agreement regarding the purpose and content of their discussion. Will the subordinate provide feedback to the supervisor, or will the discussion be one way? Will the subordinate be asked to provide a self-assessment, or will they talk about only the supervisor's perspective? Will the discussion be restricted to evaluating past performance or to mapping out a strategy for future performance, or will both topics be covered? By discussing these issues before the actual interview, both participants have time to prepare.

INTERNET RESOURCES   11.B

Conducting Performance Appraisals and Providing Feedback

At our Web site, http://jackson.swcollege.com/, you can:

1. Learn about appraisal for improvement at some of the firms discussed in this section by visiting their company home pages:

   Etec Systems

   L.L. Bean

   Con-Way

   CNF Transportation

2. View an outline of a training program for managers on how to give feedback to see what topics should be covered.

3. Take a quiz designed to assess whether you would be a good candidate to receive personal coaching as a means to improve your performance.

Content of Discussion

Initiating and carrying out an effective feedback session requires both coaching and counseling skills. Supervisors need to listen to and reflect back what subordinates say with regard to performance, its causes, and its consequences. Too often, the feedback process breaks down and supervisors end up telling employees how well or poorly they're doing and selling them on the merits of setting specific goals for improvement. This may seem efficient for the supervisors, but subordinates feel frustrated trying to convince their superiors to listen to justifications for their performance levels. As a result, they discount feedback and become entrenched in past behavior.

A more effective approach is to use the feedback session for solving problems and planning the future. Problem solving involves diagnosing the causes of performance. Planning for the future involves agreeing to address problems that were revealed in the diagnosis and setting goals. The effort pays off if employees get feedback they find useful, as such feedback is more likely to motivate employees to improve.[58]

Diagnosis. The objective of diagnosis is to understand the factors that affect an employee's performance. Diagnosis is particularly important for employees who do not perform as well as required, but it also can be useful even for employees who have performed well. Usually, even the best performers experience roadblocks that, if removed, would allow them to do even better.

The model of motivation described earlier and shown in Exhibit 11.2 suggests a number of factors that can impede performance. To determine whether any of these are causing problems for an employee, the manager and employee together can consider questions such as those listed in Exhibit 11.12. Sharing perceptions and identifying solutions should be the focus. This type of discussion is difficult for most supervisors, so prior training in problem solving and in giving and receiving feedback should be provided.

Removing Roadblocks. Based on what is learned from the diagnostic process, both the supervisor and subordinate should agree to an action plan.

ex 11.12 Checklist for Diagnosing the Causes of Performance Deficiencies

Check the determinants of performance or behavior that apply to the situation you are analyzing.

		Yes	No
I. Competencies			
A.	Does the employee have the competencies needed to perform as expected?	____	____
B.	Has the employee performed as expected before?	____	____
C.	Does the employee believe he or she has the competencies needed to perform as desired?	____	____
D.	Does the employee have the interest to perform as desired?	____	____
II. Goals for the Employee			
A.	Were the goals communicated to the employee?	____	____
B.	Are the goals specific?	____	____
C.	Are the goals difficult but attainable?	____	____
III. Certainty for the Employee			
A.	Has desired performance been clearly specified?	____	____
B.	Have rewards or consequences for good or bad performance been specified?	____	____
C.	Is the employee clear about her or his level of authority?	____	____
IV. Feedback to the Employee			
A.	Does the employee know when he or she has performed correctly or incorrectly?	____	____
B.	Is the feedback diagnostic so that the employee can perform better in the future?	____	____
C.	Is there a delay between performance and the receipt of the feedback?	____	____
D.	Can performance feedback be easily interpreted?	____	____
V. Consequences to the Employee			
A.	Is performing as expected punishing?	____	____
B.	Is not performing poorly more rewarding than performing well?	____	____
C.	Does performing as desired matter?	____	____
D.	Are there positive consequences for performing as desired?	____	____
VI. Power for the Employee			
A.	Can the employee mobilize the resources to get the job done?	____	____
B.	Does the employee have the tools and equipment to perform as desired?	____	____
C.	Is performance under the control of the employee?	____	____

The specific content of the plan depends on both organizational needs and information from the diagnosis. In general, the action plan for the supervisor should address problems such as lack of resources, providing additional information and training, and improving ongoing communications and feedback. The action plan for the subordinate should address behavioral changes that may be needed, career development activities, and specific performance goals.

Goal Setting. Goals are a necessary part of an action plan when the MBO approach is used, but they also are appropriate in organizations that use other performance measurement formats. Goals affect motivation in two ways: by increasing the amount of effort people choose to exert and by directing or channeling that effort. When employees accept a goal as something to strive for and then commit to achieving that goal, they essentially agree to exert the amount of effort required to do so. Numerous studies have documented that performance is improved when employees are guided by specific and difficult goals.[59] If a goal is specific, employees can quickly judge whether their efforts are paying off in terms of performance. Employees can then use this feedback to decide whether to continue using the same methods or try new approaches.[60]

Regardless of the goal or performance standard chosen, it will be effective only if the employee accepts it and feels a commitment to trying to attain it.[61] For some employees, goals assigned by managers may be effective, but many managers believe that goals work best when the employee participates in goal setting. Doing so increases the employee's willingness to accept goals, which is essential for the goals to be motivating.

Follow-Up

Follow-up is essential to ensuring that the behavioral contract negotiated during the feedback session interview is fulfilled. Supervisors should verify that subordinates know what is expected and realize the consequences of good or poor performance.

When behavioral changes are needed, the action plan may involve developing a strategy to reinforce the desired new behavior and stamp out problematic behaviors.

Reinforcement. Reinforcement can be as simple as a pat on the back or a compliment ("That was nice work, George"), or as tangible as a note placed in the employee's file.[62] For some behaviors, constant monitoring may be needed. Consider this example:

I'm inclined to yell. I know I shouldn't. So I got a gadget, a mechanical daisy with sunglasses and a guitar that sits in a glass and oscillates with the volume of my voice. It tells me when I'm yelling. Also, I instructed my secretary to hold up a stop sign when I'm screaming at someone. Like a recovering alcoholic, I take it one day at a time. Patience, patience. Tolerance, tolerance.

—A 49-year-old banker

Positive reinforcement involves the use of positive rewards to increase the occurrence of the desired performance. It's based on two fundamental principles: (1) people perform in ways that they find most rewarding to them; and (2) by providing the proper rewards, it's possible to improve performance. Positive reinforcement focuses on the job behavior that leads to desired results, rather than on the results directly. It uses rewards rather than punishment or the threat of punishment to influence that behavior, and is generally a very effective method for creating behavioral changes.[63]

Punishment. When behavioral problems persist, formal disciplinary action is needed. The objective of punishment is to decrease the frequency of an undesirable behavior. **Punishments** can include material consequences, such as a cut in pay, a disciplinary layoff without pay, a demotion, or, ultimately, termination. Organizations frequently use punishment because it can achieve relatively immediate results. Besides alerting the marginal employee to the fact that his or her low performance is unacceptable, punishment has vicarious power. When one person is punished, it signals other employees regarding expected performance and behavioral conduct. In addition, when other employees view the punishment as appropriate, it may increase their motivation, morale, and performance.

Punishment can also have undesirable side effects, however. For example, an employee reprimanded for low performance may become defensive and angry toward the supervisor and the organization. As many news reports attest, this anger may result in sabotage (destroying equipment, passing trade secrets) or retaliation (shooting the supervisor). Punishment also frequently leads only to a short-term suppression of the undesirable behavior, rather than its elimination. Another concern is that control of the undesirable behavior becomes contingent on the presence of the punishing agent. When the manager isn't present, the behavior is likely to be displayed.

Because the immediate supervisor or manager plays the integral role in administering discipline, the human resource department should educate managers and supervisors about the organization's disciplinary policies and train them to administer the policies.[64]

> "When people identify something that they need to work on, it's usually what everyone else wishes they'd work on too."
>
> Darcy Hitchcock
> Consultant

Self-Management. Self-management is a relatively new approach to resolving performance discrepancies. It teaches people to exercise control over their own behavior. **Self-management** begins when people assess their own problems and set specific (but individual), hard goals in relation to those problems. Next, they discuss ways in which the environment facilitates or hinders goal attainment. The challenge is to develop strategies that eliminate blocks to performance success. Put another way, self-management teaches people to observe their own behavior, compare their results to their goals, and administer their own reinforcement to sustain goal commitment and performance.[65]

LeRoy Pingho, a vice president at Fannie Mae, is a model self-manager. He began his own personal crusade to collect 360-degree feedback about his own performance and then use it to improve. He selects a cross-section of colleagues and asks them to assess his performance. He also chooses a few people each year to work with him on his "flat spots"—areas where he finds it difficult to improve on his own even when he tries. His helpers don't deliver rewards or punishments; they simply tell him when he's engaging in a behavior he has told them he wants to change. Pingho limits the number of areas targeted for improvement to only about four at a time.

When Nothing Else Works

Helping employees—especially problem ones—to improve their work performance is a tough job. It's easy to get frustrated and to wonder if we are just spinning our wheels. Even when we want our efforts to work, they sometimes don't. Still, when we conclude that "nothing works," we are really saying that it's no longer worth our time and energy to help the employee improve. This conclusion shouldn't be made in haste, because the organization has already invested a great deal of time and money in the selection and training of its employees. Nevertheless, some situations may require drastic steps, including when

- performance actually gets worse,
- the problem behavior changes a little—but not enough,
- the problem behavior doesn't change, or

- drastic changes in behavior occur immediately, but improvements don't last.

If, after repeated warnings and counseling, performance doesn't improve, then three last recourses are available.

Transfer. Sometimes, the employee and the job are just not well matched. If the employee has useful skills and abilities, it may be beneficial to transfer her or him. Transferring is appropriate if the employee's performance deficiency would have little or no effect on the new position. The concern is that a job must be available for which the problem employee is qualified.

Neutralize. Neutralizing a problem employee involves restructuring that employee's job in such a way that his or her areas of needed improvement have as little effect as possible. It means assigning noncritical tasks in which the employee can be productive. Because group morale may suffer when an ineffective employee is given special treatment, neutralizing should be avoided whenever possible. However, temporary neutralizing may be practical and even benevolent for a valued employee who is close to retiring or suffering unusual personal distress due to illness or family problems.[66]

Terminate. Termination is generally warranted for dishonesty, habitual absenteeism, substance abuse, insubordination (including flat refusals to do certain things requested), and consistently low productivity that can't be corrected through training. Termination, even for legitimate reasons, is unpleasant. In addition to the administrative hassles, documentation, and paperwork, supervisors often feel guilty. The thought of sitting down with an employee and delivering the bad news makes most supervisors anxious, so they put off firing and justify the delay by saying that they won't be able to find a "better" replacement. Still, when one considers the consequences of errors, drunkenness, or being under the influence of drugs on the job, firing may be cost-effective. Ensuring that the process is seen as fair will go a long way toward getting even this unfavorable decision accepted.[67]

INTERNET RESOURCES 11.C

When Nothing Else Works

At our Web site, http://jackson.swcollege.com/, you can:

1. Learn more out about Employee Assistance Programs.

2. Find out what services consulting firms offer to assist with employee discipline.

   RHR Associates

   Business Owners' Toolkit

3. See information provided by the American Arbitration Association that is useful when employee termination is involved.

TEAM APPRAISAL AND FEEDBACK

As organizations restructure around teams, responsibility for performance management is shifting from supervisors to team members. Experienced teams frequently take full responsibility for constructing and conducting their own performance appraisal and feedback process.

Team members are well acquainted with each other's strengths and weaknesses, so it makes sense that they become the primary performance evaluators. Simply knowing that team members will be called on to rate one's performance may in itself be motivation to perform up to the level of one's full potential. Conversely, if an organization trumpets the importance of teamwork but never asks team members to assess each other's performance, employees might reasonably wonder how important teamwork really is.

Team appraisal and feedback is fraught with challenges. In addition to all the challenges of traditional appraisal and feedback are two others that create particular problems for teams: establishing criteria and diagnosing problems.

Team Effectiveness Criteria

The first step in fostering team effectiveness involves knowing how to assess team performance. Exhibit 11.13 shows several team performance criteria as well as individual performance criteria for members of a team. As is true for individuals, whether the work team is viewed as effective overall depends on the team's performance against various performance criteria as well as the weightings of those criteria.

When work is done by a team, clear goals and objectives may be given to the team as a whole with the expectation that the team will work out the specific responsibilities of individual members. In many teams, the responsibilities of individuals are very fluid. They shift as team members come and go, as customers come and go, and as the preferences of the team fluctuate. If the team never clarifies the responsibilities of individual members, the process of rating individuals against specific individual performance criteria is likely to create anxiety on the part of raters and ratees alike. Ensuring that teams develop a set of appraisal criteria—including both behaviors and results—early on is one way out of this dilemma. Regardless of the criteria developed by the team, the process of defining standards benefits the team by clarifying performance standards while also creating greater cohesiveness among members.[68]

Diagnosing Problems

Achieving team effectiveness involves knowing about the various factors that determine how well the team is doing with respect to the effectiveness critieria. Several factors work in combination to determine work team effectiveness. These factors include the external context in which the team operates, team design, and internal team processes. When teams are ineffective, managers and team members must be able to diagnose and correct the causes of the teams' problems and poor team performance.[69]

Internal team processes may be the most immediate cause of performance problems. When a team experiences internal problems, however, the root cause of those problems may lie elsewhere. The team members may be doing the best they can but under adverse circumstances. Their internal problems may be due to aspects of the external context.

Internal Team Processes. **Internal team processes** include the development of the work team over time, personal feelings, and behavioral norms. In effective work teams, these processes support cooperation among team members and coordination of their work.[70] When a team leader and individual team

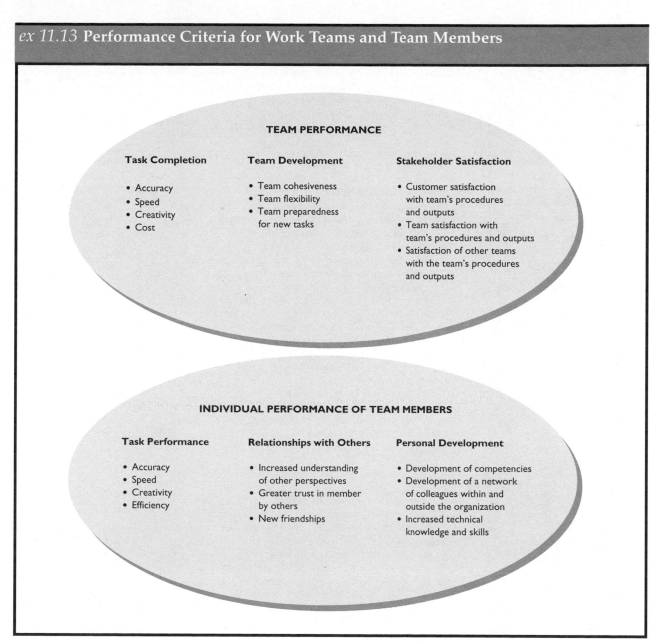

ex 11.13 **Performance Criteria for Work Teams and Team Members**

TEAM PERFORMANCE

Task Completion

- Accuracy
- Speed
- Creativity
- Cost

Team Development

- Team cohesiveness
- Team flexibility
- Team preparedness for new tasks

Stakeholder Satisfaction

- Customer satisfaction with team's procedures and outputs
- Team satisfaction with team's procedures and outputs
- Satisfaction of other teams with the team's procedures and outputs

INDIVIDUAL PERFORMANCE OF TEAM MEMBERS

Task Performance

- Accuracy
- Speed
- Creativity
- Efficiency

Relationships with Others

- Increased understanding of other perspectives
- Greater trust in member by others
- New friendships

Personal Development

- Development of competencies
- Development of a network of colleagues within and outside the organization
- Increased technical knowledge and skills

members learn how to manage the team's internal processes, they improve the likelihood of the team's being effective.

People with little experience working in teams often expect a team to be fully functioning immediately, but that rarely happens. Team members usually need to spend some time together before the team can jell—knowing this fact of team life reduces needless frustration. The establishment of trust and clear behavioral norms usually precede effective task completion.[71] A tool for assessing a work team's internal processes is presented in the feature, "Managing Teams: Diagnosing Team Processes." If you were using this survey in an organization, you would want to ask *all* members of the team you described to complete the survey.[72]

MANAGING TEAMS

Diagnosing Team Processes

This survey can be used to help a team assess its internal processes. It should be completed individually by each team member, who should indicate the extent to which he or she thinks the team exhibits the following characteristics and behaviors.

Questions	To a Very Small Extent		To Some Extent		To a Very Large Extent
1. Team members understand the range of backgrounds, skills, preferences, and perspectives in the team.	1	2	3	4	5
2. Team member differences and similarities have been effectively focused on achieving team goals.	1	2	3	4	5
3. The team cannot integrate diverse viewpoints.	5	4	3	2	1
4. Members view themselves as a team, not as a collection of individuals with their own particular jobs to do (e.g., they work interdependently, have joint accountability, and are committed to joint goals).	1	2	3	4	5
5. Team members have articulated a clear set of goals.	1	2	3	4	5
6. The team's goals are not motivating to members.	5	4	3	2	1
7. Team members agree on what goals and objectives are important.	1	2	3	4	5
8. The team has an effective work structure. It understands what work needs to be done, when work needs to be completed, and who is responsible for what.	1	2	3	4	5
9. It is not clear what each person in the team is supposed to do.	5	4	3	2	1
10. Team members have devised effective timetables and deadlines.	1	2	3	4	5
11. Team members have a clear set of norms that cover most aspects of how to function.	1	2	3	4	5
12. Team members take arguments personally and get angry easily.	5	4	3	2	1
13. Every team member does his or her fair share of the work.	1	2	3	4	5
14. A few members do most of the work.	5	4	3	2	1
15. A few people shirk responsibility or hold the team back.	5	4	3	2	1
16. Team members are imaginative in thinking about new or better ways to perform team tasks.	1	2	3	4	5
17. All team members participate in decision making.	1	2	3	4	5
18. Team members have the resources, information, and support they need from people outside team boundaries.	1	2	3	4	5
19. Team meetings are well organized.	1	2	3	4	5
20. Team meetings are not productive.	5	4	3	2	1
21. Coordination among members is a problem. People seem not to know what to do and when to do it for smooth team functioning.	5	4	3	2	1
22. Team members express their feelings freely in the team.	1	2	3	4	5
23. Team members support each other.	1	2	3	4	5
24. Team members are not effective at decision making.	5	4	3	2	1

Scoring and Interpretation

To assess the overall quality of the team's internal processes, simply add all the numbers you circled and divide by 24 (the total number of items in the survey). A score of 4 or higher indicates that you judge the team's internal processes as generally quite positive. A score less than 4 but greater than 2.5 indicates that you feel the team is doing satisfactorily overall but that several areas need improvement. A score of 2.5 or lower indicates that you believe the team's internal functioning is quite poor.

The team leader should compute the team's average score for each question. For example, suppose that a team had four members and that they gave these responses to question 1: The first person circled 3, the second person circled 4, the third person circled 5, and the fourth person circled 4. Then the team's average for question 1 is (3 + 4 + 5 + 4)/4 = 4.

After computing the average score for each question, the team leader should provide feedback to the team. Effective feedback involves acknowl-

MANAGING TEAMS

edging the things that the team seems to be doing well (e.g., questions with an average of 4 or higher), and identifying the things that need to be improved immediately (e.g., questions with an average of 2.5 or lower).

After setting priorities for the areas needing improvement, the team leader and team members should agree on a schedule for making those improvements. At the end of that time, the leader should again ask team members to respond to the Team Assessment Survey. When the reassessment results have been calculated, team members should determine whether satisfactory progress has been made in addressing the issues previously identified. If they find that it hasn't, they should continue to make adjustments and reassessments, as needed.

Teams don't exist in a vacuum, and their internal processes don't unfold in isolation. The external forces acting on a team may also be the cause of team performance problems. The external system comprises outside conditions and influences that exist before and after the team is formed. As Exhibit 11.14 shows, important features of the external system to consider include culture, team member selection, team training, and the reward system.[73] The issues of selection, training, and rewards are addressed in other chapters. Here we comment briefly on culture as a potential explanation for team performance problems.

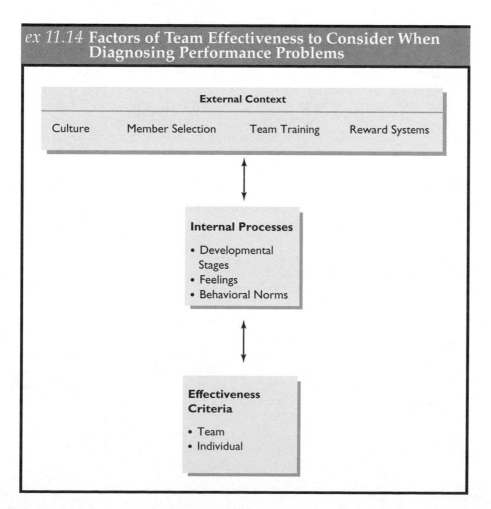

ex 11.14 **Factors of Team Effectiveness to Consider When Diagnosing Performance Problems**

External Context

| Culture | Member Selection | Team Training | Reward Systems |

Internal Processes
- Developmental Stages
- Feelings
- Behavioral Norms

Effectiveness Criteria
- Team
- Individual

Culture. Both the societal and organizational cultures within which work teams operate are important aspects of their external contexts. Differences in norms for team behavior often reflect differences in national culture. In some cultures, such as China, Malaysia, and Thailand, societal values support striving for harmony and cohesiveness and avoiding open conflict. In the more individualistic cultures of the United States and Canada, people feel more comfortable when they are able to express their opinions and have their views taken seriously by other team members. At the same time, however, U.S. and Canadian cultures value friendly relationships among coworkers, so too much conflict feels uncomfortable.[74] In an international work team, the natural tendency of team members is to behave according to the norms of their countries. When different cultures are present, misunderstandings are the likely result if team members are not familiar with the cultures represented on the team.

Even within the United States, norms vary greatly between teams. A study of executive teams revealed that norms concerning conflict differed greatly from one team to the next. About half the teams studied reported that the team members argued most of the time. In these teams, everyone felt free to voice opinions and share ideas. One executive described his team's pattern for handling conflict this way: "We scream a lot, then laugh, and then resolve the issues." In several other teams, however, there was little open conflict—in fact, some teams actually had too little conflict.[75]

Regardless of national cultures, work teams can function well if they are supported by the organization's culture. Organizations that support participation by lower-level employees increase the likelihood that work teams will embrace organizational goals and authority relations, rather than attempt to undermine them.[76] When individualistic employees are empowered through self-managing work teams, they gain more control and influence over their work. Because having control is important in individualistic cultures, employees working in self-managing teams often report being very satisfied with their work.[77]

Team Feedback

When team members evaluate each other, how should they use the information to provide feedback? Should someone outside the team conduct the appraisal interview? Should a team leader be designated for this task? Or should everyone on the team be involved in every feedback session? The reality is that different teams handle feedback in different ways. At Con-Way, everyone on the team participates in providing feedback to everyone else, and feedback is provided in a group discussion format. The goal is to incorporate feedback sessions into the normal work routine. Many other organizations provide feedback in a more private setting. Often the manager to whom the team reports is responsible for collecting performance information from the team and discussing it with each team member.

More important than who delivers the feedback is it is delivered. Ideally, anyone who gives feedback has been trained in how to do so effectively. At Con-Way, teams are learning this invaluable skill by involving a professional facilitator in their feedback sessions. With sufficient practice and guidance, Con-Way teams will develop enough skill and self-confidence to hold feedback sessions spontaneously and unassisted.

In choosing who delivers team feedback and how, cultures again may come into play. Although there is little research documenting cultural differences in how teams handle feedback, it is likely that members of a culturally diverse team will have varying expectations about how feedback should be given.[78] Thus, regardless of the method chosen, some members are likely to find it uncomfortable and unfamiliar.

ROLES AND RESPONSIBILITIES OF THE HR TRIAD

Performance management systems often fall short of achieving strategic objectives. One reason for this is the ambiguity around who owns responsibility for managing the process. Does performance management fall in the domain of human resource departments or line departments? But debates about who is responsible miss the point. Line managers, HR professionals, and employees all need to work together to ensure that appraisals are effective and fair to everyone concerned as described in the feature "The HR Triad: Roles and Responsibilities for Managing Performance and Providing Feedback."

HR Professionals

As is true for other aspects of managing human resources, the responsibilities of the HR professionals include ensuring that the organization's performance management practices are designed to be aligned with the internal organizational contexts, reflect state-of-the art knowledge, and meet legal standards. HR professionals also help ensure that well-designed practices are implemented appropriately. The role of HR professionals in designing performance management practices is similar to their role in designing other aspects of the HR systems, as discussed in prior chapters. Rather than review those responsibilities here, we provide a few comments about the role of HR professionals in the implementation of a performance management system.

Support for Managers. Organizations are not always successful in using performance measurement and feedback strategically, and one reason is that line managers do not fully understand and appreciate the basic principles. Most managers spend far more time acquiring technical competencies (e.g., in the areas of accounting, marketing, and operations management) for entry into an organization than they do learning to manage human resources. Yet, skillfully managing the performance of others is necessary for managers to achieve their corporate mandate to get things done through other people. Managers must accept responsibility for improving their competencies in the areas of performance measurement and feedback. HR professionals should be proactive in developing the organization's performance management capability. They can help by teaching managers about the objectives of the organization's performance management system and helping them develop the skills they need to implement it.

Accountability of Managers. A common roadblock to the effective use of performance measurement and feedback is that managers fail to see the pay-

THE HR TRIAD — Roles and Responsibilities for Managing Performance and Providing Feedback

LINE MANAGERS	HR PROFESSIONALS	EMPLOYEES
• Work with HR professionals and employees to develop relevant performance measures that meet legal guidelines. • Develop an understanding of how common appraisal rating errors can be avoided. • Measure employee performance conscientiously and keep accurate records. • Give constructive and honest feedback to employees. • Seek and accept constructive feedback about own performance. • Use performance information for decision making. • Diagnose individual and team performance deficiencies. • Work with employees to develop performance improvement strategies. • Provide resources and remove constraints as needed for improvement.	• Work with line managers, providing job analysis data to use to develop relevant and legal performance measures. • Train everyone who provides appraisal information (e.g., peers, subordinates, and supervisors) how to avoid appraisal rating errors. • Coordinate the administrative aspects of performance measurement and feedback. • Train line managers to give feedback. • May train self-managing teams to give feedback. • Monitor managerial decisions to ensure they're performance based. • May train self-managing teams to diagnose performance deficiencies. • Ensure managers and employees are aware of all possible ways to deal with performance deficiencies. • Provide personal assistance to employees if requested. Develop and administer appeals process.	• Work with line managers and HR professionals to set performance expectations. • Candidly appraise the work of other employees (boss, peers, etc.). • Participate in self-appraisal. • Seek and accept constructive and honest feedback. • Learn to give constructive and honest feedback to others. • Develop accurate understanding of performance expectations and criteria. • Learn to diagnose causes of performance deficiencies for self and team. • Work with managers to develop performance improvement strategies. • Develop goal-setting and self-management skills.

off for conducting them. As expectancy theory makes clear, this situation is not optimal! Nevertheless, most organizations offer no obvious incentives for managers to do a good job of measuring employee performance and providing useful feedback to employees. Many managers so dislike these activities that they try to avoid the process entirely.[79] Thus, another role for HR professionals is ensuring that managers' performance evaluations include assessments of their performance in this domain.

Support for Employees. Through their influence on the design of an organization's performance measurement and feedback system, HR professionals provide indirect support to employees, but they can also provide more direct support. In many organizations, HR professionals are available to talk to employees about performance problems they may be having and provide informal assistance. If necessary, they can also assist the employee by recommending other sources of professional assistance—for example, by helping the employee understand and use the organization's Employee Assistance Program (EAP). EAPs were originally created to battle alcoholism but have since expanded to address family, financial, and legal problems—all of which can cause unsatisfactory work performance. In addition, when employees feel their performance evaluations are unfair, HR professionals can assist them in using the organization's appeal process (described in Chapter 3).

Managers

Usually, managers are responsible for measuring the performance of their subordinates, communicating performance evaluations to their subordinates, and helping their subordinates improve in the future. Regardless of how performance is measured, managers are expected to review performance results with their employees and explain any consequences that may follow (e.g., pay raises, disciplinary action, training). These discussions serve to inform employees about their status in the organization, but that is not the only objective. Performance measurement isn't an end to be achieved. Rather, it's a means for moving into a more productive future. For performance evaluations to be useful, employees must *act* on them. Thus, one of a manager's major responsibilities is ensuring that employees accept the feedback they receive and use it as a basis for improving in the future.[80]

Employees

The primary performance management responsibilities of employees are seeking honest feedback and using it to improve their performance. Prior to discussions about their performance, employees often are asked to participate by first providing their own assessment of their performance. In addition, all employees—even those with no managerial responsibilities—share responsibility for evaluating the performance of others and providing them with feedback. The example of Con-Way Transportation Services described at the beginning of this chapter is typical of how team-oriented organizations involve employees in performance management. The growing use of upward performance assessment and feedback is aimed at improving the performance of their managers.

As this chapter reveals, developing an effective performance management system requires involvement and buy-in from everyone affected by the system. Achieving this ideal takes time and determination. But for companies like Cendant Mortgage and others that want to be seen as an "employer of choice," taking this time and having this determination are worthwhile and necessary.

> *"Managers are solely responsible for evaluating their employees. No specific, companywide evaluation forms are used for salespeople and managers. Rather, each manager designs his or her own evaluation system."*
>
> Mary Kim Stuart
> HR Manager
> Nordstrom

> *"Managing people fairly means giving everyone objective appraisals and honest and direct feedback."*
>
> Paris Couturiaux
> Cendant Mortgage

SUMMARY

Human variability is a fact of life, especially in organizational life. Much of human resource management involves attending to this variability. This chapter and the next discuss how organizations manage performance variability and use that variability as the basis for making employment decisions.

The strategic use of performance management seeks to direct and motivate employees to invest effort that contributes to the achievement of business objectives. Employees tend to do what is expected and what they believe is valued by "the system," as generally defined by the performance management system. When firms develop performance appraisal criteria that communicate the company's concerns about teamwork and customer satisfaction, they're more likely to get teamwork and customer satisfaction from their employees.

The activities of performance measurement and feedback are part of a performance management system. Such systems usually are premised on the belief that individuals can exert some influence over their performance. Performance appraisals are the most common method of performance measurement. Performance appraisal serves two purposes: (1) an evaluative purpose of letting people know where they stand and (2) a developmental purpose of providing specific information and direction to individuals, so that they can improve their performance. Performance appraisal and feedback, therefore, are linked to many other human resource management activities. The importance of using job analysis results to develop job-related performance criteria can't be emphasized too much. In general, the more subjective the performance appraisal approach, the more vulnerable the performance appraisal system is to legal challenge.

Despite well-laid plans for a performance management system, human resource professionals are often frustrated by the failure of line managers to conduct performance appraisals consistently. A number of obstacles contribute to resistance from managers: they may not have opportunities to observe subordinates' performance; they may not have clearly specified performance standards to use when making judgments; as human judges, they realize they are prone to errors and may be concerned about how these errors translate into consequences for their subordinates' lives; and they may view performance appraisal as a conflict-producing activity to be avoided.

The dual purposes of evaluation and development mean conflicts in the appraisal and feedback process are inevitable. Effective performance management practices minimize conflicts by (1) focusing on behavior and results rather than on subjective traits; (2) using multiple sources to improve reliability and validity and thus ensure that the process is fair; and (3) conducting effective problem-solving feedback sessions. Effective problem-solving involves identifying the causes of performance and making plans for ensuring effective performance in the future. These principles apply to managing individual performance as well as to managing team performance. In addition, however, teams face additional challenges. Perhaps the most difficult challenge for teams is that managing their performance involves managing the team as a whole as well as the individuals who make up the team.

TERMS TO REMEMBER

360-degree appraisal
adaptive performance
anniversary approach
behavioral criteria
behavioral observation scale (BOS)
behaviorally anchored rating scales (BARS)
contaminated
deficient
direct index approach
expectancy
expectancy theory
focal-point approach

forced distribution method
graphic rating scales
instrumentality
internal team processes
Management by Objectives (MBOs)
motivation
norm-referenced format
organizational citizenship
rater errors
results criteria
results-based formats
performance appraisal
performance criteria

performance management systems straight ranking
positive reinforcement   stretch goals
punishments   trait-based criteria
self-appraisal   upward appraisal
self-management   valence

DISCUSSION QUESTIONS

1. What are the advantages and disadvantages of Con-Way's approach to performance measurement and feedback?
2. Assume, in turn, the identity of each of the following persons: a subordinate, a supervisor, and a human resource professional. Answer this question for each person: "What purpose can a performance appraisal serve for me?" Are the purposes served by a performance appraisal for these three people congruent or conflicting? Explain.
3. Why is job analysis essential for the development of a performance appraisal?
4. Would you prefer to have an appraisal of your performance based on a graphic rating scale, BARS, or BOS? Explain the reasons for your preference. Does the type of job you have matter in choosing one format over the other?
5. What are the advantages and disadvantages of having a 360-degree feedback system?
6. Why do employees differ in their performance levels even after they have successfully passed rigorous selection procedures and have been trained adequately? How can a performance management system address this performance variability?
7. What are the possible causes of performance deficiencies? What strategies can be used to correct those performance deficiencies?
8. Assume you are supervising employees who fall into one of three categories: (1) effective performers who have lots of potential for advancement; (2) effective performers who lack motivation or ability, or both, for potential advancement; and (3) ineffective performers. It's performance appraisal time, and you are preparing for your discussions with subordinates from each of these three categories. Will you have different objectives for different types of employees? Explain how your discussions will be similar and how they will be different.
9. What is the appropriate role for a supervisor of a self-managing team? (Assume the supervisor is not a member of the team.)
10. Imagine you are the team leader of a multicultural team. What special issues will you face regarding performance measurement and feedback? How can you prepare yourself to be effective in such a role?

PROJECTS TO EXTEND YOUR LEARNING

1. *Managing Diversity.* As the HR director for one of the major public accounting firms, you've been concerned about the turnover rates for women and people of color. You know that the college graduates hired into the firm are all equally qualified. You also know that, on objective performance measures, they continue to perform equally well. Yet for some reason, women and people of color are promoted more slowly. Understandably, many get frustrated and leave to work elsewhere. You've been conducting exit interviews and believe that the slower

promotion rates reflect problems with the performance appraisal and feedback process. People who leave complain that their managers don't appreciate their efforts and seem to base promotion decisions too much on "personality." Describe how you'll proceed to address this issue. You aren't sure whether you need to make fundamental changes to the performance appraisal process. Perhaps managers simply need to be trained in how to conduct appraisals and provide feedback. Or, perhaps the problem is that managers aren't using performance appraisal results when making key employment decisions.

2. *Managing Globalization.* You work for Teresa's Tee's, which makes promotional T-shirts that sport unusually high-quality artwork. Demand for the shirts is strong, with orders now coming in from all over the world. To get closer to its customers, the company has decided to go international and open offices in several foreign countries. You plan to employ host-country nationals for all positions. Staff from headquarters will help each location get started, but then local managers will take over. The company is organized around customer-focused teams. You use 360-degree appraisals for everyone in the company, including top-level executives. The results are used for developmental purposes only, but, in the future, it's likely that the company will begin using the results for pay and promotion decisions. The CEO is committed to using 360-degree appraisals at all international locations. You're responsible for ensuring that the performance appraisal and feedback process is effective. Your first international assignment is Mexico, where you'll be staying for six months. Map out a detailed plan of action. State the objectives that you need to accomplish during your six-month assignment.

3. *Integration and Application.* Review the cases of Lincoln Electric and Southwest Airlines at the end of the text.

   a. Compare Lincoln Electric and Southwest Airlines with respect to the major purposes of performance appraisal. Which organization seems more concerned with traits? With behavior? With results? What uses does performance appraisal serve in these two companies?

   b. For Lincoln Electric, how well do the performance criteria seem to fit with the company's strategic objectives? Identify potential sources of deficiency and contamination in the company's performance measures.

   c. Compare the sources of appraisal information used at Lincoln Electric and Southwest Airlines. Would you recommend that these organizations use 360-degree feedback? Why or why not?

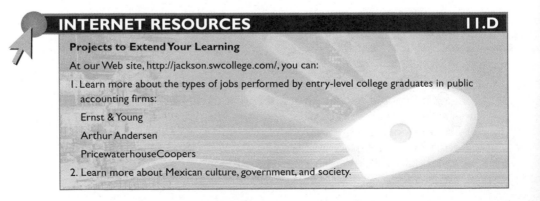

INTERNET RESOURCES   **11.D**

Projects to Extend Your Learning

At our Web site, http://jackson.swcollege.com/, you can:

1. Learn more about the types of jobs performed by entry-level college graduates in public accounting firms:

   Ernst & Young

   Arthur Andersen

   PricewaterhouseCoopers

2. Learn more about Mexican culture, government, and society.

case study

SO YOU WANT TO BE A MANAGER?

Wally Reibstein is beginning to get the hang of his job, having survived a grueling six months as a newly appointed division engineering manager for a large aerospace firm located on the West Coast. Wally graduated with a degree in engineering from Rensselaer Polytechnic Institute in the early 1980s. He worked first for an industrial fan manufacturer located in the Midwest, the closest job he could find related to his aeronautical engineering training. When his wife decided to pursue an advanced degree in economics at a prestigious West Coast university, Wally found employment with his current employer, and they moved.

During the first five years, Wally demonstrated considerable skill in working with others and successfully completed three different projects on time. One year ago, he was promoted to project engineering manager. Within six months, his immediate boss, a division head, was selected for promotion and recommended Wally to fill his position. Because of his past successes, he got the job, and as division manager he is in charge of a staff of over 50 professional and technical personnel. Five of these professionals are designated as project engineers responsible for specific contracts. The remaining staff of engineers and technicians are about equally distributed over five projects.

Wally has a challenging week ahead of him. He has decided that this is the week for "the rubber to meet the road" in his performance as a division manager. He has scheduled two performance appraisal interviews that promise to challenge his human relation skills. The first review is scheduled on Tuesday with Jerry Masters, a 52-year-old project engineering manager with a Ph.D. in electrical engineering and two master's degrees in computer science and business administration. In Wally's estimation, Jerry is a degree collector and a poor manager. Jerry's project has fallen far behind schedule and is headed for disaster. After reading performance reviews from Jerry's personnel folder, Wally has decided that Jerry must be reassigned. Jerry's past reviews indicate that he seldom met stated objectives despite repeated verbal counseling. Wally's former boss confided that he would have reassigned Jerry himself, but his head count was frozen and he had no one readily available to replace him. Wally has no such constraints. His overhead budget has been increased 10 percent as a result of three consecutive successful quarters of billings for his division. He has also recently interviewed a 45-year-old engineer who, in his judgment, possesses all the qualities needed to succeed where Jerry is failing.

Wally agrees with his former boss's counsel that Jerry is a valued citizen but terribly mismatched in his job; he simply can't manage a project. Tuesday morning arrives, and Wally decides to level with Jerry and tell him that he isn't working out and that he will be reassigned to another project. When informed of his reassignment, Jerry reacts by launching into a protracted emotional outburst accusing Wally of violating the trust he (Jerry) had placed in him to support his efforts. Jerry reminds Wally of his 12 years of service and the considerable influence he wields. Storming out, Jerry informs Wally that he intends to write a letter to the division president detailing the shoddy treatment he has received. Great, thought Wally, just what I need to make an impression on the top brass.

QUESTIONS

1. Is Jerry justified in his emotional outburst?
2. How should Wally have told Jerry about the reassignment?
3. Where did Wally go wrong?
4. What would you have done if you were in Jerry's shoes?

ENDNOTES

1 G. Imperato, "How to Give Good Feedback," *Fast Company* (September 1998): 144–156.

2 For a recent review, see R. D. Arvey and K. R. Murphy, "Performance Evaluation in Work Settings," *Annual Review Psychology* 49 (1998): 141–168.

3 Based on J. N. Cleveland, K. R. Murphy, and R. E. Williams, "Multiple Uses of Performance Appraisal: Prevalence and Correlates," *Journal of Applied Psychology* 74 (1989): 130–135.

4 For a detailed discussion of factors that affect employees' reactions, see L. M. Keeping and P. E. Levy, "Performance Appraisal Reactions: Measurement, Modeling, and Method Bias," *Journal of Applied Psychology* 85(5) (2000): 708–723.

5 D. Clutterbuck, "Mentoring and Coaching at the Top," *Financial Times* (January 8, 2001): 14–15; L. Gratton, V. Hope-Hailey, P. Stiles, and C. Truss, "Linking Individual Performance to Business Strategy: The People Process Model," *Human Resource Management* 38(1) (Spring 1999):

17–31; T. Minton-Eversole, "Performance Management Gaps Need Filled, Survey Says," *HR News* (November 2000): 14, 21.

6 A. Staijkovic and F. Luthans, "Self-Efficacy and Work-Related Performance: A Meta-Analysis," *Psychological Bulletin* 124(2) (1998): 240–261; W. Van Erde and H. Thierry, "Vroom's Expectancy Models and Work-Related Criteria: A Meta-Analysis," *Journal of Applied Psychology* 81 (1996): 575–586.

7 D. Fenn, "Personnel Best," *Inc.* (February 2000): 75–83.

8 D. H. Lindsley, D. J. Brass, and J. B. Thomas, "Efficacy-Performance Spirals: A Multilevel Perspective," *Academy of Management Review* 20 (1995): 645–678; R. W. Griffeth and P. W. Hom, "The Employee Turnover Process," *Research in Personnel and Human Resources Management* 13 (1995): 245–293. Note, however, that the link between satisfaction and turnover may be weaker for employees with high financial requirements. See J. F. Brett, W. L. Cron, and J. W. Slocum, Jr., "Economic Dependency on Work: A Moderator of the Relationship Between Organizational Commitment and Performance," *Academy of Management Journal* 38 (1995): 261–271.

9 P. Sellers, "Pepsi Opens a Second Front," *Fortune* (August 8, 1994): 71–76; J. R. Fulkerson and R. S. Schuler, "Managing Worldwide Diversity at Pepsi-Cola International," in S. E. Jackson (ed.), *Diversity in the Workplace: Human Resources Initiatives* (New York: Guilford, 1992).

10 S. B. Malos, "Current Legal Issues in Performance Appraisal," in J. W. Smither (ed.), *Performance Appraisal: State of the Art in Practice* (San Francisco: Jossey-Bass, 1998): 49–94; H. J. Bernardin and W. F. Cascio, "Performance Appraisal and the Law," in R. S. Schuler, S. A. Youngblood, and V. L. Huber (eds.), *Readings in Personnel and Human Resource Management*, 3rd ed. (St. Paul: West, 1988): 239.

11 M. S. Taylor, M. K. Renard, and K. B. Tracy, "Managers' Reactions to Procedurally Just Performance Management Systems," *Academy of Management Journal* 41 (1998): 565–579.

12 S. Lam, C. Hui, and K. Law, "Organizational Citizenship Behavior: Comparing Perspectives of Supervisors and Subordinates Across Four International Samples," *Journal of Applied Psychology* 84(4) (1999): 594–601; P. M. Podsakoff, M. Ahearne, and S. B. MacKenzie, "Organizational Citizenship Behavior and the Quantity and Quality of Work Group Performance," *Journal of Applied Psychology* 82 (1997): 262–270; T. D. Allen and M. C. Rush, "The Effects of Organizational Citizenship Behavior on Performance Judgments: A Field Study and a Laboratory Experiment," *Journal of Applied Psychology* 83 (1998): 247–260.

13 W. C. Borman and S. J. Motowidlo, "Expanding the Criterion Domain to Include Elements of Contextual Performance," in N. Schmitt et al. (eds.), *Personnel Selection in Organizations* (San Francisco: Jossey-Bass, 1993): 71–99; J. W. Johnson, "The Relative Importance of Task and Contextual Performance Dimensions to Supervisor Judgments of Overall Performance," *Journal of Applied Psychology* 86 (2001): 984–996.

14 H. S. Field and W. H. Holley, "The Relationship of Performance Appraisal System Characteristics to Verdicts in Selected Employment Discrimination Cases," *Academy of Management Journal* (1982): 392–406.

15 J. P. Campbell et al., "A Theory of Performance," in N. Schmitt and W. C. Borman (eds.), *Personnel Selection in Organizations* (San Francisco: Jossey-Bass, 1993): 35–70.

16 E. D. Pulakos, S. Arad, M. A. Donovan, and K. E. Plamondon, "Adaptability in the Workplace: Development of a Taxonomy of Adaptive Performance," *Journal of Applied Psychology* 85 (2000): 612–624.

17 V. U. Druskat and S. Wolff, "Effects and Timing of Development Peer Appraisals in Self-Managing Work Groups," *Journal of Applied Psychology* 84(1) (1999): 38–74.

18 A. G. Cohen, "Worker Watchers," *Fortune* (Summer 2001): 70–80; M. L. Ambrose and G. Adler, "Designing, Implementing, and Utilizing Computerized Performance Monitoring: Enhancing Organizational Justice," *Research in Personnel and Human Resource Management* 18 (2000): 187–219; S. Greengard, "The High Cost of Cyberslacking," *Workforce* (December 2000): 22–24.

19 S. Gruner, "Feedback from Everyone," *Inc.* (February 1997): 102–103; "Teams Introduce 360-degree Feedback for Employees After a Corpo-

rate Culture Change at Porsche Cars," *Human Resource Executive* (September 1997): C10; "Despite Hitches, Multisource Feedback Moves Ahead," *Bulletin to Management* 47 (January 18, 1996): 17.

20 Note, however, that research on managers suggests that subordinates and peers often agree in the evaluations. See T. J. Maurer, N. S. Raju, and W. C. Collins, "Peer and Subordinate Performance Appraisal Measurement Equivalence," *Journal of Applied Psychology* 83 (1998): 693–702; J. D. Facteau and S. Craig, "Are Performance Appraisal Ratings From Different Sources Comparable?" *Journal of Applied Psychology* 86(2) (2001): 215–227.

21 C. Viswesvaran, D. S. Ones, and F. L. Schmidt, "Comparative Analysis of the Reliability of Job Performance Ratings," *Journal of Applied Psychology* 81 (1996): 557–574.

22 S. J. Ashford, "Self-Assessments in Organizations: A Literature Review and Integrative Model," *Research in Organizational Behavior* 11 (1989): 133–374; T. H. Shore, L. M. Shore, and G. C. Thornton III, "Construct Validity of Self- and Peer Evaluations of Performance Dimensions in an Assessment Center," *Journal of Applied Psychology* 77 (1992): 42–54; J. L. Farh, G. H. Dobbins, and B. S. Cheng, "Cultural Relativity in Action: A Comparison of Self-Ratings Made by Chinese and U.S. Workers," *Personnel Psychology* 44 (1991): 129–147.

23 J. Dulebohn and G. Ferris, "The Role of Influence in Perceptions of Performance Evaluations' Fairness," *Academy of Management Journal* 42(3) (1999): 288–303; B. D. Cawley, L. M. Keeping, and P. E. Levy, "Participation in the Performance Appraisal Process and Employee Relations: A Meta-Analytic Review of Field Investigations," *Journal of Applied Psychology* 83 (1998): 615–633; M. A. Korsgaard, L. Roberson, and R. D. Rymph, "What Motivates Fairness? The Role of Subordinate Assertive Behavior on Managers' Interactional Fairness," *Journal of Applied Psychology* 83 (1998): 731–744.

24 F. J. Yammarino and L. E. Atwater, "Do Managers See Themselves as Others See Them? Implications of Self-Other Rating Agreement for Human Resources Management," *Organizational Dynamics* (Spring 1997): 35–44; A. H. Church, "Managerial Self-Awareness in High-Performing Individuals in Organizations," *Journal of Applied Psychology* 82 (1997): 281–292; K. M. Nowack, "Congruence Between Self-Other Ratings and Assessment Center Performance," *Journal of Social Behavior and Personality* 12 (1997): 145–166.

25 S. Weisband and L. E. Atwater, "Evaluating Self and Others in Electronic and Face-to-Face Groups," *Journal of Applied Psychology* 84(4) (1999): 632–639; R. Jelley and R. Goffin, "Can Performance-Feedback Accuracy be Improved? Effects of Rater Priming and Rating-Scale Format on Rating Accuracy," *Journal of Applied Psychology* 86(1) (2001): 134–144; J. E. Johnson and K. Ferstl, "The Effects of Interrater and Self-Other Agreement of Performance Improvement Following Upward Feedback," *Personnel Psychology* 52 (1999): 271–303; L. E. Atwater, C. Ostroff, F. J. Yammarino, and J. W. Fleenor, "Self-Other Agreement: Does It Really Matter?" *Personnel Psychology* 51 (1998): 577–598.

26 Shore, Shore, and Thornton, "Construct Validity of Self- and Peer Evaluations"; R. Saavedra and S. K. Kwun, "Peer Evaluation in Self-Managing Work Groups," *Journal of Applied Psychology* 78 (1993): 450–462.

27 J. Katzenbach and D. Smith, "The Discipline of Teams," *Harvard Business Review* (March–April 1993): 111–120; P. E. Levy, "The Nut Island Effect: When Good Teams Go Wrong," *Harvard Business Review* (March 2001): 51–59; T. J. Maurere, N. S. Raju, and W. C. Collins, "Peer and Subordinate Performance Appraisal Measurement Equivalence," *Journal of Applied Psychology* 83 (1998): 693–702.

28 Farh, Dobbins, and Cheng, "Cultural Relativity in Action," J. Zhou and J. Martocchio, "Chinese and American Managers' Compensation Award Decisions: A Comparative Policy-Capturing Study," *Personnel Psychology* 54 (2001): 115–145.

29 T. Schwartz, "It Takes a Strong Stomach to Listen to How Other People See You," *Fast Company* (March 2000): 264–268; "Upward Appraisals Rate Highly," *Bulletin to Management* (March 31, 1994): 104.

30 D. Antonioni and H. Park, "The Relationship Between Rater Affect and Three Sources of 360-Degree Feedback Ratings," *Journal of Management* 27 (2001): 479–495; D. Antonioni, "The Effects of Feedback Accountability on Upward Appraisal Ratings," *Personnel Psychology* 47 (1994): 349–360.

31 A. J. Walker and J. Smither, "A Five-Year Study of Upward Feedback: What Managers Do with Their Results Matters," *Personnel Psychology* 52 (1999): 393–423.

32 G. Huet-Cox, T. Nielsen, and E. Sundstrom, "Get the Most from 360-Degree Feedback: Put It on the Internet," *HR Magazine* (May 1999): 92–103; D. A. Waldman and L. E. Atwater, *The Power of 360 Feedback: How to Leverage Performance Evaluations for Top Productivity* (Houston, TX: Gulf, 1998); A. H. Church and D. W. Bracken (eds.), *360-Degree Feedback Systems* (Thousand Oaks, CA: Sage, Special Issue of Group & Organization Management, June 1997); R. Lepsinger and A. D. Lucia, *The Art and Science of 360° Feedback* (San Francisco: Pfeiffer, 1997).

33 M. R. Edwards and A. J. Ewen, *Providing 360-Degree Feedback: An Approach to Enhancing Individual and Organizational Performance* (Scottsdale, AZ: American Compensation Association, 1996).

34 In some forms of BARS, the anchors are stated as expected behaviors (e.g., "Could be expected to develop loan documentation accurately"). When expected behaviors are included, the BARS is more appropriately labeled a BES—Behavioral Expectation Scale. For further discussion, see F. J. Landy and J. L. Farh, "Performance Rating," *Psychological Bulletin* (January 1980): 72–107; K. R. Murphy and J. I. Constans, "Behavioral Anchors as a Source of Bias in Rating," *Journal of Applied Psychology* (November 1987): 573.

35 Adapted from V. L. Huber, *Validation Study for Electronics Maintenance Technical Positions* (Washington, DC: Human Resource Development Institute, AFL-CIO, 1991).

36 To learn more about how goals setting improves performance, see E.A. Locke and G. P. Latham, *A Theory of Goal Setting and Task Performance* (Englewood Cliffs, NJ: Prentice-Hall, 1990); R. E. Wood and E.A. Locke, "Goal Setting and Strategy Effects on Complex Tasks," *Research in Organizational Behavior* 12 (1990): 73–109; C. E. Shalley, "Effects of Productivity Goals, Creativity Goals, and Personal Discretion on Individual Creativity," *Journal of Applied Psychology* 76 (1991): 179–185; T. R. Mitchell and W. S. Silver, "Individual and Group Goals When Workers Are Interdependent: Effects on Task Strategies and Performance," *Journal of Applied Psychology* 75 (1990): 185–193; J. M. Phillips and S. M. Gully, "Role of Goal-Orientation, Ability, Need for Achievement, and Locus of Control in the Self-Efficacy and Goal-Setting Process," *Journal of Applied Psychology* 5 (1997): 792–802.

37 For a comprehensive review, see R. Rodgers and J. E. Hunter, "Impact of Management by Objectives on Organizational Productivity," *Journal of Applied Psychology* 76 (1991): 322–336.

38 E. Matson. "The Discipline of High Tech Leaders," *Fast Company* (April/May 1997): 34–36.

39 A. S. DeNisi and K. Williams, "Cognitive Approaches to Performance Appraisal," in G. R. Ferris and K. M. Rowland (eds), *Research in Personnel and Human Resource Management* (Greenwich, CT: JAI Press, 1988): 109–156; A. S. DeNisi, T. P. Cafferty, and B. M. Meglino, "A Cognitive View of the Appraisal Process: A Model and Research Propositions," *Organizational Behavior and Human Performance* 33 (1984): 360–396.

40 J. Segal, "86 Your Appraisal Process?" *HR Magazine* (October 2000): 199–206; J. N. Cleveland and K. R. Murphy, "Analyzing Performance Appraisal as Goal-Directed Behavior," *Research in Personnel and Human Resource Management* 10 (1992): 121–185; T. A. Judge and G. R. Ferris, "Social Context of Performance Evaluation Decisions," *Academy of Management Journal* 36 (1993): 80–105.

41 DeNisi and Williams, "Cognitive Approaches to Performance Appraisal"; D. R. Ilgen and J. M. Feldman, "Performance Appraisal: A Process Focus," in B. Staw and L. Cummings (eds.), *Research in Organizational Behavior* (Greenwich, CT: JAI Press, 1983): 141–197.

42 A. L. Solomonson and C. E. Lance, "Examination of the Relationship Between True Halo and Halo Error in Performance Ratings," *Journal of Applied Psychology* 82 (1997): 665–674; M. Foschi, "Double Standards in the Evaluation of Men and Women," *Social Psychology Quarterly* 59 (1996): 237–254; S. J. Wayne and R. C. Liden, "Effects of Impression Management on Performance Ratings: A Longitudinal Study," *Academy of Management Journal* 38 (1995): 232–260; K. R. Murphy, R. A. Jako, and R. L. Anhalt, "Nature and Consequences of Halo Error: A Critical Analysis," *Journal of Applied Psychology* 78 (1993): 218–225; C. E. Lance, J. A. LaPointe, and A. M. Stewart, "A Test of the Context Dependency of Three Causal Models of Halo Rater Error," *Journal of Applied Psychology* 79 (1994): 332–340; W. K. Balzer and L. M. Sulsky, "Halo and Performance Appraisal Research: A Critical Examination," *Journal of Applied Psychology* 77 (1992): 975–985; I. M. Jawahar and C. R. Williams, "Where All the Children Are Above Average: The Performance Appraisal Purpose Effect," *Personnel Psychology* 50 (1997): 905–926; J. S. Kane, H. J. Bernadin, P. Villanova, and J. Peyrefitte, "Stability of Rater Leniency: Three Studies," *Academy of Management Journal* 38 (1995): 1036–1051.

43 R. L. Dipboye, "Some Neglected Variables in Research on Discrimination in Appraisals," *Academy of Management Review* (January 1985): 118–125; B. R. Nathan and R. A. Alexander, "The Role of Inferential Accuracy in Performance Rating," *Academy of Management Review* (January 1985): 109–117.

44 T. J. Maurer, J. K. Palmer, and D. K. Ashe, "Diaries, Checklists, Evaluations, and Contrast Effects in Measurement of Behavior," *Journal of Applied Psychology* 78 (1993): 226–231.

45 H. J. Bernadin, M. R. Buckley, C. Tyler, and D. S. Wiese, "A Reconsideration of Strategies in Rater Training," *Research in Personnel and Human Resource Management* 18 (2000): 221–274; N. M. A. Hauenstein, "Training Raters to Increase Accuracy of Appraisals and the Usefulness of Feedback," in J. W. Smither (ed.), *Performance Appraisal: State of the Art in Practice* (San Francisco: Jossey-Bass, 1998): 404–442.

46 D. T. Stamoulis and N. M. A. Hauenstein, "Rater Training and Rating Accuracy: Training for Dimensional Accuracy versus Training for Ratee Differentiation," *Journal of Applied Psychology* 78 (1993): 994–1003; D. V. Day and L. M. Sulsky, "Effects of Frame-of-Reference Training and Information Configuration on Memory Organization and Rating Accuracy," *Journal of Applied Psychology* 80 (1995): 158–167; L. M. Sulsky and D.V. Day, "Frame-of-Reference Training and Cognitive Categorization: An Empirical Investigation of Rater Memory Issues," *Journal of Applied Psychology* 77 (1992): 501–510.

47 K. R. Murphy and J. N. Cleveland, *Understanding Performance Appraisal: Social, Organizational, and Goal-Based Perspectives* (Thousand Oaks, CA: Sage, 1995); C. G. Banks and K. R. Murphy, "Toward Narrowing the Research-Practice Gap in Performance Appraisal," *Personnel Psychology* 38 (1985): 335–345.

48 M. K. Mount, M. R. Sytsma, J. Fisher Hazucha, and K. E. Holt, "Rater-Ratee Race Effects in Developmental Performance Ratings of Managers," *Personnel Psychology* 50 (1997): 51.

49 K. R. Murphy, "Difficulties in the Statistical Control of Halo," *Journal of Applied Psychology* 67 (1982): 161–164; L. Hirshhord, *Meaning in the New Team Environment* (Reading, MA: Addison-Wesley, 1991); Murphy and Cleveland, *Understanding Performance Appraisal.*

50 R. F. Martell and M. R. Borg, "A Comparison of the Behavioral Rating Accuracy of Groups and Individuals," *Journal of Applied Psychology* 78 (1993): 43–50; see also J. F. Brett and L. E. Atwater, "360° Feedback: Accuracy, Reactions, and Perceptions of Usefulness," *Journal of Applied Psychology* 86 (2001): 930–942.

51 R. Mayer and J. Davis, "The Effect of the Performance Appraisal System on Trust for Management: A Field Quasi-Experiment," *Journal of Applied Psychology* 84(1) (1999): 123-136; L. E. Atwater, P. Roush, and A. Fischthal, "The Influence of Upward Feedback on Self- and Follower Ratings of Leadership," *Personnel Psychology* 48 (1995): 35–59.

52 M. London, *Job Feedback: Giving, Seeking, and Using Feedback for Performance Improvement* (Mahwah, NJ: Lawrence Erlbaum, 1997).

53 A. Nease, B. Mudgett, and M. A. Quinones, "Relationships Among Feedback, Self-Efficacy, and Acceptance of Performance Feedback," *Journal of Applied Psychology* 84(5) (1999): 806–814; A. Staijkovic and F. Luthans, "Self-Efficacy and Work-Related Performance: A Meta-Analysis," *Psychological Bulletin* 124(2) (1998): 240–261; M. Beer, "Performance Appraisal: Dilemmas and Possibilities," *Organizational Dynamics* (Winter 1981): 26; A. Zander, "Research on Self-Esteem, Feedback and Threats to Self-Esteem," in A. Zander (ed.), *Performance Appraisals: Effects on Employees and Their Performance* (New York: Foundation for Research in Human Behavior, 1963).

54 M. Ross and G. J. O. Fletcher, "Attribution and Social Perception," in G. Lindzey and E. Aronson (eds.), *Handbook of Social Psychology*, 3rd ed., Vol. II (New York: Random House, 1985): 73–122.

55 V. L. Huber, P. Podsakoff, and W. D. Todor, "An Investigation of Biasing Factors in the Attributions of Subordinates and Their Supervisors," *Journal of Business Research* 4 (1986): 83–97.

56 K. Renk, "I Want My TV," *Awards & Incentives* (2000): 158–162; K. Kirkland and S. Manoogian, *Ongoing Feedback: How to Get It, How to Use It* (Greensboro, NC: Center for Creative Leadership, 1998).

57 P. J. Kiger, "Frequent Employee Feedback Is Worth the Cost and Time," *Workforce* (March 2001): 62–65.

58 L. E. Atwater, D. A. Waldman, D. Atwater, and P. Cartier, "An Upward Feedback Field Experiment: Supervisors' Cynicism, Reactions, and Commitment to Subordinates," *Personnel Psychology* 53 (2000): 275–297.

59 E. A. Locke, "Motivation, Cognition, and Action: An Analysis of Studies of Task Goals and Knowledge," *Applied Psychology: An International Review* 49 (2000): 408–429; E. A. Locke and G. P. Latham, *A Theory of Goal Setting and Task Performance* (Englewood Cliffs, NJ: Prentice-Hall, 1990).

60 G. P. Latham and G. H. Seijts, "The Effects of Proximal and Distal Goals on Performance on a Moderately Complex Task," *Journal of Organizational Behavior* 20 (1999): 421–429. Also see P. M. Gollwitzer, "Implementation Intentions: Strong Effects of Simple Plans," *American Psychologist* 54 (1999): 493–503; D. VandeWalle, W. L. Cron, and J. W. Slocum, Jr., "The Role of Goal Orientation Following Performance Feedback," *Journal of Applied Psychology* 86 (2001): 629–640.

61 A. D. Stajkovic and F. Luthans, "Self-Efficacy and Work-Related Performance: A Meta-Analysis," *Psychological Bulletin* 124 (1998): 240–261.

62 M. M. Kennedy, "So How'm I Doing?" *Across the Board* (June 1997): 53–54.

63 A. Bandura, *Principles of Behavior Modification* (New York: Holt, Rinehart & Winston, 1969); R. W. Beatty and C. E. Schneier, "A Case for Positive Reinforcement," *Business Horizons* 2 (April 1975): 57–66.

64 "Policy Guide: 'Positive Discipline' Replaces Punishment," *Bulletin to Management* (April 27, 1995): 136; L. K. Trevino, "The Social Effects of Punishment in Organizations: A Justice Perspective," *Academy of Management Review* 17 (1992): 647–676; R. Bennett and L. L. Cummings, "The Effects of Schedule and Intensity of Aversive Outcomes on Performance: A Multitheoretical Perspective," *Human Performance* 4 (1991): 155–169.

65 C. Frayne and G. P. Latham, "The Application of Social Learning Theory to Employee Self-Management of Attendance," *Journal of Applied Psychology* 72 (1987): 387–392; F. H. Kanfer, "Self-Management Methods," in P. Karoly and A. Goldstein (eds.), *Helping People Change: A Textbook of Methods* (New York: Pergamon Press, 1980): 334–389; P. Karoly and F. H. Kanfer, *Self-Management and Behavior Change: From Theory to Practice* (New York: Pergamon Press, 1986).

66 B. P. Sunoo, "This Employee May Be Loafing, Can You Tell? Should You Tell?" *Personnel Journal* (December 1996): 54–62; "Jury Awards Manager Accused of Theft $25 Million," *Bulletin to Management* (March 27, 1997): 97; P. Carbonara, "Fire Me. I Dare You!" *Inc.* (March 1997): 58–64.

67 See F. T. Coleman, *Ending the Employment Relationship without Ending Up in Court* (Washington, DC: Society for Human Resource Management, 2001).

68 Exhibit 11.13 is adapted from D. Hellriegel, S. E. Jackson, and J. W. Slocum, Jr. *Management: A Competency-Based Approach* (Cincinnati, OH: South-Western, 2002); S. Scott and W. Einstein, "Strategic Performance Appraisal in Team-Based Organizations: One Size Does Not Fit All," *Academy of Management* 15(2) (2001): 107–116; K. A. Guion, "Performance Management for Evolving Self-Directed Work Teams," *ACA Journal* (Winter 1995): 67–75; R. Wageman, "How Leaders Foster Self-Managing Team Effectiveness: Design Choices Versus Hands-On Coaching," *Organization Science* 12 (September–October, 2001): 559–577.

69 B. D. Janz, J. A. Colquitt, and R. A. Noe, "Knowledge Worker Team Effectiveness: The Role of Autonomy, Interdependence, Team Development, and Contextual Support Variables," *Personnel Psychology* 50 (1997): 877–904; G. L. Stewart and M. R. Barrick, "Team Structure and Performance: Assessing the Mediating Role of Intrateam Process and the Moderating Role of Task Type," *Academy of Management Journal* 43 (2000):

146–163. For extensive descriptions of research relevant to each of the four components, see M. A. West (ed.), *Handbook of Work Group Psychology* (Chichester, UK: Wiley, 1996).

70 M. D. Zalezny, E. Salas, and C. Prince, "Conceptual and Measurement Issues in Coordination: Implications for Team Behavior and Performance," in K. Rowland and G. Ferris (eds.), *Research in Personnel and Human Resource Management* 13 (1995): 81–115; D. E. Hyatt and T. M. Ruddy, "An Examination of the Relationship Between Work Group Characteristics and Performance: Once More into the Breech," *Personnel Psychology* 59 (1997) 553–573.

71 K. T. Dirks, "The Effects of Interpersonal Trust on Work Group Performance," *Journal of Applied Psychology* 84 (1999): 445–555; A. Edmondson, "Psychological Safety and Learning Behavior in Work Teams," *Administrative Science Quarterly* 44 (1999): 350–383; T. L. Simons and R. S. Peterson, "Task Conflict and Relationship Conflict in Top Management Teams: The Pivotal Role of Intragroup Trust," *Journal of Applied Psychology* 85 (2000): 102–111.

72 Copyright © South-Western College Publishing. All rights reserved. The items listed here are based on a version of this survey that appears in South-Western's *Team Handbook*, 1996.

73 S. Adams and L. Kydoniefs, "Making Teams Work: Bureau of Labor Statistics Learns What Works and What Doesn't," *Quality Progress* (January 2000): 43–48; R. Ginnett, "The Essentials of Leading a High-Performance Team," *Leadership in Action* 18(6) (1999): 1–5; P. E. Tesluk and J. E. Mathieu, "Overcoming Roadblocks to Effectiveness: Incorporating Management of Performance Barriers into Models of Work Group Effectiveness," *Journal of Applied Psychology* 84 (1999): 200–217; V. U. Druskat and D. C. Kayes, "The Antecedents of Team Competence: Toward a Fine-Grained Model of Self-Managing Team Effectiveness," *Research on Managing Groups and Teams* 2 (1999): 221–231.

74 For a comparison of the United States and several European countries, see J. B. Leslie and E. Van Velsor, *A Cross-National Comparison of Effective Leadership and Teamwork: Toward a Global Workforce* (Greensboro, NC: Center for Creative Leadership, 1998).

75 K. M. Eisenhardt, J. L. Kahwajy, and L. J. Bourgeois III, "Conflict and Strategic Choice: How Top Management Teams Disagree," *California Management Review* 39 (1997): 42–62.

76 A. Sagie, "Participative Decision Making and Performance: A Moderator Analysis," *Journal of Applied Behavioral Science* 30 (1994): 227–246; W. A. Kahn and K. E. Kram, "Authority at Work: Internal Models and Their Organizational Consequences," *Academy of Management Review* 19 (1994): 17–50.

77 For a discussion of the consequences of mixing employees from different cultures within a single team, see E. Elron, "Top Management Teams Within Multinational Corporations: Effects of Cultural Heterogeneity," *Leadership Quarterly* 8(4) (1997): 393–412; J. A. Wagner III, "Studies of Individualism–Collectivism: Effects on Cooperation in Groups," *Academy of Management Journal* 38 (1995): 152–172; P. C. Earley and E. M. Mosakowski, "Creating Hybrid Team Cultures: An Empirical Test of International Team Functioning," *Academy of Management Journal* 43 (2000): 26–49.

78 M. F. S. De Luque and S. M. Sommer, "The Impact of Culture on Feedback-Seeking Behavior: An Integrated Model and Propositions," *Academy of Management Review* 25 (2000): 829–849.

79 D. Kiker and S. J. Motowidlo, "Main and Interaction Effects of Task and Contextual Performance on Supervisory Reward Decisions," *Journal of Applied Psychology* 84(4) (1999): 602–609; H. Findley, W. Giles, and K. W. Mossholder, "Performance Appraisal and System Facets: Relationships with Contextual Performance," *Journal of Applied Psychology* 85(4) (2000): 634–640; D. Grote, "The Secrets of Performance Appraisal," *Across the Board* (May 2000): 14–20; R. D. Pritchard, *Measuring and Improving Organizational Productivity: A Practical Guide* (New York: Praeger, 1990).

80 L. Grensing-Potphal, "Motivate Managers to Review Performance," *HR Magazine* (March 2001): 45–48; J. Conway, "Distinguishing Contextual Performance from Task Performance for Managerial Jobs," *Journal of Applied Psychology* 84(1) (1999): 3–13; H. Lancaster, "Your Year-End Review Doesn't Have to Be Quite That Horrible," *Wall Street Journal* (December 23, 1997): B2.

CHAPTER

12

USING PERFORMANCE-BASED PAY TO ENHANCE MOTIVATION

" The Incentive Performance System primarily attributed to James F. Lincoln has been in Lincoln Electric since the early twentieth century. It has resulted in one of the oldest 'pay for performance' systems in the country, and is frequently used for benchmarking by other businesses and studied by academics around the world."

Lincoln Electric Home Page

MANAGING THROUGH STRATEGIC PARTNERSHIPS

Lincoln Electric

When Donald Hastings became CEO of Lincoln Electric Co., he brought with him a passion for total quality management. His goal was to build quality into the production process rather than test it at the end of the production line. Donald Hastings's efforts paid off. Today, employees assume responsibility for quality. With employee-caused errors down by 50 percent, fewer inspectors are used. This saves the company and customers both time and money. Because quality is such an important part of Lincoln's strategy, both under Donald Hastings and the current CEO Anthony Massaro and president John Stropki, employees are rewarded for their efforts to maximize quality. Quality is one of the four criteria included in the performance rating system.

Output is another criterion for rating performance. To keep costs low, Lincoln Electric needs highly productive workers, and it has them. Lincoln's productivity level is two to three times that of comparable organizations. High productivity benefits customers and employees alike. Customers like the lower prices, and employees like the profits the company is able to generate. Average employee compensation is $55,000. More unusual is how much variation there is in the pay received by production workers. Some earn only $40,000 while others earn over $100,000. These differences in pay reflect substantial differences in the employees' productivity. Most of the variation in pay reflects differences in how efficient employees are on their jobs (how many pieces per hour they produce) and differences in their overall performance rating, which determines the size of their year-end bonus.

Lincoln Electric is careful in its selection of new workers because it counts on employees working overtime to keep up with demand and willingly moving from job to job as business demand changes. The company does everything possible not to bulk up with more employees as a means to meet demand. Why? Because the company also believes in employment security. Lincoln guarantees workers that they will have a job even during economic downturns. It does not cope with lean times by laying people off. In order for the company to keep its promise of employment security, however, it must also be able to count on workers to work harder and longer when demand for products is high. When business activity exceeds the number of workers, the incentive system encourages workers to work overtime.[1]

PERFORMANCE-BASED PAY WITHIN AN INTEGRATED HR SYSTEM

"The No. 1 concern when it comes to paying employees is that the relationship between performance and pay is not strong enough."

Sandra Griffin
Partner, Human Capital Services Division
Arthur Andersen

As Chapter 10 explained, an organization's total compensation system can be understood as comprising three basic components: base pay, incentive pay, and employee benefits and services. When establishing base pay rates, organizations focus on the pay rates for *jobs*. The base pay (wages and salaries) that employees receive for performing their jobs reflects conditions in the external labor market and the relative value of jobs within a specific organization. In contrast, performance-based or incentive pay—the focus of this chapter—reflects the specific performance levels of employees. **Performance-based pay** recognizes that people working in the same job can differ greatly in terms of the value they contribute to the organization and seeks to provide employees with an incentive for maximizing the value they contribute.

Link to Performance Measurement and Feedback

As explained in Chapter 11, the use of performance-based pay is one of two major components of an organization's performance management system. Linking performance to outcomes that are valued by employees is important in order to sustain acceptable levels of employee motivation and productivity. In order to create an effective linkage between performance and outcomes, employers must develop appropriate and valid performance measures. In addition, feedback should be given to employees telling them how they are doing and how they can improve in order for performance-based pay to have its intended effects.

Integrating Performance-Based Pay with Other HR Practices

The example of Lincoln Electric illustrates the importance of designing a performance-based pay system that is aligned with the organizational environment and integrated with other components of the HR system.

Internally Aligned with Organization. According to Paul J. Beddia, who was vice president of human resources for several years, the company's pay-for-performance system is just one element in a larger plan for maintaining a highly motivated and productive workforce. "To explain why our workers are as motivated as they are requires an understanding of our basic philosophy, which is centered around the importance of people. Our main employment focus is to encourage growth by involvement, participation and teamwork. Thus, *we strive to create an environment where employees can achieve company goals and personal goals simultaneously.*"

Critics of performance-based pay often view such systems as exploiting employees—always driving them to work harder and harder for a company's benefit. The Lincoln Electric philosophy is grounded in a very different point of view, which asserts that performance-based pay serves the needs of *both* employees and employers. One way that Lincoln's pay system meets the goals of employees is by allowing those who are extremely motivated to make very large amounts of money—much more than they could make doing similar work at other companies. High pay is not automatic, of course. The company cannot afford to pay employees at such high levels unless their productivity merits such high pay. Another way the company helps employees achieve their personal goals is by providing employment security. Employment security would not be possible, however, unless employees agreed to reduce their work schedules during slow times and remain flexible to accepting different job assignments.

Integrated HR System. As these examples illustrate, the performance-based pay system is a cornerstone in the total HR system at Lincoln Electric, but it does not hold up the entire organization. It takes several HR practices working together to achieve highly effective employee behavior, as shown in Exhibit 12.1.[2] For example, consider these other aspects of Lincoln's approach to managing human resources:

- Since 1914, an elected advisory board has ensured that all employees have direct and open communication with senior managers.
- The decision of whether to allocate profit-sharing bonuses is made annually at the discretion of the board of directors.
- Employees are guaranteed employment security, but only after three years of service. The company has not exercised the layoff options in the U.S. operations since 1948.
- A 401(k) plan offers employees a variety of pretax investment options.

No one HR practice accounts for the high levels of motivation and productivity found at Lincoln Electric. It is the system as a whole that produces the desired results. Using well-defined incentives, Lincoln encourages and rewards individual initiative and responsibility. Working together, employees continually reduce costs and improve quality, creating a more profitable company. And employees share in the success of the company according to their own contributions to that success.

"Our famous incentive pay plan is just part of the story."

Paul J. Beddia
Former Vice President of Human Resources
Lincoln Electric

ex 12.1 Use of Performance-Based Pay within an Integrated HR System

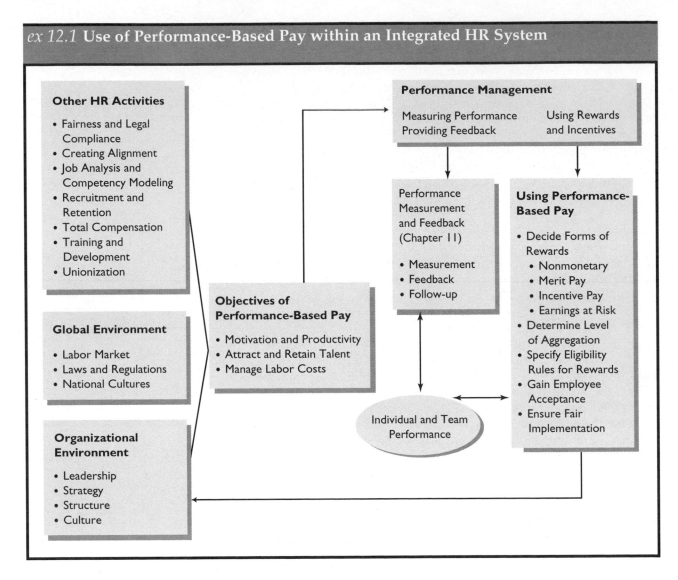

Other HR Activities

- Fairness and Legal Compliance
- Creating Alignment
- Job Analysis and Competency Modeling
- Recruitment and Retention
- Total Compensation
- Training and Development
- Unionization

Global Environment

- Labor Market
- Laws and Regulations
- National Cultures

Organizational Environment

- Leadership
- Strategy
- Structure
- Culture

Objectives of Performance-Based Pay

- Motivation and Productivity
- Attract and Retain Talent
- Manage Labor Costs

Performance Management

Measuring Performance   Using Rewards
Providing Feedback   and Incentives

Performance Measurement and Feedback (Chapter 11)

- Measurement
- Feedback
- Follow-up

Individual and Team Performance

Using Performance-Based Pay

- Decide Forms of Rewards
  - Nonmonetary
  - Merit Pay
  - Incentive Pay
  - Earnings at Risk
- Determine Level of Aggregation
- Specify Eligibility Rules for Rewards
- Gain Employee Acceptance
- Ensure Fair Implementation

Role of the External Environment

Throughout this chapter, we emphasize the importance of designing performance-based pay that fits the organizational environment—especially its corporate culture and business strategy. It is worth noting, however, that the external environment also influences the use of performance-based pay. For example, currently the general trend in both the United States and Europe has been toward increasing use of incentive pay. This is illustrated in Exhibit 12.2, which also reveals that the use of incentive pay is much more widespread in the United States than in Europe.[3]

Over the course of the past century, employers have preferred different performance-based pay approaches at different points in time. At the beginning of the 20th century, piece-rate pay systems were predominant. Following the Great Depression and a period of substantial labor unrest, these systems started to be replaced by guaranteed wages and less use of incentives.

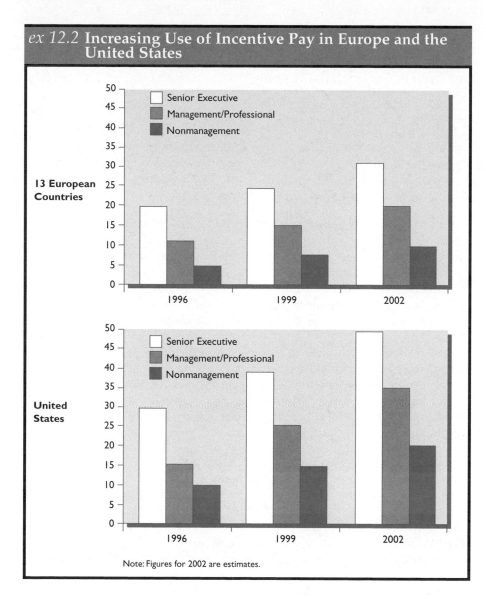

ex 12.2 **Increasing Use of Incentive Pay in Europe and the United States**

Note: Figures for 2002 are estimates.

Labor-friendly legislation such as the *Fair Labor Standards Act* and successful union organizing efforts meant that the pay received by nonmanagerial employees was often based on union settlements arrived at through negotiation. During the middle of the 20th century, merit pay plans became firmly established rates—so much so that they now are generally referred to as "traditional" pay.[4]

As we begin the 21st century, employers' use of performance-based pay is a significant aspect of the changes occurring within many companies. Sometimes referred to as "new pay" plans, the performance-based pay systems gaining popularity today have much in common with those from a much earlier era. The pendulum is swinging back in favor of the more aggressive performance-based systems that were popular several decades ago.

Throughout the past century, the shifting popularity of different approaches to performance-based pay has reflected changes in economic conditions, fluctuations in union activity, and the enactment of various new laws and regulations. Of course, for global firms, national differences in all of these external forces, as well as general cultural differences, also influence the design of performance-based pay. Although all of these external factors play a role in shaping how an employer uses performance-based pay, employers have a great deal of latitude to design a system that fits their particular organization.

Design Choices for Performance-Based Pay

Lincoln Electric's use of performance-based pay is just one of many approaches available for employers who wish to reward employees for performance. As shown in Exhibit 12.1, the use of performance-based pay involves several choices.

Monetary and Nonmonetary Rewards. One key choice concerns the extent to which the company offers monetary rewards versus other outcomes that employees may value. Theoretically, organizations could choose to give employees no monetary rewards for performing well in their jobs. Instead, they could offer only nonmonetary rewards, such as recognition and praise. Among U.S. employers, however, this approach is extremely rare. Most employers make some attempt to provide monetary rewards for better performance.

In deciding to offer monetary rewards, an organization does not exclude the use of nonmonetary rewards. Other valued outcomes can be tied to employee performance, including opportunities for career development, special assignments, and even simply praise for a job done well. When reading about the alternative approaches to performance-based pay described in this chapter, readers should keep in mind that monetary rewards are one of several forms of reward that employees may value.

Forms of Performance-based Pay. Assuming an employer decides that some monetary performance-based pay will be offered, another decision concerns which basic method to adopt for allocating monetary rewards. The major categories here are merit pay, incentive pay, and/or putting earnings at risk.

With **merit pay plans**, base pay (the pay to be received regardless of performance) is set at a market rate and a small pool of money is allocated for distributing annual raises that reflect the past year's performance of each employee. The differences in merit pay received by employees in the same job and with the same length of tenure in the job are usually quite small, for example, 5 percent.

Like merit pay plans, **incentive pay plans** peg base pay at the market rate. Additional compensation is available through bonuses or other forms of payment for peak performance. In recent years, incentive pay has been used by many companies as a means of motivating managers to achieve goals that support the firm's commitment to managing diversity more effectively. Examples of this use of incentive pay are described in the feature, "Managing Diversity: Incentive Pay for Meeting Diversity Goals."[5]

The value of incentive pay that an excellent performer can earn in a given year is greater than the size of a merit increase (e.g., 10 to 20 percent). With incentive pay, there is no permanent adjustment made in an employee's base pay as a reward for past performance. Under this system, an employee whose performance has been "excellent" for the past five years receives the

"Often, it seems that the best managerial intentions wash away into flat, indistinct merit increases for performers who meet expectations and those who exceed them."

Steve Scholl
Compensation Director
Allstate Insurance Company[8]

Incentive Pay for Meeting Diversity Goals

MANAGING
DIVERSITY

According to a study by the Society for Human Resource Management, most *Fortune* 500 companies either do not measure performance against diversity goals or they measure this performance but do not use compensation to reward success. Apparently, these organizations simply hope that the use of fair hiring methods and sending managers to diversity training programs will produce a truly multicultural organization. But about 30 percent of the *Fortune* 500 and (and about 10 percent of firms in general) take a bold, more controversial approach: They pay managers to achieve diversity objectives.

Tenneco, the oil company, was one of the mavericks. Back in the mid-1980s, Tenneco was among the first organizations to link a portion of managers' bonuses to how many women and people of color they hired and moved up the ladder. Since then, the number of professional women and people of color in the company has more than doubled. At the same time, some managers lost out when it came time for bonuses: "We've all had some of our bonus subtracted because of this program," explained one human resource manager.

Managers who are perfectly comfortable using performance-based pay plans to achieve other types of strategic objectives—such as increasing ROI and improved customer satisfaction—often balk at this practice. For some critics, the practice seems misguided because it ties pay to something other than improved financial performance. Measuring the bottom-line consequences of diversity is difficult. Companies that link bonuses to effective diversity management are saying they value this objective even if the financial benefits of diversity can't be directly measured.

Deloitte & Touche, the accounting firm, also uses performance-based pay to achieve diversity goals. Within two years of tying managers' bonuses to increasing the rate at which women were promoted, the company experienced a 50 percent increase in the number of women partners in the firm. At Motorola, a belief in the strategic importance of managing diversity is reflected in the CEO's bonus formula, which includes goals for managing diversity, EEO, and affirmative action. Some experts think the practice is just another fad. Others predict it will eventually become a standard feature in the performance management systems of leading firms.

same base pay as one whose performance has been average. However, the excellent employee will have received substantially more incentive pay during the five years. Thus, with incentive pay, there is little downside risk for employees and there is more upside potential.

Sometimes employers provide rewards for performance without specifying in advance the specific goals that must be achieved. For example, at the end of a good year, all employees may receive bonuses. The size of the bonus pool may be decided on by top management on a yearly basis. Because employees do not know the expectations in advance, this type of incentive system may not be effective in achieving specific strategic objectives.

Earnings-at-risk plans, also called pay-at-risk, involve reductions in base pay to below-market levels. In essence, employees must earn their way back to the level that would have been guaranteed under a traditional or incentive pay plan. Offsetting this risk of a possible loss in pay is an opportunity to earn much more than the market is paying. If designed appropriately, there is no economic reason to place a cap on the earnings of employees who work under these plans. Such plans may not be acceptable to employees who are used to more traditional reward structures that ensure earnings stability.[6] Yet, for salespeople who work on straight commission, placing their earnings at risk is just considered normal. Increasingly, top-level executives are being asked to accept compensation packages that put greater portions of their earnings at risk.[7] By putting pay at risk, employers effectively buy insurance that protects the company from precipitous declines in performance.

The basic differences in these three forms of pay are illustrated in Exhibit 12.3. From the employee's perspective, the degree of upside and downside risk is a key factor that differs among these three performance-based approaches. From the employer's perspective, a major difference is the degree to which labor costs fluctuate with productivity. For each of these forms of pay, employers have many specific design choices, as explained later in this chapter.

Aggregation. Independent of the degree to which pay depends on performance is the question of whether the performance measure reflects the performance of an individual, a work team, or the business as a whole. In merit plans and most commission systems, measures of individual performance are used to determine pay. In contrast, bonuses often are used to reward teams for achieving their goals. With profit-sharing plans, the rewards employees receive depend on the performance of the company as a whole.

Clearly, the choice of whether to tie pay to individual, team, or companywide performance depends upon the strategic objectives of the company and the way work is structured within the organization. For employees working in jobs where individual efforts are the primary determinants of their performance, it is appropriate to base rewards on individual performance. For employees working in self-managed teams, however, team-based performance measures and rewards may be more appropriate. For executives who are responsible for the performance of an entire business unit, companywide measures may be appropriate. Finally, in many companies a mix of individual, team, and companywide performance measures is used to allocate monetary rewards.

THE STRATEGIC IMPORTANCE OF USING PERFORMANCE-BASED PAY TO ENHANCE MOTIVATION

Perhaps the most important reason for the increasing popularity of performance-based pay is the belief that it can improve an organization's ability to achieve its strategic objectives. At Lincoln Electric, for example, the pay system supports three key strategic objectives: controlling costs, producing high-quality products, and being flexible in the face of fluctuating demand for the company's products. During the dot-com frenzy of the late 1990s, a key strategic objective for many high-tech start-up companies was creating and sustaining rapid growth. This could be achieved only by attracting excellent talent—yet most dot-com start-ups had no history of success, no high-status reputation, and little cash. The strategic objectives will be different at other companies, but the principle of using pay to drive performance against strategic objectives may be equally applicable to many situations.

Satisfying Employees

Throughout this book, we have emphasized the importance of HR practices for attracting and retaining talented employees. Creating a pay system that the best performers find attractive is one objective that drives many organizations to experiment with new forms of performance-based pay. With traditional pay plans, differences in the compensation received by the best and

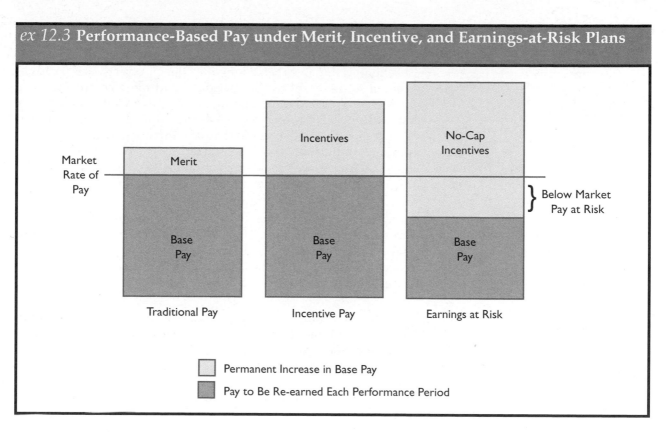

ex 12.3 Performance-Based Pay under Merit, Incentive, and Earnings-at-Risk Plans

worst performers are quite small. This is demotivating for high performers, who perceive the small differences in pay as inequitable. Recall that perceptions of equity are based on employees' comparisons of their inputs and outcomes relative to those of others. When high performers believe that they contribute more (inputs) but do not receive proportionately greater rewards (outcomes), they experience feelings of inequity and become dissatisfied (see Exhibit 11.2 in Chapter 11).[9] Dissatisfaction, in turn, may result in a decision to leave the organization or in reduced effort—in either case, the organization loses the potential benefit of those employees.

In addition to affecting the satisfaction of current employees, incentive plans can influence whether applicants apply for a position and whether they accept an offer of employment. As explained in Chapter 10, early in the life cycle of companies, risk is high, sales growth is slow, and earnings are low, so companies offer base pay that is below the market. To attract talent, performance-based pay is offered, and usually the rewards are based on companywide performance. Because there are few employees, it is assumed that the company's success will depend on the talents and efforts of each and every person. For potential employees, the attractive possibility is that they may become very wealthy as the company grows and succeeds. During the high-tech boom of the 1990s, this attractive scenario was realized by thousands of employees working for start-up firms in Silicon Valley. For mature companies, performance-based pay linked to company growth is much less likely to attract outstanding talent, because growth at this stage is likely to be slow.

Creating Internal Alignment

Growing awareness that traditional pay plans often do a poor job of aligning employee behavior with strategic objectives is probably the most important reason that more and more companies have introduced incentive pay. If organizations are to achieve their strategic objectives, then pay needs to be linked to performance in such a way that it aligns the goals of individual employees with the goals of the organization. To illustrate how performance-based pay can be used to create internal alignment, we provide two examples here. Many other examples will be given throughout this chapter.

Commenting on the shift to performance-based pay: *"[it's] absolutely gut-wrenching. Some people hate it."*

Lisa Weber
Executive Vice President of HR
MetLife

Managing Change. During times of strategic change, the misalignment between an organization's pay system and the behaviors needed from employees is often inescapable. The feature "Managing Change: A New Pay Plan for Owens Corning" describes how performance-based pay can be especially useful to organizations in transformation.[10]

Diversification. As industries change and new business opportunities arise, many firms continue to grow by entering new lines of business and gradual diversification. For example, chemical companies invest in or acquire biotech firms, retail stores open e-commerce sites, and utilities pursue opportunities in deregulated markets. To align the behaviors and effort of employees, goals are set that fit the needs of the new business and bonuses are offered for achieving those goals. If separate divisions are formed, performance-based pay may be linked to performance of the division. Or, performance-based pay may be offered to teams working on key projects, such as the development or marketing of a new product.[11] Through carefully designed incentive programs, employers can direct the behavior of some employees in one direction (e.g., innovation), and at the same time reward a different set of behaviors for employees working in other areas with different strategic priorities (e.g., cutting costs or providing reliable service).

Managing Labor Costs

As noted earlier, employers have always recognized the importance of rewarding employees for good performance. For the past several decades, the most widespread method for achieving this goal has been the merit raise. Merit raises are intended to reward performance, but in the long run, they can be costly. Suppose Rhonda Brown, an X-ray technician at Community General Hospital, is earning $20 an hour. At her annual performance review, her supervisor gives her an overall performance rating of 6 on a 7-point scale. Subsequently, she receives a 10 percent pay raise. Rhonda will now always be paid at the higher rate, regardless of her performance levels in the future. For whatever reasons, Rhonda may not perform as well next year or the year after that. Nevertheless, as long as Rhonda continues to perform satisfactorily and remains with the company, her prior salary raise increases her employer's permanent costs.

In order to deal with the problem of rising compensation costs that are unrelated to improvements in employee performance, many companies are replacing merit pay raises with other forms of performance-based pay. A

A New Pay Plan for Owens Corning

Back in the early 1990s, Toledo-based Owens Corning (the company with the Pink Lion) was in a bit of trouble. Glen Hiner, the new CEO, walked into a company that had seen sales of construction materials decline. Costly asbestos litigation had strained both cash flow and employee morale. As part of his turnaround strategy, Hiner created a new set of corporate goals, referred to as Vision 2000. The vision included achieving a $5 billion sales target and changing the culture to one that valued customer satisfaction, employee dignity, and shareholder value.

The HR group looked at the new business plan and decided they should reconsider their entire HR system. "We started with a very simple, systematic strategy that begins with the business results we want to produce. Then [we] used all of the human resource systems and processes as levers for change or drivers of the business strategy," explained Greg Thomson, senior vice president of HR. Naturally, the compensation system was included as a candidate for change. Rick Tober was the team leader in charge of redesigning compensation. "We looked at all the programs, threw them in the hopper and asked ourselves how we could design an overall compensation plan that met our guiding principle," explained Tober. To cut fixed costs, the company made several changes in its benefits program. To counterbalance those changes, it added new ways for employees to share in the future successes of the company. For example, the company contributed less to the employees' long-term savings, and counterbalanced this change with the addition of a profit-sharing that linked payouts to individual performance. It reduced its total expenditures for benefits by offering a cafeteria-style plan, and counterbalanced this change by adding a broad-based stock option plan. It converted retirement benefits to a cash balance plan with a guaranteed annual interest rate, and counterbalanced this with stock bonuses tied to company performance.

So far, the new approach seems to be working. Whether it will succeed in the long run remains to be seen. The biggest challenge may be the complexity of the changes. Developing understanding and buy-in from the entire HR staff, all the line managers, and all employees is an enormous communication task. According to one staff member, "They're starting to get it, but it takes time."

key objective is to ensure that any increases in compensation costs are paid for by improvements in productivity or profitability.

Cost considerations become more and more salient as more and more of the budget is spent on compensation. In service companies, compensation costs account for up to 80 percent of the operating budget. Thus, banks, hospitals, and other labor-intensive service providers place high priority on controlling compensation costs and using compensation wisely. Similarly, proportionately more of a company's total compensation costs go to paying upper-level executives. Consequently, executive pay plans typically include more aggressive use of performance-based pay compared with pay plans for employees at lower levels.

Due in part to the very high costs associated with executive compensation, shareholders and other external stakeholders have shown particular sensitivity to the issue of a strong link between the performance of executives and the pay they receive. In Chapter 10, we noted that executive pay levels have been rising faster than the pay levels for employees at lower levels in U.S. companies. Defenders of the increases seen in executive pay have argued that the rising pay levels reflect improvements in the performance of companies and thus are both justified and cost-effective. However, research indicates that CEO pay is more closely related to a company's size than its performance.[12] Later in this chapter, we will return to the issue of how so-called performance-based executive pay plans affect a company's costs.

DESIGNING PERFORMANCE-BASED PAY SYSTEMS

FAST FACT

A survey by Hewitt Associates revealed that 8 in 10 companies had some form of variable pay in 2001. In 1990 the figure was fewer than 5 in 10.

Substantial research supports the conclusions that performance-based pay can improve productivity. For example, when a major retailer introduced an incentive plan into half its outlets, those outlets experienced increased sales, customer satisfaction, and profits. The positive effects of performance-based pay were especially great for outlets experiencing intense competition.[13] Numerous other studies have found similar results. However, research also shows that, under some conditions, performance-based pay has no effects or even detrimental effects.[14] Results from these latter studies serve as ammunition for critics of performance-based pay.

Compensation specialist Alfie Kohn has been a particularly vocal critic, stating that "any incentive or pay-for-performance system tends to make people less enthusiastic about their work and therefore less likely to approach it with a commitment to excellence."[15] Although it has been widely publicized, Kohn's assertion is not consistent with the findings of empirical research. While it's true that performance-based pay does not always improve performance, the research indicates that ineffective reward systems are due to poor design and implementation; their failure is not due to a widespread negative psychological effect of performance-based pay.[16]

To be effective, performance-based pay systems must successfully deal with six major issues: (1) specifying and measuring performance, (2) specifying the method for linking pay to performance, (3) specifying the level of aggregation for reward distribution, (4) specifying the type of reward, (5) specifying eligibility for performance-based pay, and (6) gaining employee acceptance.[17] Of course, decisions about each of these issues also must be sensitive to legal considerations.

"If you can't measure it, you can't manage it, and if you can't do either, you sure as heck shouldn't pay for it."

Steven J. Berman
Managing Director
PricewaterhouseCoopers

Specifying and Measuring Performance

A valid and transparent performance measurement system is central to any system that links pay to performance. The practice of linking pay to performance can quickly highlight and exacerbate any flaws in the performance measurement system.

What Gets Measured Gets Rewarded. A company may tell employees that speed, efficiency, quality, and customer satisfaction warrant equal attention, and it may really mean it. But if speed and efficiency are easier to measure than quality and customer satisfaction, the pay plan weights them more heavily, leading employees to give them priority when situations force a trade-off. If the performance measurement system focuses on one component of performance and rewards are given for a different component, employees will be confused and managers will wonder why the rewards do not work. In recent years, the use of the balanced scorecard approach to measuring organizational performance has put the spotlight on precisely this issue. When it comes to paying for performance, many companies have relied heavily on financial performance measures while ignoring other performance indicators that reflect the perspectives of employees, customers, and other strategic partners. The result is a mismatch between the incentive system and the company's full understanding of what it takes to be effective in the long run.[18]

Measuring Results versus Measuring Behaviors. When the Fibers Department of E. I. DuPont de Nemours initiated a major change in its pay system, it intended to improve the relationship between pay and performance on tasks that were considered to be of strategic importance. The department shifted from straight hourly- or salary-based pay to an incentive plan that tied employees' compensation to their unit's overall performance. Employees were viewed as stakeholders. Managers thought that incentive pay would reinforce this stakeholder philosophy and build a greater sense of teamwork. The compensation plan, which took a 13-member task force two years to design, tied an individual's pay to the department's profits and losses. One of the 20,000 employees covered by the plan described it as a shift from being paid for "coming to work" to being paid for how well a business unit succeeds. The plan sounded good in theory, but it was soon scrapped. To cope with a downturn in business, the company had to reduce the workforce by 25 percent. Those who remained worked harder than ever to turn things around. Despite their efforts, however, employees fell short of their profit goal. Rather than withhold the 6 percent pay-for-performance bonus it had designed, DuPont pulled the plug on the plan to avoid demoralizing its workforce.

As DuPont's experience illustrates, the strategic value of incentive pay depends on whether the pay plan supports the behaviors that are most important to the company's success. During an economic recession, DuPont needed employees who would put in their best efforts, even if that effort didn't immediately translate into increased profitability. An incentive plan that defined the strategic objectives of smaller work groups and tied pay to outcomes that workers really could control might have worked more effectively for DuPont.

TRW ensures that employees can control the results on which their rewards depend by using behavior-based goals rather than results-based goals. In their Cleveland-based automotive plant, project teams start up and disband as project needs come and go. To support team efforts, team members establish specific behavioral goals that are tightly related to the team goals. Incentives ranging in size from 10 to 25 percent of base pay are tied to the team-driven individual goals.[19]

"We use the scorecard system to ensure that our employees deliver customer satisfaction. For example, the incentive compensation of everyone in the company—the salespeople, the service people, the engineers, the product marketing people, everyone—is based on these same satisfaction scores."

Tom Siebel
CEO
Siebel Systems

"We practice a conscious form of organizational behaviorism. We structure the compensation plan to drive the kind of behavior we need."

Tom Siebel
Siebel Systems

Short-Term versus Long-Term Perspective. As more and more companies consider paying for knowledge or skill acquisition, they come face to face with the question of how much value they should place on performance in the current job versus behaviors that prepare employees for future jobs. Motorola discovered this conflict when it introduced pay for developing reading and math skills. Team members resented it when their colleagues disappeared to school for weeks, at full pay, leaving the teams weaker. The workers complained about the mixed message they were getting and the conflict between self-development and teamwork. They went to the compensation director and said, "Would you guys get a grip? Make up your minds what you really want from us."[20]

Finding the appropriate balance between rewarding for current performance versus rewarding for long-term performance is a difficult balancing act. Many critics of performance-based incentive plans point to this as a common problem. Executive pay plans that focus attention on short-term movements in the company's stock price, for example, may lead managers to make decisions that protect the stock price in the short term but have negative longer-term consequences. In sales jobs, balancing short-term and long-term performance objectives also poses a challenge. Traditional commissions focus the attention of a sales staff on the short-term objective of selling goods and services, and do nothing to ensure the customer is satisfied with the purchase. Yet building customer loyalty and repeat business are important strategic objectives for most organizations. Thus, performance-based pay plans for sales organizations increasingly include measures of customer satisfaction.[21]

Specifying the Method for Linking Pay to Performance

As described earlier in this chapter and as shown in Exhibit 12.3, three basic approaches to linking pay to performance are available. Compensation specialists use the terms *merit, incentive,* and *at-risk* to describe different philosophies about how much risk employees should be exposed to. These approaches differ in the level of guaranteed base pay, the relationship of base pay to the market, the amount of performance pay, the method used to allocate performance pay, the permanence of performance-based pay, and the portion of total pay that's at risk.

In practice, however, the differences among pay plans are matters of degree. For example, to deal with the problem of escalating pay, some organizations have adopted merit pay plans that allocate zero raises to poorly performing employees, and they then force managers to identify a specific percentage of poorly performing employees.[22] These merit pay plans function very much like an incentive plan. Similarly, it is sometimes difficult to tell the difference between incentive pay and plans that put earnings at risk. How far below the market must a company set its policy line before we say they have adopted an earnings-at-risk approach: 5 percent? 10 percent? 20 percent? And under what conditions do employees really feel that their pay is "at risk"? Lincoln Electric employees clearly work under an earnings-at-risk plan (although it is usually referred to as an incentive system). Yet, year after year, most employees know that they can expect above-market compensation. From the employees' perspective, perceptions of risk reflect not only the formal plan but also their beliefs about how likely it is that they will perform at the level needed to ensure they will be compensated at or above the average market level.

Specifying the Level of Aggregation for Reward Distribution

Performance can be measured at the individual, work team, department, plant, strategic business unit, or organization level. Thus, rewards can be linked to the performance of individuals or to the performance of groups in which employees are members. Two factors that influence this choice are the objectivity of available performance measures and the types of behaviors needed from employees to achieve strategic objectives.

Objectivity. If individual performance can be measured only through subjective appraisals, it may not be appropriate to tie performance-based pay to individual performance. The more subjective the performance measure is, the less likely it is that employees who receive low ratings will accept the measure as valid. Tying pay to subjective measures exacerbates the problem because more is at stake for the employee. Often, more objective performance measures can be obtained when performance is measured at a higher level of aggregation—for example, the team or strategic business unit. The trade-off is that the tie to individual performance is less direct; the gain is that the tie to achieving the company's business objectives is clearer.[23]

Team-based pay systems are proving to be quite effective. In a recent Hay survey, respondents rated the effectiveness of several forms of performance-based pay. As Exhibit 12.4 reveals, team-based pay was consistently viewed as helpful, while ratings of other approaches showed mixed results.[24]

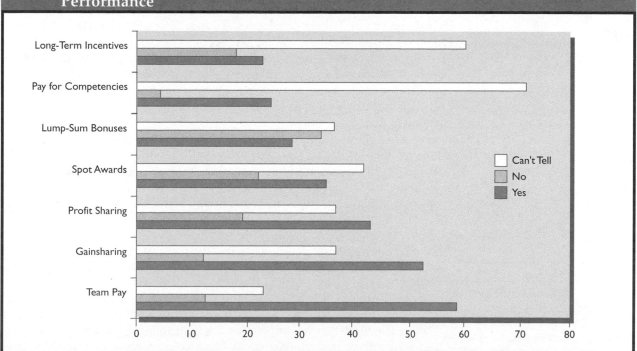

ex 12.4 **Responses of Managers When Asked Whether Each Pay Practice Improved Performance**

Behaviors. Nordstrom's managers want their salespeople to be entrepreneurs. Therefore, they use individual incentive plans, which produce greater competition, increased performance pressure, and greater risk taking.[25] Not surprisingly, when monetary rewards are tied to one's own job performance, concern about organizational citizenship fades. Pay plans that pit employees against each other in order to win rewards are likely to cut off information sharing and other forms of coworker support.[26] In some contexts, this may not be a major problem, but usually cooperation among employees is beneficial and direct competition is somewhat dysfunctional.

> *"Individuals don't accomplish anything, teams do."*
>
> The late W. Edwards Deming
> TQM Guru

One way to avoid the problem of competition among employees is to have employees compete against objective performance goals, rewarding everyone who achieves the goal. Often, this is more easily done when goals are set for teams, departments, or business units. Incentive plans that reward employees for the performance of a larger group reinforce behaviors that promote collective success. They encourage each team member to help the team attain its objectives.

Specifying the Type of Reward

Rewards for performance can be of many types, ranging from a feeling of personal satisfaction, to public recognition and small tokens, all the way to substantial monetary payments and stock ownership.

Form of Payment. Besides cash, a company may choose to give employees large prizes (e.g., all-expenses-paid vacations), direct stock awards, stock options, or any combination of these. All of these are considered monetary rewards. The terms *performance-based pay* and *incentive pay* are generally *not* used to refer to rewards that consist mostly of social recognition. In practice, however, no clear lines separate social rewards from those that are primarily monetary.

Au Bon Pain uses mystery customers to evaluate the performance of its restaurants and their employees. To establish a direct relationship between performance and rewards, managers whose employees score 100 percent in all 12 of the categories that are evaluated receive an on-the-spot bonus of 20 Club Excellence Dollars—dubbed CDs. These dollars can be traded for items in a company catalog. Most items are in the $10 to $70 range and include such things as Au Bon Pain sunglasses and portable cassette players. In addition, winner's names are posted on the store's bulletin board next to a list of the criteria for the program, and all winners receive personal letters of congratulation from company officials. It isn't clear whether Au Bon Pain's employees are motivated more by the monetary worth of these rewards or by the social recognition that goes with them. Most likely some employees like the money more while others place more value on praise and recognition.

Size of Reward. Regardless of the specific form of the reward, for it to be effective, it must be valued by employees. Because the value of a reward is only partly a function of its monetary worth, judging "how much is enough" is mostly a matter of speculation or trial and error. Companies clearly make different choices in the sizes of the monetary rewards they offer.[27] Although the average for nonexecutives is about 7 percent, at Lincoln Electric monetary rewards

> **FAST FACT**
>
> Nucor, the largest U.S. steel producer, has the lowest labor costs per ton in the American steel interest. It also pays the most, including bonuses of up to 60% of base pay.

can amount to 100 percent. Even within the same company, employees in different jobs usually have different percentages of their pay placed "at risk." The general pattern is that proportionately more of an employee's total pay is put at risk as one moves up in the hierarchy. Exhibit 12.5 illustrates this pattern.

Timing of Rewards. Generally speaking, the more quickly rewards follow desirable behavior, the more potent the rewards are in evoking subsequent desirable behavior.[28] Delayed rewards may decrease desired behavior because the employee doesn't see an immediate consequence. Delayed rewards also may increase dissatisfaction and frustration among high performers. On the other hand, by delaying the payment of rewards, a company may be able to reduce the cost of its incentive plan. The longer the company delays paying the incentive, the longer it can use the money for its own purposes. Also, by delaying the payment of rewards, the company reduces the chances of rewarding employees who are about to leave the organization. In most companies, incentive pay is received from several weeks to a year after the performance being rewarded.

International Considerations. Predicting in advance how employees in different countries will react to different pay plans is seldom easy. When international management professor Chao Chen at New York University compared the preferences of American and Chinese employees, he expected to find that the Americans would prefer unequal, performance-based distribution of rewards and the Chinese would prefer more equal distribution. Instead, his research showed that Chinese and Americans both preferred to have material rewards distributed unequally, based on performance. To his surprise, the Chinese also preferred

FAST FACT
Sixty percent of MNCs in China give discretionary bonuses to local employees.

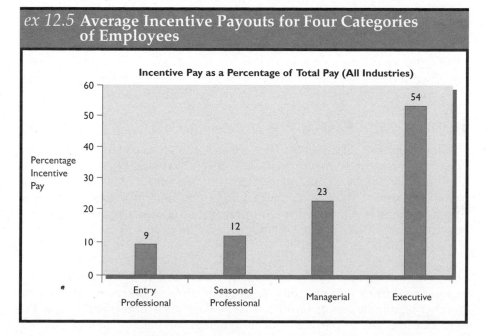

ex 12.5 **Average Incentive Payouts for Four Categories of Employees**

Incentive Pay as a Percentage of Total Pay (All Industries)

Percentage Incentive Pay

Entry Professional: 9
Seasoned Professional: 12
Managerial: 23
Executive: 54

to see socioemotional awards—such as parties and managerial friendliness—distributed unequally, whereas the Americans felt these socioemotional awards should be distributed to everyone equally.[29] Similarly, one might predict that Americans and Russians would have different preferences for how to allocate rewards, but recent research suggests that managers in both countries place primary emphasis on individual performance when allocating rewards, while showing less concern for treating everyone equally or worrying about how the reward allocations might affect coworker relations.[30]

To date, there has been relatively little systematic research investigating cultural differences in how employees react to alternative forms of performance-based pay. Thus, companies are learning on their own. When HR professionals at Motorola conducted their own research on attitudes toward pay-at-risk plans, they found that such plans were acceptable to employees in many countries—and the pattern of findings was not always what they expected. Exhibit 12.6 summarizes the conclusions Motorola reached about which countries were most accepting of pay-at-risk.[31]

Specifying Eligibility for Performance-Based Pay

As is true for many other HR practices, different parts of an organization may be subjected to differing forms of performance-based pay. As described in Chapter 10, for example, the percentage of total pay earned in the form of base pay generally decreases as one moves from lower to higher levels in the organization. Conversely, the percentage of pay that is clearly tied to performance generally increases as one moves up the organizational hierarchy. Another common pattern is to offer higher-level employees—but not lower-level employees—rewards for improved organizational performance.

The rules used to determine which employees are covered by various components of a total pay plan are called **eligibility rules**. Many of the ongoing changes in the use of performance-based pay reflect changes in the eligibility rules used by employers rather than the introduction of truly new forms of pay. When companywide profit sharing is adopted, for example, the change usually involves going from a situation in which only a limited pool of employees share the profits (top-level executives) to making all employees eligible to receive this form of pay. The same is true for other forms of performance-based pay, such as bonuses and stock options.

Gaining Employee Acceptance

Employee opposition can be a major obstacle to the successful implementation of performance-based pay, especially incentive plans. Several conditions that improve employee acceptance and thus the effectiveness of incentive pay are shown in Exhibit 12.7.[32] Particularly important for success is effective communication, which can dispel employees' fears, enhance their trust, and improve their understanding of how performance-based pay plans may affect their future earnings.

Fear. Employees may worry that performance-based pay plans will result in work speedups or will put some percentage of the workforce out of a job. Another legitimate concern may be that performance targets will be too difficult or out of the employees' control. When group performance serves as a

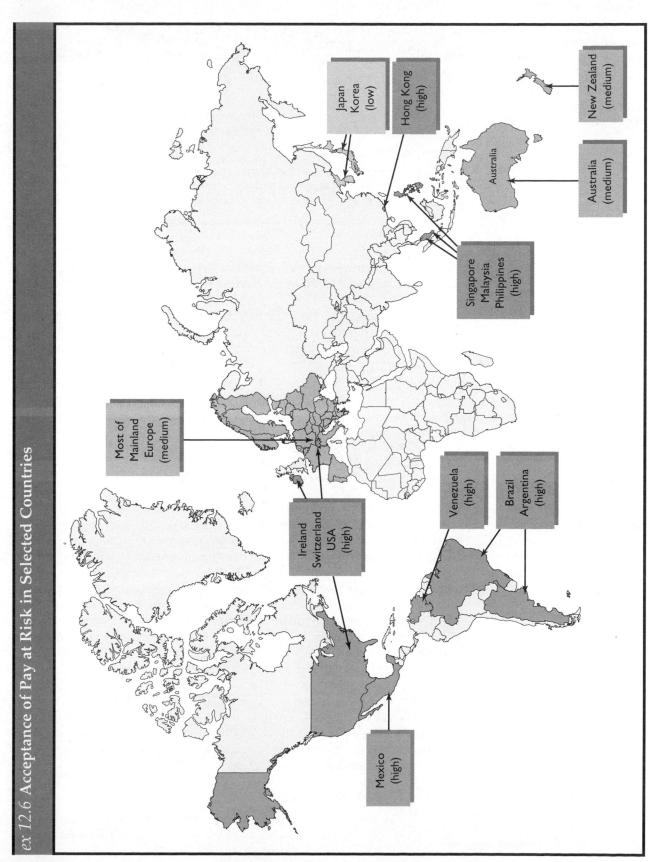

ex 12.6 Acceptance of Pay at Risk in Selected Countries

Japan
Korea
(low)

Hong Kong
(high)

New Zealand
(medium)

Australia
(medium)

Australia

Singapore
Malaysia
Philippines
(high)

Most of
Mainland
Europe
(medium)

Venezuela
(high)

Brazil
Argentina
(high)

Ireland
Switzerland
USA
(high)

Mexico
(high)

ex 12.7 Conditions That Build Employee Acceptance of Performance-Based Pay

Creating Understanding

- The plan is clearly communicated.
- The plan is understood, and bonuses are easy to calculate.
- The employees have a hand in establishing and administering the plan.

Ensuring Fairness

- The employees believe they're being treated fairly.
- Bonuses are awarded as soon as possible after the desired performance.
- The employees have an avenue of appeal if they believe they're being treated unfairly.

criterion for incentive pay, individualistic U.S. employees may fear that their pay will be decreased because they have to depend on others for their rewards.

Distrust. Some approaches to performance-based pay tie the size of rewards employees receive to managerial decisions about what the company can afford to pay in a given year. For example, at Lincoln Electric, the size of the year-end bonus pool is set by the top management team. If trust in management is low, employees may not believe the figures when management tells them how the financial performance of their business unit translates into the size of the pool available for bonuses. Regularly providing detailed financial information about business performance is one way to deal with this concern. Another is to tie managers' rewards to the same pool of funds used to pay other employees. When separate pools of funds are set aside for managerial and nonmanagerial employees, distrust is likely to increase.[33]

Misunderstanding. For employers who use an intranet to communicate with employees about compensation and benefits, many convenient software tools can be used to improve employees' understanding of performance-based pay plans and their consequences for an employee's income stream. Towers Perrin, a consulting firm with expertise in compensation systems, advocates setting up a system that allows employees to recalculate estimates of their likely annual income at least once per month. This can be especially useful for employees who (potentially) receive large annual bonuses. The size of an annual bonus often depends on both the performance of the employee and the performance of the firm. Because indicators of the firm's performance fluctuate throughout the year, employees often experience a great deal of uncertainty. A sophisticated HRIM system with the appropriate software makes it possible for employees to calculate what their bonuses would be under various "what-if?" scenarios. Such calculations can quickly become complicated, depending on the design of the pay plan. Scenarios can help employees see how changes in their performance, as well as changes in the firm's performance, may impact their earnings.[34]

Legal Considerations

FAST FACT

Until recently, Japanese companies were not permitted to issue their stock as compensation.

Legal considerations must also be taken into account when designing pay-for-performance systems. Issues of discrimination and tax laws are particularly important.

Discrimination. Under Title VII of the *Civil Rights Act* and the *Equal Pay Act*, a supervisor may be charged with unlawful discrimination by an employee in a protected group who believes that a pay raise, bonus, or other monetary reward was denied on a basis not related to performance. Such problems are most likely to arise when performance measures are subjective and when the size of rewards given to individuals is left to managerial discretion rather than being driven by a fixed formula.[35] Thus, when awarding performance-based pay, applying the same decision rules to all employees is essential. Data showing persistent pay differences between men and women and among employees from differing ethnic backgrounds cause many people to believe that unfair pay discrimination persists in many organizations today. Although some of the pay differentials can be explained by years in the labor market, study after study has shown that human capital variables such as education, experience, and performance do not fully account for these pay differences.[36]

Taxes and Accounting Rules. Tax and accounting rules also are worthy of some comment here, although a full discussion of these is beyond the scope of this chapter. Particularly in the specialized arena of executive compensation, changes in taxation and accounting rules can dramatically alter the methods companies use to administer performance-based pay. For example, when tax rates for long-term capital gains are low relative to tax rates for ordinary income, stock options become more popular. But when the differential is removed, cash becomes more popular than stock options. Likewise, laws that require taxes to be paid at the time a stock option is granted—as is true in Norway—discourage the use of stock as a form of reward; laws that defer taxation until the option is exercised have the opposite effect. In the United States, recent changes in the IRS code mean that the cost to employees of some stock plans have increased approximately 15 percent because these are no longer sheltered from payroll taxes.

> **FAST FACT**
>
> After 30 years of not assessing payroll taxes on incentive stock options and employee stock purchase plans, employers began including these compensation components when paying payroll taxes in 2002, due to new federal regulations.

INTERNET RESOURCES 12.B

Designing Performance-Based Pay Systems

At our Web site, http://jackson.swcollege.com/, you can:

1. Learn about rewarding performance at some of the firms discussed in this section by visiting their company home pages:

   Siebel Systems

   Lincoln Electric

   Deloitte & Touche

   Owens Corning

2. Find out more about the services offered by consulting groups who specialize in compensation, including

   Zigon Performance Group

   William M. Mercer

3. Find out about current pay surveys and the information they provide regarding the use of incentives at WorldatWork.

4. Visit the Institute of Management and Administration to read the latest issue of IOMA's Pay for Performance Report, a monthly report devoted to pay for performance issues.

MERIT PAY PLANS

Merit pay plans have been the cornerstone of public and private compensation systems for many years. Many organizations use some form of merit pay, but the plans differ along two key dimensions. First, some plans use only subjective performance measures and/or include factors other than performance when making pay raise decisions, which weakens the link between performance and pay raises. Second, plans differ in the way the merit increase is calculated—some award an absolute amount, others award a percentage of base salary, still others rely on merit grids.[37]

The Performance-to-Pay Link

Much of the dissatisfaction with merit pay plans stems from the fact that they link performance rewards to subjective performance measures. The criteria may be contaminated or deficient. Supervisors all too frequently evaluate incumbents according to preconceived biases. Regardless of the appraisal form—whether it's based, for instance, on behavior, output, or traits—rating errors such as leniency and halo are rampant. Therefore, supervisors and employees often disagree on evaluation results. As explained in Chapter 11, valid performance measures are essential to creating a strong link between performance and rewards (instrumentality). These problems are compounded when annual pay raises also take into account other factors, such as cost of living, job or organizational seniority, or current position in the salary range.

Calculating the Merit Raise

Under merit pay plans, department heads usually recommend raises for the employees they supervise within the constraints of a merit pool budget. Since the total of all increases can't exceed the budget percentage for the department, small merit pay pools are problematic. Charles Peck, a compensation expert with The Conference Board, based in New York, explained some of the other problems often associated with merit plans:

> **FAST FACT**
>
> About 40% of companies boost merit increases in a good financial year, while 45% reduce merit increases in a poor year.

Merit increases tend to be expensive and, contrary to their intent, not strongly related to performance. Usually everybody gets something. This so dilutes the salary increase budget that the top performer's increase isn't large enough to be significant (especially after it is prorated over the number of pay periods in the year and subjected to withholding). On the other hand, the poor performer is getting more than he or she should have, which is nothing. The result of all this is that the employees who are most dissatisfied are the ones the company wants satisfied—the top performers. If the concept of pay for performance is rigorously applied, there must be zero pay for zero performance.[38]

Allstate's Monoline Matrix Merit Guidelines illustrate this principle.[39] They assign merit increases as follows:

Performance Level	Merit Increase
Performance consistently and significantly exceeds position requirements	6% or more
Performance consistently meets position requirements	0–4%
Performance requires improvement to meet position requirements.	0%

Managerial Discretion. In this system, managers have considerable discretion. To help managers use their discretion wisely, Allstate provides them with a table that clearly lays out several different reward allocation scenarios. Using the table, managers can easily figure out how to fund larger merit raises for outstanding performers by allocating smaller increases for average and poor performers. Suppose the budget provides for an average merit increase of 4 percent. One option for the manager would be to distribute merit increases as follows:

OPTION 1

	Exceeds	Meets	Requires Improvement
Percentage of employees at the performance level	40%	55%	5%
Average percentage increase given to employees with this level of performance	6.0%	2.9%	0.0%

In this scenario, the best performers receive the minimum required increase of 6 percent. But suppose a manager feels this is too little. Can funds be allocated to give the best performers as much as an 8 percent increase? The answer is yes. Two possible ways to do it follow:

OPTION 2

	Exceeds	Meets	Requires Improvement
Percentage of employees at the performance level	30%	70%	0%
Average percentage increase given to employees with this level of performance	8.0%	2.3%	0.0%

OPTION 3

	Exceeds	Meets	Requires Improvement
Percentage of employees at the performance level	40%	55%	5%
Average percentage increase given to employees with this level of performance	8.0%	1.5%	0.0%

Employee's Position in Range. Exhibit 12.8 illustrates a more complex system, which allocates raises based on both performance and an individual's position in the salary range. At any performance rating higher than Unacceptable, employees with lower base pay will receive larger increases compared with employees at higher levels of base pay. Note, however, that although the percentage of merit increase (in dollars) is greater in the lower quartiles, the absolute size of the merit increase is often larger in the higher quartiles, provided the merit budget is large enough and the grid is designed correctly.

Employees may perceive this approach as unfair because equally performing employees do not get equal percentage increases in pay. Although employee education may help to minimize this problem, a more practical approach is to uncouple performance-based and range-based pay adjustments and award each type of increase separately.

Critics of merit pay contend that even the best-designed merit pay systems are ineffective. According to Edward E. Lawler III, an expert on reward

ex 12.8 Merit Increase Based on Current Position in the Salary Range

Performance Rating	PERCENTAGE INCREASE IN ANNUAL SALARY			
	First Quartile	Second Quartile	Third Quartile	Fourth Quartile
1. Unacceptable	0%	0%	0%	0%
2. Below Average	2%	0%	0%	0%
3. Competent	8%	6%	4%	2%
4. Above Average	10%	8%	6%	4%
5. Superior	12%	10%	8%	6%

system design, merit increases don't work well because they're plugged into antiquated pay systems. He believes that the one thing shown by 40 years of researching reward systems is that merit pay isn't effective for increasing productivity—particularly for the service, information-processing, and high-technology industries of the 21st century. Still, many U.S. workers are paid under merit systems. Many others, however, work in organizations that have abandoned the use of merit increases in favor of incentive pay plans.

INCENTIVE PAY PLANS

A major difference between merit pay and incentive pay is that merit pay is a permanent increase but incentive pay is a one-time increase. Measurements of performance often differ, also. Whereas merit pay plans typically rely on subjective performance appraisal ratings, incentive pay is often based on performance that can be quantified more easily. As is true for merit pay, performance measures used for incentive pay should be based on a clear vision of the organization's strategy and culture—that is, they should tie rewards to behaviors and outcomes that support business priorities. Finally, compared with merit pay plans, incentive plans often give managers more latitude to make large distinctions in the rewards received by employees, and in any one pay episode, they offer employees the opportunity to earn relatively larger performance-based pay.

While recognizing that distinguishing incentive pay from earnings at risk is not straightforward, in this section we review the following: individual incentives, team incentives, special achievement awards, profit sharing, and gainsharing. Typically, these forms of incentives reward employees for performance that has occurred within the time frame of one year or less.

Individual Incentives

"Fifth Third is more like Southwest Airlines or Nordstrom than a bank in terms of customer service and sales culture."

Charles Wendel
President
Financial Institutions Consulting

Individual incentives are among the oldest and most popular form of incentive pay. With this type of plan, individual standards of performance are established and communicated in advance, and rewards are based on individual output. Individual incentives are used by a significant minority of companies in all industry groups except utilities. Utility firms have been slow to implement such plans owing to their history of regulation, which limits workforce autonomy.

Fifth Third Bank is an aggressive user of individual incentives. Just about anyone can earn extra cash by persuading someone to apply for a credit card (up to $25), consumer loan ($25), or mortgage (up to $75). Branch managers can earn 20 percent above their base salary for meeting all of their goals. In addition, the 75 top-producing managers win all-expenses-paid trips to luxury resorts.[40]

A variety of individual incentive plans exist. These plans differ in terms of the method of rate determination. When the work cycle is short, units of production generally serve as the method of rate determination. For long-cycle jobs, the standard is typically based on the time required to complete a unit. Individual incentive systems also vary with regard to the constancy with which pay is a function of production level. One option is to pay a consistent amount at all production levels, for instance, $0.25 a carton for all cartons shipped. Alternatively, pay may vary as a function of production level. For example, employees may be paid $0.25 a carton for up to 1,000 units a day, and $0.37 a carton beyond this threshold.

Piecework. Piecework, like Lincoln Electric's, is the most common type of individual incentive pay. In this plan, employees are paid a certain rate for each unit of output. Under **straight piecework plans**, employees are guaranteed a standard pay rate for each unit. The standard pay rate is based on the standard output and the base wage rate. For example, if the base pay of a job is $40 a day and the employee can produce at a normal rate 20 units a day, the standard rate may be established at $2 a unit. The normal rate is more than what time-and-motion studies indicate is typical because it is supposed to represent 100 percent efficiency. The standard rate that is agreed to may also reflect the bargaining power of the employees, the economic conditions of the organization and industry, and the amount the competition is paying.

In **differential piece rate plans**, more than one rate of pay is set for the same job. This plan can be set up in several different ways. Taylor Differential Plans are one example. In Taylor plans, employees receive a higher rate of pay for work completed in a set period of time. For work that takes longer to complete, the rate of pay is lower. For example, employees may be paid $2 per piece if they complete five pieces per hour, but they would be paid only $1.80 per piece if they completed only four pieces per hour.

When used appropriately, piecework pay can be very effective in raising individual performance, but there is no panacea. Consider what happened when a group of bank processing operators went to a per-item-processed reward system. The staff of 12 operators increased the items processed from an average of 980 items per hour to more than 3,000 items per hour. Their take-home pay increased an average of 50 percent over their former hourly pay. The program seemed to be a success—until the bank president made a visit to the unit. One operator cut off her conversation with the president after a brief time, telling him that he was costing her money. The president also could see that operators were unwilling to help each other out because it would reduce their own pay. As in this case, when piece-rate incentives reward individual employees without regard to the consequences for the larger organization, their disadvantages may outweigh any benefits.[41]

Standard Hour Plans. **Standard hour plans** are the second most common type of individual incentives. This approach is based on setting a standard time for each unit of production. Tasks are broken down by the amount of time it takes to complete them, which can be determined by historical records, time-and-motion studies, or both. The normal time to perform each task becomes a standard.

If you go into an automobile repair shop, you will probably see a chart indicating the labor rates associated with various types of repair. These reflect the use of standard hour plans. Each rate includes the rate paid to the mechanic who does the work plus the premium charged by the owner of the shop. The rate is fixed regardless of how long it actually takes to do the repair. Thus, the mechanic and the shop owner both have incentives to ensure that the work is completed in a shorter amount of time than that used to set the standard rate. Consider a standard time of two hours and a rate of $16 an hour, of which the mechanic is paid $12 an hour. In this system, the mechanic receives $24 for each unit of work completed, regardless of the actual time spent. If the mechanic completes six units in an eight-hour day, he receives $6 \times $24, or $144. This is substantially more than $96, which would be the "expected" rate of pay for eight hours based on four units.

Executive Incentives. As already noted, individual incentives are commonly used to award top-level managers. Executive incentive plans use a formula to relate incentives to the attainment of corporate or strategic business unit goals, with the various goals weighted. In addition to cash, incentive pay includes such things as restricted stock grants (free shares given to the CEO for staying with the company), performance shares or performance units (free shares or cash for achieving multiyear goals), and stock option grants.[42]

Debate over the effectiveness of executive incentives has raged for many years. Two different issues fuel these debates—the size of incentive rewards received and the (small) role of performance in determining executive pay.

The pay of U.S. executives seems excessive relative to the pay of rank-and-file employees and of CEOs in other countries. The pay of the top-earning CEOs regularly makes news. Consider this: Even in an off year (2001), the average total compensation of the 15 highest earners was $88.7 million.[43] That same year, the ratio of the pay of CEOs to the pay of rank-and-file employees was more than 70 to 1 in the United States, compared with 17 to 1 in Germany and only 10 to 1 in Japan. These are the types of figures that make news, but "the relentless focus on how much CEOs are paid diverts public attention away from the real problem—how CEOs are paid," according to compensation experts Michael Jensen and Kevin J. Murphy. After studying the pay of CEOs in 1,400 companies over an eight-year period, the researchers contend that the "incentive" compensation of top executives is virtually independent of corporate performance and is no more variable than that of hourly workers. Another study found that company size—not performance—was the most important factor determining the total compensation received by CEOs.[44]

CEOs would seem to be prime candidates for compensation that puts earnings at risk. But incentive pay for CEOs too often is treated as an entitlement program rather than as a way to motivate outstanding performance. To rectify the problem, the researchers recommend building greater performance variability into executive pay, restructuring incentive pay so that salaries, bonuses, and stock options provide big rewards for superior performance and big penalties for poor performance.[45]

As is true for other employees, a fundamental challenge in designing executive incentive plans is choosing the most appropriate way to measure performance. The performance measures that drive executive incentive pay, and thus performance, are as varied as those that drive nonexecutive pay. One approach that's gained popularity in recent years is paying executives for the value they create for shareholders. This approach was popularized by the consulting firm Stern Stewart & Co., which developed a performance indica-

"It's the underlying philosophy which is the key thing. Three years ago we paid bonuses on sales. Then we moved to profit. Now we're looking for something which more accurately reflects the shareholder's position."

Andrew Higgins
Finance Director
Burton (a UK retailer)

tor called Economic Value Added (EVA). Those who champion the use of EVA as a basis for awarding executive pay argue that it's the best way to align the interests of managers with those of shareholders. Compared with other financial performance measures—including return on equity, operating margins, and earnings per share—EVA is more closely aligned with shareholders' net return on capital. Among the many companies that use EVA measures as a basis for incentive pay are Coca-Cola, AT&T, Quaker Oats, and CSX.[46]

Team Incentives

Team incentives fall somewhere between individual plans and whole-organization plans such as gainsharing and profit sharing. Performance goals are tailored specifically to what the work team needs to accomplish. Strategically, they link the goals of individuals to those of the work group, which, in turn, are usually linked to financial goals.[47]

Exhibit 12.9 shows the performance measures used by a manufacturer for awarding incentives to employees working in its plants. In this plan, separate incentives exist for work teams within a plant (40 percent weight) and for a plant as a whole (60 percent weight).

When designed appropriately, team-based incentives offer four major advantages compared with individual incentive systems. First, the mere presence of team members who have some control over rewards evokes more vigorous and persistent behavior than is evidenced when individuals work alone. Second, the likelihood that conflicting contingencies (peer pressure) will evoke counterproductive behavior is reduced. Third, the strength of the rewards is increased, since they're now paired with group-administered rewards, such as praise and camaraderie. Research also suggests that the performance of a group is higher than that attained by individual group members—although not as high as that of the best person in the group. Fourth, the performance of another group member (usually the high performer) can serve as a model, encouraging other team members to imitate successful behavior.[48]

At Sears, Roebuck and Company, this approach to team incentive pay is called **goalsharing,** because employees receive financial rewards for achieving team goals. At Sears, the team is usually defined as an individual store. The feature "Managing Teams: Goalsharing at Sears" describes this approach in more detail.[49]

> **FAST FACT**
>
> Recent surveys of employers indicate that team-based incentives are used by 37% of companies in Europe and 59% of companies in the United States.

ex 12.9 Example of Incentives Used by a Manufacturer to Reward Team and Plant Performance

Strategic Objective	How Measured (weight)	Level of Aggregation	Goals to Determine Payouts		
			Threshold	**Target**	**Maximum**
Improve productivity	Ratio of units produced over labor hours goal (40%)	Team	.75 against goal	.85 against goal	.95 against goal
Reduce defects	Percent units with quality defects (40%)	Plant	5%	3%	1%
Reduce waste	Cost of waste as a percentage of sales	Plant	3%	2%	1%

MANAGING TEAMS

Goalsharing at Sears

As Sears, Roebuck and Company has learned, team goals work well and team rewards also work well. But goalsharing, which combines both, works even better. When Sears management compared stores that used goalsharing with those that didn't, it found that stores with goalsharing had 10 percent lower turnover among employees and similar improvements in customer service and sales performance.

At Sears, goalsharing is voluntary. If managers or employees are against the idea, top management doesn't impose goalsharing on them. According to Jane Floyd, Sears's director of strategic initiatives, goalsharing doesn't work if employees participate just because the boss tells them to. Employees need to believe in the process and feel committed to it.

Stores that choose to use goalsharing get to set their own goals. They do so by committee, with each store's committee representing a "diagonal slice" of employees from each level and functional area. As part of the process of communicating the team goals, employees attend sessions to discuss how achieving their goals will affect business results. Although goals differ somewhat from store to store, most stores have goals for improving customer service and satisfaction.

Consistent with good goal-setting practices, Sears also provides regular feedback, so the team knows how well it's doing. For example, if a store is focusing on improving customer service, the results of weekly customer satisfaction surveys are posted. If sales goals have been set, posted sales figures provide feedback. By measuring their performance against the goals, employees can see what they've achieved. Floyd also says that she can see results beyond those being measured. "You see ownership, people growing in ways they never would," she says. "It's been difficult, but it's been worth it."

"Our experience has been that the group award alone does not do enough. Individuals want to be rewarded for group performance and for the individual contribution as well."

Judy H. Edge
Compensation Manager
FedEx

Types of Teams. As more and more companies restructure work around teams, new team structures are likely to proliferate. Different team structures may require different forms of pay. For example, three types of teams are commonly found in today's organizations:

- **Parallel Teams.** These teams operate in a structure that functions in parallel to the regular organization chart. Often staffed by volunteers who serve the team on a temporary assignment, the typical tasks of such teams include creating reports and making suggestions for improvements in the company. The team's work is usually a small portion of each member's full responsibility.
- **Project Teams.** Project teams may operate in a parallel structure or they may be integrated as part of the formal organization structure. Such teams often have a somewhat stable core of members with diverse areas of specialized expertise. They often are self-managing and have a broad mandate to develop innovative products or services. The team's work may be a part- or full-time responsibility for each member.
- **Work Teams.** Work teams are fully integrated into the organization structure. They have clear, narrow mandates, which usually focus on producing products or providing services. Membership in these teams is usually stable and the team's work is each member's full-time responsibility.

The very different natures of these team types mean that no single approach to rewarding the performance of team members would fit all three. Exhibit 12.10 shows how two leading experts recommend structuring the performance-based pay for these three types of teams.[50] In many organizations, multiple team types operate side by side. By implication, multiple forms of team pay should also be used.

Team Pay Design Issues. Although team-based incentives are promising, they involve administrative responsibilities that are as great as those

ex 12.10 Pay Systems for Different Types of Teams

	TYPE OF TEAM		
Feature	Parallel	Project	Work
Base pay	Job based	Skill based	Skill based
Pay for performance			
Individual	Merit pay for job performance	Possible if team assessed	Unusual but possible if team assessed
Team	Recognition or cash for suggestions	Possible at end of project	Possible if team independent
Unit	Possible gainsharing	Profit sharing or gainsharing	Profit sharing or gainsharing
Participation	Design of gainsharing plan	Assessment of individuals	All aspects of design and administration
Communication	Open about rewards for improvement	Open about skill plan and rewards for performance	Highly open

associated with individual incentive plans. Job analysis is still necessary to identify how to structure the teams and to ensure that workloads are equivalent among teams.[51] Also, team incentives may produce unintended side effects, including competition between groups, that may or may not complement goal attainment. Exhibit 12.11 summarizes several issues to be addressed when designing performance-based pay for teams.[52]

To date, research on how to best design performance-based pay for work teams is scarce, so it's difficult to propose solutions to the challenges.[53] However, case studies of the experiences in two companies—Solectron California and XEL Communications—provide several insights. For example, one solution to the challenges of changing team membership, multiple team memberships, and interteam relationships is to fund the incentive pool at the business unit level. This reminds employees that ultimately, their team should strive to enhance the organization's performance. Another lesson suggested by the experiences of these companies is that it's best to keep the pay system simple and plan to make adjustments to it as the team and company gain more experience with this approach to pay. Third, using 360-degree appraisals as the basis for developing or evaluating individuals should be resisted early in the life of the team. Until a team has matured and developed a level of trust in the team-based incentives, 360-degree appraisals may be threatening to employees, resulting in lack of candor and/or low team cohesiveness.[54]

Special Achievement Awards

Awards for achievement usually target performance in areas of particular strategic value, such as safety, customer service, productivity, quality, or attendance. Recipients typically are nominated by peers or supervisors to receive awards including gifts, savings bonds, dinner certificates, and cash incentives ranging from $150 to more than $1,000. When designed well, the activities associated with these bonuses effectively focus attention on core values and business objectives.

Recognition Awards. Data I/O Corporation, an electronics manufacturing company in Redmond, Washington, makes extensive use of achievement

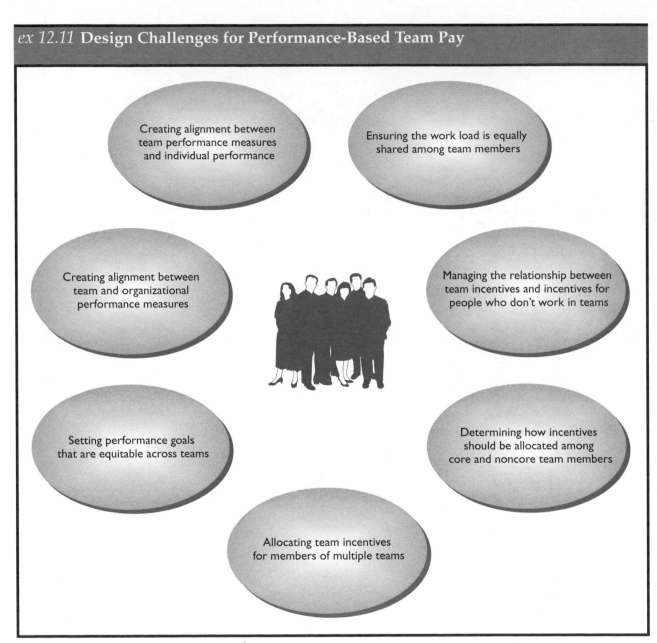

ex 12.11 **Design Challenges for Performance-Based Team Pay**

Creating alignment between team performance measures and individual performance

Ensuring the work load is equally shared among team members

Creating alignment between team and organizational performance measures

Managing the relationship between team incentives and incentives for people who don't work in teams

Setting performance goals that are equitable across teams

Determining how incentives should be allocated among core and noncore team members

Allocating team incentives for members of multiple teams

bonuses. For example, all members of a computer-aided electronics software development team—such as engineers, technical writers, shippers, and quality assurance personnel—garnered $60 dinner certificates when the product was released. Two high achievers also earned weekend trips for two to San Francisco, including $1,500 in airline and motel expenses. On other occasions, recognition plaques, mugs, T-shirts, and pen sets have been distributed. Monthly, an employee is recognized for her or his contribution to Data I/O. Recognition brings a parking place by the front door, an engraved plaque, and verbal acknowledgment in a company meeting. The feature "Managing Teams: Rewards for a Team Culture at Valassis" describes one company that uses recognition as well as other rewards to support a performance-driven culture.

Rewards for a Team Culture at Valassis

As one of the nation's leading marketing services companies, Valassis Communications offers a variety of door-to-door marketing services for consumer package goods companies and franchise retailers. Accounting for more than 75 percent of the company's revenues is its flagship product, Free-Standing Inserts (FSIs). These are four-color booklets containing coupons and other promotional offers from leading consumer package goods companies. Through its FSIs, Valassis reaches almost 60 million households each week via Sunday newspapers and distributes nearly 90 percent of all coupons in the United States.

The Valassis Impact Promotions (VIP) division provides franchise retailers with a variety of specialty promotions that can be customized in unique shapes and sizes, highly targeted, and distributed by a variety of methods (e.g., zoned newspapers and direct mail). The VIP customer base includes food services, telecommunications, and retail franchises. Through its Targeted Marketing Services division, Valassis provides newspaper-delivered product samples and advertising. Recently, Valassis expanded into Internet services by taking a 50 percent ownership in an on-line coupon site. Supporting all of the company's activities are teams of employees who are organized to serve the company's many customers.

According to *Fortune* magazine, Valassis is also one of the "100 Best Companies" to work for in the United States. The achievement is due largely to the company's highly motivating and enjoyable workplace. Valassis management views its key to success as having a culture that is fun and where goal-oriented individuals and teams are rewarded for achieving their goals. The environment embraces flexibility and change, which are consistent with the creativity needed to succeed in this industry.

The Valassis culture emphasizes having fun, but having fun is not the sole objective. This is a performance-driven company. Its executives want all employees to feel and behave as though they are owners of the company and to believe that they will share in the rewards of the company. Supporting this culture is a total compensation plan that includes profit sharing, stock purchases, and "champion pay"—rewards for outstanding achievements. But pay is not the only reward for employees at Valassis. In fact, other rewards seem much more important to satisfying employees' desire for enjoyable work. Festive occasions are used to celebrate past achievements, employees work in modern and comfortable facilities, and recognition awards are given often and with fanfare. In these and many other ways, Valassis ensures that employees enjoy coming to work and brag about their employer in their community.

MANAGING TEAMS

Suggestion Systems. To encourage more innovative ideas, many companies have suggestion systems that involve some form of instant incentive. According to the National Association of Suggestion Systems, its 900 members received nearly 1 million suggestions from their employees, resulting in savings of over $2 billion annually. Crowley Maritime Corporation's "Ship Us an Idea" is typical of most suggestion plans. The shipping company receives an average of 20 suggestions a month from its 1,000 employees. Employees earn between $50 and $150 for most ideas and may earn up to 10 percent of the cost savings for significant ideas. A presidential award of $1,000 is given annually for the best idea. According to Moon Hui Kim, program developer, the benefits far outweigh the $6,000 to $10,000 annual program administration costs.[55]

> **FAST FACT**
>
> In 2000, at the Bic Corporation, 577 out of 684 hourly workers submitted 2,999 suggestions, of which 2,368 were implemented.

Innovations and Patents. For some companies, new inventions and patents are essential to success. Motorola is one such company. It consistently ranks among the top 10 companies awarded U.S. patents each year. To encourage inventors, Motorola pays bonuses to employees when a patent is filed and again when a patent is issued. For inventors receiving their 10th patent, another bonus is awarded. Depending on the company's estimate of the invention's value, these lump sum awards may be in the range of $10,000 to $20,000.[56]

> *"Intellectual property is a relatively new [business] concept, but it's as real and valuable as tangible assets."*
>
> Gary Hoshizaki
> Director of Intellectual Property
> Motorola

Profit Sharing

Introduced first in the Gallatin glasswork factory in New Geneva, Pennsylvania, in 1794, **profit-sharing plans** in American business now number approximately half a million. As defined by the Council of Profit Sharing Industries, these plans include any procedure under which an employer pays or makes available to regular employees, special current or deferred sums based on the profits of the business, in addition to their regular pay.[57]

Economic Objectives. Profit-sharing plans are designed to pay out incentives when the organization is most able to afford them. The plans fall into three categories. **Current distribution plans** provide a percentage of profits to be distributed quarterly or annually to employees. **Deferred distribution plans** place earnings in an escrow fund for distribution upon retirement, termination, death, or disability. These are the fastest-growing type of plan owing to tax advantages. About 20 percent of firms with profit-sharing programs have **combined distribution plans**. These distribute a portion of profits immediately to employees, setting the remaining amount aside in a designated account.

Strategic Objectives. Other than sharing profits, these plans often do not have clear strategic objectives. Furthermore, the motivational potential of deferred plans is questionable because employees may not see the relationship between their performance and the profitability of the firm.

Critics of profit sharing argue that tying pay to achieving more specific strategic objectives is preferable to tying pay directly to profitability. For example, over a period of 14 years, Springfield Remanufacturing has selected 14 different goals based on its analysis of the key weaknesses that interfere with profitability. Each time a new goal is adopted, employees learn about why achieving the goal is important to long-term profitability and what they can do to help the company achieve the goal.[58]

Rob Rodin, CEO of Marshall Industries, argues that it is exactly because so many different specific goals must be met that profit sharing is the way to go. "How do you design an incentive system robust enough to accommodate every change in every customer and every product and every market every day?" he asks. "You can't—you'd be designing it the rest of your life," he concludes. That's why Rodin eliminated all incentives, commissions, bonuses, and achievement awards and replaced them with a simple profit-sharing plan. After six years of experience with profit sharing, he still loves the system. In his mind it has helped rid the organization of all the gamesmanship he used to see—shipping early to meet quotas, pushing costs to the next quarter, and fighting over how to allocate computer system costs, just to name a few.[59]

Egon Zehnder, founder of an international executive recruiting firm, agrees that profit sharing is an effective pay strategy. In his view, it is an excellent way to attract employees who are willing to work for the good of the firm as a whole and screen out self-aggrandizing individuals. Zehnder needs employees who will share information, not hoard it. His firm's compensation plan is simple. In addition to base pay, employees receive equal shares of equity. In addition, they receive pay from two profit-sharing pools.

"At most professional firms, people are paid according to the size of their client billings and how good they are at bringing in new clients. We prefer to [pay] base salaries and share profits."

Egon Zehnder
Founder and Former Chairman
Egon Zehnder International

The profit-sharing pool equals 90 percent of annual profits (10% of profits are put back into the firm). Of the total profit-sharing pool, 60 percent is distributed in equal portions to all employees. The remaining 40 percent is distributed to reward employees for the length of time they have been with the firm. Each year of service (up to a maximum of 15 years) results in a proportionately greater share of profits for the employee. After 37 years of experience with this profit-sharing plan, Zehnder is convinced it's the best way to pay. He acknowledges, however, that recruiting and hiring the right people is also essential to the success of this simple approach to compensation.[60]

> **FAST FACT**
>
> In 2002, WorldatWork estimated that 77% of hourly employees participate in profit-sharing, up from 52% in 1997.

Gainsharing

Gainsharing plans are premised on the assumption that it's possible to reduce costs by eliminating wasted materials and labor, developing new or better products or services, or working smarter. Typically, gainsharing plans involve all employees in a work unit or firm. The median gainsharing payout is 3 percent, substantially less than the average 5 percent merit increase.[61]

The term *gainsharing* was first introduced in 1889 to describe an approach to pay that involved measuring a work unit's costs and productivity and then sharing future gains with employees. The introduction of gainsharing plans has been found to improve productivity in a variety of settings. Presumably, this approach to performance-based pay is effective in part because of the motivational value of the rewards, and in part because employees become actively involved in suggesting new approaches for doing their work more efficiently.[62] Since they were first introduced more than a century ago, three generations of gainsharing plans have evolved.

First-Generation Plans. Two plans—Scanlon and Rucker—were developed in the Depression Era. Both focus on cost savings relative to historical standards. The **Scanlon and Rucker Plans** are built around the following four principles:

- A management philosophy emphasizing employee participation
- A formula to share the benefits of productivity-generated savings among employees and the employer
- Employee committees to evaluate ideas
- A formal system for gathering and implementing employee suggestions on ways to increase productivity or reduce costs.[63]

Even though the Scanlon and Rucker Plans share a common philosophy, they differ in one important aspect: the Scanlon Plan focuses only on labor cost savings. Suppose that the historical costs of labor for your firm are $1 million a year. If actual labor costs are less than anticipated costs ($800,000), a portion ($50,000) of the money saved is placed in a set-aside fund in case labor costs soar in subsequent quarters. The remaining savings ($150,000) is split among the company and the employees. In contrast, the Rucker Plan ties incentives to a wide variety of savings. A ratio is calculated that expresses the value of production required for each dollar of total wages.

Both plans are appropriate in small, mature firms employing fewer than 500 workers. Since standards are based on past performance, simple and accurate measures of performance are needed. Because of the heavy involvement of all employees, the culture must be open, trusting, and participative.[64]

Second-Generation Plans. Beginning in the 1960s, a second generation of gainsharing plans began to emerge. These differ from first-generation plans in several respects. First, they focus on labor *hours* saved, rather than labor *costs* saved. Detailed time-and-motion studies are conducted to develop engineered standards of physical production. Because of the depth of analysis required, employees typically aren't involved in the development of the plan. This may reduce perceptions of fairness.

Unlike first-generation plans, second-generation plans include non-production workers in the measurement of the organization's productivity and in the distribution of variable pay, realized from cost savings. **Improshare** (which stands for improved production through sharing) is typical of second-generation plans. Developed by industrial engineer Mitchell Fein, Improshare has been adopted in a wide array of firms, including service-sector firms such as hospitals and financial institutions. Exhibit 12.12 compares the details of the calculations of the Scanlon, Rucker, and Improshare plans.

FAST FACT

Over 2,000 companies in the United States use gainsharing plans as a form of performance-based pay.

Third-Generation Plans. According to Marc Wallace, who studied new pay practices in 46 firms, a third generation of gainsharing plans emerged during the 1980s. These plans are "so different from first and second generation models that the term gainsharing may no longer be appropriate."[65] Third-generation plans encompass a much broader range of organizational goals. They have definite terms, which support the current business plan.

A plan adopted by a Cleveland steel manufacturer called L-S Electro-Galvanizing Co. illustrates these new plans. L-SE, as the company is known, is a joint venture between the American steel company LTV Corp. and Japan's Sumitomo. The two firms joined forces after American automakers made known their intention to use rust-resistant, electro-galvanized steel in their cars. The technology was available only in Japan at the time the venture was created. L-SE began as a nontraditional workplace with high levels of participation. An important motivator was a gainsharing plan administered by a labor-management committee and applied to all team members equally. The plan capped payouts at 25 percent of an employee's wages and overtime. Objectives, which were defined twice annually and amended if necessary, reflected goals considered important by management and reasonable by employees. Gainsharing payouts have been based largely on production levels. Over time, as productivity levels improved, the formula was gradu-

---

ex 12.12 **Calculations for Selected Gainsharing Plans**

Scalon Plan Base Ratio

[(Sales Dollars – Returned Goods) + Inventory] ÷ [(Cost of Work and Nonwork Time Paid + Pension + Insurance)]

Rucker Plan Base Ratio

(Cost of All Wages and Benefits) ÷ (Sales Dollar Value of Product – Goods Returned – Supplies, Services, and Material)

Improshare Plan Base Formula

[(Standard Value Hours Earned, Current Period) x (Total Actual Hours Worked, Base Period ÷ Total Standard Value Hours Earned, Base Period)] ÷ [(Total Hours Worked, Current Period)] ally adjusted.[66] This tailored approach to the design of gainsharing plans is widespread. The new plans have their roots in Scanlon, Rucker, and Improshare plans, but the variations that have been introduced yield so many different approaches that customized plans are now almost idiosyncratic to each company.[67]

As with Lincoln Electric's plan, this method of compensation works because of other aspects of the total system used for managing human resources in the company. The conditions that support the use of gainsharing include team-based work, broadly defined job responsibilities, and a management philosophy that values employee involvement.

PAY THAT PUTS EARNINGS AT RISK

Merit-based and incentive-based pay systems apply to a large percentage of the workforce. However, sales personnel and high-level executives more frequently have their earnings placed at risk.

Some companies have pushed the notion of at-risk pay throughout the organization. Nucor, a steel mill, is a well-known pioneer of this approach. Factory workers at Nucor's steel mills earn wages set at less than half the typical union rate. At year's end, the company distributes 10 percent of pretax earnings to employees. Bonuses based on the number of tons of acceptable quality steel produced bump up total pay to about 10 percent more than that of comparable unionized workers. The bonuses reflect company productivity levels, but they also encourage individuals to behave responsibly. Workers who are late lose their bonus for the day; workers who are more than 30 minutes late lose their bonus for the week. Managers at Nucor earn bonuses also. The bonuses of department managers are based on return on plant assets and those of plant managers are based on return on equity. The system seems to work. Nucor turns out more than twice as much steel per employee than larger steel companies.[68]

Arguably, Lincoln Electric's pay plan also puts employees' earnings at risk, as does any incentive plan that does not guarantee income that's near the market average. In other words, earnings at risk is a matter of degree. Usually, the degree of risk is most extreme for employees paid on commissions.

Implementing an earnings-at-risk pay plan can be difficult, especially when employees are not familiar with the concept. Thus, prudent organizations introduce such changes cautiously. The feature "Managing Change: Bankers Prefer to Avoid Risk" describes the experience of one organization that experimented with putting pay at risk.

Commissions

Because a large part of a salesperson's job is unsupervised, performance-based compensation programs are useful in directing sales activities.

FAST FACT

With commissions, a men's clothing salesperson at Nordstrom can earn $90,000 even without a profit-sharing bonus.

As companies rethink their strategic objectives, they often evaluate their current pay system for salespeople, who represent the company to their valued customers. IBM's restructuring provides a vivid example. Under Lou Gerstner, IBM has stressed the importance of both customer satisfaction and increased profits. To implement the company's strategy, Gerstner needed salespeople to begin thinking about the implications for IBM of the deals they cut with customers. Simply making a sale to generate revenue wasn't sufficient. To focus the attention of the sales force, IBM

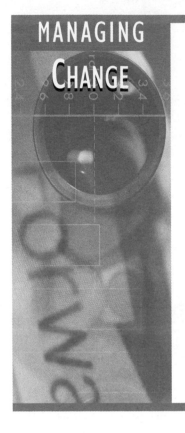

MANAGING CHANGE

Bankers Prefer to Avoid Risk

Earnings-at-risk (EAR) systems have gained popularity in many industries including retail banking because of their potential to reduce fixed costs and ensure long-term employment stability. When a large, publicly held retail bank decided to implement a new EAR pay plan, its financial health was very good, but it anticipated changes in the wind. Consolidation within the industry had begun and only the strongest institutions would survive in the long run. By changing its pay plan, the bank officers hoped they could boost productivity and strengthen the bank's position in the market.

Before the new pay plan was introduced, a traditional "upside earnings" incentive pay plan was in place. Employees received a base salary set at the market rate and they were eligible for quarterly bonuses based on branch performance. While the old plan was still in effect, the bank employees responded to a survey asking about their pay satisfaction. They completed a second survey six months after the new plan went into effect.

The first survey showed that employees were moderately satisfied with how much they earned before the EAR system was implemented (Average = 4.43). They were significantly less satisfied once the EAR was in place (Average = 3.05). The change in pay administration procedures also led Time 2 Average = 2.88). Under the old system, employees were more satisfied with how much they earned than with the pay administration process. Under the new system, employees were equally dissatisfied with both how much they earned and how the pay system was administered. Employees who had been with the bank a long time showed the biggest declines in satisfaction. Surprisingly, dissatisfaction was just as great among employees who were making more money under the new system, compared with those making the same or less.

Further analysis of the survey results showed that, under the EAR plan, employees no longer felt that their individual efforts determined how much pay they earned. They found it difficult to understand how their behavior affected the financial performance measures that were used to measure the organization's success. Based on the level of dissatisfaction revealed by the surveys, the bank officers discontinued the EAR plan and reinstated the incentive pay plan that was previously in effect.

restructured their commission system. Instead of tying only 6 percent of commission pay to profits, the new system tied 60 percent of pay to profits. The other 40 percent was tied to customer satisfaction, in order to reduce the temptation to simply push fast-turnover, high-profit products. The firm supports the pay system by giving salespeople access to relevant information—such as margins for the products they sell. Exhibit 12.13 shows the types of performance results used in pay plans for salespeople.[69] About 30 percent of all sales personnel are paid a straight salary, approximately 20 percent are paid by straight incentives, and more than 50 percent are subject to plans that include a combination of salary and individual or group incentives.[70]

Straight Salary. Paying a salary instead of commissions may be appropriate when the major function of the salesperson is providing customer service or "prospecting new accounts under low-success conditions." Straight salary plans are also appropriate in jobs demanding high technical expertise but little ability to close sales. Consider the job of a product engineer for a software publishing house. Duties of this job might include developing and executing sales and product training programs, participating in trade shows, promoting new products, and meeting with distributors to encourage them to push product lines. In such jobs, a high salary to attract technically competent individuals is more critical than incentives to close the sale.

The advantages of a straight salary program are several. From the salesperson's viewpoint, it takes the ambiguity out of the salary process. If nonsales functions (e.g., paperwork and customer support) are important, salaried sales personnel are more willing to perform them. The drawback is

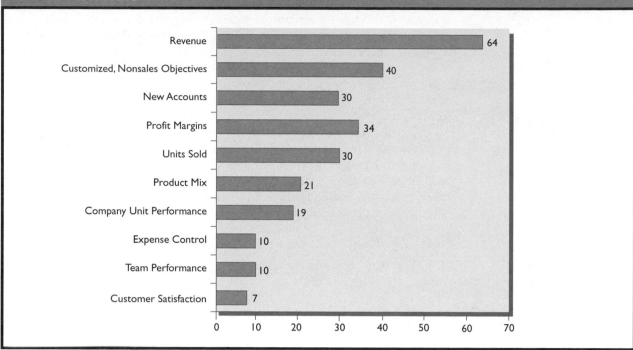

ex 12.13 Performance Results Used to Determine Incentive Pay for Field Sales Personnel

that straight salaries reduce the connection between performance and pay. Commissions make this link directly.

Straight Commission. Usually, the term **commission** refers to pay based on a percentage of the sales price of the product. The percentage received by the salesperson depends on the product being sold, industry practices, the organization's economic conditions, and special pricing during sales promotions. In establishing a sales commission program, the following questions need answering:

- What are the strategic objectives to be achieved?
- What criteria will be used to measure performance?
- Are territories equivalent in sales potential?
- Will commission rates vary by product or vary depending on sales level?
- Will earnings have a cap?
- What will be the timing of commission payments (e.g., monthly or quarterly)?

Under straight commission plans, responsibility for generating an income rests directly on the salesperson. The more sales, the greater the earnings; no sales means no income. When employees accept these as legitimate pay plans, their effect on behavior is enormous. At Nordstrom, where salespeople work entirely on commission, the salespeople earn about twice what they would at a rival's store. Unfortunately, such incentives can be so powerful that they elicit unintended behaviors, as when Sears Auto Centers in California were caught making unnecessary repairs on customers' cars.

Combined Plans. Because of concerns about the negative effects of straight commission plans, more than half of all sales compensation plans combine base salary and commissions. In setting up a combined plan, the critical question is, "What percentage of total compensation should be salary and what percentage should be commission?" The answer depends on the availability of sales criteria (e.g., sales volume, units sold, product mix, retention of accounts, and number of new accounts) and the number of nonsales duties in the job. Commonly, these plans are based on an 80-to-20 salary-to-commission mix. However, organizations wishing to push sales over customer service functions may utilize different ratios: 60-to-40 or even 50-to-50.

The commission portion of the sales compensation can be established in two ways. The simplest is to combine the commission with a draw. The salesperson receives the draw, or specific salary, each payday. Quarterly or monthly, the total commission due the salesperson is calculated. The amount taken as a draw is deducted, with the salesperson receiving the remainder. Alternatively, bonuses can be given when sales reach a specific level.

Stock Ownership

> **FAST FACT**
>
> When Howard Schultz founded Starbucks, he offered stock options to *all* employees as a way to enhance employees' self-esteem.

Companies use many different approaches to encourage their employees to own company stock and so take part as an owner of the company. One approach is to simply give employees stock awards outright, for example upon being hired, on their annual anniversary date, as an award for achieving a goal, and so on. Another approach is to grant a **stock option,** which gives the employee a right to buy stock during a specified time period or under other specified conditions. Only some uses of stock awards and stock options represent performance-based pay plans, however. And fewer still truly qualify as earnings-at-risk pay plans. Nevertheless, we discuss them here because a company often *claims* that stock options issued to executives put their earnings at risk and are a form of performance-based pay.

Broad-Based Plans. **Broad-based stock ownership plans** are designed to make stock ownership appealing to all employees. The National Center for Employee Ownership defines a plan as broad based if the company grants stock to at least 50 percent of the workforce. UPS has a broad-based stock ownership plan. Each year, 15 percent of UPS's pretax profit is used to buy company stock and distribute it to entry-level supervisors on up. Other companies with broad-based stock ownership plans include PepsiCo, Starbucks, and Whirlpool.[71]

Employee stock ownership plans (ESOPs) are one type of broad-based stock ownership plan. ESOPs grant shares of stock to employees as a means of long-term savings and retirement. They usually do not link the amount of stocks that can be purchased or the purchase price to individual or group performance indicators. Thus, ESOPs are usually treated as an employee benefit rather than as a performance-based reward. Currently, about 11,000 ESOP plans are in place within the United States, covering about 9 million employees. This benefit can be of considerable value to employees who work in companies that perform well. At Home Depot, for example, more than 1,000 employees became millionaires in a single year recently.[72]

> **FAST FACT**
>
> High-tech stock prices plunged in 2000, and so did the value of employees' stock options. At Amazon.com, the drop was 70%; at Yahoo!, 60%; at Dell and Microsoft, 50%; at Intel, 40%.

In contrast to ESOPs, stock option plans give employees the opportunity to buy the organization's stock at a later date but at a price established when the option is granted. Over a period of years, employees are given the right to buy stock in the future at today's price. Most options last 10 years, with executives typically allowed to exercise half their options after two years and the entire grant after three.[73] Companies with broad-based stock option plans include Pfizer and Eli Lilly. Broad-based stock option plans—that is, those designed to distribute stock as a reward for all employees—seldom put earnings at risk. At best, such plans use stock options as an incentive that's added on to a pay plan that pegs base pay at near-market rates.

> **FAST FACT**
>
> About 30% of large U.S. companies have established broad-based stock option plans but only about 10% have implemented them.

Stock Options for Executives. The backbone of executive compensation programs, the awarding of stock options, is premised on the assumption that the plans encourage executives to "think like owners." After all, they profit only if the stock price goes up. In recent years the size of stock options has exploded. For senior executives, the total value of stock awards often exceeds the combined value of their base salaries and all annual incentives. Another trend is the increased eligibility for stock options among employees at deeper levels in the organization. These trends are fueled partly by advantageous accounting and tax rules, and partly by a belief in the motivational value of stock ownership.[74]

> **FAST FACT**
>
> A survey of nearly 3,000 companies revealed that more than 50% give stock grants to officers and executives, fewer than 10% give them to nonexempt employees, and about 25% give them to exempt employees.

Exhibit 12.14 lists several forms of stock-based pay.[75] Note that the various plans differ with regard to the time frame for vesting, whether vesting is contingent on attaining performance goals, and pricing. When stock option plans use performance measures to determine the distribution or vesting of stock options, they're using stock ownership as a form of pay for performance. The performance measures used most frequently to award stock options are traditional accounting measures, such as cumulative profit and return on equity. When such stocks also represent a substantial portion of pay, they put earnings at risk.

> **FAST FACT**
>
> Stock options of some sort are offered by most major companies in the United States and in France, but they are seldom offered in Japan and Mexico.

Time-Restricted Stock Options. Companies may place a variety of restrictions to limit the conditions under which stocks become vested with employees. **Time-restricted stock options** require some time to elapse after the stock is granted before vesting occurs, and during that time the employee must remain at the company. In most cases, employees are required to work three to five years before they are vested in the plan. If the employee leaves the company before the required time of service elapses, the stock must be returned to the company. The intent of time restrictions is usually to deter turnover.

Performance-Based Plans. Vesting may also be restricted based on performance.[76] Three common approaches to performance-based options are performance vesting, premium-priced options, and indexed options.

With **performance-vested stock options**, vesting occurs upon achieving specified goals. Often the goals are defined as changes in the price of the company's stock. Pegging the vesting schedule to growth in earnings per share is another method. For example, 1,000 options could be vested according to a schedule determined by increases in the price of the stock. The first 200 shares might vest after a $5 increase in stock price, the next 200 might vest after a $10 increase, and so on. Though straightforward, the problem with this approach is that, under current accounting rules, performance-based vesting requires a charge to earnings, while time-based vesting does not. Nevertheless, about half of the firms in the *Fortune* 250 have adopted this

ex 12.14 Explanation of Selected Stock-Based Pay Awards

Type of Plan	How It Works
Time-Restricted Stock Option	The basic "plain vanilla" plan: for a given period of time, employee may purchase a stock at a specified price.
Time-Based Restricted Stock	Award of shares with restrictions that require a predetermined length of service to elapse before vesting occurs. If employee leaves, stock is returned to the company.
Performance-Vested Stock Option	A stock option that vests upon the achievement of specified goals.
Performance-Vested Restricted Stock	Award of shares with restrictions that requires the achievement of prespecified goals. Failure to attain goals in a specified time period may result in forfeiture.
Performance-Accelerated Stock Option	Award of shares that has a set vesting schedule but vesting may occur more rapidly if specified performance goals are met. If performance goals are not achieved, stock becomes vested with employee nevertheless.
Indexed Stock Option	Employee has the option to purchase stock at a price that fluctuates based on a specified standard index or a group of peer companies.
Premium-Priced Stock Option	Stock options with an exercise price that is above the market price at the time of the grant.

approach. Dow Chemical is an example. Dow adopted performance-vested stock options for its top 100 executives in the mid-1990s to support its strategic objective of aggressive growth.[77]

To take advantage of the tax laws while also rewarding performance rather than length of tenure, some companies use **performance-accelerated stock options**. With this approach, the basis for vesting is still defined by length of service, but the length of service required before vesting is shortened if performance hurdles are met. In recent years, about 10 percent of *Fortune* 200 companies used performance vesting or performance-accelerated vesting. Typical performance hurdles include stock price and performance relative to peer companies.

The principle behind **premium-priced stock options** is similar to performance vesting, but the mechanism is slightly different. With this method, employees are granted options at an above-market price. Thus, employees won't want to exercise their option until the price advances to a level above that price. For example, if options are granted with an exercise price of $50, but the current market price is only $40, employees would not be able to realize any reward until shareholders realized a 25 percent gain. To further motivate employees, the company might place a time limit on the performance goal. For example, the option could expire in five years if the premium price hasn't been obtained. This approach is used by about 5 percent of *Fortune* 200 companies.

Indexed stock options are designed to ensure that employees are not rewarded (or, in theory, punished) merely due to a robust or retreating economy. They achieve this by indexing the exercise price to an external standard, such as the Russell 2000, the S&P 500, or the Dow Jones Industrial Average. This approach would seem to be the best method for motivating employees to ensure that shareholders receive the best possible return on their investment. But it is seldom used, presumably because it requires a charge to earnings and so does not enjoy the tax advantages associated with other approaches.

> **FAST FACT**
>
> Companies such as Kellogg's, Alcoa and Citi-Group reload options; that is, when an executive exercises options (s)he gets another equal amount of options.

Underwater Stock Options. Stock options are attractive when a company's value is on the rise, but steep declines in stock prices create special problems. Underwater stock options have an exercise price that is above the market value of a company's stocks. In this situation, the paper value of a reward that was granted in the past declines. Underwater stocks are especially problematic for employers who use stock options as a means of hanging on to employees. Thinking that employees may be more likely to leave when the paper value of their options declines, many companies responded by repricing employees' options or making new grants priced at a much lower level. Defenders of these tactics argue that employers have little choice if they want to hold on to their employees. Critics contend that repricing defeats the original purpose. As one person put it, "It's a case of heads I win, tails I win." Furthermore, the practice appears to be ineffective for retaining key executives.[78]

> **FAST FACT**
>
> At Bay State Gas Co., nobody gets any options unless the company's total return to shareholders beats that of at least half of 30 other comparable utility companies for at least three years.

INTERNET RESOURCES 12.C

Incentive Plans and Earnings at Risk

At our Web site, http://jackson.swcollege.com/, you can:

1. Learn about using incentive pay at some of the firms discussed in this section by visiting their company home pages:

   Continental Airlines

   Valassis

   Starbucks

2. Learn more about using merit pay and incentives to pay educators based on performance, an issue that has been discussed at length in the field of education, by visiting the home pages of

   The American Federation of Teachers

   The National Education Association

3. Learn more about ESOPs from the National Council on Employee Ownership.

4. See information about goalsharing, gainsharing, Scanlon Plans, and related forms of performance-based pay, available from

   Scanlon Leadership

   The ESOP Association

   The Employee Involvement Association

   The European Association of Shareownership

THE HR TRIAD AT WORK

As the discussion so far illustrates, designing and administering an effective performance-based pay system requires close cooperation among all players in the HR Triad. In particular, line managers and HR professionals must work together to ensure that performance-based pay practices support the overall strategic objectives of the organization, as well as the specific strategic goals of smaller units and teams within the organization.

Changes in strategic objectives often trigger organizations to scrutinize and redesign their compensation systems. In recent years, changes in total compensation systems have often been directed toward creating a tighter link between performance and pay. In many organizations, such efforts represent major changes in the organization's culture. Thus, for many line managers and HR professionals, the roles and responsibilities associated with performance-based pay systems include those associated with creating organizational change, as described in Chapter 5.

As is true for any component of the HR system, the ultimate effectiveness of any performance-based pay system depends on whether employees fully understand and accept the system. Thus, seeking and using the input of the employees who will be affected by performance-based pay is an important responsibility of line managers and HR professionals. The importance of involving employees in the design of performance-based systems is amplified when the employees who will be affected come from diverse national cultures. Continuous monitoring of employee satisfaction levels as well as changes in key behaviors and performance results is needed in order to detect whether an incentive system is having its intended effects. The introduction of new performance-based pay systems often has unintended consequences, which can be quite disruptive if not detected quickly. These issues are summarized in the feature "The HR Triad: Roles and Responsibilities for Using Performance-Based Pay to Enhance Motivation."

SUMMARY

Performance-based pay systems continue to attract the attention of many human resource managers, and line managers continue to ask whether pay can be used to motivate their employees. The success of many incentive plans indicates that pay can motivate job performance. Nevertheless, many problems can arise because of the myriad issues associated with the design and implementation of performance-based pay systems.

To be effective, performance-based pay systems must successfully address several challenges. Perhaps most importantly, a valid and fair performance measurement system serves as the foundation of a performance-based pay system. Other challenges include aligning employee behaviors and performance with the organization's strategic objectives, gaining employee acceptance and buy-in for the system, and accurately predicting the cost implications of performance-based pay. If an organization has valid performance measures, and if everyone thinks the system is fair and tied to the objectives of the organization, paying for performance should increase profitability.

Performance-based pay can take many forms. Some forms link pay to the performance of individuals, while others link pay to the performance of

Roles and Responsibilities for Using Performance-Based Pay to Enhance Motivation

THE HR TRIAD

LINE MANAGERS	HR PROFESSIONALS	EMPLOYEES
• Work with HR professionals to establish the strategic objectives of performance-based pay (PBP). • Work with HR professionals to establish the performance criteria to be linked to pay and the methods to assess performance. • Understand the alternative methods of PBP. • Assist with communicating the objectives and processes for PBP. • Work with HR professionals to ensure strategic alignment and integration among all PBP plans used throughout the organization. • Implement PBP fairly. • Assist HR in monitoring and revising PBP as needed.	• Work with line managers to establish the strategic objectives of PBP. • Work with line managers to establish the performance criteria to be linked to pay and the methods to assess performance. • Provide expert knowledge regarding the available methods of PBP. • Work with accounting and finance staff to assess the cost implications of PBP. • Monitor the effects of PBP on employee satisfaction, behavior, and results, and recommend revisions to the PBP system as needed. • Ensure the PBP system is integrated and consistent with other components of the total HR system. • Develop and deliver training and communications to ensure that line managers and other employees understand the PBP system's objectives and procedures.	• Develop a comprehensive understanding of the strategic objectives of PBP. • Make sure you accurately understand the performance criteria that will be used to determine your PBP. • Assist line managers and HR professionals in identifying potential negative consequences of specific PBP plans. • Be alert to dysfunctional attempts to "game" PBP systems, and work to improve PBP that causes such dysfunction. • Perhaps assist in administering PBP for team members. • Suggest improvements in the components of the total PBP. • Adapt to needed changes in the PBP.

teams or the entire organization. Some forms permanently affect the base pay of employees, while others have no implications for base pay. Some forms create opportunities for upside rewards without creating any downside risks, while others put substantial portions of an employee's expected pay at risk. Some forms emphasize short-term performance and offer employees immediate rewards, while others focus employees on longer-term results and defer rewards far into the future.

Choosing the best methods of performance-based pay can be difficult. The effects of any of the available methods depend on many factors, including the level at which job performance can accurately be measured (individual, department, or organization); the extent of cooperation needed between departments; the willingness of managers to take the time needed to design, implement, monitor, and continuously improve one or several systems; and the culture and degree of trust in the organization. Add to these the need to ensure alignment between the performance-based pay system and all other components of the HR system, and the true magnitude of the challenge becomes apparent. Nevertheless, if the current trend continues, employees in many different industries can expect to see increasing use of performance-based pay.

TERMS TO REMEMBER

broad-based stock ownership plans
combined distribution plans
commission
current distribution plans
deferred distribution plans
differential piece rate plans
earnings-at-risk plans
eligibility rules
employee stock ownership plans
   (ESOPs)
gainsharing plans
goalsharing
Improshare
incentive pay plans
indexed stock options

merit pay plans
performance-accelerated stock
   options
performance-based pay
performance-vested stock options
premium-priced stock options
profit-sharing plans
Scanlon and Rucker Plans
standard hour plans
stock option
straight piecework plans
team incentives
time-restricted stock options
underwater stock options

DISCUSSION QUESTIONS

1. Describe in detail all the parts of compensation linked to performance at Lincoln Electric. How much credit for Lincoln's success do you give to the company's performance-based pay system?
2. What are the major disadvantages of the three major forms of performance-based pay for employees (merit, incentives, earnings at risk)?
3. Describe an experience you have had in which pay was linked to your performance. Explain the key features of the system used to determine your performance and pay. Did the system work? If not, why not?
4. Under what conditions would you expect a performance-based pay system to have the greatest likelihood of success?
5. Debate the following assertion: If selection and placement decisions are made effectively, differences in the level of performance exhibited by employees should be relatively small; therefore, a performance-based pay system isn't needed and may even be disruptive.
6. When you work on projects as a member of a team, what percentage of the rewards you receive do you prefer to have depend on your own individual performance versus the performance of the team as a whole? Explain why. Does the type of team or the type of project affect your preference? Explain.
7. What does it mean to put earnings at risk? List the potential costs and benefits of placing a substantial percentage of pay at risk for *all* employees in the following types of organizations: a hospital, a restaurant, a brokerage firm, a fashion design house.
8. Is repricing an appropriate response to underwater stock options? If yes, under what conditions do you think it is appropriate? If no, explain your logic.

PROJECTS TO EXTEND YOUR LEARNING

1. *Managing Diversity.* Interview two or three employees of a company in your area. Ask whether they are paid on the basis of their performance. If so, ask how performance is measured and what percentage of total pay is based on performance. If they are not so paid, find out if the

employees would like to be paid for performance, and if so, under what type of plan—merit, incentive, or earning at risk. Identify the reasons why employees prefer one type of plan over another.

2. *Integration and Application*

    a. Compare and contrast the use of incentive pay at Lincoln Electric and Southwest Airlines. Overall, which plan do you think is more effective? Why?

    b. Anthony Massaro has said that Lincoln Electric may gradually move toward having a more traditional pay plan. What do you think he means by this? What strategic objectives would lead this company to conclude that a more traditional pay plan would be more effective? How do you think Lincoln Electric's employees would react to such a change? Why?

THE TIME CLOCK

case study

Susan Crandall was feeling good about her new position at Western National Bank. Susan, a seven-year employee at Western, had come a long way from her starting position as a teller to her present position as human resource manager, thanks in many respects to her predecessor, Anna Bavetti.

Anna had recently resigned from the bank to take a position with a local computer software company that was experiencing explosive growth. This company recognized that it needed to systematize its staffing practices, so when Anna learned of the opportunity, she jumped. Anna was frustrated by what she considered conservative and stodgy management at the bank, so a change in scenery was a welcome relief.

Anna had begun at Western as an assistant to the then HR manager Nancy Hyer. Anna had an MBA degree from North Carolina and an undergraduate degree from Grinnell College. Anna quickly realized that her technical skills were superior to Nancy's, but she admired Nancy's street smarts and willingness to battle the CEO of the bank over new initiatives in the HR area. Nancy had put in a performance appraisal plan and an absenteeism plan before transferring to the trust department with what was touted as a promotion.

Anna, though, didn't see the move as a promotion. In her estimation, Nancy had gotten too strong and was creating a lot of waves for the top brass at the bank, who were unwilling to move at the pace that Nancy had set. When the president of Western, Larry Wilson, asked Anna to assume the role of assistant vice president of personnel, Anna welcomed the opportunity to continue the initiatives begun by Nancy.

Anna decided that she was going to undertake two goals immediately. First, she was going to begin developing Susan. Nancy was too hard on Susan, in Anna's estimation. Although Susan didn't have a college degree (she had had to drop out because her mother was ill), she had common sense and extremely good people skills. Over the next year, Anna progressively increased Susan's responsibilities by involving her in applicant screening and interviewing and including her on project assignments. Over time, Susan and Anna developed a teamlike approach to their work and learned to rely on each other to keep the HR management office functioning smoothly.

When Susan learned of Anna's departure, she was saddened but not surprised. Anna always seemed too liberal and progressive for upper management of the bank. Anna valued people and looked for the best in them. Anna, more than the other officers at the bank, seemed genuinely concerned about the welfare of the employees, especially the mostly nonexempt employee workforce. Susan was flabbergasted, though, when Larry Wilson called her into his office and asked her to assume Anna's job. Her pay would increase by 150 percent. Although the job would mean longer hours and more responsibilities, under Anna's tutelage, Susan felt confident that she could rise to the occasion.

Susan wanted more than anything to carry through on Anna's second goal, which was to link the performance evaluation system developed by Nancy to the annual pay increases. The bank had entered an era of competition with other banks and savings and loans, so productivity was a major concern for the bank. Besides cutting staff to the minimum, Susan believed that in the long run, linking pay to effort and performance would encourage productivity among all employees. Susan believed that Western's staff were hard working and would welcome the opportunity to see their pay linked to their performance.

Susan noticed it was almost 5 P.M. and she needed to speak with Gerry Latham, vice president for operations, regarding her proposed merit plan, which would influence his group the most. As she passed the elevators, she noticed several employees waiting beside the time clock. It was common practice for the nonexempts to wait for a seemingly inordinate amount of time for the elevator to arrive on the fifth floor of the bank building. A common practice was to wait until the elevator bell chimed and the doors began to open before clocking out.

As several of the employees hurriedly punched the clock and dashed to the elevator, Larry Wilson appeared behind Susan. Larry called out to Susan, who was deep in thought about how to present her merit plan to Gerry Latham. "Susan, did you see that?" questioned Larry. "I'm sorry, Larry, I was lost in thought. What are you talking about?" replied Susan. As the elevator doors closed, Larry picked up his voice in obvious irritation. "I think those employees would just as soon cheat us if they're charging their wait time on the elevators. How do we know that they're not trying to cheat us in the morning when they clock in or when they return from lunch late and have a coworker punch them in? Susan, I want you to investigate this tomorrow, first thing. This kind of fraud has got to stop immediately." Oh boy, thought Susan. How am I going to defuse this bomb? As Susan started back down the hall toward Gerry Latham's office, she began to understand the frustration that had occasionally leaked through Anna's otherwise calm exterior when she occupied Susan's job.

QUESTIONS

1. What strategic considerations support the concept of a performance-based pay plan in banking?

2. At a minimum, what HR activities must exist prior to implementing a performance-based pay plan in a bank or elsewhere?

3. Does the culture at Western support a performance-based pay plan?

4. How should Susan respond to Larry's directive to investigate the time clock fraud?

ENDNOTES

1 B. Kraretnik, "That Money Show" (PBS Program, August 20, 2001); Personal conversation between authors and Lincoln Electric officials, August 27, 2001; R. Hodgetts, "A Conversation with Donald F. Hastings of the Lincoln Electric Company," *Organizational Dynamics* (Winter 1997): 68–74; C. Wiley, "Incentive Plan Pushes Production," *Personnel Journal* (August 1993): 86–92.

2 J. Juergens, "When the Going Gets Tough Incentives Get Going," *Awards & Incentives* (July 2001): 84–89; J. E. Juergens, "Motivating Survivors," *Awards & Incentives* (July 2001): 92–99; E. E. Lawler, III, *Rewarding Excellence* (San Francisco: Jossey-Bass, 2000); B. L. Hopkins and T. C. Mawhinney, *Pay for Performance: History, Controversy and Evidence* (Binghamton, NY: Haworth Press, 1992).

3 D. Brown, "The Third Way: The Future of Pay and Reward Strategies in Europe," *WorldatWork Journal* (Second Quarter 2000): 15–25.

4 For an excellent brief historical summary, see G. T. Milkovich and J. Stevens, "From Pay to Rewards: 100 Years of Change," *ACA Journal* (First Quarter 2000): 6–18.

5 P. Digh, "The Next Challenge: Holding People Accountable," *HR Magazine: Diversity Agenda* (October 1998): 63–69; S. N. Mehta, "Diversity Pays," *Wall Street Journal* (April 11, 1996): R12.

6 K. A. Brown and V. L. Huber, "Lowering Floors and Raising Ceilings: A Longitudinal Assessment of the Effects of an Earnings-at-Risk Plan on Pay Satisfaction," *Personnel Psychology* 45 (June 1992): 279–311.

7 I. T. Kay, "High CEO Pay Helps the U.S. Economy Thrive," *Wall Street Journal* (February 23, 1998): A22.

8 S. Scholl, "Allstate Pay for Performance Methodology Rewards Excellence," *ACA News* (September 1998): 28–31.

9 G. D. Jenkins, Jr., A. Mitra, N. Gupta, and J. D. Shaw, "Are Financial Incentives Related to Performance? A Meta-Analytic Review of Empirical Research," *Journal of Applied Psychology* 83(5) (1998): 777–787; J. S. Kane and K. A. Freeman, "A Theory of Equitable Performance Standards," *Journal of Management* 23(1) (1997): 37–58.

10 C. M. Solomon, "Using Cash Drives Strategic Chance," *Workforce* (February 1998): 77–81; P. K. Zingheim and J. R. Schuster, "Pay People Right," *WorldatWork Journal* (Second Quarter 2000): 42–50. For recent research on how the change orientation of a firm's strategy is related to the use of incentives, see B. K. Boyd and A. Salamin, "Strategic Reward Systems: A Contingency Model of Pay System Design," *Strategic Management Journal* 22 (2001): 777–792.

11 R. Ferracone and B. Masuda, "It's the New Economy: Who Said Anything About Returns?" *WorldatWork Journal* (Fourth Quarter 2000): 55–60.

12 H. L. Tosi, S. Werner, J. P. Katz, and L. R. Gomez-Mejia, "How Much Does Performance Matter? A Meta-Analysis of CEO Pay Studies," *Journal of Management* 26 (2000): 301–339.

13 R. D. Banker, S-Y Lee, G. Potter, and D. Srinivasan, "Contextual Analysis of Performance Impacts of Outcome-Based Incentive Compensation," *Academy of Management Journal* 39 (1996): 920–948.

14 J. R. Deckop, R. Mangel, and C. Cirka, "Getting More than You Pay For: Organizational Citizenship Behavior and Pay-for-Performance Plans,"

Academy of Management Journal 41 (1999): 420–428; G. D. Jenkins, Jr. et al., "Are Financial Incentives Related to Performance? A Meta-Analytic Review"; N. Gupta and A. Mitra, "The Value of Financial Incentives," *ACA Journal* (Autumn 1998): 58–65.

15 L. Lavelle, "Undermining Pay for Performance," *Business Week* (January 15, 2001): 70–71; A. Kohn, "Why Incentive Plans Cannot Work," *Harvard Business Review* (September-October 1993): 54–63.

16 E. Deci, R. Koestner, and R. Ryan, "A Meta-Analytic Review of Experiments Examining the Effects of Extrinsic Rewards on Intrinsic Motivation," *Psychological Bulletin* 125(6) (1999): 627–668; E. Deci, R. Koestner, and R. Ryan, "The Undermining Effect Is a Reality After All—Extrinsic Rewards, Task Interest, and Self-Determination: Reply to Eisenberger, Pierce, and Cameron (1999) and Lepper, Henderlong, and Gingras (1999)," *Psychological Bulletin* 125(6) (1999): 692–700; R. Eisenberger, W. Pierce, and J. Cameron, "Effects of Reward on Intrinsic Motivation—Negative, Neutral, and Positive: Comment on Deci, Koestner, and Ryan (1999)," *Psychological Bulletin* 125(6) (1999): 677–691; M. Lepper, J. Henderlong, and I. Gingras, "Understanding the Effects of Extrinsic Rewards on Intrinsic Motivation—Uses and Abuses of Meta-Analysis: Comment on Deci, Koestner, and Ryan (1999)," *Psychological Bulletin* 125(6) (1999): 669–676; R. Eisenberger and J. Cameron, "Detrimental Effects of Reward," *American Psychologist* 51 (November 1996): 1153–1166; see also W. Van Eerde and H. Thierry, "Vroom's Expectancy Models and Work-Related Criteria: A Meta-Analysis," *Journal of Applied Psychology* 81 (1996): 575–586.

17 J. Van Scotter, S. J. Motowidlo, and T. Cross, "Effects of Task Performance and Contextual Performance on Systemic Rewards," *Journal of Applied Psychology* 85(4) (2000): 526–535; P. R. J. Greene, "Effective Variable Compensation Plans," *ACA Journal* (Spring 1997): 32–39.

18 S. J. Berman, "Using the Balance Scorecard in Strategic Compensation," *ACA News* (June 1998): 16–19.

19 P. Pascarella, "Compensating Teams," *Across the Board* (February 1997): 16–22; see also D. Knight, C. Durham, and E. E. Locke, "The Relationship of Team Goals, Incentives, and Efficacy to Strategic Risk, Tactical Implementation, and Performance," *Academy of Journal Management* 44(2) (2001): 326–338.

20 J. Fierman, "The Perilous New World of Fair Pay," *Fortune* (June 13, 1994): 58–59.

21 J. B. Wood, "Customer Satisfaction and Loyalty," *ACA Journal* (Summer 1998): 48–60.

22 R. J. Greene, "Improving Merit Pay Plan Effectiveness," *ACA News* (April 1998): 26–29.

23 B. Gerhart, "Designing Reward Systems: Balancing Result and Behaviors," in C. H. Fay, M. A. Thompson, and D. Knight, *The Executive Handbook on Compensation: Linking Strategic Rewards to Business Performance* (New York: Free Press, 2001): 214–237.

24 Hay Group, *The Hay Report: Compensation and Benefits for 1998 and Beyond* (New York: The Hay Group, 1998).

25 J. Kerr, "Diversification Strategies and Managerial Rewards: An Empirical Study," *Academy of Management Journal* 28 (1985): 155–179; G. T. Milkovich and J. M. Newman, *Compensation* (Homewood, IL: BPI-Irwin, 1999); E. E. Lawler III, *Pay and Organizational Development* (Reading, MA: Addison-Wesley, 1981).

26 C. Gomez, B. Kirkman, and D. Shapiro, "The Impact of Collectivism and In-Group/Out-Group Membership on the Evaluation Generosity of Team Members," *Academy of Management Journal* 43(6) (2000): 1097–1106; F. Moussa, "Determinants, Process, and Consequences of Personal Goals and Performance," *Journal of Management* 26(6) (2000): 1259–1285; P. M. Wright et al., "Productivity and Extra-Role Behavior: The Effects of Goals and Incentives on Spontaneous Helping," *Journal of Applied Psychology* 78 (1993): 374–381.

27 L. Lavelle, "The Gravy Train Is Slowing," *Business Week* (April 2, 2001): 44; B. Sosnin, "A Pat(ent) on the Back," *HR Magazine* (March 2000): 107–112; B. Gerhart and G. T. Milkovich, "Organizational Differences in Managerial Compensation and Financial Performance," *Academy of Management Review* 33 (1990): 663–691.

28 K. Bradsher, "Efficiency on Wheels," *New York Times* (June 16, 2000): C1, C8; B. Flannigan, "Turnaround from Feedback," *HR Focus* (October 1997): 3.

29 S. Gates, "Aligning Performance Measures and Incentives in European Companies," *WorldatWork Journal* (Third Quarter 2000): 19–26; C. C. Chen, "New Trends in Rewards Allocation Preferences: A Sino-U.S. Comparison," *Academy of Management Journal* 38 (1995): 408–428; see also Y. P. Hau and R. M. Steers, "Cultural Influences on the Design of Incentive Systems: The Case of East Asia," *Asia Pacific Journal of Management* 10 (1996): 71–85; C. E. Rusbult, C. A. Insko, and Y-H W. Lin, "Seniority-Based Reward Allocation in the United States and Taiwan," *Social Psychology Quarterly* 58 (1995): 13–30.

30 J. K. Giacobbe-Miller, D. J. Miller, and V. V. Victorov, "A Comparison of Russian and U.S. Pay Association Decisions, Distributive Justice Judgments, and Productivity Under Different Pay Conditions," *Personnel Psychology* 51 (1998): 137–163.

31 D. G. Goodall, "Global Employee-Based Equity Plans—Can They Work for Your Company?" in C. Reynolds (ed.), *Guide to Global Compensation and Benefits,* 2d ed. (New York: Harcourt, 2001): 121–158.

32 "Policy Guide: Incentive Pay Can Bring Many Rewards," *Bulletin to Management* (June 5, 1997): 184; "Policy Guide: Employers Use Pay to Lever Performance," *Bulletin to Management* (August 21, 1997): 272.

33 C. M. Ellis and C. L. Palus, "Blazing a Trail to Broad-Based Incentives: Lessons from Two Leading Manufacturing Companies," *WorldatWork Journal* (Fourth Quarter 2000): 33–41.

34 M. Frase-Blunt, "What Goes Up May Come Down," *HR Magazine* (August 2001): 85–90.

35 R. Gherson, "Getting the Pay Thing Right," *Workspan* (June 2000): 47–51; G. Flynn, "Your Grand Plan for Incentive Compensation May Yield a Grand Lawsuit," *Workforce* (July 1997): 89–92.

36 R. Sharpe, "As Leaders, Women Rule," *Business Week* (November 20, 2000): 75–84; T. Lewin, "Women Losing Ground to Men in Widening Income Difference," *New York Times* (September 15, 1997): A1, A6.

37 R. L. Heneman, "Merit Pay," in C. H. Fay et al., *The Executive Handbook on Compensation,* 447–465; P. Burrows, "A Self-Inflicted Bonus Cut," *Business Week* (December 18, 2000): 12; R. Wood, P. Atkins, and J. Bright, "Bonuses, Goals, and Instrumentality Effects," *Journal of Applied Psychology* 84 (1999): 703–720; D. Eskew and R. L. Heneman, "A Survey of Merit Pay Plan Effectiveness: End of the Line for Merit Pay or Hope for Improvement?" *Human Resource Planning* 19(2) (1996): 11–18.

38 C. Peck, *Variable Pay: New Performance Rewards* (New York: The Conference Board, 1990).

39 S. Scholl, "Allstate Pay for Performance Methodology Rewards Excellence," *ACA News* (September 1998): 28–31.

40 P. D. Sweeney, "Counting the Till, Then Trolling for New Accounts," *New York Times* (June 14, 2000): B2.

41 W. B. Abernathy, "Linking Performance Scorecards to Profit-Indexed Performance Pay," *ACA News* (April 1998): 23–25.

42 I. T. Kay, "High CEO Pay Helps the U.S. Economy Thrive," *Wall Street Journal* (February 2, 1998): A22.

43 L. Lavelle, "The Gravy Train Is Slowing," *Business Week* (April 2, 2001): 44.

44 M. Jensen and K. Murphy, "Performance Pay and Top Management Incentives," *Journal of Political Economy* 98(2) (1990): 225–264; M. Bloom and G. T. Milkovich, "Relationships Among Risks, Incentive Pay and Organizational Performance," *Academy of Management Journal* 41 (1998): 283–297.

45 G. E. Ledford and E. Hawk, "Compensation Strategy: A Guide for Senior Managers," *ACA Journal* (First Quarter 2000): 28–38; J. Reingold, "Executive Pay: Tying Pay to Performance Is a Great Idea. But Stock-Option Deals Have Compensation Out of Control," *Business Week* (April 21, 1997): 58–66; T. A. Stewart, "CEO Pay: Mom Wouldn't Approve,"

Fortune (March 31, 1997): 119-120; J. Reingold, "Even Executives Are Wincing at Executive Pay," *Business Week* (May 12, 1997): 40–43; J. A. Byrne, "Smoke, Mirrors, and the Boss's Paycheck," *Business Week* (October 13, 1997): 63; W. Sanders, "Behavioral Responses of CEOs to Stock Ownership and Stock Option Pay," *Academy of Management Journal* 44(3) (2001): 477–492.

46 S. Tully, "A Better Taskmaster Than the Market?" *Fortune* (October 26, 1998): 277, 286; T. Jackson, "How EVA Measures Up," *Financial Times* (October 7, 1996): 10; S. Tully, "The Real Key to Creating Wealth," *Fortune* (September 20, 1993): 38–44.

47 S. E. Gross and S. P. Leffler, "Team Pay," in C. H. Fay et al., *The Executive Handbook on Compensation,* 465–485; E. E. Lawler III and S. G. Cohen, "Designing Pay Systems for Teams," *ACA Journal* (Autumn 1992): 6–18; C. Meyer, "How the Right Measures Help Teams Excel," *Harvard Business Review* (May/June 1994): 95–103.

48 J. Davis, "Retaining Your Hot Skills Employees—Use Dollars AND Sense," *ACA Journal* (First Quarter 2000): 47–56; B. Nelson, "Does One Reward Fit All?" *Workforce* (February 1997): 67–70.

49 C. Garvey, "Goalsharing Scores," *HR Magazine* (April 2000): 99–106.

50 Lawler and Cohen, "Designing Pay Systems for Teams," 6–16.

51 E. Hollensbe and J. Guthrie, "Group Pay-For-Performance Plans: The Role of Spontaneous Goal Setting," *Academy of Management Review* 25(4) (2000): 854–872; J. S. DeMatteo, L. T. Eby, and E. Sundstrom, "Team-Based Rewards: Current Empirical Evidence and Directions for Future Research," *Research in Organizational Behavior* 20 (1998): 141–183; P. K. Zingheim and J. R. Schuster, "Best Practices for Small-Team Pay," *ACA Journal* (Spring 1997): 40–49; J. S. DeMatteo, M. C. Rush, E. Sundstrom, and L. T. Eby, "Factors Related to the Successful Implementation of Team-Based Rewards," *ACA Journal* (Winter 1997): 16–27.

52 R. K. Platt, "Driving Change—'Account Teams' Help Company to Fly into the Next Century," *ACA News* (January 1996): 17–21.

53 There have been hundreds of laboratory studies on the effects of team-based rewards, and these suggest that they can be effective. But studies in the field show mixed results, due perhaps to challenges in addressing all of the key design issues. For a complete review, see J. S. DeMatteo, L. T. Eby, and E. Sundstrom, "Team-Based Rewards: Current Empirical Evidence and Directions for Future Research," 141–183.

54 P. K. Zingheim and J. R. Schuster, "Best Practices for Small-Team Pay."

55 J. Flaherty, "Suggestions Rise from the Floors of U.S. Factories," *New York Times* (April 18, 2001): C1, C7; R. Rose, "Kentucky Plant Workers Are Cranking Out Good Ideas," *Wall Street Journal* (August 13, 1996): B1; J. Birnbaum, "Recognition Programs Are Widespread," *HR News* (November 1991): 2.

56 B. Sonsin, "A Pat(ent) on the Back," *HR Magazine* (March 2000): 107.

57 Bureau of National Affairs, "Incentive Pay Schemes Seen as a Result of Economic Employee Relation Change," *BNA Daily Report* (October 9, 1984): 1; G. T. Milkovich and J. M. Newman, *Compensation*; G. W. Florkowski, "The Organizational Impact of Profit Sharing," *Academy of Management Review* (October 1987): 622–636.

58 J. Stack, "The Problem with Profit Sharing," *Inc.* (November 1996): 67–69.

59 G. Colvin, "What Money Makes You Do," *Fortune* (August 17, 1998): 213–214.

60 E. Zehnder, "A Simple Way to Pay," *Harvard Business Review* (April 2001): 53–71.

61 A concise discussion is provided by B. Graham-Moore, "Gainsharing," in C. H. Fay et al., *The Executive Handbook on Compensation,* 527–538.

62 J. B. Arthur and L. Aidman-Smith, "Gainsharing and Organizational Learning: An Analysis of Employee Suggestions Over Time," *Academy of Management Journal* 44 (2001): 737–754.

63 B. E. Moore and T. L. Ross, *The Scanlon Way to Improved Productivity: A Practical Guide* (New York: Wiley, 1978); R. J. Schulhof, "Five Years with a Scanlon Plan," *Personnel Administrator* (June 1979): 55–63; L. S. Tyler and B. Fisher, "The Scanlon Concept: A Philosophy as Much as a System," *Personnel Administrator* (July 1983): 33–37.

64 B. Graham-Moore and T. Ross, *Productivity Gainsharing* (Englewood Cliffs, NJ: Prentice-Hall, 1983); R. J. Bullock and E. E. Lawler III, "Gainsharing: A Few Questions and Fewer Answers," *Human Resource Management* 23 (1984): 23–40; D-O Kim, "Factors Influencing Organizational Performance in Gainsharing Programs," *Industrial Relations* 35 (April 1996): 227.

65 M. J. Wallace, *Rewards and Renewal: America's Search for Competitive Advantage through Alternative Pay Strategies* (Scottsdale, AZ: American Compensation Association, 1990): 15. See also R. Balu, "Bonuses Aren't Just for the Bosses," *Fast Company* (December 2000): 74–76; K. Paulsen and D. Westman, "Using Gainsharing to Motivate," *ACA News* (July/August, 1999): 44–48.

66 "Work Redesign, Empowerment Touted," *Bulletin to Management* (August 4, 1994): 248.

67 K. Paulsen and D. Westman, "Using Gainsharing to Motivate Generation X," *ACA News* (July/August 1999): 44–48; T. M. Welbourne and L. R. Gomez-Mejia, "Gainsharing: A Critical Review and a Future Research Agenda," *Journal of Management* 21 (1995): 559–609.

68 "A Tricky Business," *Economist* (June 30, 2001): 55–56; S. Baker, "Why Steel Is Looking Sexy," *Business Week* (April 4, 1994): 106–108.

69 Based on a survey conducted by Hewitt Associates, as represented in G. Fuchsberg, "Selling Isn't Everything," *Wall Street Journal* (April 1994): R8; see also J. A. Colletti and M. S. Fiss, "Rewarding New Sales Roles with Incentive Pay," *ACA Journal* (Autumn 1998): 45–57.

70 P. D. Sweeney, "Counting the Till, Then Trolling for New Accounts," *New York Times* (June 14, 2000): A14; R. Wood, O. Atkins, and J. Bright, "Bonuses, Goals, and Instrumentality Effects," *Journal of Applied Psychology* 84(5) (1999): 703–720; C. F. Schultz, "Compensating the Sales Professional," in Balkin and Gomez-Mejia (eds.), *New Perspectives on Compensation* (Englewood Cliffs, NJ: Prentice-Hall, 1987): 250–258.

71 W. J. Duncan, "Stock Ownership and Work Motivation," *Organizational Dynamics* 30(1) (2001): 1–11.

72 F. Amato, "Employee Stock Ownership: Gaining a Foothold Worldwide," *ACA News* (February 2000): 34–36; B. W. Aisenbrey, "Global Stock Options in U.S. Companies," in C. Reynolds (ed.), *Guide to Global Compensation and Benefits* (San Diego, CA: Harcourt, 2001): 159–181; B. R. Ellig, "Broad-based Stock Ownership," in C. H. Fay et al., *The Executive Handbook on Compensation,* 580–595.

73 J. B. Fox, "The Amazing Stock Option Sleight of Hand," *Fortune* (June 25, 2001): 86–92; S. J. Wells, "Stock Incentives Remain Preferred Compensation Option," *HR News* (September 2000): 9, 17; Bureau of Labor Statistics, "BLS Reports on Non-Executive Employee Stock Options," *Workspan* (January 2001): 13; T. Buyniski and D. Silver, "Determining the Compensation Value of Stock Options, " *ACA Journal* (First Quarter 2000): 66–73; J. Dolmat-Connell, "Magic Potion . . . or Passing Fad?" *ACA News* (April 2000): 38–49; S. Kuczynski, "Taking Stock," *HR Magazine* (February 2000): 50–56; G. Morgenson, "Investors May Now Eye Costs of Stock Options," *New York Times* (August 29, 2000): C1, C8; National Center for Employee Ownership, "NCEO Releases Initial Results of Stock Survey," *Workspan* (January 2001): 13–14.

74 E. Ofek and D. Yemack, "Taking Stock: Equity-Based Compensation and the Evolution of Managerial Ownership," *Journal of Finance* 55 (2000): 1367–1384; P. Sparrow, "The Psychological Consequences of Employee Ownership: On the Role of Risk, Reward, Identity and Personality," *Trends in Organizational Behavior* 8 (2001): 79–90; J. Handel, "Take a Deep Breath: Dealing with Underwater Options," *Workspan* (January 2001): 40–43; L. Lavelle, "When Good Options Go Bad," *Business Week E.Biz* (December 11, 2000): 96–98; P. T. Chingos and M. M. Engel, "Trends in Stock Option Plans and Long-Term Incentives," *ACA Journal* (Spring 1998): 13–18.

75 Based on D. G. Goodall, "Global Employee-Based Equity Plans—Can They Work for Your Company?" in C. Reynolds (ed.), *Guide to Global Compensation and Benefits* (San Diego, CA: Harcourt, 2001): 121–158; G. Paulin, "Using Stock to Retain Key Employees," *WorldatWork Journal* (Third Quarter 2000): 45–51; P. L. Gilles, "Your Stock Price Dropped by 30%! Now What?" *ACA News* (April 2000).

76 This section is based on data reported in M. J. Halloran, "Performance-Based Options: An Upcoming Debate," *ACA News* (Spring 1998): 28–30.

77 R. Gotcher, "PBE Plans More Flavorful than Vanilla Equity," *Workspan* (January 2001): 46–48; G. Koretz, "Why Options Are Repriced," *Business Week* (August 13, 2001): 24.

78 L. Lavelle, "When Good Options Go Bad," *Business Week E.Biz* (December 11, 2000): 96–98; E. Schatzker, "What Tech Bust?" *Bloomberg Markets* (April 2001): 65–68; P. L. Gilles, "Your Stock Price Dropped by 30%! Now What?" *ACA News* (April 2000).

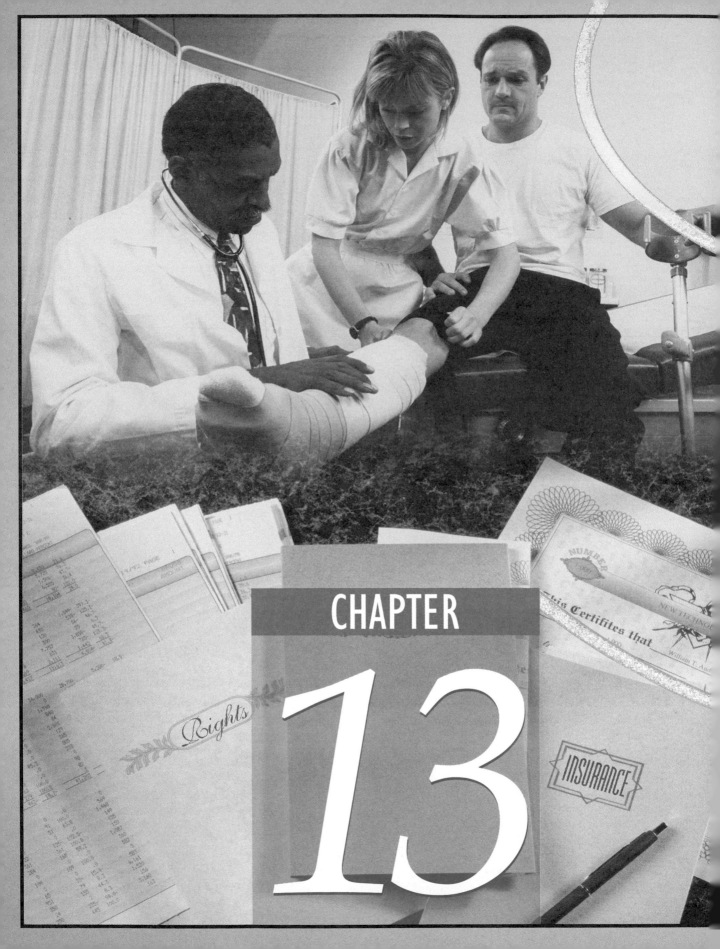

CHAPTER

13

Providing Benefits and Services

"People come here for the benefits, and they stay for them. . . . Turnover is very expensive, and our benefits keep our turnover rate down."

Bradley Honeycut
Director of Compensation and Benefits
Starbucks Coffee Company[1]

MANAGING THROUGH STRATEGIC PARTNERSHIPS

Steelcase

Steelcase, headquartered in Grand Rapids, Michigan, for 90 years, is the world's leading provider of high-performance workplaces. It serves virtually every country of the world through 800 independently owned dealers. Its own workforce of almost 21,000 employees is also spread throughout the world. It has over 50 manufacturing plants in the United States, six in France, three in the United Kingdom, and one each in seven other countries, including Mexico, Japan, and Germany, and over 650 independent dealers.

Steelcase is a business totally focused on the customer, quality improvement, and continuous innovation. This focus translates into its mission: "We are committed to helping your people work more effectively. How? By integrating the goals of your organization, the technology you use, and how your people work in the space they occupy. This focus governs all our research efforts and the products, services, and expertise we provide through our independent, worldwide dealer network."

Although Steelcase is a big operation with almost $4.0 billion in sales, it has many competitors. One of its most significant competitors is another Michigan-based firm, Herman Miller. Others include Haworth, Inc., and Hon, Inc. To compete effectively, Steelcase must continually manage and reduce its costs. During the past decade, it has focused on reducing the costs of workers' compensation claims, essentially the costs associated with having people hurt, injured, and out of work. Under medical services and the safety director, Steelcase developed and implemented a "return-to-work" program that has reduced the average cost per claim. The plan has two major concepts:

- A medical review board systematically examines the injured person and the injury situation to make the correct diagnosis of the claim. The intent here is to uncover all the facts and build an atmosphere of trust and understanding between worker and company.
- A return-to-work component enables workers to get back to work as soon as possible: once an injury is diagnosed, the biggest manageable expense is the time in getting the worker back to work. By setting up therapy centers and accommodating working conditions, Steelcase reduced time away from work for most injuries by 50 percent in six years.

This program has resulted in cost savings of over $50 million since the program's inception. Little wonder it has received the strong support of Jim Hackett, the current president and CEO, and Nancy Hickey, Senior VP for HR.[2]

The opening feature describes how Steelcase is addressing a mounting crisis in cost containment for American business. As international competition increases, U.S. firms struggle to contain their costs. For many firms, total compensation costs are a significant part of the problem. Steelcase's approach is an excellent example of what firms can do to reduce their workers' compensation costs. Other firms reduce compensation costs by asking workers to pay some of the expenses or by just cutting back on the benefits and services that they offer to employees.

Although the specific elements of plans vary, **employee benefits and services** are generally defined as in-kind payments to employees for their membership or participation in the organization. These payments provide protection against health and accident-related problems and ensure income at retirement. Legally required **public protection programs** include Social Security, unemployment compensation, and workers' compensation. **Private protection programs**, which are voluntary, include health care, life insurance, and long-term disability insurance, pensions, and other forms of retirement savings plans. Benefits and services also include pay for time not at work—for instance, vacations, holidays, sick days and absences, breaks, and washup and cleanup. Although these are not legally mandated, benefits such as these are usually considered to be mandatory from the employees' perspective. In unionized settings, they may be covered by formal contracts.

> **FAST FACT**
>
> Steelcase was recognized by *Industry Week* as one of the 100 best-managed companies in the world.

A growing category of voluntary benefits and services enables employees to enjoy a better lifestyle or to meet social or personal obligations while minimizing employment-related costs. Discounts, educational assistance, and child and elder care fall into this category.

EMPLOYEE BENEFITS AND SERVICES WITHIN AN INTEGRATED HR SYSTEM

Exhibit 13.1 shows the major elements of employee benefits and services, and the primary linkages between these and other HR practices. Also shown are the factors in the global and organization environments that have the most impact on employee benefits and services.

ex 13.1 Employee Benefits and Services within an Integrated HR System

Other HR Activities
- Fairness and Legal Compliance
- Creating Alignment
- Recruitment and Retention
- Total Compensation
- Promoting Safety and Health
- Unionization and Collective Bargaining

Global Environment
- Economic Conditions
- Labor Market
- Laws and Regulations
- National Cultures

Organizational Environment
- Strategy
- Corporate Culture

Objectives for Offering Benefits and Services
- Communicate Organization's Values
- Support Strategic Objectives
- Attract and Retain
- Motivate
- Contain Costs

Provide Mandatory Benefits and Services (Public Protection Programs)
- Social Security System
- Unemployment Compensation
- Workers' Compensation and Disability Insurance

Provide Voluntary Benefits and Services (Private Protection Programs)
- Retirement Savings and Pensions
- Medical Care
- Paid Leave
- Life Cycle Benefits

Communicate and Administer Plan

Monitor Costs and Satisfaction

Links with Other HR Practices

As described in Chapter 10, employee benefits and services are one component of a total compensation package. Indeed, as Exhibit 13.2 illustrates, approximately one-third of a company's total labor costs is due to the costs associated with the benefits and services offered to employees.[3]

Especially when the labor market is tight, employers often provide generous benefits and services in an effort to attract and retain needed talent. An employer's choice of benefits and services to offer is usually shaped by other aspects of the organization, however. Choosing benefits and services that are aligned with other practices and with the strategy is important, given the significant costs involved. At Ernst & Young, flexible work arrangements are a service that many employees value. The firm considers its flex policy to be a strategic tool that enables this professional services firm to be more competitive. The firm's results-based performance management system is important to the success of the program, however. The program is described in "Managing Diversity: Flexible Arrangements at Ernst & Young."[4]

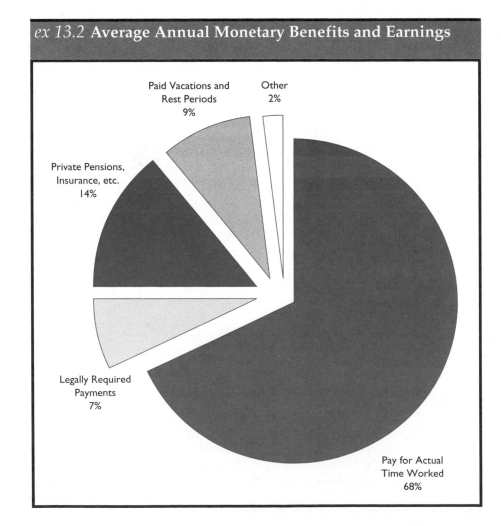

ex 13.2 **Average Annual Monetary Benefits and Earnings**

Paid Vacations and Rest Periods 9%
Other 2%
Private Pensions, Insurance, etc. 14%
Legally Required Payments 7%
Pay for Actual Time Worked 68%

Flexible Arrangements at Ernst & Young

MANAGING DIVERSITY

Ernst & Young employees are empowered to decide how, when, and where to get their jobs done. The company's flexible schedule options have been in place since the mid-1990s, when the initiative was launched in response to employees' concerns about work–life balance. Although fewer than 1 percent of employees use the flexible work arrangement (FWA) option , those who do value it greatly. According to a survey of those using FWA at the firm, 84 percent say this service is the primary reason they stay at Ernst & Young.

One novel feature of the initiative is the FWA electronic site and database, which employees can use to learn more about the realities of such arrangements. From the electronic site, employees can access a database containing profiles of existing flextimers and quotes about their experiences. Employees also can use links to the firm's formal policies and participate in discussions with FWA experts. As an educational tool, the electronic site has proved useful for flextimers as well as their colleagues and supervisors. For those interested in pursuing FWA, a self-assessment tool is available to help employees evaluate whether they have the skills and personality needed to succeed on a flexible schedule.

Employees who decide to apply for FWA must be able to make an adequate business case for their situation. The electronic site offers a Road Map to help employees think concretely about FWAs and assist with the preparation of the business case. The key objective in preparing the business case is to provide a concrete plan for how FWA will be used and how the employee will manage his or her job performance under the arrangements. Twelve experts also are available to provide assistance.

Due in part to its FWA service, Ernst & Young is one of only 16 companies included in the "100 Best" lists of both *Working Mother* and *Fortune*.

Two other sets of HR practices that are intertwined with benefits and services are (a) safety and health and (b) unionization and collective bargaining. These linkages are described in more detail in subsequent chapters that address these practices.

The Global Environment

The growth in the types and costs of employee benefits and services can be traced to several environmental trends.

Economic Conditions. Under normal business conditions, employers compete for labor primarily through the wages they offer. During times of major crisis, such as World War II and the Korean War, the government curtailed such activity in order to prevent runaway inflation. Throughout the 20th century, the imposition of wage controls in times of war forced organizations to offer more and greater benefits and services in place of wage increases, to attract new employees.

More recently, the most important economic factor has been rising health care costs. In 1940, U.S. health care expenses were $4 billion, about 4 percent of the GDP. In 2000, they were more than $1 trillion, or almost 20 percent of the GDP. For employers, the average health benefits cost for each employee was almost $4,000 in 2000. Regardless of their causes, these increases have major consequences for employee benefits and services.[5]

Inflation levels also come into play. Employee benefits and services managers, more so than compensation managers, must anticipate the effects of inflation on medical service, education, and pension benefits. For example, double-digit inflation in the 1980s eroded the purchasing power of some retirees' benefits and resulted in adjustments in the retirees' levels of bene-

"At Ernst & Young the focus is on results, not face time."

Denny Marcel
Office of Retention
Ernst & Young

fits. Inflation has been much lower in recent years, but companies must nevertheless anticipate changing inflation rates and their implications. Similarly, employers' benefits and services packages regularly change as the tax codes change, because tax rules for benefits can substantially influence both their real cost for employers and their real value to employees.

Union Bargaining. From 1935 into the 1970s, unions were able to gain steady increases in wages and benefits for their members. Practically all benefits and services are now mandatory bargaining items, which means that employers must bargain in good faith on union proposals to add them. Companies without union representation may offer similar benefits and services in order to remain attractive to job applicants.

Laws and Regulations. A variety of laws significantly affect the administration and offering of monetary benefits, including the *Family and Medical Leave Act of 1993*, the *Americans with Disabilities Act of 1990*, the *Employee Retirement Income Security Act of 1974 (ERISA)*, and the *Social Security Act of 1935*. When Congress initiated the *Social Security Act*, it covered only 60 percent of all workers. Subsequently, the scope of these benefits and the percentage of eligible workers has increased substantially. Today 95 percent of all workers are eligible for Social Security benefits, including disability benefits, health benefits, and retirement pay.

The Organization Environment

Initiatives such as major medical insurance, long-term disability plans, and child and elder care allowances reflect a general concern for employees. All were implemented by organizations in response to employee needs. Provisions such as educational assistance benefits, employee assistance programs, and wellness programs have been inspired by pressures to improve productivity and worker skills. More recently, benefits and services such as auto and home insurance, matching funds for charitable giving, and work–life balance programs have been prompted by private businesses' desire to be socially responsible and attract good workers.[6]

Traditionally, employers have adopted a "father-knows-best" attitude toward benefits; the company has assumed it knows what is the most appropriate coverage for its employees. As we begin the 21st century, this attitude is being replaced with one of high employee involvement and choice, consistent with employee empowerment. "Choice accounts" that provide various benefits and services options and allow employees, rather than the company, to allocate benefits dollars are increasingly popular.[7] Exhibit 13.3 shows how employees evaluate the importance of several benefits and services.[8]

> **FAST FACT**
>
> Employers are now offering defined contribution health care coverage that gives the employee more choice in health care options.

Corporate Culture. An organization's fundamental values set the stage for developing an approach to managing employee benefits and services. The benefits and services manager must understand the underlying basis of the philosophy and the extent to which management supports human resources generally and benefits and services specifically. Some firms adopt an egalitarian approach to benefits and services by insisting that the same ones be provided to all employees. Other firms offer different benefits and services to employees at different levels or in different jobs within the organization. Some firms, like Ernst & Young, adapt their benefits and services to the needs

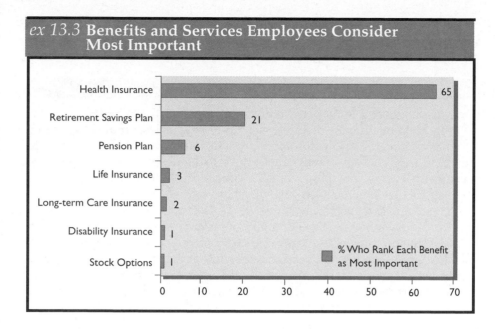

ex 13.3 Benefits and Services Employees Consider Most Important

of their workers in order to attract and retain them.[9] A similar philosophy drives Lincoln Electric's approach, but the resulting benefits and services look very different at this firm. Lincoln's approach is to offer essentially no voluntary benefits and services, and instead use the savings to fund the company's profit-sharing bonus pool. The company does make it easy for employees to participate in a group insurance plan, but doing so is completely voluntary on the part of employees.

The desire to create a more friendly corporate culture is also what led Avon Products, Inc., in New York City to develop a new retirement program. Most Avon employees are engaged in sales and marketing of beauty products; and about 75 percent of the workforce is female. In these jobs, Avon found, employees tend to move in and out of the workforce. As a result, they never were able to qualify for the traditional defined benefit retirement plans. In other words, the workers were never able to gain a benefit that most people now regard when making the decision to work for a company. Recognizing that it was competing for labor in a tight "part-timers" market, Avon remodeled its retirement benefits to make them available to a broader range of employees. It also made the retirement benefits more portable.

Portable benefits refer to those that employees can take with them when they leave the firm. With the increasing mobility of workers, portability has become a major issue. Under Avon's new plan, retirement savings are immediately vested and the benefits are available to anyone chosen by the employee, not just the surviving spouse. The new plan better serves the needs of Avon's workforce, and this in turn will help Avon better serve its customers and stockholders.

Strategy. Human resource planning involves assessing external threats and internal forces, setting and ranking goals, establishing timetables, and integrating benefits and services planning with human resource planning specifically. These in turn can be linked with the company's strategic direction and specific

FAST FACT

Employers can get lean without being mean by asking employees which perks are most important.

business objectives, such as reducing costs while also retaining valued employees. Exhibit 13.4 provides several examples of business objectives and the ways in which benefits and services can be used to address them.

THE STRATEGIC IMPORTANCE OF EMPLOYEE BENEFITS AND SERVICES

Driving the desire to offer better employee benefits and services is the desire to attract and retain valued employees. Controlling costs, on the other hand, is a major counterbalancing force that pressures employers to look for ways to cut costs. Thus, the key strategic challenge is to offer benefits and services that maximally leverage the employer's investments. Due to numerous laws and regulations that affect employee benefits and services, employers must carefully plan how to meet this challenge while also ensuring legal compliance.

Unlike other elements of total compensation, employee benefits and services are not generally considered effective tools for improving an employee's motivation and productivity while at work. This is because, generally, benefits and services are not tied to employee performance. Instead, most benefits and services are available on a noncontingent basis—as long as an employee remains employed, he or she receives the same benefits and services regardless of job performance.

Recruiting and Retaining Talent

In their recruitment ads and literature, most companies label their benefits and services packages as competitive. Owing to increased competition, being competitive without spending more often means developing innovative packages to attract and retain employees. Wellness programs, health screenings, stock options, and employee assistance programs are examples of relatively new benefits and services being offered by the leading firms. Other responses to competitive pressures include flexible benefits plans and cash options offered in place of prepaid benefits packages.[10]

ex 13.4 Business Objectives Addressed by Benefits and Services

Business Objective	Benefits Response
1. To unify the company acquired from the merger, from independent subsidiary to integrated division status, by year-end.	1. Perform an analysis of an immediate versus a gradual transfer of subsidiary employees into the corporate benefits plan.
2. To develop a working environment that is founded on integrity, open communication, and individual growth.	2. Develop an employee career-counseling system that provides employees with an opportunity to assess skills and develop competencies. Establish a tuition reimbursement program.
3. To establish the division as a recognized leader in support of its community.	3. Establish a corporate-giving matching fund.
4. To complete the downsizing of the company by the end of the third quarter.	4. Develop various termination subsidies such as severance pay, outplacement assistance, and early retirement benefits.
5. To cut accident rates 10 percent by year-end.	5. Establish an employee assistance program by year-end. Set up a free literacy training program to ensure that all employees can read job safety signs.

Communication. Many organizations pump so much money into benefits and services programs because they believe that it helps enhance the organization's image among employees and in the business community. For wisely used programs, this may be true. On the other hand, ample research demonstrates that these objectives are not always attained. Many, perhaps most, employees don't really know which benefits they receive or their worth. Realizing this, firms such as Hewlett-Packard and Starbucks aggressively market their benefits and services packages to tell employees what the company provides to them. If employees don't know they receive a benefit, they won't stay with the company in order to retain that benefit.

Entitlement. Benefits and services also may fail to help a company achieve its objectives if employees regard them as a condition of employment to which they are entitled. Rather than appreciate their employer's concern, employees may view benefits as a social responsibility the employer is obligated to provide.[11]

Relative Value. Even when employee benefits and services succeed in attracting applicants, their importance relative to other job factors—for example, opportunity for advancement, salary, geographic location, responsibilities, and prestige—may be low. Furthermore, some of the potential value of a company's benefits and services plan often is lost because each employee values only some of the benefits and services offered, and may even resent the company's decision to spend money on benefits and services used only by other employees. Allowing employees to personalize their benefits and services is one solution to this problem. As some firms reduce or even eliminate benefits and services and ask workers to share or even assume their costs, many employees are beginning to realize how expensive benefits and services can be.[12] Also, they are forced to decide which benefits and services are of most personal value.

Controlling Costs

Prior to the recent economic boom, employers were relatively generous—a growing economy meant that simply finding enough people to staff organizations required focusing less on controlling costs. Furthermore, during the mid-1990s, the rate of growth for health care costs began to slow, as employers found more economical ways to provide health insurance. As we begin the 21st century, however, the tide seems to have shifted (of course, it may have shifted again by the time you read this), and costs again are a major concern.

In 1929, total benefits payments averaged 5 percent of total pay. By 2000, they had risen to an average of about 30 percent of wages and salaries, or roughly $15,000 a year for each employee. Although these numbers vary across industries and by type of worker, the cost of benefits and services to organizations is, in general, enormous.[13] While wages and salaries are 40 times greater than 60 years ago, benefits and services are 500 times greater.[14] As will soon become apparent, some of these costs cannot easily be avoided, due to governmental mandates. Many costs are due to voluntary benefits and services, however, and so are a target of cost-cutting efforts.

Addressing Employees' Concerns

Many protection programs are designed to assist employees and their families if and when the employees' income (direct compensation) is terminated,

> Sharing costs is *"a way of getting the workforce involved in the effects of health care delivery costs. If it's a free lunch, people tend to treat it that way."*
>
> Don Morford
> Director of Benefits
> Kmart

> *"Balancing the benefit needs of both the company and employees can certainly be a challenge, but the rewards of sound, cost-effective benefits programs, and employee understanding and appreciation are certainly worth the effort."*
>
> Cherly Poulson
> Management of Benefits Planning
> GlaxoSmithKline

FAST FACT

Workers at a Guinness packaging plant in Ireland, which is set to close, accepted severance packages that include payments of up to $150,000; health benefits; and 10 years' worth of free beer. Eligible employees will receive about 14 bottles of beer a week and more on holidays twice a year.

and to alleviate the burden of health care expenses. Examples of public protection programs required by the government and those voluntarily offered by organizations are listed in Exhibit 13.5. As is clear from this list, benefit programs address a number of employee concerns, including those related to their health, welfare, and education. In many cases, employee benefits also address the concerns of the extended families of employees, including spouses, children, parents, and others who may be legal dependents.

PUBLIC PROTECTION PROGRAMS

Benefits provisions grew rapidly during the Depression, when the needs of large numbers of unemployed people were inescapable. The *Social Security Act*, passed in 1935, provided old-age, disability, survivors', and health benefits and established the basis for federal and state unemployment programs. The *Wagner Act*, or *National Labor Relations Act of 1935 (NLRA)*, helped ensure the growth of benefits by strengthening the union movement in the United States. Both the *Social Security Act* and the *Wagner Act* continue to play significant roles in the administration of benefits.

Since the 1960s, Congress has passed several acts that make this legal environment more complex, including the *Equal Pay Act of 1963*, the *Americans with Disabilities Act of 1990*, and the *Age Discrimination in Employment Act of 1967*, as discussed in previous chapters. These laws have rather broad implications, affecting many aspects of human resource management. In addition to these are several laws that focus more specifically on employee benefits and services. These are described in this section.

Social Security

Protection programs are designed to assist employees and their families if and when the employees' income (direct compensation) is terminated, and to alleviate the burden of health care expenses. Protection programs required by the federal and state governments are referred to as public protection programs, and those voluntarily offered by organizations are called private protection programs. Examples of each are listed in Exhibit 13.5.

ex 13.5 Public and Private Protection Programs

Issue	Public Programs	Private Programs
Retirement	• Social Security old-age benefits	• Defined benefit pensions • Defined contribution pensions • Money purchase and thrift plans [401(k)s and ESOPs]
Death	• Social Security survivors' benefits • Workers' compensation	• Group term life insurance (including accidental death and travel insurance • Payouts from profit-sharing, pension, or thrift plans, or any combination of these • Dependent survivors' benefits
Disability	• Workers' compensation • Social Security disability benefits • State disability benefits	• Short-term accident and sickness insurance • Long-term disability insurance
Unemployment	• Unemployment benefits	• Supplemental unemployment benefits or severance pay, or both
Medical and dental expenses	• Workers' compensation	• Hospital surgical insurance • Other medical insurance • Dental insurance

Public protection programs are the outgrowth of the *Social Security Act of 1935*. This act initially set up systems for retirement benefits, disability, and unemployment insurance. Health insurance, particularly Medicare, was added in 1966 to provide hospital insurance to almost everyone age 65 and older.

Funding of the Social Security system is provided by equal contributions from the employer and employee under terms of the *Federal Insurance Contributions Act (FICA)*. Initially, employee and employer each paid 1 percent of the employee's income up to $3,000. Today companies each pay 6.2 percent of the first $84,900 of the employee's income for retirement and disability and 1.45 percent of the total income for hospital insurance through Medicare. The average annual Social Security benefit is about $9,100 for a single person and about $15,500 for a married couple, with adjustments routinely made for increases in the consumer price index.[15]

FAST FACT

Only about 50% of workers have any idea how much they need to save for retirement.

FAST FACT

Only about 40% of adults think Social Security will have the money for their retirement; fortunately only 15% think of it as a major source of retirement money.

Unemployment Compensation Benefits

To control costs, the *Social Security Act* dictates that unemployment compensation programs be jointly administered through the federal and state governments. The federal rate is the same for everyone. But because income levels vary from state to state, unemployment compensation also varies by state. The level of benefits paid to unemployed workers ranges from 50 percent to 70 percent of base salary up to a specified maximum weekly amount, which also varies by state. Since passage of the *Tax Reform Act of 1986*, unemployment compensation has been fully taxable, making actual benefit levels much lower.[16]

Corresponding to variations in compensation paid to unemployed workers are variations in the total tax liability of employers. The tax rates for employers vary according to the number of unemployed people drawing from the fund. Consequently, employers who dismiss many workers who later draw unemployment benefits pay higher taxes than employers with better employment records.

Workers' Compensation and Disability

At Steelcase and other companies, workers' compensation costs are a major concern. Of the more than 6 million job-related injuries reported annually in the private sector, about half are serious enough for the injured worker to lose work time or experience restricted work activity, or both. In addition, hundreds of thousands of new occupational illness cases are reported each year. More than 90 percent of these illnesses are associated with repetitive motions such as vibration, repeated pressure, and movements that cause carpal tunnel syndrome. Most require medical care and result in lost work time.[17]

When injuries or illnesses occur as a result of on-the-job events, workers may be eligible for workers' compensation benefits. Administered at the state level and fully financed by employers, these benefits cover costs and lost income due to temporary and permanent disability, disfigurement, medical care, and medical rehabilitation. Survivors' benefits are provided following fatal injuries.

Proactive workers' compensation administrators such as Libby Child at Steelcase are applying a variety of health care cost-containment strategies to workers' compensation, such as

- developing networks of preferred provider organizations,
- specifying fees for treating workers' compensation claimants,
- limiting payments to medically necessary or reasonable procedures,
- requiring precertification of hospital admissions,
- establishing concurrent review of inpatient hospital stays, and
- routinely auditing hospital and health care bills.[18]

More broadly, workers' compensation managers are seeing the value of combining workers' compensation with disability management for

injuries that occur on the job and off the job (for which workers' compensation claims may not be paid). In this way companies may be able to get their injured or sick employees back to health and back to work more quickly. This boosts workers' incomes and can help companies meet their staffing needs.

Pregnancy Discrimination Act of 1978

The *Pregnancy Discrimination Act of 1978* states that pregnancy is a disability and qualifies a person to receive the same benefits and services as afforded for any other disability. Applying this statute, a state appeals court in Michigan ruled that a labor contract between General Motors and the United Auto Workers was illegal. The contract provided sickness and accident benefits of up to 52 weeks but limited childbearing disability to 6 weeks.[19]

Although the *Pregnancy Discrimination Act* does not explicitly address the issue of gender equity, it has been interpreted as requiring companies to offer the same pregnancy benefits program to wives of male employees and to husbands of female employees. The U.S. Supreme Court ruled in *Newport News Shipbuilding and Dry Dock Company v. EEOC* (1983) that employers who provide to spouses of employees health care insurance that includes complete coverage for all disabilities except pregnancy are violating Title VII of the *Civil Rights Act of 1964*. In essence, employers must provide equal benefits and services coverage for all spouses.

Family and Medical Leave Act of 1993

The *Family and Medical Leave Act of 1993* requires employers with 50 or more workers to grant an employee up to 12 weeks' unpaid leave annually "for the birth or adoption of a child, to care for a spouse or an immediate family member with a serious health condition, or when unable to work because of a serious health condition. Employers covered by the law are required to maintain any preexisting health coverage during the leave period."[20] The employee taking leave must be allowed to return to the same job or a job of equivalent status and pay—with the exception of some highly paid executives.

> **FAST FACT**
>
> When 750 human resource managers were asked in a survey if they have had to grant FMLA requests that they felt were not legitimate, 52% said yes.

To be eligible for FMLA benefits, employees must have worked at a company for at least 12 months and have put in at least 1,250 hours in the year before the leave.[21] Some 67 million employees are eligible for family leave, if and when they need it, and two out of five working Americans anticipate needing family and medical leave over the next five years.

Economic Recovery Tax Act of 1981

A major provision of the *Economic Recovery Tax Act of 1981* was that employees were allowed to make tax deductible contributions to (a) an employer-sponsored pension, profit-sharing, or savings account, or (b) an individual retirement account (IRA). The act also made it possible for employers to provide company stock to employees and pay for it with tax credits or to establish a payroll-based plan that facilitates employee stock ownership. By providing tax relief for private retirement savings accounts, this tax law and its subsequent revisions stimulated the growth of new private protection programs that give employees more control over their retirement investments. It also stimulated the use of broad-based stock ownership. As described in Chapter 12, stock ownership is appealing to employees when a company's stock price is rising. But stock ownership is not risk free; employees' paper wealth can

> **FAST FACT**
>
> Most of the 11,000 employee-owned companies in the United States have fewer than 500 employees and only 5% are unionized.

quickly fade in a declining market. Furthermore, when employees own a significant share of their companies, they may want a voice in corporate governance, as happened at United Airlines and Northwest Airlines. The increasing use of stock ownership that resulted from this tax law has had major implications for the organizational environment at some firms.[22]

Health Insurance Portability and Accountability Act of 1996

The provisions of this act aid workers in keeping track of their health care coverage and in transferring this coverage to another employer. By receiving certificates of coverage when they leave their jobs, employees can more easily obtain individual or group health insurance without restrictions on pre-existing conditions or coverage gaps.[23] This law laid the foundation for the development of cash balance plans, which are described later.

Economic Growth and Tax Relief Reconciliation Act of 2001

In addition to enacting an across-the-board federal income tax rate cut, the *Economic Growth and Tax Relief Reconciliation Act* affects employee benefits in several ways:

- raises the contribution limits for IRAs and employer-sponsored retirement plans such as 403(b) and the 401(k) plans,
- reduces from five years to three years the length of service required before employer contributions to employer-sponsored retirement programs must be available,
- shortens pension vesting waiting periods, and
- eliminates federal taxes on withdrawals from college savings plan accounts.

The law also contains a "sunset" provision, which means that it will expire in 2010 when the previous laws will be reinstated unless Congress decides otherwise.

Limits to contributions that can be made to 401(k) and 403(b) retirement plans, under this law, are raised from $10,500 per year to $15,000 in 2006. Contribution limits to IRAs are increased from $2,000 yearly to $5,000 yearly in 2008.

PRIVATE PROTECTION PROGRAMS

"We're looking at how we can improve our human resource operations, particularly the key component: benefits. Hugely expensive and getting more expensive."

Coretha Rushing
Senior Vice President of HR
Coca-Cola

Private protection programs are offered by organizations but are not required by law. They include retirement income plans, capital accumulation plans, savings and thrift plans, and supplemental unemployment benefits and guaranteed pay. Some firms also offer work options for retirees, including temporary full-time and permanent part-time employment.

The various retirement income plans can be classified in terms of whether they are qualified or nonqualified. A **qualified plan** covers a broad class of employees (e.g., not just executives), meets Internal Revenue Code requirements, and consequently is qualified to receive favorable tax treatment. For example, contributions to a qualified plan typically are tax deductible for employers for the current year, and for employees taxes are deferred until retirement. **Nonqualified plans** don't adhere to the strict tax regulations, cover only select groups of employees, and consequently don't receive favorable tax treatment. By designing benefits and services that qualify for favorable tax treatment, employers can stretch the value of their investments considerably.

ERISA and Private Employers' Pensions

Building on the foundation of the *Revenue Act of 1942,* the *Employee Retirement Income Security Act of 1974* was designed to protect the interests of workers covered by private retirement plans, especially plans that promise the workers a certain monthly dollar amount upon retirement. It does not require an employer to offer a pension fund. When companies offer private pension plans, employees are eligible for fund participation after one year of service or at age 25. ERISA also established provisions regarding **vesting,** which refers to the time when the employer's contribution belongs to the employee.

In the past, some companies set up pension funds but then, when necessary, drew upon those funds to pay for operating expenses. Such activity put employees' pensions at great risk. To protect employees against such risk, ERISA prohibits the use of unfunded pension programs that rely on the goodwill of the employer to pay retirement benefits out of current operating funds when needed. Money paid into a pension fund must be earmarked for retirees, whether paid in part by the employee or paid solely by the employer (as in noncontributory programs).

Under ERISA, employers are not required to accommodate new or transferred employees who wish to deposit funds into their retirement plans. On a voluntary basis, employers can allow employees to transfer money to individual retirement accounts. When this occurs, the pension funds are said to be portable. Increasingly, employers are making it possible for employees to transfer their retirement funds to another firm.

Because ERISA covered only single-employer plans, the *Multi-Employer Pension Plan Amendment Act of 1980* was passed to broaden the definition of defined benefit plans to include multiemployer plans. If employers withdraw from multiemployer plans, they, rather than the employees, face liability for doing so and must reimburse employees for money lost.[24]

Pension Plans

The largest category of private protection plans is pensions. Four out of five employees in medium and large firms are covered by some type of private pension or capital accumulation plan and rely on these plans to provide future security. A less well known fact is that the 20 largest pension funds, 13 of them for public employees, hold one-tenth of the equity capital of America's publicly owned companies. All told, institutional investors—primarily pension funds—control close to 40 percent of the common stock of the country's largest businesses. Pension funds also hold 40 percent or more of the medium- and long-term debt of the country's bigger companies. Thus, employees, through their pension funds, have become America's largest retirement bankers, lenders, and business owners.[25]

> **FAST FACT**
>
> The pension coverage rate is 24% of workers in small firms and 68% in larger firms (over 100 employees).

Defined Benefit and Cash Plans. With a **defined benefit pension plan**, the actual benefits received upon retirement vary with the employee's age and length of service. For example, an employee may receive $50 a month for each year of company service. Some employers and unions prefer defined benefit plans because they produce predictable, secure, and continuing income. As described above, the *Employee Retirement Income Security Act* regulates such plans in order to protect employees and prevent employers from using pension funds for other purposes. Employers must adhere to stringent reporting rules, disclosure guidelines, fiduciary standards, plan participation rules, and vesting standards. In addition, defined benefit plans must adhere to specific funding-level requirements and be insured against termination due to economic hardship, misfunding, or corporate buyouts. The **Pension Benefit Guaranty Corporation (PBGC)** administers the required insurance program and guarantees the payment of basic retirement benefits to participants if a plan is terminated. The PBGC also can terminate seriously underfunded pension funds.

Traditional defined benefit plans helped retain employees because the value of these plans built up with age and tenure in the organization. At the same time, they discouraged or penalized employee mobility. Given the reality of employee mobility in the 21st century, such "benefits" are no longer as desirable as they were when employees enjoyed more job security. For this and other reasons, many employers are phasing out defined benefits and replacing them with cash balance plans.

A **cash balance plan** pays a specified lump sum of cash to employees upon their departure from the company. These plans are more profitable for employees who work for several employers over the course of their careers. While there are serious issues in converting defined benefit to cash balance plans, conversion appears to be a trend.[26]

Exhibit 13.6 uses a hypothetical example to illustrate the differing benefits that an employee would receive under a cash balance plan versus the typical defined benefit plan.[27] The example assumes that the employee enters at age 25 and retires at age 65 from the same organization. The dashed line shows the relative disadvantage of a cash balance plan for an employee who stays in the same organization for the full 40 years. Early in an employee's career, the retirement benefits that have accrued under the cash balance plan are large. However, by age 45, the advantages of a cash balance plan begin to erode. By age 65, the cash balance plan provides nearly 35 percent less benefit to the employee. However, the picture is very different if the employee changes jobs instead of staying with the same employer for 40 years. As the solid line shows, for the more mobile employee, a cash balance plan always results in greater

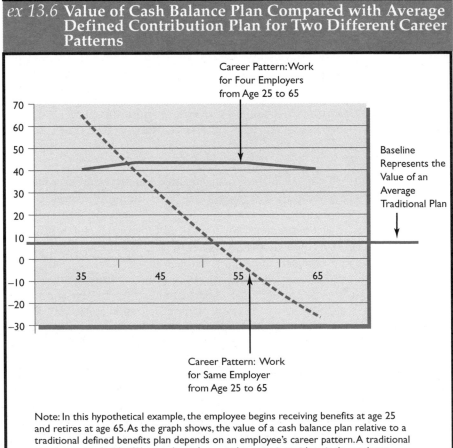

ex 13.6 Value of Cash Balance Plan Compared with Average Defined Contribution Plan for Two Different Career Patterns

Career Pattern: Work for Four Employers from Age 25 to 65

Baseline Represents the Value of an Average Traditional Plan

Career Pattern: Work for Same Employer from Age 25 to 65

Note: In this hypothetical example, the employee begins receiving benefits at age 25 and retires at age 65. As the graph shows, the value of a cash balance plan relative to a traditional defined benefits plan depends on an employee's career pattern. A traditional plan is more valuable if the employee has very long service with a single employer. A cash balance plan is better if the employee moves around among several employers.

accrued benefits. By age 65, a cash balance plan provides 40 percent greater benefit compared with an average traditional plan.

Defined Contribution Plans. With a **defined contribution plan**, each employee has a separate account to which employee and employer contributions are added. If only the employer contributes, it's a **noncontributory plan**. When both contribute, it's a **contributory plan**. Typically, the employee must activate a contributory plan by agreeing to contribute a set amount of money; the employer then matches the percentage contribution to a specific level, for example 5 percent of the employee's salary from each.

The two most common types of defined contribution plans are money purchase and tax-deferred profit-sharing plans. With **money purchase plans**, the employer makes fixed, regular contributions for participants, usually a percentage of total pay. Employees may also make voluntary contributions. The maximum amount for any employee is equal to 25 percent of earned income, up to a maximum of $30,000 for all defined contribution plans combined. Monies are held in trust funds, and the employee is given several investment options that differ in terms of the degree of risk and growth potential. At retirement, accumulated funds are used to provide annuities. In some cases, lump-sum distributions may be made.

Tax-deferred profit-sharing plans allow employees to share in company profits using a predetermined formula. Monies contributed to these plans are set aside until retirement, when the employees can cash in their profits. From the employer's perspective, tax-deferred profit-sharing plans are useful because employers may deduct up to 15 percent of each participant's compensation (up to an income level of $200,000) for contributions. In addition, the employer passes on the investment risk to employees.[28]

Supplemental Plans

In addition to Social Security and standard pension plans, large firms often offer a supplemental defined contribution plan or a supplemental savings plan. Currently, more than 30 percent of all employees participate in supplemental plans, which function as the third leg of the retirement income stool. Supplemental plans can provide additional retirement income or serve as a source for accumulating funds to meet short-term needs and goals. These plans take one of two forms: savings plans that work as defined contribution plans, called 401(k) plans, and employee stock and stock option plans.[29]

401(k) Plans. With a **401(k) plan** both the employer and the employee contribute to a fund, and the employee is responsible for investment decisions. The total amount both can contribute is increasing to about $30,000. By investing successfully, an employee can have a sizeable retirement allowance. For public employees, a **403(b) plan** functions in the same way, although slightly different rules apply.

Employee Stock and Stock Option Plans. Until recently, stock awards or stock options have been benefits reserved mainly for senior managers. As described in Chapter 12, however, many corporations have recently begun broad-based stock and stock option programs that cover almost all employees. The Starbucks program,

> **FAST FACT**
>
> Each year more and more workers become owners of companies through investment of their pension money (primarily through 401(k) plans). This, however, leaves them undiversified and vulnerable to large losses like the Enron employees in 2001.

> **FAST FACT**
>
> The turnover rate at Starbucks is 60% per year versus 300% for the industry, in part due to the feeling of ownership from stock options.

INTERNET RESOURCES   13.B

Legal Issues for Public and Private Protection Programs

At our Web site, http://jackson.swcollege.com/, you can:

1. Find out about integrated disability management from the Integrated Benefits Institute.

2. Learn about pensions from several government Web sites.

BEAN STOCK, covers virtually all of its 30,000 employees.[30] With a tight labor market, firms are finding that offering stock and stock options is a competitive necessity. As noted in Chapter 12, the motivational value of stocks and stock options fluctuates with the stock market, while the true costs of such plans fluctuate with changes in the tax code.

HEALTH CARE BENEFITS AND SERVICES

Coverage for medical expenses—including hospital charges, home health care, physician charges, and other medical services—is the core of a group health plan. Companies also may provide wellness programs, employee assistance programs, and short- and long-term disability insurance. Health benefits—particularly medical insurance—cost far less than what employees would pay on their own. Most employees underestimate the cost of health benefits to the organization and view coverage as an entitlement rather than a discretionary benefit offered by employers .

FAST FACT

In the past 10 years, there has been a sharp decline in health insurance provided by small businesses to their employees.

In reality, health care costs more than $1 trillion, and that figure continues to rise faster than inflation. Health care consumed about 14 percent of the U.S. gross domestic product in the mid-1990s; today, the figure is about 30 percent. Companies that buy health insurance for their employees spend, on average, more than 13 cents of every dollar they make to pay for this coverage. As illustrated in Exhibit 13.7, this is 35 to 40 percent more than in other industrialized countries. As a consequence, some companies have been very aggressive at reducing health care expenses, sometimes at the cost of reducing employee choice and even coverage.[31]

FAST FACT

The cost of health care for each citizen in the United States is $2,668. In Great Britain, it's $1,043, and in Canada, it's $1,915.

ex 13.7 Health Care Costs for Seniors as a Percentage of GDP (Selected Countries)

Country	Percent of Population Age 65 or Older	HEALTH OUTLAYS ON ELDERLY Share of GDP	Per Capita
United States	12.5%	5.0%	$12,090
Canada	12.9%	3.6%	$6,764
France	16.0%	3.4%	$4,717
Britain	16.1%	2.8%	$3,612
Germany	16.8%	3.5%	$4,993
Japan	17.5%	3.4%	$5,258

Medical Care

Employers usually finance and provide medical expense benefits to employees and their dependents through insurance companies. However, a variety of other approaches are gaining in popularity as businesses attempt to thwart rising costs.

Insurance Companies. Insurance carriers offer a broad range of health care services from which employers can select coverage. Premiums are set and adjusted depending on usage rates and increases in health care costs. The insurance company administers the plan, handling all the paperwork, approvals, and problems. Proponents of this approach argue that insurers protect the plan sponsor against wide fluctuations in claim exposure and costs and offer opportunities for participation in larger risk pools. Insurance companies also have administrative expertise related to certification reviews, claim audits, coordination of benefits, and other cost-containment services.

> **FAST FACT**
>
> Only 51% of the 37 million workers in companies with fewer than 25 employees have company-paid health insurance.

On the downside, the insurance company, not the employer, makes decisions regarding covered benefits. Its decisions may go against the corporation's ethics and sense of social responsibility. Companies that subscribe to a specific insurance plan don't have the luxury of ignoring the insurer's advice and doing what they feel is ethical. The insurance company makes all the tough calls.

> **FAST FACT**
>
> Some 41% of full-time workers are without health insurance.

Provider Organizations. Blue Cross and Blue Shield are nonprofit organizations that operate within defined geographic areas. Blue Cross plans cover hospital expenses, and Blue Shield plans cover charges by physicians and other medical providers. Typically, these associations negotiate arrangements with their member providers to reimburse the providers at a discounted rate when a subscriber incurs a charge. As originally established, the rate represented full payment for the service and no additional charge was levied. However, as a result of skyrocketing health care costs, employees may now be asked to pay deductibles ($50 to $250 a year for each person) or a share of the cost of service (10 to 20 percent), or both.

Health Maintenance Organizations. About one-third of all eligible employees, or about 60 million people, participate in **health maintenance organization (HMO)** plans.[32] The growth in HMOs was stimulated by the passage of the *Health Maintenance Organization Act of 1973*. This act requires that companies with at least 25 employees living in an HMO service area must offer membership in that organization as an alternative to regular group health coverage, provided the HMO meets federal qualification requirements. HMO amendments of 1988 relaxed many of the federal rules governing HMOs and specifically repealed the dual-choice mandate, effective October 1995. This shift in legislative direction is designed to make the HMO field more competitive and, as a result, employers more receptive to using HMOs.

> **FAST FACT**
>
> More employees with health insurance coverage are joining managed care programs: 48% in 1992 versus 85% in 2000.

One successful HMO is operated by John Deere and Company, a farm machinery manufacturer. Realizing 20 years ago that its own health care costs were skyrocketing, Deere brought its health care operations in-house and thereby established its own HMO, called John Deere Health. Deere has been so successful that it has attracted more than 300 other company clients.[33]

Preferred Provider Networks. The **preferred provider organization (PPO)** is another form of managed health care delivery. Introduced in the 1980s, these plans covered over 100 million participants in 2000. With these programs, employers contract directly or indirectly through an insurance company with health care providers (physicians, dentists, laboratories, hospitals, and so forth) to deliver discounted services to program participants. Because the rates and requirements for these plans are relatively unregulated, employers have a great deal of flexibility in structuring an arrangement.

Unlike HMO participants, employees in a PPO are not required to use the plan's providers exclusively. However, they are usually offered incentives, such as a lower deductible or lower cost-sharing percentage, to use a PPO provider. For example, the employer may cover all the costs of health care provided by a PPO but only 80 percent of the costs of health care provided by physicians outside the PPO network.[34]

Self-Funded Plans. Like Steelcase, a growing number of companies are opting for self-insured or self-funded plans as a way to control medical plan costs and gain relief from state insurance regulations. By eliminating or reducing insurance protection, the employer saves on carrier retention charges (the amount of money not utilized to pay claims), such as state premium taxes, administrative costs, risk and contingency expenses, and reserve requirements. Typically, the employer creates a voluntary employee beneficiary association and establishes a trust whose investment income is tax exempt as long as it's used to provide benefits to employees and their dependents.

> **FAST FACT**
>
> The Camberley Hotel in Atlanta reduced health care costs and employee turnover when it became self-insured.

Cost Containment Strategies. To further control health care costs, firms employ a variety of other strategies such as the following:

- *Hospital utilization programs.* Employers set up a system to review the necessity and appropriateness of hospitalization prior to admission, during a stay, or both.
- *Coordination of benefits.* Employers coordinate their benefits with those of other providers to prevent duplicate payment for the same health care service.
- *Data analysis.* Employers analyze the available information to determine the most viable cost management approach. Simulations and experience-based utilization assumptions are used to develop models.
- *Case management.* Many employers are active participants in case management. Medical procedures may include requirements for second opinions and peer reviews.
- *Cost sharing with employees.* By raising deductibles and contribution levels, employers hold the line on overall expenses.
- *Incentives to take care.* By offering incentives, such as bonuses to employees who lose weight, some firms hope to change employees' behaviors so they are healthier.[35]

> *"Large portions of the health care industry have undergone revolutionary change, and not for the purpose of improving health care, but in order to reduce the cost of doing business for large corporations."*
>
> New England Journal of Medicine

Wellness Programs

Frustrated with efforts to manage health care costs for employees who already are sick, a growing number of employers are taking proactive steps to prevent health care problems. Wellness programs may include exercise classes held at on-site fitness facilities, training in stress management, assistance in quitting smoking, free health screening clinics, practices to promote healthy eating, and a variety of other programs. A handful of firms implement well-designed wellness programs to produce significant savings on the bottom line.[36]

Coors Brewing Company spent 10 years fine-tuning its wellness program. For every $1.00 spent on wellness, Coors sees a return of $6.15, including $1.9 million annually in decreased medical costs, reduced sick leave, and increased productivity. According to William Coors, past chairman and CEO, the secret to Coors's success is really no secret: "Wellness is an integral part of the corporate culture." Coors's commitment to wellness includes a health risk assessment, nutritional counseling, stress management, and programs for smoking cessation, weight loss, and orthopedic rehabilitation.

Overweight Coors employees learn about the long-term risks associated with their condition through a health hazard survey. They are educated about the effect of excess weight on the cardiovascular, endocrine, and musculoskeletal systems. Then they receive an individual plan that may include individual counseling, group classes, and medical programs. The company even gives employees a financial incentive if they participate in the program and achieve and maintain their weight loss goal during a 12-month period. To further encourage involvement, classes are held on site.

Coors has been sensitive to the ADA requirements (a) that entry into a wellness program can't be a condition for passing a medical exam and (b) that facilities must be accessible to all. "At Coors Co. persons with disabilities have complete access to all of the company's facilities and its wellness center," says corporate communications manager Joe Fuentes. Part of the wellness program includes a medical questionnaire that determines employees' "health age" in relation to their chronological age. The program is totally voluntary for employees. The questionnaire asks employees whether they smoke, wear a seat belt, have high blood pressure, and exercise, and also includes questions about the employees' medical history. All Coors employees are covered by their health insurance at 85 percent. Employees who pass the questionnaire are then covered at 90 percent. If employees fail the test, they can have a plan of action recommended by the community outreach person who runs the program. Test results are confidential and made available only to the community outreach person who administers the survey. Employees can choose not to follow up on the test results.[37]

Employee Assistance Programs

Whereas wellness programs attempt to prevent the development of health problems, **employee assistance programs (EAPs)** are designed to assist employees with chronic personal problems that hinder their job performance and attendance. EAPs often serve employees with alcohol or drug dependencies, or both, or those with severe domestic problems. EAPs also help employees cope with mental disorders, financial problems, stress, eating disorders, smoking cessation, dependent care, bereavement, and AIDS. Because the job may be partly responsible for these problems, some employers are taking the lead in establishing EAPs for affected workers. As many employers learned following the World Trade Center tragedy, helping employees cope with stress is

> **FAST FACT**
>
> Whole Foods Market, a grocery chain specializing in natural foods, added a perk: acupuncture coverage.

> **FAST FACT**
>
> Some 60% of adults are overweight. And that costs companies an estimated $5.5 billion yearly in lost productivity.

> **FAST FACT**
>
> Dow's "Backs in Action" program encourages exercise, dieting, and ergonomics. The company has decreased on-the-job strains and sprains up to 90%.

> **FAST FACT**
>
> In the two weeks following the attack on the World Trade Center (9/11/01), counselors from Crisis Management International did six months' worth of work.

essential to companies that experience major catastrophes, even when the employer is not at fault.[38] Thus, EAPs are a service that helps individual employees, their families, and the firm.

PAID LEAVE

Paid leave isn't as complex to administer as benefits from protection programs, but it's more costly, accounting for more than 10 percent of the total payroll. If absenteeism policies are not designed correctly, costs may escalate even further. The two major categories of paid leave are time not worked while off the job and time not worked while on the job.

Off the Job

The most common paid-off-the-job times are vacations, holidays, sick leaves, and personal days. The challenge in administering these benefits is to contain costs while seeking better ways to tailor the benefits and services to fit employees' needs and preferences.

> **FAST FACT**
>
> More than 80% of workers received paid holidays and vacations in 2000, but less than 10% of those in the bottom tenth received paid leave of any kind.

Vacations and Holidays. Vacations give employees time to recuperate from the physical and mental demands of work. Vacation time is also viewed as an appropriate reward for service and commitment to the organization. Recently, a small number of firms have granted sabbaticals to employees (similar to those in academia), which, after a stated period of service, can be used for self-improvement, community work, or teaching. Tandem Computers, for example, grants six-week sabbaticals plus normal vacation time at full pay. Tandem found that in the short term, such programs have a negative effect on productivity, but in the long term, they enhance productivity.

In setting up vacation programs, several issues need to be addressed: (1) Will vacation pay be based on scheduled hours or on hours actually worked? (2) Under what circumstances can an employee be paid in lieu of a vacation? (3) Can vacations be deferred, or will they be lost if not taken? (4) What pay rate applies if an employee works during a vacation? The trend is toward vacation banking, with employees able to roll over a specified period of unused vacation days into a savings investment plan. Keep in mind that in the U.S. firms are not legally required to offer vacation days. In other countries, however, the government mandates the minimum number of vacation days per year. International differences in vacation policies are described in the feature "Managing Globalization: Vacationing Around the World."[39]

Paid Absences. On any given day, 1 million American workers who are otherwise employed won't attend work; they will be absent. In the United States, the daily absenteeism rate ranges from 2 percent to 3 percent of total payroll, but some organizations report absenteeism in excess of 20 percent. Employees fail to show up for work for many reasons—health problems, family problems, bad weather, transportation difficulties, and so forth. Nevertheless, absences are greatly influenced by an organization's formal policies. As the number of paid days off increases, the number of days of actual absence increases proportionally. Because of lax policies, many organizations unwittingly not only tolerate or accept absenteeism but actually reward it. Their policies make it easier to be absent than to come to work.

Vacationing Around the World

For employees who work in global firms, vacation policies and practices are among the visible differences in benefits and services enjoyed by employees around the world. Countries differ substantially in terms of what the government mandates as well as whether and how employees actually use their vacation time. In the United States, in addition to national and local holidays, full-time employees typically receive a week's vacation after one year of service and two weeks after two years. However, there are no government regulations mandating that employees receive time off, or that they be paid when they take vacations. Countries also differ in terms of whether employees actually use their vacation days to take a vacation. Many Europeans would never consider not using all of their vacation time, while Americans often take fewer days than they are entitled to. The chart below suggests some of the general differences in vacations taken by employees around the world.

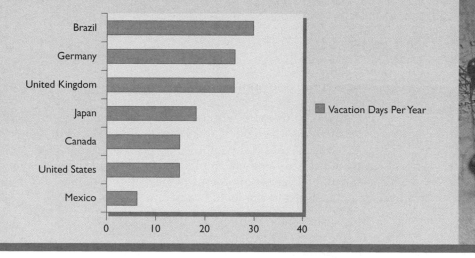

Vacation Days Per Year

Negative strategies to control absenteeism include disciplinary procedures against employees who are absent once a week or once every two weeks without a physician's excuse, before or after a holiday, after payday, without calling in, or for personal business. This discipline ranges from oral warnings for first offenses to discharge. Unfortunately, these policies appear to be generally ineffective in controlling absenteeism among habitual offenders.

Programs that reward attendance—with, for instance, cash prizes, bonuses, or conversion of a proportion of unused absence days to vacation days—appear more promising. To prevent unscheduled absenteeism, many organizations grant personal days, or personal time off (PTO). The employees can use these days during the year for any reason. The logic here is that employees must notify supervisors in advance that they will be absent. Self-management programs for habitual offenders also offer some hope for controlling excessive absenteeism.

On the Job

Time not worked on the job includes rest periods, lunch periods, washup times, and clothes-changing and getting-ready times. Together, these are the fifth most expensive benefit. Another benefit that's growing in popularity is paid time for physical fitness. This is clearly pay for time not worked, but organizations often offer it because of its on-the-job benefit: healthy workers.

In response to a growing number of single-parent families, two-earner families, aging parents in need of care, and nontraditional families, employers are expanding their benefits and services packages to address new priorities.[40] Some of these benefits and services are offered by only a handful of firms. However, employers are realizing that a failure to address these needs in the future may restrict their ability to compete. Thus, it's anticipated that many employers will add these benefits and services to assist employees in balancing work and life.[41]

Child Care Services

FAST FACT

At J&J, employees can bring their infants in for free tests and checkups six times annually. Prevention saves $13 million a year.

Recognizing that child care is a shared responsibility, more and more employers are providing some type of child care assistance to their employees. In fact, a survey of more than 10,000 firms employing 10 or more workers showed that 63 percent of those firms offered some type of assistance benefits, scheduling help, or services related to child care.[42] Thus, to be competitive in the labor market, firms at least need to survey their employees to find out their preferences and may need to offer a variety of options to meet employee needs.[43] Options employers may want to develop include any or all of the following:

- Scholarships for dependents
- Summer employment for dependents
- Subsidized tutoring for dependents
- Sick-child care
- Back-up care
- Flexible scheduling
- Child care referrals
- Family care leave
- Adoption benefits[44]

Some employers fear that childless employees may resent progressive policies to assist families. In fact, the formation of The Childfree Network, which is an advocacy group that serves as a voice for childless workers, is one indication that there is good reason to be prepared for some possible backlash from employees who feel they are not able to benefit as much as their peers who can utilize these valuable services. A recent study of employee attitudes revealed some disparity in the reactions of employees with and without children. However, the study failed to find any evidence that the more negative attitudes of the childless employees translated into concrete behaviors.[45] Other research indicates that any backlash that occurs tends to be of limited scope and does not create generalized job dissatisfaction.[46]

FAST FACT

MBNA Bank offers up to $20,000 support for adoption.

Even if some backlash occurs, the benefits and services associated with child care initiatives may outweigh the disadvantages. Prudential Insurance Company estimates that its child care center saves the company $80,000 annually through reduced absenteeism.[47] Families and society as a whole reap even more valuable gains. A recent study of nine Western European countries indicates that parental leave-taking is correlated with children's health and survival. In the countries studied, on average, eligible employees (men and women) used 32 weeks of parental leave benefits. Longer leaves significantly reduced deaths among infants and young children.[48]

Dependent Care Reimbursement Accounts. Dependent care reimbursement accounts have become the most prevalent type of child care benefit in the early 2000s. According to a survey by Buck Consultants, this benefit is offered by nearly 60 percent of medium- and large-sized companies.[49] These accounts allow employees to pay for qualified expenses with pretax dollars subject to a use-it-or-lose-it rule. They benefit employees greatly, yet involve minimal administrative costs for the sponsoring organization. The maximum amount an employee can channel into one of these accounts is $5,000 a year. For an employee to participate in a reimbursement account, the child must be under the age of 13. The expense must be necessary to permit an employee to work, to permit both husband and wife to work, or to permit a spouse to attend school full-time.[50]

> **FAST FACT**
>
> Serving a largely female workforce, First Chicago pays for about 800 deliveries a year. Coaching pregnant women has drastically reduced C-sections and underweight babies.

Resource and Referral Programs. Twenty-nine percent of firms offer child care information and referral assistance. These company-sponsored programs counsel employees about day care options and refer them to prescreened local providers. Prescreening helps to ensure that the centers in the network meet minimum care standards and are financially responsible.

On-Site Care Facilities. By 2000, thousands of employer-sponsored on-site or near-site care centers were in operation. In San Francisco, office and hotel complexes with more than 50,000 square feet must either provide an on-site facility or pay into a city child care fund. Although the operation of such centers can be costly, a growing number of employers now accept it as a social and business necessity.

Consider the comments of Dick Parker, director of administrative services for Merck and Company, at groundbreaking ceremonies for its $8 million child care center: "You don't provide child care just because you want to be a good guy. You do it for business reasons. Merck decided to build the center for three reasons: retention, recruitment, and productivity. Child care will become more and more of a recruitment issue in the future. If employees are worried about their child care services[,] that will affect their productivity and retention."[51]

> **FAST FACT**
>
> Cisco constructed a $16 million child care center for 432 children. Web cameras give parents a real-time window on their children.

Campbell Soup Company's child care center is located across the street from its corporate headquarters and cares for 110 children. Contending that on-site care cuts absenteeism, reduces distractions for employees, and helps with hiring, the company picks up 40 percent of the weekly expense for each child.[52] The Hacienda Child Development Center in Pleasanton, California, serves multiple employers, including Hewlett-Packard, Computerland Corporation, and Prudential Insurance Company. Operating costs are funded from parent fees and business fees.

Elder Care Services

Twenty-eight percent of employees over the age of 30 spend an average of 10 hours a week giving care to an older relative. For a significant fraction, this commitment equals a second job. Some 12

> **FAST FACT**
>
> One out of four households provides informal care to a relative or friend age 50 or older.

percent of workers who care for aging parents are forced to quit their jobs to do so. With aging of the baby boomers, more and more employers are considering ways to help workers who are caring for elderly relatives. Assistance ranges from information and referral programs to specialized care insurance. The *Family and Medical Leave Act of 1993* supports employee time off for both child care and elder care.

Information and Referral Programs. In 1990, only 11 percent of employers offered information and referral programs for elder care; now the number exceeds 50 percent. Like dependent care referral programs, company-operated elder care referral programs are designed to help the caregiver identify appropriate community resources.[53]

Long-Term Care Insurance. One new and fast-growing option for elder care is long-term care insurance. Although fewer than 15 percent of firms offered this benefit in the mid-1990s, nearly 70 percent offer it now. This type of insurance covers medical, social, custodial, and personal services for people who suffer from chronic physical or mental illnesses or disabling injury or disease over an extended period of time. Typically, coverage is offered to employees on an employee-pay-all basis. Premium rates are age based, and some plans set a maximum age (typically 79) for participation. Benefit maximums are related to care site (e.g., nursing home versus day care center) and include lifetime limits.

OTHER BENEFITS AND SERVICES

With demographic and value shifts, a wider array of lifestyle choices is now available. As a consequence, a rising percentage of workers—such as unmarried couples, divorced people, and single parents—don't fit into conventional benefits and services packages. Recognizing that people are assets to the organization and that the world of work can never be fully separated from the rest of life, companies on the cutting edge are redesigning their benefits and services packages to address the needs of all employees.[54]

Benefits for Spousal Equivalents

"Domestic partner benefits isn't a gay and lesbian issue. It's a business issue. We believe that by providing domestic partners access, we are enhancing our ability to recruit and retain the best employees."

Bill Shelley
Health and Welfare Supervisor
Pacific Gas & Electric

As of 1997, about 10 percent companies had extended "spousal" benefits to same-sex partners and to unmarried opposite-sex partners. By 2002, just five years later, this figure had increased to 22 percent. Among those who did not offer such benefits, 35 percent were considering doing so. The reasons firms gave for providing these benefits (also referred to as domestic partner benefits) are shown in Exhibit 13.8.[55] Notice that one important reason is complying with local government regulations. Federal laws do not require employers to provide domestic partner benefits, but some local ordinances do.

In 1997, the San Francisco Board of Supervisors mandated that all employers who do business with the city must offer registered domestic partners—who may be either same-sex or opposite-sex couples—the same benefits they offer married couples. The San Francisco 49ers football team, television stations, airlines that lease space at the airport, and many other employers have been affected. During the 1980s and early 1990s, many employers shunned domestic partner benefits, due in part to cost concerns.

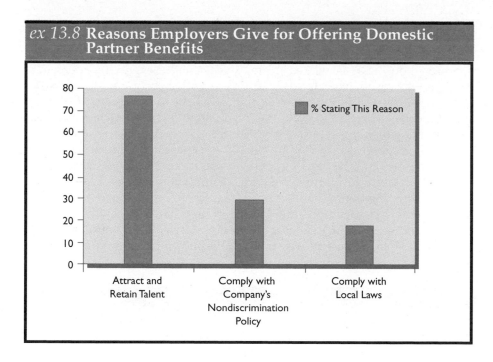

ex 13.8 **Reasons Employers Give for Offering Domestic Partner Benefits**

Back then, insurance companies often added surcharges for domestic partner coverage, because they thought that costs would go up. Since then, however, data have become available and they show the surcharges were unnecessary. Surcharges have largely disappeared, making domestic partner benefits no more expensive than benefits for spouses.[56] Lotus, now a unit of IBM, modified its insurance and benefits policy to offer gay and lesbian partners the same benefits accorded heterosexual spouses. According to Russell J. Campanello, vice president for human resources, "This is fair and equal." To be eligible, unmarried partners of the same sex must live together and share financial obligations. If they break up, the employee must wait one year before registering a new partner. In addition to health care, the plan includes life insurance, relocation expenses, bereavement leave, and a death benefit.[57] Such benefits are optional for most employers, but they are required for some.

> **FAST FACT**
>
> Three percent of the employees at Timberland Boot Company use domestic partner benefits.

Educational Expense Allowances

Faced with skill obsolescence, downsizing, and retraining demands, most medium and large firms provide some form of educational expense assistance. Most plans cover registration fees, and some assist with graduation, laboratory, entrance examination, professional certification, and activity fees. Typically, these programs require a relationship between the course and some phase of company operations. For example, National Healthcorp, which is headquartered in Murfreesboro, Tennessee, offers tuition assistance to any aide who wishes to become a nurse. The company will pay for up to two years of school in exchange for the aide's promise to stay on staff that long after graduation.

Relocation and Housing Assistance

As housing costs continue to soar, more employers are considering housing assistance as an employee benefit. Seventy-five percent of surveyed New Jersey employers with 500 or more employees attributed hiring and retention problems to the high cost of housing; 71 percent of surveyed California manufacturers said high housing costs were limiting their business expansion abilities.[58]

Relocation assistance traditionally has consisted of financial help for travel expenses and the cost of moving possessions. If needed, the company might also pay for furniture storage for a limited time as well as for temporary housing. A growing number of firms also offer a variety of allowances and services for transferred employees and high-demand new hires. These benefits and services include cost allowances for selling a house, expenses for finding a new residence, assistance in finding employment for a spouse, and temporary living expenses.

ADMINISTRATIVE ISSUES

Effectively administering employee benefits and services is a complicated challenge. In addition to deciding which benefits and services to offer, employers must work to ensure that employees understand both the content of the plan and its economic cost/value.

Determining the Benefits and Services Package

The benefits and services package should be selected on the basis of what is good for the employee as well as for the employer. Knowing employee preferences can often help organizations determine what benefits and services to offer, but decisions about what to offer must also take into account the costs relative to the benefits for employers.

Employee Preferences. Employees in one company indicated a strong preference for dental insurance over life insurance, even though dental insurance was only one-fourth the cost to the company. By providing the less expensive benefit, the employer cut costs while increasing employee satisfaction.

Employers who assume that the best way to satisfy employees' preferences is by spending more money undoubtedly are wasting some of that money.

Individual differences appear to play a large role in determining which benefits and services employees prefer. Clearly, when it comes to benefits and services, one size does not fit all employees! The differences in employees' preferences was recently demonstrated in a study of more than 2,400 employees working in 60 different companies. Employees were presented with three alternative retirement plan options, including a traditional defined benefit plan, a cash balance plan, and a hybrid plan that had elements of both. The study found that it was difficult to predict which plan a employee would prefer based on demographic characteristics (e.g., age, gender, education). Instead, preferences for the different plans depended upon how much value an employee placed on various plan features. Some employees valued portability, others valued being in control of their investments, and some preferred to avoid risk.[59]

Employer's Ability to Pay. Even if employers know what employees prefer, they may not be able to offer it. According to Jordan Shields, owner of a consulting firm specializing in benefits and services, a company's size may constrain the benefits and services it can provide. Companies with fewer than 10 employees may have difficulty finding an insurance carrier. Dental and vision care insurance options aren't very good. Disability plans for these small companies will be either very restrictive or very expensive. Only after a company has at least 25 employees can it begin to offer a choice of medical plans, according to some experts.

Companies having more than 50 employees, and certainly those with more than 100, have more options and can even participate in partial self-insurance programs. When an employer self-insures, it acts partially as the insurance company. This means that, if employees stay fairly healthy and don't file a lot of claims, the employer won't pay as much in premiums. A firm that has 300 to 400 employees can choose from among many options and carriers and can establish a large plan that can be modified easily. However, a firm that grows from 10 to 150 employees within a year or two will have major changes to make. Unfortunately, like many other functions at young, fast-growing firms, benefits and services management tends to lag behind the more urgent line functions.[60]

Corporate Strategy and Culture. As is true for other HR practices, an organization's decisions about which benefits and services to offer are driven by many internal factors. For a labor-intensive organization pursuing a low-cost strategy, providing expensive benefits and services may not be an option. Conversely, when labor costs are a relatively minor portion of an organization's total costs, providing unusually good benefits may provide a competitive advantage that ensures the company gets the best possible employees. For knowledge-intensive companies that compete on the basis of innovation and intellectual capital, the importance of attracting and retaining the best talent may be of such high priority that cost considerations are not a determinant of what benefits and services are offered.

An organization's culture may also influence decisions about which benefits and services to offer. At Starbucks, for example, teamwork is an important ingredient. The benefits and services it offers to employees support a team-based culture, as described in the feature "Managing Teams: Starbucks' Blend for Benefits and Services."[61]

Providing Flexibility

When employees can design their own benefits and services packages, both they and the company come out ahead. At least that's the experience at companies such as Quaker Oats, Ex-Cello, TRW Incorporated, Educational Testing Service (ETS), and Morgan Stanley.[62] ETS provides a core package of benefits and services to all employees, covering basic needs such as personal medical care, dental care, disability, vacation, and retirement. In addition, each individual can choose, cafeteria style, from optional benefits and services or can increase those in the core package. Employees are allowed to change their packages once a year.

At Morgan Stanley, about two-thirds of all eligible employees elect their own benefits and services package over the standard no-choice plan.

MANAGING TEAMS

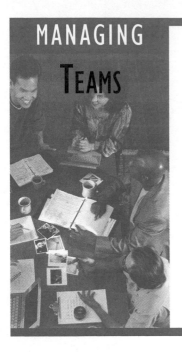

Starbucks' Blend for Benefits and Services

Headquartered in Seattle, Starbucks has grown from a local coffee hangout to a global one. With more than 27,000 employees working in more than 1,700 stores around the world, Starbucks seeks to create a spirit of camaraderie and fun. Supporting this effort, the company provides generous benefits to both full-time and part-time employees, including health and dental coverage, a pension plan, and disability and life insurance. At headquarters, employees enjoy on-site fitness services. And employees everywhere can access the company's Info-line to link up with other employees with shared interests and hobbies, or gather information about child care and elder care. Because of their relatively young workforce, Starbucks enjoys comparatively low health care costs—about 20 percent below the national average. And the costs of many of the other services it provides also are minimal. The pay-off seems to

justify the costs incurred. It has been ranked by *Fortune* as one of the best companies to work for. Its turnover rate of 60 percent annually is well below the industry average of 300 percent. Because people stay longer, recruiting and training costs also are relatively low compared with the industry.

To stay attuned to employees' concerns, Starbucks regularly conducts surveys and solicits employees' ideas. In response to what it was hearing, the company recently introduced flexible work schedules as a component of its work/life program and beefed up referral services for employees facing various life issues—which vary tremendously depending on age, family responsibilities, and other individual circumstances. Through all of these efforts, Starbucks communicates that it cares about the needs of employees and respects them as members of the company's team of key players.

"American companies have failed to realize that there's tremendous value in inspiring people to share a common purpose of self-esteem, self-respect and appreciation."

Howard Schultz
Chairman
Starbucks

The options themselves were developed by the employees, working in small discussion groups. This is happening in many companies today because their workforces are becoming so diverse, and their needs for benefits and services rather varied. For this reason, and because providing flexibility is so effective, most companies now offer at least some variable benefits and services.[63] Having benefits and services accessible through call centers or on an intranet makes it easier than ever to offer this flexibility.

Increasingly, information about benefits and services is being communicated electronically. At Oracle, Boeing, and Charles Schwab, workers can surf company intranets to learn about and self-manage 401(k) plans, health care benefits, and even tax withholding options. Hard Rock Café International makes information available through an interactive CD that can be played at publicly available monitors in the employee break rooms.

Outside the United States, flexible benefits and services are less common. In some countries, high levels of mandatory benefits make flexibility less feasible. In other countries, there are fewer sophisticated service providers to offer the full range of services that employees might desire. In some countries, restrictive tax laws reduce the appeal of offering a wide range of benefits and services.

Communicating the Benefits and Services Package

Considering that most benefits and services program objectives are not attained, assessment of communication effectiveness would probably produce unfavorable results. This may be partly due to the communication techniques used. Almost all companies use impersonal, passive booklets and brochures to convey information; only a few use more personal, active media, such as slide presentations and regular employee meetings. An especially good technique communicates the total compensation components every day. Increasingly, firms are offering voice response systems, or call centers. Employees in firms such as Cummins Engine Company in Columbus, Indiana, telephone in to learn about and manage their benefits and services. Employees can also manage their own benefits and services through intranet Web sites that describe the firms' benefits and services program.[64]

Through communicating the benefits and services package and providing flexibility, the positive image of the company can be increased. Hewitt Associates found that 75 percent of all employees who understand its compensation program perceive it as fair, whereas only about 33 percent of all employees who do not understand the system think it's fair. Providing clear information about how to file claims and where to get services tends to bring more employees into the positive-perception camp.

Managing and Reducing Costs

The trend is clear: more and more organizations are managing and reducing the costs associated with offering employees nonmandatory benefits and services. Managing costs may mean having second opinions and fewer choices in health care coverage. It may mean making sure that a disability is really a disability and that workers get back to work as soon as possible. It may mean being proactive and seeking ways to prevent sickness and injury, as well as helping employees recover more quickly by offering more home health care.[65] But it also may mean trying to provide benefits and services that really matter so as to increase the value of those benefits and services.

Does managing and reducing costs mean eliminating benefits and services? Certainly, firms are asking workers to share the expenses of their own health care and even retirement. This is a very big issue in the automobile industry. It's consistent with employee empowerment and self-management. Workers are capable of understanding business and cost conditions. By having benefits and services information, they may be able to help reduce costs without eliminating benefits and services. For coverage that each individual needs, employers are likely to find ways to not only reduce costs but also maintain employee commitment to the organization. Experiences at Steelcase, Johnson & Johnson, Levi Strauss, and Deere show that win-win situations, with extensive employee involvement and understanding, are possible.

Employers in the United States are not the only ones dealing with costs. The issue is also of growing importance in Europe, although employers there face a somewhat different situation. In Europe, governments provide most of the health care and pensions. Today, however, these governments are seeking ways to balance their budgets, and one way is to get out of the health care– and pension-providing roles. If they do this, employees and governments are likely to look to employers for relief at a time when many of those employers are already paying some of the highest wages in the world. Thus, the pressure on European employers to manage and reduce costs is likely to be even greater than it is on U.S. employers.

FAST FACT

At Sky Chefs Kitchen in El Paso, Texas, each morning begins with an employee-led stretching session designed to curb back injuries.

FAST FACT

Quaker grants bonuses of as much as $500 for families who exercise, shun smoking, and wear seat belts. Employees can keep the money or invest in added benefits.

FAST FACT

Don't even think about cutting benefits if employee retention is important:
- 401(k) matching funds
- Medical/dental benefits
- Day care
- Flextime

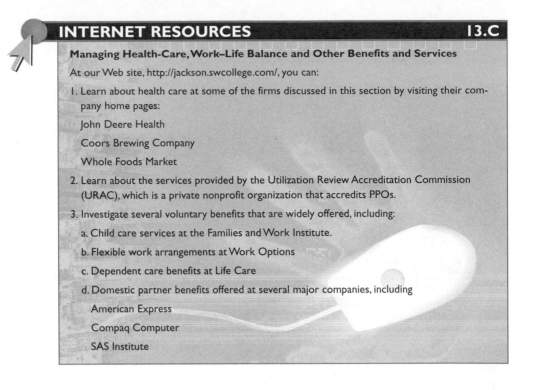

INTERNET RESOURCES   **13.C**

Managing Health-Care, Work–Life Balance and Other Benefits and Services

At our Web site, http://jackson.swcollege.com/, you can:

1. Learn about health care at some of the firms discussed in this section by visiting their company home pages:

   John Deere Health

   Coors Brewing Company

   Whole Foods Market

2. Learn about the services provided by the Utilization Review Accreditation Commission (URAC), which is a private nonprofit organization that accredits PPOs.

3. Investigate several voluntary benefits that are widely offered, including:

   a. Child care services at the Families and Work Institute.

   b. Flexible work arrangements at Work Options

   c. Dependent care benefits at Life Care

   d. Domestic partner benefits offered at several major companies, including

      American Express

      Compaq Computer

      SAS Institute

SUMMARY

From the mid-1940s to the mid-1990s, the costs of benefits and services grew substantially more than the costs of direct compensation. The increase occurred despite the lack of evidence that increased investment in benefits and services results in improved productivity. For many firms, the growing difficulty of simply attracting talent resulted in increased spending on benefits and services believed to be attractive to employees. Unfortunately, the specific benefits and services offered by employers may not be highly valued by all employees. Worse yet, employees may not even know which benefits and services their employer provides, nor do they appreciate the costs of many benefits and services.

To better align benefits and services with the preferences of employees, some employers now solicit employee opinions about their preferences for and levels of satisfaction with various benefits and services. Thus, the move has been away from the traditional paternalistic approach, toward increasing the level of employee involvement, participation, and self-determination. Organizations are also becoming more concerned with the communication of their benefits programs. Current evidence suggests that employees' lack of awareness of the contents and value of their benefits programs may partially explain why these programs are not always perceived favorably.

Besides considering employees' preferences, employers must consider the costs of various benefits and services. Tax laws can greatly affect the cost of some benefits and services, as well as their value to employees. By designing benefits and services that are eligible for favorable tax treatment, employers can more effectively leverage their investments in benefits and services. Legal considerations have also played a role in causing employers to shift away from offering traditional defined benefit pension plans toward increasing use of cash balance plans. Due to the complexity of economic and legal issues surrounding the design and administration of benefits and services, organizations face significant challenges when attempting to design a benefits and services package that addresses the strategic concerns of attracting and retaining talent, maximizing productivity, reducing costs, and ensuring legal compliance.

TERMS TO REMEMBER

401(k) plan
403(b) plan
cash balance plan
contributory plan
defined benefit pension plan
defined contribution plan
EAP (employee assistance program)
employee benefits and services
HMO (health maintenance
    organization)
money purchase plan
noncontributory plan

nonqualified plan
Pension Benefit Guaranty
    Corporation
portable benefits
PPO (preferred provider
    organization)
private protection programs
public protection programs
qualified plan
tax-deferred profit-sharing plans
vesting

DISCUSSION QUESTIONS

1. What is Steelcase doing to manage its workers' compensation costs?
2. As a manager, how can you use benefits and services to improve productivity?
3. Describe the various components of benefits and services.
4. Distinguish between public and private protection programs, and give examples of each.
5. How are unemployment benefits derived? What is the status of unemployment compensation?
6. How would you rationalize to your employer the costs of providing a physical fitness facility? How would you assess whether or not to provide various other voluntary benefits and services, taking into account the costs?
7. Should more companies follow the example of Coors and establish a wellness program? Why or why not?
8. As employers strive to offer benefits to an increasingly diverse workforce, they sometimes encounter backlash from employees who resent their policies. For example, some employees may not approve of spending on child care facilities, given that they benefit some employees and not others. Or, some employees may not approve of policies that give equal treatment to spouses and "nonspousal equivalents" or domestic partners. Make a list of the advantages and disadvantages of providing a broad range of benefits and services versus adopting a "bare-bones" approach. Which approach would you recommend? Why?

PROJECTS TO EXTEND YOUR LEARNING

1. *Managing Through Strategic Partnerships.* Your company is debating whether or not to offer stock options to all of its employees. Currently, only senior managers receive them, as is typical in many U.S. companies. The CEO and senior management think that granting options might increase the feeling of ownership and thus result in a greater commitment to work harder for the company, as it seems employees do at Southwest Airlines. However, some managers are concerned that granting options might backfire if the company's stock price does not increase. Without the increases, employees may feel less commitment to work hard. A question raised by some is "Do employees really think that they have control or influence over the price of the stock or is it really subject to broader market forces?" Furthermore, some ask, "Once employees start owning stock, will they be more interested in watching the price of the stock than in working hard?" What are your recommendations?

2. *Managing Teams.* A problem that some companies have is the lack of awareness and understanding among employees of the value and cost of the benefits and services they receive. In some cases, employees don't even know what benefits and services they receive or what they are entitled to receive. With the cost of benefits and services so high, companies are literally throwing away good money! So your first assignment is to change this situation in your company. You are now a firm believer in partnership in managing human resources. You know that through partnership better practices can be developed. You also believe that partnership is a good way to spread the understanding and awareness of what human resource practices exist. Therefore, you decide to establish a team to work on the general assignment of increasing all employees' awareness and understanding of the value and cost of the benefits and services provided by the company. Who will be on the team? What will they do? When and to whom will they report? How will you manage conflicts that might result from differences in worker age, functional area, or level in the company?

3. *Integration and Application.* After reviewing the Lincoln Electric and Southwest Airlines cases at the end of the book, answer the following questions.
   a. What are the objectives of the company's approach to benefits and services?
   b. How well are the benefits and services packages being offered serving the business objectives and the needs of employees? Which package would you prefer? Explain why.
   c. Could Southwest Airlines adopt the approach to benefits and services used at Lincoln Electric? What would be the advantages and disadvantages for Southwest Airlines of adopting the Lincoln Electric approach? Be sure to consider how various stakeholders would be affected by such a change.

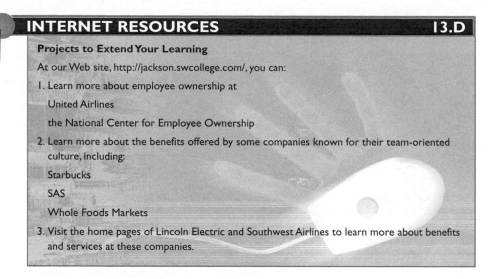

INTERNET RESOURCES

13.D

Projects to Extend Your Learning

At our Web site, http://jackson.swcollege.com/, you can:

1. Learn more about employee ownership at

   United Airlines

   the National Center for Employee Ownership

2. Learn more about the benefits offered by some companies known for their team-oriented culture, including:

   Starbucks

   SAS

   Whole Foods Markets

3. Visit the home pages of Lincoln Electric and Southwest Airlines to learn more about benefits and services at these companies.

case study

WHO'S BENEFITING?

Jack Parks is a benefits and services manager in the auto electronics division of USA Motors, a major manufacturer of audio systems and auto electronic ignition systems. He is very concerned after analyzing the impact of absenteeism on the division's staffing costs for the previous quarter. What troubles Jack is an agreement that the national union negotiated with USA Motors 10 years ago that, in effect, paid workers for being absent. Of course, the "paid absence" agreement was not supposed to work quite that way. In theory, workers were given one week of paid absence against which they could charge their personal absences. Presumably, this system would encourage workers to notify their supervisors so that staffing arrangements could be made and production maintained.

In practice, workers discovered that by not charging off any "paid absences," they could receive a full week's pay in June when the company paid off the balance of the unused paid absences for the previous year. This cash bonus, as workers had come to think of it, often coincides with the summer vacation taken by many of the 8,000 hourly employees when USA Motors shuts down for inventory.

As Jack learned, employees with chronic absentee records had figured out how to charge off absences using the regular categories, which permit sick days and excused and unexcused absences. In Jack's mind, USA Motors might just as well have negotiated a cash bonus for hourly workers or given them another 10 to 15 cents per hour.

After reviewing the division's absenteeism rates for controllable absences—that is, those categories of absences believed to be of the employee's own choice—Jack concludes that the company could reduce this rate from the previous year's figure of 11 percent. And then Jack has a brainstorm: What USA Motors needs to negotiate is an incentive plan for reducing absenteeism. The plan Jack has in mind entails a standard for the amount of controllable absence deemed acceptable. If a chronically absent employee exceeds the standard, then vacation, holiday, and sickness/accident pay would be cut by 10 percent during the next six months. If worker absence continues to exceed the allowable limits, then vacation, holiday, and sickness pay would be cut during the next six months by the actual percentage of absent days incurred by the chronic absentee. Hence, if a worker misses 15 percent of scheduled workdays during the first six-month period, vacation pay for the next six-month period would be reduced by 10 percent. If the employee continues to be absent at the 15 percent rate, then vacation pay would be reduced by 15 percent during the next six months.

Jack immediately drafts a memorandum outlining the program and submits it to the corporate

HR manager of USA Motors for inclusion in the upcoming bargaining session. To Jack's surprise and delight, the memorandum receives strong corporate support and is scheduled as a high priority bargaining topic for the fall negotiations.

QUESTIONS

1. Will the incentive plan to reduce absenteeism succeed?
2. How much absenteeism is really under the employee's control?
3. Why didn't the "paid absence" plan work?
4. What plan would you suggest to USA Motors?

ENDNOTES

1 R. McGarvey, "Something Extra," *Entrepreneur* (May 1995): 70; further details of Starbucks benefits, such as BEAN STOCK, are in N. Weiss, "How Starbucks Impassions Workers to Drive Growth," *Workforce* (August 1998): 60–64.

2 Personal communication with Libby Child, Manager, Managed Claims and Disability Management Services, Steelcase (October 1998 and April 2001).

3 "Chamber of Commerce Benefits Survey," *Bureau of National Affairs* (2001).

4 S. F. Gale, "Formalized Flextime: The Perk That Brings Productivity," *Workforce* (February 2001): 39–42.

5 "Americans' Views on Health Care, Costs," *Workspan* (February 2001): 76–78; "Health Care Costs to Keep Rising at Double-Digits Rates," *HR Magazine* (2001): 32; J. Bruner, "Value of Health Coverage: As Costs Rise and Employee Satisfaction Slumps, Businesses Look for Better Returns," *ACA Journal* (First Quarter 2000): 57–65; "Health-Care Inflation Kept in Check in '97," *Wall Street Journal* (January 20, 1998): B6; "Slow Rise in Health Care Costs Continues," *Bulletin to Management: Policy Guide* (February 6, 1997): 48; "Health Benefit Costs Hold Steady," *Bulletin to Management: Policy Guide* (January 29, 1998): 32.

6 B. Leonard, "Employers' and Employees' Benefits Priorities Differ," *HR Magazine* (February 2001): 31; J. Cole, "Auto and Home Insurance: The New Employee Benefit," *HR Focus* (December 1997): 9; J. Landauer, "Bottom-Line Benefits of Work/Life Programs," *HR Focus* (July 1997): 3.

7 S. LoJacono, "Back-Up Care: The New Benefits Tie Breaker," *Workspan* (January 2001): 16–20; J. Stanger and T. Sawyer, "A Win/Win Addition to Employee Benefits," *ACA Journal* (First Quarter 2000): 19–27; "Benefits Values from the Employee's Perspective," *ACA News* (June 1998): 14–16; A. M. Rappaport, "The New Employment Contract and Employee Benefits: A Road Map for the Future," *ACA Journal* (Summer 1997): 6–15; A. Karr, "They're Young, But New College Grads Value Retirement, Health Benefits," *Wall Street Journal* (May 5, 1998): A1; A. R. McIlvaine, "In The Mainstream," *Human Resource Executive* (August 1997): 48–49.

8 Based on responses to a survey by WorldatWork conducted in 2000, as reported in R. Platt, "Values of Benefits Remains Constant," *Workspan* (June 2000): 34–39.

9 P. Cappelli, "A Market-Driven Approach to Retaining Talent," *Harvard Business Review* (January–February 2000): 103–111; R. K. Platt, "Aligning Benefits with Employee, Organizational Goals," *ACA News* (June 1998): 11–13.

10 R. Levering and M. Moskowitz, "The 100 Best Companies to Work For," *Fortune* (January 8, 2001): 148–156; M. L. Williams and G. F. Dreher, "Compensation System Attributes and Applicant Pool Characteristics," *Academy of Management Journal* 35 (1992): 571–595.

11 "Dr. Goodnight's Company Town," *Business Week* (June 19, 2000): 193–200; Society for Human Resource Management, "The Labor Shortage," *Workplace Visions* 4 (2000): 1–8; L. Gaughan and J. Kasparek, "The Employee as Customer," *Workspan* (September 2000): 30–37; P. Kruger, "Jobs for Life," *Fast Company* (May 2000): 236–252; J. Pfeffer, "SAS Insti-

tute (B): The Decision to Go Public," Graduate School of Business, Stanford University, Case Number: HR-6B (July 2000): 1–12.

12 K. Madigan, "Here Come Hefty Hikes in Benefits," *Business Week* (May 18, 1998): 170; "Employer-Based Health Coverage Declining," *Bulletin to Management: Datagraph* (June 23, 1994): 196–197; T. Thomason, T. Schmidle, and J. F. Burton, Jr. *Workers' Compensation: Benefits, Costs, and Safety Under Alternative Insurance Arrangements* (Kalamazoo, MI: W. E. Upjohn Institute for Employment Research, 2001).

13 "Chamber of Commerce Benefits Survey;" P. Passell, "Benefits Dwindle Along with Wages for the Unskilled," *New York Times* (June 14, 1998): A1.

14 B. Beam and J. McFadden, *Employee Benefits* (Chicago: Real Estate Education Company, 2001); L. Johnson and J. Rich, "Dealing with Employee Benefit Issues in Mergers and Acquisitions," *Legal Report* (March–April 2000): 1–8; "Employee Benefits," *Workforce* (May 2000): 91–96; L. Uchitelle, "For Employee Benefits, It Pays to Wear the Union Label," *New York Times* (July 16, 1995): F10.

15 M. McNamee, "Yes: The Private Market Offers Better Returns," *Business Week* (March 23, 1998): 36; C. Farrell, "No: Why Let Wall Street Gamble with Our Nest Egg," *Business Week* (March 23, 1998): 37; G. Koretz, "How Not to Fix Social Security," *Business Week* (March 23, 1998): 24; R. J. Barro, "Don't Tinker with Social Security, Reinvent It," *Business Week* (June 8, 1998): 24; K. Feldstein, "Social Security's Gender Gap," *New York Times* (April 13, 1998): A27; "Calculating Social Security Benefits," *Bulletin to Management: Datagraph* (March 27, 1997): 100.

16 P. Carroll, "Integrated Benefits Plans Offer Companies Key Advantages," *ACA News* (March 2000): 29–32; "State Unemployment Insurance Funds," *Bulletin to Management: Datagraph* (October 2, 1997): 316.

17 T. Vander Neut, "Charting the Tides," *Human Resource Executive* (November 1997): 60–61; R. Kirsch, "Oh My Achin . . ." *Human Resource Executive* (June 6, 1997): 25; M. Weinstein, "Ably Assisted," *Human Resource Executive* (June 6, 1997): 27; J. A. Nixon, "Protected Plans," *Human Resource Executive* (June 6, 1997): 30–32; "Paradigm Shift," *Human Resource Executive* (June 6, 1997): 36–37; J. G. Kilgour, "Twenty-Four Hour Coverage: Melding Group Health Insurance with Workers' Compensation," *ACA Journal* (Spring 1997): 56–64.

18 Libby Child, personal conversation with authors, April 7, 2001; J. J. Laabs, "Steelcase Slashes Workers' Comp Costs," *Personnel Journal* (February 1993): 72–87. See also "Workers' Comp Strategy Saves $4 Million Yearly," *Personnel Journal* (January 1993): 55; T. Vander Neut, "Step by Step," *Human Resource Executive* (September 1998): 86–88; B. A. Morris, "Injury 101," *Human Resource Executive* (September 1998): 77.

19 Society for Human Resource Management, "FMLA Still Poses Implementation Problems, Employers Say," *HR News* (February 2001): 3–12.

20 B. P. Noble, "Interpreting the Family Leave Act," *New York Times* (August 1, 1993): F24. See also D. Gunsch, "The Family Leave Act: A Financial Burden?" *Personnel Journal* (September 1993): 48–57; "Companies Willing to Stretch Employees Still Further," *HR Reporter* (March 1993): 5–6.

21 J. W. Papa, "Sizing Up the FMLA," *Workforce* (August 1998): 38–43; E.

Paltell, "FMLA: After Six Years, a Bit More Clarity," *HR Magazine* (September 1999): 144–150.

22 T. A. Stewart, "Will the Real Capitalist Please Stand Up?" *Fortune* (May 11, 1998): 189; D. Leonhardt, "At Northwest, an ESOP in Name Only," *Business Week* (September 14, 1998): 63; D. Leonhardt and A. Bernstein, "Not So United at United These Days," *Business Week* (May 4, 1998): 50.

23 L. Strazewski, "HIPAA Hangover," *Human Resource Executive* (May 5, 1998): 40–41.

24 L. Zuckerman, "Divided, an Airline Stumbles," *New York Times* (March 14, 2001): C1, C6; J. A. LoCicero, "How to Cope with the Multi-Employer Pension Plan Amendments Act of 1980," *Personnel Administrator* (May 1981): 51–54, 68; C. Del Valle, "Harsh Medicine for Ailing Pension Plans," *Business Week* (September 19, 1994): 91–94; M. Rowland, "An Unseen Trap in Pension Funds," *New York Times* (August 28, 1994): F13; R. D. Hylton, "Don't Panic about Your Pension—Yet," *Fortune* (April 18, 1994): 121–128; "ERISA's Effects on Pension Plan Administration," *Bulletin to Management* (August 9, 1984): 1–2.

25 Hylton, "Don't Panic about Your Pension—Yet"; P. F. Drucker, "Reckoning with the Pension Fund Revolution," *Harvard Business Review* (March–April 1991): 106–114.

26 R. Clark and S. Schieber, "The Shifting Sands of Retirement Plans," *WorldatWork Journal* (Fourth Quarter 2000): 6–14; S. Armour, "IBM Takes a Beating," *USA Today* (September 15, 1999): B1, B2; G. Flynn, "Out of the Red, Into the Blue," *Workforce* (March 2000): 50–52; J. Gould, "Aetna Inc.'s Evolution to Cash Balance Plans," *ACA Journal* (Fourth Quarter 1999): 34–37; V. Infante, "Retirement Plan Trends," *Workforce* (November 2000): 69–76; R. Inglis and S. Vernon, "Building a Better Retirement Plan," *HR Magazine* (August 1999): 90–96; R. Inglis and R. Joss, "Smoothing the Way for Cash Balance Plans," *HR Magazine* (December 1999): 77–84; N. B. Kurland and D. Bailey, "The Advantages and Challenges of Working Here, There, Anywhere, and Anytime," *Organizational Dynamics* (Autumn 1999): 53–67; J. O'Rourke, "Retirement Benefits Innovation: Carving New Solutions for Today's Changing Work Force," *ACA News* (February 2000): 14–18; S. Poe, "Retirement Strategies Going Global with Businesses," *ACA News* (April 2000): 12; M. W. Walsh, "No Time to Put Your Feet Up as Retirement Comes in Stages," *New York Times* (April 15, 2001): A1, A18; "Retirement Options: A Primer," *Workforce* (March 2001): 67–72.

27 J. VanDerhei, "The Controversy of Traditional vs. Cash Balance Plans," *ACA News* (Fourth Quarter 1999): 7–26.

28 D. E. Logue and J. S. Rader, *Managing Pension Plans* (Boston: Harvard Business School Press, 1998); S. Blakely, "Pension Power," *Nation's Business* (July 1997): 12–20; Martin E. Segal Co., *Pension Issues: A Fifty Year History and Outlook*, newsletter 33, no. 3 (February 1990); T. F. Duzak, "Defined Benefit and Defined Contribution Plans: A Labor Perspective," *Economic Survival in Retirement* (New York: Salisbury Publishing, 1990): 69; U.S. Department of Labor, Bureau of Labor Statistics, *Employee Benefits in Medium and Large Firms, 1989* (Washington, DC, June 1990).

29 U.S. Department of Labor, "A Look at 401(k) Plan Fees," *Workforce Supplement* (September 1999): 5; "Employee Attraction Retention Drive 401(k) Plans," *Workspan* (February 2001): 10–12; "They Want Their 401(k)s," *Workforce* (December 2000): 68–73; R. Kuttner, "Pensions: How Much Risk Should Workers Have to Bear?" *Business Week* (April 16, 2001): 23; E. Hoffman, "Self-Directed Accounts: 401(k)s with a View," *HR Magazine* (March 2000): 115–124; H. Gleckman, "Gephardt Has a Great Program—For the 30s," *Business Week* (August 14, 1995): 75; J. M. Laderman and M. McNamee, "That 401(k) May Cost More Than You Think," *Business Week* (November 10, 1997): 130; D. L. Browning, "Fortune Tellers," *Human Resource Executive* (November 1997): 1; A. Bernstein, "United We Own: Employee Ownership Is Working at the Airline. Can It Travel?" *Business Week* (March 18, 1996): 96–102; "A New Look at Employee Ownership," *Business Week* (March 18, 1996): 124; W. Zellner, "Heavy Weather at American," *Business Week* (January 27, 1997): 32–33; S. Gruner, "You Can't Fire Me, I'm an Owner!" *Inc.* (June 1997): 102.

30 "Broad-Based Stock Options on the Rise," *Bulletin to Management* (July 9, 1998): 216; L. Sierra, "Growth Strategies: Finding Ways to Create Value," *ACA News* (November/December 1997): 13–16; M. A. Bennett, "Making the Case for Ownership: Employing Workers' Hearts, Not Just Their Hands," *ACA News* (November/December 1997): 18–21; "Employee Stock Options Fact Sheet," [nceo.org/library/optionfact.html]; J. Fox, "The Next Best Thing to Free Money," *Fortune* (July 7, 1997): 52–62; "Taking Stock of Employee Stock Options," *HR Executive Review* 6(1) (1998); E. J. Cripe, "Making Performance Management a Positive Experience," *ACA News* (November/December 1997): 22–26; P. D. Dowling, D. E. Welch, and R. S. Schuler, *International Dimensions of Human Resource Management*, 3rd ed. (Cincinnati: South-Western College Publishing, 1999).

31 C. Hirschman, "More Choices, Less Cost?" *HR Magazine* (January 2002): 38–41; M. J. Mandel, "Health Care May Be Just What the Economy Ordered," *Business Week* (September 17, 2001): 49; M. Boyle, "How to Cut Perks Without Killing Morale," *Fortune* (February 19, 2001): 241–244; M. Freudenheim, "Cuts in Health Benefits Squeeze Retirees' Nest Eggs," *New York Times* (December 31, 2000): BU 8; J. Weber, "Canada's Health-Care System Isn't a Model Anymore," *Business Week* (August 31, 1998): 36; "Cost-Cutting Secrets Unveiled," *Bulletin to Management* 48 (May 8, 1997): 152; "Health Benefit Costs Rise Only Slightly," *Workforce* (April 1998): 19; K. H. Hammonds, "The Healers' Revenge," *Business Week* (June 15, 1998): 68–73; "Managing Control," *Human Resource Executive* (September 1997): 94.

32 W. Atkinson, "Care vs. Cost," *HR Magazine* (November 2000): 66–72; E. Ginzberg, "Healthy Debate," *Human Resource Executive* (May 5, 1998): 57–58; A. Doan, "Unhealthy Premiums," *San Francisco Chronicle* (August 15, 1998): D2; "Benefit Policies: Enrollment in Managed Care Plans," *Bulletin to Management* 47 (August 1, 1996): 247; "Trends: Finding Enough Skilled Trained Workers," *Bulletin to Management* 47 (August 1, 1996): 247.

33 B. O'Reilly, "Health Care: Taking on the HMOs," *Fortune* (February 16, 1998): 96–104; B. J. Feder, "Deere Sees a Future in Health Care," *New York Times* (July 1, 1994): D1; J. J. Laabs, "Deere's HMO Turns Crisis into Profit," *Personnel Journal* (October 1992): 82–89.

34 T. Lieberman, "HMO or PPO: Are You in the Right Plan?" *Consumer Reports* (October 2001): 27–29; M. Freudenheim, "(Loosely) Managed Care Is in Demand," *New York Times* (September 29, 1998): C1, C4; "Benefit Policies: Enrollment in Managed Care Plans," *Bulletin to Management* 49 (August 1, 1996): 247.

35 J. Weber, M. Arndt, and L. Cohen, "America, This Is Really Gonna Hurt," *Business Week* (September 17, 2001): 46–48; P. Kerr, "Betting the Farm on Managed Care," *New York Times* (June 27, 1993): 1, 6; "An Incentive a Day Can Keep Doctor Bills at Bay," *Business Week* (April 29, 1991): 22.

36 B. Kirsch, "Working Well," *Human Resource Executive* (May 5, 1998): 45–47; N. A. Jeffrey, "'Wellness Plans' Try to Target the Not-So-Well," *Wall Street Journal* (June 20, 1996): B1, B10; B. P. Sunoo and C. M. Solomon, "Wellness Begins with Compassion," *Personnel Journal* (April 1996): 79–89; "Policy Guide: Wellness Programs Offer Healthy Returns," *Bulletin to Management* (March 7, 1996): 80.

37 "Wellness Plans and the Disabilities Act," *Bulletin to Management* (May 27, 1993): 168.

38 C. Fishman, "Crisis at Ground Zero," *Fast Company* (December 2001): 109–113. D. L. Browning, "Mood Indigo," *Human Resource Executive* (January 1997): 60–61; C. M. Steele and R. A. Josephs, "Alcohol Myopia: Its Prized and Dangerous Effects," *American Psychologist* (August 1990): 921–933.

39 "Americans Work; Europeans Play," *Workforce* (July 2001): 19; "Less Rest Assured," *AAA World* (September/October 2001): 13; P. D. Dowling, D. E. Welch, and R. S. Schuler. *International Dimension of Human Resource Management*, 3rd ed. (Cincinnati, OH: South-Western College Publishing, 1999).

40 C. Fishman, "Moving Toward a Balanced Work Life," *Workforce* (March 2000): 38–42; R. Gerbman, "Elder Care Takes America by Storm," *HR Magazine* (May 2000): 51–58; S. Lambert, "Added Benefits: The Link Between Work-Life Benefits and Organizational Citizenship Behavior," *Academy of Management Journal* 43(5) (2000): 801–815; B. Parus, "Measuring the ROI of Work/Life Programs," *Workspan* (September 2000): 50–54; Society for Human Resource Management "Experts Say Work/Life Benefits Are Here to Stay," *HR News* (June 2000): 1, 4, 13; S. Zedeck (ed.), *Work, Families, and Organizations* (San Francisco: Jossey-Bass, 1992).

41 A. Poe, "The Baby Blues," *HR Magazine* (July 2000): 79–84; S. Friedman and J. H. Greenhaus, *Work and Family—Allies or Enemies?* (London: Oxford University Press, 2000); E. E. Kossek, J. A. Colquitt, and R. A. Noe, "Caregiving Decisions, Well-Being, and Performance: The Effects of Place and Provider as a Function of Dependent Type and Work-Family Climates," *Academy of Management Journal* 44(1) (2001): 29–44; J. Perry-Smith and T. Blum, "Work-Family Human Resource Bundles and Perceived Organizational Performance," *Academy of Management Journal* 43(6) (2000): 1107–1117; N. Woodward, "Child Care to the Rescue," *HR Magazine* (August 1999): 82–88.

42 E. E. Kossek and V. Nichol, "The Effects of On-Site Child Care on Employee Attitudes and Performance," *Personnel Psychology* 45 (1992): 485–509; B. Parus, "Measuring the ROI of Work/Life Programs," *Workspan* (September 2000): 50–54.

43 "Family Friendly Benefits Have Spread Greatly," *Bulletin to Management* 47 (March 7, 1996): 73; A. Halcrow, "Optimas Reflects Changes in HR," *Personnel Journal* (January 1994): 50.

44 S. LoJacono, "Back-Up Care: The New Benefits Tie Breaker," *Workspan* (January 2001): 16–20; Society for Human Resource Management "Experts Say Work/Life Benefits are Here to Stay," *HR News* (June 2000): 1, 4, 13; Society for Human Resource Management "FMLA Still Poses Implementation Problems, Employers Say," *HR News* (February 2001): 3–12.

45 A. Hayashi, "Mommy-Track Backlash," *Harvard Business Review* (March 2001): 33–42; A. R. McIlvaine, "Drawing the Lines," *Human Resource Executive* (September 1997): 84.

46 T. J. Rothauser, J. A. Gonzalez, N. E. Clarke, and L. L. O'Dell, "Family-Friendly Backlash—Fact or Fiction? The Case of Organizations' On-Site Child Care Centers," *Personnel Psychology* 51 (1998): 685–706.

47 S. VanDerWall, "Survey Finds Unscheduled Absenteeism Hitting Seven-Year High," *HR News* (November 1998): 14.

48 "Parental Leave: Healthier Kids," *Business Week* (January 18, 1999): 30.

49 Buck Consultants, *The 1998 Benefits Survey* (Secaucus, NJ: Buck Consultants, 1998).

50 L. Mansnerus, "It Takes a Village to Make an Office. Ask Mother Merck," *New York Times* (November 21, 1999): 14:1, 8; S. J. Goff, M. K. Mount, and R. L. Jamison, "Employer Supported Child Care, Work/Family Conflict, and Absenteeism: A Field Study," *Personnel Psychology* 43 (1990): 793–809; S. Zedeck and K. L. Mosier, "Work in the Family and Employing Organization," *American Psychologist* (February 1990): 240–251.

51 C. M. Loder, "Merck and Co. Breaks New Ground for Employee Child Care Centers," *Star Ledger* (May 1990): 12.

52 S. J. Wells, "The Elder Care Gap," *HR Magazine* (May 2000): 39–46; J. J. Laabs, "How Campbell Manages Its Rural Health Care Dollars," *Personnel Journal* (May 1992): 74–81; "Campbell Soup Co.," *Personnel Journal* (January 1992): 56.

53 K. H. Hammonds, "Balancing Work and Family," *Business Week* (September 16, 1996): 74–80; B. Michaels, "A Global Glance at Work and Family," *Personnel Journal* (April 1995) 85–93; E. Smith, "First Interstate Finds an Eldercare Solution," *HR Magazine* (July 1991): 152; A. E. Scharlach, B. F. Lowe, and E. L. Schneider, *Elder Care and the Work Force* (Lexington, MA: Lexington Books, 1991).

54 Hay Group, *Compensation & Benefits for 2001 & Beyond* (Philadelphia, PA: Hay Group, 2001); K. Mills, "Domestic Partner Benefits," *Workspan*

(August 2000): 32–35; A. Vincola, "Cultural Change Is the Work/Life Solution," *Workforce* (October 1998): 70–72; E. Sullivan, "Basket Case?" *Human Resource Executive* (May 5, 1998): 42–43.

55 "Domestic Partner Benefits" http://www-2.cs.cmu.edu/afs/cs/user/dtw/www/companies (September 21, 2001); "Domestic Partner Benefits Have Doubled Since 1997," *Workspan* (February 2001): 13. "IBM Extends Benefits to Gay Workers' Domestic Partners," *Bulletin to Management* 47 (September 26, 1996): 305; D. J. Jefferson, "Gay Employees Win Benefits for Partners at More Corporations," *Wall Street Journal* (March 18, 1994): A1, A2; K. S. Robinson, "California Legislature Exercises Muscle in Workplace," *HR News* (December 2001): 5.

56 L. Holyoke, "San Francisco's Mandate Forces Domestic-Partner Benefits Mainstream," *Workforce* (June 1997): 34–41; A. D. Sherman, "Domestic Partner Benefits: Why They Can Succeed," *ACA News* (June 1997): 20.

57 L. Strazewski, "One for All," *Human Resource Executive* (May 5, 1998): 51–53; "Lotus Opens a Door for Gay Partners," *Business Week* (November 4, 1991): 80–81. See also D. Anfuso, "Soul-Searching Sustains Values at Lotus Development," *Personnel Journal* (June 1994): 54–61; M. Rowland, "Hurdles for Unmarried Partners," *New York Times* (May 22, 1994): F15.

58 D. G. Albrecht, "Are You Prepared to Relocate," *Workforce* (June 1997): 44–50; J. J. Laabs, "Smooth Moves," *Personnel Journal* (February 1994): 68–76; G. Flynn, "Relocation Has a New Look," *Personnel Journal* (February 1995): 48–60.

59 J. Dulebohn, B. Murray, and M. Sun, "Selection Among Employer-Sponsored Pension Plans: The Role of Individual Differences," *Personnel Psychology* 53 (2000): 405–432.

60 S. F. Gale, "How Three Companies Shave Health Costs," *Workforce* (August 2001): 78–83; A. Poe, "Time for a Change," *HR Magazine* (August 1999): 77–88; A. Poe, "When in Rome . . . " *HR Magazine* (November 1999): 61–64; S. J. Wells, "A Benefit Built for 2," *HR Magazine* (August 1999): 68–74; S. White, "Re-entry Means Resetting Their Sights," *New York Times* (January 30, 2001): C12; A. Martin and J. Eller, "DOL Issues Significant New Guidance on Plan Expenses," *Legal Report* (March–April 2001): 3–6.

61 N. Weiss, "How Starbucks Impassions Workers to Drive Growth," *Workforce* (August 1998): 60–64.

62 A. Vincola, "Taking Your Work/Life Policy Abroad," *Global Workforce* (July 1998): 24–27; J. E. Santora, "Employee Team Designs Flexible Benefits Program," *Personnel Journal* (April 1994): 30–39.

63 M. M. Markowich and J. Dortch, "Employees Can Be Smart Benefits Shoppers. Really," *Workforce* (September 1998): 64–70.

64 E. Blizinsky, "Good Things Come in Small Packages," *ACA News* (February 2000): 19–21; S. Greenhouse, "Temp Workers at Microsoft Win Lawsuit," *New York Times* (December 13, 2000): C1, 7; B. Leonard, "Recipes for Part-Time Benefits," *HR Magazine* (April 2000): 56–62; D. Pickle, "Using Employee Benefit Plan Assets to Pay for Administration," *Legal Report* (November–December 2000): 1–4; D. Sandler, "The Doubt About Your Benefits," *HR Magazine* (December 2000): 78–82; B. A. Morris, "Healthier Education," *Human Resource Executive* (May 5, 1998): 36–38; S. Greengard, "Steer Workers: Toward Wise Investments," *Workforce* (April 1998): 71-77; L. Strazewski, "Spreading the Word," *Human Resource Executive* (January 1998): 48–50.

65 N. Jackson, "Health Care on the Home Front," *Workforce* (March 1998): 30–34.

CHAPTER

14

PROMOTING WORKPLACE SAFETY AND HEALTH

"In my opinion, the area that requires the greatest attention is this issue of health and safety."

Bennett R. Cohen
Co-founder
Ben and Jerry's Homemade Incorporated

Ben and Jerry's Homemade

Health and safety get a great deal of attention, yet injuries remain stubbornly high. Any manufacturing company runs the risk, if not certainty, of injury to workers, and Ben and Jerry's of Vermont is primarily a manufacturing company. The type of manufacturing done at the company's three plants offers ample opportunity to hurt a back or to drop a heavy object on a foot or toe. Ben and Jerry's managers have instituted fairly rigorous training methods to prevent these kinds of accidents. But in some areas of the operation, particularly in the Springfield, Vermont, plant, jobs involve motions that are repeated all day long, day in and day out, which can lead to other types of injuries. This is especially true with regard to the manufacture of novelty lines such as Peace Pops and Brownie Bars.

Repetitive motion injuries were first recognized more than 200 years ago. In modern parlance, these are called cumulative trauma disorders. They result from motions that, although innocent in themselves, are chronically repeated, usually in an awkward or forceful manner, resulting in musculoskeletal disease, pain, or injury. You don't have to work in a factory to get them. Office workers are at risk, and so too are tennis players and runners. But at Ben and Jerry's, work on the manufacturing line is the primary cause.

Injuries of this sort are the most common workplace injuries, and during the working years, between ages 18 and 64, they are the most common reason for lost work time. Ben and Jerry's had experienced a very high number of workers' compensation claims for these injuries, higher than those of Steelcase.

One reason Ben and Jerry's may have had higher numbers than other companies is, ironically, because people want to be employed there—so much so that workers repeatedly don't report injuries in the early stages for fear of loss of employment. Employees don't fear termination from their job, but some have reported the concern that if they left the company because of disabilities, they might never again get a job that paid as well. Where people have been reluctant to report medical problems, injuries worsened, resulting in longer lost time and greater medical bills.

To address the reluctance to report injuries, Ben and Jerry's began emphasizing and encouraging early reporting of injuries so as to prevent more serious, chronic injuries later on. New employees who suffer injuries are the beneficiaries of a generous short-term disability insurance program. The company also discovered, to its chagrin, that posting consecutive workdays where no one was injured resulted not in greater incentives toward safety, but in an atmosphere where injuries were covered up so as not to break the record.

These experiences and lessons of the early 1990s encouraged Ben and Jerry's to institute a number of changes during the 1990s as Steelcase did. The company has discontinued its emphasis on the record of workdays without injuries and is now embarking on education, training, and meetings to encourage early reporting of potential injuries. Furthermore, the company has hired a number of consultants who specialize in ergonomics to visit all the plants' operations and revise tools, posture, seating, and activities so as to prevent repetitive motion injuries. Consequently the rate of injuries per worker recently began to decline. Nevertheless, the rate is still higher than the industry average. Several significant steps were taken in 1997 to improve safety performance in 1998. The Waterbury production area was upgraded with new equipment and improved line layouts that have improved working conditions. Several material handling issues, such as palletizing, were addressed via new equipment or improved procedures.[1] Improvements continue although Ben and Jerry's is now a part of Unilever, the large Anglo-Dutch multinational corporation.

PROMOTING HEALTH AND SAFETY WITHIN AN INTEGRATED HR SYSTEM

The opening feature describing Ben and Jerry's Homemade illustrates some crucial issues about occupational safety and health. One is the increased emphasis firms are putting on safety programs. The benefits associated with workplace safety include employees who are healthy and productive and lower workers' compensation payments made to the state. These both translate into lower prices for customers.

Elements of Workplace Safety and Health

Workplace safety and health refers to the physical and psychological conditions of a workforce that result from the work environment provided by the organization. If an organization takes effective safety and health measures, fewer of its employees will have short- or long-term ill effects as a result of being employed at that organization.[2]

Physical conditions include occupational diseases and accidents such as actual loss of life or limb, repetitive motion injuries, back pain, carpal tunnel syndrome, cardiovascular diseases, various forms of cancer such as lung cancer and leukemia, emphysema, and arthritis. Other conditions that are known to result from an unhealthy work environment include white lung disease, brown lung disease, black lung disease, sterility, central nervous system damage, and chronic bronchitis.

> **FAST FACT**
>
> Each year there are about 500,000 cases of job-related illnesses and 5.5 million injuries. These have been on the decline for the past 10 years.

Psychological conditions result from organizational stress and a low quality of working life. These encompass dissatisfaction, apathy, withdrawal, projection, tunnel vision, forgetfulness, inner confusion about roles and duties, mistrust of others, vacillation in decision making, inattentiveness, irritability, procrastination, and a tendency to become distraught over trifles.

This chapter describes the costs associated with unsafe and unhealthy work environments as well as the strategies that can be used to effectively promote workplace safety and health.

The Importance of Other HR Practices

As the example of Ben and Jerry's highlights, promoting safety and health involves many other HR practices. The linkages between other HR practices and workplace safety and health are illustrated in Exhibit 14.1.

As described in Chapter 6, job analysis procedures can be used to identify aspects of a job that may contribute to workplace injuries, and ergonomic principles can be applied to redesign the work environment. At some companies, the selection process might also be affected by the desire to promote workplace safety and health. Research indicates that some personality characteristics predict workplace accidents, while others predict stress-related symptoms. Some employers use their selection procedures to screen out employees with tendencies that are contrary to a safe and healthy workplace. As noted in Chapter 15, managing employee relationships in unionized environments often involves negotiating over issues of safety. In both unionized and nonunionized environments, employees participate in training in order to learn about safety policies. Training may also teach employees behaviors that reduce on-the-job accidents, and it may be needed to teach employees how to use new equipment intended to protect them from workplace hazards. When safety and health are viewed as issues of strategic importance, they become central to the entire performance management process as well. Performance measures monitor how well managers are doing against their goals, and both managers and other employees may be offered monetary incentives for reducing accidents and improving safe behaviors on the job. Despite all of these efforts, however, some employees may be victims of workplace accidents, injuries, and illness. Thus, employers provide services and benefits to assist these employees.

The Organization Environment

In some industries, where workplace hazards are an inevitable reality, issues of safety and health are of such great importance that top managers promote the development of a safety-conscious organiza-

> **FAST FACT**
>
> The Department of Labor estimates that 40% of workplaces have some sort of ergonomic plan in place.

ex 14.1 Workplace Safety and Health within an Integrated HR System

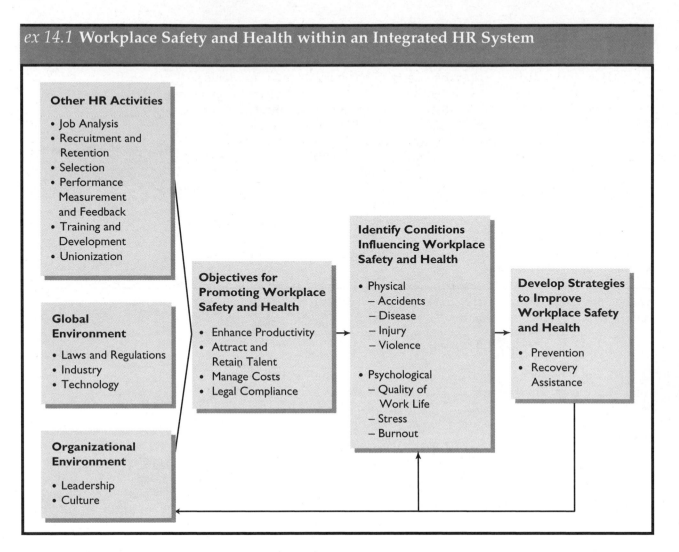

tion culture. During the strategic planning process, line managers promote safety through the development of policies and goals. In order for such policies and goals to have an effect, however, everyone in the organization must work toward creating a culture where safety is valued. In organizations where safety is embedded in the organization's culture, employees benefit by experiencing fewer injuries.[3] Creating a safety-driven culture requires visible leadership from top-level managers, but it also means that supervisors and managers at all levels must make promoting safety and health a natural part of their daily activities. Employee involvement may be used to encourage employees to identify safety and health problems and develop solutions to address them. This is the approach used at John Deere, as described in "Managing Change: John Deere Steers Clear of Workplace Injuries."[4]

The Global Environment

The external forces that are most important to workplace safety and health include the laws and regulations that govern this aspect of work, evolving technologies, industry conditions, and collective bargaining in unionized settings (described in Chapter 15).

John Deere Steers Clear of Workplace Injuries

Terry Hardy is a toolmaker at a John Deere tractor plant in Dubuque, Iowa. He's also a member of the plant's ergonomics team. In addition to all the normal tasks of a toolmaker, Terry is responsible for helping develop solutions that will reduce the incidents of workplace injuries in the plant. He and other members of the team receive no extra compensation for this—just the satisfaction of helping improve the quality of work life for themselves and the other 2,200 employees in the plant.

John Deere has been involving workers in finding solutions to workplace injuries—especially those caused by repetitive motions—since 1993. When employees experience significant pain while working, they can summon the ergonomics team. Terry carries a beeper for this purpose. When it goes off, he rushes to the scene of the latest backache or painful wrist. He and other members of the

team may consult with the employee to find a quick fix for the problem, or the team may take days to come up with a feasible solution. An example of a quick fix would be to put a riser on the bench that holds the pieces employees work on, in order to eliminate the need for them to bend over to do their work. The solution Terry is most proud of, however, was more complicated. The problem was for workers who screwed parts onto tractor frames while "standing" on ladders. But they weren't actually standing, according to Terry. They were dangling as they stretched to reach various positions. To solve the problem, Terry created a device that tips the tractors into position, alleviating the need for employees to tip themselves into position! He's pleased to have been able to help. "It's nice that people don't have to work so hard that they crawl out of here on their hands and knees," he says.

Laws and Regulations. As described in Chapter 3, the *Occupational Safety and Health Act* regulates workplace conditions and provides employees protection against workplace injuries and illness. The significant role of the legal environment is described in detail near the end of this chapter.

Technology. New technologies also influence workplace safety and health, sometimes in nonobvious ways. In manufacturing environments, the introduction of new technologies often greatly improves workplace safety and health. By introducing the latest manufacturing equipment, including robotics, employers often can eliminate the need to expose employees to unsafe conditions.

On the other hand, some new technologies introduce new hazards into the workplace. For example, new buildings often do not allow employees to open their windows, making them completely dependent on ventilation systems for the provision of clean air. Office equipment that makes the workplace more efficient may emit fumes that induce illness. As jobs of all types become increasingly dependent on computers, employees of all types are subjected to conditions that put them at greater risk of repetitive motion injuries, such as carpal tunnel syndrome.

> **FAST FACT**
>
> Carpal tunnel syndrome accounts for $\frac{1}{3}$ of workplace injuries in the United States and costs about $20 billion yearly.

Industry. For some industries, safety and health issues rise to the level of strategic importance, while in others these issues are of less concern. For example, the accident rate for 100,000 workers in the United States is 7, but for workers in Alaska's fishing industry, it's nearly 700. Another dangerous industry is construction, which places "workers in a constantly changing raw environment where one misstep or forgetful moment can snuff out a life or crush a limb. Pressures to finish a job quickly often push foremen and workers to take risks, industry experts say, amid a macho culture of muscle, sweat, and swagger that tends to belittle safety measures and confuse caution with timidity." Construction, mining, and agriculture are typically the three most dangerous industries nationwide, with yearly deaths for every 100,000 employees around 32, 43, and 40, respectively.[5]

The HR Triad

As is true of other HR practices, promoting safety and health involves everyone in the organization. Although not directly involved in the organization's operations themselves, managers play a key role by setting the tone and making safety and health a priority. As will become clear later in this chapter, HR professionals are responsible for monitoring and recording workplace incidents, as well as for developing HR practices that promote safety and health.[6]

Perhaps most importantly, employees must be actively committed to creating a safe and healthy workplace. Like Terry Hardy at John Deere, employees can spot problems and help to develop solutions. In addition, when solutions are found, employees often must be willing to adapt and change how they do their work. Finally, employees must be willing to draw attention to problems when they experience pains or other symptoms. Unfortunately, some employees would rather suffer in silence than admit to experiencing physical symptoms. These and other roles and responsibilities are summarized in "The HR Triad: Roles and Responsibilities in Safety and Health."

INTERNET RESOURCES   14.A

Workplace Safety and Health within the HR System

At our Web site, http://jackson.swcollege.com/, you can:

1. Learn about health and safety at some of the firms discussed in this section by visiting their company home pages:

   Ben & Jerry's

   Unilever

   John Deere

THE STRATEGIC IMPORTANCE OF WORKPLACE SAFETY AND HEALTH

Some observers feel that U.S. companies don't pay enough attention to safety and health issues:

We've reached an accommodation with blue-collar death. Forget that a U.S. worker is five times more likely to die than a Swede. . . . Forget that a U.S. worker is three times more likely to die than a Japanese. The sad reality is that blue-collar blood pours too easily. [Occupational Safety and Health Administration] fines amount to mere traffic tickets for those who run our companies. The small fines are simply buried in the cost of production. Blood can be cash accounted, given a number, and factored with other costs. . . . This has tremendous implications for the union-management relationship, not to mention costs from poor worker morale, lower productivity, and mounting litigation.[7]

As the preceding quote implies, some people feel that health and safety issues are neglected because they often do not affect those with the most power in organizations. But blue-collar workers aren't the only ones who suffer from workplace hazards. White-collar workers, including managers, also do so.[8]

Roles and Responsibilities in Safety and Health

THE HR TRIAD

LINE MANAGERS	HR PROFESSIONALS	EMPLOYEES
• Recognize the strategic consequences of improved workplace safety and health as objectives. • Support the HR professionals' efforts to train all employees in safety and health. • Encourage employees to report unsafe conditions and suggest how to improve workplace safety and health. • Avoid creating incentives for unsafe behaviors.	• Educate managers to understand the long-term value of improved safety and health. • Ensure that accidents and health-related incidents are accurately monitored, reported, and recorded. • Work with other professionals such as medical doctors and industrial engineers to develop new programs. • Create HR programs that train employees for safe and healthy behaviors and reward them for their success.	• Participate in the development and administration of safety and health programs. • Perform in accordance with established safety and health guidelines. • Take an active role in promoting changes that will enhance workplace safety and health. • Promote work group norms that value safety and health. • Exercise and stay in shape.

The traditional ill effects on the white-collar workforce have been psychological. Recently, however, concern has been growing over physical conditions related to the unforeseen effects of the computers—these include eyestrain, back strain, miscarriages, and carpal tunnel syndrome. White-collar workers also suffer from poor air quality, which is common in closed office buildings. Chemical components from sources such as carpeting and structural materials build up and are circulated through the ventilation system.[9] Infectious diseases also spread more quickly through these environments, putting everyone at risk.

"Once something as infectious as a flu-like symptom enters the workplace, it's an epidemic."

Dr. Alan Roberts
Occupational Medicine Physician
Sunshine Medical Center

The Benefits of a Safe and Healthy Work Environment

If organizations can reduce the rates and severity of their occupational accidents, diseases, workplace violence, and stress-related illnesses, and improve the quality of work life for their employees, they can only become more effective. Such an improvement can result in (1) more productivity owing to fewer lost workdays, (2) increased efficiency and quality from a more committed workforce, (3) reduced medical and insurance costs, (4) lower workers' compensation rates and direct payments because of fewer claims being filed, (5) greater flexibility and adaptability in the workforce as a result of increased participation and an increased sense of ownership, and (6) better selection ratios because of the enhanced image of the organization. Companies can thus increase their profits substantially and better serve the objectives of all their stakeholders.[10]

FAST FACT

Each year nearly 1 million workers become victims of workplace violence, resulting in almost 2 million days of lost work.

The Costs of an Unsafe and Unhealthy Work Environment

The costs of poor safety and health are numerous. They include the human costs of injuries and death as well as economic costs.

Injuries. Back injuries are the most prevalent of all workplace injuries. Every year an estimated 10 million employees in the United States encounter back pain that impairs their job performance. Approximately 1 million employees file workers' compensation claims for back injuries. Billions of dollars are spent each year to treat back pain—$5 billion in workers' compensation payments alone.[11] Also common are eye injuries, which cost employees about $4 billion in lost productivity each year.

Mental Health. The physical injuries that employees suffer at work may be easier to count and quantify than psychological injuries, but mental health is just as important as physical health. For some employees, the workplace is a source of substantial mental strain. As noted in Chapter 3, for example, employees who suffer harassment at work may suffer psychological symptoms that affect not only their productivity but also the quality of their lives away from work. Mental health may also suffer when employees' jobs subject them to heavy emotional workloads, or when there is simply too much work that needs to be done.

Deaths. Estimates of workplace deaths range from 2,800 to around 10,000 yearly. Workplace-related deaths were about 7 per 100,000 employees in 2000. This is much better than in 1970, when the rate was about 18 per 100,000 employees.[12] Worldwide, about 220,000 workers die around the world every year in work accidents or from illness contracted at work.

FAST FACT

Of the 6 million workplace injuries in the U.S., about half result in lost work time.

Economic Costs. The economic cost of workplace deaths and injuries is estimated to be more than $50 billion. Similar costs are estimated for the more than 100,000 workers who annually succumb to occupational diseases. Enormous costs are also associated with psychological conditions. For example, alcoholism, often the result of attempts to cope with job pressures, costs organizations and society over $65 billion annually. Of this, $20 billion is attributed to lost productivity and the remainder to the direct costs of insurance, hospitalization, and other medical items. Perhaps more difficult to quantify, but just as symptomatic of stress and a poor quality of working life, are workers' feelings of lack of meaning and involvement in their work and loss of importance as individuals.

INTERNET RESOURCES   14.B

Strategic Importance of Safety and Health

At our Web site, http://jackson.swcollege.com/, you can:

1. Find out about safety and health statistics at the ILO, the Bureau of Labor Statistics, OSHA, and the National Safety Council.

2. Learn about OSHA's record-keeping requirements for businesses, which were revised as of January 2002.

HAZARDS IN OCCUPATIONAL SAFETY AND HEALTH

As Exhibit 14.1 shows, both physical and psychological aspects of the workplace environment affect occupational safety and health. Traditionally, hazards in the physical environment have received greater attention. Increasingly, however, both employers and the **Occupational Safety and Health Administration (OSHA)**, which administers the Occupational Safety Health Act, recognize that psychological conditions greatly affect health and safety, and they are doing

FAST FACT

The costs of a safety program can be far outweighed by the expenses saved from lower insurance premiums.

something about it. At Hoffman-LaRoche, a pharmaceutical company, employees receive after-hours instruction in stress management methods such as meditation, breathing exercises, and biofeedback. Today, efforts to improve occupational safety and health aren't complete without a strategy for reducing psychological work-related stress.

Occupational Accidents

At AES, a global power company, top management is so concerned about safety that it holds everyone in the company accountable for reducing accidents. Under normal circumstances, the company may distribute as much as a 12% bonus for reaching safety-related goals. When the company experienced four fatalities worldwide, the bonus was reduced to 10%. By significantly penalizing poor safety performance, AES intends to motivate its employees to examine the causes of accidents and institute changes to prevent them in the future. At AES and elsewhere, the causes of organizational accidents are many, so eliminating them completely represents a major challenge.

Organizational Qualities. Accident rates vary substantially by industry. Firms in the construction and manufacturing industries have higher accident rates than do firms in services, finance, insurance, and real estate. But some high-risk firms are taking steps to beat the odds. Barden Bearings Corporation, in Danbury, Connecticut, is one of them. Over the years, Barden employees assumed that, because they work in a metal shop, people were going to get hurt. Then Barden created a Safety and Health Committee, which meets monthly to consider its safety and health performance. One of the major objectives is developing programs that strengthen safety awareness and performance. An example of one change made was to eliminate the safety engineering position and transfer its accountabilities to the Medical Department. The occupational health nurse in that department had shown considerable knowledge about safety matters and she aggressively investigated accidents and near misses. The occupational health nurse was promoted to a new position entitled manager of employee health and safety.[13]

Small (those with fewer than 50 employees) and large organizations (those with more than 250 employees) have lower incidence rates than medium-sized organizations. This may be because supervisors in small organizations are better able to detect safety hazards and prevent accidents than those in medium-sized ones. And larger organizations have more resources to hire staff specialists who can devote all their efforts to safety and accident prevention.

In general, however, the working conditions (e.g., vehicle driving, desk work), the tools and technology available to do the job (e.g., heavy machinery, ladders, personal computers), and availability of guns brought to work most affect **occupational accidents**. Next in line are the workers themselves.

The Unsafe Employee. Some experts point to the employee as the pivotal cause of accidents. Accidents depend on the behavior of the person, the degree of hazard in the work environment, and pure chance. The degree to which a person contributes to an accident can be an indication of the individual's proneness to accidents. No stable set of personal characteristics *always*

> *"At some of our plants, if there is one accident, everyone's bonus is cut by 25%, two accidents means a 50% cut, and three accidents means no bonus for anyone."*
>
> Dennis Bakke
> CEO
> AES

FAST FACT

Nationwide injury rates are higher for medium-sized companies employing 50 to 249 workers.

contributes to accidents. Nevertheless, certain psychological and physical characteristics seem to make some people *more susceptible* to accidents. For example, employees who are emotionally "high" have fewer accidents than those who are emotionally "low," and employees who have fewer accidents are more optimistic, trusting, and concerned for others than those who have more accidents. Employees under greater stress are likely to have more accidents than those under less stress. Substance abusers also experience more job-related injuries, and this is true regardless of whether the substance abuse takes place at work or off the job. Older workers may be less likely to have accidents, but more likely to suffer fatalities and recover more slowly.[14] As a consequence the issue of older workers in the workplace is a significant one. This is described more in the feature "Managing Diversity: Safety Issues and the Aging Workforce."[15] People who are quicker at recognizing visual patterns than at making muscular manipulations are less likely to have accidents than those who are just the opposite.

Many psychological conditions that may be related to accident-proneness—for instance, hostility and emotional immaturity—may be temporary states. Thus, they are difficult to detect until at least one accident has occurred. Because these characteristics aren't related to accidents in all work environments and because they aren't always present in employees, selecting and screening job applicants on the basis of accident-proneness is difficult.

The Violent Employee. Workplace violence is growing rapidly, and employers are being held responsible. Homicide is a major cause of death in the workplace today.[16] Homicide, as well as other less serious forms of violence, can be triggered by a number of forces, including being treated unfairly, an organizational culture that accepts aggressive behavior as normal, layoffs and downsizing, and even anger at being monitored too closely.[17] Although it may be difficult to identify the violent employee before the fact, employers are urged to be on the lookout for some common signs such as these:

- **Verbal Threats:** Individuals often talk about what they may do. An employee might say, "Bad things are going to happen to so-and-so," or "That propane tank in the back could blow up easily."
- **Physical Actions:** Troubled employees may try to intimidate others, gain access to places they don't belong, or flash a concealed weapon in the workplace to test reactions.
- **Frustration:** Most cases of workplace violence don't involve a panicked individual who perceives the world as falling apart. A more likely scenario involves an employee who has a frustrated sense of entitlement to a promotion, for example.
- **Obsession:** An employee may hold a grudge against a coworker or supervisor, which in some cases can stem from a romantic interest.[18]

These may be early warning signals for other acts of violence, including assault against coworkers and property damage. Employers may be held liable for the violent action of an employee if they knew, or should have known, that the employee was at risk for committing violence. Like other forms of unacceptable performance on the job, the options for how to deal with violent employees include employee assistance programs, training in conflict management, and termination.

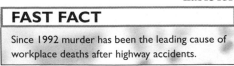

Safety Issues and the Aging Workforce

"I'm 51 years old, and I know for a fact that there's more risk for me to climb to the top of a rail car today than there was when I was younger and more agile," says Wayne Gordon, general manager of Farmers Cooperative Association in Jackson, Minnesota. Mr. Gordon indicates, however, that it's difficult to get other older workers to always agree with him: "Individuals have a tendency to think they can still do things they did 20 years ago." While he feels that it might be in the worker's interest to be prevented from performing a specific job, it might also violate age discrimination laws. The *Age Discrimination in Employment Act of 1967* means that employers can't automatically exclude workers from jobs solely because of age. Older workers, in fact, are among the best performers many companies have. Nevertheless, safety data give employers and society some concern. Federal studies show that older workers (above 54 years and particularly above 64 years of age) are 5 times more likely to die of a fatal transportation accident and 3.8 times as likely to be killed by objects and equipment than are younger workers. There also appear to be significant medical differences between older and younger workers: as a group, older workers take nearly twice as long to mend and are more likely to die from injuries than younger workers; and the average per-person cost of health claims per year for workers, 65 to 69 years old is more than double that for 45 to 59-year olds.

Especially given that the number of older workers is rising (from 3 million to 3.8 million people became 65 each year during the past 10 years), the question remains, "What can be done about this?" Studies by the *American Journal of Industrial Medicine* suggest that only about 30 percent of those older workers injured in work accidents received safety training. Other studies suggest that relatively simple workplace modifications would be helpful, such as painting the steps of ladders with bright colors. Clearly, the answers aren't easily forthcoming. Older workers have better attendance and accident records, argues the AARP, so tread carefully in labeling older workers "those more likely to be more costly to employ."

Occupational Diseases

Potential sources of work-related diseases are as distressingly varied as the symptoms of those diseases. Several federal agencies have systematically studied the workplace environment, and they have identified the following disease-causing hazards: arsenic, asbestos, benzene, bichloromethylether, coal dust, coke-oven emissions, cotton dust, lead, radiation, and vinyl chloride. Workers likely to be exposed to those hazards include chemical and oil refinery workers, miners, textile workers, steelworkers, lead smelters, medical technicians, painters, shoemakers, and plastics industry workers. Continued research will no doubt uncover additional hazards that firms will want to diagnose and remedy for the future well-being of their workforces.[19]

Categories of Occupational Diseases. In the long term, environmental hazards in the workplace have been linked to **occupational diseases** such as thyroid, liver, lung, brain, and kidney cancer; white, brown, and black lung disease; leukemia; bronchitis; emphysema; lymphoma; aplastic anemia; central nervous system damage; and reproductive disorders (e.g., sterility, genetic damage, miscarriages, and birth defects). Chronic bronchitis and emphysema are among the fastest-growing diseases in the United States, doubling every five years since World War II; they account for the second highest number of disabilities under Social Security. Cancer tends to receive the most attention, however, since it's a leading cause of death in the United States (second after heart disease). Many of the known causes of cancer are physical and chemical agents in the environment. And because these agents are theoretically more controllable than human behavior, the Occupational Safety and Health Administration's emphasis is often on eliminating them from the workplace.

OSHA is also concerned with the following categories of occupational diseases and illnesses: occupation-related skin diseases and disorders, dust diseases of the lungs, respiratory conditions due to toxic agents, poisoning (the systematic effect of toxic materials), disorders due to physical agents, disorders associated with repeated trauma, and all other occupational illnesses. OSHA, therefore, requires employers to keep records on all these diseases.

Occupational Groups at Risk. Miners, firefighters, construction and transportation workers, and blue-collar and low-level supervisory personnel in manufacturing industries experience the majority of both occupational diseases and occupational injuries. In addition, large numbers of petrochemical and oil refinery workers, dye workers, dye users, textile workers, plastics industry workers, painters, and industrial chemical workers are also particularly susceptible to some of the most dangerous health hazards. Skin diseases are the most common of all reported occupational diseases; leather workers are the group most affected.

> **FAST FACT**
>
> On September 11, 2001, more than 300 firefighters and police officers lost their lives in the World Trade Center disaster.

Nevertheless, occupational diseases aren't exclusive to blue-collar workers and manufacturing industries. The "cushy office job" has evolved into a veritable nightmare of physical and psychological ills for white-collar workers in the expanding service industries. Among the common ailments are varicose veins, bad backs, deteriorating eyesight, migraine headaches, hypertension, coronary heart disorders, and respiratory and digestive problems. The causes of these include too much noise, interior air pollutants, uncomfortable chairs, inactivity, poor office design, and electronic office technology.

> **FAST FACT**
>
> On September 11, 2001, an estimated 3,000 white-collar workers lost their lives.

A Low Quality of Working Life

For many workers, a **low quality of working life** is associated with workplace conditions that fail to satisfy important preferences and interests such as a sense of responsibility, desire for empowerment and job involvement, challenge, meaningfulness, self-control, recognition, achievement, fairness or justice, security, and certainty.[20] Organizational conditions and practices that contribute to a low quality of working life include the following:

- jobs with low levels of task significance, variety, identity, autonomy, and feedback;
- minimal involvement of employees in decision making and a great deal of one-way communication with employees;
- pay systems not based on performance, or based on performance that isn't objectively measured or under employee control;
- supervisors, job descriptions, and organizational policies that fail to convey to the employee what is expected and what is rewarded;
- unfair treatment and lack of due process procedures;
- human resource policies and practices that are discriminatory and of low validity;
- temporary employment conditions, where employees are dismissed at will (employee rights don't exist); and

- corporate cultures that aren't supportive of employee empowerment and job involvement.

Conditions that tend to create feelings of poor work life quality for one individual may not do so for another individual, because of differences in preferences, interests, and perceptions of uncertainty in the environment.

Organizational Stress

Prevalent forms of **organizational stress** include "the four Ss," organizational change, work pacing, the physical environment, stress-prone employees, and job burnout.[21]

The Four Ss. Common stressors for many employees include the supervisor, salary, security, and safety.[22] Petty work rules and relentless pressure for more production are major stressors that employees associate with supervisors. Both deny worker needs to control the work situation and to be recognized and accepted. Salary is a stressor when it's perceived as being distributed unfairly. Many blue-collar workers feel they are underpaid relative to their white-collar counterparts. Teachers may think they are underpaid relative to people with similar education who work in private industry. Employees experience stress when they aren't sure whether they will have their jobs next month, next week, or even tomorrow. For many employees, lack of job security is even more stressful than lack of safety—at least, with an unsafe job, they know the risks, whereas with an insecure job, they are in a continual state of uncertainty.[23]

Fear of workplace accidents and the resulting injury or death can also be stressful for many workers. When pressure for production is increased, the fear regarding workplace safety can rise to the point where production decreases rather than increases. This result, in turn, may lead to a vicious cycle that's counterproductive for the workers and the organization.

> **FAST FACT**
>
> Managers run double their usual risk of a heart attack during the week after they have fired an employee.

> **FAST FACT**
>
> Some 70% of workers report high or moderate workplace stress.

Organizational Change. Changes made by organizations usually involve something important and are accompanied by uncertainty, such as potential downsizing and layoffs. Many changes are made without official warning. Although rumors often circulate that a change is coming, the exact nature of the change is left to speculation. People become concerned about whether the change will affect them, perhaps by displacing them or by causing them to be transferred. Those remaining wonder how they will do all the work! The result is that many employees suffer stress symptoms.[24] As a consequence, many companies have adopted stress management programs. An example is described in the feature "Managing Change: Stress Management at Adolph Coors Co."[25]

> *"The principle cause of stress at work is bad management."*
>
> Dr. Robert Hogan
> President
> Hogan Assessment Systems

Work Pacing. **Work pacing** may be controlled by machines or people. **Machine pacing** gives control over the speed of the operation and of the work output to something other than the individual. **Employee pacing** gives that control to the individual. The effects of machine pacing are severe, because the individual is unable to satisfy a crucial need for control of the situation. It has been reported that workers on machine-paced jobs feel exhausted at the end of their shifts and are unable to relax soon after work because of increased adrenaline

> **FAST FACT**
>
> The number of hours worked per year by the average American rose by 66 hours between the late 1960s and early 2000s.

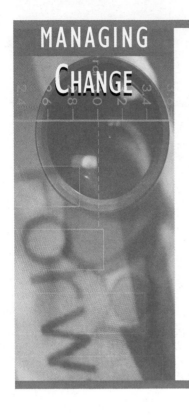

MANAGING CHANGE

Stress Management at Adolph Coors Co.

A stress management program at Adolph Coors Co., a brewery based in Golden, Colorado, has expanded to help workers cope with increasing workforce changes. A downsizing of 643 employees through voluntary separations, followed by corporate reorganization, led to a rethinking throughout the company on Coors's direction, says Bob Tank, Jr., manager of counseling services.

Originally, the stress management program included only a course on anger management and an exercise component. Now, both group programs and individualized help in managing stress are offered through the employee assistance plan, says Tank. He notes that group programs help employees see that they are "not alone" in their need to reduce stress.

Coors's stress management program currently features 27 different courses that address family and personal concerns as well as workplace issues such as communication, self-esteem, and how to work together. The program also can be "customized" to address specific problems. For example, a work group requested training because it

had been struggling with bickering, strife, and management/worker dysfunction, says Tank. Instruction was aimed at clarifying roles and redirecting energies. Feedback following the classes showed success in deflating the dysfunctional processes and clarifying team operations.

With so much going on in the company this year, employee participation in the stress management program has dropped off in every area except for a tremendously popular course on dealing with corporate change, Tank notes. To boost participation, Coors integrates more programs into the workplace, makes programs user-friendly, and makes them available to production areas. In addition, information on stress reduction is made available through open houses and notices in cafeterias and individual work sites.

Outreach programs can be an effective, less formal way to help employees deal with change, Tank adds. Companies today need to stay flexible to adapt and do what is necessary to thrive, he says. Coors wants its employees to be able to do the same.

secretion on the job. In a study of 23 white- and blue-collar occupations, assembly workers reported the highest level of severe stress symptoms.[26]

Physical Environment. Although office automation is a way to improve productivity, it has stress-related drawbacks. One aspect of office automation with a specific stress-related characteristic is the computer keyboard. Other parts of the work environment associated with stress are crowding, noise, lack of privacy, and lack of control—for example, the inability to move a desk or chairs or even to hang pictures in a work area in an effort to personalize it.[27] Poor indoor air quality is another aspect of the work environment that employees report being a source of stress. According to one survey, about one out of three managers believe that poor air quality is a significant cause of both illness among employees and lost productivity.[28]

Stress-Prone Employees. People differ in the ways they respond to organizational stressors. A classic difference is referred to as Type A versus Type B behavior. Type A people like to do things their way and are willing to exert a lot of effort to ensure that even trivial tasks are performed in the manner they prefer. They often fail to distinguish between important and unimportant situations. They are upset, for instance, when they have to wait 15 minutes to be seated in a restaurant, since this isn't in compliance with their idea of responsive service. In short, Type A people spend much of their time directing energy toward noncompliances in the environment. Still, Type A people are "movers and shakers." They enjoy acting on their environment and modifying the behavior of other people. They are primarily rewarded by compliance and punished by noncompliance.

Type B people are generally much more patient. They aren't easily frustrated or easily angered, nor do they expend a lot of energy in response to noncompliance. Type B people may be excellent supervisors to work for—that is, until you need them to push upward in the organization on your behalf. They probably will permit their subordinates a lot of freedom but also might not provide the types of upward support necessary for effective leadership.[29]

Job Burnout

Job burnout is a particular type of stress that seems to be experienced by people who work in jobs in health care, education, police work, customer response centers, and the airline industry. This type of reaction to one's work includes attitudinal and emotional reactions that a person goes through as a result of job-related experiences.

Emotional Exhaustion. Often the first sign of burnout is a feeling of being emotionally exhausted by one's work. An emotionally exhausted employee might express feelings of being drained, used up, at the end of his or her rope, or physically fatigued. Waking up in the morning may be accompanied by a feeling of dread at the thought of having to put in another day on the job. For someone who was once enthusiastic about the job and idealistic about what could be accomplished, feelings of emotional exhaustion may come somewhat unexpectedly, though to an outsider looking at the situation, emotional exhaustion would be seen as a natural response to an extended period of intense interaction with people and their problems.

Depersonalization. One common response to emotional exhaustion is to put psychological distance between one's self and one's clients and to decrease one's personal involvement with them. In moderation, this reaction may be an effective method for creating "detached concern," but when engaged in to excess, the employee may begin to dehumanize or depersonalize the clients. People who have reached the extreme end of the depersonalization continuum report feeling they have become calloused by their jobs and that they have grown cynical about their *clients.*

Feelings of Low Accomplishment. A third aspect of burnout is a feeling of low personal accomplishment. Many human service professionals begin their careers with great expectations that they will be able to improve the human condition through their work. After a year or two on the job, they begin to realize they aren't living up to these expectations. There are many systemic reasons for the gap that exists between the novice's goals and the veteran's accomplishments. These include unrealistically high expectations due to a lack of exposure to the job during training, constraints placed on the worker through the rules and regulations of an immutable bureaucracy, inadequate resources for performing one's job, clients who are frequently uncooperative and occasionally rebellious, and a lack of feedback about one's successes. These and other characteristics of human service organizations almost guarantee that employees will be frustrated in their attempts to reach their goals, yet the workers may not recognize the role of the system in producing this frustration. Instead the worker may feel personally responsible and begin to think of himself or herself as a failure. Feelings of low personal accomplishment may reduce motivation to a point where performance is in fact impaired, leading to further experienced failure.

Deteriorated Performance. Burned out employees may perform more poorly on the job compared with their counterparts who are still "fired up." Consider as an example the job of an intake interviewer in a legal aid office. For the organization, the intake interview serves as a screening device through which all potential clients must pass. Specific information about the nature and details of a case must be assessed and an evaluation of the "appropriateness" of the case for the office must be made. Since as many as 40 intake interviews may be conducted per day, it's important that the interviewer work as efficiently as possible. To the extent time is spent talking about problems not relevant for these forms, efficiency decreases.

Now consider the client's perspective. Upon arriving for an interview, the client is likely to be rehearsing the injustices done and planning for retaliation. The client does not consider the precise statutes encompassing the problem nor the essential details that make the case worthy of attention. The client's primary concern is to return emotional and physical life to normal—the law seems to offer a solution. The intake interview may be the first chance to explain the problems the client is facing. From this perspective, good job performance is displayed by an interviewer who lends a sympathetic ear.

How will the interviewer handle this situation? Typically, the person doing the interview will be a relatively recent graduate of law school with little experience. Socialization has emphasized the supremacy of objectivity. But an objective, analytic attitude combined with the pressure to efficiently fill out forms does not add up to a sympathetic ear. The objective interviewer appears unconcerned and the client becomes frustrated. The emotional client becomes an obstacle to detached efficiency, frustrating the interviewer. Whether or not open hostility erupts, both participants are aware of the antagonistic relationship they have formed.

Deteriorated Coworker Relations. Another unfortunate consequence of burnout is a deterioration of one's relationships with coworkers. A study of mental health workers found that people who were experiencing calloused feelings toward their clients also complained more about their clients to their coworkers, thereby generating a negative atmosphere within the work unit. These burned out mental health workers were also absent from work more often and took more frequent work breaks.[30]

FAST FACT

Burnout has a negative impact on the customer as well as the employee.

INTERNET RESOURCES   14.C

Understanding Workplace Hazards and Diseases

At our Web site, http://jackson.swcollege.com/, you can:

1. Learn about activities to promote safety and health at some of the firms discussed in this section by visiting their company home pages:

   AES

   Barden Bearings

   Adolph Coors Co.

   Steelcase

   Haworth

2. Find out about the AARP's positions on safety and health.

3. Find out about disease statistics at the Center for Disease Control.

STRATEGIES FOR IMPROVEMENT

Once the cause of a work hazard is identified, strategies can be developed for eliminating or reducing it. Several alternative strategies are summarized in Exhibit 14.2. To determine whether a strategy is effective, organizations can compare the incidence, severity, and frequency of illnesses and accidents before and after the intervention. OSHA has approved methods for establishing these rates.

Monitoring Safety and Health Rates

OSHA requires organizations to maintain records of the incidence of injuries and illnesses. Some organizations also record the severity and frequency of each.[31]

FAST FACT
Companies with 10 or fewer employees are not required to keep records on job-related illnesses or injuries.

Incidence Rate. The most explicit index of industrial safety is the incidence rate, which reflects the number of injuries and illnesses in a year. It's calculated by the following formula:

$$\text{Incidence Rate} = (\text{Number of Injuries and Illnesses} \times 200,000) / \text{Number of Employee Hours Worked}$$

The base for 100 full-time workers is 200,000 (40 hours a week times 50 weeks). Suppose an organization had 10 recorded injuries and illnesses and 500 employees. To calculate the number of employee hours worked, multiply the number of employees by 40 hours and by 50 weeks: $500 \times 40 \times 50 = 1,000,000$. The incidence rate thus is 2 for every 100 workers a year: $(10 \times 200,000) / 1,000,000 = 2$.

Frequency Rate. The frequency rate reflects the number of injuries and illnesses for every million hours worked, rather than in a year as with the incidence rate. It's calculated as follows:

---

ex 14.2 Sources and Strategies for Improving Occupational Safety and Health

SOURCE	STRATEGY
Physical Work Environment	
Occupational accidents	Record the accident
	Resdesign the work environment
	Set goals and objectives
	Establish safety committees
	Provide training and financial incentives
Occupational diseases	Record the disease
	Measure the work environment
	Communicate information
	Set goals and objectives
Psychological Work Environment	
Stress and burnout	Establish organizational stress programs
	Increase employees' participation in decision making
	Establish individual stress programs
	Provide adequate leave and vacation benefits
	Encourage employees to adopt healthy lifestyles

$$\textbf{Frequency Rate} = (\text{Number of Injuries and Illnesses} \times 1{,}000{,}000 \text{ hours}) / \text{Number of Employee Hours Worked}$$

Severity Rate. The severity rate reflects the hours actually lost owing to injury or illness. It recognizes that not all injuries and illnesses are equal. Four categories of injuries and illnesses have been established: deaths, permanent total disabilities, permanent partial disabilities, and temporary total disabilities. An organization with the same number of injuries and illnesses as another but with more deaths would have a higher severity rate. The severity rate is calculated by this formula:

$$\textbf{Severity Rate} = (\text{Total Hours Charged} \times 1{,}000{,}000 \text{ Hours}) / \text{Number of Employee Hours Worked}$$

Controlling Accidents

Designing the work environment to make accidents unlikely is perhaps the best way to prevent accidents and increase safety. Among the safety features that can be designed into the physical environment are guards on machines, handrails in stairways, safety goggles and helmets, warning lights, self-correcting mechanisms, and automatic shutoffs. The extent to which these features will actually reduce accidents depends on employee acceptance and use of company policies. For example, eye injuries will be reduced by the availability of safety goggles only if employees wear the goggles correctly.[32] This is more likely when employees accept the responsibility for safety, as is the trend in some firms. Du Pont employees understand that they bear responsibility for their safety. This responsibility has grown as the company has reduced its organizational levels, which means less supervision and a more participatory approach to management. With self-management and teamwork comes the burden on individuals to assume more responsibility. Teams are expected to work toward common objectives, and these objectives should include excellent safety performance.[33]

"We teach employees to look for potential issues, listen to their bodies, work with team leaders and see if they can resolve the issues. If they can't resolve them, they call the ergonomics committee."

Bradley Joseph
Manager of Ergonomics
Ford Motor Company

Ergonomics. Another way to improve safety is to make the job itself more comfortable and less fatiguing, through **ergonomics**. Ergonomics considers changes in the job environment in conjunction with the physical and physiological capabilities and limitations of the employees.[34]

In an effort to reduce the number of back injuries, the Ford Motor Company and FedEx Corporation are redesigning workstations and tasks that may be causing musculoskeletal problems for workers. For instance, lifting devices are being introduced on the assembly line to reduce back strain, and walking and working surfaces are being studied to see if floor mats can reduce body fatigue. Videotapes that feature Ford employees performing their jobs both before and after ergonomic redesign are used in training.[35]

In an effort to reduce back injuries, FedEx instituted a three-pronged prevention program stressing education, exercise, and the use of back belts for thousands of package handlers. The program begins by using training to raise overall awareness about back injuries through safety training. Awareness is further heightened through tips printed in employee newsletters and weekly group meetings that discuss safe lifting techniques. The second component of the program prepares workers physically. Employees participate in a pre-shift mandatory stretching routine designed for all workers whose jobs involve lifting. Third, all package handlers use flexible back supports. These provide direct protection while also serving as a constant reminder to lift safely.[36]

Safety Committees. Another strategy for accident prevention is the use of **safety committees**, as at the Barden Bearings Corporation. The HR department can serve as the coordinator of a committee composed of several employee representatives. Where unions exist, the committee should have union representation as well. Often, organizations have several safety committees at the department level for implementation and administration, and one larger committee at the organization level for policy formulation.

Behavior Modification. Employers have known for a long time that a small percentage of their workforce is responsible for the majority of their health insurance claims. Originally, they tried to encourage their employees to be healthy by offering to subsidize health club memberships and building exercise facilities and jogging trails, but the results were disappointing. Now, many companies are implementing incentive-based health care programs.

Reinforcing behaviors that reduce the likelihood of accidents can be highly successful. Reinforcers can range from nonmonetary rewards (such as positive feedback) to activity rewards (such as time off) to material rewards (such as company-purchased doughnuts during a coffee break) to financial rewards (such as bonuses for attaining desired levels of safety).

The behavioral approach relies on measuring performance before and after the intervention, specifying and communicating the desired performance to employees, monitoring performance at unannounced intervals several times a week, and reinforcing desired behavior several times a week with performance feedback.

In two food processing plants, behavior was monitored for 25 weeks—before, during, and after a safety training program. Slides were used to illustrate safe and unsafe behaviors. Employees were also given data on the percentage of safe behaviors in their departments. A goal of 90 percent safe behaviors was established. Supervisors were trained to give positive reinforcement when they observed safe behavior. Following the intervention, the incidence of safe behavior increased substantially—from an average of 70 percent to more than 95 percent in the wrapping department and from 78 percent to more than 95 percent in the makeup department. One year after the program, the frequency rate of lost-time injuries was fewer than 10, a substantial decline from the preceding year's rate of 53.8.[37]

Reducing the Incidence of Diseases

Occupational diseases are far more costly and harmful overall to organizations and employees than are occupational accidents. Because the causal relationship between the physical environment and occupational diseases is often subtle, developing strategies to reduce their incidence is generally difficult.

Record Keeping. At a minimum, OSHA requires that organizations measure the chemicals in the work environment and keep records on these measurements. The records must also include precise information about ailments and exposures. Such information must be kept for as long as the incubation period of the specific disease—even as long as 40 years. If the organization is sold, the new owner must assume responsibility for storing the old records and continuing to gather the required data. If the company goes out of business, the administrative director of OSHA must be told where the records are.[38] Guidelines for record keeping are given in Exhibit 14.3.

Monitoring Exposure. The obvious approach to controlling occupational illnesses is to rid the workplace of chemical agents or toxins; an alternative approach is to monitor and limit exposure to hazardous substances. Some organizations now monitor genetic changes due to exposure to carcinogens—for example, benzene, arsenic, ether, and vinyl chloride. Samples of blood are obtained from employees at fixed intervals to determine whether the employees' chromosomes have been damaged. If damage has occurred, the affected employee is placed in a different job and, where feasible, conditions are modified.

Genetic Screening. Genetic screening is the most extreme, and consequently the most controversial, approach to controlling occupational disease. By using genetic testing to screen out individuals who are susceptible to certain ailments, organizations lower their vulnerability to workers' compensation claims and problems. As discussed in Chapter 3, opponents of genetic screening contend that it measures predisposition to disease, not the actual presence of disease, and therefore violates an individual's rights.[39]

Controlling Stress and Burnout

Increasingly, organizations are offering training programs designed to help employees deal with work-related stress. For example, companies such as J. P. Morgan Chase offer stress management programs as part of a larger supervisory and management development curriculum. Available to supervisors, professional staff, and officers, these courses are designed to introduce supervisory and management material, information skills, and role definition. The emphasis is on providing concrete information to reduce the ambiguity associated with fast-paced, changing work roles.[40]

Increasing Participation in Decision Making. The importance of being able to control or at least predict future outcomes is well recognized. Having opportunities to be self-determining, combined with the freedom and the ability to influence events in one's surroundings, can be intrinsically motivating and highly rewarding. When opportunities for control are absent and people feel trapped in an environment that's neither controllable nor predictable, both psychological and physical health are likely to suffer.[41]

In most organizations, employees are controlled by organizational rules, policies, and procedures. Often these rules and procedures are creations from an earlier era of the organization and are no longer as effective as they once were. Nevertheless, their enforcement continues until new rules are developed. Most often, the new rules are created by people in the highest levels of the organization and then imposed upon people at the lower levels. Sometimes the new rules are an improvement over the old rules, other times they aren't. Regardless of whether they are an improvement, the new rules or

ex 14.3 OSHA Guidelines for Recording Cases

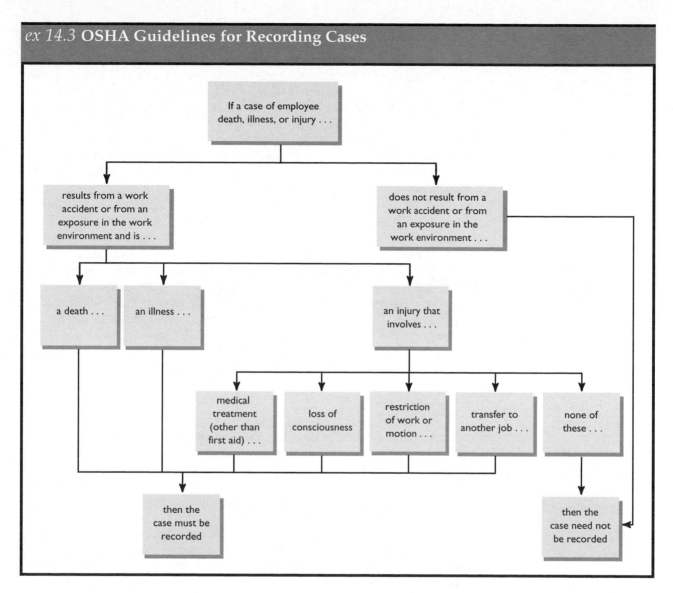

procedures are likely to be experienced as another event in the organization over which the employees had no control.

Besides giving workers a feeling of control, participation in decision making and empowerment gives them the power they need to remove obstacles to effective performance, thereby reducing frustration and strain. One effective use of influence would be to persuade others to change their conflicting role expectations for one's own behavior. Through the repeated interchanges required by participative decision making, members of the organization can also gain a better understanding of the demands and constraints faced by others. When the conflicts workers face become clear, perhaps for the first time, negotiation is likely to begin over which expectations should be changed in order to reduce inherent conflicts. There is another important conse-

FAST FACT

When supervisors empower their workers, they give the workers a sense of control over their workplace, and this reduces some stress.

quence of the increased communication that occurs when an organization uses participative decision making: people become less isolated from their coworkers and supervisors. Through their discussions, employees learn about the formal and informal expectations held by others. They also learn about the formal and informal policies and procedures of the organization. This information can help reduce feelings of role ambiguity. It also makes it easier for one to perform his or her job effectively.

Finally, participation in decision making helps prevent stress and burnout by encouraging the development of a social support network among coworkers. Social support networks help people cope effectively with the stresses they experience on the job.[42]

Individual Stress Management Strategies. Time management can be an effective individual strategy to deal with organizational stress. It's based in large part on an initial identification of an individual's personal goals. Other strategies that should be part of individual stress management include following a good diet, getting regular exercise, monitoring physical health, and building social support groups. Many large organizations such as Coors encourage employees to enroll in regular exercise programs, where their fitness and health are carefully monitored. Finally, encouraging employees to use, not bank, their vacation time and regular days off appears to be another strategy for managing stress and burnout.[43]

> **FAST FACT**
>
> About 20% of firms have an on-site fitness center.

Developing Occupational Health Policies

> **FAST FACT**
>
> A safe and healthy workplace is a corporate value at Weyerhaeuser Company. They say that "All employees are accountable for a safe, clean workplace and are empowered to challenge any activity that compromises safety and/or cleanliness."

As scientific knowledge accumulates and liabilities rise, more and more organizations are developing policy statements regarding occupational hazards. These statements grow out of a concern that organizations should be proactive in dealing with health and safety problems. For example, Dow Chemical's policy states, "No employee, male or female, will knowingly be exposed to hazardous levels of materials known to cause cancer or genetic mutations in humans."[44]

An example of the growing complexity of the problems associated with workplace hazards is the debate over whether women of childbearing age should be allowed to hold jobs in settings that could endanger fetuses. Johnson Controls Incorporated of Milwaukee, Wisconsin, which makes lead automobile batteries for such customers as Sears and the Goodyear Tire and Rubber Company, responded to this issue by restricting women's access to jobs in its Bennington, Vermont, plant. Johnson's management claimed that the factory's air contained traces of lead and lead oxide. Although presumably not high enough to harm adults, the toxin levels were dangerous for children and fetuses. Thus, women were allowed to work in the plant, but only if they were unable to bear children (either because of surgery to prevent pregnancies or because they were too old to have children). According to the company, "The issue was protecting the health of unborn children." Women's advocates and union leaders argued that the firm was guilty of sex discrimination. Specifically, they claimed that lead levels were too high for men as well; that the firm was deciding for women rather than allowing women to decide for themselves whether to take the risk; that such rules invade women's privacy; and, finally, that the restrictions denied women access to high-paying jobs (a typical factory job for women in Bennington paid $6.35 an hour, versus $15.00 an hour in the Milwaukee plant).[45]

The situation was made more complex by the reluctance of many workers to leave their jobs to avoid occupational exposure unless they were guaranteed that their income would not suffer. Some workers went so far as to have themselves sterilized to protect their jobs. When the Supreme Court heard this case, it ruled in favor of the workers, thus striking down the company's fetal protection policy (*United Auto Workers v. Johnson Controls*, 1991).

Establishing Wellness Programs

Corporations are increasingly focusing on keeping employees healthy rather than helping them get well.[46] They are investing in wellness programs at record rates, and such programs appear to be paying off in terms of morale, performance, absentee rates, and health care costs.[47]

FAST FACT

DaimlerChrysler/UAW's National Wellness program lowers health risks and saves hundreds of thousands of dollars in health care costs.

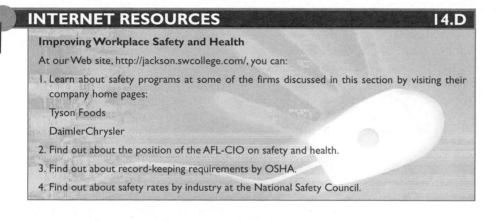

INTERNET RESOURCES   14.D

Improving Workplace Safety and Health

At our Web site, http://jackson.swcollege.com/, you can:

1. Learn about safety programs at some of the firms discussed in this section by visiting their company home pages:

   Tyson Foods

   DaimlerChrysler

2. Find out about the position of the AFL-CIO on safety and health.

3. Find out about record-keeping requirements by OSHA.

4. Find out about safety rates by industry at the National Safety Council.

LEGAL CONSIDERATIONS

The legal framework for occupational safety and health can be divided into four major categories: the Occupational Safety and Health Administration, workers' compensation programs, the common-law doctrine of torts, and local initiatives.

Occupational Safety and Health Administration

The federal government's primary response to the issue of safety and health in the workplace has been the *Occupational Safety and Health Act of 1970*, which created the Occupational Safety and Health Administration and calls for safety and health inspections of organizations regardless of size, reporting by employers, and investigations of accidents and allegations of hazards. OSHA is responsible for establishing and enforcing occupational safety and health standards and for inspecting and issuing citations to organizations that violate these standards. Two other organizations support the role of OSHA: the National Institute for Occupational Safety and Health (NIOSH) and the Occupational Safety and Health Review Commission (OSHRC). The commission reviews appeals made by organizations that received citations from OSHA inspectors for alleged safety and health violations.[48]

Regardless of whether organizations are inspected, they are required to keep safety and health records so that OSHA can compile accurate statistics on work injuries and illnesses. These records should cover all disabling, serious, or significant injuries and illnesses, whether or not they involve loss of time from work. Excluded are minor injuries that require only first aid and don't involve medical treatment, loss of consciousness, restriction of work or motion, or transfer to another job. Falsification of records or failure to keep adequate records can result in substantial fines. However, the record-keeping requirement was recently qualified.

An employer may withhold injury and illness records from federal safety investigators if it has a legitimate need to keep the records private, and the Occupational Safety and Health Administration has failed to obtain a warrant granting it access to such documents, the Occupational Safety and Health Review Commission (OSHRC) ruled. Rejecting the principle that OSHA compliance officers have unlimited rights to make warrantless examinations of an employer's records, the commission held that the employer has a reasonable expectation of privacy in safeguarding the information in its injury records. Such documents, OSHRC points out, may contain proprietary information on operations and manufacturing processes that employers may want to keep confidential (*Kings Island Division of Taft Broadcasting Co.*, 1987).

The *Access to Employee Exposure and Medical Records Regulation of 1980* requires employers to show or give employees, their designated representatives, and OSHA the employees' on-the-job medical records. This regulation also requires employers to provide access to records of measurements of employee exposure to toxic substances.

Communication Is Key. The employee's right to know was also strengthened by the Hazard Communication Standard, which went into effect in 1986. Under this standard, employers are required to provide workers with information and training on hazardous chemicals in their work area at the time of their initial assignment and whenever a new hazard is introduced. According to OSHA, effective communication is the real key and should include information for employees on

- the standard's requirements and workplace operations that use hazardous chemicals,
- proper procedures for determining the presence of chemicals and detecting hazardous releases,
- protective measures and equipment that should be used,
- the location of written hazard communication programs, and
- workers' compensation programs.[49]

Workers' Compensation Programs

Whereas OSHA was established to provide protection against accidents and diseases for workers on the job, workers' compensation provides financial aid for those unable to work because of accidents and diseases. For many years, workers' compensation awards were granted only to workers unable to work because of physical injury or damage. Since 1955, however, court decisions have either caused or enticed numerous states to allow workers' compensation payment in job-related cases of anxiety, depression, and mental disorders.

In 1955, the Texas Supreme Court charted this new direction in workers' compensation claims by stating that an employee who became terrified, highly anxious, and unable to work because of a job-related accident had a compensable claim even though he had no physical injury *(Bailey v. American General Insurance Company*, 1955). In another court ruling, *James v. State Accident Insurance Fund* (1980), an Oregon court ruled in favor of a worker's claim for compensation for inability to work due to job stress resulting from conflicting work assignments.

Determining responsibility is sometimes difficult because determining cause-and-effect relationships is difficult, especially since reactions such as asbestosis or hypertension take a long time to develop or occur only in some people working under the same conditions as others.

Common-Law Doctrine of Torts

Much of the legal discussion on human resource management is based on statutory law, that is, the body of laws passed by legislatures at the federal and state levels. For example, the *Civil Rights Act of 1991*, the *Americans with Disabilities Act of 1990*, and the *Occupational Safety and Health Act of 1970* are statutory laws. But the **common-law doctrine of torts** also plays a role. This body of law consists of court decisions regarding wrongful acts such as personal injuries that were committed by an employee against another employee against even a customer and resulted in a lawsuit against the employer.

Employees and customers can obtain damage awards if they demonstrate that the employer engaged in reckless or intentional infliction designed to degrade or humiliate. Few such cases have been successful, in part because workers' compensation programs were designed to remove workplace accidents and injuries from litigation. The cases that have been successfully brought against employers are notable because of the costs involved. For example, consider the customer in a car rental office who argued with the rental agent. The employee struck the customer with a blow to his head, knocking him to the floor. As the customer lay on the floor, the employee repeatedly kicked him and pummeled him with "judo chops." The customer filed a civil lawsuit for negligent retention. The evidence showed that the employee had a history of blowing up at and threatening customers. The rental company had not disciplined the employee either before or after the incident. A jury awarded the customer $350,000 in compensatory damages and $400,000 in punitive damages *(Greenfield v. Spectrum Inv. Group*, 1985).

> *"The law is clear that a landowner does not have a duty to provide for the safety of independent contractors."*
>
> U.S. Seventh Circuit Court of Appeals

Local Initiatives

State, municipal, and city governments may pass their own safety and health laws and regulations that go beyond the coverage of OSHA. Consequently, employers need to be aware of local regulations. Sometimes, these local initiatives offer a glimpse as to what other area governments or even the federal government might do in the future.

Americans with Disabilities Act (ADA)

Employee layoffs and discharges (terminations) constitute 50 percent of all claims filed under the ADA, and 15 percent of these are for back pain. Victims are entitled to sue for up to $300,000, and many employers are tempted to settle before going to trial in hopes of reaching smaller settlements. Thus, the ADA gives organizations another reason to seek ways to remove hazardous conditions from the work environment.[50]

SUMMARY

Employers are keenly aware of the cost of ill health and the benefits of having a healthy workforce. The federal government, through OSHA, is also making it more necessary for employers to be concerned with employee health. The government's current concern is primarily with occupational accidents and diseases, both aspects of the physical environment. However, organizations can choose to become involved in programs dealing with the psychological as well. If organizations choose not to become involved with improving psychological issues, the government may prescribe mandatory regulations. Thus, it pays for organizations to be concerned with both aspects of work. Effective programs for both environments can significantly improve both employee health and the effectiveness of the organization.

When the adoption of improvement programs is being considered, employee involvement isn't only a good idea but also is likely to be desired by employees. Many things can be done to improve both the physical and psychological work environments, each of which has its own unique components. Some improvement strategies may work well for one component, but not for others. A careful diagnosis is required before programs are selected and implemented.

Assuming that a careful diagnosis indicates the need for a stress management program, the challenge is selecting one from the many available. Programs such as time management or physical exercise can be set up so that employees can help themselves cope, or the organization can alter the conditions that are associated with stress. The latter approach requires a diagnosis of what is happening, where, and to whom before making a decision on how to proceed. Because so many possible sources of stress exist, and because not all people react the same way to them, implementing individual stress management strategies may be more efficient. However, if many people are suffering similar stress symptoms in a specific part of the organization, an organizational strategy is more appropriate.

For many aspects of safety and health, either pertinent information does not exist or organizations are unwilling to gather or provide it. From a legal as well as a humane viewpoint, it's in the best interests of organizations to seek and provide more information so that more effective strategies for improving safety and health can be developed and implemented. Failure to do so may result in costly legal settlements against organizations or further governmental regulation of workplace safety and health.

TERMS TO REMEMBER

common-law doctrine of torts
employee pacing
ergonomics
frequency rate
incidence rate
job burnout
low quality of working life
machine pacing
occupational accidents
occupational diseases

Occupational Safety and Health
    Administration (OSHA)
organizational stress
physical conditions
psychological conditions
safety committees
severity rate
work pacing
workplace safety and health

DISCUSSION QUESTIONS

1. In what ways are safety and health important issues at Ben and Jerry's?
2. How can strategies to improve the physical work environment and the psychological work environment be assessed?
3. The United States prides itself on freedom, democracy, and free labor markets. Thus, employees should be made responsible for health and safety. In other words, employers who offer riskier employment should simply pay workers more for bearing the risk (a wage premium), and the workers can in turn buy more insurance coverage to cover this risk. Discuss the advantages and disadvantages of this approach.
4. Who is responsible for workplace safety and health? The employer? The employee? The federal government? Judges and juries? Explain.
5. How are physical hazards distinct from psychological hazards? What implications do these differences have for programs to deal with these two categories of hazards?
6. Is there such a thing as an unsafe worker? Assuming that accident-prone workers exist, how can effective human resource activities address this problem?
7. Is accident-proneness a reliable trait? If not, does that mean organizations can't control it? Explain.
8. What incentives does OSHA provide the employer for promoting workplace safety? Explain.
9. How might a company's strategy to prevent occupational accidents differ from a program to prevent occupational disease? In what ways might the programs be similar?
10. Should all employers institute wellness programs for their employees?

PROJECTS TO EXTEND YOUR LEARNING

1. *Managing Teams.* Stress in organizations is a major concern: it can result in ill health and workplace accidents. Thus successful stress management activities are very desirable. Extensive research has shown that teams can be an excellent way for employees to manage the stress at work as well as to perform a multitude of complex tasks. Teams perform this helpful role in stress management by offering "social support." As you now know, it's predicted that if stress is managed well, illness and workplace accidents are likely to be reduced. You can investigate the extent of these relationships by identifying companies that are team based and those that are not. Then relate their illness measures and their accident rates to whether or not they are team based. You might consider using firms that use TQM principles versus those that don't.

2. *Managing Change.* Organizational change is a major event in the lives of many employees. It means that their organizational life will be different. Thus it would seem reasonable for employees to be told about the change that's coming. Such advance notification would help employees deal with one of the biggest sources of resistance to change: uncertainty and fear of the unknown. This uncertainty and fear are the heart of the stress that most of us feel when confronted with organizational change. Little wonder that we tend to prefer the "old" way to the "new" way. At least with the old way we know what to expect, we're certain about it, even if it's not a bed of roses. But with the new way, even though it might

be better, if we don't know this, then we are uncertain about the future. In reality, most of us like predictability. With this is mind, determine the policies and practices that organizations can use for informing their employees of forthcoming organizational changes. Find out why they choose to inform them or why they don't. Scan issues of the *Training and Development Magazine* for stories and visit the home page of the American Society for Training and Development.

3. *Integration and Application.* After reviewing the Lincoln Electric and Southwest Airlines cases at the end of the text, compare and contrast the threats to health and safety at these companies. Choose one company and describe the safety and health programs that you believe should be in place. Be specific about the objectives of the programs and be sure to state who should be responsible for them.

WHO'S THERE ON THE LINE?

The telecommunications field is changing very rapidly. In perhaps no other field has the impact of technology had such a significant effect on the jobs of so many workers. Mitch Fields, for example, still remembers that tragic day in November 1963 when President Kennedy was assassinated while Mitch was pulling the afternoon shift as a switchman for Midwest Telephone Company (MTC). As Mitch described it, it sounded like 30 locomotives hammering their way through a large room filled with walls of mechanical switches putting phone calls through to their destination. Today, that room of switches has been replaced by a microchip. Mitch himself has undergone extensive training to operate a computer console used to monitor and diagnose switching problems.

The job of operator has changed from sitting in long rows operating equipment attached to walls of jacks and cords to individual work stations that look like command centers out of a Star Trek spaceship. In addition, the competitive environment of telephone services has changed dramatically because of deregulation and competition from other phone companies offering similar services. The new thrust now is to shift operator performance from being not just fast and friendly but profitable as well, by marketing the company ("Thank you for using MTC") and selling high-profit-margin services ("Is there someone else you would like to talk to? The person-to-person rate is only additional for the first minute").

The operator's job at MTC remains unchanged in two respects: (1) operators will talk to nearly 600 people in a typical day, some of whom are still abusive, and (2) operator job performance is monitored. Technological innovation has enabled MTC to monitor each operator by computer to produce statistics on numbers of calls handled per shift, speed of the call, and amount of revenue generated by the calls. In addition to computer monitoring, supervisors may also listen in on operators to ensure that proper operator protocol is followed. For example, customers are never told they dialed the "wrong" number, obscene calls are routed to supervisors, and one learns to say "hold the line" or "one moment please" instead of "hang on."

Meeting performance standards based on these criteria does not typically lead to large rewards. A beginning operator usually earns about $12,000 a year working swing shifts that may begin at 8:30 A.M., noon, 2:00 P.M., 4:30 P.M., 8:30 P.M., or 2:00 A.M. Only the highest-rated operators have the opportunity to be transferred, promoted, or receive educational benefits.

Steve Buckley, training and development manager for MTC, knows that to change the fast and friendly MTC operator of the past to one who is fast, friendly, and profitable as well is going to be a real challenge. Steve has not figured out yet how to get the operators to conclude each transaction by saying "thank you for using MTC." A recent clandestine supervisor survey revealed that fewer than 20 percent of the operators were using the requested reply. Steve is also being pressured by the local union leaders who represent the telephone operators to reduce the job stress brought on by the high volume of people transactions and the constant, computer-assisted surveillance. One thing is for sure, however—Steve must implement a plan for improvement.

QUESTIONS

1. Can Steve really change the behavior of the operators?

2. How can Steve succeed in getting the operators to say "thank you for using MTC?"
3. Is computer monitoring the answer?
4. Should the operators really decide on the change?

ENDNOTES

1 From Ben and Jerry's *Annual Reports* 1992 to 2000; G. Smith, "A Famous Brand on the Rocky Road," *Business Week* (November 17, 2000): 54; "Ben & Jerry's Sacred Cow" http://cgi.cnnfn.com (December 3, 1999); B. Cohen and J. Greenfield, *Ben & Jerry's Double Dip* (New York: Simon & Schuster, 1997); L. Johnson, "Preventing Injuries: The Big Payoff," *Personnel Journal* (April 1994): 61–64.

2 For detailed discussions of this topic, see C. Neck and K. Cooper, "The Fit Executive: Exercise and Diet Guidelines for Enhancing Performance," *Academy of Management Executive* 14(2) (May 2000): 72–83; K. Danna and R. Griffin, "Health and Well-Being in the Workplace: A Review and Synthesis of the Literature," *Journal of Management* 25(3) (1999): 357–384; S. Cartwright, "BUPA's CEO Val Gooding on Maximizing Employee Health," *Academy of Management Executive* 14(2) (May 2000): 12–15; J. M. Harrington, *Occupational Health* (London: Blackwell, 1998); S. Sadhra and K. G. Rampal, *Occupational Health: Risk Assessment and Management* (London: Blackwell, 1999); M. A. Friend, *Fundamentals of Occupational Safety and Health* (Rockville, MD: ABS Consulting, 2001).

3 D. Zohar, "A Group-Level Model of Safety Climate: Testing the Effect of Group Climate on Microaccidents in Manufacturing Jobs," *Journal of Applied Psychology* 85(4) (2000): 587–596.

4 E. Tahmincioglu, "Battling Job-Related Aches and Pains," *New York Times* (January 3, 2001): G1.

5 T. Kelly, "For Hard Hats, a Confusion of Tongues," *New York Times* (December 15, 1999): G1; M. Westman and D. Etzion, "The Crossover of Strain from School Principals to Teachers and Vice Versa," *Journal of Occupational Health Psychology* 4(3) (1999): 269–278; S. R. King, "Nursing Homes Draw Attention as Worker-Safety Focus Shifts," *New York Times* (August 7, 1996): D1, D5; B. Saporito, "The Most Dangerous Jobs in America," *Fortune* (May 31, 1993): 131–140; "Occupational Injuries and Illnesses," *Bulletin to Management* (January 6, 1994): 4–6. These estimates could be regarded as conservative because they do not include the costs due to stress and to a low quality of working life. See also A. J. Kinicki, F. M. McKee, and K. J. Wade, "Annual Review, 1991–1995: Occupational Health," *Journal of Vocational Behavior* 49(2) (October 1996): 190–220; D. A. Hofmann and A. Stetzer, "A Cross-Level Investigation of Factors Influencing Unsafe Behaviors and Accidents," *Personnel Psychology* 49 (1996): 307.

6 B. P. Sunoo, "Over the Border," *Workforce* (July 2000): 41–44; M. Schweitzer and J. Kerr, "Bargaining Under the Influence: The Role of Alcohol Negotiations," *Academy of Management Executive* 14(2) (May 2000): 47–57; C. Cohen, "When an Employee's Crisis Becomes HR's Problem," *Workforce* (January 2001): 64–69.

7 J. A. Kinney, "Why Did Paul Die?" *Newsweek* (September 10, 1990): 11. See also B. J. Feder, "A Spreading Pain, and Cries for Justice," *New York Times* (June 5, 1994): 3-1, 3-6.

8 M. Conlin, "Is Your Office Killing You?" *Business Week* (June 5, 2000): 114–124; S. Cartwright, "Taking the Pulse of Executive Health in the U.K.," *Academy of Management Executive* 14(2) (May 2000): 16–24; J. Veiga, "AME's Executive Advisory Panel Goes for a Check-Up," *Academy of Management Executive* 14(2) (May 2000): 25–27; M. Cavanaugh, W.

Boswell, M. Rochling, and J. W. Boudreau, "An Empirical Examination of Self-Reported Work Stress Among U.S. Managers," *Journal of Applied Psychology* 85(1) (2000): 65–74; G. Evans and D. Johnson, "Stress and Open-Office Noise," *Journal of Applied Psychology* 85(5) (2000): 779–783; W. Atkinson, "When Stress Won't Go Away," *HR Magazine* (December 2000): 105–110; P. McCurry, "Safe Here, Perilous There," *HR World* (July/August 1999): 51; L. McClure, *Anger and Conflict in the Workplace: Spot the Signs, Avoid the Trauma* (New York: Impact Publications, 2000).

9 R. Grossman, "Back with a Vengeance," *HR Magazine* (August 2001): 36–46; S. Greenhouse, "Ergonomics Report Cites Job Injuries," *New York Times* (January 18, 2001): C6; R. Grossman, "Make Ergonomics," *HR Magazine* (April 2000): 36–42; M. Conlin, "Is Your Office Killing You?" *Business Week* (June 5, 2000): 114–124; M. Minehan, "OSHA Ergonomics Regs Draw Immediate Fire," *HR News* (January 2001): 1, 3; K. Tyler, "Sit Up Straight," *HR Magazine* (September 1998): 121–128.

10 J. Leigh, S. Markowitz, M Fahs, and P. Landrigan, *Costs of Occupational Injuries and Illnesses* (Ann Arbor: University of Michigan Press, 2000); R. Shindledecker, "Health and the Bottom Line," *Workspan* (September 2000): 6–8; W. Altman, "Health and Safety Commission Chair Bill Callaghan on 'Good Health Is Good Business,'" *Academy of Management Executive* 14(2) (May 2000): 8–11; J. Quick, J. Gavin, C. L. Cooper, and J. D. Quick, "Executive Health: Building Strength, Managing Risks," *Academy of Management Executive* 14(2) (May 2000): 34–46; W. Atkinson, "Safety—at a Price," *HR Magazine* (November 1999): 52–59; M. Arndt, "It Pays to Tell the Truth," *Business Week* (June 5, 2000): 128–130; R. Grossman, "Out with the Bad Air . . . ," *HR Magazine* (October 2000): 37–45; L. Grensing-Pophal, "Clearing the Air," *HR Magazine* (August 2000): 64–70; J. J. Laabs, "Cashing in on Safety," *Workforce* (August 1997): 53–57; E. Raimy, "Safety Pays," *Human Resource Executive* (November 1996): 1, 21–23; C. A. Bacon, "Is There a Nurse in the Office?" *Workforce* (June 1997): 107–113.

11 W. Atkinson, "Is Workers Comp Changing?" *HR Magazine* (July 2000): 50–61; U. Lundberg, I. Dohns, B. Melin, L. Sandsjö, G. Palmerud, T. Kadefors, M. Elkström, and D. Parr, "Psychophysiological Stress Responses, Muscle Tension, and Neck and Shoulder Pain Among Supermarket Cashiers," *Journal of Occupational Health Psychology* 4(3) (1999): 245–255; V. Infante, "The Irony of Ergonomic Regulation," *Workforce* (January 2001): 26; P. Leigh et al., *Cost of Occupational Injuries and Illnesses.*

12 J. Adams, "Workplace Deaths Decline, Co-Worker Homicides Rise," *HR Magazine* (February 2001): 12; "Occupational Injuries and Illnesses," *Bulletin to Management* (January 15, 1998): 13; "Datagraph: Workplace Fatalities—1997," *Bulletin to Management* (August 28, 1997): 276–277; "Datagraph: Occupational Injuries and Illnesses Down in 1995," *Bulletin to Management* (April 3, 1997): 108–109; "Datagraph: Workplace Issues Then and Now," *Bulletin to Management* (December 25, 1997): 412–413. See also "ILO Releases New Version of Health and Safety Encyclopedia," *International HR Update* (July 1998): 3. Visit the home page of the Bureau of Labor Statistics and the National Safety Council.

13 Personal correspondence with Donald Brush, President, Bearings Division, Barden Corporation.

14 K. Parkes, "Shiftwork, Job Type, and the Work Environment as Joint Pre-

dictors of Health-Related Outcomes," *Journal of Occupational Health Psychology* 4(3) (1999): 256–268; S. Jex and P. Bliese, "Efficacy Beliefs as a Moderator of Impact of Work-Related Stressors: A Multilevel Study," *Journal of Applied Psychology* 84(3) (1999): 349–361; M. R. Frone, "Predictors of Work Injuries Among Employed Adolescents," *Journal of Applied Psychology* 83 (1998): 565–576.

15 "Facing Middle-age Injuries," http://cgi.cnnfn.com (July 18, 2000): 1–3; M. Moss, "For Older Employees, On-the-Job Injuries Are More Often Deadly," *Wall Street Journal* (June 17, 1997): A1; "Workplace Deaths Unchanged; Homicides at Six-Year Low," *Bulletin to Management: Facts and Figures* (August 27, 1998): 269; "Occupational Injuries and Illnesses," *Bulletin to Management: Facts and Figures* (January 15, 1998): 13.

16 "Violence in the Workplace," *Workforce* (January 2002): 46; L. McClure, *Anger and Conflict in the Workplace*; K. Tyler, "Targets Behind the Counter," *HR Magazine* (August 1999): 106–111; G. Flynn, "Employers Can't Look Away from Workplace Violence," *Workforce* (July 2000): 68–73; M. France, "After the Shooting Stops," *Business Week* (March 12, 2001): 98–100; R. Denenberg and M. Braverman, *The Violence-Prone Workplace: A New Approach to Dealing with Hostile, Threatening and Uncivil Behavior* (Ithaca, NY: Cornell University Press, 1999); E. Licking, "Taking Stock of the Devastation," *Business Week* (July 17, 2000): 84–86; S. A. Baron, S. Hoffman, and J. Merrill, *When Work Equals Life: The Next Stage of Workplace Violence* (San Francisco: Pathfinder Publishing of California, 2000); T. D. Schneid, *Occupational Health Guide to Violence in the Workplace* (Chelsea, MI: Lewis, 1998).

17 S. C. Douglas and M. J. Martinko, "Exploring the Role of Individual Differences in Predicting Workplace Aggression," *Journal of Applied Psychology* 86(4) (2001): 547–559; J. H. Neuman and R. A. Baron, "Workplace Violence and Workplace Aggression: Evidence Concerning Specific Forms, Potential Causes and Preferred Targets," *Journal of Management* 24(3) (1998): 391–419; G. R. VanderBos and E. Q. Bulatao (eds.), *Violence on the Job: Identifying Risks and Developing Solutions* (Washington, DC: American Psychological Association, 1996); A. M. O'Leary-Kelly, R. W. Griffin, and D. J. Glew, "Organization-Motivated Aggression: A Research Framework," *Academy of Management Review* 21 (1996): 225–253.

18 S. A. Baron et al., *When Work Equals Life*; S. Caudron, "Target: HR," *Workforce* (August 1998): 44–52; J. J. Laabs, "What Goes Down When Minimum Wages Go Up," *Workforce* (August 1998): 54–58; "Preventing Workplace Violence," *Bulletin to Management* (June 10, 1993): 177.

19 Visit the Web site of the National Safety Council and the National Center for Health Statistics for the latest information.

20 S. Melamed, I. Ben-Avi, J. Luz, and M. S. Green, "Objective and Subjective Work Monotony: Effects on Job Satisfaction, Psychological Distress, and Absenteeism in Blue-Collar Workers," *Journal of Applied Psychology* 80(1) (1995): 29–42; P. L. Perrewe (ed.), *Handbook on Job Stress: Special Issue of Journal of Social Behavior and Personality* 6(1) (1991). "Charges of Emotional Distress: A Growing Trend," *Fair Employment Practices Guidelines* 284 (1989): 1–4.

21 For a recent summary, see R. DeFrank, R. Konopaske, and J. M. Ivancevich, "Executive Travel Stress: Perils of the Road Warrior," *Academy of Management Executive* 14(2) (May 2000): 58–71; J. Kline and L. Sussman, "An Executive Guide to Workplace Depression," *Academy of Management Executive* 14(3) (2000): 103–112; R. S. DeFrank and J. M. Ivancevich, "Stress on the Job: An Executive Update," *Academy of Management Executive* 12(3) (1998): 55–66.

22 A. B. Shostak, *Blue Collar Stress* (Reading, MA: Addison-Wesley, 1980).

23 M. A. Gowan, C. Riordan, and R. D. Gatewood, "Test of a Model of Coping with Involuntary Job Loss Following a Company Closing," *Journal of Applied Psychology* 84(1) (1999): 75–86; C. Smith, C. Robie, S. Folkard, J. Barton, I. Macdonald, L. Smith, E. Spelten, P. Totterdell, and G. Costa, "A Process Model of Shiftwork and Health," *Journal of Occupational Health Psychology* 4(3) (1999): 207–218; S. Carpenter, "Workplace Safety Tied to Job Security," *Monitor on Psychology* (April 2001): 14.

24 S. Cohen and G. M. Williamson, "Stress and Infectious Disease in Humans," *Psychological Bulletin* 109 (1991): 5–24; S. R. Barley and D. B. Knight, "Toward a Cultural Theory of Stress Complaints," *Research in Organizational Behavior* 14 (1992): 1–48; R. Martin and T. D. Wall, "Attentional Demand and Cost Responsibility as Stressors in Shopfloor Jobs," *Academy of Management Journal* 32 (1989): 69–86; C. A. Higgins and L. E. Duxbury,

"Work-Family Conflict in the Dual-Career Family," *Organizational Behavior and Human Decision Processes* 51 (1992): 51–75.

25 Adapted from "Personnel Shop Talk," *Bulletin to Management* (September 4, 1994): 282.

26 M. Frankenhaeuser and B. Gardell, "Underload and Overload in Working Life: Outline of Multidisciplinary Approach," *Journal of Human Stress* 2 (1976): 36–45; M. Pesci, "Stress Management: Separating Myth from Reality," *Personnel Administrator* (January 1982): 57–67.

27 C. Garvey, "Companies Sponsor Noise Awareness Day Events to Remind Workers to Protect Hearing," *HR News* (June 2000): 13; M. Johnson, "All Quiet on the Western Front," *HR World* (July/August 1999): 52; B. Jordan, "Quiet, For Now," *HR World* (July/August 1999): 61; R. Rudman, "Hailstones and Earthquakes," *HR World* (July/August 1999): 55.

28 "Please, Somebody! Open a Window!" *Business Week* (January 18, 1999): 8; see also G. Swartz, *Job Hazard Analysis: A Guide to Identifying Risks in the Workplace* (Rockville, MD: ABS Consulting, 2001).

29 M. Friedman and R. Roseman, *Type A Behavior and Your Heart* (New York: Knopf, 1974).

30 M. Maslach and M. P. Leiter, *The Truth About Burnout: How Organizations Cause Personal Stress and What to Do About It* (San Francisco: Jossey-Bass, 1997); C. L. Cordes and T. W. Dougherty, "A Review and Integration of Research on Job Burnout," *Academy of Management Review* 18 (1993): 621–656.

31 R. Thompson, "Setting OSHA's Agenda," *HR Magazine* (December 1999): 94–103; W. Atkinson, "When OSHA Comes Knocking," *HR Magazine* (October 1999): 35–50. For an overview of OSHA's Strategic Plan for 1997–2002 see its Web site.

32 M. W. Walsh, "Keeping Workers Safe, but at What Cost?" *New York Times* (December 20, 2000): G1; L. Miller, "People on the Move Are Going Back to Driving School," *Wall Street Journal* (May 20, 1997): A1; "Safety: A Quick Pay-Off, a Long-Term Commitment," *HR Reporter* (October 1990): 6; R. Pater, "Safety Leadership Cuts Costs," *HR Magazine* (November 1990): 46–47.

33 D. Zohar, "A Group-Level Model of Safety Climate: Testing the Effect of Group Climate on Microaccidents in Manufacturing Jobs," *Journal of Applied Psychology* 85(4) (2000): 587–596; B. Leonard, "Mission Possible: Fighting Fire with Teamwork," *HR Magazine* (December 2000): 46–48.

34 T. Bland and P. Forment, "Navigating OSHA's Ergonomics Rule," *HR Magazine* (February 2001): 61–67; M. Moss, "For Older Employees, On-the-Job Injuries Are More Often Deadly," *Wall Street Journal* (June 17, 1997): A1; D. P. Levin, "The Graying Factor," *New York Times* (February 20, 1994): 3-1, 3-3.

35 J. R. Hollenbeck, D. R. Ilgen, and S. M. Crampton, "Lower Back Disability in Occupational Settings: A Review of the Literature from a Human Resource Management View," *Personnel Psychology* 45 (1992): 247–278. See also K. Tyler, "Sit Up Straight."

36 "Personnel Shop Talk," *Bulletin to Management* (April 25, 1994): 266.

37 J. Komaki, K. D. Barwick, and L. Scott, "Pinpointing and Reinforcing Safe Performance in a Food Manufacturing Plant," *Journal of Applied Psychology* 63 (1978): 434–445. See also G. M. Ritzky, "Turner Bros. Wins Safety Game with Behavioral Incentives," *HR Magazine* (June 1998): 79–83; R. Allen, "Playing It Safe," *Human Resource Executive* (August 1997): 1, 26–30.

38 H. M. Taylor, "Occupational Health Management-by-Objectives," *Personnel* (January–February 1980): 58–64.

39 T. Minton-Eversole, "Impact of Genetic Information in Workplace Explored," *HR News* (September 2000): 1, 15; K. Ridder, "Genetic Testing Raises Fears of Workplace Bias," *Dallas Morning News* (April 26, 1998): 8H; S. Greengard, "Genetic Testing: Should You Be Afraid? It's No Joke," *Workforce* (July 1997): 38–44.

40 J. C. Erfurt, A. Foote, and M. A. Heirich, "The Cost-Effectiveness of Worksite Wellness Programs for Hypertension Control, Weight Loss, Smoking Cessation and Exercise," *Personnel Psychology* 45 (1992): 5–27;

D. L. Bebhardt and C. E. Crump, "Employee Fitness and Wellness Programs in the Workplace," *American Psychologist* (February 1990): 262–272.

41 K. Roberts and R. Bea, "Must Accidents Happen? Lessons for High-Reliability Organizations," *Academy of Management Executive* 15 (2001): 70–78; J. Forster, "When Workers Just Can't Cope," *Business Week* (October 30, 2000): 100–102; K. Tyler, "The Difference Between Life and Death," *HR Magazine* (November 2000): 107–117; D. H. Shapiro, Jr., C. E. Schwartz, and J. A. Astin, "Controlling Ourselves, Controlling Our World," *American Psychologist* 51 (December 1996): 1213–1230; T. D. Ludwig and E. S. Geller, "Assigned Versus Participative Goal Setting and Response Generalization: Managing Injury Control Among Professional Pizza Deliverers," *Journal of Applied Psychology* 82 (1997): 253–261; J. Schaubroeck and D. E. Merritt, "Divergent Effects of Job Control on Coping with Work Stressors: The Key Role of Self-Efficacy," *Academy of Management Journal* 40 (1997): 738–754.; D. C. Ganster, M. L. Fox, and D. J. Dwyer, "Explaining Employers' Health Care Costs: A Perspective Examination of Stressful Job Demands, Personal Control, and Physiological Reactivity," *Journal of Applied Psychology* 86 (2001): 954–964.

42 M. Frese, "Social Support as a Moderator of the Relationship Between Work Stressors and Psychological Dysfunctioning: A Longitudinal Study with Objective Measures," *Journal of Occupational Health Psychology* 4(3) (1999): 179–192; E. Diener, E. Suh, R. Lucas, and H. Smith, "Subjective Well-Being: Three Decades of Progress," *Psychological Bulletin* 125(2) (1999): 276–302; D. Hoffman and F. Morgeson, "Safety-Related Behavior as a Social Exchange: The Role of Perceived Organizational Support and Leader-Member Exchange," *Journal of Applied Psychology* 84(2) (1999): 286–296; L. Belkin, "If Chocolate Doesn't Work," *New York Times* (January 31, 2001): G1.

43 A. Higbie, "Quick Lessons in the Fine Old Art of Unwinding," *New York Times* (February 25, 2001): BU10; M. Freudenheim, "Employers Focus on Weight as Workplace Health Issue," *New York Times* (September 6, 1999): A15; D. Etzion, D. Eden, and Y. Lapidot, "Relief from Job Stressors and Burnout: Reserve Service as a Respite," *Journal of Applied Psychology* 83 (1998): 577–585; M. Westman and D. Eden, "Effects of Vacation on Job Stress and Burnout: Relief and Fade Out," *Journal of Applied Psychology* 82 (1997): 516–527.

44 M. Conlin, "What's That Smell?" *Business Week* (December 11, 2000): 76–84; "Fetal Protection Policy Struck Down," *Fair Employment Practices Guidelines* (May 1991): 1–2; "Fetal Protection Ruling," *Fair Employment Practices Guidelines* (March 28, 1991): 31.

45 R. Winslow, "Air Polluted by Carbon Monoxide Poses Risk to Heart Patients, Study Shows," *Wall Street Journal* (September 4, 1990): B4; R. Winslow, "Safety Group Cites Fatalities Linked to Work," *Wall Street Journal* (August 31, 1990): B8; C. Trost, "Business and Women Anxiously Watch Suit on 'Fetal Protection,'" *Wall Street Journal* (October 8, 1990): 1.

46 J. Adkins, "Ceridian Performance Partners' President Linda Hall Whitman on Navigating Work and Life," *Academy of Management Executive* 14(2) (May 2000): 28–33; B. Leonard, "Employees Are Searching for a Healthier Lifestyle," *HR Magazine* (July 2000): 32; C. Hill, "Online Wellness Programs Offer Healthy Choices," *Workspan* (January 2001): 22–25; A. Hosking, "Precautionary Tales," *HR World* (July/August 1999): 59; S. Suri, "Fly Me to Hospital," *HR World* (July/August 1999): 63; C. Winters, K. Stangler, A. L. Shaffer, and B. A. Morris, "Corporate Wellness," *Human Resource Executive* (September 1997): 47–60; "Personnel Shop Talk," *Bulletin to Management* 48 (December 18, 1997): 402.

47 D. A. Harrison and J. J. Martocchio, "Time for Absenteeism: A 20-year Review of Origins, Offshoots, and Outcomes," *Journal of Management* 24 (1998): 305–350; "Injury Rates: An Incentive to Cheat?" *Bulletin to Management* (September 17, 1998): 292; M. R. Edwards, "Measuring Team Performance Through a Balanced Model," *ACA News* (November/December 1996): 17–18.

48 "OSHA Levies Second Big Ergo Fine," *Bulletin to Management* 49 (January 8, 1998): 4; "Safety Rule on Respiratory Protection Issued," *Bulletin to Management* 49(1)(January 8, 1998): 1; "Enforcement Activity Increased in 1997," *Bulletin to Management* (January 29, 1998): 28; "OSHA Seeks 'Cooperative Compliance,'" *Bulletin to Management* (September 4, 1997): 288; "OSHA's Cooperative Program Shoves Off," *Bulletin to Management* (December 25, 1997): 416; "OSHA to Address Ruling on Protective Equipment," *Bulletin to Management* 48(52) (December 25, 1997): 409; "Settling Safety Violations Has Benefits," *Bulletin to Management* (July 31, 1997): 248.

49 C. Patton, "Gray Matters," *Human Resource Executive* (November 1997): 64–68; P. A. Susser, "Update on Hazard Communication," *Personnel Administrator* (October 1985): 57–61; M. G. Miner, "Legal Concerns Facing Human Resource Managers: An Overview," in R. S. Schuler, S. A. Youngblood, and V. L. Huber (eds.), *Readings in Personnel and Human Resource Management*, 3rd ed. (St. Paul, MN: West Publishing, 1988); "Hazard Communication Training: Compliance Cues," *Bulletin to Management* (March 13, 1986): 81.

50 L. Greenhouse, "Justices Accept 2 Cases to Clarify Protection for Disabled," *New York Times* (April 17, 2001): A13.

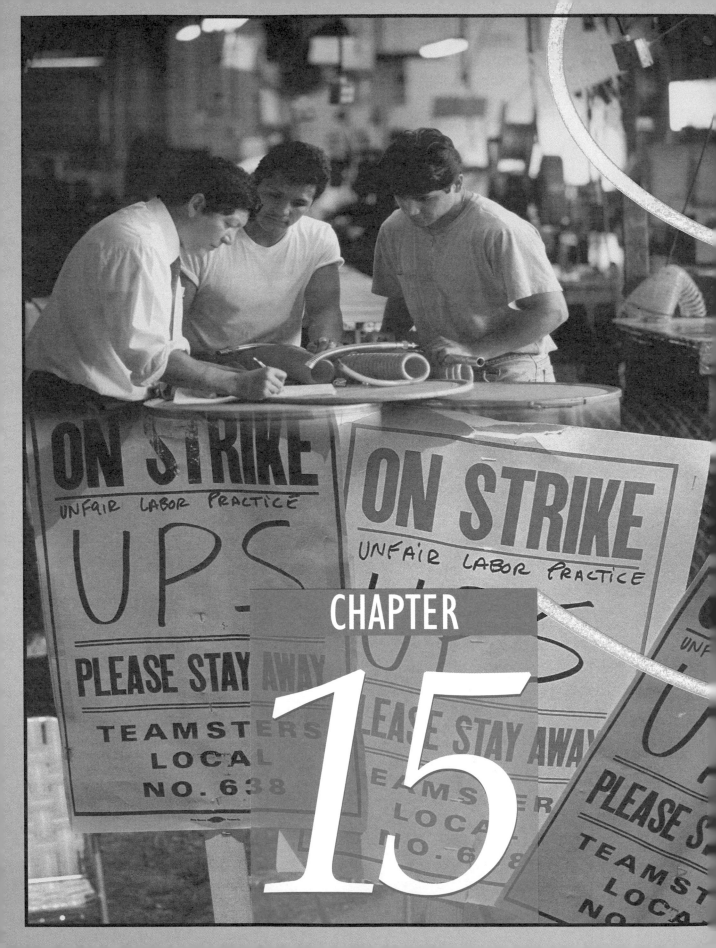

CHAPTER

15

UNDERSTANDING UNIONIZATION AND COLLECTIVE BARGAINING

"You can be a good Teamster and a good UPSer."

Jim Casey
UPS Founder[1]

MANAGING THROUGH STRATEGIC PARTNERSHIPS

UPS and the Teamsters

UPS, an employee-owned company, is the third largest private employer in the United States. It has also been rated as the top in its industry in *Fortune*'s "Most Admired Companies to Work For." Represented by the Teamsters union, the company's 300,000 employees are the highest paid in the industry and have a relatively low turnover rate. Senior managers receive modest pay compared with those in most other *Fortune* 500 companies. Clearly the history of UPS indicated a strong desire to work in partnership with the employees and the Teamsters union. When the union went on strike in August 1997, it came as a surprise to many observers. The Teamsters had worked collaboratively with the company for more than 80 years, guided by UPS founder Jim Casey's philosophy that "You can be a good Teamster and a good UPSer." What went wrong? What were the issues that divided them? Was the strike worth it?

The two most significant issues were the multiemployer pension plan and the increasing reliance on part-time workers. The pension plan was one in which several companies contributed. UPS's share to the total plan was about $1 billion yearly, a cost it thought it could reduce by administering its own plan. The Teamsters wanted to protect the retirement benefits of the UPS workers as well as the benefits for the other companies in the plan. In another attempt to cut costs, UPS had been hiring more part-time workers. The Teamsters wanted the company to hire more full-time workers who would receive better wages and benefits. To settle the strike, UPS agreed to increase salaries over the five-year life of the agreement by $3.10 per hour for full-timers and by $4.10 per hour for part-timers, combine part-time positions into 10,000 new full-time jobs, and remain in the multiemployer pension plan.

Judging by its ranking in *Fortune*, it appears that UPS has bounced back. It seems that UPS has learned from this experience. Now it realizes that all parties need to work in partnership to make sure that all is well. Perhaps UPS had underestimated the union's resolve and the workers' belief in the importance of the issues. It certainly underestimated the public support that the union members received. The legacy of this situation is that other companies thinking strategically about the use of part-timers may need to think again.[2]

FAST FACT

Unions are present in 28 of *Fortune*'s "100 Most Admired Companies."

In retrospect, the events at UPS are a good reminder of how valuable union-management cooperation can be. For more than 80 years, UPS and the Teamsters union had worked together, producing an employment relationship that benefited both workers and the company. Over the years, service quality had been excellent, absenteeism was low, employees were relatively satisfied with their jobs, they enjoyed employment security and received continual training, and the result was a profitable company. But maintaining such a positive and cooperative relationship takes constant work from everyone involved. Among the roles and responsibilities to be fulfilled are those shown in the feature "The HR Triad Extended: Roles and Responsibilities in Unionization and Collective Bargaining."

As conditions continue to change in the 21st century, the union-management relationship will likely also change. Changes are likely to occur both in unionization efforts and in the bargaining relationships between existing unions and management. For example, the UAW is extending its efforts to unionize nonteaching employees in universities. Changes are also occurring within unions as they consider offering alternative forms of membership such as an associate status.[3] To put into perspective these aspects of union-management relationships, this chapter describes the process of forming a union (unionization) and the characteristics of administering an agreement reached between the union and management (collective bargaining).

Roles and Responsibilities in Unionization and Collective Bargaining

THE HR TRIAD Extended

Line Managers	HR Professionals	Employees	Unions
• Know and appreciate the historical context of union-management relations and the current contract. • Understand why employees are likely to join a union. • Support the efforts of HR professionals in making policies and programs for good working conditions. • Manage employees with respect and equality. • Know what can and can't be said to employees regarding unionization during an organizing campaign. • Work with HR professionals in developing an effective relationship with union representatives. • Work with HR professionals and union representatives in resolving grievances.	• Train line managers in the legal considerations protecting the unionization rights of employees. • Develop HR policies and programs that make for good working conditions. • Continually survey employees' attitudes so that management knows employees' views and opinions. • Work with line managers in dealing effectively with union representatives. • Develop mechanisms for effective grievance resolution. • Move along such issues as total quality management and quality-of-work-life programs. • Work with line managers in the grievance process.	• Present views about working conditions to HR professionals and line managers. • Express views on work place conditions, wages, and working hours. • Bargain in good faith through union representatives with line managers and HR professionals. • Fulfill rights and responsibilities in the union contract. • Use mechanisms for grievances as appropriate. • Be aware of the issues management and labor leaders are discussing. • Stay involved in the grievance process as appropriate.	• Seek to represent the employees' views to the company. • Offer to improve wages and working conditions for members. • Offer to work with management to improve company profitability and survival. • Bargain with line managers and HR professionals. • Seek improvements in conditions and wages. • Be willing to adapt to local conditions and changes in technology and economic conditions. • Ensure grievances are processed fairly.

THE STRATEGIC IMPORTANCE OF UNIONIZATION AND COLLECTIVE BARGAINING

Unionization is the effort by employees and outside agencies (unions or associations) to act as a single unit when dealing with management over issues relating to their work. When recognized by the National Labor Relations Board (NLRB), a union has the legal authority to negotiate with the employer on behalf of employees—to improve wages, hours, and conditions of employment—and to administer the ensuing agreement.[4] The process of unionization is illustrated in Exhibit 15.1.

The core of union-management relations is **collective bargaining**. Collective bargaining generally includes two types of interaction. The first is the negotiation of work conditions that, when written up as the collective agreement (the contract), become the basis for employee-employer relationships on the job. The second includes activities related to interpreting and enforcing the collective agreement (contract administration) and resolving any conflicts arising from it.[5]

For employers, the existence of or possibility of a union can significantly influence an employer's ability to manage its vital human resources. Unions can help employees get what they want—for example, high wages and job security—from their employers. For management, unionization may result in less flexibility in hiring new workers, making job assignments, and introduc-

> **FAST FACT**
>
> In Seattle, the Communication Workers of America (CWA) teamed with Cisco to build a lab to house Web programming classes.

> *"My greatest regret was the relationship, for one reason or another, between myself and the unions."*
>
> Robert L. Crandell
> Retired CEO
> American Airlines

ex 15.1 Unionization and Collective Bargaining within an Integrated HR System

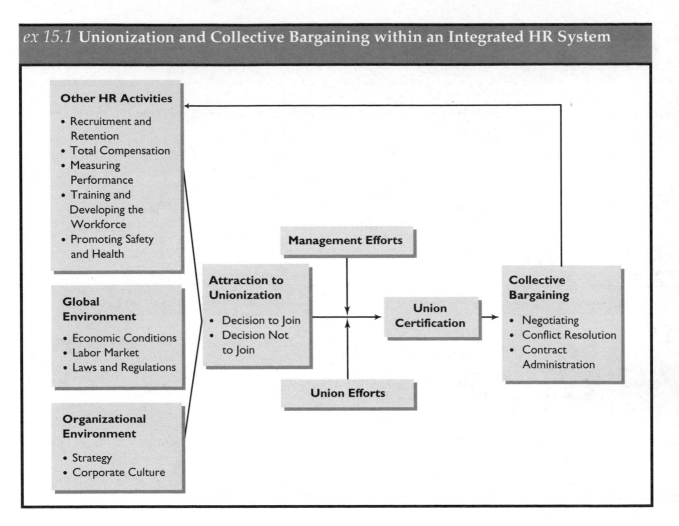

ing new work methods such as automation; a loss of control; inefficient work practices; and an inflexible job structure. It may result, however, in greater workforce cooperation with programs such as total quality management.[6]

Unions obtain rights for their members that employees without unions don't legally have. This, of course, forces unionized companies to consider their employees' reactions to a wide variety of decisions. Nevertheless, in some cases, employers who are nonunion and want to remain that way give more consideration and benefits to their employees. Consequently, it may or may not be more expensive for a company to operate with unionized rather than nonunionized employees.[7]

Unions assist employers through wage concessions or cooperation in joint workplace efforts, such as teamwork programs or Scanlon Plans, allowing employers to survive particularly difficult times and, in fact, remain profitable and competitive. This has been particularly true in the automobile, steel, and airline industries. Unions can also help identify workplace hazards and improve the quality of work life for employees.[8] Clearly, unions have an important role to play in the strategic issues of a company. These are described more in the feature "Managing Change: Unions Get Involved."[9]

Unions Get Involved

Labor costs are critical to the success of many companies vis-à-vis their competitors. Wage reductions reached between unions and management help to lower costs. During the 1980s, American Airlines, Boeing, and Ingersoll-Rand negotiated two-tier wage systems to help reduce total costs by reducing labor costs. In the 1990s, Southwest Airlines got concessions from its pilots and machinists to hold down wage costs. Without these jointly negotiated systems, these companies might not have survived. Thus, a company's relationship with its union can be critical to its survival, and the better its relationship, the more likely the company is to gain a competitive advantage.

Ford Motor Company has engaged in a program of more worker involvement and more cooperative labor relations with the United Auto Workers. The results of this program were higher product quality for Ford than for its competitors, and a marketing campaign centered on the slogan "Quality Is Job One." This program of more worker involvement gained competitive advantage through higher product quality and improved efficiencies. Similar results have been obtained at Eaton Corporation, Saturn, AT&T, Xerox, and the Mass Transportation Authority of Flint, Michigan. In these companies, gains in quality and efficiency have resulted from employee involvement. These companies have also experienced fewer grievances, reduced absenteeism and turnover, lower design costs, higher engineering productivity, and fewer costly changes in design cycles.

It is likely that we will continue to see this strategic involvement. It may, however, also take another form: workers actually taking over the company or assuming part of its equity ownership. The pilots at Southwest Airlines and Northwest Airlines got a stake in the company for granting wage concessions. At National Steel Corporation, Wheeling-Pittsburgh Steel Corporation, and the LTV Corporation, wage concessions resulted in board membership. Giving unions access to the board room is common in Europe, where the unions are stronger, but is still quite novel in the United States. It has generally only been entertained by troubled companies that have had to work closely with their unions to avert bankruptcy or liquidation. Only the future will tell if non-troubled companies also elect to bring worker representation onto their boards.

MANAGING CHANGE

The Importance of Other HR Practices

As the story of UPS highlights and Exhibit 15.1 illustrates, unionizing and collective bargaining activities often involve other HR practices. In the UPS example, benefits and services and wages were an important part of the strike between the Teamsters and UPS. While pension contributions are an important concern to union leadership and their members, so are traditional concerns like cost-of-living increases, working conditions, and health and safety. Unions are increasingly concerned about training and educational benefits for their members. They recognize the need for companies to remain competitive in this global market and the need to utilize the most current technologies available that often require additional training and education. Unions are also concerned about performance appraisal measurement and compensation plans that are tied to employee performance. They want to ensure that these HR activities are implemented with fairness and respect for each employee. In many respects they can work with the company and its HR professionals to help design, as well as implement, many HR practices. Many unions have worked with companies to help design and implement programs in total quality management, safety and health, and worker education.

Unions as organizations themselves are involved in all the HR practices described in this book. They need to plan for their own staffing needs, recruit and retain their own employees, and train, appraise, and compensate them. Unions are concerned about having a workforce that is diverse, well educated, and able to serve the needs of the membership. Thus their own HR

"You would see a more militant and adversarial relationship come back if the unemployment rate were two or three percentage points higher than it is today."

Larry Gigerich
President
Indianapolis Economic Development
Corporation

departments play a vital role in the success of unions in the attainment of their own strategic objectives, such as increasing membership.

Deciding to Join a Union

Unions were originally formed in response to the exploitation and abuse of employees by management. To understand the union movement today, we need to examine why employees decide to join unions and why they decide not to. Three separate conditions strongly influence an employee's decision to join a union: dissatisfaction, lack of power, and union instrumentality.[10]

Dissatisfaction. When an individual takes a job, certain conditions of employment (wages, hours, and type of work) are specified in the employment contract. A **psychological contract** also exists between employer and employee, consisting of the employee's unspecified expectation about reasonable working conditions, requirements of the work itself, the level of effort that should be expended on the job, and the nature of the authority the employer should have in directing the employee's work.[11] These expectations are related to the employee's desire to satisfy certain personal preferences in the workplace. The degree to which the organization fulfills these preferences determines the employee's level of satisfaction. Dissatisfaction with the implicit terms and conditions of the employment will lead employees to attempt to improve the work situation, often through unionization. If management wants to make unionization less attractive to employees, it must make work conditions more satisfying.

Lack of Power. Unionization is seldom the first recourse of employees who are dissatisfied with some aspect of their jobs. The first attempt to improve the work situation is usually made by an individual acting alone. Someone who has enough power or influence can effect the necessary changes without collaborating with others. The amount of power the jobholder has in the organization is determined by **exclusivity**, or how difficult it is to replace the person, and **essentiality**, or how important or critical the job is to the overall success of the organization. An exclusive employee with an essential task may be able to force the employer to make a change. If, however, the employee can easily be replaced and the employee's task is not critical, other means, including collective action, must be considered in order to influence the organization.[12]

Union Instrumentality. When employees are dissatisfied with aspects of a work environment—such as pay, promotion opportunity, treatment by supervisor, the job itself, and work rules—they may perceive a union as being able to help improve the situation. If they believe that the union may be able to help, they then weigh the value of the benefits to be obtained through unionization against unionization's costs, such as a lengthy organizing campaign and bad feelings between supervisors, managers, and other employees who don't want a union. Finally, the employees weigh the costs and benefits against the likelihood of a union's being able to obtain the benefits. In other words, they determine **union instrumentality**.[13] The more that employees believe a union can obtain positive work aspects, the more instrumental employees perceive the union to be in removing the causes of dissatisfaction. When the benefits exceed the costs and union instrumentality is high, employees are more likely to be will-

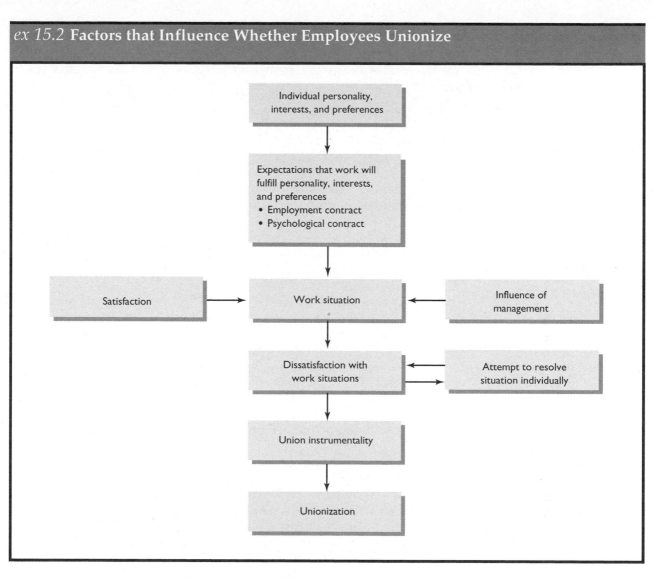

ex 15.2 **Factors that Influence Whether Employees Unionize**

ing to support a union.[14] However, research suggests that employees' willingness to support a union is also affected by general attitudes about unions formed early in life.[15] Exhibit 15.2 summarizes these reasons for joining a union.

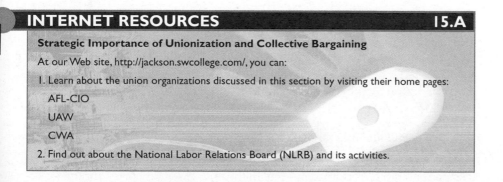

INTERNET RESOURCES   **15.A**

Strategic Importance of Unionization and Collective Bargaining

At our Web site, http://jackson.swcollege.com/, you can:

1. Learn about the union organizations discussed in this section by visiting their home pages:

   AFL-CIO

   UAW

   CWA

2. Find out about the National Labor Relations Board (NLRB) and its activities.

THE HISTORICAL CONTEXT AND UNIONS TODAY

A better understanding of the attitudes and behaviors of both unions and management can be gained through a knowledge of past union-management relations.

The Early Days

The beginning of the labor union movement in the United States can be traced back to the successful attempt of journeymen printers to win a wage increase in 1778. By the 1790s, unions of shoemakers, carpenters, and printers had appeared in Boston, Baltimore, New York, and other cities. The Federal Society of Journeymen Cordwainers, for example, was organized in Philadelphia in 1794, primarily to resist employers' attempts to reduce wages. Other issues of concern to these early unions were union shops (companies using only union members) and the regulation of apprenticeships to prevent the replacement of journeymen employees.

The early unions had methods and objectives that are still in evidence today. Although there was no collective bargaining, the unions did establish a price below which members would not work. Strikes were used to enforce this rate. These strikes were relatively peaceful and for the most part successful.

"The union is very important to me. With unions, you get your managers to treat you with respect, and you get a worthwhile salary."

Dora Guzman
Food Server
Los Angeles International Airport

One negative characteristic of early unions was their susceptibility to depressions. Until the late 1800s, most unions thrived in times of prosperity but died off during depressions. Part of this problem may have been related to the insularity of the unions. Aside from sharing information on strikebreakers or scabs, the unions operated independently of each other. The work situation had undergone several important changes by the end of the 19th century. Transportation systems (canals, railroads, and turnpikes) expanded the markets for products and increased worker mobility. Increases in capital costs prevented journeymen from reaching the status of master craftworker (that is, from setting up their own businesses), thereby creating a class of skilled workers. Unionism found its start in these skilled occupations.

Unions continued to experience ups and downs that were largely tied to economic conditions. Employers took advantage of the depressions to combat unions: In "an all out frontal attack . . . they engaged in frequent lockouts, hired spies . . . summarily discharged labor 'agitators,' and [engaged] the services of strikebreakers on a widespread scale."[16] These actions, and the retaliations of unions, established a tenor of violence and lent a strong adversarial nature to union-management relations, the residual effects of which are still in evidence today.

Unions Today

Today, the adversarial nature of the union-management relationship has been replaced to a certain extent by a more cooperative one. This change toward relying on collective bargaining has been dictated in part by current trends in union membership, including the shifting distribution of the membership.

Decline in Membership

Union membership in the United States has declined steadily from its high of 35.5 percent of the workforce in 1945. In the mid-1950s, 35 percent of the work-

Unions Reach Out

Linda Chavez-Thompson is the first female executive vice president of the AFL-CIO, a position critical to the future of the union movement. President John J. Sweeney has stated that the union movement has changed, and the union needs to be more responsive in organizing women and minorities, the fastest growing groups of union membership. According to Sweeney, the election of Chavez-Thompson is very significant: "I wanted someone who knew what it was like to go door-to-door organizing and to come home at night dead-tired and foot-sore." In addition to including a greater variety of groups in the top management of the AFL-CIO, the union movement has sought to include more groups in the grassroots of labor. It

has expanded its organizing efforts in the South, has increased efforts to organize construction and kitchen workers in Las Vegas, has signed up asbestos cleanup crews in New York, and has signed up more farm workers in California. It is doing this in part with a new crop of workers/organizers who are young, ambitious, college-educated people with a passion for the union movement. "They get to know every nuance of a company's operations and target the weak managers' departments as a way to appeal to employees who may be willing to organize." And with the real wages of many workers remaining stagnant, the voice of appeal may fall on an increasing number of willing ears, and especially white-collar workers such as those in the dot-coms.

force was unionized; in 1970, the percentage was 25; in 1980 it was 23. In 2001 approximately 13.5 percent of all workers—10 percent in the private sector and 30 percent in the public sector—were represented by unions.[17] This number constitutes about 16.3 million people. These percentage declines resulted in part from an increase in service sector employment, high technology jobs, and white-collar jobs—all of which historically have had a low proportion of union members. Other contributing circumstances are a decline in employment in industries that are highly unionized, increased decertification of unions, and management initiatives. To counter these trends, union leadership, particularly the AFL-CIO, has increased its efforts to expand its membership base.[18] The feature "Managing Diversity: Unions Reach Out" illustrates some recent union efforts to expand membership.[19]

To gain more organizational ability, power, and financial strength, several unions have merged. Although mergers may not automatically increase membership, they can mean more efficiency in union-organizing efforts and an end to costly jurisdictional disputes between unions. Increased organizational strength from mergers may also enable unions to cover industries and occupations previously underrepresented in union membership, such as health care and telecommunications workers.

FAST FACT

New York and Hawaii have the highest percentage of unionization: about 28%. South Carolina is the lowest at 3.8%.

FAST FACT

The rates of unionization around the world vary greatly:

- Australia   35%
- Brazil   44%
- Denmark   80%
- France   9%
- Japan   24%
- Mexico   43%
- UK   33%

Distribution of Membership

Historically, membership has been concentrated in a small number of large unions. In 1976, 16 unions represented 60 percent of union membership, and 85 unions represented just 2.4 percent. Similarly, the National Education Association accounted for 62 percent of all teaching association members. Many employee associations are small because they are state organizations; therefore, their membership potential is limited. Unions today are exhibiting a substantial and increasing amount of diversification of membership. The most pronounced diversification has occurred in manufacturing.[20]

The Structure of American Unions

The basic unit of labor unions in the United States is the national (or international) union, a body that organizes, charters, and controls member locals. National unions develop the general policies and procedures by which locals operate and help locals in areas such as collective bargaining. National unions provide clout for locals because they control a large number of employees and can influence large organizations through national strikes or slowdown activities.

The major umbrella organization for national unions is the **American Federation of Labor and Congress of Industrial Organizations (AFL-CIO)**. It represents about 85 percent of the total union membership. Every two years, the AFL-CIO holds a convention to develop policy and amend its constitution. Each national union is represented in proportion to its membership. Between conventions, an executive council (the governing body) and a general board direct the organization's affairs; a president is in charge of day-to-day operations.

The executive council's activities include evaluating legislation that affects labor and watching for corruption within the AFL-CIO. Standing committees are appointed to deal with executive, legislative, political, educational, organizing, and other activities. The department of organization and field services, for instance, focuses its attention on organizing activities. Three structures organize the local unions: the trade department and the industrial department represent many of the craft unions, and the remaining locals are organized directly as part of the national unions, being affiliated with AFL-CIO headquarters but retaining independence in dealing with their own matters.

About 60 national unions, representing 4.5 million workers, operate independently of the AFL-CIO, which has about 13 million members. The two largest unions in the AFL-CIO are the Teamsters and the American Federation of State, County and Municipal Employees. In 2001, the United Brotherhood of Carpenters and Joiners pulled out of the AFL-CIO, taking about 300,000 members.

At the heart of the labor movement are the 70,000 or so local unions, varying in size up to 40,000 members. The locals represent the workers at the workplace, where much of the day-to-day contact with management and the human resource department takes place. Most locals elect a president, a secretary-treasurer, and perhaps one or two other officers from the membership. In the larger locals, a **business representative** is hired as a full-time employee to handle grievances and contract negotiation. Locals also have a **steward**—an employee elected by her or his work unit to act as the union representative at the workplace and to respond to company actions against employees that may violate the labor agreement. The steward protects the rights of the worker by filing grievances when the employer has acted improperly.

FAST FACT

The confederation of unions in Mexico is Concamin.

FAST FACT

The George Meany Center for Labor Studies offers many educational opportunities.

FAST FACT

The Amalgamated Engineering and Electrical Union has a single union deal with Nissan in Sunderland, England. By comparison, U.K. firms typically deal with multiple unions in one location.

How Unions Operate

The activities of union locals revolve around collective bargaining and grievance handling. In addition, locals hold general meetings, publish newsletters, and otherwise keep their members informed. Typically, however, the membership is apathetic about union involvement. Unless a serious problem

Unionization in Mexico and Canada

In Mexico, unions have the right to organize workers at a business, but only one union represents a given location, covering all employees at that location. When a strike is called, the workplace is closed until the strike is settled—picket lines are unknown.

In case of a dispute, the burden of proof is always on the employer. Also, the labor law is part of Mexico's constitution, and workers aren't allowed to renounce these rights. Therefore, any individual employment contracts or collective agreements that limit these rights are considered invalid.

Since the advent of NAFTA, union organizations in the United States have seen relations with Mexico as a strategic opportunity and necessity. Many U.S. firms such as GE and General Motors have increased operations in Mexico. The U.S. unions active in these companies are providing support to the local unions in Mexico, such as the Authentic Workers Front, that are trying to organize the workers of these companies. The U.S. union movement is also trying to work through NAFTA to help improve wages and working conditions in Mexico. NAFTA legislation empowers the secretaries of labor in Canada, the United States, and Mexico to impose fines on a country that fails to enforce its labor laws.

Approximately one-third of the Canadian labor force is unionized. About three-fourths of the union members are affiliated with the Canadian Labor Congress (CLC). As in the United States, the union local is the basic local unit. The CLC is the dominant labor group at the national level. Its political influence may be compared with that of the AFL-CIO.

The labor laws in Canada are similar to those in the United States, with noteworthy differences. For example, Canadian labor laws require frequent interventions by governmental bodies before a strike can take place. In the United States, such intervention is largely voluntary. For the Canadian union movement as a whole, the trend toward concessionary bargaining to avoid layoffs and plant closings appears to be less evident than it is in the United States. At the same time, Canadian labor organizations affiliated with unions dominated by labor organizations in the United States are becoming increasingly autonomous. This trend was highlighted when the United Auto Workers in Canada became independent from the same union in the United States.

MANAGING GLOBALIZATION

exists, attendance at meetings is usually low, and the election of officers often draws votes from less than one-fourth of the membership.[21]

At headquarters, the AFL-CIO staff and committees work on a wide range of issues, including civil rights, job security, community service, economic policy, union-management cooperation, education, ethical practices, housing, international affairs, legislation, public relations, health care, research, safety, Social Security, and veterans' affairs. A publications department produces a variety of literature for the membership and outsiders. National union headquarters also provides specialized services to regional and local bodies. People trained in organizing, strikes, legal matters, public relations, and negotiations are available to individual unions.

FAST FACT

The AFL-CIO's Office of Investment keeps track of CEO compensation levels. It believes that excessive CEO pay is a point around which it can rally the workers.

National unions and the AFL-CIO are also active in the political arena. Labor maintains a strong lobbying force in Washington, D.C., and is involved in political action committees at the state and local levels. Some large national unions have been active in international politics. The United Auto Workers lobbied in Washington, D.C., to

FAST FACT

The AFL-CIO has organized many garment factory workers in Cambodia.

restrict car imports in an attempt to bolster U.S. automakers and increase jobs. It lobbied against NAFTA and for health care reform. To help their membership, unions are expanding their activities on all levels and, in some cases, working with other organizations to attain mutual goals. Unions are also trying to do a more effective job in their organizing campaigns. Descriptions of these activities in Mexico and Canada are offered in the feature "Managing Globalization: Unionization in Mexico and Canada."[22]

THE ORGANIZING CAMPAIGN

FAST FACT

Union salting refers to the practice of union organizers seeking employment in companies without disclosing their true backgrounds in order to establish a base for union organizing activities.

One major function of the National Labor Relations Board is to conduct the process in which a union is chosen to represent employees. This is accomplished through a certification election to determine if the majority of employees want the union. The process by which a single union is selected to represent all employees in a particular unit is crucial to the American system of collective bargaining. If a majority of those voting opt for union representation, all employees are bound by that choice and the employer is obligated to recognize and bargain with the chosen union.[23]

Because unions may acquire significant power, employers may be anxious to keep them out. Adding to this potential union-management conflict is the possibility of competition and conflict between unions if more than one union is attempting to win certification by the same group of employees. The certification process has several stages, as outlined in Exhibit 15.3.[24]

Soliciting Employee Support

In the campaign to solicit employee support, unions generally attempt to contact the employees, obtain a sufficient number of authorization cards, and request an election from the NLRB.[25]

Establishing Contact Between the Union and Employees

Contact between the union and employees may be initiated by either party. National unions usually contact employees in industries or occupations in which they have an interest or are traditionally involved. The United Auto Workers, for example, has contacted nonunion employees in the new automobile plants that have been built in the South by German and Japanese auto companies.

In other cases, employees may approach the union, and the union is usually happy to oblige. Employees may have strong reasons for desiring

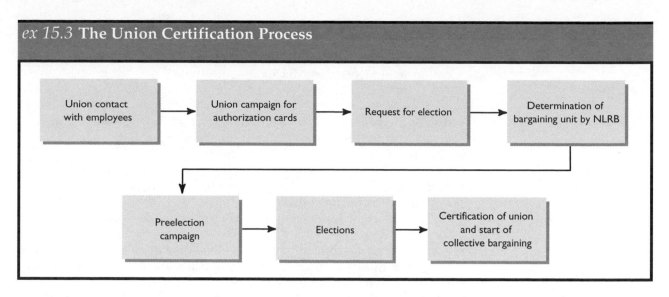

ex 15.3 **The Union Certification Process**

this affiliation—low pay, poor working conditions, and other issues relating to dissatisfaction. Because workers generally tend to be apathetic toward unions, however, their concern must become quite serious before they will take any action.

At the point that contact occurs between the union and employees, the company must be careful to avoid committing unfair labor practices. Accordingly, *employers should not*:

- **Misrepresent the facts.** Any information management provides about a union or its officers must be factual and truthful.
- **Threaten employees.** It is unlawful to threaten employees with losses of their jobs or transfers to less desirable positions, income reductions, or losses or reductions of benefits and privileges. The use of intimidating language to dissuade employees from joining or supporting a union also is forbidden. In addition, supervisors may not blacklist, lay off, discipline, or discharge any employee because of union activity.
- **Promise benefits or rewards.** Supervisors may not promise a pay raise, additional overtime or time off, promotions, or other favorable considerations in exchange for an employee's agreement to refrain from joining a union or signing a union card, to vote against union representation, or to otherwise oppose union activity.
- **Make unscheduled changes in wages, hours, benefits, or working conditions.** Any such changes are unlawful unless the employer can prove they were initiated before union activity began.
- **Conduct surveillance activities.** Management is forbidden to spy on employees' union activities or to request antiunion workers to do so, or to make any statements that give workers the impression they are being watched. Supervisors also may not attend union meetings or question employees about a union's internal affairs. They also may not ask employees for their opinions of a union or its officers.
- **Interrogate workers.** Managers may not require employees to tell them who has signed a union card, voted for union representation, attended a union meeting, or instigated an organization drive.

- **Prohibit solicitation.** Employees have the right to solicit members on company property during their nonworking hours, provided this activity does not interfere with work being performed, and to distribute union literature in nonwork areas during their free time.[26]

Employers can

- discuss the history of unions and make factual statements about strikes, violence, or the loss of jobs at plants that have unionized,
- discuss their own experiences with unions,
- advise workers about the costs of joining and belonging to unions,
- remind employees of the company benefits and wages they receive without having to pay union dues,
- explain that union representation won't protect workers against discharge for cause,
- point out that the company prefers to deal directly with employees (not through a third party) in settling complaints about wages, hours, and other employment conditions,
- tell workers that, in negotiating with the union, the company is not obligated to sign a contract or accept all the union's demands, especially those that aren't in its economic interests,
- advise employees that unions often resort to work stoppages to press their demands and that such tactics can cost workers money, and
- inform employees of the company's legal right to hire replacements for workers who go out on strike for economic reasons.[27]

Authorization Cards and the Request for Elections. Once contact has been made, the union begins the campaign to collect sufficient authorization cards, or signatures of employees interested in having union representation. This campaign must be carried out within the constraints set by law. If the union obtains cards from 30 percent of an organization's employees, it can petition the NLRB for an election. (Procedures in the public sector are similar.) If the NLRB determines there is indeed sufficient interest, it will schedule an election. If the union gets more than 50 percent of the employees to sign authorization cards, it may petition the employer as the bargaining representative. Usually employers refuse, whereupon the union petitions the NLRB for an election.

The employer usually resists the union's card-signing campaign. For instance, companies often prohibit solicitation on the premises. However, employers are legally constrained from interfering with an employee's freedom of choice. Union representatives have argued that employers ignore this law because the consequences are minimal—and by doing so, they can effectively discourage unionism.

During the union campaign and election process, it is important that the HR manager caution the company against engaging in unfair labor practices. Unfair labor practices, when identified, generally cause the election to be set aside. Severe violations by the employer can result in certification of the union as the bargaining representative, even if it has lost the election.

Determination of the Bargaining Unit

When the union has gathered sufficient signatures to petition for an election, the NLRB will identify the bargaining unit, the group of employees that will be represented by the union. This process can determine the quality of labor-management relations in the future: At the heart of labor-management relations is the bargaining unit. The bargaining unit must be truly appropriate and not contain a mix of antagonistic interests or submerge the legitimate interests of a small group of employees in the interest of a larger group.[28]

To ensure the fullest freedom of collective bargaining, legal constraints and guidelines exist for the unit. Professional and nonprofessional groups can't be included in the same unit, and a craft unit can't be placed in a larger unit unless both units agree to it. Physical location, skill levels, degree of ownership, collective bargaining history, and extent of organization of employees are also considered.

From the union's perspective, the most desirable bargaining unit is one whose members are pro-union and will help win certification. The unit also must have sufficient influence in the organization to give the union some power once it wins representation. Employers generally want a bargaining unit that's least beneficial to the union; this will help maximize the likelihood of failure in the election and minimize the power of the unit.

Preelection Campaign

After the bargaining unit has been determined, both union and employer embark on a **preelection campaign**. Unions claim to provide a strong voice for employees, emphasizing improvement in wages and working conditions and the establishment of a grievance process to ensure fairness. Employers emphasize the costs of unionization—dues, strikes, and loss of jobs. Severe violations of the legal constraints on behavior, such as the use of threats or coercion, are prevented by the NLRB, which watches the preelection activity.

Election, Certification, and Decertification

Generally, elections are part of the process of determining if unions will win the right to represent workers. Elections can also determine if unions will retain the right to represent employees.

Election and Certification. The NLRB conducts the **certification election**. If a majority votes for union representation, the union will be certified. If the union does not get a majority, another election won't be held for at least a year. Generally, about one-third to one-half of all certification elections certify the union, with less union success in larger companies. Once a union has been certified, the employer is required to bargain with that union.

Decertification Elections. The NLRB also conducts **decertification elections** that can remove a union from representation. If 30 percent or more of the employees in an organization request such an election, it will be held. Decertification elections most frequently occur in the first year of a union's representation when the union is negotiating its first contract. During this period, union strength has not yet been established, and employees are readily discouraged by union behavior.

THE COLLECTIVE BARGAINING PROCESS

Collective bargaining is a complex process in which union and management negotiators maneuver to win the most advantageous contract. How the issues involved are settled depends on

- the quality of the union-management relationship,
- the processes of bargaining used by labor and management,
- management's strategies in collective bargaining, and
- the union's strategies in collective bargaining.

"If you can bargain for it, you should get it," is how this union leader justifies some pilot salaries of $400,000.

Duane E. Woerth
President
Air Line Pilots Association

The labor relations system is composed of three subunits: employees, management, and the union, with the government influencing interaction between the three. Employees may be managers or union members, and some union members are part of the union management system (local union leaders). Each of the three interrelationships in the model is regulated by specific federal statutes.

Each group in the labor relations model typically has different goals. Workers are interested in improved working conditions, wages, and opportunities. Unions are interested in these as well as their own survival, growth, and acquisition of power, which depend on their ability to maintain the support of the employees by providing for their needs. Management has overall organizational goals (e.g., increasing profits, market share, and growth rates) and also seeks to preserve managerial prerogatives to direct the workforce and to attain the personal goals of the managers (e.g., promotion or achievement). Government is interested in a stable and healthy economy, protection of individual rights, and safety and fairness in the workplace. All of these factors influence the roles that these groups play.

Adversarial Relationship

The goals of workers, unions, management, and governments were often seen as incompatible. Thus, an adversarial relationship emerged, with labor and management attempting to get a bigger cut of the pie, while government oversaw its own interests. In an adversarial relationship between union and management, the union's role is to gain concessions from management during collective bargaining and to preserve those concessions through the grievance procedure. The union is an outsider and critic.[29]

"What we're seeing is a complete lack of respect for workers, for the jobs they do. We're seeing so many examples of how insensitive corporate America can be to their workers."

John Sweeney
President
AFL-CIO

Historically, unions have adopted an adversarial role in their interactions with management. Their focus has been on wages, hours, and working conditions as they attempt to get "more and better" from management. This approach works well in economic boom times but encounters difficulties when the economy is not healthy. High unemployment and the threat of continued job losses induces unions to expand their role, especially since many of their traditional goals have already been achieved. Consequently, some unions have begun to enter into new, collaborative efforts with employers, which result in a cooperative relationship.

Cooperative Relationship

In a cooperative relationship, the union's role is that of a partner, not a critic, and the union is jointly responsible with management for reaching a suitable solution to business challenges. Thus, a cooperative relationship requires that union and management solve problems, share information, and integrate outcomes.[30]

Cooperative systems have not been a major component of labor relations in the United States, although they have been built into labor relations in other countries such as Sweden and Germany.[31] Increasingly, however, U.S. management and labor are working together cooperatively. Management recognizes that most of the programs it undertakes to improve its organization need the acceptance of the union to be successful. Active involvement of the union is a good way to gain this acceptance.[32]

At most firms, teamwork is critical to improving quality. Unions such as the UAW and the CWA, and firms such as Ford and AT&T are recognizing how important quality is to survival.[33] Consequently, they favor "workplace reforms," and unions are working together with management to design and implement them.[34]

Cooperative agreements are particularly fragile: "A lot of times when they break down it's not because of new economic circumstances. An individual can make a difference—a new plant manager, a new local president."

Douglas Fraser
Past President
UAW

Types of Bargaining

Five types of bargaining are used in contract negotiations: distributive, integrative, concessionary, continuous, and intraorganizational.

Distributive Bargaining. **Distributive bargaining** takes place when the parties are in conflict over the issue, and the outcome represents a gain for one party and a loss for the other. Each party tries to negotiate for the best possible outcome. The process is outlined in Exhibit 15.4.[35] On any particular issue, union and management negotiators each have three identifiable positions. The union has an *initial demand point,* which is generally more than it expects to get; a *target point,* which is its realistic assessment of what it may be able to get; and a *resistance point,* or the lowest acceptable level for the issue. Management has three similar points: an *initial offer point,* which is usually lower than the expected settlement; a *target point,* at which it would like to reach agreement; and a *resistance point,* or its upper acceptable limit. If, as shown in Exhibit 15.4, management's resistance point is greater than the union's, a *positive settlement range* exists. If, however, management's resistance point is below the union's, a *negative settlement range,* or bargaining impasse, exists, and there is no common ground for negotiation.[36] For example, on the issue of wages, the union may have a resistance point of $8.40 an hour, a target of $8.60, and an initial demand point of $8.75. Management may offer $8.20, have a target of $8.45 and a resistance point of $8.55. The positive settlement range is between $8.40 and $8.55, and this is where the settlement will likely be. However, only the initial wage demand and offer are made public at the beginning of negotiations.

Because many issues are involved in a bargaining session, the actual process is much more complicated. Although each issue can be described by the above model, in actual negotiations the issues are negotiated simultaneously, so the process is more complex than depicted. Union concessions on one issue may be traded for management concessions on another. Thus the total process is dynamic.[37]

Integrative Bargaining. When more than one issue needs to be resolved, integrative agreements may be pursued. **Integrative bargaining** focuses on

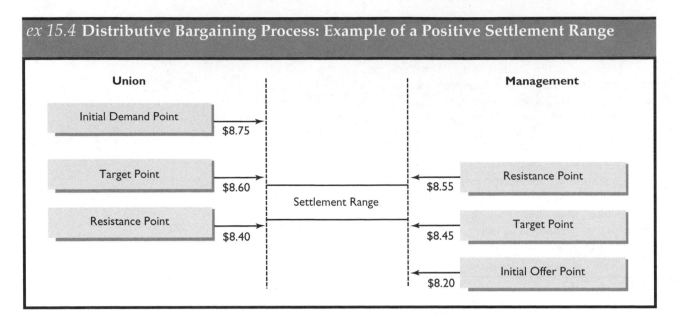

ex 15.4 **Distributive Bargaining Process: Example of a Positive Settlement Range**

creative solutions that reconcile (integrate) the parties' interests and yield high joint benefit. It can occur only when negotiators have an "expanding-pie" perception—that is, when the two parties (union and management) have two or more issues and are willing to develop creative ways to satisfy both parties.[38]

Concessionary Bargaining. Distributive and integrative bargaining are the primary approaches to bargaining; **concessionary bargaining** often occurs within these two frameworks. Concessionary bargaining may be prompted by severe economic conditions faced by employers. Seeking to survive and prosper, employers seek givebacks or concessions from the unions, promising job security in return. In the early 1990s, this type of bargaining was prevalent, especially in the smokestack industries such as automobiles, steel, and rubber, and to some extent in the transportation industry. In these groups of enterprises, concessions sought by management from the unions included wage freezes, wage reductions, work rule changes or elimination, fringe benefit reductions, COLA delays or elimination, and more hours of work for the same pay. Two-tier wage systems were tried in some industries, but problems of inequity and lower worker morale offset much of the savings from lower labor costs.[39] In addition, available evidence suggests that these agreements erode union solidarity, leadership credibility, and control, as well as union power and effectiveness.

Continuous Bargaining. As affirmative action, safety and health requirements, and other governmental regulations continue to complicate the situation for both unions and employers, and as the rate of change in the environment continues to increase, some labor and management negotiators are turning to **continuous bargaining**. In this process, joint committees meet on a regular basis to explore issues and solve problems of common interest. These committees have appeared in the retail food, over-the-road trucking, nuclear power, and men's garment industries.[40] Several characteristics of continuous bargaining are

- frequent meetings during the life of the contract,
- a focus on external events and problem areas rather than on internal problems,
- use of the skills of outside experts in decision making, and
- use of a problem-solving (integrative) approach.[41]

The intention of continuous bargaining is to develop a union-management structure that's capable of adapting positively and productively to sudden changes in the environment. This approach is different from, but an extension of, the emergency negotiations that unions have insisted on when inflation or other circumstances have substantially changed the acceptability of the existing agreement. Continuous bargaining is a permanent arrangement intended to help avoid the crises that often occur under traditional collective bargaining systems.

Intraorganizational Bargaining. During negotiations, the bargaining teams from both sides may have to engage in **intraorganizational bargaining**—that is, confer with their constituents over changes in bargaining positions. Management negotiators may have to convince management to change its position on an issue—for instance, to agree to a higher wage settlement. Union negotiators must eventually convince their members to accept the negotiated contract, so they must be sensitive to the demands of the membership, as well as realistic. When the membership votes on the proposed package, it will be strongly influenced by the opinions of the union negotiators.

NEGOTIATING THE AGREEMENT

Once a union is certified as the representative of a bargaining unit, it becomes the only party that can negotiate an agreement with the employer for all members of that work unit, whether they are union members or not. Technically, however, individuals within the unit can still negotiate with the employer personal deals that give them more than the other members receive, particularly if the agreement is silent on this issue.

The union serves as a critical link between employees and employer. It is responsible to its members to negotiate for what they want, and it has the duty to represent all employees fairly. The quality of its bargaining is an important measure of union effectiveness.

Negotiating Committees

The employer and the union select their own representatives for the negotiating committee. Neither party is required to consider the wishes of the other. For example, management negotiators can't refuse to bargain with representatives of the union because they dislike them or don't think they are appropriate.

Union negotiating teams typically include representatives of the union local—often the president and other executive staff members. In addition, the national union may send a negotiating specialist, who is likely to be a labor lawyer, to work with the team. The negotiators selected by the union don't have to be members of the union or employees of the company. The general goal is to balance skill and experience in bargaining with knowledge and information about the specific situation.

At the local level, when a single bargaining unit is negotiating a contract, the company is usually represented by the manager and members of the labor relations or human resource staff. Finance and production managers may also be involved. When the negotiations are critical, either because the bargaining unit is large or because the effect on the company is great, specialists such as labor lawyers may be included on the team.

In national negotiations, top industrial relations or human resource executives frequently head a team of specialists from corporate headquarters and perhaps managers from critical divisions or plants within the company. Again, the goal is to have expertise along with specific knowledge about critical situations.

The Negotiating Structure

Most contracts are negotiated by a single union and a single employer. In some situations, however, different arrangements can be agreed on. When a single union negotiates with several similar companies, for instance, firms in the construction industry, the employers may bargain as a group. At the local level, this is called **multiemployer bargaining**; at the national level, it is referred to as **industrywide bargaining.** Industrywide bargaining occurs in the railroad, coal, wallpaper, and men's suits industries. When several unions bargain jointly with a single employer, they engage in **coordinated bargaining**. Although not as common as the multiemployer and industrywide bargaining, coordinated bargaining appears to be increasing, especially in the public sector. One consequence of coordinated and industrywide bargaining is often **pattern settlements**, where similar wage rates are imposed on the companies whose employees are represented by the same union within a given industry.

In the contract construction industry, a **wide-area** and **multicraft bargaining** structure arose in response to the unionized employers' need to be more price competitive and to have fewer strikes, and in response to the unions' desire to gain more control at the national level. Consequently, the bargaining is done on a regional (geographic) rather than local basis, and it covers several construction crafts simultaneously. The common contract negotiations resulting from wide-area and multicraft bargaining help lessen the opportunity for unions to **whipsaw** the employer. Whipsawing occurs when one contract settlement is used as a precedent for the next, which then forces the employer to get all contracts settled in order to have all the employees working. As a result of whipsawing, an employer frequently agrees to more favorable settlements on all contracts, regardless of the conditions and merits of each one, just to keep all employees working.[42]

Preparation for Bargaining

Prior to the bargaining session, management and union negotiators need to develop the strategies and proposals they will use.

Management Strategies. For negotiations with the union, management needs to complete four different tasks:

1. preparation of specific proposals for changes in contract language;
2. determination of the general size of the economic package that the company anticipates offering during the negotiations;

3. preparation of statistical displays and supportive data that the company will use during negotiations; and
4. preparation of a bargaining book for use by company negotiators that compiles the information on issues that will be discussed, giving an analysis of the effect of each clause, its use in other companies, and other facts.[43]

The relative cost of pension contributions, pay increases, health benefits, and other bargaining provisions should be determined prior to negotiations. Other costs should also be considered. For instance, management might ask itself, "What is the cost of union demands for changes in grievance and discipline procedures or transfer and promotion provisions?" The goal is to be as well prepared as possible by considering the implications and ramifications of the issues that will be discussed and by being able to present a strong argument for the position taken.

Union Strategies. Like management, unions need to prepare for negotiations by collecting information. Because collective bargaining is the major means by which a union can convince its members of its effectiveness and value, this is a critical activity. Unions collect information on

- the financial situation of the company and its ability to pay;
- the attitude of management toward various issues, as reflected in past negotiations or inferred from negotiations in similar companies; and
- the attitudes and desires of the employees.

The first two areas give the union an idea of what demands management is likely to accept. The third area is sometimes overlooked. It involves awareness of the preferences of the union membership. For instance, the union might ask, "Is a pension increase preferred over increased vacation or holiday benefits?" Membership preferences will vary with the characteristics of the workers. Younger workers are more likely to prefer more holidays, shorter workweeks, and limited overtime, whereas older workers are more likely interested in pension plans, benefits, and overtime. The union can determine these preferences by using questionnaires and meetings to survey its members.

Issues for Negotiation

The issues that can be discussed in collective bargaining sessions are specified by the *Labor-Management Relations Act*. This act has established three categories of issues for negotiation: mandatory, permissive, and prohibited.[44]

Employers and employee representatives (unions) are obligated to meet and discuss "wages, hours, and other terms and conditions of employment." These are the mandatory issues. These critical elements in the bargaining process include the issues that may affect management's ability to run the company efficiently or may clash with the union's desire to protect jobs and workers' standing in their jobs.

Permissive issues are those not specifically related to the nature of the job but still of concern to both parties. For example, decisions about price, product design, and new jobs may be subject to bargaining if the parties agree to it. Permissive issues usually develop when both parties see that mutual discussion and agreement will be beneficial, which may be more likely when a cooperative relationship exists between union and management. Management and union negotiators can't refuse to agree on a contract if they fail to settle a permissive issue.[45]

"We no longer accept the view that the only way to make money as shareholders is to ignore the needs of working Americans and their communities."

John Sweeney
President
AFL-CIO

Prohibited issues are those concerning illegal or outlawed activities, such as the demand that an employer use only union-produced goods or, where it is illegal, that it employ only union members. Such issues may not be discussed in collective bargaining sessions.

Total Compensation. Wage conflicts are a leading cause of strikes. Difficulties arise here because a wage increase is a direct cost to the employer, whereas a wage decrease is a direct cost to the employee. As discussed in Chapter 10, rates of pay are influenced by a variety of issues, including the going rate in an industry, the employer's ability to pay, the cost of living, and productivity. All these subjects are often debated and discussed in negotiations.

FAST FACT

The wages and benefits of German workers in manufacturing average $30 per hour. However, the rate of unemployment is 10%.

Benefits and Services. Because the cost of benefits and services can run as high as 40 percent of the total cost of wages, it is a major concern in collective bargaining. Benefit provisions are very difficult to remove once they are in place, so management tends to be cautious about agreeing to them. Some commonly negotiated forms of benefits and services are pensions, paid vacations, paid holidays, sick leave, health care and life insurance, dismissal or severance pay, and supplemental unemployment benefits.

Hours of Employment. Although organizations are already required by federal labor law to pay overtime for work beyond 40 hours a week, unions continually try to reduce the number of hours worked each week. Negotiations may focus on including the lunch hour in the eight-hour-day requirement, or on providing overtime after any eight-hour shift rather than after a 40-hour workweek.

Institutional Issues. Some issues are not directly related to jobs but are nevertheless important to both employees and management. Institutional issues that affect the security and success of both parties include:

- *Union Security.* About two-thirds of the major labor contracts stipulate that employees must join the union after being hired into its bargaining unit. This arrangement is called a **union shop**. However, 20 states that traditionally have low levels of unionization have **right-to-work laws** outlawing union membership as a condition of employment.
- *Checkoff.* Unions have attempted to arrange for payment of dues through deduction from employees' paychecks. By law, employees must agree in writing to a dues checkoff. A large majority of union contracts contain a provision for this agreement.
- *Strikes.* The employer may insist that the union agree not to strike during the life of the contract, typically when a cost-of-living clause has been included. The agreement may be unconditional, allowing no strikes at all, or it may limit strikes to specific circumstances.
- *Managerial Prerogatives.* More than half the agreements today stipulate that certain activities are the right of management. In addition, management in most companies argues that it has "residual rights"—that rights not specifically limited by the agreement belong to management.

Administrative Issues. Administrative issues concern the treatment of employees at work. These issues include:

- *Breaks and Cleanup Time.* Some contracts specify the time and length of coffee breaks and meal breaks for employees. In addition, jobs requiring cleanup may have a portion of the work period set aside for this procedure.

- *Job Security.* Job security is perhaps the issue of most concern to employees and unions. Employers are concerned with a restriction of their ability to lay off employees. Changes in technology or attempts to subcontract work impinge on job security. The International Longshoremen's Association (ILA) in the late 1960s demonstrated a typical union response to technological change when containerized shipping was introduced. The union operated exclusive hiring halls, developed complex work rules, and negotiated a guaranteed annual income for its members. Job security continues to be a primary issue for most unions.

- *Seniority.* Length of service is used as a criterion for many human resource decisions in most collective agreements. Layoffs are usually determined by seniority. "Last hired, first fired" is a common situation. Seniority is also important in transfer and promotion decisions. The method of calculating seniority is usually specified in order to clarify the relative seniority of employees.

> **FAST FACT**
>
> Harry Bridges, when head of the ILA, was in favor of containerized shipping to reduce the workload on his members.

- *Discharge and Discipline.* Termination and discipline are tough issues, and, even when an agreement addresses these problems, many grievances are filed concerning the way they are handled.

- *Safety and Health.* Although the *Occupational Safety and Health Act* specifically deals with worker safety and health, some contracts have provisions specifying that the company will provide safety equipment, first aid, physical examinations, accident investigations, and safety committees. Hazardous work may be covered by special provisions and pay rates. Often, the agreement will contain a general statement that the employer is responsible for the safety of the workers, so that the union can use the grievance process when any safety issues arise.

- *Production Standards.* The level of productivity or performance of employees is a concern of both management and the union. Management is concerned with efficiency, and the union is concerned with the fairness and reasonableness of management's demands. Increasingly, both are concerned about total quality and quality of work life.

- *Grievance Procedures.* The contract usually outlines a process for settling disputes that may arise during its administration.

- *Training.* The design and administration of training and development programs and the procedure for selecting employees for training may also be bargaining issues. This is particularly important when the company is pursuing a strategy of total quality management.

- *Duration of the Agreement.* Agreements can last for one year or longer, with the most common period being three years.

Factors Affecting Bargaining

The preceding discussion suggests that negotiations proceed in a rational manner and end in resolution when there is a positive contract zone, a set of outcomes that is preferred to the imposition of a strike. Unfortunately, negotiators often fail to reach agreement, even when a positive contract zone exists.

To fully understand the negotiation process, it is important to examine the decision processes of negotiators. If the biases of negotiators can be identified, then prescriptive approaches and training programs can be developed to improve negotiations. The following are common cognitive or mental limitations on negotiator judgments.[46]

The Mythical Fixed Pie. All too frequently, negotiators believe that their interests automatically conflict with the other party's interests. In other words, what one side wins, the other side loses. However, most conflicts usually have more than one issue at stake, with the parties placing different values on the different issues. Consequently, the potential usually exists for integrative agreements. A fundamental task in training negotiators lies in identifying and eliminating this false "fixed pie" assumption and preparing them to look for trade-offs between issues of different value to each side.

Framing. Consider the following bargaining situation. The union claims that its members need a raise to $12 an hour and that anything less will represent a loss due to inflation. Management argues that the company can't pay more than $10 an hour and that anything more would impose an unacceptable loss. If each side had the choice between settling at $11 an hour or going to binding arbitration, they are likely to take the risk and move toward arbitration rather than settlement.

Changing the frame of the situation to a positive one results in a very different outcome. If the union can view anything above $10 an hour as a gain, and if management can view anything under $12 as a gain, then a negotiated settlement at $11 is likely.

As the preceding example emphasizes, the frame (positive or negative) of negotiators can make the difference between settlement and impasse. One solution, then, to impasses is to alter the frame of reference such that it is positive rather than negative.[47]

CONFLICT RESOLUTION

Although the desired outcome of collective bargaining is agreement on the conditions of employment, on many occasions negotiators are unable to reach such an agreement at the bargaining table. In these situations, several alternatives are used to break the deadlock. The most dramatic response is a strike or lockout; indirect responses are also used, and third-party interventions such as mediation and arbitration are common as well.

Strikes and Lockouts

When the union is unable to get management to agree to a demand it believes is critical, it may tell employees to refuse to work at the company. This is called a **strike**. When management refuses to allow employees to work, the situation is called a **lockout**.[48]

In order to strike, the union usually holds a vote to gain members' approval. Strong membership support for a strike strengthens the union negotiators' position. If the strike takes place, union members picket the employer, informing the public about the existence of a labor dispute and preferably, from the union's point of view, convincing it to avoid this company during the strike. Union members commonly refuse to cross the picket line of another striking union, which gives added support to the striking union.

Employers usually attempt to continue operations while a strike is in effect. They either run the company with supervisory personnel and people not in the bargaining unit or hire replacements for the striking employees. At the conclusion of the strike, employers will be expected to (1) reinstate strikers in all the positions that remain unfilled, unless they have substantial business reasons for doing otherwise, and (2) establish a preferential hiring list for displaced strikers to facilitate their recall as new openings occur.

FAST FACT

Some of the biggest strikes in the past five years have occurred at General Motors, Northwest Airlines, and UPS.

The success of a strike depends on its ability to cause economic hardship to the employer. Severe hardship usually causes the employer to concede to the union's demands.[49] Thus, from the union's point of view, the cost of the company's lack of production must be high. The union, therefore, actively tries to prevent replacement employees from working. Although it appears that the company can legally hire replacements, the union reacts strongly to the employment of scabs, as these workers are called, and the replacement employees may be a cause of increasingly belligerent labor relations. The hiring of replacement workers has reached a level where companies are keeping them even after the strike is settled—if the strike is settled at all. This tactic has given employers even more power in a strike situation. Thus, the union movement seeks a law to prevent replacement workers from becoming permanent workers.

The timing of the strike is also often critical. The union attempts to hold negotiations just before the employer has a peak demand for its product or services, when a strike will have the maximum economic effect.

Although strikes have been on the decline, they are costly to both the employer, who loses revenue, and employees, who lose income. If a strike is prolonged, the cost to employers will likely never be fully recovered by the benefits gained. In part because of this, employers seek to avoid strikes. Moreover, the public interest is generally not served by strikes. They are often an inconvenience and can have serious consequences for the economy as a whole.

Slowdowns. Short of an actual strike, unions may invoke a **work slowdown**. At the Caterpillar plant, Lance Vaughan usually installed a set of small and large hoses on huge off-highway trucks—small hoses first, then the big hoses. But when a slowdown started, he began to install the big hoses first, and then reach awkwardly around them to attach the other smaller hoses. The result was lost production time. Technically, Vaughan was just doing his job. The instructions furnished by Caterpillar's engineers describe the inefficient procedure. Normally, Vaughan ignores such instructions and makes a note to himself to tell the engineers to fix the mistake. When the slowdown began, he stopped speaking up and began working according to the rules furnished by the company. "I used to give the engineers ideas," explained Vaughan, who has worked at Caterpillar for 20 years. "We showed them how to eliminate some hose clips and save money. And I recommended larger bolts that made assembly easier and faster, and were less likely to come loose."[50]

FAST FACT

At Caterpillar, workers engaged in a slowdown by just following what was written in their job descriptions.

At Caterpillar, the slowdown was referred to as an "in-plant strategy." Regardless of the name, the result is the same: a reduction of work output, physically and mentally. Slowdowns can be more effective than actual strikes.

Primary Boycotts. Unions sometimes want to make the public more aware of their cause. As a consequence, they may engage in a **primary boycott**. For instance, a union that is striking a soda-bottling company may set up an informational picket line at grocery stores that sell the bottler's products. It has generally been ruled that as long as the picket line is directed at the bottling company, asking customers not to buy its soda, it constitutes a primary boycott and thus is legal. The picket line becomes illegal, however, when it tries to prevent customers from shopping at the grocery store. This action is called a **secondary boycott**, and it is illegal because it can harm an innocent third party—the grocery store.

Corporate Campaigns. In a corporate campaign, a union may ask the public and other unions to write letters to a company, asking it to change the way it bargains with the union.[51]

Mediation

"A tremendous amount of negotiation and dispute resolution is already occurring by means of the Internet."

David Lipsky
Director, Institute for Conflict Resolution
Cornell University

Mediation is a procedure in which a neutral third party helps the union and management negotiators reach a voluntary agreement.[52] Having no power to impose a solution, the mediator attempts to facilitate the negotiations between union and management. The mediator may make suggestions and recommendations and perhaps add objectivity to the often emotional negotiations. To have any success at all, the mediator must have the trust and respect of both parties and have sufficient expertise and neutrality to convince the union and employer that she or he will be fair and equitable.

The U.S. government operates the Federal Mediation and Conciliation Service (FMCS) to make experienced mediators available to unions and companies. A program called Relationships by Objective is offered by the FMCS to eliminate the causes of recurrent impasses. It uses aspects of attitudinal structuring to increase the likelihood of a cooperative relationship between union and management.

Arbitration

FAST FACT

The real power of the arbitrator's decision was established by three Supreme Court decisions in 1960 referred to as the Trilogy cases and all involving the United Steelworkers.

Arbitration is a procedure in which a neutral third party studies the bargaining situation, listens to both parties and gathers information, and then makes a determination that is binding on the parties. The arbitrator, in effect, determines the conditions of the agreement.

In final-offer arbitration, the arbitrator can choose between the final offer of the union and the final offer of the employer. The arbitrator can't alter these offers but must select one as it stands. Since the arbitrator chooses the offer that appears most fair, and since losing the arbitration decision means settling for the other's offer, each side is pressured to make as good an offer as possible. By contrast, in conventional arbitration, the arbitrator is free to fashion any award deemed appropriate.

The arbitration process that deals with the contract terms and conditions is called interest arbitration. This type of arbitration is relatively infrequent in the private sector; it is more common in the public sector, where it becomes a necessary quid pro quo for forgoing the strike option.[53] Only about 20 states have compulsory interest arbitration procedures.

Once the contract impasse is removed, union and management have an agreement. Abiding by it is the essence of contract administration; however, at times, arbitration will again be necessary, namely when a grievance is filed. This type of arbitration is referred to as rights arbitration or grievance arbitration.

CONTRACT ADMINISTRATION

Once signed, the collective agreement becomes the contract that governs daily work life.[54] That is, the daily operation and activities in the organization are subject to the conditions of the agreement. Because of the difficulty of writing an unambiguous agreement anticipating all the situations that will occur over its life, disputes will inevitably occur over the contract's interpretation and application. The most common method of resolving these disputes is a grievance procedure. Virtually all agreements negotiated today provide for a grievance process to handle employee complaints.

Grievance Procedures

Basically, a grievance is a charge that the union-management contract has been violated.[55] A grievance may be filed by the union for employees, or by employers, although management rarely does so. The grievance process is designed to investigate the charges and to resolve the problem. Common sources of grievances are

- outright violation of the agreement,
- disagreement over facts,
- dispute over the meaning of the agreement,
- dispute over the method of applying the agreement, and
- argument over the fairness or reasonableness of actions.[56]

Grievance procedures typically involve several stages. The collective bargaining agreement specifies the maximum length of time that can elapse between the incident that is the subject of the dispute and the filing of a grievance on that incident. The most common grievance procedure, shown in Exhibit 15.5,[57] involves the following four steps:

STEP 1. An employee who feels that the labor contract has been violated usually contacts the union steward, and together they discuss the problem with the supervisor involved. If the problem is simple and straightforward, it is often resolved at this level.

STEP 2. If agreement cannot be reached at the supervisor level, or if the employee is not satisfied, the complaint can enter the second step of the grievance procedure. Typically, a human resource representative of the company now seeks to resolve the grievance.

STEP 3. If the grievance is sufficiently important or difficult to resolve, it may be taken to the third step. Although contracts vary, they usually specify that top-level management and union executives be involved at this stage. These people have the authority to make the major decisions that may be required to resolve the grievance.

STEP 4. If a grievance cannot be resolved at the third step, an arbitrator will likely need to consider the case and reach a decision. The arbitrator is a neutral, mutually acceptable individual who may be appointed by the FMCS or some private agency. The arbitrator holds a hearing, reviews the evidence, and then rules on the grievance. The decision of the arbitrator is usually binding.

Because the cost of arbitration is shared by the union and employer, some incentive exists to settle the grievance before it goes to arbitration. An added incentive in some cases is the requirement that the loser pay for the arbitration. The expectation behind these incentives is that the parties will

"This company is one of the greatest in the world. If they go back to where they were before the strike, to where they were employing people and asking for their input, there's no company that can compete with us."

Michael Surges
Driver
UPS

ex 15.5 Typical Union-Management Grievance Procedure

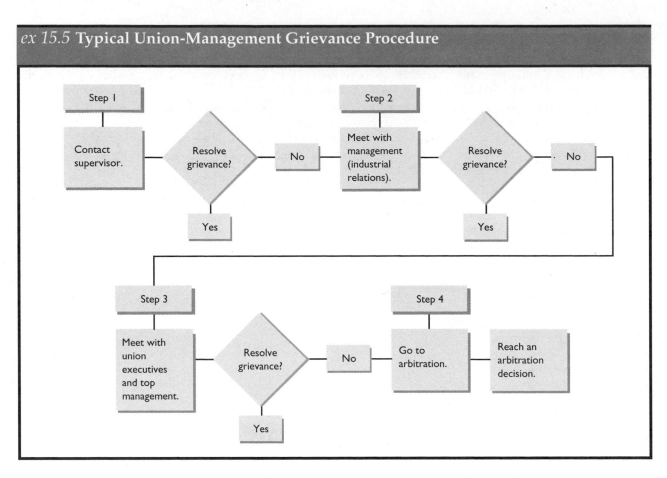

screen or evaluate grievances more carefully because pursuing a weak grievance to arbitration will be expensive.

Occasionally, the union will call a strike over a grievance in order to
resolve it. This may happen when the issue at hand is so important that the
union feels that it cannot wait for the slower arbitration process. Such an
"employee rights" strike may be legal; however, if the contract specifically
forbids strikes during the tenure of the agreement, it is not legal and is called
a wildcat strike. Wildcat strikes are not common; most grievances are settled
through arbitration.

Grievance Issues

Grievances can be filed over any workplace issue that is subject to the collective agreement, or they can be filed over interpretation and implementation
of the agreement itself. The most common type of grievance reaching the
arbitration stage involves discipline and discharge, although many
grievances are filed over other issues.

Absenteeism can be grounds for discharge, and a grievance procedure may be used to determine whether the absenteeism in question is excessive. Insubordination is either failure to do what
the supervisor requests or the outright refusal to do it. If the supervisor's
orders are clear, explicit, and legal, and if the employee is warned of the con-

sequences, discipline for refusal to respond is usually acceptable. The exception is when the employee feels that the work endangers health.

Because seniority is usually used to determine who is laid off, bumped from a job to make way for someone else, or rehired, its calculation is of great concern to employees. Seniority is also used as one of the criteria to determine eligibility for promotions and transfers, so management must be careful in this area in order to avoid complaints and grievances.

Compensation for time away from work, vacations, holidays, or sick leave is also a common source of grievances. Holidays cause problems because special pay arrangements often exist for people working on those days.

Wage and work schedules may also lead to grievances. Disagreements often arise over interpretation or application of the agreement relating to such issues as overtime pay, pay for reporting, and scheduling. Grievances have been filed over the exercise of such management rights as the right to introduce technological changes, use subcontractors (outsource), or change jobs in other ways. This type of behavior may also be the source of charges of unfair labor practices, since these activities may require collective bargaining.

The *Taft-Hartley Act* gives unions the right to file grievances on their own behalf if they feel their rights have been violated. It also gives unions access to information necessary to process the grievance or to make sure the agreement is not being violated. In addition, unions may file grievances for violations of union shop or checkoff provisions. On the other hand, employees have the right to present their *own* grievances on an individual basis, and the employer can resolve that grievance without the union's presence. The only qualifying items are that adjustments cannot abrogate the collective agreement, and the union must be given an opportunity to participate in the grievance proceedings at some point prior to the adjustment.

Occasionally, other activities prompt grievances. Wildcat strikes or behavior that functions as a strike (mass absences from work, for example) can result in a management grievance. Increasingly, outsourcing and replacement workers are issues resulting in grievances.

Management Procedures

Management can significantly affect the grievance rate by adopting proper procedures for taking action against an employee. One of the most important procedures involves discipline and discharge. The issue of just cause and fairness is central to most discipline grievances. Employers must ensure that the employee is adequately warned of the consequences, that the rule involved is related to operation of the company, that a thorough investigation is undertaken, and that the penalty is reasonable. In areas outside of discipline and discharge, management can avoid grievance problems by educating supervisors and managers about labor relations and about the conditions of the collective agreement. It has been found that supervisors with labor knowledge are an important factor in the reduction of grievances.

Union Procedures

The union has an obligation to its members to provide them fair and adequate representation and to process and speedily investigate grievances brought by its members. Thus it should have a grievance-handling procedure that aids in effectively processing grievances without being guilty of unfair representation. Unfair representation, according to the NLRB, is usually related to one of four types of union behavior:

1. *Improper motives.* The union cannot refuse to process a grievance because of the employee's race or gender or because of the employee's attitude toward the union.
2. *Arbitrary conduct.* Unions cannot dismiss a grievance without investigating its merits.
3. *Gross negligence.* The union cannot recklessly disregard the employee's interests.
4. *Union conduct after filing the grievance.* The union must process the grievance to a reasonable conclusion.[58]

Because the employer can also be cited for unfair representation, management should attempt to maintain a fair grievance process. Company labor relations managers should avoid taking advantage of union errors in handling grievances so that this action does not affect fair representation.

Another important influence on the grievance process is the union steward. Since the union steward is generally the first person to hear about an employee's grievance, the steward has substantial influence on the grievance process. A steward can either encourage an employee to file a grievance, suggest that the problem is really not a grievance, or informally resolve the problem outside the grievance procedure. The personalities of stewards may, in fact, influence the number of grievances filed.[59] Because stewards are selected from the ranks of employees and may have little knowledge of labor relations, the union should train them to improve their effectiveness. The company can also be liable in a fair-representation suit and therefore should support such training.

ASSESSMENT OF COLLECTIVE BARGAINING

The effectiveness of the entire collective bargaining process and the union-management relationship can be measured by the extent to which each party attains its goals, but this approach has its difficulties. Because goals are incompatible in many cases and can therefore lead to conflicting estimates of effectiveness, a more useful measure may be the quality of the system used to resolve conflict. Conflict is more apparent in the collective bargaining process, where failure to resolve the issues typically leads to strikes. Another measure of effectiveness is the success of the grievance process, or the ability to resolve issues developing from the bargaining agreement.

Effectiveness of Negotiations

Because the purpose of negotiations is to achieve an agreement, the agreement itself becomes an overall measure of bargaining effectiveness. A healthy and effective bargaining process encourages the discussion of issues and problems and their subsequent resolution at the bargaining table. In addition, the effort required to reach agreement is a measure of how well the process is working. Some indications of this effort are the duration of negotiations, the outcome of member ratification votes, the frequency and duration of strikes, the use of mediation and arbitration, the need for government intervention, and the quality of union-management relations (whether conflict or cooperation exists). Joint programs for productivity and quality-of-work-life improvements could be regarded as successes resulting from effective union-management relations.

Effectiveness of Grievance Procedures

The effectiveness of a grievance procedure may be assessed from different perspectives. Management may view a small number of grievances filed or a large number settled in its favor as indicating success. Unions may also consider these numbers, but from their point of view, a large number filed and a large number settled in their favor indicate success.

An overall set of measures to gauge grievance procedure effectiveness may be related to the disagreements between managers and employees. Measures that might be included are frequency of grievances; the level in the grievance procedure at which grievances are usually settled; the frequency of strikes or slowdowns during the term of labor agreements; the rates of absenteeism, turnover, and sabotage; and the necessity for government intervention.

The success of arbitration is often judged by the acceptability of the decisions, the satisfaction of the parties, the degree of innovation, and the absence of bias in either direction. The effectiveness of any third-party intervention rests in part on how successfully strikes are avoided, because the motivation for such intervention is precisely to avert this extreme form of conflict resolution.

SUMMARY

Line managers and HR professionals need to know as much as possible about unionization because the stakes are substantial. Employees are generally attracted to unionization because they are dissatisfied with work conditions and feel powerless to change them. By correcting unsatisfactory work conditions, or by not allowing them to occur in the first place, organizations help prevent unions from becoming attractive. However, once a union-organizing campaign begins, a company cannot legally stop it without committing an unfair labor practice.

Historically, unions and management have operated as adversaries because many of their goals are in conflict, but effective labor relations have been established to reduce conflict that is detrimental to both management and unions. Although cooperation is not widespread, it may be the style of union-management relations in the future. Its effects are particularly apparent in collective bargaining, contract negotiation, and grievance processing.

The quality of the union-management relationship can have a strong influence on contract negotiations. Labor and management each select a bargaining committee to negotiate the new agreement. The negotiations may be between a single union and a single company or multiple companies, or between multiple unions and a single company. Bargaining issues are mandatory, permissive, or prohibited. Mandatory issues must be discussed, permissive issues can be discussed if both parties agree to do so, and prohibited issues can't be discussed. The issues can be grouped into wage, economic supplement, institutional, and administrative issues.

Almost all labor contracts outline procedures for handling employee complaints. The most common grievance is related to discipline and discharge, although wages, promotions, seniority, vacations, holidays, and management and union rights are also sources of complaints.

The effectiveness of collective bargaining and contract administration is usually assessed by measures of how well the process is working. Bargaining can be evaluated using measures such as the duration of negotiations, the frequency of strikes, the use of third-party intervention, and the need for government intervention. The effectiveness of the grievance process can be assessed by the number of grievances; the level in the grievance process at which settlement occurs; the frequency of strikes or slowdowns; the rates of absenteeism, turnover, and sabotage; and the need for government intervention.

Finally, as economic conditions in the world have changed substantially, so have union-management relations. Much more cooperation exists. Management sees cooperative relationships as instrumental in the implementation of quality-improvement strategies, while unions see them as instrumental in protecting the jobs and incomes of their members. And society as a whole sees cooperation as necessary and appropriate in these times of intense global competition. Thus, with some exceptions, we are likely to see cooperative relationships continue throughout the 21st century.

TERMS TO REMEMBER

AFL-CIO (American Federation of Labor/Congress of Industrial Organizations)	mediation
	multicraft bargaining
	multiemployer bargaining
arbitration	pattern settlements
business representative	preelection campaign
certification election	primary boycott
collective bargaining	psychological contract
concessionary bargaining	right-to-work laws
continuous bargaining	secondary boycott
coordinated bargaining	steward
decertification election	strike
distributive bargaining	union instrumentality
essentiality	union salting
exclusivity	union shop
industrywide bargaining	unionization
integrative bargaining	whipsaw
intraorganizational bargaining	wide-area bargaining
lockout	work slowdown

DISCUSSION QUESTIONS

1. How can the UAW and UPS work together even more effectively than they do today?
2. Identify and discuss the conditions that make unionization attractive to employees. Are these conditions different today than they were 50 years ago?
3. What is a certification election? A decertification election?
4. What is the structure of unionization in the United States today?
5. What is a bargaining unit? Why is its formation important?
6. Why has there been a trend toward cooperation between unions and management?
7. What are the steps in a typical grievance procedure?

8. Distinguish among mandatory, permissive, and prohibited bargaining issues.

9. Distinguish mediation from arbitration. How does a grievance procedure differ from interest arbitration? What is final-offer arbitration?

PROJECTS TO EXTEND YOUR LEARNING

1. *Managing Through Strategic Partnerships.* At Southwest Airlines almost 80 percent of its employees are members of unions. Yet, the employees are among the most productive in the industry and have a tremendous sense of pride and respect for the company and for Herb Kelleher. The company puts a great deal of value on the employees and the unions as key stakeholders in the success of the airlines. And it treats the employees and deals with the unions as if it means it! This fits with the overall model the company uses: employee satisfaction leads to customer satisfaction which leads to profitability. Employees and the unions are strategic partners at Southwest Airlines. Identify other companies that are similar. Perhaps start your search in *Fortune* magazine's "Most Admired" companies. Look at the names of the companies in Robert Levering's book, *The 100 Best Companies to Work for in America.* Determine what makes company-employee-union relationships so good.

2. *Managing Change.* Today's environment requires that firms not only be global, but that they are able to change rapidly. This means they need to move people around, train their employees to have new skills, and manage their employees so they aren't only able to change but willing to change as well. What's the role of the union here? Should companies that are unionized work closely with the union so that together they create a workforce that's ready and willing to change and adapt to new conditions? Are unions responsible for making sure that companies don't expect more from their employees than they are capable of providing? Companies like Ford and Cadillac have successfully adopted total quality management principles working with the unions. What did they do to help ensure that the process went smoothly? Identify companies that have been changing and determine what they do with the unions to help ensure a true cooperative partnership in navigating through organizational change.

3. *Managing Diversity.* What position should the union take regarding a firm's effort at developing a highly diverse organization? If it wants to be helpful, what can it do? Should it at least serve as a role model, that is, be highly diverse and manage diversity well? What type of diversity do unions have today? Contact local or national unions such as the AFL-CIO, the Teamsters, or the United Auto Workers to discuss these questions.

4. *Integration and Application.* Using the cases at the end of the text, compare and contrast Lincoln Electric and Southwest Airlines with regard to
    *   the views of management regarding union representation of its workers,
    *   the views of employees regarding union representation, and
    *   the consequences of these views for cooperation and conflict between employees and management.
    What changes in the environment or the company might lead Lincoln Electric's employees to become more interested in unionization? How likely do you think such changes are to occur?

THE UNION'S STRATEGIC CHOICE

Maria Dennis sits back and thoughtfully reads through the list of strategies that the union's committee gave her this morning. If her union is to rebuild the power it has lost over the past few years, it's time to take drastic action. If the union continues to decline as it has the last few years, it won't be able to represent the members who voted for it to be their exclusive bargaining representative.

Maria was elected two years ago, at her union's convention, to be the international president of the Newspaper Workers International Union (NWIU). At the time, she knew it would not be an easy job, and she eagerly looked forward to taking on a new challenge. But she had no idea just how difficult it would be to get the union back on its feet again.

The NWIU was founded in the late 1890s, made up of newspaper typographers who were responsible for such tasks as setting type on linotype machines, creating the layout of the newspaper, proofing the articles, and printing the newspaper. Members of the union typically completed a six-year apprenticeship, learning all the different tasks involved in the printing process. Before 1960, printing professionals were considered the elite of the industrial workforce. The craft demanded that typographers be literate at a time when even the middle and upper classes were not. Furthermore, printing was a highly skilled, highly paid craft.

Since the 1980s, however, the union has declined. Literacy is no longer a unique characteristic, and automation has led to a de-skilling of the craft. The introduction of video display terminals, optical character recognition scanners, and computerized typesetting has eliminated substantial composing room work, and the demand for skilled union workers has been reduced. The union experienced its peak membership of 120,000 in 1975. During the 1980s, membership began a substantial decline, and in 1998, the total membership was only 40,000. The reduced membership has resulted in other problems for the union. First, fewer members mean fewer dues, which are the union's main source of revenue. Consequently, the union is having some serious financial problems and is being forced to cut some of its services to members.

Second, the union is experiencing a significant loss in bargaining power with newspaper management. In the past, the printers were fairly secure in their jobs because there was a good demand in the labor market for individuals who could run the complicated printing equipment. But the recent switch to automation has eliminated many jobs and has also made it possible for employers to easily replace union employees. Anyone can be trained in a short time to use the new printing equipment. Therefore, if union members decide to strike for better wages, hours, and working conditions, management could easily, and legally, find replacements for them. In essence, the union is unable to fulfill its main mission, which is to collectively represent the employees who voted for it.

To solve the current crisis, Maria is considering five options:

1. Implement an associate member plan through which any individual could join the union for a fee of $50 a year. Although these members would not be fully represented on the job, they would get an attractive package of benefits, such as low-cost home, health, and auto insurance.

2. Attempt some cooperative labor-management

relations programs, such as getting member representation on newspaper boards of directors or employee participation programs in the workplace.

3. Put more effort into political action. For example, lobby for labor law reform or for new laws more favorable to unions. Initiate action that would result in harsher penalties against employers that practice illegal union-avoidance activities, such as threatening to move the business if a union is voted in or firing pro-union employees.

4. Appeal to community leaders to speak out in favor of the union in order to improve public relations, to help recruit new members, and to encourage employers to bargain fairly when negotiating with the union.

5. Search for another union with which the printing professionals might merge, thus increasing their membership, strengthening their finances, increasing their bargaining power, and obtaining economies of scale.

Maria realizes that each of these options could have both positive and negative results, and is unsure which strategy, if any, she should recommend for the union to pursue. In less than three hours, however, she will have to present the list to the council with her recommendations.

QUESTIONS

1. What are the strengths and weaknesses of each strategy?
2. What strategies could be employed to get new bargaining units?
3. What other types of services could the union offer to its members?
4. What would be your final recommendation? Justify your response.

Source: K. Stratton-Devine, University of Alberta.

ENDNOTES

1 R. J. Grossman, "Trying to Heal the Wounds," *HR Magazine* (September 1998): 85–92.

2 R. J. Grossman, "Trying to Heal the Wounds;" D. A. Tosh, "After the UPS Strike," *ACA News* (October 1997): 11–14; C. Haddad, "How UPS Delivered Through the Disaster," *Business Week* (October 1, 2001): 66.

3 "GM Saturn Workers Weigh Innovative Labor Accord," *Wall Street Journal* (February 18, 1998): B6; R. Kuttner, "Unions Are Good for the U.S.—and Clinton Should Say So," *Business Week* (October 7, 1996): 23; A. R. McIlvaine, "The Comeback Trail," *Human Resource Executive* (November 1997): 55–58.

4 For a more extensive discussion of unionization and the entire union-management relationship, see P. Clark, *Building More Effective Unions* (Ithaca, NY: ILR Press, 2000); J. A. Fossum, *Labor Relations: Development, Structure, Process*, 8th ed. (New York: Irwin McGraw-Hill, 2002).

5 For an overview and in-depth discussion of collective bargaining, see H. C. Katz and T. A. Kochan, *An Introduction to Collective Bargaining and Industrial Relations* (New York: Irwin McGraw-Hill, 2000).

6 M. France, "After the Shooting Stops," *Business Week* (March 12, 2001): 98–99; J. Nee, P. Kennedy, and D. Langham, "Increasing Manufacturing Effectiveness Through Joint Union/Management Cooperation," *Human Resource Management* 38(1) (Spring 1999): 77–85; D. A. Tosh, "After the UPS Strike;" M. J. Koch and G. Hundley, "The Effects of Unionism on Recruitment and Selection Methods," *Industrial Relations* 36(3) (July 1997): 349.

7 L. Balliet, *Survey of Labor Relations* (Washington, DC: Bureau of National Affairs, 1981).

8 D. P. Twomey, *Labor Law and Legislation* (Cincinnati, OH: South-Western, 1998).

9 P. Elstrom, "Needed: A New Union for the New Economy," *Business Week* (September 4, 2000): 48; C. McDonald, "U. S. Union Membership in

Future Decades: A Trade Unionist's Perspective," *Industrial Relations* (Winter 1992): 13–30; A. Gladstone et al. (eds.), *Labour Relations in a Changing Environment* (New York: Walter de Gruyter, 1992); M. Bognanno and M. Kleiner, "Introduction: Labor Market Institutions and the Future Role of Unions," *Industrial Relations* (Winter 1992): 1–12; T. A. Kochan and P. Osterman, *The Mutual Gains Enterprise: Forging a Winning Partnership among Labor, Management, and Government* (Boston: Harvard Business School Press, 1994); T. A. Kochan, R. B. McKersie, and P. Cappelli, "Strategic Choice and Industrial Relations Theory," *Industrial Relations* (Winter 1984): 16–38; A. L. Cowan, "Steel Pact Lets Union Name a Board Member," *New York Times* (August 1, 1993): L34.

10 J. Barling, E. K. Kelloway, and E. H. Bremermann, "Preemployment Predictors of Union Attitudes: The Role of Family Socialization and Work Beliefs," *Journal of Applied Psychology* 75(5) (1991): 725–731; S. Mellor, "The Relationship between Membership Decline and Union Commitment: A Field Study of Local Unions in Crisis," *Journal of Applied Psychology* 75(3) (1990): 258–267; C. Fullagar and J. Barling, "A Longitudinal Test of a Model of the Antecedents and Consequences of Union Loyalty," *Journal of Applied Psychology* 74(2) (1989): 213–227; S. P. Deshpande and J. Fiorito, "Specific and General Beliefs in Union Voting Models," *Academy of Management Journal* 32(4) (1989): 883–897; G. E. Fryxell and M. E. Gordon, "Workplace Justice and Job Satisfaction as Predictors of Satisfaction with Union and Management," *Academy of Management Journal* 32(4) (1989): 851–866.

11 A. Bernstein, "The Amalgamated Doctors of America?" *Business Week* (June 28, 1999): 36; S. Greenhouse, "The First Unionization Vote by Dot-Com Workers Is Set," *New York Times* (January 9, 2001): C4; C. Hirschman, "Overtime Overload," *HR Magazine* (December 2000): 84–92; M. Conlin, "Labor Laws Apply to Dot-Coms? Really?" *Business Week* (February 26, 2001): 96–98.

12 A. Ritter, "Are Unions Worth the Bargain?" *Personnel* (February 1990): 12–14.

13 S. A. Youngblood et al., "The Impact of Work Attachment, Instrumentality Beliefs, Perceived Labor Union Image, and Subjective Norms on

Union Voting Intentions and Union Membership," *Academy of Management Journal* (1984): 576–590.

14 Katz and Kochan, *An Introduction to Collective Bargaining and Industrial Relations*.

15 P. Bamberger, A. Kluger, and R. Suchard, "The Antecedents and Consequences of Union Commitment: A Meta-Analysis," *Academy of Management Journal* 42(3) (1999): 304–318; J. Barling, E. K. Kelloway, and E. H. Bremermann, "Preemployment Predictors of Union Attitudes: The Role of Family Socialization and Work Beliefs," *Journal of Applied Psychology* 75(5) (1991): 725–731.

16 A. A. Sloane and F. Witney, *Labor Relations* (Englewood Cliffs, NJ: Prentice-Hall, 1985): 62; see also J. Rosenfeld, "Free Agents in the Olde World," *Fast Company* (May 2001): 136–140.

17 "The Labor Movement," *Workforce* (January 2002): 27; J. W. Wimberly, "State of the Unions," *Human Resource Executive* (September 1998): 90–91; G. Burkins, "Union Membership Fell Further in 1997," *Wall Street Journal* (March 18, 1998): A2, A8; S. Greenhouse, "Gains Put Unions at Turning Point, Many Experts Say," *New York Times* (September 1, 1997): A1, A20; "Union Membership Fell Again in 1997," *Bulletin to Management* (February 26, 1998): 61; "Union Membership by State and Industry," *Bulletin to Management* (June 12, 1997): 188–189; "Union Membership by State and Industry," *Bulletin to Management* (May 29, 1997): 172-173; "Union Membership and Earnings," *Bulletin to Management* (February 13, 1997): 52-53. For an extensive presentation of union membership data, see C. D. Gifford (ed.), *Directory of U.S. Labor Organizations*, 1997–98 Edition (Washington, DC: Bureau of National Affairs, 1998); and B.T. Hirsch and D.A. Macpherson, *Union Membership and Earnings Data Book*, 1998 Edition (Washington, DC: Bureau of National Affairs, 1998).

18 S. Greenhouse, "During a Blue-Collar Upswing, Labor Seeks a Lift," *New York Times* (December 5, 2001): A16; D. Whitford, "Labor's Lost Chance," *Fortune* (September 28, 1998): 177–182; S. Greenhouse, "Despite Efforts to Organize, Union Rosters Have Declined," *New York Times* (March 22, 1998): 21; "More Women Leading Unions," *Fair Employment Practices Guidelines* (November 22, 1990): 141; J. G. Kilgour, "The Odds on White-Collar Organizing," *Personnel* (August 1990): 29–34.

19 C. Daniels, "Watch for Rallies in the Valley," *Fortune* (April 2, 2001): 36; M. B. Regan, "Shattering the AFL-CIO's Glass Ceiling," *Business Week* (November 13, 1998): 46; A. Bernstein, "Sweeney's Blitz," *Business Week* (February 17, 1997): 56–62; A. Bernstein, "Andy Stern's Mission Impossible," *Business Week* (June 10, 1996): 73; A. Bernstein, "Wireless Workers Get Connected," *Business Week* (May 26, 1997): 160; J. E. Lyncheski and J. M. McDermott, "Unions Employ New Growth Strategies," *HR Focus* (September 1996): 22–23.

20 C. D. Gifford, *Directory of U. S. Labor Organizations, 2001–2002 Edition* (Washington, DC: Bureau of National Affairs, 2002); D. Whitford, "Carpenter Gives AFL-CIO Labor Pains," *Fortune* (July 23, 2001): 44–46.

21 Balliet, *Survey of Labor Relations*, 72–105.

22 M. Maynard, "U.S. and Canadian Unions Look at Plans Differently," *New York Times* (January 12, 2002): C3; G. Gori, "Strike at VW 1 Mexico Ends Unusually," *New York Times* (September 6, 2001): W1; S. Greenhouse, "In U.S. Unions, Mexico Finds Unlikely Ally on Immigration," *New York Times* (July 19, 2001): A1, A21; M. Maynard, "Canada Vote May Bring Union to Japan Carmaker," *New York Times* (July 6, 2001): C1, C11; G. Flynn, "HR in Mexico: What You Should Know," *Personnel Journal* (August 1994): 34; C. R. Greer and G. K. Stephens, "Employee Relations Issues for U.S. Companies in Mexico," *California Management Review* 38(3) (Spring 1996): 121–145.

23 B. P. Noble, "At the Labor Board, New Vigor," *New York Times* (September 4, 1994): F21.

24 Prepared for this chapter by William D. Todor, Professor of HRM, The Ohio State University.

25 S. Greenhouse, "Unions Predict Gain from Boeing Strike," *New York Times* (March 21, 2000): A14; "Unions Won More Representation Elections Than They Lost in 1997," *Bulletin to Management* (June 4, 1998): 173; G. Burkins, "Labor Plans to Shift to Its Foot Soldiers in 1998's Congres-

sional Campaigns," *Wall Street Journal* (January 20, 1998): A20; S. Greenhouse, "Renewed Push in New York: More Union Cards in Wallets," *New York Times* (May 30, 1997): A1, B2.

26 M. Bryant and R. Gilson, "Unions Can Organize Temporary Employees Along with Regular Workforce," *Legal Report* (November–December 2000): 7–8; G. Flynn, "When the Unions Come Calling," *Workforce* (November 2000): 82–87; C. R. Fine, "Beware the Trojan Horse," *Workforce* (May 1998): 45–51.

27 J. Hoerr, "The Strange Bedfellows Backing Workplace Reform," *Business Week* (April 20, 1990): 57. See also R. Koenig, "Quality Circles Are Vulnerable to Union Tests," *Wall Street Journal* (March 28, 1990): B1; L. E. Hazzard, "A Union Says Yes to Attendance," *Personnel Journal* (November 1990): 47–49; Twomey, *Labor Law and Legislation*, 134.

28 J. R. Getman, J. B. Goldberg, and J. B. Herman, *Union Representation Elections: Law and Reality* (New York: Russell Sage, 1976): 72.

29 J. B. Fuller, Jr., and K. Hester, "A Closer Look at the Relationship Between Justice Perceptions and Union Participation," *Journal of Applied Psychology* 86 (2001): 1096–1105; R. Peterson and D. Lewin, "Research on Unionized Grievance Procedures: Management Issues and Recommendations," *Human Resource Management* 39(4) (Winter 2000): 395–406; W. Zellner, "Congestion at the Bargaining Table, Too," *Business Week* (March 19, 2001): 46; J. M. Brett, "Behavioral Research on Unions and Union-Management Systems," *Research in Organizational Behavior* 2 (1980): 200.

30 J. Hutchins, "Labor and Management Build a Prescription for Health," *Workforce* (March 2001): 50–52; "This Is Not Your Father's Bargaining Agreement," *HR Magazine* (March 2001): 31–32; J. Muller, "Will the UAW Be Chrysler's Friend in Need?" *Business Week* (December 18, 2000): 94; M. Estes, "Adversaries Find Common Ground," *Workforce* (March 1997): 97–102; A. Bernstein, "Look Who's Pushing Productivity," *Business Week* (April 7, 1997): 72–73; V. Zinno, "Relations in Labor," *Human Resource Executive* (August 1996): 28–30. See N. Herrick, *Joint Management and Employee Participation: Labor and Management at the Crossroads* (San Francisco: Jossey-Bass, 1990); Brett, "Behavioral Research on Unions and Union-Management Systems;" Brett, "Why Employees Want Unions," 45–59.

31 C. Hirschman, "When Operating Abroad, Companies Must Adopt European-Style HR Plan," *HR News* (March 2001): 1, 6; R. Meredith, "Saturn Union Votes to Retain Its Cooperative Company Pact," *New York Times* (March 12, 1998): D1, D4.

32 J. T. Delaney, "Workplace Cooperation: Current Problems, New Approaches," *Journal of Labor Research* 17(1) (Winter 1996): 45–61; T.A. Kochan, "Creating a Labor Policy for the 1990s," *Boston Globe* (September 12, 1995): 40.

33 K. Bradsher, "Efficiency on Wheels: US Auto Industry Is Catching Up with the Japanese," *New York Times* (June 16, 2000): C1, C8; B. Vlasic and W. C. Symonds, "Sweet Deal," *Business Week* (September 30, 1996): 32–33; J. Flynn, S. Reed, and A. Barrett, "Give a Little, Get a Little in Detroit," *Business Week* (November 18, 1996): 56–57; K. Bradsher, "U.A.W.'s Pact at Ford Aims At Downsizing," *New York Times* (September 18, 1996): A1, D6; B. P. Noble, "More than Labor Amity at AT&T," *New York Times* (March 14, 1993): F25. See also Chapter 6 in J. Pfeffer, *Competitive Advantage through People* (Boston: Harvard Business School Press, 1994).

34 H. Campbell, "Adventures in Teamland," *Personnel Journal* (May 1996): 56–62.

35 Adapted from R. E. Walton and R. B. McKersie, *A Behavioral Theory of Labor Negotiations* (New York: McGraw-Hill, 1965): 43.

36 J. A. Fossum, *Labor Relations: Development, Structure, Process*, 8th ed. (Plano, TX: Business Publications, 2002).

37 A. Blum, "Collective Bargaining: Ritual or Reality?" *Harvard Business Review* (November–December 1961): 64.

38 M. H. Bazerman, *Judgment in Managerial Decision Making* (New York: Wiley, 1986); M. H. Bazerman and J. S. Carroll, "Negotiator Cognition," in Cummings and Staw (eds.), *Research in Organizational Behavior*, Vol. 9

(Greenwich, CT: JAI Press, 1987); M. H. Bazerman, T. Magliozzi, and M. A. Neale, "The Acquisition of an Integrative Response in a Competitive Market," *Organizational Behavior and Human Decision Processes* 34 (1985): 294–313.

39 M. Winerip, "A Union Standing Fast Now Stands to Lose," *New York Times* (June 12, 1996): A16; K. Jennings and E. Traynman, "Two-Tier Plans," *Personnel Journal* (March 1988): 56–58.

40 Sloan and Witney, *Labor Relations.*

41 Fossum, "Labor Relations," in S. J. Carroll and R. S. Schuler (eds.), *Human Resource Management in the 1980s* (Washington, DC: Bureau of National Affairs, 1983): 395–396.

42 P. Hartman and W. Franke, "The Changing Bargaining Structure in Construction: Wide-Area and Multicraft Bargaining," *Industrial and Labor Relations Review* (January 1980): 170–184.

43 Sloan and Witney, *Labor Relations,* 59.

44 Hartman and Franke, "The Changing Bargaining Structure in Construction."

45 Fossum, *Labor Relations.*

46 M. F. Bazerman and M. A. Neale, "Heuristics in Negotiation: Limitations to Effective Dispute Resolution," in M. Bazerman and R. J. Lewicki (eds.), *Negotiating in Organizations,* (Beverly Hills, CA: Sage, 1983): 51–67; M. E. Gordon et al., "Laboratory Research in Bargaining and Negotiations: An Evaluation," *Industrial Relations* (Spring 1984): 218–223; R. E. Walton and R. B. McKersie, *A Behavioral Theory of Labor Negotiations* (New York: McGraw-Hill, 1965).

47 M. A. Neale, V. L. Huber, and G. Northcraft, "The Framing of Negotiations: Contextual versus Task Frame," *Organizational Behavior and Human Decision Processes* 39 (1987): 228–241.

48 "Union Growth—Learn the Signs and How to Prevent It," *HR Reporter* 14(12) (December 1997): 5.

49 C. Giambusso, "Delta's Labor Troubles: View from the Cockpit," *New York Times* (January 7, 2001): BU 6; W. Zellner, "Up Against the Wal-Mart," *Business Week* (March 13, 2000): 76–78; E. Zimmerman, "HR Lessons from a Strike," *Workforce* (November 2000): 36–42; S. Greenhouse, "Unions, Growing Bolder, No Longer Shun Strikes," *New York Times* (September 7, 1998): A12; B. P. Sunoo, "Managing Strikes, Minimizing Loss,"

Personnel Journal (January 1995): 50–60; J. E. Martin and R. R. Sinclair, "A Multiple Motive Perspective on Strike Prosperities," *Journal of Organizational Behavior* 22 (2001): 387–407.

50 D. Weimer, "A New Cat on the Hot Seat," *Business Week* (March 9, 1998): 56–61; A. Bernstein, "Why Workers Still Hold a Weak Hand," *Business Week* (March 2, 1998): 98; "Tentative Deal Reached by Caterpillar and the UAW," *Bulletin to Management* 49(7) (February 19, 1998): 49.

51 J. Tasini, "For the Unions, a New Weapon," *New York Times Magazine* (June 12, 1988): 24–25, 69–71; C. Perry, *Union Corporate Campaigns* (Philadelphia: Wharton Industrial Relations Center, 1987).

52 S. Briggs, "Labor/Management Conflict and the Role of the Neutral," in R. S. Schuler, S. A. Youngblood, and V. L. Huber (eds.), *Personnel and Human Resource Management,* 3rd ed. (St. Paul, MN: West Publishing Co., 1988); R. J. Weinstein, *Meditation in the Workplace: A Guide for Training Practices* (Westport, CT: Quorum, 2001); C. Patton, "Net Negotiations," *Human Resource Executive* (March 1, 2001): 92–95.

53 "Collective Bargaining through Diplomacy," *Bulletin to Management* (January 25, 1990): 32.

54 R. J. Colon, "Grievances Hinge on Poor Contract Language," *Personnel Journal* (September 1990): 32–36.

55 K. E. Boroff and D. Lewin, "Loyalty, Voice, and Intent to Exit a Union Firm: A Conceptual and Empirical Analysis," *Industrial and Labor Relations Review* 51(1) (October 1997): 50–63; S. Slichter, J. Healy, and E. Livernash, *The Impact of Collective Bargaining on Management* (Washington, DC: Brookings Institution, 1960): 694.

56 B. Bemmels and J. R. Foley, "Grievance Procedure Research: A Review and Theoretical Recommendations," *Journal of Management* 22(3) (1996): 359–384.

57 Prepared by William D. Todor, Professor of HRM, The Ohio State University, for this chapter.

58 Memorandum 79-55, National Labor Relations Board (July 7, 1979); C. Shrout, "Some Issues Are Off-Table for Collective Bargaining," *HR News* (July 2001): 19.

59 D. R. Dalton and W. D. Todor, "Manifest Needs of Stewards: Propensity to File a Grievance," *Journal of Applied Psychology* (December 1979): 654–659.

CHAPTER

16

Understanding the HR Profession

"We discovered that you almost can't get HR involved too early. From a Gillette perspective, the human resource organization is a key partner in everything we do."

Tom Webber
Director of HR for Manufacturing
Gillette

MANAGING THROUGH STRATEGIC PARTNERSHIPS

Cisco Systems

Mergers and acquisitions that cross country borders are likely to accelerate the blending of domestic and international HR activities. Cisco has pursued the acquisition strategy as well as any company as a means of expanding its product lines. John Chambers, CEO of Cisco, says very clearly that integrating the newly acquired company into the Cisco culture is very important. In fact, Cisco even evaluates the culture of the companies it is thinking about acquiring. This is done through the involvement of the senior V. P. of HR, Barbara Beck. The culture for them represents the values of the company and the way it treats people. Given that Cisco manages its people to (1) allow them to be rewarded for their performance; (2) encourage them to be creative; and (3) facilitate their working effectively in teams, Cisco evaluates the companies it may acquire on these same cultural dimensions. Certainly this is a clear role for the human resource manager and one the company takes very seriously. When put in a global context with national cultural, language, and legal differences, this cultural evaluation audit becomes even more complex and challenging, and so are the potential costs of any misjudgments.[1]

As the experience of Cisco highlights in this feature and the opener in Chapter 1, the HR profession can contribute to—even determine—the success (or failure) of an organization. Members of a company's HR staff, working with external HR consultants and vendors, can help ensure that the needs of the business *and* the needs of employees are reflected in HR policies, mission statements, and practices. These are central to the coordination and operation of an organization. At Cisco, HR professionals help the firm satisfy its key stakeholders.

> ### FAST FACT
>
> At Spectrum Signal Processing Inc., there is no HR department. Instead, the 180 employees serve as rotating members of the company's HR committee.

The human resource department is the group formally established by an organization to help manage the organization's people as effectively as possible for the good of the employees, the company, and society. HR professionals include external consultants and service providers with HR expertise. As we have emphasized throughout this book, the managing of human resources gets done through a working partnership of HR professionals, line managers, and employees. At times, this partnership extends outside the organization—for example, as the firm strives to forge better working relationships with its suppliers.[2] It may also venture into local education facilities as the HR staff works with schools to prepare students for internships in the firm. And, increasingly, companies use HR consultants to help with activities such as compensation, benefits, training, recruiting and selection, and implementing large-scale organizational change.[3]

HUMAN RESOURCE PROFESSIONALS PLAY MANY ROLES

According to a poll of HR professionals, a meeting between the head of HR and the CEO occurs at least every day for one-third of companies, several times per week for about one-third of companies and less than once per week for one-third of companies.

Charles Nielson, former vice president of human resources at Texas Instruments, has watched the profession's evolution for more than three decades: "I've been involved in the people business in one way or another for 35 years, and I'm having more fun today than I've ever had. . . . In the past, the HR function has been like a spare tire kept in the trunk. In an emergency, it's taken out, but as soon as the emergency's over, it's put away. Now I feel that we're a wheel running on the ground. We're not the HR we used to be, but in terms of partnering and helping our companies become competitive, we've only just begun. There are fun times ahead," he says.[4]

The fun comes in part from performing a broad variety of activities and playing a variety of roles. The effectiveness with which HR professionals play all these roles depends on the leadership and staffing of the department and the positioning of the department within the organization.

Effective firms in the highly competitive environments of today encourage their HR professionals to play many roles. The more roles HR professionals play well, the better they will serve all of the organization's stakeholders. Janet Brady, vice president of human resources at The Clorox Co., understands how challenging it can be to address the concerns of many different stakeholders:

I serve the board of directors, executive management, general office employees, retirees, production and salespeople across the country, every type of function—and they all view HR slightly differently based on their backgrounds, their needs and their histories. That has told me there isn't a one-size-fits-all solution. I've got to listen and ask questions, so that we can ultimately do something that's fair for everybody. HR can be very challenging because what we do can affect people at the most personal level and we can't lose sight of that.[5]

The major roles for the most effective HR departments and their HR leaders are shown in Exhibit 16.1.

Strategic Management Role

Traditionally, HR departments often had limited involvement in the company's business affairs and goals. HR managers were often only concerned with making staffing plans, providing specific job training programs, or running annual performance appraisal programs (the results of which were sometimes put in the files, never to be used). They focused on the short-term—perhaps day-to-day—needs of human resources.

With the growing importance of human resources to the firm's success, HR managers and their departments are deeply involved in the business. They know the needs of the business and understand how the organization's approach to managing human resources can help address the concerns of all stakeholders.[6] The involvement of HR professionals includes planning the longer-term, strategic directions of the organization as well as planning and implementing more tactical activities in the short term.

At the strategic level, HR departments and their professionals get involved in broader decisions—those that provide overall direction and vision for the organization. Being a strategic partner requires an understanding of how the business functions, the strategic objectives of the company, the products and services it offers, who the customers are, and how the company is positioned competitively in the marketplace. This is why we discussed the organizational environment so extensively in Chapter 4 and the global environment in Chapter 2. The process of linking a firm's HR policies and practices to the broader, longer-term needs of the firm and its stakeholders is the essence of *strategic* human resource management.[7]

"HR people first get involved in strategic planning in areas that are most closely aligned with HR issues."

Diana Lewis
Vice President of HR
EcoLab

ex 16.1 Key Roles for HR Professionals

KEY ROLES	WHAT IS EXPECTED ON THE JOB
Strategic Management Role	• Understands the global and organizational environment • Knows the market and what the business is • Has a long-term vision of where the business is headed • Knows strategy formulation and implementation • Assists with mergers, acquisitions, and IJVs • Shows concern for bottom-line results
Enabler and Consultant Role	• Works in partnership with line managers • Develops and administers specific HR practices and policies • Provides HR information and advice to line managers • Provides counsel and advice to employees • Knows the employees and understands their needs • Adopts a customer orientation
Monitoring and Maintaining Role	• Takes responsibility for ensuring the organization's approaches to managing human resources meet the highest standards for fair and ethical practice • Ensures employment laws are known and observed • Ensures the organization attends to both "soft" and "hard" data when evaluating its HR policies and practices • Helps the organizational morale, sense of purpose, and optimism • Monitors employees' attitudes and concerns in crisis situations
Innovator Role	• Initiates; does not wait for others to call attention to the need for action • Seeks ways to better satisfy stakeholders • Creatively measures effectiveness throughout the company • Is proactive in recommending how new technology can be used effectively in the management of human resources • Continually revises and updates HR policies and practices
Change and Knowledge Facilitator Role	• Can create a sense of urgency • Can think conceptually and articulate thoughts • Has a sense of purpose—a steadfast focus, a definite value system • Foresees the talent needed for executing future strategies • Moves knowledge around the company • Is capable of educating line managers and mobilizing them to educate others • Recognizes people with outstanding potential and anticipates their concerns

FAST FACT

In a recent survey of HR professionals, 41.8% said they spend 2 to 3 hours a day on strategic issues and 38.8% said they spend less than an hour a day.

Typically, strategic business needs arise from decisions such as what products and services to offer and on what basis to compete—quality, cost, or innovation, or for purposes of survival, growth, adaptability, and profitability. These decisions are associated with the formulation and implementation of the organization's strategy, as described in Chapter 5.[8]

Strategy formulation includes

- deciding what business the company will be in, forming a vision, committing to a set of values and a general strategy;
- identifying strategic business issues and setting strategic business objectives; and
- crafting corporate and business-level plans of action.

Strategy implementation includes

- developing functional and operational plans of action; and
- measuring, evaluating, revising and refocusing for the future.[9]

The process of strategy formulation leads to stating specific strategic objectives, which serve as the basis for the strategic management implementation activities. An illustration of these activities is shown in Exhibit 5.3 (in Chapter 5).

Setting the Direction. The activities involved in establishing the vision, mission, and values and then identifying the strategic business objectives were described in Chapter 5. While the process of identifying and setting strategic business objectives is likely to highlight numerous implications for human resource management, these remain rather unspecified until they are developed in the strategic plans.

Crafting Corporate- and Business-Level Plans. Crafting strategic plans involves deciding how the vision, mission, and strategic objectives are going to be obtained. Typically, a good strategic plan includes

- analysis of the economy and industry in which the firm competes;
- identification of the sources of competitive advantage and the critical success factors;
- analysis of existing and potential competition;
- assessment of company strengths, weaknesses, and core competencies; and
- plans of actions.

Making the strategic plan a bit more complex is the reality that there are two levels of strategy formulation: corporate and business. Corporate strategy concerns how a diversified company intends to establish business positions in different industries and the actions and approaches it employs to improve the performance of the full group of businesses held within the corporation. Business-level strategy lays out the actions and the approaches crafted by management to produce successful performance in one specific line of business: the central business strategy issue is how to build a stronger long-term competitive position.

Developing and Implementing Functional Plans. The specific implications of corporate and business-level strategies for managing human resources often become crystallized in the organization's functional plans. Each function has to identify the implications of the corporate and business-level plans for its activities. Strategy implementation is often about change. Not surprisingly, managing the change process—both at the individual and the organizational levels—is seen by HR professionals as one of their most significant and challenging activities. By way of example, take the strategic business objective of "enhancing customer focus by adopting a 'solutions' orientation." For the human resource function, this objective may suggest the need to develop plans that will result in a new vision, statement of values, and culture for the company. The objective may also imply the need to develop a plan for how to "customerize" the HR department, for example, by restructuring the department into teams of HR professionals assigned to serve specific groups of internal customers within the firm.

Customerization means the state of viewing everybody, whether inside or outside the organization, as a customer and then putting that

> *"There was a time when the HR department was the last to know. Now, the first thing you do is call human resources and say, 'Can you help me do things properly?'"*
>
> Richard A. Zimmerman
> Former CEO
> Hershey Foods

FAST FACT

HR adds 60% of its value through strategic activities yet these are only 10% of HR costs.

> *"We exist because of customers. They are our raison d'etre."*
>
> Michael Mitchell
> Former Vice President of Human Resources
> Tiffany & Company

customer first. For human resource professionals, customers include other line and staff managers as well as all of the organization's individual employees. Essential to customerization is the realization that all HR professionals produce and deliver products and services for "customers."[10] Customerization also means recognizing that customers are more likely to be satisfied with the products and services delivered by HR when they are involved in the design of those products and services. Together, in partnership, the customer and HR professional determine what is best for the situation.

Measure, Evaluate, Revise, and Refocus. The final task of the strategic management task is reviewing what has been done against the strategic plans, deciding upon corrective actions, and establishing new courses of action to take should the situation warrant it. Reviewing and evaluating depend upon having stated criteria against which to compare results. Shortcomings in the attainment of the strategic plan triggers problem diagnosis to determine the reasons for the deficiencies. Revised action plans are then formulated.

Enabler and Consultant Role

In reality, human resource policies and practices succeed because line managers make them succeed. The HR professional's bread-and-butter job, therefore, is to enable line managers to make things happen. In designing and helping to carry out activities such as recruiting, selecting, training, evaluating, rewarding, and promoting safety and health, HR professionals are basically providing a service to line managers. As part of the assistance, HR professionals may provide training that enables line managers to be more effective. Common topics that HR managers cover in the training they provide to line managers include equal employment opportunity legislation, performance management, and safety and health standards. When line managers conclude that changes are needed in order to improve any aspect of HR management, HR professionals serve as consultants to line managers. In this role, they often help line managers diagnose problems and develop solutions that incorporate state-of-the-art HR practices.

The enabler and consultant role also applies to the HR professional's relationship with employees. To fulfill their responsibilities, HR professionals must be accessible to all members of the workforce and attuned to their changing needs and concerns.

Monitoring and Maintaining Role

Although HR professionals may delegate much of the implementation of HR activities to line managers, they remain responsible for seeing that HR programs are implemented fairly and consistently. Meeting this obligation requires monitoring the outcomes and effectiveness of all HR activities. Various state and federal regulations make sophisticated demands on organizations to monitor many elements of the human resource management system. Compliance with these regulations generally requires giving responsibility for these tasks to a central group, such as the HR department.

Monitoring the organization's compliance with legal regulations is not the only aspect of this role, however. As we have emphasized throughout the preceding chapters, HR professionals should continuously monitor the

"If you become over-focused on the [bottom-line results], you can get to a point at which you need to do a ROI (a return on investment analysis) to make sure it's worth the time spent measuring results— it can get a little crazy."

Mark Teachout, Ph.D.
Executive Director of Learning and
Performance Technology
USAA

"One of the biggest challenges for us is that the HR department is centralized. We service 30,000 people in 56 different cities and about one-third of our people are flying around in big metal tubes all day. It's challenging to be available and accessible to our people."

Libby Sartain
Former Vice President of People
Southwest Airlines

effectiveness of HR activities to ensure they are meeting the various and changing needs of both line managers and other employees.

HR professionals have an important role to play when it comes to making sure that the organization maintains it overall morale and esprit de corps. This role is particularly acute during difficult times including natural disasters such as flooding, hurricanes, major fires, and earthquakes. It is also important during terrorist activities such as those carried out on the World Trade Center and the Pentagon in September 2001. During such events, HR professionals provide needed counseling and advice to employees and their families. They can provide advice ranging from information about psychological coping to employees' rights to pay and benefits. Of course, advice and counsel such as this is equally important to all employees. By providing timely assistance to employees in times of distress, HR professionals make it easier for employees to cope with the events and to be productive upon returning to work.

Organizations are also finding that providing advice to employees is important during times of major organizational changes, downsizings, and general uncertainty. Doubtless, these are difficult and challenging activities for HR professionals, but ones that are important in maintaining the overall health and effectiveness of both individual employees and the organization as a whole.

"My boss, as the CEO, views my job as equivalent in value to the CFO, to the VP of engineering, to the VP of manufacturing, and expects me to deliver the same amount of value."

David Lietzke
Vice President of HR
Bay Networks (now a part of Nortel)

Innovator Role

Today, managers turn to HR professionals for innovative approaches and solutions to improve productivity and the quality of work life while complying with the law in an environment of high uncertainty, energy conservation, and intense international competition. And they demand solutions that can be justified in dollars and cents. Simply doing things the way they have always been does not make the cut in this environment; innovation is not optional, it is necessary.[11]

As part of the innovator role, HR professionals should do more than help others innovate—they should serve as a role model. HR managers face the same demands as other managers in the organizations. They must continually streamline their operations and redesign the way work gets done. Not waiting for mandated cutbacks, they review and evaluate expenses and implement incremental changes to become, and stay, lean. Flexible HR managers aggressively seek to be perceived as "bureaucracy busters," setting an example for other staff functions and line organizations.

Change and Knowledge Facilitator Role

It is increasingly necessary for organizations to adapt new technologies, structures, processes, cultures, and procedures to meet the demands of stiffer competition. Organizations look to the human resource department for the skills to facilitate organizational change and to maintain organizational flexibility and adaptability. One consequence of this change facilitator role is the need to focus on the future. As the global environment and business strategies change, new skills and competencies are needed. To ensure that the right skills and competencies are available at the appropriate time, HR professionals must anticipate change. In addition, they must guide the discussion and flow of knowledge, information, and learning throughout the organization.

"We need to understand where our business is going 5 to 6 years down the road, and HR is crucial to understanding the changing demographics and expectations of our workforce."

Mike Goodrich
CEO
BE&K

THE HR TRIAD

Responsibility for effectively managing human resources does not rest with HR professionals alone. All managers are responsible for leading people. Regardless of whether a line manager ever holds a formal position in human resource management, she or he will be accountable for the task of managing people.

As we have said from the very first chapter of this book, the responsibilities of line managers and HR professionals are especially great, but the triad involves even more sharing of responsibility. Employees in the organization, regardless of their particular jobs, also share responsibility for effective human resource management. An illustration of how all members of the triad can share responsibility is provided by the W. L. Gore company, as described in the feature "Managing Teams: HR Teams Fit the Pattern at Gore."[12]

INTERNET RESOURCES   16.A

Roles for HR Professionals

At our Web site, http://jackson.swcollege.com/, you can:

1. Learn about the HR professionals and the roles they play at some of the firms mentioned in this section by visiting their company home pages:

    Levi Strauss

    Cisco Systems

    Texas Instruments

    Gillette

    W. L. Gore

STAFFING THE HUMAN RESOURCE DEPARTMENT

Effective management of an organization's human resources depends in large part on the knowledge, skills, and abilities of the people in the human resource department, particularly the HR leader, HR generalists, and HR specialists—collectively referred to as HR professionals. The top human resource leaders and staff members must be capable administrators, functional experts, business consultants, and problem solvers with global awareness. Management expects the HR staff "to have it all." Administrative skills are essential for efficiency. Specialized expertise also is important, particularly in combination with business knowledge and perspective. In flexible organizations, problem-solving and consulting skills are vital in guiding and supporting new management practices.

On the topic of effective HR leaders: *"To succeed, you must have the ability to be persuasive, move the organization forward and influence key business decisions."*

Mike Bowlin
Former CEO
ARCO

The Human Resource Leader

For the HR department to perform all its roles effectively, it needs a very special leader. The leader must be knowledgeable in HR activities and also well versed in topics such as mergers and acquisitions, productivity, and total quality efforts. He or she must be familiar with the needs of the business and able to work side by side as a partner with line managers. An example of a job description for an HR leader is shown in Exhibit 16.2.[13]

Personal Qualities. The most effective person to head an HR department is an outstanding performer in the organization, with both HR expertise and

HR Teams Fit the Pattern at Gore

W. L. Gore & Associates, the company that manufactures GoreTex® and other fabric-based materials, doesn't have bosses and it doesn't have employees. Instead, consistent with its flat structure and culture of creativity, it employs sponsors and associates who have no specified job titles. When Bill Gore, a research chemist, founded the company, he worked out of his home's basement. Now, more than 50 years later, some 200 Gore manufacturing plants with more than 6,000 employees operate in 45 countries. Regardless of their location, all Gore work sites reflect the company's core values:

1. Fairness to each other and everyone with whom we come in contact.
2. Freedom to encourage, help, and allow other associates to grow knowledge, skill, and scope of responsibility.
3. The ability to make one's own commitments and keep them.
4. Consultation with other associates before undertaking actions that could impact the reputation of the company by hitting it "below the water line."

HR professionals serve as caretakers of these values.

At W. L. Gore, each plant is essentially self-sufficient, with at least one dedicated HR generalist located on-site. In addition to serving as a member of the leadership team, the HR generalist is responsible for workforce development, staff allocation, and conflict resolution. "They're the ones who make sure we're being fair (value #1) and creating an environment people want to work in,

which is critical to getting business results," observed business leader Terri Kelly. Supporting the HR generalists are specialists located at the headquarters office. Gore refers to this structure as a "Lattice." Just as a garden trellis might support the growth of a rambling rose, Gore's Lattice structure is designed to support the growth and development of HR practices and decisions that complement the needs of the business.

To understand how the Lattice structure works, consider what happens when a plant leadership position needs to be filled. Recruitment and hiring for the position is carried out by a team that includes other plant leaders, the HR generalist at the plant, and one or more specialists from headquarters. The business leaders define their needs and the HR professionals help them meet those needs through the use of effective recruitment and selection procedures. Those procedures recognize the importance of finding talent that is both technically competent and appropriate for the culture. HR knows that the needs of the business are changing rapidly, so new hires must be agile and willing to learn new skills. When people are hired, they make commitments to perform within a general functional area (value #3)—they aren't hired to fill a specific job title. In these and other ways, employees also join the organization as a team member who agrees to collaborate with others and adapt as needed to changing situations.

This democratic, high-involvement approach to HR has costs as well as benefits. Conducting HR through partnership takes time and costs money. But in the end, Gore believes "the quality of life is far better than what you'll find in a dictatorship."

---

line management experience. According to Libby Sartain, former vice president of the People Department at Southwest Airlines,

Those who are most effective HR leaders lead because of their strong desire and need to serve others. To be a strong leader one must have a lot of guts—when I say that, I mean two kinds, first, you have to stand up for what is right when others might not think the same. Sometimes you will make others uncomfortable and be unpopular, but when it is the right thing to do, you have to be able to stick your neck out. The other kind of guts is that "gut feeling." A great HR leader has to have a superior ability to evaluate people and situations. This instinctive ability is partially innate and partially develops and grows over time, but the best of the best have it. HR leaders must also be good businesspeople and understand the [industry] they are in. Without this, you have no chance to have a seat at the table on the senior leadership team. And, of course, great HR leaders have to be able to kick back and have fun. There are many difficult and serious issues we deal with on a daily basis. A positive outlook and the ability to lighten up on a regular basis are essential.[14]

ex 16.2 Position Description and Candidate Specifications

Position:	Vice President, Human Resources
Company:	Nationwide Clothing Retailer
Location:	Midwestern United States
Reports to:	President and CEO

Company

Is an exciting, high growth, publicly held specialty retailer of quality casual, classic American sportswear that appeals to customers of all ages yet specifically targets people in their 20s. As the "keeper of the culture," the ideal candidate must strongly embody and reinforce the unique brand image, which is casual, classic, and all-American.

Given the Company's distinctive culture and strong brand image, the Human Resource Department is critical to the continued success of the Company. The ideal candidate will bring a fresh and creative approach to the Human Resource Department to further the brand position through the recruitment, training, and motivation of all employees. The candidate must also be nonpolitical and able to diplomatically voice his/her opinions while operating in a team-oriented environment.

Ideal Candidate Specifications

- Build upon a premier recruiting program that reflects energy, vitality and a team-oriented atmosphere.
- Establish a process to identify and recruit the very best brand representatives (sales associates) to assure an ongoing flow of future talent for the business.
- Institute a program of design training and establish a reputation in programs that assures that the Company becomes the number one choice of design graduates from the best schools in the country.

Professional Characteristics

- Has built a strong career with either a "best of class" consumer or technology company that places a premium on attracting top talent or a premier organizational consulting firm that has a strong human resource focus.
- Quickly understands the critical organizational structure and the unique culture to assure the future growth of the business and its supporting mechanisms, i.e., recruiting, training, and succession planning and other key human resource aspects to accomplish this objective.
- Successfully tailors a new compensation program that reflects shareholder value, corporate profitability and individual unit/group objectives.
- Able to partner with top management to bring a critical human resources perspective that complements the strategic, merchandising, business, and financial acumen of the Company.

Personal Characteristics

- Has a passion for the Company's distinctive and powerful lifestyle brand.
- Has a "sixth sense" which allows the candidate to grasp the inherent uniqueness of the Company's brand image and identify those same great qualities in prospective employees at all levels of the organization.
- Thrives in a team-oriented and creative atmosphere, yet also has the ability to bring a tough perspective to top management in human resources and other business issues.
- Takes a creative approach as a leader and partner with the Company's top management team.

Education. To be a true professional with expert knowledge about the full range of HR activities virtually requires obtaining an advanced degree in the subject and working full time in the field. Many aspects of managing human resources have become incredibly complicated because of their close connection to strategic, legal, and financial matters. In this book, we have just begun to lay out the many issues involved in managing human resources. For each topic to which we devoted a single chapter, an entire textbook is required to provide the level of detailed explanation that is needed by someone who wishes to claim expertise in the area.

Business Experience. In addition to understanding the full range of technical issues, an HR leader spends a significant amount of time helping line managers solve problems. To be effective here, it is not enough for senior HR managers to have worked in different areas of the HR function; they also need some line experience to gain first-hand familiarity with the business operations.[15] Line experience gives the HR leader an understanding of the needs of the business and the needs of the department's customers. To prepare potential HR leaders, the HR department's staff should rotate through various line positions over several years. Short of actually serving as a line manager, HR professionals can prepare for the HR leader role by serving as special assistants to line managers or heading up a special task force for a companywide project. In other words, the development of an HR leader involves the same types of career planning and attention to career management as is required for any other type of organizational leader (see Chapter 9).

Competencies. To effectively play the roles described in Exhibit 16.1, the HR leader in a highly competitive environment needs the following competencies and knowledge:

Strategic Management Competencies
- Industry and environment knowledge
- Company understanding
- Financial understanding
- Global perspective/knowledge
- Strategic visioning
- Triad orientation
- Multiple stakeholder sensitivity
- E-business orientation and thinking

Leadership, Managerial, and Innovation Competencies
- Strategic analysis
- Diversity management
- Problem solving
- Ability to create learning culture
- Decision making
- Planning skills
- Adaptability
- Resource allocation
- Value-shaping skills

Change and Knowledge Management Competencies
- Consulting and communicating
- Group process facilitation
- Organization diagnosis
- Partnering and relationship building
- Designing and monitoring planned change efforts
- Assessing impact
- Managing learning transfer
- Negotiating

Professional and Technical Competencies
- Organization and job design
- Workforce planning, staffing, and workflow management

> *"We do have a fair amount of interchange, especially at the entry level between manufacturing operations and HR. We see HR as an integral part of the technical and manufacturing operation. We feel the same about financial and engineering."*
>
> Mike Cowhing
> Senior VP, Manufacturing and Technical Operations
> Gillette

> *"The model I use in leadership is to try to paint a picture. I try to get people to think about what things could look like, so they can visualize it, too."*
>
> Janet M. Brady
> Vice President Human Resources
> The Clorox Co.

- Performance management
- Education/training/development
- Compensation/reward/recognition systems
- Employee communications and involvement
- Succession planning
- Employee and labor relations
- Safety/health/wellness
- Diversity management
- Technological awareness
- Strong personal and professional ethics

Some firms are now adopting procedures to identify competencies for their HR staff. At Weyerhaeuser, each major division, led by its human resources director, is responsible for developing a list of specific, required competencies. The HR directors generate a slate of competencies based on their interviews with the "customers" in the organization, other HR professionals, and their own requirements. The corporation is also aiming to predict future HR issues as a basis for developing future competency requirements for HR staff. The senior HR professionals at Deutsche Bank (DB) went through a similar process. In their efforts to help DB become more globally competitive, the members of the HR department realized they needed to develop new competencies as described in the feature "Managing Change: The New HR Roles at Deutsche Bank."[16]

The systematic preparation of a job description that captures all the required competencies helps firms like Weyerhaeuser and Deutsche Bank that want to select and develop their HR leaders from outside the organization.

The Human Resource Staff

As the HR department and HR leader begin to play many of the roles listed in Exhibit 16.1, staff members must adapt accordingly. After all, the leader is playing these roles because of the need to form a better link to the business, to be more effective, and to establish a partnership with the employees and the line managers. Although they may not play the same roles to the same depth as their leader, the staff members need to know the business, facilitate change, be conscious of costs and benefits, and work with line managers (although this is probably more true for the generalist than for the specialist). The HR staff is active at the operational level and the managerial level, whereas most of the leader's time is spent at the strategic level and some at the managerial level.

In effective organizations, managers like the HR staff to work closely with them in solving people-related business challenges. Although line managers may best understand their own people, many appreciate the more distant perspective of HR staff in handling problems. As the HR staff actively builds working relationships with line management, the managers will find it easier to work with them as partners.

HR specialists and HR generalists are types of staff positions typically found in larger organizations. **Human resource specialists** typically focus on one aspect of HR practice. They can pursue their fields of specialization within a company or sell their expertise to organizations as consultants. Areas of specialization include recruitment and selection; training and development; managing organization change; performance management; benefits and services;

The New HR Roles at Deutsche Bank

Deutsche Bank (DB) has more than 90,000 employees organized into five globally operating business divisions and a corporate center. Although successful by traditional standards, in 1999, after successfully acquiring and integrating Bankers Trust, it was faced with a new reality: If it didn't change rather dramatically, it would soon lose its position in the industry. The new reality was being created by events such as disintermediation, deconstruction, deregulation, and e-business. All of these events were making traditional business models obsolete.

In order to help DB deal with the changes needed for success in the new business environment, the HR professionals recognized that they would have to become strategic partners—linked to the business and to the line managers who had to execute new business models and strategies. The HR department identified the major aspects of the environment facing DB and started a global transformation program for 1,600 HR professionals. The program was designed to create an HR department that could respond more strategically and more capably to the rest of the bank's management and employees.

The global transformation had four parts: strategy, structure, management, and competency. These parts recognized that for the bank to succeed it needed to have great human resources. So the HR department had to link its activities with the needs of the business. To do so effectively, it had to change its structure and it had to manage itself like a business unit. Critical to these changes in the HR department were the changes in the roles and competencies of the HR professionals. In essence, the 1,600 HR professionals realized they had to play all the roles shown in Exhibit 16.1 and they needed to develop the competencies to play them as well as possible. Together with HR consultants, the senior HR leaders developed a learning program. Taught at Deutsche Bank University, the learning program helps HR professionals obtain the competencies they need in their new roles. As of 2002, the program is successful, even though the business environment remains very challenging!

MANAGING CHANGE

health and safety; international HRM; and industrial relations. **Human resource generalists** have broad knowledge and experience. They may be responsible for serving all of the human resource management needs of a business unit or small organization. Usually, generalists are needed for higher-level positions within an HR department. They also serve on companywide task forces for special issues such as downsizing or capital improvement projects. Finally, as U.S. organizations become more global, opportunities for careers in international HR management will increase.[17] Most U.S. firms see growth coming from abroad, so having overseas assignments may be a typical part of any manager's career.

Human Resource Generalists. Line management positions are one source for human resource generalists. HR generalists come from a variety of backgrounds: some are career HR professionals with specialized degrees in human resource management, industrial relations, general business, or psychology; some are former line managers who have switched fields; and some are line managers who are on a required tour of duty. As the value of human resources is more widely recognized by organizations, required tours of duty by line managers will become more frequent. A brief tour by a line manager in an HR staff position conveys the knowledge, language, needs, and requirements of the line in a particularly relevant way. As a result, the HR department can more effectively fill its roles.

Human Resource Specialists. Human resource specialists should have skills related to a particular specialty, an awareness of the relationship of that specialty to other HR activities, and knowledge of where the specialized activity fits in the organization. Since specialists may work at almost any human resource activity, qualified applicants can come from specialized programs in law, organizational and industrial psychology, labor and industrial relations, HR management, counseling, organizational development, and medical and health science. In addition, specialists are needed in the areas of total quality management, Web creation and Internet management, service technologies, and information systems. With such rapid changes occurring in hardware and software technologies, the HR information systems manager is a particularly important HR specialist.

Typically, when organizations create an HRIM system, they use a specialist to manage the area. Over the years, the role of this leader has changed from that of a project manager to that of a systems manager and now to that of a strategic change partner. An emerging trend is to see the specialist who manages the HRIM system as playing a strategic rather than technical role. This new role asks the HRIM manager to be concerned not with how efficiently the department can store and retrieve information but with how the HRIM manager can be a strategic partner and manage organizational change.[18]

The role changes for the HRIM manager have paralleled those for the HR manager. Not surprisingly, they have also produced the same need for new competencies. Today's HRIM manager must be aware of the global environment and of the organization's approach to balancing globalization with local sensitivity and responsiveness. An HRIM system can enable managers worldwide to tap into a database giving information about candidates to run an operation in a distant country, without their even knowing the candidates. The availability of such powerful technology means it is essential that line managers understand issues of information privacy and security.[19]

The names of employees, where they work, and what they do can be valuable information to other companies, especially competitors. Such information can be used to plan recruiting efforts to lure these people from their current employment. Organizations that value openness and access to information are especially vulnerable to this threat.[20] Yet, if companies are to empower people, they often need to be open and allow access to information. Tandem Computers in Cupertino, California, handles this concern by

- creating an awareness among managers and employees that others could gain access to company information and data;
- tightening telephone security so that callers need to identify themselves and respond to the right screening questions;
- weeding out bogus job candidates—that is, those who are only going through the motions in order to gain access to information;
- adding more restrictions in confidentiality agreements; for example, when individuals join the firm, they can be asked to sign agreements not to reveal company secrets to others at any time, even if they leave; and
- classifying information and restricting access using a need-to-know basis.

Not only can these programs limit the leakage of corporate information but they also can prevent unauthorized people from obtaining personal information about individual employees—not a trivial concern in today's atmosphere of rising employee violence and credit card scams.

Some say that restricting the type and amount of information collected reduces the potential for invasion of privacy. This solution has to be balanced against the HR department's need for information for its various

---

FAST FACT

The HR reengineering effort at Texas Instruments' was a total redesign of its HR systems. It now has a distributed, decentralized system, rather than a mainframe system, throughout its global operations.

"When corporate spies want confidential information, they often infiltrate HR departments first. A well-structured information-security program can keep spies from obtaining your company's secrets."

Marc Tanzer
President of an information security firm
Portland, Maine

programs. Family-friendly activities such as drug and alcohol abuse programs cannot take place without a sound database. Nor can an organization's numerous legal obligations be fulfilled without an effective HRIM system. Striking the proper balance may be challenging, but as is true in many other endeavors, the best defense is a good offense.

Compensation of HR Staff

Human resource management is becoming very attractive as a field of employment. On average, HR salaries have been increasing between 4 and 5 percent a year, which is above the overall U.S. average. The results of a 2001 compensation survey, by types of jobs in a human resource department, show that HR jobs pay well.[21] In that survey, salaries were generally higher for individuals in larger organizations, for those with more experience, and for those with more education. In addition, salaries were higher in the South and Midwest. In other surveys, the senior HR person, sometimes called senior vice president, was the highest paid individual in the survey, earning about $201,500 on average, including salary plus cash bonus and profit sharing.

As is true for other managerial jobs, incentive pay is becoming a bigger part of the picture for top-level HR executives: about 50 percent of the corporate labor relations and industrial relations executives are eligible for long-term incentive pay and 86 percent of the corporate international HR executives. In comparison, between 15 and 44 percent of other HR managers are eligible for long-term incentive pay. Short-term incentive pay is more common: 84 percent of senior-level jobs are eligible and 55 to 79 percent of those at the HR manager level.[22]

INTERNET RESOURCES   **16.B**

Staffing the HR Department

At our Web site, http://jackson.swcollege.com/, you can:

1. Find out about compensation of HR professionals at SHRM and the Bureau of National Affairs.

2. Read about HR jobs that are available at the Society for Human Resource Management.

PROFESSIONALISM IN HUMAN RESOURCE MANAGEMENT

Like any profession, HR management follows a code of ethics and has an accreditation institute and certification procedures. Together, these provide standards for behavior that serve as useful guides to professionals.

Ethical Issues

The code of ethics for human resource management states that:

Practitioners must regard the obligation to implement public objectives and protect the public interest as more important than blind loyalty to an employer's preferences.

More specifically, in daily practice, HR professionals are expected to

- thoroughly understand the problems assigned and undertake whatever study and research are required to ensure continuing competence and the best of professional attention;

"I went through a period of really agonizing over the behavior I was seeing—things I didn't expect to encounter."

Anonymous
HR Professional

- maintain a high standard of personal honesty and integrity in every phase of daily practice;
- give thoughtful consideration to the personal interest, welfare, and dignity of all employees who are affected by their prescriptions, recommendations, and actions; and
- make sure that the organizations that represent them maintain a high regard and respect for the public interest and that they never overlook the importance of the personal interests and dignity of employees.[23]

Increasingly, HR professionals are becoming involved in ethical issues. Some of the most serious issues center around differences in the way people are treated because of favoritism or a relationship to top management. In a survey conducted by the Society for Human Resource Management (SHRM) and the Commerce Case Clearing House (CCCH), HR professionals agreed that workplace ethics requires people to be judged solely on job performance. Ethics requires managers to eliminate such things as favoritism, friendship, sex bias, race bias, or age bias from promotion and pay decisions (it is, of course, also unlawful to take sex, race, or age into account).[24]

Is ethics a "bottom line" issue? It becomes one when we consider that by acting in an ethical manner, companies will, in fact, hire, reward, and retain the best people. This will, in turn, help assure that the company has the best workforce possible to achieve its business goals.[25] By adopting a definition of workplace ethics that centers on job performance, HR professionals may be in a better position to persuade others in the organization that making ethical behavior a priority will produce beneficial results.

Not all ethical issues affect the bottom line in the way that favoritism versus employee performance does, however, and to assume that a single policy can be devised to ensure that everyone in the organization always behaves ethically is unrealistic. People with different perspectives will inevitably view some situations differently. Even when they agree about basic values, such as the right of employees to be treated fairly, they may disagree about what constitutes fairness. For example, a Catholic nurse in Erie, Pennsylvania, who was fired for refusing to hand out birth control pills and condoms felt she was unfairly terminated because of her religious beliefs, but her employer felt the nurse's behavior was unfair to patients. Such situations are common and unavoidable. Nevertheless, business ethics can be improved in a number of ways.

A good starting point for managing ethical issues is for top management to critically examine such practices as such reward systems, managerial style, and decision-making processes. In some organizations, the reward system promotes unethical behavior by encouraging the achievement of organizational goals at almost any cost. Because of HR's traditional involvement in reward systems, HR has a natural role in encouraging ethical behavior.[26] But in the spirit of partnership, encouraging ethical behavior is a responsibility of all parties—the employees, line managers, and HR professionals. A result of this partnership might be the creation of an easy-to-use hot line and dissemination of standards that offer guidance on issues of ethical behavior.

"It's comforting to know that ethical issues are out there and I'm not alone. But it's disheartening to know that they're so commonplace."

Participant
On-line ethics bulletin board

Professional Certification

The Society for Human Resource Management (SHRM) has established the Human Resource Certification Institute to certify human resource professionals. The institute's purposes are to

FAST FACT

Approximately 175,000 HR professionals are members of SHRM.

- recognize individuals who have demonstrated expertise in particular fields;
- raise and maintain professional standards;
- identify a body of knowledge as a guide to practitioners, consultants, educators, and researchers;
- help employers identify qualified applicants; and
- provide an overview of the field as a guide to self-development.

The certification institute has two levels of **accreditation**: basic (PHR) and senior (SPHR). The basic accreditation is the professional in human resources (PHR). The examinations for the PHR and SPHR focus on the same six major areas, giving different weights to each area in each examination. The six major areas and the weights given to each for the PHR and the SPHR are shown in Exhibit 16.3.

Detailed contents of each area are provided at the Institute's Web site. You will see that the contents are consistent with the materials covered in all the chapters of this textbook. The senior-level accreditation is designed for the senior professional in human resources and focuses more on the strategic/policy aspects of managing human resources.

The Human Resources Certification Institute recommends that HR professionals pursuing the SPHR designation have six to eight years of professional work experience before taking the examination, but two years is the minimum requirement.

Toward Defining Global Competencies for HR Professionals

The globalization of business is putting HR professionals from around the world in almost daily contact with each other and with line managers representing many different countries and cultures. Coinciding with this globalization of business is the globalization of the HR profession. The World Federation of Personnel Management Associations (WFPMA) links together country- and region-specific professional associations such as SHRM around the world. As a service to its members, the WFPMA investigated the question of how the work of HR professionals is similar and different around the world. Its research helped develop an understanding of global HR competencies. Another study done by Cranfield University for the Institute of Personnel Development in England found that within many countries HR competencies reflect the roles that HR professionals need to play, which are determined in part by the environment.[27]

INTERNET RESOURCES   16.C

Professionalism

At our Web site, http://jackson.swcollege.com/, you can:

1. Learn more the HR code of ethics at SHRM.

2. Learn what is required to obtain HR accreditation from HRCI.

3. Read more about the World Federation of Personnel Management Associations.

4. Find out about the professional HR societies in England and Australia.

ORGANIZING THE HUMAN RESOURCE DEPARTMENT

In traditional, bureaucratic organizations, HR professionals resided almost exclusively within a centralized functional department. As organizations

ex 16.3 Sample of the Test Areas of the PHR and SPHR Certification Examinations and Their Relative Weights

AREA	% PHR EXAM	% SPHR EXAM
Strategic Management	12%	26%

Responsibilities in Strategic Management

- Interpret information related to the organization's operations from internal sources, including financial/accounting, marketing, operations, information technology, and individual employees, in order to participate in strategic planning and policy making.
- Participate as a partner in the organization's strategic planning process.
- Provide direction and guidance during changes in organizational processes, operations, and culture that balances the expectations and needs of the organization, its employees, and other stakeholders (including customers).
- Cultivate leadership and ethical values in self and others through modeling and teaching.
- Monitor legislative environment for proposed changes in law and take appropriate action to support, modify, or stop the proposed action (for example, write to a member of Congress, provide expert testimony at a public hearing, lobby legislators).

Knowledge in Strategic Management

- Knowledge of internal and external environmental scanning techniques.
- Knowledge of strategic planning process and implementation.
- Knowledge of techniques to sustain creativity and innovation.

Workforce Planning and Employment	26%	16%

Responsibilities in Workforce Planning and Employment

- Identify staffing requirements to meet the goals and objectives of the organization.
- Conduct job analyses to write job descriptions and develop job competencies.
- Develop a succession planning process.
- Establish hiring criteria based on the competencies needed.
- Assess internal workforce, labor market, and recruitment agencies to determine the availability of qualified applicants.
- Knowledge of immigration laws (for example, visas, I-9).
- Knowledge of recruitment methods and sources.
- Knowledge of staffing alternatives (for example, telecommuting, outsourcing).
- Knowledge of planning techniques (for example, succession planning, forecasting).
- Knowledge of reliability and validity of selection tests/tools/methods.
- Knowledge of impact of compensation and benefits plans on recruitment and retention.
- Knowledge of international HR and implications of international workforce for workforce planning and employment.
- Knowledge of downsizing and outplacement.

Human Resource Development	15%	13%

Responsibilities in Human Resource Development

- Conduct needs analyses to identify and establish priorities regarding human resource development activities.
- Develop training programs.
- Implement training programs.
- Evaluate training programs.

Knowledge in Human Resource Development

- Knowledge of training methods, programs, and techniques.
- Knowledge of performance appraisal and performance management methods.

ex 16.3 Sample of the Test Areas of the PHR and SPHR Certification Examinations and Their Relative Weights (continued)

AREA	% PHR EXAM	% SPHR EXAM
Compensation and Benefits	20%	16%

Responsibilities in Compensation and Benefits

- Analyze, select, implement, maintain, and administer executive compensation, stock purchase, stock options, and incentive and bonus programs.
- Analyze, develop, implement, and maintain compensation policies and a pay structure consistent with the organization's strategic objectives.

Knowledge in Compensation and Benefits

- Knowledge of federal, state, and local compensation and benefit laws (for example, FLSA, ERISA, and COBRA).
- Knowledge of accounting practices related to compensation and benefits (for example, excess group term life, compensatory time).
- Knowledge of job evaluation methods.
- Knowledge of benefit plans (for example, health insurance, pension, education, health club).
- Knowledge of international compensation laws and practices (for example, expatriate compensation, socialized medicine, mandated retirement).
- Knowledge of job pricing and pay structure.
- Knowledge of incentive and variable pay methods.

Employee and Labor Relations	21%	24%

Responsibilities for Employee and Labor Relations

- Promote, monitor, and measure the effectiveness of employee relations activities.
- Assist in establishing work rules and monitor their application and enforcement to ensure fairness and consistency (for union and nonunion environments).
- Develop grievance and disciplinary policies and procedures to ensure fairness and consistency.

Knowledge in Employee and Labor Relations

- Knowledge of applicable federal, state, and local laws affecting employment in union and nonunion environments, such as antidiscrimination laws, sexual harassment, labor relations, and privacy.
- Knowledge of individual employment rights issues and practices (for example, employment-at-will, negligent hiring, defamation, employees' rights to bargain collectively).

Occupational Health, Safety, and Security	6%	5%

Responsibilities in Occupational Health, Safety, and Security

- Ensure compliance with all applicable federal, state, and local workplace health and safety laws and regulations.
- Implement injury/occupational illness prevention program.
- Implement workplace injury/occupational illness procedures (for example, workers' compensation, OSHA).

Knowledge in Occupational Health, Safety, and Security

- Knowledge of potential violent behavior and workplace violence condition.
- Knowledge of workplace injury and occupational illness compensation laws and programs (for example, workers' compensation).
- Knowledge of employee assistance programs.

have restructured into a variety of newer forms, however, they have often reevaluated this approach. As is true for many support functions, much experimentation is currently going on to find the most effective way to organize the HR function.[28] When considering new organizational forms, one needs to address two major questions:

1. Where are the HR decisions made?
2. What level of investment will the company make?

The first question has to do with the advantages and disadvantages of centralized and decentralized organizations. The second question has to do with budgets and compensation.

Centralization versus Decentralization

Centralization means structuring the organization so that essential decision making and policy formulation are conducted at one location (at headquarters); **decentralization** means that essential decision making and policy formulation are conducted at several locations (in various divisions or departments of the organization).

Alternatives. Organization of HR departments differs widely from one company to another not only because of the differing requirements of various industries but also because of differing philosophies, cultures, and strategic plans of individual organizations. Compare the centralized structure of Merck with the decentralized structure of TRW. At Merck, large, specialized corporate staffs formulate and design human resource strategies and activities, which are then communicated to the small HR staffs of operating units for implementation. High levels of consistency and congruence with corporate goals are thus attained. At TRW, small corporate staffs manage HR systems only for executives and act as advisers only to operating units. This organization tends to operate with a wider divergence in practices and a greater flexibility in addressing local concerns.[29]

The organizational structures used by Merck and TRW are very appropriate for their respective types of businesses. TRW, a high-technology company with a diverse array of businesses, cannot use the consistent, stable approach to HR that Merck, with a more singular product focus, is able to employ.[30]

Trends. Because of today's rapidly changing and highly competitive business environment, the trend seems to be toward greater decentralization. This entails a greater delegation of responsibilities to lower HR levels and to the operating units and line managers themselves. Along with this is a trend toward less formalization of policies—that is, fewer rules that are seen as bureaucratic hurdles. Human resource departments and their organizations thus have greater flexibility to cope with the continually changing environment. Diminished bureaucratization can also lead to a greater openness in approaches to problems. On the other hand, it tends to reduce the consistency of HR practices found throughout an organization. When HR practices vary dramatically across different units within an organization, it may become more difficult to maintain a common corporate culture. To address this concern, decentralized organizations generally strive to develop broad policy statements that state basic principles to be followed by everyone and then allow local units to develop practices that fit their specific contexts.

Controlling Costs

The amount of money that organizations allocate to their HR departments generally rises yearly. In 2000, the median budget allocated to the human resource department for each employee was $787. Not surprisingly, department expenditures per employee decrease steadily with company size. For all firms, the median ratio of HR department staff members to workers in 2000 was 1.0 to 100. Among firms with fewer than 250 employees, the median ratio was 1.3 staff for every 100 workers, and among companies with 250 to 499 employees it was 1.0 for every 100 employees. The ratio was substantially lower in organizations with 500 to 999 employees, at 0.9 for every 100 workers, .6 for organizations of 1,000 to 2,499 employees, and lowest among employers with 2,500 or more workers, at 0.5 for every 100 employees.[31]

Information Technology. As we have described throughout this book, using information technology is one approach to controlling costs associated with administering HR policies and practices. On-line recruiting, for example, greatly speeds up the process of filling positions while reducing paperwork and the time needed to conduct basic screening of candidates. For large organizations, the cost of developing electronic training materials may be justified by the savings associated with individualized e-training at the job site. In benefits and services, information technology makes it possible for employees to access personal information directly and even enter new information into their files. In these and other ways, information technology can reduce administrative costs and free up HR staff members for other more strategic activities.

Shared Services. Larger organizations generally have been able to spend less per employee because they have taken advantage of the efficiencies associated with standardized policies and practices. As organizations attempt to decentralize their HR function, many find that their administrative costs begin to increase. In order to keep administrative costs under control, some organizations have adopted a structure that includes **shared services**. Like a traditional functional department, a shared services unit provides service to units throughout the entire organization. But a major difference is that costs associated with shared services usually are allocated to the specific units that use the services.

Service Centers. One approach to shared services is to create **service centers** that handle transaction-based activities such as processing medical claims, answering questions related to retirement planning, and handling tuition reimbursement programs. Within the company they are also referred to as self-service and call centers. Such transactions can be efficiently carried out by one unit for the entire firm, often over the telephone or on-line. IBM's Human Resources Service Center (HRSC) for its North American operations is located in Raleigh, North Carolina. Its mission is to be the "premier centralized service channel for the competitive delivery and administration of HR policies, programs, processes, applications, and database management in support of IBM's quest for industry leadership." The HRSC's 400 employees serve more than 700,000 current and former employees, handling more than 7 million transactions annually via the phone, e-mail, and the Service Center's intranet site. Among the many

> **FAST FACT**
>
> AT&T created an Employee Services intranet where employees have access to important training, benefits, pension, and payroll information.

activities handled by the service center are payroll transactions, benefits management and problem solving, the design and management of a self-service HR Web site, establishment of affirmative action plans, OFCCP compliance reviews, processing of job applications, and the dissemination and analysis of employee surveys. IBM's HRSC is considered to be among the best in the world, serving as a benchmark target for other firms. Established in 1995, it has continually evolved over time—leveraging new technologies, adding new services, and at the same time reducing costs.

Centers of Excellence. An alternative way to reduce costs within a decentralized structure is through the use of **centers of excellence**. A center of excellence typically houses a variety of HR specialists who have in-depth expertise in activities that are of significant value to the firm. Such activities include recruitment and selection, compensation, job redesign, reengineering, organizational change, and measuring organizational effectiveness. These specialists essentially work as internal consultants, providing service only to the units that request (and are willing to pay for) them.[32] Like shared services, the objective behind organizing HR activities into centers of excellence is to improve efficiency while also allowing for flexibility and decentralization of HR practices. In 1999, AT&T reorganized its HR function from a highly decentralized model to a new structure that utilizes both shared services and centers of excellence.

According to William M. Mercer, an HR consulting firm, changes such as those under way at IBM and AT&T reflect the newly emerging HR organizational model. "The traditional design typically includes a vice president of HR, then a manager of benefits and compensation, a manager of HR information systems and payroll, a manager of employment, and so on," explained associate David Hilborn. "However, the emerging model is more like a three-legged stool." One leg is a service center focused on efficiently performing administrative tasks. A second leg is a center of excellence that focuses on designing the most effective approaches to HR, given the organization's needs. The services provided by these two legs are shared throughout the company. The third leg houses the HR generalists who report directly to line managers within the businesses. They focus on creating strategic fit at the business unit level and report secondarily to HR. Seated at the top of this three-legged stool is the HR leadership team. They're responsible for coordinating these various activities and ensuring that pressures for centralization and cost reduction are balanced appropriately with the need for flexibility and change.[33]

Reengineering and Outsourcing

Reengineering the HR department basically means reconsidering what the department is doing to see whether it can do it better and more effectively.[34] Customerization is consistent with this process because it asks, "What are we doing for our customers, what do they want, and how can we fill in the gaps between what they get and what they want?" But reengineering goes much further. It seeks to examine all the parts of the department, asking, "What is the purpose of this group, what does it do and how does it do it, and can it improve the way it does things? The reengineering process should identify what counts, what adds value, and what can best be done by someone else—particularly a consulting firm that specializes in supplying HR activities, such as pension plan administration.

"The optimist says the glass is half full, the pessimist says the glass is half empty, the re-engineer says the glass is too big."

Michael Hammer
Coauthor
Re-engineering the Corporation

Reengineering may lead to a decision to outsource some HR activities.[35] Novell, like many other companies, decided that some of its responsibilities were better left to outside vendors. According to Theresa Dadone, director of compensation and benefits for Novell:

It wasn't long ago that employees had to come to HR and request a loan from their 401(k) plan. They had to talk to an HR person and fill out papers. A committee then had to review the request and decide whether or not to grant the loan. Well, that's not in keeping with customer service. That's treating our employees like children. So, we outsourced that responsibility to an HR consulting firm. There's now a toll-free number for employees to call so they don't have to involve HR in their personal finances. We're out of the loop . . . that isn't where our value is. Our value is in helping employees understand the plan.

Educational assistance is another responsibility that's been outsourced. Employees used to have to come to HR and request approval of a course and receive reimbursement. Today, an HR consulting firm takes care of it. Employees don't have to come begging to HR, hat in hand, to process something. We now spend our time helping employees understand the benefits of educational assistance and how it can serve them in their personal and professional lives.[36]

During the 1990s, many firms began **outsourcing** a variety of staff functions, including HR. Forecasters predict that as many as 40 percent of firms will outsource all or part of the HR department by the year 2003. The logic underlying this trend is that outside vendors, who might serve dozens of organizations, should be more efficient. Consequently, the cost per employee for their services should be lower. But after a few years of experience, many companies have discovered that outsourcing often results in higher costs.[37] At the same time, service levels from outside vendors often don't match the level formerly provided by the company's own staff. Like all other decisions regarding how to manage human resources, organizations can avoid some of the disappointments associated with outsourcing by treating outsourcing as a key strategic move. Exhibit 16.4, entitled "Avoiding Common Outsourcing Pitfalls," summarizes several challenges that must be met in order to reap the potential benefits of outsourcing.[38]

"About 25 percent of the people who've outsourced [HR activities] that we've talked to this year indicate they've experienced disappointment."

Jack Walsh
Consulting Practice Leader
The Segal Company

Globalization

The 1990s and 2000s have seen dramatic changes in international trade and business. Once-safe markets are now fierce battlegrounds where firms aggressively fight for their share against both foreign and domestic competitors. It is, therefore, not surprising to find that in an increasing number of firms, a large proportion of the workforce is located in other countries.

When it comes to operating in a global context, most organizations and most HR professionals are at an early stage of learning. Globalization is forcing managers to grapple with complex issues as they seek to gain or sustain a competitive advantage. Faced with unprecedented levels of foreign competition at home and abroad, operating an international business is high on the list of priorities for top management. So are finding and nurturing the human resources required to implement an international or global strategy.

ex 16.4 Avoiding Common Outsourcing Pitfalls

Common Mistakes	Recommended Solutions
• Begin outsourcing as a tactical solution to an immediate problem. • Fail to anticipate resistance to change.	• Adopt a strategic perspective. Consider what HR should be like 5 or 10 years from now. • Recognize that outsourcing is a form of major organization change and must be managed accordingly.
• Do not measure, or ignore, current costs *and* service levels. • Fail to fully design and specify the "ideal" service delivery model to be achieved. • Do not learn about the outsourcing market in advance. • Choose a vendor that doesn't perform satisfactorily.	• Document current costs and service levels for use in future evaluations of outsourcing effectiveness. • Specify the roles and relationships of all partners involved *before* evaluating and contracting with specific vendors. • Thoroughly research alternative vendors. Understand their differences in business philosophies, technologies, and long-term plans. • Using a cross-functional team, develop a vendor selection model that includes specific, objective criteria that have been prioritized according to their importance. At the same time, develop performance indicators and a process for evaluating subsequent vendor performance. Then, repeat the competitive bidding process every 3 to 5 years.
• Mismanage the contract negotiation, which can be costly, cause delays, and damage relationships. • Underestimate the time and resources required for implementation.	• Use experienced negotiators. Be sure that at least one member of the selection design team is involved in the vendor negotiations. • Establish an implementation team to develop a project plan that includes a clear statement of goals, roles and responsibilities, realistic time lines, and target milestones.
• Underestimate the need for frequent communications with the vendor and for vendor management. • Do not anticipate failure.	• Identify someone to be responsible for vendor management and clearly specify that person's roles and activities. • Consider what can go wrong, identify warning symptoms to watch for, and develop contingency plans.

HR professionals play a critical role in the globalization process by helping companies evaluate the human resource prospects and possibilities involved in moving to different regions of the world. The HR department of Novell helped its senior management decide to establish a technical center in Australia. According to Tim Harris, Novell's former HR head:

We were debating between establishing the center in Australia or Singapore. We had to evaluate local employment laws, the cost and availability of housing and what it would cost to recruit and relocate the multilingual employees needed to staff the center. We also researched tax issues, the competitive salary structure, medical facilities and the healthcare system. There's a myriad of decisions in which HR must participate to go back to the business unit and say: "This is what you should do, this is what it will cost, and this is how long it will take to get the new business or division up and running."[39]

The complexities of operating in different countries with different cultures, religions, and laws, and of employing people of different nationalities, are the main issues that differentiate domestic and international HR management. Many companies underestimate these complexities, and some evidence suggests that business failures in the international arena often are due to ineffective or inappropriate human resource management practices.

The primary causes of failure in multinational ventures stem from a lack of understanding of the essential differences in managing human resources, at all levels, in foreign environments. Certain management philosophies and techniques have proved successful in the domestic environment, yet their application in a foreign environment too often leads to frustration, failure, and underachievement. These "human" considerations are as important as the financial and marketing criteria upon which so many decisions to undertake multinational ventures depend.[40]

Increasingly, domestic HR is taking on an international flavor as the workforce becomes more and more diverse. Despite the merging of domestic and international concerns, several issues differentiate international HR from domestic HR. In the future, more and more HR professionals will find that being effective in an international HR work setting is required for success in their profession. A consideration of how international and domestic HR differ today provides a glimpse of the future.[41]

> **FAST FACT**
>
> Helping expatriate families adjust to a new culture helps make the expatriate employees more successful.

More Functions and Activities. To operate in an international environment, the HR department must engage in a number of activities that would not be necessary in a domestic environment: international taxation, international relocation and orientation, administrative services for expatriates, host-government relations, and language translation services.

Broader Perspective. Domestic managers generally administer programs for a single national group of employees who are covered by a uniform compensation policy and who are taxed by one government. International managers face the problem of designing and administering programs for more than one national group of employees, and they must therefore take a more global view of issues.

More Involvement in Employees' Lives. A greater degree of involvement in employees' personal lives is necessary for the selection, training, and effective management of expatriate employees. The international HR department needs to ensure that the expatriate employee understands housing arrangements, health care, and all aspects of the compensation package provided for the assignment.

More Risk Exposure. Frequently, the human and financial consequences of failure are more severe in the international arena than in domestic business. For example, expatriate failure (the premature return of an expatriate from an international assignment) is a persistent, high-cost problem for international companies. Another aspect of risk exposure that is relevant to international HR is terrorism. Major multinational companies must now routinely consider this element when planning international meetings and assignments.

More External Influences. Other forces that influence the international arena are the type of host government, the state of its economy, and business practices that may differ substantially from those of the originating country. A host government can, for example, dictate hiring procedures or insist on a company providing training to local workers. Local cultural and religious practices may make it necessary to modify the company's local approach to managing human resource practices.

INTERNET RESOURCES   16.D

Organizing the Department

At our Web site, http://jackson.swcollege.com/, you can:

1. Learn about HR at some of the firms discussed in this section by visiting their company home pages.

   Bank of America

   Merck

   TRW

   IBM

2. Find out about outsourcing at the Outsourcing Institute.

SUMMARY

Because of the increasing complexity of managing human resources, nearly all mid- to large-size companies employ human resource professionals—as full-time employees, as vendors with long-term contracts, or as consultants who work on short-term projects. The ways organizations allocate responsibility for HR activities are many. They vary from firm to firm, and even over time within the same firm. Regardless of how HR activities are structured, however, companies that value their human resources seek professionals who effectively perform across several roles: strategic management, enabler and consultant, monitoring and maintaining, innovator, and change and knowledge management. In these roles, HR professionals help organizations serve many stakeholders. In doing so, they demonstrate their own value to the organization.

Going forward, human resource professionals will increasingly be called upon to perform their roles in a global context. Globalization adds additional challenges for the HR profession and it may ultimately reshape the professional's role. Regardless of how the roles of HR professionals shift, however, getting everyone involved in human resource management will continue to be essential. Employees, line managers, and HR professionals need to work together in order for organizations to manage human resources effectively.

TERMS TO REMEMBER

accreditation   human resource generalists
centers of excellence   human resource specialists
centralization   outsourcing
code of ethics   service centers
customerization   shared services
decentralization

DISCUSSION QUESTIONS

1. How does Cisco link its HR activities to the needs of the business?
2. Is the HR profession essential to the success of organizations? Explain your opinion.

3. How do the roles of the HR leader and the HR staff differ?
4. Why are some human resource management departments centralized and others decentralized?
5. Is outsourcing of HR activities likely to increase or decrease during the next 10 years? Explain your opinion.
6. How is the role of HR professionals likely to change as organizations move toward globalization?

PROJECTS TO EXTEND YOUR LEARNING

1. *Managing Through Strategic Partnerships.* Your company would like you to link the way it manages its people more closely with the needs of the business, as Southwest Airlines and Lincoln Electric do. They want you to be as thorough as possible. As far as you know, when the strategy of the company was formulated two years, the human resource department was not involved. Consequently, you may wish to start with an understanding of the strategy of the firm and work through the implications for human resource management. Your company is a relatively new one and is based on the concept that some people would rather take the bus than the train or plane, but bus service just isn't fun, nor very efficient. You strongly believe that your company, Funways, definitely can do a better job of linking the people with the needs of the business and serve the needs of the customers. You can't do everything at once, but to start, outline the types of behaviors the company needs from most of its employees and then identify what human resource practices would help attain these behaviors. First you may want to read the next project on **Managing Teams**.

2. *Managing Teams.* You know the value of teams and the importance of partnership in human resource management. In order to identify the behaviors needed by the employees of Funways to successfully implement the company's strategy and serve the customers, you decide to form a team. This team might also be used to help you gain a much better understanding of the company's strategy and what human resource management practices would be acceptable to the company. So with this team you will fulfill the needs of the first exercise, **Managing Through Strategic Partnerships**. Accordingly, identify the members of the team and describe how they would work together. What incentives would you give them to be members of the team? How would you motivate them to do a great job?

3. *Integration and Application.* After reviewing the cases at the end of the text, describe the following for each company (Lincoln Electric and Southwest Airlines):
    a. the degree of partnership in managing human resources,
    b. the role/importance of the HR department,
    c. the value that the company places on its people, and
    d. the competencies of the human resource professionals.

ENDNOTES

1 L. Grensing-Pophal, "What's Your HR Creed?" *HR Magazine* (June 2001): 145–153; C. Hirschman, "For PEOs, Business is Booming," *HR Magazine* (February 2000): 43-48; B. Leonard, "Ready to Soar," *HR Magazine* (January 2001): 52–56; A. Kupfer, "Cisco Systems," *Fortune* (Sep- tember 7, 1998): 85–94; P. Nakache, "Cisco's Recruiting Edge," *Fortune* (September 29, 1997): 275–276; J. A. Byrne, "The Corporation of the Future," *Business Week* (August 31, 1998): 102–106; C. M. Solomon, " Corporate Pioneers Navigate Global Mergers," *Global Workforce* (Sep-

tember 1998): 12–17; "HR Has Role in Mergers," *Bulletin to Management* (August 13, 1998): 256; R. E. Numerof and M. N. Abrams, "Integrating Corporate Culture from International M&As," *HR Focus* (June 1998): 11–12.

2 R. S. Schuler and I. C. MacMillan, "Gaining Competitive Advantage Through Human Resource Management Practices," *Human Resource Management* 23 (1994): 241–255.

3 C. R. Greer, S. A. Youngblood, and D. Gray, "Human Resource Management Outsourcing: The Make or Buy Decision," *Academy of Management Executive* 13(3) (1999): 85–96; M. F. Cook, *Outsourcing Human Resources Functions* (New York: AMACOM, 1999).

4 L. Bossidy, "The Job No CEO Should Delegate," *Harvard Business Review* (March 2001): 47–49; C. Joinson, "The Best of Both Worlds," *HR Magazine* (September 1999): 50–58; C. Joinson, "Changing Shapes," *HR Magazine* (March 1999): 41–47; *Bulletin to Management* (Washington, DC: Bureau of National Affairs, Inc., 1999); *Bulletin to Management* 51(26) Part 2 (Washington, DC: Bureau of National Affairs, June 29, 2000); S. Caudron, "HR Leaders Brainstorm," *Personnel Journal* (August 1994): 53–62.

5 L. Davidson, "Survey Results Show HR's Progress," *Workforce* (August 1999): 68–74; J. J. Laabs, "Painting a Vivid Picture of HR," *Workforce* (October 1998): 26-30.

6 M. Kirk, "Source of Strength," *Human Resource Executive* (June 16, 2000): 102–106; P. W. Wright, L. Dyer, and M. Takala, *Execution: The Critical "What's Next?" in Strategic Human Resource Management* (Ithaca, NY: Cornell University, 1999).

7 B. Calandra, "Razor Sharp," *Human Resource Executive* (June 4, 1999): 1, 5, 6; L. Broedling, "Applying a Systems Approach to Human Resource Management," *Human Resource Management* 38(3) (Fall 1999): 269–278.

8 J. J. Laabs, "Thinking Outside the Box at the Container Store," *Workforce* (March 2001): 34; C. Artis, B. E. Becker, and M. A. Huselid, "Strategic Human Resource Management at Lucent," *Human Resource Management* 38(4) (Winter 1999): 309–313.

9 R. S. Schuler, S. E. Jackson, and J. Storey, "HRM and Its Link with Strategic Management," *Human Resource Management: A Critical Text*, 2d ed. (London: ITL, 2001); R. S. Schuler and S. E. Jackson, *Strategic Human Resource Management* (London: Blackwell, 1999).

10 M. Lengnick-Hall and C. Lengnick-Hall, "Expanding Customer Orientation in the HR Function," *Human Resource Management* 38(3) (Fall 1999): 201–214; M. Voves, "Blazing the HR Trail Alone," *Personnel Journal* (December 1996): 39–45; "Customers for Keeps: Training Strategies," *Bulletin to Management* (March 31, 1988): 8.

11 B. Leonard, "Straight Talk," *HR Magazine* (January 2002): 46–51; W. Brockbank, "If HR Were Really Strategically Proactive: Present and Future Directions in HR's Contribution to Competitive Advantage," *Human Resource Management* 38(4) (Winter 1999): 337–352; J. Dysart, "Powering a Systems Overhaul," *HR Magazine* (July 2000): 121–128; J. J. Laabs, "Why HR Can't Win Today," *Workforce* (May 1998): 62–74; S. Caudron, "Team Staffing Requires New HR Role," *Personnel Journal* (May 1994): 88–94; E. E. Lawler III and J. R. Galbraith, "Staff Organizations: New Directions," *Organizing for the Future: New Approaches to Managing Complex Organizations* (San Francisco: Jossey-Bass, 1995).

12 T. M. Welbourne and L. Cyr, "The Human Resource Executive Effects in Initial Public Offering Firms," *Academy of Management Journal* 42(6) (1999): 616–629; D. Anfuso, "Core Values Shape W. L. Gore's Innovative Culture," *Workforce* (March 1999): 48–53.

13 B. Acosta, "A Portal to Online," *Workspan* (February 2001): 16–19; based on N. D. Johnson, "Positioning Your HR Organization to Become a Strategic Business Partner," *ACA News* (March 1998) 20–23; D. Ulrich, M. Losey, and G. Lake (eds.), *Tomorrow's HR Management: 48 Thought Leaders Call for Change* (New York: Wiley, 1997).

14 N. Wong, "Let Spirit Guide Leadership," *Workforce* (February 2000): 33–36; J. Wiscombe, "Your Wonderful, Terrible HR Life," *Workforce* (June 2001): 32–38.

15 "How to Make HR a Profit Center," *Workforce* (February 2001):

14–18; E. E. Lawler, III, and S. A. Mohrman, "Beyond the Vision: What Makes HR Effective?" *Human Resource Planning* 23(4) (2000): 10–20; C. Solomon, "Putting HR on the Score Card," *Workforce* (March 2000): 94–98; B. E. Becker, M. A. Huselid, and D. Ulrich, *The HR Scorecard: Linking People, Strategy, and Performance* (Boston: Harvard Business School Press, 2001); M. A. Huselid, S. E. Jackson, and R. S. Schuler, "Technical and Strategic Human Resource Management Effectiveness as Determinants of Firm Performance," *Academy of Management Journal* 40 (1997): 171–188; L. Davidson, "Measure What You Bring to the Bottom Line," *Workforce* (September 1998): 34–40.

16 M. Svoboda and S. Schroder, "Transforming Human Resources in the New Economy: Developing the Next Generation of Global HR Managers at Deutsche Bank," *Human Resource Management* (Fall 2001): 261–273.

17 N. Wong, "Mark Your Calendar! Important Tasks for International HR," *Workforce* (April 2000): 72–74; J. Fitz-enz, "Proven Change," *Workforce* (May 2000): 82–89; L. Grensing-Pophal, "Flying Solo," *HR Magazine* (August 1999): 34–40; L. Grensing-Pophal, "Getting to the Top: Advice from Those Who've Made It," *HR Magazine* (December 2000): 96-102; H. Lancaster, "Mike Bowlin Started His Path to Arco CEO from a Personnel Job," *Wall Street Journal* (September 3, 1996): B1.

18 K. Baeman and A. J. Walker, "Globalizing HRIS: The New Transnational Model," *IHRIM Journal* (October–December 2000): 30–43; S. Greengard, "Handing Off Your HRMS: What You Need to Know," *Workforce* (February 2001): 50–54; V. Y. Haines and A. Petit, "Conditions for Successful Human Resource Information Systems," *Human Resource Management* 36(2) (Summer 1997): 261–276.

19 T. Loofbourrow, "Smartening Your HR Intranet," *Human Resource Executive* (June 18, 1999): 61–66; T. Starner, "The Effect of 'e,' " *Human Resource Executive* (March 1, 2001): 44–51.

20 M. Tanzer, "Keep Spies Out of Your Company," *Personnel Journal* (May 1993): 45–51.

21 P. Schaeffer, "HR Pay Keeps Rising," *HR Magazine* (October 2000): 78–83; "Human Resource Compensation," *Bulletin to Management* (September 30, 1998): 252–253; A. R. McIlvaine, "Show Me the Money," *Human Resource Executive* (March 19, 1998): 66–68; "Datagraph: Human Resource Compensation Survey," *Bulletin to Management* (September 18, 1997): 300–301.

22 "Human Resource Activities, Budgets and Staffs, 2000–2001," SHRM-BNA Survey No. 66 (Washington, DC: BNA): June 28, 2001; P. Schaeffer, "HR Pay Keeps Rising;" T. Philbin, "Give Your Movers a Performance Review," *HR Magazine* (January 2001): 81–105; M. Avery, "HR Pay Growth Accelerates," *HR Magazine* (November 1998): 122–126; P. Schaeffer, "HR Compensation: A Mixed Bag," *HR Magazine* (October 2001): 56–63.

23 J. Walker and W. Stopper, "Developing Human Resource Leaders," *Human Resource Planning* (1999): 38–44; M. Langbert, "Professors, Managers, and Human Resource Education," *Human Resource Management* 39(1) (Spring 2000): 65–78; F. Shipper and J. Dillard, "A Study of Impending Derailment and Recovery of Middle Managers Across Career Stages," *Human Resource Management* 39(4) (Winter 2000): 331–345.

24 S. H. Applebaum, *1991 SHRM/CCCH Survey* (June 26, 1991); M. T. Brown, *Working Ethics: Strategies for Decision Making and Organizational Responsibility* (San Francisco: Jossey-Bass, 1990).

25 D. Patel, "Ethics in HR Practices Good for Bottom Line, Research Suggests," *HR News* (July 2001): 14; L. Grensing-Pophal, "Walking the Tightrope," *HR Magazine* (October 1998): 112–119; M. T. Brown, *Working Ethics*; L. L. Nash, *Good Intentions Aside: A Manager's Guide to Resolving Ethical Problems* (Boston: Harvard Business School Press, 1990).

26 "HR Staff Feeling, Seeing Ethics Pressure," *Bulletin to Management* 49(6) (February 12, 1998): 41.

27 C. Brewster, E. Farndale, and J. van Ommeren, "HR Competencies and Professional Standards," *World Federation of Personnel Management Associations* (June 2000).

28 R. S. Schuler and S. E. Jackson, "HR Roles, Competencies, Partnerships and Structure," M. Warner and M. Poole, *International Encyclopedia of Business and Management,* 2d ed. (London: ITL, 2001).

29 L. Morgan, "Technology: Changing the Role of Human Resources," *ACA News* (March 2000): 17–22; C. Joinson, "The Best of Both Worlds," *HR Magazine* (September 1999): 50–58; J. J. Laabs, "Stay a Step Ahead," *Workforce* (October 1997): 56–65; R. A. Eisenstat, "What Corporate Human Resources Brings to the Picnic: Four Models for Functional Management," *Organizational Dynamics* (Autumn 1996): 7–21; C. Gedvilas, "The HR Organization for the Future," *ACA News* (March 1997): 14–15.

30 "Special PPF Survey Report: A Profile of Human Resource Executives," *Bulletin to Management* 48(25) (June 19, 1997): 1–8.

31 "SHRM-BNA Survey No. 63, Human Resource Activities, Budgets, and Staffs: 1997–1998," *Bulletin to Management* 49(24) (June 18, 1998): 1–27; "SHRM-BNA Survey No. 62, Human Resource Activities, Budgets, and Staffs: 1996–1997," *Bulletin to Management* 48(26) (June 26, 1997): 1–20.

32 F. Fox, "HR Knowledgebases: Stepping Beyond Self-Service," *HR Magazine* (January 2001): 119–128; M. C. Ciccarelli, "Calling All Computers," *Human Resource Executive* (March 5, 1998): 32–35; D. Ulrich, "Shared Services: From Vogue to Value," *Human Resource Planning* 18(3) (1995): 12–23.

33 A. Wellner, "Entrepreneurial HR," *HR Magazine* (March 2000): 53–58; F. Jossi, "Asking ASPs the Right Questions," *HR Magazine* (February 2001): 117–122; C. D. Johnson, "Changing Shapes: As Organizations Evolve, HR's Form Follows Its Functions," *HR Magazine* (March 1999): 41–48.

34 L. Davidson, "Cut Away Noncore HR," *Workforce* (January 1998): 41–45; F. Kemske, "HR's Role Will Change. The Question Is How. HR 2008," *Workforce* (January 1998): 47–60; J. A. Byrne, "Has Outsourcing Gone Too Far?" *Business Week* (April 1, 1996): 26–28; "Outsourcing Offers Strategic Advantage," *Bulletin to Management* (June 29, 1995): 208; "HR's Advances in Reengineering and Restructuring," *Personnel Journal* (January 1996): 60.

35 J. Rogier, "Making Every Minute Count," *Workforce* (May 1998): 31–33; R. K. Platt, "Outsourcing the HR Function," *ACA News* (June 1996): 12–15.

36 A. Halcrow, "Survey Shows HR in Transition," *Workforce* (June 1998): 73–80; Caudron, "HR Leaders Brainstorm," 59–60.

37 "Outsourcing: Not Always What It's Cracked Up to Be," *Workforce* (August 1998): 23.

38 D. Garr, "Inside Out-sourcing," *Fortune* (Summer 2001): 85–92; E. Zimmerman, "B of A and Big-Time Outsourcing," *Workforce* (April 2001): 51–54; B. Mcmenamin, "Payroll Paternalism," *Forbes* (April 16, 2001): 114–120; C. R. Greer, S. A. Youngblood, and D. Gray, "Human Resource Management Outsourcing: The Make or Buy Decision," *Academy of Management Executive* 13(3) (1999): 85–96; J. J. Laabs, "The Dark Side of Outsourcing," *Workforce* (September 1998): 42–48; K. S. Wallace, "Avoid the Ten Major Pitfalls of Outsourcing," *Workforce* (September 1998): 44–45; C. M. Solomon, "Protect Your Outsourcing Investment," *Workforce* (October 1998): 130–132.

39 Caudron, "HR Leaders Brainstorm," 57; B. P. Sunoo, "Amgen's Latest Discovery," *Personnel Journal* (February 1996): 38–45.

40 F. Luthans, P. A. Marsnik, and K. W. Luthans, "A Contingency Matrix Approach to IHRM," *Human Resource Management* 36(2) (Summer 1997): 183–200; P. J. Dowling, D. E. Welch, and R. S. Schuler, *International Dimensions of Human Resource Management,* 3rd ed. (Cincinnati, OH: South-Western, 1999).

41 M. S. Schnell and C. M. Solomon, "Global Culture: Who's the Gatekeeper," *Workforce* (November 1997): 35–39; J. J. Laabs, "Getting Ahead by Going Abroad," *Global Workforce* (January 1998): 10–11; J. J. Laabs, "HR Pioneers Explore the Road Less Traveled," *Personnel Journal* (February 1996): 70–78.

THE LINCOLN ELECTRIC COMPANY

People are our most valuable asset. They must feel secure, important, challenged, in control of their destiny, confident in their leadership, be responsive to common goals, believe they are being treated fairly, have easy access to authority and open lines of communication in all possible directions. Perhaps the most important task Lincoln employees face today is that of establishing an example for others in the Lincoln organization in other parts of the world. We need to maximize the benefits of cooperation and teamwork, fusing high technology with human talent, so that we here in the USA and all of our subsidiary and joint venture operations will be in a position to realize our full potential.

George Willis, former CEO, The Lincoln Electric Company

Introduction

Today, the Lincoln Electric Company, under the leadership of Anthony Massaro, is the world's largest manufacturer of arc-welding products and a leading producer of industrial electric motors. The firm employs almost 6,300 workers in three U.S. factories near Cleveland and sites in 18 other countries. The company's U.S. market share (for arc-welding products) is estimated at more than 40 percent.[1]

The Lincoln incentive management plan has been well known for many years. Many college management texts make reference to the Lincoln plan as a model for achieving higher worker productivity. Certainly, the firm has been successful according to the usual measures.

James F. Lincoln died in 1965 and there was some concern, even among employees, that the management system would fall into disarray, that profits would decline, and that year-end bonuses might be discontinued. Quite the contrary; since Lincoln's death, the company appears as strong as ever. Each year, except the recession years 1982 and 1983, has seen high profits and bonuses. In 1995, Lincoln Electric's centennial, sales for the first time surpassed $1 billion. While there was some employee discontent about relatively flat bonuses in 1995, employee morale and productivity remain very good.[2] Employee turnover is almost nonexistent except for retirements. Lincoln's market share is stable. The historically high stock dividends continue.

A Historical Sketch

In 1895, after being "frozen out" of the depression-ravaged Elliott-Lincoln Company, a maker of Lincoln-designed electric motors, John C. Lincoln took out his second patent and began to manufacture his improved motor. He opened his new business, unincorporated, with $200 he had earned redesigning a motor for young Herbert Henry Dow, who later founded the Dow Chemical Company.

Started during an economic depression and cursed by a major fire after only one year in business, the company grew, but hardly prospered, through its first quarter century. In 1906, John C. Lincoln incorporated the business and moved from his one-room, fourth-floor factory to a new three-story building he erected in east Cleveland. He expanded his workforce to 30 and sales grew to over $50,000 a year. John preferred being an engineer and inventor rather than a manager, though, and it was to be left to another Lincoln to manage the company through its years of success. In 1907, after a bout with typhoid fever forced him from Ohio State University in his senior year, James F. Lincoln, John's younger brother, joined the fledgling company. In 1914 he became the active head of the firm, with the titles of general manager and vice president. John remained president of the company for some years but became more involved in other business ventures and in his work as an inventor.

One of James Lincoln's early actions was to ask the employees to elect representatives to a committee that would advise him on company operations. This "Advisory Board" has met with the chief executive officer every two weeks since that time. This was only the first of a series of innovative personnel policies that have, over the years, distinguished Lincoln Electric from its competitors.

The first year the Advisory Board was in existence, working hours were reduced from 55 per week, then standard, to 50 hours a week. In 1915, the company gave each employee a paid-up life insurance policy. A welding school, which continues today, was begun in 1917. In 1918, an employee bonus plan was attempted; it was not continued, but the idea was to resurface later.

The Lincoln Electric Employees Association was formed in 1919 to provide health benefits and social activities. This organization continues today and has assumed several additional functions over the years. In 1923, a piecework pay system was in effect, employees got two weeks' paid vacation each year, and wages were adjusted for changes in the Consumer Price Index. Approximately 30 percent of the common stock was set aside for key employees in 1914, and a stock purchase plan for all employees was begun in 1925.

The board of directors voted to start a suggestion system in 1929. The program is still in effect, but cash awards, a part of the early program, were discontinued several years ago. Now, the company rewards suggestions by giving "additional points" that increase year-end bonuses.

The legendary Lincoln bonus plan was proposed by the Advisory Board and accepted on a trial basis in 1934. The first annual bonus amounted to about 25 percent of wages. There has been a bonus every year since then. The bonus plan has been a cornerstone of the Lincoln management system and recent bonuses have approximated annual wages.

By 1944, Lincoln employees enjoyed a pension plan, a policy of promotion from within, and continuous employment. Base pay rates were determined by formal job evaluation and a merit rating system was in effect.

In the prologue of James F. Lincoln's last book, Charles G. Herbruck writes regarding the foregoing personnel innovations:

They were not to buy good behavior. They were not efforts to increase profits. They were not antidotes to labor difficulties. They did not constitute a "do-gooder" program. They were an expression of mutual respect for each person's importance to the job to be done. All of them reflect the leadership of James Lincoln, under whom they were nurtured and propagated.

During World War II, Lincoln prospered as never before. By the start of the war, the company was the world's largest manufacturer of arc-welding products. Sales of about $4 million in 1934 grew to $24 million by 1941. Productivity per employee more than doubled during the same period. The Navy's Price Review Board challenged the high profits, and the Internal Revenue Service questioned the tax deductibility of employee bonuses, arguing they were not "ordinary and necessary" costs of doing business. But the forceful and articulate James Lincoln was able to overcome the objections.

Certainly since 1935 and probably for several years before that, Lincoln's productivity has been well above the average for similar companies. The company claims levels of productivity more than twice those for other manufacturers from 1945 onward. Information available from outside sources tends to support these claims.

Company Philosophy

James F. Lincoln was the son of a Congregational minister, and Christian principles were at the center of his business philosophy. The confidence that he had in the efficacy of Christ's teachings is illustrated by the following remark taken from one of his books:

The Christian ethic should control our acts. If it did control our acts, the savings in cost of distribution would be tremendous. Advertising would be a contact of the expert consultant with the customer, in order to give the customer the best product available when all of the customers' needs are considered. Competition then would be in improving the quality of products and increasing efficiency in producing and distributing them; not in deception, as is now too customary. Pricing would reflect efficiency of production; it would not be a selling dodge that the customer may be sorry he accepted. It would be proper for all concerned and rewarding for the ability used in producing the product.

There is no indication that Lincoln attempted to evangelize his employees or customers—or the general public for that matter. Neither the former chairman of the board and chief executive, George Willis, nor his successors, mentions the Christian gospel in their speeches and interviews. The company motto, "The actual is limited, the possible is immense," is prominently displayed, but there is no display of religious slogans, and there is no company chapel.

Attitude Toward the Customer

James Lincoln saw the customer's needs as the raison d'etre for every company. He wrote, "When any company has achieved success so that it is attractive as an investment, all money usually needed for expansion is supplied by the customer in retained earnings. It is obvious that the customer's interests, not the stockholder's, should come first." In 1947 he said, "Care should be taken . . . not to rivet attention on profit. Between 'How much do I get?' and 'How do I make this better, cheaper, more useful?' the difference is fundamental and decisive." Willis, too, ranked the customer as management's most important constituency. This is reflected in Lincoln's policy to "at all times price on the basis of cost and at all times keep pressure on our cost. . . ." Lincoln's goal, often stated, is "to build a better and better product at a lower and lower price." James Lincoln said, "It is obvious that the customer's interests should be the first goal of industry."

This priority, and the priority given to other groups, is reflected in the Mission and Values Statement and the set of Goals shown in Appendix 1.

Attitude Toward Stockholders

Stockholders are given last priority at Lincoln. This is a continuation of James Lincoln's philosophy: "The last group to be considered is the stockholders who own stock because they think it will be more profitable than investing money in any other way." Concerning division of the largess produced by incentive management, he wrote, "The absentee stockholder also will get his share, even if undeserved, out of the greatly increased profit that the efficiency produces."

Attitude Toward Unionism

There has never been a serious effort to organize Lincoln employees. While James Lincoln criticized the labor movement for "selfishly attempting to better its position at the expense of the people it must serve," he still had kind words for union members. He excused abuses of union power as "the natural reactions of human beings to the abuses to which management has subjected them." Lincoln's idea of the correct relationship between workers and managers is shown by this comment: "Labor and management are properly not warring camps; they are parts of one organization in which they must, and should, cooperate fully and happily."

Beliefs and Assumptions About Employees

If fulfilling customer needs is the desired goal of business, then employee performance and productivity are the means by which this goal can best be achieved. It is the Lincoln attitude toward employees, reflected in the following comments by James Lincoln, which is credited by many with creating the success the company has experienced:

He is just as eager as any manager is to be part of a team that is properly organized and working for the advancement of our economy. He has no desire to make profits for those who do not hold up their end in production, as is true of absentee stockholders and inactive people in the company.

If money is to be used as an incentive, the program must provide that what is paid to the worker is what he has earned. The earnings of each must be in accordance with accomplishment.

Status is of great importance in all human relationships. The greatest incentive that money has, usually, is that it is a symbol of success. The resulting status is the real incentive. Money alone can be an incentive to the miser only.

There must be complete honesty and understanding between the hourly worker and management if high efficiency is to be obtained.

These beliefs and assumptions have helped shaped Lincoln's human resource objectives. These are shown in Appendix 2.

Lincoln's Business

Arc welding has been the standard joining method in shipbuilding for decades and is the predominant way of connecting steel in the construction industry.

Most industrial plants have their own welding shops for maintenance and construction. Manufacturers of tractors and all kinds of heavy equipment use arc welding extensively in the manufacturing process. Many hobbyists have their own welding machines and use them for making metal items such as patio furniture and barbecue pits. The popularity of welded sculpture as an art form is growing.

While advances in welding technology have been frequent, arc-welding products, in the main, have hardly changed. Lincoln's Innershield process is a notable exception. This process, described later, lowers welding cost and improves quality and speed in many applications. The most widely used Lincoln electrode, the Fleetweld 5P, has been virtually the same since the 1930s. The most popular engine-driven welder in the world, the Lincoln SA-200, has been a gray-colored assembly including a four-cylinder continental Red Seal engine and a 200-ampere direct-current generator with two current-control knobs for at least four decades. A 1989 model SA-200 even weighed almost the same as the 1950 model, and it certainly was little changed in appearance.

The company's share of the U.S. arc-welding products market appears to have been about 40 percent for many years. The welding products market has grown somewhat faster than the level of industry in general. The market is highly price competitive, with variations in prices of standard items normally amounting to only a percent or two. Lincoln's products are sold directly by its engineering-oriented sales force and indirectly through its distributor organization. Advertising expenditures amount to less than three-fourths of a percent of sales, but research and development expenditures typically range from $10 million to $12 million, considerably more than competitors.

The other major welding process, flame welding, has not been competitive with arc welding since the 1930s. However, plasma arc welding, a relatively new process that uses a conducting stream of super-heated gas (plasma) to confine the welding current to a small area, has made some inroads, especially in metal tubing manufacturing, in recent years. Major advances in technology that will produce an alternative superior to arc welding within the next decade or so appear unlikely. Also, it seems likely that changes in the machines and techniques used in arc welding will be evolutionary rather than revolutionary.

It is also reasonable to observe that Lincoln Electric's business objectives, shown in Appendix 3, are likely to change in an evolutionary rather than a revolutionary way.

Products

The company is primarily engaged in the manufacture and sale of arc-welding products—electric welding machines and metal electrodes. Lincoln also produces electric motors ranging from one-half horsepower to 200 horsepower. Motors constitute about 8 to 10 percent of total sales. Several million dollars has recently been invested in automated equipment that will double Lincoln's manufacturing capacity for one-half to 20-horsepower electric motors. The electric welding machines, some consisting of a transformer or motor and generator arrangement powered by commercial electricity and others consisting of an internal combustion engine and generator, are designed to produce 30 to 1,500 amperes of electrical power. This electrical current is used to melt a consumable metal electrode, with the molten metal being transferred in super hot spray to the metal joint being welded. Very high temperatures and hot sparks are produced, and operators usually must wear special eye and face protection and leather gloves, often along with leather aprons and sleeves. Lincoln and its competitors now market a wide range of general purpose and specialty electrodes for welding mild steel, aluminum, cast iron, and stainless and special steels. Most of these electrodes are designed to meet the standards of the American Welding Society, a trade association. They are thus essentially the same as to size and composition from one manufacturer to another. Every electrode manufacturer has a limited number of unique products, but these typically constitute only a small percentage of total sales.

Welding electrodes are of two basic types: coated "stick" electrodes and coiled wire. Coated "stick" electrodes, usually 14 inches long and smaller than a pencil in diameter, are held in a special insulated holder by the operator, who must manipulate the electrode in order to maintain a proper arc-width and pattern of deposition of the metal being transferred. Stick electrodes are packaged in 6- to 50-pound boxes.

Thin coiled wire is designed to be fed continuously to the welding arc through a "gun" held by the operator or positioned by automatic positioning equipment. The wire is packaged in coils, reels, and drums weighing from 14 to 1,000 pounds and may be solid or flux-cored.

For more information on products visit the Web site, **http://www.lincolnelectric.com/**.

Manufacturing Process

The main plant is in Euclid, Ohio, a suburb on Cleveland's east side. The layout of this plant is shown in Exhibit 1. There are no warehouses. Materials flow from the half-mile-long dock on the north side of the plant through the production lines to a very limited storage and loading area on the south side.

Materials used on each work station are stored as close as possible to the work station. The administrative offices, near the center of the factory, are entirely functional. A corridor below the main level provides access to the factory floor from the main entrance near the center of the plant. *Fortune* declared the Euclid facility one of America's 10 best-managed factories.

Another Lincoln plant, in Mentor, Ohio, houses some of the electrode production operations, which were moved from the main plant. Electrode manufacturing is highly capital intensive. Metal rods purchased from steel producers are drawn down to smaller diameters, cut to length, and coated with pressed-powder "flux" for stick electrodes or plated with copper (for conductivity) and put into coils or spools for wire. Lincoln's Innershield wire is hollow and filled with a material similar to that used to coat stick electrodes. As mentioned earlier, this represented a major innovation in welding technology when it was introduced. The company is highly secretive about its electrode production processes, and outsiders are not given access to the details of those processes.

Lincoln welding machines and electric motors are made on a series of assembly lines. Gasoline and diesel engines are purchased partially assembled, but practically all other components are made from basic industrial products, for example, steel bars and sheets and bar copper conductor wire.

Individual components, such as gasoline tanks for engine-driven welders and steel shafts for motors and generators, are made by numerous small "factories within a factory." The shaft for a certain generator, for example, is made from raw steel bar by one operator who uses five large machines, all running continuously. A saw cuts the bar to length, a digital lathe machines different sections to varying diameters, a special mining machine cuts a slot for the keyway, and so forth, until a finished shaft is produced. The operator moves the shafts from machine to machine and makes necessary adjustments. Another operator punches, shapes, and paints sheetmetal cowling parts. One assembles steel laminations onto a rotor shaft, then winds, insulates,

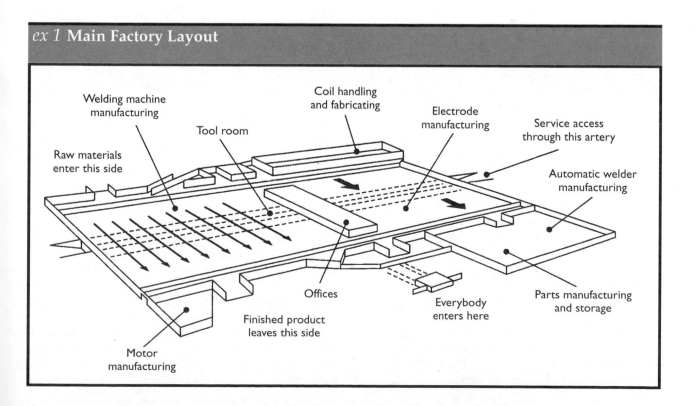

ex 1 **Main Factory Layout**

Welding machine manufacturing

Coil handling and fabricating

Electrode manufacturing

Service access through this artery

Tool room

Raw materials enter this side

Automatic welder manufacturing

Parts manufacturing and storage

Offices

Everybody enters here

Finished product leaves this side

Motor manufacturing

and tests the rotors. Finished components are moved by crane operators to the nearby assembly lines.

Worker Performance and Attitude

Exceptional worker performance at Lincoln is a matter of record. The typical Lincoln employee earns about twice as much as other factory workers in the Cleveland area. Yet the company's labor cost per sales dollar is well below industry averages. Worker turnover is practically nonexistent except for retirements and departures by new employees. Turnover is less than 4 percent for employees who have been on the job for at least 18 months.[3]

Sales per Lincoln factory employee currently exceed $150,000. An observer at the factory quickly sees why this figure is so high. Each worker is proceeding busily and thoughtfully about the task at hand. There is no idle chatter. Most workers take no coffee breaks. Many operate several machines and make a substantial component unaided. The supervisors are busy with planning and record-keeping duties and hardly glance at the people they "supervise." The manufacturing procedures appear efficient—no unnecessary steps, no wasted motions, no wasted materials. Finished components move smoothly to subsequent work stations. Appendix 4 includes summaries of interviews with employees.

Organizational Structure

Lincoln has never allowed development of a formal organization chart. The objective of this policy is to ensure maximum flexibility. An open door policy is practiced throughout the company, and personnel are encouraged to take problems to the persons most capable of resolving them. Once, Harvard Business School researchers prepared an organization chart reflecting the implied relationships at Lincoln. The chart became available within the company, and present management feels that had a disruptive effect. Therefore, no organizational chart appears in this case.

Perhaps because of the quality and enthusiasm of the Lincoln workforce, routine supervision is almost nonexistent. A typical production foreman, for example, supervises as many as 100 workers, a span of control that does not allow more than infrequent worker-supervisor interaction.

Position titles and traditional flows of authority do imply something of an organizational structure, however. For example, the vice president, Sales, and the vice president, Electrode Division, report to the president, as do various staff assistants such as the personnel director and the director of purchasing.

Using such implied relationships, it has been determined that production workers have two or, at most, three levels of supervision between themselves and the president.

Human Resource Practices

As mentioned earlier, it is Lincoln's remarkable human resource practices that are credited by many with the company's success.

Recruitment and Selection

Every job opening is advertised internally on company bulletin boards and any employee can apply for any job so advertised. External hiring is permitted only for entry-level positions. Selection for these jobs is done on the basis of personal interviews—there is no aptitude or psychological testing. A committee consisting of vice presidents and supervisors interviews candidates initially cleared by the Personnel Department. Final selection is made by the supervisor who has a job opening. Nonetheless, it is increasingly desirable that factory workers have some advanced math skills and understand the use of computers. Out of over 20,000 applications received by the Personnel Department during a recent period, relatively few were hired in 1994–1995. Consequently, Lincoln's expansion is becoming increasingly dependent upon getting employees qualified to work in the Lincoln environment, within the famous incentive system.[4]

Job Security

In 1958 Lincoln formalized its guaranteed continuous employment policy, which had already been in effect for many years. There have been no layoffs since World War II. Since 1958, every worker with over two years' longevity has been guaranteed at least 30 hours per week, 49 weeks per year.

The policy has never been so severely tested as during the 1981–1983 recession. As a manufacturer of capital goods, Lincoln's business is highly cyclical. In previous recessions the company was able to avoid major sales declines. However, sales plummeted 32 percent in 1982 and another 16 percent the next year. Few companies could withstand such a revenue collapse and remain profitable. Yet, not only did Lincoln earn profits, but no employee was laid off and year-end incentive bonuses continued. To weather the storm, management cut most of the nonsalaried workers back to 30 hours a week for varying periods of time. Many employees were reassigned, and the total workforce was slightly reduced through normal attrition and restricted hiring. Many employees grumbled at their unexpected misfortune, probably to the surprise and dismay of some Lincoln managers. However, sales and profits—and employee bonuses—soon rebounded.

Performance Evaluation

Each supervisor formally evaluates subordinates twice a year using the cards shown in Exhibit 2. The employee performance criteria, "quality," "dependability," "ideas and cooperation," and "output" are considered to be independent of each other. Marks on the cards are converted to numerical scores that are forced to average 100 for each evaluating supervisor. Individual merit rating scores normally range from 80 to 110. Any score over 110 requires a special letter to top management. These scores (over 110) are not considered in computing the required 100-point average for each evaluating supervisor.

Suggestions for improvements often result in recommendations for exceptionally high performance scores. Supervisors discuss individual performance marks with the employees concerned. Each warranty claim is traced to the individual employee whose work caused the defect. The employee's performance score may be reduced, or the worker may be required to repay the cost of servicing the warranty claim by working without pay.

Compensation

Basic wage levels for jobs at Lincoln are determined by a wage survey of similar jobs in the Cleveland area.[5] These rates are adjusted quarterly in accordance with changes in the Cleveland area wage index. Insofar as possible, base wage rates are translated into piece rates. Today the average Lincoln factory worker earns $16.54 an hour versus the average $14.25 manufacturing wage in the Cleveland area. Practically all production workers and many others—for example, some forklift operators—are paid by piece rate. Once established, piece rates are never changed unless a substantive change in the way a job is done results from a source other than the worker doing the job.

In December of each year, a portion of annual profits is distributed to employees as bonuses. Incentive bonuses since 1934 have averaged about 90 percent of annual wages. Individual bonuses are proportional to merit-rating scores. For example, assume the amount set aside for bonuses is 80 percent of total wages paid to eligible employees. A person whose performance score is 95 will receive a bonus of 76 percent (0.80 × 0.95) of annual wages. While these percentages have often resulted in high total compensation, some employees believe that their bonuses are not rising fast enough, despite rising profits. This reflects the firm's decision to use profits to expand the operations rather than put them into higher bonuses. It also reflects the fact that there are more workers today sharing in a bonus pool that is only a little higher than in many years in the 1980s.[6]

Vacations

The company is shut down for two weeks in August and two weeks during the Christmas season. Vacations are taken during these periods. For employees with over 25 years of service, a fifth week of vacation may be taken at a time acceptable to superiors.

Work Assignments

Management has authority to transfer workers and to switch between overtime and short time as required. Supervisors have undisputed authority to assign specific parts to individual workers, who may have their own preferences due to variations in piece rates. During the 1982–1983 recession, 50 factory workers volunteered to join sales teams and fanned out across the country to sell a new welder designed for automobile body shops and small machine shops. The result: $10 million in sales and a hot new product.

Employee Participation in Decision Making

Thinking of participative management usually evokes a vision of a relaxed, nonauthoritarian atmosphere. This is not the case at Lincoln. Formal authority is quite strong. "We're very authoritarian around here," says Willis. James F. Lincoln placed a good deal of stress on protecting management's authority. "Management in all successful departments of industry must have complete power," he said. "Management is the coach who must be obeyed. The men, however, are the Players who alone can win the game." Despite this attitude, there are several ways in which employees participate in management at Lincoln.

Richard Sabo, former assistant to the chief executive officer, relates job enlargement/enrichment to participation. He said, "The most important participative technique that we use is giving more responsibility to employees. We give a high school graduate more responsibility than other companies give their

ex 2 Merit Rating Cards

→ **Increasing Quality** →

This card rates the QUALITY of work you do.

It also reflects your success in eliminating errors and in reducing scrap and waste.

QUALITY

This rating has been done jointly by your department head and the Inspection Department in the shop and with other department heads in the office and engineering.

→ **Increasing Dependability** →

This card rates how well your supervisors have been able to depend on you to do those things that have been expected of you without supervision.

It also reflects your ability to supervise yourself including your work safety performance, your orderliness, care of equipment, and the effective use you make of your skills.

DEPENDABILITY

This rating has been done by your department head.

→ **Increasing Output** →

This card rates your Cooperation, Ideas, and Initiative.

IDEAS & COOPERATION

→ **Increasing Output** → Days Absent

This card rates HOW MUCH PRODUCTIVE WORK you actually turn out. It also reflects your willingness not to hold back and recognizes your attendance record.

New ideas and new methods are important to your company in our continuing effort to reduce costs, increase output, improve quality, work safety, and improve our relationship with our customers. This card credits you for your ideas and initiative used to help in this direction.

It also rates your cooperation—how you work with others as a team. Such factors as your attitude toward supervision, coworkers and the company, your efforts to share knowledge with others, and your cooperation in installing new methods smoothly, are considered here.

OUTPUT

This rating has been done jointly by your department head and the Production Control Department in the shop and with other department heads in the office and engineering.

foremen." Management puts limits on the degree of participation that is allowed, however. In Sabo's words:

When you use "participation," put quotes around it. Because we believe that each person should participate only in those decisions he is most knowledgeable about. I don't think production employees should control the decisions of the chairman. They don't know as much as he does about the decisions he is involved in.

The Advisory Board, elected by the workers, meets with the chairman and the president every two weeks to discuss ways of improving operations. As noted earlier, this board has been in existence since 1914 and has contributed to many innovations. The incentive bonuses, for example, were first recommended by this committee. Every employee has access to Advisory Board members, and answers to all Advisory Board suggestions are promised by the following meeting. Willis, Hastings, and Massaro are quick to point out, though, that the Advisory Board only recommends actions. "They do not have direct authority," Willis says, "and when they bring up something that management thinks is not to the benefit of the company, it will be rejected."

Under the early suggestion program, employees were awarded one-half of the first year's savings attributable to their suggestions. Now, however, the value of suggestions is reflected in performance evaluation scores, which determine individual incentive bonus amounts.

Training and Education

Production workers are given a short period of on-the-job training and then placed on a piecework pay system. Lincoln does not pay for off-site education, unless very specific company needs are identified. The idea behind this latter policy, according to Sabo, is that everyone cannot take advantage of such a program, and it is unfair to expend company funds for an advantage to which there is unequal access. Recruits for sales jobs, already college graduates, are given on-the-job training in the plant followed by a period of work and training at one of the regional sales offices. Today, Lincoln Electric conducts a large number of training programs. Visit its Web site to review them all and you may be very impressed!

Fringe Benefits and Executive Perquisites

A medical plan and a company-paid retirement program have been in effect for many years. A plant cafeteria, operated on a break-even basis, serves meals at about 60 percent of usual costs. The Employee Association, to which the company does not contribute, provides disability insurance and social and athletic activities. The employee stock ownership program has resulted in employee ownership of about 50 percent of the common stock. Under this program, each employee with more than two years of service may purchase stock in the corporation; the price of these shares is established at book value. Stock purchased through this plan may be held by employees only. Dividends and voting rights are the same as for stock that is owned outside the plan. Approximately 75 percent of the employees own Lincoln stock.

As to executive perquisites, there are none—crowded, austere offices, no executive washrooms or lunchrooms, and no reserved parking spaces. Even the top executives pay for their own meals and eat in the employee cafeteria. If the CEO arrives late due to a breakfast speaking engagement, he has to park far away from the factory entrance.

Financial Policies

James F. Lincoln felt strongly that financing for company growth should come from within the company—through initial cash investment by the founders, through retention of earnings, and through stock purchases by those who work in the business. He saw the following advantages of this approach:

1. Ownership of stock by employees strengthens team spirit. "If they are mutually anxious to make it succeed, the future of the company is bright."
2. Ownership of stock provides individual incentive because employees feel that they will benefit from company profitability.
3. "Ownership is educational." Owner-employees "will know how profits are made and lost; how success is won and lost. There are few socialists in the list of stockholders of the nation's industries."
4. "Capital available from within controls expansion." Unwarranted expansion would not occur, Lincoln believed, under his financing plan.
5. "The greatest advantage would be the development of the individual worker. Under the incentive of ownership, he would become a greater man."
6. "Stock ownership is one of the steps that can be taken that will make the worker feel that there is less of a gulf between him and the boss. Stock

ownership will help the worker to recognize his responsibility in the game and the importance of victory."

Until 1980, Lincoln Electric borrowed no money. Even now, the company's liabilities consist mainly of accounts payable and short-term accruals. The unusual pricing policy at Lincoln was succinctly stated by Willis: "At all times price on the basis of cost and at all times keep pressure on our cost." This policy resulted in the price for the most popular welding electrode then in use going from 16 cents a pound in 1929 to 4.7 cents in 1938. More recently, the SA-200 welder, Lincoln's largest-selling portable machine, decreased in price from 1958 through 1965. According to Dr. C. Jackson Grayson of the American Productivity Center in Houston, Texas, Lincoln's prices increased only one-fifth as fast as the Consumer Price Index from 1934 to about 1970. This resulted in a welding products market in which Lincoln became the undisputed price leader for the products it manufactures. Not even the major Japanese manufacturers, such as Nippon Steel for welding electrodes and Saka Transformer for welding machines, were able to penetrate this market.

Substantial cash balances accumulated each year preparatory to paying the year-end bonuses. Modest success with international expansion put some pressure on what was basically a conservative financial philosophy. However, the company borrowed money in 1992 to pay for employee bonuses in the United States. In 1995 Lincoln issued $119 million of new stock. This sale created greater public ownership. As a consequence, Don Hastings remarked that the company must now consider not only the employees but its shareholders, customers, and suppliers.[7] For more current financial information, visit Lincoln's Web site.

How Well Does Lincoln Serve Its Stakeholders?

Lincoln Electric differs from most other companies in the importance it assigns to each of the groups it serves. Hastings identifies these groups, in the order of priority ascribed to them, as (1) customers, (2) employees, and (3) stockholders. As suggested, the 1995 stock issue increased the salience of the stockholders.

Certainly the firm's customers have fared well over the years. Lincoln prices for welding machines and welding electrodes are acknowledged to be the lowest in the marketplace. Quality has consistently been high. The cost of field failures for Lincoln products was recently determined to be a remarkable 0.04 percent of revenues. The Fleetweld electrodes and SA-200 welders have been the standard in the pipeline and refinery construction industry, where price is hardly a criterion, for decades. A Lincoln distributor in Monroe, Louisiana, says that he has sold several hundred of the popular AC-225 welders, which are warranted for one year, but has never handled a warranty claim.

Perhaps best-served of all management constituencies have been the employees. Not the least of their benefits, of course, are the year-end bonuses, which effectively double an already average compensation level. The foregoing description of the personnel program and the comments in Appendix 4 further illustrate the desirability of a Lincoln job.

While stockholders were relegated to an inferior status by James F. Lincoln, they have done very well indeed. Recent dividends exceeded $11 a share and earnings per share have approached $30. In January 1980, the price of restricted stock, committed to employees, was $117 a share. By 1989, the stated value, at which the company will repurchase the stock if tendered, was $201. A check with the New York office of Merrill Lynch, Pierce, Fenner and Smith at that time revealed an estimated price on Lincoln stock of $270 a share, with none being offered for sale. Technically, this price applies only to the unrestricted stock owned by the Lincoln family, a few other major holders, and employees who have purchased it on the open market. Risk associated with Lincoln stock, a major determinant of stock value, is minimal because of the small amount of debt in the capital structure, because of an extremely stable earnings record, and because of Lincoln's practice of purchasing the restricted stock whenever employees offer it for sale. The 1995 stock sale has changed this situation dramatically. The stock now trades freely on the NASDAQ stock exchange.

A Concluding Comment

It is easy to believe that the reason for Lincoln's success is the excellent attitude of the employees and their willingness to work harder, faster, and more intelligently than other industrial workers. However, Sabo suggests that appropriate credit be given to Lincoln executives, whom he credits with carrying out the following policies:

1. Management has limited research, development, and manufacturing to a standard product line designed to meet the major needs of the welding industry.

2. New products must be reviewed by manufacturing and all producing costs verified before being approved by management.

3. Purchasing is challenged to not only procure materials at the lowest cost but also to work closely with engineering and manufacturing to assure that the latest innovations are implemented.

4. Manufacturing supervision and all personnel are held accountable for reduction of scrap, energy conservation, and maintenance of product quality.

5. Production control, material handling, and methods engineering are closely supervised by top management.

6. Management has made cost reduction a way of life at Lincoln, and definite programs are established in many areas, including traffic and shipping, where tremendous savings can result.

7. Management has established a sales department that is technically trained to reduce customer welding costs. This sales approach and other real customer services have eliminated nonessential frills and resulted in long-term benefits to all concerned.

8. Management has encouraged education, technical publishing, and long-range programs that have resulted in industry growth, thereby assuring market potential for the Lincoln Electric Company.

Sabo writes, "It is in a very real sense a personal and group experience in faith—a belief that together we can achieve results which alone would not be possible. It is not a perfect system and it is not easy. It requires tremendous dedication and hard work. However, it does work and the results are worth the effort."

As Lincoln Electric has increased its global presence it has learned just how much it can use its same philosophy of managing human resources. The company has learned that countries have important legal, cultural, and political conditions that can influence the effectiveness and applicability of some of their practices and that the company needs to either adapt to them or locate in places where the differences with the United States are more modest.

Credits: This case was written by Arthur Sharplin and appears in P. D. Buller and R. S. Schuler (eds.), *Managing Organizations: Cases in Management, Organizational Behavior and Human Resource Management*, 6th ed. (Cincinnati, OH: South-Western, 2000). It is adapted here by R. S. Schuler and used with the permission of Arthur D. Sharplin.

ENDNOTES

1 In 2002, *Workforce* magazine cited Lincoln Electric's innovative human resource management practices as one of the most significant influences from the 20th century that shape how companies manage human resources in the 21st century. See the company's Web site for the most current information on all issues and topics addressed in this case.

2 T. W. Gerdel, "Lincoln Electric Experiences Season of Worker Discontent," *Plain Dealer* [Cleveland] (December 10, 1995): 1-C.

3 Z. Schiller, "A Model Incentive Plan Gets Caught in a Vise," *Business Week* (January 22, 1996): 89, 92.

4 R. Narisetti, "Job Paradox: Manufacturers Decry a Shortage of Workers While Rejecting Many," *Wall Street Journal* (September 8, 1995): A4.

5 Schiller, "A Model Incentive Plan Gets Caught in a Vise," 89, 92.

6 Gerdel, "Lincoln Electric Experiences Season of Worker Discontent."

7 Gerdel, "Lincoln Electric Experiences Season of Worker Discontent."

8 R. M. Hodgetts, "A Conversation with Donald F. Hastings of the Lincoln Electric Company," *Organizational Dynamics* (Winter 1997): 68–74; M. Gleisser, "Lincoln CEO's Formula: Mutual Trust and Loyalty," *Plain Dealer* [Cleveland] (June 22, 1996): 2-C.

app 1 Mission and Values Statement of the Lincoln Electric Company

MISSION AND VALUES STATEMENT

The mission of The Lincoln Electric Company is to earn and retain global leadership as a total quality supplier of superior products and services.

OUR CORE VALUES

As a responsible and successful company in partnership with our customers, distributors, employees, shareholders, suppliers, and our host communities, we pledge ourselves to conduct our business in accordance with these core values:
- Respond to our customers' needs and expectations with quality, integrity, and value.
- Recognize people as our most valuable asset.
- Maintain and expand the Lincoln Incentive Management philosophy.
- Practice prudent and responsible financial management.
- Strive continually to be environmentally responsible.
- Support communities where we operate and industries in which we participate.

TO REALIZE OUR MISSION AND SUPPORT OUR CORE VALUES, WE HAVE ESTABLISHED THE FOLLOWING GOALS:

Respond to Our Customers' Needs and Expectations with Quality, Integrity, and Value

- Assure value through innovative, functional, and reliable products and services in all the markets we serve around the world.
- Exceed global standards for products and service quality.
- Provide our customers with personalized technical support that helps them achieve improvements in cost reduction, productivity, and quality.
- Lead the industry in aggressive application of advanced technology to meet customer requirements.
- Invest constantly in creative research and development dedicated to maintaining our position of market leadership.
- Achieve and maintain the leading market share position in our major markets around the world.

Recognize People as Our Most Valuable Asset

- Maintain a safe, clean, and healthy environment for our employees.
- Promote employee training, education, and development, and broaden skills through multidepartmental and international assignments.
- Maintain an affirmative action program and provide all employees with opportunities for advancement commensurate with their abilities and performance regardless of race, religion, national origin, sex, age, or disability.
- Maintain an environment that fosters ethical behavior, mutual trust, equal opportunity, open communication, personal growth, and creativity.
- Demand integrity, discipline, and professional conduct from our employees in every aspect of our business and conduct our operations ethically and in accordance with the law.
- Reward employees through recognition, "pay for performance," and by sharing our profits with incentive bonus compensation based on extraordinary achievement.

Maintain and Expand the Lincoln Incentive Management Philosophy

Promote dynamic teamwork and innovation as the most profitable and cost-effective way of achieving:
- A committed work ethic and positive employee attitudes throughout the Company.
- High-quality, low-cost manufacturing.
- Efficient and innovative engineering.
- Customer-oriented operation and administration.
- A dedicated and knowledgeable sales and service force.
- A total organization responsive to the needs of our worldwide customers.

Practice Prudent and Responsible Financial Management

- Establish attainable goals, strategic planning, and accountability for results that enhance shareholder value.
- Promote the process of employee involvement in cost reductions and quality improvements.
- Recognize profit as the resource that enables our Company to serve our customers.

app 1 Mission and Values Statement of the Lincoln Electric Company (continued)

Strive Continually to Be Environmentally Responsible
- Continue to pursue the most environmentally sound operating practices, processes, and products to protect the global environment.
- Maintain a clean and healthy environment in our host communities.

Support Communities Where We Operate and Industries in Which We Participate
- Invest prudently in social, cultural, educational, and charitable activities.
- Contribute to the industries we serve and society as a whole by continuing our leadership role in professional organizations and education.
- Encourage and support appropriate employee involvement in community activities.

app 2 Lincoln Electric's HR Objectives

What Are the HR Objectives of Lincoln Electric?
- To maintain and expand the Lincoln Incentive Management Philosophy
- To recognize people as [the company's] most valuable asset
- To promote training, education, and development that broaden employee skills
- To maintain an affirmative action program and provide all employees with opportunities for advancement commensurate with their abilities and performance regardless of race, religion, national origin, sex, age, or disability

app 3 Lincoln Electric's Business Objectives

Business Objectives of Lincoln Electric
- To be a global leader in price and quality and serve the customers first
- To achieve and retain global leadership as a total quality supplier of superior products and services
- To respond to our customers with quality, integrity, and value
- To practice prudent and responsible financial management
- To strive continually to be environmentally responsible
- To support communities where we operate and industries in which we participate
- To maintain an environment that fosters ethical behavior, mutual trust, equal opportunity, open communication, personal growth, and creativity.
- To promote feedback
- To demand integrity, discipline, and professional conduct from our employees in every aspect of our business and conduct operations ethically and in accordance with the law
- To reward employees through recognition, pay for performance, and by sharing profits with incentive bonus compensation based on extraordinary achievement as a means of motivation
- To promote dynamic teamwork and innovation

app 4 Employee Interviews

Typical questions and answers from employee interviews are presented here. In order to maintain each employee's personal privacy, fictitious names are given to the interviewees.

Interview I

Betty Stewart, a 52-year-old high school graduate who had been with Lincoln 13 years, was working as a cost accounting clerk at the time of the interview.

Q: What jobs have you held here besides the one you have now?
A: I worked in payroll for a while, and then this job came open and I took it.
Q: How much money did you make last year, including your bonus?
A: I would say roughly around $25,000, but I was off for back surgery for a while.
Q: You weren't paid while you were off for back surgery?
A: No.
Q: Did the Employees Association help out?
A: Yes. The company doesn't furnish that, though. We pay $8 a month into the Employee Association. I think my check from them was $130.00 a week.
Q: How was your performance rating last year?
A: It was around 100 points, but I lost some points for attendance for my back problem.
Q: How did you get your job at Lincoln?
A: I was bored silly where I was working, and I had heard that Lincoln kept their people busy. So I applied and got the job the next day.
Q: Do you think you make more money than similar workers in Cleveland?
A: I know I do.
Q: What have you done with your money?
A: We have purchased a better home. Also, my son is going to the University of Chicago, which costs $13,000 a year. I buy the Lincoln stock which is offered each year, and I have a little bit of gold.
Q: Have you ever visited with any of the senior executives, like Mr. Willis or Mr. Hastings?
A: I have known Mr. Willis for a long time.
Q: Does he call you by name?
A: Yes. In fact, he was very instrumental in my going to the doctor that I am going to with my back. He knows the director of the clinic.
Q: Do you know Mr. Hastings?
A: I know him to speak to him, and he always speaks, always. But I have known Mr. Willis for a good many years. When I did Plant Two accounting I did not understand how the plant operated. Of course you are not allowed in Plant Two, because that's the Electrode Division. I told my boss about the problem one day and the next thing I knew Mr. Willis came by and said, "Come on, Betty, we're going to Plant Two." He spent an hour and a half showing me the plant.
Q: Do you think Lincoln employees produce more than those in other companies?
A: I think with the incentive program the way that it is, if you want to work and achieve, then you will do it. If you don't want to work and achieve, you will not do it no matter where you are. Just because you are merit rated and have a bonus, if you really don't want to work hard, then you're not going to. You will accept your 90 points or 92 or 85 because, even with that you make more money than people on the outside.
Q: Do you think Lincoln employees will ever join a union?
A: I don't know why they would.
Q: So you say that money is a very major advantage?
A: Money is a major advantage, but it's not just the money. It's the fact that having the incentive, you do wish to work a little harder. I'm sure that there are a lot of men here who, if they worked some other place, would not work as hard as they do here. Not that they are overworked—I don't mean that—but I'm sure they wouldn't push.
Q: Is there anything that you would like to add?
A: I do like working here. I am better off being pushed mentally. In another company if you pushed too hard you would feel a little bit of pressure, and someone might say, "Hey, slow down, don't try so hard." But here you are encouraged, not discouraged.

app 4 Employee Interviews (continued)

Interview 2
Ed Sanderson, a 23-year-old high school graduate who had been with Lincoln four years, was a machine operator in the Electrode Division at the time of the interview.

Q: How did you happen to get this job?
A: My wife was pregnant, and I was making three bucks an hour and one day I came here and applied. That was it. I kept calling to let them know I was still interested.
Q: Roughly, what were your earnings last year including your bonus?
A: $45,000.
Q: What have you done with your money since you have been here?
A: Well, we've lived pretty well and we bought a condominium.
Q: Have you paid for the condominium?
A: No, but I could.
Q: Have you bought your Lincoln stock this year?
A: No, I haven't bought any Lincoln stock yet.
Q: Do you get the feeling that the executives here are pretty well thought of?
A: I think they are. To get where they are today, they had to really work.
Q: Wouldn't that be true anywhere?
A: I think more so here because seniority really doesn't mean anything. If you work with a guy who has 20 years here, and you have two months and you're doing a better job, you will get advanced before he will.
Q: Are you paid on a piece-rate basis?
A: My gang does. There are nine of us who make the bare electrode, and the whole group gets paid based on how much electrode we make.
Q: Do you think you work harder than workers in other factories in the Cleveland area?
A: Yes, I would say I probably work harder.
Q: Do you think it hurts anybody?
A: No, a little hard work never hurts anybody.
Q: If you could choose, do you think you would be as happy earning a little less money and being able to slow down a little?
A: No, it doesn't bother me. If it bothered me, I wouldn't do it.
Q: Why do you think Lincoln employees produce more than workers in other plants?
A: That's the way the company is set up. The more you put out, the more you're going to make.
Q: Do you think it's the piece rate and bonus together?
A: I don't think people would work here if they didn't know that they would be rewarded at the end of the year.
Q: Do you think Lincoln employees will ever join a union?
A: No.
Q: What are the major advantages of working for Lincoln?
A: Money.
Q: Are there any other advantages?
A: Yes, we don't have a union shop. I don't think I could work in a union shop.
Q: Do you think you are a career man with Lincoln at this time?
A: Yes.

Interview 3
Roger Lewis, a 23-year-old Purdue graduate in mechanical engineering who had been in the Lincoln sales program for 15 months, was working in the Cleveland sales office at the time of the interview.

Q: How did you get your job at Lincoln?
A: I saw that Lincoln was interviewing on campus at Purdue, and I went by. I later came to Cleveland for a plant tour and was offered a job.
Q: Do you know any of the senior executives? Would they know you by name?
A: Yes, I know all of them—Mr. Hastings, Mr. Willis, Mr. Sabo.

app 4 Employee Interviews (continued)

Q: Do you think Lincoln sales representatives work harder than those in other companies?

A: Yes. I don't think there are many sales reps for other companies who are putting in 50- to 60-hour weeks. Everybody here works harder. You can go out in the plant, or you can go upstairs, and there's nobody sitting around.

Q: Do you see any real disadvantage of working at Lincoln?

A: I don't know if it's a disadvantage, but Lincoln is a spartan company, a very thrifty company. I like that. The sales offices are functional, not fancy.

Q: Why do you think Lincoln employees have such high productivity?

A: Piecework has a lot to do with it. Lincoln is smaller than many plants, too; you can stand in one place and see the materials come in one side and the product go out the other. You feel a part of the company. The chance to get ahead is important, too. They have a strict policy of promoting from within, so you know you have a chance. I think in a lot of other places you may not get as fair a shake as you do here. The sales offices are on a smaller scale, too. I like that. I tell someone that we have two people in the Baltimore office, and they say, "You've got to be kidding." It's smaller and more personal. Pay is the most important thing. I have heard that this is the highest paying factory in the world.

Interview 4

Jimmy Roberts, a 47-year-old high school graduate who had been with Lincoln 17 years, was working as a multiple-drill press operator at the time of the interview.

Q: What jobs have you had at Lincoln?

A: I started out cleaning the men's locker room in 1967. After about a year I got a job in the flux department, where we make the coating for welding rods. I worked there for seven or eight years and then got my present job.

Q: Do you make one particular part?

A: No, there are a variety of parts I make—at least 25.

Q: Each one has a different piece rate attached to it?

A: Yes.

Q: Are some piece rates better than others?

A: Yes.

Q: How do you determine which ones you are going to do?

A: You don't. Your supervisor assigns them.

Q: How much money did you make last year?

A: $53,000.

Q: Have you ever received any kind of award or citation?

A: No.

Q: Was your rating ever over 110?

A: Yes. For the past five years, probably, I made over 110 points.

Q: Is there any attempt to let the others know . . . ?

A: The kind of points I get? No.

Q: Do you know what they are making?

A: No. There are some who might not be too happy with their points and they might make it known. The majority, though, do not make it a point of telling other employees.

Q: Would you be just as happy earning a little less money and working a little slower?

A: I don't think I would, not at this point. I have done piecework all these years, and the fast pace doesn't really bother me.

Q: Why do you think Lincoln productivity is so high?

A: The incentive thing—the bonus distribution. I think that would be the main reason. The paycheck you get every two weeks is important too.

Q: Do you think Lincoln employees would ever join a union?

A: I don't think so. I have never heard anyone mention it.

Q: What is the most important advantage of working here?

A: Amount of money you make. I don't think I could make this type of money anywhere else, especially with only a high school education.

Q: As a black person, do you feel that Lincoln discriminates in any way against blacks?

app 4 Employee Interviews (continued)

A: No. I do not think any more so than any other job. Naturally, there is a certain amount of discrimination, regardless of where you are.

Interview 5
Joe Trahan, a 58-year-old high school graduate who had been with Lincoln 39 years, was employed as a working supervisor in the tool room at the time of the interview.

Q: Roughly what was your pay last year?
A: Over $56,000, salary, bonus, stock dividends.
Q: How much was your bonus?
A: About $26,000.
Q: Have you ever gotten a special award of any kind?
A: Not really.
Q: What have you done with your money?
A: My house is paid for, and my two cars. I also have some bonds and the Lincoln stock.
Q: What do you think of the executives at Lincoln?
A: They're really top notch.
Q: What is the major disadvantage of working at Lincoln Electric?
A: I don't know of any disadvantage at all.
Q: Do you think you produce more than most people in similar jobs with other companies?
A: I do believe that.
Q: Why is that? Why do you believe that?
A: We are on the incentive system. Everything we do, we try to improve to make a better product with a minimum of outlay. We try to improve the bonus.
Q: Would you be just as happy making a little less money and not working quite so hard?
A: I don't think so.
Q: Do you think Lincoln employees would ever join a union?
A: I don't think they would ever consider it.
Q: What is the most important advantage of working at Lincoln?
A: Compensation.
Q: Tell me something about Mr. James Lincoln, who died in 1965.
A: You are talking about Jimmy Sr. He always strolled through the shop in his shirt sleeves. Big fellow. Always looked distinguished. Gray hair. Friendly sort of guy. I was a member of the Advisory Board one year. He was there each time.
Q: Did he strike you as really caring?
A: I think he always cared for people.
Q: Did you get any sensation of a religious nature from him?
A: No, not really.
Q: And religion is not part of the program now?
A: No.
Q: Do you think Mr. Lincoln was a very intelligent man, or was he just a nice guy?
A: I would say he was pretty well educated. A great talker—always right off the top of his head. He knew what he was talking about all the time.
Q: When were bonuses for beneficial suggestions done away with?
A: About 18 years ago.
Q: Did that hurt very much?
A: I do not think so, because suggestions are still rewarded through the merit rating system.
Q: Is there anything you would like to add?
A: It's a good place to work. The union kind of ties other places down. At other places, electricians only do electrical work, carpenters only do carpentry work. At Lincoln Electric we all pitch in and do whatever needs to be done.
Q: So a major advantage is not having a union?
A: That's right.

app 5 Letter from the CEO

To Our Shareholders

Each of you is aware that your company faced enormous challenges in 1993. Those challenges required a focused, creative and positive leadership approach on the part of your management team. As I write this, first quarter 1994 results indicate that the domestic economy is continuing its upward surge. Because of the many tough decisions we had to make in 1993, we are now poised to take advantage of an improved economic climate. Even though much of my personal time has been devoted to overseeing the situation in Europe, excellent results are being achieved in the U.S.A. and Canada.

During 1993, a thorough strategic assessment of our foreign operations led to the conclusion that Lincoln Electric lacked the necessary financial resources to continue to support 21 manufacturing sites. We did not have the luxury of time to keep those plants operating while working to increase our sales and profitability. As a result, with the endorsement of our financial community, the Board of Directors approved management's recommendation to restructure operations in Europe, Latin America, and Japan.

The restructuring included closing the Messer Lincoln operations in Germany, reducing employment throughout Lincoln Norweld, which operates plants in England, France, the Netherlands, Spain, and Norway; and closing manufacturing plants in Venezuela, Brazil, and Japan. The result was a workforce reduction totaling some 770 employees worldwide. We are not abandoning these markets by any means. Rather, the restructuring will allow us to retain and increase sales while relieving us of the high costs associated with excess manufacturing capacity. Now that the restructuring has been accomplished, we operate fifteen plants in ten countries. This capacity will be adequate to supply the inventory needed to support our customers and an increasingly aggressive marketing strategy. We are internationally recognized for outstanding products and service, and we have been certified to the international quality standard ISO-9002.

It was not easy for Lincoln Electric to eliminate manufacturing capacity and jobs. However, I must point out that the overseas companies were given repeated opportunities to turn their performance around. In all fairness, no one anticipated the depth of the recession that continues to devastate Europe, and particularly Germany. But we could not in good conscience, risk both the continuous erosion of shareholder value and the jobs of our dedicated U.S. employees, by remaining unprofitable in these manufacturing operations.

For the second year in the history of this company, it was necessary to take restructuring charges that resulted in a consolidated loss. The restructuring charge totaled $70,100,000 ($40,900,000 after tax), and contributed to a consolidated net loss for 1993 of $38,100,000, compared to a $45,800,000 consolidated loss in 1992.

In 1993 our U.S. and Canadian operations achieved outstanding results with increased levels of sales and profitability and a significant gain in market share. We made a huge step forward by concentrating on the "Top Line" to meet one of our major goals—manufacturing and selling $2.1 million worth of product from our Ohio company each billing day from June 1 through the end of the year. Our Canadian company also made significant contributions with a 38 percent increase in sales. The bottom line automatically moved into greater profitability.

These impressive gains were not made without sacrifice. Lincoln manufacturing people voluntarily deferred 614 weeks of vacation, worked holidays, and many employees worked a seven-day-a-week schedule to fill the steady stream of orders brought in by the sales department as we capitalized on an emerging domestic economy that we felt was being largely ignored by our major competitors.

This remarkable achievement would never have been possible without the expert management of your President and Chief Operating Officer Frederick W. Mackenbach. His leadership consistently inspired our employees and management team alike. The U.S. company's extraordinary performance encouraged the Board of Directors to approve a gross bonus of $55 million, and to continue the regular quarterly dividend payment throughout the year. As you know, the usual course of action for a company reporting a consolidated loss is to cut or defer bonuses and dividends. That these were paid is a tribute to our Board and their steadfast belief in the long-range, proven benefits of the Incentive Management System.

Thinking in the long term is critical to our progress in a world that too often seems to demand instant solutions to complex problems. Your Chairman, your Board, and your management team are determined to resist that impulse. Currently, Lincoln people around the world are working diligently to formulate a Strategic Plan that will carry this company into the next century. An important element of this business plan will be our new state-of-the-art motor manufacturing facility, which is on schedule. Furthermore, we have strengthened our international leadership with the addition of executives experienced in global management to our Board and to key management posts.

app 5 Letter from the CEO (continued)

While your company is indeed emerging from a very challenging period in its history, we project excellent results for 1994, with strong sales, increased profits, and the benefits of those developments accruing to shareholders, customers, and employees. As the year proceeds, we will be looking forward to our Centennial in 1995. I am confident that you and I will enjoy celebrating that event together.

Sincerely,

Donald E. Hastings
Chairman and Chief Executive Officer (Retired May 1997)

Postscript: In Lincoln Electric's centennial year, 1995, sales topped $1 billion for the first time. It was also the year that Hastings eliminated the two-tier wage plan that was instituted in 1993. Under this plan, new hires started at 75 percent of the normal pay rate. This plan increased the turnover among the new hires and was regarded as unfair by senior workers. According to one of them, "If an individual shows he can handle the workload, he should be rewarded." As of 1997, Lincoln Electric appears to be back on track, committed as ever to its philosophy and values.[8] Although Donald F. Hastings has been replaced by Anthony A. Massaro, he continues to be an inspiration for the direction and spirit of Lincoln Electric.

SOUTHWEST AIRLINES

The tale of two men, one airline, and a cocktail napkin . . . "Let's start our own airline," Rollin W. King said to his friend Herb Kelleher in a bar years ago. "Convince me," Herb replied. Rollin drew a triangle connecting Texas's major cities on a cocktail napkin. He said, "We could offer fares so low people would fly instead of drive." Herb paused, placed his drink on the napkin, then spoke. "Rollin, you're crazy. Let's do it."[1]

Introduction

Southwest Airlines is currently facing a multitude of challenges to its historically successful business strategy that has created concerns about its ability to grow in the future. These challenges are both external and internal. External challenges include competition and price pressures, current conditions in the airline industry stemming from deregulation and competitors' continued access to short-haul markets that have long provided the company with significant profitability and competitive advantage. Internally the company faces challenges such as finding continued access to talent that is selected very carefully, and at the same time is compensated very competitively, resulting in relatively low labor costs for the company. The continued access to and availability of talent directly impacts Southwest's operating strategy of being the cheapest and most efficient airline, which in turn depends upon highly motivated employees who deliver outstanding customer service.

Southwest's former CEO and current chairman, Herb Kelleher, has created a unique culture that has been sustained during the company's 30-year life. He is the figurehead that embodies the company's greatest strengths. The unique culture that has been created by Southwest and championed by its chairman has been able, thus far, to sustain its recruitment and retention goals for the types of employees it targets. Employee ownership has been used extensively to tie the fortunes of the company with those responsible for it and to retain employees who might otherwise look to Southwest's competitors. Employee satisfaction and the recognition that Southwest is one of the best companies for attracting, developing, and retaining talented people makes it a well-oiled industry leader.

The question is whether Southwest can continue its profitability, outstanding level of customer service, and reputation for being low cost, on time, and safe in the context of a limited pool of market talent, which is at the heart of its competitive advantage. Can the company maintain its relatively low turnover rate even though the demand for skilled labor has put significant pressures on recruitment and retention of employees? Can the firm continue to spend so much time and money on recruitment and training and remain competitive and equally profitable with all of the external conditions applying pressure on its business at the same time? Will the fact that Herb Kelleher is no longer Southwest's CEO and James Parker has assumed the position hurt the company's reputation in the marketplace and cause it to lose its unique identity and cachet?

In addition to these questions, all of the external environmental issues such as more direct competition, weakened labor relations, and the change from a short-haul airline to a longer-haul airline will have an impact on the future growth and success of the company. The strategies that have been so successful in the past will have to be modified to allow the company to grow into other markets, and these modifications will come with all their accompanying challenges. The key to these challenges may be the company's understanding and appreciation of its People.

Background

Few industries have experienced the turmoil faced by the U.S. domestic airline business during the past two decades. Once characterized by high wages, stable prices, and choreographed competition, the industry changed swiftly and dramatically when deregulation took effect in 1978. Several of the strongest and greatest airlines (e.g., Pan Am, Eastern) disappeared through mergers or bankruptcies. Strikes and disruptions interfered with companies' attempts to reduce costs. New competitors aggressively swooped into the marketplace; the majority failed.

The industry is again in a period of high demand and expanding profitability. Despite the volatile conditions and many organizational failures, one carrier grew and prospered throughout this entire period—Southwest Airlines.

Southwest was controversial from its inception. Although the Texas Aeronautics Commission approved Southwest's petition to fly on February 20, 1968, the nascent airline was locked in legal battles for three years because competing airlines—Braniff, TransTexas, and Continental—fought through political and legal means to keep it out of the market. Through the efforts of Herb Kelleher, a New York University law school graduate and the airline's former chief executive officer and current chairman of the board, Southwest finally secured the support of both the Texas Supreme Court and the U.S. Supreme Court.

Southwest emerged from these early legal battles with its now famous underdog fighting spirit. The company built its initial advertising campaigns around a prominent issue of the time as well as its airport location. Thus "Make Love, Not War" became the airline's theme, and the company became the "Love" airline. Fittingly, *LUV* was chosen as the company's stock ticker symbol. Southwest went on to see successful growth through three distinct periods. The "Proud Texan" period (1971–1978) saw the establishment of a large city-service network

within its home state of Texas. Because it did not engage in interstate commerce, the fledgling carrier was not subject to many federal regulations, particularly those imposed by the Civil Aeronautics Board (CAB). The second phase, "Interstate Expansion" (1978–1986), was characterized by the opening of service to 14 other states. Interstate expansion was made possible by, and thus coincided with, the deregulation of the domestic airline industry. The most recent phase, "National Achievement" (1987–present) has been a time of considerable growth, distinguished recognition, and success.

Despite its past success, Southwest Airlines now faces new challenges that raise concerns about its continued ability to grow. Ironically, many of these concerns are a result of changes brought about by Southwest itself. Some of them are external, such as imitation by competitors who are becoming more efficient and the limited size of the shorter-haul flight markets in which Southwest developed a core competency. Others are internal, including the emergent problems of managing a larger, more complex organization, and a culture that might have been dependent on the charisma of a single individual, Herb Kelleher, or that may not play well to the new audiences needed for future growth. Will Southwest Airlines be able to continue its remarkable success or will emerging conditions seriously threaten Southwest's future prosperity?

The Airline Industry

The competitive environment in which Southwest operates can be subdivided into different value-added stages, customer and service segments, and competitor groups.

Airlines engage in several value-adding activities. These include aircraft procurement, aircraft maintenance, reservation systems, schedule and route planning, in-flight services, and post-flight services. Competitors may differ in their involvement in these activities. For example, Southwest performs some in-house maintenance but offers no post-flight services. By contrast, American Airlines owns and markets its own reservation system, and Allegis, as United Airlines was known briefly in 1987, at one time operated a car rental agency (Hertz) and two hotel chains (Hilton and Westin). (To improve your understanding of key terms used in the airline industry, refer to Exhibit 1.)

Airlines compete for three primary types of customers: travel agents, corporate travel managers,

ex 1 Glossary of Terms

ARC	Airline Reporting Corporation. An organization owned by the airlines that serves as a clearinghouse for processing airline tickets.
ASM	Available Seat Mile. One ASM is one sellable seat, flown for one mile. For example, a 138-seat Boeing 737 traveling 749 miles from LGA to ORD (LaGuardia to O'Hare) represents 103,362 ASMs.
Class of Service	The fare level at which a ticket is sold. This does not refer to the cabin in which the passenger flies. For example, a United Airlines' availability display shows the following classes of service for coach: Y B M H Q V. By subdividing coach into classes, airlines can control inventory and manage yield.
Code Share	An interline agreement by which two carriers are able to apply their flight numbers to the same plane. This often includes an interline connection. For example, American Airlines and South African Airlines code share on SAA's flight to JHB (Johannesburg). The flight has an AA flight number and an SAA flight number. AA can sell it as an American Airlines flight.
CRS	Computer Reservation System. Allows airlines and travel agents to reserve and sell seats on airline flights. CRS companies include Apollo, Sabre, System One, and Worldspan.
Direct Flight	Any flight designated by a single flight number. Direct flights can include multiple stops and even changes of aircraft. For example, Pan Am Flight 1 at one time made 11 stops as it flew "round the world" direct from LAX to JFK.
Full Fare	Designated as "Full Y." The undiscounted first, business, or coach fare. For domestic fares, this is used to calculate the level of discounted fares. Full Y is rarely paid for domestic flights, but is common on international flights when inventory is scarce.
Interline Agreement	Refers to various agreements between carriers. Common interline agreements concern the transfer of baggage, the endorsement and acceptance of tickets, and joint airfares (for example, a passenger flies USAir from Albany to JFK and then SAS to Copenhagen).
Inventory	The number of seats available for each class of service for a given flight. For example, a USAir flight may have no K inventory available (seats to sell at K class fare levels) although higher-priced H seats may be available. Both seats are in coach.
Load Factor	The percentage of ASMs that are filled by paying passengers. Can be calculated by dividing RPMs by ASMs.
O&D	Origin and Destination. Refers to the originating and terminating airports of an itinerary segment. Connection points are not counted in O&Ds. This is different from city-pair, which refers to the origination and termination of a flight segment. For example, for a passenger traveling on NW from HPN (White Plains) to SMF (Sacramento), the O&D market is HPN-SMF. The city-pairs flown will be HPN-DTW and DTW-SMF (White Plains-Detroit, Detroit-Sacramento).
Restricted Fare	Any fare that has restrictive rules attached to it. Common restrictions include Saturday Night Stayover, Advance Purchase, Day/Time of Travel, Non-Refundability, and Class of Service. Generally, lower fares have greater restrictions.
RPM	Revenue Passenger Mile. One passenger paying to fly one mile. For example, a passenger who pays to fly from LGA to ORD represents 749 RPMs. The class of service and fare paid are not considered in calculating RPMs.
Stage Length	The length of a flight segment. The stage length between LGA and ORD is 749 miles.
Unrestricted Fare	A fare with no restrictions. Often, this is not the full fare. For example, American's Y26 fare is an unrestricted fare, but still lower than the full Y fare.
Yield	Measured as revenue per RPM.

and individual travelers. The two major categories of passengers are leisure travelers, who tend to be quite price sensitive, and business travelers, who are more concerned with convenience. To satisfy the different needs of some or all of these groups, airlines present a wide variety of services, depending on their strategy.

Passenger service can be categorized along a number of dimensions. For example, airlines differ by geographical coverage; some specialize in short-haul service while others provide a vast network of interconnected long-haul and short-haul flights on a global basis through a network of strategic alliances. They also differ in how their routes are structured within the territories they serve. The two extremes are point-to-point and hub-and-spoke. The former is characterized by direct service between two points. The latter is characterized by complex, coordinated routes and schedule structures that channel passengers from numerous far-flung airports (the spokes) through a central airport (the hub). The hub itself has many costly infrastructure requirements (baggage handling systems, large terminals, maintenance facilities, and parts inventories). To address the pricing complexity created by multiple traffic flows through a hub, hub-and-spoke carriers conduct complicated yield and inventory management calculations. The result of this complexity is that the hub-and-spoke pricing structure is systematically different from point-to-point pricing. These added complexities allow a carrier to offer flights between more "city-pairs" than it could under a point-to-point network. For a company that relies on a network, like an airline or telephone company, competitive advantage accrues from economies of scope, that is, the geographic reach of that network. Economies of scope do not necessarily complement economies of scale, and in fact are often achieved at the expense of scale economies and vice versa. Thus, although the hub-and-spoke system is driven by economies of scope, each strategy, hub-and-spoke or point-to-point, has its own inherent cost and organizational implications.

Passenger service can also be characterized in terms of breadth. An airline may choose to provide a broad gamut of services including meals, advance seat assignments, and frequent flier programs (full service), or it can offer only Spartan services (no-frills). A further differentiation is the number of service classes offered. Most airlines have two classes of service, First and Coach. Some offer three classes, First, Business, and Coach (United and American on select flights), others offer only Coach (Southwest), and a few offer only First Class (Midwest Express). In addition to the direct cost of providing differentiated service, amenities such as First Class seating and in-flight meals indirectly affect the cost structure of an airline by limiting the number of seats its aircraft can hold. Because Southwest does not currently offer meals or First Class service, its 737-300 holds 137 seats, whereas a United Airlines 737-300 holds only 128 seats.

U.S. airlines can be categorized into three major competitor groups based on geographical coverage. First are the "major" national airlines. They include America West Airlines, American Airlines, Continental Airlines, Delta Airlines, Northwest Airlines, United Airlines, and Southwest Airlines. Second are the regionals, which include Airtran (formerly ValuJet), Frontier Airlines, Alaska Airlines/Horizon Air, and many others. Third are the commuter or "feed" carriers, most of which operate as extensions of the majors. These carriers use mostly turboprop or regional jet equipment and fly routes that are generally less than 500 miles. Some of these carriers include Atlantic Coast Airlines, which operates as United Express; Atlantic Southeast Airlines, which operates as Delta's Business Express; Comair Holdings, another Delta commuter; and Mesa Air Group, which operates its own flights as well as feeder flights for United, SkyWest, Inc., and numerous others.

Competitive Environment

The *Airline Deregulation Act of 1978* redefined the industry by eliminating the ability of the CAB to set fares, allocate routes, and control entry into and exit from markets. Unfortunately, most airlines were hamstrung by high cost structures, including exorbitant labor costs, and highly inefficient planes and infrastructure facilities. After the complete removal of entry and price controls by 1980, competition intensified considerably as new entrants cherry-picked the large carriers' most profitable routes. This led to an extended period of severe industry shake-out and consolidation.

Industry Characteristics

The industry's structural characteristics make it a tough place to be very profitable. The overall industry is not highly concentrated, although it has become more concentrated since deregulation. Nevertheless, most discrete markets are served by a limited number of carriers. In the oligopolistic markets in which most airlines compete, the pricing actions of one company affect the profits of all competitors. Intense price wars have been frequent in the industry. Because competition varies from route to route, a carrier can dominate one market, be dominated in another, and face intense rivalry in a third. As a result of the hub-and-spoke system, airlines face head-to-head competition with more carriers in more markets.

Suppliers tend to have relatively high bargaining power. Certain unions are in a position to shut down airlines. Airplane manufacturers (Boeing, Airbus) have considerable power in altering the terms of purchase for planes. Furthermore, the business is capital intensive and requires very large expenditures for airplanes and other infrastructure.

Despite difficult economics, the industry is still attractive to new entrants. There are few substitutes for long-haul air travel. In addition, most of the incumbents have high cost structures that are exceedingly difficult to improve significantly. Carrier failures and downsizing have also created a large supply of relatively new "used" aircraft, and the cost of acquiring aircraft is reduced further by the practice of aircraft leasing. Given high debt levels and low profitability in comparison with other industries, most airlines, including Southwest, have begun to lease their planes rather than purchase them. In light of high debt and low profits, the depreciation tax shield is not as valuable to the airlines. By leasing, carriers can "sell" that tax shield to the leasing company, actually creating value for the carrier. As a result, entry barriers are not as high as one would expect in other capital-intensive industries.

Furthermore, new entrants generally gain significant cost advantage by securing lower labor costs because they are not burdened by the unfavorable union contracts that affect many older airlines. Many of the union contracts agreed to by the major airlines call for higher pay and contain work rule provisions that reduce labor productivity. In addition, new entrants are sometimes able to gain favorable terms by purchasing excess capacity of other airlines, such as training and maintenance.

Profitability

In order to survive and profit in this tough environment, airlines attempt to manipulate three main variables: cost, calculated as total operating expenses divided by available seat miles (ASM); yield, calculated as total operating revenues divided by the number of revenue passenger miles (RPM); and load factor, calculated as the ratio between RPMs and ASMs, which measures capacity utilization. Thus,

profitability, defined as income divided by ASM, is computed as:

$$Profitability = [yield \times load\ factor] - cost$$

The major airlines have faced intensive competition from low-priced airlines during the past 10 to 15 years. While these low-priced airlines expanded the market for air travel, they also placed great downward pressure on the prices of the majors, thereby reducing their yields. To compete, the majors engaged in great cost-cutting efforts.

Capacity

J. P. Morgan Chase analysts believe that the most important factor influencing pricing in the long-term will be the falling industry cost curve. They point out that low-cost airlines have already lowered and inverted the traditionally downward-sloping industry cost curve. "With it they have pressured fares industry-wide, but particularly in short-haul markets where their impact on costs have been most dramatic . . . the airlines that are increasing capacity are those lowest on the industry's cost curve."[2] This shift has occurred because of the growth in low-cost, short-haul travel.

Outlook

Lehman Brothers analysts concluded that the U.S. airline industry was entering a mature and more stable phase, as the major restructuring it required was largely accomplished. In their view, this restructuring was driven by two key developments. First was the retrenchment of the majors into their core hubs. Second was technology diffusion, which occurred when the weaker airlines upgraded their systems technology regarding pricing and yield management and eliminated many disparities among major carriers.

Arenas of competition have also shifted. This trend was heightened by the events of September 11, 2001, and the public's concern about flying. Low-cost carriers, including Southwest Airlines and Shuttle by United, dominate short-haul capacity in the West. Expansion of the low-cost carriers now seems to be increasing, and competition appears to be increasing. Meanwhile the East Coast is still dominated by high-cost carriers such as Delta and Continental, although they are facing significant profitability issues. Consequently, it is not surprising that the low-cost airlines have targeted the east as a major arena for expansion. Southwest's invasion of Florida and Providence, Rhode Island is a noteworthy example. In the Northeast, capacity reduction by high-cost competitors such as American and Continental has also enhanced the opportunities for low-cost airlines such as JetBlue, which now has a hub at JFK and wants to add a plane a week to its fleet from now until 2008! As carriers learn to adapt the low-cost formula to the geographic, climatic, and market intricacies of the Northeast, low-cost operations will likely continue to expand.[3]

Southwest Airlines' Mission and Objectives

Southwest Airlines' mission focuses to an unusually large degree on customer service and employee commitment. According to its annual report, the mission of Southwest Airlines is "dedication to the highest quality of Customer Service delivered with a sense of warmth, friendliness, individual pride, and Company Spirit." Indeed, Southwest proudly proclaims, "We are a company of People, not planes. That is what distinguishes us from other airlines and other companies." In many respects, the vision that separates Southwest from many of its competitors is the degree to which it is defined by a unique partnership with, and pride in, its employees. As stated in its *Annual Report*:

At Southwest Airlines, People are our most important asset. Our People know that because that's the way we treat them. Our People, in turn, provide the best Customer Service in the airline industry. And that's what we are in business for—to provide Legendary Customer Service. We start by hiring only the best People, and we know how to find them. People want to work for a "winner," and because of our success and the genuine concern and respect we have for each of our Employees, we have earned an excellent reputation as a great place to work. As a result, we attract and hire the very best applicants. Once hired, we train, develop, nurture, and, most important of all, support our People! In other words, we empower our Employees to effectively make decisions and to perform their jobs in this very challenging industry.

The airline's goal is to deliver a basic service very efficiently and safely. This translates into a number of fundamental objectives. A central pillar of its approach is to provide safe, low-price transportation in conjunction with maximum customer convenience. The airline provides a high frequency of flights with consistent on-time departures and arrivals. Southwest's employees also aspire to make this commodity service a "fun" experience. Playing games is encouraged, such as "guess the weight of the gate agent." The fun spirit is tempered so that it is never in poor taste and does not alienate business travelers.

Southwest Airlines' Strategy

Southwest Airlines is categorized as a Low Fare/No Frills airline. However, its size and importance have led most analysts to consider it one of the major airlines despite its fit in the low-fare segment. In a fundamental sense, Southwest's business-level strategy is to be the cheapest and most efficient operator in specific domestic regional markets, while continuing to provide its customers with a high level of convenience and service leveraged off its highly motivated employees. Essentially, Southwest's advantage is its low cost and good safety reputation.

Cost Leadership

Southwest operates the lowest-cost major airline in the industry. The airline devised a number of clever stratagems to achieve this low-cost structure. For example, by serving smaller, less congested secondary airports in larger cities, which tend to have lower gate costs and landing fees, Southwest can maintain schedules cheaply and easily. Southwest's approach is also facilitated by its focus on the Southwest and other locations with generally excellent weather conditions, which leads to far fewer delays. Moreover, by following a point-to-point strategy, Southwest need not coordinate flight schedules into connecting hubs and spokes, which dramatically reduces scheduling complexity and costs.

Route Structure

Historically, Southwest has specialized in relatively short-haul flights and has experienced considerable threat from providers of ground transportation (cars, trains, and buses) because the buyers of these short-haul services tend to be quite price sensitive. Southwest has widened the market for air travel by attracting large numbers of patrons who previously relied on ground transportation. For example, before it entered the Louisville to Chicago market, weekly traffic totaled 8,000 passengers. After Southwest entered the market, that number grew to over 26,000. This increase in traffic is now recognized as "The Southwest Effect." Emphasis on short-haul flights has also allowed it to pare costly services such as food, which passengers demand on longer flights. Passengers are provided with only an "extended snack"—cheese, crackers, and a Nutri-Grain bar.

Turnaround Time

Its route structure has helped Southwest to experience the most rapid aircraft turnaround time in the industry (15 to 20 minutes versus an industry average of 55 minutes). Interestingly, Southwest's "20 Minute Turnaround" can be traced directly to the carrier's first days of operation in Texas when financial pressures forced the company to sell one of the four Boeing 737s it had purchased for its initial service. Having only three planes to fly three routes necessitated very rapid turnaround.

Rapid turnaround time is essential for short-haul flights because airplanes are airborne for a smaller percentage of time than on long-haul flights. Faster turnaround also allows Southwest to fly more daily segments with each plane, which in turn increases its assets' turnover. Its ability to maintain this practice is being challenged by the increased security requirements, but so far it seems to be doing well. Experience will show the exact impact of the *Airline Security Act* signed into law by President Bush on November 19, 2001.

Fleet Composition

Southwest has the simplest fleet composition among the major airlines. The company flies only Boeing 737 planes and has committed to fly the 737 exclusively through 2004.

In choosing the fuel-efficient 737, Southwest developed a close relationship with Boeing that enabled it to receive comparatively favorable purchase terms. Although Southwest flies a number of model variations of the 737, the cockpits of the entire fleet are standardized. Therefore, any pilot can fly any plane, and any plane can be deployed on any route. In addition to helping capture scale economies at a much smaller size than its larger competitors, the homogeneous fleet composition reduces the complexities of training, maintenance, and service. It is difficult to calculate the large savings associated with this approach, but they exist in almost all operating areas including scheduling, training, aircraft deployment and use, wages and salaries, maintenance, and spare parts inventories.

Travel Agency Exposure

According to its annual report, Southwest sells over 70 percent of its seats directly rather than through travel agents (compared with the industry average of 20 to 25 percent), thereby saving the 10 percent commission paid to travel agents. This also alleviates the need to participate in many of the travel agent reservation systems.

While this reduces the company's breadth of distribution, it helps to reduce commission payments and Computer Reservation System (CRS) fees, which are approximately $2.50 per flight segment.

Gates

Access to gates is often a constraining factor in the ability of airlines to expand, because major airports have limited numbers of gates and most are already taken by other airlines. An emphasis on less-crowded secondary airports has alleviated this problem for Southwest. Southwest purchases or leases gates at airports, as opposed to renting the gates of other airlines, which enables the airline to use its own ground crews.

Connections

Southwest does not offer connections to other airlines, which simplifies its ground operations. However, this also limits access for many passengers, particularly from international flights.

Fare Structure

Southwest also controls costs through its simplified fare structure. While Southwest's major competitors have complex fare structures and use computers and artificial intelligence programs to maximize passenger revenues, Southwest offers no special business or first-class seating. Rather, it generally offers a regular coach fare and a limited number of discounted coach fares.

Labor

Labor is the largest cost component of airlines despite the heavy capital investment demanded in the industry. Southwest's labor costs are roughly 30 percent of revenues and 40 percent of all expenses. This represents about 8 cents per seat mile. About 82 percent of Southwest's employees are unionized. Given the ability of unions to bring carrier operations to a halt, it is not surprising that they wield considerable power. The International Association of Machinists and Aerospace Workers (IAM) represents customer service and reservation employees; the Transportation Workers Union of America (TWU) represents flight attendants; the Southwest Airline Pilots' Association (SWAPA) represents pilots; and the International Brotherhood of Teamsters (IBT) represents aircraft cleaners, mechanics, flight training instructors, and others. There are also some other smaller unions.

In an industry where unions and management have often been at war—and where unions have the power to resist essential changes—the quality of their relationship is a crucial issue. Perhaps one of the best examples of this is the 1994 agreement between Southwest Airlines and SWAPA. The pilots agreed to keep pay rates at existing levels for 5 years, with increases of 3 percent in 3 of the last 5 years of the 10-year deal (5-year base term, with an additional 5 years unless it is terminated by the union). Pilots can earn additional pay based on company profits. The pilots also obtained options to acquire up to 1.4 million shares of company stock in each of the 10 years, in accord with market prices on the date of the deal. Pilots hired between 1996 and 2003 obtain lesser amounts of options at 5 percent over the then market value of the stock. Maximum pilot salary at Southwest is $148,000 yearly, while at United it is $290,000 yearly. At JetBlue it is $115,000.

Customer Service
Southwest's approach to customer service is one of its core strategies. Its "Positively Outrageous Service" (POS) is different from the customer service associated with other major airlines. Service is provided with friendliness, caring, warmth, and company spirit—staff go out of their way to be helpful. This approach to service leverages Southwest's outstanding relationship with its employees. However, this stellar customer service does not include costly amenities like reserved seats or food service, and offers only very limited automatic baggage rechecking. By emphasizing flight frequency and on-time performance, Southwest has redefined the concept of quality air service. This unusual approach has allowed Southwest to differentiate its service while maintaining its cost leadership strategy.

Marketing
Marketing savvy also plays a key role in Southwest's strategy. Since Southwest's inception, the major elements of the product offering have been price, convenience, and service. As a Texas native serving mostly Texas markets, it has played the role of the hometown underdog, fighting against the majors. Now, when Southwest enters a new market, it uses a sophisticated combination of advertising, public relations, and promotions in the belief that once people fly Southwest they will be hooked.

Growth
Despite its remarkable growth in what had been until recently a relatively moribund industry, Southwest has not emphasized growth as an objective. In fact, Herb Kelleher has expressed a "go-slow" phi-losophy. For example, Southwest will not enter markets unless it perceives favorable conditions, which range from the wishes of the local community to the availability of an appropriate labor supply. Given its record of success and its reputation, it is not surprising that many communities want Southwest to serve their markets. After all, good air service is considered by most communities to be an essential aspect of economic development. However, Southwest's policy prohibits accepting monetary subsidies or other incentives that cities and airports offer to gain air service. Southwest has also demonstrated a remarkable ability to manage its growth, an essential commodity in an industry known for its complexity. The inability to manage rapid growth has been blamed for the failure of many carriers, including Braniff, PeopleExpress, and ValuJet.

Organization

Structure
Southwest, like most airlines, is a formal and centralized organization. Organizationally, Southwest is structured according to functions. The nature of operations in the airline business is quite mechanical. That is, airline operations naturally aim for efficiency and consistency. They are not spontaneous—they value clocklike behavior. Planes must be in certain places at certain times and must be operated safely and efficiently. Safety itself requires following very rigorous procedures to ensure proper maintenance and training. The reputation of an airline can be severely damaged by only one or two serious accidents. Therefore, the organization of Southwest is characterized by a high degree of formalization and standardization.

Reporting to Vice Chairman of the Board and Chief Executive Officer (CEO) James Parker are Colleen Barrett, president and chief operating officer, and Gary Kelly, executive vice president and chief financial officer. Perhaps the most influential is Colleen C. Barrett, who is in charge of such key functions as marketing, sales, advertising, human resources, customer relations, and governmental affairs. John G. Denison is executive vice president in charge of corporate services, which includes finance, legal, facilities, reservations, revenue management (pricing), and systems (including computer services and telecommunications). There is one other vice president reporting to Parker, Al Davis, who is in charge of internal auditing and special projects. For operations controller functions he reports to Gary Kelly.

How has Southwest Airlines maintained high levels of customer and employee satisfaction in the context of a functional organization? The company uses a number of mechanisms to allow employee participation. The fundamental concept is the notion of a "loose-tight" design. Within the context of tight rules and procedures, employees are encouraged to take a wide degree of leeway. The company maintains rather informal job descriptions and decentralizes decision making regarding customer service. So while standardization is very high regarding operations, it is low with respect to customer service. Employees are empowered to do what is necessary to satisfy customers. Flight attendants are allowed to improvise cabin instructions and use their judgment in addressing passengers' needs. The company management operates with an informal open door policy that allows employees to circumvent the formal hierarchy. Employees are encouraged to try things, knowing they will not be punished.

Southwest's organization is considerably simpler than its major competitors. Most of its competitors must manage the spatial complexity of far-flung international operations and contend with the added intricacies of hub-and-spoke systems. These large international carriers are also involved in complex alliances with other airlines in foreign markets to augment the scope of their services. They manage code sharing arrangements with small regional domestic carriers. In short, the large carriers are complex networks, with more complicated organizational management issues.

Size

Southwest operates in more than 57 cities in 29 states and employs over 30,000 people. As of 2001, this consists of approximately 6,228 flight personnel, 1,049 maintenance workers, 13,148 in ground customer service, and 2,519 in management, marketing, accounting, and clerical positions. Southwest has become such a popular employer that it received 216,000 resumes in the year 2000 and hired 5,134 new employees. Southwest is still a relatively small company compared with the other major airlines. It ranks eighth in revenues and fifth in passenger boardings. Southwest's Available Seat Miles (ASMs) total less than a quarter that of American Airlines, and it operates a fleet of only 352 aircraft compared with about 700 aircraft for American. Nevertheless, Southwest is the largest carrier in a significant number of the markets in which it flies and the dominant airline in the short-haul niche of the airline business.

Adaptability

Southwest has been a very nimble organization, quick to take advantage of market opportunities. For example, when American Airlines and USAir scaled back their California operations, Southwest quickly took over the abandoned gates, acquired more planes, and now has 50 percent of the California market. Another example is Southwest's expansion into the Chicago Midway market following the collapse of Midway Airlines. Much of this flexibility stems from the company's remarkable labor relations. In addition, although Southwest is still purely a domestic carrier, it is developing a strategic alliance with Icelandair, a small North European carrier.

Human Resource Management

At Southwest Airlines the human resource function is called the People Department. According to the department's mission statement: "recognizing that our people are the competitive advantage, we deliver the resources and services to prepare our people to be winners, to support the growth and profitability of the company, while preserving the values and special culture of Southwest Airlines." The crucial importance of human resources to the strategy of Southwest has made the People Department more organizationally central to the company than its counterparts are at its competitors. Given Southwest's reputation as a great place to work, it is no wonder that so many people apply for each job opening

Unique Approach Aligned with Culture

Southwest Airlines distinguishes itself from its competitors by doing many things differently. One of the most striking differences is how it goes through the selection process. It begins with Chairman Herb Kelleher, who states, "We like mavericks—people who have a sense of humor. We look for attitude. We'll train you on whatever you need to do, but the one thing we can't do is change inherent attitudes."[4] Libby Sartain, Southwest's former vice president of People, remarked that the company has had to become more and more creative in how it finds candidates.[5] In a typical year, she noted, the company hires 4,000 to 5,000 people. In the past, about one out of four applicants would be interviewed and less than 3 percent would actually be hired. In theory, the odds of getting into Harvard are higher. [6]

Hire Based on Attitude

What does Southwest look for in the selection process? The approach places great emphasis on hiring based on attitude. During the interview process, there may not be a fixed set of skills or experiences that are examined.[7] The search is for something that Southwest considers to be much more elusive and important—a blend of energy, humor, team spirit, and self-confidence. These key predictors are used by Southwest to indicate how well applicants will perform and fit in with its own unique culture.

The hiring process at Southwest also emphasizes the importance of hiring people who are inclined toward teamwork. Ann Rhodes, former vice president of People, stated that one of the important unwritten rules at Southwest was that "you can't be an elitist." Southwest actually uses a personality test to rate candidates (on a scale from one to five) on seven separate traits.[8] The seven areas are cheerfulness, optimism, decision-making skills, team spirit, communication, self-confidence, and self-starter skills. Anything less than a three is considered cause for rejection. With this methodology, the airline has chosen to use a multiple hurdles approach where an applicant must exceed fixed levels of proficiency on all of the predictors in order to be accepted. With this approach a higher rating in one area will not compensate for a lower score on one of the other predictors. Southwest believes in these seven predictors, and that failing to make the grade in even one will guarantee that the person will be unsuccessful on the job.

Interview Based on Strategy

The process of selection based on the seven predictors applies to everyone from pilots to mechanics. In the words of Libby Sartain, "we would rather go short and work overtime than hire one bad apple." In addition to the evaluation of the seven predictors, Southwest uses other methods in the selection process. The process begins as in most companies with an interview. The interviewer looks for team-oriented people with prior work experiences that match. A common theme in screening all candidates revolves around people skills. According to Gittell,[9] the easiest way to get in trouble at Southwest is to offend another employee. Even when pilots are interviewed, the airline goes out of its way to find candidates who lack an attitude of superiority and who seem likely to treat coworkers with respect. Southwest's system for selecting its people is time intensive but based on a history of bringing in people that fit into the culture of the company.

Southwest publicly explains almost every detail of the practices it uses to select employees. In theory, any company could attempt to copy the process and claim it as its own. It would probably fail for a number of reasons. First, Southwest expends much more energy and time than most companies do. In order to find the right people it spends the money up front on the selection process in the belief that it becomes worthwhile over time. So, not every company would be willing or able to make that type of investment. Second, Southwest's selection process matches the culture of the company. It values people and "walks the talk" when it comes to finding the right employees. (See Exhibits 2 and 3.) Some additional quotes from Herb Kelleher back this up:

Other companies don't value attitude. They don't pay all that much attention to it. They don't make it a priority. I've been with companies where they have an opening, and you know what they consider the function of the Personnel Department? To plug a hole as quickly as they possibly can. That's quite different from what we do in many cases. Some years ago our VP of the People Department told me they had interviewed 34 people for a ramp agent position in Amarillo, Texas, and she was a little embarrassed about the amount of time it was taking and the implied cost of it, and my answer was: if you have to interview 134 people to get the right attitude on the ramp in Amarillo, Texas, do it.

Developing the Process

The People Department, which is the HR function at Southwest Airlines, developed its interview process in collaboration with Development Dimensions International, a consulting firm that specializes in designing sound selection procedures. The procedures at Southwest Airlines adhere to the basic principles of good interview design: structured questions, systematic scoring, multiple interviewers, and interviewer training.

Benefits of Centralization and Role of the People Department

The overall selection and placement process at Southwest is centralized like the rest of the organizational structure of the airline. The centralization of this process helps make the best candidate available for the right job (that is, it makes the placement process successful and feasible). Having trained people involved in the selection and placement decision improves the efficiency of the process and also reduces the risk of bias or unfair judgments. It also helps the operating managers to concentrate on their

ex 2 Interview with an Employee in the Marketing Division

Interview of Joanna DePinto, employee in marketing division of Southwest Airlines, conducted by the team by telephone on March 23, 2001.

1. **When you got hired, what was the process?**

   I was an intern in Austin, when I applied. I got interviewed by a bunch of people many times. Group interviews are a big deal at Southwest. They see your ability to communicate well and get along with other people. You meet the group you will be working with and they see how you get on with them.

2. **Do you know of any other companies, which have the same selection process?**

   No! Well not exactly the same selection process. Some companies like Compac and Cisco are trying to emulate us. They are hiring people not just for technical skills but also for their people skills.

3. **Who do you think makes the final decision about selection?**

   The applicants work with a recruiter through all rounds of interviews, but I think the final decision is made by the manager of the department and the director.

4. **What impacts the decision-making process most at Southwest?**

   Everyone works towards the good of the company. It all comes down to what is best for the company. Cost saving is very important. As far as hiring is concerned, it is definitely about the kind of person you are. They hire for personality and train for skill.

5. **So attitude and personality are the key drivers at Southwest?**

   Oh! Absolutely!

6. **What about internal politics in hiring and selection?**

   There is no infighting or disagreement. People really try and do what is best for the company. I don't think there is any internal politics that affects decision making. People enjoy coming to work everyday, there is no cut-throat competition or anything.

7. **What is Herb like?**

   Oh! He is awesome! He is a wonderful man, very reachable. The first day I went to work, he got into the same elevator as me and kissed me! I got like quite excited, "Herb Kelleher kissed me." When I reached my office I told my colleagues about it and they said, "Oh! But he kisses everyone!"

---

job while remaining involved in selection and placement decisions without personally formulating the process. This of course is a huge benefit in terms of keeping decisions and policies consistent throughout the organization.

The People Department at Southwest enjoys an extremely important role in its selection and placement process. This kind of centralized process helps the organization because the applicants have to go to one place to apply for any position, and specialists trained in selection techniques can assist in the process of deciding which candidates should be hired and where they ought to be placed. Southwest keeps the line managers and other employees involved in the process, which serves to its benefit for a number of reasons. Employees who get the opportunity to contribute in the selection of their team members also become more committed to helping them succeed and feel a sense of urgency. The involvement of all levels of management and employees along with the HR department in the selection and placement process helps Southwest build a strong network of employees, who can then successfully forward the organization's mission of providing the right attitude and service to its customers.

ex 3 Interview with an Employee in the University of People

Question 1A: Describe the Hiring Process at Southwest

Southwest Airlines tries to fill all vacancies from within the Company if at all possible. The reason for this is because we are making the assumption that someone who is already employed by us has the "spirit" and attitude and work ethics we want, whereas we would be taking a chance by hiring from outside. The theory is that we will hire for attitude and train for skill. Obviously, there are times when we must hire from outside. First, of course, we do as close a match as possible for the job requirements—although if an internal doesn't meet all the requirements but does meet most of them and has a great attitude/spirit, we will give them a chance at interviewing for the position.

Our interview process can be quite strenuous. We do group interviews for some frontline positions such as Flight Attendant or Reservation Sales Agent. This would consist of a team of interviewers and each asks questions that the applicants respond to. Then each interviewer gets to cast a vote for or against bringing each applicant back for a second interview. From this point on the process is similar for all job applicants. The second interview (for those who participated in group interviews) and the first interview for other applicants usually consists of a smaller interview team. The questions are asked by all of the interviewers but they are basically "behavior based" questions. This means that applicants will be asked to describe a time in their past work life when they were faced with a certain situation. The response should include what the situation was, what the applicant did or how they handled it, and finally what was the result. For example, if the job required good conflict management skills, an interviewer might ask the applicant to describe a time when they were in a heated disagreement with a coworker—what was the situation, how did you handle it, and what was the result. The response from the applicant is a predictor of the behavior this potential employee would use in the future on this job if hired.

When the interview is over, all interview team members must come to a consensus as to whether to hire this individual or, as is frequently necessary, to bring the applicant back for a third interview. If there is a third interview, the next higher level of leadership will be involved. Sometimes, depending on the position being interviewed for, interviews can continue all the way through the vice president. An example of that is that anyone taking a position within our People Department (human resources) or even just moving from one position to another within the People Department will interview first with a recruiter and interview team consisting of peers and first-level leadership for that position, and continue all the way through our vice president of People.

This is time consuming; however, we are more confident of getting the right person in the right position. Also, you should be aware that we frequently start with a pool of applicants but end up reposting the job. The reasons this happens is that we do not take the best person in the pool; instead we are looking for the best person for the job and if we don't find him or her in the pool, then we start over. An empty desk for a period of time is sometimes a price we pay in order to find the best fit.

Question 1B: Can Any Company Duplicate What Southwest Does? Have Any Tried or Benchmarked and Then Launched Their Own?

Many companies have benchmarked Southwest for numerous reasons. In fact, SWA at one time hosted a "Culture Day" for outside companies because we had so many requests. We have stopped doing this because it got so big, it was taking us away from what we should be doing. I'm sure that some of those organizations have listened to what they were told and did try to implement some of what we do. However, I do not know who did not do it, nor do I have information on how successful they were. Obviously, there is a down side to the way we approach hiring. Lots of organizations probably decided not to put the extra burden on other employees by having a position vacant for very long and using resources in the hiring process for such a long interview process.

Question 2: Who Makes the Selection and Placement Decisions at Southwest?

I believe I answered this question in 1A above. To recap, the decision is a joint decision of the interview team if it is a frontline position. If not frontline, then not only does the interview team have to be in agreement, but all the leaders involved in the interview process. If any one of them kicks back on an application, it can take that applicant out of the running.

Question 3: What Impacts the Decision-Making Process the Most at Southwest? Do Politics Impact the Process?

The hire/no hire decision is based on how well of a match the applicant is to the requirements of the job PLUS their attitude/spirit—it takes both! As far as politics are concerned, even Herb stays out of the hiring process. It is the least political, buddy-buddy system that it can be.

ex 3 Interview with an Employee in the University of People (continued)

Question 4: How Important Is the Selection and Placement Process to Southwest's Success?
Southwest Airlines has a unique culture and our financial success as an airline is founded on that culture; it is what makes us "different." We like to have fun, we love a challenge, we are made up of people who take accountability for their actions and for the success of our airline—we, therefore, believe in hard work/hard play. We like people who are willing to work outside the lines and are willing to step up to the plate and make a decision. We don't like people who take themselves too seriously, are complainers or not willing to "do whatever it takes." Not everyone is fit for this environment. If we do not continue to employ "the right stuff," our culture, overall, could fail. How important is the selection and placement process to Southwest's success? I don't know a word descriptive enough! Let's just say it is crucial!

—Pat Janson, Facilitator
University of People, Career Development Services
People Department, Southwest Airlines
March 27 and April 4, 2001

The Decision-Making in Selection and Placement

The People Department has sound procedures in place for any level of selection, be it in the form of interviews or written assessments. The selection and placement decisions would, however, finally be made by a combined panel of line managers and specialized representatives from the People Department. Going by Chairman Herb Kelleher's deep involvement and his interpersonal demeanor in the management of Southwest, one could also assume that he would have the final say in any placement and selection decisions. In his own words, "My name is Herb/Big Daddy—O/You should all know me/I run this show."[11] Selection and placement decisions at Southwest seem to be made by line managers and senior management with full participation of present employees in the spirit of true partnership. The People Department is responsible for designing the process and is largely responsible for attracting, helping to select and place, and retaining a strong set of employees.

All of the various applications go through the People Department and prospective candidates are then interviewed and tested for *aptitude and attitude* by a panel of interviewers, in keeping with a consistent process that is developed by the HR function. Once selection decisions are made, placement of the right individual in the right position is once again done with the involvement of all levels of employees from that department along with specialists.

As mentioned earlier, though, while em-ployees and their feedback are valued at Southwest, it seems from the workings of the management headed by Herb Kelleher that final decision-making powers are largely vested with the management of the company. This process seems to have worked quite well for Southwest Airlines.

The vice president of People, and her team have spent years analyzing the staff at Southwest and have calibrated their questions to the specific needs and requirements of each job, as well as attributes like judgment and decision-making skills. The process can take up to six weeks before anybody is hired. About 20 percent of recruits fail to make it through the training period at the University for People in Dallas.

The time and money spent on the recruitment process has resulted in a turnover rate of 9 percent, the lowest in the industry. Traditionally, the HR department does not do much to endear itself to finance. However, Southwest's CFO, Gary Kelly, believes investing in hiring is vital. "If you are not going to work hard to get people who are a good fit, it will hurt you. For example, we have never had a strike. What airline is even close to being able to say that?"

The predictor most stringently used for selection and placement of employees is personality and values. A panel of representatives from the People Department and the Inflight Department first interviews the candidates for flight attendant jobs. Before the selection process is finished, they will also have one-on-one interviews with a recruiter or supervisor from the hiring department and a peer. The selection is highly systematic and a multiple hurdles approach combined with a good interview design: structured questions, systematic scoring, multiple interviews, and interviewer training implies that only the best candidates are selected. The selection of candidates that fit the organizational culture of Southwest is undoubtedly critical to the success of Southwest.

This has enabled Southwest to maintain a strong, unified culture in the face of enormous growth and to groom management talent within it. This is reflected at the senior management level, where promotions within the ranks have led to all but five positions being occupied by insiders, some of them having started their careers in entry-level positions. Internal politics is not apparent from the sources available to us. We can, however, make the assumption that the involvement of politics in decision making is always a possibility.

As Southwest grows, sustaining this zeal is likely to get harder. Previously, the question that was frequently asked was: After Kelleher, who? According to Bob Crandell, former CEO of American Airlines, "The kind of contribution Kelleher can make to Southwest is to select the next leader and help the next leader make a successful transition." Well, he did just that in 2001. James Parker, formerly the vice president, took over as the CEO. It is yet to be seen whether Parker and his team can continue the growth and success Southwest has been enjoying for the past three decades. Now everyone will be watching to see if the success of SWA has been a function of the unique person or not.

Training

In an organization where attitudes, culture, and fit are so important, it is natural that the company places such a great emphasis on socialization and training. McDonald's has its Hamburger University, Southwest has its University for People. Everyone at Southwest has a responsibility for self-improvement and training. Once a year, all Southwest employees, including all senior management, are required to participate in training programs designed to reinforce shared values. Except for flight training, which is regulated and certified, all training is done on the employee's own time. Nonetheless, the training department operates at full capacity, seven days a week. The fun spirit of Southwest emerges in graduates very early. For example, a class of new pilots stumbled into Kelleher's office wearing dark glasses and holding white canes.

Labor Relations

The importance of labor relations cannot be underestimated in a company that is about 82 percent unionized. Here again Kelleher's unusual abilities emerged. Somehow he was able to convince union members and officials to identify with the company. Time will tell whether Parker can have the same success. So far, especially during the difficult time in 2001, success continues. This is further described in the section below entitled "Southwest Airlines Performance Indicators."

Compensation

It is also noteworthy that in an era when chief executive pay has escalated to huge amounts, Kelleher was named one of the lowest-paid chief executive officers in Dallas on a performance-adjusted basis. Furthermore, company officers do not get the perks often enjoyed by their counterparts in comparable organizations—no cars or club memberships—and they even stay in the same hotels as flight crews. Southwest has refused to compete for executive talent based on salary.

Culture

The most distinguishing feature of Southwest Airlines is its culture. When competitors and outside observers describe Southwest, they tend to focus on its cultural attributes. Herb Kelleher made the development and maintenance of culture one of his primary duties. The culture permeates the entire organization and sends clear signals about the behavior expected at Southwest. To promote employee awareness of the effects of their efforts on the company's bottom line, *LUV Lines* (the company newsletter) reports break-even volumes per plane. The newsletter informs employees not only of Southwest's issues but competitor news as well. The belief is that informed employees are better equipped to make decisions.

One of the shared values is the importance of having fun at work. Humor is a significant aspect of the work environment. Such attributes are believed by senior management to enhance a sense of community, trust, and spirit and to counterbalance the stress and pressures of the mechanistic demands of airline operations.

Another characteristic is the cooperative relationship among employee groups. This can be an advantage in functional structures, which are notorious for generating coordination problems. In other airlines, work procedures clearly demarcate job duties. However, at Southwest everyone pitches in regardless of the task. Stories abound of pilots helping with baggage and of employees going out of their way to help customers. In one particularly bizarre story, an agent baby-sat a passenger's dog for two weeks so that the customer could take a flight on which pets were not allowed. Employee cooperation impacts the bottom line. When pilots help flight attendants clean the aircraft and check in passengers at the gate, turnaround time, a cornerstone of the low-cost structure, is expedited.

Because of its team-oriented culture, Southwest is not stifled by the rigid work rules that characterize most competitors. As a result, Southwest has tempered the stringent demands of a functional structure with the liberating force of an egalitarian culture. One excerpt from Southwest's "The Book on Service: What Positively Outrageous Service Looks Like at Southwest Airlines" is rather instructive:

"Attitude breeds attitude . . ." If we want our customers to have fun, we must create a fun-loving environment. That means we have to be self-confident enough to reach out and share our sense of humor and fun—with both our internal and external customers. We must want to play and be willing to expend the extra energy it takes to create a fun experience with our customers.

Just as the words "it's not my job" can take away the source of life for a consumer-oriented business, the words "it's just a job" are equally as dangerous. Positively Outrageous Service cannot be learned from a book or manual; it cannot be artificially manufactured; and it is not required by law. It is born and bred in each individual according to his or her experiences, attitude, and genuine desire to succeed—both personally and professionally. Service does not start at the beginning of each work day, nor does it end when you go home. It is a very real part of you . . . it's your company; your success; your future.

This approach certainly contributes significantly to the lowest employee turnover rate in the industry (7 percent) and the highest level of consumer satisfaction.

Despite all of the freedom that the culture permits, in some areas the company also employs very stringent controls. Perhaps the best example is that Herb Kelleher himself had to approve all expenditures over $1,000!

Forged over 30 years, Southwest's culture has been a source of sustainable competitive advantage. A Bankers Trust analyst put it this way:

Southwest has an indefinably unique corporate culture and very special management/employee relationship that has taken years to cultivate. Employees have long had a significant stake in the company; employee ownership and employee contribution to wealth creation are not ideas that are alien to the workforce of Southwest Airlines since it is emphatically not "just a job." Then, too, the relationship is not merely spiritual—the employees have come to trust the only company that has a record of 23 consecutive years of earning stability combined with an impressive record of stock appreciation unmatched by virtually any company . . . within or beyond the airline industry. The pilots are well compensated relative to the industry average, and they understand that. The challenge was to find creative ways to tie together the fortunes of the company with those responsible for it without risk or destruction of shareholder value . . . and, unlike the employee groups at other major airlines, the Southwest pilots understand that.[12]

Management

Until Parker arrived as CEO, there was no doubt as to who is in charge at Southwest. In this respect Southwest is like most of the other airlines, centralized with a very strong, if not dominating, CEO. What set Herb Kelleher apart was his charismatic nature. His friendly, participative, deeply involved, and caring approach was and is revered throughout the organization. A very large number of employees know the chairman, and he is reputed to know thousands of them by name. Nonetheless, it is also known that behind the scenes he can be extremely tough, implying that his public and private personae can be quite different.

Herb Kelleher, age 68, started Southwest with a former client, Rollin King, who is still a member of the board of directors. King supposedly presented his idea for a low-cost Texas-only airline based on the success of Pacific Southwest Airlines in California to Kelleher over dinner at the St. Antony Club in San Antonio. The original "Love Triangle," the foundation of Southwest's strategy, was drawn on a cocktail napkin.

Kelleher's management style, which had been described as a combination of Sam Walton's thriftiness and Robin Williams's wackiness,[12] seems to have been consistent right from the beginning. Direct, visible, and, some would say, even bizarre, he has attended company parties dressed in drag and appeared in a company ad as Elvis. Known for constantly showing the flag in the field and interacting with large numbers of employees and customers,

Kelleher is reputed to have engaged people in conversations for hours, at all hours, about company and industry issues, often with a drink in his hand. He almost always seems ready for a party, and this fun-oriented atmosphere pervades the organization. The company newspaper, *LUV Lines*, has a column, "So, What Was Herb Doing All This Time?" recounting the CEO's activities. Following his example, Southwest employees are well known for going the extra mile. Among the stories of such behavior is that of a customer service representative who stayed overnight at a hotel with an elderly woman who was afraid to stay alone when her flight was grounded due to fog. The agent "knew" that was what Herb would have done.

Kelleher replaced formal strategic planning with "future scenario generation," arguing that "reality is chaotic, and planning is ordered and logical. The meticulous nit-picking that goes on in most strategic planning processes creates a mental straightjacket that becomes disabling in an industry where things change radically from one day to the next."[13] It seems likely that Parker will continue these practices, but his style may be quite different.

One of the most powerful departments is the Customer Department headed by Colleen Barrett, executive vice president, and Parker's right-hand. She is the senior female in the airline industry and provided the organizational balance for Kelleher. She is known to be a stickler for details. She plays another unofficial role, acting as an ombudsman for customers and an internal management expert.

In the early 1990s Barrett set up a company culture committee, composed of people from all geographic areas and levels of the company. The committee, which meets four times a year, is charged with preserving and enhancing the company culture. One of the committee's successes is illustrated by the company organization. It is well known that functional structures such as Southwest's are designed to promote specialization and scale economies, but often at the expense of teamwork and coordination. As these organizations grow they become even more difficult to operate in an integrated manner. The committee developed a number of initiatives to improve cross-functional cooperation. One example is that all company officers and directors have to spend one day every quarter in the field—working a real "line job."

Technology

Like all airlines, Southwest is a very heavy user of computer-related technology. This technology supports all activities from scheduling to reservations to general operations support. The network is built on four superservers and a reservations subsystem that connects more than 5,000 PCs and terminals across the country. Remote locations communicate with the servers using TCP/IP across Novell LANs.

This network supports a reservation system that has enabled Southwest to be the first carrier to offer ticketless travel on all of its flights. Over 80 percent of Southwest's seats are now sold ticketless. The ticketless system offers significantly improved customer service by eliminating lines at ticket counters. The system also reduces costs; it is estimated that it costs an airline from $15 to $30 to produce and process a single paper ticket.

Customers using the Southwest ticketless system can purchase a seat on a Southwest flight by telephone or on the Internet. Customers receive a confirmation code, which is traded for a boarding pass at the airport. The concept of ticketless travel originated at Morris Air, a Salt Lake City airline acquired by Southwest in 1993. Although policy and operational differences prevented Southwest from adopting the Morris system, the company was able to accelerate the development of its own system with the assistance of Evan Airline Information Services, a consulting firm that helped to develop Morris Air's system. The first ticketless passenger boarded a Southwest plane only four months after development began.

All Internet activities are concentrated under Kevin Krone, vice president—Interactive Marketing. Marketing activities explicitly build on the Internet as a primary marketing channel. Southwest was the first carrier to host a Web site, **http://www.southwest.com**, which was deemed "Best Airline Web Site" by Air Transport World. It recently launched a joint venture with Worldview Systems to enhance its Internet presence.

Southwest Airlines Performance Indicators

Many different criteria can be used to evaluate Southwest's success in achieving its basic objectives. Certainly Southwest's different constituencies look at its performance in different ways. Southwest takes particular pride in the following accomplishments:

- 30 years of safe, reliable operations;
- number one in fewest customer complaints for the last nine consecutive years in the Department of Transportation's Air Travel Consumer Report;
- in the top five of *Fortune*'s "100 Best Companies to Work for in America" for the past four years;

- five consecutive years of Triple Crown Customer Service;
- nine consecutive years of increased profits and 28 years of profitability;
- recognition as one of the top 10 places to work in Robert Levering and Milton Moscowitz's book, *The Best 100 Companies to Work for in America*;
- top ranking in the Airline Quality Survey conducted by the National Institute for Aviation Research for two of the last three years;
- consistent financial success that provides thousands of jobs in the aerospace industry; and
- a route system that has grown to 58 airports in 29 states, carrying more than 60 million customers on 352 Boeing 737 aircraft.

(Check the magazine stories and the Web site regularly to update these performance figures.)

No issue is more important than safety and security. One need only study the checkered history of ValuJet or Air Florida to see what one catastrophic crash can do to an airline when the airline is perceived to have been at fault. Meanwhile, Southwest maintains a 30-year safety record and is generally acknowledged to be one of the world's safest airlines.

Of course, Southwest's customers remain one of the company's main constituencies. Despite its "no-frills" orientation, Southwest consistently receives the highest rankings for customer satisfaction. This is achieved through the successful management of customer expectations. By emphasizing low price and consistency, Southwest has successfully redefined the concept of quality airline service. For example, the "Triple Crown Award" goes to the airline, if any, that has the best on-time record, best baggage handling, and fewest customer complaints according to statistics published in the Department of Transportation (DOT) Air Travel Consumer Reports. Southwest won the award first in 1988 and every year since 1992. No other airline has ranked on top in all three categories for even a single month, although Continental Airlines is catching up fast!

Given its mission, employee satisfaction is another important indicator of company success. Personnel are a crucial determinant of organizational performance throughout the industry. Labor costs are about 40 percent of operating costs in the industry, while at Southwest they are considerably lower. As noted, labor relations is an important determinant of company survival. Southwest has one of the lowest personnel turnover ratios in the industry. It began the first profit-sharing plan in the industry, and employees now own about 12 percent

of the stock. *Fortune* has named Southwest one of the best companies for attracting, developing, and keeping talented people. In 1997, *Fortune* ranked Southwest first on its list of the "100 Best Companies to Work for in America," and Southwest has been in the top five for the past four years.

Southwest has had generally peaceful and cooperative labor relations throughout most of its history. One salient result of management-labor harmony is that Southwest employees are the most productive in the industry. A single agent usually staffs gates, where competitors commonly use two or three. Ground crews are composed of six or fewer employees, about half the number used by other carriers. Despite the lean staffing, planes are turned around in half the time of many rivals. Southwest pays its pilots wages that are comparable to the major carriers, but pilot productivity (e.g., number of flights per day, number of hours worked) is considerably higher.

Despite its low-cost structure, Southwest is not able to control all costs. Perhaps the most important uncontrollable element is fuel, which has varied from 78.7 cents per gallon in 2000 to 55.2 cents per gallon in 1995. One advantage that larger, broader-scope carriers have is a more limited exposure to fuel price volatility. Broader scope allows them to take advantage of geographic differences in fuel prices, and deeper pockets allow them to hedge against future price increases. However, Southwest does have the advantage of a younger and more fuel-efficient fleet than its larger competitors.

Market share is another indicator of an organization's performance. By this criterion, Southwest also ranks at the top of the industry. For example, it consistently ranks first in market share in 80 to 90 of its top 100 city-pair markets, and overall has 60 to 65 percent of total market share. Because of the "Southwest Effect," the carrier gains this share by growing the size of each of its markets—this is achieved by a fare structure that is on average $60 lower than the majors.

The Challenges Ahead

Southwest Airlines is no Johnny-come-lately. Its basic strategy of consistent low-cost, no-frills, high-frequency, on-time air transportation with friendly service is a recipe that has been refined throughout the company's 30-year life. It has worked for the company in periods of catastrophic losses for the industry as well as in times of abundance. Southwest has been able to compete successfully both with the major airlines and with those that have been formed to copy its formula.

Opportunities for Growth

Southwest apparently recognizes the potential saturation of its historic markets and the limited number of attractive short-haul markets. Therefore, it has expanded into some longer-haul markets. Longer-haul not only provides avenues for future growth but also provides potentially higher margins. On average, the company's cost per ASM is about 8 cents. However, on its longer routes costs are as low as 4 cents per ASM. Furthermore, as mentioned, the 10 percent ticket tax has been replaced with a combination ticket tax and takeoff fee. This increases the attractiveness of longer-haul flights.

Analysts see growth directions in the invasion of new markets, such as Florida, as well as in the addition of new city-pairs to Southwest's point-to-point network. In 2000, Southwest began service in Albany and Buffalo, and in 2001, entered West Palm Beach.

Limits to Growth

As critics have noted, there are many challenges on the horizon. Southwest will eventually saturate its historic niche. The company currently flies into 58 airports with more than 2,700 flights per day. Its old strategy of focusing on good climates and smaller, less congested airports has contributed to Southwest's low costs. Many believe that poor weather conditions can affect Southwest's ability to maintain on-time performance and can significantly impact down-line operations. This is magnified by a schedule based on a rapid turnaround, which leaves little leeway for flight delays. Southwest entered and then left the Denver market when bad weather forced an unacceptable number of delays and canceled flights.

This puts a limit on growth because there are only a finite number of markets that can satisfy these criteria. Thus, Southwest has begun to enter markets in poorer climates and to introduce longer-haul flights. Providence, Rhode Island, one of the newer locations, is not a good weather location. There are about 56 airports in good weather locations with populations of over 100,000. Southwest currently serves 36. It is unclear how much demand for point-to-point service exists in the remaining 20.

If Southwest decides to introduce food services as an amenity for longer-haul flights, it would require galleys and onboard services that would significantly boost the cost of operation of those airplanes. Longer flights also result in fewer flights per day and may serve to drive down yield. A mixture of galleyed and nongalleyed aircraft will also make fleet scheduling less flexible. Furthermore, there will be a greater need for functions in the organization responsible for new elements such as national marketing, the frequent flyer program, interline agreements, new geographic operations, and possibly food services.

People and culture also are major concerns in further expansion. Southwest is highly selective; it consequently needs a large pool of applicants in order to find a few people good enough for the culture. With labor shortages across the country, it may be difficult to attract large pools of applicants. Without the selectivity, Southwest may not be able to get the human resources it needs in order to differentiate itself from others. The unique culture of Southwest helps make the company really fly. As companies expand, particularly in geographic location, they often find that it becomes increasingly more difficult to maintain the same culture. This is particularly true if the culture is built around the persona of one major leader such as Herb.

Competition

During the last several years, the gap between Southwest and the rest of the majors has narrowed as other carriers have attempted to emulate Southwest's formula. Larger airlines have developed lower-cost short-haul divisions. Continental, United, and Delta have all introduced an "airline within an airline" to lower costs for short-haul flights. These separate divisions may hire their own pilots and ground support at much lower costs under separate contractual relations with unions. Under these arrangements pilots can often be employed for less than half the cost of the parent airline. This, not surprisingly, has led to some bitter disputes between management and unions. For example, at American Airlines the unions have seen this as a management tactic for shifting their members from high- to low-paying jobs with the same duties.

At the same time, Southwest has adopted many of the features that the majors use to support their large networks. As Southwest has grown in scope, it has introduced national advertising, including NFL sponsorship; a frequent flyer program, including a branded credit card; and interline and marketing agreements with international carriers. Southwest's operations at Nashville are developing into a hub. The carrier's average stage length has also increased over the last several years. Southwest has now expanded into geographic markets and climates that are not as compatible with its original fair-weather, low-congestion strategy. Its flights now compete head-to-head with some of the major carriers.

Recent successes of Continental Airlines under the leadership of Gordon Bethune are most impressive. He has virtually turned the airline around 180 degrees. In the near term Continental seems likely to be one of SWA's strongest competitors, in addition to JetBlue.[14] JetBlue, under the leadership of David Neeleman, the opposite in personality from Herb Kelleher, is fast becoming a no-frills airline for Southwest to take seriously. It has a philosophy similar to SWA's, for example, it has just one type of plane, the Airbus A320, and doesn't serve meals. It does, however, let passengers pick their seats, and has leather upholstery, free satellite TV, and a frequent-flier program. Neeleman has big plans that SWA cannot afford to ignore.[15]

While SWA and JetBlue are just thinking about going global, Ryanair and EasyJet, based in Britain, are expanding their networks out of Britain and setting up bases in Europe where low-fare airlines are few and far between. Crossair is now a player in this important market along with Virgin Express. These two carriers are now in a regulatory environment that SWA faced in 1978, that is, one that is becoming much more deregulated thanks to the EU legislation that took full effect in 1997 that allows any qualified airline to fly anywhere within the EU without government approval. Although both these low-fare airlines are copying much of the SWA model, greater social costs and much more attractive high-speed rail alternatives make running a low-cost operation successfully in Europe a bit more challenging, as Virgin Express and Debonair have learned. Nonetheless, low-fare air travel is growing 25 percent yearly in Europe![16]

Credits: Ari Ginsberg and Richard Freedman prepared the original version of this case with the research assistance of Bill Smith. It is used here with their permission. They thank Myron Uretsky, Eric Greenleaf, and Bethany Gertzog for their valuable comments and suggestions. They also appreciate the careful review, corrections, and helpful recommendations made by Susan Yancey of Southwest Airlines on an earlier version. The case is intended to serve as the basis for class discussion rather than to illustrate either effective or ineffective handling of an administrative situation. A glossary of their key terms appears in Appendix 2A.

The case was updated in 2001 by Randall S. Schuler, Susan E. Jackson, and Kristin Nordfors. Materials to update this case were taken from the Web site of SWA and the case materials (including appendixes 2B and 2C) of Megha Channa, Olympia Cicchino, Shirish Grover, Mohini Mukherjee, and Drew Von Tish, all students in the Rutgers University Master's of HRM program, and are used with their permission. Additional materials and insights provided by the students at the GSBA-Zurich.

ENDNOTES

1 K. Brooker, "The Chairman of the Board Looks Back," *Fortune* (May 28, 2001): 63–76.

2 J. P. Morgan, Short-Haul Competitive Update (April 16, 1996): 3; _____, "Snip, Snip, Snip," *Economist* (October 13, 2001): 59–60.

3 E. Brown, "A Smokeless Herb," *Fortune* (May 28, 2001): 78–79; L. Zuckerman, "Airline Based at Kennedy Expands West," *New York Times* (May 23, 2001): C1, C6.

4 CEO Profile of Herb Kelleher, *Chief Executive Magazine* (March 2000).

5 N. Wong, "Let Spirit Guide Leadership" *Workforce* (February 2000): 33–36; G. Donnelly, "Recruiting, Retention & Returns," *CFO* (March 1, 2000).

6 J. H. Gittell, "Paradox of Coordination and Control," *California Management Review* (Spring 2000): 101–117. Libby Sartin moved to the same position at Yahoo!.

7 P. Carbonara, "Hire for Attitude, Train for Skill," *Fast Company* (August 1996): 73–78.

8 K. Brooker, "Can Anyone Replace Herb?" *Fortune* (April 17, 2000): 186–192.

9 J. H. Gittell, "Paradox."

10 K. Jones, "Herb's Flight Plan," *Texas Monthly* (March 1999); W. Zellner, "Southwest: After Kelleher, More Blue Skies," *Business Week* (April 2, 2001): 45.

11 V. Lee, "Impacts of Deregulation and Recent Trends on Aviation Industry Management," *Bankers Trust Research* (August 30, 1996): 16; S. Tully, "From Bad to Worse," *Fortune* (October 15, 2001): 119–128; M. Conlin, "Where Layoffs Are a Last Resort," *Business Week* (October 8, 2001):42; J. Ewing, D. Fairlamb, and K. Capell, "The Fallout in Europe," *Business Week* (October 8, 2001): 52–53.

12 A. R. Myerson, "Air Herb," *New York Times Magazine* (November 9, 1997): 36.

13 J. Freiberg and K. Freiberg, *NUTS! Southwest Airlines' Crazy Recipe for Business and Personal Success* (Austin, TX: Bard Books, 1996); R. Oppel, "Southwest Manages to Keep Its Balance," *New York Times* (September 25, 2001): C6.

14 "Outlaw Flyboy CEOs," *Fortune* (November 13, 2000): 237–250.

15 E. Brown, "A Smokeless Herb"; L. Zuckerman, "JetBlue, Exception Among Airlines, Is Likely to Post a Profit," *New York Times* (November 7, 2001): C3.

16 "The Squeeze on Europe's Air Fares," *The Economist* (May 26, 2001): 57–58; K. Done, "Ryanair Continues to Escape Turbulence," *Financial Times* (November 6, 2001): 23.

Statistics for Managing Human Resources

Throughout, this book refers to numerous research studies that provide documentation for its assertions. Readers who wish to learn more about the studies cited are encouraged to consult the original sources listed in the notes for each chapter. Much of this literature requires some basic familiarity with the statistics and research methods used in human resource management. This appendix describes some of the basic concepts needed to understand the original research reports. Although this appendix uses examples relevant to selection and placement (described in Chapter 8), the basic concepts described here also apply to research on most other topics.

MEASUREMENT

Regardless of the method or site used to study human resource issues, researchers need to be concerned about the reliability and validity of measurement devices. *Reliability* refers to the consistency of measurement and *validity* relates to the truth or accuracy of measurement. Both are expressed by a *correlation coefficient* (denoted by the symbol r).

Correlation Coefficient

A correlation coefficient expresses the degree of linear relationship between two sets of scores. A positive correlation exists when high values on one measure (e.g., a job knowledge test) are associated with high scores on another measure (e.g., overall ratings of job performance). A negative correlation exists when high scores on one measure are associated with low scores on another measure. The range of possible correlation coefficients is from $+1$ (a perfect positive correlation coefficient) to -1 (a perfect negative correlation coefficient). Several linear relationships represented by plotting actual data are shown in Exhibit A.1.

    The correlation between scores on a predictor (x) and a criterion (y) is typically expressed for a sample as r_{xy}. If we did not have a sample but were able to compute our correlation on the population of interest, we would express the correlation as ρ_{xy} (ρ is the Greek letter *rho*). In almost all cases, researchers do not have access to the entire population. Therefore, they must estimate the population correlation coefficient based on data from a sample of the population. For instance, an organization may desire to know the correlation between a test for computer programming ability (scores on a predictor, x) and job performance (scores on a performance appraisal rating form, y) for all its computer programmers, but decides it cannot afford to test all computer programmers (i.e., the population of interest). Instead, the organization may select a sample of computer programmers and estimate the correlation coefficient in the population (ρ_{xy}) based on the observed correlation in the sample (r_{xy}).

    For each scatterplot in Exhibit A.1, a solid line represents the pattern of data points. Each line is described by an equation, which takes the general form for a straight line: $y = a + bx$, where a is the point at which the line intercepts the y-axis and b is the slope of the line. Such equations, called *prediction equations*, allow researchers to estimate values of y (the criterion) from their knowledge of x (the predictor). For example, we may conduct a study

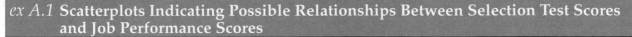

ex A.1 Scatterplots Indicating Possible Relationships Between Selection Test Scores and Job Performance Scores

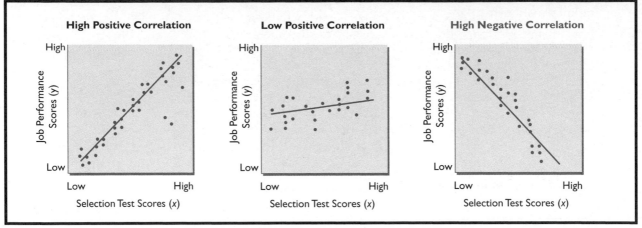

to determine the correlation between sales performance (i.e., dollar sales volume) and number of years of sales experience, for a group of salespeople. Once we have developed a prediction equation, we can then estimate how well a sales applicant might perform on the job.[1] The equation might read,

Dollar Sales per Month = $50,290 + $2,000 × Years of Sales Experience

Using this equation, we would predict that a salesperson with 10 years of experience will generate $70,290 a month in sales. A new salesperson with only 1 year of experience will be expected to generate only $52,290 a month in sales.

As you might expect, decision makers often employ more than one predictor in their equations. For example, organizations often use multiple predictors when making selection and placement decisions. Similar to that of the single-predictor approach, the purpose of multiple prediction is to estimate a criterion (y) from a linear combination of predictor variables: $y = a + b_1x_1 + b_2x_2 + \ldots + b_mx_m$). Such equations are called *multiple-prediction equations* or *multiple-regression equations*. The bs are the regression weights applied to the predictor measures. The relationship between the predictors and the criterion score is referred to as the *multiple-correlation coefficient* (denoted by the symbol R).[2]

For example, suppose a manager believed that sales were a function of years of experience, education, and shyness (scored 0 for people who are not very shy to 7 for people who are very shy). To determine whether the manager's intuition was correct, we might conduct a research study. Information on each of these predictors could be collected, along with sales performance, or criterion, data. A multiple-regression equation such as the following could be generated:

Dollar Sales per Month = $25,000 + ($1,500 × Years of Experience) + ($500 × Years of Schooling) − ($25 × Score on Shyness)

This equation would indicate that a salesperson who scored low on shyness (1) and had 10 years of experience plus a college degree (16 years of schooling) will be expected to generate $47,975 in sales [$25,000 + ($1,500 × 10) + ($1,500 × 16) − (25 × 1)].

Multiple-regression analysis has been used to determine how to combine information from multiple selection devices. Multiple regression has also been used to assess such things as the effects of rater and ratee characteristics (e.g., sex, experience, prior performance rating, and rate of pay) on performance appraisal and pay decisions and to measure the effects of organizational characteristics (e.g., size, industry, and sales) on human resource planning and policies.

Reliability

If a measure such as a selection test is to be useful, it must yield reliable results. The reliability of a measure can be defined and interpreted in several ways. Each of these methods is based on the notion that observed scores (x) comprise true scores (T) plus some error (E) or $x = T + E$ where T is the expected score if there were no error in measurement.[3] To the extent that observed scores on a test are correlated with true scores, a test is said to be reliable. That is, if observed and true scores could be obtained for every individual who took a personnel selection test, the squared correlation between observed and true scores in the population is (ρ^2_x) and would be called the reliability coefficient for that selection test.

One means of estimating reliability is *test-retest reliability* (ρ_{xx}). This method is based on testing a sample of individuals twice with the same measure and then correlating the results to produce a reliability estimate.

Another means of estimating the reliability of a measure is to correlate scores on alternate forms of the measure. *Alternate test forms* are any two test forms that have been constructed in an effort to make them parallel; their observed score means, variances (i.e., measures of the spread of scores about the means), and correlations with other measures may be equal or very similar.[4] They are also intended to be similar in content.

A problem with test-retest reliability and alternate forms reliability is the necessity of testing twice. In contrast, *internal consistency reliability* is estimated based on only one administration of a measure. The most common method, *coefficient* α (alpha), yields a *split-half reliability* estimate. That is, the measure (e.g., a test) is divided into two parts, which are considered alternate forms of each other, and the relationship between these two parts is an estimate of the measure's reliability.

Researchers are interested in assessing the reliability of measures based on one or more of these methods because reliability is a necessary condition for determining validity. The reliability of a measure sets a limit on how highly the measure can correlate with another measure, because it is very unlikely that a measure will correlate more strongly with a different measure than with itself.

Estimating Population Coefficients

If we were able to assess the relationship between a predictor and a criterion in a population of interest with no measurement error, then we would have computed the true correlation coefficient for the population, ρ_{xy}. Because we almost never have the population available and almost always have measurement error, our observed correlation coefficients underestimate the population coefficients. That is, predictor and criterion unreliability are statistical artifacts that lower predictor-criterion relationships.[5]

Two other statistical artifacts that obscure true relationships are sampling error and range restriction. A *sampling error* is an inaccuracy resulting from the use of a sample that is smaller than the population when computing the validity coefficient. A *range restriction* is a correlation or validity coefficient computed between the predictor and criterion scores for a restricted group of individuals. For example, suppose you were interested in determining the correlation between height and weight. If you had data that reflected the entire range of human variability, the correlation would be fairly substantial. However, if you studied only retired adult men, the correlation would be artificially low owing to the restricted range of heights and weights represented in your sample.

Formulas have been developed to remove the effects of predictor unreliability, criterion unreliability, and range restriction, and to determine sampling error variance. Researchers can use these correction formulas to remove the influence of statistical artifacts and, consequently, obtain a better idea of the predictor-criterion relationship in the relevant population. A number of studies have examined the effects of variations in sample size, range restriction, and reliability on the size and variability of observed validity coefficients. These studies have improved our understanding of how observed validity coefficients are affected by measurement error and statistical artifacts.

Validity

As defined in the American Psychological Association's *Principles for the Validation and Use of Personnel Selection Procedures*, validity is the degree to which inferences from scores on tests or assessments are supported by evidence. This means that validity refers to the inferences made from the use of a measure, not to the measure itself. Two common strategies used to justify the inferences made from scores on measures are criterion-related validation and content-oriented validation.

Criterion-Related Validation. Criterion-related validation empirically assesses how well a predictor measure forecasts a criterion measure. Usually, predictor measures are scores on one or more selection "tests" (e.g., a score from an interview or a score to reflect the amount of experience), and criteria measures represent job performance (e.g., dollar sales per year or supervisory ratings of performance). Two types of criterion-related validation strategies are concurrent validation and predictive validation. These are shown in Exhibit A.2. *Concurrent validation* evaluates the relationship between a predictor and a criterion for all participants in the study at the same time. For example, the HR department could use this strategy to determine the correlation between years of experience and job performance. The department would collect from each person in the study information about years of experience and performance scores. All persons in the study would have to be working in similar jobs, generally in the same job family or classification. Then, a correlation would be computed between the predictor scores and criterion scores.

The steps in determining predictive validity are similar, except that the predictor is measured sometime before the criterion is measured. Thus, *predictive validity* is determined by measuring an existing group of employees on a predictor and then later gathering their criterion measures.

ex A.2 Criterion-Related Validation Strategies

CONCURRENT STUDY

Time I	**Time I**	**Time I**
Test (predictor) scores are gathered.	Criterion scores are gathered.	The correlation between scores on predictor measures (x) and criterion measures (y), r_{xy}, is calculated.

PREDICTIVE STUDY

Time I	**Time 2**	**Time 2**
Test (predictor) scores are gathered.	Criterion scores are gathered.	The correlation between scores on predictor measures (x) and criterion measures (y), r_{xy}, is calculated.

The classic example of a predictive validation analysis is AT&T's Management Progress Study.[6] In that study, researchers at AT&T administered an assessment center to 422 male employees. Then, they stored the scores from the assessment center and waited. After eight years, they correlated the assessment center scores with measures of how far the same individuals progressed in AT&T's management hierarchy. For a group of college graduates, the predictions were highly accurate; a correlation of .71 was obtained between the assessment center predictions and the level of management achieved.

Content-Oriented Validation. On many occasions, employers are not able to obtain sufficient empirical data for a criterion-related study. Consequently, other methods of validation are useful. One of the most viable is *content-oriented validation*. It differs from a criterion-related strategy in that it uses subjective judgments and logic as the basis for arguing that a predictor is likely to be effective in forecasting a criterion. To employ a content validation strategy, one must know the duties of the actual job. As discussed in Chapter 6, information about job tasks and duties can be obtained using one or more job analysis procedures. Once the duties are known, then logic is used to argue that a predictor is relevant to performance in the job. For example, if a job analysis showed that word processing duties were a substantial portion of a job, then you might logically conclude that a test of word processing skills would be a valid predictor of job performance. For this type of validation, the most important data are job analysis results.

Validity Generalization

Since the mid-1900s, hundreds of criterion-related validation studies have been conducted in organizations to determine the predictive effectiveness of HR measures (e.g., ability tests) for selecting and placing individuals. Often, the validity coefficients for the same or a similar predictor-criterion relationship differed substantially from one setting to another. Although researchers were aware that these differences were affected by range restriction, predictor unreliability, criterion unreliability, and sampling error, only recently were corrections for these statistical artifacts integrated into systematic procedures for estimating to what degree true validity estimates for the same predictor-criterion relationship generalize across settings.

A series of studies has applied validity generalization procedures to validity coefficient data for clerical jobs, computer programming jobs, petroleum industry jobs, and so on.[7] In general, these investigations showed that the effects of range restriction, predictor unreliability, criterion unreliability, and sample size accounted for much of the observed variance in validity coefficients for the same or similar test-criterion relationship within an occupation (i.e., a job grouping or job family). Thus, the estimated true (corrected) validity coefficients were higher and less variable than the observed (uncorrected) validity coefficient.

The implication of these findings is that inferences (predictions) from scores on selection tests can be transported across situations for similar jobs. That is, if two similar jobs exist in two parts of an organization, a given selection test may have approximately the same validity coefficients for both jobs. If validity generalization can be successfully argued, an organization can save a great deal of time and money developing valid, job-related predictors when the inferences from a predictor for a job have already been established.

The concept of validity generalization, or *meta-analysis*, has also been applied to other areas of HR research.[8] Such research has led to a better understanding of the effectiveness of interventions such as training programs, goal-setting programs, and performance measurement (appraisal) programs.

Cross-Validation

HR researchers are also interested in how stable their prediction equations are across samples. Cross-validation studies address this concern. For the prediction equations developed by researchers to be of any practical use, they must produce consistent results. *Cross-validation* is a procedure for determining how much capitalization on chance has affected the prediction equation, (or *regression weights*). In the case of HR selection research, for example, one is interested in how well the regression weights estimated in a sample of job incumbents will predict the criterion value of new job applicants not tested in the sample.

Traditional or empirical cross-validation typically involves holding out some of the data from the initial sample and then applying the equation developed in the initial sample to the holdout sample to evaluate the equation's stability. In general, this procedure is less precise than one using a formula for estimating the stability of regression equations. The reason for this is that in formula-based estimates, all the available information (the total sample) is used at once in estimating the original weights.[9]

UTILITY ANALYSIS

Armed with tools to determine the reliability and validity of measurement devices, researchers have become concerned about demonstrating the usefulness of the methods and procedures they use. This is particularly important when human resource activities and programs are vying for scarce financial resources. To justify funding, human resource activities must be cost-effective. The process used to assess the costs and benefits of human resource programs is called *utility analysis*. Although it is not yet used by many organizations, utility analysis helps human resource managers compare the economic consequences of two alternative HR practices. For example, you might compare the consequences of relying on a single interview to select people for a job, versus giving applicants a written ability test. Or you might compare the economic consequences of a three-week off-site training session versus a six-month on-the-job approach to training.[10]

In HR selection, most applications of utility analysis are premised on the assumption that supervisors can estimate the dollar values associated with performance at the 50th percentile, the 85th percentile, and the 15th percentile. This is called the *standard deviation* (SD_y) of the performance in dollars. Studies have been conducted in which supervisors have provided estimates of the SD_y for such jobs as sales manager, computer programmer, insurance counselor, and entry-level park ranger. The research indicates that the SD_y usually ranges from 16 to 70 percent of wages, with values most often being in the 40 to 60 percent range. This means that an estimate of the SD_y for a job paying \$40,000 a year typically ranges from \$16,000 to \$24,000. Utility analysis also considers other variables (e.g., the number of employees, tax rates, and the validity coefficient of the selection device) that affect the value or utility of a selection process. The following equation, which incorporates these economic concepts, can be employed when comparing two alternative selection procedures or other human resource options:

$$\Delta U = N_s \sum_{t=1}^{T} = \{[1/(1 + i)^t]SD_y(1 + V)(1 - TAX)(\rho_1 - \rho_2)z_s\} - \{(C_1 - C_2)(1 - TAX)\}$$

where

ΔU = The total estimated dollar value of replacing one selection procedure (1) with another procedure (2) after variable costs, taxes, and discounting

N_s = The number of employees selected

T = The number of future time periods

t = The time period in which a productivity increase occurs

i = The discount rate

SD_y = The standard deviation of job performance in dollars

V = The proportion of SD_y represented by variable costs

TAX = The organization's applicable tax rate

ρ_1 = The estimated population validity coefficient between scores on one selection procedure and the criterion

ρ_2 = The estimated population validity coefficient between scores on an alternative selection procedure and scores on the criterion

z_s = The mean standard score on the selection procedure of those selected (this is assumed to be equal in this equation for each selection procedure)

C_1 = The total cost of the first selection procedure

C_2 = the total cost of the alternative selection procedure[11]

For illustration, let us employ a portion of the utility analysis information collected at a large international manufacturing company, which we will call company A. Company A undertook a utility analysis to obtain an estimate of the economic effect of its current procedure for selecting sales managers as compared with that of its previous program. The current procedure is a managerial assessment center. Although the assessment center had been in operation for seven years at the time of the utility analysis, a value of four years was used because this was the average tenure (T) for the 29 sales managers (N_s) who had been selected from a pool of 132 candidates. A primary objective of the utility analysis was to compare the estimated dollar value of selecting these managers using the assessment center with what the economic gain would have been if the managers had been selected by an interviewing program.

The values $-.05$ for V and $.49$ for TAX were provided by the accounting and tax departments, respectively. V was the proportion of dollar sales volume compared with operating costs. Its value was negative because a positive relationship existed between combined operating costs (e.g., salaries, benefits, supplies, and automobile operations) and sales volume. The value for i, $.18$, was based on an examination of corporate financial documentation. The accounting department also provided the figure for C_1 (the total cost of the assessment center), $263,636. Based on 29 selected individuals, the cost of selecting one district sales manager was computed to be about $9,091. The estimated total cost to select 29 sales managers by the previous one-day interviewing program (C_2) was $50,485.

The estimated population validity coefficient for the assessment center, ρ_1, was obtained by correlating five assessment dimension scores (i.e., scores for planning and organizing, decision making, stress tolerance, sensitivity, and persuasiveness) with an overall performance rating. The multiple correlation between the measures was $.61$. Next, the cross-validated multiple correlation for the population was calculated, using the appropriate formulas. The resulting value, $.41$, was corrected for range restriction and criterion reliability to yield an estimated value of $.59$ for ρ_1.

Because Company A had not conducted a criterion-related validity study for the interviewing selection program, a value was obtained from the validity generalization literature; the resulting ρ_2 for the interviewing program was $.16$. In addition, the standard score on the predictor, (z_s) was determined to be $.872$. This value was assumed to be the same for both the assessment center and the interviewing program.

The final, and traditionally the most difficult, component to estimate in the equation was SD_y. This expression is an index of the variability of job performance in dollars in the relevant population. The relevant population for evaluating a selection procedure is the applicant group exposed to that procedure. When we evaluate the economic utility of organizational interventions, however, the relevant group is current employees. Because the intervention at Company A would be applied to current employees, the appropriate value of SD_y was for this group. Thus, if SD_y were estimated from the applicant group, it could be an overestimate. Consequently, the approximate value for a sales manager, $30,000, was used for SD_y.

Placing all these values into the utility analysis equation gave approximately $316,460 as the estimated present value, over four years, to the organization from the use of the assessment center in place of an interviewing program to select 29 sales managers. Although the cost of the interviewing program was only about one-fifth that of the assessment center, the estimated dollar gain from use of the assessment center instead of the interviewing program was substantial. This result was primarily due to the greater predictive effectiveness (i.e., higher validity coefficient) of the assessment center.

Despite the potential usefulness of utility analysis, very few firms have adopted its procedures. Several circumstances may explain this failure. First, practice tends to lag theory. Because utility analysis is rather new, it may not yet have filtered down to organizations. Second, opponents of utility analysis question the viability of measuring the standard deviation of performance by using managerial estimates. However, this concern may be alleviated by a utility approach that does not require the direct estimation of SD_y.[12] Finally, as noted in Chapter 8, validation studies have not been conducted as often as they should be. Without information regarding the validity of selection, training, safety, or absenteeism programs, utility analysis cannot be conducted.

ENDNOTES

1 For a summary of the conditions under which each type of correlation coefficient is used, refer to M. J. Allen and W. M. Yen, *Introduction to Measurement Theory* (Monterey, CA: Brooks/Cole, 1979), 36–41.

2 G. V. Glass and J. C. Stanley, *Statistical Methods in Education and Psychology* (Englewood Cliffs, NJ: Prentice-Hall, 1970).

3 F. M. Lord and M. R. Novick, *Statistical Theories of Mental Test Scores* (Reading, MA: Addison-Wesley, 1968).

4 E. E. Ghiselli, J. P. Campbell, and S. Zedeck, *Measurement Theory for the Behavioral Sciences* (San Francisco: Freeman, 1981).

5 P. Bobko, "An Analysis of Correlations Corrected for Attenuation and Range Restriction," *Journal of Applied Psychology* 68 (1983): 584–589; R. Lee, R. Miller, and W. Graham, "Corrections for Restriction of Range and Attenuation in Criterion-Related Validation Studies," *Journal of Applied Psychology* 67 (1982): 637–639.

6 A. Howard, "College Experience and Managerial Performance," *Journal of Applied Psychology* 53 (1968): 530–552. For a discussion of the AT&T Management Progress Study, as well as an overview of assessment centers, see A. Howard, "An Assessment of Assessment Centers," *Academy of Management Journal* 17(71) (1974): 115–134. See also A. Howard and D. W. Bray, *Managerial Lives in Transition: Advancing Age and Changing Times* (New York: Guilford, 1988).

7 For a review of validity generalization research, see M. J. Burke, "A Review of Validity Generalization Models and Procedures," in R. S. Schuler, S. A. Youngblood, and V. L. Huber (eds.), *Readings in Personnel and Human Resource Management*, 3rd ed. (St. Paul, MN: West Publishing Co., 1988). See also F. L. Schmidt and J. E. Hunter, "Development of a General Solution to the Problem of Validity Generalization," *Journal of Applied Psychology* 62 (1977): 529–540. Alternative validity generalization procedures have been presented in J. C. Callender and H. G. Osburn, "Development and Test of a New Model for Validity Generalization," *Journal of Applied Psychology* 65 (1980): 543–558; N. S. Raju and M. J. Burke, "Two New Procedures for Studying Validity Generalization," *Journal of Applied Psychology* 68 (1982): 382–395. For a discussion of the practical usefulness of utility analysis, see D. P. Skarlicki, G. P. Latham, and G. Whyte, "Utility Analysis: Its Evolution and Tenuous Role in Human Resource Management Decision Making," *Canadian Journal of Administrative Science* 13(1) (1996): 13–21;

G. P. Latham and G. Whyte, "The Futility of Utility Analysis," *Personnel Psychology* 47 (1994): 31–46; G. Whyte and G. P. Latham, "The Futility of Utility Revisited: When Even an Expert Fails," *Personnel Psychology* 50 (1997): 601–610; S. F. Cronshaw, "Lo! The Stimulus Speaks: The Insider's View on Whyte and Latham's 'The Futility of Utility Analysis,'" *Personnel Psychology* 50 (1997): 611–615; M. C. Sturman, "Implications of Utility Analysis Adjustments for Estimates of Human Resource Intervention Value," *Journal of Management* 26 (2000): 281–299.

8 G. V. Glass coined the term *meta-analysis* to refer to the statistical analysis of the findings of many individual studies, in "Primary, Secondary, and Meta-Analysis of Research," *Educational Researcher* 5 (1976): 3–8. Numerous articles and books have been written on the subject of meta-analysis (of which validity generalization can be considered a subset); two original and frequently cited texts in this area are G. V. Glass, B. McGaw, and M. L. Smith, *Meta-Analysis in Social Research* (Beverly Hills, CA: Sage, 1981), and J. E. Hunter, F. L. Schmidt, and G. Jackson, *Meta-Analysis: Cumulating Research Findings across Settings* (Beverly Hills, CA: Sage, 1982).

9 P. Cattlin, "Estimations of the Predictive Power of a Regression Model," *Journal of Applied Psychology* 65 (1980): 407–414; J. G. Claudy, "Multiple Regression and Validity Estimation in One Sample," *Applied Psychological Measurement* 2 (1978): 595—607; K. R. Murphy, "Cost-Benefit Considerations in Choosing among Cross-Validation Methods," *Personnel Psychology* 37 (1984): 15–22.

10 W. F. Cascio, *Costing Human Resource Management*, 3rd ed. (Boston: PWS-Kent, 1991); G. R. Jones and P. M. Wright, "An Economic Approach to Conceptualizing the Utility of Human Resource Management Practices," in K. Rowland and G. Ferris (eds.), *Research in Personnel and Human Resource Management*, 10th ed. (Greenwich, CT: JAI Press, 1992), 271–299.

11 A study that employed this full equation and provides useful information for estimating economic components as well as true validity coefficients is presented in M. J. Burke and J. T. Frederick, "A Comparison of Economic Utility Estimates for Alternative *SD* Estimation Procedures," *Journal of Applied Psychology* 71 (1986): 334–339.

12 N. S. Raju, M. J. Burke, and J. Normand, "A New Approach for Utility Analysis," *Journal of Applied Psychology* 75(1) (1990): 3–12.